www.wadsworth.com

wadsworth.com is the World Wide Web site for
Wadsworth Publishing Company and is your direct
source to dozens of online resources.

At *wadsworth.com* you can find out about
supplements, demonstration software, and
student resources. You can also send e-mail to
many of our authors and preview new publications
and exciting new technologies.

wadsworth.com
Changing the way the world learns®

Philosophical Problems in the Law

Third Edition

DAVID M. ADAMS

California State Polytechnic University, Pomona

Australia • Canada • Denmark • Japan • Mexico • New Zealand • Philippines
Puerto Rico • Singapore • South Africa • Spain • United Kingdom • United States

Philosophy Editor: Peter Adams
Assistant Editor: Kerri Abdinoor
Editorial Assistant: Mindy Newfarmer
Marketing Manager: Dave Garrison
Print Buyer: April Reynolds
Permissions Editor: Robert Kauser
Production: Matrix Productions, Inc.
Copyeditor: Jill Saxton
Cover Design: Jennifer Sweeting
Cover Image: © Earl Dotter
Compositor: Pre-Press Company, Inc.
Printer: Webcom

Printed in Canada

1 2 3 4 5 6 03 02 01 00 99

For permission to use material from this
text, contact us:
   Web: www.thomsonrights.com
   Fax: 1-800-730-2215
   Phone: 1-800-730-2214

Wadsworth/Thomson Learning
10 Davis Drive
Belmont, CA 94002-3098
USA
www.wadsworth.com

International Headquarters
Thomson Learning
290 Harbor Drive, 2nd Floor
Stamford, CT 06902-7477
USA

UK/Europe/Middle East
Thomson Learning
Berkshire House
168-173 High Holborn
London WC1V 7AA
United Kingdom

Asia
Thomson Learning
60 Albert Street #15-01
Albert Complex
Singapore 189969

Canada
Nelson/Thomson Learning
1120 Birchmount Road
Scarborough, Ontario M1K 5G4
Canada

Library of Congress Cataloging-in-Publication Data
Philosophical problems in the law / [compiled by] David M.
Adams—3rd ed.
     p.   cm.
     Includes bibliographical references.
     ISBN 0-534-51903-2
     1. Law—United States.   2. Law—Philosophy.   3. Law—
United States—Interpretation and construction.   I. Adams,
David M., 1953-
KF379.P455   1999   99-19935
340'.1—dc21

 This book is printed on acid-free recycled paper.

Contents

Chapter II   *Law, Liberty, and Morality   193*

Chapter III   *Equality and the Law*   *303*

Preface

Challenges and Aims

This text began in frustration. Teaching a course in the philosophy of law to undergraduates at a four-year college or university presents challenges philosophy instructors often do not face in their other courses. These challenges derive from two basic features of a course in the philosophy of law. First, although the course normally draws some philosophy majors, the largest constituency frequently consists of a diverse audience of prelaw students majoring in everything from business administration and criminal justice to history and English literature. For many students, this course is their first exposure to philosophy. Second, the primary source materials for the course—judicial opinions and commentaries upon these opinions—are written in a drab, technical vocabulary for an audience of trained professionals. As such, the materials presuppose substantial specialized knowledge.

The instructor thus faces two challenges: (1) to teach students of varying ability levels and disciplinary backgrounds without presupposing too much sophistication with either philosophy or law and legal institutions, and (2) to motivate students, many of whom most likely are not philosophy majors, to care about the philosophical problems the law raises and to promote philosophical engagement with the law and legal texts. These challenges in turn generate two others: to balance the exploration of contemporary issues and cases with an examination of broader philosophical problems and to provide enough and the right kind of primary source material.

Philosophical Problems in the Law, both in content and in organization, addresses the foregoing challenges and implements their ensuing objectives: to reach a diverse audience and to motivate philosophical puzzlement about the law.

Content and Organization

Like its predecessors, the third edition of *Philosophical Problems in the Law* is designed for use in introductory-level courses in philosophy of law or jurisprudence, with selections chosen for both overall accessibility and philosophical merit. Where difficult philosophical or legal concepts or arguments are involved, they are first presented and explained in chapter introductions.

The organization of both individual chapters and the entire text reflects the aim of making the material more readily "teachable." Instead of being structured around explicitly philosophical theories and debates (with which students are unlikely to be familiar), the text is organized around general areas of law—constitutional, criminal, civil—and within each area more specifically around particular issues and questions. The present edition continues the aim of earlier editions to motivate engagement with abstract topics and problems (the nature of law and legal reasoning, the limits of free expression, the purposes of criminal punishment) by situating them within a concrete context of controversial cases and emerging issues (the legality of "war crimes" trials, indecency on the Internet, the death penalty, and so on).

Most chapters begin with an illustrative case or recent controversy; all chapters include both an introductory overview and two or more sets of Study Questions that test students' knowledge and provoke them to apply and extend insights gained from the readings. Each chapter contains several Cases for Further Reflection to be used as vehicles for classroom discussion or in connection with assigned written work.

Four other learning aids are included. *Appendices* explaining legal citations and published law reports and presenting Amendments to the U.S. Constitution continue to appear. They are supplemented now with a third appendix providing a brief review of legal resource information available on the Internet and other World Wide Web sites. A *glossary of legal terms* provides easy reference to frequently used legal terminology.

Third Edition

This edition of *Philosophical Problems in the Law* incorporates numerous changes. As was true for earlier editions, the experience and insights of colleagues who worked with the text have been most helpful. Coverage of certain theories and issues has been expanded and deepened, and new selections (both cases and essays) have been included.

Revisions/Expansions. The chapters on the nature of law, on liberty and morality, and on criminal law and tort law have been expanded significantly.

Chapter One, on the nature of law and legal reasoning, now begins with an entirely new section of text, which provides a brief overview of the law and of philosophy and moral theory. Presented within the context of a hypothetical case concerning a sinking lifeboat, the section reviews differing sources of law (legislative; adjudicative; constitutional); substantive versus procedural law; and the structure of the courts and legal system. The second half of the section constitutes a short introduction to moral theory, with an emphasis on consequentialism and deontology.

Selections from Aquinas and John Austin now appear in Chapter One; the section on legal realism now features an excerpt from Karl Llewellyn. The section on contemporary theories of law has been significantly expanded, with new material on each of the following: critical legal studies, law and economics, critical race theory, and feminist jurisprudence. The section on legal reasoning and constitutional interpretation contains new essays on originalism.

Chapter Two has been retitled "Law, Liberty, and Morality" and now has excerpts from famous essays by Patrick Devlin and H. L. A. Hart, as well as a case dealing with civil disobedience. An entirely new section on freedom of religion has also been added. Chapter Four, on criminal law, features expanded coverage of both the theory of punishment and the death penalty.

Updated Selections. As was true in earlier editions, new selections, both cases and essays, have been included in each chapter of the book. Material on such topics as indecent speech on the Internet, gay rights, age discrimination, and the Bosnian war crimes trials are now covered.

Current Cases. New cases appearing in this edition include: the case of the slave ship *Amistad;* two recent affirmative action cases, *Adarand* and *Hopwood;* the Supreme Court's opinion in the *VMI* case; the case of the convicted Unabomber, Theodore Kazczynski; and cases involving Howard Stern, Hooters Restaurants, and other lively topics.

A new appendix appears at the back of the book, providing basic information on legal source material available on the Internet and over the World Wide Web. Virtual law libraries, general legal search engines and web sites, as well as sites dealing specifically with selected areas of the law are included.

Alternative Paths

As before, the text remains structured in five chapters, each as self-contained as possible. This allows the instructor to pursue alternative paths through the text. Some instructors, for example, may want to begin with Chapter Two, on law, liberty, and morality, move through the chapters on criminal and tort law, and then return to the more heavily theoretical problems dealt with in Chapter One. This strategy enables students to encounter first a variety of more specific issues and to read a number of judicial opinions, building up to an understanding of what is at stake in debates over the proper methods of legal reasoning or debates between naturalist and positivist theories of law.

Contributors

Like the contributors to the first and second editions, contributors to the third edition represent a broad spectrum of scholars and practitioners, embracing the work of legal academics, political theorists, and members of the bench and bar in addition to well-known philosophers. New selections by those working in feminist jurisprudence, critical legal studies, and critical race theory are included. The third edition continues to incorporate the work of more women and people of color.

Acknowledgments

I am greatly indebted to many for their kind help in the preparation of this edition. The list includes Robert Ashmore, Marquette University; Karen Bell, California State University, Fresno; Raymond Belliotti, State University College, Fredonia; James Drier, Brown University; Gerald Dworkin, University of Illinois, Chicago; Charles Evans, City College, CUNY; Leslie Francis, University of Utah; Ann Garry, California State University, Los Angeles; Jim Momarkay, Tennessee State University; Jack Musselman, Indiana University; Jim Nickel, University of Colorado at Boulder; Heather Poole, New York Law School; Don Scheid, Winona State University; Michael Shapiro, University of Southern California Law Center; Roger Shiner, University of Alberta; Laurie Shrage, California State Polytechnic University, Pomona; Tom Simon, Illinois State University; Larry Solum, Loyola Law School; Julie Van Camp, California State University, Long Beach; Jeff Vanderpool, California State University, Fullerton.

Bibliographical Note

David M. Adams is Professor of Philosophy and Director of the Institute for Ethics and Public Policy at the California State Polytechnic University, Pomona. He is also a clinical bioethicist and an adjunct member of the Department of Medicine at Pomona Valley Hospital Medical Center, Pomona, California. He is a graduate of the University of California at Berkeley and the University of Washington (Ph.D.) and holds a master's degree in law from Stanford Law School. His publications include articles in legal theory, ethics, social philosophy, and bioethics. He is the co-author (with Edward L. Maine) of Business Ethics for the 21st Century.

Chapter I

The Nature of Law and Legal Reasoning

The rule of law is something with which we daily live, but which we rarely pause to try to understand. We know that we must pay our taxes, stop at red lights, and refrain from stealing other people's property. We know that if we are being threatened with a lawsuit we had better get a lawyer, and that if the suit is filed we may well wind up in court before a judge. We know that the judge's job is to apply something called "the law," as opposed to simply doing as he or she pleases, and we have a vague sense that this requirement is part of what it means to live in a society governed by the "rule of law," as opposed to the "rule of men." But what does living under the rule of law really mean? Why do we think it is better to live in a society in which there are statutes and judges than one in which these are absent?

Most of us are aware of the old theory that a regime of law is necessary to keep us in line, to prevent the "war of all against all" that some warn would immediately follow upon the breakdown of "law and order." Is law then exclusively about power, control over others? If so, who (or what) holds that power? Those who "make" the law? If so, how is the rule of law different from the rule of men? When the

Allied nations, at the conclusion of World War II, put on trial the highest-ranking officials of the German government, was this merely (as some critics contended) the arbitrary exercise of naked power, an organized act of revenge? Or was it an attempt to reassert the primacy of law? If, as many people believed, punishing the Nazi leaders was the morally right thing to do, does this fact itself mean that the Nuremberg trials were genuine *legal* proceedings? What is the relationship between that which is morally right and that which is the law? It is obvious to most people that not everything that is morally wrong is also "against the law"; and similarly, not everything that is illegal is "wrong" in a moral sense. Do legality and morality have any more than a coincidental connection? Can a system of immoral rules and principles be a *legal* system? These are the questions and issues explored in Chapter One.

Because this text does not assume any previous study of either philosophy or of the law, the first section offers an overview of both, beginning with an imaginary case that presents a number of issues both legal and philosophical. Basic features of the law and the legal system are reviewed, followed by an

1

introduction to some theories in the philosophical field of ethics that will have particular relevance to many of the topics covered in
this book.

The second section provides a concrete
context within which to approach questions
about the nature of law and legality: the so-
called Nuremberg trials, held at the close of
World War II. Robert Jackson and Charles
Wyzanski debate the nature of the "law" to
which the Nazi leaders were subjected; the report of the United Nations Secretary General
on the former Yugoslavia demonstrates the
continuing relevance of the Nuremberg debate for basic questions in international law.
Author Neil Kritz argues that the ideal of the
rule of law exercises a powerful influence on
emerging democracies around the world. The
third section of the chapter explores two classical theories of law: legal positivism and natural law theory. The excerpt from theologian
and philosopher St. Thomas Aquinas presents
the classic formulation of the natural law position. English legal theorists John Austin and
H. L. A. Hart defend versions of legal positivism; Lon Fuller responds with his own
conception of legal naturalism. Section D examines two further views of the nature of law,
each with roots in the twentieth century:
American legal realism, represented here by
Oliver Wendell Holmes and Karl Llewellyn;
and the interpretive theory of contemporary
legal philosopher Ronald Dworkin. Section E
looks at several recently emerging philosophies of law. The selections by Mark Tushnett
and Andrew Altman outline themes basic to

the critical legal studies movement; federal
judge and legal scholar Richard Posner argues
on behalf of the law and economics movement; Angela Harris and Margaret Radin
articulate and defend forms of feminist
jurisprudence; and Derrik Bell's essay represents the concerns of scholars working in critical race theory. The last section of this chapter
explores the complexities of constitutional interpretation as a vehicle for understanding the
nature and processes of legal reasoning.

The readings are followed by several
Cases for Further Reflection. The case of *Riggs
v. Palmer* presents a classic confrontation between legal positivism and natural law in a
case involving an heir who murders his
grandfather to get rich. This case is followed
by two more from the first half of the nineteenth century involving the legality of the
slave trade. Named after the slave ships involved—*The Antelope* and *The Amistad*—the
cases became famous through the story told in
Steven Spielberg's film *Amistad*. The "Problem
of the Grudge Informer," written by Lon
Fuller, nicely portrays the clash of various jurisprudential perspectives in an imaginary
state making the transition to democratic rule
after years of dictatorial oppression at the
hands of the Fascist "Purple Shirts." *People v.
Hall* concludes the cases. Decided by the
Supreme Court of California in 1854, the case
shows how legal reasoning can be used to
achieve a result many people today would
find morally objectionable.

A. *Philosophy and the Law*

The Case of the Overcrowded Lifeboat

In this section, we will cover some basics, the nuts and bolts of the law and the legal system, and the general areas of philosophy most relevant to the study of law. Both to focus our discussion and to illustrate the relevance of philosophy and the law, let's begin with a hypothetical case study, which we can call "The Case of the Overcrowded Lifeboat."

You are a judge faced with the following case: Several months ago, a 40-foot chartered yacht left Long Beach headed for Hawaii. On-board were about forty passengers and crew. The cruise proceeded without incident for two days, but the third saw the yacht confront a terrific storm of unexpected strength and severity. The yacht was badly damaged by smashing waves and eventually began to list and then sink. Because the ship's radio was knocked out soon after the storm hit, the crew were unable to call for help. The captain and some of the passengers were swept away and drowned. The first mate, two crew members, and a number of passengers managed to clamber into a lifeboat and weather the tail end of the storm. (The yacht regularly kept two lifeboats, but during the emergency one was found to be unseaworthy and thus could not be used.)

Adrift in the lifeboat, the remnant of the crew surveyed the situation: the boat could seat twenty people comfortably; twenty-four could ride in the boat without serious danger of causing the craft to founder. Every additional passenger added above twenty-four, however, significantly increased the risk that the boat would capsize or sink (especially in rough seas); yet there was no way of telling precisely how many more people the boat could accommodate while still affording those aboard any real chance of survival. The total number of people now in the boat was twenty-three.

The ship had sunk during the early hours of the morning, and with the first light it immediately became apparent to those in the boat that some survivors still lived and were swimming in the water nearby. When these unfortunates saw that a lifeboat had endured the ordeal, they made for it as quickly as they could. Soon six desperate souls were yelling to those in the boat, asking to be helped aboard. The first mate now had a dilemma: how many, if any, of the swimmers should he try to save? After some moments of seemingly agonizing reflection on his part, the first mate himself reached out and helped aboard the strongest among those in the water. Many of the people already in the boat were older—retirees on their way to lounge in the lazy Hawaiian sun. The mate knew that their only hope was to row toward to the main shipping route (from which they had been blown some distance by the storm) in hopes of being spotted. He needed, he felt, a robust man to help row; hence his choice. The mate refused the remaining five permission to enter. At one point, when two swimmers tried to climb aboard anyway, the mate ordered two crew members to push them off. This they did. The bodies of the five were found later by the search-and-rescue team. One of the deceased was a woman three weeks pregnant.

After three days of hard rowing and a narrow escape from a sudden squall, the lifeboat was spotted by a commercial fishing boat and all aboard were returned safely to shore. After investigating the matter, the Coast Guard took the first mate and the two crew members into custody; they were eventually turned over to civil authorities and indicted in state court on six counts of murder.

Because of the unusual nature of the case, the defendants waived their right to a jury trial, and the case is brought before you. The relevant law in this case consists of two statutes, one relating to the crime charged and one concerning the defense relied upon by the mate and crew:

(1) In your state, the penal code defines murder as follows: "Murder is the unlawful killing of a human being with malice aforethought" (that is, with the purpose or intent to kill).

(2) Your state defines the defense of "general justification" as follows: " Conduct that the actor believes to be necessary to avoid a harm or evil to himself or to another is justifiable, provided that the harm or evil sought to be avoided by such conduct is greater than that sought to be prevented by the law defining the offense charged."

One further item is relevant to your deliberations. Like many questions of law, that presented here may be affected to one degree or another by prior rulings. Your preliminary investigation turns up one such prior case: *United States v. Holmes* 1 Wall Jr. 1, 226 Fed. Cas. (1842). The case involved a sailing ship, the *William Brown*, which set sail from Liverpool bound for Philadelphia carrying British immigrants to the United States. Off Newfoundland, the ship struck an iceberg and quickly began to sink. The captain, crew, and passengers abandoned ship. Most of the survivors, the ship's mate and several sailors wound up in a "longboat" (about 22 1/2 feet long). Soon overcrowded, the boat held forty-one, but was meant for only a fraction of that number.

On the second day adrift, the sea grew rough, several holes appeared in the overstrained seams, and the mate at last gave the order "men, fall to work, the boat must be lightened or we will all be lost." One robust sailor, Holmes, went to work. Vowing not to throw over any women or children and "not to part man and wife," Holmes and his fellow crewmen threw overboard close to a dozen men. Subsequently, the survivors were rescued and Holmes charged with murder. Holmes was convicted on the grounds that, although "the law overlooks the taking of life under circumstances of imperious necessity," passengers must be given priority over sailors, and lots must be cast in determining who should be sacrificed. Neither principle had been honored.

Based on these facts, how would you decide the case before you, and on what grounds?

Before we explore this question further, let's look at the law and then at philosophy.

Sources of Law

The law has many sources. For our purposes, we can boil these down to four: *legislative* law; *constitutional* law; *judicial* law; and *administrative* law. Legislative law, or what is sometimes called *statutory* law, consists of the enactments of an elected, legislative body, such as the California State Assembly or the United States Congress. An *ordinance* is another form of written, legislative law, usually referring to the laws passed by a local government body, such as a city council, or county board of supervisors. After being passed, statutes and ordinances remain in force until they are either repealed by the legislative body that created them or ruled unconstitutional by a state or federal court (explained below). Two such statutes are at stake in our lifeboat case: a statute defining "murder," and a statute defining a defense to criminal charges based on "general justification."

Judicial law derives from the process of *adjudication*, that is, the process by which courts apply statutes, ordinances, or constitutional provisions to the facts of a particular case. Courts must apply the language drafted by legislatures to a variety of circumstances, some of which may well not have been fully anticipated by the law's drafters. This means that courts often must interpret what a legislature has said—the rules, of course, cannot apply themselves. As an example, consider the second of the two statutes in our lifeboat case. As the judge in the case, you must decide whether the facts warrant the appeal to "general justification." This may not be an easy matter (we'll look at that in a moment). Just how courts should go about interpreting the written law is a fascinating and contentious issue, which we explore later in this chapter.

The process of adjudication calls upon courts to issue rulings based upon the application of the written law to various circumstances. In this way, courts may develop new legal doctrines that, in turn, also become part of "the law." Lawyers sometimes call judge-made law *case law* or *common law*, to distinguish it from legislative sources. A central element of case law is the principle of *stare decisis*— the process of following the points of law established by other courts in earlier cases. Courts apply *stare decisis* by attempting to use previous decisions as points of reference to guide their decision in a new case. This process is known as following *precedent,* where precedent refers to the authority of a prior ruling in a similar case. By following precedent, courts may actually extend the law to fit unanticipated or new facts. Like the interpretation of written law, however, the process of identifying and following relevant precedent is not necessarily easy. Consider the precedent given in our lifeboat case, which is *U.S. v. Holmes.* In determining whether to follow the guidance afforded by the decision in *Holmes*, you must first decide how closely the facts of our case match the facts of that one. What are the similarities? What are the differences? And are the differences significant legally?

Constitutional law is perhaps best thought of as a kind of hybrid of legislative and judicial law, since it borrows from both. Each state, as well as the federal government, possesses a written constitution, which sets out the basic structure of the state or national government. Consider the federal Constitution. The various "articles" of this document provide for the creation of Congress, of the executive branch of government (the presidency), and for a system of federal courts, topped by the U.S. Supreme Court. The original articles have been

supplemented by written "amendments," dealing both with procedural matters (such as the election of senators) and with fundamental rights (such as the right to "equal protection of the laws"). Constitutional law is similar to legislative law in that it exists in the form of a written document; however, much of what lawyers study in law school under the heading of "constitutional law" is really judicial or case law—decisions of courts like the U.S. Supreme Court, where when one or another provision of the written Constitution has been interpreted and applied. So, for example, cases involving free speech on the internet, abortion, and discrimination against gays in employment have all been decided under the Constitution and have become part of constitutional law, even though none of these specific topics were included by the framers in the original Constitution of 1789.

One further and very important feature of constitutional law links adjudication and legislation. Courts have the power to invalidate legislative enactments that violate provisions of a state or federal constitution. This power, known as *judicial review,* was not explicitly assigned to the courts by the federal Constitution; nonetheless, the Supreme Court inferred that such a power is implicit in the so-called "supremacy clause" of the Constitution, which declares itself the "supreme law of the land."

A fourth type of law, administrative law, comprises all of the regulations, standards, and decisions that derive from the many administrative agencies created by Congress and the executive branch. These agencies, such as the Federal Communications Commission, the Environmental Protection Agency, and the Food and Drug Administration, were created to regulate certain areas of social life. Such agencies have the authority to issue regulations that have the force of law.

Substantive Law

Regardless of its source, the law can usefully be sorted into one of two types: *substantive* or *procedural.* The principal areas of substantive law are *civil* law and *criminal* law. Civil law is typically defined as law regarding private disputes between parties over property, business transactions, accidents and injuries, and so on. In this sense, "private party" can mean an individual person, a small company, or a huge multinational corporation. "Private," in other words, simply means that the entity involved is not governmental. The category of civil law includes everything from sexual harassment claims to suits for breach of contract to multimillion-dollar legal actions against tobacco companies or breast-implant manufacturers. Personal injury lawsuits, involving the law of *tort,* make up an increasing number of civil cases.

Criminal law is defined as law concerning wrongs against the state, rather than against a private party. When someone commits a robbery or a murder, the perpetrator has wronged us all, violating the rules by which we have all agreed to abide. Criminal law is probably the most visible aspect of the law for most people, endlessly dramatized in movies and on TV. The substantive criminal law is, of course, the law at stake in the lifeboat case with which we began.

Procedural Law

Where substantive law deals with the actual rights and wrongs of life, procedural law is, in effect, the legal referee. Procedural law regulates the process of resolving a civil lawsuit or criminal case. For example, procedural regulations in every state stipulate how an initial complaint in a lawsuit is to be filed, how pretrial motions and fact-finding are to be conducted, how evidence is to be gathered, shared, and then presented at trial, and how appeals are to be handled.

Procedure in civil and in criminal cases are largely similar, the differences being attributable in many cases to special rights and protections afforded to criminal defendants under state and federal constitutions. In a typical civil case, the official proceedings begin with the *pleadings,* that is, the documents filed in court by the plaintiff (lodging a complaint) and by the defendant (responding to a complaint). Following the submission of pleadings, the process of *discovery* commences. During this phase, evidence is gathered by both sides, involving, among other things, depositions (sworn testimony) and requests for documents, results of medical examinations, and the like. A *pretrial* hearing is usually conducted by the judge assigned to the case to determine whether

the parties are prepared to go to trial. After a jury is selected, a trial is conducted, at the conclusion of which the jury reaches a verdict for the plaintiff or for the defendant.

Procedure in criminal cases is similar, prefaced by the steps necessary to process a crime. When a suspect in a criminal case has been arrested, he or she typically makes an initial appearance in court and is apprised of his or her legal rights, including the right to have an attorney. A *preliminary hearing* is often called to examine the basis for the charges against the defendant, although this step may be waived by the accused. This hearing offers the accused the opportunity to challenge the prosecution's case before the court. If the judge determines that sufficient evidence exists to send the case to trial, the defendant will then face an *indictment,* or formal presentation of the charges against him or her. At an *arraignment,* the defendant must then enter a plea to the charges in the indictment. Criminal defendants have three pleas available to them: (1) A plea of *not guilty* results in a trial. (2) In a *guilty* plea, the defendant admits the commission of the crime and awaits a sentence imposed by the court. As a practical matter, the great majority of guilty pleas are the result of a *plea bargain* or arrangement in which the defendant agrees not to contest the charges if the prosecutor will agree to a lesser sentence. (3) A third plea, less frequently used, is called *nolo contendere* (literally "I do not contest"). This plea is functionally equivalent to a guilty plea but does not actually admit culpability. A plea of nolo contendere cannot be used in later civil or criminal proceedings as an admission of guilt.

In both civil and criminal cases, the losing party has the right to *appeal* a verdict. An appeal asks another court—an *appellate* court—to examine whether an error occurred in the proceeding in which the losing party lost. Appellate courts do not retry the facts or hear evidence. The role of the appellate court is simply to review the allegation that an error took place at the trial level. Given their place in the system, appellate courts frequently set precedent that then becomes part of the law.

In addition to regulating the trial process, as outlined above, procedural law sets out the roles and functions of the various participants involved in a court proceeding. The job of the judge is to oversee courtroom procedure and to serve as the determiner of the law. The judge is the authority on what the law requires in a given case, and he or she must rule on many different requests from the parties to a civil or criminal proceeding. The parties to a legal case are referred to by standard designations: the *plaintiff* is the person who files a complaint in a civil case; hence the plaintiff could be an individual or a corporation. The *defendant* in a civil case is the person against whom a complaint has been lodged. In criminal law, the defendant is the person charged with an offense.

Whether a proceeding is civil or criminal, the parties involved have lawyers. The basic role of the attorney, according to *Model Rules of Professional Conduct* of the American Bar Association, is one who "zealously asserts the client's position under the rules of the adversary system." What does this mean? Ours is an *adversary* system of law, based on a concept of justice that assumes that the truth is most effectively discovered and justice best obtained by trials in which two opponents vie with each other, clashing before an impartial tribunal, each side testing the other's merits as thoroughly as possible. In this way, it is assumed, all of the facts relevant to an issue will be brought to light and a just verdict thereby rendered. In this light, serving the interests of one's client and serving the "system" are thought to be one and the same.

The final part of the court system consists of the jurors. The jury in a civil or criminal case is composed of citizens who are to serve as the "triers of fact"—the people who sift through the evidence, listen to both sides, and determine what the facts actually are. The jury receives instructions from the judge about the law and must then determine the facts and apply the law to them in order to reach a verdict. Sometimes the roles of the judge and jury are consolidated. In this proceeding, known as a "bench trial," the defendant typically has waived his or her right to a trial by jury, and it falls to the judge to function as both the "finder of fact" and the authority on the law.

The Structure of the Legal System

In the largest sense, the legal system includes everyone who has a role in creating, maintaining, enforcing, changing, or in some way supporting the law. Because most of the issues and questions of philosophical interest in the law have to do with its

meaning and interpretation, our primary focus within the legal system will be the courts.

The court system comprises two parallel tracks: federal and state. There are three levels of federal courts in the United States. The first level consists of U.S. District Courts. Currently more than ninety such courts function as the trial courts of the federal system. The U.S. Circuit Courts of Appeal, numbering thirteen, review appeals on all matters of federal law. The U.S. Supreme Court is the final authority on all cases arising under the Constitution, federal statutes, or administrative laws. Most states have a three-tier system of courts that parallels the federal system.

Courts differ also as to their jurisdiction. *Jurisdiction* refers to the power or authority to pass judgment on a given type of case and with respect to certain parties. If a court lacks jurisdiction over persons or issues, it cannot hear the dispute involved. Federal and state courts have differing jurisdictions. In the federal system, cases can be presented when a federal statute, administrative regulation, or provision of the Constitution is involved, or when parties from differing states are embroiled in a controversy. State courts, by contrast, have jurisdiction over the great majority of civil and criminal cases that arise on a daily basis, and over the interpretation and application of their own state constitutions.

Philosophy and Ethics

Suppose you are asked to look at some problem "philosophically." What does that mean? For most people, such a request would be taken as an invitation to get some perspective, to look at the "big picture," to reflect on a variety of factors. In one sense, this reaction captures what it means to have a philosophical attitude. Philosophers try to adopt that frame of mind with regard to a number of fundamental questions. Philosophers wonder what any of us is doing here, about the ultimate purpose of life. Why, philosophers ask, does the universe exist at all? How much, if anything, can we truly know about the world around us? What is truth? Love? Time? Philosophy is concerned with these kinds of fundamental questions and is an attempt to reflect upon them in a sustained and critical way.

Recall now the lifeboat case with which we began this section. It is important to see that several of the legal questions that you, as the judge, must resolve, lead directly into philosophical questions about knowledge, reality, and right and wrong. Consider, for example, the language of the murder statute: "killing a human being with malice afore-thought." One obvious problem here is whether the mate and the crew "killed" anyone. Certainly people died, but saying that they were killed seems to ascribe some connection between the mate's actions and the deaths. Did the mate "kill" the swimmers, or did he simply leave them to die? What, exactly, is the difference? And why is the difference important? Trying to puzzle out this problem involves issues in the philosophical field of *metaphysics* —the study of the basic nature of reality. A fundamental part of our picture of the world—which the law assumes—says that persons exist as agents who can act on and cause changes to occur in the world, and for which they can then (at least sometimes) be held responsible. However, this metaphysical picture does not always fit our experience easily. In the lifeboat case, for example, the prosecution will undoubtedly insist that the deceased would not have died but for the neglect of the first mate and crew. But again, for all we know, they would not have died but for the terrible storm that swamped the yacht. The defense attorneys will claim that the swimmers died from exposure; or they might confess that it was an "act of God" for which no person is responsible. But couldn't the mate have intervened by his own agency and saved at least some of the swimmers? Recall also that the crew, at one point, pushed off several swimmers who had tried to climb aboard. Is "pushing some-one off" the boat an action for which the crew is re-sponsible? Or should it be viewed merely as failing to rescue the swimmers? This is a crucial question, as it turns out, for as we will learn in Chapter Five, the law traditionally has held people accountable only for their acts, not for their omissions.

A further question is whether the crew acted with "malice aforethought." As we will discover in Chapter Four, this term refers to the state of mind of the crew at the time. Specifically, did the crew, when they refused the swimmers permission to enter the boat, intend for them to die? Or did they intend merely that the swimmers stay out of the

boat? The defense will maintain the latter, stating that the crew merely intended that the swimmers remain in the water and out of the boat; maybe they even hoped that the swimmers could miraculously survive. The prosecution, however, will insist that the obvious and easily foreseeable consequence of remaining in the water was death, and that the crew therefore must have intended for the victims to die. After all, if I point a loaded gun to your head and pull the trigger, I can't realistically say that I didn't intend to kill you, but only to pass a bullet through your head, hoping for a miracle. These is-sues turn, ultimately, on questions that involve metaphysics and *epistemology*— the theory of knowledge. How do we know what the crew really intended? How do we describe their state of mind?

Some of the most profound philosophical questions raised by our lifeboat case fall within the field of *ethics* or moral philosophy—philosophical reflection upon the values and standards that shape our lives and guide our actions. What makes life worthwhile? What are the really important values? Does being moral lead to happiness? Is morality simply a matter of self-interest, obeying the rules and doing what you should simply to avoid hassles or punishment? What rules, principles, or stan-dards should we live by? What validates or justifies the principles I choose to follow? Are those stan-dards relative to my culture or time or place, or are there "objective" moral truths applicable to all cul-tures and times? Facing up to these questions and trying to think them through as carefully as possi-ble comprises the task of philosophical ethics.

There are many ways of thinking philosophi-cally about moral issues, and to review all of them would transform this into a textbook in ethics. However, at least two general approaches to moral questions have particular relevance to the philoso-phy of law. It is useful, therefore, to look at each of these approaches briefly.

Utilitarianism and the Greater Good

The first approach to moral issues is illustrated by a common reaction to the lifeboat case: namely, that the mate and crew did the right thing, since they *acted for the greater good*. Think, for example, of the numbers of lives involved. The boat could hold only so many people; too many and the boat would sink. Assuming that everyone would have died had all five of the swimmers been welcomed into the boat, what reason would there be to prefer twenty-nine deaths to the deaths of five (or six, if we count the fetus)? The underlying appeal here is to the good consequences that would flow from the actions taken by the crew. Philosophically, the idea could be put this way: *The morally right act is that which will produce the best consequences for all affected.* Philosophers call such an outlook *consequentialist* because it makes the consequences of an act the key to understanding its moral status. Philosophers have attempted in several ways to make the basic idea behind consequentialist thinking more precise. For our purposes, however, it suffices to focus on just one of these attempts, and that is the theory called *Utilitarianism.*

The most prominent philosophers to write extensively on utilitarianism were British philosophers in the eighteenth and nineteenth centuries: Jeremy Bentham (1748–1832) and John Stuart Mill (1806–1873). Bentham regarded utilitarianism as an important tool for social and legal reform—a blueprint for legislation. Bentham ridiculed the criminal justice system of England at the time, calling it excessively brutal and outdated. A person's action is criminal, Bentham reasoned, only if it produces genuinely harmful consequences for others. Bentham's cause was taken up by Mill. Mill's book *Utilitarianism*, published in 1863, became a classic statement of the view.

According to utilitarianism, the central moral requirement, sometimes called the "Principle of Utility," can be stated in this way: *Always act so as to bring about the greatest net good for all of those affected by your actions.* Several aspects of this statement must be carefully examined. To begin with, the principle of utility demands that we strive for the greatest *net* good. This reference is meant, of course, to recognize that we may on some occasions be forced to choose between alternatives that each have bad consequences as well as good. In such a case, utilitarianism says, we must choose the course of conduct that has the greatest amount of good or the least amount of bad. Secondly, utilitarianism insists that we do that which will produce the most good. But what do "good" and "bad" mean here? Just what is the "good" that is to be

maximized? Plainly, the utilitarian must answer this question, and Bentham, Mill, and later utilitarians have realized this, although not all have agreed on the best response.

Bentham and Mill both believed that the good we must seek to maximize and the bad that we must minimize, reduce, in the final analysis, to pleasure and pain. The theory that explains the good in terms of pleasure and the bad in terms of pain is called *hedonism*. Hedonism holds that pleasure (and the avoidance of pain) is the only thing of intrinsic value or worth—that is, the only thing worth having just for what it is. All of the other things that we humans want—money, cars, fame—are valuable only as a means to obtain pleasure or avoid pain. Imagine, for example, asking someone to explain why she wants a university degree. "To get a good job," she answers. But why do you want that? "So I can make more money." But why do you want more money? "So I can buy things that give me pleasure." Why do you want more pleasure? Most people would find the last question rather strange: everybody wants pleasure just because it is what it is—pleasurable. Here we seem to come to a point at which the thing we desire or seek is sought just for itself, not as a means to get something further. This is the good that Bentham and Mill believed all of us want, ultimately, to get the most of.

Not all utilitarians are hedonists, however, and this is explained by the fact that hedonism itself raises further questions, not all of which have found satisfactory answers. For example, are all pleasures to be regarded as on a par? Is the pleasure derived from donating money to a museum or writing a great novel really no better than the pleasure associated with getting drunk or staring vacantly at the television for hours? Although Bentham seemed willing to accept this consequence, Mill and other utilitarians were less comfortable with it. Mill tried to distinguish between "higher" and "lower" pleasures, insisting that the higher pleasures were more desirable. Philosophers are divided over whether Mill's effort to establish this point is convincing. Others have accused hedonists of placing the cart before the horse. What human beings truly seek, these critics argue, are the things that enable us to lead genuinely and uniquely human lives—for example, friendship, love, and the pursuit of knowledge. These are the good things of life that human beings need, and pleasure usually accompanies them. However, the pleasure such things bring is not what we ultimately seek; in fact, it is often only when we don't specifically aim at getting pleasure that we find it.

If pleasure is not the good that the principle of utility instructs us to maximize, what then is the good to which it refers? Some utilitarians have tried to avoid the problematic implications of hedonism by talking in terms of "happiness" and "unhappiness": the principle of utility entreats us always to act so as to produce the "greatest happiness," leaving it undetermined exactly how happiness is to be cashed out. Other utilitarians have spoken of "satisfying people's preferences" as the good to be maximized in the utilitarian calculus. *Preference utilitarianism*, as it is sometimes called, asks us to take account of the preferences or interests of all of those affected by our conduct; the goal is then to bring about the greatest net satisfaction of preferences.

Two further aspects of the principle of utility are important. Utilitarianism requires that it be possible, at least in principle, to identify and aggregate or add up all of the relevant preferences (or, in the hedonistic version, pleasures and pains) of all of those affected by one's actions. This may strike you as not being terribly realistic, and for several reasons. Are the preferences people have really comparable items? How can the pleasure I derive from one course of action really be compared to the pain you might derive from it? How is the judge or legislator supposed to know whose preference is stronger, or whose pain is greater? Moreover (and this raises a related concern for utilitarians) how can any of us know the precise impact that our actions will have? Wouldn't I need to have the power to see far into the future to know just what consequences my actions might have? To these kinds of questions, utilitarians have responded variously. Some, most notably Bentham, thought it actually possible to quantify episodes of pain and pleasure, and to devise an interpersonal scale or metric against which to compare one person's pleasure with that of another. To many, this view has seemed to require heroic assumptions that just are not realistic. Other utilitarians have responded more circumspectly, claiming only that it is possible to make at least some assumptions allowing for com-

parisons (for example, that most people prefer the pleasures of friendship or good health over the pleasure of scratching an itch or watching TV). Many utilitarians would insist that omniscience and clairvoyance are not necessary to apply the principle of utility: no one can appreciate in advance all of the consequences of his or her actions, so the best anyone can be expected to do is to judge in light of the best understanding possible at the time. We are all human, after all, and we have to live with our limitations.

One of the most common objections to the moral theory of utilitarianism concerns what the principle of utility might allow—or even require—people to do, under certain circumstances. One complaint is that the principle of utility might, on some occasions, ask too much of us. Suppose for a moment that you are a passenger on the lifeboat. Suppose also that you are a football player weighing 250 pounds and that you notice that two of the swimmers in the water are half your weight. If you were to jump into the water (and thus end your life), two people might be welcomed into the boat in your place without affecting the overall load in the boat. From a purely numerical standpoint, it might seem that it would be better for everyone concerned (although certainly not for you in particular) if you were simply to end your own life. The greater good, in other words, might be best served through the self-sacrifice of your life. Yet, even if the principle of utility appears to demand this course of action, this would seem to many to be asking too much. In fact, some might object that you have a duty to live, and that any principle is just wrong if it seems to suggest otherwise. (We'll return to the subject of duty in a moment.)

The flip side of the complaint that utilitarianism may require too much of us is that it may demand a course of action that seems simply to be wrong. This, of course, is a serious charge for any moral theory—that is, any theory that purports to capture and explain what is most important in moral life. To understand this charge, consider the following case: A rash of violent crimes has plagued a community for some time. Law enforcement officials are baffled as to the perpetrator. Public outrage at the crimes is rising to fever-pitch, and something must be done to calm the public. The police decide to frame an innocent man for the crimes. A trial is held, and the man is convicted on phony evidence. The public anger is quelled and the community and law enforcement are content, but an innocent person's rights have been violated. One could argue, say critics of utilitarianism, that the greater good was best served in this case. However, a grave injustice has been done. Most of us, the critics contend, would insist that to sacrifice an innocent person in this way is wrong, regardless of the benefits to be gained from doing so.

How might a utilitarian respond to these charges? Each of these major arguments against the principle of utility turns on showing that the principle can require that people do something that would otherwise be believed to be wrong. The utilitarian might reply that utilitarianism, properly understood, does not lead to these counterintuitive results. Demanding that people kill themselves or that they be sacrificed in some way to the greater good are not, in fact, actions that would be legitimated or condoned by the principle of utility, despite what the critics say. Utilitarians who make this move often insist that careful attention be paid to the level on which the principle of utility is to be applied. The utilitarian weighing of costs and benefits is not to be undertaken merely on a case-by-case, short-term basis. Any rational person, the utilitarian might claim, must realize the importance of looking at the larger picture. Sacrificing yourself or others to the common good are not actions that have overall positive consequences in the long term. Using people as scapegoats in the name of the greater good does not maximize happiness over time. This is because much unhappiness and distress would be present in a society in which no one could feel safe or secure—in which no one could rely upon others to respect their rights. The utilitarian in this way argues that the principle of utility does not so much apply to individual actions at a particular time and place, but rather to social rules or conventions that are applicable broadly. Rules such as "Do not punish the innocent," which set standards valid in all situations, are justified on utilitarian grounds since the general observance of such rules produces the most good overall in the long run. This version of utilitarianism, often called *rule utilitarianism*, contrasts with *act utilitarianism*, the view that the principle of utility is to be applied to individual actions.

Let's return now to the case of the lifeboat. As we have seen, one way to defend the actions of the crew in refusing to rescue the swimmers is to appeal to a utilitarian calculation: better that five die than everyone perish. How might the prosecution respond? Aside from questioning whether the course of action taken was the one that actually promoted the greater good in the long run, the prosecuting lawyers are likely to ask what right the mate and crew had to decide who would live and who would die. This rhetorical question actually rests on a serious point, for the mate and crew arguably acted in ways that took innocent lives. They, like all of us, the prosecution might argue, had a duty to respect the lives of others. In this they failed. Let's look more closely at the moral outlook reflected in these arguments.

Deontology and Rights

The arguments of the prosecution in the case of the overcrowded lifeboat reflect an underlying approach to moral thinking contrasting sharply with the utilitarian. This view, often called *deontology*, insists that the central fact about moral life is that we all have *duties* or *obligations* to treat others in certain ways, and that these duties are based upon something other than the consequences of our or others' actions. The word 'deontology' comes from the Greek root 'deon,' which means 'duty.' What makes a decision or an action morally worthwhile or right, according to deontologists, is not the effect it has or the consequences it produces, but rather the fact that it was the right decision to make, the right thing to do. Where consequentialists tend to be forward-looking—estimating the future impact of present actions—deontologists are more likely to look to other ways, examining actions already undertaken or relationships already formed as a basis for obligations in the present. That I have made a promise or a commitment to someone in the past, for example, might be for a deontologist a ground for a moral duty that I must fulfill to that person, regardless of whatever consequences would result from my keeping or breaking the promise.

Deontologism is part of a way of thinking about morality that has a long history, although we cannot examine that history here. It is enough to point out that the writings of contemporary deontologists have been influenced by several sources. One such source is the *natural law* philosophy of the Greek and Roman Stoic philosophers—a school of thought that flourished in the few centuries before and after the birth of Christ and (as we will see later in this chapter) continues to be a significant part of jurisprudential debate. Other sources of deontology are the Hebrew and Christian moral traditions. The common thread running throughout these views is the belief that there exist moral rules or standards of conduct that are universally valid and applicable to all human beings and that can be ascertained by us, at least in principle, through the use of our ability to reason. This universal or common moral code is variously referred to as 'moral law' or 'natural law.' Many Jewish and Christian philosophers explicitly linked this idea of a moral law valid for everyone with their own religious doctrines of God, creation, and human destiny. According to these views, the supreme principle of morality might be "Do whatever God commands." Other deontological philosophers, however, have tried to argue that the validity of these ultimate principles can be seen independently of more specific religious beliefs. One of the most influential of these philosophers was Immanuel Kant (1724–1804). It is especially instructive to consider Kant's version of deontology because he tried with great care to reconstruct this traditional way of thinking about morality and make explicit what it says and the assumptions upon which it rests. Moreover, Kant's theory has been enormously influential on philosophers of law.

Several concepts are important in understanding the deontological ethic defended by Kant. A review of these will make his theory more understandable and the contrast between deontology and consequentialism sharper. To begin with, Kant disagreed strongly with the hedonism of some of the utilitarians. Pleasure is not, Kant claimed, of intrinsic or inherent value. Nor, he insisted, does the moral value or worth of an action lie in the effects or in the results it produces, whether these are measured by units of pleasure, satisfaction of interests, or what have you. Second, and more fundamentally, Kant disagreed with the basic premises of all consequentialist theories—namely, that the moral value of an action is a function of its results. To understand Kant's reasons for this disagreement, consider another case of possible rescue. John Doe is sitting by the edge of a small lake, enjoying some relaxing sunshine. It is a weekday afternoon; Doe appears to be alone at the lake. He notices a figure down at the shore—a small child who appears to be in trouble in the water. No one else is around. Doe is an excellent swimmer, and the water in the lake is quite shallow. Doe wades into the water and rescues the child. Later we discover that the apparent hero in fact acted only because the child's parents owe him money and he believed that the "good deed" would hasten the repayment. If this is what Doe supposes, he should think twice. Kant would claim that the situation is not one of which Doe can be proud. Outwardly, Kant would say, Doe may have done the "right" thing, but surely he did not do it for the right reason. He acted selfishly, hence his actions really have no moral value. An action is right, Kant claims, only if it is done just because it is the right thing to do, not because doing so will get you something you want, whether that be money, fame, or the pleasure of thinking yourself a hero.

But how, according to the deontologist, can I know that my actions are right? How can I know what my moral duties to others are? To grasp Kant's answers to these questions, we have to explore a further aspect of his view.

Deontology and the Categorical Imperative

Kant assumed that whenever any of us does something deliberately, it is as if we were endorsing a private rule that we are choosing to follow. If I discover that my employer is in violation of state pollution laws and I decide to "blow the whistle" on him by writing to state authorities, I am effectively operating on the basis of a rule that says "When I am convinced that my employer is violating the law, I will alert law enforcement." I may not say this to myself in so many words, of course, but that is the rule I am implicitly endorsing. Kant called all such private rules "maxims," and he believed that those who take morality seriously would never follow a maxim that did not conform to the most basic of all moral principles, which Kant called the *categorical imperative.*

An imperative is a command of the form "You should do this," or "You ought not to do that." Some commands or imperatives, Kant observed, are *hypothetical*, or conditional upon some fact or preference. Examples of hypothetical imperatives include: "If you want to be hired you should dress professionally"; "If you desire a raise, you ought to increase your productivity"; and "If you want to avoid liability, you should not act negligently." Each of these hypothetical imperatives takes as a given some end or goal already accepted or desired. Moral principles cannot command us in these merely hypothetical ways, Kant thought, since the demands of morality are not dependent upon how we feel or what we want. Feelings and desires are far too flimsy a basis for morality. After all, if the only reason you should act morally is that you feel like doing so or that you desire something in return, what happens when your feelings change (as they often do) or when your desire dissipates? Feelings and preferences are transient and thus too undependable a foundation for genuine moral principles. Hypothetical imperatives can even take the form of immoral demands, followed by people pursing their own ends. An example is an unscrupulous corporate executive who reasons "If we are to stay competitive, we must break any laws that get in our way." For all of these reasons, Kant concluded, a moral imperative must be categorical or absolute: it must be unconditional, providing an enduring incentive to act rightly. It is a mark of a genuine moral command that it tells us what we must do regardless of whether we want to do it.

The moral duties we have, then, as delineated in the deontological theory of Kant, are defined by the categorical imperative. Kant's discussion of the categorical imperative is notoriously complicated, and he himself reformulated the idea in several ways throughout his writings. The essence of his thinking, however, can be stated fairly straightforwardly. According to Kant, the basic and categorical rule behind all moral thinking says that one ought *always to act only on that maxim that one can will to be a universal law*, or, more simply, *act only in ways that you can imagine everyone acting*. This basic principle is one, Kant was convinced, upon which we all rely, whether we are conscious of it or not, in our everyday moral thinking. This is the principle we have in mind when we reprove people who act wrongly with the question "How would you like it if everyone did that?" The moral education of children often proceeds on this basis, getting the child to place herself in the other person's shoes.

To determine whether an action is morally right, I must articulate the maxim upon which it relies and then ask whether I could conceive of this maxim being a "universal law," that is, a rule for everyone. Recall, once more, the case of John Doe, the would-be rescuer. Let's modify the original facts. Suppose that, although he is an excellent swimmer and the water in the lake is quite shallow, Doe decides to leave, telling himself that he doesn't want to get involved. The child survives but is injured. If he were to think deontologically, Doe might pause to consider whether, if the situation were reversed, he would want a potential rescuer to leave him in the water. Kant argued that his deontological concept of morality convincingly explains the judgment that Doe would be acting wrongly in abandoning the struggling child. In the modified case, Doe acts on the basis of a maxim that could be expressed this way: "If it is inconvenient for me, I will refuse to help another, even when doing so would be easy and safe." Remember that Kant's idea is to determine whether someone's action is morally right by asking what it would be like if his maxim were to be universal, that is, if everyone were to act upon it. Kant observed that no one could actually will a maxim of "nonhelpfulness" to be a universal practice, for the world is such that we can be reasonably certain that we shall one day be on the receiving end of such beneficent gestures.

Consider one other example, involving the ethical standards of medical professionals. Imagine that you are a physician and that you have an elderly patient whom you have diagnosed with a terminal illness. You have just told the members of the patient's immediate family the truth about her condition; they now request that you keep the truth from the patient herself. "It will make her final days easier," they plead. Uncertain how to proceed, you delay informing the patient of her status. The patient, however, soon realizes that she is not improving, and one day she confronts you: "What's going to happen to me doctor? Am I going to die"?

What should you say? To act as the family had requested would be tantamount to acting on a maxim that could be expressed this way: "If deceiving my patient will keep him or her from possible suffering and make others happy, I will do so." Could you "will" this maxim to be a universal practice? A Kantian moralist might well respond that you could not, that no rational person would want to live in a world where this practice was the norm. To see why the Kantian would likely give such an answer, we must look at one last aspect of Kant's deontologism.

Deontology and Autonomy

We began our discussion of Kant by noting that acting morally, in his view, means doing what is right just because it is right: this is the only basis for action that has intrinsic worth and unconditional value. Kant tried to connect this idea with the claim that humans are rational beings to explain the value and importance of human life. Kant claimed that each person has an absolute worth, that each rational being exists as an "end in itself," that is, valuable simply by virtue of being what it is. Each of us has an intrinsic value; we do not exist or have importance only because others can use us to suit their purposes. It is for this reason that Kant restates the categorical imperative as follows: *Always act so as to treat others as an end and never as a means alone.* Now, notice that Kant is not saying that we may never use others as a means to something we might want. In fact, we use others all the time: commuters use the bus driver to get them to work; shoppers use manufacturers to supply goods for purchase; workers use their employers as a source of income; and so on. What Kant says is forbidden is treating others *only* as a means: You may use the bus driver as a way to get to around, but you must also acknowledge the driver as a person, not just a uniform—as an individual with a life that matters. Kant's point here is sometimes put by saying that we must always respect the *autonomy* of others. By 'autonomy' Kant means the ability to take charge of one's own life and to live in accordance with valid moral principles, rather than being led around by desires. Kant maintained that only human beings have the capacity intentionally to act in ways that

are motivated by an awareness of moral duties. Autonomy is also often expressed in terms of the idea of self-determination: an autonomous person is a determiner of his or her own destiny, and moral relationships depend upon mutual respect for the autonomy of all rational beings. This suggests that respect for others involves, for example, helping them to further their own ends and goals.

The demand that we respect the dignity and worth of each and every person, as autonomous beings, may explain why no rational being could conceive of living in a world where lying to a dying person is a universal practice. To deceive the patient in this way, a deontologist could argue, is an affront to his or her dignity as an autonomous person. We can now fully appreciate the contrast between Kant's deontologism and the consequentialism of the utilitarians. The centerpiece of Kant's ethic is that to act morally is to act on principle—to do the right thing because it is right. This kind of deontological view insists that certain acts simply must not be done, regardless of the consequences that might flow from them. Even if it would make others extremely happy, it might still be wrong to conceal the truth or to break a promise. To lie to or deceive another would be to use that person as a means to the happiness of others—and this one must not do.

This point connects with another that is often made by deontologists. What Kant says about autonomy and treating other persons with dignity and respect is frequently expressed in the language of *rights* : To say that we must respect the lives of other autonomous beings is to say that they are entitled to or have a right to be so treated. A right typically is a claim that others do something for the person who holds the right (or that they refrain from doing something to him), and thus it correlates with a duty or obligation to act accordingly: if X owes money to Y, Y has a right to the money and X has a duty to pay; if I have a duty to rescue you by pulling you into the lifeboat, you have a duty to be so rescued.

The language of rights seems to presuppose a division between the public boundaries limiting your actions—boundaries set by everyone's respective rights—and a private realm of choice within which each of us is free to develop and pursue our own plans and projects in life. To have a right is to occupy a kind of moral space within which one can operate as one pleases, to enjoy a sphere of autonomy or a realm of protected choices and interests. Deontologists sometimes describe this power of right by saying that rights are like trump cards in a game of bridge: they take priority over other factors. (This is not always the case, of course, and few deontologists would declare that any given right is absolute, taking priority over everything else, including other rights.) As we will see, appeals to individual rights and respect for autonomy play a large part in the legal, as well as the moral assessment of many issues and problems covered in this text.

Objections to Deontology

Deontology, like consequentialism, has its critics. One of the most common complaints concerning Kant's deontology centers on what some perceive to be the excessive formality and abstraction of his view. Insisting that moral credit is to be awarded only to those who act solely for the sake of duty is often scorned as an arid and puritanical position, unconnected to any of the particular duties that arise out of the richness and diversity of human relationships; and while Kant may have shown us what morality is like when it is based purely on reason alone, few people actually live their moral lives in this fashion. Defenders of Kant respond that, although one must perform an action from duty to be morally worthy, this is not inconsistent with being a compassionate and loving individual. The happiness and satisfaction that come from doing good for others is not banned from Kant's deontology, as long as they are accompanied by the proper motive for moral action.

More specific criticisms focus on the categorical imperative itself. Critics question, for example, whether the categorical imperative always recommends one best course of action as the "right" one under the circumstances. Isn't it possible that different people, evaluating the same situation (evaluating, that is, the same maxim) might conclude that the categorical imperative demands two or more different actions? Kant seems to have thought that this would not happen, and in this he doubtless shared in the belief of many living during the so-called "Enlightenment" that human reason is universal, with requirements that are the same for everyone. These are overly optimistic assumptions, say the critics, and the categorical imperative is so general and abstract that its requirements can easily be read in differing ways. Nor does it help to invoke the language of rights. Much of contemporary moral and social life is punctuated by appeals to "his right to this" and "her right to that," without any clear sense of how these often conflicting rights are to be weighed or measured against each other, or how conflicts between them are to be resolved. Utilitarians point out that a moral world in which people think only of exercising their rights is not necessarily a better world: a wealthy corporate executive may have the right to donate large amounts of money to the Ku Klux Klan or to groups of neo-Nazis; this fact, of course, is no guarantee that doing so would be the right thing to do. Rights can be exercised in a way that actually increases the unhappiness and disvalue in the world. Utilitarians might question whether the value of individual autonomy and choice is always such as to outweigh the disvalue that exercising rights can create.

Conclusion

We began this section with what seemed to be a straightforward story of a tragedy at sea. We quickly discovered, however, that many of the aspects of that story raised issues that were deeply philosophical. Just as significantly, we learned that the simple exhortation to solve this case by "applying the law" is deeply problematic as well. What really is "the law," after all? It is to this question that we turn in the next section.

B. *What Is Law?*

The Nuremberg Trial

On July 30, 1993, the Supreme Court of Israel reversed the conviction of a man the court conceded was a Nazi war criminal. John Demjanjuk, a retired autoworker from Cleveland, had been stripped of his U.S. citizenship in 1981 and extradited to (surrendered to authorities of) Israel in 1986. The Israelis claimed to possess overwhelming evidence that the inconspicuous-looking Demjanjuk was in reality the sadistic "Ivan the Terrible" of Treblinka, a Nazi officer during World War II, posted to one of Hitler's most infamous death camps—a man who eagerly sent thousands to their deaths in the gas chambers. Convicted and sentenced to death in 1988, Demjanjuk successfully appealed his conviction with the aid of exculpatory evidence gleaned from KGB files after the collapse of the Soviet Union. Reviewing that evidence, which pointed to another man as "Ivan," the judges of the Israeli Supreme Court conceded that "doubt began to gnaw at our judicial consciences; perhaps the appellant was not Ivan the Terrible of Treblinka."[1] In an ironic twist, the Court also found that the evidence exonerating Demjanjuk of the "Ivan" charge "proved the appellant's participation in the extermination process" by confirming that Demjanjuk had worked at another extermination camp in Poland.[2] Because the basis for his extradition to Israel had been the sole charge of being Ivan, the Court argued, there was no basis for further prosecution of Mr. Demjanjuk and he was released and returned to the United States in 1993. (A U.S. court of appeals subsequently quashed Demjanjuk's extradition on grounds that U.S. prosecutors had ear-

lier knowingly suppressed exculpatory evidence then in their possession.) Mr. Demjanjuk now lives in Ohio. As of 1998, Mr. Demjanjuk remained unsuccessful in persuading the U.S. government to have his citizenship restored.

For many, the Demjanjuk case raised serious questions about the ability of the law to do justice; for others it reawakened memories of the horrors of the Nazi regime; and the controversy surrounding Demjanjuk's trial in Israel recalled the debate sparked by similar trials held nearly forty years previously, at the German town of Nuremberg. The problems raised and questions posed by the Nuremberg and similar trials provide an illuminating perspective from which to view the fundamental controversy over the nature of law.

At the conclusion of World War II, the Allied powers were faced with the problem of what to do with the senior officials of the Nazi government and with the highest-ranking officers in the Nazi military. It was decided, after some debate, that they should be brought to trial in the first in a series of international legal proceedings. Before the proceedings were over, several series of trials had been held in which German industrialists, judges, lawyers, and businessmen, in addition to military and political leaders, were tried. The first and most dramatic of these trials began in October 1945 and lasted until October of the following year. Twenty-two of the highest-ranking Nazi civilian and military leaders were tried; three were completely exonerated, seven received prison terms, and twelve were handed death sentences and executed.

The Trial of the Major War Criminals proceeded pursuant to an agreement signed by the Allied powers on August 8, 1945: the Treaty of London. This agreement created what became the Charter for the International Military Tribunal at Nuremberg. The Charter specified three categories

---

[1] *New York Times,* 30 July 1993, sec. 1, p. 21.
[2] *Ibid.*

of criminal activity, for violation of each of which at least several of the twenty-two defendants were charged:

> Crimes Against Peace: namely, planning, preparation, initiation or waging a war of aggression, or a war in violation of international treaties, agreements, or assurances, or participation in a Common Plan or Conspiracy for the accomplishment of the foregoing . . . ;
>
> War Crimes: namely, violations of the laws or customs of war. Such violations shall include . . . murder, ill-treatment or deportation to slave labor or for any other purpose of civilian population of or in occupied territory, murder or ill-treatment of prisoners of war . . . wanton destruction of cities, towns, or villages, or devastation not justified by military necessity. . . ;
>
> Crimes Against Humanity: namely, murder, extermination, enslavement, deportation, and other inhumane acts committed against any civilian population, before or during the war, or persecutions on political, racial, or religious grounds . . . whether or not in violation of domestic law of the country where perpetrated.[3]

Based on these definitions, the Allied prosecutors at the Tribunal indicted the Nazis on four counts: conspiracy to wage aggressive war; waging an aggressive war; commission of war crimes; and perpetration of crimes against humanity.

The evidence presented at the trial overwhelmingly implicated many of the defendants in acts of systematic and deliberate barbarism. It would not have been sufficient for their purposes, however, for the American, British, French, and Soviet prosecutors simply to have condemned the Nazis *morally;* for this was to be a *legal* proceeding, and the Nazis were therefore to be punished (if at all) for having violated the *law,* however much

what they did (or instructed others to do) was regarded by everyone involved as grossly immoral. The Nazis were to be sent to prison—or to the hangman—for conduct that was *illegal;* and it is here that serious questions were raised, and continue to be raised, about the Nuremberg trials. These questions, which we will explore throughout this chapter, converge on a core philosophical issue: What was the status of the "law" under which the Nazi leaders were prosecuted? What was the *legal* basis for the categories of criminality and standards of individual liability endorsed by the Charter? Is the Charter itself valid "law"? If so, by virtue of what?

Controversies Regarding Nuremberg

Two opposing responses to these questions—two different conceptions of the trials themselves—are represented in our selections by Robert Jackson, chief American prosecutor of Nuremberg (then on leave from the United States Supreme Court), and Charles Wyzanski, a noted Massachusetts judge.

Wyzanski questions the legality of the Charter's basic provisions with the charge that the Charter created "new law" *ex post facto,* "after the fact." As Wyzanski implies, the Charter and the Tribunal were legal novelties in at least two ways: one party to the proceeding became prosecutor, judge, and jury; and the Charter sought to combine elements from both Anglo-American and Continental legal systems. The last proved especially difficult as the two systems differ, both from the standpoint of legal procedure and as regards the content of the (substantive) law. In the English and American systems, as most of us are aware, trials proceed according to a strict division of function. Each of the opposing sides has the responsibility to make the best possible case it can for its position by uncovering all of the facts it believes to be relevant and by noting all of the pertinent legal issues and authorities bearing on the dispute. The role of the judge is essentially that of an umpire, reminding each side of what the proper procedures are and penalizing one or the other for violations of the rules. In many European courtrooms, however, this rigid division of labor is not observed; the effort to discover the

---

[3] See *Nazi Conspiracy and Aggression,* Vol. 1, Office of the United States Chief of Counsel for Prosecution of Axis Criminality (Washington, D.C.: U.S. Government Printing Office, 1946), pp. 5–12.

truth and arrive at a just verdict is conducted in a more collaborative way, with the judge in particular playing a much more active and inquisitorial role than would be permitted in the United States or Britain.

The German defense attorneys at Nuremberg complained bitterly that they were hampered by the Tribunal's decision to rely for the most part upon the Anglo-American procedural system. They also complained that the accusation of participation in a "conspiracy" or "common plan" to start a war had no counterpart in, and was not recognized by, the law of Germany. Wyzanski raises a deeper problem: The Tribunal's "law" effectively permitted it to hold anyone who joined in the Nazi war effort personally liable for anything done by anyone else similarly engaged, and this, Wyzanski insists, was fundamentally unjust.

Behind Wyzanski's specific complaints lies a general concern with the conditions under which an action or decision can be said to be in accord with the rule of law. Wyzanski accuses the Allies of abrogating or negating a principle that is fundamental to the ideas of law and legality: *nullum crimen et nulla poena sine lege*, "[there can be] no crime and no penalty without a[n already existing] law." The Charter creates *ex post facto* law, making something punishable after it has been done. Such laws are forbidden by the United States Constitution; and Wyzanski seems to think that the Charter loses in a crucial way its status as "law" by including *ex post facto* provisions.

Wyzanski also questions the wisdom of trials such as those at Nuremberg. If, as seems likely, the Allies never intended that the Nazis go free, are they not reducing a legal proceeding to a propaganda device? This "debases justice" and suggests the same kind of hypocrisy of which the Allies accused the Hitler regime.

In his opening address before the Tribunal, Robert Jackson responds to the objections raised by Wyzanski. Waging an aggressive war was a crime in international law long before the start of World War II, Jackson claims, and the Germans knew this. Jackson notes several international treaties and agreements, signed by numerous nations in the early part of this century which, he claims, had the effect of outlawing aggressive warfare. Aggressive

warfare was made illegal by these agreements and by international custom; moreover, Jackson adds, the nations of the world have a right to create new customs, to enter into new agreements and understandings that can then serve as a further platform for the development and growth of international law. We cannot allow the defendants to take refuge, Jackson argues, behind the hope that international law will continue to "lag so far behind the moral sense of mankind." To agree with the assertion that the Charter is not law because its core provisions are *ex post facto* would be foolish, for the claim is both empty and hypocritical. How could anyone be surprised to discover that genocide and torture are crimes? And how could those guilty of such atrocities have the gall to hide behind the principles of the moral and legal order that their actions sought so completely to repudiate?

Wyzanski believes that Jackson and the Tribunal have sacrificed the principle of *nullum crimen* on the altar of "higher justice." He suggests that international law, as it stood at the time the Nazis began the war, did not unequivocally make aggressive warfare a crime for which individual persons could be held liable. After all, no leading Western nation, in the period from the early 1920s to 1939, condemned any war as an illegal act of aggression. Yet, Wyzanski assumes, someone must have been an aggressor in the confrontations that took place during that time. Shocking and immoral as it was, Wyzanski concludes, the conduct of the Nazis was not for that reason also a contravention of law.

The Continuing Relevance of Nuremberg

The arguments that took place at Nuremberg concerning the nature of law are just as alive today as they were fifty years ago. Questions about the meaning and value of the rule of law continue to inform both scholarly debate and practical decision making in the field of international law.

In 1998, Goran Jelisic, 29, a Bosnian Serb, was captured by NATO forces in Bosnia-Herzegovina and transported to The Hague, in the Netherlands, to stand trial for the war crime of genocide. Jelisic was to be brought before the International Criminal

Tribunal for the Former Yugoslavia, created by U.N. Security Council Resolution 808, passed in 1993. The charge of the Tribunal is to seek justice for those victimized by acts of ethnic cleansing, deportation, and summary execution occurring during the nearly four-year war in Bosnia. These war crimes prosecutions were the first such international trials since Nuremberg. Under the Tribunal's statute, defendants can be tried for violations of treaties and international conventions, and for crimes against humanity as recognized by the Nuremberg charter. There are differences between the two tribunals and their authority, however. Unlike the Nuremberg Tribunal, the Hague Tribunal lacks direct power to obtain physical custody over the more than seventy persons indicted—as of mid-1998, only twenty-one people had turned themselves in or been arrested. Evidence is more difficult to obtain in Bosnia than it was for the Allies after WW II, and the Hague Tribunal cannot try defendants *in absentia*. There is no death penalty for those convicted by the Hague Tribunal; yet the list of war crimes includes rape, which was not included at Nuremberg. Most significantly, the Hague Tribunal is restricted to punishing crimes alleged to have taken place in the former Yugoslavia after 1991. International officials debate whether this means that some incidents in which atrocities are alleged to have occurred are not subject to international law since they may have been internal to Yugoslavia before Bosnia and Croatia were acknowledged as independent nations.[4]

The Report of the Secretary General on Resolution 808, excerpted in your readings, is noteworthy for its reliance upon the precedent of Nuremberg.

Yet, as the Report makes clear, drafters of the charter for the Hague Tribunal were particularly concerned to avoid the charge leveled by Wyzanski and others at Nuremberg: namely, that such trials amount to the imposition of *ex post facto* "victor's justice" in violation of the ideal of the rule of law. For this reason, the Report stresses that the Hague Tribunal will be applying standards that are beyond any doubt part of the "customary law of nations."

The question of how best to respect the value of the rule of law is now being faced by nations from Africa to Latin America to Asia. The overthrow of military juntas and quasi dictatorships frequently exposes a sordid history of torture, political murders, and other human rights violations in many countries. As these oppressive regimes topple and are replaced by elected governments seeking to implement constitutional reforms, these democracies must determine how best to bring justice to those associated with the wrongs of the prior regime. If those who earlier committed atrocities did so under the cover that such actions were "lawful," according to the statutes and court rulings of that government, how can a democratic administration hold such persons legally accountable for their actions? International law scholar Neil Kritz closes this section by outlining the nature of this dilemma in the selection included here. Kritz discusses several examples of such dilemmas, including one that faced courts in Germany following the reunification of the nation in 1990. That case, the Trial of Border Guards, opens the readings for this chapter.

---

[4] See "Bosnia: The New Nuremberg," *National Law Journal*, 26 Sept. 1994, p. A1.

1. Trial of Border Guards

During the time between August 1961 and November, 1989, it is estimated that over two hundred people were shot and killed by border guards of the German Democratic Republic (East Germany) as they sought to flee the communist bloc into West Germany. On February 5, 1989, two East Germans, Chris Gueffroy and Christian Gaudian attempted to escape the GDR. Although they successfully crossed several barriers constructed by the East German government, they were spotted by members of the East German border guard and shot as they tried to climb the final border fence. Gueffroy was killed; Gaudian was wounded and arrested. Subsequent to the reunification of Germany in 1990, public pressure mounted to punish those responsible for border killings. Four guards involved in the shooting of Gueffroy and Gaudian were placed on trial in 1991. Below are excerpts from the court's ruling.

The 23rd Grand Criminal Court—Court of Assizes—of the Berlin State Court, . . . ruled as follows during the Court Session of 20 January 1992:

The following are hereby sentenced:

Defendant H for homicide to a prison sentence of 3 (three) years and six months,

Defendant K for two crimes, committed as combined act, involving attempted homicide, to a prison sentence of 2 (two) years, whose enforcement is suspended for probation.

Defendants Sch and S are acquitted, Defendant H is also acquitted in as much as he was charged with another offense of attempted homicide. . . .

Legal Assessment

. . . The punishability of the defendants is to be judged primarily according to the law of the scene of the act as it applied in the former GDR (Article 2,

Berlin State Court, Docket No. (523) 2 Js 48/90 (9/91)

Paragraph 1, Criminal Code). According to . . . the Unification Treaty of 6 September 1990 . . .—apart from a few exceptions—the Criminal Code of the Federal Republic of Germany took effect on 3 October 1990 in the former territory of the GDR . . . at the same time, the Criminal Code of the GDR— apart from some exceptions that are not significant here—has been invalidated. According to . . . the Unification Treaty, Article 2, Criminal Code, with the measures regulated in Article 315 . . . is applicable to acts committed in the GDR prior to the date of effectiveness of the entry of the GDR in the Federal Republic, in other words, prior to 3 October 1990.

The acts committed by the defendants therefore are to be judged first of all according to GDR criminal law which was applicable at the scene of the action at the time of the action (Article 2, Paragraph 1, Criminal Code) and they are thus to be gauged in favor of the defendants in the light of the criminal law of the Federal Republic which has taken its place since. . . .

In the case at hand . . . the punishment threatened under the Criminal Code [of the Federal Republic] is less and therefore . . . this is to be applicable.

The following applies to the individual defendants:

[*Defendant* H]

a) With the aimed round fired, single-shot, from the Kalashnikov submachine gun, from a range of less than 40 m, in the manner described above, at the upper part of the body of Chris Gueffroy, who was standing at the border fence, facing toward him, Defendant H killed a human being without being a murderer (Article 212, Criminal Code). Chris Gueffroy died on the spot within a few minutes as a consequence of the round which passed through the heart. Even immediate medical assistance could not have prevented the occurrence of death.

b) Chris Gueffroy's killing was unlawful; the defendant did not have any legally justifying grounds on his side. . . .

According to [the] Border Protection Act, the use of firearms while on Border Guard duty was justified if it served the purpose of preventing the immediately impending execution or continuation of a criminal act which, according to the circumstances, looked like a crime or for the apprehension of persons who were compellingly suspected of a crime. Unlawful border crossing . . . however, was to be classified as a crime only in serious cases. . . . In the case at hand, according to GDR law, there was a serious case of attempted border crossing because the act was committed together with others . . . and because the act was accomplished along with the use of dangerous means or methods, that is to say, with the use of the grappling hook. . . .

. . . In contrast to GDR law, only really grave offenses are qualified as crimes in the Federal Republic. In the then GDR, however, a mere act of "unlawful border crossing" could already become a "crime" if—as in this case—it was committed by at least two persons simultaneously or, to mention another provision that is particularly flexible, "with particular intensity." . . . Firing was permitted in all of these cases; just as to how this was to be done, the law only says: "The life of persons is to be spared to the extent possible." . . .

Within the practice of law, such as it was in effect at the time of the action in what then was the GDR, . . . the soldiers however repeatedly were given the general suggestion during "guard mount"—according to witness Fabian—that no escapee was allowed to slip through and that a "breach of the border" would have to be prevented at all costs. In this way, many soldiers were bound to get the impression and indeed could get the impression that a dead escapee was always better than an escaped escapee with the consequence that their inhibition threshold—when it came to firing their submachine guns at unarmed people—was lowered.

That this is something the superiors wanted in this way is documented particularly clearly by the testimony of witness Fabian according to which soldiers were praised even if they had fired only at a single escapee although, even according to GDR law applicable at that time, it would not have been permitted to fire on him. In such cases, the soldiers were given to understand from the very beginning that they probably just saw a shadow and that nothing would happen to them as a result of unjustified use of firearms.

The case at hand also confirms that the use of firearms in the final analysis was always considered to be justified; there was no investigation at all as to the legality of firearm use; instead, the defendants were praised and rewarded with special leave and monetary bonuses. But if one wished to accept the reality, which corresponded to the legal situation at that time and to what the law was really like in the GDR, . . . then one would indeed have to note that, in Article 30, the GDR Constitution granted its citizens protection of life, physical integrity, and health. . . . From this, one can deduce that government interference in these assets within the context of a legally permissible use of firearms, was bound to be guided strictly by the principle of proportionality, such as it is also spelled out in the Border Protection Act, although inadequately, at that. . . .

In looking into the question as to whether it may be permissible to threaten with death the person who does not want to abide by the exit prohibition and, disregarding it, wants to cross the border, and whether it may if necessary also be permissible to kill him, we run into the question as to whether everything that is formal and that was considered as a right by virtue of interpretation is indeed rightful.

On this score, it has been recognized in Supreme Court jurisprudence, that there is a certain core area of law which no law and no sovereign act may touch according to the legal consciousness of the general public.

On that point, it says the following in a ruling handed down by the Federal Court in 1952 . . . :

"The freedom of a State to determine, for its area, what is lawful and what is unlawful, no matter how widely it is determined, however, is not unlimited. In the consciousness of all civilized nations, with all of their differences revealed by the various national bodies of law, there is a certain nucleus of the law which, according to general legal concepts, must not be violated by any law and by any other sovereign State measure. It encompasses certain basic principles of human behavior that are considered untouchable and that have taken shape with the passage of time among all cultured nations on the fertile ground of coincident basic moral views and which are considered to be legally binding, regardless of whether individual regulations in national bodies of law seem to allow that they be disregarded" . . .

"Particularly strict requirements must be established when attacks against human life are involved. It is in keeping with jurisprudence such as it prevails among all cultured nations, later on also expressed in the Convention for the Protection of Human Rights, that the individual's right to life must be protected to a greater degree. Killings without a court verdict accordingly are permissible only if they result from an absolutely required use of force."

The Federal Constitutional Court also recognizes the basic principle that laws, which interfere in the described core area of the law, are null and void: . . .

"It was especially the time of the National Socialist regime in Germany that taught us that the legislator can also legislate injustice, in other words, if practical legal usage is not to stand defenseless against such historically thinkable developments, there must be a possibility, in extreme cases, to evaluate the basic principle of material justice more highly than the principle of legal certainty, such as it is expressed in the applicability of positive law for routine cases."

As a criterion for the existence of such a special case, the Federal Constitutional Court points to the formulation by Gustav Radbruch, . . . according to which such a case does exist when the contradiction between positive law and justice has reached such an unbearable degree that the law must yield to justice since it is "incorrect law." The rule of law includes not only certainty and safety under the law but also material justice. . . .

These legal principles, to be sure, were developed on the occasion of the crimes of the National Socialist regime of injustice in Germany which, in the monstrosity of their scope, cannot be compared to the situation under discussion here. Nevertheless, the court has no objection in following this jurisdiction also in the case at hand; this is because the protection of human life applies quite generally and cannot depend on the materialization of a certain number of killings. . . .

. . .

Defendant cannot claim Article 258, Criminal Code/GDR.

According to this regulation, a soldier was not liable under criminal law for an action which he carried out by way of execution of an order given by a superior, unless the execution of the order obviously clashed with recognized standards of international law or if it violated criminal laws.

. . .

[Even] if one were to construe—as "order" within the meaning of Article 258, Criminal Code/GDR—the generally stated requirement that none must be allowed to get through, the results still would not be any different. Such an order would be unlawful and would not have deserved any obedience because this would have been an invitation to commit crimes, that is to say, the unlawful and intentional killing of people, and the execution of the order would have violated criminal laws (Arts. 112, 113, Criminal Code/GDR). . . .

Shooting at people, which may lead to killing, that is to say, people who merely wanted to leave the territory of the then GDR, constitutes such a violation of the standards of ethics and human coexistence that—even considering indoctrination, education, and training in the former GDR—one really cannot visualize that the defendant, considering his origin, his schooling, and his personality, as regards the action against the escapees with which he is charged, was in a state of prohibition misinterpretation that would rule out any guilt on his part. In the case of the defendant, one cannot assume that he was unable to recognize the few basic principles that are indispensable for human coexistence and that belong to the untouchable basic assets and core of the law, such as it lives in the legal consciousness of all cultured nations—perhaps because he had not been educated in a knowledge of these principles. Justice and humanity were explained and pictured as ideals also in the then GDR. To that extent, generally adequate ideas as to the basis of natural justice were indeed disseminated. That this is so is pointed up also by the circumstance that a considerable multitude of inhabitants of the former GDR considered action against so-called border violators along the Berlin Wall and along the inner-German boundary to be unjust. The background of the accused, his schooling, and his comment on the motives and assessments of the conflicts, in which so-called border violators were enmeshed, show that he did have and could have available the fundamentals of a normal legal consciousness. He had every reason to think deeply as to whether it was permitted to happen that people may, if necessary, be shot down along the border only because they wanted to leave the GDR without official permission. He had sufficient references and if he had thought about them carefully, he could have figured out for himself that an event, such as it is to be judged here, was not compatible with the set of values prevailing in his environment. In making this examination, one of course cannot consider as representatives of the environment—as the defense argues—those pillars of the system of justice of the then GDR, such as members of the State Security Ministry, judges, or prosecutors; instead, what is important here is to find out whether the "people of the State" of the GDR did or did not approve the procedures under discussion here.

The realization that deadly shots along the border were a crass injustice and that they were in crying contradiction to the generally recognized basic principles of law and justice should and could have been a matter of general knowledge and usage if the Border Guard soldiers and their superiors had developed the proper conscience.

. . .

Apportionment of Punishment

. . . It follows from the considerations given below that we are dealing here with an "otherwise less grave case" within the meaning of Art. 213, Criminal Code:

The acts carried out by the defendants must be viewed against the background of the inhuman system of compulsion prevailing in the then GDR which educated the defendants, with all means of mass psychology, to blind onesidedness and imparted a restricted image of the world which the defendants, in terms of their personality and education, had little to counter with.

Here again, one had to keep in mind that all those who contributed to the distortion of the legal consciousness of the Border Guard soldiers—be it in school, in the so-called mass organizations, or in political indoctrination sessions in the military— cannot be made liable for this under criminal law because the law does not know any criminal action facts in this context.

. . .

Weighing all of the circumstances that speak for and against the defendants, the administration of the following penalties was quite in keeping with the guilt but it was also required in order impressively to make them aware of the injustice of their actions:

In the case of Defendant H, a prison sentence of 3 years and 6 months.

2. *Opening Address for the United States, Nuremberg Trials*

ROBERT H. JACKSON

May it please Your Honors,

The privilege of opening the first trial in history for crimes against the peace of the world imposes a grave responsibility. The wrongs which we seek to condemn and punish have been so calculated, so malignant and so devastating, that civilization cannot tolerate their being ignored because it cannot survive their being repeated. That four great nations, flushed with victory and stung with injury stay the hand of vengeance and voluntarily submit their captive enemies to the judgment of the law is one of the most significant tributes that Power ever has paid to Reason.

This tribunal, while it is novel and experimental, is not the product of abstract speculations nor is it created to vindicate legalistic theories. This inquest represents the practical effort of four of the most mighty of nations, with the support of seventeen more, to utilize International Law to meet the greatest menace of our times—aggressive war. The common sense of mankind demands that law shall not stop with the punishment of petty crimes by little people. It must also reach men who possess themselves of great power and make deliberate and concerted use of it to set in motion evils which leave no home in the world untouched. It is a cause of this magnitude that the United Nations will lay before Your Honors.

In the prisoners' dock sit twenty-odd broken men. Reproached by the humiliation of those they have led almost as bitterly as by the desolation of those they have attacked, their personal capacity for evil is forever past. It is hard now to perceive in these miserable men as captives the power by which as Nazi leaders they once dominated much of the world and terrified most of it. Merely as individuals, their fate is of little consequence to the world.

What makes this inquest significant is that those prisoners represent sinister influence that will lurk in the world long after their bodies have returned to dust. They are living symbols of racial hatreds, or terrorism and violence, and of the arrogance and cruelty of power. They are symbols of fierce nationalisms and militarism, of intrigue and war-making which have embroiled Europe generation after generation, crushing its manhood, destroying its homes, and impoverishing its life. They have so identified themselves with the philosophies they conceived and with the forces they directed that any tenderness to them is a victory and an encouragement to all the evils which are attached to their names. Civilization can afford no compromise with the social forces which would gain renewed strength if we deal ambiguously or indecisively with the men in whom those forces now precariously survive.

What these men stand for we will patiently and temperately disclose. We will give you undeniable proofs of incredible events. The catalogue of crimes will omit nothing that could be conceived by a pathological pride, cruelty, and lust for power. These men created in Germany, under the *Fuehrerprinzip*, a National Socialist despotism equalled only by the dynasties of the ancient East. They took from the German people all those dignities and freedoms that we hold natural and inalienable rights in every human being. The people were compensated by inflaming and gratifying hatreds toward those who were marked as "scape-goats." Against their opponents, including Jews, Catholics, and free labor the Nazis directed such a campaign of arrogance, brutality, and annihilation as the world has not witnessed since the pre-Christian ages. They excited the German ambition to be a "master race," which of course implies serfdom for others. They led their people on a mad gamble for domination. They diverted social energies and resources to the creation of what they thought to be an invincible war machine. They overran their neighbors. To sustain the "master race" in its [war-making], they enslaved millions of human beings and brought them into Germany, where these hapless creatures now wander as "displaced persons." At length bestiality and bad faith reached such excess that they aroused the sleeping strength of imperiled civilization. Its united efforts have ground the German war machine to fragments. But the struggle has left Europe a liberated yet prostrate land where a demoralized society struggles to survive. These are the fruits of the sinister forces that sit with these defendants in the prisoners' dock.

In justice to the nations and the men associated in this prosecution, I must remind you of certain difficulties which may leave their mark on this case. Never before in legal history has an effort been made to bring within the scope of a single litigation the developments of a decade, covering a whole Continent, and involving a score of nations, countless individuals, and innumerable events. Despite the magnitude of the task, the world has demanded immediate action. This demand has had to be met, though perhaps at the cost of finished craftsmanship. In my country, established courts, following familiar procedures, applying well thumbed precedents, and dealing with the legal consequences of local and limited events seldom commence a trial within a year of the event in litigation. Yet less than eight months ago today the courtroom in which you sit was an enemy fortress in the hands of German SS troops. Less than eight months ago nearly all our witnesses and documents were in enemy hands. The law had not been codified, no procedure had been established, no Tribunal was in existence, no usable courthouse stood here, none of the hundreds of tons of official German documents had been examined, no prosecuting staff had been assembled, nearly all the present defendants were at large, and the four prosecuting powers had not yet joined in common cause to try them. I should be the last to deny that the case may well suffer from incomplete researches and quite likely will not be the example of professional work which any of the prosecuting nations would normally wish to sponsor. It is, however, a completely adequate case to the judgment we shall ask you to render, and its full development we shall be obliged to leave to historians.

Before I discuss particulars of evidence, some general considerations which may affect the credit of this trial in the eyes of the world should be candidly faced. There is a dramatic disparity between the circumstances of the accusers and of the accused that might discredit our work if we should falter, in even minor matters, in being fair and temperate.

Unfortunately, the nature of these crimes is such that both prosecution and judgment must be by victor nations over vanquished foes. The worldwide scope of the aggressions carried out by these men has left but few real neutrals. Either the victors must judge the vanquished or we must leave the defeated to judge themselves. After the First World War, we learned the futility of the latter course. The former high station of these defendants, the notoriety of their acts, and the adaptability of their conduct to provoke retaliation make it hard to distinguish between the demand for a just and measured retribution, and the unthinking cry for vengeance which arises from the anguish of war. It is our task, so far as humanly possible, to draw the line between the two. We must never forget that the record on which we judge these defendants today is the record on which history will judge us tomorrow. To pass these defendants a poisoned chalice is to put it to our own lips as well. We must summon such detachment and intellectual integrity to our task that this trial will commend itself to posterity as fulfilling humanity's aspirations to do justice.

At the very outset, let us dispose of the contention that to put these men to trial is to do them an injustice entitling them to some special consideration. These defendants may be hard pressed but they are not ill used. Let us see what alternative they would have to being tried.

More than a majority of these prisoners surrendered to or were tracked down by forces of the United States. Could they expect us to make American custody a shelter for our enemies against the just wrath of our Allies? Did we spend American lives to capture them only to save them from punishment? Under the principles of the Moscow Declaration, those suspected war criminals who are not to be tried internationally must be turned over to individual governments for trial at the scene of their outrages. Many less responsible and less culpable American-held prisoners have been and will be turned over to other United Nations for local trial. If these defendants should succeed, for any reason, in escaping the condemnation of this

Tribunal, or if they obstruct or abort this trial, those who are American-held prisoners will be delivered up to our continental Allies. For these defendants, however, we have set up an International Tribunal and have undertaken the burden of participating in a complicated effort to give them fair and dispassionate hearings. That is the best known protection to any man with a defense worthy of being heard.

If these men are the first war leaders of a defeated nation to be prosecuted in the name of the law, they are also the first to be given a chance to plead for their lives in the name of the law. Realistically, the Charter of this Tribunal, which gives them a hearing, is also the source of their only hope. It may be that these men of troubled conscience, whose only wish is that the world forget them, do not regard a trial as a favor. But they do have a fair opportunity to defend themselves—a favor which these men, when in power, rarely extended to their fellow countrymen. Despite the fact that public opinion already condemns their acts, we agree that here they must be given a presumption of innocence, and we accept the burden of proving criminal acts and the responsibility of these defendants for their commission.

When I say that we do not ask for convictions unless we prove crime, I do not mean mere technical or incidental transgression of international conventions. We charge guilt on planned and intended conduct that involves moral as well as legal wrong. And we do not mean conduct that is a natural and human, even if illegal, cutting of corners, such as many of us might well have committed had we been in the defendants' positions. It is not because they yielded to the normal frailties of human beings that we accuse them. It is their abnormal and inhuman conduct which brings them to this bar.

We will not ask you to convict these men on the testimony of their foes. There is no count of the Indictment that cannot be proved by books and records. The Germans were always meticulous record keepers, and these defendants had their share of the Teutonic passion for thoroughness in putting things on paper. Nor were they without vanity. They arranged frequently to be photographed in action. We will show you their own films. You will see their own conduct and hear their own voices as these defendants reenact for you,

from the screen, some of the events in the course of the conspiracy.

We would also make clear that we have no purpose to incriminate the whole German people. We know that the Nazi Party was not put in power by a majority of the German vote. We know it came to power by an evil alliance between the most extreme of the Nazi revolutionists, the most unrestrained of the German reactionaries, and the most aggressive of the German militarists. If the German populace had willingly accepted the Nazi program, no Stormtroopers would have been needed in the early days of the Party and there would have been no need for concentration camps or the Gestapo, both of which institutions were inaugurated as soon as the Nazis gained control of the German state. Only after these lawless innovations proved successful at home were they taken abroad.

The German people should know by now that the people of the United States hold them in no fear, and in no hate. It is true that the Germans have taught us the horrors of modern warfare, but the ruin that lies from the Rhine to the Danube shows that we, like our Allies, have not been dull pupils. If we are not awed by German fortitude and proficiency in war, and if we are not persuaded of their political maturity, we do respect their skill in the arts of peace, their technical competence, and the sober, industrious and self-disciplined character of the masses of the German people. In 1933, we saw the German people recovering prestige in the commercial, industrial and artistic world after the set-back of the last war. We beheld their progress neither with envy nor malice. The Nazi regime interrupted this advance. The recoil of the Nazi aggression has left Germany in ruins. The Nazi readiness to pledge the German word without hesitation and to break it without shame has fastened upon German diplomacy a reputation for duplicity that will handicap it for years. Nazi arrogance has made the boast of the "master race" a taunt that will be thrown at Germans the world over for generations. The Nazi nightmare has given the German name a new and sinister significance throughout the world which will retard Germany a century. The German, no less than the non-German world, has accounts to settle with these defendants.

The fact of the war and the course of the war, which is the central theme of our case, is history. From September 1st, 1939, when the German armies crossed the Polish frontiers, until September, 1942, when they met epic resistance at Stalingrad, German arms seemed invincible. Denmark and Norway, the Netherlands and France, Belgium and Luxembourg, the Balkans and Africa, Poland and the Baltic States, and parts of Russia, all had been overrun and conquered by swift, powerful, well-aimed blows. That attack upon the peace of the world is the crime against international society which brings into international cognizance crimes in its aid and preparation which otherwise might be only internal concerns. It was aggressive war, which the nations of the world had renounced. It was war in violation of treaties, by which the peace of the world was sought to be safeguarded.

This war did not just happen—it was planned and prepared for over a long period of time and with no small skill and cunning. The world has perhaps never seen such a concentration and stimulation of the energies of any people as that which enabled Germany twenty years after it was defeated, disarmed, and dismembered to come so near carrying out its plan to dominate Europe. Whatever else we may say of those who were the authors of this war, they did achieve a stupendous work in organization, and our first task is to examine the means by which these defendants and their fellow conspirators prepared and incited Germany to go to war.

In general, our case will disclose these defendants all uniting at some time with the Nazi Party in a plan which they well knew could be accomplished only by an outbreak of war in Europe. Their seizure of the German state, their subjugation of the German people, their terrorism and extermination of dissident elements, their planning and waging of war, their calculated and planned ruthlessness in the conduct of warfare, their deliberate and planned criminality toward conquered peoples, all these are ends for which they acted in concert; and all these are phases of the conspiracy, a conspiracy which reached one goal only to set out for another and more ambitious one. We shall also trace for you the intricate web of organizations which these men formed and utilized to accomplish these ends. We will show how the entire structure of offices and officials was dedicated to the criminal purposes and committed to use of the criminal methods planned by these defendants and their co-conspirators, many of whom war and suicide have put beyond reach.

It is my purpose to open the case, particularly under Count One of the Indictment, and to deal with the common plan or conspiracy to achieve ends possible only by resort to crimes against peace, war crimes, and crimes against humanity. My emphasis will not be on individual barbarities and perversions which may have occurred independently of any central plan. One of the dangers ever present is that this trial may be protracted by details of particular wrongs and that we will become lost in a "wilderness of single instances." Nor will I now dwell on the activity of individual defendants except as it may contribute to exposition of the common plan.

The case as presented by the United States will be concerned with the brains and authority back of all the crimes. These defendants were men of a station and rank which does not soil its own hands with blood. They were men who knew how to use lesser folk as tools. We want to reach the planners and designers, the inciters and leaders without whose evil architecture the world would not have been for so long scourged with the violence and lawlessness, and wracked with the agonies and convulsions of this terrible war.

. . .

Even the most warlike of peoples have recognized in the name of humanity some limitations on the savagery of warfare. Rules to that end have been embodied in international conventions to which Germany became a party. This code had prescribed certain restraints as to the treatment of belligerents. The enemy was entitled to surrender and to receive quarter and good treatment as a prisoner of war. We will show by German documents that these rights were denied, that prisoners of war were given brutal treatment and often murdered. This was particularly true in the case of captured airmen, often my countrymen.

. . .

Civilized usage and conventions to which Germany was a party had prescribed certain immunities for civilian populations unfortunate enough to dwell in lands overrun by hostile armies. The German occupation forces, controlled or commanded by men on trial before you, committed a long series of outrages against the inhabitants of occupied territory that would be incredible except for captured orders and the captured reports showing the fidelity with which these orders were executed.

. . .

The end of the war and capture of these prisoners presented the victorious Allies with the question whether there is any legal responsibility on high-ranking men for acts which I have described. Must such wrongs either be ignored or redressed in hot blood? Is there no standard in the law for a deliberate and reasoned judgment on such conduct?

The Charter of this Tribunal evidences a faith that the law is not only to govern the conduct of little men, but that even rulers are, as Lord Chief Justice Coke put it to King James, "under God and the law." The United States believed that the law long has afforded standards by which a juridical hearing could be conducted to make sure that we punish only the right men and for the right reasons. Following the instructions of the late President Roosevelt and the decision of the Yalta conference, President Truman directed representatives of the United States to formulate a proposed International Agreement, which was submitted during the San Francisco Conference to Foreign Ministers of the United Kingdom, the Soviet Union, and the Provisional Government of France. With many modifications, that proposal has become the Charter of this Tribunal.

But the Agreement which sets up the standards by which these prisoners are to be judged does not express the views of the signatory nations alone. Other nations with diverse but highly respected systems of jurisprudence also have signified adherence to it. These are Belgium, The Netherlands, Denmark, Norway, Czechoslovakia, Luxembourg, Poland, Greece, Yugoslavia, Ethiopia, Australia, Haiti, Honduras, Panama, New Zealand, Venezuela, and India. You judge, therefore, under an organic act which represents the wisdom, the sense of justice, and the will of twenty-one governments, representing an overwhelming majority of all civilized people.

The Charter by which this Tribunal has its being embodies certain legal concepts which are inseparable from its jurisdiction and which must govern its decision. These, as I have said, also are conditions attached to the grant of any hearing to defendants. The validity of the provisions of the Charter is conclusive upon us all whether we have accepted the duty of judging or of prosecuting under it, as well as upon the defendants, who can point to no other law which gives them a right to be heard at all. My able and experienced colleagues believe, as do I, that it will contribute to the expedition and clarity of this trial if I expound briefly the application of the legal philosophy of the Charter to the facts I have recited.

While this declaration of the law by the Charter is final, it may be contended that the prisoners on trial are entitled to have it applied to their conduct only most charitably if at all. It may be said that this is new law, not authoritatively declared at the time they did the acts it condemns, and that this declaration of the law has taken them by surprise.

I cannot, of course, deny that these men are surprised that this is the law; they really are surprised that there is any such thing as law. These defendants did not rely on any law at all. Their program ignored and defied all law. That this is so will appear from many acts and statements, of which I cite but a few. In the Fuehrer's speech to all military commanders on November 23, 1939, he reminded them that at the moment Germany had a pact with Russia, but declared, "Agreements are to be kept only as long as they serve a certain purpose." Later on in the same speech he announced, "A violation of the neutrality of Holland and Belgium will be of no importance" (*789-PS*). A Top Secret document, entitled "Warfare as a Problem of Organization," dispatched by the Chief of the High Command to all Commanders on April 19, 1938, declared that "the normal rules of war toward neutrals may be considered to apply on the basis whether operation of rules will create greater advantages or disadvantages for belligerents" (*L-211*). And from the files of the German Navy Staff, we have a "Memorandum on Intensified Naval War," dated October 15, 1939, which begins by stating a desire to comply with International Law. "However," it continues, "if decisive successes are expected from any measure considered as a war necessity, it must be carried through even if it is not in agreement with international law" (*UK-65*). International Law, natural law, German law, any law at all was to these men simply a propaganda device to be invoked when it helped and to be ignored when it would condemn what they wanted to do. That men may be protected in relying upon the law at the time they act is the reason we find laws of retrospective operation unjust. But these men cannot bring themselves within the reason of the rule which in some systems of jurisprudence prohibits *ex post facto* laws. They cannot show that they ever relied upon International Law in any state or paid it the slightest regard.

The Third Count of the Indictment is based on the definition of war crimes contained in the Charter. I have outlined to you the systematic course of conduct toward civilian populations and combat forces which violates international conventions to which Germany was a party. Of the criminal nature of these acts at least, the defendants had, as we shall show, clear knowledge. Accordingly, they took pains to conceal their violations. It will appear that the defendants Keitel and Jodl were informed by official legal advisors that the orders to brand Russian prisoners of war, to shackle British prisoners of war, and to execute commando prisoners were clear violations of International Law. Nevertheless, these orders were put into effect. The same is true of orders issued for the assassination of General Giraud and General Weygand, which failed to be executed only because of a ruse on the part of Admiral Canaris, who was himself later executed for his part in the plot to take Hitler's life on July 20, 1944 (*Affidavit A*).

The Fourth Count of the Indictment is based on crimes against humanity. Chief among these are mass killings of countless human beings in cold blood. Does it take these men by surprise that murder is treated as a crime?

The First and Second Counts of the Indictment add to these crimes the crime of plotting and waging wars of aggression and wars in violation of nine treaties to which Germany was a party. There was a time, in fact I think the time of the [F]irst World War, when it could not have been said that war-inciting or war-making was a crime in law, however reprehensible in morals.

Of course, it was under the law of all civilized peoples a crime for one man with his bare knuckles to assault another. How did it come that multiplying this crime by a million, and adding fire arms to bare knuckles, made a legally innocent act? The doctrine was that one could not be regarded as criminal for committing the usual violent acts in the conduct of legitimate warfare. The age of imperialistic expansion during the Eighteenth and Nineteenth Centuries added the foul doctrine, contrary to the teachings of early Christian and International Law scholars such as Grotius, that all wars are to be regarded as legitimate wars. The sum of these two doctrines was to give [war-making] a complete immunity from accountability to law.

This was intolerable for an age that called itself civilized. Plain people, with their earthly common sense, revolted at such fictions and legalisms so contrary to ethical principles and demanded checks on war immunity. Statesmen and international lawyers at first cautiously responded by adopting rules of warfare designed to make the conduct of war more civilized. The effort was to set legal limits to the violence that could be done to civilian populations and to combatants as well.

The common sense of men after the First World War demanded, however, that the law's condemnation of war reach deeper, and that the law condemn not merely uncivilized ways of waging war, but also the waging in any way of uncivilized wars—wars of aggression. The world's statesmen again went only as far as they were forced to go. Their efforts were timid and cautious and often less explicit than we might have hoped. But the 1920's did outlaw aggressive war.

The reestablishment of the principle that there are unjust wars and that unjust wars are illegal is traceable in many steps. One of the most significant is the Briand-Kellogg Pact of 1928, by which Germany, Italy, and Japan, in common with practically all the nations of the world, renounced war as an instrument of national policy, bound themselves to seek the settlement of disputes only by pacific means, and condemned recourse to war for the solution of international controversies. This pact altered the legal status of a war of aggression. As Mr. Stimson, the United States Secretary of State put it in 1932, such a war "is no longer to be the source and subject of rights. It is no longer to be the principle around which the duties, the conduct, and the rights of nations revolve. It is an illegal thing. . . . By that very act, we have made obsolete many legal precedents and have given the legal profession the task of reexamining many of its codes and treaties."

The Geneva Protocol of 1924 for the Pacific Settlement of International Disputes, signed by the representatives of forty-eight governments, declared that "a war of aggression constitutes . . . an international crime." The Eighth Assembly of the League of Nations in 1927, on unanimous resolution of the representatives of forty-eight member nations, including Germany, declared that a war of aggression constitutes an international crime. At the Sixth Pan-American Conference of 1928, the twenty-one American Republics unanimously adopted a resolution stating that "[a] war of aggression constitutes an international crime against the human species."

A failure of these Nazis to heed, or to understand the force and meaning of this evolution in the legal thought of the world is not a defense or a mitigation. If anything, it aggravates their offense and makes it the more mandatory that the law they have flouted be vindicated by juridical application to their lawless conduct. Indeed, by their own law—had they heeded any law—these principles were binding on these defendants. Article 4 of the Weimar Constitution provided that "The generally accepted rules of international law are to be considered as binding integral parts of the law of the German Reich" (*2050-PS*). Can there by any doubt that the outlawry of aggressive war was one of the "generally accepted rules of international law" in 1939?

Any resort to war—to any kind of a war—is a resort to means that are inherently criminal. War inevitably is a course of killings, assaults, deprivations of liberty, and destruction of property. An honestly defensive war is, of course, legal and saves those lawfully conducting it from criminality. But inherently criminal acts cannot be defended by showing that those who committed them were engaged in a war, when war itself is illegal. The very minimum legal consequence of the treaties making aggressive wars illegal is to strip those who incite or wage them of every defense the law ever gave,

and to leave warmakers subject to judgment by the usually accepted principles of the law of crimes.

But if it be thought that the Charter, whose declarations concededly bind us all, does contain new law I still do not shrink from demanding its strict application by this Tribunal. The rule of law in the world, flouted by the lawlessness incited by these defendants, had to be restored at the cost to my country of over a million casualties, not to mention those of other nations. I cannot subscribe to the perverted reasoning that society may advance and strengthen the rule of law by the expenditure of morally innocent lives but that progress in the law may never be made at the price of morally guilty lives.

It is true, of course, that we have no judicial precedent for the Charter. But International Law is more than a scholarly collection of abstract and immutable principles. It is an outgrowth of treaties and agreements between nations and of accepted customs. Yet every custom has its origin in some single act, and every agreement has to be initiated by the action of some state. Unless we are prepared to abandon every principle of growth for International Law, we cannot deny that our own day has the right to institute customs and to conclude agreements that will themselves become sources of a newer and strengthened International Law. International Law is not capable of development by the normal processes of legislative authority. Innovations and revisions in International Law are brought about by the action of governments designed to meet a change in circumstances. It grows, as did the Common Law, through decisions reached from time to time in adapting settled principles to new situations. The fact is that when the law evolves by the case method, as did the Common Law and as International Law must do if it is to advance at all, it advances at the expense of those who wrongly guessed the law and learned too late their error. The law, so far as International Law can be decreed, had been clearly pronounced when these acts took place. Hence, I am not disturbed by the lack of judicial precedent for the inquiry we propose to conduct.

3. Nuremberg: A Fair Trial?

CHARLES E. WYZANSKI, JR.

1

The Nuremberg War Trial has a strong claim to be considered the most significant as well as the most debatable event since the conclusion of hostilities. To those who support the trial it promises the first effective recognition of a world law for the punishment of malefactors who start wars or conduct them in bestial fashion. To the adverse critics the trial appears in many aspects a negation of principles which they regard as the heart of any system of justice under law.

This sharp division of opinion has not been fully aired largely because it relates to an issue of foreign policy upon which this nation has already acted and on which debate may seem useless or, worse, merely to impair this country's prestige and power abroad. Moreover, to the casual newspaper reader the long-range implications of the trial are not obvious. He sees most clearly that there are in the dock a score of widely known men who plainly deserve punishment. And he is pleased to note that four victorious nations, who have not been unanimous on all post-war questions, have, by a miracle of administrative skill, united in a proceeding that is overcoming the obstacles of varied languages, professional habits, and legal traditions. But the more profound observer is aware that the foundations of the Nuremberg trial may mark a watershed of modern law.

Before I come to the discussion of the legal and political questions involved, let me make it clear that nothing I may say about the Nuremberg trial should be construed as a suggestion that the individual Nuremberg defendants or others who have done grievous wrongs should be set at liberty. In my opinion there are valid reasons why several thousand Germans, including many defendants at Nuremberg, should either by death or by imprisonment be permanently removed from civilized society. If prevention, deterrence, retribution, nay even vengeance are ever adequate motives for punitive action, then punitive action is justified against a substantial number of Germans. But the question is: Upon what theory may that action properly be taken?

The starting point is the indictment of October 18, 1945, charging some twenty individuals and various organizations, in four counts, with conspiracy, crimes against peace, war crimes, and crimes against humanity. Let me examine the offenses that are called in Count 3 of the indictment "war crimes," in the strict sense.

It is sometimes said that there is no international law of war crimes. But most jurists would agree that there is at least an abbreviated list of war crimes upon which the nations of the world have agreed. Thus in Articles 46 and 47 of the Hague Convention of 1907, the United States and many other countries accepted the rules that in an occupied territory of a hostile state "family honour and rights, the lives of persons, and private property, as well as religious conviction and practice, must be respected. Private property cannot be confiscated. Pillage is formally forbidden." And consistently the Supreme Court of the United States has recognized that rules of this character are part of our law. In short, there can be no doubt of the legal right of this nation prior to the signing of a peace treaty to use a military tribunal for the purpose of trying and punishing a German if, as Count 3 charges, in occupied territory he murdered a Polish civilian, or tortured a Czech, or raped a Frenchwoman, or robbed a Belgian. Moreover, there is no doubt of the military tribunal's parallel right to try and to punish a German

From *The Atlantic Monthly*, Vol. 177 (April 1946), pp. 66–70. Reprinted with permission of *The Atlantic Monthly* and the Wyzanski Estate.

if he has murdered, tortured, or maltreated a prisoner of war.

In connection with war crimes of this sort there is only one question of law worth discussing here: Is it a defense to a soldier or civilian defendant that he acted under the order of a superior?

The defense of superior orders is, upon the authorities, an open question. Without going into details, it may be said that superior orders have never been recognized as a complete defense by German, Russian, or French law, and that they have not been so recognized by civilian courts in the United States or the British Commonwealth of Nations, but they tend to be taken as a complete excuse by Anglo-American military manuals. In this state of the authorities, if the International Military Tribunal in connection with a charge of a war crime refuses to recognize superior orders as a defense, it will not be making a retroactive determination or applying an *ex post facto* law. It will be merely settling an open question of law as every court frequently does.

The refusal to recognize the superior-order defense not only is not repugnant to the *ex post facto* principle, but is consonant with our ideas of justice. Basically, we cannot admit that military efficiency is the paramount consideration. And we cannot even admit that individual self-preservation is the highest value. This is not a new question. Just as it is settled that X is guilty of murder if, in order that he and Y, who are adrift on a raft, may not die of starvation, he kills their companion, Z; so a German soldier is guilty of murder if, in order that he may not be shot for disobedience and his wife tortured in a concentration camp, he shoots a Catholic priest. This is hard doctrine, but the law cannot recognize as an absolute excuse for a killing that the killer was acting under compulsion—for such a recognition not only would leave the structure of society at the mercy of criminals of sufficient ruthlessness, but also would place the cornerstone of justice on the quicksand of self-interest.

Of course, there always remains the fundamental separateness of the problem of guilt and the problem of treatment. And no one would expect a tribunal to mete out its severest penalty to a defendant who yielded to wrongdoing only out of fear of loss of his life or his family's.

2

In addition to "war crimes," the indictment, in Count 4, charges the defendants with "crimes against humanity." This count embraces the murder, torture, and persecution of minority groups, such as Jews, inside Germany both before and after the outbreak of war. It is alleged in paragraph X of the indictment that these wrongs "constituted violations of international conventions, of internal penal laws, of the general principles of criminal law as derived from the criminal law of all civilized nations and were involved in and part of a systematic course of conduct."

I shall pass for the time being the last phrase just quoted, for that is merely a way of saying that the Nazis persecuted the minority German groups to harden the German will for aggression and to develop an issue that would divide other countries. In other words, the legal validity of that phrase rests upon the same considerations as the validity of the charge of "crimes against the peace."

I consider first the legal validity of the other phrases upon which is premised the charge that murdering, torturing, and persecuting German Jews and other non-Nazis from 1933 to 1939 as well as from 1939 to 1945 are crimes. And before I say anything of the legal question, let me make it abundantly clear that as a human being I regard these murders, tortures, and persecutions as being morally quite as repugnant and loathsome as the murders, tortures, and persecutions of the civilian and military personnel of American and Allied nations.

In paragraph X of the indictment, reference is first made to "international conventions." There is no citation of any particular international convention which in explicit words forbids a state or its inhabitants to murder its own citizens, in time either of war or of peace. I know of no such convention. And I, therefore, conclude that when the draftsman of the indictment used the phrase "international conventions" he was using the words loosely and almost analogously with the other phrase, "general principles of criminal law as derived from the criminal law of all civilized nations." He means to say that there exists, to cover the most atrocious conduct, a broad principle of universal international criminal law which is according to the law of most penal codes and public sentiment in most places, and for violations of which an offender may be tried by any new court that one or more of the world powers may create.

If that were the only basis for the trial and punishment of those who murdered or tortured German citizens, it would be a basis that would not satisfy most lawyers. It would resemble the universally condemned Nazi law of June 28, 1935, which provided: "Any person who commits an act which the law declares to be punishable or which is deserving of penalty according to the fundamental conceptions of the penal law and sound popular feeling, shall be punished." It would fly straight in the face of the most fundamental rules of criminal justice—that criminal laws shall not be *ex post facto* and that there shall be *nullum crimen et nulla poena sine lege*—no crime and no penalty without an antecedent law.

The feeling against a law evolved after the commission of an offense is deeply rooted. Demosthenes and Cicero knew the evil of retroactive laws: philosophers as diverse as Hobbes and Locke declared their hostility to it; and virtually every constitutional government has some prohibition of *ex post facto* legislation, often in the very words of Magna Carta, or Article I of the United States Constitution, or Article 8 of the French Declaration of Rights. The antagonism to *ex post facto* laws is not based on a lawyer's prejudice encased in a Latin maxim. It rests on the political truth that if a law can be created after an offense, then power is to that extent absolute and arbitrary. To allow retroactive legislation is to disparage the principle of constitutional limitation. It is to abandon what is usually regarded as one of the essential values at the core of our democratic faith.

But, fortunately, so far as concerns murders of German minorities, the indictment was not required to invent new law. The indictment specifically mentions "internal penal laws." And these laws are enough in view of the way the question would arise in a criminal proceeding.

Under universally accepted principles of law, an occupying belligerent power may and indeed often does establish its own tribunals to administer the domestic law of the occupied country for the in-habitants. Thus if Adolph killed Berthold before the American Army occupied Munich, it would be normal for the United States government to set up a military tribunal to try and to punish Adolph.

But suppose Adolph raised as a defense the contention that he was acting pursuant to orders from superiors which were the law of Germany. If that defense were raised, and if we assume (contrary to what some German jurists tell us) that in Germany there were on the statute books pertinent exculpatory laws, nonetheless under well-known principles of German law, going back to the Middle Ages and differing from current Anglo-American theories, the superior order could be disregarded by a court applying German law, on the ground that it was so repugnant to "natural law" as to be void. That is, perhaps a German tribunal or one applying German law can disregard an obviously outrageous statute or executive order as offensive to natural law just as the Supreme Court of the United States can disregard a statute or executive order as offensive to the United States Constitution.

But further suppose that Adolph raised as a defense the point that the wrong was so old as to be barred by some statute of limitations. If there is such a statute in Germany, the limitation may be set aside without involving any violation of the *ex post facto* principle. As our own Supreme Court has pointed out, to set aside a statute of limitation is not to create a new offense.

3

I turn now to Count 2 of the indictment, which charges "crimes against peace." This is the count that has attracted greatest interest. It alleges that the defendants participated "in the planning, preparation, initiation and waging of wars of aggression, which were also wars in violation of international treaties, agreements and assurances."

This charge is attacked in many quarters on the ground it rests on *ex post facto* law. The reply has been that in the last generation there has accumulated a mounting body of international sentiment which indicates that wars of aggression are wrong and that a killing by a person acting on behalf of an aggressor power is not an excusable homicide. Reference is made not only to the Briand-Kellogg Pact of August 27, 1928, but to deliberations of the League of Nations in 1924 and subsequent years—all of which are said to show an increasing awareness of a new standard of conduct. Specific treaties outlawing wars of aggression are cited. And, having regard to the manner by which all early criminal law evolves and the manner by which international law grows, it is claimed that now it is unlawful to wage an aggressive war and it is criminal to aid in preparing for such a war, whether by political, military, financial, or industrial means.

One difficulty with that reply is that the body of growing custom to which reference is made is custom directed at sovereign states, not at individuals. There is no convention or treaty which places obligations explicitly upon an individual not to aid in waging an aggressive war. Thus, from the point of view of the individual, the charge of a "crime against peace" appears in one aspect like a retroactive law. At the time he acted, almost all informed jurists would have told him that individuals who engaged in aggressive war were not in the legal sense criminals.

Another difficulty is the possible bias of the Tribunal in connection with Count 2. Unlike the crimes in Counts 3 and 4, Count 2 charges a political crime. The crime which is asserted is tried not before a dispassionate neutral bench, but before the very persons alleged to be victims. There is not even one neutral sitting beside them.

And what is most serious is that there is doubt as to the sincerity of our belief that all wars of aggression are crimes. A question may be raised whether the United Nations are prepared to submit to scrutiny the attack of Russia on Poland, or on Finland, or the American encouragement to the Russians to break their treaty with Japan. Every one of these actions may have been proper, but we hardly admit that they are subject to international judgment.

These considerations make the second count of the Nuremberg indictment look to be of uncertain foundation and uncertain limits. To some the count may appear as nothing more than the ancient rule that the vanquished are at the mercy of the victor. To others it may appear as the mere declaration of

an always latent doctrine that the leaders of a nation are subject to outside judgment as to their motives in waging war.

The other feature of the Nuremberg indictment is Count 1, charging a "conspiracy." Paragraph III of the indictment alleges that the "conspiracy embraced the commission of Crimes against Peace; . . . it came to embrace the commission of War Crimes . . . and Crimes against Humanity."

In international as well as in national law there may be for almost any crime what the older lawyers would have called principal offenders and accessories. If Adolph is determined to kill Sam, and talks the matter over with Berthold, Carl, and Dietrich, and Berthold agrees to borrow the money to buy a pistol, and Carl agrees to make a holster for the pistol, and all of them proceed as planned and then Adolph gives the pistol and holster to Dietrich, who goes out alone and actually shoots Sam without excuse, then, of course, Adolph, Berthold, Carl, and Dietrich are all guilty of murder. They should not be allowed to escape with the plea Macbeth offered for Banquo's murder, "Thou canst not say I did it."

If the conspiracy charge in Count 1 meant no more than that those are guilty who plan a murder and with knowledge finance and equip the murderer, no one would quarrel with the count. But it would appear that Count 1 means to establish some additional separate substantive offense of conspiracy. That is, it asserts that there is in international law a wrong which consists in acting together for an unlawful end, and that he who joins in that action is liable not only for what he planned, or participated in, or could reasonably have foreseen would happen, but is liable for what every one of his fellows did in the course of the conspiracy. Almost as broad a doctrine of conspiracy exists in municipal law.

But what is the basis for asserting so broad a substantive crime exists in international law? Where is the treaty, the custom, the academic learning on which it is based? Is this not a type of "crime" which was first described and defined either in London or in Nuremberg sometime in the year 1945?

Aside from the fact that the notion is new, is it not fundamentally unjust? The crime of conspiracy was originally developed by the Court of Star Chamber on the theory that any unlicensed joint action of private persons was a threat to the public, and so if the action was in any part unlawful it was all unlawful. The analogies of the municipal law of conspiracy therefore seem out of place in considering for international purposes the effect of joint political action. After all, in a government or other large social community there exists among the top officials, civilian and military, together with their financial and industrial collaborators, a kind of overall working arrangement which may always be looked upon, if its invidious connotation be disregarded, as a "conspiracy." That is, government implies "breathing together." And is everyone who, knowing the purposes of the party in power, participates in government or joins with officials to be held for every act of the government?

To take a case which is perhaps not so obvious, is everyone who joins a political party, even one with some illegal purposes, to be held liable to the world for the action that every member takes, even if that action is not declared in the party platform and was not known to or consented to by the person charged as a wrongdoer? To put upon any individual such responsibility for action of the group seems literally to step back in history to a point before the prophet Ezekiel and to reject the more recent religious and democratic teachings that guilt is personal.

4

Turning now from the legal basis of the indictment, I propose briefly to consider whether, quite apart from legal technicalities, the procedure of an international military tribunal on the Nuremberg pattern is a politically acceptable way of dealing with the offenders in the dock and those others whom we may legitimately feel should be punished.

The chief arguments usually given for this quasi-judicial trial are that it gives the culprits a chance to say anything that can be said on their behalf, that it gives both the world today and the world tomorrow a chance to see the justice of the Allied cause and the wickedness of the [Nazis] and that it sets a firm foundation for a future world

order wherein individuals will know that if they embark on schemes of aggression or murder or torture or persecution they will be severely dealt with by the world.

The first argument has some merit. The defendants, after hearing and seeing the evidence against them, will have an opportunity without torture and with the aid of counsel to make statements on their own behalf. For us and for them this opportunity will make the proceeding more convincing. Yet the defendants will not have the right to make the type of presentation that at least English-speaking persons have thought the indispensable concomitant of a fair trial. No one expects that Ribbentrop will be allowed to summon Molotov to disprove the charge that in invading Poland Germany started an aggressive war. No one anticipates that the defense, if it has the evidence, will be given as long a time to present its evidence as the prosecution takes. And there is nothing more foreign to those proceedings than either the presumption that the defendants are innocent until proved guilty or the doctrine that any adverse public comment on the defendants before the verdict is prejudicial to their receiving a fair trial. The basic approach is that these men should not have a chance to go free. And that being so, they ought not to be tried in a court of law.

As to the second point, one objection is purely pragmatic. There is a reasonable doubt whether this kind of trial, despite the voluminous and accessible record it makes, persuades anyone. It brings out new evidence, but does it change men's minds? Most reporters say that the Germans are neither interested in nor persuaded by these proceedings, which they regard as partisan. They regard the proceedings not as marking a rebirth of law in Central Europe but as a political judgment on their former leaders. The same attitude may prevail in future because of the departure from accepted legal standards.

A more profound objection to the second point is that to regard a trial as a propaganda device is to debase justice. To be sure, most trials do and should incidentally educate the public. Yet any judge knows that if he, or counsel, or the parties regard a trial primarily as a public demonstration, or even as a general inquest, then there enter considerations which would otherwise be regarded as improper. In a political inquiry and even more in the spread of propaganda, the appeal is likely to be to the unreflecting thought and the deep-seated emotions of the crowd, untrammeled by any fixed standards. The objective is to create outside the courtroom a desired state of affairs. In a trial the appeal is to the disinterested judgment of reasonable men guided by established precepts. The objective is to make inside the courtroom a sound disposition of a pending case according to settled principles.

The argument that these trials set a firm foundation for a future world legal structure is perhaps debatable. The spectacle of individual liability for a world wrong may lead to future treaties and agreements specifying individual liability. If this were the outcome and if, for example, with respect to wars of aggression, war crimes, and use of atomic energy the nations should agree upon world rules establishing individual liability, then this would be a great gain. But it is by no means clear that this trial will further any such program.

At the moment, the world is most impressed by the undeniable dignity and efficiency of the proceedings and by the horrible events recited in the testimony. But, upon reflection, the informed public may be disturbed by the repudiation of widely accepted concepts of legal justice. It may see too great a resemblance between this proceeding and others which we ourselves have condemned. If in the end there is a generally accepted view that Nuremberg was an example of high politics masquerading as law, then the trial instead of promoting may retard the coming of the day of world law.

Quite apart from the effect of the Nuremberg trial upon the particular defendants involved, there is the disturbing effect of the trial upon domestic justice here and abroad. "We but teach bloody instructions, which, being taught, return to plague the inventor." Our acceptance of the notions of *ex post facto* law and group guilt blunt much of our criticism of Nazi law. Indeed our complaisance may mark the beginning of an age of reaction in constitutionalism in particular and of law in general. Have we forgotten that law is not power, but restraint on power?

If the Nuremberg trial of the leading Nazis should never have been undertaken, it does not follow that we should not have punished these men. It would have been consistent with our philosophy and our law to have disposed of such of the defendants as were in the ordinary sense murderers by individual, routine, undramatic military trials. This was the course proposed in the speeches of the Archbishop of York, Viscount Cecil, Lord Wright, and others in the great debate of March 20, 1945, in the House of Lords. In such trials the evidence and the legal issues would have a stark simplicity and the lesson would be inescapable.

For those who were not chargeable with ordinary crimes but only with political crimes such as planning an aggressive war, would it not have been better to proceed by an executive determination—that is, a proscription directed at certain named individuals? The form of the determination need not have been absolute on its face. It might have been a summary order reciting the offense and allowing the named persons to show cause why they should not be punished, thus giving them a chance to show any mistake of identification or gross mistake of fact.

There are precedents for such executive determination in the cases of Napoleon and of the Boxer rebels. Such a disposition would avoid the inevitably misleading characteristics of the present proceedings, such as a charge presented in the form of an "indictment," the participation of celebrated civil judges and the legal formalities of rulings on evidence and on law. It is these characteristics which may make the Nuremberg trial such a potential danger to law everywhere. Moreover, if it were generally felt that we ought not to take a man's life without the form of a trial, then the executive determination could be limited to imprisonment. The example of Napoleon shows that our consciences would have no reason to be disturbed about the removal from society and the permanent detention of irresponsible men who are a threat to the peace of the world.

To be sure, such an executive determination is *ex post facto*. Indeed, it is a bill of attainder. To be sure, it is also an exhibition of power and not of restraint. But its very merit is its naked and unassumed character. It confesses itself to be not legal justice but political. The truthful facing of the character of our action would make it more certain that the case would not become a precedent in domestic law.

As Lord Digby said in 1641 regarding the Strafford bill of attainder, "There is in Parliament a double Power of Life and Death by Bill, a Judicial Power, and a legislative; the measure of the one, is what is legally just; of the other, what is Prudentially and Politickly fit for the good and preservation of the whole. But these two, under favour, are not to be confounded in Judgment: We must not piece up want of legality with matter of convenience, nor the defailance of prudential fitness with a pretense of Legal Justice."

This emphasis on procedural regularity is not legalistic or, as it is sometimes now said, conceptualistic. If there is one axiom that emerges clearly from the history of constitutionalism and from the study of any bill of rights or any charter of freedom, it is that procedural safeguards are the very substance of the liberties we cherish. Not only the specific guarantees with respect to criminal trials, but the general promise of "due process of law,"

have always been phrased and interpreted primarily in their procedural aspect. Indeed it hardly lies in the mouth of any supporter of the Nuremberg proceedings to disparage such procedural considerations; for may it not be said that the reason that the authors of those proceedings cast them in the form of a trial was to persuade the public that the customary safeguards and liberties were preserved?

It is against this deceptive appearance, big with evil consequences for law everywhere, that as a matter of civil courage all of us, judges as well as lawyers and laymen, however silent we ordinarily are, ought to speak out. It is for their silence on such matters that we justly criticize the Germans. And it is the test of our sincere belief in justice under law never to allow it to be confused with what are merely our interest, our ingenuity, and our power.

---

4. *Report of the* U.N. *Secretary General: War Crimes Tribunal for the Former Yugoslavia*

United Nations Security Council

Introduction

By paragraph 1 of resolution 808 (1993) of 22 February 1993, the Security Council decided "that an international tribunal shall be established for the prosecution of persons responsible for serious viola-

S/25704

3 May 1993, Report of the Secretary-General pursuant to Paragraph 2 of Security Council Resolution 808 (1993).

tions of international humanitarian law committed in the territory of the former Yugoslavia since 1991".

By paragraph 2 of the resolution, the Secretary-General was requested "to submit for consideration by the Council at the earliest possible date, and if possible no later than 60 days after the adoption of the present resolution, a report on all aspects of this matter, including specific proposals and where appropriate options for the effective and expeditious implementation of the decision (to establish an international tribunal), taking into account suggestions put forward in this regard by Member States."

The present report is presented pursuant to that request.

Resolution 808 (1993) represents a further step taken by the Security Council in a series of resolutions concerning serious violations of international humanitarian law occurring in the territory of the former Yugoslavia.

. . .

In resolution 771 (1992) of 13 August 1992, the Security Council expressed grave alarm at continuing reports of widespread violations of international humanitarian law occurring within the territory of the former Yugoslavia and especially in Bosnia and Herzegovina, including reports of mass forcible expulsion and deportation of civilians, imprisonment and abuse of civilians in detention centres, deliberate attacks on non-combatants, hospitals and ambulances, impeding the delivery of food and medical supplies to the civilian population, and wanton devastation and destruction of property. The Council strongly condemned any violations of international humanitarian law, including those involved in the practice of "ethnic cleansing," and demanded that all parties to the conflict in the former Yugoslavia cease and desist from all breaches of international humanitarian law. It called upon States and international humanitarian organizations to collate substantiated information relating to the violations of humanitarian law, including grave breaches of the Geneva Conventions, being committed in the territory of the former Yugoslavia and to make this information available to the Council.

. . .

The Security Council's decision in resolution 808 (1993) to establish an international tribunal is circumscribed in scope and purpose: the prosecution of persons responsible for serious violations of international humanitarian law committed in the territory of the former Yugoslavia since 1991.

. . .

It should be pointed out that, in assigning to the International Tribunal the task of prosecuting persons responsible for serious violations of international humanitarian law, the Security Council would not be creating or purporting to "legislate" that law. Rather, the International Tribunal would have the task of applying existing international humanitarian law.

. . .

Competence of the International Tribunal

Competence Ratione Materiae (Subject-Matter Jurisdiction)

According to paragraph 1 of resolution 808 (1993), the international tribunal shall prosecute persons responsible for serious violations of international humanitarian law committed in the territory of the former Yugoslavia since 1991. This body of law exists in the form of both conventional law and customary law. While there is international customary law which is not laid down in conventions, some of the major conventional humanitarian law has become part of customary international law.

In the view of the Secretary-General, the application of the principle *nullum crimen sine lege* requires that the international tribunal should apply rules of international humanitarian law which are beyond any doubt part of customary law so that the problem of adherence of some but not all States to specific conventions does not arise. This would appear to be particularly important in the context of an international tribunal prosecuting persons responsible for serious violations of international humanitarian law.

The part of conventional international humanitarian law which has beyond doubt become part of international customary law is the law applicable in armed conflict as embodied in: the Geneva Conventions of 12 August 1949 for the Protection of War Victims;[1] the Hague Convention (IV) Respecting the Laws and Customs of War on Land and the Regulations annexed thereto of 18 October 1907;[2] the Convention on the Prevention and Punishment of the Crime of Genocide of 9 December 1948;[3] and the Charter of the International Military Tribunal of 8 August 1945.[4]

. . .

The Geneva Conventions constitute rules of international humanitarian law and provide the core of the customary law applicable in international armed conflicts. These Conventions regulate the conduct of war from the humanitarian perspective by protecting certain categories of persons: namely, wounded and sick members of armed forces in the field; wounded, sick and shipwrecked members of armed forces at sea; prisoners of war, and civilians in time of war.

Each Convention contains a provision listing the particularly serious violations that qualify as "grave breaches" or war crimes. Persons committing or ordering grave breaches are subject to trial and punishment. The lists of grave breaches contained in the Geneva Conventions are reproduced in the article which follows.

The Security Council has reaffirmed on several occasions that persons who commit or order the commission of grave breaches of the 1949 Geneva Conventions in the territory of the former Yugoslavia are individually responsible for such breaches as serious violations of international humanitarian law.

. . .

The Nürnberg Tribunal recognized that many of the provisions contained in the Hague Regulations, although innovative at the time of their adoption were, by 1939, recognized by all civilized nations and were regarded as being declaratory of the laws and customs of war. The Nürnberg Tribunal also recognized that war crimes defined in article 6(b) of the Nürnberg Charter were already recognized as war crimes under international law, and covered in the Hague Regulations, for which guilty individuals were punishable.

Crimes against humanity were first recognized in the Charter and Judgement of the Nürnberg Tribunal, as well as in Law No. 10 of the Control Council for Germany. Crimes against humanity are aimed at any civilian population and are prohibited regardless of whether they are committed in an armed conflict, international or internal in character.[5]

Crimes against humanity refer to inhumane acts of a very serious nature, such as wilful killing, torture or rape, committed as part of a widespread or systematic attack against any civilian population on national, political, ethnic, racial or religious grounds. In the conflict in the territory of the former Yugoslavia, such inhumane acts have taken the form of so-called "ethnic cleansing" and widespread and systematic rape and other forms of sexual assault, including enforced prostitution.

Endnotes

[1] Convention for the Amelioration of the Condition of the Wounded and Sick in Armed Forces in the Field of 12 August 1949, Convention for the Amelioration of the Condition of the Wounded, Sick and Shipwrecked Members of Armed Forces at Sea of 12 August 1949, Convention relative to the Treatment of Prisoners of War of 12 August 1949, Convention relative to the Protection of Civilian persons in Time of War of 12 August 1949 (United Nations, *Treaty Series*, vol. 75, No. 970-973).

[2] Carnegie Endowment for International Peace, *The Hague Conventions and Declarations of 1899 and 1907* (New York, Oxford University Press, 1915), p. 100.

[3] United Nations, *Treaty Series*, vol. 78, No. 1021.

[4] The Agreement for the Prosecution and Punishment of the Major War Criminals of the European Axis, signed at London on 8 August 1945 (United Nations, *Treaty Series*, vol. 82, No. 251); see also Judgement of the International Military Tribunal for the Prosecution and Punishment of the Major War Criminals of the European Axis (United States Government Printing Office, *Nazi Conspiracy and Aggression, Opinion and Judgement*) and General Assembly resolution 95 (I) of 11 December 1946 on the Affirmation of the Principles of International Law Recognized by the Charter of the Nürnberg Tribunal.

[5] In this context, it is to be noted that the International Court of Justice has recognized that the prohibitions contained in common article 3 of the 1949 Geneva Conventions are based on "elementary considerations of humanity" and cannot be breached in an armed conflict, regardless of whether it is international or internal in character. *Case concerning Military and Paramilitary Activities in and against Nicaragua (Nicaragua v. United States of America), Judgement of 27 June 1986: I. C. J. Reports 1986*, p. 114.

5. *The Dilemmas of Transitional Justice*

Neil J. Kritz

. . . In recent years, particularly during the past decade, there has been a remarkable movement in various regions of the world away from undemocratic and repressive rule towards the establishment of constitutional democracies.

In nearly all instances, the displaced regimes were characterized by massive violations of human rights and undemocratic systems of governance. In their attempt to combat real or perceived opposition, they exercised authority with very little regard to accountability. . . .

Ironically, the advent of democracy has also put the welcome endeavors for national consensus to a test. In South Africa, for instance, it has highlighted the deep divisions that have existed within society.

As all these countries recover from the trauma and wounds of the past, they have had to devise mechanisms not only for handling past human rights violations, but also to ensure that the dignity of victims, survivors, and relatives is restored. In the context of this relentless search for appropriate equilibria, profound issues of policy and law have emerged. They have arisen out of the question of how a country in transition should respond to allegations of gross human rights violations by individuals of either the predecessor or extant authority. The issue that has concerned the international community is the problem created by the incompatibility of such amnesties with a state's international obligations.

Nelson Mandela
President of the Republic of South Africa

Criminal Sanctions

A basic question confronting all transitional governments, of course, is whether to undertake the prosecution of the leaders of the ousted regime or their henchmen for the abuses they inflicted upon the nation. Some will argue that trial and punishment of these people is not only essential to achieve some degree of justice, but that a public airing and condemnation of their crimes is the best way to draw a line between the old and new governments, lest the public perceives the new authorities as simply more of the same. Others will claim that these are simply show trials unbefitting a democracy, that they are manifestations of victor's justice, that the best way to rebuild and reconcile the nation is to leave the past behind by means of a blanket amnesty. In some cases, abuses have been committed both by the former government and by its opponents, and it can be argued that the best approach is to forgive the sins of both sides.

The debate recurs time and again. Following the death of Franco, the relatively peaceful Spanish transition was marked by such a mutual amnesty. In Greece, nearly twenty years after the conviction of junta leaders who had overseen the torture of hundreds, plans to release them from prison still prompted huge protests. In newly democratic Argentina and Chile, the prospect of trials for the gross violations of human rights that had occurred under the old regime provoked bald threats of military intervention and a return to the terror of the past. In post-apartheid South Africa, disagreements at the end of 1994 regarding amnesty were reported to threaten the stability of the new coalition government. International standards are evolving which help deal with this question; there is a growing consensus that, at least for the most heinous violations of human rights and international humanitarian law, a sweeping amnesty is impermissible.

When a decision is made to prosecute, the desire to use criminal sanctions against those who served the old regime may run directly counter to the development of a democratic legal order. The principles of *ex post facto* and *nulla poena sine lege*, for example, form one of the basic concepts of that legal order, barring the prosecution of anyone for an act which was not criminal at the time it was committed. At the very time that countries emerging from repressive regimes are committing themselves to these basic principles, the reality is that many of the acts that they desire to punish today were not crimes when they were committed under the former regime; they were often laudable and encouraged under the old system. In post-war France, for example, this issue was fiercely debated. Ultimately, thousands of people were prosecuted under a 1944 law establishing the new offense of "national indignity" for acts they had committed prior to the law's adoption. In the immediate post-communist period, largely owing to this same *ex post facto* dilemma, German officials initiated proceedings against Erich Mielke, the former head of East Germany's Stasi secret police, not for any abuses of the hated Stasi, but for a murder he had allegedly committed half a century earlier—based on evidence extracted by Nazi police. Although some sort of justice might have been served by this trial, the Mielke prosecution could not provide for East Germans the kind of catharsis that would be achieved through a public airing and trial of secret police wrongdoing.

Some of the worst abuses inflicted by former regimes *were* crimes under the old system, but they were obviously not prosecuted. If the statute of limitations for these crimes has already elapsed by the time of the transition, can the new authorities still hold the perpetrators accountable for their deeds? In both Hungary and the Czech Republic, post-communist legislators argued that since these crimes (particularly those committed to suppress dissent in 1956 and 1968 respectively) had not been prosecuted for wholly political reasons, it was legitimate to hold that the statute of limitations had not been in effect during the earlier period. Now, freed of political obstacles to justice, the statutory period for these crimes could begin anew, enabling the new authorities to prosecute these decades-old crimes. Legislation was adopted accordingly. In both countries, the matter was put to the newly created constitutional court for review. In a fascinating pair of rulings, each court handed down a decision which eloquently addressed the need to view this question of legacy and accountability in the context of the new democracy's commitment to the rule of law. On this basis—with plainly similar fact patterns—the Czech constitutional court upheld the re-running of the statute of limitations for the crimes of the old regime as a requirement of justice; the Hungarian court struck down the measure for violating the principle of the rule of law.

How widely should the net be cast in imposing sanctions on those who served the former regime? How high up the chain of command should superiors be responsible for abuses inflicted by their underlings? What standard of evidence is required to demonstrate that, rather than random events, these acts of persecution, corruption, and violence were designed, or at least condoned, by those at the top? Conversely, how far down the chain should soldiers or bureaucrats be held liable for following the orders of their superiors in facilitating these abuses? In dealing with the legacy of the former East Germany, several young border guards were prosecuted in 1991 for implementing shoot-to-kill orders that produced nearly 600 deaths of East Germans attempting to escape across the border. Many criticized the first of these trials for punishing the "small fry" at the end of the chain of responsibility who actually pulled the trigger, while leaving untouched the party leaders who had designed the repugnant system and given the orders. (In January 1995, seven former senior East German officials *were* eventually charged, in a 1,600-page indictment, with manslaughter and attempted manslaughter for their roles in developing and overseeing the system.) In Rwanda, after ousting a regime that organized genocidal killings of at least half a million people, if the new government were to undertake prosecution of every person who participated in this heinous butchery, some 30,000–100,000 Rwandan citizens could be placed in the dock—a situation that would be wholly unmanageable and extremely destabilizing to the transition. Moving the nation forward toward both justice and reconciliation plainly precludes an absolutist approach to the chain of responsibility.

In bringing those who served the former regime to account for their actions, what kind of deeds should be scrutinized? Should prosecution be limited to egregious violations of human rights? Should they be extended to charges of corruption and economic mismanagement? In Bulgaria, for instance, several former officials were convicted because of their role in specific foreign aid decisions that contributed to the country's economic ruin.

Should there be limits on the penalties imposed in these criminal cases? Some will argue that, even in those countries in which capital punishment is used, it should not be available in transitional purge trials. Given the high emotion and political pressures inherent in these trials, they suggest that use of the death penalty will further aggravate tensions within the society.

The temptation of victims of ghastly human rights violations under the old regime to make short shrift of the criminal procedural rights of those put in the dock for the crimes of that regime—to pay them back for the abuses they inflicted—is certainly understandable. Providing yesterday's dictators and torturers with the judicial guarantees and procedural protections that they never afforded their victims may be a source of short-term frustration during the transition, prompting cynicism of the sort expressed by an East German activist: "what we wanted was justice; what we got was the rule of law." Nonetheless, if these defendants are not afforded all the same rights granted to common defendants in a democratic order, the rule of law does not exist and the democratic foundation of the new system is arguably weakened.

Non-Criminal Sanctions

At least as great a challenge to the installation of democracy and the rule of law comes in the context of administrative penalties. Most frequently, the issue is that of purging from the public sector those who served the repressive regime. In post-war France, the process was called *epuration*; in the Czech and Slovak Federal Republic, *lustration*. A variety of effective arguments are made in favor of this process. The new democratic authorities must find ways to restore public confidence in the institutions of government. The public may reasonably be skeptical when told they will now be treated differently, if these institutions simply retain all their existing personnel. These, after all, are the same people who kept the engine of the repressive state operating; it is unlikely that many of them have undergone a sudden epiphany that has turned them into committed democrats. Even if they do not actively attempt to sabotage the changes undertaken by the new authorities, these people are set in the old ways and will serve as obstacles to the process of democratic reform. Finally, jobs in public service, whether as senior ministers or as clerks, should be granted first and foremost to those who have demonstrated loyalty to the democratic ideals of the new order.

Depending on the country, those perceived as having supported the old regime might include senior officials and architects of the system, bureaucrats who implemented the old policies and may continue to be obstacles to reform, members of the military or police, paid or volunteer collaborators with the secret police, or even simply party members. Perhaps the most difficult of these categories in one country after another is the vague description of "collaborators." In some emerging democracies, those who fit into one of these categories potentially comprise more than half the population.

On the other hand, particularly in those countries where the ousted regime was in power for many years, these people may be the only ones with the knowledge and experience to staff the ministries and the banks and the other institutions without which the national infrastructure would surely collapse. Practical considerations may make them indispensable.

How to undertake such a purge while rebuilding on the basis of democratic principles? These programs of administrative sanctions do not, as a rule, provide individuals with the same level of due process protections from which they would benefit in a criminal proceeding. Driven by the fact that they involve a large number of people, purges tend to be conducted in summary fashion. Beyond procedural considerations, the rule of law rejects collective punishment and discrimination on the basis of political opinion or affiliation. In establishing accountability, even in a non-criminal proceeding, the burden of proof should be on the authorities making the accusation, not on the accused to prove his or her innocence. When large numbers of people are removed from their places of employment purely because they had worked there under the old system or because of their membership in a political party, without any demonstration of individual wrongdoing, they may legitimately cry foul and question the democratic underpinnings of the new government. Rather than contributing to reconciliation and rebuilding, the result may be the creation of a substantial ostracized opposition that threatens the stability of the new system.

In much of the former communist bloc, the issue of lustration was a source of great controversy during the first years after the revolutions of 1989. In Poland, for example, only 38 percent of those polled in late 1991 supported creation of a system for disqualification of former communists, officials, and collaborators from public offices; a March 1992 poll showed an increase to 64 percent in favor of disqualification. Some observers suggested that the trend was related to the complex questions of privatization and redistribution of wealth: necessary austerity programs and wrenching efforts to overhaul the entire economic system result in many people becoming more impoverished, and the desire consequently grows to assign blame for society's ills. In addition, a perception exists that many former communist officials gave themselves "golden parachutes" as they exited their government posts, in the form of embezzled funds and property or controlling interests in the newly privatized companies; rather than being punished, in other words, the old guard had won once again.

The courts reflect an interesting problem relative to the purge process. On the one hand, the rule of law requires an independent judiciary insulated from political pressures. This generally means that judges are not easily removable from their posts. Even if judges were easily purged, it might take years to train a qualified class of new lawyers and judges to replace them on the bench. On the other hand, in most cases of transition from totalitarian or authoritarian regimes, the judiciary was severely compromised and was very much a part of the old system, implementing the repressive policies and wrapping them in the mantle of law. In post-war Germany, when victims of Nazi persecution were authorized to file claims for damages, some of them were stunned to find their claims assigned to the very same judge who had sentenced the claimants or their relatives in the first place. In order to enhance the power and independence of the judiciary as part of the democratization process in post-communist Poland, a law was enacted establishing the irremovability of judges. One consequence, subsequently recognized, was that many tainted communist judges thereby became entrenched in the "new" court system. An effort followed to create a system for the verification of judges based on their past activity and affiliation, and apply that system to both prospective new judges and those already in office.

In Ethiopia, it was proposed that all members of the former ruling party be denied the right to vote in elections. Such denial of suffrage based on previous party affiliation has occurred in other places, such as Norway after World War II. Other countries may attempt to ban the former ruling party and its successor parties. In Russia, President Boris Yeltsin's decree banning the Communist Party and seizing its assets was hotly debated and resulted in a closely watched case before the country's new constitutional court, which ultimately struck down half of the ban while leaving significant elements of it intact.

Once again, these efforts can rub against the intention to create a new, freer society wholly unlike the old regime. Administrative purge programs can easily be abused for purely political motives. In many cases, the old regime actually used the same methods, banning political parties, denying people a say in choosing their government. Citizens' rights to vote, to run for office, or to exercise their freedom of association are fundamental elements of a democracy. The balancing act for countries feeling their way through transitional justice is not an easy one.

Acknowledging the Past

In all cases of transition from a repressive regime, history has been controversial. Even after its ouster, the old guard will still have its defenders, who will deny that the evil acts of which it is accused ever took place, or will claim that they were actually perpetrated by others, or will suggest that they were justified by exigent circumstances. If left uncontested, these claims may undermine the new government and strengthen the hand of those determined to return the former regime to power. They will also add insult to the injury already inflicted on the victims.

Establishing a full, official account of the past is increasingly seen as an important element to a successful democratic transition. Criminal trials are one way in which the facts and figures of past abuses may be established. The establishment of a "truth commission" . . . is another. Following the initial phase of transition, this history may be reaffirmed in the long-term through national days of remembrance, the construction of museums and commemorative monuments, and the incorporation of this recent history into the curriculum of the nation's schools. . . .

. . .

As a rule, these are not problems that disappear quickly or easily. A half-century after the Second World War, the scars of Nazism are still felt in Germany. After the fall of the Berlin Wall and reunification, many acknowledged that the debate over decommunization was in many ways a shadow debate among East and West Germans over the success of denazification and was significantly colored by a desire to "do it better this time." The trials of Klaus Barbie and Paul Touvier for their crimes as part of the Vichy regime exposed still-raw nerves and soul-searching in France some fifty years after the facts in question. In Namibia, several years after the transition, officials claim that it is still too soon for an investigation and accounting of those who disappeared on both sides of the conflict, that such an effort would threaten Namibian stability; others argue that this past will haunt the country until it is dealt with. And in Cambodia, talk of bringing charges against leaders of the Khmer Rouge for the genocide they inflicted on their country twenty years ago will continue to affect the reconstruction process.

This is, of course, an ongoing process. A full accounting is yet to be written of transitional justice in countries such as South Africa, El Salvador, or Ethiopia. The current global trend from totalitarian and authoritarian systems to democratic ones will

hopefully continue, producing new cases of transitional justice in the years to come. . . . [We] can hope that positive lessons will be derived from past experience, that future transitions will bolster their own stability by achieving justice and reconciliation through the rule of law.

Study Questions

1. Jackson claims that the international community has the right to institute new customs that will form the basis for expanding international law. Do you agree?

2. What are some of the specific grounds on which Jackson bases his claim that aggressive warfare was a violation of international law even prior to the formulation of the Nuremberg Charter? Do you find them convincing?

3. In his opening statement at Nuremberg, Jackson asks (rhetorically): "Does it take these men by surprise that murder is treated as a crime?" In what sense is Jackson using "crime" here? Could the force of his remark be trading on an equivocation between crime as a *moral* wrong and crime as a *legal* wrong?

4. In August 1998, representatives of more than 100 nations from across the world voted to support a treaty that, if ratified, would create a permanent, international criminal court, or ICC, with broad powers to try war criminals and those accused of crimes against humanity. The United States, in a break with virtually all of its allies, refused to support the court. U.S. officials cited primarily political reasons for opposing the treaty; but significant legal obstacles stand in the way of such an undertaking. Which legal system should a world criminal court employ? What procedural rules (covering everything from motions and indictments to introduction of evidence and composition of juries) should be followed? Should trials *in absentia* be allowed? Which crimes would fall within the court's jurisdiction? How should crimes of genocide, for example, be defined? Should other serious crimes, such as drug traf-

ficking, be punishable by the ICC? Should the death penalty be available? Imagine that you are designing an authorizing statute for a court like the ICC. How would you resolve these issues? And given that no nation currently has laws that can be expected to match completely the rules any such international court would follow, could individuals brought before the ICC claim that they were being subjected to "new" law in violation of the principles of legality and the rule of law?

5. In what ways, according to Wyzanski, did the Nuremberg Charter create "new" law?

6. During the Persian Gulf War, then-President Bush repeatedly called Iraq's Saddam Hussein "a new Hitler," and some people suggested that Hussein be captured and placed on trial for committing war crimes against the inhabitants of Kuwait. Would Nuremberg have been a sound precedent for such a trial? Could Saddam Hussein have raised the *ex post facto* objection first raised by the Nazis?

7. Why is an appeal to principles of justice or human rights embedded in "the law of civilized nations" necessarily an *ex post facto* appeal? Usually a law is *ex post facto* if what a person did was not a crime at the time he or she did it. But, Jackson might argue, these basic ideals had been around for a long time; they weren't invented in 1945. How would you respond?

8. Some of the Nazi defendants at Nuremberg raised the defense of obedience to superior orders: "I was ordered to kill the civilians." Assuming that such orders were given by Hitler or his top aides, were such orders legal, given a natural law theory? Given a positivist theory?

9. Imagine that you are a judge at Nuremberg on the panel hearing the case against the Nazis. Jackson and Wyzanski have each presented their case before you. Assuming that the evidence in support of Nazi atrocities is strong, would you rule that they have broken "the law"? How would you defend your answer?

10. A classic treatise on the subject defined international law as "the body of rules and principles of actions which are binding upon civilized states in their relations with one another" (Brierly, J. *The Law of Nations*, 6th ed. [Oxford: Oxford University Press, 1963]). How would you go about determining what such "law" contains? Was Robert Jackson's argument before the Nuremberg Tribunal an appeal to some such broad definition?

11. Is international "law" really law at all? Can a legal system really exist in the absence of courts with compulsory jurisdiction to resolve disputes and without a centralized police authority to enforce the courts' decrees? Is international law based upon the *consent* of various states to be bound by the terms of treaties and customs? If so, what makes such acts of consent legally binding?

12. In July 1994, the United Nations Security Council determined that unrest in the island nation of Haiti was a threat to peace and security in the region. A multinational task force was dispatched, including U.S. troops, to end the military dictatorship on the island. Members of the Army's 10th Mountain Division, including Capt. Lawrence Rockwood, entered Haiti in September. Rockwood, a Buddhist, was personally concerned about intelligence reports of human rights violations at Haiti's National Penitentiary, in the city of Port au Prince. Rockwood attempted to initiate a task force inspection of prison conditions; he raised the issue with his superiors, the Judge Advocate General's (JAG) office, and the division chaplain. Failing to secure recognition of his concerns, Capt. Rockwood, without command authorization, personally went to the prison to inspect it. Rockwood was subsequently detained and charged with willful disobedience of a superior officer. In his defense, Rockwood claimed that his otherwise criminal acts were justified because he had a personal legal duty as a member of U.S. forces and under international law to prevent human rights violations. Rockwood alleged that he would be liable under the Nuremberg Charter for failing to act. A military Court of Criminal Appeals rejected Rockwood's arguments. Rockwood, the court maintained, had

not been asked to do anything that would be a violation of international law, and the failure of his superiors to act on his concerns, even if illegal under international law, relieved Rockwood of any responsibility for wrongs occur-

ring at the prison. Was Rockwood's case correctly decided? What "law" should take priority in this case?

C. *Classical Theories of Law*

Natural Law Versus Positivism

On trial at Nuremberg, Nazi officials and officers sought to use a variety of defenses. One defense was presented by Professor Hermann Jahrreiss, an associate defense attorney. Jahrreiss argued that the Enabling Act of March 24, 1933, authorized Adolf Hitler to rule by decree: "Now in a state in which the entire power to make final decisions is concentrated in the hands of a single individual, the orders of this one man are absolutely binding on the members of the hierarchy. This individual is their sovereign . . ."[1] Behind Jahrreiss' argument lay a view of law familiar to the average person: A statement or rule becomes a rule of *law* only if it is a *command,* an order backed up by the threat of force and issued by someone in absolute control. Law is erected on a power relationship: the commander issues an order, and the commanded must comply. Hitler's orders were law, Jahrreiss stated, and the Nuremberg defendants were simply obeying their sovereign.

The Nuremberg tribunal rejected the arguments of Jahrreiss: "That a soldier was ordered to

kill or torture in violation of the international law of war has never been recognized as a defense to such acts of brutality. . . ."[2] Although the defense was rejected, the idea of law as an order backed by force has a long history. An opposing view of law has an equally long record. In Sophocles' play *Antigone,* the ancient Greek playwright describes the dilemma confronted by the daughter of the tragic Oedipus. Antigone's brothers have killed each other, and Creon, king of Thebes, has issued an order forbidding the burial of one brother, Polynices. Antigone's sister reminds Antigone that this "law is strong, we must give in to the law."[3] Antigone, who is determined to do what is right and bury her brother properly, rebukes her sister, observing that "apparently the laws of the gods mean nothing to you."[4] Antigone insists that law is what is just, proper, or right—not merely whatever a dictator demands. Antigone sacrifices her life out of fidelity to this ideal.

The history of legal philosophy is importantly shaped by the conflict between these two opposing general conceptions of law and legality: law as power and law as justice. These general views

---

[1] Quoted in Stanley Paulson, "Classical Legal Positivism at Nuremberg," *Philosophy & Public Affairs,* Vol 4 (1975), p. 144.

[2] *Ibid.*

[3] Dudley Fitts and Robert Fitzgerald (trans.), *Sophocles: The Oedipus Cycle* (New York: Harcourt, Brace, and Co., 1949), p. 188.

[4] *Ibid.*

have, of course, been much debated and refined. Our discussion begins with two specific forms of these broad approaches: *legal positivism* and *natural law theory.*

Natural law theory, or simply *naturalism,* holds that the phenomenon we call "law" can adequately be understood only in relation to a certain view about the nature of *moral* judgments and standards. What we recognize and venerate as law, according to naturalism, is both essentially connected to and grounded in a "natural moral order"—that is, principles and standards not simply made up by humans but rather part of an objective moral order present in the universe and accessible to human reason. Naturalism holds that human practices and institutions are to be measured against these "higher" standards, and where they fall short of the mark, specific human arrangements, whether statutes, executive orders, or constitutions, fail fully to have the character of law.

Positivism, by contrast, holds that the phenomenon of law is best understood as a system of orders, commands, or rules enforced by power. For the positivist, law is that which has been "posited," that is, made, enacted, or laid down in some prescribed fashion. It is as such a purely human product, "artificial," rather than "natural." Moreover, for the positivist, a rule of law need have no connection with what is morally right or correct or true in order to qualify as law: there is no necessary connection between what law is and what it ought to be.

Legal Positivism

As H. L. A. Hart points out in his selection, positivism came into its own as a distinct and well-formulated legal theory in the late eighteenth and early nineteenth centuries in the writings of two British philosophers, Jeremy Bentham and John Austin. Central to the legal theory of both was the conviction that law as it is is not necessarily law as it ought to be. It does not, they believed, follow from the fact that because a statute or an ordinance is valid law it is also morally good or right. A statute *could,* of course, coincide with what is right, but the fact of its being the "law" does not guarantee this. The morality and legality of a rule are in this way distinct and separate. This "separability

thesis," as later positivists have come to call it, led both Bentham and Austin to distinguish sharply between the task of giving an accurate, descriptive account of what law is—"expository" or "analytical" jurisprudence—and the task of evaluating the law morally, stating what it *ought to be*—"censorial" or "normative" jurisprudence.

As Hart makes clear, in addition to their commitment to positivism, Bentham and Austin shared an allegiance to a general moral and political outlook known as *utilitarianism.* We will have occasion to encounter utilitarianism more later; for now it is enough to note its basic features. Utilitarianism is one among several ethical theories or views of moral life that regard the *consequences* of an act as the sole or exclusive factor to be weighed in determining whether the act is morally right or good. More specifically, utilitarians such as Bentham argue that an action is right or good only if it brings more overall happiness (or at least less unhappiness) into the world than any alternative course of action open to a person at a given time. Bentham appealed to this "Principle of Utility" frequently when it came to evaluating the law from a moral standpoint, and he often found the laws of the England of his time sadly lacking from the perspective of bringing about the greatest happiness.

The work of contemporary positivist H. L. A. Hart is widely regarded as a central statement of modern positivism. Although not all contemporary positivists agree with Hart, all acknowledge that he has largely set the terms in which the contemporary debate about positivism has taken place. Much of what Hart has to say is written against a background of familiarity with the basic outlines of the theories of Bentham and especially Austin. It is therefore useful to acquaint ourselves briefly with the outlines of Austin's account and with the deficiencies that Hart and others have noted in it.

In the selection from his book, *The Province of Jurisprudence Determined,* Austin makes it clear he has little patience for talk of the "natural law," "moral law," or "the law of God." Along with customs and international agreements, these can be called "law" only in an improper sense. What is law? According to Austin, law "properly so called" is something established by a political superior over subjects and takes the form of a command issued by a sovereign. What is a command? It is a signification of desire, backed by a credible threat of punishment, a threat that can in all likelihood be carried out. Is anyone's command a law? No; only the command of the "sovereign" can be certified as law. Who (or what) is the sovereign? Austin makes no attempt to define the sovereign in terms of some normative or value-laden criterion, such as "he who has the right to rule" or "he who legitimately rules." Instead, Austin argues that the sovereign is the person or group of persons that is habitually obeyed by the bulk of a given population but that does not in fact habitually obey anyone else; the sovereign is the "unobeying obeyed." If some person, X, is habitually obeyed by the bulk of the population and yet does not in fact habitually obey anyone else, that person is the sovereign. If X then expresses the desire that certain things be done (or not done) and makes a credible threat that failure to comply will be punished, X has issued a command and his or her command is law. Finally, Austin makes it very clear that just because a law, in the sense that he has defined, exists, there is no guarantee that such a law is fair, just, or right.

Austin's model is elegant in its simplicity; but it is open to seemingly decisive objections, as Hart and others have pointed out. The most fundamental of these objections has to do with the notions of command and sovereign. A command is a desire backed by a threat. Do all laws fit this model? Do all laws have sanctions? Austin's model makes some sense if the paradigm of law is, for example, criminal law. But what about other types of law? What about the law of contracts or of wills? What about American constitutional law? If I enter into a contract with you or write a will leaving you all my money, am I being commanded? By whom? And to do what? Austin tried to deal with these and similar cases by claiming that there *is,* after all, a sanction with which I am being threatened in these cases, what Austin called the "sanction of nullity": the sovereign will "punish" me by not giving effect to my will or my contract in the event that, for example, I don't fill them out properly. But this seems contrived. Isn't the situation better described by saying that the laws of wills and contracts *empower* me to do certain things (for example, sell my house) or bring about certain effects (for example, give all my property to my wife)? The aim here isn't to punish but to facilitate.

The laws of our own Constitution don't command us to continue their observance. If the citizens of what is now the United States were overwhelmingly to decide to repudiate the Constitution in its entirety next Friday at noon, would we all be punished for doing so? It seems not; but that fact does not incline us to say that the Constitution is not "law," at least in some sense. It merely shows that the Constitution is not law as a command (or series of commands) but rather is law as a structure or system of relative powers and competencies designed to facilitate or effect certain aims.

Austin's conception of sovereignty raises further difficulties. Do all legal systems necessarily have Austinian sovereigns? Consider again our own constitutional democracy. Do we have a sovereign? Who is it? To the extent that we can think in these terms at all, we view *ourselves* ("*we* the people") as those in charge. Austin, it seems, would have us then say that we (the people) in our constitution-enacting-and-maintaining role are sovereign over ourselves in our role as citizens. But does this preserve any of the simplicity of Austin's initial model? Furthermore, in our constitutional democracy we have grown accustomed to thinking of ours as a *limited* government. But can Austin's model make sense of limitations upon the power of sovereigns? To do so, Austin would have to argue that sovereigns, in their sovereign capacity, issue commands to themselves in their capacity as citizens. But then, of course, what distinguishes between these two aspects of sovereigns must be some notion of *official* capacity, and this idea cannot be spelled out in terms of Austin's theory.

To see why this last is so, consider the following problem. All persons who presently serve as United States senators meet at a football field on a holiday and "vote" to make themselves "kings" of the states from which they come (forget about the problem of having two kings from each state). None of us would be prepared to say that this vote has made "law," because (we would explain) the senators were not acting in their "official" capacity. But Austin has no room for official capacity; his theory sees only these individuals, who are after all the same people (and people habitually obeyed, though not on this occasion) whether in or out of the Senate chamber.

Hart's Theory

In his central work, *The Concept of Law*[5], Hart attempted to give a fresh start to positivism by resolving the problems implicit in Austin's theory. Austin conceived of law and of a legal system on the analogy of a holdup by an armed robber: orders backed by threats. Law is merely the "gunman situation writ large." Hart argued that this view confuses two quite different states of affairs: being *obliged* to give my money to the robber (to avoid being hurt) and being legally *obligated* to pay my taxes by April 15 (to avoid a penalty). Feeling obliged is just that—a feeling, a psychological state. But being under an obligation is a feature of life that is *social* and that essentially involves the idea of a social rule. Hart argued that a shared activity or practice cannot constitute a social rule unless the people whose rule it is manifest a certain attitude toward it, specifically, that they accept and use the rule to guide their conduct. In this sense, "Pay your taxes by April 15" is a social rule because most of us use it (however reluctantly!) to guide our conduct and help us plan. "Give me your money or else" is, on the other hand, plainly not such a rule.

Hart summarized his own theory of law as the view that law is a union of primary and secondary rules. *Primary rules* are those social rules that concern themselves directly with the way we live and behave. "No one may drive faster than 55 mph" or "Pay your taxes by April 15" are just such rules. *Secondary rules*, on the other hand, are "secondary" in the sense that their subject matter is not human behavior but rather the primary rules themselves. "The traffic code is exclusively the jurisdiction of the state" and "Proposed changes in the tax code must be approved by Congress" are examples of secondary rules. In order for a body of rules to qualify as *legal* rules, according to Hart, there must be secondary rules to supplement the primary ones. Of particular interest here is Hart's notion of a *rule of recognition*. This is a secondary rule that specifies criteria for what counts as a primary rule. "Whatever the chief utters is law" or "Whatever

the legislatures enact consistently with the Constitution is law" are examples of rules of recognition. "Pay your taxes by April 15" is then a valid rule of law because it was created (enacted by a legislature) in the way specified by the ultimate rule of recognition of our legal system.

Much debate has accompanied what Hart says about the existence of rules of recognition. What does it mean for such rules to exist? To say that the rule of recognition exists cannot mean that it is valid because it is enacted in accordance with a procedure laid down in the rule of recognition; plainly, the rule cannot validate itself. The existence of the rule of recognition must be a matter of descriptive fact; it simply *is* the rule acknowledged by most legal actors within a given system.

In his essay "Positivism and the Separation of Law and Morals," included here, Hart notes that critics of positivism sometimes conflate the separability thesis—the claim that legality and morality are separate issues—with Austin's command theory of law, reasoning that since the latter is open to serious objections, so must be the former. Hart believes, however, that it is possible to adhere to the separability thesis (and to a utilitarian moral outlook) and still reject Austin's command model; and this is indeed Hart's position.

Hart considers several objections to the separation of law and morals so important to positivism. Some critics argue that law and morality cannot be separated for the reason that legal rules cannot always say how they are to be applied. For example, the general rule "No vehicles in the park" cannot be applied to the specific situation of my rocket-powered skateboard without the exercise of moral judgment: Should I be allowed to ride through the park on my skateboard? Any positivists who think differently, so these critics say, are guilty of the error of "formalism," the belief that all rules of law can be unambiguously and straightforwardly applied to any situation with complete logical certainty. Hart responds that this criticism relies on a false dilemma: we can, Hart believes, adhere to the separability thesis and yet not fall victim either to a direct appeal to moral values when interpreting a rule such as "No vehicles in the park" nor to the silliness of formalism. Judges can resolve these "penumbral," or "fuzzy," cases by appeal to accepted social policies and purposes.

---

[5]H. L. A. Hart, *The Concept of Law* (Oxford: Clarendon Press, 1961).

A further objection to the positivistic insistence that a rule can still be a rule of law even if it is immoral is made by those who have lived under evil legal regimes such as that in effect in Germany during the Nazi period. These critics complain that the positivist separation of law and morals can have (and has had) pernicious effects: by insisting that laws remain valid even if immoral, positivism has been easily exploited by corrupt "law-and-order" regimes eager to exact compliance with their regulations. Hart tries to argue that the proper response to these critics is not to reject the separability thesis but to recognize that although they may still be the law, some rules or regulations may simply be too morally outrageous to obey.

Hart does make one seeming concession to the natural law position. We do have, Hart admits, an obvious need for a system of legal protections and regulations with some minimal moral content. Legal rules prohibiting physical violence are necessary, for example, not because the presence of such values is entailed by the very idea of something's being the law, but simply given the contingent fact that human beings are vulnerable to physical harm and abuse. This, says Hart, is the core of good sense in the naturalist position; but it is an error to mistake the necessity for such laws for a truth about the nature of law as such.

Natural Law Theory

Naturalism has a rich and varied history, extending back to the ancient Greeks and Romans. One of the most elaborate and thorough expositions of the naturalist position was given by thirteenth-century Catholic theologian Thomas Aquinas. [6]

St. Thomas Aquinas

In the brief selection included here from his great work, the *Summa Theologica*, Aquinas argues, first, that law necessarily involves rules that (given that they have their source in reason) must have some

---

[6] See Anton C. Pegis, ed. *Summa Theologica, The Basic Writings of Saint Thomas Aquinas,* Vol. 2, (New York: Random House, 1945), pp. 742ff.

purpose or goal. Following Greek philosopher Aristotle, Aquinas insists that this goal must be overall happiness or the "common good." Laws must be "promulgated" or made clear to those who are subject to them, Aquinas continues, and this means that God is the ultimate source of such promulgating authority.

Aquinas sets out his famous typology of four distinct kinds of law: eternal, divine, natural, and human. Eternal law represents God's overall plan for the universe. Divine law was for Aquinas the revealed word of God, the principles revealed by Scripture. Divine law is necessary, so Aquinas thought, because human beings have a supernatural destiny to which we must be guided, our native intellect being inadequate to reveal to us the nature of this destiny and how to secure it. Human law, by contrast with eternal and divine law, is created by us for the purpose of carrying out the requirements of natural law.

What, then, is natural law? Aquinas argued that because all things are subject to divine providence and thus are "ruled and measured" by eternal law, all things "partake" in some way of eternal law. Aquinas believed that humans, as rational beings, occupy a special place in God's eternal plan, in that we can understand eternal law as it applies to us and can allow that understanding to guide our conduct. Eternal law, as it applies to human conduct, Aquinas calls "natural law."

What does natural law tell us to do? In answering this question, Aquinas invoked (as he often did) a distinction drawn by Greek philosopher Aristotle. Aristotle had distinguished between two kinds of reason: speculative and practical. Speculative reason is the capacity we have as reasoning beings to apprehend or understand certain truths, such as the truths of mathematics and geometry. Practical reason is not concerned with these abstract matters but rather with human action. Practical reason tells us what things we should value, what goods we should seek in life, and how to obtain them. Aquinas and Aristotle held that, in both speculative and practical reason, certain principles are *per se nota*, known through themselves. These are self-evident propositions, requiring no proof (in the sense of being derivable from something else). As examples of self-evident principles of speculative reason, Aquinas included the principle of non-contradiction ("What is, is, and what is not, is not") and certain truths of mathematics and geometry. Turning to practical reason, Aquinas claimed that the first and most fundamental principle or "precept" of natural law is "Good is to be done and evil avoided." Other examples he gives include "One should not kill one's father"; and "God's precepts are to be obeyed."

How does natural law relate to human law? Aquinas maintained that human law is necessary to implement and adapt the basic precepts of natural law, which are quite general, to the changing needs and contexts of human societies. The basic precepts are the same for everyone and do not change, but the detailed conclusions drawn from these basic precepts may differ from place to place and time to time, and human law reflects this fact. "Goods held in trust for another should be returned" is, according to Aquinas, a requirement of natural law, but it should not be followed when the good is a gun and the person to whom it should be returned is in a homicidal frenzy. Human law must adjust the principles of natural law to specific situations. Moreover, since human communities need many detailed regulations and ordinances simply to function (for example, tax and traffic laws), natural law requires that they be made, although it does not, of course, dictate their particular content (for example, natural law does not require that we drive on the right; only that the community establish some rule so as to meet the fundamental requirement that health and safety be protected).

What about a situation in which human law fails to conform to natural law? It is here that Aquinas's naturalism has potentially far-reaching consequences. As he makes clear in the reading, the force of a human law necessarily depends upon its justice: human enactments or measures that contravene natural law are not laws "but a perversion of law"; they are "acts of violence" and do not bind in conscience. Although it is still debated exactly what Aquinas meant by such statements, these remarks have seemed to many to imply that any human "laws" at odds with natural law have no legal validity. Even entire legal systems, Aquinas suggests, if they are evil "perversions" of natural law (for example, the legal regime of the Nazis) may stand invalidated on that ground.

Fuller and the Internal Morality of Law

The selection by late Harvard jurist Lon Fuller, while careful not to endorse the classical natural law theory of Aquinas, nonetheless bears a recognizable "naturalistic" stamp in its insistence that "law" and "what is morally right" are in an important sense inseparable. In his other writing, Fuller had been especially interested in the legal problems that arose in Germany after the Nazi period, represented, for example, by the case of the housewife-turned-informer. According to Fuller, Hart wrongly assessed these cases, assuming that something persisted throughout the Nazi reign that deserved the name of "law" in a way that makes meaningful the ideal of *fidelity to law*. Fidelity to law, as Fuller understood it, meant that a statute or an ordinance is deserving of loyalty and respect simply by virtue of its being the law. Fuller maintained that positivism could not explain or make sense of the ideal of *fidelity to law* and that positivism was therefore descriptively false or inaccurate. Fuller conceded that a particular rule of law can still be law even if it is immoral, but he denied that such rules could remain law if they were part of an entire legal system that was itself deeply evil and unjust.

In our selection, Fuller uses a fictional story of a king named Rex to illustrate his view that for a system of *legal* rules to exist certain minimum *moral* demands must be met; because Rex failed to heed these demands, Fuller argues, he failed to make "law." Fuller details the demands that form his "internal morality of law" and distinguishes his "procedural" version of natural law from the "substantive" view of classical naturalists like Aquinas.

6. What Is Law?
From Summa Theologiae

ST. THOMAS AQUINAS

Question 90

Law is a rule and measure of acts, whereby man is induced to act or is restrained from acting; for *lex [law]* is derived from *ligare [to bind]*, because it binds one to act. Now the rule and measure of human acts is the reason, which is the first principle of human acts. . . . For it belongs to the reason to direct to the end, which is the first principle in all matters of action, according to [Aristotle]. . . . Reason has its power of moving from the will, . . . for it is due to the fact that one wills the end, that the reason issues its commands as regards things ordained to the end. But in order that the volition of what is commanded may have the nature of law, it needs to be in accord with some rule of reason. And in this sense is to be understood the saying that the will of the sovereign has the force of law; or otherwise the sovereign's will would savor of lawlessness rather than of law.

[Now] the first principle in practical matters, which are the object of the practical reason, is the last end: and the last end of human life is happiness or beatitude. . . . Consequently, law must . . . concern itself mainly with the order that is in beatitude. Moreover, since every part is ordained to the whole as the imperfect to the perfect, and since one man is a part of the perfect community, law must . . . concern itself properly with the order directed to universal happiness. Therefore Aristotle mentions both happiness and the body politic, since he says that we call those legal matters *just which are adapted to produce and preserve happiness and its parts for the body politic.*

Now in every genus, that which belongs to it chiefly is the principle of the others, and the others belong to that genus according to some order towards that thing. Thus fire, which is chief among

hot things, is the cause of heat in mixed bodies, and these are said to be hot in so far as they have a share of fire. Consequently, since law is chiefly ordained to the common good, any other precept in regard to some individual work must . . . be devoid of the nature of law, save in so far as it regards the common good. Therefore every law is ordained to the common good.

Just as nothing stands firm with regard to the speculative reason except that which is traced back to the first indemonstrable principles, so nothing stands firm with regard to the practical reason, unless it be directed to the last end which is the common good. Now whatever stands to reason in this sense has the nature of a law.

[A] private person cannot lead another to virtue efficaciously; for he can only advise, and if his advice be not taken, it has no coercive power, such as the law should have, in order to prove an efficacious inducement to virtue. . . . But this coercive power is vested in the whole people or in some public personage, to whom it belongs to inflict penalties. . . . Therefore the framing of laws belongs to him alone.

[A] law is imposed on others as a rule and measure. Now a rule or measure is imposed by being applied to those who are to be ruled and measured by it. Therefore, in order that a law obtain the binding force which is proper to a law, it must . . . be applied to the men who have to be ruled by it. But such application is made by its being made known to them by promulgation. Therefore promulgation is necessary for law to obtain its force.

Thus, . . . Law is nothing else than an ordinance of reason for the common good, promulgated by him who has the care of the community.

The natural law is promulgated by the very

fact that God instilled it into man's mind so as to be known by him naturally. . . . The promulgation that takes place in the present extends to future time by reason of the durability of written characters, by which means it is continually promulgated.

Question 91

Every act of reason and will in us is based on that which is according to nature. . . . For every act of reasoning is based on principles that are known naturally, and every act of appetite in respect of the means is derived from the natural appetite in respect of the last end. Accordingly, the first direction of our acts to their end must . . . be through the natural law.

[Augustine] distinguishes two kinds of law, the one eternal, the other temporal, which he calls human. . . . Just as in the speculative reason, from naturally known indemonstrable principles we draw the conclusions of the various sciences, the knowledge of which is not imparted to us by nature, but acquired by the efforts of reason, so too it is that from the precepts of the natural law, as from common and indemonstrable principles, the human reason needs to proceed to the more particular determination of certain matters. These particular determinations, devised by human reason, are called human laws, provided that the other essential conditions of law be observed.

Question 94

[The] precepts of the natural law are to the practical reason what the first principles of demonstrations are to the speculative reason, because both are self-evident principles. . . . Now as *being* is the first thing that falls under the apprehension absolutely, so *good* is the first thing that falls under the apprehension of the practical reason, which is directed to action (since every agent acts for an end, which has the nature of good). Consequently, the first principle in the practical reason is one founded on the nature of the good, viz., that *good is that which all things seek after*. Hence this is the first precept of law, that *good is to be promoted, and evil is to be avoided*. All other precepts of the natural law are based on this; so that all things which the practical reason naturally apprehends as man's good belong to the precepts of the natural law under the form of things to be done or avoided.

Question 95

[As] Augustine says, *that which is not just seems to be no law at all*. Hence the force of a law depends on the extent of its justice. Now in human affairs a thing is said to be just from being right, according to the rule of reason. But the first rule of reason is the law of nature. . . . Consequently, every human law has just so much of the nature of law as it is derived from the law of nature. But if in any point it departs from the law of nature, it is no longer law but a perversion of law.

[The] common principles of the natural law cannot be applied to all men in the same way because of the great variety of human affairs; and hence arises the diversity of positive laws among various people. . . . In this respect, there are various human laws according to the various forms of government. . . . Tyrannical government, which is altogether corrupt, . . . has no corresponding law.

Question 96

The natural law is a participation in us of the eternal law, while human law falls short of the eternal law. For Augustine says, *The law which is framed for the government of states allows and leaves unpunished many things that are punished by divine providence. Nor, if this law does not attempt to do everything, is this a reason why it should be blamed for what it does.* Therefore, human law likewise does not prohibit everything that is forbidden by the natural law.

[Laws] framed by man are either just or unjust. If they be just, they have the power of binding the conscience from the eternal law whence they are derived. . . . On the other hand, laws may be unjust in two ways: first, by being contrary to human good, . . . as when an authority imposes on his subjects burdensome laws, conducive, not to the common good, but rather to his own cupidity or vainglory. . . . Such are acts of violence rather than laws, because, as Augustine says, *a law that is not just seems to be no law at all.* Therefore, such laws do not bind in conscience. . . .

Secondly, laws may be unjust through being opposed to the divine good. . . . Laws of this kind must in no way be observed, because . . . *we ought to obey God rather than men.*

7. *Legal Positivism*

JOHN AUSTIN

Lecture 1

The matter of jurisprudence is positive law: law, simply and strictly so called: or law set by political superiors to political inferiors. . . .

A law, in the most general and comprehensive acceptation in which the term, in its literal meaning, is employed, may be said to be a rule laid down for the guidance of an intelligent being by an intelligent being having power over him. Under this definition are included, and without impropriety, several species. It is necessary to define accurately the line of demarcation which separates these species from one another, as much mistiness and intricacy has been infused into the science of jurisprudence by their being confounded or not clearly distinguished. In the comprehensive sense above indicated, or in the largest meaning which it has, without extension by metaphor or analogy, the term *law* embraces the following objects:—Laws set by God to his human creatures, and laws set by men to men.

The whole or a portion of the laws set by God to men is frequently styled the law of nature, or natural law: being, in truth, the only natural law of which it is possible to speak without a metaphor, or without a blending of objects which ought to be distinguished broadly. But, rejecting the appellation Law of Nature as ambiguous and misleading, I name those laws or rules, as considered collectively or in a mass, the *Divine law*, or the *law of God.*

Laws set by men to men are of two leading or principal classes: classes which are often blended, although they differ extremely; and which, for that reason, should be severed precisely, and opposed distinctly and conspicuously.

Of the laws or rules set by men to men, some are established by *political* superiors, sovereign and subject: by persons exercising supreme and subordinate *government*, in independent nations, or independent political societies. The aggregate of the rules thus established, or some aggregate forming a portion of that aggregate, is the appropriate matter of jurisprudence, general or particular. To the aggregate of the rules thus established, or to some aggregate forming a portion of that aggregate, the term *law*, as used simply and strictly, is exclusively applied. . . . As contradistinguished to the rules which I style *positive morality*, and so on which I shall touch immediately, the aggregate of the rules, established by political superiors, may also be marked commodiously with the name of *positive law.* . . .

Though *some* of the laws or rules, which are set by men to men, are established by political superiors, *others* are *not* established by political superiors, or are *not* established by political superiors, in that capacity or character.

Closely analogous to human laws of this second class, are a set of objects frequently but *improperly* terms *laws*, being rules set and enforced by *mere opinion*, that is, by the opinions or sentiments held or felt by an indeterminate body of men in regard to human conduct. Instances of such a use of the term *law* are the expressions—"The law of honour"; "The law set by fashion"; and rules of this species constitute much of what is usually termed "International law."

The aggregate of human laws properly so called belonging to the second of the classes above mentioned, with the aggregate of objects *improperly* but by *close analogy* termed laws, I place together in a common class, and denote them by the term *positive morality*. The name *morality* severs them from *positive law*, while the epithet *positive* disjoins them from the *law of God*. And to the end of obviating confusion, it is necessary or expedient that they *should* be disjoined from the latter by that distinguishing epithet. For the name *morality* (or *morals*), when standing unqualified or alone, denotes indifferently either of the following objects: namely, positive morality *as it is*, or without regard to its merits; and positive morality *as it would be*, if it conformed to the law of God, and were, therefore, deserving of *approbation*.

. . . I shall now state the essentials of *a law* or *rule* (taken with the largest signification which can be given to the term *properly*).

Every *law* or *rule* (taken with the largest signification which can be given to the term *properly*) is a *command*. Or, rather, laws or rules, properly so called, are a *species* of commands.

. . . A command is distinguished from other significations of desire, not by the style in which the desire is signified, but by the power and the purpose of the party commanding to inflict an evil or pain in case the desire be disregarded. If you cannot or will not harm me in case I comply not with your wish, the expression of your wish is not a command, although you utter your wish in imperative phrase. . . .

A command, then, is a signification of desire. But a command is distinguished from other significations of desire by this peculiarity: that the party to whom it is directed is liable to evil from the other, in case he comply not with the desire.

Being liable to evil from you if I comply not with a wish which you signify, I am *bound* or *obliged* by your command, or I lie under a *duty* to obey it. If, in spite of that evil in prospect, I comply not

with the wish which you signify, I am said to disobey your command, or to violate the duty which it imposes.

Command and duty are, therefore, correlative terms: the meaning denoted by each being implied or supposed by the other. Or (changing the expression) wherever a duty lies, a command has been signified; and whenever a command is signified, a duty is imposed.

. . . The greater the eventual evil, and the greater the chance of incurring it, the greater is the efficacy of the command, and the greater is the strength of the obligation. . . .

Rewards are, indisputably, *motives* to comply with the wishes of others. But to talk of commands and duties as *sanctioned* or *enforced* by rewards, or to talk of rewards as *obliging* or *constraining* to obedience, is surely a wide departure from the established meaning of the terms. . . .

It appears, then, from what has been premised, that the ideas or notions comprehended by the term *command* are the following. 1. A wish or desire conceived by a rational being, that another rational being shall do or forbear. 2. An evil to proceed from the former, and to be incurred by the latter, in case the latter comply not with the wish. 3. An expression or intimation of the wish by words or other signs.

It also appears from what has been premised, that *command*, *duty*, and *sanction* are inseparably connected terms: that each embraces the same ideas as the others, though each denotes those ideas in a peculiar order or series. . . .

Now where it obliges *generally* to acts or forbearance of a *class*, a command is a law or rule. But where it obliges to a *specific* act or forbearance, or to acts or forbearance which it determines *specifically* or *individually*, a command is occasional or particular. . . .

If you command your servant to go on a given errand, or *not* to leave your house on a given evening, or to rise at such an hour on such a morning, or to rise at that hour during the next week or month, the command is occasional or particular. For the act or acts enjoined or forbidden are specially determined or assigned.

If you command him *simply* to rise at that hour, or to rise at that hour *always*, or to rise at that hour *till further orders*, it may be said, with propriety, that you lay down a *rule* for the guidance of your servant's conduct. For no specific act is assigned by the command, but the command obliges him generally to acts of a determined class.

If a regiment be ordered to attack or defend a post, or to quell a riot, or to march from their present quarters, the command is occasional or particular. But an order to exercise daily till further orders shall be given would be called a *general order*, and *might* be called a *rule*.

If Parliament prohibited simply the exportation of corn, either for a given period or indefinitely, it would establish a law or rule: a *kind* or *sort* of act being determined by the command, and acts of that kind or sort being *generally* forbidden. But an order issued by Parliament to meet an impending scarcity, and stopping the exportation of corn *then shipped and in port*, would not be a law or rule, though issued by the sovereign legislature. . . .

Now the lawgiver determines a class or description of acts; prohibits acts of the class generally and indefinitely; and commands, with the like generality, that punishment shall follow transgression. The command of the lawgiver is, therefore, a law or rule. But the command of the judge is occasional or particular. For he orders a specific punishment, as the consequence of a specific offence. . . .

It appears, from what has been premised, that a law, properly so called, may be defined in the following manner.

A law is a command which obliges a person or persons.

But, as contradistinguished or opposed to an occasional or particular command, a law is a command which obliges a person or persons, and obliges *generally* to acts or forbearances of a *class*.

In language more popular but less distinct and precise, a law is a command which obliges a person or persons to a *course* of conduct.

Laws and other commands are said to proceed from *superiors*, and to bind or oblige *inferiors*. I will, therefore, analyze the meaning of those correlative expressions; and will try to strip them of a certain mystery, by which that simple meaning appears to be obscured.

Superiority is often synonymous with *precedence or excellence*. . . .

But, taken with the meaning wherein I here understand it, the term *superiority* signifies *might*: the power of affecting others with evil or pain, and of forcing them, through fear of that evil, to fashion their conduct to one's wishes.

For example, God is emphatically the *superior* of Man. For His power of affecting us with pain, and of forcing us to comply with His will, is unbounded and resistless.

To a limited extent, the sovereign One or Number is the superior of the subject or citizen: the master, of the slave or servant: the father, of the child.

In short, whoever can *oblige* another to comply with his wishes, is the *superior* of that other, so far as the ability reaches: The party who is obnoxious to the impending evil, being, to that same extent, the *inferior*.

The might or superiority of God, is simple or absolute. . . .

A member of a sovereign assembly is the superior of the judge: the judge being bound by the law which proceeds from that sovereign body. But, in his character of citizen or subject, he is the inferior of the judge: the judge being the minister of the law, and armed with the power of enforcing it.

It appears, then, that the term *superiority* (like the terms *duty* and *sanction*) is implied by the term *command*. For superiority is the power of enforcing compliance with a wish: and the expression or intimation of a wish, with the power and the purpose of enforcing, are the constituent elements of a command.

"That *laws* emanate from *superiors*" is, therefore, an identical proposition. For the meaning which it affects to impart is contained in its subject. . . .

According to an opinion which I must notice *incidentally* here, though the subject to which it relates will be treated *directly* hereafter, *customary laws* must be excepted from the proposition "that laws are a series of commands."

By many of the admirers of customary laws . . . they are thought to oblige legally (independently of the sovereign or state), *because* the citizens or subjects have observed or kept them. . . .

At its origin, a custom is a rule of conduct which the governed observe spontaneously, or not in pursuance of a law set by a political superior. The custom is transmitted into positive law, when it is adopted as such by the courts of justice, and when the judicial decisions fashioned upon it are enforced by the power of the state. But before it is adopted by the courts, and clothed with the legal sanction, it is merely a rule of positive morality: a rule generally observed by the citizens or subjects; but deriving the only force, which it can be said to possess, from the general disapprobation falling on those who transgress it.

Now when judges transmute a custom into a legal rule (or make a legal rule not suggested by a custom), the legal rule which they establish is established by the sovereign legislature. A subordinate or subject judge is merely a minister. The portion of the sovereign power which lies at his disposition is merely delegated. The rules which he makes derive their legal force from authority given by the state: an authority which the state may confer expressly, but which it commonly imparts in the way of acquiescence. For, since the state may reverse the rules which he makes, and yet permits him to enforce them by the power of the political community, its sovereign will "that his rules shall obtain as law" is clearly evinced by its conduct, though not by its express declaration. . . .

Lecture 5

. . . Now it follows from these premises, that the laws of God, and positive laws are laws proper, or laws properly so called.

The laws of God are laws proper, inasmuch as they are *commands* express or tacit, and therefore emanate from a *certain* source.

Positive laws, or laws strictly so called, are established directly or immediately by authors of three kinds:—by monarchs, or sovereign bodies, as supreme political superiors: by men in a state of subjection, as subordinate political superiors: by subjects, as private persons, in pursuance of legal rights. But every positive law, or every law strictly so called, is a direct or circuitous command of a monarch or sovereign number in the character of political superior: that is to say, a direct or circuitous command of a monarch or sovereign number to a person or persons in a state of subjection to its author. And being a *command* (and therefore

flowing from a *determinate* source), every positive law is a law proper, or a law properly so called.

Besides the human laws which I style positive law, there are human laws which I style positive morality, rules of positive morality, or positive moral rules.

The generic character of laws of the class may be stated briefly in the following negative manner.—No law belonging to the class is a direct or circuitous command of a monarch or sovereign number in the character of political superior. In other words, no law belonging to the class is a direct or circuitous command of a monarch or sovereign number to a person or persons in a state of subjection to its author. . . .

The existence of law is one thing; its merit or demerit is another. Whether it be or be not is one enquiry; whether it be or be not conformable to an assumed standard, is a different enquiry. A law, which actually exists, is a law, though we happen to dislike it, or though it vary from the text, by which we regulate our approbation and disapprobation. This truth, when formally announced as an abstract proposition, is so simple and glaring that it seems idle to insist upon it. But simple and glaring as it is, when enunciated in abstract expressions the enumeration of the instances in which it has been forgotten would fill a volume.

Sir William Blackstone, for example, says in his "Commentaries," that the laws of God are superior in obligation to all other laws; that no human laws should be suffered to contradict them; that human laws are of no validity if contrary to them; and that all valid laws derive their force from that Divine original.

Now, he *may* mean that all human laws ought to conform to the Divine laws. If this be his meaning, I assent to it without hesitation. The evils which we are exposed to suffer from the hands of God as a consequence of disobeying His commands are the greatest evils to which we are obnoxious; the obligations which they impose are consequently paramount to those imposed by any other laws, and if human commands conflict with the Divine law, we ought to disobey the command which is enforced by the less powerful sanction; this is implied in the term *ought*: the proposition is identical, and therefore perfectly indisputable—it is our interest to choose the smaller and more uncertain evil, in preference to the greater and surer. If this be Blackstone's meaning, I assent to his proposition, and have only to object to it, that it tells us just nothing.

Perhaps, again, he means that human lawgivers are themselves obliged by the Divine laws to fashion the laws which they impose by that ultimate standard, because if they do not, God will punish them. To this also I entirely assent. . . .

But the meaning of this passage of Blackstone, if it has a meaning, seems rather to be this: that no human law which conflicts with the Divine law is obligatory or binding; in other words, that no human law which conflicts with the Divine law *is a law*, for a law without an obligation is a contradiction in terms. I suppose this to be his meaning, because when we say of any transaction that it is invalid or void, we mean that it is not binding: as, for example, if it be a contract, we mean that the political law will not lend its sanction to enforce the contract.

Now, to say that human laws which conflict with the Divine law are not binding, that is to say, are not laws, is to talk stark nonsense. The most pernicious laws, and therefore those which are most opposed to the will of God, have been and are continually enforced as laws by judicial tribunals. Suppose an act innocuous, or positively beneficial, be prohibited by the sovereign under the penalty of death; if I commit this act, I shall be tried and condemned, and if I object to the sentence, that it is contrary to the law of God, who has commanded that human lawgivers shall not prohibit acts which have no evil consequences, the Court of Justice will demonstrate the inconclusiveness of my reasoning by hanging me up, in pursuance of the law of which I have impugned the validity. An exception, demurrer, or plea, founded on the law of God was never heard in a Court of Justice, from the creation of the world down to the present moment.

But this abuse of language is not merely puerile, it is mischievous. When it is said that a law ought to be disobeyed, what is meant is that we are urged to disobey it by motives more cogent and compulsory than those by which it is itself sanctioned. If the laws of God are certain, the motives which they hold out to disobey any human command which is at variance with them are para-mount to all others. But the laws of God are not always certain. . . . In quiet times the dictates of utility are fortunately so obvious that the anarchical doctrine sleeps, and men habitually admit the validity of laws which they dislike. To prove by pertinent reasons that a law is pernicious is highly useful, because such process may lead to the abrogation of the pernicious law. To incite the public to resistance by determinate views of *utility* may be useful, for resistance, grounded on clear and definite prospects of good, is sometimes beneficial. But to proclaim generally that all laws which are pernicious or contrary to the will of God are void and not to be tolerated, is to preach anarchy, hostile and perilous as much to wise and benign rule as to stupid and galling tryanny. . . .

Lecture 6

. . . Every positive law, or every law simply and strictly so called, is set by a sovereign person, or a sovereign body of persons, to a member or members of the independent political society wherein that person or body is sovereign or supreme. Or (changing the expression) it is set by a monarch, or sovereign number, to a person or persons in a state of subjection to its author. Even though it sprung directly from another fountain or source, it *is* a positive law, or a law strictly so called, by the institution of that present sovereign in the character of political superior. . . .

The superiority which is styled sovereignty, and the independent political society which sovereignty implies, is distinguished from other superiority, and from other society, by the following marks or characters.—1. The bulk of the given society are in a *habit* of obedience or submission to a *determinate* and *common* superior: let that common superior be a certain individual person, or a certain body or aggregate of individual persons. 2. That certain individual, or that certain body of individuals, is *not* in a habit of obedience to a determinate human superior. Laws (improperly so called) which opinion sets or imposes, may permanently affect the conduct of that certain individual or body. To express or tacit commands of other determinate parties, that certain individual or body may yield occasional submission. But there is no determinate person, determinate aggregate of persons, to whose commands, express or tacit, that certain individual or body renders habitual obedience. . . . By "an independent political society," or "an independent and sovereign nation," we mean a political society consisting of a sovereign and subjects, as opposed to a political society which is merely subordinate: that is to say, which is merely a limb or member of another political society, and which therefore consists entirely of persons in a state of subjection.

In order that a given society may form a society political and independent, the two distinguish-ing marks which I have mentioned above must unite. The *generality* of the given society must be in the *habit* of obedience to a *determinate* and *common* superior: whilst that determinate person, or determinate body of persons must *not* be habitually obedient to a determinate person or body. It is the union of that positive, with this negative mark, which renders that certain superior sovereign or supreme, and which renders that given society (including that certain superior) a society political and independent.

---

8. *Positivism and the Separation of Law and Morals*

H. L. A. HART

In this article I shall discuss and attempt to defend a view which Mr. Justice Holmes, among others, held and for which he and they have been much criticized. . . . Contemporary voices tell us we must recognize something obscured by the legal "positivist" whose day is now over: that there is a "point of intersection between law and morals," or that what *is* and what *ought to* be are somehow indissolubly fused or inseparable, though the positivists denied it. What do these phrases mean? Or rather which of the many things that they *could* mean, *do* they mean? Which of them do "positivists" deny and why is it wrong to do so?

1

I shall present the subject as part of the history of an idea. At the close of the eighteenth century and the beginning of the nineteenth the most earnest thinkers in England about legal and social problems and the architects of great reforms were the great utilitarians. Two of them, Bentham and Austin, constantly insisted on the need to distinguish, firmly and with the maximum of clarity, law as it is from law as it ought to be. This theme haunts their work, and they condemned the natural-law thinkers precisely because they had blurred this apparently simple but vital distinction. By contrast, at the present time in this country and to a lesser extent in England, this separation between law and morals is held to be superficial and wrong. Some critics have thought that it blinds men to the true nature of law and its roots in social life. Others have thought it not only intellectually

From *Harvard Law Review*, Vol. 71 (1958), pp. 593–629. Copyright (c) 1958 by the Harvard Law Review Association. Reprinted with permission of the *Harvard Law Review*.

misleading but corrupting in practice, at its worst apt to weaken resistance to state tyranny or absolutism, and at its best apt to bring law into disrespect. The nonpejorative name "legal positivism," like most terms which are used as missiles in intellectual battles, has come to stand for a baffling multitude of different sins. One of them is the sin, real or alleged, of insisting, as Austin and Bentham did, on the separation of law as it is and law as it ought to be.

How then has this reversal of the wheel come about? What are the theoretical errors in this distinction? Have the practical consequences of stressing the distinction as Bentham and Austin did been bad? Should we now reject it or keep it? In considering these questions we should recall the social philosophy which went along with the utilitarians' insistence on this distinction. They stood firmly but on their own utilitarian ground for all the principles of liberalism in law and government. No one has ever combined, with such even-minded sanity as the utilitarians, the passion for reform with respect for law together with a due recognition of the need to control the abuse of power even when power is in the hands of reformers. . . . Here are liberty of speech, and of press, the right of association, the need that laws should be published and made widely known before they are enforced, the need to control administrative agencies, the insistence that there should be no criminal liability without fault, and the importance of the principle of legality, *nulla poena sine lege* [no punishment without law]. Some, I know, find the political and moral insight of the utilitarians a very simple one, but we should not mistake this simplicity for superficiality nor forget how favorably their simplicities compare with the profundities of other thinkers. Take only one example: Bentham on slavery. He says the question at issue is not whether those who are held as slaves can reason, but simply whether they suffer. Does this not compare well with the discussion of the question in terms of whether or not there are some men whom Nature has fitted only to be the living instruments of others? We owe it to Bentham more than anyone else that we have stopped discussing this and similar questions of social policy in that form.

So Bentham and Austin were not dry analysts fiddling with verbal distinctions while cities burned, but were the vanguard of a movement which laboured with passionate intensity and much success to bring about a better society and better laws. Why then did they insist on the separation of law as it is and law as it ought to be? What did they mean? Let us first see what they said. Austin formulated the doctrine:

> The existence of law is one thing; its merit or demerit is another. Whether it be or be not is one enquiry; whether it be or be not conformable to an assumed standard, is a different enquiry. A law, which actually exists, is a law, though we happen to dislike it, or though it vary from the text, by which we regulate our approbation and disapprobation. This truth, when formally announced as an abstract proposition, is so simple and glaring that it seems idle to insist upon it. But simple and glaring as it is, when enunciated in abstract expressions the enumeration of the instances in which it has been forgotten would fill a volume.
>
> Sir William Blackstone, for example, says in his "Commentaries," that the laws of God are superior in obligation to all other laws; that no human laws should be suffered to contradict them; that human laws are of no validity if contrary to them; and that all valid laws derive their force from that Divine original.
>
> Now, he *may* mean that all human laws ought to conform to the Divine laws. If this be his meaning, I assent to it without hesitation. . . . Perhaps, again, he means that human lawgivers are themselves obliged by the Divine laws to fashion the laws which they impose by that ultimate standard, because if they do not, God will punish them. To this also I entirely assent. . . .
>
> But the meaning of this passage of Blackstone, if it has a meaning, seems rather to be this: that no human law which conflicts with the Divine law is obligatory or binding; in other words, that no human law which conflicts with the Divine law *is a law.* . . .

Austin's protest against blurring the distinction between what law is and what it ought to be is quite general; it is a mistake, whatever our standard of what ought to be, whatever "the text by which we regulate our approbation or disapprobation." His examples, however, are always a confusion between law as it is and law as morality would require it to be. For him, it must be remembered, the fundamental principles of morality were God's commands, to which utility was an "index": besides this there was the actual accepted morality of a social group or "positive" morality. . . .

In view of later criticisms it is also important to distinguish several things that the utilitarians did not mean by insisting on their separation of law and morals. They certainly accepted many of the things that might be called "the intersection of law and morals." First, they never denied that, as a matter of historical fact, the development of legal systems had been powerfully influenced by moral opinion, and, conversely, that moral standards had been profoundly influenced by law, so that the content of many legal rules mirrored moral rules or principles. . . .

Secondly, neither Bentham nor his followers denied that by explicit legal provisions moral principles might at different points be brought into a legal system and form part of its rules, or that courts might be legally bound to decide in accordance with what they thought just or best. . . .

What both Bentham and Austin were anxious to assert were the following two simple things: first, in the absence of all expressed constitutional or legal provision, it could not follow from the mere fact that a rule violated standards of morality that it was not a rule of law; and, conversely, it could not follow from the mere fact that a rule was morally desirable that it was a rule of law. . . .

2

So much for the doctrine in the heyday of its success. Let us turn now to some of the criticisms.

. . . We must remember that the utilitarians combined with their insistence on the separation of law and morals two other equally famous but distinct doctrines. One was the important truth that a purely analytical study of legal concepts, a study of the meaning of the distinctive vocabulary of the law, was as vital to our understanding of the nature of law as historical or sociological studies, though

of course it could not supplant them. The other doctrine was the famous imperative theory of law—that law is essentially a command.

These three doctrines constitute the utilitarian tradition in jurisprudence; yet they are distinct doctrines. It is possible to endorse the separation between law and morals and to value analytical inquiries into the meaning of legal concepts and yet think it wrong to conceive of law as essentially a command. One source of great confusion in the criticism of the separation of law and morals was the belief that the falsity of any one of these three doctrines in the utilitarian tradition showed the other two to be false; what was worse was the failure to see that there were three quite separate doctrines in this tradition. . . . [Some] critics . . . have thought that the inadequacies of the command theory which gradually came to light were sufficient to demonstrate the falsity of the separation of law and morals.

This was a mistake, but a natural one. To see how natural it was we must look a little more closely at the command idea. The famous theory that law is a command was a part of a wider and more ambitious claim. Austin said that the notion of a command was "the *key* to the sciences of jurisprudence and morals," and contemporary attempts to elucidate moral judgments in terms of "imperative" or "prescriptive" utterances echo this ambitious claim. But the command theory, viewed as an effort to identify even the quintessence of law, let alone the quintessence of morals, seems breathtaking in its simplicity and quite inadequate. There is much, even in the simplest legal system, that is distorted if presented as a command. Yet the utilitarians thought that the essence of a legal system could be conveyed if the notion of a command were supplemented by that of a habit of obedience. The simple scheme was this: What is a command? It is simply an expression by one person of the desire that another person should do or abstain from some action, accompanied by a threat of punishment which is likely to follow disobedience. Commands are laws if two conditions are satisfied: First, they must be general; second, they must be commanded by what (as both Bentham and Austin claimed) exists in every political society whatever its constitutional form, namely, a person or a group of persons who are in receipt of habitual obedience from most of the society but pay no such obedience to others. These persons are its sovereign. Thus law is the command of the uncommanded commanders of society—the creation of the legally untrammeled will of the sovereign who is by definition outside the law.

It is easy to see that this account of a legal system is threadbare. One can also see why it might seem that its inadequacy is due to the omission of some essential connection with morality. The situation which the simple trilogy of command, sanction, and sovereign avails to describe, if you take these notions at all precisely, is like that of a gunman saying to his victim, "Give me your money or your life." The only difference is that in the case of a legal system the gunman says it to a large number of people who are accustomed to the racket and habitually surrender to it. Law surely is not the gunman situation writ large, and legal order is surely not to be thus simply identified with compulsion.

This scheme, despite the points of obvious analogy between a statute and a command, omits some of the most characteristic elements of law. Let me cite a few. It is wrong to think of a legislature (and a fortiori an electorate) with a changing membership, as a group of persons habitually obeyed: this simple idea is suited only to a monarch sufficiently long-lived for a "habit" to grow up. Even if we waive this point, nothing which legislators do makes law unless they comply with fundamental accepted rules specifying the essential lawmaking procedures. This is true even in a system having a simple unitary constitution like the British. These fundamental accepted rules specifying what the legislature must do to legislate are not commands habitually obeyed, nor can they be expressed as habits of obedience to persons. They lie at the root of a legal system, and what is most missing in the utilitarian scheme is an analysis of what it is for a social group and its officials to accept such rules. This notion, not that of a command as Austin claimed, is the "key to the science of jurisprudence," or at least one of the keys.

Again, Austin, in the case of a democracy, looked past the legislators to the electorate as "the sovereign" (or in England as part of it). He thought that in the United States the mass of the electors to the state and federal legislatures were the sovereign whose commands, given by their "agents" in the legislatures, were law. But on this footing the whole notion of the sovereign outside the law being "habitually obeyed" by the "bulk" of the population must go: for in this case the "bulk" obeys the bulk, that is, it obeys itself. Plainly the general acceptance of the authority of a lawmaking procedure, irrespective of the changing individuals who operate it from time to time, can be only distorted by an analysis in terms of mass habitual obedience to certain persons who are by definition outside the law, just as the cognate but much simpler phenomenon of the general social acceptance of a rule, say of taking off the hat when entering a church, would be distorted if represented as habitual obedience by the mass to specific persons.

Other critics dimly sensed a further and more important defect in the command theory, yet blurred the edge of an important criticism by assuming that the defect was due to the failure to insist upon some important connection between law and morals. This more radical defect is as follows. The picture that the command theory draws of life under law is essentially a simple relationship of the commander to the commanded, of superior to inferior, of top to bottom; the relationship is vertical between the commanders or authors of the law conceived of as essentially outside the law and those who are commanded and subject to the law. In this picture no place, or only an accidental or subordinate place, is afforded for a distinction between types of legal rules which are in fact radically different. Some laws require men to act in certain ways or to abstain from acting whether they wish to or not. The criminal law consists largely of rules of this sort: like commands they are simply "obeyed" or "disobeyed." But other legal rules are presented to society in quite different ways and have quite different functions. They provide facilities more or less elaborate for individuals to create structures of rights and duties for the conduct of life within the coercive framework of the law. Such are the rules enabling individuals to make contracts, wills, and trusts, and generally to mould their legal relations with others. Such rules, unlike the criminal law, are not factors designed to obstruct wishes and choices of an antisocial sort. On the contrary, these rules provide facilities for the realization of wishes and choices. They do not say (like commands) "do this whether you wish it or not," but rather "if you wish to do this, here is the way to do it." Under these rules we exercise powers, make claims, and assert rights. These phrases mark off characteristic features of laws that confer rights and powers; they are laws which are, so to speak, put at the disposition of individuals in a way in which the criminal law is not.

. . . Rules that confer rights, though distinct from commands, need not be moral rules or coincide with them. Rights, after all, exist under the rules of ceremonies, games, and in many other spheres regulated by rules which are irrelevant to the question of justice or what the law ought to be. Nor need rules which confer rights be just or morally good rules. The rights of a master over his slaves show us that. "Their merit or demerit," as Austin termed it, depends on how rights are distributed in society and over whom or what they are exercised. These critics indeed revealed the inadequacy of the simple notions of command and habit for the analysis of law; at many points it is apparent that the social acceptance of a rule or standard of authority (even if it is motivated only by fear or superstition or rests on inertia) must be brought into the analysis and cannot itself be reduced to the two simple terms. Yet nothing in this showed the utilitarian insistence on the distinction between the existence of law and its "merits" to be wrong.

3

I now turn to a distinctively American criticism of the separation of the law that is from the law that ought to be. It emerged from the critical study of the judicial process with which American jurisprudence has been on the whole so beneficially occupied. The most skeptical of these critics—the loosely named "Realists" of the 1930s—perhaps too naively accepted the conceptual framework of the natural sciences as adequate for the characterization of law and for the analysis of rule guided action of which a living system of law at least partly consists. But they opened men's eyes to what actually goes on when courts decide cases, and the contrast they drew between the actual facts of judicial decision and the traditional terminology for describing it as if it were a wholly logical operation was usually illuminating; for in spite of some exaggeration the "Realists" made us acutely conscious of one cardinal feature of human language and human thought, emphasis on which is vital not only for the understanding of law but in areas of philosophy far beyond the confines of jurisprudence. The insight of this school may be presented in the following example. A legal rule forbids you to take a vehicle into the public park. Plainly this forbids an automobile, but what about bicycles, roller skates, toy automobiles? What about airplanes? Are these, as we say, to be called "vehicles" for the purpose of the rule or not? If we are to communicate with each other at all, and if, as in the most elementary form of law, we are to express our intentions that a certain type of behavior be regulated by rules, then the general words we use—like "vehicle" in the case I consider—must have some standard instance in which no doubts are felt about its application. There must be a core of settled meaning, but there will be, as well, a penumbra of debatable cases in which words are neither obviously applicable nor obviously ruled out. These cases will each have some features of common with the standard case; they will lack others or be accompanied by features not present in the standard case. Human invention and natural processes continually throw up such variants on the familiar, and if we are to say that these ranges of facts do or do not fall under existing rules, then the classifier must make a decision which is not dictated to him, for the facts and phenomena to which we fit our words and apply our rules are as it were *dumb*. The toy automobile cannot speak up and say, "I am a vehicle for the purpose of this legal rule," nor can the roller skates chorus, "We are not a vehicle." Fact situations do not await us neatly labeled, creased, and folded, nor is their legal classification written on them to be simply read off by the judge. Instead, in applying legal rules, some one must take the responsibility of deciding that words do or do not cover some case in hand with all the practical consequences involved in this decision.

We may call the problems which arise outside the hard core of standard instances or settled meaning "problems of the penumbra"; they are always with us whether in relation to such trivial things as the regulation of the use of the public park or in relation to the multidimensional generalities of a constitution. If a penumbra of uncertainty must surround all legal rules, then their application to specific cases in the penumbral area cannot be a matter of logical deduction, and so deductive reasoning, which for generations has been cherished as the very perfection of human reasoning, cannot serve as a model for what judges, or indeed anyone, should do in bringing particular cases under general rules. In this area men cannot live by deduction alone. And it follows that if legal arguments and legal decisions of penumbral questions are to be rational, their rationality must lie in something other than a logical relation to premise. So if it is rational or "sound" to argue and to decide that for the purposes of this rule an airplane is not a vehicle, this argument must be sound or rational without being logically conclusive. What is it then that makes such decisions correct or at least better than alternative decisions? Again, it seems true to say that the criterion which makes a decision sound in such cases is some concept of what the law ought to be; it is easy to slide from that into saying that it must be a moral judgment about what law ought to be. So here we touch upon a point of necessary "intersection between law and morals" which demonstrates the falsity or, at any rate, the misleading character of the utilitarians' emphatic insistence on the separation of law as it is and ought to be. Surely, Bentham and Austin could only have written as they did because they misunderstood or neglected this aspect of the judicial process, because they ignored the problems of the penumbra.

The misconception of the judicial process which ignores the problems of the penumbra and which views the process as consisting preeminently in deductive reasoning is often stigmatized as the error of "formalism" or "literalism." My question now is, how and to what extent does the demonstration of this error show the utilitarian distinction to be wrong or misleading? Here there are many issues which have been confused, but I can only disentangle some. The charge of formalism has been leveled both at the "positivist" legal theorist and at the courts, but of course it must be a very different charge in each case. Leveled at the legal theorist, the charge means that he has made a theoretical mistake about the character of legal decision; he has thought of the reasoning involved as consisting in deduction from premises in which the judges' practical choices or decision play no

part. It would be easy to show that Austin was guiltless of this error; only an entire misconception of what analytical jurisprudence is and why he thought it important has led to the view that he, or any other analyst, believed that the law was a closed logical system in which judges deduced their decisions from premises. On the contrary, he was very much alive to the character of language, to its vagueness or open character; he thought that in the penumbral situation judges must necessarily legislate, and, in accents that sometimes recall those of the late Judge Jerome Frank, he berated the common-law judges for legislating feebly and timidly and for blindly relying on real or fancied analogies with past cases instead of adapting their decisions to the growing needs of society as revealed by the moral standard of utility. The villains of this piece, responsible for the conception of the judge as an automaton, are not the utilitarian thinkers. The responsibility, if it is to be laid at the door of any theorist, is with . . . Blackstone's "childish fiction" (as Austin termed it) that judges only "find," never "make," law.

But we are concerned with "formalism" as a vice not of jurists but of judges. What precisely is it for a judge to commit this error, to be a "formalist," "automatic," a "slot machine"? . . . It is clear that the essence of his error is to give some general term an interpretation which is blind to social values and consequences (or which is in some other way stupid or perhaps merely disliked by critics). But logic does not prescribe interpretation of terms; it dictates neither the stupid nor intelligent interpretation of any expression. Logic only tells you hypothetically that *if* you give a certain term a certain interpretation then a certain conclusion follows. Logic is silent on how to classify particulars—and this is the heart of a judicial decision. So this reference to logic and to logical extremes is a misnomer for something else, which must be this. A judge has to apply a rule to a concrete case—perhaps the rule that one may not take a stolen "vehicle" across state lines, and in this case an airplane has been taken. He either does not see or pretends not to see that the general terms of this rule are susceptible of different interpretations and that he has a choice left open uncontrolled by linguistic conventions. He ignores, or is blind to, the fact that he is in the area of the penumbra and is not dealing with a standard case. Instead of choosing in the light of social aims, the judge fixes the meaning in a different way. He either takes the meaning that the word most obviously suggests in its ordinary nonlegal context to ordinary men, or one which the word has been given in some other legal context, or, still worse, he thinks of a standard case and then arbitrarily identifies certain features in it—for example, in the case of a vehicle, (1) normally used on land, (2) capable of carrying a human person, (3) capable of being self propelled—and treats these three as always necessary and always sufficient conditions for the use in all contexts of the word "vehicle," irrespective of the social consequences of giving it this interpretation. This choice, not "logic," would force the judge to include a toy motor car (if electrically propelled) and to exclude bicycles and the airplane. In all this there is possibly great stupidity but not more "logic," and no less, than in cases in which the interpretation given to a general term and the consequent application of some general rule to a particular case is consciously controlled by some identified social aim.

Decisions made in a fashion as blind as this would scarcely deserve the name of decisions; we might as well toss a penny in applying a rule of law. But it is at least doubtful whether any judicial decisions (even in England) have been quite as automatic as this. Rather either the interpretations stigmatized as automatic have resulted from the conviction that it is fairer in a criminal statute to take a meaning which would jump to the mind of the ordinary man at the cost even of defeating other values, and this itself is a social policy (though possibly a bad one); or much more frequently, what is stigmatized as "mechanical" and "automatic" is a determined choice made indeed in the light of a social aim but of a conservative social aim. Certainly many of the Supreme Court decisions at the turn of the century which have been so stigmatized represent clear choices in the penumbral area to give effect to a policy of a conservative type. . . .

But how does the wrongness of deciding cases in an automatic and mechanical way and the rightness of deciding cases by reference to social purposes show that the utilitarian insistence on the distinction between what the law is and what it ought to be is wrong? I take it that no one who wished to use these vices of formalism as proof that

the distinction between what is and what ought to be is mistaken would deny that the decisions stigmatized as automatic are law; nor would he deny that the system in which such automatic decisions are made is a legal system. Surely he would say that they are law, but they are bad law, they ought not to be law. But this would be to use the distinction, not to refute it; and of course both Bentham and Austin used it to attack judges for failing to decide penumbral cases in accordance with the growing needs of society.

Clearly, if the demonstration of the errors of formalism is to show the utilitarian distinction to be wrong, the point must be drastically restated. The point must be not merely that a judicial decision to be rational must be made in the light of some conception of what ought to be, but that the aims, the social policies and purposes to which judges should appeal if their decisions are to be rational, are themselves to be considered as part of the law in some suitably wide sense of "law" which is held to be more illuminating than that used by the utilitarians. This restatement of the point would have the following consequence: Instead of saying that the recurrence of penumbral questions shows us that legal rules are essentially incomplete, and that, when they fail to determine decisions, judges must legislate and so exercise a creative choice between alternatives, we shall say that the social policies which guide the judges' choice are in a sense there for them to discover; the judges are only "drawing out" of the rule what, if it is properly understood, is "latent" within it. To call this judicial legislation is to obscure some essential continuity between the clear cases of the rule's application and the penumbral decisions. I shall question later whether this way of talking is salutary, but I wish at this time to point out something obvious, but likely, if not stated, to tangle the issues. It does not follow that, because the opposite of a decision reached blindly in the formalist or literalist manner is a decision intelligently reached by reference to some conception of what ought to be, we have a junction of law and morals. We must, I think, beware of thinking in a too simpleminded fashion about the word "ought." This is not because there is no distinction to be made between law as it is and ought to be. Far from it. It is because the distinction should be between what is and what from many different points of view ought to be. The word "ought" merely reflects the presence of some standard of criticism; one of these standards is a moral standard but not all standards are moral. We say to our neighbour, "You ought not to lie," and that may certainly be a moral judgment, but we should remember that the baffled poisoner may say, "I ought to have given her a second dose." The point here is that intelligent decisions which we oppose to mechanical or formal decisions are not necessarily identical with decisions defensible on moral grounds. We may say of many a decision: "Yes, that is right; that is as it ought to be," and we may mean only that some accepted purpose or policy has been thereby advanced; we may not mean to endorse the moral propriety of the policy or the decision. So the contrast between the mechanical decision and the intelligent one can be reproduced inside a system dedicated to the pursuit of the most evil aims. It does not exist as a contrast to be found only in legal systems which, like our own, widely recognize principles of justice and moral claims of individuals.

An example may make this point plainer. With us the task of sentencing in criminal cases is the one that seems most obviously to demand from the judge the exercise of moral judgement. Here the factors to be weighed seem clearly to be moral factors: society must not be exposed to wanton attack; too much misery must not be inflicted on either the victim or his dependents; efforts must be made to enable him to lead a better life and regain a position in the society whose laws he has violated. To a judge striking the balance among these claims, with all the discretion and perplexities involved, his task seems as plain an example of the exercise of moral judgment as could be; and it seems to be the polar opposite of some mechanical application of a tariff of penalties fixing a sentence careless of the moral claims which in our system have to be weighed. So here intelligent and rational decision is guided however uncertainly by moral aims. But we have only to vary the example to see that this need not necessarily be so and surely, if it need not necessarily be so, the utilitarian point remains unshaken. Under the Nazi regime men were sentenced by courts for criticism of the regime. Here the choice of sentence might be guided exclusively by consideration of what was needed to maintain

the state's tyranny effectively. What sentence would both terrorize the public at large and keep the friends and family of the prisoner in suspense so that both hope and fear would cooperate as factors making for subservience? The prisoner of such a system would be regarded simply as an object to be used in pursuit of these aims. Yet, in contrast with a mechanical decision, decision on these grounds would be intelligent and purposive, and from one point of view the decision would be as it ought to be. Of course, I am not unaware that a whole philosophical tradition has sought to demonstrate the fact that we cannot correctly call decisions or behavior truly rational unless they are in conformity with moral aims and principles. But the example I have used seems to me to serve at least as a warning that we cannot use the errors of formalism as something which per se demonstrates the falsity of the utilitarian insistence on the distinction between law as it is and law as *morally* it ought to be.

We can now return to the main point. It is true that the intelligent decision of penumbral questions is one made not mechanically but in the light of aims, purposes, and policies, though not necessarily in the light of anything we would call moral principles, is it wise to express this important fact by saying that the firm utilitarian distinction between what the law is and what it ought to be should be dropped? Perhaps the claim that it is wise cannot be theoretically refuted for it is, in effect, an *invitation* to revise our conception of what a legal rule is. We are invited to include in the "rule" the various aims and policies in the light of which its penumbral cases are decided on the ground that these aims have, because of their importance, as much right to be called law as the core of legal rules whose meaning is settled. But though an invitation cannot be refuted, it may be refused and I would proffer two reasons for refusing this invitation. First, every thing we have learned about the judicial process can be expressed in other less mysterious ways. We can say laws are incurably incomplete and we must decide the penumbral cases rationally by reference to social aims. I think Holmes, who had such a vivid appreciation of the fact that "general propositions do not decide concrete cases," would have put it that way. Second, to insist on the utilitarian distinction is to emphasize that the hard core of settled meaning is law in some centrally important sense and that even if there are borderlines, there must first be lines. If this were not so the notion of rules controlling courts' decisions would be senseless as some of the "Realists"—in their most extreme moods, and, I think, on bad grounds—claimed.

By contrast, to soften the distinction, to assert mysteriously that there is some fused identity between law as it is and as it ought to be, is to suggest that all legal questions are fundamentally like those of the penumbra. It is to assert that there is no central element of actual law to be seen in the core of central meaning which rules have, that there is nothing in the nature of a legal rule inconsistent with *all* questions being open to reconsideration in the light of social policy. Of course, it is good to be occupied with the penumbra. Its problems are rightly the daily diet of the law schools. But to be occupied with the penumbra is one thing, to be preoccupied with it another. And preoccupation with the penumbra is, if I may say so, as rich a source of confusion in the American legal tradition as formalism in the English. Of course we might abandon the notion that rules have authority; we might cease to attach force or even meaning to an argument that a case falls clearly within a rule and the scope of a precedent. We might call all such reasoning "automatic" or "mechanical," which is already the routine invective of the courts. But until we decide that this is what we want; we should not encourage it by obliterating the utilitarian distinction. . . .

4

The third criticism of the separation of law and morals is of a very different character; it certainly is less an intellectual argument against the utilitarian distinction than a passionate appeal supported not by detailed reasoning but by reminders of a terrible experience. For it consists of the testimony of those who have descended into Hell, and, like Ulysses or Dante, brought back a message for human beings. Only in this case the Hell was not beneath or beyond earth, but on it; it was a Hell created on earth by men for other men.

This appeal comes from those German thinkers who lived through the Nazi regime and re-

flected upon its evil manifestations in the legal system. One of these thinkers, Gustav Radbruch, had himself shared the "positivist" doctrine until the Nazi tyranny, but he was converted by this experience and so his appeal to other men to discard the doctrine of the separation of law and morals has the special poignancy of a recantation. What is important about this criticism is that it really does confront the particular point which Bentham and Austin had in mind in urging the separation of law as it is and as it ought to be. . . .

. . . Austin, it may be recalled, was emphatic in condemning those who said that if human laws conflicted with the fundamental principles of morality then they cease to be laws, as talking "stark nonsense."

> The most pernicious laws, and therefore those which are most opposed to the will of God, have been and are continually enforced as laws by judicial tribunals. Suppose an act innocuous, or positively beneficial, be prohibited by the sovereign under the penalty of death; if I commit this act, I shall be tried and condemned, and if I object to the sentence, that it is contrary to the law of God . . . the court of justice will demonstrate the inconclusiveness of my reasoning by hanging me up, in pursuance of the law of which I have impugned the validity. An exception, demurrer, or plea, founded on the law of God was never heard in a Court of Justice, from the creation of the world down to the present moment.

These are strong, indeed brutal words, but we must remember that they went along—in the case of Austin and, of course, Bentham—with the conviction that if laws reached a certain degree of iniquity then there would be a plain moral obligation to resist them and to withhold obedience. We shall see, when we consider the alternatives, that this simple presentation of the human dilemma which may arise has much to be said for it. . . .

It is impossible to read without sympathy [the] passionate demand that the German legal conscience should be open to the demands of morality and [the] complaint that this has been too little the case in the German tradition. On the other hand there is an extraordinary naïveté in the view that insensitiveness to the demands of morality and subservience to state power in a people like the Germans should have arisen from the belief that law might be law though it failed to conform with the minimum requirements of morality. Rather this terrible history prompts inquiry into why emphasis on the slogan "law is law," and the distinction between law and morals, acquired a sinister character in Germany, but elsewhere, as with the utilitarians themselves, went along with the most enlightened liberal attitudes. . . . Let me cite briefly one of these cases.

In 1944 a woman, wishing to be rid of her husband, denounced him to the authorities for insulting remarks he had made about Hitler while home on leave from the German army. The wife was under no legal duty to report his acts, though what he had said was apparently in violation of statutes making it illegal to make statements detrimental to the government of the Third Reich or to impair by any means the military defense of the German people. The husband was arrested and sentenced to death, apparently pursuant to these statutes, though he was not executed but was sent to the front. In 1949 the wife was prosecuted in a West German court for an offense which we would describe as illegally depriving a person of his freedom (*rechtswidrige Freiheitsberaubung*). This was punishable as a crime under the German Criminal Code of 1871 which had remained in force continuously since its enactment. The wife pleaded that her husband's imprisonment was pursuant to the Nazi statutes and hence that she had committed no crime. The court of appeal to which the case ultimately came held that the wife was guilty of procuring the deprivation of her husband's liberty by denouncing him to the German courts, even though he had been sentenced by a court for having violated a statute, since, to quote the words of the court, the statute "was contrary to the sound conscience and sense of justice of all decent human beings." This reasoning was followed in many cases which have been hailed as a triumph of the doctrines of natural law and as signaling the overthrow of positivism. The unqualified satisfaction with this result seems to me to be hysteria. Many of us might applaud the objective—that of punishing a woman for an outrageously immoral act—but this was secured only by declaring a statute estab-

lished since 1934 not to have the force of law, and at least the wisdom of this course must be doubted. There were, of course, two other choices. One was to let the woman go unpunished; one can sympathize with and endorse the view that this might have been a bad thing to do. The other was to face the fact that if the woman were to be punished it must be pursuant to the introduction of a frankly retrospective law and with a full consciousness of what was sacrificed in securing her punishment in this way. Odious as retrospective criminal legislation and punishment may be, to have pursued it openly in this case would at least have had the merits of candour. It would have made plain that in punishing the woman a choice had to be made between two evils, that of leaving her unpunished and that of sacrificing a very precious principle of morality endorsed by most legal systems. Surely if we have learned anything from the history of morals it is that the thing to do with a moral quandary is not to hide it. Like nettles, the occasions when life forces us to choose between the lesser of two evils must be grasped with the consciousness that they are what they are. The vice of this use of the principle that, at certain limiting points, what is utterly immoral cannot be law or lawful is that it will serve to cloak the true nature of the problems with which we are faced and will encourage the romantic optimism that all the values we cherish ultimately will fit into a single system, that no one of them has to be sacrificed or compromised to accommodate another.

. . . If with the utilitarians we speak plainly, we say that laws may be law but too evil to be obeyed. This is a moral condemnation which everyone can understand and it makes an immediate and obvious claim to moral attention. If, on the other hand, we formulate our objection as an assertion that these evil things are not law, here is an assertion which many people do not believe, and if they are disposed to consider it at all, it would seem to raise a whole host of philosophical issues before it can be accepted. So perhaps the most important single lesson to be learned from this form of the denial of the utilitarian distinction is the one that the utilitarians were most concerned to teach: when we have the ample resources of plain speech we must not present the moral criticism of institutions as propositions of a disputable philosophy.

9. The Morality of Law

Lon L. Fuller

[A] law which a man cannot obey, nor act according to it, is void and no law: and it is impossible to obey contradictions, or act according to them.

Vaughan, C. J.

Thomas v. Sorrell, 1677

It is desired that our learned lawyers would answer these ensuing queries . . . whether ever the Commonwealth, when they chose the Parliament, gave them a lawless unlimited power, and at their pleasure to walk contrary to their own laws and ordinances before they have repealed them?

Lilburne

England's Birth-Right Justified, 1645

This chapter will begin with a fairly lengthy allegory. It concerns the unhappy reign of a monarch who bore the convenient, but not very imaginative and not even very regal sounding name of Rex.

Eight Ways to Fail to Make Law

Rex came to the throne filled with the zeal of a reformer. He considered that the greatest failure of his predecessors had been in the field of law. For generations the legal system had known nothing like a basic reform. Procedures of trial were cumbersome, the rules of law spoke in the archaic tongue of another age, justice was expensive, the judges were slovenly and sometimes corrupt. Rex was resolved to remedy all this and to make his name in history as a great lawgiver. It was his unhappy fate to fail in this ambition. Indeed, he failed spectacularly, since not only did he not succeed in introducing the needed reforms, but he never even succeeded in creating any law at all, good or bad.

His first official act was, however, dramatic and propitious. Since he needed a clean slate on which to write, he announced to his subjects the immediate repeal of all existing law, of whatever kind. He then set about drafting a new code. Unfortunately, trained as a lonely prince, his education had been very defective. In particular he found himself incapable of making even the simplest generalizations. Though not lacking in confidence when it came to deciding specific controversies, the effort to give articulate reasons for any conclusion strained his capacities to the breaking point.

Becoming aware of his limitations, Rex gave up the project of a code and announced to his subjects that henceforth he would act as a judge in any disputes that might arise among them. In this way under the stimulus of a variety of cases he hoped that his latent powers of generalization might

From Lon Fuller, *The Morality of Law.* © 1969 Yale University Press. Reprinted by permission of the publisher.

develop and, proceeding case by case, he would gradually work out a system of rules that could be incorporated in a code. Unfortunately the defects in his education were more deep-seated than he had supposed. The venture failed completely. After he had handed down literally hundreds of decisions neither he nor his subjects could detect in those decisions any pattern whatsoever. Such tentatives toward generalization as were to be found in his opinions only compounded the confusion, for they gave false leads to his subjects and threw his own meager powers of judgment off balance in the decision of later cases.

After this fiasco Rex realized it was necessary to take a fresh start. His first move was to subscribe to a course of lessons in generalization. With his intellectual powers thus fortified, he resumed the project of a code and, after many hours of solitary labor, succeeded in preparing a fairly lengthy document. He was still not confident, however, that he had fully overcome his previous defects. Accordingly, he announced to his subjects that he had written out a code and would henceforth be governed by it in deciding cases, but that for an indefinite future the contents of the code would remain an official state secret, known only to him and his scrivener. To Rex's surprise this sensible plan was deeply resented by his subjects. They declared it was very unpleasant to have one's case decided by rules when there was no way of knowing what those rules were.

Stunned by this rejection Rex undertook an earnest inventory of his personal strengths and weaknesses. He decided that life had taught him one clear lesson, namely, that it is easier to decide things with the aid of hindsight than it is to attempt to foresee and control the future. Not only did hindsight make it easier to decide cases, but—and this was of supreme importance to Rex—it made it easier to give reasons. Deciding to capitalize on this insight, Rex hit on the following plan. At the beginning of each calendar year he would decide all the controversies that had arisen among his subjects during the preceding year. He would accompany his decisions with a full statement of reasons. Naturally, the reasons thus given would be understood as not controlling decisions in future years, for that would be to defeat the whole purpose of the new

arrangement, which was to gain the advantages of hindsight. Rex confidently announced the new plan to his subjects, observing that he was going to publish the full text of his judgments with the rules applied by him, thus meeting the chief objection to the old plan. Rex's subjects received this announcement in silence, then quietly explained through their leaders that when they said they needed to know the rules, they meant they needed to know them in advance so they could act on them. Rex muttered something to the effect that they might have made that point a little clearer, but said he would see what could be done.

Rex now realized that there was no escape from a published code declaring the rules to be applied in future disputes. Continuing his lessons in generalization, Rex worked diligently on a revised code, and finally announced that it would shortly be published. This announcement was received with universal gratification. The dismay of Rex's subjects was all the more intense, therefore, when his code became available and it was discovered that it was truly a masterpiece of obscurity. Legal experts who studied it declared that there was not a single sentence in it that could be understood either by an ordinary citizen or by a trained lawyer. Indignation became general and soon a picket appeared before the royal palace carrying a sign that read, "How can anybody follow a rule that nobody can understand?"

The code was quickly withdrawn. Recognizing for the first time that he needed assistance, Rex put a staff of experts to work on a revision. He instructed them to leave the substance untouched, but to clarify the expression throughout. The resulting code was a model of clarity, but as it was studied it became apparent that its new clarity had merely brought to light that it was honeycombed with contradictions. It was reliably reported that there was not a single provision in the code that was not nullified by another provision inconsistent with it. A picket again appeared before the royal residence carrying a sign that read, "This time the king made himself clear—in both directions."

Once again the code was withdrawn for revision. By now, however, Rex had lost his patience with his subjects and the negative attitude they seemed to adopt toward everything he tried to do for them. He decided to teach them a lesson and put an end to their carping. He instructed his experts to purge the code of contradictions, but at the same time to stiffen drastically every requirement contained in it and to add a long list of new crimes. Thus, where before the citizen summoned to the throne was given ten days in which to report, in the revision the time was cut to ten seconds. It was made a crime, punishable by ten years' imprisonment, to cough, sneeze, hiccough, faint or fall down in the presence of the king. It was made treason not to understand, believe in, and correctly profess the doctrine of evolutionary, democratic redemption.

When the new code was published a near revolution resulted. Leading citizens declared their intention to flout its provisions. Someone discovered in an ancient author a passage that seemed apt: "To command what cannot be done is not to make law; it is to unmake law, for a command that cannot be obeyed serves no end but confusion, fear and chaos." Soon this passage was being quoted in a hundred petitions to the king.

The code was again withdrawn and a staff of experts charged with the task of revision. Rex's instructions to the experts were that whenever they encountered a rule requiring an impossibility, it should be revised to make compliance possible. It turned out that to accomplish this result every provision in the code had to be substantially rewritten. The final result was, however, a triumph of draftsmanship. It was clear, consistent with itself, and demanded nothing of the subject that did not lie easily within his powers. It was printed and distributed free of charge on every street corner.

However, before the effective date for the new code had arrived, it was discovered that so much time had been spent in successive revisions of Rex's original draft, that the substance of the code had been seriously overtaken by events. Ever since Rex assumed the throne there had been a suspension of ordinary legal processes and this had brought about important economic and institutional changes within the country. Accommodation to these altered conditions required many changes of substance in the law. Accordingly as soon as the new code became legally effective, it was subjected to a daily stream of amendments. Again popular discontent mounted; an anony-

mous pamphlet appeared on the streets carrying scurrilous cartoons of the king and a leading article with the title: "A law that changes every day is worse than no law at all."

Within a short time this source of discontent began to cure itself as the pace of amendment gradually slackened. Before this had occurred to any noticeable degree, however, Rex announced an important decision. Reflecting on the misadventures of his reign, he concluded that much of the trouble lay in bad advice he had received from experts. He accordingly declared he was reassuming the judicial power in his own person. In this way he could directly control the application of the new code and insure his country against another crisis. He began to spend practically all of his time hearing and deciding cases arising under the new code.

As the king proceeded with this task, it seemed to bring to a belated blossoming his long dormant powers of generalization. His opinions began, indeed, to reveal a confident and almost exuberant virtuosity as he deftly distinguished his own previous decisions, exposed the principles on which he acted, and laid down guidelines for the disposition of future controversies. For Rex's subjects a new day seemed about to dawn when they could finally conform their conduct to a coherent body of rules.

This hope was, however, soon shattered. As the bound volumes of Rex's judgments became available and were subjected to closer study, his subjects were appalled to discover that there existed no discernible relation between those judgments and the code they purported to apply. Insofar as it found expression in the actual disposition of controversies, the new code might just as well not have existed at all. Yet in virtually every one of his decisions Rex declared and redeclared the code to be the basic law of his kingdom.

Leading citizens began to hold private meetings to discuss what measures, short of open revolt, would be taken to get the king away from the bench and back on the throne. While these discussions were going on Rex suddenly died, old before his time and deeply disillusioned with his subjects.

The first act of his successor, Rex II, was to announce that he was taking the powers of government away from the lawyers and placing them in the hands of psychiatrists and experts in public relations. This way, he explained, people could be made happy without rules.

The Consequences of Failure

Rex's bungling career as legislator and judge illustrates that the attempt to create and maintain a system of legal rules may miscarry in at least eight ways; there are in this enterprise, if you will, eight distinct routes to disaster. The first and most obvious lies in a failure to achieve rules at all, so that every issue must be decided on an ad hoc basis. The other routes are: (2) a failure to publicize, or at least to make available to the affected party, the rules he is expected to observe; (3) the abuse of retroactive legislation, which not only cannot itself guide action, but undercuts the integrity of rules prospective in effect, since it puts them under the threat of retrospective change; (4) a failure to make rules understandable; (5) the enactment of contradictory rules or (6) rules that require conduct beyond the powers of the affected party; (7) introducing such frequent changes in the rules that the subject cannot orient his action by them; and, finally, (8) a failure of congruence between the rules as announced and their actual administration.

A total failure in any one of these eight directions does not simply result in a bad system of law; it results in something that is not properly called a legal system at all, except perhaps in the Pickwickian sense in which a void contract can still be said to be one kind of contract. Certainly there can be no rational ground for asserting that a man can have a moral obligation to obey a legal rule that does not exist, or is kept secret from him, or that came into existence only after he had acted, or was unintelligible, or was contradicted by another rule of the same system, or commanded the impossible, or changed every minute. It may not be impossible for a man to obey a rule that is disregarded by those charged with its administration, but at some point obedience becomes futile—as futile, in fact, as casting a vote that will never be counted. As the sociologist Simmel has observed, there is a kind of reciprocity between government and the citizen with respect to the observance of rules.[1] Government says to the citizen in effect, "These are the rules we expect you to follow. If you follow them, you have our assurance that they are the rules that will be applied to your conduct." When this bond of reciprocity is finally and completely ruptured by government, nothing is left on which to ground the citizen's duty to observe the rules.

The citizen's predicament becomes more difficult when, though there is no total failure in any direction, there is a general and drastic deterioration in legality, such as occurred in Germany under Hitler.[2] A situation begins to develop, for example, in which though some laws are published, others, including the most important, are not. Though most laws are prospective in effect, so free a use is made of retrospective legislation that no law is immune to change ex post facto if it suits the convenience of those in power. For the trial of criminal cases concerned with loyalty to the regime, special military tribunals are established and these tribunals disregard, whenever it suits their convenience, the rules that are supposed to control their decisions. Increasingly the principal object of government seems to be, not that of giving the citizen rules by which to shape his conduct, but to frighten him into impotence. As such a situation develops, the problem faced by the citizen is not so simple as that of a voter who knows with certainty that his ballot will not be counted. It is more like that of the voter who knows that the odds are against his ballot being counted at all, and that if it is counted, there is a good chance that it will be counted for the side against which he actually voted. A citizen in this predicament has to decide for himself whether to stay with the system and cast his ballot as a kind of symbolic act expressing the hope of a better day. So it was with the German citizen under Hitler faced with deciding whether he had an obligation to obey such portions of the laws as the Nazi terror had left intact.

In situations like these there can be no simple principle by which to test the citizen's obligation of fidelity to law, any more than there can be such a principle for testing his right to engage in a general revolution. One thing is, however, clear. A mere respect for constituted authority must not be confused with fidelity to law. Rex's subjects, for example, remained faithful to him as king throughout his long and inept reign. They were not faithful to his law, for he never made any. . . .

Legal Morality and Natural Law

. . . The first task is to relate what I have called the internal morality of the law to the ages-old tradition of natural law. Do the principles expounded in my second chapter represent some variety of natural law? The answer is an emphatic, though qualified, yes.

What I have tried to do is to discern and articulate the natural laws of a particular kind of human undertaking, which I have described as "the enterprise of subjecting human conduct to the governance of rules." These natural laws have nothing to do with any "brooding omnipresence in the skies." Nor have they the slightest affinity with any such proposition as that the practice of contraception is a violation of God's law. The remain entirely terrestrial in origin and application. They are not "higher" laws; if any metaphor of elevation *is* appropriate they should be called "lower" laws. They are like the natural laws of carpentry, or at least those laws respected by a carpenter who wants the house he builds to remain standing and serve the purpose of those who live in it.

Though these natural laws touch one of the most vital of human activities they obviously do not exhaust the whole of man's moral life. They have nothing to say on such topics as polygamy, the study of Marx, the worship of God, the progressive income tax, or the subjugation of women. If the question be raised whether any of these subjects, or others like them, should be taken as objects of legislation, that question relates to what I have called the external morality of law.

As a convenient (though not wholly satisfactory) way of describing the distinction being taken we may speak of a procedural, as distinguished from a substantive natural law. What I have called the internal morality of law is in this sense a procedural version of natural law, though to avoid misunderstanding the word "procedural" should be assigned a special and expanded sense so that it would include, for example, a substantive accord between official action and enacted law. The term "procedural" is, however, broadly appropriate as indicating that we are concerned, not with the substantive aims of legal rules, but with the ways in which a system of rules for governing human conduct must be constructed and administered if it is to be efficacious and at the same time remain what it purports to be. . . .

Legal Morality and the Concept of Positive Law

. . . The only formula that might be called a definition of law offered in these writings is by now thoroughly familiar: law is the enterprise of subjecting human conduct to the governance of rules. Unlike most modern theories of law, this view treats law as an activity and regards a legal system as the product of a sustained purposive effort. Let us compare the implications of such a view with others than might be opposed to it.

The first such theory I shall consider is one that in mood and emphasis stands at the opposite pole from these chapters and yet, paradoxically, advances a thesis that is easily reconciled with my own. This is Holmes' famous predictive theory of law: "The prophecies of what the courts will do in fact, and nothing more pretentious, are what I mean by law."[3]

Now clearly the ability to prophesy presupposes order of some sort. The predictive theory of law must therefore assume some constancy in the influences that determine what "the courts will do in fact." Holmes chose to abstract from any study of these influences, concentrating his attention on the cutting edge of the law.

He himself explained that he made this abstraction in order to effect a sharp distinction between law and morality. But he could think he had succeeded in this objective only by refraining from any attempt to describe the actual process of prediction itself. If we are to predict intelligently what the courts will do in fact, we must ask what they are trying to do. We must indeed go further and participate vicariously in the whole purposive effort that goes into creating and maintaining a system for directing human conduct by rules. If we are to understand that effort, we must understand that many of its characteristic problems are moral in nature. Thus, we need to put ourselves in the place of the judge faced with a statute extremely vague in its operative terms yet disclosing clearly enough in its preamble an objective the judge considers plainly unwise. We need to share the anguish of the weary legislative draftsman who at 2:00 A.M. says to himself, "I know this has got to be right and if it isn't people may be hauled into court for things we don't mean to cover at all. But how long must I go on rewriting it?"

A concentration on the order imposed by law in abstraction from the purposive effort that goes into creating it is by no means a peculiarity of Holmes' predictive theory. Professor Friedmann, for example, in an attempt to offer a neutral concept of law that will not import into the notion of law itself any particular ideal of substantive justice, proposes the following definition:

> the rule of law simply means the "existence of public order." It means organized government, operating through the various instruments and channels of legal command. In this sense, all modern societies live under the rule of law, fascist as well as socialist and liberal states.[4]

Now it is plain that a semblance of "public order" can be created by lawless terror, which may serve to keep people off the streets and in their homes. Obviously, Freidmann does not have this sort of order in mind, for he speaks of the "organized government, operating through the various instruments and channels of legal command." But beyond this vague intimation of the kind of order he has in mind he says nothing. He plainly indicates, however, a conviction that, considered just "as law," the law of Nazi Germany was as much law as that of any other nation. This proposition, I need not say, is completely at odds with the analysis presented here.

Endnotes

[1] The *Sociology of Georg Simmel* (1950), trans. Wolff, §4, "Interaction in the Idea of 'Law,'" pp. 186–89; see also Chapter 4, "Subordination under a Principle," pp. 250–67. Simmel's discussion is worthy of study by those concerned with defining the conditions under which the ideal of "the rule of law" can be realized.

[2] I have discussed some of the features of this deterioration in my article, "Positivism and Fidelity to Law," 71 *Harvard Law Review* 630, 648–57 (1958). This article makes no attempt at a comprehensive survey of all the postwar

judicial decisions in Germany concerned with events occurring during the Hitler regime. Some of the later decisions rested the nullity of judgments rendered by the courts under Hitler not on the ground that the statutes applied were void, but on the ground that the Nazi judges misinterpreted the statutes of their own government. See Pappe, "On the Validity of Judicial Decisions in the Nazi Era," 23 *Modern Law Review* 260–74 (1960). Dr. Pappe makes more of this distinction than seems to me appropriate. After all, the meaning of a statute depends in part on accepted modes of interpretation. Can it be said that the postwar German court gave full effect to Nazi laws when they interpreted them by their own standards instead of the quite different standards current during the Nazi regime? Moreover, with statutes of the kind involved, filled as they were with vague phrases and unrestricted delegations of power, it seems a little out of place to strain over questions of their proper interpretation.

[3] "The Path of the Law," 10 *Harvard Law Review* 457–78, at p. 461 (1897).

[4] *Law and Social Change* (1951), p. 281.

Study Questions

1. In what ways does the positivist separation of law and morals help to clarify the kind of dilemma faced by the postwar German courts in the grudge-informer cases, as Hart claims?

2. How does Fuller's naturalism differ from that of Aquinas?

3. In *The Province of Jurisprudence Determined,* Austin insists that "the existence of law is one thing; its merit or demerit is another. Whether it be or be not is one enquiry; whether it be or be not conformable to an assumed standard, is a different enquiry. A law, which actually exists, is a law, though we happen to dislike it, or though it vary from the text, by which we regulate our approbation or disapprobation." Does this statement reflect your understanding of "law"? Given this view, how could Austin explain or account for the idea that there is a moral obligation to obey the law? Does the claim that something is the "law" or is "lawful" carry with it any moral or normative connotation? Does the mere fact that

something is the law supply a reason for compliance with it?

4. How does Hart explain the difference between "primary" and "secondary" rules? In what ways do secondary rules cure the defects present in a society with only primary rules?

5. Does Fuller's claim that Rex failed to make law support his contention that there is an internal morality of law? Why or why not? Why is Fuller entitled to say that Rex failed to make law, rather than simply that Rex failed to make *good* (or sensible) law?

6. By 1998, King Bhumibol Adulyadej had served as monarch of Thailand for more than fifty years—he was the world's longest-reigning monarch. Since 1932, Thailand has had seventeen coups, twenty-three prime ministers, and sixteen constitutions. Under the current constitution, the King has few clearly defined powers, but he wields tremendous influence. Disruptive student demonstrations ended when he appeared on television and asked for order; violent clashes between prodemocracy groups and the military stopped when the leaders of the respective groups prostrated themselves before the King to receive a public scolding; governmental turmoil over the appointment of a new prime minister was resolved when rumors were circulated that the King was ill (the illness ceased when the dispute was settled); and during a recent hospitalization, 100,000 Thais came to his hospital to pray for the King's recovery. Is King Bhumibol a "sovereign," as Austin understands that term? Could Thailand have more than one sovereign? Try to imagine how Austin would respond to questions.

7. What is the difference between human law and the natural law, according to Aquinas?

8. Give an example of each of Aquinas' four types of laws.

D. *Modern Theories of Law*

American Legal Realism

The theories of law we have so far examined, positivism and naturalism, are undeniably abstract and seemingly far removed from the day-to-day activities of lawyers, judges, and police officers that most of us would at least initially identify as comprising the "law." During the first several decades of this century, a group of American legal scholars defended an approach to the study of law and legal systems quite unlike that found in Aquinas and Austin. These scholars, who later came to be called *legal realists*, wrote with the explicit aim of understanding the law in its daily operation by focusing on what judges and lawyers (and others) actually *do*, rather than what they, or theorists like Aquinas and Austin, *say* they do. The concern of the legal realists lay with the "law in action," not with the "law in books." In this section, we encounter the views of two prominent theorists associated with the realist movement.

Holmes and the "Bad Man"

Oliver Wendell Holmes's career spanned a vast period in American history, from before the Civil War to the New Deal. Holmes was a teacher, writer, judge, and justice of the United States Supreme Court, and while he has always defied neat classification into one or another jurisprudential camp, his essay "The Path of the Law," reprinted here, became a classic statement of several key realist themes. To appreciate fully what Holmes has to say, we need a clearer sense of the context within which he and other realists wrote, and in particular a clearer understanding of the concept of law against which he and they were reacting.

The nineteenth century saw a tremendous growth and expansion of the traditional sciences, as well as the birth of new realms of scientific investigation, such as psychology and biology. The growing social and intellectual prestige of the sciences fueled the desire of legal scholars to make law a "scientific" discipline. In 1870, the new dean of Harvard Law School, Christopher Columbus Langdell, instituted a series of reforms in legal education, with the aim of teaching law as a science. Prominent among these reforms was the introduction of the "case method" of legal study: the student was to confront and analyze the opinions written by judges deciding particular disputes in order to extract from them the fundamental principles of law. Behind Langdell's case method stood a conception of the nature of law that Langdell shared with other influential scholars and teachers, including James Barr Ames, Joseph Beale, and Samuel Williston. According to these men, law is a completely self-contained and thoroughly consistent and systematic body of principles and rules. After a judge or student extracts the rule from the authoritative sources, he or she can logically deduce what conclusion that rule requires in any given case. In this way, every possible legal dispute has a uniquely correct solution that can be rigorously deduced from a coherent set of basic axioms. Law becomes a kind of social geometry.

No sooner was this vision articulated than realists like Holmes began to assail it. They attacked the formalism of the "law-as-science" theorists: "The life of the law has not been logic, it has been experience," as Holmes famously remarked. And the experience that is most relevant here is the experience and perspective of the "bad man," the cynic whose only concern is with the bottom line: How much can I get away with before bringing the power of the state down upon me? Holmes provides several examples of this bad-man perspective in "The Path of the Law" as, for example, in his theory of contract. A contract, says Holmes, is not a moral commitment that the law wants me to keep. This is shown, for example, by the fact that I may be sued for breach of contract even though I intended to make no such commitment. A contract is merely what the bad man would take it to be: a choice to perform as promised or ignore the promise and pay the penalty. In a similar fashion, when I injure another through my negligent behavior, the law of tort requires that I pay damages to the person affected. From the perspective of the bad man, such a penalty is no different from a tax: each is a negative consequence brought on by my conduct. To understand the law, then, is to be able to predict when and under what circumstances one's conduct will trigger society's response. By thus washing the law in "cynical acid," Holmes seeks to boil law down to its bare essentials.

The realists attacked the formalism of the Langdellian legal scholars in another way: by insisting that judges and courts deciding actual disputes do not reason in a logically rigorous fashion from general principles of legal doctrine to particular conclusions in specific situations. As Holmes notes, law and legal doctrine develop only slowly and as a result of judges' decisions; and this development is embedded in history and tradition in a way far deeper than the law-as-science people were willing to admit. Since law develops in this way, the realists claimed, it is futile to seek or expect much "logic" in it. The law is not a rigid body of fixed and unchanging rules but a shifting and flexible social institution, with sufficient play to accommodate the balancing of various and competing interests within a society.

Rationalization and Rule-Skepticism

Holmes and other realists had to admit, of course, that judges and lawyers often write and talk *as if* they were deciding a case, or arguing for a particular position, by deducing conclusions from "rules of law" in a straightforward fashion. But the statements made by judges in their opinions, many realists insisted, are frequently little more than rationalizations for decisions that they had already arrived at on grounds or for reasons other than that the "rules" required them to decide in a particular way. Realists like Jerome Frank argued that legal reasoning characteristically proceeds "backwards," beginning with an intuitive judgment or "gut feeling" that a particular decision is correct or right and proceeding to a rationalization of that decision so cast in legal jargon that it appears to follow from the rules in a logical way.[1]

Coupled with their theory of legal reasoning as rationalization stands the realist's *rule-skepticism.* "The law . . . consists of *decisions,* not of rules."[2] By denying that the law consists of rules, some realists pushed their doctrine of the flux and flexibility of the law to the limit. Frank, in particular, challenged the concept of *stare decisis* or the doctrine of precedent. This is the idea that a court's decision in one case can serve to guide the decision of future cases that are similar to the original one in relevant ways. (For more on the concept of "following precedent," see Section E in this chapter.) The realists repeatedly emphasized the indeterminacy or looseness of *stare decisis* by pointing out that a particular ruling in one case never binds a decision maker in any future case, because the future decision maker can always find some aspect of the later case that can serve as a ground for differentiating or "distinguishing" it from the prior one.

The bottom line for the realists was that law is a matter of *prediction:* "The prophecies of what the courts will do in fact, and nothing more pretentious are what I mean by the law";[3] "Law . . . as to any given situation is either (a) actual law, i.e., a specific past decision, as to that situation, or (b) probable law, i.e., a guess as to a specific future decision."[4] Accordingly, many realists advocated the study of judicial behavior, arguing that to understand law you must concentrate on the patterns of decisions revealed in actual cases as these are the most reliable guides to, and the most accurate basis for, prediction of what future courts will do.

---

[1] See Jerome Frank, *Law and the Modern Mind* (New York: Anchor Books/Doubleday, 1963).

[2] *Ibid.,* p. 50.

[3] Holmes, "The Path of the Law," *infra.*

[4] Frank, *Law and the Modern Mind,* pp. 50–51.

Legal Reasoning and Intuition

Central to the realist criticism of legal reasoning as a rational procedure bound by rules was the conviction, expressed by Holmes, that "general propositions do not decide concrete cases." Cases, not rules, were for the realists the only source of law. A few judges even came openly to express this view. Joseph Hutcheson, for example, recounted how his training in a mechanical, "slot-machine" view of the law had given way in the face of his many years in the courtroom to the realization that good judges, like good jurors, "feel" their way to a just decision by waiting for the "hunch" or flash of insight that will light the way, the intuition that will point in the right direction.[5] The rest of what the judge typically does, the lengthy opinion that he or she provides as a preface to the decision, was, according to Hutcheson, mere rhetoric. Supporting the hunch with appropriate legal jargon is necessary, however, to disguise its arbitrary nature. The task of the judge is therefore to reason backward from an intuition of the "desirable" result to a rationalization that will fit it. In these ways, Hutcheson agreed with other realists, many of whom argued that judges deciding particular disputes should be guided by the aim of responding to the real human needs before them, not by the slavish following of inferences from the abstract categories and distinctions embedded in "the rules."

The last point is made very clearly in the excerpt included here from a prominent realist, Karl Llewellyn. Llewellyn frames his discussion as a response to the work of Roscoe Pound, himself an influential figure in American jurisprudence and one-time Dean of Harvard Law School. Llewellyn views Pound as representative of a traditional, stuffy, established way of thinking about the law, which held that the law consists of precepts or rules, formulated in the canonical verbiage of legal doctrine. The trouble with such a view, Llewellyn insisted, is that such rules and doctrines do not relate to society, to the "real" world. Instead, legal formulas are mistakenly viewed as having a life of their own, apart from the actions and experiences of prosecutors, magistrates, and appellate judges that

---

[5] See Joseph Hutcheson, "The Judgment Intuitive," *Cornell Law Quarterly* 14 (1929): pp. 274–288.

create them. The "rules on paper" exist only insofar as they describe the judgments actually made in particular legal disputes. But, Llewellyn observes, this reality is often reversed: the behavior of officials within the legal system is measured against a rule that is assumed already to exist. Judges are even criticized for failing to see that a given rule is "controlling" or must be followed in a specific case. Real laws, according to Llewellyn, are descriptive claims about the practices of courts and "their effects upon the conduct and expectations" of citizens.

If a judge's actual decision or judgment, rather than the verbiage surrounding it, accurately states the law on a given subject, those seeking to predict what the judge will do in the future should look to any and all of those factors likely to influence his or her decision. This conclusion led some legal realists to advocate an empirical or even anthropological study of judges and their decisions, focusing on the collection of data regarding their lifestyle, social status, political affiliation, and even diet, in an effort to account for all factors that could conceivably influence a judge's behavior.

"Legal reasoning" for many of the realists, then, was something of a misnomer. What a judge does when faced with a difficult case is much closer to an art or craft than to compliance with a stable, logical procedure.

Law as Interpretation

One of the most widely debated theories of law to have emerged in recent years has been defended and refined by Oxford legal philosopher Ronald Dworkin. Published in a number of essays and books, Dworkin's jurisprudence has undergone several changes, at least some of which are briefly noted here.

Dworkin's Critique of Positivism

In one of his earliest and most influential works, Dworkin summarized what he took to be the essential commitments of Hart's positivism: (1) The law of a community consists of a body of rules identifiable as legal based on their "pedigree," how they came about. (2) If a given case is not covered by a

"pedigreeable" rule, the court must exercise discretion by going beyond the law to reach a decision. (3) Since legal rights can be specified only by rules, in any case that is not covered by rules, the court's resolution of the case cannot involve enforcing anyone's *legal* rights.[6]

One of Dworkin's primary jurisprudential concerns has been to develop and defend a theory of adjudication: an account of how courts can and ought to reason to a conclusion in those "hard" cases in which no settled rule applies. And it is this concern that animated Dworkin's critique of Hart's positivism. Dworkin's core insight was that when courts reason about hard cases, they appeal to standards other than positivistic rules: they appeal to *principles.* Unlike rules, principles have no discernible "pedigree" in Hart's sense. Principles function as a reason in favor of a particular decision but do not compel a result in the way a rule does. Moreover, a principle such as "No one should profit from his own wrongdoing," invoked in the famous *Riggs* case (reprinted at the end of this chapter), can remain a principle of our law despite the fact that it is not always followed. Finally, principles frequently give expression to underlying or background *rights* held by one of the parties to a dispute, and such rights frequently "trump" or take priority over other considerations.

Are principles part of the law? Or do they stand outside it? Hart's theory, says Dworkin, must treat principles as extralegal standards to which judges could appeal when the rules have run out, so that the court is then no longer bound by any standards set by the authority of law. Dworkin regards Hart's picture as both *descriptively* inaccurate and *normatively* (or from a moral point of view) unattractive. It is inaccurate since courts do, Dworkin thinks, invoke principles and background rights; it is morally unattractive since the model of the judge enjoying broad discretion after the genuine rules have run out suggests that he or she can and should ignore, or at least significantly downplay, the rights of litigants and focus instead on policy considerations, asking, for example, what decision will be best for society as a whole.

---

[6] See *Taking Right Seriously* (Cambridge: Harvard University Press, 1977).

Dworkin's Theory of Law

In "'Natural' Law Revisited," reprinted here, Dworkin restates his theories of law and adjudication so as to show how the question "What is law?" depends for its solution on correct answers to moral questions. At the same time, Dworkin tries to situate his theory within the context of recent work by various legal scholars who compare literary texts and the approaches to interpreting and reasoning about them with legal texts and the processes of legal reasoning. A central controversy in both literary and legal theory has turned on the extent to which textual interpretation, whether it be of a novel or a constitution, is merely a "subjective" process in which the interpreter imposes whatever meaning he or she chooses. Is there any sense in which textual interpretation can be said to be "objective"? And what would that mean? Are there meaningful constraints upon interpretive activity? These questions take on particular significance in the law as they intersect with the common assumption that legal reasoning must be conceived as a special form of interpretive activity, distinct from political decision making. Dworkin's discussion of these issues in our selection presents in outline the theory developed at much greater length in his book, *Law's Empire*.

Adjudication, according to Dworkin, is a form of interpretive activity. Judges are like contributors to a "chain novel": they must take the statutes, prior cases, and other legal materials before them and try to make sense of them in a way that allows them to continue to extend whatever "story" the materials tell in a definite direction. In *Law's Empire*, Dworkin argues that this concept of judicial interpretation follows from a more general view of what it means to *interpret* anything, be it a text, a work of art, or what have you. This general view says that in order for me to interpret a theatrical play, for example, I must seek to understand it "from the inside out," trying to grasp what it means to the "society" (actors, audience, critics) whose play it is.

Similarly, the interpretation of a social practice such as law involves the attempt to understand it as a way of life created and sustained by its participants, people who see themselves as part of a larger community ("community of principle," "interpretive community") held together by a commitment to the rule of law. And this means, Dworkin believes, that interpretation cannot simply involve discovering the intent of the author of the play or the drafter of a statute. Instead, interpretation must be *constructive*. This means that interpreters must try to see the play or the law in its best light, as the coherent embodiment of a unifying theme or point. For judges trying to interpret a series of earlier precedents, this means that they must seek to state the best constructive interpretation of the legal doctrine of their community as it is expressed in those precedents. And this will require that judges, at some point, rely upon their own opinions and convictions as they attempt to find the best interpretation of the existing law.

Dworkin cautions us not to misunderstand the last point. Because interpretation is not a mechanical process, the interpreters' own opinions must inevitably shape their interpretations to some degree, but this does not mean that judges can, for example, simply do whatever they please when faced with a hard case. Part of understanding and interpreting the law of their communities requires that judges respect values that are deeply rooted in their society. Values of fairness and democratic rule, for example, require that they must balance their own opinions against public opinion (as expressed, say, by the votes of representatives in Congress); and the value of due process requires that judges protect people's expectation by not allowing the judges' interpretations of the law to deviate radically or break too decisively with the past.

Judges, then, look for a "reading" or interpretation that will contribute to the legal "story" by portraying the law in its best light. But what if several competing interpretations or readings of that past are possible? Here interpreters must measure and compare these readings along two dimensions. First, the dimension of "fit": How well and to what degree does a particular reading explain all of the fundamental features of our law? Second, the dimension of value: How well does that reading present our law as something coherent and worthwhile? Whichever interpretation succeeds best on both of these scorecards becomes the interpretation judges must choose and enforce. Dworkin sums up his overall theory by calling it "law as integrity": The law is the product of the interpretation that most faithfully sums up the texts, principles, and values of a given community into a coherent and morally attractive whole.

Although he does not object to the label "naturalism" to describe this view, Dworkin makes it clear that this is a naturalism of a very different sort from that defended by Aquinas . Dworkin's judges are not free to follow just any normative or moral principle, nor do the principles to which they do appeal derive their validity from a natural moral order. Dworkin's judges are permitted to recognize only the moral principles and values "present," either explicitly or implicitly, in the legal history and tradition of their communities and to recognize them only for that reason, not because they have some independent moral or religious basis.

---

10. *The Path of the Law*

Oliver Wendell Holmes

When we study law we are not studying a mystery but a well-known profession. We are studying what we shall want in order to appear before judges, or to advise people in such a way as to keep them out of court. The reason why it is a profession, why people will pay lawyers to argue for them or to advise them, is that in societies like ours the command of the public force is intrusted to the judges in certain cases, and the whole power of the state will be put forth, if necessary to carry out their judgments and decrees. People want to know under what circumstances and how far they will run the risk of coming against what is so much stronger than themselves, and hence it becomes a business to find out when this danger is to be feared. The object of our study, then, is prediction, the prediction of the incidence of the public force through the instrumentality of the courts.

The means of the study are a body of reports, of treatises, and of statutes, in this country and in England, extending back for six hundred years, and now increasing annually by hundreds. In these sibylline leaves are gathered the scattered prophecies of the past upon the cases in which the axe will fall. These are what properly have been called the oracles of the law. New effort of legal thought is to make these prophecies more precise, and to generalize them into a thoroughly connected system. The process is one, from a lawyer's statement of a case, eliminating as it does all the dramatic elements with which his client's story has clothed it, and retaining only the facts of legal import, up to the final analyses and abstract universals of theoretic jurisprudence. The reason why a lawyer does not mention that his client wore a white hat when he made a contract, while Mrs. Quickly would be sure to dwell upon it along with the parcel gilt goblet and the seacoal fire, is that he foresees that the public force will act in the same way whatever his client had upon his head. It is to make the prophecies easier to be remembered and to be understood that the teachings of the decisions of the past are put into general propositions and gathered into text-books, or that statutes are passed in a general form. The primary rights and duties with which jurisprudence busies itself again are nothing but prophecies. One of the many evil effects of the confusion between legal and moral ideas, about which I shall have something to say in a moment, is that theory is apt to get the cart before the horse, and to consider the right or the duty as something existing apart from and independent of the consequences of its breach, to which certain sanctions are added afterward. But, as I shall try to show, a legal duty so called is nothing but a prediction that if a man does or omits certain things he will be made to suffer in this or that way by judgment of the court; and so of a legal right.

The number of our predictions when generalized and reduced to a system is not unmanageably large. They present themselves as a finite body of dogma which may be mastered within a reasonable time. It is a great mistake to be frightened by the ever-increasing number of reports. The reports of a given jurisdiction in the course of a generation take up pretty much the whole body of the law, and restate it from the present point of view. We could reconstruct the corpus from them if all that went before were burned. The use of the earlier reports is mainly historical, a use about which I shall have something to say before I have finished.

I wish, if I can, to lay down some first principles for the study of this body of dogma or systematized prediction which we call the law, for men who want to use it as the instrument of their business to enable them to prophesy in their turn, and, as bearing upon the study, I wish to point out an ideal which as yet our law has not attained.

The first thing for a business-like understanding of the matter is to understand its limits, and therefore I think it desirable at once to point out and dispel a confusion between morality and law, which sometimes rises to the height of conscious theory, and more often and indeed constantly is making trouble in detail without reaching the point of consciousness. You can see very plainly that a bad man has as much reason as a good one for wishing to avoid an encounter with the public force, and therefore you can see the practical importance of the distinction between morality and law. A man who cares nothing for an ethical rule which is believed and practised by his neighbors is likely nevertheless to care a good deal to avoid being made to pay money, and will want to keep out of jail if he can.

I take it for granted that no hearer of mine will misinterpret what I have to say as the language of cynicism. The law is the witness and external deposit of our moral life. Its history is the history of the moral development of the race. The practice of it, in spite of popular jests, tends to make good citizens and good men. When I emphasize the difference between law and morals I do so with reference to a single end, that of learning and understanding the law. For that purpose you must definitely master its specific marks, and it is for that I ask you for the moment to imagine yourselves indifferent to other and greater things.

I do not say that there is not a wider point of view from which the distinction between law and morals becomes of secondary or no importance, as all mathematical distinctions vanish in presence of the infinite. But I do say that that distinction is of the first importance for the object which we are here to consider—a right study and mastery of the law as a business with well understood limits, a body of dogma enclosed within definite lines. I have just shown the practical reason for saying so. *If you want to know the law and nothing else, you must look at it as a bad man, who cares only for the material consequences which such knowledge enables him to predict*, not as a good one, who finds his reasons for conduct, whether inside the law or outside of it, in the vaguer sanctions of conscience. The theoretical importance of the distinction is no less, if you would reason on your subject aright. The law is full of phraseology drawn from morals, and by the mere force of language continually invites us to pass from one domain to the other without perceiving it, as we are sure to do unless we have the boundary constantly before our minds. The law talks about rights and duties, and malice, and intent, and negligence, and so forth, and nothing is easier, or, I may say, more common in legal reasoning, than to take these words in their moral sense, at some stage of the argument, and so to drop into fallacy. For instance, when we speak of the rights of man in a moral sense, we mean to mark the limits of interference with individual freedom which we think are prescribed by conscience, or by our ideal, however reached. Yet it is certain that many laws have been enforced in the past, and it is likely that some are enforced now, which are condemned by the most enlightened opinion of the time, or which at all events pass the limit of interference as many consciences would draw it. Manifestly, therefore, nothing but confusion of thought can result from assuming that the rights of man in a moral sense are equally rights in the sense of the Constitution and the law. No doubt simple and extreme cases can be put of imaginable laws which the statute-making power would not dare to enact, even in the absence of written constitutional prohibitions, because the community would rise in rebellion and fight; and this gives some plausibility to the proposition that the law, if not a part of morality, is limited by it. But this limit of power is not coextensive with any system of morals. For the most part it falls far within the lines of any such system, and in some cases may extend beyond them, for reasons drawn from the habits of a particular people at a particular time. I once heard the late Professor Agassiz say that a German population would rise if you added two cents to the price of a glass of beer. A statute in such a case would be empty words, not because it was wrong, but because it could not be enforced. No one will deny that wrong statutes can be and are enforced, and we should not all agree as to which were the wrong ones.

The confusion with which I am dealing besets confessedly legal conceptions. Take the fundamental question, What constitutes the law? You will find some text writers telling you that it is something different from what is decided by the courts of Massachusetts or England, that it is a system of reason, that it is a deduction from principles of ethics or admitted axioms or what not, which may or may not coincide with the decisions. But if we take the view of our friend the bad man we shall find that he does not care two straws for the axioms or deductions, but that he does want to know what the Massachusetts or English courts are likely to do in fact. I am much of his mind. The prophecies of what the courts will do in fact, and nothing more pretentious, are what I mean by the law.

Take again a notion which as popularly understood is the widest conception which the law contains—the notion of legal duty, to which already I have referred. We fill the word with all the content which we draw from morals. But what does it mean to a bad man? Mainly, and in the first place, a prophecy that if he does certain things he will be subjected to disagreeable consequences by way of imprisonment or compulsory payment of money. But from his point of view, what is the difference between being fined and being taxed a certain sum for doing a certain thing? That his point of view is the test of legal principles is shown by the many discussions which have arisen in the courts on the very

question whether a given statutory liability is a penalty or a tax. On the answer to this question depends the decision whether conduct is legally wrong or right, and also whether a man is under compulsion or free. Leaving the criminal law on one side, what is the difference between the liability under the mill acts or statutes authorizing a taking by eminent domain and the liability for what we call a wrongful conversion of property where restoration is out of the question. In both cases the party taking another man's property has to pay its fair value as assessed by a jury, and no more. What significance is there in calling one taking right and another wrong from the point of view of the law? It does not matter, so far as the given consequence, the compulsory payment, is concerned, whether the act to which it is attached is described in terms of praise or in terms of blame, or whether the law purports to prohibit it or to allow it. If it matters at all, still speaking from the bad man's point of view, it must be because in one case and not in the other some further disadvantages, or at least some further consequences, are attached to the act by the law. The only other disadvantages thus attached to it which I ever have been able to think of are to be found in two somewhat insignificant legal doctrines, both of which might be abolished without disturbance. One is, that a contract to do a prohibited act is unlawful, and the other, that, if one of two or more joint wrongdoers has to pay all the damages, he cannot recover contribution from his fellows. And that I believe is all. You see how the vague circumference of the notion of duty shrinks and at the same time grows more precise when we wash it with cynical acid and expel everything except the object of our study, the operations of the law.

Nowhere is the confusion between legal and moral ideas more manifest than in the law of contract. Among other things, here again the so called primary rights and duties are invested with a mystic significance beyond what can be assigned and explained. The duty to keep a contract at common law means a prediction that you must pay damages if you do not keep it—and nothing else. If you commit a tort, you are liable to pay a compensatory sum. If you commit a contract, you are liable to pay a compensatory sum unless the promised event comes to pass, and that is all the difference. But such a mode of looking at the matter stinks in the nostrils of those who think it advantageous to get as much ethics into the law as they can. It was good enough for Lord Coke, however, and here, as in many other cases, I am content to abide with him. In *Bromage v. Genning*,[1] a prohibition was sought in the King's Bench against a suit in the marches of Wales for the specific performance of a covenant to grant a lease, and Coke said that it would subvert the intention of the covenantor, since he intends it to be at his election either to lose the damages or to make the lease. Sergeant Harris for the plaintiff confessed that he moved the matter against his conscience, and a prohibition was granted. This goes further than we should go now, but it shows what I venture to say has been the common law point of view from the beginning, although Mr. Harriman, in his very able little book upon Contracts has been misled, as I humbly think, to a different conclusion.

I have spoken only of the common law, because there are some cases in which a logical justification can be found for speaking of civil liabilities as imposing duties in an intelligible sense. These are the relatively few in which equity will grant an injunction, and will enforce it by putting the defendant in prison or otherwise punishing him unless he complies with the order of the court. But I hardly think it advisable to shape general theory from the exception, and I think it would be better to cease troubling ourselves about primary rights and sanctions altogether, than to describe our prophecies concerning the liabilities commonly imposed by the law in those inappropriate terms.

I mentioned, as other example of the use by the law of words drawn from morals, malice, intent, and negligence. It is enough to take malice as it is used in the law of civil liability for wrongs—what we lawyers call the law of torts—to show that it means something different in law from what it means in morals, and also to show how the difference has been obscured by giving to principles which have little or nothing to do with each other the same name. Three hundred years ago a parson preached a sermon and told a story out of Fox's *Book of Martyrs* of a man who had assisted at the torture of one of the saints, and afterward died, suffering compensatory inward torment. It happened that Fox was wrong. The man was alive and chanced to hear the sermon, and thereupon he sued the parson. Chief Justice Wray instructed the jury that the defendant was not liable, because the story was told innocently, without malice. He took malice in the moral sense, as importing a malevolent motive. But nowadays no one doubts that a man may be liable, without any malevolent motive at all, for false statements manifestly calculated to inflict temporal damage. In stating the case in pleading, we still should call the defendant's conduct malicious; but, in my opinion at least, the word means nothing about motives, or even about the defendant's attitude toward the future, but only signifies that the tendency of his conduct under the known circumstances was very plainly to cause the plaintiff temporal harm.[2]

In the law of contract the use of moral phraseology has led to equal confusion, as I have shown in part already, but only in part. Morals deal with the actual internal state of the individual's mind, what he actually intends. From the time of the Romans down to now, this mode of dealing has affected the language of the law as to contract, and the language used has reacted upon the thought. We talk about a contract as a meeting of the minds of the parties, and thence it is inferred in various cases that there is no contract because their minds have not met; that is, because they have intended different things or because one party has not known of the assent of the other. Yet nothing is more certain than that parties may be bound by a contract to things which neither of them intended, and when one does not know of the other's assent. Suppose a contract is executed in due form and in writing to deliver a lecture, mentioning no time. One of the parties thinks that the promise will be construed to mean at once, within a week. The other thinks that it means when he is ready. The court says that it means within a reasonable time. The parties are bound by the contract as it is interpreted by the court, yet neither of them meant what the court declares that they have said. In my opinion no one will understand the true theory of contract or be able even to discuss some fundamental questions intelligently until he has understood that all contracts are formal, that the making of a contract depends not on the agreement of two minds in one intention, but on the agreement of two sets of external signs—not on the parties' having *meant* the same thing but on their having *said* the same thing. Furthermore, as the signs may be addressed to one sense or another—to sight or to hearing—on the nature of the sign will depend the moment when the contract is made. If the sign is tangible, for instance, a letter, the contract is made when the letter of acceptance is delivered. If it is necessary that the minds of the parties meet, there will be no contract until the acceptance can be read—not, for example, if the acceptance be snatched from the hand of the offerer by a third person.

This is not the time to work out a theory in detail, or to answer many obvious doubts and questions which are suggested by these general views. I know of none which are not easy to answer, but what I am trying to do now is only by a series of hints to throw some light on the narrow path of legal doctrine, and upon two pitfalls which, as it seems to me, lie perilously near to it. Of the first of these I have said enough. I hope that my illustrations have shown the danger, both to speculation and to practice, of confounding morality with law, and the trap which legal language lays for us on that side of our way. For my own part, I often doubt whether it would not be a gain if every word of moral significance could be banished from the law altogether, and other words adopted which should convey legal ideas uncolored by anything outside the law. We should lose the fossil records of a good deal of history and the majesty got from ethical associations, but by ridding ourselves of an unnecessary confusion we should gain very much in the clearness of our thought.

So much for the limits of the law. The next thing I wish to consider is what are the forces which determine its content and its growth. You may assume, with Hobbes and Bentham and Austin, that all law emanates from the sovereign, even when the first human beings to enunciate it are the judges, or you may think that law is the voice of the Zeitgeist, or what you like. It is all one to my present purpose. Even if every decision required the sanction of an emperor with despotic power and a whimsical turn of mind, we should be interested none the less, still with a view to prediction, in discovering some order, some rational explanation, and some principle of growth for the rules which he laid down. In every system there are such explanations and principles to be found. It is with regard to them that a second fallacy comes in, which I think it important to expose.

The fallacy to which I refer is the notion that the only force at work in the development of the law is logic. In the broadest sense, indeed, that notion would be true. The postulate on which we think about the universe is that there is a fixed quantitative relation between every phenomenon and its antecedents and consequents. If there is such a thing as a phenomenon without these fixed quantitative relations, it is a miracle. It is outside the law of cause and effect, and as such transcends our power of thought, or at least is something to or from which we cannot reason. The condition of our thinking about the universe is that it is capable of being thought about rationally, or, in other words, that every part of it is effect and cause in the same sense in which those parts are with which we are most familiar. So in the broadest sense it is true that the law is a logical development, like everything else. The danger of which I speak is not the admission that the principles governing other phenomena also govern the law, but the notion that a given system, ours, for instance, can be worked out like mathematics from some general axioms of conduct. This is the natural error of the schools, but it is not confined to them. I once heard a very eminent judge say that he never let a decision go until he was absolutely sure that it was right. So judicial dissent often is blamed, as if it meant simply that one side or the other were not doing their sums right, and, if they would take more trouble, agreement inevitably would come.

This mode of thinking is entirely natural. The training of lawyers is a training in logic. The processes of analogy, discrimination, and deduction are those in which they are most at home. The language of judicial decision is mainly the language of logic. And the logical method and form flatter that longing for certainty and for repose which is in every human mind. But certainty generally is illusion, and repose is not the destiny of man. Behind the logical form lies a judgment as to the relative worth and importance of competing legislative grounds, often an inarticulate and unconscious judgment, it is true, and yet the very root and nerve of the whole proceeding. You can give any conclusion a logical form. You always can imply a condition in a contract. But why do you imply it? It is because of some belief as to the practice of the community or of a class, or because of some opinion as to policy, or, in short, because of some attitude of yours upon a matter not capable of exact quantitative measurement, and therefore not capable of founding exact logical conclusions. Such matters really are battle grounds where the means do not exist for determinations that shall be good for all time, and where the decision can do no more than embody the preference of a given body in a given time and place. We do not realize how large a part of our law is open to reconsideration upon a slight change in the habit of the public mind. No concrete proposition is self evident, no matter how ready we may be to accept it, not even Mr. Herbert Spencer's "Every man has a right to do what he wills, provided he interferes not with a like right on the part of his neighbors."

Why is a false and injurious statement privileged, if it is made honestly in giving information about a servant? It is because it has been thought more important that information should be given freely, than that a man should be protected from what under other circumstances would be an actionable wrong. Why is a man at liberty to set up a business which he knows will ruin his neighbor? It is because the public good is supposed to be best subserved by free competition. Obviously such judgments of relative importance may vary in different times and places. Why does a judge instruct a jury that an employer is not liable to an employee for an injury received in the course of his employment unless he is negligent, and why do the jury generally find for the plaintiff if the case is allowed to go to them? It is because the traditional policy of our law is to confine liability to cases where a prudent man might have foreseen the injury, or at least the danger, while the inclination of a very large part of the community is to make certain classes of persons insure the safety of those with whom they deal. Since the last words were written, I have seen the requirement of such insurance put forth as part of the programme of one of the best known labor organizations. There is a concealed, half conscious battle on the question of legislative policy, and if any one thinks that it can be settled deductively, or once for all, I only can say that I think he is theoretically wrong, and that I am certain that his conclusion will not be accepted in practice *semper ubique et ab omnibus.*

Indeed, I think that even now our theory upon this matter is open to reconsideration, although I am not prepared to say how I should decide if a re-

consideration were proposed. Our law of torts comes from the old days of isolated, ungeneralized wrongs, assaults, slanders, and the like, where the damages might be taken to lie where they fell by legal judgment. But the torts with which our courts are kept busy to-day are mainly the incidents of certain well known businesses. They are injuries to person or property by railroads, factories, and the like. The liability for them is estimated, and sooner or later goes into the price paid by the public. The public really pays the damages, and the question of liability, if pressed far enough, is really the question how far it is desirable that the public should insure the safety of those whose work it uses. It might be said that in such cases the chance of a jury finding for the defendant is merely a chance, once in a while rather arbitrarily interrupting the regular course of recovery, most likely in the case of an unusually conscientious plaintiff, and therefore better done away with. On the other hand, the economic value even of a life to the community can be estimated, and no recovery, it may be said, ought to go beyond that amount. It is conceivable that some day in certain cases we may find ourselves imitating, on a higher plane, the tariff for life and limb which we see in the *Leges Barbarorum.*

I think that the judges themselves have failed adequately to recognize their duty of weighing considerations of social advantage. The duty is inevitable, and the result of the often proclaimed judicial aversion to deal with such considerations is simply to leave the very ground and foundation of judgments inarticulate, and often unconscious, as I have said. When socialism first began to be talked about, the comfortable classes of the community were a good deal frightened. I suspect that this fear has influenced judicial action both here and in England, yet it is certain that it is not a conscious factor in the decisions to which I refer. I think that something similar has led people who no longer hope to control the legislatures to look to the courts as expounders of the Constitutions, and that in some courts new principles have been discovered outside the bodies of those instruments, which may be generalized into acceptance of the economic doctrines which prevailed about fifty years ago, and a wholesale prohibition of what a tribunal of lawyers does not think about right. I cannot but believe that if the training of lawyers led them habitually to consider more definitely and explicitly the social advantage on which the rule they lay down must be justified, they sometimes would hesitate where now they are confident, and see that really they were taking sides upon debatable and often burning questions.

. . .

Endnotes

[1] Roll. Rep. 368.

[2] See *Hanson v. Globe Newspaper Co.*, 159 Mass. 293, 302.

---

11. A *Realistic Jurisprudence*—The Next Step

KARL N. LLEWELLYN

. . .

When men talk or think about law, they talk and think about *rules.* "Precepts" as used by Pound, for instance, I take to be roughly synonymous with rules and principles, the principles being wider in scope and proportionately vaguer in connotation, with a tendency toward idealization of some portion of the *status quo* at any given time. And I think you will find as you read Pound that the precepts are *central* to his thinking about law. Along with rules and principles—along with precepts proper, may I say?—he stresses for instance "standards" as a part of the subject matter of law. These standards seem to be those vague but useful pictures with which one approaches a wide and varied field of conduct to measure the rights of a particular situation: a conception of what a reasonable man would do in the circumstances, or of what good faith requires, and similar pictures. They differ from rules, though not from principles, partly in their vagueness, they differ from both in being not propositions in themselves, but normative approaches to working out the application of some one *term* in a major proposition. The principle, let us say, would read: a man must answer for what good faith requires. But a standard (like a concept, like any class-term, loose or sharp) functions chiefly or exclusively as *part* of a precept. Consequently, it belongs in much the same

This article originally appeared at *30 Colum. L. Rev. 431* (1930). Reprinted with permission.

world. It, too, *centers* on precepts. But Pound mentions more as law than precepts and standards. Along with the standards he stresses also ideals as to "the end" of law. These I take to be in substance standards on a peculiarly vague and majestic scale; standards, perhaps, to be applied to rules rather than to individual transactions. Finally, he stresses— and we meet here a very different order of phenomena—"the traditional techniques of developing and applying" precepts. Only a man gifted with insight would have added to the verbal formulae and verbalized (though vague) conceptual pictures thus far catalogued, such an element *of practices*, of habits and techniques of action, of *behavior*. But only a man partially caught in the traditional precept-thinking of an age that is passing would have focussed that behavior on, have given it a major reference to, have belittled its importance by dealing with it as a phase of, those merely verbal formulae: precepts. I have no wish to argue the point. It will appeal, or it will not, and argument will be of little service. But not only this particular bit of phrasing (which might be accidental), but the use made in Pound's writings of the idea, brings out vigorously the limitations of rules, of precepts, of *words*, when made the focus, the *center of reference*, in thinking about law.

. . .

I see no value to be gained from the interests-rights and rules-remedies set up except to bring out, to underscore, that law is not all, nor yet the major part of, society; and to force attention to the relations and interactions of law and the rest of society; and as a matter of method, to provide words which keep legal and non-legal aspects of the situation and the interactions distinct. And it would seem to go without demonstration that *the most significant* (I do *not* say the *only* significant) aspects of the relations of law and society lie in the field of behavior, and that words take on importance either because and insofar as they are behavior, or because and insofar as they demonstrably reflect or influence other behavior. This statement seems not worth making. Its truth is absurdly apparent. For all that, it reverses, it upsets, the whole traditional approach to law. It turns accepted theory on its head. The traditional approach is in terms of words; it centers on words; it has the utmost difficulty in getting beyond words. If nothing be said about behavior, the *tacit* assumption is that the words do reflect behavior, and if they be the words of rules of law, do influence behavior, even influence behavior effectively and precisely to conform completely to those words. Here lies the key to the muddle. The "rules" are laid down; in the typecase they are "ought" rules, prescriptive rules: the writer's prescriptions, the writer's oughts, individually proclaimed oughts—the true rule is that judges should give judgment for the plaintiff on these facts. From this we jump without necessary notice into equivalent oughts as *accepted* in the legal system under discussion: prevailing oughts—the authorities agree that judges should give judgment for the plaintiff on these facts. Here, again without notice and without inquiry, we *assume* that *practice* of the judges conforms to the accepted oughts on the books; that the verbal formulations of oughts *describe* precisely the is-es of practice; that they *do* give such judgment on such facts. A toothed bird of a situation, in law or any other walk of life. Where is men's ideology about their doing, about what is good practice—where is that ideology or has it ever been an adequate description of their *working* practice?

This is the first tacit imputation of factuality to the rules of ought. A second such imputation follows forthwith—again without explicitness, again without inquiry, again (save in odd instances) without challenge or suggestion or doubt. The paper rule of ought which has not been *assumed* to *describe* the judges' *working* rule of ought (*i.e.*, to correspond with the judges' practice of decision) is now further

assumed to *control* the practice of the interested layman, to *govern* people's conduct. Pray for the storm-tossed mariner on a night like this! What hope is there for clarity of reasoning with such a waste of billowing to build on?

Do I suggest that (to cut in at one crucial point) the "accepted rules," the rules the judges say that they apply, are without influence upon their actual behavior? I do not. I do not even say that, *sometimes* these "accepted rules" may not be a very accurate description of the judges' actual behavior. What I say is that such accuracy of description is rare. The question is how, and how much, and in what direction, do the accepted rule and the practice of decision diverge? More: how, and how much, *in each case*? You cannot generalize on this, *without investigation*. Your guesses may be worth something, in the large. *They are worth nothing at all, in the particular*. The one thing we know now for certain is, that different rules have totally different relations to the behavior of judges, of other officials, and of the particular persons "governed" (optimistic word!) by those different rules. The approach here argued for admits, then, out of hand, *some* relation between *any* accepted rule and judicial behavior; and then proceeds to deny that that admission involves anything but a problem for investigation in the case in hand; and to argue that the significance of the particular rule will appear only *after* the investigation of the vital, focal, phenomenon: the behavior. And if an empirical *science* of law is to have any realistic basis, any responsibility to the facts, I see no escape from moving to this position. . . .

. . .

What now, is the place of rules and rights, under such an approach? To attempt their excision from the field of law would be to fly in the face of fact. I should like to begin by distinguishing real "rules" and rights from paper rules and rights. The former are conceived in terms of behavior; they are but other names, convenient shorthand symbols, for the remedies, the actions of the courts. They are descriptive, not prescriptive, except in so far as there may occasionally be implied that courts *ought* to continue in their practices. "Real rules," then, if I had my way with words, would by legal scientists be called the practices of the courts, and not "rules" at all. And statements of "rights" would be statements of likelihood that in a given situation a certain type of court action loomed in the offing. Factual terms. No more. . . . This concept of "real rule" has been gaining favor since it was first put into clarity by Holmes. "Paper rules" are what have been treated, traditionally, as rules of law: the accepted *doctrine* of the time and place—what the books there say "the law" is. The "real rules" and rights—"what the courts will do in a given case, and nothing more pretentious"— are then predictions. They are, I repeat, on the level of isness and not of oughtness; they seek earnestly to go no whit, in their suggestion, beyond the remedy actually available. Like all shorthand symbols, they are dangerous in connotation, when applied to situations which are not all quite alike. But their intent and effort is to describe. And one can borrow for them Max Weber's magnificent formulation in terms of probability; a right (or practice, or "real rule") exists *to the extent that* a likelihood exists that A can induce a court to squeeze, out of B, A's damages; more: *to the extent that* the likely collections will cover A's damage. In this aspect *substantive* rights and "rules," as distinct from adjective, simply disappear—on the descriptive level. The measure of a "rule," the measure of a right, becomes what can be done about the situation. *Accurate* statement of a "rule rule" or of a right includes all procedural limitations on what can be done about the situation. What is left, in the realm of *description,* are at the one end the facts, the groupings of conduct (and demonstrable expectations) which may be claimed to constitute an interest; and on the other the practices of courts in their effects upon the conduct and expectations of the laymen in question. Facts, in the world of isness, to be compared directly with other facts, also in the world of isness.

A reversion, do you say, to the crude and outmoded thinking of rules in terms of remedies only, to confining legal thinking to the vagaries of traditions-bound procedure? Not quite. It is a reversion to the realism of that primitive point of view. But a sophisticated reversion to a sophisticated realism. Gone is the ancient assumption that law is because law is; there has come since, and remains, the inquiry into the purpose of what courts are doing, the criticism in terms of searching out purposes and criticizing means. Here value-judgments reenter the picture, and should. Observing

particular, concrete facts of conduct and of expectation which suggests the presence of "an interest," one arrives at his value conclusion that something in those facts calls for protection at the hands of state officials. What protection is called for, and called for in terms of what *action* of the state officials? Again a matter of judgment—but a matter of judgment which at least foots on reality and comes to results in terms of action. With that hypothetical action, the actual conduct of those officials can be directly compared. Room for error, in plenty, in diagnosing interests, and in imagining the forms of official conduct suited to their protection. But realism in discussion; realism at each end of the comparison; a narrowing as far as the present state of knowledge will permit, of the field for obstructing eyes with words that masquerade as things without a check-up.

. . .

Like rules, concepts are not to be eliminated; it cannot be done. Behavior is too heterogeneous to be dealt with except after some artificial ordering. The sense impressions which make up what we call observation are useless unless gathered into some arrangement. Nor can thought go on without categories.

A realistic approach would, however, put forward two suggestions on the making of such categories. The first of them rests primarily upon the knowledge that to classify is to disturb. It is to build emphases, to create stresses, which obscure some of the data under observation and give fictitious value to others—a process which can be excused only insofar as it is necessary to the accomplishing of a purpose. The data to be singled out in reference to that purpose are obviously those which appear most relevant. But true relevancy can be determined only as the inquiry advances. For this reason a realistic approach to any new problem would begin by skepticism as to the adequacy of the *received* categories for ordering the phenomena effectively toward a solution of the new problem. It is quite possible that the received categories as they already stand are perfect for the purpose. It is, however, altogether unlikely. The suggestion then comes to this: that with the new purpose in mind one approach the data afresh, taking them in as raw a condition as possible, and discovering how far and how well the available traditional categories really cover the most relevant of the raw data. And that before proceeding one undertake such modifications in the categories as may be necessary or look promising. In view of the tendency toward over-generalization in the past this is likely to mean the making of smaller categories—which may be either sub-groupings inside the received categories, or may cut across them.

The other suggestion of a realistic approach rests on the observation that categories and concepts, once formulated and once they have entered into thought processes, tend to take on an appearance of solidity, reality and inherent value which has no foundation in experience. More than this: although originally formulated on the model of at least some observed data, they tend, once they have entered into the organization of thinking, both to suggest the presence of corresponding data when these data are not in fact present, and to twist any fresh observation of data into conformity with the terms of the categories. This has been discussed above in its application to rules; it holds true, however, of any concept. It is peculiarly troublesome in regard to legal concepts, because of the tendency of the crystallized legal concept to persist after the fact model from which the concept was once derived has disappeared or changed out of recognition. A simple but striking instance is the resistance opposed by the "master-servant" concept to each readjustment along the lines of a new industrial labor situation. The counsel of the realistic approach here, then, would be the constant back-checking of the category against the data, to see whether the data are still present *in the form suggested by the category-name.* This slows up thinking. But it makes for results which mean something when one gets them.

. . .

Discussions of law, like discussions of "social control," tend a little lightly to assume *"a society"* and to assume the antecedent discovery of "social" objectives. Either is hard to find in any sense which corresponds with the facts of control. Where is the unity, the single coherent group? Where is the demonstrable objective which is social, and not opposed by groups well nigh as important as those which support it? And law in particular presents over most, if not all of its bulk, the phenomenon of clashing interests, of antagonistic persons or groups, with officials stepping in to favor some as against some others. Either to line up the dissenter in the interests of his own group; that is one broad phase. Or to regulate the relations between two groups, or to alter the terms of the struggle (competitive or other) between them.

One matter does need mention here, however the eternal dilemma of the law, indeed of society, and of the law because the law purports peculiarly among our institutions to "represent" the whole. There is, amid the welter of self-serving groups, clamoring and struggling over this machine that will give power over others, the recurrent emergence of some wholeness, some sense of responsibility which outruns enlightened self-interest, and results in action apparently headed (often purposefully) for the common good. To affirm this is to confess no Hegelian mysticism of the State. It leaves quite open any question of the existence of some "life principle" in a society. It merely notes that, lacking such a self-sanation in terms of the whole, the whole would not indefinitely continue as a whole. And to deny that would be folly. It would be to carry emancipation from the idle ideology of "representation of the whole" into blindness to the half-truth around which that once-precious ideology was built. But to deny the emancipation, to worship the half truth without dire and specific concern for the details of the welter, would be a folly quite as great.

12. *"Natural" Law Revisited*

Ronald A. Dworkin

What Is Naturalism?

Everyone likes categories, and legal philosophers like them very much. So we spend a good deal of time, not all of it profitably, labeling ourselves and the theories of law we defend. One label, however, is particularly dreaded: no one wants to be called a natural lawyer. Natural law insists that what the law is depends in some way on what the law should be. This seems metaphysical or at least vaguely religious. In any case it seems plainly wrong. If some theory of law is shown to be a natural law theory, therefore, people can be excused if they do not attend to it much further.

In the past several years, I have tried to defend a theory about how judges should decide cases that some critics (though not all) say is a natural law theory and should be rejected for that reason. I have of course made the pious and familiar objection to this charge, but it is better to look at theories than labels. But since labels are so much a part of our common intellectual life it is almost as silly to flee as to hurl them. If the crude description of natural law I just gave is correct, that any theory which makes the content of law sometimes depend on the correct answer to some moral question is a natural law theory, then I am guilty of natural law. I am not now interested, I should add, in whether this crude characterization is historically correct, or whether it succeeds in distinguishing natural law from positivist theories of law. My present concern is rather this. Suppose this *is* natural law. What in the world is wrong with it?

A. Naturalism

I shall start by giving the picture of adjudication I want to defend a name, and it is a name which accepts the crude characterization. I shall call this picture naturalism. According to naturalism, judges should decide hard cases by interpreting the political structure of their community in the following, perhaps special way: by trying to find the best *justification* they can find, in principles of political morality, for the structure as a whole, from the most profound constitutional rules and arrangements to the details of, for example, the private law of tort or contract. Suppose the question arises for the first time, for example, whether and in what circumstances careless drivers are liable, not only for physical injuries to those whom they run down, but also for any emotional damage suffered by relatives of the victim who are watching. According to naturalism, judges should then ask the following questions of the history (including the contemporary history) of their political structure. Does the best possible justification of that history suppose a principle according to which people who are injured emotionally in this way have a right to recover damages in court? If so, what, more precisely, is that principle? Does it entail, for example, that only immediate relatives of the person physically injured have that right? Or only relatives on the scene of the accident, who might themselves have suffered physical damage?

Of course a judge who is faced with these questions in an actual case cannot undertake anything like a full justification of all parts of the constitutional arrangement statutory system and judicial precedents that make up his "law." I had to invent a mythical judge, called Hercules, with superhuman powers in order even to contemplate what a full justification of the entire system would be like.[1] Real judges can attempt only what we might call a partial justification of the law. They can try to justify, under some set of principles, those parts of the legal background which seem to them immediately relevant, like, for example, the prior judicial decisions about recovery for various sorts of damage in automobile accidents. Nevertheless it is useful to describe this as a partial justification—as a part of what Hercules himself would do—in order to emphasize that, according to this picture, a judge should regard the law he mines and studies as embedded in a much larger system, so that it is always relevant for him to expand his investigation by asking whether the conclusions he reaches are consistent with what he would have discovered had his study been wider.

It is obvious why this theory of adjudication invites the charge of natural law. It makes each judge's decision about the burden of past law depend on his judgment about the best political justification of that law, and this is of course a matter of political morality. Before I consider whether this provides a fatal defect in the theory, however, I must try to show how the theory might work in practice. It may help to look beyond law to other enterprises in which participants extend a discipline into the future by re-examining its past. This process is in fact characteristic of the general activity we call interpretation, which has a large place in literary criticism, history, philosophy and many other activities. Indeed, the picture of adjudication I have just sketched draws on a sense of what interpretation is like in these various activities, and I shall try to explicate the picture through an analogy to literary interpretation.[2] I shall, however, pursue that analogy in a special context designed to minimize some of the evident differences between law and literature, and so make the comparison more illuminating.

B. The Chain Novel

Imagine, then, that a group of novelists is engaged for a particular project. They draw lots to determine the order of play. The lowest number writes the opening chapter of a novel, which he then sends to the next number who is given the following assignment. He must add a chapter to that novel, which he must write so as to make the novel being constructed the best novel it can be. When he completes his chapter, he then sends the two chapters to the next novelist, who has the same assignment, and so forth. Now every novelist but the first has the responsibility of interpreting what has gone before in the sense of interpretation I described for a naturalist judge. Each novelist must decide what

the characters are "really" like; what motives in fact guide them; what the point or theme of the developing novel is; how far some literary device or figure consciously or unconsciously used can be said to contribute to these, and therefore should be extended, refined, trimmed or dropped. He must decide all this in order to send the novel further in one direction rather than another. But all these decisions must be made, in accordance with the directions given, by asking which decisions make the continuing novel better as a novel.

Some novels have in fact been written in this way (including the soft-core pornographic novel NAKED CAME THE STRANGER) though for a debunking purpose, and certain parlor games, for rainy weekends in English country houses, have something of the same structure. But in this case the novelists are expected to take their responsibilities seriously, and to recognize the duty to create, so far as they can, a single unified novel rather than, for example, a series of independent short stories with characters bearing the same names. Perhaps this is an impossible assignment; perhaps the project is doomed to produce, not simply an impossibly bad novel, but no novel at all, because the best theory of art requires a single creator, or if more than one, that each have some control over the whole. (But what about legends and jokes? What about the Old Testament, or, on some theories, the ILIAD?) I need not push that question further, because I am interested only in the fact that the assignment makes sense, that each of the novelists in the chain can have some sense of what he or she is asked to do, whatever misgivings each might have about the value or character of what will then be produced.

The crucial question each must face is this. What is the difference between continuing the novel in the best possible way, by writing plot and development that can be seen to flow from what has gone before, and starting a fresh novel with characters having the same names? Suppose you are a novelist well down the chain, and are handed several chapters which are, in fact, the first sections of the Dickens short novel, A CHRISTMAS CAROL. You consider these two interpretations of the central character: that Scrooge is irredeemably, inherently evil, and so an example of the degradation of which human nature is intrinsically capable, or that Scrooge is inherently good, but progressively corrupted by the false values and perverse demands of high capitalist society. The interpretation you adopt will obviously make an enormous difference in the way you continue the story. You aim, in accordance with your instructions, to make the continuing novel the best novel it can be; but you must nevertheless choose an interpretation that makes the novel a single work of art. So you will have to respect the text you have been given, and not choose an interpretation that you believe the text rules out. The picture that text gives of Scrooge's early life, for example, might be incompatible with the claim that he is inherently wicked. In that case you have no choice. If, on the other hand, the text is equally consistent with both interpretations, then you do have a choice. You will choose the interpretation that you believe makes the work more significant or otherwise better, and this will probably (though not inevitably) depend on whether you think people like Scrooge are in fact, in the real world, born bad or corrupted by capitalism.

Now consider a more complex case. Suppose the text does not absolutely rule out either interpretation, but is marginally less consistent with one, which is, however, the interpretation you would pick if they both fit equally well. Suppose you believe that the original sin interpretation (as we might call it) is much the more accurate depiction of human nature. But if you choose that interpretation you will have to regard certain incidents and attributions established in the text you were given as "mistakes." You must then ask yourself which interpretation makes the work of art better *on the whole*, recognizing, as you will, that a novel whose plot is inconsistent or otherwise lacks integrity is thereby flawed. You must ask whether the novel is still better as a novel, read as a study of original sin, even though it must now be regarded as containing some "mistakes" in plot, than it would be with fewer "mistakes" but a less revealing picture of human nature. You may never have reflected on that question before, but that is no reason why you may not do so now, and once you make up your mind you will believe that the correct interpretation of Scrooge's character is the interpretation that makes the novel better on the whole.

C. The Chain of Law

Naturalism is a theory of adjudication not of the interpretation of novels. But naturalism supposes that common law adjudication is a chain enterprise sharing many of the features of the story we invented. According to naturalism, a judge should decide fresh cases in the spirit of a novelist in the chain writing a fresh chapter. The judge must make creative decisions, but must try to make these decisions "going on as before" rather than by starting in a new direction as if writing on a clean slate. He must read through (or have some good idea through his legal training and experience) what other judges in the past have written, not simply to discover what these other judges have said, or their state of mind when they said it, but to reach an opinion about what they have collectively *done*, in the way that each of our novelists formed an opinion about the collective novel so far written. Of course, the best interpretation of past judicial decisions is the interpretation that shows these in the best light, not aesthetically but politically, as coming as close to the correct ideals of a just legal system as possible. Judges in the chain of law share with the chain novelists the imperative of interpretation, but they bring different standards of success—political rather than aesthetic—to bear on that enterprise.

The analogy shows, I hope, how far naturalism allows a judge's beliefs about the personal and political rights people have "naturally"—that is, apart from the law—to enter his judgments about what the law requires. It does not instruct him to regard these beliefs as the only test of law. A judge's background and moral convictions will influence his decisions about what legal rights people have under the law. But the brute facts of legal history will nevertheless limit the role these convictions can play in those decisions. The same distinction we found in literary interpretation, between interpretation and ideal, holds here as well. An Agatha Christie mystery thriller cannot be interpreted as a philosophical novel about the meaning of death even by someone who believes that a successful philosophical novel would be a greater literary achievement than a successful mystery. It cannot be interpreted that way because, if it is, too much of the book must be seen as accidental, and too little as integrated, in plot, style and trope, with its alleged genre or point. Interpreted that way it becomes a shambles and so a failure rather than a sucess at anything at all. In the same way, a judge cannot plausibly discover, in a long and unbroken string of prior judicial decisions in favor of the manufacturers of defective products, any principle establishing strong consumers' rights. For that discovery would not show the history of judicial practice in a better light; on the contrary it would show it as the history of cynicism and inconsistency, perhaps of incoherence. A naturalist judge must show the facts of history in the best light he can, and this means that he must not show that history as unprincipled chaos.

Of course this responsibility, for judges as well as novelists, may best be fulfilled by a dramatic reinterpretation that both unifies what has gone before and gives it new meaning or point. This explains why a naturalist decision, though it is in this way tied to the past, may yet seem radical. A naturalist judge might find, in some principle that has not yet been recognized in judicial argument, a brilliantly unifying account of past decisions that shows them in a better light than ever before. American legal education celebrates dozens of such events in our own history. In the most famous single common law decision in American jurisprudence, for example, Cardozo reinterpreted a variety of cases to find, in these cases, the principle on which the modern law of negligence was built.[3]

Nevertheless the constraint, that a judge must continue the past and not invent a better past, will often have the consequence that a naturalist judge cannot reach decisions that he would otherwise, given his own political theory, want to reach. A judge who, as a matter of political conviction, believes in consumers' rights may nevertheless have to concede that the law of his jurisdiction has rejected this idea. It is in one way misleading to say, however, that he will be then forced to make decisions *at variance with* his political convictions. The principle that judges should decide consistently with principle, and that law should be coherent, is part of his convictions, and it is this principle that makes the decision he otherwise opposes necessary.

D. Interpretation in Practice

In this section I shall try to show how a self-conscious naturalist judge might construct a working approach to adjudication, and the role his background moral and political convictions would play in that working approach. When we imagined you to be a novelist in the chain novel, several pages ago, we considered how you would continue the first few chapters of A CHRISTMAS CAROL. We distinguished two dimensions of a successful interpretation. An interpretation must "fit" the data it interprets, in order not to show the novel as sloppy or incoherent, and it must also show that data in its best light, as serving as well as can be some proper ambition of novels. Just now, in noticing how a naturalist judge who believed in consumers' rights might nevertheless have to abandon the claim that consumers' rights are embedded in legal history, . . . the same distinction between these two dimensions was relied upon. A naturalist judge would be forced to reject a politically attractive interpretation, we supposed, simply because he did not believe it fit the record well enough. If fit is indeed an independent dimension of success in interpretation, then any judge's working approach would include some tacit conception of what "fit" is, and of how well a particular interpretation must fit the record of judicial and other legal decisions in order to count as acceptable.

This helps us to explain why two naturalist judges might reach different interpretations of past judicial decisions about accidents, for example. They might hold different conceptions of "fit" or "best fit," so that, for instance, one thinks that an interpretation provides an acceptable fit only if it is supported by the opinions of judges in prior cases, while the other thinks it is sufficient, to satisfy the dimension of fit, that an interpretation fit the actual decisions these judges reached even if it finds no echo in their opinions. This difference might be enough to explain, for example, why one judge could accept an "economic" interpretation of the accident cases—that the point of negligence law is to reduce the overall social costs of accidents— while another judge, who also found that interpretation politically congenial, would feel bound by his beliefs about the requirement of fit to reject it.

At some point, however, this explanation of differences between two judges' theories of the same body of law would become strained and artificial. Suppose Judge X believes, for example, that pedestrians ought to look out for themselves, and have no business walking in areas in which drivers are known normally to exceed the legal speed limit. He might rely on this opinion in deciding that "our law recognizes no general right to recover whenever someone is injured by a speeding driver while walking on a highway where most drivers speed." If Judge Y reaches a different judgment about what the law is, because he believes that pedestrians should be entitled to assume that people will obey the law even when there is good evidence that they will not, then it would strain language to explain this difference by saying that these judges disagree about the way or the degree in which an interpretation of the law must fit past decisions. We would do better to say that these judges interpret the law differently, in this instance, because they bring different background theories of political morality to their interpretations just as two art critics might disagree about the correct interpretation of impressionism because they bring different theories about the value of art to that exercise.

Any naturalist judge's working approach to interpretation will recognize this distinction between two "dimensions" of interpretations of the prior law, and so we might think of such a theory as falling into two parts. One part refines and develops the idea that an interpretation must fit the data it interprets. This part takes up positions on questions like the following. How many decisions (roughly) can an interpretation set aside as mistakes, and still count as an interpretation of the string of decisions that includes those "mistakes"? How far and in what way must a good interpretation fit the opinions judges write as well as the decisions they make? How far must it take account of popular morality contemporary with the decisions it offers to interpret? A second part of any judge's tacit theory of interpretation, however, will be quite independent of these "formal" issues. It will contain the substantive ideals of political morality on which he relies in deciding whether any putative interpretation is to be preferred because it shows legal practice to be better as a matter of substantive justice. Of course, if any working approach to interpretation has these two parts, then it must also have principles that combine or adjudicate between them.

This account of the main structure of a working theory of interpretation has heuristic appeal. It provides judges, and others who interpret the law, with a model they might use in identifying the approach they have been using, and self-consciously to inspect and improve that model. A thoughtful judge might establish for himself, for example, a rough "threshold" of fit which any interpretation of data must meet in order to be "acceptable" on the dimension of fit, and then suppose that if more than one interpretation of some part of the law meets this threshold, the choice among these should be made, not through further and more precise comparisons between the two along that dimension, but by choosing the interpretation which is "substantively" better, that is, which better promotes the political ideals he thinks correct. Such a judge might say, for example, that since both the foreseeability and the area-of-physical-risk interpretations rise above the threshold of fit with the emotional damage cases I mentioned earlier, foreseeability is better *as an interpretation* because it better accords with the "natural" rights of people injured in accidents.

The practical advantages of adopting such a threshold of fit are plain enough. A working theory need specify that threshold in only a rough and impressionistic way. If two interpretations both satisfy the threshold, then, as I said, a judge who uses such a theory need make no further comparisons along that dimension in order to establish which of them in fact supplies the "better" fit, and he may therefore avoid many of the difficult and perhaps arbitrary decisions about better fit that a theory without this feature might require him to make. But there are nevertheless evident dangers in taking the device too seriously, as other than a rule-of-thumb practical approach. A judge might be tricked into thinking that these two dimensions of interpretation are in some way deeply competitive with one another, that they represent the influence of two different and sometimes contradictory ambitions of adjudication.

He will then worry about those inevitable cases in which it is unclear whether some substantively attractive interpretation does indeed meet the threshold of fit. He will think that in such cases he must define that threshold, not impressionistically, as calling for a "decent" fit, but precisely, perhaps everything will then turn on whether that interpretation in fact just meets or just fails the crucial test. This rigid attitude toward the heuristic distinction would miss the point that any plausible theory of interpretation, in law as in literature, will call for some cross influence between the level of fit at which the threshold is fixed and the substantive issues involved. If an interpretation of some string of cases is far superior "substantively" it may be given the benefit of a less stringent test of fit for that reason.

For once again the underlying issue is simply one of comparing two pictures of the judicial past to see which offers a more attractive picture, from the standpoint of political morality, overall. The distinction between the dimensions of fit and substance is a rough distinction in service of that issue. The idea of a threshold of fit, and therefore of a lexical ordering between the two dimensions, is simply a working hypothesis, valuable so far as the impressionistic characterization of fit on which it depends is adequate, but which must be abandoned in favor of a more sophisticated and piece-meal analysis when the occasion demands.

Of course the moment when more sophisticated analysis becomes necessary, because the impressionistic distinction of the working theory no longer serves, is a moment of difficulty calling for fresh political judgments that may be hard to make. Suppose a judge faces, for the first time, the possibility of overruling a narrow rule followed for some time in his jurisdiction. Suppose, for example, that the courts have consistently held, since the issue was first raised, that lawyers may not be sued in negligence. Our judge believes that this rule is wrong and unjust, and that it is inconsistent in principle with the general rule allowing actions in negligence against other professional people like doctors and accountants. Suppose he can nevertheless find some putative principle, in which others find though he does not, which would justify the distinction the law has drawn. Like the principle, for example, that lawyers owe obligations to the courts or to abstract justice, it would be unfair to impose on the many legal obligations of due care to their clients. He must ask whether the best interpretation of the past includes *that* principle in spite of the fact that he himself would reject it.

Neither answer to this question will seem wholly attractive to him. If he holds that the law does include this putative principle, then this argument would present the law, including the past decisions about suits against lawyers as coherent; but he would then expose what he would believe to be a flaw in the substantive law. He would be supposing that the law includes a principle he believes is wrong, and therefore has no place in a just and wise system. If he decides that the law does not include the putative principle, on the other hand, then he can properly regard this entire list of cases about actions against lawyers as mistakes, and ignore or overrule them; but he then exposes a flaw in the record of a different sort, namely that past judges have acted in an unprincipled way, and a demerit in his own decision, that it treats the lawyer who loses the present case differently from how judges have treated other lawyers in the past. He must ask which is, in the end, the greater of these flaws; which way of reading the record shows it, in the last analysis, in the better and which in the worse light.

It would be absurd to suppose that all the lawyers and judges of any common law community share some set of convictions from which a single answer to that question could be deduced. Or even that many lawyers or judges would have ready at hand some convictions of their own which could supply an answer without further ado. But it is nevertheless possible for any judge to confront issues like these in a principled way, and this is what naturalism demands of him. He must accept that in deciding one way rather than another about the force of a line of precedents, for example, he is developing a working theory of legal interpretation in one rather than another direction, and this must seem to him the right direction as a matter of political principle, not simply an appealing direction for the moment because he likes the answer it recommends in the immediate case before him. Of course there is, in this counsel, much room for deception, including self-deception. But in most cases it will be possible for judges to recognize when they have submitted some issue to the discipline this description requires and also to recognize when some other judge has not.

Let me recapitulate. Interpretation is not a mechanical process. Nevertheless, judges can form working styles of interpretation, adequate for routine cases, and ready for refinement when cases are not routine. These working styles will include what I called formal features. They will set out, impressionistically, an account of fit, and may characterize a threshold of fit an interpretation must achieve in order to be eligible. But they will also contain a substantive part, formed from the judge's background political morality, or rather that part of his background morality which has become articulate in the course of his career. Sometimes this heuristic distinction between fit and substantive justice, as dimensions of a successful interpretation, will itself seem problematic, and a judge will be forced to elaborate that distinction by reflecting further on the full set of the substantive and procedural political rights of citizens a just legal system must respect and serve. In this way any truly hard case develops as well as engages a judge's style of adjudication.

Endnotes

[1] R. Dworkin, Taking Rights Seriously 105–130 (1977).

[2] R. Dworkin, *Law and Interpretation*, Critical Inquiry (1982).

[3] *McPherson v. Buick*, 217 N.Y. 328, 111 N.E. 1050 (N.Y. 1916).

Study Questions

1. Holmes attempts to show that concepts such as law, contract, and malice (as in "malice aforethought"), even though they appear at first to contain or imply moral or value judgments, can be explained without reference to moral notions from the perspective of the bad man (or woman). Do you find his attempt successful?

2. Holmes claims that "the prophecies of what the courts will do in fact, and nothing more pretentious, are what I mean by the law." Suppose that you are a judge on the highest court in the land. How would Holmes' claim guide your understanding of what you should do in deciding a legal question?

3. Realists such as Llewellyn and Joseph Hutcheson insist that (in Hutcheson's words) "the judge does not decide causes by the abstract application of rule of just . . . but having heard the cause and determined that the decision ought to go this way or that way" he looks for "some category of the law into which the case will fit" in order to "support his desired result" ("The Judgment Intuitive"). In *The Com-*

mon Law Tradition, Llewellyn argued that same point: lawyers must seek an understanding of the law, not in the *ratio decidendi* (the reasoning) of a case, but in patterns of results or actual judgments, all the while making the results *look* inevitable. If the realists are correct and the process of trying to reason within the concepts of the law is a fake, why should lawyers or judges continue to do it? Can the realist explain what value might attach to continuing such a pretense?

4. The legal realists emphasize the role of "intuition," or "insight"—a hunch—in the process of resolving legal cases. Llewellyn argues that the best judges operate in what he calls the "Grand Style," by appealing to "situation sense" to craft their decisions. Is there a danger in allowing judges to follow their feelings and hunches openly and candidly in this way? What if their feelings lead to evil decisions? Do Llewellyn and Hutcheson assume that the judges' hunches or situation sense will guide them to just and "right" results? If so, is the assumption likely to be correct?

5. It has been suggested that the realist insistence on the almost complete indeterminacy of the law resulted from a distorted or skewed perspective, one explained by the so-called *selection hypothesis:* Cases that reach the appellate court level, and upon which legal scholars (like the realists) tend to focus, are just the cases in which the law is uncertain and in which the opposing arguments are fairly equally balanced. However, the great bulk of the law, the argument continues, is far more stable and determinate than the realists would admit. Does this explanation undermine legal realism?

6. Does the realist indeterminacy thesis express a necessary feature of law or legality? Or is it simply a contingent claim about a specific legal system or legal culture, namely, our own?

7. Dworkin argues that the "law" as it applies to any given case is more than simply the positive rules, encompassing as it does all of the principles and ideals that are part of the best or soundest overall justification or interpretation

of the existing rules. Could there be such a "best" theory? And if so, could any of us come to know it?

8. Dworkin argues that the task of a court is always to search for the interpretation of the existing state of the law that depicts it in the best moral light. How would this procedure apply to a judge in Nazi Germany who rejects the Nazi laws as immoral?

9. Dworkin refined and elaborated upon his basic interpretive theory in subsequent work. In *Law's Empire,* Dworkin argues that legal theory must be interpretive because useful theories of law must try to understand the "argumentative character" of legal practice—that is, the fact that people debate about what their law means. Taking up this "internal" perspective on law means that the interpretation of law must be "constructive," it must try to see the law as if it expressed a unifying vision or ideal. What could Dworkin say to a legal realist or other skeptic who challenges the assumption that such an "internal" perspective is the best one from which to understand what law is?

10. Is Llewellyn accepting the positivist claim that the law as it "ought to be" is distinct (or should be viewed as distinct) from the law "as it is"?

11. Llewellyn argues that the "received" categories around which the law is structured must be replaced with categories arrived at from a "fresh look" at the "raw data." What are such categories going to look like? Can we tell? Why won't those categories also fall prey to the tendency to "take on a life of their own"?

12. Read *People v. Hall* (included under "Cases for Further Reflection" at the end of this chapter). Imagine that you are a judge faced with deciding this case and that you also subscribe to Dworkin's concept of law as interpretation. Is there any way to depict the legal situation in *Hall* in a good light? If not, what should a Dworkinian judge do in a case like *Hall*?

E. *Contemporary Perspectives*

Contemporary legal scholarship covers a broad array of fascinating perspectives upon and activism with regard to the law. In addition to the work of such theorists as Ronald Dworkin, positivists Joseph Raz, and natural law scholar John Finnis, several newly emerging "schools" of legal thought have captured much attention in the last two decades.[1] Included within this category are the Critical Legal Studies movement; the Law and Economics movement; Feminist Jurisprudence; and Critical Race Theory. This section of Chapter One provides a brief overview of these philosophies of the law.

Critical Legal Studies

Throughout this chapter, we have been concerned with the questions, What does it mean to live under the "rule of law" as opposed to the "rule of men,"

---

[1] See Ronald Dworkin, *Law's Empire* (Cambridge: Harvard University Press, 1986); Joseph Raz, *The Authority of Law* (Oxford: Oxford University Press, 1979); John Finnis, *Natural Law and Natural Rights* (Oxford: Clarendon Press, 1982).

and What is legality and how does it differ from morality? We have so far examined several theories that try to answer these questions by offering accounts of the nature of law and the value of legality. The newly emerging schools of legal theory each challenge the assumptions about the nature and importance of the rule of law held, so it is claimed, by many representatives of the established theories.

Many members of the *critical legal studies* (CLS) movement have challenged the very possibility of a society based upon the "rule of law." They perceive a deep inconsistency between the concept of the rule of law and the theory of political liberalism with which that concept has come to be associated. The work of one prominent critical legalist, Roberto Unger, illustrates the CLS position.[2]

The "theory" of CLS is in some ways hard to pin down precisely, for in many ways CLS focuses upon the fragmentary character of the law—the fact that it doesn't really "hang together" very well (if at all). We will see what that means in a moment; for now it is best to try to get our bearing by comparing CLS with legal realism.

CLS scholars share with legal realists the basic conviction that the rules that (when seen as a system) are taken by positivists to form the essence of law are in fact inherently indeterminate; that is, without a clear, fixed meaning. Critical legalists also share the moral skepticism of some of the realists, rejecting the notion of a natural or rational moral order that could serve as the basis for a natural law theory. The critical scholars similarly reject the formalistic theory of law defended by Langdell (see section D). And, like the realists, CLS proponents are deeply skeptical about the doctrine of following precedent, claiming that it provides very little in the way of constraining or challenging legal reasoning. Both legal realists and CLS scholars place more of an emphasis on the role played by factors other than the written law in the shaping of court decisions. CLS theorists have, for example, argued that economic interests have driven many changes in the law: the development of personal in-

jury law in the ninteenth century can be explained, according to one prominent critical scholar, as an effort to further the expansion of large industries.

Proponents of CLS (or "crits") do disagree with the legal realists on some key points. For the crits, the realists did not go far enough in terms of developing a thorough "critique" of the ideological bias concealed within legal doctrines and procedures. The realists were too willing to trust to the social sciences as a way to reform law and legal practice, but even these assumptions, say the realists, must be critiqued.

The central challenge of CLS is directed at the assumption—centrally a part of legal positivism—that the law consists of clear rules that can be applied in an objective and neutral fashion to reach predictable, correct results in a given case. What lawyers and judges call "rules" of law are often vague and indeterminate, in a way that conveniently hides their ultimately political nature. Nor do CLS theorists accept Dworkin's view that an expanded concept of "law"—consisting of rules and principles—can yield right answers in legal cases through Dworkin's process of interpretation. Indeed, many of the crits seem to reject any theory of legal reasoning at all, arguing against any attempt to make sense of adjudication as a rationally defensible process in a way that distinguishes it from a purely political act. Courts do not, as positivists such as Hart would say, legislate only in the restricted "penumbral" zone, but all the time.

The assertion that law is thoroughly political is a direct attack upon the possibility of a society based on the "rule of law," and it is therefore not surprising that much critical literature has focused on this ideal. The most familiar concept of the rule of law, according to CLS scholars such as Roberto Unger, presupposes a society characterized by certain features: a pervasive belief in the "subjectivity" of values; a concomitant pluralism and diversity of moral, religious, and political viewpoints; and the conviction that the government must (given the foregoing facts) remain scrupulously neutral on questions dealing with the "best" way to live. The presence of these conditions, some crits believe, gives rise to two problems that the idea of the rule of law is supposed to solve: how to form and sustain a workable social order under conditions of

---

[2] See Roberto Unger, *Knowledge and Politics* (New York: Free Press, 1975); *The Critical Legal Studies Movement* (Cambridge: Harvard University Press, 1983).

deep moral and political disagreement, and how to do this in a way that won't amount simply to domination of one group through subjugation to the values of another. The attempt to solve these problems gives rise to the ideal of the rule of law, the view that the exercise of collective force should be regulated by general, clear, and authoritative norms that have been set out in advance and are made applicable to all.

The fundamental critical objection to this "liberal legalism" is that the very conditions that give rise to the need for the rule of law also make it impossible. The rule of law requires government neutrality in both the enactment and the interpretation of law, neutrality in both legislation and adjudication. However, statutes and ordinances invariably are colored by the value biases of those with sufficient political power to get them voted into law, and the interpretation of such laws, once established, inevitably relies on the subjective views and values of the interpreter (usually a judge). Since there can be no neutral process either for the enactment or for the interpretation of law, a paradox is concealed in the very idea of legality. As an example of this critique, some CLS writers have pointed to the debate over the proper interpretation of the U.S. Constitution (see the next section for material on that debate). Some crits have argued that no defensible theory of legal reasoning—no interpretive methodology—about the meaning of the Constitution has been or can be produced that would account to or legitimate the "discovery" of fundamental rights in the Constitution—rights such as the right to privacy.

A further and central preoccupation of the crits lies with the manipulable and indeterminate or vague character of legal doctrine. The critical point here is not simply that the "law on the books" isn't the whole story; the point is rather that it isn't a coherent story at all. Legal doctrines, concepts, and cases can be read and interpreted in almost any way a judge wishes, according to one main CLS argument. At its most radical, some crits try to "deconstruct" or "trash" the law by seeking to expose it as a tangled mess; at the very least, most critical legalists believe that the law is a collection of not entirely compatible moral, social, and political perspectives.

Many of the aspects of CLS just outlined can be unified around one theme: an attack upon what has been called "liberal legalism": the view that the concepts and rules of the law are required to be neutral as between differing religious, political, and social ideals or views about what is good in life. Law, in this view, is a neutral playing field that secures equal rights and freedoms for everyone. This ideal is fatally flawed, according to the critical legalists, since the law simply cannot be neutral or objective in any meaningful sense.

In the selections included here, CLS scholar Mark Tushnet looks more specifically at the ways in which CLS is an outgrowth of the concerns of the legal realists. Tushnet argues that a core part of the theory of CLS is the rejection of the "policy analysis" so prevalent in the law today. An ordinary lawyer or judge, Tushnet maintains, has very likely been taught to argue and decide cases in a way that best balances the competing interests that are always at stake in legal disputes. As Tushnet observes, this approach to law and adjudication is itself one of the long-lasting effects of legal realism—part of the realists' "constructive program." Tushnet then looks at what he calls the "dominant" project within the CLS movement and the ways in which it "deconstructs" and "critiques" the reigning views of the law.

Philosopher Andrew Altman argues that the position of CLS is best conceived as an attack on the ideal of the rule of law—an ideal according to which political power is confined and channeled in a way that promotes the liberal values of liberty, toleration, and individuality. Altman distinguishes moderate from more radical versions of CLS and sketches some objections to the more radical form.

Law and Economics

One characteristic of many new fields of jurisprudence is the effort to look at the law from a different perspective, whether it be the "outsider" perspective of a person of color victimized by discriminatory laws, or the perspective of a different academic discipline, such as women's studies. One of the most successful of such recent interdisciplinary efforts is the *law and economics* movement.

The many writers who have contributed to this view of the law again make it somewhat difficult to generalize; nonetheless, the theory of law and economics has at least two basic dimensions: one descriptive the other *prescriptive* (or *normative*). In its descriptive form, law and economics say that an economic analysis of the formation and function of legal rules and doctrines provides the best explanation for the law as it exists. "The logic of the law is economics," as economics scholar and federal judge Richard Posner has claimed. In its normative dimension, the theory of law and economics says that an economic analysis of the law is the one that should be used by lawyers and judges to work out the meaning and application of legal doctrine.

A concept basic to the law and economics perspective is that of *economic efficiency*. In a very rough sense, we can say that a legal rule or arrangement is economically efficient when no one can be made better off except at another's expense. The efficiency of a law is to be measured, according to Posner, by first assuming (as economists do) that people act rationally when they act to increase their own wealth. Wealth here is not simply to be equated to money; rather, it has to do with the satisfaction of one's interests or preferences: wealth is increased to the extent that one's preferences are fulfilled. A further assumption is then made: that when each individual acts to maximize his or her own welfare or wealth, the wealth of society as a whole is thereby also maximized. Thus, where laws are concerned, an economically efficient situation is one in which wealth is optimized or maximized.

The work of law and economics scholars has largely tracked these basic assumptions. Under the descriptive heading, law and economics proponents ask: What behavioral incentives will a particular rule of law have? And would those incentives push society in the direction of greater efficiency? So, for example, a law and economics scholar might ask whether allowing consumers to sue manufacturers over inadequate warning labels on consumer goods would promote overall efficiency. On the normative or prescriptive side, law and economics theorists want the law, whether it be the law of personal injury, commercial contracts, or antitrust, to encourage goods and services to end up in the control of those who value them the most.

As an example of how the law and economics theory is supposed to work, consider the law or personal injury—what lawyers call the law of *tort* (see also Chapter Five). According to economic analyses of tort law, the purpose of tort is to bring about an efficient allocation of resources with regard to absorbing the cost of accidents which result in injury. In this view, tort law treats the occurrence of accidents as a problem of *social cost*.

Suppose O is the owner of a steel mill. The mill produces a useful commodity (steel) and an undesirable by-product (pollution). One effect of the process—steel—is positive; the other—pollution—is a negative effect, representing a cost (social cost) borne by everyone. H is a homeowner living adjacent to the mill. H sues O for failure to abate the nuisance of filthy smoke and other pollutants drifting across his (H's) property. Should O be held liable? It is of course true that the nuisance to H would not have occurred but for the conduct of O; yet it is equally true that H's decision to live where he does is also a necessary condition of the injury. And it will get us nowhere, the economic theorists reason, to ask whether O caused H's loss, as this is just a disguised way of re-asking the basic question of whether O should be made to pay. The idea of holding liable the one who *caused* the injury is therefore of little help. What the courts must do instead is view the problem as one of *social cost*: to adjust the law's response to suits like H's by attempting to strike a cost-efficient balance between the amount of benefit conferred by the factory's total product—steel-plus-pollution—against the amount of costs generated, the most efficient allocation of the joint resources of O and H.

A simple example illustrates how the economic theory is supposed to work. Suppose that O receives $5,000 per ton for the first 100 tons of steel manufactured; and suppose that this 100 tons of steel imposes a total cost upon H and his neighbors of $550 per ton. Clearly the net result for society as a whole is a benefit of $4,500. Under these circumstances, the economic theory says the courts should find that O has not been negligent and should not be liable for damage to H. Suppose, on the other hand, that the manufacture of ten thousand tons of steel brings only $1,500 per ton for O (given the marginal decline in the value of every extra lot of

200 tons produced), but that, because the factory's pollution-control equipment becomes less efficient at higher volume, it imposes a cost upon residents of the surrounding community of $1,800 per ton. Here the production of so much polluting steel is not cost-justified on an overall basis, so the law must find O liable as a way of forcing him to absorb the excess cost imposed on the community and thereby return the overall level of social expenditures to an efficient point. The question of whether the defendant caused the plaintiff's injury drops out of the picture altogether.

In the economic view, the question is not so much who is responsible or should be blamed for pollution, but rather, how overall social wealth can be maximized.

In our selection, judge and scholar Richard Posner defends the economic approach to law. The actions of legislators and the decisions of judges do, Posner thinks, facilitate wealth-maximizing transactions; and many common-law doctrines can be explained on the assumption that they are wealth maximizing. Posner examines the objection that, even if the idea of wealth maximization accurately describes what many courts and legislators have done in fashioning the law, the criterion of wealth-maximization is not one that *should* serve in this capacity. One important criticism of law and economics insists that the goal of wealth maximization is totalistic, looking only to the attainment of prosperity for the society as a whole, and thus seemingly unconcerned with the welfare, rights, or entitlements of individuals. Posner responds to this objection and argues for a pragmatic response to it.

Feminist Jurisprudence

According to one of its principal spokespersons, feminist legal theory is defined by two central tasks: the exposure ("unmasking") and critique of patriarchy underlying purportedly neutral and ungendered legal doctrine and legal theory—revealing the "male tilt" in existing law; and the attempt to reconceive law on the basis of categories and concepts distinctively rooted in "women's voice."[3] According advocates of a feminist jurisprudence, the job of the philosopher of law is to uncover the myriad of ways in which the law wrongly assumes, reflects, and builds upon the experiences of men.

Much early work in feminist legal theory owed its inspiration to the path-breaking work of psychologist Carol Gilligan.[4] Gilligan sought to describe, in broad outline, two distinct moral outlooks or perspectives that she argued, corresponded roughly to the perspectives of men and of women.

The typically "male" outlook, according to Gilligan, tends to regard the moral and social worlds legalistically, and to be preoccupied with rules and rule following and with appeals to basic principles of justice and rights. The male social world is hierarchical and competitive, formal and abstract. Women's voice, according to Gilligan, speaks differently. Women tend to emphasize nurturance and care over competition, and networks of relationships with others over hierarchy. Women generally approach moral and social problems contextually, seeking to embed the dilemma within a larger story or narrative that may then point to some kind of resolution that will preserve the ties and relationships already intact. Where men frequently appeal to "universalizable" principles and rules, women look to more context-relative moral and political considerations. Although Gilligan's work has been enormously influential, some recent feminist lawyers have taken issue with her assumptions: scholars such as Catherine MacKinnon have argued that Gilligan's analysis is flawed because it tends to identify "women's voice" with a concept of "the feminine" that is itself a gender stereotype sustained by a patriarchal society.

Other feminist writers question whether there even can be one "woman's voice."

It is not news, of course, that the opportunities, goals, and hopes women could enjoy and entertain were long restricted by the law openly and blatantly (see Chapter 3 for examples). However, the subordination and devaluation of women, feminist legal theorists argue, is still very much apparent in the laws of sexual harassment and rape, spousal

---

[3] Robin West, "Jurisprudence and Gender," *University of Chicago Law Review* 55 (1988), pp. 1–72.

[4] See Carol Gilligan, *In A Different Voice* (Cambridge: Harvard University Press, 1982).

abuse, and discrimination in the workplace. To reveal the erroneous and "gendered" assumptions upon which many of these mistaken legal doctrines are based, feminist legal theorists have urged an appeal to the individual experiences of particular women, and to the traits with which women (according to Gilligan and others) are especially endowed—empathy, sensitivity, and a disdain for abstract and formal solutions to legal disputes.

Not all feminist legal scholars agree, of course. One principal source of disagreement turns on how radically the law must be reformed in order to eliminate the patriarchy implicit in the law. One view argues for the elimination of specific instances of obvious gender bias in, for example, the law of rape. A different, and more radical, critique of patriarchy insists that feminist legal theory must reconceive whole areas of law with an understanding of how existing doctrines silence and subordinate women, trivialize their abuse, and elevate male dominance to appear natural or inevitable. (See, for example, MacKinnnon's critique of pornography law in Chapter Two).

Another debate that separates adherents to feminist legal theory is sometimes referred to as the "special" treatment versus "equal" treatment debate, or the "asymmetrical" versus the "symmetrical" approaches to feminism in the law. According to one writer:

> [T]he asymmetrical approach contends that it is crucial to recognize women's unique needs and to value their special contributions. It contends that the best way to do this is by means of sex-specific laws and policies that treat women differently than men. The ... symmetrical approach argues that women are best served by making sex irrelevant to all decisions governing opportunities available to women and men. It contends that the best way to secure this is by sex-neutral statutes and regulations that stress the analogies between the life-situations of women and men.[5]

The symmetrical approach had been apparent in the 1960s and 70s in arguments for equal pay, equal work, and the proposed Equal Rights Amendment to the Constitution. The asymmetrical model has been urged more recently by those concerned that women have special needs concerning, for example, pregnancy, child care, and work hours, that cannot be assimilated to parallel needs of men. The law must, therefore, make special accommodation for the "real difference" between men and women.

Theorists of the symmetrical approach argue that the moral (and constitutional) ideal of sexual equality is best understood as one of complete gender neutrality or "assimilationism," in which sex-based biological differences are assimilated to that of (say) eye color, so that they become insignificant with regard to the distribution of social goods. Advocates of the asymmetrical approach—sometimes called "difference" theorists—on the other hand, argue that an ideal of gender neutrality cannot bring about a condition of substantive equality when the allegedly "neutral" state of affairs against which moral and social progress is to be judged itself conceals a bias against women. Difference theorists argue that assimilationism ignores real differences between men and women, for instance, the unique needs of women arising out of pregnancy and childbirth. A specific issue in labor law can be used to help students see the relevance of the "sameness/difference" controversy: How should employers respond to the needs of female workers regarding pregnancy and childbirth? Should women be allowed only as much of a "disability" leave as would a man with, say, a hernia, with the consequence that pregnant women and new mothers may, upon returning to work, face hardships (loss of benefits, demotion) not encountered by men? Or should pregnancy be treated as a special "condition," for which employers should be required to give leaves of a certain length whether or not leaves with similar conditions are given to men with disabilities? (Is pregnancy a "disability"?) What do "equal protection" or "equal treatment" in this context amount to?

Two selections included here explore aspects of feminist legal theory. Margaret Radin argues that the philosophical tradition of pragmatism can illuminate and clarify the aims of feminist jurisprudence. Radin sees the primary problem of women

---

[5] J. Ralph Lindgren, "Strategic Themes in Recent Feminist Legal Literature," *American Philosophical Association Newsletter on Feminism and Law* 94 (1995), p. 55.

and the law as one of a "double-bind": an impasse created when one way of using the law to improve the condition of women has a "backlash" effect, worsening women's prospects in other ways. Following American pragmatist philosophers such as William James and John Dewey, Radin claims that such double-binds must be dealt with by "dissolving" or side-stepping the legal and conceptual frameworks that give rise to them. Radin goes on to claim that pragmatism in philosophy and feminism in legal theory hold several methodological views in common: a commitment to seeking knowledge in the situated particulars of actual experience; a concept of truth as provisional; a rejection of sharp dichotomies (reason versus feeling; theory versus practice, and so on). Radin explores the pragmatist notion of truth as coherence among beliefs and questions whether such a view is compatible with the activist and progressive dimension of a feminist jurisprudential outlook.

Angela Harris takes a different point of view, looking at the nature and limits of feminist jurisprudence from the standpoint of critical race theory (see below). Harris attacks what she calls "essentialism": the assumption, quite apparent in feminist theory, that there is one and only one "women's voice," one and only one set of experiences that qualify as "women's experience." Harris tries to show how such gender essentialism is presupposed by the work of other feminist scholars, and she explains the connection between gender essentialism and "racial essentialism," the idea that the experience of white women stands for that of all women. For Harris, racial essentialism wrongly excludes the experience of people of color.

Critical Race Theory

The last of the jurisprudential movements to be covered in this chapter is *critical race theory*. While sharing some of the same convictions about law and its manipulability as CLS lawyers and scholars,

critical race theorists agree that CLS does not get at a crucial fact of American law and culture: its racial stratification. Critical race theorists seek to focus attention on the extent to which racial categories deeply affect not only the way that the law is realized in the streets, but also how the law itself is structured and administered. Just as feminist legal scholars have tried to call attention to the gendered nature of many legal statutes and doctrines, critical race scholars have worked to show the various ways in which the law supports racial hierarchies that subordinate people of color, while concealing this fact under the guise of allegedly "neutral" laws. Such laws—the backbone of traditional civil rights doctrine—are not equipped, critical race theorists argue, fully to expose the ways in which people can be discriminated against, or the manner in which a person's race can be used as a weapon to harm him or her.

In the selection included here, law professor Derrick Bell advocates the need for a "racial realism" in legal thought. Bell outlines an agenda for critical race theory that parallels that of legal realism. The realists, as we have seen, attacked the idea of law as a set of neutrally defined rights, adjudicated through an apolitical and objective form of legal reasoning. Realism exposed ways in which this myth of formalism was used to perpetrate the economic status quo in the early part of the twentieth century. In the same way, Bell suggests, racial realism can expose how law is used to preserve a status quo regarding the oppression of Blacks and other people of color. Contemporary civil rights law, Bell contends, has been co-opted to perpetuate racism in less overt forms than the outright segregation prevalent in many parts of the nation in the past. It is these forms that a racial realism seeks to unmask.

13. *Critical Legal Studies: An Introduction to Its Origins and Underpinnings*

Mark Tushnet

These comments take on the task of explaining why Critical Legal Studies (CLS) forms an appropriate part of a jurisprudence course. Additionally, it provides an overview of what might be included in that part of the course. Material from CLS is already infiltrating the materials used in the first-year curriculum, and at least one prominent British text on jurisprudence has included a brief discussion of CLS in its chapter on American Legal Realism. As that discussion suggests, Legal Realism is one of the intellectual origins of CLS; the other is the progressive tradition in American historiography.

In many ways CLS is a direct descendant of American Legal Realism, which flourished in the 1920s and 1930s and left an important legacy to all legal thought. CLS interprets Legal Realism along the following lines. The Realists offered a critical analysis of law as they saw it. At the time the Realists wrote, many lawyers, judges, and scholars seemed to think that they could draw on a relatively small collection of fairly abstract concepts—CLS has focused on "liberty of contract" and "property rights"—as the basis for decisions in particular cases. Results could either be deduced from the necessary meanings of the concepts or intuited from the social understanding of their meanings. The critical dimensions of Legal Realism established that these assumptions were unfounded. The concepts were so abstract that they led to contradictory conclusions, and because of social divisions—between employers and organized labor, for example—there could be no broadly shared social understandings on which intuitions could properly be based.

The second intellectual source of CLS is the progressive tradition in American historiography. Like Legal Realism, progressive historiography flourished in the 1920s and 1930s. The progressive historians, including Charles Beard and Vernon Parrington, argued that the best way to understand the course of American history was to pay attention to the play of interest groups in American society. Much of their work was devoted to debunking the claims of filiopietistic writers that the best way to understand the course of American history was as the working out of the idea of progress within a generally liberal political framework. The progressive historians looked at American policies and politics and saw much more of economic interest at work; for that they were, rather like CLS people today, called Marxists.

. . .

The Realists made another important point, which was constructive rather than critical. They argued that deduction and intuition had to be replaced by explicit and fairly systematic policy analysis. This constructive program had three elements. First, decision-makers, whether judges, legislators, or lawyers advising clients, had to identify those social interests actually at issue in a particular controversy, and had to think about how those interests might be affected by the various courses of action that might be pursued. Understanding the consequences of legal decisions required studying the actual operation of the legal system, drawing on sociology and political science for organizing concepts. This study came to be called policy analysis, and it is now so widely accepted a way of thinking about law that the forms for student evaluation of teaching routinely ask whether the teacher adequately explored policy issues in the course.

Second, according to the Realists, although lawyers should abandon abstract legal concepts as the basis for decision, they should still pay attention to some important but nonetheless abstract social interests, such as promoting human freedom and

Reprinted by permission of the Journal of Legal Education.

material well-being. For while people might disagree about *how* those interests should be advanced and *whether* other particular values ought to be promoted, no one would disagree *that* these most fundamental values are important. Thus policy analysis could be grounded on these newly identified and broadly shared social understandings.

The third element in the Realists' constructive program was a method of legal analysis, the method of balancing. Once the precise interests at stake have been identified and their relation to the broad social values understood, decision-makers should balance the interests to arrive at an appropriate decision.

The Realists' constructive program provides the framework for most legal thought today. One need only read a randomly selected law review article or—perhaps a better indicator of what we teach our students—a randomly selected student note of comment to find that the right answer to the question at issue can be found by balancing the interests identified in the appropriate three-part test.

CLS accepts the critical aspect of Legal Realism but challenges its constructive program. Because it does so by using the critical techniques developed by the Realists, CLS is in this sense a true descendant of Realism. The way in which CLS is concerned with the political dimensions of law and domination can be explored by examining the CLS attack on policy analysis, balancing, and shared social values—that is, on the constructive program of Legal Realism.

The CLS attack on policy analysis has focused on what is at present the most popular systematic form of policy analysis, law-and-economics. Law-and-economics attempts to identify what the most efficient solution to a legal problem is. That is, suppose we know how wealth is distributed in a particular society and the preferences of its members. Law-and-economics attempts to determine what rule will allow that society to achieve the most of what its members want, given the existing distribution of wealth. Everyone knows that many interesting questions are assumed away when law-and-economics takes the distribution of wealth as a given. But its proponents claim that answers to many questions are insensitive to the distribution of wealth—there could be large changes in that distribution and no changes in the efficient rules—and

that, in any event, if you care about wealth distribution, it is pretty silly to worry about tort or contract law rather than, for example, the tax system.

CLS has attacked law-and-economics in a number of ways. I am not competent to evaluate the technical attack, but I can describe it: The legal system, through its rules of property, contract, and tort, creates a set of entitlements. These entitlements consitute the pattern of wealth-holding in the society. If you are trying to figure out what the efficient rule of contract law is, you cannot take the distribution of wealth as given, because the rule you come up with defines the distribtion of wealth. A second line of attack is that economic analysis —and by extention policy analysis more generally—neccessarily proceeds by making simplifying assumptions about the world. Law-and-economics has increasingly relaxed those assumptions to make the economic models more realistic. But as the realism of the models increases the conclusions that we draw become weaker and weaker.

. . .

The most sophisticated economic analyses end up where the Legal Realists began, with a list of things we ought to think about. The third attack on policy analysis is still more general. Legal rules, and the distribution of wealth, do not merely *reflect* individual preferences. To some degree the rules shape those preferences. Decision-makers must therefore ask not only "What can we do to provide what people want" but, "How will what we do affect what people want?"

The Legal Realists' constructive program answered this question by offering its method of balancing. Sensible decision-makers, brought up in their society and sensitive to its present desires and its aspirations, would be able to take into account everything that policy analysis identified and could come up with the right answers. Here CLS makes a simple point. In our society the class of decision-makers is not representative enough to provide the assurance the Realists wanted. Decision-makers are an elite, demographically unrepresentative and socialized into a set of beliefs about society and technology that skew the balance that they reach. The CLS challenge to balancing, then, is the claim that balancing is a social process that needs to be examined sociologically. The concern for sociological analysis of the actual exercise of power is one part of the legacy of progressive historiography. Sociological analysis inevitably raises political questions. For example, CLS argues that the Realists did not go far enough in demanding a democratization of law and, notably, that neither the New Deal nor the present Democratic Party does so either.

Concern for the politics of legal thought is even more evident in the most fundamental part of the CLS challenge to the Legal Realists' constructive program. The Realists wanted lawyers to worry about how the legal system promoted broadly shared social values. Parts of the CLS argument here are simple applications of the Realists' critical arguments: The social values are described so abstractly that they could justify any decision, and there is some disagreement even about these abstract values—consider the environmentalists' challenge to arguments for increasing a society's material wealth. But the more important part of the CLS argument goes deeper. CLS insists that the social values, on which there may well be agreement, are not valuable in some abstract and timeless sense. They are values because our society is structured to produce in its members just that set of values. But if that is so, the entire constructive enterprise collapses on itself, because you cannot think about altering legal rules to conform to a society's values when those values are constructed partly on the basis of the legal rules themselves.

Taken together, the CLS arguments are bound to be unsettling. If the argument about the social construction of values is correct, people who talk about radical changes in social organization are likely to seem at least weird and off-the-wall. CLS tries to put into question the deepest values of a society: Because there is nothing timeless about those values, we might simply decide to abandon them. CLS might not be able to make much headway with these arguments were it not aided by developments in other disciplines such as philosophy and sociology, whose important thinkers have also argued that social reality is itself socially constructed.

. . .

I turn now to a description of the current state of CLS. First, however, I must interject a number of qualifications. CLS is a developing body of thought, and it would be unsound to attempt to freeze it with an absolutely precise description. Further, different participants in the effort to push CLS ahead have different opinions, and as one of the participants, I have my own views on matters in controversy.

One issue should be mentioned, only to be put aside. It seems to be a standard line in statements by critics of CLS that CLS has no constructive program. As I will indicate at the conclusion of these remarks, there is a deep sense in which that is correct. But in the superficial sense that these critics appear to intend, their comments are simply wrong. CLS offers many proposals for alternative programs. These proposals run from the mundane, such as William Simon's suggestion that a random selection of welfare determinations be automatically subjected to review on appeal,[1] to the grandiose, such as Roberto Unger's description of various forms of public control over investment.[2] I suppose that the critics' point is that, though they can *read* these statements about what ought to be done, they cannot quite understand how those practical proposals are related to the critical or theoretical dimensions of CLS.

Here I will give the short answer to this criticism and will devote the rest of my paper to explaining that answer. The short answer is that the point of the proposals is to continue the critique of existing society, not to get these particular proposals adopted in the short run. This position is, as I will now try to argue, related to ongoing discussions within CLS.

To illustrate this relation, I will describe what is, or at least what was, probably the central debate within CLS. The early position in CLS was that one could say something systematic about the relation between legal rules and power—for example, we can say, though with many qualifications, that the legal system is tilted in favor of capitalism. So long as it is not bound by too many qualifications, that statement or some variant has a fairly obvious intuitive appeal.

The dominant position responds by identifying—or perhaps more precisely by stressing more strongly than the early position—the difficulties inherent even in heavily qualified versions of the early formulations. Three of its arguments have been particularly effective. The first emphasizes the Legal Realists' skepticism about rules, which made it impossible to say that "the legal system" is tilted in any direction at all: If decision-makers can in principle reach any conclusion they wish within the legal system, "the system" cannot be tilted, though of course the decision-makers might be biased. The second argument is that no one has shown that any particular aspect of the legal system, or even the legal system as a whole, serves the interests of capitalism better than do obvious alternatives, including wholesale rejection of vast bodies of law. For any particular rule in the law of contracts in some state in the United States which might be thought to support capitalism, there is a precisely contrary rule, within an equally capitalist system, that is, in another state. International comparisons demonstrated that capitalist economic systems could be found in countries with widely divergent legal systems. The final argument against tilt is that the legal system in fact has little direct impact on the maintenance of capitalism. It provides a framework within which bargains can be struck, and its rules are a sort of disaster insurance against unforseen calamities. But it is difficult to see how an institution whose purposes are so limited could have much of systemic impact.

These arguments have forced a reformulation of the early position. Agreeing that tilt could not be found systematically in the rules of the legal system, the reformulation argued that it is located in the construction of the categories used to organize legal thought and in the construction of the operations used to relate those categories. This seems to me the present state of the position: It claims an analytic program, but has not yet made much progress in demonstrating the program's power.

The renunciation of the theoretical dimension of the initial project of CLS helps explain an otherwise curious characteristic of recent critical legal scholarship. Although it devotes a great deal of attention to phenomena that occurred in the past, much of the work is relentlessly ahistorical. It focuses synchronically on particular moments in the past or offers a sort of comparative statics, but never gives a diachronic account of transformation over time. I believe that this ahistoricism is linked to the critique of social theory, because diachronic accounts explicitly or implicitly rely on social theory to give them coherence. One tradition in the philosophy of history holds that narratives must draw on covering laws—the generalizations of social theory—of which sequences of particular

events are specific instances based on identified initial conditions. Another tradition is less explicitly theoretical and claims only that historians provide narratives of past events. But the selection of the events that are placed in the narrative's sequence, out of all the possible events that could be used, seems to require some (usually implicit) theoretical account, if only the common sense theories held by well-socialized readers of historical narratives. Having renounced social theory, CLS is barred/precluded from using these standard traditions of historical writing—thus its characteristic ahistoricism.

Alternatively, one could provide a multitude of competing stories about how things changed, while insisting that none of the stories has the sort of epistemological priority that social theories gives to the narratives of the standard traditions. Or one could rely on the critique of social theory as a background against which only one account was offered, demanding that readers abjure the usual expectations they might hold about the epistemological claims implicit in such narratives. Either of these courses—the many stories or the one told with a raised eyebrow—could force readers to consider what might be the basis for the critical legal scholar's choice or stories to tell. And that would bring the politics of CLS directly into the discussion.

The view of historical analysis that I have just sketched is implicit in much recent critical legal scholarship, but I believe that the body of work would be strengthened by explicit discussions of these issues. More often the issues have been taken up in the use of structuralist and deconstructionist methods. These methods lie behind much of the currently dominant practice. As soon as an analyst offers a systematic explanation of something, the dominant strain in CLS decenters the explanation, rearranging the terms and categories used in the explanation to demonstrate that the reorganized explanation is just as good as the original one. This decentering project has no termination.

The use of deconstruction has developed its insistence that general social-theoretical explanations are unavailable into the position that all one can do is provide minutely detailed maps or descriptions of phenomena. At this point the open question for the dominant view arises. In general, though it has abandoned the search for social theory, it has not abandoned the view that social power (illegitimate hierarchy) exists. Somehow the detailed descriptions are to reveal how power actually operates. They do so not by invoking social theory of covering laws, but by educing, in an essentially intuitive way, understanding out of the reader's immersion in details. But we need to ask, how is this understanding supposed to emerge?

One possible answer is that the dominant program does not really aim at understanding in the usual sense. Rather, this view maintains, proponents of the dominant program have made a strategic judgment that in the present circumstances their political goals are more likely to be reached by using deconstructive methods. This view breaks the connection between the analytic program and the politics of critical legal studies.

A second possibility is that understanding emerges because of the essentially literary techniques used by those presenting the detailed descriptions. It might be that these techniques operate in a sphere epistemologically distinct from that in which social theory is thought to operate. If so, the emptiness of social theory need not imply that we cannot gain knowledge via deconstruction.

A third possibility, and the one that I believe many critical legal scholars would prefer to pursue, is that we can analyze the ways in which intuitive understanding emerges from detailed descriptions. The anthropologist Clifford Geertz has argued that all knowledge is this sort of "local knowledge."[3] But neither Geertz nor anyone who has appropriated his terminology has done much to explain the sense in which "local knowledge" is knowledge. The effort to do so seems sensible for two reasons. First, we know that people sometimes have different intuitions about a particular problem, and we ought to be curious about how and why intuitive understandings are sometimes shared and sometimes divergent. Second, the analytic effort may be required by the CLS emphasis on domination and illegitimate hierarchy. These terms have normative connotations that suggest that any accurate understanding of hierarchal situations would refer to domination. But that judgment plainly needs some sort of defense.

One line of defense, which appears in some works, is to rely on an essentially romantic view of

human nature. Joseph Singer, for example, counters hard-nosed views that "what people *really* like is doing horrible things to each other" with the sensible response that they "do not want just to be beastly to each other. . . . [T]hey also want not to harm others."[4] The difficulty is that as Singer pursues his analysis, he forgets the implication of the "not just" and "also"; in other words, he forgets that people do indeed sometimes want to be beastly. What to those on the bottom is an illegitimate hierarchy is to those on the top a perfectly sensible one. The romantic view of human nature denies that anyone could hold the latter belief in good faith, but, in the absence of a fairly elaborate late Sartrean exposition of the concept of bad faith, the denial is unpersuasive.

A second line of defense for judgments about domination can be called strategic silence. Gary Peller's analysis of the reification of consent in the law of rape provides a useful example.[5] In a standard deconstructive analysis, Peller argues that the concept of consent can be applied in particular settings only by "construct[ing] the context which is supposed to provide the ground for representing the event," a course that "promises total circularity."[6] Peller's aim is to demonstrate that the use of consent as a defense in the law of rape projects "the ideological message . . . that consensual sexuality is consistent with male domination in society.[7] But it should be clear that the same analysis could be used to explain what might be called the Maileresque assessment that female domination requires men to engage in sexual behavior that society creates to be coercive. The technique of deconstruction, that is, cannot in itself support the political conclusions implicit in the use of the term "domination" as applied to particular arrangements. Because the political open-endedness of the deconstructive technique is so obvious, the silence about it in the CLS literature should be understood as strategic, designed to place on the table the political judgments implied by any use of language.

But strategic silence only raises the political issues; it does not explain why one ought to adopt the feminist interpretation of consent and reject the Maileresque interpretation of coercion. This fact suggests that the idea of strategic silence could be extended. The extension would hold that there is nothing beyond that silence, that the process of decentering our understandings is indeed interminable. One offers the feminist interpretation of rape because one has made a political judgment that in our society congealed forms of domination are more likely to be broken up by that interpretation than by the Maileresque alternative. But that is an ungrounded political judgment, open to discussion and alteration as times, circumstances, and understandings change.

The critique of social theory thus replaces one form of political analysis with another. Instead of having political positions flow from social theory, the dominant CLS project simply takes political positions. But not just any political positions. The politics of the dominant position is the politics of decentering, disrupting whatever understandings happen to be settled, criticizing the existing order whatever that order is. Some CLS proponents are attracted to small-scale decentralized socialism. But that attraction must be understood as the embodiment of a critique of large-scale centralized capitalism. It cannot set forth a permanent program, the realization of which would be the end of politics. In fact, in a socialist society, the critical legal scholar would criticize socialism as denying the importance of individual achievement, and decentralization as an impediment to material and spiritual achievement. Roberto Unger captured this dimension of the irrationalist project in his description of destabilization rights, "claims to the disruption of established institutions ... that have ... contributed to the very kind of crystallized plan of social hierarchy and division that the entire constitution wants to avoid."[8]

With all this in hand, we can in conclusion turn to the implications of the critique of social theory for the future of CLS. Of course the Legal Realist analysis of rules will continue to be used; the legal academy's commitment to the coherence of rules is strong enough to require repeated assaults. It might be useful as well to develop detailed analyses of how law and beliefs about law are implicated in practices of domination and liberation, but the institutional impediments to sustained empirical research by legal academics are so substantial that it is unlikely that critical legal scholars will produce much along these lines.

I should mention too that one part of the future of CLS is continued institutionalization as part of the pluralist intellectual world of the legal academy. It now seems to be a more or less standard practice in symposia and workshops to include someone from CLS, or at least to feel bad if you do not manage to round one up (or if you willfully ignore them).

But the most important implication of the dominant CLS analysis is that any critique of the existing order is consistent with the project of CLS. Statistical studies, casual empiricism, classical social theory, the most old-fashioned doctrinal analysis—all might be critical legal studies so long as three conditions are met. First, the work should not be defended on grounds that suggest that something more enduring than interminable critique might result from following it through. Second, it must be designed as a critique rather than as a defense of the existing order—or of a slightly modified version of the existing order that, once modified, would be the end of politics. Finally, the work should actually operate as a critique.

Perhaps the program of interminable critique swallows itself. If it is widely accepted, people may at first resign themselves to their inability to transcend critique. But they may come to see that inability is itself transcendent, creating a new form of life in which the terms on which critique must proceed today have become unintelligible.

I would like to close by elaborating this point about interminable critique. I will do so by describing one of the more controversial CLS arguments, which has been called the critique of rights. According to this argument, it would seem that we could abandon such valued rights as the constitutional protections our society gives to free speech and to the antidiscrimination principle. The CLS argument has two parts. The first applies the critique of legal concepts to the concepts embodied in these ideas about rights. Here the critique argues that the rights are defined on too abstract a level to be helpful in resolving the claims presented in particular cases. Nor will recourse to underlying values or to a balancing process help, for reasons I have already reviewed. This aspect of the argument is not unusual or, in itself, particularly bothersome, because it relies on positions for which the Realists were thought to have adequate answers.

One person to whom the critique of rights was described reacted by called the world that it depicted "Kafkaesque." According to the critique of rights, people cannot know what rights they have, and there are no political methods that guarantee those rights. The term "Kafkaesque" is perfectly appropriate and provides a clue to the justification for the constructive program—or for the program of interminable critique. For by invoking Kafka's vision, the term allows CLS to say that it, like Kafka, is describing the condition of the modern world. Those reared in, or attracted to, premodernist traditions may well find the world so described quite distasteful. But the point of modernism is precisely that that is just the way things are these days.

CLS is thus the form that modernism takes in legal thought. Like modernism in philosophy and sociology, it displaces settled understandings, insisting that whatever we have is something we create and re-create daily. As a form of modernism, CLS argues that our lives are structured by institutions that we create and sustain, and that our lives have no meaning outside those institutions and the processes by which we create them—and create ourselves. So, in part, the CLS program is justified in the way all modernist programs are: The program consists of shattering congealed forms of life

by showing that they have no particular integrity. And whatever makes that demonstration effective—utopian yearnings, close analysis of legal texts, concrete proposals—is part of the program.

Perhaps this analysis could be continued indefinitely. But if the CLS critique is interminable, this article is not.

Endnotes

[1] William Simon, Legality, Bureaucracy, and Class in the Welfare System, 92 Yale L. J. 1198, 1267–68 (1983).

[2] Roberto Unger, The Critical Legal Studies Movement, 96 Harv. L. Rev. 561, 596–97 (1983).

[3] Clifford Geertz, Local Knowledge (New York, 1983).

[4] Joseph Singer, The Player and the Cards: Nihilism and Legal Theory, 94 Yale L.J. 1, 54 (1984).

[5] Peller, *supra* note 22, at 1187–91.

[6] *Id.* at 1189–90.

[7] *Id.* at 1191.

[8] Unger, *supra* note 12, at 600, 611–15.

14. *Critical Legal Studies and Liberalism*

Andrew Altman

The Rule of Law

The CLS movement is a trend in legal scholarship that has developed over the last decade or so in a large number of law-review articles and in a few key books. Its ideas have proved to be unusually controversial, leading the dean at a major American law school to declare that adherents to CLS are not

fit to teach in law schools.[1] The controversy stems in large part from the movement's challenge to some of the most cherished ideals of modern liberal thought. In particular, CLS represents a challenge to a principle central to liberal legal thought—the rule of law. The central contention of CLS is that the rule of law is a myth.

Undoubtedly, I have put this contention in a form that is too crude and calls for clarification and qualification. Yet ii is an appropriate first approximation of the heart of the CLS view and serves to draw the main battle line along which CLS has chosen to wage its campaign against liberal legal philosophy. Its critique of liberal legal thought largely stands or falls with the success of its attack on the idea of the rule of law as it is understood by liberal thought.

There can be no doubt that a vital element of liberal legal philosophy is the principle that a society ought to operate under the rule of law. Its commitment to the rule of law originates with the birth of modern liberalism in the seventeenth century and remains as strong as ever in contemporary liberal theory. And the terms in which the rule of law is endorsed by liberals have remained remarkably constant throughout rather substantial changes in certain aspects of liberal theory and some rather deep disagreements among liberals themselves. In his *Second Treatise of Government*, Locke expressed his commitment in these words:

> [F]reedom of men under government is to have a standing rule to live by, common to every one of that society and made by the legislative power erected in it, a liberty to follow my own will in all things where the rule prescribes not, and not to be subject to the inconstant, uncertain, unknown, arbitrary will of another man.[2]

Locke went on to argue that

> the legislative or supreme authority cannot assume to itself a power to rule by extemporary, arbitrary decrees, but is bound to dispense justice and to decide the rights of the subject by promulgated, standing laws, and known authorized judges.[3]

And the importance of the rule of law to Locke's thinking is concisely formulated in his *Letter Concerning Toleration*: "There are two sorts of contests amongst men; the one managed by law, the other by force: and these are of that nature, that where the one ends, the other always begins."[4]

Several centuries later, Hobhouse argued for the reconstruction of liberal theory, implicitly and explicitly rejecting significant elements of Locke's early version. Hobhouse argued that the state should adopt economic policies calculated to reduce the vast inequalities generated by the operation of the market. He called for social control over basic economic resources and rejected what he re-

garded as traditional liberalism's excessive reliance on private ownership and the market mechanism. Yet the ringing endorsement of the rule of law remains the same:

> [T]he first condition of free government is government not by the arbitrary determination of the ruler, but by fixed rules of law, to which the ruler himself is subject.[5]

A few decades after Hobhouse's classic reformulation of liberalism, Hayek repudiated the tendency toward socialism and state economic planning that Hobhouse's liberalism embodied, which was gaining wide acceptance in Western liberal democracies. Yet Hayek too endorsed the principle of the rule of law and even proceeded to claim that socialist economic policies were to be rejected because they were necessarily inconsistent with it:

> Nothing distinguishes more clearly conditions in a free country from those in a country under arbitrary government than the observance in the former of the great principles known as the Rule of Law. Stripped of all technicalities, this means that government in all its actions is bound by rules fixed and announced beforehand—rules which make it possible to foresee with fair certainty how the authority will use its coercive powers in given circumstances and to plan one's individual affairs on the basis of this knowledge.[6]

In recent years, Joseph Raz has rejected Hayek's argument against socialistic economic policies, suggesting that Hayek exaggerated the importance of punctiliously observing the rule of law. But it is manifest that Raz himself places great value on its observance and stands squarely in the liberal tradition when he declares that "it is clear that deliberate disregard for the rule of law violates human dignity."[7]

Finally, we may cite the two most influential American legal philosophers of the last half century, Lon Fuller and Ronald Dworkin. The work of these important liberal thinkers embodies a strong commitment to the rule of law. Fuller writes:

> Surely the very essence of the Rule of Law is that in acting upon the citizen (by putting

him in jail, for example, or declaring invalid a deed under which he claims title to property) a government will faithfully apply rules previously declared as those to be followed by the citizen and determinative of his rights and duties. . . . Applying rules faithfully implies, in turn, that rules will take the form of general declarations. . . . [T]he basic principle of the Rule of Law [is] that the acts of a legal authority toward the citizen must be legitimated by being brought within the terms of a previous declaration of general rules.[8]

And Dworkin describes the rule of law in its most general form in this way:

> [T]he most abstract and fundamental point of legal practice is to guide and constrain the power of government. . . . Law insists that force not be used or withheld, no matter how useful that would be to ends in view, no matter how beneficial or noble these ends, except as licensed or required by individual rights and responsibilities flowing from past political decisions about when collective force is justified.
>
> The law of a community on this account is the scheme of rights and responsibilities that meet that complex standard: they license coercion because they flow from past decisions of the right sort.[9]

In citing this line of liberal thinkers from Locke through Dworkin, I do not meant to suggest that they all have precisely the same conception of the rule of law. There are important differences. . . . Yet there is a remarkable similarity of conceptions and commitments, given the immense span of years and the wide divergence on issues in political philosophy that otherwise divide these thinkers.

The rule of law plays such a central and abiding role in the theories of liberal thinkers because they judge it to be an indispensable institutional mechanism for securing the dominant value cherished by their tradition—individual liberty—and those values that are intertwined with it, such as toleration, individuality, privacy, and private property. The liberal believes that in the absence of the rule of law, there would be no way to secure in practice the individual liberty that he cherishes in theory. The law is an indispensable mechanism for regulating public and private power in a way that effectively helps to prevent the oppression and domination of the individual by other individuals and by institutions. Law as such is not sufficient to accomplish this purpose, and every liberal will also concede that oppressive laws are not only a logical possibility but a historical reality as well. But liberal legal thought holds that the rule of law is, in the world of the modern nation-state at least, a necessary condition for securing a sufficiently wide zone of individual liberty. Moreover, it is a necessary condition that in practice, takes us a significant way toward the goal of preventing the oppression or domination of the individual. The rule of law can do this, according to liberal thought, because the law has the power to constrain, confine, and regulate the exercise of social and political power.

The CLS *Attack*

There are three main prongs to the CLS attack on the liberal embrace of the rule of law, three main elements to the CLS charge that the rule of law, as liberal theory conceptualizes it, is a myth. . . .

The first prong hinges on the claim that the rule of law is not possible in a social situation where the kind of individual freedom endorsed by the liberal view reigns. Such a situation would be characterized by a pluralism of fundamentally incompatible moral and political viewpoints. The establishment of the rule of law under the conditions of pluralism would require some mode of legal reasoning that could be sharply distinguished from moral and political deliberation and choice. There would have to be a sharp distinction, so the argument goes, between law, on one side, and both morals and politics, on the other. Without such a distinction, judges and other individuals who wield public power could impose their own views of the moral or political good on others under the cover of law. Such impositions, however, would destroy the rule of law and the liberal freedom it is meant to protect.

Thus, the liberal view requires that legal reasoning—that is, reasoning about what rights persons have under the law and why—be clearly distinguished from reasoning about political or ethical values. Legal reasoning is not to be confused with deciding which party to a case has the best moral or political argument. Yet it is precisely this kind of legal reasoning that is impossible in a setting of moral and political pluralism, according to CLS. The law-politics distinction collapses, and legal reasoning becomes tantamount to deciding which party has the best moral or political argument. Karl Klare puts the CLS position concisely: "This [liberal] claim about legal reasoning—that it is autonomous from political and ethical choice—is a falsehood."[10]

Duncan Kennedy is even more blunt, but the essential point is the same:

> Teachers teach nonsense when they persuade students that legal reasoning is distinct, *as a method for reaching correct results*, from ethical or political discourse in general. . . . There is never a "correct legal solution" that is other than the correct ethical or political solution to that legal problem.[11]

The second prong of the CLS attack on the rule of law revolves around the claim that the legal doctrines of contemporary liberal states are riddled by contradictions. The contradictions consist of the presence of pairs of fundamentally incompatible norms serving as authoritative elements of legal doctrine in virtually all departments of law. These contradictions are thought to defeat the notion that the rule of law actually reigns in those societies that most contemporary liberal philosophers regard as leading examples of political societies operating under the rule of law. Kennedy contends that the contradictions are tied to the fact that legal doctrine does not give us a coherent way to talk about the rights of individuals under the law: "Rights discourse is internally inconsistent, vacuous, or circular. Legal thought can generate plausible rights justifications for almost any result."[12] Klare echoes Kennedy's claim: "Legal reasoning is a texture of openness, indeterminacy, and contradiction."[13]

As Klare and Kennedy suggest, the CLS view is that the consequence of these doctrinal contradictions is pervasive legal indeterminacy—that is, the widespread inability of the authoritative rules and doctrines to dictate a determinate outcome to legal cases. The contradictions enable lawyers and judges to argue equally well for either side of most legal cases, depending on which of two contradictory legal norms they choose to rely upon. Moreover, the existence of indeterminacy is tied to the collapse of the distinction between law and politics. Judges can and do covertly rely on moral and political considerations in deciding which of two incompatible legal norms they will base their decisions upon. In existing liberal states, we have not the rule of law but the rule of politics. Joseph Singer sums up this phase of the CLS attack on the rule of law nicely:

> While traditional legal theorists acknowledge the inevitability and desirability of some indeterminacy, traditional legal theory requires a relatively large amount of determinacy as a fundamental premise of the rule of law. Our legal system, however, has never satisfied this goal.[14]

Closely associated with the first two prongs of the CLS attack on the rule of law is the thesis that the very idea of the rule of law serves as an instrument of oppression and domination. David Kairys expresses the general idea in a manner characteristic of much CLS writing:

> The law is a major vehicle for the maintenance of existing social and power relations. . . . The law's perceived legitimacy confers a broader legitimacy on a social system . . . characterized by domination. This perceived legitimacy of the law is primarily based . . . on the distorted notion of government by law, not people.[15]

In the CLS view, then, the idea that our political society operates under the rule of law serves to perpetuate illegitimate relations of power. Exposing the rule of law as a myth is thought of in the CLS movement as an essential part of a strategy designed to undermine those relations of power. . . .

The third prong of the CLS attack focuses on the idea that law is capable of constraining the exercise of social and political power. The contention is made that to think of law as capable of such constraint is to adopt a form of fetishism—to be guilty of regarding a human creation as though it were an independent power capable of controlling those who in fact have created and sustained it. This form of fetishism disempowers human beings; it places them in thrall to forces over which they can and should be the masters. In this CLS view, then, the idea of the rule of law must be criticized as part of a general attack on ideas that disempower humans.

The Totalitarian Charge

In light of the CLS attack on the rule of law, it should not be surprising that the movement has generated an unusual degree of controversy and opposition among legal theorists. There is, however, another source of controversy. The CLS literature is often construed by its opponents as strongly inclined toward a total rejection of liberal values. The attack on law is seen as one phase of a more general totalitarian tilt against the individual freedoms associated with the tradition of liberal political philosophy. I do not believe that a fair examination of the CLS literature can support such an interpretation. It is, at best, a gross caricature. Many CLS authors often do argue that liberal values present only one side of the human story, that there are things people do and should cherish that are either omitted or distorted in the liberal picture. Solidarity and community are the values most often invoked in this regard. However, it is a mistake to infer some sort of totalitarian tilt in CLS from its talk of solidarity, community, and so forth; its thinkers are strongly committed to the essential individual freedoms that liberals have fought to secure against their absolutist, fascist, and totalitarian foes. The words of three prominent CLS authors testify to this conclusion.

First, consider the single most important text in the CLS literature, Roberto Unger's *Knowledge and Politics*. This work has been interpreted as a total rejection of liberal values. It is true that Unger repeatedly insists that what is needed is a "total criticism" of liberalism rather than the "partial criticisms" which many thinkers have offered hitherto.[16] However, Unger does not equate "total criticism" with "total rejection."[17] As Unger uses the term, a *total criticism* of liberalism is one that sees liberalism as a whole, as a single, interconnected system of principles and postulates about human psychology, morality, law, and politics. Unger explicitly states that the liberal value of individual freedom is a part of the liberal system that must be cherished and preserved. And in allusion to the great English liberals—including Locke, Bentham, and Mill—Unger declares:

> Many of the liberal thinkers were devoted to freedom. . . . If for no other reason than for this devotion, they will rank forever as heroes and teachers of the human race, and all the sins of England will be forgiven because of her services to liberty.[18]

Unger's purpose is not to reject the liberal devotion to individual liberty but to claim that there are other aspects of human life that ought to be cherished for which liberal theory does not adequately account. It may be wrong that liberalism cannot adequately account for community, solidarity and the like. But it is instructive that liberal philosophers do not reject the importance of those values; rather, they argue that liberal theory can adequately account for them.[19] The propensity of liberal theorists to make such arguments testifies to the fallacy of inferring that CLS is guilty of a totalitarian tilt against individual freedoms because it insists on acknowledging the central importance of community and solidarity in human life.

Another CLS author, Mark Tushnet, echoes Unger's view that liberal values are not to be rejected but are to be seen as part of a fuller account of what humans do and should cherish. For Tushnet, it is the civic republican tradition in modern political thought that provides the needed supplement. He claims that "just as the republican tradition correctly emphasizes our mutual dependence, the liberal tradition correctly emphasizes our individuality and the threats we pose to one another."[19] And Duncan Kennedy is also not hesitant to embrace liberal freedom. In a discussion of the liberal conception of individual rights, Kennedy claims, "Embedded in the rights notion is a liberating accomplishment of our culture: the affirmation of free human subjectivity against the constraints of group life, along with the paradoxical countervision of a group life that creates and nurtures individuals capable of freedom."[20]

These statements by three of the leading critics hardly evidence a commitment to the totalitarian repudiation of individual liberty. To be sure, liberal theorists will see a threat to liberty in the CLS effort to brand the rule of law a myth. But that view hinges on a particular answer to one of the points of contention between the two groups. CLS does not deny the importance of individual liberty, contrary to the claims of those who intimate that the movement is tainted by totalitarianism. Rather, CLS denies that the rule of law does, or could, protect such liberty and so asserts that other social mechanisms must be invented for such protection. I will argue that the CLS position is unsound, but my argument is wholly consistent with recognizing that individual liberty holds a key place in CLS thinking.

Conflict within CLS

It would be a mistake to complete this overview of the CLS–liberalism debate without introducing some of the disagreements that divide the CLS movement. The movement is by no means monolithic, and there are fundamental differences that divide it into various wings. I am especially concerned with two incompatible strands of thinking that run through the CLS literature, one of which may be characterized as *radical*, the other as *moderate*. The radical strand combines a position on the meanings of legal terms and norms that can loosely be described as *deconstructionist* with the idea that there is no objective structure to the law or any social institution. The position on meaning holds that the words that constitute legal norms and doctrines have no stable or fixed meanings, but are rather "empty vessels" into which the individual may pour whatever meaning he or she chooses. This view is conjoined to the position that it is an illusion to see the law, or any other element of social reality, as having a structure independent of any individual's perception of it. Tushnet expresses the radical position on the structure of legal doctrine in the course of endorsing a certain strand of thinking in the American legal realist movement:

> The materials of legal doctrine are almost measureless, and the acceptable techniques of legal reasoning—distinguishing on the basis of the facts, analogizing to other areas of law where cognate problems arise, and the like—are so flexible that they allow us to assemble diverse precedents into whatever pattern we choose.[21]

The moderate strand of CLS rejects the deconstructionist position on meaning and the view that law and social reality have no objective structure. It holds instead that words do have a settled core of meaning but that the interpretations required to render legal decisions are inescapably responsive to the individual's moral and political beliefs. It holds that our law does have an objective structure but that this structure is a function of a certain controversial and inadequate ethical perspective. Unger gives the most consistent and systematic expression to the moderate strand in CLS. He has never even flirted with deconstructionism, and the social theory that he has recently developed involves a clear rejection of the view that social reality and law are not constituted by objective structures. Unger describes the kinds of explanations offered by his social theory by claiming that they

> assign central importance to the distinction between routine deals or quarrels and the recalcitrant institutional and imaginative frameworks in which they ordinarily occur. . . . In the contemporary Western democracies the social framework includes legal rules that use property rights as the instrument of economic decentralization [and] constitutional arrangements that provide for representation while discouraging militancy.[22]

Unger's idea of a social and legal framework that shapes and guides routine activities and is resistant to change rests on a rejection of the radical premise that social reality and law do not consist of structures independent of the way any particular individual chooses to think about them.

These important differences between the radical and moderate wings of CLS lead to differences in argument when it comes to the three main elements of the attack on the rule of law as the liberal conceptualizes it. The radical wing attacks on the basis of its deconstructionism and its view that law has no objective structure. The moderate wing attacks on the basis of its claims about legal interpretation and the relation of the existing structure of law to a certain (allegedly) deficient ethical viewpoint.

My strategy in defending liberal legal philosophy can now be concisely stated, albeit in a slightly oversimplified form. On the one hand, the strategy aims to show that the radical arguments of CLS rest on flawed theoretical premises regarding language and law: The deconstructionist position on meaning and the idea that law and social reality have no objective structure are both indefensible. On the other hand, my strategy aims to show that the theoretical premises of the moderate wing are basically sound but do not entail any serious deficiency in the liberal conception of the rule of law. There are indeed certain forms of liberal theory whose conceptions of the rule of law are arguably inconsistent with the ideas of the moderate wing, but that is only to say that certain forms of liberal theory are weaker and more vulnerable to criticism than others. The basic ideas of the moderate wing, to the extent that they are sound, are fully consistent with stronger liberal conceptions of the rule of law. . . .

Endnotes

[1] Paul Carrington, "Of Law and the River," *Journal of Legal Education* 34 (1984): 227.

[2] John Locke, *Second Treatise of Government* (Indianapolis: Bobbs-Merrill, 1952), p. 15.

[3] *Ibid.*, p. 77.

[4] John Locke, *A Letter Concerning Toleration* (Indianapolis: Hackett, 1983), p. 49.

[5] L. T. Hobhouse, *Liberalism* (New York: Oxford University Press, 1964), p. 17.

[6] Friedrich Hayek, *The Road to Serfdom* (Chicago: University of Chicago Press, 1944), p. 72.

[7] Joseph Raz, *The Authority of Law* (New York: Oxford University Press, 1979), p. 221.

[8] Lon Fuller, *The Morality of Law*, rev. ed. (New Haven: Yale University Press, 1964), pp. 209–10, 214.

[9] Dworkin, *Law's Empire*, p. 93.

[10] Karl Klare, "The Law School Curriculum in the 1980s: What's Left? *Journal of Legal Education* 32 (1982): 340.

[11] Duncan Kennedy, "Legal Education as Training for Hierarchy," in Kairys, *Politics of Law*, p. 47.

[12] *Ibid.*, p. 48.

[13] Klare, "Law School Curriculum," p. 340.

[14] Joseph Singer, "The Player and the Cards: Nihilism and Legal Theory," *Yale Law Journal* 94 (1984): 13.

[15] David Kairys, "Introduction," in *Politics of Law*, pp. 5–6.

[16] Roberto Unger, *Knowledge and Politics* (New York: Free Press, 1975). pp. 1–3, 10, 15, 17–18.

[17] Karsten Harries appears to misinterpret Unger on this point. See Harries, "The Contradictions of Liberal Thought," *Yale Law Journal* 85 (1975–1976): 842.

[18] Unger, *Knowledge and Politics*, p. 277

[19] Tushnet, *Red, White, and Blue*, p. 23.

[20] Duncan Kennedy, "Critical Labor Law Theory: A Comment," *Industrial Relations Law Journal* 4 (1981): 506.

[21] Tushnet, *Red, White, and Blue*, pp. 191–92.

[22] Roberto Unger, *Social Theory: Its Situation and Its Task* (New York: Cambridge University Press, 1987), p. 3.

15. *The Economic Approach to Law*

Richard A. Posner

The most ambitious and probably the most influential effort in recent years to elaborate an overarching concept of justice that will both explain judicial decision making and place it on an objective basis is that of scholars working in the interdisciplinary field of "law and economics," as economic analysis of law is usually called. I am first going to describe the most ambitious version of this ambitious effort and then use philosophy to chip away at it and see what if anything is left standing.

The Approach

The basic assumption of economics that guides the version of economic analysis of law that I shall be

Reprinted by permission of the publisher from *The Problems of Jurisprudence* by Richard Posner, Cambridge, MA: Harvard University Press, © 1990 by the President and Fellows of Harvard College.

presenting is that people are rational maximizers of their satisfactions—*all* people (with the exception of small children and the profoundly retarded) in *all* of their activities (except when under the influence of psychosis or similarly deranged through drug or alcohol abuse) that involve choice. Because this definition embraces the criminal deciding whether to commit another crime, the litigant deciding whether to settle or litigate a case, the legislator deciding whether to vote for or against a bill, the judge deciding how to cast his vote in a case, the party to a contract deciding whether to break it, the driver deciding how fast to drive, and the pedestrian deciding how boldly to cross the street, as well as the usual economic actors, such as businessmen and consumers, it is apparent that most activities either regulated by or occurring within the legal system are grist for the economic analyst's mill. It should go without saying that nonmonetary as well as monetary satisfactions enter into the individual's calculus of maximizing (indeed, money for most people is a means rather than an end) and that decisions, to be rational, need not be well thought out at the conscious level—indeed, need not be conscious at all. Recall that "rational" denotes suiting means to ends, rather than mulling things over, and that much of our knowledge is tacit.

Since my interest is in legal doctrines and institutions, it will be best to begin at the legislative (including the constitutional) level. I assume that legislators are rational maximizers of their satisfactions just like everyone else. Thus nothing they do is motivated by the public interest as such. But they want to be elected and reelected, and they need money to wage an effective campaign. This money is more likely to be forthcoming from well-organized groups than from unorganized individuals. The rational individual knows that his contribution is unlikely to make a difference; for this reason and also because voters in most elections are voting for candidates rather than policies, which further weakens the link between casting one's vote and obtaining one's preferred policy, the rational individual will have little incentive to invest time and effort in deciding whom to vote for. Only an organized group of individuals (or firms or other organizations—but these are just conduits for individuals) will be able to overcome the informational and free-rider problems that plague collec-

tive action. But such a group will not organize and act effectively unless its members have much to gain or much to lose from specific policies, as tobacco farmers, for example, have much to gain from federal subsidies for growing tobacco and much to lose from the withdrawal of those subsidies. The basic tactic of an interest group is to trade the votes of its members and its financial support to candidates in exchange for an implied promise of favorable legislation. Such legislation will normally take the form of a statute transferring wealth from unorganized taxpayers (for example, consumers) to the interest group. If the target were another interest group, the legislative transfer might be effectively opposed. The unorganized are unlikely to mount effective opposition, and it is their wealth, therefore, that typically is transferred to interest groups.

On this view, a statute is a deal. . . . But because of the costs of transactions within a multi-headed legislative body, and the costs of effective communication through time, legislation does not spring full-grown from the head of the legislature; it needs interpretation and application, and this is the role of the courts, They are agents of the legislature. But to impart credibility and durability to the deals the legislature strikes with interest groups, courts must be able to resist the wishes of current legislators who want to undo their predecessors' deals yet cannot do so through repeal because the costs of passing legislation (whether original or amended) are so high, and who might therefore look to the courts for a repealing "interpretation." The impediments to legislation actually facilitate rather than retard the striking of deals, by giving interest groups some assurance that a deal struck with the legislature will not promptly be undone by repeal. An independent judiciary is one of the impediments.

Judicial independence makes the judges imperfect agents of the legislature. This is tolerable not only for the reason just mentioned but also because an independent judiciary is necessary for the resolution of ordinary disputes in a way that will encourage trade, travel, freedom of action, and other highly valued activities or conditions and will minimize the expenditure of resources on influencing governmental action. Legislators might appear to have little to gain from these widely diffused rule-of-law virtues. But if the aggregate benefits from a particular social policy are very large and no interest group's ox is gored, legislators may find it in their own interest to support the policy. Voters understand in a rough way the benefits to them of national defense, crime control, dispute settlement, and the other elements of the night watchman state, and they will not vote for legislators who refuse to provide these basic public services. It is only when those services are in place, and when (usually later) effective means of taxation and redistribution develop, that the formation of narrow interest groups and the extraction by them of transfers from unorganized groups become feasible.

The judges thus have a dual role: to interpret the interest-group deals embodied in legislation and to provide the basic public service of authoritative dispute resolution. They perform the latter function not only by deciding cases in accordance with preexisting norms, but also—especially in the Anglo-American legal system—by elaborating those norms. They fashioned the common law out of customary practices, out of ideas borrowed from statutes and from other legal systems (for example, Roman law), and out of their own conceptions of public policy. The law they created exhibits, according to the economic theory that I am expounding, a remarkable (although not total—remember the extension of the rule of capture to oil and gas) substantive consistency. It is as if the judges *wanted* to adopt the rules, procedures, and case outcomes that would maximize society's wealth.

I must pause to define "wealth maximization," a term often misunderstood. The "wealth" in "wealth maximization" refers to the sum of all tangible and intangible goods and services, weighted by prices of two sorts: offer prices (what people are willing to pay for goods they do not already own); and asking prices (what people demand to sell what they do own). If A would be willing to pay up to $100 for B's stamp collection, it is worth $100 to A. If B would be willing to sell the stamp collection for any price above $90, it is worth $90 to B. So if B sells the stamp collection to A (say for $100, but the analysis is qualitatively unaffected at any price between $90 and $100—and it is only in that range that a transaction will occur), the wealth of society will rise by $10. Before the transaction A had $100 in cash and B had a stamp collection worth $90 (a total of $190); After the transaction A has a stamp

collection worth $100 and B has $100 in cash (a total of $200). The transaction will not raise measured wealth—gross national product, national income, or whatever—by $10; it will not raise it at all unless the transaction is recorded, and if it is recorded it is likely to raise measured wealth by the full $100 purchase price. But the real addition to social wealth consists of the $10 increment in *nonpecuniary* satisfaction that A derives from the purchase, compared with that of B. This shows that "wealth" in the economist's sense is not a simple monetary measure. . . .

[I]f I am given a choice between remaining in a job in which I work forty hours a week for $1,000 and switching to a job in which I would work thirty hours for $500, and I decide to make the switch, the extra ten hours of leisure must be worth at least $500 to me, yet GNP will fall when I reduce my hours of work. Suppose the extra hours of leisure are worth $600 to me, so that my full income rises from $1,000 to $1,100 when I reduce my hours. My former employer presumably is made worse off by my leaving (else why did he employ me?), but not more than $100 worse off; for if he were, he would offer to pay me a shade over $1,100 a week to stay—and I would stay. (The example abstracts from income tax.)

Wealth is *related* to money, in that a desire not backed by ability to pay has no standing—such a desire is neither an offer price nor an asking price. I may desperately desire a BMW, but if I am unwilling or unable to pay its purchase price, society's wealth would not be increased by transferring the BMW from its present owner to me. Abandon this essential constraint (an important distinction, also, between wealth maximization and utilitarianism—for I might derive greater utility from the BMW than its present owner or anyone else to whom he might sell the car), and the way is open to tolerating the crimes committed by the passionate and the avaricious against the cold and the frugal.

The common law facilitates wealth-maximizing transactions in a variety of ways. It reognizes property rights, and these facilitate exchange. It also protects property rights, through tort and criminal law. (Although today criminal law is almost entirely statutory, the basic criminal protections—for example, those against murder, assault, rape, and theft—have, as one might expect, common law origins.) Through contract law it protects the process of exchange. And it establishes procedural rules for resolving disputes in these various fields as efficiently as possible.

The illustrations given thus far of wealth-maximizing transactions have been of transactions that are voluntary in the strict sense of making everyone affected by them better off, or at least no worse off. Every transactions has been assumed to affect just two parties, each of whom has been made better off by it. Such a transaction is said to be Pareto superior [i.e., at least one person is better off, and nobody is worse off], but Pareto superiority is not a necessary condition for a transaction to be wealth maximizing. Consider an accident that inflicts a cost of $100 with a probability of .01 and that would have cost $3 to avoid. The accident is a wealth-maximizing "transaction" . . . because the expected accident cost ($1) is less than the cost of avoidance. (I am assuming risk neutrality. Risk aversion would complicate the analysis but not change it fundamentally.) It is wealth maximizing even if the victim is not compensated. The result is consistent with Learned Hand's formula, which defines negligence as the failure to take cost-justified precautions. If the only precaution that would have averted the accident is not cost-justified, the failure to take it is not negligent and the injurer will not have to compensate the victim for the costs of the accident.

If it seems artificial to speak of the accident as the transaction, consider instead the potential transaction that consists of purchasing the safety measure that would have avoided the accident. Since a potential victim would not pay $3 to avoid an expected accident cost of $1, his offer price will be less than the potential injurer's asking price and the transaction will not be wealth maximizing. But if these figures were reversed—if an expected accident cost of $3 could be averted at a cost of $1—the transaction would be wealth maximizing, and a liability rule administered in accordance with the Hand formula would give potential injurers an incentive to take the measures that potential victims would pay them to take if voluntary transactions were feasible. The law would be overcoming transaction-cost obstacles to wealth-maximizing transactions—a frequent office of liability rules.

The wealth-maximizing properties of common law rules have been elucidated at considerable length in the literature of the economic analysis of law. Such doctrines as conspiracy, general average (admiralty), contributory negligence, equitable servitude, employment at will, the standard for granting preliminary injunctions, entrapment, the contract defense of impossibility, the collateral-benefits rule, the expectation measure of damages, assumption of risk, attempt, invasion of privacy, wrongful interference with contract rights, the availability of punitive damages in some cases but not others, privilege in the law of evidence, official immunity, and the doctrine of moral consideration have been found—at least by some contributors to this literature—to conform to the dictates of wealth maximization. . . . It has even been argued that the system of precedent itself has an economic equilibrium. Precedents are created as a by-product of litigation. The greater the number of recent precedents in an area, the lower the rate of litigation will be. In particular, cases involving disputes over legal as distinct from purely factual issues will be settled. The existence of abundant, highly informative (in part because recent) precedents will enable the parties to legal disputes to form more convergent estimates of the likely outcome of a trial, and . . . if both parties agree on the outcome of trial they will settle beforehand because a trial is more costly than a settlement. But with less litigation, fewer new precedents will be produced, and the existing precedents will obsolesce as changing circumstances render them less apt and informative. So the rate of litigation will rise, producing more precedents and thereby causing the rate of litigation again to fall.

This analysis does not explain what drives judges to decide common law cases in accordance with the dictates of wealth maximization. Prosperity, however, which wealth maximization measures more sensitively than purely monetary measures such as GNP, is a relatively uncontroversial policy, and most judges try to steer clear of controversy: their age, method of compensation, and relative weakness vis-à-vis the other branches of government make the avoidance of controversy attractive. It probably is no accident, therefore, that many common law doctrines assumed their modern form in the nineteenth century, when laissez-faire ideology, which resembles wealth maximization, had a strong hold on the Anglo-American judicial imagination. . . .

It may be objected that in assigning ideology as a cause of judicial behavior, the economist strays outside the boundaries of his discipline; but he need not rest on ideology. The economic analysis of legislation implies that fields of law left to the judges to elaborate, such as the common law fields, must be the ones in which interest-group pressures are too weak to deflect the legislature from pursuing goals that are in the general interest. Prosperity is one of these goals, and one that judges are especially well equipped to promote. The rules of the common law that they promulgate attach prices to socially undesirable conduct, whether free riding or imposing social costs without corresponding benefits. By doing this the rules create incentives to avoid such conduct, and these incentives foster prosperity. In contrast, judges can, despite appearances, do little to redistribute wealth. A rule that makes it easy for poor tenants to break leases with rich landlords, for example, will induce landlords to raise rents in order to offset the costs that such a rule imposes, and tenants will bear the brunt of these higher costs. Indeed, the principal redistribution accomplished by such a rule may be from the prudent, responsible tenant, who may derive little or no benefit from having additional legal rights to use against landlords—rights that enable a tenant to avoid or postpone eviction for nonpayment of rental—to the feckless tenant. That is a capricious redistribution. Legislatures, however, have by virtue of their taxing and spending powers powerful tools for redistributing wealth. So an efficient division of labor between the legislative and judicial branches has the legislative branch concentrate on catering to interest-group demands for wealth distribution and the judicial branch on meeting the broad-based social demand for efficient rules governing safety, property, and transactions. Although there are other possible goals of judicial action besides efficiency and redistribution, many of these (various conceptions of "fairness" and "justice") are labels for wealth maximization, or for redistribution in favor of powerful interest groups; or else they are too controversial in a heterogeneous society, too ad hoc, or insufficiently developed to provide judges who desire a reputation for objectivity and disinterest with adequate grounds for their decisions.

Finally, even if judges have little commitment to efficiency, their inefficient decisions will, be definition, impose greater social costs than their efficient ones will. As a result, losers of cases decided mistakenly from an economic standpoint will have a greater incentive, on average, to press for correction through appeal, new litigation, or legislative action than losers of cases decided soundly from an economic standpoint—so there will be a steady pressure for efficient results. Moreover, cases litigated under inefficient rules tend to involve larger stakes than cases litigated under efficient rules (for the inefficient rules, by definition, generate social waste), and the larger the stakes in a dispute the likelier it is to be litigated rather than settled; so judges will have a chance to reconsider the inefficient rule.

Thus we should not be surprised to see the common law tending to become efficient, although since the incentives of judges to perform well along any dimension are weak (this is a by-product of judicial independence), we cannot expect the law ever to achieve perfect efficiency. Since wealth maximization is not only a guide in fact to common law judging but also a genuine social value and the only one judges are in a good position to promote, it provides not only the key to an accurate description of what the judges are up to but also the right benchmark for criticism and reform. If judges are failing to maximize wealth, the economic analyst of law will urge them to alter practice or doctrine accordingly. In addition, the analyst will urge—on any legislator sufficiently free of interest-group pressures to be able to legislate in the public interest—a program of enacting only legislation that conforms to the dictates of wealth maximization.

Besides generating both predictions and prescriptions, the economic approach enables the common law to be reconceived in simple, coherent terms and to be applied more objectively than traditional lawyers would think possible. From the premise that the common law does and should seek to maximize society's wealth, the economic analyst can deduce in logical—if you will, formalist—fashion (economic theory is formulated nowadays largely in mathematical terms) the set of legal doctrines that will express and perfect the inner nature of the common law, and can compare these doctrines with the actual doctrines of common law. After translating from the economic vocabulary back into the legal one, the analyst will find that most of the actual doctrines are tolerable approximations to the implications of economic theory and so far formalistically valid. Where there are discrepancies, the path to reform is clear—yet the judge who takes the path cannot be accused of making rather than finding law, for he is merely contributing to the program of realizing the essential nature of the common law.

The project of reducing the common law—with its many separate fields, its thousands of separate doctrines, its hundreds of thousands of reported decisions—to a handful of mathematical formulas may seem quixotic, but the economic analyst can give reasons for doubting this assessment. Much of the doctrinal luxuriance of common law is seen to be superficial once the essentially economic nature of the common law is understood. A few principles, such as cost-benefit analysis, the prevention of free riding, decision under uncertainty, risk aversion, and the promotion of mutually beneficial exchanges, can explain most doctrines and decisions. Tort cases can be translated into contract cases by recharacterizing the tort issue as finding the implied pre-accident contract that the parties would have chosen had transaction costs not been prohibitive, and contract cases can be translated into tort cases by asking what remedy if any would maximize the expected benefits of the contractual undertaking considered ex ante. The criminal's decision whether to commit a crime is no different in principle from the prosecutor's decision whether to prosecute; a plea bargain is a contract; crimes are in effect torts by insolvent defendants because if all criminals could pay the full social costs of their crimes, the task of deterring antisocial behavior could be left to tort law. Such examples suggest not only that the logic of the common law really is economics but also that the teaching of law could be simplified by exposing students to the clean and simple economic structure beneath the particolored garb of legal doctrine.

If all this seems reminiscent of Langdell, it differs fundamentally in being empirically verifiable. The ultimate test of a rule derived from economic theory is not the elegance or logicality of the derivation but the rule's effect on social wealth. The extension of the rule of capture to oil and gas was subjected to such a test, flunked, and was replaced (albeit through legislative rather than judicial ac-

tion) by efficient rules. The other rules of the common law can and should be tested likewise. . . .

Criticisms of the Normative Theory

The question whether wealth maximization *should* guide legal policy, either in general or just in common law fields (plus those statutory fields where the legislative intent is to promote efficiency—antitrust law being a possible example), is ordinarily treated as separate from the question whether it *has* guided legal policy, except insofar as the positive theory may be undermined by the inadequacies of the normative theory. Actually the two theories are not as separable as this, illustrating again the lack of a clear boundary between "is" and "ought" propositions. One of the things judges ought to do is follow precedent, although not inflexibly; so if efficiency is the animating principal of much common law doctrine, judges have some obligation to make decisions that will be consistent with efficiency. This is one reason why the positive economic theory of the common law is so contentious.

The normative theory has been highly contentious in its own right. Most contributors to the debate over it conclude that it is a bad theory, and although many of the criticisms can be answered, several cannot be, and it is those I shall focus on.

The first is that wealth maximization is inherently incomplete as a guide to social action because it has nothing to say about the distribution of rights—or at least nothing we want to hear. Given the distribution of rights (whatever it is), wealth maximization can be used to derive the policies that will maximize the value of those rights. But this does not go far enough, because naturally we are curious about whether it would be just to start off with a society in which, say, one member owned all the others. If wealth maximization is indifferent to the initial distribution of rights, it is a truncated concept of justice.

Since the initial distribution may dissipate rapidly, this point may have little practical significance. Nor is wealth maximization completely silent on the initial distribution. If we could compare two otherwise identical nascent societies, in one of which one person owned all the others and in the other of which slavery was forbidden, and could repeat the comparison a century later, almost certainly we would find that the second society was wealthier and the first had abolished slavery (if so, this would further illustrate the limited effect of the initial distribution on the current distribution). Although it has not always and everywhere been true, under modern conditions of production slavery is an inefficient method of organizing production. The extensive use of slave labor by Nazis during World War II may seem an exception—but only if we disregard the welfare of the slave laborers.

This response to the demand that wealth maximization tell us something about the justice of the initial distribution of rights is incomplete. Suppose it were the case—it almost surely *is* the case—that some people in modern American society would be more productive as slaves than as free persons. These are not antisocial people whom we want to punish by imprisoning (a form of slavery that is tolerated); they are not psychotic or profoundly retarded; they just are lazy, feckless, poorly organized, undisciplined people—people incompetent to manage their own lives in a way that will maximize their output, even though the relevant output is not market output alone but also leisure, family associations, and any other sources of satisfaction to these people as well as to others. Wealth would be maximized by enslaving these people, provided the costs of supervision were not too high—but the assumption that they would not be too high is built into the proposition that their output would be greater as slaves than as free persons, for it is net output that we are interested in. Yet no one thinks it would be right to enslave such people, even if there were no evidentiary problems in identifying them, the slave masters could be trusted to be benign, and so on; and these conditions, too, may be implicit in the proposition that the net social output of some people would be greater if they were slaves.

It is no answer that it would be inefficient to enslave such people unless they consented to be enslaved, that is, unless the would-be slave master met the asking price for their freedom. The term *"their* freedom" assumes they have the property right in their persons, and the assumption is arbitrary. We can imagine assigning the property rights in persons (perhaps only persons who appeared

likely to be unproductive) to the state to auction them to the highest bidder. The putative slave could bid against the putative master, but would lose. His expected earnings, net of consumption, would be smaller than the expected profits to the master; otherwise enslavement would not be efficient. Therefore he could not borrow enough—even if capital markets worked without any friction (in the present setting, even if the lender could enslave the borrower if the latter defaulted!)—to outbid his master-to-be.

This example points to a deeper criticism of wealth maximization as a norm or value: like utilitarianism, which it closely resembles, or nationalism, or Social Darwinism, or racialism, or organic theories of the state, it treats people as if they were the cells of a single organism; the welfare of the cell is important only insofar as it promotes the welfare of the organism. Wealth maximization implies that if the prosperity of the society can be promoted by enslaving its least productive citizens, the sacrifice of their freedom is worthwhile. But this implication is contrary to the unshakable moral intuitions of Americans, and . . . conformity to intuition is the ultimate test of a moral (indeed of any) theory.

[We can] provide illustrations of collisions between, on the one hand, moral intuitions that have been influential in law and, on the other hand, wealth maximization. Recall, first, that the idea of corrective justice may well include the proposition that people who are wronged are entitled to some form of redress, even in cases when from an aggregate social standpoint it might be best to let bygones be bygones. Such an idea has no standing in a system powered by wealth maximization. Second, the . . . lawfulness of confessions in a system single-mindedly devoted to wealth maximization would depend entirely on the costs and benefits of the various forms of coercion, which range from outright torture to the relatively mild psychological pressures that our legal system tolerates. Cost-benefit analysis might show that torture was rarely cost-effective under modern conditions, being a costly method of interrogation (especially for the victim, but perhaps also for the torturer) that is apt to produce a lot of false leads and unreliable confessions. Nevertheless, even the most degrading forms of torture would not *necessarily* be ruled out, even in the investigation of ordinary crimes. . . .

[C]ost-benefit thinking has made inroads into coerced-confession law, but at some point these inroads would collide with, and be stopped by, strong moral intuitions that seem incompatible with economic thinking.

Or suppose it were the case—it may be the case—that some religious faiths are particularly effective in producing law-abiding, productive, healthy citizens. Mormonism is a plausible example. Would it not make sense on purely secular grounds, indeed on purely wealth-maximizing grounds, for government to subsidize these faiths? Practitioners of other religious faiths would be greatly offended, but from the standpoint of wealth maximization the only question would be whether the cost to them was greater than the benefits to the country as a whole.

Consider now a faith that both has few adherents in the United States and is feared or despised by the rest of the population. (The Rastafarian faith is a plausible example.) Such a faith will by assumption be imposing costs on the rest of the community, and given the fewness of its adherents, the benefits conferred by the faith may, even when aggregated across all its adherents, be smaller than the costs. It could then be argued that wealth maximization warranted or even required the suppression of the faith. This example suggests another objection to wealth maximization, one alluded to in the discussion of slavery: its results are sensitive to assumptions about the initial distribution of rights—a distribution that is distinct from the initial distribution of wealth (which is unlikely to remain stable over time), but about which wealth maximization may again have relatively little to say. If Rastafarians are conceived to have a property right in their religion, so that the state or anyone else who wants to acquire that right and suppress the religion must meet their asking-price, probably the right will not be sold. Asking prices can be very high—in principle, infinite: how much would the average person sell his life for, if the sale had to be completed immediately? But if rights over religious practices are given to the part of the populace that is not Rastafarian, the Rastafarians may find it impossible to buy the right back; their offer price will be limited to their net wealth, which may be slight.

No doubt in this country, in this day and age, religious liberty is the cost-justified policy. The broader point is that a system of rights—perhaps the system we have—may well be required by a *realistic* conception of utilitarianism, that is, one that understands that given the realities of human nature a society dedicated to utilitarianism requires rules and institutions that place checks on utility-maximizing behavior in particular cases. For example, although one can imagine specific cases in which deliberately punishing an innocent person as a criminal would increase aggregate utility, one has trouble imagining a system in which government officials could be trusted to make such decisions. "Wealth maximizing" can be substituted for "utilitarian" without affecting the analysis. Religious liberty may well be both utility maximizing and wealth maximization, and this may even be why we have it. And if it became *too* costly, probably it would be abandoned; and so with the prohibition of torture, and the other civilized political amenities of a wealthy society. If our crime rate were much lower than it is, we probably would not have capital punishment—and if it gets much higher, we surely will have fewer civil liberties.

But at least in the present relatively comfortable conditions of our society, the regard for individual freedom appears to transcend instrumental considerations; freedom appears to be valued for itself rather than just for its contribution to prosperity—or at least to be valued for reasons that escape the economic calculus. Is society really better off in a utilitarian or wealth-maximizing sense as a result of the extraordinarily elaborate procedural safeguards that the Bill of Rights gives criminal defendants? This is by no means clear. Are minority rights welfare maximizing—when the minority in question is a small one? That is not clear either, as the Rastafarian example showed. The main reasons these institutions are valued seem not to be utilitarian or even instrumental in character. *What* those reasons are is far from clear; indeed, "noninstrumental reason" is almost an oxymoron. And as I have suggested, we surely are not willing to pay an infinite price, perhaps not even a very high price, for freedom. While reprobating slavery we condone similar (but more efficient) practices under different names—imprisonment as punishment for crime, preventive detention, the authority of parents and school authorities over children, conscription, the institutionalization of the insane and the retarded. The Thirteenth Amendment has been read narrowly. Although the only stated exception is for punishment for crime ("neither slavery nor involuntary servitude, except as a punishment for crime whereof the party shall have been duly convicted, shall exist within the United States, or any place subject to their jurisdiction"), laws requiring jury service, military service, and even working on the public roads have been upheld. We reprobate the infliction of physical pain as a method of extracting confessions or imposing punishment but, perhaps in unconscious tribute to the outmoded dualism of mind and body, condone the infliction of mental pain for the same purposes.

Still, hypocritical and incoherent as our political ethics may frequently be, we do not permit degrading invasions of individual autonomy merely on a judgment that, on balance, the invasion would make a net addition to the social wealth. And whatever the philosophical grounding of this sentiment, it is too deeply entrenched in our society at present for wealth maximization to be given a free rein. The same may be true of the residue of corrective-justice sentiment.

I have said nothing about the conflict between wealth maximization and equality of wealth, because I am less sure of the extent of egalitarian sentiment in our society than that of individualistic sentiment (by "individualism" I mean simply the rivals to aggregative philosophies, such as utilitarianism and wealth maximization). Conflict there is, however, and it points to anther important criticism of wealth maximization even if the critic is not an egalitarian. Imagine that a limited supply of growth hormone, privately manufactured and sold, must be allocated. A wealthy parent wants the hormone so that his child of average height will grow tall; a poor parent wants the hormone so that his child of dwarfish height can grow to normal height. In a system of wealth maximization the wealthy parent might outbid the poor parent and get the hormone. This is not certain. Amount of wealth is only one factor in willingness to pay. The poor parent might offer his entire wealth for the hormone, and that wealth, although meager, might exceed the amount of money the wealthy parent was willing to pay, given alternative uses to which he could put his money. Also, altruists might help the poor parent bid more than he could with only his own

resources. The poor might actually be better off in a system in which the distribution of the hormone were left to the private market, even if there were no altruism. Such a system would create incentives to produce and sell the hormone sooner, and perhaps at a lower price, than if the government controlled its distribution; for the costs of production would probably be lower under private rather than public production, and even a monopolist will charge less when his costs fall.

But what seems impossible to maintain convincingly in the present ethical climate is that the wealthy parent has the *right* to the hormone by virtue of being willing to pay the supplier more than the poor parent can; more broadly, that consumers have a right to purchase in free markets. These propositions cannot be derived from wealth maximization. Indeed, they look like propositions about transactional freedom rather than about distribution only because I have assumed that the growth hormone is produced and distributed exclusively through the free market. An alternative possibility would be for the state to own the property right in the hormone and to allocate it on the basis of need rather than willingness to pay. To argue against this alternative (socialist medicine writ small) would require an appeal either to the deeply controversial idea of a natural right to private property, or to purely instrumental considerations, such as the possibility that in the long run the poor will be better off with a free market in growth hormone—but to put the question *this* way is to assume that the poor have some sort of social claim by virtue of being poor, and thus to admit the relevance of egalitarian considerations and thereby break out of the limits of wealth maximization.

A stronger-seeming argument for the free-enterprise solution is that the inventor of the hormone should have a right to use it as he wishes, which includes the right to sell it to the highest bidder. But this argument seems stronger only because we are inclined to suppose that what has happened is that *after* the inventor invented it the government decided to rob him of the reward for which he had labored. If instead we assume that Congress passes a law in 1989 which provides that after the year 2000 the right to patent new drugs will be conditioned on the patentee's agreeing to limit the price he charges, we shall have difficulty objecting to the law on ethical, as distinct from practical, grounds. It would be just one more restriction on free markets.

. . . [A] quest for a natural-rights theory of justice is unlikely to succeed. Although the advocate of wealth maximization can argue that to the productive should belong the fruits of their labor, the argument can be countered along the lines . . . that . . . production is really a social rather than individual effort—to which it can be added that wealth may often be due more to luck (and not the luck of the genetic lottery, either) than to skill or effort. Furthermore, if altruism is so greatly admired, as it is by conservatives as well as by liberals, why should not its spirit inform legislation? Why should government protect only our selfish instincts? To this it can be replied that the spirit of altruism is voluntary giving. But the reply is weak. The biggest reason we value altruism is that we *desire* some redistribution—we may admire the altruist for his self-sacrifice but we would not admire him as much if he destroyed his wealth rather than giving it to others—and we think that voluntary redistribution is less costly than involuntary. If redistribution is desirable, some involuntary redistribution may be justifiable, depending on the costs, of course, but not on the principle of the thing.

There is a still deeper problem with founding wealth maximization on a notion of natural rights. The economic perspective is thoroughly (and fruitfully) behaviorist. "Economic man" is not, as vulgarly supposed, a person driven by purely pecuniary incentives, but he is a person whose behavior is completely determined by incentives; his rationality is no different from that of a pigeon or a rat. The economic task from the perspective of wealth maximization is to influence his incentives so as to maximize his output. How a person so conceived could be thought to have a *moral* entitlement to a particular distribution of the world's goods— an entitlement, say, to the share proportional to his contribution to the world's wealth—is unclear. Have marmots moral entitlements? Two levels of discourse are being mixed.

By questioning anti-egalitarian arguments I do not mean to be endorsing egalitarian ones. . . . The egalitarian is apt to say that differences in intelligence, which often translate into differences in productivity, are the result of a natural lottery and

therefore ought not guide entitlements. But if differences in intelligence are indeed genetic, as the argument assumes, then liberal and radical arguments about the exploitiveness of capitalist society are undermined. A genetic basis for intellectual differences and resulting differences in productivity implies that inequality in the distribution of income and wealth is to a substantial degree natural (which is not to say that it is morally good), rather than a product of unjust social and political institutions. It also implies that such inequality is apt to be strongly resistant to social and political efforts to change it.

The strongest argument for wealth maximization is not moral, but pragmatic. Such classic defenses of the free market as chapter 4 of Mill's *On Liberty* can easily be given a pragmatic reading. We look around the world and see that in general people who live in societies in which markets are allowed to function more or less freely not only are wealthier than people in other societies but have more political rights, more liberty and dignity, are more content (as evidenced, for example, by their being less prone to emigrate)—so that wealth maximization may be the most direct route to a variety of moral ends. The recent history of England, France, and Turkey, of Japan and Southeast Asia, of East versus West Germany and North versus South Korea, of China and Taiwan, of Chile, of the Soviet Union, Poland, and Hungary, and of Cuba and Argentina provides striking support for this thesis.

Writing in the early 1970s, the English political philosopher Brian Barry doubted the importance of incentives. "My own guess," he said, "is that enough people with professional and managerial jobs really like them (and enough others who would enjoy them and have sufficient ability to do them are waiting to replace those who do not) to enable the pay of these jobs to be brought down considerably. . . . I would suggest that the pay levels in Britain of schoolteachers and social workers seem to offer net rewards which recruit and maintain just enough people, and that this provides a guideline to the pay levels that could be sustained generally among professionals and managers." He rejected the "assumption that a sufficient supply of highly educated people will be forthcoming only if lured by the anticipation of a higher income afterwards as a result," adding that "it would also be rash to assume that it would be an economic loss if fewer sought higher education." He discussed with approval the Swedish experiment at redistributing income and wealth but thought it hampered by the fact that "Sweden still has a privately owned economy." He worried about "brain drain" but concluded that it was a serious problem only with regard to airline pilots and physicians; and a nation can do without airlines and may be able to replace general practitioners "with people having a lower (and less marketable) qualification." (Yet Barry himself was soon to join the brain drain, and he is neither a physician nor an airline pilot.) He proposed "to spread the nastiest jobs around by requiring everyone, before entering higher education or entering a profession, to do, say, three years of work wherever he or she was directed. (This would also have educational advantages.) To supplement this there could be a call-up of say a month every year, as with the Swiss and Israeli armed forces but directed towards peaceful occupations."

At least with the benefit of hindsight we can see that Barry wrote a prescription for economic disaster. It may be impossible to lay solid philosophical foundations under wealth maximization,

just as it may be impossible to lay solid philosophical foundations under the natural sciences, but this would be a poor reason for abandoning wealth maximization, just as the existence of intractable problems in the philosophy of science would be a poor reason for abandoning science. We have reason to believe that markets work—that capitalism delivers the goods, if not the Good—and it would be a mistake to allow philosophy to deflect us from the implications. . . .

A sensible pragmatism does not ignore theory. The mounting evidence that capitalism is more efficient than socialism gives us an additional reason for believing economic theory (not every application of it, to be sure). The theory in turn gives us greater confidence in the evidence. Theory and evidence are mutually supporting. From the perspective of economic theory, brain drain is not the mysterious disease that Barry supposes it to be; it is the rational response to leveling policies by those whose incomes are being leveled downward.

. . .

16. *The Pragmatist and the Feminist*

MARGARET JANE RADIN

I want to discuss pragmatism and feminism. I undertake this project not because I have read everything considered feminist or pragmatist by its writers or readers, although I wish I had, but rather because I have discovered that in my own work I am speaking both of pragmatism and feminism. I desire to explore how pragmatism and feminism cohere, if they do, in my own thought, and I write with the hope that what I find useful will be useful for others as well. . . .

I. *The Double Bind*

I begin at the point it became clear to me that I was combining pragmatism and feminism. That point was in my thinking about the transition problem of the double bind in the context of contested commodification of sexuality and reproductive capacity. If the social regime permits buying and selling of sexual and reproductive activities, thereby treating them as fungible market commodities given the current capitalistic understandings of monetary exchange, there is a threat to the personhood of women, who are the "owners" of these "commodities." The threat to personhood from commodification arises because essential attributes are treated as severable fungible objects, and this denies the integrity and uniqueness of the self. But if the social regime prohibits this kind of commodification, it denies women the choice to market their sexual or reproductive services, and given the current feminization of poverty and lack of avenues for free choice for women, this also poses a threat to the personhood of women. The threat from enforced noncommodification arises because narrowing women's choices is a threat to liberation, and because their choices to market sexual or reproductive services, even if nonideal, may represent the best alternatives available to those who would choose them.

Thus the double bind: both commodification and noncommodification may be harmful. Harmful, that is, under our current social conditions. Neither one need be harmful in an ideal world. The fact that money changes hands need not necessarily contaminate human interactions of sharing, nor must the fact that a social order makes nonmonetary sharing its norm necessarily deprive or subordinate anyone. That commodification now tends toward fungibility of women and noncommodification now tends toward their domination and continued subordination are artifacts of the current social hierarchy. In other words, the fact of oppression is what gives rise to the double bind.

Thus, it appears that the solution to the double bind is not to solve but to dissolve it: remove the oppressive circumstances. But in the meantime, if we are practically limited to those two choices, which are we to choose? I think that the answer must be pragmatic. We must look carefully at the nonideal circumstances in each case and decide which horn of the dilemma is better (or less bad), and we must keep redeciding as time goes on.

To generalize a bit, it seems that there are two ways to think about justice. One is to think about justice in an ideal world, the best world that we can now conceive. The other is to think about nonideal justice: given where we now find ourselves, what is the better decision? In making this decision, we

think about what actions can bring us closer to ideal justice. For example, if we allow commodification, we may push further away any ideal of a less commodified future. But if we enforce noncommodification, we may push further away any ideal of a less dominated future. In making our decisions of nonideal justice, we must also realize that these decisions will help to reconstitute our ideals. For example, if we commodify all attributes of personhood, the ideal of personhood we now know will evolve into another one that does not conceive fungibility as bad. The double bind, then, is a problem involving nonideal justice, and I think its only solution can be pragmatic. There is no general solution; there are only piecemeal, temporary solutions.

I also think of the double bind as a problem of transition, because I think of nonideal justice as the process by which we try to make progress (effect a transition) toward our vision of the good world. I think we should recognize that all decisions about justice, as opposed to theories about it, are pragmatic decisions in the transition. At the same time we should also recognize that ideal theory is also necessary, because we need to know what we are trying to achieve. In other words, our visions and nonideal decisions, our theory and practice, paradoxically constitute each other.

Having discovered the double bind in true pragmatic fashion, by working on a specific problem, I now see it everywhere. The double bind is pervasive in the issues we have thought of as "women's issues." The reason it is pervasive is to be sought in the perspective of oppression. For a group subject to structures of domination, all roads thought to be progressive can pack a backlash. I shall mention here a few other examples of the double bind: the special treatment/equal treatment debate, affirmative action, the understanding of rape, and the idea of marriage as a contract.

When we single out pregnancy, for example, for "special treatment," we fear that employers will not hire women. But if we do not accord special treatment to pregnancy, women will lose their jobs. If we grant special treatment, we bring back the bad old conception of women as weaker creatures; if we do not, we prevent women from becoming stronger in the practical world. Feminist theory that tends toward the ideal, the visionary side of our thought about justice, has grasped the point that the dilemma must be dissolved because its framework is the conceptual framework of the oppressors (who define what is "special" and what is "equal"). But feminist theory that tends toward the nonideal practical side of our thought about justice has also realized that if the dominant conceptions are too deeply held at this time, trying to implement an alternative vision could be counterproductive. My personal view is that in the case of pregnancy, the time has come to convince everyone that both men and women should have the opportunity to be parents in a fulfilling sense, and that the old conceptions of the workplace now can begin to give way. But I think that each women's issue situation, such as pregnancy, workplace regulation to protect fetuses, and height and weight restrictions, will have to be evaluated separately, and continually reevaluated.

If there is a social commitment to affirmative action, in this nonideal time and place, then a woman or person of color who holds a job formerly closed to women and people of color is likely to be presumed to be underqualified. More women and people of color will hold jobs, but few will be allowed to feel good about it. The dominant group will probably be able to make women and people of color meet higher standards than those applicable to white males, and yet at the same time convince everyone, including, often, the beneficiaries of affirmative action themselves, that as beneficiaries they are inferior. But what is our alternative? If there is no affirmative action commitment in place, far fewer women and people of color will hold these jobs; yet those who do, whatever vicissitudes they endure, will not endure this particular backlash. The pragmatic answer in most cases, I believe, is that backlash is better than complete exclusion, as long as the backlash is temporary. But if backlash can keep alive the bad old conceptions of women and people of color, how will we evolve toward better conceptions of the abilities of those who have been excluded?

Our struggle with how to understand rape seems to be another instance of the double bind. MacKinnon's view—or perhaps an oversimplified version of her view—is that under current conditions of gender hierarchy there is no clear dividing line between the sort of heterosexual intercourse that is genuinely desired by women and the sort that is unwelcome. There can be no clear line because our very conception of sexuality is so deeply intertwined with male dominance that our desires as we experience them are problematic. Our own desires are socially constituted to reinforce patterns of male dominance against our own interest.[1] "Just say no" as the standard for determining whether rape has occurred is both under- and overinclusive. It is under-inclusive because women who haven't found their voices mean "no" and are unable to say it; and it is over-inclusive because, like it or not, the way sexuality has been constituted in a culture of male dominance, the male understanding that "no" means "yes" was often, and may still sometimes be, correct. MacKinnon's view is painful. If there is no space for women to experience heterosexuality that is not suspect, what does that do to our self-esteem and personhood in a social setting in which sex is important to selfhood?

The other prong of the double bind—roughly represented by the views of Robin West—is that we should greet all of women's subjective experience with acceptance and respect.[2] That view is less threatening to personhood in one way but more so in another. How can we progress toward a social conception of sexuality that is less male-dominated if we do not regard with critical suspicion some of the male-dominated experiences we now take pleasure in?

The last example of the double bind I want to mention is the conceptualization of marriage. Is marriage to be considered a contract in which certain distributions of goods are agreed to between autonomous bargaining agents? Upon divorce, such a conception of marriage makes it difficult for oppressed women who have not bargained effectively to obtain much. Or is marriage to be considered a noncontractual sharing status in which the partners' contributions are not to be monetized? Upon divorce, such a conception makes it difficult for oppressed women who have contributed unmonetized services to their husbands' advantage to obtain much. The idea of contractual autonomy may be more attractive in our nonideal world if the alternative is to be submerged in a status that gives all power to men. Yet the autonomy may be illusory because oppression makes equal bargaining power impossible. At the same time, the reinforcement of individualist bargaining models of human interaction is contrary to our vision of a better world and may alter that vision in a way we do not wish.

Perhaps it is obvious that the reason the double bind recurs throughout feminist struggles is that it is an artifact of the dominant social conception of the meaning of gender. The double bind is a series of two-pronged dilemmas in which both prongs are, or can be, losers for the oppressed. Once we realize this, we may say it is equally obvious that the way out of the double bind is to dissolve these dilemmas by changing the framework that creates them. That is, we must dissolve the prevalent conception of gender.

Calling for dissolution of the prevalent conception of gender is the visionary half of the problem: we must create a new vision of the meaning of male and female in order to change the dominant social conception of gender and change the double bind. In order to do that, however, we need the social empowerment that the dominant social conception of gender keeps us from achieving.

Then how can we make progress? The other half of the problem is the nonideal problem of transition from the present situation toward our ideal. Here is where the pragmatist feminist comes into her own. The pragmatist solution is to confront each dilemma separately and choose the alternative that will hinder empowerment the least and further it the most. The pragmatist feminist need not seek a general solution that will dictate how to resolve all double bind issues. Appropriate solutions may all differ, depending on the current stage of women's empowerment, and how the proposed solution might move the current social conception of gender and our vision of how gender should be reconceived for the future. Indeed, the "same" double bind may demand a different solution tomorrow from the one we find best today.

II. *The Perspective of Domination and the Problem of Bad Coherence*

. . .

Over the past few years I have been continually struck with some points of resonance between the methodology and commitments of many who call themselves feminists and those of certain impor-

tant figures in the new wave of pragmatism. It now seems to me that the points of resonance between feminism and pragmatism are worthy of some exploration.

I begin with an awareness that there is something problematic about my ambition to talk theoretically about pragmatism and feminism together. I want to avoid the type of exercise that tries to define two "isms" and then compare and contrast them. Insomuch as they are lively, these "isms" resist definition. There are a number of pragmatisms. At least there are distinctive strains stemming from Charles Sanders Peirce, William James, and John Dewey, and the new wave may be considered a fourth pragmatism. There are also a number of feminisms. One recent survey of feminist thought lists them as liberal, Marxist, radical, socialist, psychoanalytic, existentialist, and postmodern.[3]

One way to frame the investigation I have in mind would be to start with the question, Is feminism "really" pragmatism? (Or, is pragmatism "really" feminism?) If this is the question, one way to respond to it—a way I think would be both unpragmatic and unfeminist—is to ask what commitments or characteristics are common to all the pragmatisms we are certain are pragmatisms, and ask what commitments or characteristics are common to all the feminisms we are certain are feminisms. We would then see whether the feminist list includes both the necessary criteria for being pragmatist and enough or important enough criteria to be sufficient for being pragmatist, or whether the pragmatist list includes the necessary and sufficient criteria for being feminist. This definitional response is a blueprint of conceptualist methodology, an abstract exercise in reification that promises little of interest to a pragmatist or a feminist.

In a more pragmatic and feminist spirit of inquiry, we might ask instead another question. Of what use might it be to think of feminism and pragmatism as allied, as interpenetrating each other? In this . . . essay I will pursue this question in various ways. In order to do so I still have to engage in some problematic cataloguing, but at least it will be easier to deal with the inescapable incompleteness of that way of seeing matters. I can explore how in some ways it might be useful to consider pragmatism and feminism together, without having to have a definite answer to the (to a pragmatist inapposite) question of what pragmatism and feminism "really are." Feminism and pragmatism are not things; they are ways of proceeding. The pragmatists were famous for their theory of truth without the capital T—their theory that truth is inevitably plural, concrete, and provisional. John Dewey wrote, "Truth is a collection of truths; and these constituent truths are in the keeping of the best available methods of inquiry and testing as to matters of fact."[4] Similarly, William James wrote:

> Truth for us is simply a collective name for verification processes, just as health, wealth, strength, etc., are names for other processes connected with life, and also pursued because it pays to pursue them. Truth is *made*, just as health, wealth and strength are made, in the course of experience.[5]

Pragmatism and feminism largely share, I think, the commitment to finding knowledge in the particulars of experience. It is a commitment against abstract idealism, transcendence, foundationalism, and a temporal universality; and in favor of immanence, historicity, concreteness, situatedness, contextuality, embeddedness, narrativity of meaning.

If feminists largely share the pragmatist commitment that truth is hammered out piecemeal in the crucible of life and our situatedness, they also share the pragmatist understanding that truth is provisional and ever-changing. Too, they also share the pragmatist commitment to concrete particulars. Since the details of our life are connected with what we know, those details matter. Thus, the pragmatist and the feminist both arrive at an embodied perspectivist view of knowledge.

It is not surprising that pragmatists have stressed embodiment more than other philosophers, nor that feminists have stressed it even more. Once we understand that the details of our embodiment matter for what the world is for us (which in some pragmatist views is all the world is), then it must indeed be important that only one half of humans directly experience menstruation, pregnancy, birth, and lactation. So it is no wonder that feminists write about prostitution, contract motherhood, rape, child care, and the PMS defense. It is not just the fact that these are women's issues that makes these writings feminist—they are after all human issues—but specifically the instantiation of the perspective of female embodiment.

Another pragmatist commitment that is largely shared by feminists is the dissolution of traditional dichotomies. Pragmatists and feminists have rejected the dichotomy between thought and action, or between theory and practice. John Dewey especially made this his theme; and he also rejected the dichotomies of reason and feeling, mind and body, nature and nurture, connection and separation, and means and ends. In a commitment that is not, at least not yet, shared by modern pragmatists, feminists have also largely rejected the traditional dichotomy of public (man) and private (woman). For these feminists, the personal is political.

One more strong resonance between the pragmatist and the feminist is in concrete methodology. The feminist commitment to learning through consciousness raising in groups can be regarded as the culmination of the pragmatist understanding that, for consciousness to exist at all, there must be shared meaning arising out of shared interactions with the world. A particularly clear statement of this pragmatist position is found in Dewey's *Experience and Nature*. Dewey's treatment is suffused with the interrelationship of communication, meaning, and shared group experience. In one representative passage, Dewey says:

> The heart of language is not "expression" of something antecedent, much less expression of antecedent thought. It is communication; the establishment of cooperation in an activity in which there are partners, and in which the activity of each is modified and regulated by that partnership.[6]

The modern pragmatists' stress on conversation or dialogue stems from the same kind of understanding.

The special contribution of the methodology of consciousness raising is that it makes new meaning out of a specific type of experience, the experience of domination and oppression. In order to do so, it must make communication possible where before there was silence. In general, rootedness in the experiences of oppression makes possible the distinctive critical contribution that feminism can make to pragmatism. Feminist methodology and perspective make it possible to confront the problem of bad coherence, as I will now try to explain.

Pragmatists have tended toward coherence theories of truth and goodness. Coherence theories tend toward conservativism, in the sense that when we are faced with new experiences and new beliefs, we fit them into our web with as little alteration of what is already there as possible. James said that "in this matter of belief we are all extreme conservatives."[7] According to James, we will count a new idea as true if we can use it to assimilate a new experience to our old beliefs without disturbing them too much.

> That new idea is truest which performs most felicitously its function of satisfying our double urgency. It makes itself true, gets itself classed as true, by the way it works; grafting itself then upon the ancient body of truth, which thus grows much as a tree grows by the activity of a new layer of cambium.[8]

James also said that truth is what is good in the way of belief, meaning that we should, and do, believe those things that work best in our lives.

To those whose standpoint or perspective—whose embodied contextuality—is the narrative of domination and oppression, these coherence theories raise a question that is very hard for the pragmatist to answer. Is it possible to have a coherent system of belief, and have that system be coherently bad? Those who have lived under sexism and racism know from experience that the answer must be yes. We know we cannot argue that any given sexist decision is wrong simply because it does not fit well with all our history and institutions, for the problem is more likely that it fits only too well. Bad coherence creates the double bind. Everywhere we look we find a dominant conception of gender undermining us.

But how can the pragmatist find a standpoint from which to argue that a system is coherent but bad, if pragmatism defines truth and good as coherence? Inattention to this problem is what makes pragmatism seem complacent, when it does. One answer to the problem of bad coherence, which the pragmatist will reject, is to bring back transcendence, natural law, or abstract idealism. Another answer, which the pragmatist can accept, is to take the commitment to embodied perspective very seriously indeed, and especially the commitment to the perspective of those who directly experience domination and oppression.

What this leads to, first, is either an expansive view of coherence that leaves room for broad critique of the dominant understandings and the status quo, or else, perhaps, to denial that pragmatism espouses coherence theory. Its other consequences need exploring. It seems that a primary concomitant of the commitment to perspectivism might be a serious pluralism. "We" are looking for coherence in "our" commitments, but the most important question might be, Who is "we"? A serious pluralism might begin by understanding that there can be more than one "we." One "we" can have very different conceptions of the world, selves, communities, than another. Perhaps, at least practically speaking, each "we" can have its own coherence. Dominant groups have tended to understand themselves without question as the only "we," whereas oppressed groups, simply by virtue of recognizing themselves as an oppressed group, have understood that there can be plural "we's." Perhaps, then, we should understand the perspective of the oppressed as making possible an understanding that coherence can be plural.

A serious pluralism must also find a way to understand the problem of transition, as the "we" of an oppressed group seeks to change dominant conceptions in order to make possible its own empowerment. One important problem of transition is false consciousness. If the perspective of the oppressed includes significant portions of the dominant conception of the world, and of the role of the oppressed group in it, then the oppressed perspective may well be incoherent, rather than a separate coherence to be recognized as a separate "reality." If this is a useful way to view the matter, then we can say that the perspective of the oppressed struggles to make itself coherent in order to make itself real.

What leads some pragmatists into complacency and over-respect for the status quo is partly the failure to ask, Who is "we"? And what are "our" material interests? Why does it "work" for "us" to believe this? It is not necessary for pragmatists to make this mistake. Dewey, especially, understood the connection between truth, goodness, and liberation. He argued cogently that many of philosophy's earlier errors, such as belief in eternal abstract forms, were expressions of the social position of philosophers as an elite leisure class. But the mistake is tempting for a pragmatist whose perspective is that of a member of the dominant group, because from that perspective it seems that one has "the" perspective. I suggest that feminism, in its pragmatic aspect, can correct this complacent tendency. The perspective of domination, and the critical ramifications it must produce once it is taken seriously, seem to be feminism's important contribution to pragmatism.

. . .

Endnotes

1. MacKinnon, "Feminism, Marxism, Method, and the State," 533–542; MacKinnon, *Feminism Unmodified*, 85–92.

2. See Robin West, "The Difference in Women's Hedonic Lives," *Wisconsin Women's Law Journal* 3 (1987): 81–145.

3. Rosemarie Tong, *Feminist Thought: A Comprehensive Introduction* (Boulder, Colo: Westview Press, 1989).

4. John Dewey, *Experience and Nature*, 2nd ed., (New York: Dover, 1929), 410.

5. William James, *Pragmatism*, ed. Fredson Bowers, (Cambridge, Mass.: Harvard University Press, 1975), 104.

6. Dewey, *Experience and Nature*, 179.

7. William James, *Pragmatism*, 35.

8. *Ibid.*, 36 and 104 (where James elaborates on how we choose what theories to class as true).

---

17. *Race and Essentialism in Feminist Legal Theory*

Angela P. Harris

In *Funes the Memorious*, Borges tells of Ireneo Funes, who was a rather ordinary young man (notable only for his precise sense of time) until the age of nineteen, when he was thrown by a half-tamed horse and left paralyzed but possessed of perfect perception and a perfect memory. . . .

Funes tells the narrator that after his transformation he invented his own numbering system. "In place of seven thousand thirteen, he would say (for example) Maximo Perez; in place of seven thousand fourteen, The Railroad; other numbers were Luis Melian Lafinur, Olimar, sulphur, the reins, the whale, the gas, the caldron, Napoleon, Agustin de Vedia." The narrator tries to explain to Funes "that this rhapsody of incoherent terms was precisely the opposite of a system of numbers. I told him that saying 365 meant saying three hundreds, six tens, five ones, an analysis which is not found in the 'numbers' The Negro Timoteo or meat blanket.

Funes did not understand me or refused to understand me."

In his conversation with Funes, the narrator realizes that Funes' life of infinite unique experiences leaves Funes no ability to categorize: "With no effort, he had learned English, French, Portuguese and Latin. I suspect, however, that he was not very capable of thought. To think is to forget differences, generalize, make abstractions. In the teeming world of Funes, there were only details, almost immediate in their presence." For Funes, language is only a unique and private system of classification, elegant and solipsistic. The notion that language, made abstract, can serve to create and reinforce a community is incomprehensible to him. . . .

Describing the voice that speaks the first sentence of the Declaration of Independence, James Boyd White remarks:

> It is not a person's voice, not even that of a committee, but the "unanimous" voice of "thirteen united States" and of their "people." It addresses a universal audience—

Republished with permission of the *Stanford Law Review*, 559 Nathan Abbot Way, Palo Alto, CA 94305.

nothing less than "mankind" itself, located neither in space nor in time—and the voice is universal too, for it purports to know about the "Course of human events" (all human events?) and to be able to discern what "becomes necessary" as a result of changing circumstances.

The Preamble of the United States Constitution, White argues, can also be heard to speak in this unified and universal voice. This voice claims to speak

> for an entire and united nation and to do so directly and personally, not in the third person or by merely delegated authority. . . . The instrument thus appears to issue from a single imaginary author, consisting of all the people of the United States, including the reader, merged into a single identity in this act of self-constitution. "The People" are at once the author and the audience of this instrument.

Despite its claims, however, this voice does not speak for everyone, but for a political faction trying to constitute itself as a unit of many disparate voices; its power lasts only as long as the contradictory voices remain silenced.

. . .

The metaphor of "voice" implies a speaker. I want to suggest, however, that both the voices I have described come from the same source, a source I term "multiple consciousness." It is a premise of this article that we are not born with a "self," but rather are composed of a welter of partial, sometimes contradictory, or even antithetical "selves." A unified identity, if such can ever exist, is a product of will, not a common destiny or natural birthright. Thus, consciousness is "never fixed, never attained once and for all"; it is not a final outcome or a biological given, but a process, a constant contradictory state of becoming, in which both social institutions and individual wills are deeply implicated. A multiple consciousness is home both to the first and the second voices, and all the voices in between.

As I use the phrase, "multiple consciousness" as reflected in legal or literary discourse is not a golden mean or static equilibrium between two extremes, but rather a process in which propositions are constantly put forth, challenged, and subverted.

. . .

The need for multiple consciousness in feminist movement—a social movement encompassing law, literature, and everything in between—has long been apparent. Since the beginning of the feminist movement in the United States, black women have been arguing that their experience calls into question the notion of a unitary "women's experience." In the first wave of the feminist movement, black women's realization that the white leaders of the suffrage movement intended to take neither issues of racial oppression nor black women themselves seriously was instrumental in destroying or preventing political alliances between black and white women within the movement. In the second wave, black women are again speaking loudly and persistently, and at many levels our voices have begun to be heard. Feminists have adopted the notion of multiple consciousness as appropriate to describe a world in which people are not oppressed only or primarily on the basis of gender, but on the bases of race, class, sexual orientation, and other categories in inextricable webs. Moreover, multiple consciousness is implicit in the precepts of feminism itself. . . .

In feminist legal theory, however, the move away from univocal toward multivocal theories of women's experience and feminism has been slower than in other areas. In feminist legal theory, the pull of the second voice, the voice of abstract categorization, is still powerfully strong: "We the People" seems in danger of being replaced by "We the Women." And in feminist legal theory, as in the dominant culture, it is mostly white, straight, and socioeconomically privileged people who claim to speak for all of us. Not surprisingly, the story they tell about "women," despite its claim to universality, seems to black women to be peculiar to women who are white, straight, and socioeconomically privileged—a phenomenon Adrienne Rich terms "white solipsism."

. . .

The notion that there is a monolithic "women's experience" that can be described independent of other facets of experience like race, class, and sexual orientation is one I refer to in this essay as "gender essentialism." A corollary to gender essentialism is "racial essentialism"—the belief that there is a monolithic "Black Experience," or "Chicano Experience." The source of gender and racial essentialism (and all other essentialisms, for the list of categories could be infinitely multiplied) is the second voice, the voice that claims to speak for all. The result of essentialism is to reduce the lives of people who experience multiple forms of oppression to addition problems: "racism + sexism = straight black women's experience," or "racism + sexism + homophobia = black lesbian experience." Thus, in an essentialist world, black women's experience will always be forcibly fragmented before being subjected to analysis, as those who are "only interested in race" and those who are "only interested in gender" take their separate slices of our lives.

Moreover, feminist essentialism paves the way for unconscious racism.

In a racist society like this one, the storytellers are usually white, and so "woman" turns out to be "white woman."

Why, in the face of challenges from "different" women and from feminist method itself, is feminist essentialism so persistent and pervasive? I think the reasons are several. Essentialism is intellectually convenient, and to a certain extent cognitively ingrained. Essentialism also carries with it important emotional and political payoffs. Finally, essentialism often appears (especially to white women) as the only alternative to chaos, mindless pluralism (the Funes trap), and the end of the feminist movement. In my view, however, as long as feminists, like theorists in the dominant culture, continue to search for gender and racial essences, black women will never be anything more than a crossroads between two kinds of domination, or at the bottom of a hierarchy of oppressions; we will always be required to choose pieces of ourselves to present as wholeness.

Essentialism in feminist theory has two characteristics that ensure that black women's voices will be ignored. First, in the pursuit of the essential feminine, Woman leached of all color and irrelevant social circumstance, issues of race are bracketed as belonging to a separate and distinct discourse—a process which leaves black women's selves fragmented beyond recognition. Second, feminist essentialists find that in removing issues of "race" they have actually only managed to remove black women—meaning that white women now stand as the epitome of Woman. Both processes can be seen at work in dominance theory.

[The] essentialist approach recreates the paradigmatic woman in the image of the white woman, in the name of "unmodified feminism." As in the dominant discourse, black women are relegated to the margins, ignored or extolled as "just like us, only more so." But "Black women are not white women with color." Moreover, feminist essentialism represents not just an insult to black women, but a broken promise—the promise to listen to women's stories, the promise of feminist method.

. . .

[Robin] West argues that the biological and social implications of motherhood shape the selfhood of all, or at least most, women. This claim involves at least two assumptions. First, West assumes (as does the liberal social theory she criticizes) that everyone has a deep, unitary "self" that is relatively stable and unchanging. Second, West assumes that this "self" differs significantly between men and women but is the same for all women and for all men despite differences of class, race, and sexual orientation: that is, that this self is deeply and primarily gendered.

. . .

In this society, it is only white people who have the luxury of "having no color"; only white people have been able to imagine that sexism and racism are separate experiences. Far more for black women than for white women, the experience of self is precisely that of being unable to disentangle the web of race and gender—of being enmeshed always in multiple, often contradictory, discourses of sexuality and color. The challenge to black women has been the need to weave the fragments, our many selves, into an integral, though always changing and shifting, whole: a self that is neither "female" nor "black," but both-and. West's insistence that every self is deeply and primarily gendered, then, with its corollary that gender is more important to personal identity than race, is finally another example of white solipsism. By suggesting that gender is more deeply embedded in self than race, her theory privileges the experience of white people over all others, and thus serves to reproduce relations of domination in the larger culture.

. . .

In my view, there are at least three major contributions that black women have to offer postessentialist feminist theory: the recognition of a self that is multiplicitous, not unitary; the recognition that differences are always relational rather than inherent; and the recognition that wholeness and commonality are acts of will and creativity, rather than passive discovery.

Black women experience not a single inner self (much less one that is essentially gendered), but many selves. This sense of a multiplicitous self is not unique to black women, but black women have expressed this sense in ways that are striking, poignant, and potentially useful to feminist theory.

A post-essentialist feminism can benefit not only from the abandonment of the quest for a unitary self, but also from Martha Minow's realization that difference—and therefore identity—is always relational, not inherent. Zora Neale Hurston's work is a good illustration of this notion.

In an essay written for a white audience, *How It Feels to Be Colored Me*, Hurston argues that her color is not an inherent part of her being, but a response to her surroundings. She recalls the day she "became colored"—the day she left her home in an all-black community to go to school: "I left Eatonville, the town of the oleanders, as Zora. When I disembarked from the river-boat at Jacksonville, she was no more. It seemed that I had suffered a sea change. I was not Zora of Orange County any more, I was now a little colored girl." But even as an adult, Hurston insists, her colored self is always situational: "I do not always feel colored. Even now I often achieve the unconscious Zora of Eatonville before the Hegira. I feel most colored when I am thrown against a sharp white background."

. . .

Thus, "how it feels to be colored Zora" depends on the answer to these questions: "Compared to what? As of when? Who is asking? In what context? For what purpose? With what interests and presuppositions?" What Hurston rigorously shows is that questions of difference and identity are always functions of a specific interlocutionary situation—and the answers, matters of strategy rather than truth." Any "essential self" is always an invention; the evil is in denying its artificiality.

To be compatible with this conception of the self, feminist theorizing about "women" must similarly be strategic and contingent, focusing on rela-

tionships, not essences. One result will be that men will cease to be a faceless Other and reappear as potential allies in political struggle. Another will be that women will be able to acknowledge their differences without threatening feminism itself. In the process, as feminists begin to attack racism and classism and homophobia, feminism will change from being only about "women as women" (modified women need not apply), to being about all kinds of oppression based on seemingly inherent and unalterable characteristics. We need not wait for a unified theory of oppression; that theory can be feminism.

. . .

Finally, black women can help feminist movement move beyond its fascination with essentialism through the recognition that wholeness of the self and commonality with others are asserted (if never completely achieved) through creative action, not realized in shared victimization.

. . .

[T]he recognition of the role of creativity and will in shaping our lives is liberating, for it allows us to acknowledge and celebrate the creativity and joy with which many women have survived and turned existing relations of domination to their own ends. Works of black literature like *Beloved*, *The Color Purple*, and *Song of Solomon*, among others, do not linger on black women's victimization and misery; though they recognize our pain, they ultimately celebrate our transcendence.

Finally, on a collective level this emphasis on will and creativity reminds us that bridges between women are built, not found. The discovery of shared suffering is a connection more illusory than real; what will truly bring and keep us together is the use of effort and imagination to root out and examine our differences, for only the recognition of women's differences can ultimately bring feminist movement to strength. This is hard work, and painful work; but it is also radical work, real work.

. . .

I have argued in this article that gender essentialism is dangerous to feminist legal theory because in the attempt to extract an essential female self and voice from the diversity of women's experience, the experiences of women perceived as "different" are ignored or treated as variations on the (white) norm. Now I want to return to an earlier point: that legal theory, including feminist legal theory, has been entranced for too long and to too great an extent by the voice of "We the People." In order to energize legal theory, we need to subvert it with narratives and stories, accounts of the particular, the different, and the hitherto silenced.

Whether by chance or not, many of the legal theorists telling stories these days are women of color. Mari Matsuda calls for "multiple conscious-

ness as jurisprudential method"; Patricia Williams shows the way with her multilayered stories and meditations. These writings are healthy for feminist legal theory as well as legal theory more generally. In acknowledging "the complexity of messages implied in our being," they begin the task of energizing legal theory with the creative struggle between Funes and We the People: the creative struggle that reflects a multiple consciousness.

18. *Racial Realism*

DERRICK A. BELL, JR.

The struggle by black people to obtain freedom, justice, and dignity is as old as this nation. At times, great and inspiring leaders rose out of desperate situations to give confidence and feelings of empowerment to the black community. Most of these leaders urged their people to strive for racial equality. They were firmly wedded to the idea that the courts and judiciary were the vehicle to better the social position of blacks. In spite of dramatic civil rights movements and periodic victories in the legislatures, black Americans by no means are equal to whites. Racial equality is, in fact, not a realistic goal. By constantly aiming for a status that is unobtainable in a perilously racist America, black Americans face frustration and despair. Over time, our persistent quest for integration has hardened into self-defeating rigidity.

Black people need reform of our civil rights strategies as badly as those in the law needed a new way to consider American jurisprudence prior to the advent of the Legal Realists. By viewing the law—and, by extension, the courts—as instruments for preserving the status quo and only periodically and unpredictably serving as a refuge of oppressed

people, blacks can refine the work of the Realists. Rather than challenging the entire jurisprudential system, as the Realists did, blacks' focus must be much narrower—a challenge to the principle of racial equality. This new movement is appropriately called "Racial Realism," and it is a legal and social mechanism on which blacks can rely to have their voice and outrage heard.

Reliance on rigid application of the law is no less damaging or ineffectual simply because it is done for the sake of ending discriminatory racial practices. Indeed, Racial Realism is to race relations what "Legal Realism" is to jurisprudential thought. The Legal Realists were a group of scholars in the early part of the twentieth century who challenged the classical structure of law as a formal group of common law rules that, if properly applied to any given situation, lead to a right—and therefore just—result.

The Realists comprised a younger generation of scholars—average age forty-two—who were willing to challenge what they viewed as the rigid ways of the past. More than their classical counterparts, they had been influenced by the rapid spread of the scientific outlook and the growth of social sciences. Such influence predisposed them to accept a critical and empirical attitude toward the law, in contrast to the formalists who insisted that

Reprinted by permission of the publisher from *Connecticut Law Review* Vol. 24, 1992.

law was logically self-evidence, objective, a priori valid, and internally consistent. The great majority of the movement's pioneers had practical experience, which strengthened their awareness of the changing and subjective elements in the legal system. This awareness flew in the face of the Langdellian conception of law as unchanging truth and an autonomous system of rules.

The Realists took their cue from Oliver Wendell Holmes, who staged a fifty-year battle against legalistic formalism. According to Holmes's scientific and relativistic lines of attack, judges settled cases not by deductive reasoning, but rather by reliance on value-laden, personal beliefs. To Holmes, such judges engineered socially desirable policies based on these beliefs, which, like all moral values, were wholly relative and determined by one's particular environment. Realist notions also were grounded in the views of the Progressives during the 1890s. Concerned with social welfare legislation and administrative regulation, the Progressives criticized the conceptualization of property rights being expounded by the United States Supreme Court. Creating a remedy based upon the finding of a property right was the court's way of subtly imposing personal and moral beliefs; abstraction was the method it used to accomplish its purpose. The Realists stressed the *function* of law, however, rather than the *abstract conceptualization* of it.

The Realists also had a profound impact by demonstrating the circularity of defining rights as "objective," which definition depended, in large part, on a distinction between formalistically bounded spheres between public and private. Classical judges justified decisions by appealing to these spheres. For example, an opinion would justify finding a defendant liable because she had invaded the (private) property rights of the plaintiff; but such a justification, the Realists pointed out, was inevitably circular because there would be such a private property right if and only if the court found for the plaintiff or declared the statute unconstitutional. The cited reasons for decisions were only results, and as such served to obscure the extent to which the state's enforcement power through the courts lay behind private property and other rights claims.

Closely linked with the Realists' attack on the logic of rights theory was their attack on the logic of precedent. No two cases, the Realists pointed out, are ever exactly alike. Hence, a procedural rule from a former case cannot simply be applied to a new case with a multitude of facts that vary from the former case. Rather, the judge must choose whether or not the ruling in the earlier case should be extended to include the new case. Such a choice basically is about the relevancy of facts, and decisions about relevancy are never logically compelled. Decisions merely are subjective judgments made to reach a particular result. Decisions about the relevance of distinguishing facts are value-laden and dependent upon a judge's own experiences.

The imperatives of this Realist attack were at least two. First, to clear the air of "beguiling but misleading conceptual categories"[1] so that thought could be redirected toward facts (rather than nonexistent spheres of classism) and ethics. If social decision-making was inevitably moral choice, policymakers needed some ethical basis upon which to make their choices. And second, the Realists' critique suggested that the whole liberal worldview of private rights and public sovereignty mediated by the rule of law needed to be exploded. The Realists argued that a worldview premised upon the public and private spheres is an attractive mirage that masks the reality of economic and political power. This two-pronged attack had profoundly threatening consequences: it carried with it the potential collapse of legal liberalism. Realism, in short, changed the face of American jurisprudence by exposing the result-oriented, value-laden nature of legal decision-making. Many divergent philosophies emerged to combat, not a little defensively, the attack on law as instrumental, not self-evidently logical, and "made" by judges, rather than simply derived from transcendent or ultimate principles.

As every civil rights lawyer has reason to know—despite law school indoctrination and belief in the "rule of law"—abstract principles lead to legal results that harm blacks and perpetuate their inferior status. Racism provides a basis for a judge to select one available premise rather than another when incompatible claims arise. A paradigm example presents itself in the case of *Regents of the University of California v. Bakke.*[2] Relying heavily on the formalistic language of the Fourteenth Amendment and utterly ignoring social questions about which race in fact has power and advantages and which race has been denied entry for centuries into academia, the court held that an affirmative action policy may not unseat white candidates on the basis of their race. By introducing an artificial and inappropriate parity in its reasoning, the court effectively made a choice to ignore historical patterns, to ignore contemporary statistics, and to ignore flexible reasoning. Following a Realist approach, the court would have observed the social landscape and noticed the skewed representation of minority medical school students. It would have reflected on the possible reasons for these demographics, including inadequate public school systems in urban ghettos, lack of minority professionals to serve as role models, and the use of standardized tests evaluated according to "white" criteria. Taking these factors into consideration, the court very well may have decided *Bakke* differently.

Bakke serves as an example of how formalists can use abstract concepts, such as equality, to mask policy choices and value judgments. Abstraction, in the place of flexible reasoning, removes a heavy burden from a judge's task; at the same time, her opinion appears to render the "right" result. Thus, cases such as *Bakke* should inspire many civil rights lawyers to reexamine the potential of equality jurisprudence to improve the lives of black Americans.

The protection of whites' race-based privilege, so evident in the *Bakke* decision, has become a common theme in civil rights decisions, particularly in many of those decided by an increasingly conservative Supreme Court. The addition of Judge Clarence Thomas to that court, as the replacement for Justice Thurgood Marshall, is likely to add deep insult to the continuing injury inflicted on civil rights advocates. The cut is particularly unkind because the choice of a black like Clarence Thomas replicates the slave masters' practice of elevating to overseer and other positions of quasi-power those slaves willing to mimic the masters' views, carry out orders, and by their presence provide a perverse legitimacy to the oppression they aided and approved.

For liberals in general, and black people in particular, the appointment of Thomas to the Supreme Court, his confirmation hearings, and the nation's reaction to Professor Anita Hill's sexual harassment charges, all provide most ominous evidence that we are in a period of racial rejection, a time when many whites can block out their own justified fears about the future through increasingly blatant forms of discrimination against blacks.

The decline of black people is marked by a precipitous collapse in our economic status and the frustration of our political hopes. An ultimate rebuff and symbol of our powerlessness is President Bush's elevation of one of us who is willing to denigrate and disparage all who look like him to gain personal favor, position, and prestige.

. . .

Beyond symbolism though, the message of the Thomas appointment virtually demands that equality advocates reconsider their racial goals. This is not, as some may think, an overreaction to a temporary setback in the long "march to freedom" that blacks have been making since far before the Emancipation Proclamation. Rather, the event is both a reminder and a warning of the vulnerability of black rights and of the willingness of powerful whites to sacrifice and subvert these rights in furtherance of political or economic ends. I speak here not of some new prophetic revelation. Rather, these are frequently stated yet seldom acknowledged truths that we continue to ignore at our peril.

What was it about our reliance on racial remedies that may have prevented us from recognizing that abstract legal rights, such as equality, could do little more than bring about the cessation of one form of discriminatory conduct, which soon appeared in a more subtle though no less discriminatory form? I predict that this examination will require us to redefine goals of racial equality and opportunity to which blacks have adhered with far more simple faith than hardheaded reflection.

I would urge that we begin this review with a statement that many will wish to deny, but none can refute. It is this: Black people will never gain full equality in this country. Even those herculean efforts we hail as successful will produce no more than temporary "peaks of progress," short-lived victories that slide into irrelevance as racial patterns adapt in ways that maintain white dominance. This is a hard-to-accept fact that all history verifies. We must acknowledge it and move on to adopt policies based on what I call "Racial Realism." This mind-set or philosophy requires us to acknowledge the permanence of our subordinate status. That acknowledgment enables us to avoid despair and frees us to imagine and implement racial strategies that can bring fulfillment and even triumph.

Legal precedents we thought permanent have been overturned, distinguished, or simply ignored. All too many of the black people we sought to lift through law from a subordinate status to equal opportunity are more deeply mired in poverty and despair than they were during the "separate but equal" era.

Despite our successful effort to strip the law's endorsement from the hated Jim Crow signs, contemporary color barriers are less visible but no less real or less oppressive. Today, one can travel for thousands of miles across this country and never come across a public facility designated for "colored" or "white." Indeed, the very absence of visible signs of discrimination creates an atmosphere of racial neutrality which encourages whites to believe that racism is a thing of the past.

Today, blacks experiencing rejection for a job, a home, a promotion anguish over whether race or individual failing prompted their exclusion. Either conclusion breeds frustration and eventually despair. We call ourselves "African Americans," but despite centuries of struggle, none of us—no matter our prestige or position—is more than a few steps away from a racially motivated exclusion, restriction, or affront.

There is little reason to be shocked at my prediction that blacks will not be accepted as equals, a status that has eluded us as a group for more than three hundred years. The current condition of most blacks provides support for this position. It is surely possible to use statistics to distort, and I do wish for revelations showing that any of the dreadful data illustrating the plight of so many black people is false or misleading. Yet there is little effort to discredit the shocking disparities contained in these reports. Even so, the reports have little effect on policymakers or the society in general.

Statistics and studies reflect racial conditions that transformed the "we have a dream" mentality of the sixties into the trial by racial ordeal so many blacks are suffering in the nineties. The adverse psychological effects of nonexistent opportunity are worse than the economic and social loss. As the writer Maya Angelou, put it recently: "In these bloody days and frightful nights when an urban warrior can find no face more despicable than his own, no ammunition more deadly than self-hate and no target more deserving of his true aim than his brother, we must wonder how we came so late and lonely to this place."[3]

As a veteran of a civil rights era that is now over, I regret the need to explain what went wrong. Clearly, we need to examine what it was about our reliance on racial remedies that may have prevented us from recognizing that these legal rights could do little more than bring about the cessation of one form of discriminatory conduct, which soon appeared in a more subtle though no less discriminatory form. The question is whether this examination requires us to redefine goals of racial equality and opportunity to which blacks have adhered for more than a century. The answer, must be a resounding yes.

Traditional civil rights law is highly structured and founded on the belief that the Constitution was intended—at least after the Civil War amendments—to guarantee equal rights to blacks. The belief in eventual racial justice, and the litigation and legislation based on that belief, was always dependent on the ability of believers to remain faithful to their creed of racial equality while rejecting the contrary message of discrimination that survived their best efforts to control or eliminate it.

Despite the Realist challenge that demolished its premises, the basic formalist model of law survives, although in bankrupt form. *Bakke*, as well as numerous other decisions that thwart the use of affirmative action and set-aside programs, illustrates that notions of racial equality fit conveniently into the formalist model of jurisprudence. Thus, a judge may advocate the importance of racial equality while arriving at a decision detrimental to black Americans. In fact, racial equality can be used to keep blacks out of institutions of higher education, such as the one at issue in *Bakke*. By reasoning that race-conscious policies derogate the meaning of racial equality, a judge can manipulate the law and arrive at an outcome based upon her worldview, to the detriment of blacks seeking enrollment.

The message the formalist model conveys is that existing power relations in the real world are by definition legitimate and must go unchallenged. Equality theory also necessitates such a result.

Nearly every critique the Realists launched at the formalists can be hurled at advocates of liberal civil rights theory. Precedent, rights theory, and objectivity merely are formal rules that serve a covert purpose; even in the context of equality theory, they will never vindicate the legal rights of black Americans.

Outside of the formalistic logic in racial equality cases, history should also trigger civil rights advocates to question the efficacy of equality theory. After all, it is an undeniable fact that the Constitution's Framers initially opted to protect property, including enslaved Africans in that category, through the Fifth Amendment. Those committed to racial equality also had to overlook the political motivations for the Civil War amendments—self-interested motivations almost guaranteeing that when political needs changed, the protection provided the former slaves would not be enforced. Analogize this situation with that presented in *Bakke:* arguably the court rules as it did because of the anti-affirmative action rhetoric sweeping the political landscape. In conformation with past practice, protection of black rights is now predictably episodic. For these reasons, both the historic pattern and its contemporary replication require review and replacement of the now-defunct, racial equality ideology.

Racism translates into a societal vulnerability of black people that few politicians—including our last two presidents—seem able to resist. And why not? The practice of using blacks as scapegoats for failed economic or political policies works every time. The effectiveness of this "racial bonding" by whites requires that blacks seek a new and more realistic goal for our civil rights activism. It is time we concede that a commitment to racial equality merely perpetuates our disempowerment. Rather, we need a mechanism to make life bearable in a society where blacks are a permanent, subordinate class. Our empowerment lies in recognizing that Racial Realism may open the gateway to attaining a more meaningful status.

Some blacks already understand and act on the underlying rationale of Racial Realism. Unhappily, most black spokespersons and civil rights organizations remain committed to the ideology of racial equality. Acceptance of the Racial Realism concept would enable them to understand and respond to recurring aspects of our subordinate status. It would free them to think and plan within a context of reality rather than idealism. The reality is that blacks still suffer disproportionately higher rates of poverty, joblessness, and insufficient health care than other ethnic populations in the United States. The ideal is that law, through racial equality, can lift them out of this trap. I suggest we abandon this ideal and move on to a fresh, realistic approach.

Casting off the burden of equality ideology will lift the sights, providing a bird's-eye view of situations that are distorted by race. From this broadened perspective on events and problems, we can better appreciate and cope with racial subordination.

While implementing Racial Realism we must simultaneously acknowledge that our actions are not likely to lead to transcendent change and, despite our best efforts, may be of more help to the system we despise than to the victims of that system we are trying to help. Nevertheless, our realization, and the dedication based on that realization, can lead to policy positions and campaigns that are less likely to worsen conditions for those we are trying to help and more likely to remind those in power that there are imaginative, unabashed risk-takers who refuse to be trammeled upon. Yet confrontation with our oppressors is not our sole reason for engaging in Racial Realism. Continued struggle can bring about unexpected benefits and gains that in themselves justify continued endeavor. The fight itself has meaning and should give us hope for the future.

I am convinced that there is something real out there in America for black people. It is not, however, the romantic love of integration; it is surely not the long-sought goal of equality under law, though we must maintain the struggle against racism, else the erosion of black rights will become even worse than it is now. The Racial Realism that we must seek is simply a hard-eyed view of racism as it is and our subordinate role in it. We must realize, as our slave forebears did, that the struggle for freedom is, at bottom, a manifestation of our humanity which survives and grows stronger through resistance to oppression, even if that oppression is never overcome.

A final remembrance may help make my point. The year was 1964. It was a quiet, heat-hushed evening in Harmony, a small black community near the Mississippi Delta. Some Harmony residents, in the face of increasing white hostility, were organizing to ensure implementation of a court order mandating desegregation of their schools the next September. Walking with Mrs. Biona MacDonald, one of the organizers, up a dusty, unpaved road toward her modest home, I asked where she found the courage to continue working for civil rights in the face of intimidation that included her son losing his job in town, the local bank trying to foreclose on her mortgage, and shots fired through her living room window. "Derrick," she said slowly, seriously, "I am an old woman. I lives to harass white folks."

Mrs. MacDonald did not say she risked everything because she hoped or expected to win out over the whites who, as she well knew, held all the economic and political power, and the guns as well. Rather, she recognized that—powerless as she was—she had and intended to use courage and determination as weapons "to harass white folks." Her fight, in itself, gave her strength and empowerment in a society that relentlessly attempted to wear her down. Mrs. MacDonald did not even hint that her harassment would topple whites' well-entrenched power; rather, her goal was defiance, and its harassing effect was more potent precisely because she placed herself in confrontation with her oppressors with full knowledge of their power and willingness to use it.

Mrs. MacDonald avoided discouragement and defeat because at the point that she determined to resist her oppression, she was triumphant. Nothing the all-powerful whites could do to her would diminish her triumph. Mrs. MacDonald understood twenty-five years ago the theory that I am espousing in the nineties for black leaders and civil rights lawyers to adopt. If you remember her story, you will understand my message.

Endnotes

[1] See E. Mensch, "The History of Mainstream Legal Thought," in D. Kairys, ed. in *The Politics of Law*, (1990), at 23.

[2] 438 U.S. 265 (1978).

[3] Maya Angelou, "I Dare to Hope," *New York Times* (Aug. 25, 1991), E15.

Study Questions

1. In what ways, according to Mark Tushnet, does Critical Legal Studies (CLS) differ from legal realism?

2. How, according to Tushnet, have CLS scholars attacked the premises of the law and economics movement?

3. How does Tushnet respond to the criticism that CLS has no positive or constructive agenda or outlook? Do you find his response convincing?

4. In light of your understanding of CLS from this chapter, recall Dworkin's critique of various forms of "skepticism" about law. Are Dworkin's responses to the crits convincing, in your view?

5. CLS scholar Roberto Unger argues that the resolution of cases through the neutral application of the "rules" cannot work, even in simple cases. Suppose that the law forbids "spilling of blood in the streets." Would this law prohibit a medic from performing emergency surgery at an accident scene? Because the rule itself cannot answer this question, its solution must be sought by appealing to the purposes and values that lie behind it. Yet, Unger insists, ours is a society in which shared values and beliefs are not sufficiently apparent to settle such disputes. (See Unger, *Knowledge and Politics*, pp. 63–103.) How would a legal positivist respond to this argument? How would Dworkin respond?

6. How does Posner use the example of the stamp collection to illustrate the concept of wealth maximization?

7. In what way does Posner think that the model of wealth maximization can be given a "pragmatic" justification?

8. Some critics of law and economics have argued that Posner and others have placed the cart before the horse: the fact that certain legal decisions or doctrines can be shown to promote wealth maximization does not establish

that such rulings or parts of the law are best explained by appeal to economic ideas. Moral concepts such as justice and fairness, the critics argue, may provide a better overall explanation of how the law developed and a better justification for its authority. How do you think Posner would respond to this criticism? What makes one explanation of the law better or worse than another?

9. Are the assumptions upon which the economic analysis is based too far removed from actual experiences to make them viable? Do people always act rationally in the way that Posner understands that notion? What would Posner say (for example) about seemingly altruistic behavior?

10. According to Angela Harris, what are the characteristics of the "essential woman." How have those characteristics been identified?

11. In what ways does Harris argue that the use of stories of "multiple consciousness" will improve legal theory?

12. What legal effects do you think differences between the sexes should have? Are the differences between men and women such that different legal treatment is required? Which differences? Should sex-based generalizations ever be used to set policy or to define legal doctrines? If so, under what circumstances?

13. According to Margaret Radin, what are the similarities between pragmatism and feminism?

14. What does Radin mean by the problem of "bad coherence"? How does she propose to overcome it using a pragmatic approach?

15. Why does Derrick Bell maintain that racial equality for blacks in America will never be a "realistic goal"?

16. According to Bell, how has the formalistic view of the law, attacked earlier by legal realists, persisted to this day in civil rights law?

F. Legal Reasoning and the Constitution

Constitutional Interpretation

In the summer of 1987, President Ronald Reagan nominated Judge Robert Bork, then serving as a federal circuit court of appeals judge, to fill a vacancy on the United States Supreme Court. Judge Bork, an outspoken and articulate conservative, had written and spoken widely throughout his career on matters of constitutional law and social policy and had been especially critical of many controversial Supreme Court decisions dealing with civil rights,

freedom of speech and religion, privacy, and affirmative action, among others. Although he was eventually rejected by the Senate, Bork's nomination began a discussion that continued throughout the confirmation hearings of subsequent nominees to the Court: it sparked a nationwide debate on the meaning of our law, how it is to be interpreted, and what the job of a judge should be. Have the courts acted irresponsibly, as Bork alleged, by "reading into" the Constitution their own moral, social, and political agendas? Or have they simply enforced the "true" meaning of the Constitution? What is the difference between "reading things into" the Constitution and "finding" them there already? What does it mean to interpret a constitution or a statute responsibly? How does one reason from vague and open-ended language such as "due process" or "equal protection" to concrete decisions in particular cases, from general principles to specific results? In what way are judges' decisions guided by the law, rather than by their own opinions? This section examines the nature of legal reasoning by focusing on the specific example of constitutional interpretation.

Perhaps the best way to grasp the issues around which this section turns is to begin with a brief recitation of a handful of rulings issued by the Supreme Court in the past few years. Among the more controversial holdings, then, are these (many of which we will encounter later in this text): a state that arrests and imprisons homosexuals for practicing sodomy in their bedrooms does not violate their constitutional rights; a law requiring that "creationism" be taught in the public schools violates the First Amendment because it "establishes a religion"; a statutory rape law providing that only males are punishable for rape does not violate their right to "equal protection of the laws"; there is no constitutionally protected right to use the drug peyote as part of a religious ceremony; no state may execute a person who was under the age of sixteen at the time of a capital offense; no American citizens have a right of privacy in their garbage; neither Congress nor the states may prohibit the burning of the American flag as a form of political protest; irreversibly comatose persons who have not made clearly known their wishes regarding life support have no constitutionally protected "right to die." This is, of course, but a small sampling of an increasingly long list of controversial decisions handed down by the courts each year, decisions touching freedom of speech and of the press, freedom of religion, racial and sexual equality, criminal liability and punishment, personal autonomy and privacy, and so on.

Accustomed as we are to hearing of these controversial rulings, the reaction they provoke in many of us is still the same: Who are the justices of the Supreme Court to lay down the law in a community that purports at least to be a democracy? In

making these delicate and often disturbing decisions, many say, the Supreme Court and lower courts are going too far; they are overstepping their legitimate function, which is to "apply" the law, not to "make" it. (This view has since been echoed in calls for judges who would "interpret" the Constitution and not "legislate from the bench.") This common complaint about the courts and their controversial rulings actually disguises two fundamental questions about constitutional interpretation and judicial reasoning. First, in a democracy who should have the right to issue authoritative interpretations of the Constitution? Second, what is the proper method of understanding what the Constitution requires or permits or forbids? The first of these questions has come to be called the "counter-majoritarian difficulty": What justifies permitting a body, neither elected nor otherwise politically accountable in any significant way, to overrule the judgments of the people as expressed by their representatives? Why shouldn't interpreting the Constitution itself be a democratic process?

The second question, and the one with which we shall be concerned in this section, is equally daunting. The Constitution, on its face at least, makes absolutely no reference whatever to privacy, garbage, sodomy, creationism, peyote, statutory rape, flag burning, or the irreversibly comatose. It has been made to speak to these issues only through *acts of interpretation*. But what governs or controls or constrains these acts of interpretation? What tells us whether the interpretation has been done well or badly, correctly or incorrectly? Is there any standard of "correctness" here at all? Or are constitutional decisions simply choices dictated by the private moral and political convictions of the judge?

Griswold and the Right of Privacy

No area of constitutional adjudication has posed these questions about interpretation more acutely than the Supreme Court's "privacy" rulings, dealing primarily with abortion and sexual matters. How should the text of the Constitution and the Court's subsequent decisions be interpreted in regard to privacy and personal sexual autonomy? Is there any principled interpretive methodology that can settle such cases noncontroversially? Are any of the Court's privacy rulings legitimate? Two prominent privacy cases serve as our focus for these questions, *Griswold v. Connecticut* and *Bowers v. Hardwick.*

In 1961, Griswold, the director of the Planned Parenthood League of Connecticut, was arrested for violating a state statute forbidding the dissemination of contraceptive devices and information, even to married persons. Griswold contended that the statute violated the Constitution, and the Supreme Court agreed. Writing for the majority, Justice Douglas argued that the statute violates the general right of privacy granted by the Constitution to all citizens. Douglas was aware that "privacy" occurs nowhere in the text of the Constitution; nonetheless he found a right of privacy in the "penumbras," the faint shadows of several of the amendments to the Constitution. To establish this, Douglas relied partly upon precedent, the authority of prior cases. In the *Pierce* and *Meyer* cases from the 1920s, for example, it had been held that the First Amendment protects the rights of parents to send their children to private schools and to teach them a foreign language. In *NAACP v. Alabama*, the Court had protected the freedom to associate by preventing disclosure of an organization's membership list. The Third and Fourth Amendments protect a person's interest in the privacy and sanctity of the home; and the Fifth Amendment, Douglas continued, protects people against being forced to disclose things about themselves. Douglas believed that these textual requirements and prior cases add up to a general right of privacy relating to matters of marriage, children, and family; the state of Connecticut must have a good reason for invading this zone of privacy. Douglas insisted that it did not. After all, if the purpose of the statute is to discourage illicit sexual relations (as the state claimed), why make even birth control counseling for married persons punishable?

At least two other arguments were given in *Griswold* to support the finding of a right of privacy in the Constitution. Justice Goldberg asserted one of these arguments by invoking the Ninth Amendment: "The enumeration in the Constitution, of certain rights, shall not be construed to deny or disparage others retained by the people." Goldberg believed privacy to be one of the rights "retained by the people," and he contended that the Connecticut statute violated the "due process" clause of the Fourteenth Amendment, which protects (in Harlan's language) "values implicit in the concept of ordered liberty," rights that are "fundamental." One of these values or rights, Harlan believed, is privacy in the home, and this includes marital privacy. Finally, Justice Black, in dissent, admitted that he found the Connecticut law offensive but that he could find no specific provision of the Constitution protecting a general right of privacy. The majority's arguments, he thought, are little better than a vehicle through which the justices rationalized their invalidation of a law they find personally offensive. This, Black insisted, is not their job.

A number of significant decisions extending the scope of the right of privacy followed in the wake of *Griswold*, striking down laws prohibiting interracial marriage, extending the right of privacy to include the possession of obscene materials in one's own home, reversing a conviction for public distribution of contraceptives to *unmarried* persons, and invalidating prohibitions on the sale of nonprescription contraceptives to persons under the age of sixteen.[1] By far the most controversial extension of *Griswold*, however, came in 1973 in the case of Roe v. Wade, in which the Court struck down criminal abortion statutes that prohibited abortions except to save the life of the mother. Justice Blackmun's opinion for the Court applied the privacy right to the decision to abort: "The right of privacy, whether it be founded in the Fourteenth Amendment's concept of personal liberty and restrictions upon state action, as we feel it is, or, as the District Court determined, in the Ninth Amendment's reservation of rights to the people, is broad enough to encompass a woman's decision whether or not to terminate her pregnancy."[2]

Bowers v. Hardwick, decided by the Supreme Court in 1986, raises deep questions about *Griswold* and its aftermath: What did *Griswold* really decide?

---

[1] See, respectively, *Loving v. Virginia* 388 U.S. 1 (1967); *Stanley v. Georgia* 394 U.S. 577 (1969); *Eisenstadt v. Baird* 405 U.S. 438 (1972); and *Carey v. Population Services* 431 U.S. 678 (1977).

[2] 410 U.S. 153, 164–165.

Just what is the scope of the constitutional right of privacy?

Michael Hardwick had been cited for drinking in public; he missed his first court appearance, and a warrant for his arrest was issued. Hardwick subsequently paid his fine, but the warrant was not recalled. The officer charged with executing the warrant appeared at Hardwick's home and a guest admitted him. The officer then saw Hardwick, in his bedroom, engaged in oral sex with another man, an act which is a felony in Georgia. Hardwick was arrested for violating the sodomy statute, and he challenged the law's constitutionality before the Supreme Court. Justice White, writing for the Court, framed the issue in this way: Does the Constitution confer a fundamental right to engage in homosexual sodomy? White answered no. Hardwick's conduct is not protected, White maintained, by the rationale of the line of cases stretching from *Pierce* and *Meyer* through *Griswold* and *Roe,* for those cases dealt only with intimate matters pertaining to family, marriage, and procreation, none of which are at stake in homosexual sodomy. Nor is Hardwick's sexual conduct one of the "fundamental values" or liberties "deeply rooted in our Nation's history and traditions," a point White supported by citing the long history of the criminalization of homosexual conduct. Nor can Hardwick rely on privacy in the home; as not everything that occurs in the home is constitutionally protected.

In his dissent, Justice Blackmun distinguished between two ideas or threads running throughout the privacy cases: privacy in certain decisions involving personal autonomy in intimate matters and privacy in certain locations, such as the home. Blackmun argued that both of these are implicated in *Bowers.* We protect choices regarding marriage, childbearing, and child rearing not because they are the only constitutionally important interests, but because each deals with the most fundamental ways in which individuals define themselves, with the lives that they must make for themselves. Plainly, Blackmun argued, sexual orientation and sexual conduct are crucial parts of one's self-definition. Furthermore, the incident here took place in Hardwick's bedroom, and there is a textual basis, Blackmun thought, for protecting privacy in the home, as earlier cases made clear.

Constitutional Interpretation and the Limits of Privacy

The selection by Robert Bork raises important questions about the source, legitimacy, and scope of the constitutional right of privacy. Bork is concerned with what he (and others) see as the growing politicizing, or political involvement, of the courts: the pursuit by judges of a political agenda (usually liberal), which should be voted on by legislatures rather than inserted into the law by courts. Such "activism" threatens the legitimacy of the rule of law. Bork would have courts follow "the only thing that can be called law," namely, "the principles of the text, whether Constitution or statute, as generally understood at the time of enactment."[3] This is the premise of Bork's theory of constitutional interpretation, what he calls a jurisprudence of "original understanding."

Bork roundly criticizes Douglas's argument in *Griswold,* arguing that no number of specific constitutional freedoms, even including their "penumbras," add up to a distinct and general "right of privacy," a right that Douglas created and that, Bork alleges, hovers uncertainly over the only rights with a genuine constitutional basis. Bork repeatedly presses the question of what the right of privacy includes, given that it has no actual basis in the Constitution. He concludes that no major case in the Court's privacy jurisprudence has the support, by way of precedent, of anything in the constitutional text or in the holdings or of any of the earlier cases in the series. Each is a fresh act of judicial policy making, and this is nowhere more evident, Bork believes, than in Justice Blackmun's dissent in *Bowers.*

Elsewhere, Bork asserts that the privacy decisions, along with other "activist" holdings, violate three core requirements of permissible constitutional interpretation: that constitutional principles and rights be neutrally derived, defined, and applied.[4] Privacy is not neutrally derivable from the text but read into it by judges with a particular

---

[3] Bork, *The Tempting of America* (New York: Free Press, 1990), chap. 7.

[4] *Ibid.*, chap. 7.

moral bias. Nor has constitutional privacy been neutrally defined; indeed, its scope has not been defined at all. And at what level of generality should a right like that of privacy be understood and applied? Should it be viewed narrowly, following White in *Bowers?* Or should it be viewed expansively and at a higher level of generality or abstraction, as Blackmun urges? Because the right of privacy has not been neutrally derived from the Constitution to begin with, Bork reasons, it is no wonder that these questions have no answer.

Originalism

One important theory of constitutional interpretation has a long history. This is the view often referred to as a jurisprudence of "original understanding" or more simply "originalism." The basic idea behind originalism is fairly straightforward: The courts should always strive to interpret statutory and constitutional language by seeking to discover, resurrect, and apply the intent of the authors of the statute or of the Constitution. The search for authorial intent (which has its advocates elsewhere, for example, in literary theory), although requiring the gathering of historical evidence of various kinds, relies chiefly upon the language of the written text as the most important source of evidence regarding that intent.

Originalists defend their theory as a coherent and nonarbitrary interpretive methodology: The written text has an objective meaning that can be found, not made up. Originalists such as Bork insist that "there is a historical Constitution that was understood by those who enacted it to have a meaning of its own. The intended meaning has an existence independent of anything judges may say."[5] By deriving and applying this meaning, courts can settle problems that otherwise plague current constitutional decision making, for example, the difficulty of determining at what level of generality a constitutional principle or right is to be defined. Original understanding avoids the problem, Bork claims, by "finding the level of generality that interpretation of the words, structure, and his-

tory of the Constitution fairly supports."[6] Bork sums up the view this way: "What is the meaning of a rule . . . ? It is the meaning understood at the time of the law's enactment. . . . Law is a public act. Secret reservations and intentions count for nothing. All that counts is how the words used in the Constitution would have been understood at the time. The original understanding is thus manifested in the words used and in the secondary materials, such as debates at the conventions, public discussion, newspaper articles, dictionaries in use at the time, and the like."[7]

Originalism, as an interpretive methodology, raises a number of questions and has been subjected to a variety of criticisms. The theory says that we are to look for the original intent, the intent of the "authors" of the Constitution. But this hides a crucial problem. Who are the authors? The framers of the document, those who actually wrote it in Philadelphia? Or perhaps the adopters, the people in the various colonial conventions who voted to ratify the document? There are reasons for discounting either group. It is not clear why the intent of the framers, an elite group of wealthy property owners, unelected by anyone, should be privileged in this way, especially if one of the driving forces behind originalism is to square constitutional interpretation with democracy. On the other hand, people vote for things, including constitutions, with all manner of purposes and motives. What reason is there to think that the majority of New Yorkers who voted to ratify the Constitution expressed any uniform "intention" with regard to anything on which the Constitution speaks? These are the *epistemological* difficulties posed by originalism, that is, problems dealing with what we can know of the intentions of the authors of a statute or a constitution. How can we know the intent of people who lived so long ago? And even if we could unearth their thoughts, might we not find that they neither intended nor did not intend for (say) garbage to be private or for "creationism" to be taught, that is, that they simply never thought about the constitutionality of these matters at all?

Despite its problems, the originalist theory of constitutional interpretation is a response to a seri-

---

[5] Bork, *op. cit.,* p. 176.

[6] *Ibid.,* p. 150.
[7] *Ibid.,* p. 144.

ous difficulty: If we don't look to the intent of the drafters or framers of a statute or a constitution to give meaning to vague or open-ended language, what anchors a reading or an interpretation to the text at all? Can we permit judges or other constitutional interpreters to rely solely and directly upon their own value judgments in their role as interpreters? Or to appeal to the precepts of "natural law" or the principles of "correct moral reasoning"? To invoke America's "fundamental traditions"? To defer to public consensus or majoritarian sentiment? The basic difficulty with all these ways of reasoning within and from the Constitution is, according to the originalist, the same in every case: None yields any real constraint on the task of interpreting the Constitution because each can be employed or invoked to support almost any decision. Our "traditions" are many and various, the "correct" moral theory notoriously difficult to find, and the view of the majority often that which the constitutional language (particularly in the Bill of Rights) seeks to protect us against.

Supreme Court Justice Antonin Scalia provides a defense of originalism in our readings, arguing that it is the only theory of constitutional reasoning that is consistent with the concept of judicial review—the idea that the courts have the power to review and pass constitutional judgment upon the acts of other branches of government. Scalia discusses what he takes to be the two most basic challenges to originalism: knowing how to apply correctly the original meaning of a Constitutional provision, and accepting the consequences of pursuing originalism consistently. Despite these difficulties, Scalia maintains that the problems facing nonoriginalist methods of interpretation are so severe as to be irresolvable. "Nonoriginalism" does not refer to any coherent method for reasoning about the Constitution, Scalia thinks, and it is far too prone to reliance upon the judges' own values and beliefs.

Philosopher David Lyons takes a critical view of originalism from several angles. The appeal to original intent must be justified, Lyons asserts, since the meaning of a text such as the Constitution may differ from the meaning intended by its authors. But no convincing justification is forthcoming. Lyons reviews several explanations for reliance upon the author's intentions in reasoning about a legal text, but he finds them wanting. Since many terms in the Constitution are "open-textured," Lyons argues, the document may be understandable only by appeal to arguments that go outside its "strict linguistic implications."

---

19. *Griswold v. Connecticut*

Douglas, [Justice].

Appellant Griswold is Executive Director of the Planned Parenthood League of Connecticut. Appellant Buxton is a licensed physician and a professor at the Yale Medical School who served as Medical Director for the League at its Center in New Haven—a center open and operating from

381 U.S. 479 (1965)
United States Supreme Court

November 1 to November 10, 1961, when appellants were arrested.

They gave information, instruction, and medical advice to *married persons* as to the means of preventing conception. They examined the wife and prescribed the best contraceptive device or material for her use. Fees were usually charged, although some couples were serviced free.

The statutes whose constitutionality is involved in this appeal are §§53-32 and 54-196 of the General Statutes of Connecticut (1958 rev.). The former provides: "Any person who uses any drug, medicinal article or instrument for the purpose of preventing conception shall be fined not less than fifty dollars or imprisoned not less than sixty days nor more than one year or be both fined and imprisoned."

Section 54-196 provides: "Any person who assists, abets, counsels, causes, hires or commands another to commit any offense may be prosecuted and punished as if he were the principal offender."

The appellants were found guilty as accessories and fined $100 each, against the claim that the accessory statute as so applied violated the Fourteenth Amendment. The Appellate Division of the Circuit Court affirmed. The Supreme Court of Errors affirmed that judgment. We noted probably jurisdiction. . . .

Coming to the merits, we are met with a wide range of questions that implicate the Due Process Clause of the Fourteenth Amendment. Overtones of some arguments suggest that *Lochner v. New York* should be our guide. But we decline that invitation. . . . We do not sit as a superlegislature to determine the wisdom, need, and propriety of laws that touch economic problems, business affairs, or social conditions. This law, however, operates directly on an intimate relation of husband and wife and their physician's role in one aspect of that relation.

The association of people is not mentioned in the Constitution nor in the Bill of Rights. The right to educate a child in a school of the parents' choice—whether public or private or parochial—is also not mentioned. Nor is the right to study any particular subject or any foreign language. Yet the First Amendment has been construed to include certain of those rights.

By *Pierce v. Society of Sisters* the right to educate one's children as one chooses is made applicable to the States by the force of the First and Fourteenth Amendments. By *Meyer v. Nebraska* the same dignity is given the right to study the German language in a private school. In other words, the State may not consistently with the spirit of the First Amendment, contract the spectrum of available knowledge. The right of freedom of speech and press includes not only the right to utter or to print, but the right to distribute, the right to receive, the right to read and freedom of inquiry, freedom of thought, and freedom to teach—indeed the free-

dom of the entire university community. Without those peripheral rights the specific rights would be less secure. And so we reaffirm the principle of the *Pierce* and the *Meyer* cases.

In *NAACP v. Alabama*, 357 U.S. 449 (1958), we protected the "freedom to associate and privacy in one's associations," noting that freedom of association was a peripheral First Amendment right. Disclosure of membership lists of a constitutionally valid association, we held, was invalid, "as entailing the likelihood of a substantial restraint upon the exercise by petitioner's members of their right to freedom of association." In other words, the First Amendment has a penumbra where privacy is protected from governmental intrusion. In like context, we have protected forms of "association" that are not political in the customary sense but pertain to the social, legal, and economic benefit of the members. *NAACP v. Button* 371 U.S. 415 (1963). In *Schware v. Board of Bar Examiners*, 353 U.S. 232 (1957), we held it not permissible to bar a lawyer from practice, because he had once been a member of the Communist Party. . . .

Those cases involved more than the "right of assembly"—a right that extends to all irrespective of their race or ideology. The right of "association," like the right of belief, is more than the right to attend a meeting; it includes the right to express one's attitudes or philosophies by membership in a group or by affiliation with it or by other lawful means. Association in that context is a form of expression of opinion; and while it is not expressly included in the First Amendment its existence is necessary in making the express guarantees fully meaningful.

The foregoing cases suggest that specific guarantees in the Bill of Rights have penumbras, formed by emanations from those guarantees that help give them life and substance. . . . Various guarantees create zones of privacy. The right of association contained in the penumbra of the First Amendment is one, as we have seen. The Third Amendment in its prohibition against the quartering of soldiers "in any house" in time of peace without the consent of the owner is another facet of that privacy. The Fourth Amendment explicitly affirms the "right of the people to be secure in their persons, houses, papers, and effects, against unreasonable searches and seizures." The Fifth Amendment in its Self-Incrimination Clause enables the citizen to create a zone of privacy under which government may not force him to surrender to his detriment. The Ninth Amendment provides: "The enumeration in the Constitution, of certain rights, shall not be construed to deny or disparage others retained by the people."

The Fourth and Fifth Amendments were described in *Boyd v. United States*, 116 U.S. 616 (1886), as protection against all governmental invasions "of the sanctity of a man's home and the privacies of life." We recently referred . . . to the Fourth Amendment as creating a "right to privacy, no less important than any other right carefully and particularly reserved to the people." . . .

The present case, then, concerns a relationship lying within the zone of privacy created by several fundamental constitutional guarantees. And it concerns a law which, in forbidding the use of contraceptives rather than regulating their manufacture or sale, seeks to achieve its goals by means having a maximum destructive impact upon that relationship. Such a law cannot stand in light of the familiar principle, so often applied by this Court, that a "governmental purpose to control or prevent activities constitutionally subject to state regulation may not be achieved by means which sweep unnecessarily broadly and thereby invade the area of protected freedoms." . . . Would we allow the police to search the sacred precincts of marital bedrooms for telltale signs of the use of contraceptives? The very idea is repulsive to the notions of privacy surrounding the marriage relationship.

We deal with a right of privacy older than the Bill of Rights—older than our political parties, older than our school system. Marriage is a coming together for better or for worse, hopefully enduring, and intimate to the degree of being sacred. It is an association that promotes a way of life, not causes; a harmony in living, not political faiths; a bilateral loyalty, not commercial or social projects. Yet it is an association for as noble a purpose as any involved in our prior decisions.

Reversed.

Goldberg, [Justice], joined by Warren, [Chief Justice], and Brennan, [Justice], concurring.

I agree with the Court that Connecticut's birth-control law unconstitutionally intrudes upon the right of marital privacy, and I join in its opinion

and judgment. Although I have not accepted the view that "due process" as used in the Fourteenth Amendment incorporates all of the first eight Amendments, I do agree that the concept of liberty protects those personal rights that are fundamental, and is not confined to the specific terms of the Bill of Rights. My conclusion that the concept of liberty is not so restricted and that it embraces the right of marital privacy though that right is not mentioned explicitly in the Constitution is supported . . . by the language and history of the Ninth Amendment. . . .

The Ninth Amendment . . . was proffered to quiet expressed fears that a bill of specifically enumerated rights could not be sufficiently broad to cover all essential rights and that the specific mention of certain rights would be interpreted as a denial that others were protected. . . . [T]he Framers did not intend that the first eight amendments be construed to exhaust the basic and fundamental rights which the Constitution guaranteed to the people.

. . . To hold that a right so basic and fundamental and so deep-rooted in our society as the right of privacy in marriage may be infringed because that right is not guaranteed in so many words by the first eight amendments to the Constitution is to ignore the Ninth Amendment and to give it no effect whatsoever. . . .

I do not mean to imply that the Ninth Amendment is applied against the States by the Fourteenth. Nor do I mean to state that the Ninth Amendment constitutes an independent source of rights protected from infringement by either the States or the Federal Government. Rather the Ninth Amendment simply lends strong support to the view that the "liberty" protected by the Fifth and Fourteenth Amendments from infringement by the Federal Government or the States is not restricted to rights specifically mentioned in the first eight amendments. . . .

In determining which rights are fundamental, judges are not left at large to decide cases in light of their personal and private notions. Rather, they must look to the "traditions and [collective] conscience of our people" to determine whether a principle is "so rooted [there] . . . as to be ranked as fundamental." The inquiry is whether a right involved "is of such a character that it cannot be denied without violating those 'fundamental principles of liberty and justice which lie at the base of all our civil and political institutions.'"

The entire fabric of the Constitution and the purposes that clearly underlie its specific guarantees demonstrate that the rights to marital privacy and to marry and raise a family are of similar order and magnitude as the fundamental rights specifically protected.

Although the Constitution does not speak in so many words of the right of privacy in marriage, I cannot believe that it offers these fundamental rights no protection. The fact that no particular provision of the Constitution explicitly forbids the State from disrupting the traditional relation of the family—a relation as old and as fundamental as our entire civilization—surely does not show that the Government was meant to have the power to do so. . . .

The logic of the dissents would sanction federal or state legislation that seems to me even more plainly unconstitutional than the statute before us. Surely the Government, absent a showing of a compelling subordinating state interest, could not decree that all husbands and wives must be sterilized after two children have been born to them. Yet by their reasoning such an invasion of marital privacy would not be subject to constitutional challenge because, while it might be "silly," no provision of the Constitution specifically prevents the Government from curtailing the marital right to bear children and raise a family. . . .

In a long series of cases this Court has held that where fundamental personal liberties are involved, they may not be abridged by the States simply on a showing that a regulatory statute has some rational relationship to the effectuation of a proper state purpose. "Where there is a significant encroachment upon personal liberty, the State may prevail only upon showing a subordinating interest which is compelling." . . . The law must be shown "necessary, and not merely rationally related, to the accomplishment of a permissible state policy." . . .

Although the Connecticut birth-control law obviously encroaches upon a fundamental personal liberty, the State does not show that the law serves any "subordinating [state] interest which is compelling" or that it is "necessary . . . to the accomplishment of a permissible state policy." The State, at most, argues that there is some rational relation between this statute and what is admittedly a legitimate subject of state concern—the discouraging of extra-marital relations. It says that preventing the use of birth-control devices by married persons helps prevent the indulgence by some in such extra-marital relations. The rationality of this justification is dubious, particularly in light of the admitted widespread availability to all persons in the State of Connecticut, unmarried as well as married, of birth-control devices for the prevention of disease, as distinguished from the prevention of conception. But, in any event, it is clear that the state interest in safeguarding marital fidelity can be served by a more discriminately tailored statute, which does not, like the present one, sweep unnecessarily broadly, reaching far beyond the evil sought to be dealt with and intruding upon the privacy of all married couples. . . . The State of Connecticut does have statutes, the constitutionality of which is beyond doubt, which prohibit adultery and fornication. These statutes demonstrate that means for achieving the same basic purpose of protecting marital fidelity are available to Connecticut without the need to "invade the area of protected freedoms." . . .

In sum, I believe that the right to privacy in the marital relation is fundamental and basic—a personal right "retained by the people" within the meaning of the Ninth Amendment. Connecticut cannot constitutionally abridge this fundamental right, which is protected by the Fourteenth Amendment from infringement by the States. I agree with the Court that petitioners' convictions must therefore be reversed.

. . .

Harlan, [Justice], concurring. . . .

In my view, the proper constitutional inquiry in this case is whether this Connecticut statute infringes the Due Process Clause of the Fourteenth Amendment because the enactment violates basic values "implicit in the concept of ordered liberty. . . ." For reasons state[d] at length in my dissenting opinion in *Poe v. Ullman* ([367 U.S. 487 {1961}], I believe that it does. While the relevant inquiry may be aided by resort to one or more of the provisions of the Bill of Rights, it is not dependent on them or any of their radiations. The Due Process Clause of the Fourteenth Amendment stands, in my opinion, on its own bottom.

. . .

White, [Justice], concurring. . . .

In my view, this Connecticut law as applied to married couples deprives them of "liberty" without due process of law, as that concept is used in the Fourteenth Amendment. I therefore concur in the judgment of the Court reversing these convictions under Connecticut's aiding and abetting statute. . . .

[T]his is not the first time this Court has had occasion to articulate that the liberty entitled to protection under the Fourteenth Amendment includes the right "to marry, establish a home and bring up children." . . . and "the liberty . . . to direct the upbringing and education of children," . . . and that these are among "the basic civil rights of man." . . . These decisions affirm that there is a "realm of family life which the state cannot enter" without substantial justification. . . . Surely the right invoked in this case, to be free of regulation of the intimacies of the marriage relationship, "come[s] to this Court with a momentum for respect lacking when appeal is made to liberties which derive merely from shifting economic arrangements." . . .

An examination of the justification offered, however, cannot be avoided by saying that the Connecticut anti-use statute invades a protected area of privacy and association or that it demeans the marriage relationship. The nature of the right invaded is pertinent, to be sure, for statutes regulating sensitive areas of liberty do, under the cases of this Court, require "strict scrutiny," *Skinner v. Oklahoma*, and "must be viewed in the light of less drastic means for achieving the same basic purpose." "Where there is a significant encroachment upon personal liberty, the State may prevail only upon showing a subordinating interest which is compelling." But such statutes, if reasonably necessary for the effectuation of a legitimate and substantial state interest, and not arbitrary or capricious in application, are not invalid under the Due Process Clause.

As I read the opinions of the Connecticut courts and the argument of Connecticut in this Court, the State claims but one justification for its anti-use statute. . . . [T]he statute is said to serve the State's policy against all forms of promiscuous or illicit sexual relationships, be they premarital or extramarital, concededly a permissible and legitimate legislative goal.

Without taking issue with the premise that the fear of conception operates as a deterrent to such relationships in addition to the criminal proscriptions Connecticut has against such conduct, I wholly fail to see how the ban on the use of contraceptives by married couples in any way reinforces the State's ban on illicit sexual relationships. Connecticut does not bar the importation or possession of contraceptive devices; they are not considered contraband material under state law, and their availability in that State is not seriously disputed. The only way Connecticut seeks to limit or control the availability of such devices is through its general aiding and abetting statute whose operation in this context has been quite obviously ineffective and whose most serious use has been against birth-control clinics rendering advice to married, rather than unmarried, persons. . . . Moreover, it would appear that the sale of contraceptives to prevent disease is plainly legal under Connecticut law.

In these circumstances one is rather hard pressed to explain how the ban on use by married persons in any way prevents use of such devices by persons engaging in illicit sexual relations and thereby contributes to the State's policy against such relationships. . . . At most the broad ban is of marginal utility to the declared objective. A statute limiting its prohibition on use to persons engaging in the prohibited relationship would serve the end posited by Connecticut in the same way, and with the same effectiveness, or ineffectiveness, as the broad antiuse statute under attack in this case. I find nothing in this record justifying the sweeping scope of this statute, with its telling effect on the freedoms of married persons, and therefore conclude that it deprives such persons of liberty without due process of law.

. . .

Black, [Justice], joined by Stewart, [Justice], dissenting. . . .

In order that there may be no room at all to doubt why I vote as I do, I feel constrained to add that the law is every bit as offensive to me as it is to my Brethren of the majority. . . . There is no single one of the graphic and eloquent strictures and criticisms fired at the policy of this Connecticut law either by the Court's opinion or by those of my concurring Brethren to which I cannot subscribe—except their conclusion that the evil qualities they see in the law make it unconstitutional. . . .

The Court talks about a constitutional "right of privacy" as though there is some constitutional provision or provisions forbidding any law ever to be passed which might abridge the "privacy" of individuals. But there is not. There are, of course, guarantees in certain specific constitutional provisions which are designed in part to protect privacy at certain times and places with respect to certain activities. Such, for example, is the Fourth Amendment's guarantee against "unreasonable searches and seizures." But I think it belittles that Amendment to talk about it as though it protects nothing but "privacy." . . .

One of the most effective ways of diluting or expanding a constitutionally guaranteed right is to substitute for the crucial word or words of a constitutional guarantee another word or words, more or less flexible and more or less restricted in meaning. . . . "Privacy" is a broad, abstract and ambiguous concept which can easily be shrunken in meaning but which can also, on the other hand, easily be interpreted as a constitutional ban against many things other than searches and seizures. . . . For these reasons I get nowhere in this case by talk about a constitutional "right of privacy" as an emanation from one or more constitutional provisions. I like my privacy as well as the next one, but I am nevertheless compelled to admit that government has a right to invade it unless prohibited by some specific constitutional provision. . . .

I discuss the due process and Ninth Amendment arguments together because on analysis they turn out to be the same thing—merely using different words to claim for this Court and the federal judiciary power to invalidate any legislative act which the judges find irrational, unreasonable or offensive. . . .

Of the cases on which my Brothers White and Goldberg rely so heavily, undoubtedly the reasoning of two of them supports their result here—as would that of a number of others which they do not bother to name. . . . The two they do cite and quote from, *Meyer v. Nebraska*, and *Pierce v. Society of Sisters*, were both decided in opinions by Mr. Justice McReynolds which elaborated the same natural law due process philosophy found in *Lochner v. New York*, one of the cases on which he relied in *Meyer*, along with such other long discredited decisions as, e.g., *Adkins v. Children's Hospital*. . . . Without expressing an opinion as to whether either of those cases reached a correct result in light of our later decisions applying the First Amendment to the States through the Fourteenth, I merely point out that the reasoning stated in *Meyer* and *Pierce* was the same natural law due process philosophy which many later opinions repudiated, and which I cannot accept. . . .

My Brother Goldberg has adopted the recent discovery that the Ninth Amendment as well as the Due Process Clause can be used by this Court as authority to strike down all state legislation which this court thinks violates "fundamental principles of liberty and justice," or is contrary to the "traditions and [collective] conscience of our people." He also states, without proof satisfactory to me, that in making decisions on this basis judges will not consider "their personal and private notions." One may ask how they can avoid considering them. Our Court certainly has no machinery with which to take a Gallup Poll. And the scientific miracles of this age have not yet produced a gadget which the Court can use to determine what traditions are rooted in the "[collective] conscience of our people." Moreover, one would certainly have to look far beyond the language of the Ninth Amendment to find that the Framers vested in this Court any such awesome veto powers over lawmaking, either by the States or by the Congress. . . . That Amendment was passed not to broaden the powers of this Court or any other department of "the General Government," but, as every student of history knows, to assure the people that the Constitution in all its provisions was intended to limit the Federal Government to the powers granted expressly or by necessary implication. . . .

The Due Process Clause with an "arbitrary and capricious" or "shocking to the conscience" formula was liberally used by this Court to strike down economic legislation in the early decades of this century, threatening, many people thought, the tranquility and stability of the Nation. That formula, based on subjective considerations of "natural justice," is no less dangerous when used to enforce this Court's view about personal rights than those about economic rights. . . .

20. Bowers v. Hardwick

Justice White delivered the opinion of the Court.

In August 1982, respondent Hardwick (hereafter respondent) was charged with violating the Georgia statute criminalizing sodomy by committing that act with another adult male in the bedroom of respondent's home. After a preliminary hearing, the District Attorney decided not to present the matter to the grand jury unless further evidence developed.

Respondent then brought suit in the Federal District Court, challenging the constitutionality of the statute insofar as it criminalized sodomy. He asserted that he was a practicing homosexual, that the Georgia sodomy statute, as administered by the defendants, placed him in imminent danger of arrest, and that the statute for several reasons violates the Federal Constitution. The District Court granted the defendants' motion to dismiss for failure to state a claim. . . .

A divided panel of the Court of Appeals for the Eleventh Circuit *reversed.*

. . .

. . . Relying on our decisions in *Griswold v. Connecticut*, 381 U.S. 479 . . . (1965); *Eisenstadt v. Baird*, 405 U.S. 438 . . . (1972); *Stanley v. Georgia*, 394 U.S. 557 . . . (1969); and *Roe v. Wade*, 410 U.S. 113 . . . (1973), the court went on to hold that the Georgia statute violated respondent's fundamental rights because his homosexual activity is a private and intimate association that is beyond the reach of state regulation by reason of the Ninth Amendment and the Due Process Clause of the Fourteenth Amendment.

. . . We agree with petitioner that the Court of Appeals erred, and hence reverse its judgment.

. . . This case does not require a judgment on whether laws against sodomy between consenting adults in general, or between homosexuals in par-

478 U.S. 186 (1986)
United States Supreme Court

ticular, are wise or desirable. It raises no question about the right or propriety of state legislative decisions to repeal their laws that criminalize homosexual sodomy, or of state-court decisions invalidating those laws on state constitutional grounds. The issue presented is whether the Federal Constitution confers a fundamental right upon homosexuals to engage in sodomy and hence invalidates the laws of the many States that still make such conduct illegal and have done so for a very long time. The case also calls for some judgment about the limits of the Court's role in carrying out its constitutional mandate.

We first register our disagreement with the Court of Appeals and with respondent that the Court's prior cases have construed the Constitution to confer a right of privacy that extends to homosexual sodomy and for all intents and purposes have decided this case. The reach of this line of cases was sketched in *Carey v. Population Services International*, 431 U.S. 678, 685 . . . (1977). *Pierce v. Society of Sisters*, 268 U.S. 510 . . . (1925), and *Meyer v. Nebraska*, 262 U.S. 390 . . . (1923), were described as dealing with child rearing and education; *Prince v. Massachusetts*, 321 U.S. 158 . . . (1944), with family relationships; *Skinner v. Oklahoma ex rel. Williamson*, 316 U.S. 535 . . . (1942), with procreation; *Loving v. Virginia*, 388 U.S. 1 . . . (1967), with marriage; *Griswold v. Connecticut, supra*, and *Eisenstadt v. Baird, supra*, with contraception; and *Roe v. Wade*, 410 U.S. 113 . . . (1973), with abortion. The latter three cases were interpreted as construing the Due Process Clause of the Fourteenth Amendment to confer a fundamental individual right to decide whether or not to beget or bear a child. . . .

Accepting the decisions in these cases and the above description of them, we think it evident that none of the rights announced in those cases bears any resemblance to the claimed constitutional right of homosexuals to engage in acts of sodomy that is asserted in this case. No connection between family, marriage, or procreation on the one hand and homosexual activity on the other has been demonstrated, either by the Court of Appeals or by respondent. Moreover, any claim that these cases nevertheless stand for the proposition that any kind of private sexual conduct between consenting adults is constitutionally insulated from state proscription is unsupportable. Indeed, the Court's opinion in *Carey* twice asserted that the privacy right, which the *Griswold* line of cases found to be one of the protections provided by the Due Process Clause, did not reach so far. . . .

Precedent aside, however, respondent would have us announce, as the Court of Appeals did, a fundamental right to engage in homosexual sodomy. This we are quite unwilling to do. It is true that despite the language of the Due Process Clauses of the Fifth and Fourteenth Amendments, which appears to focus only on the processes by which life, liberty, or property is taken, the cases are legion in which those Clauses have been interpreted to have substantive content, subsuming rights that to a great extent are immune from federal or state regulation or proscription. Among such cases are those recognizing rights that have little or no textual support in the constitutional language. *Meyer, Prince,* and *Pierce* fall in this category, as do the privacy cases from *Griswold* to *Carey.*

Striving to assure itself and the public that announcing rights not readily identifiable in the Constitution's text involves much more than the imposition of the Justices' own choice of values on the States and the Federal Government, the Court has sought to identify the nature of the rights qualifying for heightened judicial protection. In *Palko v. Connecticut,* 302 U.S. 319 . . . (1937), it was said that this category includes those fundamental liberties that are "implicit in the concept of ordered liberty," such that "neither liberty nor justice would exist if [they] were sacrificed." A different description of fundamental liberties appeared in *Moore v. East Cleveland,* 431 U.S. 494, 503 . . . (1977) (opinion of Powell, J.), where they are characterized as those liberties that are "deeply rooted in this Nation's history and tradition." . . .

It is obvious to us that neither of these formulations would extend a fundamental right to homosexuals to engage in acts of consensual sodomy. Proscriptions against that conduct have ancient roots. . . . Sodomy was a criminal offense at common law and was forbidden by the laws of the original thirteen States when they ratified the Bill of Rights. In 1868, when the Fourteenth Amendment was ratified, all but 5 of the 37 States in the Union had criminal sodomy laws. In fact, until 1961, all 50 States outlawed sodomy, and today, 24 States and the District of Columbia continue to provide criminal penalties for sodomy performed in private and between consenting adults. . . . Against this background, to claim that a right to engage in such conduct is "deeply rooted in this Nation's history and tradition" or "implicit in the concept of ordered liberty" is, at best, facetious.

. . . Nor are we inclined to take a more expansive view of our authority to discover new fundamental rights imbedded in the Due Process Clause. The Court is most vulnerable and comes nearest to illegitimacy when it deals with judge-made constitutional law having little or no cognizable roots in the language or design of the Constitution. That this is so was painfully demonstrated by the faceoff between the Executive and the Court in the 1930's, which resulted in the repudiation of much of the substantive gloss that the Court had placed on the Due Process Clauses of the Fifth and Fourteenth Amendments. There should be, therefore, great resistance to expand the substantive reach of those Clauses, particularly if it requires redefining the category of rights deemed to be fundamental. Otherwise, the Judiciary necessarily takes to itself further authority to govern the country without express constitutional authority. The claimed right pressed on us today falls far short of overcoming this resistance.

Respondent, however, asserts that the result should be different where the homosexual conduct occurs in the privacy of the home. He relies on *Stanley v. Georgia,* 394 U.S. 557 . . . (1969), where the Court held that the First Amendment prevents conviction for possessing and reading obscene material in the privacy of one's home: "If the First Amendment means anything, it means that a State has no business telling a man, sitting alone in his house, what books he may read or what films he may watch." . . .

Stanley did protect conduct that would not have been protected outside the home, and it partially prevented the enforcement of state obscenity laws; but the decision was firmly grounded in the

First Amendment. The right pressed upon us here has no similar support in the text of the Constitution, and it does not qualify for recognition under the prevailing principles for construing the Fourteenth Amendment. Its limits are also difficult to discern. Plainly enough, otherwise illegal conduct is not always immunized whenever it occurs in the home. Victimless crimes, such as the possession and use of illegal drugs, do not escape the law where they are committed at home. *Stanley* itself recognized that its holding offered no protection for the possession in the home of drugs, firearms, or stolen goods. . . . And if respondent's submission is limited to the voluntary sexual conduct between consenting adults, it would be difficult, except by fiat, to limit the claimed right to homosexual conduct while leaving exposed to prosecution adultery, incest, and other sexual crimes even though they are committed in the home. We are unwilling to start down that road.

. . . Even if the conduct at issue here is not a fundamental right, respondent asserts that there must be a rational basis for the law and that there is none in this case other than the presumed belief of a majority of the electorate in Georgia that homosexual sodomy is immoral and unacceptable. This is said to be an inadequate rationale to support the law. The law, however, is constantly based on notions of morality, and if all laws representing essentially moral choices are to be invalidated under the Due Process Clause, the courts will be very busy indeed. Even respondent makes no such claim, but insists that majority sentiments about the morality of homosexuality should be declared inadequate. We do not agree, and are unpersuaded that the sodomy laws of some 25 States should be invalidated on this basis.

Accordingly, the judgment of the Court of Appeals is

Reversed.

. . .

Justice Blackmun, with whom Justice Brennan, Justice Marshall, and Justice Stevens join, dissenting.

This case is no more about "a fundamental right to engage in homosexual sodomy," as the Court purports to declare, than *Stanley v. Georgia* . . . was about a fundamental right to watch obscene movies, or *Katz v. United States*, 389 U.S. 347 . . . (1967), was about a fundamental right to place

interstate bets from a telephone booth. Rather, this case is about "the most comprehensive of rights and the right most valued by civilized men," namely, "the right to be let alone." *Olmstead v. United States*, 277 U.S. 438, 478 . . . (1928) (Brandeis, [Justice], dissenting).

The statute at issue, Ga. Code Ann. § 16–6–2 (1984) denies individuals the right to decide for themselves whether to engage in particular forms of private, consensual sexual activity. The Court concludes that § 16–6–2 is valid essentially because "the laws of . . . many States . . . still make such conduct illegal and have done so for a very long time." . . . But the fact that the moral judgments expressed by statutes like § 16–6–2 may be "natural and familiar . . . ought not to conclude our judgment upon the question whether statutes embodying them conflict with the Constitution of the United States.'" *Roe v. Wade*, . . . (1973), quoting *Lochner v. New York*, 198 U.S. 45, 76 . . . (1905) (Holmes, J., dissenting). Like Justice Holmes, I believe that "[i]t is revolting to have no better reason for a rule of law than that so it was laid down in the time of Henry IV. It is still more revolting if the grounds upon which it was laid down have vanished long since, and the rule simply persists from blind imitation of the past." Holmes, "The Path of the Law," 10 *Harv. L. Rev.* 457, 469 (1897). I believe we must analyze Hardwick's claim in the light of the values that underlie the constitutional right to privacy. If that right means anything, it means that, before Georgia can prosecute its citizens for making choices about the most intimate aspects of their lives, it must do more than assert that the choice they have made is an "'abominable crime not fit to be named among Christians.'" . . .

I

In its haste to reverse the Court of Appeals and hold that the Constitution does not "confe[r] a fundamental right upon homosexuals to engage in sodomy," . . . the Court relegates the actual statute being challenged to a footnote and ignores the procedural posture of the case before it. A fair reading of the statute and of the complaint clearly reveals that the majority has distorted the question this case presents.

First, the Court's almost obsessive focus on homosexual activity is particularly hard to justify in light of the broad language Georgia has used. Unlike the Court, the Georgia Legislature has not proceeded on the assumption that homosexuals are so different from other citizens that their lives may be controlled in a way that would not be tolerated if it limited the choices of those other citizens. . . . Rather, Georgia has provided that "[a] person commits the offense of sodomy when he performs or submits to any sexual act involving the sex organs of one person and the mouth or anus of another." . . . The sex or status of the persons who engage in the act is irrelevant as a matter of state law. In fact, to the extent I can discern a legislative purpose for Georgia's 1968 enactment of §16–6–2, that purpose seems to have been to broaden the coverage of the law to reach heterosexual as well as homosexual activity. I therefore see no basis for the Court's decision to treat this case as an "as applied" challenge to §16–6–2 . . . or for Georgia's attempt, both in its brief and at oral argument, to defend §16–6–2 solely on the grounds that it prohibits homosexual activity. Michael Hardwick's standing may rest in significant part on Georgia's apparent willingness to enforce against homosexuals a law it seems not to have any desire to enforce against heterosexuals. . . . But his claim that §16–6–2 involves an unconstitutional intrusion into his privacy and his right of intimate association does not depend in any way on his sexual orientation.

. . .

II

"Our cases long have recognized that the Constitution embodies a promise that a certain private sphere of individual liberty will be kept largely beyond the reach of government." *Thornburgh v. American College of Obstetricians & Gynecologists*, 476 U.S. 747, 772 . . . (1986). In construing the right to privacy, the Court has proceeded along two somewhat distinct, albeit complementary, lines. First, it has recognized a privacy interest with reference to certain *decisions* that are properly for the individual to make. . . . Second, it has recognized a privacy interest with reference to certain *places* without regard for the particular activities in which the indi-

viduals who occupy them are engaged. . . . The case before us implicates both the decisional and the spatial aspects of the right to privacy.

A

The Court concludes today that none of our prior cases dealing with various decisions that individuals are entitled to make free of governmental interference "bears any resemblance to the claimed constitutional right of homosexuals to engage in acts of sodomy that is asserted in this case." . . . While it is true that these cases may be characterized by their connection to protection of the family, . . . the Court's conclusion that they extend no further than this boundary ignores the warning in *Moore v. East Cleveland* . . . (1977) (plurality opinion), against "clos[ing] our eyes to the basic reasons why certain rights associated with the family have been accorded shelter under the Fourteenth Amendment's Due Process Clause." We protect those rights not because they contribute, in some direct and material way, to the general public welfare, but because they form so central a part of an individual's life. . . . And so we protect the decision whether to marry precisely because marriage "is an association that promotes a way of life, not causes; a harmony in living, not political faiths; a bilateral loyalty, not commercial or social projects." *Griswold*. . . . We protect the decision whether to have a child because parenthood alters so dramatically an individual's self-definition, not because of demographic considerations or the Bible's command to be fruitful and multiply. . . . And we protect the family because it contributes so powerfully to the happiness of individuals, not because of a preference for stereotypical households. . . .

Only the most willful blindness could obscure the fact that sexual intimacy is "a sensitive, key relationship of human existence, central to family life, community welfare, and the development of human personality," *Paris Adult Theatre I v. Slaton*, 413 U.S. 49, 63 . . . (1973). . . . The fact that individuals define themselves in a significant way through their intimate sexual relationships with others suggests, in a Nation as diverse as ours, that there may be many "right" ways of conducting those relationships, and that much of the richness of a relationship will come from the freedom an individual has to *choose* the form and nature of these intensely personal bonds.

. . .

B

The behavior for which Hardwick faces prosecution occurred in his own home, a place to which the Fourth Amendment attaches special significance. The court's treatment of this aspect of the case is symptomatic of its overall refusal to consider the broad principles that have informed our treatment of privacy in specific cases. Just as the right to privacy is more than the mere aggregation of a number of entitlements to engage in specific behavior, so too, protecting the physical integrity of the home is more than merely a means of protecting specific activities that often take place there. Even when our understanding of the contours of the right to privacy depends on "reference to a 'place,'" . . . "the essence of a Fourth Amendment violation is 'not the breaking of [a person's] doors, and the rummaging of his drawers,' but rather is 'the invasion of his indefeasible right of personal security, personal liberty and private property.'" *California v. Ciraolo*, 476 U.S. 207, 226 . . . (1986) (Powell, [Justice], dissenting), quoting *Boyd v. United States*, 116 U.S. 616, 630 . . . (1886).

. . .

III

The Court's failure to comprehend the magnitude of the liberty interests at stake in this case leads it to slight the question whether petitioner, on behalf of the State, has justified Georgia's infringement on these interests. I believe that neither of the two general justifications for §16–6–2 that petitioner has advanced warrants dismissing respondent's challenge for failure to state a claim.

First, petitioner asserts that the acts made criminal by the statute may have serious adverse consequences for "the general public health and welfare," such as spreading communicable diseases or fostering other criminal activity. Inasmuch as this case was dismissed by the District Court on the pleadings, it is not surprising that the record before us is barren of any evidence to support petitioner's claims.

. . .

The core of petitioner's defense of §16–6–2, however, is that respondent and others who engage in the conduct prohibited by §16–6–2 interfere with Georgia's exercise of the "'right of the Nation and of the States to maintain a decent society.'"

. . .

. . . Essentially, petitioner argues, and the Court agrees, that the fact that the acts described in §16–6–2 "for hundreds of years, if not thousands, have been uniformly condemned as immoral" is a sufficient reason to permit a State to ban them today. . . .

I cannot agree that either the length of time a majority has held its convictions or the passions with which it defends them can withdraw legislation from this Court's scrutiny.

. . .

The assertion that "traditional Judeo-Christian values proscribe" the conduct involved . . . cannot provide an adequate justification for §16–6–2.

. . . That certain, but by no means all, religious groups condemn the behavior at issue gives the State no license to impose their judgments on the entire citizenry. The legitimacy of secular legislation depends instead on whether the State can advance some justification for its law beyond its conformity to religious doctrine.

. . .

21. *The Right of Privacy*

ROBERT BORK

The 1965 decision in *Griswold v. Connecticut*[1] was insignificant in itself but momentous for the future of constitutional law. Connecticut had an ancient statute making it criminal to use contraceptives. The state also had a general accessory statute allowing the punishment of any person who aided another in committing an offense. On its face, the statute criminalizing the use of contraceptives made no distinction between married couples and others. But the statute also had never been enforced against anyone who used contraceptives, married or not. There was, of course, no prospect that it ever would be enforced. If any Connecticut official had been mad enough to attempt enforcement, the law would at once have been removed from the books and the official from his office. Indeed, some Yale law professors had gotten the statute all the way to the Supreme Court a few years previously, and the Court had refused to decide it precisely because there was no showing that the law was ever enforced. The professors had some difficulty arranging a test case but finally managed to have two doctors who gave birth control information fined $100 apiece as accessories.

Such enforcement in the area as there was consisted of the occasional application of the accessory statute against birth control clinics, usually clinics that advertised. The situation was similar to the enforcement of many antigambling laws. They may cover all forms of gambling on their faces, but they are in fact enforced only against commercial gambling. An official who began arresting the priest at the church bingo party or friends having their monthly poker game at home would have made a most unwise career decision and would be quite

unlikely to get a conviction. There are a number of statutes like these in various state codes, such as the statutes flatly prohibiting sodomy and other "unnatural practices," which apply on their faces to all couples, married or unmarried, heterosexual or homosexual. The statutes are never enforced, but legislators, who would be aghast at any enforcement effort, nevertheless often refuse to repeal them.

There is a problem with laws like these. They are kept in the codebooks as precatory statements, affirmations of moral principle. It is quite arguable that this is an improper use of law, most particularly of criminal law, that statutes should not be on the books if no one intends to enforce them. It has been suggested that if anyone tried to enforce a law that had moldered in disuse for many years, the statute should be declared void by reason of desuetude or that the defendant should go free because the law had not provided fair warning.

But these were not the issues in *Griswold.* Indeed, getting off on such grounds was the last thing the defendants and their lawyers wanted. Since the lawyers had a difficult time getting the state even to fine two doctors as accessories, it seems obvious that the case was not arranged out of any fear of prosecution, and certainly not the prosecution of married couples. *Griswold* is more plausibly viewed as an attempt to enlist the Court on one side of one issue in a cultural struggle. Though the statute was originally enacted when the old Yankee culture dominated Connecticut politics, it was now quite popular with the Catholic hierarchy and with many lay Catholics whose religious values it paralleled. The case against the law was worked up by members of the Yale law school faculty and was supported by the Planned Parenthood Federation of America, Inc., the Catholic Council on Civil Liberties, and the American Civil Liberties Union. A ruling of unconstitutionality may have been sought as a statement that opposition to contraception is benighted and, therefore, a statement about whose cultural values are dominant. Be that as it may, the upshot was a new constitutional doctrine perfectly suited, and later used, to enlist the Court on the side of moral relativism in sexual matters.

Justice Douglas's majority opinion dealt with the case as if Connecticut had devoted itself to sexual fascism. "Would we allow the police to search the sacred precincts of marital bedrooms for telltale signs of the use of contraceptives? The very idea is repulsive to the notions of privacy surrounding the marriage relationship."[2] That was both true and entirely irrelevant to the case before the Court. Courts usually judge statutes by the way in which they are actually enforced, not by imagining horrible events that have never happened, never will happen, and could be stopped by courts if they ever seemed about to happen. Just as in *Skinner* he had treated a proposal to sterilize three-time felons as raising the specter of racial genocide, Douglas raised the stakes to the sky here by treating Connecticut as though it was threatening the institution of marriage. "We deal with a right of privacy older than the Bill of Rights—older than our political parties, older than our school system." The thought was incoherent. What the right of privacy's age in comparison with that of our political parties and school system had to do with anything was unclear, and where the "right" came from if not from the Bill of Rights it is impossible to understand. No court had ever invalidated a statute on the basis of the right Douglas described. That makes it all the more perplexing that Douglas in fact purported to derive the right of privacy not from some pre-existing right or law of nature, but from the Bill of Rights. It is important to understand Justice Douglas's argument both because the method, though without merit, continually recurs in constitutional adjudication and because the "right of privacy" has become a loose canon in the law. Douglas began by pointing out that "specific guarantees in the Bill of Rights have penumbras, formed by emanations from those guarantees that help give them life and substance." There is nothing exceptional about that thought, other than the language of penumbras and emanations. Courts often give protection to a constitutional freedom by creating a buffer zone, by prohibiting a government from doing something not in itself forbidden but likely to lead to an inva-

sion of a right specified in the Constitution. Douglas cited *NAACP v. Alabama*,[3] in which the Supreme Court held that the state could not force the disclosure of the organization's membership lists since that would have a deterrent effect upon the members' first amendment rights of political and legal action. That may well have been part of the purpose of the statute. But for this anticipated effect upon guaranteed freedoms, there would be no constitutional objection to the required disclosure of membership. The right not to disclose had no life of its own independent of the rights specified in the first amendment.

Douglas named the buffer zone or "penumbra" of the first amendment a protection of "privacy," although, in *NAACP v. Alabama*, of course, confidentiality of membership was required not for the sake of individual privacy but to protect the public activities of politics and litigation. Douglas then asserted that other amendments create "zones of privacy." These were the first, third (soldiers not to be quartered in private homes), fourth (ban on unreasonable searches and seizures), and fifth (freedom from self-incrimination). There was no particularly good reason to use the word "privacy" for the freedoms cited, except for the fact that the opinion was building toward those "sacred precincts of marital bedrooms." The phrase "areas of freedom" would have been more accurate since the provisions cited protect both private and public behavior.

None of the amendments cited, and none of their buffer or penumbral zones, covered the case before the Court. The Connecticut statute was not invalid under any provision of the Bill of Rights, no matter how extended. Since the statute in question did not threaten any guaranteed freedom, it did not fall within any "emanation." *Griswold v. Connecticut* was, therefore, not like *NAACP v. Alabama*. Justice Douglas bypassed that seemingly insuperable difficulty by simply asserting that the various separate "zones of privacy" created by each separate provision of the Bill of Rights somehow created a general but wholly undefined "right of privacy" that is independent of and lies outside any right or "zone of privacy" to be found in the Constitution. Douglas did not explain how it was that the Framers created five or six specific rights that could, with considerable stretching, be called "privacy," and, though the

Framers chose not to create more, the Court could nevertheless invent a general right of privacy that the Framers had, inexplicably, left out. It really does not matter to the decision what the Bill of Rights covers or does not cover.

Douglas closed the *Griswold* opinion with a burst of passionate oratory. "Marriage is a coming together for better or for worse, hopefully enduring, and intimate to the degree of being sacred. It is an association that promotes a way of life, not causes; a harmony in living, not political faiths; a bilateral loyalty, not commercial or social projects. Yet it is an association for as noble a purpose as any involved in our prior decisions."[4] It is almost a matter for regret that Connecticut had not threatened the institution of marriage, or even attempted to prevent anyone from using contraceptives, since that left some admirable sentiments, expressed with rhetorical fervor, dangling irrelevantly in mid-air. But the protection of marriage was not the point of *Griswold*. The creation of a new device for judicial power to remake the Constitution was the point.

The *Griswold* opinion, of course, began by denying that any such power was being assumed. "[W]e are met with a wide range of questions that implicate the Due Process Clause of the 14th Amendment. Overtones of some arguments suggest that [*Lochner v. New York*] should be our guide. But we decline that invitation. . . . We do not sit as a super-legislature to determine the wisdom, need, and propriety of laws that touch economic problems, business affairs, or social conditions."[5] *Griswold*, as an assumption of judicial power unrelated to the Constitution is, however, indistinguishable from *Lochner*. And the nature of that power, its lack of rationale or structure, ensured that it could not be confined.

The Court majority said there was now a right of privacy but did not even intimate an answer to the question, "Privacy to do what?" People often take addictive drugs in private, some men physically abuse their wives and children in private, executives conspire to fix prices in private, Mafiosi confer with their button men in private. If these sound bizarre, one professor at a prominent law school has suggested that the right of privacy may create a right to engage in prostitution. Moreover,

as we shall see, the Court has extended the right of privacy to activities that can in no sense be said to be done in private. The truth is that "privacy" will turn out to protect those activities that enough Justices to form a majority think ought to be protected and not activities with which they have little sympathy.

If one called the zones of the separate rights of the Bill of Rights zones of "freedom," which would be more accurate, then, should one care to follow Douglas's logic, the zones would add up to a general right of freedom independent of any provision of the Constitution. A general right of freedom—a constitutional right to be free of regulation by law—is a manifest impossibility. Such a right would posit a state of nature, and its law would be that of the jungle. If the Court had created a general "right of freedom," we would know at once, therefore, that the new right would necessarily be applied selectively, and, if we were given no explanation of the scope of the new right, we would know that the "right" was nothing more than a warrant judges had created for themselves to do whatever they wished. That, as we shall see in the next chapter, is precisely what happened with the new, general, undefined, and unexplained "right of privacy."

Justice Black's dissent stated: "I like my privacy as well as the next one, but I am nevertheless compelled to admit that government has a right to invade it unless prohibited by some specific constitutional provision."[6] He found none. "The Court talks about a constitutional 'right of privacy' as though there is some constitutional provision or provisions forbidding any law ever to be passed which might abridge the 'privacy' of individuals. But there is not." He pointed out that there are "certain specific constitutional provisions which are designed in part to protect privacy at certain times and places with respect to certain activities." But there was no general right of the sort Douglas had created. Justice Stewart's dissent referred to the statute as "an uncommonly silly law" but noted that its asininity was not before the Court.[7] He could "find no such general right of privacy in the Bill of Rights, in any other part of the Constitution, or in any case ever before decided by this Court." He also observed that the "Court does not say how far the new constitutional right of privacy announced today extends." That was twenty-four years ago, and the Court still has not told us.

. . .

Endnotes

[1] 381 U.S. 479 (1965).

[2] *Id.* at 485–86.

[3] 357 U.S. 449 (1958).

[4] 381 U.S. at 486.

[5] *Ibid.* at 481–482.

[6] [*Ibid.*] at 507, 508, 510 (Black, [Justice], dissenting).

[7] [*Ibid.*] at 527, 530 n. 7 (Stewart, [Justice], dissenting).

---

22. *Originalism: The Lesser Evil*

Antonin Scalia

. . .

It may surprise the layman, but it will surely not surprise the lawyers here, to learn that originalism is not, and had perhaps never been, the sole method of constitutional exegesis. It would be hard to count on the fingers of both hands and the toes of both feet, yea, even on the hairs of one's youthful head, the opinions that have in fact been rendered not on the basis of what the Constitution originally meant, but on the basis of what the judges currently thought it desirable for it to mean. That is, I suppose, the sort of behavior Chief Justice Hughes was referring to when he said the Constitution is what the judges say it is. But in the past, nonoriginalist opinions have almost always had the decency to lie, or at least to dissemble, about what they are doing—either ignoring strong evidence of original intent that contradicted the minimal recited evidence of an original intent congenial to the court's desires, or else not discussing original intent at all, speaking in terms of broad constitutional generalities with no pretense of historical support. . . The latter course was adopted, to sweep away [Justice] Taft's analysis in Humphrey's Executor, which announced the novel concept of constitutional powers that are neither legislative, nor executive, nor judicial, but "quasi-legislative" and quasi-judicial." It is only in relatively recent years, however, that nonoriginalist exegesis has, so to speak, come out of the closet, and put itself forward overtly as an intellectually legitimate device. To be sure, in support of its venerability as a legitimate interpretive theory there is often trotted out John Marshall's statement in McCulloch v. Maryland that "we must never forget it is a constitution we are expounding"—as though the implication of that statement was that our interpretation must change from age to age. But that is a canard. The real implication was quite the opposite: Marshall was saying that the Constitution had to be interpreted generously because the powers conferred upon Congress under it had to be broad enough to serve not only the needs of the federal government originally discerned but also the needs that might arise in the future. If constitutional interpretation could be adjusted as changing circumstances required, a broad initial interpretation would have been unnecessary.

Those who have not delved into the scholarly writing on constitutional law for several years may be unaware of the explicitness with which many prominent and respected commentators reject the original meaning of the Constitution as an authoritative guide. Harvard Professor Laurence H. Tribe, for example, while generally conducting his constitutional analysis under the rubric of the open-ended textual provisions such as the Ninth Amendment, does not believe that the originally understood content of those provisions has much to do with how they are to be applied today. The Constitution, he has written, "invites us, and our judges, to expand on the . . . freedoms that are uniquely our heritage,"[3] and "invites a collaborative inquiry, involving both the Court and the country, into the contemporary content of freedom, fairness, and fraternity."[4] Stanford Dean Paul Brest, having (in his own words) "abandoned both consent and fidelity to the text and original understanding as the touchstones of constitutional decisionmaking,[5] concludes that "the practice of constitutional decisionmaking should enforce those, but only those, values that are fundamental to our society.[6] While Brest believes that the "text," "original understanding," "custom," "social practices," "conventional morality, " and "precedent" all strongly inform the determination of those values, the conclusions drawn from all these sources are "defensible in the light of changing public values."[7] Yale Professor Owen Fiss asserts that , whatever the Constitution might originally have meant, the courts should give "concrete meaning and application" to those values that "give our society an identity and inner coherence [and] its distinctive public morality."[8] Oxford Professor (and expatriate American) Ronald Dworkin calls for "a fusion of constitutional law and moral theory."[9] Harvard Professor Richard Parker urges, somewhat more specifically, that constitutional law "take seriously and work from (while no doubt revising) the classical conception of a republic, including its elements of relative equality, mobilization of citizenry, and civic virtue."[10] More specifically still, New York University Professor David Richards suggests that it would be desirable for the courts' constitutional decisions to follow the contractarian moral theory set forth in Professor John Rawls' treatise, A Theory of Justice.[11] And I could go on.

The principal theoretical defect of nonoriginalism, in my view, is its incompatibility with the very principle that legitimizes judicial review of constitutionality. Nothing in the text of the Constitution confers upon the courts the power to inquire into, rather than passively assume, the constitutionality of federal statutes. That power is, however, reasonably implicit because, as Marshall said in *Marbury v. Madison*, (1) "[i]t is emphatically the province and duty of the judicial department to say what the law is, "(2)" [i]f two laws conflict with each other the courts must decide on the operation of each," and (3) "the constitution is to be considered, in court, as a paramount law." Central to that analysis, it seems to me, is the perception that the Constitution, though it has an effect superior to other laws, is in its nature the sort of "law" that is the business of the courts—an enactment that has a fixed meaning ascertainable through the usual devices familiar to those learned in the law. If the Constitution were not that sort of a "law," but a novel invitation to apply current societal values, what reason would there be to believe that the invitation was addressed to the courts rather than to the legislature? One simply cannot say, regarding that sort of novel enactment, that "[i]t is emphatically the province and duty of the judicial department" to determine its content. Quite to the contrary, the legislature would seem a much more appropriate expositor of social values, and its determination that a statute is compatible with the Constitution should, as in England, prevail.

Apart from the frailty of its theoretical underpinning, nonoriginalism confronts a practical difficulty reminiscent of the truism of elective politics that "You can't beat somebody with nobody." It is not enough to demonstrate that the other fellow's candidate (originalism) is no good; one must also agree upon another candidate to replace him. Just as it is not very meaningful for a voter to vote "non-Reagan," it is not very helpful to tell a judge to be a "non-originalist." If the law is to make any attempt at consistency and predictability, surely there must be general agreement not only that judges reject one exegetical approach (originalism), but that they adopt another. And it is hard to discern any emerging consensus among the nonoriginalists as to what this might be. Are the "fundamental values" that replace original meaning to be derived from the philosophy of Plato, or of Locke, or Mills, or Rawls, or perhaps from the latest Gallup poll? This is not to say that originalists are in entire agreement as to what the nature of their methodology is; as I shall mention shortly, there are some significant differences. But as its name suggests, it by and large represents a coherent approach, or at least an agreed-upon point of departure. As the name "nonoriginalism" suggests (and I know no other, more precise term by which this school of exegesis can be described), it represents agreement on nothing except what is the wrong approach.

Finally, I want to mention what is not a defect of nonoriginalism, but one of its supposed benefits that seems to me illusory. A bit earlier I quoted one of the most prominent nonoriginalists, Professor Tribe, to the effect that the Constitution "invites us, and our judges, to expand on the . . . freedoms that are uniquely our heritage."[12] I think it fair to say that that is a common theme of nonoriginalists in general. But why, one may reasonably ask—once the original import of the Constitution is cast aside to be replaced by the "fundamental values" of the current society—why are we invited only to "expand on" freedoms, and not to contract them as well? Last Term we decided a case, *Coy v. Iowa*,[13] in which, at the trial of a man accused of taking indecent liberties with two young girls, the girls were permitted to testify separated from the defendant by a screen which prevented them from seeing him. We held that, at least absent a specific finding that these particular witnesses needed such protection, this procedure violated that provision of the Sixth Amendment that assures a criminal defendant the right "to be confronted with the witnesses against him." Let us hypothesize, however (a hypothesis that may well be true), that modern American society is much more conscious of, and averse to, the effects of "emotional trauma" than was the society of 1791, and that it is, in addition, much more concerned about the emotional frailty of children and sensitivity of young women regarding sexual abuse. If that is so, and if the nonoriginalists are right, would it not have been possible for the Court to hold that, even though in 1791 the confrontation clause clearly would not have permitted a blanket exception for such testimony, it does so today? Such a holding, of course, could hardly be characterized as an "expansion upon" preexisting freedoms. Or let me give another example that is already history: I think it

highly probable that over the past two hundred years the Supreme Court, though not avowedly under the banner of "non-originalist" interpretation, has in fact narrowed the contract clause of the Constitution well short of its original meaning. Perhaps were all content with that development— but can it possibly be asserted that it represented an expansion, rather than a contraction, of individual liberties? Our modern society is undoubtedly not as enthusiastic about economic liberties as were the men and women of 1789; but we should not fool ourselves into believing that because we like the result the result does not represent a contraction of liberty. Nonoriginalism, in other words, is a two-way street that handles traffic both to and from individual rights.

Let me turn next to originalism, which is also not without its warts. Its greatest defect, in my view, is the difficulty of applying it correctly. Not that I agree with, or even take very seriously, the intricately elaborated scholarly criticisms to the effect that (believe it or not) words have no meaning. They have meaning enough, as the scholarly critics themselves must surely believe when they choose to express their views in text rather than music. But what is true is that it is often exceedingly difficult to plumb the original understanding of an ancient text. Properly done, the task requires the consideration of an enormous mass of material—in the case of the Constitution and its Amendments, for example, to mention only one element, the records of the ratifying debates in all the states. Even beyond that, it requires an evaluation of the reliability of that material—many of the reports of the ratifying debates, for example, are thought to be quite unreliable. And further still, it requires immersing oneself in the political and intellectual atmosphere of the time—somehow placing out of mind knowledge that we have which an earlier age did not, and putting on beliefs, attitudes, philosophies, prejudices and loyalties that are not those of our day. It is, in short, a task sometimes better suited to the historian than the lawyer.

Nowadays, of course, the Supreme Court does not give itself much time to decide cases. . . Except in those very rare instances in which a case is set for reargument, the case will be decided in the same Term in which it is first argued—allowing at best the period between the beginning of October and the end of June, and at worst the period between the end of April and the end of June. . . .

. . .

I can [now describe] what seems to me the second most serious objection to originalism: In its undiluted form, at least, it is medicine that seems too strong to swallow. Thus, almost every originalist would adulterate it with the doctrine of *stare decisis*—so that *Marbury* v. *Madison* would stand even if Professor Raoul Berger should demonstrate unassailably that it got the meaning of the Constitution wrong. (Of course recognizing *stare decisis* is seemingly even more incompatible with nonoriginalist theory: If the most solemnly and democratically adopted text of the Constitution and its Amendments can be ignored on the basis of current values, what possible basis could there be for enforced adherence to a legal decision of the Supreme Court?) But *stare decisis* alone is not enough to prevent originalism from being what many would consider too bitter a pill. What if some state should enact a new law providing public lashing, or branding of the right hand, as punishment for certain criminal offenses? Even if it could be demonstrated unequivocally that these were not cruel and unusual measures in 1791, and even though no prior Supreme Court decision had specifically disapproved them, I doubt whether any federal judge— even among the many who consider themselves originalists—world sustain them against an eighth amendment challenge. It may well be, as Professor Henry Monaghan persuasively argues, that this cannot legitimately be reconciled with originalist philosophy—that it represents the unrealistic view of the Constitution as a document intended to create a perfect society for all ages to come, whereas in fact it was a political compromise that did not pretend to create a perfect society even for its own age (as its toleration of slavery, which a majority of the founding generation recognized as an evil, well enough demonstrates).[14] Even so, I am confident that public flogging and handbranding would not be sustained by our courts, and any espousal of originalism as a practical theory of exegesis must somehow come to terms with that reality.

One way of doing so, of course, would be to say that it was originally intended that the cruel and unusual punishment clause would have an evolving content—that "cruel and unusual" originally meant "cruel and unusual for the age in ques-

tion" and not "cruel and unusual in 1791." But to be faithful to originalist philosophy, one must not only say this but demonstrate it to be so on the basis of some textual or historical evidence. Perhaps the mere words "cruel and unusual" suggest an evolutionary intent more than other provisions of the Constitution, but that is far from clear; and I know of no historical evidence for that meaning. And if the faint-hearted originalist is willing simply to posit such an intent for the "cruel and unusual punishment" clause, why not for the due process clause, the privileges and immunity clause, etc? When one goes down that road, there is really no difference between the faint-hearted originalist and the moderate nonoriginalist, except that the former finds it comforting to make up (out of whole cloth) and original evolutionary intent, and the latter thinks that superflous. It is, I think, that the fact that most originalists are faint-hearted and most nonoriginalists are moderate (that is, would not ascribe evolving content to such clear provisions as the requirement that the President be no less than thirty-five years of age) which accounts for the fact that the sharp divergence between the two philosophies does not produce an equivalently sharp divergence in judicial opinions.

Having described what I consider the principal difficulties with the originalist and nonoriginalist approaches, I suppose I owe it to the listener to say which of the two evils I prefer. It is originalism. I take the need for theoretical legitimacy seriously, and even if one assumes (as many nonoriginalists do not even bother to do) that the Constitution was originally meant to expound evolving rather than permanent values, as I discussed earlier I see no basis for believing that supervision of the evolution would have been committed to the courts. At an even more general theoretical level, originalism seems to me more compatible with the nature and purpose of a Constitution in a democratic system. A democratic society does not, by and large, need constitutional guarantees to insure that its laws will reflect "current cultures." Elections take care of that quite well. The purpose of constitutional guarantees— and in particular those constitutional guarantees of individual rights that are at the center of this controversy—is precisely to prevent the law from reflecting certain changes in original values that the society adopting the Constitution thinks fun-

damentally undesirable. Or, more precisely, to require the society to devote to the subject the long
and hard consideration required for a constitutional amendment before those particular values
can be cast aside.

I also think that the central practical defect of
nonoriginalism is fundamental and irreparable: the
impossibility of achieving any consensus on what,
precisely, is to replace original meaning, once that is
abandoned. The practical defects of originalism, on
the other hand, while genuine enough, seem to me
less severe. While it may indeed be unrealistic to
have substantial confidence that judges and lawyers
will find the correct historical answer to such refined questions of original intent as the precise content of "the executive Power," for the vast majority
of questions the answer is clear. The death penalty,
for example, was not cruel and unusual punishment because it is referred to in the Constitution
itself: and the right of confrontation by its plain language meant, at least, being face-to-face with
person testifying against one at trial. For the nonoriginalist, even these are open questions. As for the
fact that originalism is strong medicine, and that
one cannot realistically expect judges (probably myself included) to apply it without a trace of constitutional perfectionism: I suppose I must respond that
this is a world in which nothing is flawless, and fall
back upon G. K. Chesterton's observation that a
thing worth doing is worth doing badly.

It seems to me, moreover, that the practical defects of originalism are defects more appropriate
for the task at hand—that is, less likely to aggravate
the most significant weakness of the system of judicial review and more likely to produce results acceptable to all. If one is hiring a reference-room
librarian, and has two applicants, between whom
the only substantial difference is that the one's normal conversational tone tends to be too loud and
the other's too soft, it is pretty clear which of the
imperfections should be preferred. Now the main
danger in judicial interpretation of the Constitution—or, for that matter, in judicial interpretation of
any law—is that the judges will mistake their own
predilections for the law. Avoiding this error is the
hardest part of being a conscientious judge; perhaps no conscientious judge ever succeeds entirely.
Nonoriginalism, which under one or another formulation invokes "fundamental values" as the
touchstone of constitutionality, plays precisely to

this weakness. It is very difficult for a person to discern a difference between those political values that
are "fundamental to our society." Thus, by the
adoption of such a criterion judicial personalization
of the law is enormously facilitated. (One might
reduce this danger by insisting that the new "fundamental values" invoked to replace original
meaning to be clearly and objectively manifested in
the laws of the society. But among all the varying
tests suggested by nonoriginalist theoreticians, I
am unaware that that one ever appears. Most if not
all nonoriginalists, for example, would strike down
the death penalty, though it continues to be widely
adopted in both state and federal legislation.)

Originalism does not aggravate the principal
weakness of the system, for it establishes a historical criterion that is conceptually quite separate from
the preferences of the judge himself. And the principal defect of that approach—that historical
research is always difficult and sometimes inconclusive—will, unlike nonoriginalism, lead to a more
moderate rather than a more extreme result. The inevitable tendency of judges to think that the law is
what they would like it to be will, I have no doubt,
cause most errors I judicial historiography to be
made in the direction of projecting upon the age of
1789 current, modern values—so that as applied,
even as applied in the best of faith, originalism will
(as the historical record shows) end up as something
of a compromise. Perhaps not a bad characteristic
for a constitutional theory. Thus, nonoriginalists can
say, concerning the principal defect of originalism,
"Oh happy fault." Originalism is, it seems to me, the
librarian who talks too softly.

Having made that endorsement, I hasten to
confess that in a crunch I may prove a faint-hearted
originalist. I cannot imagine myself, any more than
any other federal judge, upholding a statute that
imposes the punishment of flogging. But then I
cannot imagine such a case's arising either. In any
event, in deciding the cases before me I expect I
will rarely be confronted with making the stark
choice between giving evolutionary content (not
yet required by *stare decisis*)and not giving evolutionary content to particular constitutional provisions. The vast majority of my dissents from
non-originalist thinking (and I hope at least some
of those dissents will be majorities) will, I am sure,
be able to be framed in the terms that, even if the
provision in question has an evolutionary content,

there is inadequate indication that any evolution in social attitudes has occurred. That—to conclude this largely theoretical talk on a note of reality—is the real dispute that appears in the case: not between nonoriginalists on the one hand and pure originalists on the other, concerning the validity of looking at all to current values; but rather between, on the one hand, nonoriginalists, fainthearted originalist and pure-originalists-accepting-for-the-sake-of-argument-evolutionary-content, and, on the other hand, other adherents of the same three approaches, concerning the nature and degree of evidence necessary to demonstrate that constitutional evolution has occurred.

I am left with a sense of dissatisfaction, as I am sure you are, that a discourse concerning what one would suppose to be a rather fundamental—indeed, the most fundamental—aspect of constitutional theory and practice should end so inconclusively. But it should come to no surprise. We do not yet have an agreed-upon theory for interpreting statutes, either. I find it perhaps too laudatory to say that this is the genius of the common law system; but it is at least its nature.

Endnotes

[1] *Humphrey's Executor v. United States,* 295 U.S. 602, 628, (1935).

[2] 4 Wheat. (17 U.S.) 316 (1819).

[3] L. Tribe, God Save This Honorable Court 45 (1985).

[4] L. Tribe, American Constitutional Law 771 (2d ed. 1988).

[5] Brest, The Misconceived Quest for the Original Understanding, 60 B.U.L. Rev. 204, 226 (1980).

[6] *Id.* at 227.

[7] *Id.* at 229.

[8] Fiss, The Supreme Court 1978 Term—Forward: The Forms of Justice, 93 Harv. L. Rev. 1, 9, 11 (1979).

[9] R. Dworkin, Taking Rights Seriously 149 (1977).

[10] Parker, The Past of Constitutional Theory—And Its Future, 42 OHIO St. L.J. 223, 258 n. 146 (1981).

[11] Richards, Constitutional Privacy, The Right to Die and the Meaning of Life: A Moral Analysis, 22 Wm. & Mary L. Rev. 327, 344–47 (1981).

[12] Tribe, *supra* note 3 at 45

[13] 108 5 ct. 2798 (1988).

[14] See Monaghan, "Our Perfect Constitution," 56 N. Y. U. L. Rev. 353 (1981).

---

23. *Constitutional Interpretation and Original Meaning*

David Lyons

[O]riginalism can seem to be the only plausible approach to judicial review. One might reason as follows: "A court cannot decide whether an official decision conforms to the Constitution without applying its rules. The Constitution was written down to fix its content, and its rules remain unchanged until it is amended. Courts have not been authorized to change the rules. So courts deciding cases under the Constitution should follow the rules there laid down. By what right would courts decide constitutional cases on any other grounds?"

From *Moral Aspects of Legal Theory*, pp. 141-158, 168, ©1993 by Cambridge University Press. Reprinted by permission.

That challenge is conveyed by writings on judicial review that are regarded as originalist. But it is misleading. Most of the positions that are condemned by contemporary originalists accept the authority of the Constitution. Although originalists present the issue as fidelity to the Constitution, it primarily concerns, I shall argue, how the Constitution is to be interpreted.

A distinctively originalist mode of interpretation assumes that the doctrinal content of the Constitution was completely determined when it was adopted and that constitutional doctrines can be identified by a value-free factual study of the text or of "original intent." It is part of my purpose to show that this type of theory is not only less plausible than its severest critics have suggested but that significant alternatives to it are available.

An approach to judicial review includes not only a theory of interpretation, which tells us how to understand the Constitution, but also a theory of adjudication, which tells us how to apply the Constitution so interpreted—how it should be used in constitutional cases. Originalist theory is not usually analyzed in this way, but we shall find that the distinction is needed when considering contemporary originalism.

One would expect a distinctively originalist approach to adjudication to hold that constitutional cases should be decided on the basis of doctrines in the "original" Constitution (that is, the Constitution interpreted in an originalist way), and on no other basis whatsoever. I shall show that contemporary theorists who present themselves as strict originalists accept rules for judicial review that cannot be found in or otherwise attributed to the "original" Constitution.

A third point I wish to make is that doctrines drawn from general philosophy—ideas about meaning and morals, for example—play a significant role in contemporary originalist theorizing. This point is important because these philosophical notions are dubious and controversial. It must be emphasized, however, that some of the same philosophical ideas have wide currency in legal theory generally.

Although originalism has relatively few defenders, its most prominent champions are highly placed within the federal government. These included Robert H. Bork, Judge on the United States Court of Appeals for the District of Columbia Circuit, Edwin Meese III Attorney General of The United States, and William H. Rehnquist Associate Justice of the United States Supreme Court. It is important for us to recognize the quality of the constitutional theories that are embraced by these responsible officials.

This paper is, then, a critique of constitutional originalism. We need a better theory. Although I shall not offer one here, I shall suggest some requirements for an adequate theory of constitutional adjudication.

Original Intent

... An originalist mode of interpretation holds that the doctrinal content of the Constitution was fixed when (or by the time that) the Constitution was adopted and that constitutional doctrines can be identified by a value-free factual inquiry. An intentionalist version of originalism holds that we must understand the Constitution in terms of the "intentions" of its framers, adopters, or ratifiers such as the specific applications that they had in mind, those they would have been prepared to accept, or their larger purposes.

Champions of "original intent" seem to regard that approach to constitutional interpretation as so obviously correct that it requires no justification; for none seems to be offered. So it will be useful to begin by noting some aspects of intentionalism that imply its need for justification.

Reference to "original intent" is inherently ambiguous. The following questions indicate some (but not all) of that ambiguity. Whose intentions count? The intentions of, for example, one who drafts a text or one who votes for it? Which intentions count? To establish as authoritative some particular text, or some text understood in a certain way, or to serve some identifiable larger purposes? Reference to original intent is problematic in other ways too. While two or more individuals can share an intention, it is by no means clear how (or whether it is always possible) to aggregate the relevant attitudes of the members of a group so as to determine their collective intentions.

The answer that one gives to such questions should affect originalist interpretation, so the selection of any particular criterion of original intent as the basis for interpreting the Constitution requires specific justification. In the absence of a satisfactory rationale, we should regard any particular criterion of original intent as theoretically arbitrary. Sad to say, original intent theorists generally ignore these fundamental problems, despite their having systematically been surveyed in law reviews for at least two decades.

But the differences among the various versions of originalist intentionalism do not chiefly concern us now. The point I would like to emphasize is that *any* intentionalist approach requires substantial justification. Intentionalism is a special theory of constitutional interpretation, not a platitude.

Early in our constitutional career, the Supreme Court refused to apply the Bill of Rights to the several states, holding that the first ten amendments restricted only the federal government, although their language does not explicitly limit most of those amendments in that way. In so deciding, the Court made some reference to the intentions of "the framers." Although the Court's grounds for its decision went far beyond original intent, its reference to framers' intent might suggest that the Court followed the criterion of constitutional meaning instead of the apparent meaning of the authoritative text. If that were so, the Court would have followed a special theory of constitutional interpretation, and one that requires substantial justification.

In general, we recognize that we do not always mean what we say or write; *we* may mean something different from the meaning *of the language* that we use. This is reflected in our reading of legal instruments such as wills and contracts. It has also been observed, by advocates as well as critics of intentionalism, that the surest guide to author's intent is the authoritative constitutional text itself. This is possible only because the text is understood to carry a meaning to carry a meaning that stands on its own—that is independent of its authors' intentions.

It follows that intentionalism is a special theory of constitutional interpretation, not a platitude. Either it derives from a failure to appreciate the distinction between the meaning of a text and what its authors meant to convey; or else it presupposes some reason for holding that the meaning of the constitutional text, unlike that of texts generally, is a matter of authors' intent. So intentionalism is either confused or else requires substantial justification.

What might justify intentionalist constitutional interpretation? Originalists might appeal to (1) the idea (not limited to law) that interpretation should generally be governed by authors' intentions; (2) a specifically legal canon of construction; or (3) some theory of political morality that implies that we are under an obligation to respect the intentions of the framers, adopters, or ratifiers.

(1) Intentionalism as a general approach to interpretation.

The notion that textual interpretation seeks generally to determine authors' intentions is plausible when our primary concern is what some individual had in mind, as in the case of personal communications, studies of literary figures and, in law, wills and contracts. The question is whether our proper concern when interpreting an authoritative public text such as a constitution is to determine what its authors had in mind. The suggestion seems to me implausible.

I do not wish to deny that, just as a poem can be a political statement, law can be read as literature. But law's distinctive functions are significantly different from those of literature and personal communications. Law tells us what we must or must not do, threatening punishment for disobedience. It places the coercive power of the state behind some individuals' decisions. It quite literally regulates death and taxes, war and peace, debts and compensation, imprisonment, conscription and confiscation, and innumerable other matters of direct, vital interest to individuals, communities, and often all humanity. That is the explicit, normal business of the law, including the U. S. Constitution.

An important feature of law's normal business is that it requires justification. The same applies, of course, to judicial decisions, including those that turn upon legal interpretation. They require justification, too. The justification of judicial decisions, like the justification of the normal business of the law generally, cannot be understood in narrowly legalistic terms. Adequate justification concerns not merely whether something is required or allowed by law but, also, whether what the law does is what I have elsewhere called "defensible." All of this suggests that the need for justification may properly regulate matters of legal and specifically constitutional interpretation and, thus, that these matters turn on political morality.

(2) Intentionalism as a theory of legal interpretation.

Could intentionalism be based on a general canon of construction for legal instruments? The possibility is suggested by the fact that statutory construction is said to seek out "legislative intent." But there are several difficulties here. Insofar as constitutional intentionalism relies upon a canon of construction that derives from precedent or common law, there will be some difficulty incorporating such a theory of interpretation into originalism, as I shall explain later.

Another problem is this. Conventions regulate the identification of "legislative intent," such as the authority given to official reports from legislative committees. Such conventions have only problematic application to the U. S. Constitution. The existence of such conventions suggests something else that seems important, namely, that the search for "legislative intent" is not a purely factual inquiry about a consensus that obtained at a particular historical moment. This is suggested also by the fact that statutory construction characteristically seeks to interpret legislation in as favorable a light as possible; for example, as a reasonable and legislatively legitimate means to a reasonable and legislatively legitimate end. Such a normative bias can be explained by the fact that statutory construction seeks to provide, if possible, a grounding for judicial decisions that are justified. If what counts as "legislative intent" is in fact shaped by normative considerations, it could not serve as a model for "original intent," for those who endorse the latter as the criterion of constitutional meaning regard it as a plain matter of historical fact, accessible to a value-free inquiry.

Originalists assume that the Constitution is a morally adequate basis for judicial decisions (as well as for our political arrangements generally). The normative bias within interpretation to which I refer requires that we interpret the Constitution in such a way that it is, if possible, capable of performing that function.

If statutory construction is no help to constitutional intentionalism, what about the interpretation of other legal instruments, such as wills and contracts? The first point made about "legislative intent" applies here, too: insofar as constitutional

intentionalism relies upon a canon of construction that derives from precedent or common law, there will be some difficulty incorporating such a theory of interpretation into originalism.

It might nonetheless be thought that an intentionalist interpretation of contracts could serve as a model for constitutional intentionalism. That is because political rhetoric often refers to the Constitution as the upshot of a "social contract." Now, the idea of a "social contract" is invoked to argue for obedience to law, however objectionable on other grounds it might be, so long as it does not violate constitutional restrictions. This means that a "social contract" basis for intentionalism is dependent on a theory of political morality. To accept intentionalism on this basis, we must establish the legitimacy of a "social contract" argument and its valid application to this case.

(3) Intentionalism as a theorem of political morality

Our discussion suggests that we should seek a rationale for constitutional intentionalism in the political morality of constitutional creation and application, that is, in principles that explain why the Constitution is worthy of respect and morally binding. Two ideas are provided by political rhetoric. One, already noted, refers to a "social contract." Another, asserted within as well as outside the Constitution, hold that it comes from "the people."

The latter idea is promising because contemporary originalists, like most constitutional theorist, emphasize the predominately "democratic" character of our constitutional arrangements. Representative government nicely complements popular sovereignty. Political rhetoric suggests that "the people" knowingly and freely agreed to respect government so long as it conforms to the Constitution, and that "the people" are accordingly bound by that agreement. But this does not yet yield the constitutional theory of original intent, which requires that the Constitution be understood in terms of the "intentions" of a special subclass of "the people," namely, the Framers, adopters, or ratifiers, as opposed to (say) the understanding that one might have of the Constitution based on text meaning.

The present line of reasoning requires us to suppose, then, (a) that "the people" *contracted to accept the intentions of the authors,* by reference to which the Constitution must therefore be understood, and (b) that *this* makes the Constitution binding on us now. The theory seems fatally flawed.

(a) In the first place, only a small minority of the people of that time and place were permitted to participate in the original adoption process. We lack precise figures, but it should suffice for present purposes to observe that the process excluded not only many adult white males (and, of course, children) but also women, chattel slaves, and Native Americans. It could not have included more than a small fraction of the total population, and willing contractors would have amounted to a smaller fraction still.

In the second place, it is doubtful whether any such contractors would have been morally competent to create obligations to respect political arrangements that continued chattel slavery, second-class citizenship for women, and the subjugation of Native Americans. At the very least, those subject to such arrangements could not be bound by a constitution simply because it was agreeable to others.

(b) In the third place, it is unclear how contracts made by members of earlier generations can bind succeeding generations. This is not to suggest that law can bind only those who have given their consent. But the mere fact that some people some time in the past have accepted a political arrangement cannot by itself automatically bind others. More is required than that to show that later generations are bound.

But the rhetoric of popular sovereignty is nonetheless illuminating. It suggests a commitment to popular government, however narrowly that was at first conceived. Furthermore, the Constitution is a piece of public, not private, law. Our proper concern in interpreting it is not to implement the understanding of parties to a limited, private agreement or the personal wishes of a testator, but to establish the basis for political arrangements and justified judicial decisions that legitimately concern the community as a whole. Whatever else is needed for a theory of constitutional adjudication, the legitimate interest of the entire population strongly suggests that the primary criterion of constitutional meaning should be popular understand-ing, the basic index of which must be text meaning.

Consider the alternative. Interpretation in terms of the intentions of constitutional framers or ratifiers would seem to assume a conception of law like that of the classical legal positivists Bentham and Austin, according to which an exclusive subgroup of the population makes law for others to follow. That is objectionable because of our interest in justification. Interpretation based on anything like that conception of the law will present formidable obstacles to justifying the Constitution, justifying compliance with morally deficient laws so long as they conform to the Constitution, and justifying judicial decisions that those laws require.

The upshot is that constitutional intentionalism is profoundly problematic. There is no obvious linguistic or moral basis for interpreting the Constitution by reference to the intentions for an exclusive political group, as opposed to the meaning of the text. When these considerations are combined with other substantial objections to intentionalism, the theory seems unpromising indeed.

Alternatives to Intentionalism

In this section, I agree that intentionalism does not win out by default, despite its deficiencies. According to Brest's typology, the originalist alternative to intentionalism is textualism, which comes in two varieties. "A strict textualist purports to construe words and phrases very narrowly and precisely."[1] Brest appears to argue that this is untenable both as textual interpretation and as originalism: "An originalist would hold that, because interpretation is designed to capture the original understanding, the text must be understood in the context of the society that adopted it."[2] This means that textualism must be "moderate" to be plausible. "A moderate textualist takes account of the open-textured quality of language and reads the language of provisions in their social and linguistic contexts."[3]

In other words, Brest judges the only legitimate originalist alternative to intentionalism to be a reading of constitutional language as "textured."[4] Unfortunately, Brest does not explain what he takes this to mean. But his reference to the spurious precision of "strict" textualism suggests that we might understand "moderate textualism" by reference to

Hart's use of "open-textured" when he introduced that technical term into legal theory.

Following the received wisdom of the time, Hart held that all terms in "natural" languages (which include the language of the law) are "open-textured." An "open-textured" word has a core of determinate meaning, encompassing fact situations to which it uncontroversially applies, and a "penumbra" encompassing fact situations to which the term neither clearly applies nor clearly does not apply. The idea of "open texture" assumes that the meaning of a word is indeterminate whenever there are reasons both for and against applying the word. This aspect of the theory of "open texture" provides a theoretical rationale for a view that is widely accepted by legal theorists, namely, that legal language has indeterminate meaning insofar as its proper application is unclear.

On this understanding, to characterize constitutional language as "open-textured" is to imply that the doctrines given by that language are incompletely formed. Provisions that many theorists seem to believe fit this description to an extreme degree include the so-called "vague clauses" guaranteeing "free speech," "due process," "just compensation, " "equal protection," and the like. On the "open texture" model, these provisions are seen as having tiny cores of clear (and therefore determinate) meaning and relatively wide unclear (and therefore indeterminate) penumbras.

This is a politically significant idea. For it implies that, insofar as the judicial process of "interpreting" the Constitution makes its proper application clearer, the process really *changes* the Constitution by making its meaning more determinate. The clearer doctrines resulting from such "interpretations" could not then be attributed to the "original" Constitution. That is the view of constitutional language that Brest seems to regard as the ("moderate") originalist alternative to "strict" textualism.

Given this conception of the alternatives, we can better understand why originalists regard as most significant the dividing line between "strict" and "moderate" originalism. That is because moderate originalism appears to collapse into nonoriginalism.

Originalism regards the authority of the "original" Constitution as axiomatic, whereas nonoriginalism holds that adherence to the Constitution requires justification and that principles of political morality that are capable of providing such justification might also justify deviation from it. To clarify this difference, we can distinguish two categories of doctrines that might be used in constitutional cases. Those that can and those that cannot truly be attributed to the Constitution may be called "constitutional" and "extra-constitutional," respectively. Nonoriginalism is prepared to consider using extra-constitutional doctrines in constitutional cases, whereas a distinctively originalist theory of adjudication would presumably reject any such use of them.

"Moderate" originalism regards unclear constitutional language as "open-textured," or inherently somewhat vague. It also accepts the judicial practice of deciding cases under unclear aspects of the Constitution, but it seems to regard the constitutional "interpretations" that are used as creating, and the resulting decisions as applying, doctrines that are extra-constitutional—judicial amendments to the "original" Constitution. On this view, "moderate" originalism's approach to deciding cases under unclear aspects of the Constitution *is equivalent to nonoriginalism*. Such decisions would be condemned by a "strict" originalist who holds that, as courts have no authority to amend the Constitution, they should refrain from doing so.

It must be emphasized that the line of reasoning sketched in the last few paragraphs assumes that "moderate" textualism regards the Constitution as indeterminate insofar as its proper application is unclear. But we need not assume this; we need not accept the dubious assumption that the meaning of a text is indeterminate whenever it is unclear, or whenever interpretation of it would be controversial, so that the discovery of text meaning is impossible precisely when it is needed.

Instead of discussing these issues in the abstract, it will be useful to consider an approach which agrees that such language in the "original" Constitution does *not* provide *complete* doctrines of just compensation, free speech, and the like. This approach nevertheless provides grounds for attributing the doctrines resulting from sound interpretations to the Constitution. This will provide us with all that we require for present purposes, namely, an alternative to "strict" intentionalism that might justifiably assign meaning to the Constitution and enable courts ot decide cases on constitutional grounds.

It has been suggested that the so-called "vague clauses" incorporate "contested concepts." It is the nature of such a concept to admit of competing "conceptions" and thus routinely to *require* interpretation. Contested concepts do not have built-in criteria of application; they are more abstract than that. As a result, different people can use the same (concepts, such as "right" and "wrong," "good" and "bad," "right" and "obligation," as well as more specific normative concepts, such as particular virtues and vices, are "contested" in this way. When people agree about the "facts" but disagree in their evaluations, their disagreement concerns the principles that determine the proper application of those concepts to particular cases.

The notion of a "contested concept" is explicitly used, for example, in Rawls's theory of social justice, the relevant part of which can be explained as follows. Imagine that you and I disagree about the substantive requirements of social justice. We then differ as to how the concept of justice applies; we differ, that is, about the principles of justice. This is possible if the concept of justice admits of different interpretations, or competing conceptions. That seems to be the case.

Rawls maintains that the mere concept of justice determines no detailed, substantive criteria of justice, only the skeletal requirement that there be no "arbitrary distinctions" between persons but, rather, "a proper balance between competing claims."[5] The task of a theory of justice is to show (not merely to claim) the superiority of one conception (one principle or set of principles) over competing conceptions as an interpretation of this requirement. The possibility of a uniquely correct interpretation of a provision incorporating the contested concept of justice, then, depends on the superior justifiability of a particular conception of justice.

Now consider a constitutional example. Past judicial interpretations aside, a court applying the just compensation clause would not necessarily decide a case as the original authors would have done, nor would it automatically follow a more popular consensus of the time (even if either were possible). Instead, a court would understand the Constitution to mean precisely what it says and thus to require *just compensation.* A court would

need to defend a particular conception of just compensation (that is, it would need to defend principles of justice appropriate to compensation) against the most plausible alternatives. It would then apply that conception to decide the case at bar.

Someone might be skeptical about the possibility of justifying such an interpretation. Someone might believe it is impossible to provide a rational defense of, say, principles of just compensation and might therefore claim that a court adopting this approach would inevitably impose its own arbitrary conception of just compensation instead of the conception embraced by the authors of the Constitution or by a broader "original" consensus. (It should be emphasized that, on this view, an "original" conception of just compensation is completely arbitrary and indefensible.) Someone might hold, in other words, that all such principles are inherently arbitrary, so that courts cannot possibly do what is required to implement this approach to the interpretation of "vague" constitutional language. I shall not offer a general critique of such skepticism, but I shall suggest below why it is reasonable to believe that there can be a best conception among competing conceptions of some contested concepts. I shall later show how philosophical skepticism about values is, in this context, incoherent.

Contested concepts do not seem confined to morality and law. Their properties are at any rate similar to those of concepts referring to natural substances or phenomena, such as water and heat. On a plausible understanding of the development of science, for example, the caloric and kinetic theories of heat are (or at one time were) competing conceptions of the concept heat. This is suggested by the fact that "heat" refers to a physical phenomenon that is but partially and imperfectly identified by any prescientific verbal definition of the word, and that something very much like the idea of a contested concept is required to explain how there can be two theories of heat, that is, two different conceptions of the single concept heat.

If, as most people would agree, "heat" refers to a determinate physical phenomenon, there can be, in principle, a best theory of heat. This implies that there can be a best conception of a contented concept, at least in some cases. This suggests, in turn, that contested concepts in the Constitution might have best interpretations.

The kinetic theory of heat has displaced the caloric conception and is currently our best conception of heat. As this example implies, we may be justified in using *our* best conception even if it is not in fact *the* best. Similarly, just as our best conception of heat is liable to change, so we may expect change from time to time in our best conception of, say, just compensation. This involves no moral relativism.

Now if the idea that the Constitution includes contested concepts is correct, then to apply the Constitution in terms of their best interpretation is, in effect, to apply doctrines whose application is called for by the original Constitution. But, just as interpretation of the concept heat requires more than mere reflection, any interpretation of this type inevitably draws on resources that are neither implicit in the text nor purely linguistic. It makes essential use of political argument, though at a relatively general or abstract level. So this alternative approach implies that a sound interpretation—one faithful to the meaning of the text—can include substantive doctrines that are not derivable from the text (even supplemented by its original social and linguistic context) but that are identifiable only by reasoning about political principles in the context of the federal system.

It is important to emphasize that this approach to constitutional interpretation, where applicable, requires that an interpreter go outside the "four corners" of the text, its strict linguistic implications, and the relatively specific intentions of its authors, for interpretations, and arguments supporting them. But, as this is done because it is understood to be required by the very nature of contested concepts found within the Constitution, both the strategy of argument and its results can claim fidelity to the Constitution. For this reason, the interpretive approach just sketched might reasonably be regarded as "originalist."

As usually understood, however, "originlism" assumes that constitutional doctrines must be identified by a value-free factual study of the text or of original intent and that doctrines that are not implicit in the "original" text or "understanding" cannot truly be attributed to the Constitution. It accordingly rejects without a hearing the possibility of attributing to the Constitution interpretations of those contested concepts that are in the Constitution. That possibility gives reason to withhold assent from the more familiar originalist theories.

Originalist Adjudication

The Fourteenth Amendment says that no state "shall deny to any person within its jurisdiction the equal protection of the laws." The meaning of this provision is unclear. If (as some suggest) the provision does not have any determinate meaning, how should courts deal with cases under it? The Constitution does not tell us what we should then do.

As I have suggested, a comprehensive theory of judicial review can be understood as having two parts. A theory of interpretation purports to determine constitutional meaning. If well grounded, such a theory should be welcome when the text is unclear. Furthermore, anyone who holds the text to be misleading needs a good theory to justify such a claim.

But theories about judicial review go beyond straightforward interpretation; they include theories of adjudication, which purport to determine how the Constitution should be applied. Such a theory is required if cases are decided when the meaning of the Constitution is undetermined, or to justify departure from the Constitution's implications.

To illustrate the latter possibility, consider Thayer's famous deferential doctrine.[6] Thayer argued that federal legislation should never be nullified by federal courts unless it cannot reasonably be doubted that the legislation violates the Constitution. He held that this judicial policy was needed to promote respect for federal law and to protect the courts from legislative interference. Thayer did not assume that the Constitution has no determinate meaning when there is reasonable disagreement about its meaning. On the contrary, he insisted that the judiciary should not apply its best interpretation of the Constitution but should defer whenever it is possible to regard the legislature's actions as constitutional.

> [W]hen the ultimate question is . . . . whether certain acts of another department, officer, or individual are legal or permissible, . . . *the ultimate question is not what is the true meaning of the constitution, but whether legislation is sustainable or not.*[7]

Thayer recommends, in effect, that the courts should sometimes refrain from enforcing the Constitution, even when they have a good, justifiable, and perhaps sound idea of what it means. That mounts to a special theory of adjudication (and, incidentally, one that seems decidedly extra-constitutional).

The distinctively originalist approach to adjudicating constitutional cases would seem to hold that they should be decided exclusively by doctrines that can be found in the "original" Constitution, that is, interpreted in an originalist way. There is a problem here. It is by no means clear that originalist theory can be found within the "original" Constitution. If originalism itself includes extraconstituional doctrines, then insofar as a court applied and was guided by this theory of adjudication, it would decide cases in a nonoriginalist way!

It may accordingly seem reasonable to revise the originalist theory of adjudication so that originalism does not prohibit its own application. It would be modified to say that a doctrine may be applied within judicial review if, but only if, the doctrine either is attributable to the Constitution (in the sense required by an appropriate originalist theory of interpretation) or else is a doctrine of originalism itself.

That problem seemed easily solved. But it may suggest how difficult it is to embrace originalism unqualifiedly. Take another example. Raoul Berger's attack upon judicial decisions that fail to respect "framers' intent" leads him to suggest that courts should repudiate all decisions that cannot be grounded upon the Constitution so construed, regardless of "undesirable consequences."[8] But Berger hastily retreats from this proposal, saying:

> It would, however, be utterly unrealistic and probably impossible to undo the past in the face of the expectations that the segregation decisions, for example, have aroused in our black citizenry—expectations confirmed by every decent instinct. That is more than the courts should undertake and more, I believe, than the American people would desire.[9]

Berger's retreat appears unprincipled. At best, he invokes an undefined and undefended extraconstitutional principle of constitutional adjudication, which clashes with his originalist pretensions.

Henry Monaghan appears sensitive to Berger's problem. He too says that the school desegregation decisions should not be undone. Unlike Berger, however, Monaghan suggests a judicial principle that would permit leaving those decisions undisturbed, even through he questions their constitutional warrant. His solution is to advocate a doctrine of judicial precedent.

The question now is whether a doctrine of judicial precedent can be attributed to the "original" Constitution. Monaghan appears not to think so. But he believes that such a doctrine can be justified because it serves "the long-run values of stability and predictability for ordering our most fundamental affairs."[10]

Monaghan does not seem to appreciate the awkwardness of his position. In offering a justification for a doctrine of precedent based on its desirable consequences, he commits himself to holding that judicial review may be regulated by *any* principles whose use would serve the same "long-run values." That would permit the use in judicial review of an indeterminate class of useful extraconstitutional principles.

One might, alternatively, suggest that a doctrine of precedent was in fact provided by the "original" Constitution. For the Constitution was grafted on a system whose common law heritage includes, of course, a doctrine requiring courts to respect judicial precedent. The trouble with this way of reasoning, from an originalist perspective, is that it would render the Constitution much less limited doctrinally than originalists tend to view it. It would imply that the Constitution contains a multitude of common law principles.

Monaghan's predicament suggests the instability of originalism. If an originalist believes that there is justification for respecting a judicial principle that is no more controversial than precedent, he not only runs the risk of agreeing that constitutional cases may properly be decided by doctrines that cannot be attributed to the Constitution; he may become committed to accepting a relatively indeterminate theory of judicial review, incorporating all the principles of constitutional adjudication that can be justified by the criteria that are needed to justify a doctrine of precedent.

This point is generalizable. Contemporary originalists are often preoccupied with "restraining" the federal judiciary in constitutional cases and tend to embrace theories of adjudication that are designed in part to limit judicial nullification of decisions made by elected officials. The relevant judicial principles require justification. If such principles cannot be found in the "original" Constitution, they require justification by reference to some principles of political morality. The considerations that are adduced or required to justify such doctrines are capable of justifying an indefinite class of other doctrines that are relevant to constitutional adjudication. To endorse an extra-constitutional principle is to commit oneself to endorsing any other principle that is justifiable on the same grounds that justify the one endorsed. Such an approach to constitutional adjudication is hardly consistent with the spirit of originalism.

Conclusion

Originalism seems to derive its initial plausibility from a simplified conception of how written constitutions work. Interpretation in terms of original intent promises a stable, uncontroversial version of the Constitution. But intentionalism faces overwhelming difficulties and appears to lack compensating justification, either in political or linguistic terms. Seeing no promising alternatives, opponents of strict originalism have accepted the need for extra-constitutional doctrines in constitutional adjudication. Originalists appear to reject such heterodoxy, but they unselfconsciously embrace a variety of extra-constitutional doctrines. Their theorizing about the Constitution tends toward the superficially descriptive and has yet to face the substantive value commitments implicit even in ritualistic appeals to democracy. Just as the Constitution cannot be value-free, so our understanding of it must be informed by reflection on the principles it serves.

Endnotes

[1] Brest, "The Misconceived Quest for the Original Understanding," 60 B.U.L. Rev. 204 (1980), P. 204.

[2] *Ibid.* p. 208.

[3] *Ibid.* p. 223.

[4] *Ibid.* pp. 205, 223.

[5] Rawls. *A Theory of Justice* (Cambridge: Harvard Univ. Press, (1971), pp. 5–10.

[6] Thayer, "The Origin and Scope of the American Doctrine of Constitutional Law," 7 *Harv. L. Rev.* 129 (1893).

[7] Thayer, "Origin," p. 150 (emphasis in the original).

[8] R. Berger, *Government By Judiciary* 412 (1977).

[9] *Ibid.*, pp. 412–413.

[10] Monaghan, "Our Perfect Constitution," *56 N. Y. U. L. Rev* (1981), p. 389.

Study Questions

1. Does Justice Douglas's appeal to the "penumbras and emanations" of the Bill of Rights in *Griswold* constitute good constitutional interpretation in your view? Is such an appeal a license to ignore the text of the Constitution? Why or why not? Take note of the Third Amendment, which prohibits the quartering of soldiers in someone's home without the owner's consent, and of the Fourth Amendment, which guarantees the right "of the people to be secure in their person, houses, papers, and effects, against unreasonable searches and seizures." Note that the kind of intrusion prohibited by both amendments is a physical intrusion, not a regulation of behavior. Is it stretching the meaning of these amendments to make them prohibit statutes regulating behavior, as the Connecticut statute did?

2. At various points throughout the privacy cases, appeal has been made to the Ninth Amendment: "The enumeration in the Constitution, of certain rights, shall not be construed to deny or disparage others retained by the people." The suggestion has been made that privacy is one of these "retained" rights. But the Ninth is the focus of controversy. Some scholars argue that its appearance in the text of the Constitution is prophylactic only: at the time of adoption there was some concern that the inclusion of a bill of rights would be taken to imply that the federal power (granted in section 8 of Article I) is not limited but extends all the way up to the edge of the rights enumerated; that is, that the federal government has the power to do everything except infringe upon those listed rights. The Ninth Amendment was meant merely to preclude that inference. On its face, however, the Ninth seems to be a clear invitation to look beyond the text and structure of the Constitution to locate

fundamental rights still retained by the people. The difficulty, of course, is that we are not told where to look for such rights; the text of the amendment provides no guidelines. How would you determine to what rights the Ninth Amendment refers? Should the Ninth be relied upon at all in interpreting the Constitution?

3. Concurring in *Griswold*, Justice Goldberg asserted that privacy in the marital relation is a fundamental part of our nation's traditions. Is he right? Is it part of our traditions that couples be allowed to use birth control? Do any aspects of our history dispute this?

4. Justice Blackmun, in dissent in *Bowers*, argued that the Court should protect our fundamental interests in "controlling the nature of [our] intimate associations with others." Bork objects to this formulation of the right of privacy as it would make it impossible consistently to criminalize adultery, incest, or other sex crimes so long as they are committed in the home. Is Bork correct?

5. Why, according to Bork, is the right of privacy neither neutrally derived, defined, nor applied?

6. Bork insists that the "original understanding" or original intent behind the language of the Constitution cannot be taken to reflect the specific opinions or views of any particular person or group. Why does Bork make this claim?

7. Why does Scalia think that nonoriginalist methods of constitutional interpretation are inconsistent with the idea of judicial review? The concept of judicial review itself is not, as has often been pointed out, explicitly mentioned in the Constitution. How does Scalia square the viability of judicial review with the originalist theory?

8. Scalia confesses that he would likely find public whipping to be a cruel and unusual punishment. How does he meet the criticism that a consistent application of the originalist theory would seem to require that punishments such as flogging be permitted under the Constitution? Try to imagine how an originalist would frame an argument that would show flogging to be cruel and unusual.

9. According to Lyons, what are the two political ideals of principles of political morality that could be used to justify the claim that the intentions of the authors of the Constitution should determine its meaning?

10. What positive proposal does Lyons offer for ascertaining the meaning of vague or "open-textured" phrases of the Constitution? Does Lyons's proposal overcome the defects pointed out by Scalia?

Cases for Further Reflection

24. *Riggs et al. v. Palmer*

The confrontation between naturalism and positivism is well joined in this case. As you read through the case, consider these questions: Are the precedents cited by Earl convincing? What is the source of the authoritativeness of the "fundamental maxims" of "universal law" invoked by Earl to support the judgment that Elmer Palmer must not be allowed to collect under his grandfather's will?

Earl [Judge].

On the 13th day of August, 1880, Francis B. Palmer made his last will and testament, in which he gave small legacies to his two daughters, Mrs. Riggs and Mrs. Preston, the plaintiffs in this action, and the remainder of his estate to his grandson, the defendant Elmer E. Palmer, subject to the support of Susan Palmer, his mother, with a gift over to the two daughters, subject to the support of Mrs. Palmer in case Elmer should survive him and die under age, unmarried, and without any issue. The testator, at the date of his will, owned a farm, and considerable personal property. He was a widower, and thereafter, in March, 1882, he was married to Mrs. Bresee, with whom, before his marriage, he entered into an antenuptial contract, in which it was agreed that in lieu of dower and all other claims upon his estate in case she survived him she should have her support upon his farm during her life, and such support was expressly charged upon the farm. At the date of the will, and subsequently to the death of the testator, Elmer lived with him as a member of his family, and at his death was 16 years old. He knew of the provisions made in his favor in the will, and, that he might prevent his grandfather from revoking such provisions, which he had manifested some intention to do, and to obtain the speedy enjoyment and immediate possession of his property, he willfully murdered him by poisoning him. He now claims the property, and the sole question for our determination is, can he have it?

The defendants say that the testator is dead; that his will was made in due form, and has been admitted to probate; and that therefore it must have effect according to the letter of the law. It is quite true that statutes regulating the making, proof, and effects of wills and devolution of property if literally construed, and if their force and effect can in no way and under no circumstances be controlled or modified, give this property to the murderer. The purpose of those statutes was to enable testators to dispose of their estates to the objects of their bounty at death, and to carry into effect their final wishes legally expressed; and in considering and giving ef-

22 N.E. 188 (1889)
Court of Appeals of New York

fect to them this purpose must be kept in view. It was the intention of the lawmakers that the donees in a will should have the property given to them. But it never could have been their intention that a donee who murdered the testator to make the will operative should have any benefit under it. If such a case had been present in their minds, and it had been supposed necessary to make some provision of law to meet it, it cannot be doubted that they would have provided for it. It is a familiar canon of construction that a thing which is within the intention of the makers of a statute is as much within the statute as if it were within the letter; and a thing which is within the letter of the statute is not within the statute unless it be within the intention of the makers. The writers of laws do not always express their intention perfectly, but either exceed it or fall short of it, so that judges are to collect it from probable or rational conjectures only, and this is called "rational interpretation;" and Rutherford, in his Institutes, (page 420,) says: "Where we make use of rational interpretation, sometimes we restrain the meaning of the writer so as to take in less, and sometimes we extend or enlarge his meaning so as to take in more, than his words express." Such a construction ought to put upon a statute as will best answer the intention which the makers had in view. . . . [M]any cases are mentioned where it was held that matters embraced in the general words of statutes nevertheless were not within the statutes, because it could not have been the intention of the law-makers that they should be included. They were taken out of the statutes by an equitable construction; and it is said in Bacon: "By an equitable construction a case not within the letter of a statute is sometimes holden to be within the meaning, because it is within the mischief for which a remedy is provided. The reason for such construction is that the law-makers could not set down every case in express terms. In order to form a right judgment whether a case be within the equity of a statute, it is a good way to suppose the law-maker present, and that you have asked him this question. Did you intend to comprehend this case? Then you must give yourself such answer as you imagine he, being an upright and reasonable man, would have given. If this be that he did mean to comprehend it, you may safely hold the case to be within the equity of the statute; for while you do no more than he would have done, you do not act contrary to the statute, but in conformity thereto." In some cases the letter of a legislative act is restrained by an equitable construction; in others, it is enlarged; in others, the construction is contrary to the letter. The equitable construction which restrains the letter of a statute is defined by Aristotle as frequently quoted in this manner: *Æquitas est correctio legis generaliter latæ qua parte deficit*. If the [law-makers] could, as to this case, be consulted, would they say that they intended by their general language that the property of a testator or of an ancestor should pass to one who had taken his life for the express purpose of getting his property? In 1 Bl. Comm. 91, the learned author, speaking of the construction of statutes, says: "If there arise out of them collaterally any absurd consequences manifestly contradictory to common reason, they are with regard to those collateral consequences void. [. . .] Where some collateral matter arises out of the general words, and happens to be unreasonable, there the judges are in decency to conclude that this consequence was not foreseen by the parliament, and therefore they are at liberty to expound the statute by equity, and only *quoad hoc* disregard it;" and he gives as an illustration, if an act of parliament gives a man power to try all causes that arise within his manor of Dale, yet, if a cause should arise in which he himself is party, the act is construed not to extend to that, because it is unreasonable that any man should determine his own quarrel. There was a statute in Bologna that whoever drew blood in the streets should be severely punished, and yet it was held not to apply to the case of a barber who opened a vein in the street. It is commanded in the decalogue that no work shall be done on the Sabbath, and yet giving the command a rational interpretation founded upon its design the Infallible Judge held that it did not prohibit works of necessity, charity, or benevolence on that day.

What could be more unreasonable than to suppose that it was the legislative intention in the general laws passed for the orderly, peaceable, and just devolution of property that they should have operation in favor of one who murdered his ancestor that he might speedily come into the possession of his estate? Such an intention is inconceivable. We need not, therefore, be much troubled by the gen-

eral language contained in the laws. Besides, all laws, as well as all contracts, may be controlled in their operation and effect by general, fundamental maxims of the common law. No one shall be permitted to profit by his own fraud, or to take advantage of his own wrong, or to found any claim upon his own iniquity, or to acquire property by his own crime. These maxims are dictated by public policy, have their foundation in universal law administered in all civilized countries, and have nowhere been superseded by statutes. They were applied in the decision of the case of *Insurance Co. v. Armstrong*, 117 U.S. 599, 6 Sup. Ct. Rep. 877. There it was held that the person who procured a policy upon the life of another, payable at his death, and then murdered the assured to make the policy payable, could not recover thereon. Mr. Justice FIELD, writing the opinion, said: "Independently of any proof of the motives of Hunter in obtaining the policy, and even assuming that they were just and proper, he forfeited all rights under it when, to secure its immediate payment, he murdered the assured. It would be a reproach to the jurisprudence of the country if one could recover insurance money payable on the death of a party whose life he had feloniously taken. As well might he recover insurance money upon a building he had wilfully fired." These maxims, without any statute giving them force or operation, frequently control the effect and nullify the language of wills. A will procured by fraud and deception, like any other instrument, may be decreed void, and set aside; and so a particular portion of a will may be excluded from probate, or held inoperative, if induced by the fraud or undue influence of the person in whose favor it is. *Allen v. McPherson*, 1 H. L. Cas. 191; *Harrison's Appeal*, 48 Conn. 202. So a will may contain provisions which are immoral, irreligious, or against public policy, and they will be held void.

Here there was no certainty that this murderer would survive the testator, or that the testator would not change his will, and there was no certainty that he would get his property if nature was allowed to take its course. He therefore murdered the testator expressly to vest himself with an estate. Under such circumstances, what law, human or divine, will allow him to take the estate and enjoy the fruits of his crime? The will spoke and became operative at the death of the testator. He caused that death, and thus by his crime made it speak and have operation. Shall it speak and operate in his favor? If he had met the testator, and taken his property by force, he would have had no title to it. Shall he acquire title by murdering him? If he had gone to the testator's house, and by force compelled him, or by fraud or undue influence had induced him, to will him his property, the law would not allow him to hold it. But can he give effect and operation to a will by murder, and yet take the property? To answer these questions in the affirmative it seems to me would be a reproach to the jurisprudence of our state, and an offense against public policy. Under the civil law, evolved from the general principles of natural law and justice by many generations of jurisconsults, philosophers, and statesmen, one cannot take property by inheritance or will from an ancestor or benefactor whom he has murdered. . . . In the Civil Code of Lower Canada the provisions on the subject in the Code Napoleon have been substantially copied. But, so far as I can find, in no country where the common law prevails has it been deemed important to enact a law to provide for such a case. Our revisers and law-makers were familiar with the civil law, and they did not deem it important to incorporate into our statutes its provisions upon [this] subject. This is not a *casus omissus*. It was evidently supposed that the maxims of the common law were sufficient to regulate such a case, and that a specific enactment for that purpose was not needed. For the same reasons the defendant Palmer cannot take any of this property as heir. Just before the murder he was not an heir, and it was not certain that he ever would be. He might have died before his grandfather, or might have been disinherited by him. He made himself an heir by the murder, and he seeks to take property as the fruit of his crime. What has before been said as to him as legatee applies to him with equal force as an heir. He cannot vest himself with title by crime. My view of this case does not inflict upon Elmer any greater or other punishment for his crime than the law specifies. It takes from him no property, but simply holds that he shall not acquire property by his crime, and thus be rewarded for its commission.

Our attention is called to *Owens v. Owens*, 100 N.C. 240, 6 S.E. Rep. 794, as a case quite like this. There a wife had been convicted of being an accessory before the fact to the murder of her husband, and it was held that she was nevertheless entitled to dower. I am unwilling to assent to the doctrine of that case. The [statutes] provide dower for a wife who has the misfortune to survive her husband, and thus lose his support and protection. It is dear beyond their purpose to make provision for a wife who by her own crime makes herself a widow, and willfully and intentionally deprives herself of the support and protection of her husband. As she might have died before him, and "though" never have been his widow, she cannot by her crime vest herself with an estate. The principle which lies at the bottom of the maxim *volenti non fit injuria* should be applied to such a case, and a widow should not, for the purpose of acquiring, as such, property rights, be permitted to allege a widowhood which she has wickedly and intentionally created.

Gray, [Judge] (dissenting).

The appellants' argument for a reversal of the judgment, which dismissed their complaint, is that the respondent unlawfully prevented a revocation of the existing will, or a new will from being made, by his crime; and that he terminated the enjoyment of the testator of his property, and effected his own succession to it, by the same crime. They say that to permit the respondent to take the property willed to him would be to permit him to take advantage of his own wrong. To sustain their position that the appellants' counsel has submitted an able and elaborate brief, and, if I believed that the decision of the question could be effected by considerations of an equitable nature, I should not hesitate to assent to views which commend themselves to the conscience. But the matter does not lie within the domain of conscience. We are bound by the rigid rules of law, which have been established by the legislature, and within the limits of which the determination of this question is confined. The question we are dealing with is whether a testamentary disposition can be altered, or a will revoked, after the testator's death, through an appeal to the courts, when the legislature has by its enactments prescribed exactly when and how wills may be made, altered, and revoked, and apparently, as it seems to me, when they have been fully complied with, has left no room for the exercise of an equitable jurisdiction by courts over such matters. Modern jurisprudence, in recognizing the right of the individual, under more or less restrictions, to dispose of his property after his death, subjects it to legislative control, both as to extent and as to mode of exercise. Complete freedom of testamentory disposition of one's property has not been and is not the universal rule, as we see from the provisions of the Napoleonic Code, from the systems of jurisprudence in countries which are modeled upon the Roman law, and from the statutes of many of our states. To the statutory restraints which are imposed upon the disposition of one's property by will are added strict and systematic statutory rules for the execution, alteration, and revocation of the will, which must be, at least substantially, if not exactly, followed to insure validity and performance. The reason for the establishment of such rules, we may naturally assume, consists in the purpose to create those safeguards about these grave and important acts which experience has demonstrated to be the wisest and surest. That freedom which is permitted to be exercised in the testamentary disposition of one's estate by the laws of the state is subject to its being exercised in conformity with the regulations of the statutes. The capacity and the power of the individual to dispose of his property after death, and the mode by which that power can be exercised, are matters of which the legislature has assumed the entire control, and has undertaken to regulate with comprehensive particularity. . . .

I cannot find any support for the argument that the respondent's succession to the property should be avoided because of his criminal act, when the laws are silent. Public policy does not de-

mand it; for the demands of public policy are satisfied by the proper execution of the laws and the punishment of the crime. There has been no convention between the testator and his legatee. The appellants' argument practically amounts to this: that, as the legatee has been guilty of a crime, by the commission of which he is placed in a position to sooner receive the benefits of the testamentary provision, his rights to the property should be forfeited, and he should be divested of his estate. To allow their argument to prevail would involve the diversion by the court of the testator's estate into the hands of persons whom, possibly enough, for all we know, the testator might not have chosen or desired as its recipients. Practically the court is asked to make another will for the testator. The laws do not warrant this judicial action, and mere presumption would not be strong enough to sustain it. But, more than this, to concede the appellants' views would involve the imposition of an additional punishment or penalty upon the respondent. What power or warrant have the courts to add to the respondent's penalties by depriving him of property? The law has punished him for his crime, and we may not say that it was an insufficient punishment. In the trial and punishment of the respondent the law has vindicated itself for the outrage which he committed, and further judicial utterance upon the subject of punishment or deprivation of rights is barred. We may not, in the language of the court in *People v. Thornton*, 25 Hun, 456, "enhance the pains, penalties, and forfeitures provided by law for the punishment of crime." The judgment should be affirmed, with costs.

25. The Amistad

The story of the slave ship *Amistad* was made famous in the Steven Speilberg movie. The real story of the *Amistad* raises serious issues of law, as well as the social and moral issues explored in the film.

In January 1839, African natives were sold into the Spanish slave trade and then sent by ship to Havana, Cuba. There, two Spaniards, Ruiz and Montez, who had purchased the slaves, loaded them aboard the *Amistad,* bound for another part of Cuba. Three days into this journey, a twenty-five-year-old slave (named "Cinque" by his Spanish captors), led a revolt, culminating in the death of most of the ship's crew. The two Spanish "owners" were ordered to steer the ship back to Africa, but they tricked the slaves, pretending to sail for Africa while actually seeking to sail back to Cuba. A zigzag journey of more than two months ended when the *Amistad* went aground near Long Island, in New York. The U.S. federal government seized the ship and its "cargo." The government charged the slaves with piracy and murder, and they were sent to prison pending a hearing before a federal judge.

Ruiz and Montez, the alleged "owners," argued that both slavery and the slave trade were legal in Spain; Ruiz and Montez were Spanish citizens and the *Amistad* was registered under the flag of Spain. Moreover, the slaves had been bought and sold in Cuba, which was a Spanish territory at the time. The slaves were property, they claimed, according to the law of Spain. Under U.S. law in 1841, however, the slave trade was illegal. Important for U.S. officials was whether Cinque and his followers were to be considered Spanish citizens (thus "property"), citizens of Africa, or to have some other status.

A federal district judge ruled that the slaves were free men, ordering their release from prison, and directing that the U.S. government return the Africans to their native land. The U.S. attorney argued that the federal government must be free to return the slaves to Spain, as its treaty obligations required. The case was appealed to the U.S. Supreme Court.

Excerpt of argument for the United States

. . . The only inquiries, then, that present themselves, are: 1. Has 'due and sufficient proof concerning the property thereof' been made? 2. If so, have the United States a right to interpose in the manner they have done, to obtain its restoration to the Spanish owners? If these inquiries result in the affirmative, then the decree of the circuit court was erroneous, and ought to be reversed.

I. It is submitted, that there has been due and sufficient proof concerning the property, to authorize its restoration. It is not denied, that, under the

40 U.S. 518 (1841) United States Supreme Court

laws of Spain, negroes may be held as slaves, as completely as they are in any of the states of this Union; nor will it be denied, if duly proved to be such, they are subject to restoration, as much as other property, when coming under the provisions of this treaty. Now, these negroes are declared, by the certificates of the governor-general, to be slaves, and the property of the Spanish subjects therein named. That officer (1 White's New Rec. 369, 371; 8 Pet. 310) is the highest functionary of the government in Cuba; his public acts are the highest evidence of any facts stated by him, within the scope of his authority. It is within the scope of his authority, to declare what is property, and what are the rights of the subjects of Spain, within his jurisdiction, in regard to property.

Now, in the intercourse of nations, there is no rule better established than this, that full faith is to be given to such acts—to the authentic evidence of such acts. The question is not, whether the act is right or wrong; it is, whether the act has been done, and whether it is an act within the scope of the authority. We are to inquire only whether the power existed, and whether it was exercised, and how it was exercised; not whether it was rightly or wrongly exercised. . . .

Excerpt of argument for the Africans

The American people have never imposed it as a duty on the government of the United States, to become actors in an attempt to reduce to slavery, men found in a state of freedom, by giving extra-territorial force to a foreign slave law. Such a duty would not only be repugnant to the feelings of a large portion of the citizens of the United States, but it would be wholly inconsistent with the fundamental principles of our government, and the purposes [40 U.S. 518, 551] for which it was established, as well as with its policy in prohibiting the slave-trade and giving freedom to its victims. The recovery of slaves for their owners, whether foreign or domestic, is a matter with which the executive of the United States has no concern. The constitution confers upon the government no power to establish or legalize the institution of slavery. It recognises it as existing, in regard to persons held to service by the laws of the states which tolerate it;

and contains a compact between the states, obliging them to respect the rights acquired under the slave laws of other states, in the cases specified in the constitution. But it imposes no duty, and confers no power, on the government of the United States, to act in regard to it. So far as the compact extends, the courts of the United States, whether sitting in a free state or a slave state, will give effect to it. Beyond that, all persons within the limits of a state are entitled to the protection of its laws.

If these Africans have been taken from the possession of their Spanish claimants, and wrongfully brought into the United States by our citizens, a question would have been presented similar to that which existed in the case of the *Antelope*. But when men have come here voluntarily, without any wrong on the part of the government or citizens of the United States, in withdrawing them from the jurisdiction of the Spanish laws, why should this government be required to become active in their restoration? They appear here as freemen. They are in a state where they are presumed to be free. They stand before our courts on equal ground with their claimants; and when the courts, after an impartial hearing, with all parties in interest before them, have pronounced them free, it is neither the duty nor the right of the executive of the United States, to interfere with the decision.

. . .

The Africans, when found by Lieutenant Gedney, were in a free state, where all men are presumed to be free, and were in the actual condition of freemen. The burden of proof, therefore, rests on those who assert them to be slaves. 10 Wheat, 66; 2 Mason 459. When they call on the courts of the United States to reduce to slavery men who are apparently free, they must show some law, having force in the place where they were taken, which makes them slaves, or that the claimants are entitled in our courts to have some foreign law, obligatory on the Africans as well as on the claimants, enforced in respect to them, and that by such foreign law they are slaves. It is not pretended, that there was any law existing in the place where they were found, which made them slaves, but it is claimed, that by the laws of Cuba, they were slaves to Ruiz and Montez; and that those laws are to be here enforced. But before the laws of Cuba, if any such there be, can be applied, to affect the personal status of individuals within a foreign jurisdiction, it is very clear, that it must be shown that they were domiciled in Cuba.

. . .

Story, Justice, *delivered the opinion of the court.*

. . .

If these negroes were, at the time, lawfully held as slaves, under the laws of Spain, and recognised by those laws as property, capable of being lawfully bought and sold; we see no reason whey they may not justly be deemed, within the intent of the treaty, to be included under the denomination of merchandize, and as such ought to be restored to the claimants; for upon that point the laws of Spain would seem to furnish the proper rule of interpretation. But admitting this, it is clear, in our opinion, that neither of the other essential facts and requisites has been established in proof; and the *onus probandi* of both lies upon the claimants to give rise to the *casus foederis*. It is plain, beyond controversy, if we examine the evidence, that these negroes never were the lawful slaves of Ruiz or Montez, or of any other Spanish subjects. They are natives of Africa, and were kidnapped there, and were unlawfully transported to Cuba, in violation of the laws and treaties of Spain, and the most solemn edicts and declarations of that government. By those laws and treaties, and edicts, the African slave trade is utterly abolished; the dealing in that trade is deemed a heinous crime; and the negroes thereby introduced into the dominions of Spain, are declared to be free. Ruiz and Montez are proved to have made the pretended purchase of these negroes, with a full knowledge of all the circumstances. And so cogent and irresistible is the evidence in this respect, that the district-attorney has admitted in open court, upon the record, that these negroes were native Africans, and recently imported into Cuba, as alleged in their answers to the libels in the case. The supposed proprietary interest of Ruiz and Montez is completely displaced, if we are at liberty to look at the evidence, or the admissions of the district-attorney.

If then, these negroes are not slaves, but are kidnapped Africans, who, by the laws of Spain itself, are entitled to their freedom, and were kidnapped and illegally carried to Cuba, and illegally detained and restrained on board the *Amistad*; there is no pretence to say, that they are pirates or robbers. We may lament the dreadful acts by which they asserted their liberty, and took possession of the *Amistad,* and endeavored to regain their native [40 U.S. 518, 594] country; but they cannot be deemed pirates or robbers, in the sense of the law of nations, or the treaty with Spain, or the laws of Spain itself; at least, so far as those laws have been brought to our knowledge. Nor do the libels of Ruiz or Montez assert them to be such.

It is also a most important consideration, in the present case, which ought not to be lost sight of, that, supposing these African negroes not to be slaves, but kidnapped, and free negroes, the treaty with Spain cannot be obligatory upon them; and the United States are bound to respect their rights as much as those of Spanish subjects. The conflict of rights between the parties, under such circumstances, becomes positive and inevitable, and must be decided upon the eternal principles of justice and international law. If the contest were about any goods on board of this ship, to which American citizens asserted a title, which was [40 U.S. 518, 596] denied by the Spanish claimants, there could be no doubt of the right to such American citizens to litigate their claims before any competent American tribunal, notwithstanding the treaty with Spain. *A fortiori,* the doctrine must apply, where human life and human liberty are in issue, and constitute the very essence of the controversy. The treaty with Spain never could have intended to take away the equal rights of all foreigners, who should contest their claims before any of our courts, to equal justice; or to deprive such foreigners of the protection given them by other treaties, or by the general law of nations. Upon the merits of the case, then, there does not seem to us to be any ground for doubt, that these negroes ought to be deemed free; and that the Spanish treaty interposes no obstacle to the just assertion of their rights.

26. *The Antelope*

[An opinion by legendary Chief Justice John Marshall, this early case represents yet another clash between positive and natural law, set here in the context of the law of nations. Can you explain why, if both the (positive) statutes of the United States and the principles of the "law of nature" condemn the slave trade, Marshall nonetheless orders the return of the slaves to their "owners"? Why does Marshall hold that the positive laws of nations "trumps" the positive law of the United States?]

[In 1808 the Congress prohibited the importation of slaves into the United States. Subsequent federal laws punished persons who engaged in the slave trade, requiring that their ships be forfeited and that the Negroes be returned to Africa. The slave ship *Antelope,* carrying over two hundred African slaves, was intercepted off the coast of Florida by a United States vessel for suspected violation of the slave-trade laws. The governments of Spain and Portugal insisted that the ship and its cargo be released, maintaining that the Africans were the property of Spanish and Portuguese citizens. The U.S. government resisted and presented the Supreme Court with the question of whether the U.S. federal laws applied to forfeit slaves owned by foreign nationals.]

Marshall, Chief Justice.

In prosecuting this appeal, the United States assert no property in themselves. They appear in the character of guardians, or next friends, of these Africans, who are brought, without any act of their own, into the bosom of our country, insist on their right to freedom, and submit their claim to the laws of the land, and to the tribunals of the nation. The consuls of Spain and Portugal, respectively, demand these Africans as slaves, who have, in the regular cause of legitimate commerce, been acquired as property, by the subjects of their respective sovereigns, and claim their restitution under the laws of the United States.

In examining claims of this momentous importance—claims in which the sacred rights of liberty and of property come in conflict with each other—which have drawn from the bar a degree of talent

and of eloquence, worthy of the questions that have been discussed, their court must not yield to feelings which might seduce it from the path of duty, and must obey the mandate of the law.

That the course of opinion on the slave-trade should be unsettled, ought to excite no surprise. The Christian and civilized nations of the world with whom we have most intercourse, have all been engaged in it. However abhorrent this traffic may be to a mind whose original feelings are not blunted by familiarity with the practice, it has been sanctioned, in modern times, by the laws of all nations who possess distant colonies, each of whom has engaged in it as a common commercial business, which no other could rightfully interrupt. It has claimed all the sanction which could be derived from long usage and general acquiescence. That trade could not be considered as contrary to the law of nations which was authorized and protected by the laws of all commercial nations; the right to carry on which was claimed by each, and allowed by each.

23 U.S. (19 Wheat.) 66 (1825)
United States Supreme Court

The course of unexamined opinion, which was founded on this inveterate usage, received its first check in America; and, as soon as these states acquired the right of self-government, the traffic was forbidden by most of them. In the beginning of this century, several humane and enlightened individuals of Great Britain devoted themselves to the cause of the Africans; and by frequent appeals to the nation, in which the enormity of this commerce was unveiled and exposed to the public eye, the general sentiment was at length roused against it, and the feelings of justice and humanity, regaining their long-lost ascendency, prevailed so far in the British parliament, as to obtain an act for its abolition. The utmost efforts of the British government, as well as of that of the United States, have since been assiduously employed in its suppression. It has been denounced by both, in terms of great severity, and those concerned in it are subjected to the heaviest penalties which law can inflict. In addition to these measures, operating on their own people, they have used all their influence to bring other nations into the same system, and to interdict this trade by the consent of all. Public sentiment has, in both countries, kept pace with the measures of government; and the opinion is extensively, if not universally, entertained, that this unnatural traffic ought to be suppressed. While its illegality is asserted by some governments, but not admitted by all; while the detestation in which it is held, is growing daily, and even those nations who tolerate it, in fact, almost disavow their own conduct, and rather connive at, than legalize, the acts of their subjects, it is not wonderful, that public feeling should march somewhat in advance of strict law, and that opposite opinions should be entertained on the precise cases in which our own laws may control and limit the practice of others. Indeed, we ought not to be surprised, if, in this novel series of cases, even courts of justice should, in some instances, have carried the principle of suppression further than a more deliberate consideration of the subject would justify. . . .

The question, whether the slave-trade is prohibited by the law of nations has been seriously propounded, and both the affirmative and negative of the proposition have been maintained with equal earnestness. That it is contrary to the law of nature, will scarcely be denied. That every man has a natural right to the fruits of his own labor, is generally admitted; and that no other person can rightfully deprive him of those fruits, and appropriate them against his will, seems to be the necessary result of this admission. But from the earliest times, war has existed, and war confers rights in which all have acquiesced. Among the most enlightened nations of antiquity, one of these was, that the victor might enslave the vanquished. This, which was the usage of all, could not be pronounced repugnant to the law of nations, which is certainly to be tried by the test of general usage. That which has received the assent of all, must be the law of all. Slavery, then, has its origin in force; but as the world has agreed, that it is a legitimate result of force, the state of things which is thus produced by general consent, cannot be pronounced unlawful.

Throughout Christendom, this harsh rule has been exploded, and war is no longer considered, as giving a right to enslave captives. But this triumph of humanity has not been universal. The parties to the modern law of nations do not propagate their principles by force, and Africa has not yet adopted them. Throughout the whole extent of that immense continent, so far as we know its history, it is still the law of nations, that prisoners are slaves. Can those who have themselves renounced this law, be permitted to participate in its effects, by purchasing the beings who are its victims? Whatever might be the answer of a moralist to this question, a jurist must search for its legal solution, in those principles of action which are sanctioned by the usages, the national acts, and the general assent, of that portion of the world of which he considers himself as a part, and to whose law the appeal is made. If we resort to this standard, as the test of international law, the question, as has already been observed, is decided in favor of the legality of the trade. Both Europe and America embarked in it; and for nearly two centuries, it was carried on, without opposition, and without censure. A jurist could not say, that a practice, thus supported, was illegal, and that those engaged in it might be punished, either personally or by deprivation of property. In this commerce thus sanctioned by universal assent, every nation had an equal right to engage. How is their right to be lost? Each may renounce it for its own people; but can this renunciation affect others?

No principle of general law is more universally acknowledged, than the perfect equality of nations. Russia and Geneva have equal rights. It results from this equality, that no one can rightfully impose a rule on another. Each legislates for itself, but its legislation can operate on itself alone. A right, then, which is vested in all, by the consent of all, can be divested only by consent; and this trade, in which all have participated, must remain lawful to those who cannot be induced to relinquish it. As no nation can prescribe a rule for others, none can make a law of nations; and this traffic remains lawful to those whose governments have not forbidden it. If it be consistent with the law of nations, it cannot in itself be piracy. It can be made so only by statute; and the obligation of the statute cannot transcend the legislative power of the state which may enact it.

If it be neither repugnant to the law of nations, nor piracy, it is almost superfluous to say, in this court, that the right of bringing in for adjudication, in time of peace, even where the vessel belongs to a nation which has prohibited the trade, cannot exist. The courts of no country execute the penal laws of another; and the course of the American govern-ment, on the subject of visitation and search, would decide any case in which that right had been exercised by an American cruiser, on the vessel of a foreign nation, not violating our municipal laws, against the captors. It follows, that a foreign vessel engaged in the African slave-trade, captured on the high seas, in time of peace, by an American cruiser, and brought in for adjudication, would be restored. . . .

The general question being disposed of, it remains to examine the circumstances of the particular case. [The Court denied the Portuguese claims, taking judicial notice of the fact that] Americans, and others who cannot use the flag of their own nations, carry on this criminal and inhuman traffic, under the flags of other countries. . . . [The real owner of the Africans claimed by Portugal] belongs to some other nation, and feels the necessity of concealment. [Because the Court was evenly divided over the legitimacy of the Spanish claim, it affirmed the lower court's decree, though it reduced the number of Africans to be restored to the Spanish owners.]

---

27. *The Problem of the Grudge Informer*

Lon Fuller

Fuller's imaginary case presents you with a difficult choice: What will you do as the newly elected Minister of Justice? As you read the recommendations of the various deputies, try to detect appeals to one or another of the theories about the nature of law covered in this chapter. Do any of the deputies come close to your solution?

By a narrow margin you have been elected Minister of Justice of your country, a nation of some twenty million inhabitants. At the outset of your term of office you are confronted by a serious prob-lem that will be described below. But first the background of this problem must be presented.

For many decades your country enjoyed a peaceful, constitutional and democratic government. However, some time ago it came upon bad times. Normal relations were disrupted by a deepening economic depression and by an increasing antagonism among various factional groups, formed along economic, political, and religious lines. The proverbial man on horseback appeared in the form of the Headman of a political party or society that called itself the Purple Shirts.

In a national election attended by much disorder the Headman was elected President of the Republic and his party obtained a majority of the seats in the General Assembly. The success of the party at the polls was partly brought about by a campaign of reckless promises and ingenious falsifications, and partly by the physical intimidation of night-riding Purple Shirts who frightened many people away from the polls who would have voted against the party.

When the Purple Shirts arrived in power they took no steps to repeal the ancient Constitution or any of its provisions. They also left intact the Civil and Criminal Codes and the Code of Procedure. No official action was taken to dismiss any government official or remove any judge from the bench. Elections continued to be held at intervals and ballots were counted with apparent honesty. Nevertheless, the country lived under a reign of terror.

Judges who rendered decisions contrary to the wishes of the party were beaten and murdered. The accepted meaning of the Criminal Code was perverted to place political opponents in jail. Secret statutes were passed, the contents of which were known only to the upper levels of the party hierarchy. Retroactive statutes were enacted which made acts criminal that were legally innocent when committed. No attention was paid by the government to the restraints of the Constitution, of antecedent laws, or even of its own laws. All opposing political parties were disbanded. Thousands of political opponents were put to death, either methodically in prisons or in sporadic night forays of terror. A general amnesty was declared in favor of persons under sentence for acts "committed in defending

From *The Morality of Law* (New Haven: Yale University Press, 1969), pp. 245–253. Reprinted with permission of Yale University Press.

the fatherland against subversion." Under this amnesty a general liberation of all prisoners who were members of the Purple Shirt party was effected. No one not a member of the party was released under the amnesty.

The Purple Shirts as a matter of deliberate policy preserved an element of flexibility in their operations by acting at times through the apparatus of the state which they controlled. Choice between the two methods of proceeding was purely a matter of expediency. For example, when the inner circle of the party decided to ruin all the former Socialist-Republicans (whose party put up a last-ditch resistance to the new regime), a dispute arose as to the best way of confiscating their property. One faction, perhaps still influenced by prerevolutionary conceptions, wanted to accomplish this by a statute declaring their goods forfeited for criminal acts. Another wanted to do it by compelling the owners to deed their property over at the point of a bayonet. This group argued against the proposed statute on the ground that it would attract unfavorable comment abroad. The Headman decided in favor of direct action through the party to be followed by a secret statute ratifying the party's action and confirming the titles obtained by threats of physical violence.

The Purple Shirts have now been overthrown and a democratic and constitutional government restored. Some difficult problems have, however, been left behind by the deposed regime. These you and your associates in the new government must find some way of solving. One of these problems is that of the "grudge informer."

During the Purple Shirt regime a great many people worked off grudges by reporting their enemies to the party or to the government authorities. The activities reported were such things as the private expression of views critical of the government, listening to foreign radio broadcasts, associating with known wreckers and hooligans, hoarding more than the permitted amount of dried eggs, failing to report a loss of identification papers within five days, etc. As things then stood with the administration of justice, any of these acts, if proved, could lead to a sentence of death. In some cases this sentence was authorized by "emergency" statutes; in others it was imposed without statutory warrant, though by judges duly appointed to their offices.

After the overthrow of the Purple Shirts, a strong public demand grew up that these grudge informers be punished. The interim government, which preceded that with which you are associated, temporized on this matter. Meanwhile it has become a burning issue and a decision concerning it can no longer be postponed. Accordingly, your first act as Minister of Justice has been to address yourself to it. You have asked your five Deputies to give thought to the matter and to bring their recommendations to conference. At the conference the five Deputies speak in turn as follows:

FIRST DEPUTY: "It is perfectly clear to me that we can do nothing about these so-called grudge informers. The acts they reported were unlawful according to the rules of the government then in actual control of the nation's affairs. The sentences imposed on their victims were rendered in accordance with principles of law then obtaining. These principles differed from those familiar to us in ways that we consider detestable. Nevertheless they were then the law of the land. One of the principal differences between that law and our own lies in the much wider discretion it accorded to the judge in criminal matters. This rule and its consequences are as much entitled to respect by us as the reform which the Purple Shirts introduced into the law of wills, whereby only two witnesses were required instead of three. It is immaterial that the rule granting the judge a more or less uncontrolled discretion in criminal cases was never formally enacted but was a matter of tacit acceptance. Exactly the same thing can be said of the opposite rule which we accept that restricts the judge's discretion narrowly. The difference between ourselves and the Purple Shirts is not that theirs was an unlawful government—a contradiction in terms—but lies rather in the field of ideology. No one has a greater abhorrence than I for Purple Shirtism. Yet the fundamental difference between our philosophy and theirs is that we permit and tolerate differences in viewpoint, while they attempted to impose their monolithic code on everyone. Our whole system of government assumes that law is a flexible thing, capable of expressing and effectuating many different aims. The cardinal point of our creed is that when an objective has been duly incorporated into a law or judicial decree it must be provisionally accepted even

by those that hate it, who must await their chance at the polls, or in another litigation, to secure a legal recognition of their own aims. The Purple Shirts, on the other hand, simply disregarded laws that incorporated objectives of which they did not approve, not even considering it worth the effort involved to repeal them. If we now seek to unscramble the acts of the Purple Shirt regime, declaring this judgment invalid, that statute void, this sentence excessive, we shall be doing exactly the thing we most condemn in them. I recognize that it will take courage to carry through with the program I recommend and we shall have to resist strong pressures of public opinion. We shall also have to be prepared to prevent the people from taking the law into their own hands. In the long run, however, I believe the course I recommend is the only one that will insure the triumph of the conceptions of law and government in which we believe."

SECOND DEPUTY: "Curiously, I arrive at the same conclusion as my colleague, by an exactly opposite route. To me it seems absurd to call the Purple Shirt regime a lawful government. A legal system does not exist simply because policemen continue to patrol the streets and wear uniforms or because a constitution and code are left on the shelf unrepealed. A legal system presupposes laws that are known, or can be known, by those subject to them. It presupposes some uniformity of action and that like cases will be given like treatment. It presupposes the absence of some lawless power, like the Purple Shirt Party, standing above the government and able at any time to interfere with the administration of justice whenever it does not function according to the whims of that power. All of these presuppositions enter into the very conception of an order of law and have nothing to do with political and economic ideologies. In my opinion law in any ordinary sense of the word ceased to exist when the Purple Shirts came to power. During their regime we had, in effect, an interregnum in the rule of law. Instead of a government of laws we had a war of all against all conducted behind barred doors, in dark alleyways, in palace intrigues, and prison-yard conspiracies. The acts of these so-called grudge informers were just one phase of that war. For us to condemn these acts as criminal would involve as much incongruity as if we were to attempt to apply juristic conceptions to the struggle for existence that goes on in the jungle or beneath the surface of the sea. We must put this whole dark, lawless chapter of our history behind us like a bad dream. If we stir among its hatreds, we shall bring upon ourselves something of its evil spirit and risk infection from its miasmas. I therefore say with my colleague, let bygones be bygones. Let us do nothing about the so-called grudge informers. What they did do was neither lawful nor contrary to law, for they lived, not under a regime of law, but under one of anarchy and terror."

THIRD DEPUTY: "I have a profound suspicion of any kind of reasoning that proceeds by an 'either-or' alternative. I do not think we need to assume either, on the one hand, that in some manner the whole of the Purple Shirt regime was outside the realm of law, or, on the other, that all of its doings are entitled to full credence as the acts of a lawful government. My two colleagues have unwittingly delivered powerful arguments against these extreme assumptions by demonstrating that both of them lead to the same absurd conclusion, a conclusion that is ethically and politically impossible. If one reflects about the matter without emotion it becomes clear that we did not have during the Purple Shirt regime a 'war of all against all.' Under the surface much of what we call normal human life went on— marriages were contracted, goods were sold, wills were drafted and executed. This life was attended by the usual dislocations—automobile accidents, bankruptcies, unwitnessed wills, defamatory misprints in the newspapers. Much of this normal life and most of these equally normal dislocations of it were unaffected by the Purple Shirt ideology. The legal questions that arose in this area were handled by the courts much as they had been formerly and much as they are being handled today. It would invite an intolerable chaos if we were to declare everything that happened under the Purple Shirts to be without legal basis. On the other hand, we certainly cannot say that the murders committed in the streets by members of the party acting under orders from the Headman were lawful simply because the party had achieved control of the government and its chief had become President of the Republic. If we must condemn the criminal acts of the party and its members, it would seem absurd to

uphold every act which happened to be canalized through the apparatus of the government that had become, in effect, the alter ego of the Purple Shirt Party. We must therefore, in this situation, as in most human affairs, discriminate. Where the Purple Shirt philosophy intruded itself and perverted the administration of justice from its normal aims and uses, there we must interfere. Among these perversions of justice I would count, for example, the case of a man who was in love with another man's wife and brought about the death of the husband by informing against him for a wholly trivial offense, that is, for not reporting a loss of his identification papers within five days. This informer was a murderer under the Criminal Code which was in effect at the time of his act and which the Purple Shirts had not repealed. He encompassed the death of one who stood in the way of his illicit passions and utilized the courts for the realization of his murderous intent. He knew that the courts were themselves the pliant instruments of whatever policy the Purple Shirts might for the moment consider expedient. There are other cases that are equally clear. I admit that there are also some that are less clear. We shall be embarrassed, for example, by the cases of mere busybodies who reported to the authorities everything that looked suspect. Some of these persons acted not from desire to get rid of those they accused, but with a desire to curry favor with the party, to divert suspicions (perhaps ill-founded) raised against themselves, or through sheer officiousness. I don't know how these cases should be handled, and make no recommendation with regard to them. But the fact that these troublesome cases exist should not deter us from acting at once in the cases that are clear, of which there are far too many to permit us to disregard them."

FOURTH DEPUTY: "Like my colleague I too distrust 'either-or' reasoning, but I think we need to reflect more than he has about where we are headed. This proposal to pick and choose among the acts of the deposed regime is thoroughly objectionable. It is, in fact, Purple Shirtism itself, pure and simple. We like this law, so let us enforce it. We like this judgment, let it stand. This law we don't like, therefore it never was a law at all. This governmental act we disapprove, let it be deemed a nullity. If we proceed this way, we take toward the laws and acts of the

Purple Shirt government precisely the unprincipled attitude they took toward the laws and acts of the government they supplanted. We shall have chaos, with every judge and every prosecuting attorney a law unto himself. Instead of ending the abuses of the Purple Shirt regime, my colleague's proposal would perpetuate them. There is only one way of dealing with this problem that is compatible with our philosophy of law and government and that is to deal with it by duly enacted law, I mean, by a special statute directed toward it. Let us study this whole problem of the grudge informer, get all the relevant facts, and draft a comprehensive law dealing with it. We shall not then be twisting old laws to purposes for which they were never intended. We shall furthermore provide penalties appropriate to the offense and not treat every informer as a murderer simply because the one he informed against was ultimately executed. I admit that we shall encounter some difficult problems of draftsmanship. Among other things, we shall have to assign a definite legal meaning to 'grudge' and that will not be easy. We should not be deterred by these difficulties, however, from adopting the only course that will lead us out of a condition of lawless, personal rule."

FIFTH DEPUTY: "I find a considerable irony in the last proposal. It speaks of putting a definite end to the abuses of the Purple Shirtism, yet it proposes to do this by resorting to one of the most hated devices of the Purple Shirt regime, the *ex post facto* criminal statute. My colleague dreads the conclusion that will result if we attempt without a statute to undo and redress 'wrong' acts of the departed order, while we uphold and enforce its 'right' acts. Yet he seems not to realize that his proposed statute is a wholly specious cure for this uncertainty. It is easy to make a plausible argument for an undrafted statute; we all agree it would be nice to have things down in black and white on paper. But just what would this statute provide? One of my colleagues speaks of someone who had failed for five days to report a loss of his identification papers. My col-

league implies that the judicial sentence imposed for that offense, namely death, was so utterly disproportionate as to be clearly wrong. But we must remember that at that time the underground movement against the Purple Shirts was mounting in intensity and that the Purple Shirts were being harassed constantly by people with false identification papers. From their point of view they had a real problem, and the only objection we can make to their solution of it (other than the fact that we didn't want them to solve it) was that they acted with somewhat more rigor than the occasion seemed to demand. How will my colleague deal with this case in his statute, and with all of its cousins and second cousins? Will he deny the existence of any need for law and order under the Purple Shirt regime? I will not go further into the difficulties involved in drafting this proposed statute, since they are evident enough to anyone who reflects. I shall instead turn to my own solution. It has been said on very respectable authority that the main purpose of the criminal law is to give an outlet to the human instinct for revenge. There are times, and I believe this is one of them, when we should allow that instinct to express itself directly without the intervention of forms of law. This matter of the grudge informers is already in process of straightening itself out. One reads almost every day that a former lackey of the Purple Shirt regime has met his just reward in some unguarded spot. The people are quietly handling this thing in their own way and if we leave them alone, and instruct our public prosecutors to do the same, there will soon be no problem left for us to solve. There will be some disorders, of course, and a few innocent heads will be broken. But our government and our legal system will not be involved in the affair and we shall not find ourselves hopelessly bogged down in an attempt to unscramble all the deeds and misdeeds of the Purple Shirts."

As Minister of Justice which of these recommendations would you adopt?

28. *People v. Hall*

Hall was convicted of murder, based largely on the testimony of Chinese immigrants. Hall challenged his conviction on the ground that the law in California at the time prohibited an "Indian or Negro" from testifying against a White person. The court goes to extreme lengths to show that this law also applies to ethnic Chinese. The tortuous reasoning of the court should be considered particularly in light of Dworkin's theory of adjudication. How would a judge, living at this time and confronted with such a law, interpret the statute in "its best light"? Would the "political morality" of nineteenth-century America afford a justification for this statute? What should a Dworkinian judge do when confronted with an unjust law?

Mr. Ch. J. Murray delivered the opinion of the Court, Mr. J. Heydenfeldt concurred.

The appellant, a free white citizen of this State, was convicted of murder upon the testimony of Chinese witnesses.

The point involved in this case, is the admissibility of such evidence.

The 394th section of the Act Concerning Civil Cases, provides that no Indian or Negro shall be allowed to testify as a witness in any action or proceeding in which a White person is a party.

The 14th section of the Act of April 16th, 1850, regulating Criminal Proceedings, provides that "No Black, or Mulatto person, or Indian, shall be allowed to give evidence in favor of, or against a white man."

The true point at which we are anxious to arrive, is the legal signification of the words, "Black, Mulatto, Indian and White person," and whether the Legislature adopted them as generic terms, or intended to limit their application to specific types of the human species.

[The] name of Indian, from the time of Columbus to the present day, has been used to designate, not alone the North American Indian, but the whole of the Mongolian race, and that the name, though first applied probably through mistake,

4 Cal. 399 (1854)
Supreme Court of California

was afterwards continued as appropriate on account of the supposed common origin.

That this was the common opinion in the early history of American legislation, cannot be disputed, and, therefore, all legislation upon the subject must have borne relation to that opinion.

Can, then, the use of the word "Indian," because at the present day it may be sometimes regarded as a specific, and not as a generic term, alter this conclusion? We think not; because at the origin of the legislation we are considering, it was used and admitted in its common and ordinary acceptation, as a generic term, distinguishing the great Mongolian race, and as such, its meaning then became fixed by law, and in construing Statutes the legal meaning of words must be preserved.

Again: the words of the Act must be construed in *pari materia*. It will not be disputed that "White" and "Negro," are generic terms, and refer to two of the great types of mankind. If these, as well as the word "Indian," are not to be regarded as generic terms, including the two great races which they were intended to designate, but only specific, and applying to those Whites and Negroes who were inhabitants of this Continent at the time of the passage of the Act, the most anomalous consequences would ensue. The European white man who comes here would not be shielded from the testimony of the degraded and demoralized caste, while the Negro, fresh from the coast of Africa, or the Indian of Patagonia, the Kanaka, South Sea

Islander, or New Hollander, would be admitted, upon their arrival, to testify against white citizens in our courts of law.

To argue such a proposition would be an insult to the good sense of the Legislature.

The evident intention of the Act was to throw around the citizen a protection for life and property, which could only be secured by removing him above the corrupting influences of degraded castes.

It can hardly be supposed that any Legislature would attempt this by excluding domestic Negroes and Indians, who not unfrequently have correct notions of their obligations to society, and turning loose upon the community the more degraded tribes of the same species, who have nothing in common with us, in language, country or laws.

We have, thus far, considered this subject on the hypothesis that the 14th section of the Act Regulating Criminal Proceedings, and the 394th section of the Practice Act, were the same.

As before remarked, there is a wide difference between the two. The word "Black" may include all Negroes, but the term "Negro" does not include all Black persons.

By the use of this term in this connection, we understand it to mean the opposite of "White," and that it should be taken as contradistinguished from all White persons.

In using the words, "No Black, or Mulatto person, or Indian shall be allowed to give evidence for or against a White person," the Legislature, if any intention can be ascribed to it, adopted the most comprehensive terms to embrace every known class or shade of color, as the apparent design was to protect the White person from the influence of all testimony other than that of persons of the same caste. The use of these terms must, by every sound rule of construction, exclude every one who is not of white blood.

. . .

We are of the opinion that the words "White," "Negro," "Mulatto," "Indian," and "Black person," wherever they occur in our Constitution and laws, must be taken in their generic sense, and that, even admitting the Indian of this Continent is not of the Mongolian type, that the words "Black person," in the 14th section must be taken as contradistin-guished from White, and necessarily excludes all races other than the Caucasian.

We have carefully considered all the consequences resulting from a different rule of construction, and are satisfied that even in a doubtful case we would be impelled to this decision on grounds of public policy.

The same rule which would admit them to testify, would admit them to all the equal rights of citizenship, and we might soon see them at the polls, in the jury box, upon the bench, and in our legislative halls.

This is not a speculation which exists in the excited and over-heated imagination of the patriot and statesman, but it is an actual and present danger.

The anomalous spectacle of a distinct people, living in our community, recognizing no laws of this State except through necessity, bringing with them their prejudices and national feuds, in which they indulge in open violation of law; whose mendacity is proverbial; a race of people whom nature has marked as inferior, and who are incapable of progress or intellectual development beyond a certain point, as their history has shown; differing in language, opinions, color, and physical conformation; between whom and ourselves nature has placed an impassable difference, is now presented, and for them is claimed, not only the right to swear away the life of a citizen, but the further privilege of participating with us in administering the affairs of our Government.

These facts were before the Legislature that framed this Act, and have been known as matters of public history to every subsequent Legislature.

There can be no doubt as to the intention of the Legislature, and that if it had ever been anticipated that this class of people were not embraced in the prohibition, then such specific words would have been employed as would have put the matter beyond any possible controversy.

For these reasons, we are of opinion that the testimony was inadmissible.

The judgment is reversed and the cause remanded.

Chapter II

Law, Liberty and Morality

In 1996, Congress passed and the president signed the Communications Decency Act (CDA). This act made it a federal offense to use any "interactive computer service" to send or display in a way accessible to minors under the age of eighteen "any comment, request, suggestion, proposal, image, or other communication that, in context, depicts or describes, in terms patently offensive as measured by contemporary community standards, sexual or excretory activities or organs." The CDA was a response to growing concern over easy access by children to pornographic material available on the Internet and World Wide Web. The following year, the U.S. Supreme Court ruled that the CDA was unconstitutional because it violates the "freedom of speech" protected by the First Amendment to the Constitution.

Four years before it struck down the CDA, the Supreme Court had ruled unconstitutional another law. In that case, the Court invalidated an ordinance of the City of Hialeah, Florida, which prohibited the ritual slaughter of animals. The Court found that that law, while apparently applying neutrally to everyone, was in fact targeted against practitioners of the Santeria faith, and thus violated another

clause of the First Amendment protecting "the free exercise of religion."

These two cases highlight a number of important issues: How free can I be to put into practice my religious beliefs? How free should I be to express myself in cyberspace? Or in public? Does the idea of freedom of expression protect all forms of expression? Should activities that offend others be legally prohibited? What if my conduct is viewed by others as immoral? Can the law fairly be used to impose the moral or religious views of the majority upon the minority? What would this mean? Shouldn't the law always try to enforce moral standards of behavior? Would it ever be justifiable to disobey the law on moral grounds?

The readings in this chapter explore various dimensions of these questions, beginning with a general discussion about the relationship of law to morality. The similarities and differences between law and morality are briefly outlined, followed by readings that debate the appropriate boundaries of legal enforcement of moral standards and the moral limits of obedience to the law. The classic essay by philosopher John Stuart Mill is followed by selections evaluating and criticizing

Mill's views. A contemporary classic, by Martin Luther King, Jr. defends a perspective on disobedience to law.

The selections in Section B explore the constitutional dimensions of freedom of speech and expression, with a specific focus on the difficult case of hate speech. Joel Feinberg and Catherine MacKinnon examine the recurrent and divisive issues of obscene and pornographic speech in Section C. The chapter concludes with a set of readings on the freedom of religion.

The Cases for Further Reflection at the end of this chapter involve various claims: that sunbathing nude and burning the American flag are protected forms of expression; that wearing a mask in public could be construed as hate speech; that the state must allow a Mormon man to pursue bigamy; and that Amish children must not be forced to attend public school.

A. *Boundaries of the Law: Enforcing Morality and Justifying Disobedience*

Law and Morality

Laws and moral standards differ in some significant ways. Laws, for example, come into existence when enacted by a legislature or expressed by a court; they take effect at a particular time and place and are enforced by specific procedures. Moral rules, on the other hand, don't seem to share these features. Moreover, laws may apply to activities that have no apparent moral significance. Such laws are called *mala prohibita* ("bad because forbidden") and include such laws as driving on the right side of the street and paying taxes by April 15.

Law and morality do overlap, however, and deliberately so. Both legal statutes and moral rules, for example, forbid harming others; both require that people honor their promises, and both protect rights to property, privacy, and many other things. Laws can also be brought into conformity to moral standards by being changed or repealed when they are believed to be wrong. Some would argue (as we saw in Chapter One) that areas of vagueness or open texture in the law may have to be filled in by reference to moral concepts.

More controversial than these obvious connections between law and morality is the claim that the law should be used to enforce the moral opinions of the majority concerning certain areas of social life. Often these issues concern behavior that a minority views as morally acceptable and thus not the law's business. Examples of such areas include sexual behavior, religious practices, suicide, and drug use. Questions about what this category should or should not include, how the things included are to be defined, and whether the category should exist at all are the subject of much legal and philosophical debate. Often contentious in this regard are (1) activities that allegedly harm only oneself, such as smoking or drinking, failing to wear a seat belt or motorcycle helmet, and (2) activities that offend others, as in the case of public nudity or obscene speech.

In the opening section of Chapter Two, we focus on two specific issues: the use of the law to "enforce" the moral views and beliefs of a community and the appeal to moral norms in justifying disobedience to the law.

The Bullington Case

The case of Edgar Bullington, decided by an appellate court in California, involves a man employed as an embalmer at the county morgue in Los Angeles. Circumstantial evidence pointed to Bullington as the culprit in a case of corpse desecration. Bullington's case poses fascinating issues: Did Bullington do anything wrong? Did he "mutilate" a dead body? Should the law punish his conduct? If he should be punished, is it because he "harmed" someone? Should behavior offensive to many be prohibited by law on that basis?

Mill and the Harm Principle

John Stuart Mill's famous essay "On Liberty" aims to give a broad philosophical justification for wide-ranging individual freedom of thought and action. The core of Mill's position, stated in the opening paragraph of our selection, has come to be called the "harm principle." This states that the only justification for limiting a person's freedom of thought and action is to prevent that person from harming others. His or her own good is never a sufficient reason for restricting a person's freedom, either physically or through use of the law. (Mill recognizes only two narrow exceptions to this principle: children and "backward" peoples.) Only when actions threaten to harm others is interference legitimate; where conduct is primarily "self-regarding," it cannot be prohibited. That which is primarily self-regarding defines the sphere of individual liberty.

Mill isolates three types of liberty: (1) liberty of "tastes and pursuits," the liberty to frame and pursue a plan of life, to make a variety of personal, ca-reer, and lifestyle choices; (2) liberty of "association," the freedom to come together with others for purposes anywhere from marriage to clubs, from church to business; and (3) liberty of "thought and feeling," the freedom of conscience and expression. Mill is especially concerned with the last of these because he believes it contributes crucially both to the individual and to the social good. For all we know, Mill claims, any given opinion or view may express the truth; if we squelch that opinion we are robbed of the opportunity to learn the truth, thus harming ourselves. Furthermore, the collision of differing and contrasting points of view and lifestyles is helpful in challenging us to justify our own convictions to ourselves; views that must be defended are thereby invigorated. And finally, if an opinion is false or a choice a poor one, these facts will be discovered sooner or later in their clash with contending perspectives; the truth will win out in the end.

Mill's theory firmly repudiates the view known as *paternalism*, the idea that interference with a person's liberty is justified in order to protect that person's own welfare or needs or interests; a restriction of your freedom for your own good. No one, Mill believes, should be told what to do with his or her life, assuming of course that he or she is a competent adult. Each of us has the best knowledge of what is in our own interests. The evil of paternalistic interference far outweighs any evil that a person may visit upon himself. This does not mean that Mill argues for a callous egoism: we certainly should encourage and assist others to take better care of themselves, to give up dangerous habits, to enrich their lives, but we may not coerce them into such things with the instrument of the law. Where the majority seeks to coerce the minority, Mill observes, the result is frequently intolerance, prejudice, and pain.

Some writers have suggested that the decisions of courts in many cases dealing with pornography, religious freedom, and so on, illustrate how the First Amendment "constitutionalizes" Mill's harm principle, so that the Constitution is read as an endorsement of the conception of liberty articulated by Mill. When reading the material throughout this chapter, you should ask yourself whether this is the case and whether such a reading of the Constitution is desirable.

Is it possible, for example, to frame or draft statutes or interpret constitutional language in a way that adequately defines what is to count as "harm" to another? Certain forms of harm are of course obvious and uncontroversial: deprivation of property and physical injury, for example. But to limit harm to such obvious forms would be unacceptably narrow. Most of us would agree that the law should prohibit assault (placing another in reasonable fear of imminent bodily harm) or libel (publication of facts about another with the aim of injuring his or her reputation). Plainly there are ways of "harming" someone without stealing his stereo or punching him in the nose. Harm, it seems, must include certain forms of psychological injury or distress, but this gives rise to another difficulty: How to shape the law so that further harms fall within the prohibitions of the harm principle without weakening that standard altogether by counting as "harmful" anything that displeases or offends. The freedom to do only that to which no one has any objection is limited indeed.

Responses to Mill

British judge Patrick Devlin, in a now classic work, argues that Mill's demand that society afford the maximum scope possible for individual thought and action, consistent with a prohibition on harm to others, is indefensible. The impetus for Devlin's essay stemmed from the publication in Britain of a report recommending the decriminalization of homosexual acts on grounds largely derived from Mill. Devlin used the occasion to develop a forceful critique of Mill.

In his essay, Devlin asks us to think about the idea of society. What is a society? It is not, Devlin reasons, merely a geographical locality or a political structure. A society is a community of ideas and ideals—an interconnected network of shared values and beliefs. Not only must a society have a political structure to be viable, it must also have a moral structure. This shared body of values—what Devlin calls the "public morality"—is essential to the preservation of a society. Devlin uses the institution of marriage as an example of one element of the public morality. Marriage is both a legal and a political institution. It is also the basis of various

moral prohibitions on behavior (for example, adultery and polygamy). Society may legitimately use the law to support these moral proscriptions in order to preserve an important part of the social fabric. Of course, Devlin is aware that not just any deviation from these values will pose a threat to the public morality. How, then, is it to be determined when something is so vital to the public morality that it must be protected? We must look, says Devlin, to the views of the ordinary person. We must find out, or try to imagine, what the reaction of the average, reasonable person would be to some behavior. If that person has a deep-seated feeling of revulsion or disgust at some activity, this is a signal that the limits of social toleration have been reached. Devlin elaborates on this idea by appealing to the notion of the juror in the jury room. Just as a jury typically must come to a unanimous decision, so it must be that everyone (or nearly everyone) is disgusted by some practice before society has a right to step in with the law. Also, people on a jury are supposed to deliberate calmly and carefully before reaching a verdict, rather than being carried away by their prejudices.

What does Devlin's theory mean in practical terms? Suppose Jane Roe is arrested and charged with committing acts of ritual animal sacrifice. If, upon careful reflection, nearly everyone in Jane's community is repulsed by the idea of such a practice, the community would be justified (according to Devlin) in making Jane's conduct illegal, even over her protest that animal sacrifice is part of her religion.

In a response to Devlin included here, philosopher H. L. A. Hart charges that Devlin wrongly conceives of the public morality as a kind of seamless web, so deviation from any part of it (for example, a rejection of traditional sexual mores) will create tears throughout the entire fabric. Devlin also seems mistakenly to move from the claim that a viable society must have some shared moral values to the claim that a society is identical with its shared morality as defined at a given point, so any disruption in the public morality would amount to the destruction of society. But this conception, Hart reasons, would make change within a society impossible—any change would signal the end of one society and the beginning of another. Nothing is gained by thinking about the situation in this way.

Morality and Disobedience to Law

As we have seen, the requirements imposed by the law often parallel those placed upon us by morality, and occasionally the law asks us to do things (such as drive on the right side of the road) that have no moral weight of their own. But suppose the law is deeply morally flawed, as it was, for instance, in many Southern states during the time of legal segregation of and open discrimination toward Blacks. What are a citizen's responsibilities in such a situation? Are we obligated to obey a law we deem immoral? May we deliberately violate the law in the name of a "higher" moral value or principle? If so, what are the limits to such acts of disobedience?

Here, as you can expect, questions abound: Is there an obligation to obey the law as such? If so, can such an obligation be absolute, applicable without exception in all cases? What about situations in which a moral imperative seems to outweigh the force of the law (for example, when I run a stop sign to get an injured person to the hospital)? On what grounds could even a nonabsolute obligation to obey the law be justified? On these questions, political and legal philosophers have appealed to various ideas: that a general obligation to follow the law derives from a "social contract" or agreement to obey, or that fairness demands obedience as the price for the benefits obtained by reason of others' obedience to law. We will not pursue these arguments here, but turn instead to the question of how claims to disobey the law, however obedience is explained, are themselves justified.

The case of *U.S. v. Schoon*, involves what the court calls "indirect" civil disobedience. Civil rights sit-ins at segregated lunch counters involved "direct" civil disobedience, the court reasons, because the protesters' actions were calculated to violate the very laws they sought to change. In *Schoon*, the defendants disrupted an IRS office to call attention to what they believed were unjust U.S. policies in Central America. Faced with criminal trespass and other charges, the defendants argued that their violation of the law was justified on grounds of "necessity"—the prevention of a greater evil.

In his famous "Letter from Birmingham Jail," Martin Luther King, Jr. defends disobedience to positive law by appeal to natural law (recall the theories of law covered in Chapter One). Writing from a jail cell in Alabama in 1963, King responds to criticism of his disobedience to the segregationist statutes of the South by appealing to a "higher" law—the natural law—and invokes the core naturalist claim that these human enactments, these racist statutes, have forfeited their status as "law" by virtue of their obvious immorality.

29. *The People v. Edgar S. Bullington*

Wood, J.

An information was filed against defendant charging him with the crime of violation of section

Court of Appeal of California
27 Cal. App. 2d 396
Second Appellate District, Division Two

290 of the Penal Code in that he did "feloniously mutilate the dead body of Michael Conway, a human being." At a jury trial he was found guilty and sentenced to the state penitentiary.

For about ten years defendant was employed as an embalmer at the morgue maintained by the county of Los Angeles. The work at the morgue is divided into three shifts, the first shift beginning at

9 A.M. and ending at 5 P.M., the second shift beginning at 5 P.M. and ending at 1 A.M. and the third shift beginning at 1 A.M. and ending at 9 A.M. On the day shift beginning at 9 A.M. the chief embalmer and a number of attendants are employed. On each of the other two shifts an embalmer and two mortuary attendants are employed. On January 10 and 11, 1938, defendant was the embalmer working on the shift from 5 P.M. to 1 A.M.

The body of the deceased was brought into the morgue at 6:45 A.M. January 10th, and at 8 A.M. the embalmer then on duty, one Monroe, started to embalm it. At 9 A.M. Monroe went off duty and the chief embalmer, McCue, continued with the work of embalming until it was finished at about 10 A.M. The body was embalmed with a hard fluid. A number of witnesses testified that they saw two gold crowns on the teeth of the deceased. During the preparation for the embalming the lips of the deceased were sewed together and when the embalming was finished the body was placed on a truck opposite one of the crypts. Mr. McCue testified that ten minutes before he went off duty at 5 P.M. he inspected the body and observed that the lips were still sewed together with string and that there was Vaseline on the lips to stick them together. He lifted the corner of the lips and saw that the gold crowns were still in place. During the next shift the two mortuary attendants occasionally made trips away from the morgue to bring in other bodies and during these periods defendant was alone at the morgue. Mr. Monroe returned to work at 1 A.M. on January 11th and relieved defendant. He testified that he looked at the body of the deceased and observed that the gold crowns were missing. He then took the two attendants who worked with him on this shift to observe the condition of the mouth and the absence of the crowns. When Mr. McCue returned to work at 8 A.M. on January 11th, he and Mr. Monroe looked at the body and observed that the lips were still sewed together but that the Vaseline was not upon the lips. The mortuary attendants on all of the shifts were called as witnesses and each denied that he had removed the crowns.

At 10:30 A.M. on the morning of January 11th, detectives Ledbetter and Hurst met defendant at 1045 Overton Street and informed defendant he must accompany them to the coroner's office. Defendant drove his own car and the officers followed in a different car. Defendant parked his car at the corner of Temple and Grand Avenues, about three blocks from the morgue. At that time the officers searched defendant's automobile and under the driver's wheel found a small manila envelope torn in half. This envelope was delivered to Mr. Pinker, chemist on the Los Angeles police force. In the vest pocket of defendant the officers found another and similar manila envelope containing a small piece of gold which defendant stated had been used as a filling in one of his own teeth. Defendant's statement was later verified by the dentist who had done the work on the defendant's tooth. Defendant told the officers that his cigarette package had become wet and that he had used the torn envelope found in the car in which to carry four or five cigarets. Evidence of gold in the torn envelope could not be detected by the naked eye. Mr. Pinker testified that from his microscopic examination he determined that "the interior of the envelope was contaminated with microscopic portions of a metal having a gold appearance in color. From spectrograph examination of those I determined that it was an alloy of gold and silver containing the element boron." He further testified that in dental work an alloy of silver and gold is customarily employed; "that boron can enter the metal in the form of a flux, or from the molding that is used in molding the filling or the crown." The witness further testified that jewelers use an alloy composed of gold and silver and that the gold specks found in the envelope could have come from jewelry; that jewelers use boron for a flux. The envelopes found in defendant's pocket and on the floor of his car were of the kind customarily used in the county morgue for the purpose of preserving small pieces of jewelry and cash found on the body of the deceased persons.

Two funeral directors, who had had many years of experience in embalming dead bodies, testified that if a body had been embalmed with a hard embalming fluid it would be very difficult to open the jaws seven hours after embalming; that the jaws would be set in about two hours. That it is customary to sew the mouth before embalming. That after embalming the flesh becomes rigid and hard; that the flesh can be stretched but that it is almost impossible to get it back to its original position. That after seven hours from the time of embalming any movement of the jaw or lips could not be repaired but would be discernible; that the teeth could not be taken out after embalming without breaking the strings.

Defendant now contends that the acts he is accused of having committed do not constitute a violation of section 290 of the Penal Code; and that the evidence is insufficient to justify the finding of the jury that he removed the gold crowns. Both of these contentions must be sustained.

The trial court refused to instruct the jury at the request of the defendant that the removal of the gold caps without the removal of the natural teeth of the deceased did not constitute a mutilation of the dead body but the court did instruct the jury as follows: "A removal of a crown cemented upon a tooth of the body of a dead human being constitutes a mutilation of such body. If such act be done willfully and unlawfully, it constitutes a violation of Section 290 of the Penal Code of the State of California." It will be noted that the court took from the jury the consideration of the question as to what constituted a mutilation but positively held as a matter of law that the removal of two crowns which had been cemented to the natural teeth of the body constituted a mutilation within the meaning of the code provision. Section 290 of the Penal Code is as follows: "Every person who mutilates, disinters, or removes from the place of sepulture the dead body of a human being without authority of law, is guilty of felony. But the provisions of this section do not apply to any person who removes the dead body of a relative or friend for reinterment." The legal dictionaries are in accord as to the meaning of the word "mutilate": "The term 'mutilate' as applied to a person means to 'cut off a limb or an essential part of the body', and in criminal law means 'to deprive a man of the use of those limbs which may be useful to him in fight.'" [T]o 'mutilate' is to cut off a limb or essential part of the body. Turning to the general dictionaries we find this definition: "To deprive of a limb or essential part; maim; disfigure." . . . "To cut off or remove a limb or essential part of; to maim."

The trial court instructed the jury as follows: "The word 'mutilate' as used in Section 290 of the Penal Code, means to destroy or remove a material part of, so as to render imperfect." In none of the dictionaries, either legal or general in scope, do we find a definition of the word "mutilate" as applied to the human body which is couched in the language used by the trial court or in any similar language. Without the use of the dictionaries it would be difficult to conclude that one who removes gold crowns from the teeth of a dead body could be properly accused of mutilating the body. The evidence in the case before us shows that the natural teeth were not removed or impaired and that the only act committed was the mere removal of the crowns which had been cemented to the teeth. There was no maiming or disfigurement of the teeth or of any part of the body. It could not be successfully argued that a plate of false teeth, which is frequently removed for long periods of time, is in fact a part of the body. If two teeth should be removed from the jaw of a living person and two crowns should be fashioned by the dentist in such manner that they could be used and readily removed it could not be seriously argued that the two false teeth would become a part of the body. The argument that the placing of cement on the false teeth to make them adhere to the natural teeth would result in the false teeth becoming a part of the human body seems equally unsound. An examination of all the evidence leads to the inevitable conclusion that the crime charged in the information has not been proved.

The judgement is *reversed* and the bail of appellant is exonerated.

30. *On Liberty*

JOHN STUART MILL

The object of this Essay is to assert one very simple principle, as entitled to govern absolutely the dealings of society with the individual in the way of compulsion and control, whether the means used be physical force in the form of legal penalties, or the moral coercion of public opinion. That principle is, that the sole end for which mankind are warranted, individually or collectively, in interfering with the liberty of action of any of their number, is self-protection. That the only purpose for which power can be rightfully exercised over any member of a civilized community, against his will, is to prevent harm to others. His own good, either physical or moral, is not a sufficient warrant. He cannot rightfully be compelled to do or forbear because it will be better for him to do so, because it will make him happier, because, in the opinions of others, to do so would be wise, or even right. These are good reasons for remonstrating with him, or reasoning with him, or persuading him, or entreating him, but not for compelling him, or visiting him with any evil in case he do otherwise. To justify that, the conduct from which it is desired to deter him must be calculated to produce evil to some one else. The only part of the conduct of any one, for which he is amenable to society, is that which concerns others. In the part which merely concerns himself, his independence is, of right, absolute. Over himself, over his own body and mind, the individual is sovereign.

It is, perhaps, hardly necessary to say that this doctrine is meant to apply only to human beings in the maturity of their faculties. We are not speaking of children, or of young persons below the age which the law may fix as that of manhood or womanhood. Those who are still in a state to require being taken care of by others, must be protected against their own actions as well as against external injury. For the same reason, we may leave out of consideration those backward states of society in which the race itself may be considered as in its nonage. The early difficulties in the way of spontaneous progress are so great, that there is seldom any choice of means for overcoming them; and a ruler full of the spirit of improvement is warranted in the use of any expedients that will attain an end, perhaps otherwise unattainable. Despotism is a legitimate mode of government in dealing with barbarians, provided the end be their improvement, and the means justified by actually effecting that end. Liberty, as a principle, has no application to any state of things anterior to the time when mankind have become capable of being improved by free and equal discussion. Until then, there is nothing for them but implicit obedience to an Akbar or a Charlemagne, if they are so fortunate as to find one. But as soon as mankind have attained the capacity of being guided to their own improvement by conviction or persuasion (a period long since reached in all nations with whom we need here concern ourselves), compulsion, either in the direct form or in that of pains and penalties for non-compliance, is no longer admissible as a means to their own good, and justifiable only for the security of others.

It is proper to state that I forego any advantage which could be derived to my argument from the idea of abstract right, as a thing independent of utility. I regard utility as the ultimate appeal on all ethical questions; but it must be utility in the largest sense, grounded on the permanent interests of man as a progressive being. Those interests, I contend, authorise the subjection of individual spontaneity to external control, only in respect to those actions of each, which concern the interest of other people. If any one does an act hurtful to others, there is a *prima facie* case for punishing him, by law, or, where legal penalties are not safely applicable, by general disapprobation. There are also many positive acts for the benefit of others, which he may rightfully be compelled to perform; such as to give evidence in a court of justice; to bear his fair share in the common defense, or in any other joint work necessary to the interest of the society of which he enjoys the protection; and to perform certain acts of individual beneficence, such as saving a fellow-creature's life, or interposing to protect the defenseless against ill-usage, things which whenever it is obviously a man's duty to do, he may rightfully be made responsible to society for not doing. A person may cause evil to others not only by his actions but by his inaction, and in either case he is justly accountable to them for the injury. The latter case, it is true, requires a much more cautious exercise of compulsion than the former. To make any one answerable for doing evil to others is the rule; to make him answerable for not preventing evil is, comparatively speaking, the exception. Yet there are many cases clear enough and grave enough to justify that exception. In all things which regard the external relations of the individual, he is *de jure* amenable to those whose interests are concerned, and, if need be, to society as their protector. There are often good reasons for not holding him to the responsibility; but these reasons must arise from the special expediencies of the case: either because it is a kind of case in which he is on the whole likely to act better, when left to is own discretion, than when controlled in any way in which society have it in their power to control him; or because the attempt to exercise control would produce other evils, greater than those which it would prevent. When such reasons as these preclude the enforcement of responsibility, the conscience of the agent himself should step into the vacant judgment seat, and protect those interests of others which have no external protection; judging himself all the more rigidly, because the case does not admit of his being made accountable to the judgment of his fellow-creatures.

But there is a sphere of action in which society, as distinguished from the individual, has, if any, only an indirect interest; comprehending all that portion of a person's life and conduct which affects only himself, or if it also affects others, only with their free, voluntary, and undeceived consent and participation. When I say only himself, I mean directly, and in the first instance; for whatever affects himself, may affect others *through* himself; and the objection which may be grounded on this contingency, will receive consideration in the sequel. This, then, is the appropriate region of human liberty. It comprises, first, the inward domain of consciousness; demanding liberty of conscience in the most comprehensive sense; liberty of thought and feeling; absolute freedom of opinion and sentiment on all subjects, practical or speculative, scientific, moral, or theological. The liberty of expressing and publishing opinions may seem to fall under a different principle, since it belongs to that part of the conduct of an individual which concerns other people; but, being almost of as much importance as the liberty of thought itself, and resting in great part on the same reasons, is practically inseparable from it. Secondly, the principle requires liberty of tastes and pursuits; of framing the plan of our life to suit our own character, of doing as we like, subject to such consequences as may follow; without impediment from our fellow creatures, so long as what we do does not harm them, even though they should think our conduct foolish, perverse or wrong. Thirdly, from this liberty of each individual, follows the liberty, within the same limits, of combination among individuals; freedom to unite, for any purpose not involving harm to others; the persons combining being supposed to be of full age, and not forced or deceived.

No society in which these liberties are not, on the whole, respected, is free, whatever may be its form of government; and none is completely free in which they do not exist absolute and unqualified. The only freedom which deserves the name, is that of pursuing our own good in our own way, so long as we do not attempt to deprive others of theirs, or impede their efforts to obtain it. Each is the proper guardian of his own health, whether bodily, or mental and spiritual. Mankind are greater gainers by suffering each other to live as seems good to themselves, than by compelling each to live as seems good to the rest.

Though this doctrine is anything but new, and, to some persons, may have the air of a truism, there is no doctrine which stands more directly opposed to the general tendency of existing opinion and practice. Society has expended fully as much effort in the attempt (according to its lights) to compel people to conform to its notions of personal as of social excellence. The ancient commonwealths thought themselves entitled to practise, and the ancient philosophers countenanced, the regulation of every part of private conduct by public authority, on the ground that the State had a deep interest in the whole bodily and mental discipline of every one of its citizens; a mode of thinking which may have been admissible in small republics surrounded by powerful enemies, in constant peril of being subverted by foreign attack or internal commotion, and to which even a short interval of relaxed energy and self-command might so easily be fatal that they could not afford to wait for the salutary permanent effects of freedom. In the modern world, the greater size of political communities, and, above all, the separation between spiritual and temporal authority (which placed the direction of men's consciences in other hands than those which controlled their worldly affairs), prevented so great an interference by law in the details of private life; but the engines of moral repression have been wielded more strenuously against divergence from the reigning opinion in self-regarding, than even in social matters; religion, the most powerful of the elements which have entered into the formation of moral feeling, having almost always been governed either by the ambition of a hierarchy, seeking control over every department of human conduct, or by the spirit of Puritanism. And some of those modern reformers who have placed themselves in strongest opposition to the religions of the past,

have been in no way behind either churches or sects in their assertion of the right of spiritual domination: M. Comte, in particular, whose social systems, as unfolded in his *Système de Politique Positive*, aims at establishing (though by moral more than by legal appliances) a despotism of society over the individual, surpassing anything contemplated in the political ideal of the most rigid disciplinarian among the ancient philosophers.

Apart from the peculiar tenets of individual thinkers, there is also in the world at large an increasing inclination to stretch unduly the powers of society over the individual, both by the force of opinion and even by that of legislation; and as the tendency of all the changes taking place in the world is to strengthen society, and diminish the power of the individual, this encroachment is not one of the evils which tend spontaneously to disappear, but, on the contrary, to grow more and more formidable. The disposition of mankind, whether as rulers or as fellow-citizens, to impose their own opinions and inclinations as a rule of conduct on others, is so energetically supported by some of the best and by some of the worst feelings incident to human nature, that it is hardly ever kept under restraint by anything but want of power; and as the power is not declining, but growing, unless a strong barrier of moral conviction can be raised against the mischief, we must expect, in the present circumstances of the world, to see it increase.

31. *The Enforcement of Morals*

Patrick Devlin

The report of the Committee on Homosexual Offences and Prostitution, generally known as the Wolfenden Report, is recognized to be an excellent study of two very difficult legal and social problems. But it has also a particular claim to the respect of those interested in jurisprudence; it does what

law reformers so rarely do; it sets out clearly and carefully what in relation to its subjects it considers the function of the law to be. Statutory additions to the criminal law are too often made on the simple principle that 'there ought to be a law against it'. The greater part of the law relating to sexual offences is the creation of statute and it is difficult to ascertain any logical relationship between it and the moral ideas which most of us uphold. Adultery, fornication, and prostitution are not, as the Report points out, criminal offences: homosexuality between males is a criminal offence but between females it is not. Incest was not an offence until it was declared so by statute only fifty years ago. Does the legislature select these offences haphazardly or are there some principles which can be used to determine what part of the moral law should be embodied in the criminal? There is, for example, being now considered a proposal to make A.I.D., that is, the practice of artificial insemination of a woman with the seed of a man who is not her husband, a criminal offence; if, as is usually the case, the woman is married, this is in substance, if not in form, adultery. Ought it to be made punishable when adultery is not?

This sort of question is of practical importance, for a law that appears to be arbitrary and illogical, in the end and after the wave of moral indignation that has put it on the statute book subsides, forfeits respect. As a practical question it arises more frequently in the field of sexual morals than in any other, but there is no special answer to be found in that field. The inquiry must be general and fundamental. What is the connection between crime and sin and to what extent, if at all, should the criminal law of England concern itself with the enforcement of morals and punish sin or immorality as such?

· · ·

It is true that for many centuries the criminal law was much concerned with keeping the peace and little, if at all, with sexual morals. But it would be wrong to infer from that that it had no moral content or that it would ever have tolerated the idea of a man being left to judge for himself in matters of morals. The criminal law of England has from the very first concerned itself with moral principles. A simple way of testing this point is to consider the attitude which the criminal law adopts towards consent.

Subject to certain exceptions inherent in the nature of particular crimes, the criminal law has never permitted consent of the victim to be used as a defence. In rape, for example, consent negatives an essential element. But consent of the victim is no defence to a charge of murder. It is not a defence to any form of assault that the victim thought his punishment well deserved and submitted to it; to make a good defence the accused must prove that the law gave him the right to chastise and that he exercised it reasonably. Likewise, the victim may not forgive the aggressor and require the prosecution to desist; the right to enter a *nolle prosequi* belongs to the Attorney-General alone.

Now, if the law existed for the protection of the individual, there would be no reason why he should avail himself of it if he did not want it. The reason why a man may not consent to the commission of an offence against himself beforehand or forgive it afterwards is because it is an offence against society. It is not that society is physically injured; that would be impossible. Nor need any individual be shocked, corrupted, or exploited; everything may be done in private. Nor can it be explained on the practical ground that a violent man is a potential danger to others in the community who have therefore a direct interest in his apprehension and punishment as being necessary to their own protection. That would be true of a man whom the victim is prepared to forgive but not of one who gets his consent first; a murderer who acts only upon the consent, and maybe the request, of his victim is no menace to others, but he does threaten one of the great moral principles upon which society is based, that is, the sanctity of human life. There is only one explanation of what has hitherto been accepted as the basis of the criminal law and that is that there are certain standards of behaviour or moral principles which society requires to be observed; and the breach of them is an offence not merely against the person who is injured but against society as a whole.

Thus, if the criminal law were to be reformed so as to eliminate from it everything that was not designed to preserve order and decency or to protect citizens (including the protection of youth from corruption), it would overturn a fundamental principle. It would also end a number of specific crimes. Euthanasia or the killing of another at his own request, suicide, attempted suicide, and suicide pacts, duelling, abortion, incest between brother and sister, are all acts which can be done in private and without offence to others and need not involve the corruption or exploitation of others. Many people think that the law on some of these subjects is in need of reform, but no one hitherto has gone so far as to suggest that they should all be left outside the criminal law as matters of private morality. They can be brought within it only as a matter of moral principle. It must be remembered also that although there is much immorality that is not punished by law, there is none that is condoned by the law. The law will not allow its processes to be used by those engaged in immorality of any sort. For example, a house may not be let for immoral purposes; the lease is invalid and would not be enforced. But if what goes on inside there is a matter of private morality and not the law's business, why does the law inquire into it at all?

I think it is clear that the criminal law as we know it is based upon moral principle. In a number of crimes its function is simply to enforce a moral principle and nothing else. The law, both criminal and civil, claims to be able to speak about morality and immorality generally. Where does it get its authority to do this and how does it settle the moral principles which it enforces? Undoubtedly, as a matter of history, it derived both from Christian teaching. But [the] law can no longer rely on doctrines in which citizens are entitled to disbelieve. It is necessary therefore to look for some other source.

In jurisprudence, as I have said, everything is thrown open to discussion and, in the belief that they cover the whole field, I have framed three interrogatories addressed to myself to answer:

1. Has society the right to pass judgment at all on matters of morals? Ought there, in other words, to be a public morality, or are morals always a matter for private judgment?
2. If society has the right to pass judgment, has it also the right to use the weapon of the law to enforce it?
3. If so, ought it to use that weapon in all cases or only in some; and if only in some, on what principles should it distinguish?

I shall begin with the first interrogatory and consider what is meant by the right of society to pass a moral judgment, that is, a judgment about what is good and what is evil. The fact that a majority of people may disapprove of a practise does not of itself make it a matter for society as a whole. Nine men out of ten may disapprove of what the tenth man is doing and still say that it is not their business. There is a case for a collective judgment (as distinct from a large number of individual opinions which sensible people may even refrain from pronouncing at all if it is upon somebody else's private affairs) only if society is affected. Without a collective judgment there can be no case at all for intervention. Let me take as an illustration the Englishman's attitude to religion as it is now and as it has been in the past. His attitude now is that a man's religion is his private affair; he may think of another man's religion that it is right or wrong, true or untrue, but not that it is good or bad. In earlier times that was not so; a man was denied the right to practise what was thought of as heresy, and heresy was thought of as destructive of society.

The language used in the passages I have quoted from the Wolfenden Report suggests the view that there ought not to be a collective judgment about immorality *per se*. Is this what is meant by 'private morality' and 'individual freedom of choice and action'? Some people sincerely believe that homosexuality is neither immoral nor unnatural. Is the 'freedom of choice and action' that is offered to the individual, freedom to decide for himself what is moral or immoral, society remaining neutral; or is it freedom to be immoral if he wants to be? The language of the Report may be open to question, but the conclusions at which the Committee arrive answer this question unambiguously. If society is not prepared to say that homosexuality is morally wrong, there would be no basis for a law protecting youth from 'corruption' or punishing a man for living on the 'immoral' earnings of a homosexual prostitute, as the Report recommends. This attitude the Committee makes even clearer when they come to deal with prostitution. In truth, the Report takes it for granted that there is in existence a public morality which condemns homosexuality and prostitution. What the Report seems to mean by private morality might perhaps be better described as private behaviour in matters of morals.

This view—that there is such a thing as public morality—can also be justified by *a priori* argument. What makes a society of any sort is community of ideas, not only political ideas but also ideas about the way its members should behave and govern their lives; these latter ideas are its morals. Every society has a moral structure as well as a political one: or rather, since that might suggest two independent systems, I should say that the structure of every society is made up both of politics and morals. Take, for example, the institution of marriage. Whether a man should be allowed to take more than one wife is something about which every society has to make up its mind one way or the other. In England we believe in the Christian idea of marriage and therefore adopt monogamy as a moral principle. Consequently the Christian institution of marriage has become the basis of family life and so part of the structure of our society. It is there not because it is Christian. It has got there because it is Christian, but it remains there because it is built into the house in which we live and could not be removed without bringing it down. The great majority of those who live in this country accept it because it is the Christian idea of marriage and for them the only true one. But a non-Christian is bound by it, not because it is part of Christianity but because, rightly or wrongly, it has been adopted by the society in which he lives. It would be useless for him to stage a debate designed to prove that polygamy was theologically more correct and socially preferable; if he wants to live in the house, he must accept it as built in the way in which it is.

We see this more clearly if we think of ideas or institutions that are purely political. Society cannot tolerate rebellion; it will not allow argument about the rightness of the cause. Historians a century later may say that the rebels were right and the Government was wrong and a percipient and conscientious subject of the State may think so at the time. But it is not a matter which can be left to individual judgment.

The institution of marriage is a good example for my purpose because it bridges the division, if there is one, between politics and morals. Marriage is part of the structure of our society and it is also the basis of a moral code which condemns fornication and adultery. The institution of marriage would be gravely threatened if individual judgments were permitted about the morality of adultery; on these points there must be a public morality. But public morality is not to be confined to those moral principles which support institutions such as marriage. People do not think of monogamy as something which has to be supported because our society has chosen to organize itself upon it; they think of it as something that is good in itself and offering a good way of life and

that it is for that reason that our society has adopted it. I return to the statement that I have already made, that society means a community of ideas; without shared ideas on politics, morals, and ethics no society can exist. Each one of us has ideas about what is good and what is evil; they cannot be kept private from the society in which we live. If men and women try to create a society in which there is no fundamental agreement about good and evil they will fail; if, having based it on common agreement, the agreement goes, the society will disintegrate. For society is not something that is kept together physically; it is held by the invisible bonds of common thought. If the bonds were too far relaxed the members would drift apart. A common morality is part of the bondage. The bondage is part of the price of society; and mankind, which needs society, must pay its price.

. . .

I think, therefore, that it is not possible to set theoretical limits to the power of the State to legislate against immorality. It is not possible to settle in advance exceptions to the general rule or to define inflexibly areas of morality into which the law is in no circumstances to be allowed to enter. Society is entitled by means of its laws to protect itself from dangers, whether from within or without. Here again I think that the political parallel is legitimate. The law of treason is directed against aiding the king's enemies and against sedition from within. The justification for this is that established government is necessary for the existence of society and therefore its safety against violent overthrow must be secured. But an established morality is as necessary as good government to the welfare of society. Societies disintegrate from within more frequently than they are broken up by external pressures. There is disintegration when no common morality is observed and history shows that the loosening of moral bonds is often the first stage of disintegration, so that society is justified in taking the same steps to preserve its moral code as it does to preserve its government and other essential institutions. The suppression of vice is as much the law's business as the suppression of subversive activities; it is no more possible to define a sphere of private morality than it is to define one of private subversive activity. It is wrong to talk of private morality or of the law not being concerned with immorality as such or to try to set rigid bounds to the part which the law may play in the suppression of vice. There are no theoretical limits to the power of the State to legislate against treason and sedition, and likewise I think there can be no theoretical limits to legislation against immorality. You may argue that if a man's sins affect only himself it cannot be the concern of society. If he chooses to get drunk every night in the privacy of his own home, is any one except himself the worse for it? But suppose a quarter or a half of the population got drunk every night, what sort of society would it be? You cannot set a theoretical limit to the number of people who can get drunk before society is entitled to legislate against drunkenness. The same may be said of gambling. The Royal Commission on Betting, Lotteries, and Gaming took as their test the character of the citizen as a member of society. They said: 'Our concern with the ethical significance of gambling is confined to the effect which it may have on the character of the gambler as a member of society. If we were convinced that whatever the degree of gambling this effect must be harmful we should be inclined to think that it was the duty of the State to restrict gambling to the greatest extent practicable'.

In what circumstances the State should exercise its power is the third of the interrogatories I have framed. But before I get to it I must raise a point which might have been brought up in any one of the three. How are the moral judgments of society to be ascertained? By leaving it until now, I can ask it in the more limited form that is now sufficient for my purpose. How is the law-maker to ascertain the moral judgments of society? It is surely not enough that they should be reached by the opinion of the majority; it would be too much to require the individual assent of every citizen. English law has evolved and regularly uses a standard which does not depend on the counting of heads. It is that of the reasonable man. He is not to be confused with the rational man. He is not expected to reason about anything and his judgment may be largely a matter of feeling. It is the viewpoint of the man in the street—or to use an archaism familiar to all lawyers—the man in the Clapham omnibus. He might also be called the right-minded man. For my purpose I should like to call him the man in the jury box, for the moral judgment of society must be something about which any twelve men or women

drawn at random might after discussion be expected to be unanimous. This was the standard the judges applied in the days before Parliament was as active as it is now and when they laid down rules of public policy. They did not think of themselves as making law but simply as stating principles which every right-minded person would accept as valid. It is what Pollock called 'practical morality', which is based not on theological or philosophical foundations but 'in the mass of continuous experience half-consciously or unconsciously accumulated and embodies in the morality of common sense'. He called it also 'a certain way of thinking on questions of morality which we expect to find in a reasonable civilized man or a reasonable Englishman, taken at random'.

Immorality then, for the purpose of the law, is what every right-minded person is presumed to consider to be immoral. Any immorality is capable of affecting society injuriously and in effect to a greater or lesser extent it usually does; this is what gives the law its *locus standi*. It cannot be shut out. But—and this brings me to the third question—the individual has a *locus standi* too; he cannot be expected to surrender to the judgment of society the whole conduct of his life. It is the old and familiar question of striking a balance between the rights and interests of society and those of the individual. This is something which the law is constantly doing in matters large and small. To take a very down-to-earth example, let me consider the right of the individual whose house adjoins the highway to have access to it; that means in these days the right to have vehicles stationary in the highway, sometimes for a considerable time if there is a lot of loading or unloading. There are many cases in which the courts have had to balance the private right of access against the public right to use the highway without obstruction. It cannot be done by carving up the highway into public and private areas. It is done by recognizing that each have rights over the whole; that if each were to exercise their rights to the full, they would come into conflict; and therefore that the rights of each must be curtailed so as to ensure as far as possible that the essential needs of each are safeguarded.

I do not think that one can talk sensibly of a public and private morality any more than one can of a public or private highway. Morality is a sphere in which there is a public interest and a private interest, often in conflict, and the problem is to reconcile the two. This does not mean that it is impossible to put forward any general statements about how in our society the balance ought to be struck. Such statements cannot of their nature be rigid or precise; they would not be designed to circumscribe the operation of the law-making power but to guide those who have to apply it. While every decision which a court of law makes when it balances the public against the private interest is an *ad hoc* decision, the cases contain statements of principle to which the court should have regard when it reaches its decision. In the same way it is possible to make general statements of principle which it may be thought the legislature should bear in mind when it is considering the enactment of laws enforcing morals.

. . .

This indicates a general sentiment that the right to privacy is something to be put in the balance against the enforcement of the law. Ought the same sort of consideration to play any part in the formation of the law? Clearly only in a very limited number of cases. When the help of the law is invoked by an injured citizen, privacy must be irrelevant; the individual cannot ask that his right to privacy should be measured against injury criminally done to another. But when all who are involved in the deed are consenting parties and the injury is done to morals, the public interest in the moral order can be balanced against the claims of privacy. The restriction on police powers of investigation goes further than the affording of a parallel; it means that the detection of crime committed in private and when there is no complaint is bound to be rather haphazard and this is an additional reason for moderation. These considerations do not justify the exclusion of all private immorality from the scope of the law. I think that, as I have already suggested, the test of 'private behaviour' should be substituted for 'private morality' and the influence of the factor should be reduced from that of a definite limitation to that of a matter to be taken into account. Since the gravity of the crime is also a proper consideration, a distinction might well be made in the case of homosexuality between the lesser acts of indecency and the full offense, which on the principles of the Wolfenden Report it would be illogical to do.

32. *Law, Liberty, and Morality*

H. L. A. HART

When we turn [to] the positive grounds held to justify the legal enforcement of morality it is important to distinguish a moderate and an extreme

---

*ED. James Fitzjames Stephen was a British lawyer and judge who was sharply critical of the democratic and secular society for which Mill had argued. Stephen's criticisms of Mill can be found in his book, *Liberty, Equality, Fraternity*, published in 1873.

thesis, though critics of Mill have sometimes moved from one to the other without marking the transition. Lord Devlin seems to me to maintain, for most of his essay, the moderate thesis and Stephen the extreme one.*

According to the moderate thesis, a shared morality is the cement of society; without it there would be aggregates of individuals but no society. "A recognized morality" is, in Lord Devlin's words, "as necessary to society's existence as a recognized government," and though a particular act of immorality may not harm or endanger or corrupt others nor, when done in private, either shock or give offence to others, this does not conclude the matter. For we must not view conduct in isolation from its effect on the moral code: if we remember this, we can see that one who is "no menace to others" nonetheless may by his immoral conduct "threaten one of the great moral principles on which society is based." In this sense the breach of moral principle is an offence "against society as a whole," and society may use the law to preserve its morality as it uses it to safeguard anything else essential to its existence. This is why "the suppression of vice is as much the law's business as the suppression of subversive activities."

By contrast, the extreme thesis does not look upon a shared morality as of merely instrumental value analogous to ordered government, and it does not justify the punishment of immorality as a step taken, like the punishment of treason, to preserve society from dissolution or collapse. Instead, the enforcement of morality is regarded as a thing of value, even if immoral acts harm no one directly, or indirectly by weakening the moral cement of society. I do not say that it is possible to allot to one or other of these two theses every argument used, but they do, I think characterise the main critical positions at the root of most arguments, and they incidentally exhibit an ambiguity in the expression "enforcing morality as such." Perhaps the clearest way of distinguishing the two theses is to see that there are always two levels at which we may ask whether some breach of positive morality is harmful. We may ask first, Does this act harm anyone independently of its repercussion on the shared morality of society? And secondly we may ask, Does this act affect the shared morality and thereby weaken society? The moderate thesis requires, if the punishment of the act is to be justified, an affirmative answer at least at the second level. The extreme thesis does not require an affirmative answer at either level.

Lord Devlin appears to defend the moderate thesis. I say "appears" because, though he says that society has the right to enforce a morality as such on the ground that a shared morality is essential to society's existence, it is not at all clear that for him the statement that immorality jeopardizes or weakens society is a statement of empirical fact. It seems sometimes to be an *a priori* assumption, and sometimes a necessary truth and a very odd one. The most important indication that this is so is that, apart from one vague reference to "history" showing that "the loosening of moral bonds is often the first stage of disintegration," no evidence is produced to show that deviation from accepted sexual morality, even by adults in private, is something which, like treason, threatens the existence of society. No reputable historian has maintained this thesis, and there is indeed much evidence against it. As a proposition of fact it is entitled to no more respect than the Emperor Justinian's statement that homosexuality was the cause of earthquakes. Lord Devlin's belief in it, and his apparent indifference to the question of evidence, are at points traceable to an undiscussed assumption. This is that all morality—sexual morality together with the morality that forbids acts injurious to others such as killing, stealing, and dishonesty—forms a single seamless web, so that those who deviate from any part are likely or perhaps bound to deviate from the whole. It is of course clear (and one of the oldest insights of political theory) that society could not exist without a morality which mirrored and supplemented the law's proscription of conduct injurious to others. But there is again no evidence to support, and much to refute, the theory that those who deviate from conventional sexual morality are in other ways hostile to society.

There seems, however, to be central to Lord Devlin's thought something more interesting, though no more convincing, than the conception of social morality as a seamless web. For he appears to move from the acceptable proposition that *some* shared morality is essential to the existence of any society to the unacceptable proposition that a society is identical with its morality as that is at any given moment of its history, so that a change in its morality is tantamount to the destruction of a society. The former proposition might be even accepted as a necessary rather than an empirical truth depending on a quite plausible definition of society as a body of men who hold certain moral views in common. But the latter proposition is absurd. Taken strictly, it would prevent us saying that the morality of the given society had changed, and would compel us instead to say that one society had disappeared and another one taken its place. But it is only on this absurd criterion of what it is for the same society to continue to exist that it could be asserted without evidence that any deviation from a society's shared morality threatens its existence.

It is clear that only this tacit identification of a society with its shared morality supports Lord Devlin's denial that there could be such a thing as private immorality and his comparison of sexual immorality, even when it takes place "in private," with treason. No doubt it is true if deviations from conventional sexual morality are tolerated by the law and come to be known, the conventional morality might change in a permissive direction, though this does not seem to be the case with homosexuality in those European countries where it is not punishable by law. But even if the conventional morality did so change, the society in question would not have been destroyed or "subverted." We should compare such a development not to the violent overthrow of government but to a peaceful constitutional change in its form, consistent not only with the preservation of a society but with its advance.

. . .

The extreme thesis has many variants, and it is not always clear which of them its advocates are concerned to urge. According to some variants, the legal enforcement of morality is only of instrumental value: it is merely a means, though an indispensable one, for preserving of morality, whereas the preservation of morality is the end, valuable in itself, which justifies its legal enforcement. According to other variants, there is something intrinsically valuable in the legal enforcement of morality. What is common to all varieties of the extreme thesis is that, unlike the moderate thesis, they do not hold the enforcement of morality or its preservation to be valuable merely because of their beneficial consequences in securing the existence of society.

It is to be observed that Lord Devlin hovers somewhat ambiguously between one form of the extreme thesis and the moderate thesis. For if we interpret his crucial statement that the preservation of a society's morality is necessary for its existence as a statement of fact (as the analogy with the suppression of treason suggests we should), then the continued existence of society is something distinguishable from the preservation of its morality. It is, in fact, a desirable consequence of the preservation of its morality, and, on the as-

sumption that the enforcement of morality is identical with or required for its preservation, this desirable consequence justifies the enforcement of morality. So interpreted, Lord Devlin is an advocate of the moderate thesis and his argument is a utilitarian one. The objection to it is that his crucial statement of fact is unsupported by evidence; it is Utilitarianism without benefit of facts. If, on the other hand, we interpret his statement that any immorality, even in private, threatens the existence of society, not as an empirical statement but as a necessary truth (as the absence of evidence suggests we should), then the continued existence of a society is not something different from the preservation of its morality; it is identical with it. On this view the enforcement of morality is not justified by its valuable consequences in securing society from dissolution or decay. It is justified simply as identical with or required for the preservation of the society's morality. This is a form of the extreme thesis, disguised only by the tacit identification of a society with its morality which I criticised.

Stephen is, I think, a more consistent defender of certain forms of the extreme thesis than Lord Devlin is of the moderate one.

It is important for the understanding of Stephen's views on the legal enforcement of morality to notice that he, like Lord Devlin, assumes that the society to which his doctrine is to apply is marked by a considerable degree of moral solidarity, and is deeply disturbed by infringements of its moral code. Just as for Lord Devlin the morality to be enforced by law must be "public," in the sense that it is generally shared and identifiable by the triple marks of "intolerance, indignation, and disgust," so for Stephen "you cannot punish anything which public opinion as expressed in the common practice of society does not strenuously and unequivocally condemn . . . To be able to punish a moral majority must be overwhelming." It is possible that in mid-Victorian England these conditions were satisfied in relation to "that considerable number of acts" which according to Stephen were treated as crimes merely because they were regarded as grossly immoral. Perhaps an "overwhelming moral majority" then actually did harbour the healthy desire for revenge of which he speaks and which is to be gratified by the punishment of the guilty. But it would be sociologically naïve to assume that these conditions obtain in contemporary England at least as far as sexual morality is concerned. The fact that there is lip service to an official sexual morality should not lead us to neglect the possibility that in sexual, as in other matters, there may be a number of mutually tolerant moralities, and that even where there is some homogeneity of practice and belief, offenders may be viewed not with hatred or resentment but with amused contempt or pity.

In a sense, therefore, Stephen's doctrine, and much of Lord Devlin's, may seem to hover in the air above the *terra firma* of contemporary social reality; it may be a well-articulated construction, interesting because it reveals the outlook characteristic of the English judiciary but lacking application to contemporary society.

33. *United States of America v. Gregory D. Schoon*

Boochever, Circuit Judge:

Gregory Schoon, Raymond Kennon, Jr., and Patricia Manning appeal their convictions for obstructing activities of the Internal Revenue Service Office in Tucson, Arizona, and failing to comply with an order of a federal police officer. Both charges stem from their activities in protest of United States involvement in El Salvador. They claim the district court improperly denied them a necessity defense. Because we hold the necessity defense inapplicable in cases like this, we affirm.

I.

On December 4, 1989, thirty people, including appellants, gained admittance to the IRS office in Tucson, where they chanted "keep America's tax dollars out of El Salvador", splashed simulated blood on the counters, walls, and carpeting, and generally obstructed the office's operation. After a federal police officer ordered the group, on several occasions, to disperse or face arrest, appellants were arrested.

———————

971 F.2d 193 (1992)
United States Court of Appeals
Ninth Circuit

At a bench trial, appellants proffered testimony about conditions in El Salvador as the motivation for their conduct. They attempted to assert a necessity defense, essentially contending that their acts in protest of American involvement in El Salvador were necessary to avoid further bloodshed in that country. While finding appellants motivated solely by humanitarian concerns, the court nonetheless precluded the defense as a matter of law, relying on Ninth Circuit precedent. The sole issue on appeal is the propriety of the court's exclusion of a necessity defense as a matter of law.

II.

A district court may preclude a necessity defense where the evidence, as described in the defendant's offer of proof, is insufficient as a matter of law to support the proffered defense. . . . To invoke the necessity defense, therefore, the defendants colorably must have shown that: (1) they were faced with a choice of evils and chose the lesser evil; (2) they acted to prevent imminent harm; (3) they reasonably anticipated a direct casual relationship between their conduct and the harm to be averted; and (4) they had no legal alternatives to violating the law. . . .

The district court denied the necessity defense on the grounds that (1) the requisite immediacy was lacking; (2) the actions taken would not abate the evil; and (3) other legal alternatives existed. Because the threshold test for admissibility of a necessity defense is a conjunctive one, a court may preclude invocation of the defense if proof is deficient with regard to any of the four elements.

While we could affirm substantially on those grounds relied upon by the district court, we find a deeper, systemic reason for the complete absence of federal case law recognizing a necessity defense in an indirect civil disobedience case. As used in this opinion, "civil disobedience" is the willful violation of a law, undertaken for the purpose of social or political protest. *Cf. Webster's Third New International Dictionary* 413 (unabridged, 1976) ("refusal to obey the demands or commands of the government" to force government concessions). Indirect civil disobedience involves violating a law or interfering with a government policy that is not, itself, the object of protest. Direct civil disobedience, on the other hand, involves protesting the existence of a law by breaking that law or by preventing the execution of that law in a specific instance in which a particularized harm would otherwise follow. . . . This case involves indirect civil disobedience because these protestors were not challenging the laws under which they were charged. In contrast, the civil rights lunch counter sit-ins, for example, constituted direct civil disobedience because the protestors were challenging the rule that prevented them from sitting at lunch counters. Similarly if a city council passed an ordinance requiring immediate infusion of a suspected carcinogen into the drinking water, physically blocking the delivery of the substance would constitute direct civil disobedience: protestors would be preventing the execution of a law in a specific instance in which a particularized harm—contamination of the water supply—would otherwise follow.

While our prior cases consistently have found the elements of the necessity defense lacking in cases involving indirect civil disobedience . . . we have never addressed specifically whether the defense is available in cases of indirect disobedience. . . . Today, we conclude, for the reasons stated below, that the necessity defense is inapplicable to cases involving indirect civil disobedience.

III.

Necessity is, essentially, a utilitarian defense. . . . It therefore justifies criminal acts taken to avert a greater harm, maximizing social welfare by allowing a crime to be committed where the social benefits of the crime outweigh the social costs of failing to commit the crime. . . . Pursuant to the defense, prisoners could escape a burning prison; . . . a person lost in the woods could steal food from a cabin to survive[2] . . . ; an embargo could be violated because adverse weather conditions necessitated sale of the cargo at a foreign port; . . . a crew could mutiny where their ship was thought to be unseaworthy; . . . and property could be destroyed to prevent the spread of fire.

What all the traditional necessity cases have in common is that the commission of the "crime" averted the occurrence of an even greater "harm." In some sense, the necessity defense allows us to act as individual legislatures, amending a particular criminal provision or crafting a one-time exception to it, subject to court review, when a real legislature would formally do the same under those circumstances. For example, by allowing prisoners who escape a burning jail to claim the justification of necessity, we assume the lawmaker, confronting this problem, would have allowed for an exception to the law proscribing prison escapes.

Because the necessity doctrine is utilitarian, however, strict requirements contain its exercise so as to prevent nonbeneficial criminal conduct. For example, if the criminal act cannot abate the threatened harm, society receives no benefit from the criminal conduct. . . . Similarly, to forgive a crime taken to avert a lesser harm would fail to maximize social utility. The cost of the crime would outweigh the harm averted by its commission. Likewise, criminal acts cannot be condoned to thwart threats, yet to be imminent, or those for which there are legal alternatives to abate the harm.

Analysis of three of the necessity defense's four elements leads us to the conclusion that necessity can never be proved in a case of indirect civil disobedience. We do not rely upon the imminent harm prong of the defense because we believe there can be indirect civil disobedience cases in which the protested harm is imminent.

A.

1. Balance of Harms. It is axiomatic that, if the thing to be averted is not a harm at all, the balance of harms necessarily would disfavor any criminal action. Indirect civil disobedience seeks first and foremost to bring about the repeal of a law or a change of government policy, attempting to mobilize public opinion through typically symbolic action. These protestors violate a law, not because it is unconstitutional or otherwise improper, but because doing so calls public attention to their objectives. Thus, the most im-mediate "harm" this form of protest targets is the *existence* of the law or policy. However, the mere existence of a constitutional law or governmental policy cannot constitute a legally cognizable harm. . . .

There may be, of course, general harms that result from the targeted law or policy. Such generalized "harm," however, is too insubstantial an injury to be legally cognizable. We have in the past rejected the use of the necessity defense in indirect civil disobedience cases as a "'back door' attempt to attack government programs in a manner foreclosed by [federal] standing requirements." . . . The law could not function were people allowed to rely on their *subjective* beliefs and value judgments in determining which harms justified the taking of criminal action.

The protest in this case was in the form of indirect civil disobedience, aimed at reversal of the government's El Salvador policy. That policy does not violate the Constitution, and appellants have never suggested as much. There is no evidence that the procedure by which the policy was adopted was in any way improper; nor is there any evidence that appellants were prevented systematically from participating in the democratic processes through which the policy was chosen. . . . The most immediate harm the appellants sought to avert was the existence of the government's El Salvador policy, which is not in itself a legally cognizable harm. Moreover, any harms resulting from the operation of this policy are insufficiently concrete to be legally cognizable as harms for purposes of the necessity defense.

Thus, as a matter of law, the mere existence of a policy or law validly enacted by Congress cannot constitute a cognizable harm. If there is no cognizable harm to prevent, the harm resulting from criminal action taken for the purpose of securing the repeal of the law or policy necessarily outweighs any benefit of the action.

2. Causal Relationship Between Criminal Conduct and Harm to Be Averted. This inquiry requires a court to judge the likelihood that an alleged harm will be abated by the taking of illegal action. In the sense that the likelihood of abatement is required in the traditional necessity cases, there will never be such likelihood in cases of indirect political protest. In the traditional cases, a prisoner flees a burning cell and averts death, or someone demolishes a home to create a firebreak and prevents the conflagration of an entire community. The nexus between the act undertaken and the result sought is a close one. Ordinarily it is the volitional illegal act alone which, once taken, abates the evil.

In political necessity cases involving indirect civil disobedience against congressional acts, however, the act alone is unlikely to abate the evil precisely because the action is indirect. Here, the IRS obstruction, or the refusal to comply with a federal officer's order, are unlikely to abate the killings in El Salvador, or immediately change Congress's policy; instead, it takes another *volitional* actor not controlled by the protestor to take a further step; Congress must change its mind.

3. Legal Alternatives. A final reason the necessity defense does not apply to these indirect civil disobedience cases is that legal alternatives will never be deemed exhausted when the harm can be mitigated by congressional action. As noted above, the harm indirect civil disobedience aims to prevent is the continued existence of a law or policy. Because congressional action can *always* mitigate this "harm," lawful political activity to spur such action will always be a legal alternative. On the other hand, we cannot say that this legal alternative will always exist in cases of direct civil disobedience, where protestors act to avert a concrete harm flowing from the operation of the targeted law or policy.

The necessity defense requires the absence of any legal alternative to the contemplated illegal conduct which could reasonably be expected to abate an imminent evil. . . . A prisoner fleeing a burning jail, for example, would not be asked to wait in his cell because someone might conceivably save him; such a legal alternative is ill-suited to avoiding death in a fire. In other words, the law implies a reasonableness requirement in judging whether legal alternatives exist.

Where the targeted harm is the existence of a law or policy, our precedents counsel that this reasonableness requirement is met simply by the possibility of congressional action. . . .

. . .

The real problem here is that litigants are trying to distort to their purposes an age-old common law doctrine meant for a very different set of circumstances. What these cases are really about is gaining notoriety for a cause—the defense allows protestors to get their political grievances discussed in a courtroom. . . . It is precisely this political motive that has left some courts, like the district court in this case, uneasy. . . . Because these attempts to invoke the necessity defense force the courts to choose among causes they should make legitimate by extending the defense of necessity, and because the criminal acts, themselves, do not maximize social good, they should be subject to a *per se* rule of exclusion.

Conclusion

Because the necessity defense was not intended as justification for illegal acts taken in indirect political protest, we affirm the district court's refusal to admit evidence of necessity.

Affirmed.

---

34. *Letter from Birmingham Jail*

MARTIN LUTHER KING, JR.

My dear Fellow Clergymen,

While confined here in the Birmingham city jail, I came across your recent statement calling our present activities "unwise and untimely." Seldom, if ever, do I pause to answer criticism of my work and ideas. If I sought to answer all of the criticisms that cross my desk, my secretaries would be engaged in little else in the course of the day, and I would have no time for constructive work. But since I feel that you are men of genuine good will and your criticisms are sincerely set forth, I would

like to answer your statement in what I hope will be patient and reasonable terms.

I think I should give the reason for my being in Birmingham, since you have been influenced by the argument of "outsiders coming in." I have the honor of serving as president of the Southern Christian Leadership Conference, an organization operating in every southern state, with headquarters in Atlanta, Georgia. We have some eight-five affiliate organizations all across the South—one being the Alabama Christian Movement for Human Rights. Whenever necessary and possible we share staff, educational and financial resources with our affiliates. Several months ago our local affiliate here in Birmingham invited us to be on call to engage in a nonviolent direct-action program if such were deemed necessary. We readily consented and when the hour came we lived up to our promises. So I am here, along with several members of my staff, because we were invited here. I am here because I have basic organizational ties here.

Beyond this, I am in Birmingham because injustice is here. Just as the eighth century prophets left their little villages and carried their "thus saith the Lord" far beyond the boundaries of their home-towns; and just as the Apostle Paul left his little village of Tarsus and carried the gospel of Jesus Christ to practically every hamlet and city of the Graeco-Roman world, I too am compelled to carry the gospel of freedom beyond my particular home-town. Like Paul, I must constantly respond to the Macedonian call for aid.

Moreover, I am cognizant of the interrelated-ness of all communities and states. I cannot sit idly by in Atlanta and not be concerned about what happens in Birmingham. Injustice anywhere is a threat to justice everywhere. We are caught in an inescapable network of mutuality, tied in a single garment of destiny. Whatever affects one directly affects all indirectly. Never again can we afford to live with the narrow, provincial "outside agitator" idea. Anyone who lives in the United States can never be considered an outsider anywhere in this country.

You deplore the demonstrations that are presently taking place in Birmingham. But I am sorry that your statement did not express a similar concern for the conditions that brought the demon-strations into being. I am sure that each of you would want to go beyond the superficial social an-alyst who looks merely at effects, and does not grapple with underlying causes. I would not hesi-tate to say that it is unfortunate that so-called demonstrations are taking place in Birmingham at this time, but I would say in more emphatic terms that it is even more unfortunate that the white power structure of this city left the Negro commu-nity with no other alternative.

. . .

You may well ask, "Why direct action? Why sit-ins, marches, etc.? Isn't negotiation a better path?" You are exactly right in your call for negotia-tion. Indeed, this is the purpose of direct action. Nonviolent direct action seeks to create such a crisis and establish such creative tension that a commu-nity that has constantly refused to negotiate is forced to confront the issue. It seeks so to dramatize the issue that it can no longer be ignored. I just re-ferred to the creation of tension as a part of the work of the nonviolent resister. This may sound rather shocking. But I must confess that I am not afraid of the word tension. I have earnestly worked and preached against violent tension, but there is a type of constructive nonviolent tension that is necessary for growth. Just as Socrates felt that it was necessary to create a tension in the mind so that individuals could rise from the bondage of myths and half-truths to the unfettered realm of creative analysis and objective appraisal, we must see the need for having nonviolent gadflies to create the kind of ten-sion in society that will help men to rise from the dark depths of prejudice and racism to the majestic heights of understanding and brotherhood. So the purpose of the direct action is to create a situation so crisis-packed that it will inevitably open the door to negotiation. We therefore, concur with you in your call for negotiation. Too long has our beloved Southland been bogged down in the tragic attempt to live in monologue rather than dialogue.

. . .

We know through painful experience that free-dom is never voluntarily given by the oppressor; it must be demanded by the oppressed. Frankly, I have never yet engaged in a [direct-action] move-ment that was "well-timed," according to the timetable of those who have not suffered unduly from the disease of segregation. For years now I have heard the word "Wait!" It rings in the ear of every Negro with a piercing familiarity. This "Wait" has almost always meant "Never." It has been a tranquilizing thalidomide, relieving the emotional stress for a moment, only to give birth to an ill-formed infant of frustration. We must come to see with the distinguished jurist of yesterday that "jus-tice too long delayed is justice denied." We have waited for more than 340 years for our constitu-tional and God-given rights. The nations of Asia and Africa are moving with jetlike speed toward the goal of political independence, and we still creep at horse and buggy pace toward the gaining of a cup of coffee at a lunch counter. I guess it is easy for those who have never felt the stinging darts of seg-regation to say, "Wait." But when you have seen vi-cious mobs lynch your mothers and fathers at will and drown your sisters and brothers at whim; when you have seen hate-filled policemen curse, kick, brutalize and even kill your black brothers and sisters with impunity; when you see the vast majority of your twenty million Negro brothers smothering in an airtight cage of poverty in the midst of an affluent society; when you suddenly find your tongue twisted and your speech stammering as you seek to explain to your six-year-old daughter why she can't go to the public amusement park that has just been advertised on television, and see tears welling up in her little eyes when she is told that Funtown is closed to colored children, and see the depressing clouds of inferiority begin to form in her little mental sky, and see her begin to distort her little personality by unconsciously developing a bitterness toward white people; when you have to concoct an answer for a five-year-old son asking in agonizing pathos: "Daddy, why do white people treat colored people so mean?"; when you take a cross-country drive and find it necessary to sleep night after night in the uncomfortable corners of your automobile because no motel will accept you; when you are humiliated day in and day out by nagging signs reading "white" and "colored"; when your first name becomes "nigger" and your middle name becomes "boy" (however old you are) and your last name becomes "John", and when your wife and mother are never given the respected title "Mrs."; when you are harried by day and haunted by night by the fact that you are a Negro, living constantly at tiptoe stance never quite knowing what to expect next, and plagued with inner fears and outer resentments; when you are forever fighting a degenerating sense of "nobodiness"; then you will understand why we find it difficult to wait. There comes a time when the cup of endurance runs over, and men are no longer willing to be plunged into an abyss of injustice where they experience the blackness of corroding despair. I hope, sirs, you can understand our legitimate and unavoidable impatience.

You express a great deal of anxiety over our willingness to break laws. This is certainly a legitimate concern. Since we so diligently urge people to obey the Supreme Court's decision of 1954 outlawing segregation in the public schools, it is rather strange and paradoxical to find us consciously breaking laws. One may well ask, "How can you advocate breaking some laws and obeying others?"

The answer is found in the fact that there are two types of laws: there are *just* and *unjust* laws. I would agree with Saint Augustine that "An unjust law is no law at all."

Now what is the difference between the two? How does one determine when a law is just or unjust? A just law is a man-made code that squares with the moral law or the law of God. An unjust law is a code that is out of harmony with the moral law. To put it in the terms of Saint Thomas Aquinas, an unjust law is a human law that is not rooted in eternal and natural law. Any law that uplifts human personality is just. Any law that degrades human personality is unjust. All segregation statutes are unjust because segregation distorts the soul and damages the personality. It gives the segregator a false sense of superiority, and the segregated a false sense of inferiority. To use the words of Martin Buber, the great Jewish philosopher, segregation substitutes an "I-it" relationship for the "I-thou" relationship, and ends up relegating persons to the status of things. So segregation is not only politically, economically and sociologically unsound, but it is morally wrong and sinful. Paul Tillich has said that sin is separation. Isn't segregation an existential expression of man's tragic separation, an expression of his awful estrangement, his terrible sinfulness? So I can urge men to disobey segregation ordinances because they are morally wrong.

Let us turn to a more concrete example of just and unjust laws. An unjust law is a code that a majority inflicts on a minority that is not binding on itself. This is difference made legal. On the other hand a just law is a code that a majority compels a minority to follow that it is willing to follow itself. This is sameness made legal.

Let me give another explanation. An unjust law is a code inflicted upon a minority which that minority had no part in enacting or creating because they did not have the unhampered right to vote. Who can say that the legislature of Alabama which set up the segregation laws was democratically elected? Throughout the state of Alabama all types of conniving methods are used to prevent Negroes from becoming registered voters and there are some counties without a single Negro registered to vote despite the fact that the Negro constitutes a majority of the population. Can any law set up in such a state be considered democratically structured?

These are just a few examples of unjust and just laws. There are some instances when a law is just on its face and unjust in its application. For instance, I was arrested Friday on a charge of parading without a permit. Now there is nothing wrong with an ordinance which requires a permit for a parade, but when the ordinance is used to preserve segregation and to deny citizens the First Amendment privilege of peaceful assembly and peaceful protest, then it becomes unjust.

I hope you can see the distinction I am trying to point out. In no sense do I advocate evading or defying the law as the rabid segregationist would do. This would lead to anarchy. One who breaks an unjust law must do it *openly, lovingly* (not hatefully as the white mothers did in New Orleans when they were seen on television screaming "nigger, nigger, nigger"), and with a willingness to accept the penalty. I submit that an individual who breaks a law that conscience tells him is unjust, and willingly accepts the penalty by staying in jail to arouse the conscience of the community over its injustice, is in reality expressing the very highest respect for law.

Of course, there is nothing new about this kind of civil disobedience. It was seen sublimely in the refusal of Shadrach, Meshach and Abednego to obey the laws of Nebuchadnezzar because a higher moral law was involved. It was practiced superbly by the early Christians who were willing to face hungry lions and the excruciating pain of chopping blocks, before submitting to certain unjust laws of the Roman Empire. To a degree academic freedom is a reality today because Socrates practiced civil disobedience.

We can never forget that everything Hitler did in Germany was "legal" and everything the Hungarian freedom fighters did in Hungary was "illegal." It was "illegal" to aid and comfort a Jew in Hitler's Germany. But I am sure that if I had lived in Germany during that time I would have aided and comforted my Jewish brothers even though it was illegal. If I lived in a Communist country today where certain principles dear to the Christian faith are suppressed, I believe I would openly advocate disobeying these antireligious laws. I must make two honest confessions to you, my Christian and Jewish brothers. First, I must confess that over the last few years I have been gravely disappointed with the white moderate. I have almost reached the regrettable conclusion that the Negro's great stumbling block in the stride toward freedom is not the White Citizen's Counciler or the Ku Klux Klanner, but the white moderate who is more devoted to "order" than to justice; who prefers a negative peace which is the absence of tension to a positive peace which is the presence of justice; who constantly says, "I agree with you in the goal you seek, but I can't agree with your methods of direct action"; who paternalistically feels that he can set the timetable for another man's freedom; who lives by the myth of time and who constantly advised the Negro to wait until a "more convenient season." Shallow understanding from people of good will is more frustrating than absolute misunderstanding from people of ill will. Lukewarm acceptance is much more bewildering than outright rejection.

I had hoped that the white moderate would understand that law and order exist for the purpose of establishing justice, and that when they fail to do this they become dangerously structured dams that block the flow of social progress. I had hoped that the white moderate would understand that the present tension of the South is merely a necessary phase of the transition from an obnoxious negative peace, where the Negro passively accepted his unjust plight, to a substance-filled positive peace, where all men will respect the dignity and worth of human personality. Actually, we who engage in nonviolent direct action are not the creators of tension. We merely bring to the surface the hidden tension that is already alive. We bring it out in the open where it can be seen and dealt with. Like a boil that can never be cured as long as it is covered up but must be opened with all its pus-flowing ugliness to the natural medicines of air and light, injustice must likewise be exposed, with all of the tension its exposing creates, to the light of human conscience and the air of national opinion before it can be cured.

In your statement you asserted that our actions, even though peaceful, must be condemned because they precipitate violence. But can this assertion be logically made? Isn't this like condemning the robbed man because his possession of money precipitated the evil act of robbery? Isn't this like condemning Socrates because his unswerving commitment to truth and his philosophical delvings precipitated the misguided popular mind to make him drink the hemlock? Isn't this like condemning Jesus because His unique God-consciousness and never-ceasing devotion to his will precipitated the evil act of crucifixion? We must come to see, as federal courts have consistently affirmed, that it is immoral to urge an individual to withdraw his efforts to gain his basic constitutional rights because the quest precipitates violence. Society must protect the robbed and punish the robber.

. . .

In spite of my shattered dreams of the past, I came to Birmingham with the hope that the white religious leadership of this community would see the justice of our cause, and with deep moral concern, serve as the channel through which our just grievances would get to the power structure. I had hoped that each of you would understand. But again I have been disappointed. I have heard numerous religious leaders of the South call upon their worshippers to comply with a desegregation decision because it is the *law*, but I have longed to hear white ministers say, "Follow this decree because integration is morally *right* and the Negro is your brother." In the midst of blatant injustices inflicted upon the Negro, I have watched white churches stand on the sideline and merely mouth pious irrelevancies and sanctimonious trivialities. In the midst of a mighty struggle to rid our nation of racial and economic injustice, I have heard so many ministers say, "Those are social issues with which the gospel has no real concern," and I have watched so many churches commit themselves to a completely otherworldly religion which made a strange distinction between body and soul, the sacred and the secular.

. . .

I must close now. But before closing I am impelled to mention one other point in your statement that troubled me profoundly. You warmly commended the Birmingham police force for keeping "order" and "preventing violence." I don't believe you would have so warmly commended the police force if you had seen its angry violent dogs literally biting six unarmed, nonviolent Negroes. I don't believe you would so quickly commend the policemen if you would observe their ugly and inhuman treatment of Negroes here in the city jail; if you would watch them push and

curse old Negro women and young Negro girls; if you would see them slap and kick old Negro men and young boys; if you will observe them, as they did on two occasions, refuse to give us food because we wanted to sing our grace together. I'm sorry that I can't join you in your praise for the police department.

It is true that they have been rather disciplined in their public handling of the demonstrators. In this sense they have been rather publicly "nonviolent." But for what purpose? To preserve the evil system of segregation. Over the last few years I have consistently preached that nonviolence demands that the means we use must be as pure as the ends we seek. So I have tried to make it clear that it is wrong to use immoral means to attain moral ends. But now I must affirm that it is just as wrong, or even more so, to use moral means to preserve immoral ends. Maybe Mr. Connor and his policemen have been rather publicly nonviolent, as Chief Pritchett was in Albany, Georgia, but they have used the moral means of nonviolence to maintain the immoral end of flagrant racial injustice. T. S. Eliot has said that there is no greater treason than to do the right deed for the wrong reason.

Study Questions

1. Why did the court in *Bullington* conclude that Bullington did not "mutilate" the body of the deceased? Do you agree?

2. Mill insists that even false speech must be tolerated in a free society. What grounds does Mill give for this claim?

3. Mill claims that liberty should not be restricted unless the actor threatens harm to others. What clues does Mill give as to how he thinks "harm" should be interpreted?

4. Mill rests his case for the "harm principle" on a utilitarian moral and social theory: The harm principle is "right" just because it promotes the greatest good for society overall (or at least more good than any other arrangement). Can you see problems in attempting to justify such a stringent principle on utilitarian grounds?

5. How does Devlin determine when something becomes a matter of public morality? Is the reaction of the average person on the street a reliable indicator that some standard is central to the public morality?

6. Is Devlin making a utilitarian argument that government has a right to promote virtue and condemn vice only where this will promote the good of social cohesion? Or is he arguing that society has a right to instill virtues irrespective of utility?

7. Some people would argue that the rise in divorce rates and the breakdown of the traditional nuclear family in America in the decades since Devlin wrote have contributed to a variety of other social ills: growing poverty, child neglect, increasing juvenile delinquency, joblessness, drug use, and so on. Do these trends (if correctly perceived) support Devlin's argument about the centrality of the institution of marriage to the public morality?

8. Consider the following cases: (a) You enjoy listening to rap music, particularly music by rap groups that use what some people would consider violent and lewd lyrics. Your neighbor Joe knows that you listen to such music nightly (he never hears it, though, as you never play it too loudly), and this knowledge drives him to distraction. Joe hates rap music. He believes it is the root of all evil. He can't sleep at night, lying awake greatly distressed by the thought that you are polluting your mind with the hateful chatter. (b) One day you take your portable stereo and your rap music tapes to the beach, set them up, and turn on the music while snoozing in the sun. Joe is a few yards away; he hears the music and is disgusted; his day is ruined. (c) A friend of yours joins you on the beach and is so taken by the music that she removes all of her clothing and prances about the beach naked, moving to the music. Joe witnesses this display and is, predictably, distressed and offended. Question: Have you (or your friend) "harmed" Joe in any of these cases? If not, why not? What difference is there between the psychological distress produced by assaulting or defaming someone (which most of us, and certainly the law, recognize as real

forms of harm) and the various forms of distress experienced by Joe? Many communities have ordinances prohibiting public nudity. Can such ordinances be justified on Mill's grounds?

9. Imagine that I am a budding genius at chemistry and that I discover a recipe for making a deadly nerve gas from household ingredients. I then decide to publish my results in a letter to the editor in the local newspaper. Should I be allowed to do so? On what grounds could my "speech" be curtailed?

10. Lawrence Horn and James Perry were convicted for the 1993 murders of Horn's ex-wife and disabled son. Horn arranged for Perry to do the killing so that Horn could collect insurance money. One aspect of the case raised unusual freedom-of-expression claims concerning what terrorism experts call "mayhem manuals"—books and magazines available from small, independent publishers (and increasingly on the World Wide Web) with "how to" instructions on making bombs, silencers, sniper weapons, and other devices. Police discovered in Horn's apartment a copy of a 130-page mail-order guidebook for murder—"Hit Man: A Technical Manual for Independent Contractors." In the book, the pseudonymous author announces that "the professional hit man fills a need in society and is, at times, the only alternative for personal justice." The killer need feel "no twinge of guilt," because "the hit man is merely the executioner, an enforcer who carries out the sentence." Prosecutors found that Horn and Perry had followed twenty-two of the book's steps in committing their crime. The killers used an AR-7 rifle, recommended by "Hit Man" because it "breaks down easily." The book advises that the killer fire "at least three shots to ensure quick and easy death. Aim for the head," the book suggests, "preferably the eye sockets. Close kills enable you to determine right away whether you have successfully fulfilled your part in the contract." The victims died from three shots to the face by a powerful rifle. The publisher of "Hit Man, " Paladin Press, argued that it could not be held liable for abetting the murders, because it had no knowledge of Horn's intentions. Paladin also claimed that

mystery writers and other law-abiding citizens buy "Hit Man." A number of major publishers sided with Paladin for fear that a decision against "Hit Man" would be a vote for censorship. Should the First Amendment shield the publication of such materials? Did Paladin Press, by virtue of publishing "Hit Man," incite criminal acts? Do such publications pose a "clear and present danger" of imminent lawlessness? Is there any reason for the publication of "Hit Man" other than as a manifestation of the intent to assist in the commission of murder?

11. Controversial radio talk show personality Howard Stern was the subject of a 1996 lawsuit for intentional infliction of emotional distress based on Stern's alleged handling of and remarks about the cremated remains of the plaintiff's sister. The deceased woman, Debbie Tay, had been a frequent guest on Stern's show before her death from a drug overdose. Stern persuaded a friend of Tay's, Chaunce Hayden, to appear on the show and to bring Ms. Tay's cremated remains, which he did. Hayden had been a close friend of Tay and had been given a portion of the remains by Tay's next-of-kin. Relatives of Ms. Tay alleged that Hayden appeared on the radio show on July 18, 1995, with a decorative box containing some of Ms. Tay's remains, and that Stern shook and rattled the box, played with some of the bone fragments, and joked about Ms. Tay. The deceased's relatives sued Stern, claiming that his intentional and outrageous conduct caused them emotional harm. The court dismissed the suit, finding that "while the program which is the predicate of the complaint was certainly vulgar and disrespectful, the acts complained of cannot be characterized as being beyond all bounds of decency, atrocious and utterly intolerable in a civilized society." The court also found that Stern could not be sued for inflicting emotional harm resulting from the negligent mishandling of a corpse, since the deceased had been cremated. The court further concluded that "since a gift was made [to Mr. Hayden] of Ms. Tay's remains, whatever property interest [Tay's relatives] had in [the remains] was forfeited. Mr. Hayden . . . was then free to do as he saw fit with his share of the remains." Do you agree with the court's ruling? Do you agree that Mr. Hayden is free to do anything he wishes with the remains? Can he sell them? Feed them to his dog? An unsubstantiated allegation accused Stern of daring Hayden to eat some of the remains. Should that kind of treatment of human remains be prohibited by law? If so, on what grounds? Is there any "harm" in such behavior? Does such conduct threaten the "public morality"?

12. Both Hart and Mill seem to assume that the cost of enforcing the common, public morality is necessarily too great. Are they correct, in your judgment?

13. Do you agree with the court in *Schoon* that claiming an act is necessary to avert a greater harm can never be justified in a case of "indirect" civil disobedience? Would the defendants in *Schoon* have had a better defense, according to the court, had they traveled to El Salvador and physically harassed U.S. military personnel and advisors, thus making the case closer to one of "direct" civil disobedience?

14. Is the defense of necessity a utilitarian defense, as the court in *Schoon* reasons?

15. King quotes Saint Augustine's famous remark that "an unjust law is no law at all." It has been objected that this claim is plainly false. How can something fail to be "law" simply because it is unjust or in some other way immoral? King, himself, critics point out, was punished and put in jail for, as we would say, "breaking the law." Assuming we believe that King was right and the racially discriminatory statutes and practices of the South were unjust, does the fact that King wound up in jail prove that unjust laws nonetheless remain laws? Does that fact in itself refute Augustine? If not, why not?

16. King rests his justification of civil disobedience on an explicit appeal to natural law. Must disobedience of the positive law be grounded in such an appeal? What other grounds might be offered to justify disobedience? Could those grounds, themselves, be called "legal"?

B. *Freedom of Expression and Hate-Speech*

Gangsta Rappers and Artistic Freedom

In the summer of 1998, police in Sacramento, California, arrested "Gangsta" rapper Shawn Thomas, who performs under the name C-BO, for violating conditions of parole for a previous offense. The arrest sparked controversy and outrage among advocates of free speech—for Thomas had been jailed because of violent, antipolice lyrics released on a new CD. Over his lawyer's objections, Thomas had earlier been required as a condition of parole not to record lyrics that "promote the gang lifestyle [or are] anti-law enforcement." Lyrics on the CD included the following: "You better swing, batter, batter swing/'Cause once you get your third felony,/Yeah, 50 years you gotta bring/It's a deadly game of baseball/So when they try to pull you over, shoot 'em in the face, ya'll." Police authorities insisted that the parole conditions were a justifiable effort to stem gang violence; critics argued that authorities should never have the power to jail a person based solely on the content of his or her speech.

The Thomas controversy came on the heels of a ruling by the U.S. Supreme Court on the question of whether the government may limit the content of art produced by artists who receive public arts funding. In 1990, Congress passed legislation amending the annual federal appropriations for the National Endowment for the Arts (NEA), a major source of grants to organizations and individuals working in music and the fine and performing arts. Many in Congress were outraged by the prospect of taxpayer moneys being used to support "art" that they viewed as "filth." Supporters of the legislation pointed to cases like that of gay artist and photographer Robert Mapplethorpe. Cincinnati's Contemporary Arts Center had, in 1990, been charged with violating obscenity laws with an exhibition featuring a retrospective of Mapplethorpe's work. Some of the photos, from Mapplethorpe's "X portfolio," depicted homoerotic and sadomasochistic images, including a man's fist up another man's rectum and a bullwhip protruding from a man's anus. The legislation provided that "None of the funds authorized to be appropriated for the National Endowment for the Arts . . . may be used to promote, disseminate, or produce materials which in the judgment of the [NEA] . . . may be considered obscene, including but not limited to, depictions of sadomasochism, homoeroticism, the sexual exploitation of children, or individuals engaged in sex acts and which, when taken as a whole, do not have serious literary, artistic, political, or scientific value." The NEA was forced to require that grant recipients sign a certification agreeing to comply with this requirement. Challenged by a group of performance artists, the federal law was upheld by the Supreme Court in 1998. The restriction on NEA funding, the Court reasoned, did not penalize disfavored viewpoints or suppress speech, but simply allowed decency to be taken into consideration.

Freedom of Expression and the First Amendment

The legal questions raised by the Shawn Thomas and NEA cases turn on whether artists and performers have a right to express themselves or to use public money to convey ideas that taxpayers or their authorities may find deeply offensive. But the controversy raises other questions as well: Should my creative freedom as an artist take priority over your demand that such freedom be curtailed? For what reasons, if any, may society properly restrict an artist's—or anyone's—expressive freedom? Probing further, we may ask whether the ideal of freedom of expression protects all forms of expression. What about obscene language or pornographic literature? What about racist insults? Or the symbols and chants of hate groups and bigots? What justifies the law's attempt to draw lines dividing permissible from impermissible speech? May only speech that harms others be restricted?

At the most basic philosophical level, the foregoing questions converge on the demand to know what justifies or legitimates placing coercive restraints or criminal penalties on any of the myriad ways in which people choose to act, think, or express themselves. For what reasons may society restrict my liberty to think or act as I please? Political and legal philosophers have defended a variety of answers to these most basic questions. It is always a good reason for restricting someone's liberty, the answers go, if this is necessary to (1) prevent harm to others, (2) prevent serious and profound offense to others, (3) prevent harm to the actor himself or herself, or (4) prevent the occurrence of something inherently wrong or immoral even if neither harm nor profound offense to the actor or others is likely. Which, if any, of these proffered grounds (or some combination) are sufficient to justify curtailing individual liberty? Which of these alternatives (or some combination) should we seek to implement through the vehicle of the law? In our system of jurisprudence, such basic issues concerning individual liberty and collective authority arise most sharply at the constitutional level, for example, in applying the First Amendment to the U.S. Constitution: "Congress shall make no law . . . abridging freedom of speech. . . ."

The interpretation of and rationales for a legal regime strongly protective of free speech raises many more questions. What is "speech"? Is it whatever is spoken? But surely the First Amendment applies as much to the written word as to an oral exchange. Is speech whatever is (in any way) "communicated"? This interpretation seems too broad; after all, physical assault can "communicate" ideas (on some level), but surely a robber cannot rely on the First Amendment as a defense. Yet courts have protected a range of "symbolic speech"—wearing armbands, burning flags—involving conduct commonly recognized as expressing a message. Why

should freedom of speech be protected? Is it to promote democratic self-government? How much speech would actually be covered by this rationale? Is it to generate and sustain a "marketplace of ideas"? To further the search for truth? Will truth always win out in the marketplace?

Of course, not all expression should be protected: threats, bribes, and false advertising are all forms of "speech," but no one would seriously doubt that they should properly be made illegal. Over a number of decades, the courts have fashioned a framework to distinguish protected from unprotected speech: If communication is expressive (whether spoken, written, or "symbolic"), the government may not prohibit it unless (1) the government has a compelling or overriding interest or purpose and (2) the restriction or suppression of the expression is unrelated to the content of what is said (i.e., the restriction is not based on the content of the communication). The state can prohibit bribes, for it has a compelling interest in discouraging such things; and the state can prohibit the use of loudspeakers at 2 A.M., because this limitation is imposed regardless of what I use my loudspeaker to say. Throughout this section, we will have occasion to consider how this basic framework applies to a variety of cases.

The Cohen Case

The case of Robert Cohen, included in the readings of this section, squarely raises the question: What is constitutionally protected expression? Cohen had been charged with "disturbing the peace . . . through offensive conduct" for wearing a jacket bearing the words "Fuck the draft" into the Los Angeles County courthouse. Cohen appealed the conviction, and the U.S. Supreme Court eventually overturned it. Justice Harlan, writing for the court, raised a number of points. The state cannot punish Cohen merely for the underlying content of his message (i.e., "I don't like the draft"), for to allow that would plainly violate the First Amendment. Cohen's speech did not fall within the generally recognized areas in which restrictions on speech are appropriate (for example, Cohen did not "incite a riot" or engage in "fighting words" or defamatory remarks against a specific person). Nor was

Cohen's message unavoidable to those who might be offended by it. Finally, Harlan attacks the California statute at stake in the case. That law is far too vague: What does "offensive" mean? The term is dangerously flexible, such that almost any offense or distress could become grounds for prohibition. The language of the California law is so vague that it fails to give people adequate notice of what the law requires. Harlan here appeals to a crucially important notion in the law: It is a fundamental principle that criminal offenses be specified as precisely as possible, so that people can know with reasonable certainty what is against the law and what isn't. Statutes are sometimes held "void for vagueness"—so unclear that they are unconstitutional.

Speech and Hate

Among the most recent and divisive disputes concerning the scope of freedom of expression is that over how institutions of higher learning ought to respond to the much-publicized rise in incidents of racial and sexual "hate-speech" on college and university campuses. Many college campuses in the last few years have experienced an alarming increase in various racial incidents, from racial graffiti in dorms to confrontational racial slurs and epithets in the quad. As a consequence, several campuses have experimented with policies prohibiting "discriminatory harassment" or "personal vilification." Generally, such "speech codes" have tended to fall into two categories. Some seek to suppress the broadest range of hate-speech, from the lowliest gutter epithets and slurs to more disguised, veiled, or sophisticated expressions of racial hatred and contempt. Others aim to isolate and suppress only the crudest forms of racial insults: those directed at specific persons with the intent to vilify and degrade their target.

Critics have argued that such policies run afoul of the First Amendment, and in 1988 a federal court in Michigan struck down a policy of the University of Michigan that prohibited "stigmatizing or victimizing" individuals or groups on the basis of "race, ethnicity, religion, sex, sexual orientation, creed, national origin, ancestry, age, marital status, handicap, or Vietnam-era veteran status" by creating an "intimidating, hostile, or demeaning" educational environment. The court claimed that the terms of the policy were so vague and broad as to fail to pass constitutional muster.[1]

As the readings in this section discuss, the courts have held that certain categories of expression do not deserve free-speech protection. These categories include, for example, defamatory speech, "fighting words," and speech that is "directed to inciting or producing imminent lawless action" where such lawlessness is likely. Does abusive racist speech deserve full free-speech protection? Or is it sufficiently close to one or another of the forms of expression traditionally excluded from such protection? Much of the difficulty here lies in deciding what "hate-speech" is; it is best to look at specific examples. (Warning: To discuss concrete cases, it is necessary to employ the language used by bigots. I will need to do so here.) One case involved a group of White students who trailed a Black female across campus saying "I've never tried a nigger before." Another involved a swastika and the words "die faggot" scrawled on a dormitory door. These kinds of cases are arguably close to conduct already prohibited (for example, sexual harassment or assault). Other cases are not so clear. Suppose two students, one White and the other Black, are involved in a heated classroom discussion of affirmative action (the White student is against it; the Black student supports it). At one point, the White student angrily points a finger at the Black student and says, "You just want a handout because you're a [expletive deleted] nigger, and lazy niggers always want a handout." Without more, this is not conduct rising to the level of an assault. Nor does it suffice to display a pattern of discriminatory behavior. It certainly is direct vilification based on race. If the White student defends his statement on free-speech grounds, should this defense be credited?

Should Hate-Speech Be Prohibited?

Law professor Cass Sunstein, in his essay included here, distinguishes speech at the core of the First

---

[1] See *Doe v. University of Michigan* 721 F. Supp. 852 (1989).

Amendment, deserving maximal protection, from speech at the periphery, demanding little or no protection. We must work within such a distinction, Sunstein argues, because an absolutist position on the First Amendment—that anyone can say anything anywhere—is indefensible. Sunstein theorizes that speech intended to contribute to public debate on issues is central to constitutionally protected freedom of expression, and he utilizes this claim to probe the constitutionality and wisdom of campus hate-speech restrictions. Sunstein reasons that only the most direct forms of hate-speech—epithets and slurs—would be so "low value" as to deserve no First Amendment protection; but even barring these forms of hate-speech may violate established precedents, such as the Supreme Court's recent ruling in the *R.A.V.* case. Sunstein closes with an argument supporting narrow campus restrictions on hate-speech, grounded on the idea of a university's educational mission.

The readings continue with an essay in which Richard Delgado and Jean Stefancic argue that racist insults can be profoundly harmful to those victimized by them, that the law should therefore allow victims of such hate speech to bring a lawsuit (in the law of tort) against the perpetrators of hate, and that universities should prohibit speech that "constructs a stigma picture" of a subordinate group. Delgado and Stefancic try to show how this view can be squared with the basics of First Amendment law. Finally, Nadine Strossen argues that efforts to curb racist speech run too great a risk of descending a slippery slope into unacceptable forms of censorship. Strossen argues that to protect First Amendment freedoms vigilantly, we must allow even the expression of racial hatred. No exceptions should be made to free-speech protections for racist speech.

---

35. *Cohen v. California*

Opinion of the Court

Mr. Justice Harlan delivered the opinion of the Court.

This case may seem at first blush too inconsequential to find its way into our books, but the issue it presents is of no small constitutional significance.

Appellant Paul Robert Cohen was convicted in the Los Angeles Municipal Court of violating that part of California Penal Code § 415 which prohibits "maliciously and willfully disturb[ing] the peace or quiet of any neighborhood or person . . . by . . . of-

408 U.S. 15 (1971)
United States Supreme Court

fensive conduct. . . ."[1] He was given 30 days' imprisonment. The facts upon which his conviction rests are detailed in the opinion of the Court of Appeal of California, Second Appellate District, as follows:

"On April 26, 1968, the defendant was observed in the Los Angeles County Courthouse in the corridor outside of division 20 of the municipal court wearing a jacket bearing the words 'Fuck the Draft' which were plainly visible. There were women and children present in the corridor. The defendant was arrested. The defendant testified that he wore the jacket knowing that the words were on the jacket as a means of informing the public of the depth of his feelings against the Vietnam War and the draft.

"The defendant did not engage in, nor threaten to engage in, nor did anyone as the result of his conduct in fact commit or threaten to commit any act of violence. The defendant did not make any loud or unusual noise, nor was there any evidence that he uttered any sound prior to his arrest."

In affirming the conviction the Court of Appeal held that "offensive conduct" means "behavior which has a tendency to provoke *others* to acts of violence or to in turn disturb the peace", and that the State had proved this element because, on the facts of this case, "[i]t was certainly reasonably foreseeable that such conduct might cause others to rise up to commit a violent act against the person of the defendant or attempt to forcibly remove his jacket." The California Supreme Court declined review by a divided vote. We brought the case here, postponing the consideration of the question of our jurisdiction over this appeal to a hearing of the case on the merits. We now reverse.

I

In order to lay hands on the precise issue which this case involves, it is useful first to canvass various matters which this record does *not* present.

The conviction quite clearly rests upon the asserted offensiveness of the *words* Cohen used to convey his message to the public. The only "conduct" which the State sought to punish is the fact of communication. Thus, we deal here with a conviction resting solely upon "speech," not upon any separately identifiable conduct which allegedly was intended by Cohen to be perceived by others as expressive of particular views but which, on its face, does not necessarily convey any message and hence arguably could be regulated without effectively repressing Cohen's ability to express himself. Further, the State certainly lacks power to punish Cohen for the underlying content of the message the inscription conveyed. At least so long as there is no showing of an intent to incite disobedience to or disruption of the draft, Cohen could not, consistently with the First and Fourteenth Amendments, be punished for asserting the evident position on the inutility or immorality of the draft his jacket reflected.

Appellant's conviction, then, rests squarely upon his exercise of the "freedom of speech" protected from arbitrary governmental interference by the Constitution and can be justified, if at all, only

as a valid regulation of the manner in which he exercised that freedom, not as a permissible prohibition on the substantive message it conveys. This does not end the inquiry, of course, for the First and Fourteenth Amendments have never been thought to give absolute protection to every individual to speak whenever or wherever he pleases, or to use any form of address in any circumstances that he chooses. In this vein, too, however, we think it important to note that several issues typically associated with such problems are not presented here.

In the first place, Cohen was tried under a statute applicable throughout the entire State. Any attempt to support this conviction on the ground that the statute seeks to preserve an appropriately decorous atmosphere in the courthouse where Cohen was arrested must fail in the absence of any language in the statute that would have put appellant on notice that certain kinds of otherwise permissible speech or conduct would nevertheless, under California law, not be tolerated in certain places. No fair reading of the phrase "offensive conduct" can be said sufficiently to inform the ordinary person that distinctions between certain locations are thereby created.[2]

In the second place, as it comes to us, this case cannot be said to fall within those relatively few categories of instances where prior decisions have established the power of government to deal more comprehensively with certain forms of individual expression simply upon a showing that such a form was employed. This is not, for example, an obscenity case. Whatever else may be necessary to give rise to the States' broader power to prohibit obscene expression, such expression must be, in some significant way, erotic. It cannot plausibly be maintained that this vulgar allusion to the Selective Service System would conjure up such psychic stimulation in anyone likely to be confronted with Cohen's crudely defaced jacket.

This court has also held that the States are free to ban the simple use, without a demonstration of additional justifying circumstances, of so-called "fighting words," those personally abusive epithets which, when addressed to the ordinary citizen, are, as a matter of common knowledge, inherently likely to provoke violent reaction. While the four-letter word displayed by Cohen in relation to the draft is not uncommonly employed in a personally provocative fashion, in this instance it was clearly not "directed to the person of the hearer." No individual actually or likely to be present could reasonably have regarded the words on appellant's jacket as a direct personal insult. Nor do we have here an instance of the exercise of the State's police power to prevent a speaker from intentionally provoking a given group to hostile reaction. There is, as noted above, no showing that anyone who saw Cohen was in fact violently aroused or that appellant intended such a result.

Finally, in arguments before this Court much has been made of the claim that Cohen's distasteful mode of expression was thrust upon unwilling or unsuspecting viewers, and that the State might therefore legitimately act as it did in order to protect the sensitive from otherwise unavoidable exposure to appellant's crude form of protest. Of course, the mere presumed presence of unwitting listeners or viewers does not serve automatically to justify curtailing all speech capable of giving offense. While this Court has recognized that government may properly act in many situations to prohibit intrusion into the privacy of the home of unwelcome views and ideas which cannot be totally banned from the public dialogue, we have at the same time consistently stressed that "we are often 'captives' outside the sanctuary of the home and subject to objectionable speech." The ability of government, consonant with the Constitution, to shut off discourse solely to protect others from hearing it is, in other words, dependent upon a showing that substantial privacy interests are being invaded in an essentially intolerable manner. Any broader view of this authority would effectively empower a majority to silence dissidents simply as a matter of personal predilections.

In this regard, persons confronted with Cohen's jacket were in a quite different posture than, say, those subjected to the raucous emissions of sound trucks blaring outside their residences. Those in the Los Angeles courthouse could effectively avoid further bombardment of their sensibilities simply by averting their eyes. And, while it may be that one has a more substantial claim to a recognizable privacy interest when walking through a courthouse corridor than, for example, strolling through Central Park, surely it is nothing like the interest in being free from unwanted expression in the confines of one's own home. Given the subtlety and complexity of the factors involved,

if Cohen's "speech" was otherwise entitled to constitutional protection, we do not think the fact that some unwilling "listeners" in a public building may have been briefly exposed to it can serve to justify this breach of the peace conviction where, as here, there was no evidence that persons powerless to avoid appellant's conduct did in fact object to it, and where that portion of the statute upon which Cohen's conviction rests evinces no concern, either on its face or as construed by the California courts, with the special plight of the captive auditor, but, instead, indiscriminately sweeps within its prohibitions all "offensive conduct" that disturbs "any neighborhood or person."

II

Against this background, the issue flushed by this case stands out in bold relief. It is whether California can excise, as "offensive conduct," one particular scurrilous epithet from the public discourse, either upon the theory of the court below that its use is inherently likely to cause violent reaction or upon a more general assertion that the States, acting as guardians of public morality, may properly remove this offensive word from the public vocabulary.

The rationale of the California court is plainly untenable. At most it reflects an "undifferentiated fear or apprehension of disturbance [which] is not enough to overcome the right to freedom of expression." We have been shown no evidence that substantial numbers of citizens are standing ready to strike out physically at whomever may assault their sensibilities with execrations like that uttered by Cohen. There may be some persons about with such lawless and violent proclivities, but that is an insufficient base upon which to erect, consistently with constitutional values, a governmental power to force persons who wish to ventilate their dissident views into avoiding particular forms of expression. The argument amounts to little more than the self-defeating proposition that to avoid physical censorship of one who has not sought to provoke such a response by a hypothetical coterie of the violent and lawless, the States may more appropriately effectuate that censorship themselves.

Admittedly, it is not so obvious that the First and Fourteenth Amendments must be taken to disable to States from punishing public utterance of this unseemly expletive in order to maintain what they regard as a suitable level of discourse within the body politic. We think, however, that examination and reflection will reveal the shortcomings of a contrary viewpoint.

At the outset, we cannot overemphasize that, in our judgment, most situations where the State has a justifiable interest in regulating speech will fall within one or more of the various established exceptions, discussed above but not applicable here, to the usual rule that governmental bodies may not prescribe the form or content of individual expression. Equally important to our conclusion is the constitutional backdrop against which our decision must be made. The constitutional right of free expression is powerful medicine in a society as diverse and populous as ours. It is designed and intended to remove governmental restraints from the arena of public discussion, putting the decision as to what views shall be voiced largely into the hands of each of us, in the hope that use of such freedom will ultimately produce a more capable citizenry and more perfect polity and in the belief that no other approach would comport with the premise of individual dignity and choice upon which our political system rests.

To many, the immediate consequence of this freedom may often appear to be only verbal tumult, discord, and even offensive utterance. These are, however, within established limits, in truth necessary side effects of the broader enduring values which the process of open debate permits us to achieve. That the air may at times seem filled with verbal cacophony is, in this sense not a sign of weakness but of strength. We cannot lose sight of the fact that, in what otherwise might seem a trifling and annoying instance of individual distasteful abuse of a privilege, these fundamental societal values are truly implicated. That is why "[w]holly neutral futilities . . . come under the protection of free speech as fully as do Keats' poems or Donne's sermons," *Winters v. New York*, (1948) (Frankfurter, J., dissenting), and why "so long as the means are peaceful, the communication need not meet standards of acceptability," *Organization for a Better Austin v. Keefe*, (1971).

Against this perception of the constitutional policies involved, we discern certain more particu-

larized considerations that peculiarly call for reversal of this conviction. First, the principle contended for by the State seems inherently boundless. How is one to distinguish this from any other offensive word? Surely the State has no right to cleanse public debate to the point where it is grammatically palatable to the most squeamish among us. Yet no readily ascertainable general principle exists for stopping short of that result were we to affirm the judgment below. For, while the particular four-letter word being litigated here is perhaps more distasteful than most others of its genre, it is nevertheless often true that one man's vulgarity is another's lyric. Indeed, we think it is largely because governmental officials cannot make principled distinctions in this area that the Constitution leaves matters of taste and style so largely to the individual.

Additionally, we cannot overlook the fact, because it is well illustrated by the episode involved here, that much linguistic expression serves a dual communicative function: it conveys not only ideas capable of relatively precise, detached explication, but otherwise inexpressible emotions as well. In fact, words are often chosen as much for their emotive as their cognitive force. We cannot sanction the view that the Constitution, while solicitous of the cognitive content of individual speech, has little or no regard for that emotive function which, practically speaking, may often be the more important element of the overall message sought to be communicated. Indeed, as Mr. Justice Frankfurter has said, "[o]ne of the prerogatives of American citizenship is the right to criticize public men and measures—and that means not only informed and responsible criticism but the freedom to speak foolishly and without moderation." *Baumgartner v. United States*, (1944).

Finally, and in the same vein, we cannot indulge the facile assumption that one can forbid particular words without also running a substantial risk of suppressing ideas in the process. Indeed, governments might soon seize upon the censorship of particular words as a convenient guise for banning the expression of unpopular views. We have been able, as noted above, to discern little social benefit that might result from running the risk of opening the door to such grave results.

It is, in sum, our judgment that, absent a more particularized and compelling reason for its actions, the State may not, consistently with the First and Fourteenth Amendments, make the simple public display here involved of this single four-letter expletive a criminal offense. Because that is the only arguably sustainable rationale for the conviction here at issue, the judgment below must be reversed.

Separate Opinion

Mr. Justice Blackmun, with whom The Chief Justice and Mr. Justice Black join.

I dissent, and I do so for two reasons:

1. Cohen's absurd and immature antic, in my view, was mainly conduct and little speech. The California Court of Appeal appears so to have described it, and I cannot characterize it otherwise. Further, the case appears to me to be well within the sphere of *Chaplinsky v. New Hampshire,* where Mr. Justice Murphy, a known champion of First Amendment freedoms, wrote for a unanimous bench. As a consequence, this Court's agonizing First Amendment values seems misplaced and unnecessary.

2. I am not at all certain that the California Court of Appeal's construction of § 415 is now the authoritative California construction. . . .

Endnotes

[1] The statute provides in full:

"Every person who maliciously and willfully disturbs the peace or quiet of any neighborhood or person, by loud or unusual noise, or by tumultuous or offensive conduct, or threatening, traducing, quarreling, challenging to fight, or fighting, or who, on the public streets of any unincorporated town, or upon the public highways in such unincorporated town, run any horse race, either for a wager or for amusement, or fire any gun or pistol is such unincorporated town, or use any vulgar language within the presence or hearing of women or children, in a loud and boisterous manner, is guilty of a misdemeanor, and upon conviction by any Court of competent jurisdiction shall be punished by fine not exceeding two hundred dollars, or by imprisonment in the County Jail for not more than ninety days, or by both fine and imprisonment, or either, at the discretion of the Court."

[2] It is illuminating to note what transpired when Cohen entered a courtroom in the building. He removed his jacket and stood with it folded over his arm. Meanwhile, a policeman sent the presiding judge a note suggesting that Cohen be held in contempt of court. The judge declined to do so and Cohen was arrested by the officer only after he emerged from the courtroom.

36. *Liberalism, Speech Codes, and Related Problems*

Cass R. Sunstein

The law has rarely been at odds with academic freedom. In recent years, however, the development of campus "speech codes" has created a range of new controversies. In these remarks, one of my purposes is to defend the constitutionality of narrowly drawn restrictions on hate speech, arguing in the process against the broader versions that have become popular in some institutions. My most general goal is to set the dispute over speech codes in the broader context of the liberal commitment to freedom of speech and academic pluralism. Through this approach it may be possible to overcome the "all or nothing" tone that has dominated much of public and even academic discussion. In the process of defending some narrow restrictions on hate speech, it will be necessary to say a good deal about the principle of neutrality in constitutional law, academic life, and perhaps elsewhere.

. . .

[In a well-functioning system of free expression, political speech—speech "intended and received as a contribution to public deliberation about some issue"] belongs in the top tier; more speech, not censorship, is the remedy for speech that threatens harm; only an emergency can support suppression. Nonpolitical speech is also protected, but it can be regulated on the basis of a lesser showing of harm. Here too the government must point to something other than persuasiveness or offense at the control of ideas.

We can use this discussion as a basis for exploring the complex problems resulting from recent efforts to regulate hate speech on campus. Some regulations are often associated with alleged efforts to impose an ideological orthodoxy on students and faculty, under the rubric of "political correctness." Perhaps radical left-wing campuses, under pressure from well-organized groups, are silencing people who disagree. Are the campus speech codes constitutional?

. . .

On the approach provided thus far, we can offer an important provisional conclusion: If campus speech restrictions at public universities cover not merely epithets, but speech that is part of social deliberation, they might well be seen as unconstitutional for that very reason. At least as a presumption, speech that is intended and received as a contribution to social deliberation is constitutionally protected even if it amounts to what is sometimes classified as hate speech—even if it is racist and sexist.

Consider, for example, the University of Michigan's judicially invalidated ban on "[a]ny behavior, verbal or physical, that stigmatizes or victimizes an individual on the basis of race, ethnicity, religion, sex, sexual orientation, creed, national origin, ancestry, age, marital status, handicap, or Vietnam-era veteran status, and that . . . creates an intimidating, hostile, or demeaning environment for educational pursuits. . . ." This broad ban forbids a wide range of statements that are part of the exchange of ideas. It also fails to give people sufficient notice of what statements are allowed. For both reasons, it seems invalid.

In a famous case, Justice Frankfurter, speaking for a 5–4 majority of the Supreme Court, rejected this view. *Beauharnais v. Illinois*[1] upheld an Illinois law making it unlawful to publish or exhibit any publication which "portrays depravity, criminality, unchastity, or lack of virtue of a class of citizens, which [publication] exposes the citizens of any race, color, creed or religion to contempt, derision, or obloquy or which is productive of breach of the peace or riots". The law was applied to ban circulation of a petition urging "the need to prevent the white race from becoming mongrelized by the negro," and complaining of the "aggressions, rapes, robberies, knives, guns, and marijuana of the negro."

In upholding the law, Justice Frankfurter referred to a range of factors. He pointed to the historical exclusion of libel from free speech protection; to the risks to social cohesion created by racial hate speech; and to the need for judicial deference to legislative judgments on these complex matters. Many countries in Europe accept the same analysis and do not afford protection to racial and ethnic hate speech. But most people think that after *New York Times v. Sullivan*,[2] *Beauharnais* is no longer the law. In *New York Times*, the Court indicated that the law of libel must be evaluated in accordance with the constitutional commitment to robust debate on public issues. The conventional view—which the Supreme Court has not directly addressed—is that racial hate speech contains highly political ideas, that it belongs in the free speech "core," and that it may not be suppressed merely because it is offensive or otherwise harmful.

There are real complexities here. In its strongest form, the defense of *Beauharnais* would point toward the contribution of hate speech to the maintenance of a caste system based on race and gender. A principal point here would be the effect of such speech on the self-respect of its victims and also the relationship between such speech and fears of racially-motivated violence. I cannot fully discuss this issue here; but I think that *Beauharnais* was incorrect. No one should deny that distinctive harms are produced by racial hate speech, especially when it is directed against members of minority groups. It is only obtuseness—a failure of perception or empathetic identification—that would enable someone to say that the word "fascist" or "pig" or "communist," or even "honky," produces the same feelings as the word "nigger." In view of our history, invective directed against minority groups, and racist speech in general, create fears of violence and subordination—of second-class citizenship—that are not plausibly described as mere offense. As I have noted, most European countries, including flourishing democracies committed to free speech, make exceptions for such expression. In many countries, including our own, it is possible to think that racial and ethnic hate speech is really *sui generis,* and that it is properly treated differently.

But there are strong counter-arguments. If we were to excise all of what is described as hate speech from political debate, we would severely truncate our discussion of such important matters as civil rights, foreign policy, crime, conscription, abortion, and social welfare policy. Even if speech produces anger or resentment on the basis of race, it might well be thought a legitimate part of the deliberative process, and it bears directly on politics. Foreclosure of such speech would probably accomplish little good, and by stopping people from hearing certain ideas, it could bring about a great deal of harm. These are the most conventional Millian arguments for the protection of speech.

From all this it seems that the University of Michigan ban was far too broad. On the other hand, it should be permissible for colleges and universities to build on the basic case of epithet in order to regulate certain narrowly defined categories of hate speech. Standing by themselves, or accompanied by little else, epithets are not intended and received as contributions to social deliberation about anything. We are therefore dealing with lower tier speech. The injury to dignity and self-respect is a sufficient harm to allow regulation. (See my discussion below of the Stanford regulation.)

It is now possible to offer a provisional conclusion. A public university should be allowed to regulate hate speech in the form of epithets. But it should be prohibited from reaching very far beyond epithets to forbid the expression of views on public issues, whatever those views may be.

. . .

Colleges and universities do, however, have some arguments to [consider]. . . .

1. *In General.*

The largest point here is that colleges and universities are often in the business of controlling speech, and their controls are hardly ever thought to raise free speech problems. Indeed, controlling speech is, in one sense, a defining characteristic of the university. There are at least four different ways in which such controls occur.

First, universities impose major limits on the topics that can be discussed in the classroom. Subject matter restrictions are part of education. Irrelevant discussion is banned. Students cannot discuss the presidential election, or Marx and Mill, if the subject is math. Schools are allowed to impose subject matter restrictions that would be plainly unacceptable if enacted by states or localities.

Second, a teacher can require students to treat each other with at least a minimum of basic respect. It would certainly be legitimate to suspend a student for using consistently abusive or profane language in the classroom. This is so even if that language would receive firm constitutional protection on the street corner. The educational process requires at least a measure of civility. Perhaps it would be unacceptable for universities to ban expressions of anger or intense feeling; the notion of civility should not be a disguise for forbidding irreverence or disagreement. But so long as requirements of civility are both reasonable and neutral with respect to viewpoint, a university may limit abusive or profane comments within the classroom.

The problem goes deeper, for—this is the third kind of academic control on speech—judgments about quality are pervasive. Such judgments affect admissions, evaluation of students in class and on paper, and evaluation of prospective and actual faculty as well. Academic decisions about quality will of course be based on a conception of appropriate standards of argument and justification. These standards involve judgments about merit or excellence that would of course be unacceptable in the setting of criminal punishment or civil fine, but that are a perfectly and nearly inescapable legitimate part of the educational function. At least this is so if there is no discrimination on the basis of viewpoint, that is, if the person involved in making the assessment offers judgments on the basis of standards of quality that are applied neutrally to everyone (an ambitious aspiration, and one that is conceptually complex).

But there is a fourth and more troublesome way in which universities control speech, and this involves the fact that many academic judgments are viewpoint-based, certainly in practice. In many places, a student who defends fascism or communism is unlikely to receive a good grade. In many economics departments, sharp deviation from the views of Adam Smith may well be punished. History and literature departments have their own conceptions of what sorts of arguments are retrograde or beyond the pale. Viewpoint discrimination is undoubtedly present in practice, and even if we object to it in principle, it is impossible and perhaps undesirable for outsiders to attempt to police it.

Thus far I have mostly been discussing students; but much the same is true for faculty members. Universities can impose on their faculty restrictive rules of decorum and civic participation. A teacher who refuses to teach the subject, fails to allow counter-arguments, treats students contemptuously, or vilifies them in class, can be penalized without offense to the Constitution. The job performance of teachers consists mostly of speech. When that performance is found wanting, it is almost always because of content, including judgments about subject matter and quality, and sometimes because of viewpoint.

It is worthwhile pausing over this point. Initial hirings, tenure, and promotion all involve subject matter restrictions, and sometimes viewpoint discrimination in practice. All this suggests that universities are engaged in regulating speech through content discrimination and at least implicit viewpoint discrimination. The evaluation of students and colleagues cannot occur without resort to content, and it would be most surprising if viewpoint discrimination did not affect many evaluations.

These examples do not by any means compel the conclusion that any and all censorship is acceptable in an academic setting. A university can have a good deal of power over what happens in the classroom, so as to promote the educational enterprise, without also being allowed to decree a political orthodoxy by discriminating on the basis of viewpoint. If a public university were to ban students from defending (say) conservative or liberal causes in political science classes, a serious free speech issue would be raised. There are therefore real limits to permissible viewpoint discrimination within the classroom, even if it is hard to police the relevant boundaries. Certainly the university's permissible limits over the classroom do not extend to the campus in general. We could not allow major restrictions on what students and faculty may say when they are not in class. A university could not say that outside of class, students can talk only about subjects of the university's choice.

From these various propositions, we might adopt a principle: *The university can impose subject matter or other restrictions on speech only to the extent that the restrictions are closely related to its educational mission.* This proposition contains both an authorization to the university and sharp limitations on what it may do. There is a close parallel here with decisions about what to include or exclude from libraries and about how to fund the arts; in all these contexts, certain forms of content discrimination are inescapable. But in cases in which the educational mission is not reasonably at stake, restrictions on speech should be invalidated. Certainly this would be true in cases in which a university attempts to impose a political orthodoxy, whether inside or outside the classroom. We might react to the existence of implicit viewpoint discrimination by saying that it is hard for courts to police, but nonetheless a real offense to both academic aspirations and free speech principles.

2. *Educational Requirements and Hate Speech.*

How does this proposition bear on the hate speech issue? Perhaps a university could use its frequently exercised power over speech in order to argue for certain kinds of hate speech codes. Perhaps it could say that when it legitimately controls speech, it does so in order to promote its educational mission, which inevitably entails limits on who may say what. Perhaps a university could be allowed to conclude that its educational mission requires unusually firm controls on hate speech, so as not to compromise the values of education itself.

The university might emphasize in this regard that it has a special obligation to protect all of its students as equal members of the community. This obligation calls for restrictions on what faculty members may say. The university might believe that certain narrowly defined forms of hate speech are highly destructive to the students' chance to learn. It might think that black students and women can be effectively excluded by certain forms of hate speech. Probably a university should be given more leeway to restrict hate speech than a state or locality, precisely because it ought to receive the benefit of the doubt when it invokes concerns of this kind. Surely the educational mission ought to grant the university somewhat greater room to maneuver, especially in light of the complexity and delicacy of the relevant policy questions. Courts might also hesitate before finding viewpoint discrimination or impermissible selectivity. Perhaps there should be a presumption in favor of a university's judgment that narrowly defined hate speech directed at blacks or women produces harm that is especially threatening to the educational enterprise.

This conclusion is buttressed by two additional factors. First, there are numerous colleges and universities. Many students can choose among a range of alternatives, and a restriction in one, two, or more imposes an extremely small incursion into the system of free expression. Colleges that restrict a large amount of speech may find themselves with few students, and in any case other institutions will be available. Second, the Constitution is itself committed to the elimination of second-class citizenship, and this commitment makes it hard to say that an educational judgment opposed to certain forms of hate speech is impermissibly partisan.

3. *Details.*

I think that an analysis of this kind would justify two different sorts of approaches to the issue of hate speech on campus. First, a university might regulate hate speech, narrowly defined, as simply a part of its general class of restrictions on speech that is incompatible with the educational mission. On this approach, there would be no restriction specifically directed against hate speech—no campus "speech code"—but a general, suitably defined requirement of decency and civility, and this requirement of decency would regulate hate speech as well as other forms of abuse. Just as a university might ban the use of profanity in class, or personally abusive behavior on campus, so it might stop racial epithets and similar expressions of hatred or contempt. This is not to say that students and teachers who violate this ban must be expelled or suspended. Generally informal sanctions, involving conversations rather than punishment, are much to be preferred. But the Constitution should not stand as a barrier to approaches of this sort, so long as the university is neutral in this way.

Second, courts should allow narrowly defined hate speech restrictions even if those restrictions are not part of general proscriptions on indecent or uncivil behavior. . . .

Endnotes

[1] 343 U.S. 250 (1952).

[2] 376 US 254 (1964).

37. Words That Wound

RICHARD DELGADO AND JEAN STEFANCIC

Not long ago, in *Contreras v. Crown Zellerbach, Inc.*,[1] the Washington Supreme Court held that a Mexican American's allegations that fellow employees had subjected him to a campaign of racial abuse stated a valid claim against his employer for the tort of outrage. The plaintiff alleged that he had suffered "humiliation and embarrassment by reason of racial jokes, slurs and comments"[2] and that the defendant's agents and employees had wrongfully accused him of stealing the employer's property, thereby preventing him from gaining employment and holding him up to public ridicule. Focusing on the alleged racial abuse, the court declared that "racial epithets which were once part of common usage may not now be looked upon as 'mere insulting language.'"[3]

Eleven months later, the United States Court of Appeals for the Seventh Circuit in *Collin v. Smith*[4] affirmed a federal district court's decision declaring unconstitutional certain ordinances of the village of Skokie, Illinois, which had been drafted to block a demonstration by members of the National Socialist Party of America. The village argued that the demonstration, together with the display of Nazi uniforms and swastikas, would inflict psychological trauma on its many Jewish citizens, some of whom had lived through the Holocaust. The court of appeals acknowledged that "many people would find [the] demonstration extremely mentally and emotionally disturbing."[5] Mentioning *Contreras*, the court also noted that Illinois recognizes the new tort of intentional infliction of severe emotional distress, which might well include the uttering of racial slurs. Nevertheless, the threat of criminal penalties imposed by the ordinance was held impermissibly to abridge the plaintiffs' First Amendment rights.

Should our legal system offer redress for the harm of racist speech? The first case, from a liberal state court, implies that it should—at least if the remedy takes the form of a private action, a tort suit. The second implies it should not, if the remedy takes the form of public condemnation through the criminal law—a view that has been reaffirmed more recently in the *R.A.V.* (Minneapolis cross-burning) case discussed later. Tort law, rooted in ancient Anglo-American tradition, has often served as a testing ground for new social sensibilities, which are later incorporated into our "public law," for example campus conduct codes or criminal statutes. Tort law thus serves as a kind of social laboratory, testing theories and assessing harms.

What, then, are some of the harms associated with racial insults? And how have courts viewed these harms over the years?

Psychological, Sociological, and Political Effects of Racism

American society remains deeply afflicted by racism. Long before slavery became the mainstay of the plantation society of the antebellum South, Anglo-Saxon attitudes of racial superiority left their stamp on the developing culture of colonial America. Today, over a century after the abolition of slavery, many citizens suffer from discriminatory attitudes and practices infecting our economic system, cultural and political institutions, and the daily interactions of individuals. The idea that color is a badge of inferiority and a justification for the denial of opportunity and equal treatment is deeply ingrained.

The racial insult remains one of the most pervasive channels through which discriminatory attitudes are imparted. Such language injures the dignity and self-regard of the person to whom it is addressed, communicating the message that distinctions of race are ones of merit, dignity, status, and personhood. Not only does the listener learn and internalize the messages contained in racial insults, these messages color our society's institutions and are transmitted to succeeding generations.

. . .

The Harms of Racial Insults

In addition to [the] more general harms associated with racism and racist treatment, certain specific harms result from racial *insults*. Immediate mental or emotional distress is the most obvious direct harm. Without questions, mere words, whether racial or otherwise, can cause mental, emotional, or even physical harm to their target, especially if delivered in front of others or by a person in a position of authority. Racial insults, relying as they do on the unalterable fact of the victim's race and on the history of slavery and race discrimination in this country, have an even greater potential for harm than other insults.

Although the emotional damage caused is variable and depends on many factors, only one of which is the outrageousness of the insult, a racial insult is always a dignitary affront, a direct violation of the victim's right to be treated respectfully. Our moral and legal systems recognize the principle that individuals are entitled to treatment that does not denigrate their humanity through disrespect for their privacy or moral worth. This ideal has a high place in our traditions, finding expression in such principles as universal suffrage, the prohibition against cruel and unusual punishment, the protection of the Fourth Amendment against unreasonable searches, and the abolition of slavery. A racial insult is a serious transgression of this principle because it derogates by race, a characteristic central to one's self-image.

The wrong of this dignitary affront consists of the expression of a judgment that the victim of the racial slur is entitled to less than that to which all other citizens are entitled. Verbal tags provide a convenient means of categorization so that individuals may be treated as members of a class and assumed to share all the negative attitudes imputed to the class. They thus make it easier for their users to justify their own superior position with respect to others. Racial insults also serve to keep the victim compliant. Such dignitary affronts are certainly no less harmful than others recognized by the law.

Clearly, a society whose public law recognizes harm in the stigma of separate but equal schooling and the potential offensiveness of the required display of a state motto on automobile license plates, and whose private law sees actionable conduct in an unwanted kiss or the forcible removal of a person's hat, should also recognize the dignitary harm inflicted by a racial insult.

The need for legal redress for victims also is underscored by the intentionality of racial insults. Their intentionality is obvious: what other purpose could the insult serve? There can be little doubt that the dignitary affront of racial insults, except perhaps those that are overheard, is intentional and therefore most reprehensible. Most people today know that certain words are offensive and only calculated to wound. No other use remains for such words as "nigger," "wop," "spic," or "kike."

In addition to the harms of immediate emotional distress and infringement of dignity, racial insults inflict psychological harm upon the victim. Racial slurs may cause long-term emotional pain because they draw upon and intensify the effects of the stigmatization, labeling, and disrespectful treatment that the victim has previously undergone. Social scientists who have studied the effects of racism have found that speech that communicates low regard for an individual because of race "tends to create in the victim those very traits of 'inferiority' that it ascribes to him."[6] Moreover, "even in the absence of more objective forms of discrimination—poor schools, menial jobs, and substandard housing—traditional stereotypes about the low ability and apathy of Negroes and other minorities can operate as 'self-fulfilling prophecies.' "[7] These stereotypes, portraying members of a minority group as stupid, lazy, dirty, or untrustworthy, are often communicated either explicitly or implicitly through racial insults.

Because they constantly hear racist messages, minority children, not surprisingly, come to question their competence, intelligence, and worth. Much of the blame for the formation of these attitudes lies squarely on value-laden words, epithets, and racial names. . . . If the majority "defines them and their parents as no good, inadequate, dirty, incompetent, and stupid," the child will find it difficult not to accept those judgments.[8]

Minority children possess even fewer means for coping with racial insults than do adults. "A child who finds himself rejected and attacked . . . is not likely to develop dignity and poise. . . . On the contrary he develops defenses. Like a dwarf in a world of menacing giants, he cannot fight on equal terms."[9] The child who is the victim of belittlement can react with only two unsuccessful strategies, hostility or passivity. Aggressive reactions can lead to consequences which reinforce the harm caused by the insults; children who behave aggressively in school are marked by their teachers as troublemakers, adding to the children's alienation and sense of rejection. Seemingly passive reactions have no better results; children who are passive toward their insulters turn the aggressive response on themselves; robbed of confidence and motivation, these children withdraw into moroseness, fantasy, and fear.

But Will a Tort Remedy Do Any Good?

The various and severe harms associated with racial treatment argue for some sort of social sanction. (Indeed, the following section shows that courts are already affording relief, usually by smuggling in recovery under some conventional, already recognized, legal theory such as defamation or the tort of intentional infliction of emotional distress.) But should a new, *freestanding* remedy be devised? And if so, would it do any good?

It is, of course, impossible to predict the degree of deterrence a cause of action in tort would create. However, as one leading authority has observed, "for most people living in racist societies, racial prejudice is merely a special kind of convenient rationalization for rewarding behavior."[10] In other words, in racist societies "most members of the dominant group will exhibit both prejudice and discrimination,"[11] but only in conforming to social norms. Thus, "[W]hen social pressures and rewards for racism are absent, racial bigotry is more likely to be restricted to people for whom prejudice fulfills a psychological 'need.' In such a tolerant milieu prejudiced persons may even refrain from discriminating behavior to escape social disapproval."[12] Increasing the cost of racial insults thus would certainly decrease their frequency. Laws will never prevent violations altogether, but they will deter "whoever is deterrable."[13]

Because most citizens comply with legal rules, and this compliance in turn "reinforce[s] their own sentiments toward conformity,"[14] a tort action for racial insults would discourage such harmful activity through the teaching function of the law. The establishment of a legal norm "creates a public conscience and a standard for expected behavior that check overt signs of prejudice."[15] Legislation aims first at controlling only the acts that express undesired attitudes. But "when expression changes, thoughts too in the long run are likely to fall into line."[16] "Laws . . . restrain the middle range of mortals who need them as a mentor in molding their habits."[17] Thus, "If we create institutional arrangements in which exploitive behaviors are no longer reinforced, we will then succeed in changing attitudes [that underlie these behaviors]."[18] Because racial attitudes of white Americans "typically follow rather than precede actual institutional [or legal] alteration,"[19] a tort for racial slurs is a promising vehicle for the eradication of racism.

. . .

A First Amendment View

The First Amendment appears to stand as a formidable barrier to campus rules prohibiting group-disparaging speech. Designed to assure that debate on public issues is uninhibited, robust, and wide open, the First Amendment protects speech that we hate as much as that which we hold dear. Yet racial insults implicate powerful social interests in equality and equal personhood. When uttered on university campuses, racial insults bring into play additional concerns. Few would question that the university has strong, legitimate interests in teaching students and teachers to treat each other respectfully; protecting minority-group students from harassment; and protecting diversity, which could be impaired if students of color become demoralized and leave the university, or if parents of minority race decide to send their children elsewhere.

Only on one occasion has the United States Supreme Court weighed free speech against the equal-protection values endangered by race-hate speech. In *Beauharnais v. Illinois*,[20] the defendant was convicted under a statute prohibiting dissemination of materials promoting racial or religious hatred. Citing the "fighting words" doctrine of *Chaplinsky v. New Hampshire,* Justice Frankfurter ruled that libelous statements aimed at groups, like those aimed at individuals, fall outside First Amendment protection.[21] Later decisions, notably *New York Times v. Sullivan,*[22] and *R.A.V. v. St. Paul,*[23] have increased protection for libelous speech, with the result that some commentators and courts question whether *Beauharnais* today would be decided differently. Yet, *Beauharnais* has never been overruled, and in the meantime many courts have afforded redress in tort for racially or sexually insulting language, with few finding any constitutional problem with doing so.

Moreover, over the past century the courts have carved out or tolerated dozens of "exceptions" to free speech. These exceptions include speech used to form a criminal conspiracy or an ordinary contract; speech that disseminates an official secret; speech that defames or libels someone; speech that is obscene; speech that creates a hostile workplace; speech that violates a trademark or plagiarizes another's words; speech that creates an immediately harmful impact or is tantamount to shouting fire in a crowded theater; "patently offensive" speech directed at captive audiences or broadcast on the airwaves; speech that constitutes "fighting words"; speech that disrespects a judge, teacher, military officer, or other authority figure; speech used to defraud a consumer; words used to fix prices; words ("stick 'em up—hand over the money") used to communicate a criminal threat; and untruthful or irrelevant speech given under oath or during a trial.

Much speech, then, is unprotected. The issues are whether the social interest in reining in racially offensive speech is as great as that which gives rise to these "exceptional" categories, and whether the use of racially offensive language has speech value. Because little recent Supreme Court law directly addresses these issues, one might look to the underlying policies of our system of free expression to understand how the Court may rule if an appropriate case comes before it.

[Our] system of free expression serves a number of societal and individual goals. Included are the personal fulfillment of the speaker; ascertainment of the truth; participation in democratic decision-making; and achieving a balance between social stability and change. Applying these policies to the controversy surrounding campus anti-racism rules yields little support for their detractors. Uttering racial slurs may afford the racially troubled speaker some immediate relief, but hardly seems essential to self-fulfillment in any ideal sense. Indeed, social science writers hold that making racist remarks impairs, rather than promotes, the growth of the person who makes them, by encouraging rigid, dichotomous thinking and impeding moral development. Moreover, such remarks serve little dialogic purpose; they do not seek to connect the speaker and addressee in a community of shared ideals. They divide, rather than unite.

Additionally, slurs contribute little to the discovery of truth. Classroom discussion of racial matters and even the speech of a bigot aimed at proving the superiority of the white race might move us closer to the truth. But one-on-one insults do not. They neither state nor attack a proposition; they are like a slap in the face. By the same token, racial insults do little to help reach broad social consensuses. Indeed, by demoralizing their victim they may actually reduce speech, dialogue, and participation in political life. "More speech" is rarely a solution. Epithets often strike suddenly, immobilizing their victim and rendering her speechless. Often they are delivered in cowardly, anonymous fashion—in the form of a defaced poster or leaflet slipped under a student's door, or hurled by a group against a single victim, rendering response foolhardy. Nor do they help strike a healthy balance between stability and social change. Racial epithets could be argued to relieve racial tension harmlessly and thus contribute to racial stability, but this strained argument has been called into question by social science.

Yet racial epithets are speech, and as such we ought to protect them unless there is a very good reason for not doing so. A recent book by Kent Greenawalt suggests a framework for assessing laws against insults. Drawing on First Amendment principles and case law, Greenawalt writes that the setting, the speaker's intention, the forum's interest, and the relationship between the speaker and the victim must be considered. Moreover, abusive words (like kike, nigger, wop, and faggot) are punishable if spoken with intent, cause a harm capable of formulation in clear legal language, and form a message essentially devoid of ideas. Greenawalt offers as an example of words that could be criminally punishable, "You Spic whore", uttered by four men to a woman of color at a bus stop, intended to humiliate her. He notes that such words can have long-term damaging effects on the victim and have little if any cognitive content; that meaning which the words convey may be expressed in other ways.

Under Greenawalt's test, narrowly drawn university guidelines penalizing racial slurs might well withstand scrutiny. The university forum has a strong interest in establishing a nonracist atmosphere. Moreover , most university rules are aimed at face-to-face remarks that are intentionally abusive. Most exclude classroom speech, speeches to a crowd, and satire published in a campus newspaper. Under Greenawalt's nonabsolutist approach, such rules might well be held constitutional.

An Equal Protection View

The First Amendment perspective thus yields no clear-cut result. Society has a strong interest in seeing that expression is as unfettered as possible, yet racial slurs have no great social worth and can cause serious harm. Unfortunately, looking at the problem of racist speech from the perspective of the equality-protecting amendments yields no clearer result.

Equality and equal respect are highly valued principles in our system of jurisprudence. Three constitutional provisions and a myriad of federal and state statutes are aimed at protecting the rights of racial, religious, and sexual minorities to be free from discrimination in housing, education, jobs, and many other areas of life. Moreover, universities have considerable power to enact regulations protecting minority interests. Yet the equality principle is not without limits. State agencies may not redress breaches by means that too broadly encroach on the rights of whites, or on other constitutional principles. Rigorous rules of intent, causation, standing, and limiting relief circumscribe what

may be done. New causes of action are not lightly recognized; for example, the legal system has resisted efforts by feminists to have pornography deemed a civil rights offense against women. And, as we have seen, even tort law has been slow to recognize a civil cause of action for racist speech.

Moreover, courts have held or implied that a university's power to effectuate campus policies, presumably including equality, is also limited. Cases stemming from efforts to regulate the wearing of armbands, what students may publish in the school newspaper, or their freedom to gather in open areas for worship or speech have shown that individual liberty will sometimes limit an institution's interest in achieving its educational objectives—students do not abandon all their constitutional rights at the schoolhouse door. According to the author of a leading treatise on higher-education law, rules bridling racist speech will be found constitutional if there is a local history of racial disruption; if the rules are narrowly tailored to punish only face-to-face insults and avoid encroaching on classroom and other protected speech; if they are consistently and even-handedly applied; and if due process protections such as the right to representation and a fair hearing are present. The author's guidelines seem plausible, but have yet to be tested. One set of rules was promulgated, then withdrawn; others were declared overly broad and subsequently redrafted. In several jurisdictions, the ACLU has announced that it is monitoring developments and may file suit.

In the meantime, analogous authority continues to develop. In *Bob Jones University v. United States*,[24] the Supreme Court held that universities may not discriminate in the name of religion. In *University of Pennsylvania v. EEOC*,[25] the Supreme Court held that a university's desire to protect confidential tenure files did not insulate the university from review in connection with discrimination investigations. Both cases imply that the antidiscrimination imperative will at times prevail over other strong interests, such as freedom of religion or academic freedom—and possibly speech. In the recent Minnesota "cross-burning" case (discussed later), however, the Court held that criminal laws regulating hate messages must be broadly and neutrally drawn.

Reconciling the First and Fourteenth Amendments: Stigma-Pictures and the Social Construction of Reality

Class Subordination and the Problem of Concerted Speech

As we have seen, neither the constitutional narrative of the First, nor of the Thirteenth and Fourteenth, Amendments clearly prevails in connection with campus anti-racism rules. Judges must choose. The dilemma is embedded in the nature of our system of law and politics: we want and fear both equality and liberty. We think the problem of campus anti-racism rules can yield to a postmodern insight: that speech by which society constructs a stigma picture of minorities may be regulated consistently with the First Amendment. Indeed, regulation may be necessary for full effectuation of the values of equal personhood we hold equally dear.

The first step is recognizing that racism is, in almost all its aspects, a class harm—the essence of which is subordination of one people by another. The mechanism of this subordination is a complex, interlocking series of acts, some physical, some symbolic. Although the physical acts (like lynchings and cross burnings) are often the most striking, the symbolic acts are the most insidious. By communicating and constructing a shared cultural image of the victim group as inferior, we enable ourselves to feel comfortable about the disparity in power and resources between ourselves and the stigmatized group. Even civil rights law may contribute to this stigmatization: the group is so vulnerable that it requires help. The shared picture also demobilizes the victims of discrimination, particularly the young. Indeed, social scientists have seen evidence of self-hatred and rejection of their own identity in children of color as early as age three.

The ubiquity and incessancy of harmful racial depiction are thus the source of its virulence. Like water dripping on sandstone, it is a pervasive harm which only the most hardy can resist. Yet the prevailing First Amendment paradigm predisposes us to treat racist speech as an individual harm, as though we had only to evaluate the effect of a single drop of water. This approach—corresponding to liberal, individualistic theories of self and society—systematically misperceives the experience of racism for both victim and perpetrator. This mistake is natural, and corresponds to one aspect of our natures—our individualistic selves. In this capacity, we want and need liberty. But we also exist in a social capacity; we need others to fulfill ourselves as beings. In this group aspect, we require inclusion, equality, and equal respect. Constitutional narratives of equal protection and prohibition of slavery —narratives that encourage us to form and embrace collectivity and equal citizenship for all—reflect this second aspect of our existence.

When the tacit consent of a group begins to coordinate the exercise of individual rights so as seriously to jeopardize participation by a smaller group, the "rights" nature of the first group's actions acquires a different character and dimension. The exercise of an individual right now poses a group harm and must be weighed against this qualitatively different type of threat.

Greenawalt's book has made a cautious move in this direction. Although generally a defense of free speech in its individual aspect, his book also notes that speech is a primary means by which we construct reality. Thus, a wealthy and well-regarded citizen who is victimized by a vicious defamation is able to recover in tort. His social "picture," in which he has a property interest, has been damaged, and will require laborious reconstruction. It would require only a slight extension of Greenawalt's observation to provide protection from racial slurs and hate speech. Indeed, the rich man has the dominant "story" on his side; repairing the defamation's damage will be relatively easy.

Racist speech, by contrast, is not so readily repaired—it separates the victim from the storytellers who alone have credibility. Not only does racist speech, by placing all the credibility with the dominant group, strengthen the dominant story, it also works to disempower minority groups by crippling the effectiveness of their speech in rebuttal. This situation makes free speech a powerful asset to the dominant group, but a much less helpful one to subordinate groups—a result at odds, certainly, with marketplace theories of the First Amendment. Unless society is able to deal with this incongruity, the Thirteenth and Fourteenth Amendments and our complex system of civil rights statutes will be of little avail. At best, they will be able to obtain redress for episodic, blatant acts of individual prejudice and bigotry. This redress will do little to alleviate the source of the problem: the speech that creates the stigma-picture that makes the acts hurtful in the first place, and that renders almost any other form of aid—social or legal—useless.

Operationalizing the Insight

Could judges and legislators effectuate our suggestion that speech which constructs a stigma-picture of a subordinate group stands on a different footing from sporadic speech aimed at persons who are not disempowered? It might be argued that all speech constructs the world to some extent, and that every speech act could prove offensive to someone. Traditionalists find modern art troublesome, Republicans detest left-wing speech, and some men hate speech that constructs a sex-neutral world. Yet race—like gender and a few other characteristics—is different; our entire history and culture bespeak this difference. Thus, judges easily could differentiate speech which subordinates blacks, for example, from that which disparages factory owners. Will they choose to do so? There is cause for doubt: low-grade racism benefits the status quo. Moreover, our system's winners have a stake in liberal, marketplace interpretation of law and politics—their seeming neutrality and meritocratic nature reassure the decision-makers that their social position is deserved.

Still, resurgent racism on our nation's campuses is rapidly becoming a national embarrassment. Almost daily, we are faced with headlines featuring some of the ugliest forms of ethnic conflict and the specter of virtually all-white universities. The need to avoid these consequences may have the beneficial effect of causing courts to reflect on, and tailor, constitutional doctrine. . . .

We began by pointing out a little-noticed indeterminacy in the way campus anti-racism rules are analyzed. Such rules may be seen either as posing a First Amendment problem or falling within the ambit of the equality-protecting amendments. The survey of the experience of other nations in regulating hate speech and the writings of social scientists on race and racism do not dispel this indetermi-

nacy. Each view is plausible; each corresponds to a deeply held narrative; each proceeds from one's life experiences; each is backed by constitutional case law and principle. Each lays claim to the higher education imperative that our campuses reflect a marketplace of ideas.

The gap between the two approaches can be addressed by means of a postmodern insight: racist speech is different because it is the means by which society constructs a stigma-picture of disfavored groups. It is tacitly coordinated by its speakers in a broad design, each act of which seems harmless but which, in combination with others, crushes the spirits of its victims while creating culture at odds with our national values. Only by taking account of this group dimension can we capture the full power of racially scathing speech—and make good on our promises of equal citizenship to those who have so long been denied its reality.

. . .

How the System of Free Expression Sometimes Makes Matters Worse

Speech and free expression are not only poorly adapted to remedy racism, they often make matters worse—far from being stalwart friends, they can impede the cause of racial reform. First, they encourage writers, filmmakers, and other creative people to feel amoral, nonresponsible in what they do. Because there is a marketplace of ideas, the rationalization goes, another filmmaker is free to make an anti-racist movie that will cancel out any minor stereotyping in the one I am making. My movie may have other redeeming qualities; besides, it is good entertainment and everyone in the industry uses stock characters like the black maid or the bumbling Asian tourist. How can one create film without stock characters?

Second, when insurgent groups attempt to use speech as an instrument of reform, courts almost invariably construe First Amendment doctrine against them. As Charles Lawrence points out, civil rights activists in the sixties made the greatest strides when they acted in defiance of the First Amendment as then understood. They marched, were arrested and convicted; sat in, were arrested and convicted; distributed leaflets, were arrested and convicted. Many years later, after much gallant lawyering and the expenditure of untold hours of effort, the conviction might be reversed on appeal if the original action had been sufficiently prayerful, mannerly, and not too interlaced with an action component. The history of the civil rights movement does not bear out the usual assumption that the First Amendment is of great value for racial reformers.

Current First Amendment law is similarly skewed. Consider the way the many "exceptions" to First Amendment protection favor the interests of the powerful. If one says something disparaging of a wealthy and well-regarded individual, one discovers that one's words were not free after all; that individual has a type of property interest in his or her community image, damage to which is compensable even though words were the sole instrument of the harm. Similarly, if one infringes the copyright or trademark of a well-known writer or industrialist, again it turns out that one's action is punishable. Further if one disseminates an official secret valuable to a powerful branch of the military or defense contractor, that speech is punishable. If one speaks disrespectfully to a judge, police officer, teacher, military official, or other powerful authority figure, again one discovers that one's words were not free; and so with words used to defraud, form a conspiracy, breach the peace, or untruthful words given under oath during a civil or criminal proceeding.

Yet the suggestion that we create a new exception to protect lowly and vulnerable members of our society, such as isolated, young black undergraduates attending dominantly white campuses, is often met with consternation: minorities (we say), if they knew their own self-interest, should appreciate the need for free speech even more than others. This one-sidedness of free-speech doctrine makes the First Amendment much more valuable to the majority than to the minority.

The system of free expression also has a powerful after-the-fact apologetic function. Elite groups use the supposed existence of a marketplace of ideas to justify their own superior position. Imagine a society in which all A's were rich and happy, all B's were moderately comfortable, and all C's were poor, stigmatized, and reviled. Imagine also that this society scrupulously believes in a free

marketplace of ideas. Might not the A's benefit greatly from such a system? On looking about them and observing the inequality in the distribution of wealth, longevity, happiness, and safety between themselves and the others, they might feel guilt. Perhaps their own superior position is undeserved, or at least requires explanation. But the existence of an ostensibly free marketplace of ideas renders that effort unnecessary. Rationalization is easy: our ideas, our culture competed with their more easygoing ones and won. It was a fair fight. Our position must be deserved; the distribution of social goods must be roughly what fairness, merit, and equity call for. It is up to them to change, not us.

A free market of racial depiction resists change for two final reasons. First, the dominant pictures, images, narratives, plots, roles, and stories ascribed to, and constituting the public perception of minorities, are always dominantly negative. Through an unfortunate psychological mechanism, incessant bombardment by images of the sort described above (as well as today's versions) inscribes those negative images on the souls and minds of minority persons. Minorities internalize the stories they read, see, and hear every day. Persons of color can easily become demoralized, blame themselves, not speak up vigorously. The expense of speech also precludes the stigmatized from participating effectively in the marketplace of ideas. They are often poor—indeed, one theory of racism holds that maintenance of economic inequality is its prime function—and hence unlikely to command the means to bring countervailing messages to the eyes and ears of others.

Second, even when minorities do speak they have little credibility. Who would listen to or credit a speaker or writer one associates with watermelon eating, buffoonery, menial work, intellectual inadequacy, laziness, lasciviousness, and demanding resources beyond his or her deserved share?

Our very image of the outsider shows that, contrary to the usual view, society does not really want them to speak out effectively in their own behalf, in fact cannot visualize them doing so. Ask yourself: How do outsiders speak in the dominant narratives? Poorly, inarticulately, with broken syntax, short sentences, grunts, and unsophisticated ideas. Try to recall a single popular narrative of an eloquent, self-assured black (for example) orator or speaker. In the real world, of course, they exist in profusion. But when we stumble upon them, we are surprised: "What a welcome 'exception'!"

Words, then, can wound. But the fine thing about the current situation is that one gets to enjoy a superior position and feel virtuous at the same time. By supporting the system of free expression no matter what the cost, one is upholding principle. One can belong to impeccably liberal organizations and believe one is doing the right thing, even while taking actions that are demonstrably injurious to the least privileged, most defenseless segments of our society. In time, one's actions will seem wrong and will be condemned as such, but paradigms change slowly. The world one helps to create—a world in which denigrating depiction is good or at least acceptable, in which minorities are buffoons, clowns, maids, or Willie Hortons, and only rarely fully individuated human beings with sensitivities, talents, personalities, and frailties—will survive into the future. One gets to create culture at outsiders' expense. And, one gets to sleep well at night, too.

Racism is not a mistake, not a matter of episodic, irrational behavior carried out by vicious-willed individuals, not a throwback to a long-gone era. It is ritual assertion of supremacy, like animals sneering and posturing to maintain their places in the hierarchy of the colony. It is performed largely unconsciously, just as the animals' behavior is. Racism seems right, customary, and inoffensive to those engaged in it, while bringing psychic and pecuniary advantages. The notion that more speech, more talking, and more preaching, and more lecturing can counter this system of oppression is appealing, lofty, romantic—and wrong.

Endnotes

[1] 88 Wash. 2d 735, 565 P.2d 1173 (1977) (en banc).

[2] 88 Wash. 2d at 736, 565 P.2d at 1174.

[3] *Id.* At 741, 565 P.2d at 1177.

[4] 578 F.2d 1197 (7th Cir.), *cert. denied,* 439 U.S. 916 (1978).

[5] *Id.* at 1200.

[6] M. Deutsch, I. Katz, & A. Jensen, Social Class, Race and Psychological Development 175 (1968).

[7] *Id.*

[8] K. Keniston, All Our Children 33 (1977).

[9] See G. Allport, The Nature of Prejudice 77-78 (1954) at 139.

[10] See generally A. Higginbotham, In the Matter of Color (1978).

[11] *Id.* at 20.

[12] *Id.*

[13] G. Allport, *supra* at 472.

[14] R. Williams, *supra* at 73.

[15] G. Allport, *supra* at 470.

[16] *Id.*

[17] *Id.* at 439. See also G. Allport, *Prejudice: A Problem In Psychological and Social Causation* 4, Supp. Ser. No. 4, J. Soc. Issues (1950) (examination of prejudice as a mode of mental functioning).

[18] H. Triandis, *The Impact of Social Change on Attitudes,* in Attitudes, Conflict and Social Changes 132 (1972) (quoted in Katz, *Preface,* Toward The Elimination of Racism 8 (P. Katz ed., 1976).

[19] G. Myrdal, An American Dilemma 20 (1944) (fallacy of theory that law cannot change custom).

[20] 343 U.S. 250 (1952).

[21] *Id.* at 257-58.

[22] 376 U.S. 254 (1964) (libel of public figures requires showing of actual malice); see also *Garrison v. Louisiana,* 379 U.S. 64 (1964) (overturning libel judgment won by public official by analogizing case to seditious libel).

[23] 112 S. Ct. 2538 (1992).

[24] *Bob Jones Univ. v. United States,* 461 U.S. 574 (1983) (government's "overriding interest in eradicating racial discrimination in education" outweighs institution's free exercise claim to a tax exemption); see Laycock, Tax Exemption for Religiously Discriminatory Schools, 60 Tex. L. Rev. 759 (1987).

[25] *University of Pennsylvania v. EEOC,* 110 S. Ct. 577 (1990).

38. *Regulating Racist Speech on Campus: A Modest Proposal?*

NADINE STROSSEN

Because civil libertarians have learned that free speech is an indispensable instrument for the promotion of other rights and freedoms—including racial equality—we fear that the movement to regulate campus expression will undermine equality, as well as free speech. Combating racial discrimination and protecting free speech should be viewed as mutually reinforcing, rather than antagonistic, goals. A diminution in society's commitment to racial equality is neither a necessary nor an appropriate price for protecting free speech. Those who frame the debate in terms of this false dichotomy simply drive artificial wedges between would-be allies in what should be a common effort to promote civil rights and civil liberties.

. . .

In the recent wave of college crackdowns on racist and other forms of hate speech, examples abound of attempts to censor speech conveying ideas that clearly play a legitimate role in academic discourse, although some of us might find them wrongheaded or even odious. For example, the University of Michigan's anti-hate speech policy could justify attacks on author Salman Rushdie because his book, *The Satanic Verses,* was offensive to Muslims.

In addition to their chilling effect on the ideas and expressions of university community members, policies that bar hate speech could engender broader forms of censorship. As noted by Professor William Cohen of Stanford Law School, an anti-hate speech rule such as the one adopted by his university "purports to create a personal right to be free from involuntary exposure to any form of expression that gives certain kinds of offense." Therefore, he explains, such a rule "could become a sword to challenge assigned readings in courses, the showing of films on campus, or the message of certain speakers."

Reprinted by permission of the
Duke Law Journal.

The various proposed campus hate speech regulations, including the Stanford code that Professor Lawrence endorses, are inconsistent with current Supreme Court doctrine prescribing permissible limits on speech. More importantly, they jeopardize basic free speech principles. Whereas certain conduct may be regulable, speech that advocates such conduct is not, and speech may not be regulated on the basis of its content, even if many of us strongly disagree with—or are repelled by—that content.

Civil libertarians, scholars, and judges consistently have distinguished between speech advocating unlawful conduct and the unlawful conduct itself. Although this distinction has been drawn in numerous different factual settings, the fundamental underlying issues always are the same. For example, within recent years, some pro-choice activists have urged civil libertarians and courts to make an exception to free speech principles in order to restrain the expressive conduct of anti-abortion activists. Instead, civil libertarians have persuaded courts to prohibit assaults, blockages of clinic entrances, trespasses, and other illegal conduct by anti-choice activists. Similarly, civil libertarians and courts have rejected pleas by some feminists to censor pornography that reflects sexist attitudes. Instead, civil libertarians have renewed their efforts to persuade courts and legislatures to invalidate sexist actions. A decade ago, civil libertarians and several courts—including the Supreme Court—rejected the plea of Holocaust survivors in Skokie, Illinois to prohibit neo-Nazis from demonstrating. Instead, civil libertarians successfully have lobbied for the enactment and enforcement of laws against anti-Semitic vandalism and other hate-inspired conduct.

A pervasive weakness in Professor Lawrence's analysis is his elision of the distinction between racist speech, on the one hand, and the racist conduct, on the other. It is certainly true that racist speech, like other speech, may have some causal connection to conduct. As Justice Holmes observed, "[e]very idea is an incitement" to action. However, as Justice Holmes also noted, to protect speech that advocates conduct you oppose does not "indicate that you think the speech impotent, . . . or that you do not care wholeheartedly for the result." Rather, this protection is based on the critical distinction between speech that has a direct and immediate link to unlawful conduct and all other speech, which has less direct and immediate links. In Holmes' immortal words:

> [W]e should be eternally vigilant against attempts to check the expression of opinions that we loathe and believe to be fraught with death, unless they so imminently threaten immediate interference with the lawful and pressing purposes of the law that an immediate check is required to save the country. . . . Only the emergency that makes it immediately dangerous to leave the correction of evil counsels to time warrants making any exception to the sweeping command, "Congress shall make no law . . . abridging the freedom of speech."

It is impossible to draw a bright line between speech and conduct. It also may be difficult to determine whether certain speech has a sufficiently tight nexus to conduct to justify regulating that speech. Professor Lawrence, however, abandons the attempt to make any such distinctions at all. He treats even the most extreme, blatant discriminatory conduct as speech, including slavery itself. Although undoubtedly harmful, the utterance of disparaging remarks cannot be equated fairly with the systematic denial of all rights to a group of human beings. Professor Lawrence recognizes this and appropriately chides anyone who insists that *all* racist conduct that includes an expressive component should be treated alike—namely, as protected speech. However, Professor Lawrence himself engages in precisely the same kind of oversimplification when he suggests that all conduct with an expressive component—which, in his view, includes *all* racist conduct and *all* racist speech—should be treated alike, namely, as *unprotected* speech. Those of us who reject either extreme as unreasonably rigid should join forces in undertaking the essential, albeit difficult, task of line-drawing.

It is important to place the current debate about campus racist speech in the context of earlier efforts to censor other forms of hate speech, including sexist and anti-Semitic speech. Such a broadened perspective suggests that consistent principles should be applied each time the issue resurfaces in any guise. Every person may find one particular type of speech especially odious and one message that most sorely tests his or her dedication to free speech values. But for each person who would exclude racist speech from the general proscription against content-based speech regulations, recent experience shows that there is another who would make such an exception only for anti-choice speech, another who would make it only for sexist speech, another who would make it only for anti-Semitic speech, another who would make it only for flag desecration, and so on.

The recognition that there is no principled basis for curbing speech expressing some particular ideas is reflected in the time-honored prohibition on any content-based or view-point-based regulations. As stated by Professor Tribe, "If the Constitution forces government to allow people to march, speak and write in favor of peace, brotherhood, and justice, then it must also require government to allow them to advocate hatred, racism, and even genocide."

The position stated by Professor Tribe is not just the traditional civil libertarian view, but it also is the law of the land. The courts consistently have agreed with civil libertarian claims that the first amendment protects the right to engage in racist and other forms of hate speech. Why is this so, and should it be so? Professor Lawrence rightly urges us to take a fresh look at this issue, no matter how well-settled it is as a matter of law. I have taken that invitation seriously and reflected long and hard upon his thought-provoking article and the questions it presents. Having done so, however, I conclude that the courts and traditional civil libertarians are correct in steadfastly rejecting laws that create additional new exceptions to free speech protections for racist expression.

To attempt to craft free speech exceptions only for racist speech would create a significant risk of a slide down the proverbial "slippery slope." To be sure, lawyers and judges are capable of—indeed, especially trained in—drawing distinctions between similar situations. Therefore, I agree with Professor Lawrence and other critics of the absolutist position that slippery slope dangers should not be exaggerated. It is probably hyperbole to contend that if we ever stepped off the mountaintop where all speech is protected regardless of its content, then inevitably we would end up in the abyss where the government controls all our words. On the other hand, critics of absolutism should not minimize the real danger. We would have a difficult time limiting our descent to a single downward step by attempting to prohibit only racist expression on campus. Applicable rules and supporting rationales would need to be crafted carefully to distinguish this type of speech from others.

First, we must think hard about the groups that should be protected. Should we regulate speech aimed only at racial and ethnic groups, as the University of Texas is considering? Or should we also bar insults of religious groups, women, gays and lesbians, individuals with disabilities, Vietnam War veterans, and so on, as do the rules adopted by Stanford and the University of Michigan? As the committee that formulated the University of Texas's proposed rule pointed out, each category requires a separate evaluation, since each "raise[s] different policy and legal concerns." Therefore, we should not play fast and loose with the first amendment by casually expanding the categories of proscribed hate speech.

Second, we must carefully define proscribable harassing speech to avoid encompassing the important expression that inevitably is endangered by any hate speech restriction. Censorial consequences could result from many proposed or adopted university policies, including the Stanford code, which sanctions speech intended to "insult or stigmatize" on the basis of race or other prohibited grounds. For example, certain feminists suggest that all heterosexual sex is rape because heterosexual men are aggressors who operate in a cultural climate of pervasive sexism and violence against women. Aren't these feminists insulting or stigmatizing heterosexual men on the basis of their sex and sexual orientation? And how about a Holocaust survivor who blames all ("Aryan") Germans for their collaboration during World War II? Doesn't this insinuation insult or stigmatize on the basis of national and ethnic origin? And surely we can think of numerous other examples that would have to give us pause.

. . .

An exaggerated concern with racist speech creates a risk of elevating symbols over substance in two problematic respects. First, it may divert our attention from the causes of racism to its symptoms. Second, a focus on the hateful message conveyed by particular speech may distort our view of fundamental neutral principles applicable to our system of free expression generally. We should not let the racist veneer in which expression is cloaked obscure our recognition of how important free expression is and of how effectively it has advanced racial equality.

Study Questions

1. As the readings in this section explained, the courts have found that certain forms of speech, including obscenity and "fighting words," are not deserving of First Amendment protection. Why didn't the Supreme Court find that Cohen's conduct (in *Cohen v. California*) fell within one of those categories? Explain in your own words.

2. The dissenters in *Cohen v. California* argued that the case involved "mainly conduct and little speech" and that the conduct could legitimately be prohibited as likely to provoke violence. Is wearing a jacket bearing a four-letter word "conduct," rather than "speech"? Suppose there had been evidence that someone who saw Cohen's jacket became violent. Is that a convincing argument for restricting Cohen's right to express himself (assuming that that was what he was doing)?

3. Some of the most controversial of recent cases concerning the proper limits of free expression have involved protests at abortion clinics. Opponents of abortion, such as the members of Operation Rescue, have repeatedly and aggressively challenged women attempting to enter such clinics. Abortion foes insist that their right of freedom of expression gives them a right to engage in loud, in-your-face speech in an effort to stop women from obtaining abortions. Although the courts have upheld protest-free zones within 15 feet of doors or driveways of

abortion facilities, in 1997 the Supreme Court refused to extend this zone. Arguing that there is no "generalized right to be left alone on a public street or sidewalk," Chief Justice William Rehnquist maintained that shouting, chanting, and other confrontational tactics are "classic forms of speech that lie at the heart of the First Amendment." (*Schenck v. Pro-Choice Network*, 519 U.S. 357 [1997]). The limits of aggressive speech tactics under the free speech clause have also been at issue in gay rights protests targeting Catholic Church leaders and in efforts by municipalities to control panhandling. When do such aggressive tactics become intimidation or harassment?

4. What arguments does Sunstein offer to show that the claim "all speech is on the same footing" with regard to degree of constitutional protection is false?

5. What reasons does Sunstein give for treating political speech as the focal point of the domain of protected expression?

6. Do you agree with Sunstein's claim that excluding all hate-speech from constitutional protection would "severely truncate our discussion of . . . civil rights, foreign policy, crime, conscription, abortion, and social welfare"?

7. In 1977, residents of the Chicago suburb of Skokie were shocked to learn that the American Nazi Party was planning to stage a "white-power" rally on the steps of Skokie's village hall on May 1. Nearly half of Skokie's population was at that time Jewish, and as many as twelve hundred of those were actual survivors of Hitler's persecution of European Jews. The members of the community forced village officials to obtain a court order preventing the rally and to pass ordinances prohibiting the dissemination of any material "which promotes and incites hatred against persons by reason of their race, national origin, or religion" or to "incite violence, hatred, abuse or hostility toward anyone based on race, religion, or ethnicity." Skokie maintained that neo-Nazi chants and signs or armbands bearing the swastika were racial slurs, unprotected

by the First Amendment. Frank Collin, then head of the Nazi Party, challenged the ordinances in federal court and won. The court found that the ordinances impermissibly limited freedom of speech. Collin was quoted as stating: "The key to Skokie is that the right to free speech was denied us here. . . . We fought in the courts from 1975 onward. We were constantly denied. . . . I've got to come up with something within the law, to use the law against our enemy, the Jew. . . . I used it [the First Amendment] at Skokie. I planned the reaction of the Jews. They are hysterical." [Quoted in Donald Alexander Downs, *Nazis in Skokie* (Notre Dame, Ind.: University of Notre Dame Press, 1985), p. 28.] Did the courts correctly invalidate the Skokie ordinances, in your view? Suppose the Nazis had marched through Skokie and that some of the citizens reacted violently. Would this mean that the Nazis had "incited a riot," or that their march posed a "clear and present danger" of immediate violence? Or would the violence be the fault of the onlookers who chose to react in that manner?

8. In the early 1990s, Stanford University approved a modification to university policies regarding racist speech. Titled "Free Expression and Discriminatory Harassment," the policy prevented harassment by "personal vilification," defined as "words or nonverbal symbols . . . commonly understood to convey direct and visceral hatred or contempt for human beings on the basis of their sex, race, color, handicap, religion, sexual orientation, or national and ethnic origin." The harassing conduct must have been "intended to stigmatize an individual or small number of individuals" and addressed directly to those it stigmatized. Similar antiharassment policies have been implemented at universities and colleges across the country. The Stanford policy remained in effect for five years but was invalidated by a California court after a group of students filed suit alleging that the policy prohibited speech on the basis of its content and thus was constitutionally impermissble. The court agreed, finding that "on its face, the Speech Code pro-

hibits words which will not only cause people to react violently, but also cause them to feel insulted or stigmatized . . . [Stanford] cannot proscribe speech that merely hurts the feelings of those who hear it." (*Corry v. Stanford*, No. 740309 [Cal. Super. Ct. Santa Clara County Feb. 27, 1995.]) Do you agree with the court's judgment? Should the Stanford policy have been judged constitutionally permissible? How would the Stanford policy have been evaluated under the analysis recommended by Sunstein? By Strossen? By Delgado and Stefancic?

9. Many communities now allow local organizations and businesses to contribute to road maintenance in and around their towns and cities through the "adopt a highway" program. Sponsors like the program because they are acknowledged by signs posted along the roadway—a form of publicly assisted advertising. Suppose that the Ku Klux Klan contributes to the program and demands that a sign be posted acknowledging its help: "Highway Maintenance Courtesy of the KKK." Officials refuse to honor the request. What should be the result under the First Amendment?

10. What do Delgado and Stefancic mean by a "stigma picture" of racially subordinate groups? Could such a picture be constructed or conveyed through that use of speech that should nevertheless remain constitutionally protected?

11. Are racial slurs and epithets a "class harm," as Delgado and Stefancic suggest, or are they individual harms? What would be the answer for First Amendment issues raised by hate-speech?

12. Strossen refers to a distinction between the advocacy of unlawful conduct and the unlawful conduct itself. Is it possible in many cases to distinguish these? If not, does that fact undermine Strossen's argument?

C. *Obscenity and Pornography*

Indecency on the Internet

As of September 1998, two bills were pending in Congress concerning access to obscene and pornographic material on the Internet, a worldwide network of linked computers accessible with a simple computer and modem from nearly anywhere on earth. One bill would require that Internet providers secure an adult access code before letting users view pornographic web pages; the other would require that schools and libraries receiving federal funds install software blocking minors' access to "inappropriate" material.

These bills were proposed in response to the Supreme Court's landmark 1997 ruling on the Communications Decency Act, a federal law designed to protect children from encountering "indecent" or "patently offensive" material in cyberspace. The Court's opinion, which opens the readings for this section, reasoned that limiting the access of minors to offensive material would unjustifiably suppress speech addressed to adults. The

Court struck down the law as a violation of the First Amendment. In the course of its argument, the Court usefully reviews justifications for limiting freedom of speech in cases involving speech thought to be obscene or indecent.

Legal Definitions

Many people believe that speech that is "pornographic" or "obscene" (whether the two are the same is one of the topics of this section) should not be protected by the law. Such speech might include (but would not necessarily be limited to) (1) depictions, on film or in still pictures, of human genitalia or of contact between genitals, anus, and mouth (in various combinations) or descriptions of such activities; (2) depictions or descriptions of homosexual intercourse; and (3) depictions or descriptions of bestiality. Many would also include in such prohibited categories of "speech" depictions or descriptions of violence in connection with any of the above (for example, mutilation, binding and gagging, sexual penetration with implements, drawing of blood, infliction of pain).

The term *pornography* can be broadly defined to refer to any form of sexually explicit material. In this sense, any of the items falling within the categories listed above would be "pornographic." The focus of this section is what legal implications, if any, should flow from that description. As all parties to the debate about the legality of pornography are willing to admit, existing law construes pornography as a special case of the "obscene"; and many of the pornography cases that have come before the courts in the past several decades have posed the issue of whether, and to what extent, obscenity is constitutionally protected speech. The basic standard governing current obscenity law was handed down by the Supreme Court in 1973 in *Miller v. California*. The Court held that "the basic guidelines for the trier of fact must be: (a) whether 'the average person, applying contemporary community standards,' would find that the work, taken as a whole, appeals to the prurient interest, (b) whether the work depicts or describes in a patently offensive way, sexual conduct specifically defined by the applicable state law, and (c) whether the work, taken

as a whole, lacks serious literary, artistic, political, or scientific value."[1]

The Court confined the permissible scope of the state regulation of the obscene to "works which depict or describe sexual conduct," and urged that "patently offensive representations or descriptions of ultimate sexual acts, normal or perverted, actual or simulated," or "patently offensive representations or descriptions of masturbation, excretory functions, and lewd exhibition of the genitals" would likely fall within the ambit of material deemed "obscene" by the *Miller* standard. State regulations of obscene materials have been upheld under the *Miller* test to protect audiences whose members are unwilling, "captive" (for example, prohibitions on showing pornographic films at drive-in movie theaters visible from the street or of the broadcast over the radio of "dirty words") or minors.[2] Zoning ordinances for "adult theaters" and restrictions on "live" sexual performances have also been permitted.[3] Nonetheless, a great many works that many people might find obscene (*Playboy, Hustler,* the "triple-X" film available at the local video store) are plainly at present constitutionally protected forms of expression.

The Hudnut Case

In 1984, the city of Indianapolis, Indiana, enacted an unusual antipornography ordinance. The ordinance was based on the city council's finding that pornography is "a systematic practice of exploitation and subordination based on sex which differentially harms women," and pornography was accordingly defined as "the graphic sexually explicit subordination of women, whether in pictures or in words." Based on this conception of pornography, the ordinance prohibited a variety of activities, including "trafficking" in pornography and

---

[1] 413 U.S. 15 (1973).

[2] See *Erznoznik v. Jacksonville* 422 U.S. 205 (1975), *F.C.C. v. Pacific Foundation* 438 U.S. 726 (1978), and *Pinkus v. United States* 436 U.S. 293 (1978).

[3] See *Young v. American Mini Theatres* 427 U.S. 50 (1976) and *California v. Larue* 409 U.S. 109 (1972).

"forcing" pornography on a person in any place of employment, school, home, or public place. The ordinance further prohibited "coercion into pornographic performance." The law gave to any woman aggrieved by trafficking or coercion a right to file a complaint "as a woman acting against the subordination of women."

In the *Hudnut* case, reprinted here, federal appellate judge Frank Easterbrook, writing for the court, affirms a lower court's decision that the Indianapolis ordinance was unconstitutional under the First Amendment because it discriminated on the grounds of speech content, permitting only speech "treating women in the approved way." Judge Easterbrook concedes that pornographic materials can reinforce beliefs of male domination and female submission, but, he insists, pornography's impact on people's beliefs can be only through the vehicle of ideas—ideas that must receive First Amendment protection.

Pornography and Harm

Should pornography be legally permissible? In his selection, philosopher Joel Feinberg explores various factors bearing on this question. Feinberg argues for a generally liberal position, consistent with the overall view of Mill: Pornographic works may be prohibited only if they can be shown to be directly harmful or at least profoundly offensive to many in a way that cannot be avoided. Feinberg criticizes what he takes to be the courts' confusion of pornography with the obscene. This has led, among other things, to the debates about the status of pornographic materials. Are they forms of art or literature or simply "sex aids"? The concept of the "obscene," according to Feinberg, encompasses that which is blatant, flagrant, or shameless. Can sex ever be described in these ways? Perhaps in some cases; but much pornography, Feinberg thinks, is not actually obscene.

Feinberg discusses two general grounds for banning or at least greatly restricting the production and distribution of pornographic materials: that they bring about violence and that they are profoundly offensive. With respect to the latter ground, Feinberg considers the suggestion that the prohibition of pornography could be defended by appeal to what he calls the "offense principle": the idea that conduct that is profoundly or extremely obscene, offensive, or revolting may legitimately be forbidden as a form of public nuisance (similar, for example, to creating a horrible stench), at least where the conduct is unavoidable by reasonable means. Here, of course, the question of the status of works of pornography as art or literature may be used to offset their offensiveness. However, even pornography lacking any such "redeeming" characteristics, Feinberg maintains, rarely rises to the level of revulsion necessary to be preventable under the offense principle. And even if it does, such material is usually avoidable.

Does pornography cause harm? And if so, can its production and use be restricted on Mill's grounds? It is here that Feinberg takes up the challenge of feminist arguments in favor of banning pornography. The feminist critique of pornography is, as Feinberg sees it, defended on two grounds: Pornography harms women either by "defaming" them (holding them up to ridicule and derision) as a group or by inciting violence against them (for example, rape). Feinberg responds that a connection between neither pornography and defamation nor pornography and instances of actual violence can be closely enough forged to pass muster under the harm principle, properly understood. If pornography depicts women as subordinate in a way that gives rise to a cause of action for defamation, so do many other things, from television shows to novels. On the other hand, to prohibit pornography on the ground that it brings about violence requires both a likelihood of serious harm and a direct link between the pornographic expression (the film or magazine) and the violence. The connection between pornography and violence can't be merely suggestive, it must be tight. Feinberg is doubtful that such a tight link can be established; the closest that one can come to such proof, he admits, is in the case of "violent" pornography, of which he provides several gruesome examples.

Yet even in the case of especially violent pornography the question can still be raised: Does it *cause* violence against women? No, says Feinberg, and the explanation is that the direction of causation is not from violent pornography to violent acts against women. It is, rather, that violent pornography and rape are both effects of a deeper causal agency: the "cult of macho." Pornography and rape are both products of a set of underlying beliefs about and attitudes toward women which are associated with "machismo." Pornography is a symptom, and therefore its suppression will likely have little effect. Nor is it possible to argue, by analogy to concepts in the criminal law, that the makers or distributors of pornographic materials are guilty of "incitement" to violence or "solicitation" of rape, for vendors of pornography do not counsel or advise customers to rape—not, at least, in a way the law currently would recognize.

Finally, Feinberg rejects the feminist argument that the profound offense felt by women through their awareness of degrading and humiliating pornographic films and magazines is sufficient to justify the suppression of pornography. Even if not reasonably avoidable, such feelings of offense "at the thought" that members of one's sex are being degraded fails to establish that anyone in particular is really being victimized by such portrayals.

The Feminist Critique of Pornography

In her essay, feminist legal scholar Catherine MacKinnon defends the general position taken by the Indianapolis ordinance (of which she was a principal author) addressed in the *Hudnut* case. Like Feinberg, MacKinnon also challenges the law's identification of pornography with the obscene, but for very different reasons. Equating pornography with obscenity, MacKinnon claims, obscures its true nature by representing it as just one more form of expression, one more way of conveying an idea, belief, or attitude. From a moral point of view, this reduces the debate about pornography to whether such material is in good or bad taste; legally it has the effect of making pornography an issue under the First Amendment. As against this, MacKinnon defends the "civil rights" conception of pornogra-

phy implicit in the Indianapolis law: Pornography is a discriminatory practice, not simply a certain type of offensive picture or text; pornography is not a political or social or religious "idea," and as such it does not deserve First Amendment protection, any more than does the now-outlawed practice of racial segregation. Displays of violent pornography are not invitations to engage in a dialogue with the "marketplace of ideas"; they are rather acts of disempowerment.

Pornography, MacKinnon believes, reflects and reinforces the way men in general tend to regard women; it is not linked only with a cult of machismo: even men who don't think of themselves as especially macho nonetheless participate in a culture that regards women as essentially commodities for use by men. The problem with obscenity law is that it is made by men and reflects male ideals and standards. This is especially obvious, MacKinnon thinks, in the case of the *Miller* standards: the "average person" is a male; "community standards" are already infected with sexism; "lacking serious . . . merit" effectively permits much that is demeaning to women.

At a deeper level, MacKinnon challenges Feinberg's Millian premises as they apply to the pornography question. Mill and other liberal political philosophers assume that people will not be silenced socially so long as no legal restrictions are placed upon their freedom of expression. But this, MacKinnon claims, is false: Permitting pornographers to "speak" silences women. Finally, MacKinnon argues that pornography does "contribute causally" to harm to women; and she urges that the law's understanding of "harm," derived from the simple transitive model of "A hit B," is unduly narrow and fails to account for a larger sense in which a discriminatory practice, whether it be pornography or racial segregation, can result in a "collective harm."

39. *Reno v. American Civil Liberties Union*

Justice Stevens delivered the opinion of the Court.

At issue is the constitutionality of two statutory provisions enacted to protect minors from "indecent" and " patently offensive" communications on the Internet. Notwithstanding the legitimacy and importance of the congressional goal of protecting children from harmful materials, we agree with the three-judge District Court that the statute abridges "the freedom of speech" protected by the First Amendment.

The District Court made extensive findings of fact: [The] Internet is an international network of interconnected computers [that now] enable tens of millions of people to communicate with one another and to access vast amounts of information from around the world. The Internet is "a unique and wholly new medium of worldwide human communication." The Internet has experienced "extraordinary growth." [About] 40 million people used the Internet at the time of trial, a number that is expected to mushroom to 200 million by 1999. Individuals can obtain access to the Internet from many different sources. [Most] colleges and universities provide access for their students and faculty; many corporations provide their employees with access through an office network; many communities and local libraries provide free access; and an increasing number of storefront "computer coffee shops" provide access for a small hourly fee. Several major national "online services" [offer] access to their own extensive proprietary networks as well as a link to the much larger resources of the Internet.

Anyone with access to the Internet may take advantage of a wide variety of communication and information retrieval methods. [E-mail] enables an individual to send an electronic message—generally akin to a note or letter—to another individual or to a group of addressees. [A] mail exploder is a sort of e-mail group. [Newsgroups] also serve groups of regular participants, but these postings may be read by others as well. [In] addition to positing a message that can be read later, two or more individuals wishing to communicate more immediately can enter a chat room [by] typing messages to one another that appear almost immediately on the others' computer screens.

The best known category of communication over the Internet is the World Wide Web, which allows users to search for and retrieve information stored in remote computers, as well as, in some cases, to communicate back to designated sites. [The] Web is [comparable,] from the readers' viewpoint, to both a vast library including millions of readily available and indexed publications and a sprawling mall offering goods and services. From the publishers' point of view, it constitutes a vast platform from which to address and hear from a worldwide audience of millions of readers, viewers, researchers, and buyers. Any person or organization with a computer connected to the Internet can "publish" information. Publishers include government agencies, educational institutions, commercial entities, advocacy groups, and individuals. Publishers may either make their material available to the entire pool of Internet users, or confine access to a selected group, such as those willing to pay for the privilege. "No single organization controls any membership in the Web, nor is there any centralized point from which individual Web sites or services can be blocked from the Web."

Sexually explicit material on the Internet includes text, pictures, and chat and "extends from the modestly titillating to the hardest-core." These files are created, named, and posted in the same manner as material that is not sexually explicit, and may be accessed either deliberately or unintentionally during the course of an imprecise search. "Once a provider posts its content on the Internet, it cannot prevent that content from entering any community." [Some] of the communications over the Internet that originate in foreign countries are also sexually explicit. [The] "odds are slim" that a

---

117 S. Ct. 2329 (1997).

user would enter a sexually explicit site by accident. Unlike communications received by radio or television, "the receipt of information on the Internet requires a series of affirmative steps more deliberate and directed than merely turning a dial. A child requires some sophistication and some ability to read to retrieve material and thereby to use the Internet unattended."

Systems have been developed to help parents control the material that may be available on a home computer with Internet access. A system may either limit a computer's access to an approved list of sources that have been identified as containing no adult material, it may block designated inappropriate sites, or it may attempt to block messages containing identifiable objectionable features. "Although parental control software currently can screen for certain suggestive words or for known sexually explicit sites, it cannot now screen for sexually explicit images." Nevertheless, the evidence indicates that "a reasonably effective method by which parents can prevent their children from accessing sexually explicit and other material which parents may believe is inappropriate for their children will soon be available."

The problem of age verification differs for different uses of the Internet. The District Court categorically determined that there "is no effective way to determine the identify or the age of a user who is accessing material through e-mail, mail exploders, newsgroups or chat rooms." The Government offered no evidence that there was a reliable way to screen recipients and participants in such fora for age. [Technology] exists by which an operator of a Web site may condition access on the verification of requested information such as a credit card number or an adult password. Credit card verification is only feasible, however, either in connection with a commercial transaction in which the card is used, or by payment to a verification agency. Using credit card possession as a surrogate for proof of age would impose costs on non-commercial Web sites that would require many of them to shut down. [Commercial] pornographic sites that charge their users for access have assigned them passwords as a method of age verification. The record does not contain any evidence concerning the reliability of these technologies. Even if passwords are effective for commercial purveyors of indecent material, the District Court found that an adult password re-

quirement would impose significant burdens on noncommercial sites, both because they would discourage users from accessing their sites and because the cost of creating and maintaining such screening systems would be "beyond their reach."

[Two provisions of] the "Communications Decency Act of 1996" (CDA) [are] challenged in this case. [The "indecent transmission" provision] prohibits the knowing transmission of obscene or indecent messages to any recipient under 18 years of age. . . .

The ["patently offensive display" provision] prohibits the knowing sending or displaying of patently offensive messages in a manner that is available to a person under 18 years of age. . . .

[Some] of our cases have recognized special justifications for regulation of the broadcast media that are not applicable to other speakers. . . . In these cases, the Court relied on the history of extensive government regulation of the broadcast medium; the scarcity of available frequencies at its inception; and its "invasive" nature. Those factors are not present in cyberspace. Neither before nor after the enactment of the CDA have the vast democratic fora of the Internet been subject to the type of government supervision and regulation that has attended the broadcast industry. Moreover, the Internet is not as "invasive" as radio or television. The District Court specifically found that "communications over the Internet do not 'invade' an individual's home or appear on one's computer screen unbidden. Users seldom encounter content 'by accident.' "It also found that 'almost all sexually explicit images are preceded by warnings as to the content." We distinguished *Pacifica in Sable* on just this basis, [explaining that the "dial-a-porn medium] requires the listener to take affirmative steps to receive the communication."

[Finally], unlike the conditions that prevailed when Congress first authorized regulation of the broadcast spectrum, the Internet can hardly be considered a "scarce" expression commodity. It provides relatively unlimited, low-cost capacity for communication of all kinds, [including] not only traditional print and news services, but also audio, video, and still images, as well as interactive real-time dialogue. Through the use of chat rooms, any person with a phone line can become a town crier with a voice that resonates farther than it could from any soapbox. Through the use of Web pages, mail exploders, and newsgroups, the same individual can become a pamphleteer. As the District Court found, "the content on the Internet is as diverse as human thought." We agree with its conclusion that our cases provide no basis for qualifying the level of First Amendment scrutiny that should be applied to this medium.

Regardless of whether the CDA is so vague that it violates the Fifth Amendment, the many ambiguities concerning the scope of its coverage render it problematic for purposes of the First Amendment. [The] Government argues that the statute is no more vague than the obscenity standard this court established in *Miller v. California* (1973). But that is not so. [The purportedly analogous] second prong of the *Miller* test [contains] a critical requirement that is omitted from the CDA: that the proscribed ["patently offensive"] material be "specifically defined by the applicable state law." [Moreover], the *Miller* definition is limited to "sexual conduct," whereas the CDA extends also to include "excretory activities" as well as "organs" of both a sexual and excretory nature. [Just] because a definition including three limitations is not vague, it does not follow that one of those limitations, standing by itself, is not vague. Each of *Miller's* additional two prongs—that, taken as a whole, the material appeal to the "prurient" interest, and that it "lack serious literary, artistic, political, or scientific value"—critically limits the uncertain sweep of the obscenity definition. The [latter] requirement is particularly important because, unlike the "patently offensive" and "prurient interest" criteria, it is not judged by contemporary community standards. This "societal value" requirement, absent in the CDA, allows appellate courts to impose some limitations and regularity on the definition by setting, as a matter of law, a national floor for socially redeeming value. The Government's contention that courts will be able to give such legal limitations to the CDA's standards is belied by Miller's own rationale for having juries determine whether material is "patently offensive" according to community standards: that such questions are essentially ones of fact. In contrast to *Miller* and our other previous cases, the CDA thus presents a greater threat of censoring speech that, in fact, falls outside the statute's scope. [That] danger provides further reason for insisting that the statute not be overly broad.

We are persuaded that CDA lacks the precision that the First Amendment requires when a statute regulates the content of speech. In order to deny minors access to potentially harmful speech, the CDA effectively suppresses a large amount of speech that adults have a constitutional right to receive and to address to one another. That burden on adult speech is unacceptable if less restrictive alternatives would be at least as effective in achieving the legitimate purpose that the statute was enacted to serve.

[It] is true that we have repeatedly recognized the governmental interest in protecting children from harmful materials. But that interest does not justify an unnecessarily broad suppression of speech addressed to adults. [In] arguing that the CDA does not so diminish adult communication, the Government relies on the incorrect factual premise that prohibiting a transmission whenever it is known that one of its recipients is a minor would not interfere with adult-to-adult communication. The findings of the District Court make clear that this premise is untenable. Given the size of the potential audience for most messages, in the absence of a viable age verification process, the sender must be charged with knowing that one or more minors will likely view it. Knowledge that, for instance, one or more members of a 100-person chat group will be minor—and therefore, that it would be a crime to send the group an indecent message—would surely burden communication among adults.

. . . As a practical matter, . . . it would be prohibitively expensive for noncommercial—as well as some commercial—speakers who have Web sites to verify that their users are adults. These limitations must inevitably curtail a significant amount of adult communication on the Internet.

The breadth of the CDA's coverage is wholly unprecedented. [It] is not limited to commercial speech or commercial entities. Its open-ended prohibitions embrace all nonprofit entities and individuals posting indecent messages or displaying them on their own computers in the presence of minors. The general, undefined terms "indecent" and "patently offensive" cover large amounts of nonpornographic material with serious educational or other value. Moreover, the "community standards" criterion as applied to the Internet means that any communication available to a nation-wide audience will be judged by the standards of the community most likely to be offended by the message. [The] strength of the Government's interest in protecting minors is not equally strong throughout the coverage of this broad statute. Under the CDA, a parent allowing her 17-year-old to use the family computer to obtain information on the Internet that she, in her parental judgment, deems appropriate could face a lengthy prison term. Similarly, a parent who sent his 17-year-old college freshman information on birth control via e-mail could be incarcerated even though neither he, his child, nor anyone in their home community, found the material "indecent" or "patently offensive," if the college town's community thought otherwise.

. . .

[We] agree with the District Court's conclusion that the CDA places an unacceptably heavy burden on protected speech, and that the defenses do not constitute the sort of "narrow tailoring" that will save an otherwise patently invalid unconstitutional provision. In *Sable,* we remarked that the speech restriction at issue there amounted to "'burning the house to roast the pig'." The CDA, casting a far darker shadow over free speech, threatens to torch a large segment of the Internet community.

[Finally], the Government [argues that an] interest in fostering the growth of the Internet provides an independent basis for upholding the constitutionality of the CDA. The Government apparently assumes that the unregulated availability of "indecent" and "patently offensive" material on the Internet is driving countless citizens away from the medium because of the risk of exposing themselves or their children to harmful material. We find this argument singularly unpersuasive. [The] record demonstrates that the growth of the Internet has been and continues to be phenomenal. As a matter of constitutional tradition, in the absence of evidence to the contrary, we presume that governmental regulation of the content of speech is more likely to interfere with the free exchange of ideas than to encourage it. The interest in encouraging freedom of expression in a democratic society outweighs any theoretical but unproven benefit of censorship.

[Affirmed.]

---

40. *American Booksellers Association v. Hudnut*

Easterbrook, Circuit Judge.

Indianapolis enacted an ordinance defining "pornography" as a practice that discriminates against women. "Pornography" is to be redressed through the administrative and judicial methods used for other discrimination. The City's definition of "pornography" is considerably different from

771 F. 2d 323 (1985)
United States Court of Appeals,
Seventh Circuit

"obscenity", which the Supreme Court has held is not protected by the First Amendment.

. . . To be "obscene" under *Miller v. California*, 413 U.S. 15 . . . (1973), "a publication must, taken as a whole, appeal to the prurient interest, must contain patently offensive depictions or descriptions of specified sexual conduct, and on the whole have no serious literary, artistic, political, or scientific value.". . . Offensiveness must be assessed under the standards of the community. Both offensiveness and an appeal to something other than "normal, healthy sexual desires" . . . are essential elements of "obscenity."

"Pornography" under the ordinance is "the graphic sexually explicit subordination of women, whether in pictures or in words, that also includes one or more of the following:

1. Women are presented as sexual objects who enjoy pain or humiliation; or

2. Women are presented as sexual objects who experience sexual pleasure in being raped; or

3. Women are presented as sexual objects tied up or cut up or mutilated or bruised or physically hurt, or as dismembered or truncated or fragmented or severed into body parts; or

4. Women are presented as being penetrated by objects or animals; or

5. Women are presented in scenarios of degradation, injury, abasement, torture, shown as filthy or inferior, bleeding, bruised, or hurt in a context that makes these conditions sexual; or

6. Women are presented as sexual objects for domination, conquest, violation, exploitation, possession, or use, or through postures or positions of servility or submission or display."

The Indianapolis ordinance does not refer to the prurient interest, to offensiveness, or to the standards of the community. It demands attention to particular depictions, not to the work judged as a whole. It is irrelevant under the ordinance whether the work has literary, artistic, political, or scientific value. The City and many amici point to these omissions as virtues. They maintain that pornography influences attitudes, and the statute is a way to alter the socialization of men and women rather than to vindicate community standards of offensiveness. And as one of the principal drafters of the ordinance has asserted, "if a woman is subjected, why should it matter that the work has other value?" Catherine A. MacKinnon, *Pornography, Civil Rights, and Speech*, 20 HarvCiv.Rts.—Civ.Lib.L. Rev. 1, 21 (1985).

Civil rights groups and feminists have entered this case as amici on both sides. Those supporting the ordinance say that it will play an important role in reducing the tendency of men to view women as sexual objects, a tendency that leads to both unacceptable attitudes and discrimination in the workplace and violence away from it. Those opposing the ordinance point out that much radical feminist literature is explicit and depicts women in ways forbidden by the ordinance and that the ordinance would reopen old battles. It is unclear how Indianapolis would treat works from James Joyce's *Ulysses* to Homer's *Iliad*; both depict women as submissive objects for conquest and domination.

We do not try to balance the arguments for and against an ordinance such as this. The ordinance discriminates on the ground of the content of the speech. Speech treating women in the approved way—in sexual encounters "premised on equality" (MacKinnon, *supra*, at 22)—is lawful no matter how sexually explicit. Speech treating women in the disapproved way—as submissive in matters sexual or as enjoying humiliation—is unlawful no matter how significant the literary, artistic, or political qualities of the work taken as a whole. The state may not ordain preferred viewpoints in this way. The Constitution forbids the state to declare one perspective right and silence opponents.

The ordinance contains four prohibitions. People may not "traffic" in pornography, "coerce" others into performing in pornographic works, or "force" pornography on anyone. Anyone injured by someone who has seen or read pornography has a right of action against the maker or seller.

Trafficking is defined in § 16–3(g)(4) as the "production, sale, exhibition, or distribution of pornography." The offense excludes exhibition in a public" or educational library, but a "special display" in a library may be sex discrimination. Section 16–3(g)(4)(c) provides that the trafficking paragraph "shall not be construed to make isolated passages or isolated parts actionable."

"Coercion into pornographic performance" is defined in § 16–3(g)(5) as "[c]oercing, intimidating or fraudulently inducing any person . . . into performing for pornography. . . ." The ordinance specifies that proof of any of the following "shall not constitute a defense: I. That the person is a woman; . . . VI. That the person has previously posed for sexually explicit pictures . . . with anyone . . . ; . . . VIII. That the person actually consented to a use of the performance that is changed into pornography; . . . IX. That the person knew that the purpose of the acts or events in question was to make pornography; . . . XI. That the person signed a contract, or made statements affirming a willingness to cooperate in the production of pornography; XII. That no physical force, threats, or weapons were used in the making of the pornography; or XIII. That the person was paid or otherwise compensated."

"Forcing pornography on a person," according to § 16–3(g)(5), is the "forcing of pornography on any woman, man, child, or transsexual in any place of employment, in education, in a home, or in any public place." The statute does not define forcing, but one of its authors states that the definition reaches pornography shown to medical students as part of their education or given to language students for translation. MacKinnon, *supra*, at 4–41.

Section 16–3(g)(7) defines as a prohibited practice the "assault, physical attack, or injury of any woman, man, child, or transsexual in a way that is directly caused by specific pornography."

For purposes of all four offenses, it is generally "not . . . a defense that the respondent did not know or intend that the materials were pornography. . . . " Section 16–3(g)(8). But the ordinance provides that damages are unavailable in trafficking cases unless the complainant proves "that the respondent knew or had reason to know that the materials were pornography." It is a complete defense to a trafficking case that all of the materials in question were pornography only by virtue of category (6) of the definition of pornography. In cases of assault caused by pornography, those who seek damages from "a seller, exhibitor or distributor" must show that the defendant knew or had reason to know of the material's status as pornography. By implication, those who seek damages from an author need not show this.

A woman aggrieved by trafficking in pornography may file a complaint "as a woman acting against the subordination of women" with the office of equal opportunity. Section 16–17(b). A man, child, or transsexual also may protest trafficking "but must prove injury in the same way that a woman is injured. . . ." *Ibid.* Subsection (a) also provides, however, that "any person claiming to be aggrieved" by trafficking, coercion, forcing, or assault may complain against the "perpetrators." We need not decide whether § 16–17(b) qualifies the right of action § 16–17(a).

The office investigates and within 30 days makes a recommendation to a panel of the equal opportunity advisory board. The panel then decides whether there is reasonable cause to proceed (§ 16–24(2) and may refer the dispute to a conciliation conference or to a complaint adjudication committee for a hearing (§§ 16–24(3), 16–26 (a)). The committee uses the same procedures ordinarily associated with civil rights litigation. It may make findings and enter orders, including both orders to cease and desist and orders "to take further affirmative action . . . including but not limited to the power to restore complainant's losses. . . ." Section 16–26(d). Either party may appeal the committee's decision to the board, which reviews the record before the committee and may modify its decision.

Under Indiana law an administrative decision takes effect when rendered, unless a court issues a stay. . . . The board's decisions are subject to review in the ordinary course. . . . Judicial review in pornography cases is to be de novo . . . , which provides a second complete hearing. When the board finds that a person has engaged in trafficking or that a seller, exhibitor, or distributor is responsible for an assault, it must initiate judicial review of its own decision, . . . and the statute prohibits injunctive relief in these cases in advance of the court's final decision. . . .

The district court held the ordinance unconstitutional. . . . The court concluded that the ordinance regulates speech rather than the conduct involved in making pornography. The regulation of speech could be justified, the court thought, only by a compelling interest in reducing sex discrimination, an interest Indianapolis had not established. The ordinance is also vague and overbroad, the court believed, and establishes a prior restraint of speech.

. . . "If there is any fixed star in our constitutional constellation, it is that no official, high or petty, can prescribe what shall be orthodox in politics, nationalism, religion, or other matters of opinion or force citizens to confess by word or act their faith therein. "*West Virginia State Board of Education v. Barnette*, 319 U.S. 624, 642 . . . (1943). Under the First amendment the government must leave to the people the evaluation of ideas. Bald or subtle, an idea is as powerful as the audience allows it to be. A belief may be pernicious—the beliefs of Nazis led to the death of millions, those of the Klan to the repression of millions. A pernicious belief may prevail. Totalitarian governments today rule much of the planet, practicing suppression of billions and spreading dogma that may enslave others. One of the things that separates our society from theirs is our absolute right to propagate opinions that the government finds wrong or even hateful. . . .

Under the ordinance graphic sexually explicit speech is "pornography" or not depending on the perspective the author adopts. Speech that "subordinates" women and also, for example, presents women as enjoying pain, humiliation, or rape, or even simply presents women in "positions of servility or submission or display" is forbidden, no matter how great the literary or political value of the work taken as a whole. Speech that portrays women in positions of equality is lawful, no matter how graphic the sexual content. This is thought control. It establishes an "approved" view of women, of how they may react to sexual encounters, of how the sexes may relate to each other. Those who espouse the approved view may use sexual images; those who do not, may not.

Indianapolis justifies the ordinance on the ground that pornography affects thoughts. Men who see women depicted as subordinate are more likely to treat them so. Pornography is an aspect of dominance. It does not persuade people so much as change them. It works by socializing, by establishing the expected and the permissible. In this view pornography is not an idea; pornography is the injury.

There is much to this perspective. Beliefs are also facts. People often act in accordance with the images and patterns they find around them. People raised in a religion tend to accept the tenets of that religion, often without independent examination. People taught them from birth that black people are fit only for slavery rarely rebelled against that creed; beliefs coupled with the self-interest of the masters established a social structure that inflicted great harm while enduring for centuries. Words and images act at the level of the subconscious before they persuade at the level of the conscious. Even the truth has little chance unless a statement fits within the framework of beliefs that may never have been subjected to rational study. . . .

Yet this simply demonstrates the power of pornography as speech. All of these unhappy effects depend on mental intermediation. Pornography affects how people see the world, their fellows, and social relations. If pornography is what pornography does, so is other speech. Hitler's orations affected how some Germans saw Jews. Communism is a world view, not simply a *Manifesto* by Marx and Engels or a set of speeches. Efforts to suppress communist speech in the United States were based on the belief that the public acceptability of such ideas would increase the likelihood of totalitarian government. Religions affect socialization in the most pervasive way. The opinion in *Wisconsin v. Yoder*, 406 U.S. 205 . . . 1526 . . . (1972), shows how a religion can dominate an entire approach to life, governing much more than the relation between the sexes. Many people believe that the existence of television, apart from the content of specific programs, leads to intellectual laziness, to a penchant for violence, to many other ills. The Alien and Sedition Acts passed during the administration of John Adams rested on a sincerely held belief that disrespect for the government leads to social collapse and revolution—a belief with support in the history of many nations. Most governments of the world act on this empirical regularity, suppressing critical speech. In the United States, however, the strength of the support for this belief is irrelevant. . . .

Racial bigotry, anti-Semitism, violence on television, reporters' biases—these and many more influence the culture and shape our socialization. None is directly answerable by more speech, unless that speech too finds its place in the popular culture. Yet all is protected as speech, however insidious. Any other answer leaves the government in control of all of the institutions of culture, the great censor and director of which thoughts are good for us.

Sexual responses often are unthinking responses, and the association of sexual arousal with the subordination of women therefore may have a substantial effect. But almost all cultural stimuli provoke unconscious responses. Religious ceremonies condition their participants. Teachers convey messages by selecting what not to cover; the implicit message about what is off limits or unthinkable may be more powerful than the messages for which they present rational argument.

Television scripts contain unarticulated assumptions. People may be conditioned in subtle ways. If the fact that speech plays a role in a process of conditioning were enough to permit governmental regulation, that would be the end of freedom of speech.

It is possible to interpret the claim that the pornography is the harm in a different way. Indianapolis emphasizes the injury that models in pornographic films and pictures may suffer. The record contains materials depicting sexual torture, penetration of women by red-hot irons and the like. These concerns have nothing to do with written materials subject to the statute, and physical injury can occur with or without the "subordination" of women . . . [A] state may make injury in the course of producing a film unlawful independent of the viewpoint expressed in the film.

The more immediate point, however, is that the image of pain is not necessarily pain. In *Body Double*, a suspense film, directed by Brian DePalma, a woman who has disrobed and presented a sexually explicit display is murdered by an intruder with a drill. The drill runs through the woman's body. The film is sexually explicit and a murder occurs—yet no one believes that the actress suffered pain or died. In *Barbarella* a character played by Jane Fonda is at times displayed in sexually explicit ways and at times shown "bleeding, bruised, [and] hurt in a context that makes these conditions sexual"—and again no one believes that Fonda was actually tortured to make the film. In *Carnal Knowledge* a woman grovels to please the sexual whims of a character played by Jack Nicholson; no one believes that there was a real sexual submission, and the Supreme Court held the film protected by the First Amendment . . . And this

works both ways. The description of women's sexual domination of men in *Lyistrata* was not real dominance. Depictions may affect slavery, war, or sexual roles, but a book about slavery is not itself slavery, or a book about death by poison a murder.

Much of Indianapolis's argument rests on the belief that when speech is "unanswerable," and the metaphor that there is a "marketplace of ideas" does not apply, the First Amendment does not apply either. The metaphor is honored; Milton's *Aeropagitica* and John Stuart Mill's *On Liberty* defend freedom of speech on the ground that the truth will prevail, and many of the most important cases under the First Amendment recite this position. The Framers undoubtedly believed it. As a general matter it is true. But the Constitution does not make the dominance of truth a necessary condition of freedom of speech. To say that it does would be to confuse an outcome of free speech with a necessary condition for the application of the amendment.

A power to limit speech on the ground that truth has not yet prevailed and is not likely to prevail implies the power to declare truth. At some point the government must be able to say (as Indianapolis has said): "We know what the truth is, yet a free exchange of speech has not driven out falsity so that we must now prohibit falsity." If the government may declare the truth, why wait for the failure of speech? Under the First Amendment, however, there is no such thing as a false idea, *Gertz v. Robert Welch, Inc.*, 418 U.S. 323 . . . (1974), so the government may not restrict speech on the ground that in a free exchange truth is not yet dominant.

. . .

41. *Obscenity as Pornography*

JOEL FEINBERG

1. *The Feminist Case Against Pornography*

In recent years a powerful attack on pornography has been made from a different quarter and on different, but often shifting grounds. Until 1970 or so, the demand for legal restraints on pornography came mainly from "sexual conservatives," those who regarded the pursuit of erotic pleasure for its own sake to be immoral or degrading, and its public depiction obscene. The new attack, however, comes not from prudes and bluenoses, but from women who have been in the forefront of the sexual revolution. We do not hear any of the traditional complaints about pornography from this group—that erotic states in themselves are immoral, that sexual titillation corrupts character, and that the spectacle of "appeals to prurience" is repugnant to moral sensibility. The new charge is rather that pornography degrades, abuses, and defames women, and contributes to a general climate of attitudes toward women that makes violent sex crimes more frequent. Pornography, they claim, has come to pose a threat to public safety, and its legal restraint can find justification either under the harm principle, or, by analogy with Nazi parades in Skokie and K.K.K. rallies, on some theory of profound (and personal) offense.

. . .

There is no necessity . . . that pornography *as such* be degrading to women. . . . [W]e can imagine easily enough an ideal pornography in which men and women are depicted enjoying their joint sexual pleasures in ways that show not a trace of dominance or humiliation of either party by the other. The materials in question might clearly satisfy my

previous definition of "pornography" as materials designed entirely and effectively to induce erotic excitement in observers, without containing any of the extraneous sexist elements.

. . .

. . . Some degrading pornography is also violent, glorifying in physical mistreatment of the woman, and featuring "weapons, of torture or bondage, wounds and bruises."[1] "One frightening spread from *Chic Magazine* showed a series of pictures of a woman covered with blood, masturbating with a knife. The title was "Columbine Cuts Up.'"[2] A movie called "Snuff" in which female characters (and, it is alleged, the actresses who portrayed them) are tortured to death for the sexual entertainment of the audiences, was shown briefly in a commercial New York theatre. The widely circulated monthly magazine *Hustler* once had a cover picture of a nude woman being pushed head first into a meat grinder, her shapely thighs and legs poised above the opening to the grinder in a sexually receptive posture, while the rest comes out of the bottom as ground meat. The exaggeration of numbers in Kathleen Barry's chilling description hardly blunts its horror: "In movie after movie women are raped, ejaculated on, urinated on, anally penetrated, beaten, and, with the advent of snuff films, murdered in an orgy of sexual pleasure."[3] The examples, alas, are abundant and depressing. . . .

. . .

May the law legitimately be used to restrict the liberty of pornographers to produce and distribute, and their customers to purchase and use, erotic materials that are violently abusive of women? (I am assuming that no strong case can be made for the proscription of materials that are merely degrading in one of the relatively subtle and nonviolent ways.) Many feminists answer, often with reluctance, in the affirmative. Their arguments can be divided into two general classes. Some simply invoke the harm principle. Violent pornography wrongs and harms women, according to these arguments, either by defaming them as a group, or (more importantly) by inciting males to violent crimes against them or creating a cultural climate in which such crimes are likely to become more frequent. The two traditional legal categories involved in these harm-principle arguments, then, are *defamation* and *incitement*. The other class of arguments invokes[s] the offense principle, not in order to prevent mere "nuisances," but to prevent profound offense analogous to that of the Jews in Skokie or the blacks in a town where the K.K.K. rallies.

2. *Violent Pornography, the Cult of Macho, and Harm to Women*

I shall not spend much time on the claim that violent and other extremely degrading pornography should be banned on the ground that it *defames* women. In a skeptical spirit, I can begin by pointing out that there are immense difficulties in applying the civil law of libel and slander as it is presently constituted in such a way as not to violate freedom of expression. Problems with *criminal* libel and slander would be even more unmanageable, and *group* defamation, whether civil or criminal, would multiply the problems still further. The argument on the other side is that pornography is essentially propaganda—propaganda against women. It does not slander women in the technical legal sense by asserting damaging falsehoods about them, because it *asserts* nothing at all. But it spreads an image of women as mindless playthings or "objects," inferior beings fit only to be used and abused for the pleasure of men, whether they like it or not, but often to their own secret pleasure. This picture lowers the esteem men have for women, and for that reason (if defamation is the basis of the argument) is sufficient ground for proscription even in the absence of any evidence of tangible harm to women caused by the behavior of misled and deluded men.

If degrading pornography defames (libels or slanders) women, it must be in virtue of some beliefs about women—false beliefs— that it conveys, so that in virtue of those newly acquired or reinforced false beliefs, consumers lower their esteem for women in general. If a work of pornography, for example, shows a woman (or group of women) in exclusively subservient or domestic roles, that may lead the consumer to *believe* that women, in virtue of some inherent female characteristics, are only fit for such roles. There is no doubt that much pornography does portray women in subservient positions, but if that is defamatory to women in anything like the legal sense, then so are soap commercials on TV. So are many novels, even some good ones. (A good novel may yet be about some degraded characters.) That some groups are portrayed in unflattering roles has not hitherto been a ground for the censorship of fiction or advertising. Besides, it is not clearly the *group* that is portrayed at all in such works, but only one individual (or small set of individuals) and fictitious ones at that. Are fat men defamed by Shakespeare's picture of Falstaff? Are Jews defamed by the characterization of Shylock? Could any writer today even hope to write a novel partly about a fawning corrupted black, under group defamation laws, without risking censorship or worse? The chilling effect on the practice of fiction-writing would amount to a near freeze. . . .

What looks like sexual subservience to some looks like liberation from sexual repression to others. It is hard to imagine how a court could provide a workable, much less fair, test of whether a given work has sufficiently damaged male esteem toward women for it to be judged criminally defamatory, when so much of the viewer's reaction he brings on himself, and viewer reactions are so widely variable.

It is not easy for a single work to defame successfully a group as large as 51% of the whole human race. (Could a misanthrope "defame" the whole human race by a false statement about "the nature of man"? Would every human being then be his "victim"?) Perhaps an unanswered barrage of thousands of tracts, backed by the prestige of powerful and learned persons without dissent might successfully defame any group no matter how large, but those conditions would be difficult to satisfy so long as there is freedom to speak back on the other side. In any case, defamation is not the true gravamen of the wrong that women in general suffer from extremely degrading pornography. When a magazine cover portrays a woman in a meat grinder, *all* women are insulted, degraded, even perhaps endangered, but few would naturally complain that they were *libeled* or *slandered.* Those terms conceal the point of what has happened. If women are harmed by pornography, the harm is surely more direct and tangible than harm to "the interest in reputation."

The major argument for repression of violent pornography under the harm principle is that it promotes rape and physical violence. In the United States there is a plenitude both of sexual violence against women and of violent pornography. According to the F.B.I. Uniform Crime Statistics (as of 1980), a 12-year-old girl in the United States has one chance in three of being raped in her lifetime; studies only a few years earlier showed that the number of violent scenes in hard-core pornographic books was as high as 20% of the total, the number of violent cartoons and pictorials in leading pornographic magazines was as much as 10% of the total. This has suggested to some writers that there must be a direct causal link between violent pornography and sexual violence against women; but causal relationships between pornography and rape, if they exist, must be more complicated than that.

. . .

One the other hand, there is evidence that novel ways of committing crimes are often suggested (usually inadvertently) by bizarre takes in films or TV . . . , and even factual newspaper reports of crimes can trigger the well-known "copy-cat crime" phenomenon. But if the possibility of copy-cat cases, by itself, justified censorship or punishment, we would have grounds for suppressing films of *The Brothers Karamozov* and the TV series *Roots* (both of which have been cited as influences on imitative crimes). . . . A violent episode in a pornographic work may indeed be a causally necessary condition for the commission of some specific crime by a specific perpetrator on a specific victim at some specific time and place. But for his reading or viewing that episode, the perpetrator may not have done precisely what he did in just the time, place, and manner that he did it. But so large a part of the full causal explanation of his act concerns his own psychological character and predispositions, that it is likely that some similar crime would have suggested itself to him in due time. It is not likely that non-rapists are converted into rapists *simply* by reading and viewing pornography. If pornography has a serious causal bearing on the occurrence of rape (as opposed to the trivial copy-cat effect) it must be in virtue of its role (still to be established) in implanting the appropriate cruel dispositions in the first place.

Rape is such a complex social phenomenon that there is probably no one simple generalization to account for it. Some rapes are no doubt ineliminable, no matter how we design our institutions. Many of these are the product of deep individual psychological problems, transferred rages, and the like. But for others, perhaps the preponderant number, the major part of the explanation is sociological, not psychological. In these cases the rapist is a psychologically normal person well adjusted to his particular subculture, acting calmly and deliberately rather than in a rage, and doing what he thinks is expected of him by his peers, what he must do to acquire or preserve standing in his group. His otherwise inexplicable violence is best explained as a consequence of the peculiar form of his socialization among his peers, his pursuit of a prevailing ideal of manliness, what the Mexicans have long called *machismo*, but which exists to some degree or other among men in most countries, certainly in our own.

The macho male wins the esteem of his associates by being tough, fearless, reckless, wild, unsentimental, hard-boiled, hard drinking, disrespectful, profane, willing to fight whenever his honor is impugned, and fight without fear of consequences no matter how extreme. He is a sexual athlete who must be utterly dominant over "his" females, who are expected to be slavishly devoted to him even though he lacks gentleness with them and shows his regard only by displaying them like trophies; yet he is a hearty and loyal companion to his "teammates" (he is always on a "team" of some sort). Given the manifest harm the cult of macho has done to men, women, and to relations between men and women, it is difficult to account for its survival in otherwise civilized nations. Perhaps it is useful in time of war, and war has been a preoccupation of most generations of young men, in most nations, up to the present. If so, then the persistence of *machismo* is one of the stronger arguments we have (among many others) for the obsolescence of war.

The extreme character of macho values must be understood before any sense can be made of the appeal of violent pornography. The violent porn does not appeal to prurience or lust as such. Indeed, it does not appeal at all to a psychologically normal male who is not in the grip of the macho cult. In fact these pictures, stories, and films have no other function but to express and reinforce the macho ideology. "Get your sexual kicks," they seem to say, "but make sure you get them by humiliating the woman, and showing her who's boss. Make sure at all costs not to develop any tender feelings toward her that might give her a subtle form of control over you and thus destroy your standing with the group. Remember to act in the truly manly manner of a 'wild and crazy guy.'"

In her brilliant article on this subject, Sarah J. McCarthy cites some horrible examples from *Penthouse* Magazine of the macho personality structure which is peculiarly receptive to, and a necessary condition for, the appeal of violent porn:

"There's still something to be said for bashing a woman over the head, dragging her off behind a rock, and having her," said one of the guys in the February 1980 *Penthouse.* . . . "Women Who Flirt With Pain" was the cover hype for a *Penthouse* interview with an assortment of resident Neanderthals (a name that would swell them with pride).

"We're basically rapists because we're created that way," proclaims Dale. "We're irrational, sexually completely crazy. Our sexuality is more promiscuous, more immediate, and more fleeting, possibly less deep. We're like stud bulls that want to mount everything in sight. . . . "

The letters-to-the-editor in the February *Penthouse* contains an ugly letter from someone who claims to be a sophomore at a large midwestern university and is "into throat-fucking." He writes of Kathy and how he was "ramming his huge eleven-inch tool down her throat." [Sexual bragging, pornography style.] Kathy "was nearly unconscious from coming." [Deceit and self-deception, pornography style.] Gloria Steinem writes in the May 1980 *Ms.:* "Since *Deep Throat,* a whole new genre of pornography has developed. Added to the familiar varieties of rape, there is now an ambition to rape the throat. . . . "

Another issue of *Penthouse* contains an article about what they have cleverly called "tossing." A college student from Albuquerque, who drives a 1974 Cadillac and who is "attracted to anything in a skirt," tells how it's done. "How did you get into tossing?" the *Penthouse* interviewer asks. "It just happened," says Daryl. "I was doing it in high school two years ago and didn't know what it was. I'd date a chick once, fuck her in my car, and just dump her out. Literally."[4]

These repugnant specimens are not examples of make-believe violent pornography. Rather, they are examples of the attitudes and practices of persons who are antecedently prone to be appreciative consumers of violent pornography. These grisly sentiments are perhaps found more commonly among working class youths in military barracks and factories but they are only slightly more familiar than similar bravado heard by middle class Americans in fraternity houses and dormitories. These remarks are usually taken as meant to impress their male auditors; they are uttered with a kind of aggressive pride. The quotations from *Penthouse* capture the tone exactly.

. . .

Would it significantly reduce sexual violence if violent pornography were effectively banned? No one can know for sure, but if the cult of macho is the main source of such violence, as I suspect, then repression of violent pornography, whose function is to pander to the macho values already deeply rooted in society, may have little effect. Pornography does not cause normal decent chaps, through a single exposure, to metamorphize into rapists. Pornography-reading machos commit rape, but that is because they already have macho values, not because they read the violent pornography that panders to them. Perhaps then *constant* exposure to violent porn might turn a decent person into a violence-prone macho. But that does not seem likely either, since the repugnant violence of the materials could not have any appeal in the first place to one who did not already have some strong macho predispositions, so "constant exposure" could not begin to become established. Clearly, other causes, and more foundational ones, must be at work, if violent porn is to have any initial purchase. Violent pornography is more a symptom of *machismo* than a cause of it, and treating symptoms merely is not a way to offer protection to potential victims of rapists. At most, I think there may be a small spill-over effect of violent porn on actual violence. Sometimes, a bizarre new sadistic trick (like "throat-fucking"?) is suggested by a work of violent pornography and taken up by those prone to cruel violence to begin with. More often, perhaps, the response to an inventive violent porno scene may be like that of the college *Penthouse* reader to "tossing": "I was doing it in high school two years ago, and I didn't know what it was." He read *Penthouse* and learned "what it was," but his conduct, presumably, was not significantly changed.

If my surmise about casual connections is correct they are roughly as indicated in the . . . diagram.

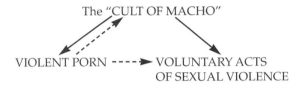

The "CULT OF MACHO"

VIOLENT PORN ----► VOLUNTARY ACTS OF SEXUAL VIOLENCE

———► = causal direction
----► = possible "spill-over effects"

The primary causal direction is not from violent pornography to violent real-life episodes. Neither is it from violent pornography to the establishment and reinforcement of macho values. Rather, the cult of macho expectations is itself the primary cause *both* of the existence of violent porn (it provides the appreciative audience) and of the real-life sexual violence (it provides the motive). The dotted arrows express my acknowledgement of the point that there might be some small spill-over effect from violent pornography back on the macho values that spawn it, in one direction, and on real-life violence in the other, but the pornography cannot be the primary causal generator. Sexual violence will continue to fester so long as the cult of macho flourishes, whether or not we eliminate legal violent pornography.

How then can we hope to weaken and then extirpate the cultish values at the root of our problem? The criminal law is a singularly ill-adapted tool for that kind of job. We might just as well legislate against entrepreneurship on the grounds that capitalism engenders "acquisitive personalities," or against the military on the grounds that it produces "authoritarian personalities," or against certain religious sects on the ground that they foster puritanism, as criminalize practices and institutions on the grounds that they contribute to *machismo*. But macho values are culturally, not instinctively, transmitted, and the behavior that expresses them is learned, not inherited, behavior. What is learned can be unlearned. Schools should play a role. Surely, learning to see through machismo and avoid its traps should be as important a part of a child's preparation for citizenship as the acquisition of patriotism and piety. To be effective, such teaching should be frank and direct, not totally reliant on general moral platitudes. It should talk about the genesis of children's attitudes toward the other sex, and invite discussion of male insecurity, resentment of women, cruelty, and even specific odious examples. Advertising firms and film companies should be asked (at first), then pressured (if necessary) to cooperate, as they did in the successful campaign to deglamorize cigarette smoking. Fewer exploitation films should be made that provide attractive models of youths flashing knives, playing chicken or Russian roulette, or "tossing" girls. Materials (especially films) should be made available to clergymen as well as teachers, youth counselors, and parole officers. A strong part of the emphasis of these materials should be on the harm that bondage to the cult of macho does to men too, and how treacherous a trap *machismo* can be. The new moral education must be careful, of course, not to preach dull prudence as a preferred style for youthful living. A zest for excitement, adventure, even danger, cannot be artificially removed from adolescent nature. Moreover, teamwork, camaraderie, and toughness of character need not be denigrated. But the cult of macho corrupts and distorts these values in ways that can be made clear to youths. The mistreatment of women, when its motivation is clearly revealed and understood, should be a sure way of eliciting the contempt of the group, not a means to greater prestige within it.

Rape is a harm and a severe one. Harm prevention is definitely a legitimate use of the criminal law. Therefore, if there is a clear enough causal connection to rape, a statute that prohibits violent pornography would be a morally legitimate restriction of liberty. But it is not enough to warrant suppression that pornography as a whole might have some harmful consequences to third parties, even though most specific instances of it do not.

. . .

Those instances of sexual violence which may be harmful side-effects of violent pornography are directly produced by criminals (rapists) acting voluntarily on their own. We already have on the statute books a firm prohibition of rape and sexual assault. If, in addition, the harm principle permits the criminalization of actions only indirectly related to the primary harm, such as producing, displaying or selling violent pornography, then there is a danger that the law will be infected with unfairness; for unless certain further conditions are fulfilled, the law will be committed to punishing some parties for the entirely voluntary criminal conduct of other parties. . . . Suppose that *A* wrongfully harms (e.g. rapes) *B* in circumstances such that (1) *A* acts fully voluntarily on his own initiative, and (2) nonetheless, but for what *C* has communicated to him, he would not have done what he did to *B*. Under what further conditions, we must ask, can *C* be rightfully held criminally responsible along with *A* for the harm to *B*? Clearly *C* can be held responsible if the information he communicated was helpful assistance to *A* and intended to be such. In that case *C* becomes a kind of collaborator. Under traditional law, *C* can also incur liability if what he communicated to *A* was some kind of encouragement to commit a crime against *B*. The clearest cases are those in which *C* solicits *A*'s commission of the criminal act by offering inducements to him. "Encouragement" is also criminal when it takes the form of active urging. Sometimes mere advice to commit the act counts as an appropriate sort of encouragement. When the encouragement takes a general form, and the harmful crime is recommended to "the general reader" or an indefinite audience, then the term "advocacy" is often used. Advocating criminal conduct is arguably a way of producing such conduct, and is thus often itself a crime. An article in a pornographic magazine advocating the practice of rape (as opposed to advocating a legislative change of the rape laws) would presumably be a crime if its intent were serious and its audience presumed to be impressionable to an appropriately dangerous degree.

Violent pornography, however, does not seem to fit any of these models. Its authors and vendors do not solicit rapes; nor do they urge or advise rapes; nor do they advocate rape. If some of their customers, some of the time, might yet "find encouragement" in their works to commit rapes because rape has been portrayed in a way that happens to be alluring to them, that is their own affair, the pornographer might insist, and their own responsibility.

. . .

3. *Violent Pornography and Profound Offense*

The harm principle grounds for legally banning pornography do not appear sufficient. Does the offense principle do any better? Pornographic displays *can* be public nuisances, of course, and when the balancing tests tip in the nuisance direction, the offending activities may fairly be prohibited, or redirected to less offensive channels. The manner in which degrading and violent pornography offends women (and men who support women's rights) is substantially different from that in which erotica as such offend the prudish. The shame, embarrassment, shock, disgust, and irritation of the latter group can be effectively avoided if the erotic displays are concealed from their view. The offense to a woman's sensibilities when her whole sex is treated as grist for the meat grinder, however, is deeply repugnant to her moral sensibilities whether out of view or not. Feminist writers often make this point by means of analogies to racist literature and films.

Suppose some unscrupulous promoters decide that they can make large profits by pandering to the latent hatred against blacks which they suppose to be endemic in a substantial minority of the white community. Since explicitly racist remarks and overt racist behavior are no longer widely acceptable in American society, many secret black-haters might enjoy an occasional night at the movies where they can enjoy to their heart's content specially made films that lampoon minstrel-style "darkies" "with wide eyes as white as moons, hair shot straight in the air like Buckwheat's, afraid of everything—spiders, [their] own shadows, ghosts."[5] So much for comic openers. The main features could be stories of uppity blacks put in their place by righteous whites, taunted and hounded, tarred and feathered, tortured and castrated, and in the climactic scenes, hung up on gallows to the general rejoicing of their betters. The aim of the films would be to provide a delicious catharsis of pent-up hatred. It would be prudent, on business grounds, to keep advertisements discreet, and to use euphemistic descriptions like "folk films" (analogous to "adult films").

I don't imagine that many blacks would be placated by the liberal lawmaker who argues in support of his refusal to enact prohibitive legislation that there is little evidence of actual harm done to blacks by the films, that they do not advocate violence to blacks or incite mobs to fury, and that for all we know they will make the racists less dangerous by providing a harmless outlet for their antisocial impulses. Neither would many blacks be assuaged by the liberal assurance that we should all be wary of possible harmful effects anyway, continue to look for evidence thereof, and use educational campaigns as a more effective means of exposing the evils of racism. "That is all well and good," the blacks might reply, "but first we must lance this painful boil on our sensibilities. The 'folk films,' whether we are in the audience or not, are morally abominable affronts to us. Their very existence in our midst is a perpetual laceration of our feelings. We aren't present to be humiliated, but they degrade the very atmosphere in which we breathe and move."

The analogy to violent pornographic films is close though not perfect. (It is an interesting fact to ponder that although there undoubtedly is a large racist underground in this country, no promoter has yet found a way of exploiting it in the manner of our example.) The pornographic films do serve an erotic interest of their customers, and that gives them, *ceteris paribus*, a personal value greater perhaps than that of the "folk films." The racist films, on the other hand, may be easier to disguise as genuine works of drama, thus making it much more difficult for a line to be drawn between them and genuine attempts at dramas about odious people

and their victims. The bare-knowledge offense in the two cases seems almost equally profound, going well beyond anything called "mere nuisance," to touch the chord of moral sensibility.

It does not express an unsympathetic attitude toward the offended parties, however, to deny a basis in either the harm or offense principles for the use of legal force to "lance the boil." Profound offense . . . , is either an impersonal and disinterested moral outrage or else an aggrieved response on one's own behalf because of the unpleasant mental states one has been forced to experience. If it is an impersonal response, then it can warrant legal force against its cause only on the basis of the principle of legal moralism which is unacceptable to liberals. We would have to argue in that case that the very showing of violent films to appreciative audiences is an evil in itself and one of such magnitude that it can be rightly prevented by legal force if necessary, even though it is not the kind of evil that *wrongs* any one. . . . If, on the other hand, the profound offense is a felt personal wrong voiced on one's own behalf as its "victim," then the complaint is that the offending materials cause one to suffer unpleasant states that are a nuisance to avoid. But that offense will not have much weight on the scales if one is not forced to witness the showings, or lurid announcements of the showings, and is not forced to take irritating and inconveniencing detours to avoid them. The offense principle, in short, will not warrant legal prohibition of the films unless the offense they cause is not reasonably avoidable. It is only in its character as disinterested moral outrage that it is not reasonably avoidable, but we cannot ban everything that is thought to be outrageous, whether right-violating or not, without recourse to legal moralism.

. . .

Racist and porno films do not directly insult specific individuals, but rather large groups, thus diluting the impact of the insult, or at least its directed personal character, proportionately. The "folk films" might be more serious affronts in this respect than the porno films since their target is a much smaller group than half of the human race, and one which has historically been brutalized by slavery and cruel repression. A black man might be more likely to feel a *personal* grievance at the folk film he does not witness than a woman would to a porno film she does not witness, for these reasons. This personal aspect of his offense would overlay the more general disinterested moral indignation he shares with the women who are offended by their bare knowledge of the existence of violent pornographic displays. Nonetheless, understandable as the black's felt grievance may be, the insulting film shown to a willing audience in a private or commercial theatre is in the same boat as the insulting conversations among willing friends in a private home or club. In both cases the conduct is morally execrable, but in neither case do liberal principles warrant state intervention to punish the mischief.

. . .

Endnotes

[1] Gloria Steinem, "Erotica and Pornography, A Clear and Present Difference," *Ms.*, November, 1978, p. 54.

[2] Lisa Lehrman, *op. cit.* (footnote 2), pp. 181–82.

[3] Kathleen Barry, *Female Sexual Slavery* (New York: Avon Books, 1979), p. 206.

[4] Sarah J. McCarthy, "Pornography, Rape, and the Cult of Macho," *The Humanist*, Sept./Oct., 1980, p. 15.

[5] *Ibid.*, p. 11.

42. *Pornography: On Morality and Politics*

Catherine MacKinnon

Possession and use of women through the sexualization of intimate intrusion and access to them is a central feature of women's social definition as inferior and feminine. Visual and verbal intrusion, access, possession, and use is predicated upon and produces physical and psychic intrusion, access, possession, and use. In contemporary industrial society, pornography is an industry that mass produces sexual intrusion on, access to, possession and use of women by and for men for profit. It exploits women's sexual and economic inequality for gain. It sells women to men as and for sex. It is a technologically sophisticated traffic in women.

This understanding of the reality of pornography must contend not only with centuries of celebratory intellectual obfuscation. It must contend with a legal tradition of neutralization through abstraction from the realities of power, a tradition that has authoritatively defined pornography as not about women as such at all, but about sex, hence about morality, and as not about acts or practices, but about ideas. Uncovering gender in this area of law reveals women to be most invisible when most exposed and most silent when used in defense of speech. In both pornography and the law of obscenity, women are seen only as sex and heard only when mouthing a sexual script. When pornography and the law of pornography are investigated together, it becomes clear that pornography is to women's status, hence its critique is to feminism, as its preservation is to male supremacy in its liberal legal guise.

The law of obscenity is the state's approach to addressing the pornography problem, which it construes as an issue of regulation of expression under the First Amendment. Nudity, explicitness, excess of candor, arousal or excitement, prurience, unnaturalness—these qualities raise concerns under obscenity law when sex is depicted or portrayed. . . . Obscenity as such probably does little harm. Pornography contributes causally to attitudes and behaviors of violence and discrimination which define the treatment and status of half the population.

Obscenity law is concerned with morality, meaning good and evil, virtue and vice. The concerns of feminism with power and powerlessness are first political, not moral. From the feminist perspective, obscenity is a moral idea; pornography is a political practice. Obscenity is abstract; pornography is concrete. Obscenity conveys moral condemnation as a predicate to legal condemnation. Pornography identifies a political practice that is predicated on power and powerlessness—a practice that is, in fact, legally protected. The two concepts represent two entirely different things.

In accounting for gender inequality as part of the socially constructed relationship between power—the political—on the one hand and knowledge of truth and reality—the epistemological—on the other, the classic description Justice Stewart once offered of the obscenity standard, "I know it when I see it,"[1] becomes even more revealing than it is usually taken to be. Taken as a statement that connects epistemology with power, if one asks, from the point of view of women's experience, does he know what women know when we see what we see, one has to doubt it, given what is on the newsstands. How does his point of view keep what is there, there? To liberal critics, his admission exposed the relativity, the partiality, the insufficient abstractness of the obscenity standard. Not to be emptily universal, to leave your concreteness showing, is a sin among men. Their problem with Justice Stewart's formulation is that it implies that anything, capriciously, could be suppressed. In fact, almost nothing is. The meaning of what his view permits, as it turns out, is anything but capricious. It is entirely systematic and determinate. His statement is precisely descriptively accurate; its candor is why it has drawn so much criticism. He admitted what courts do epistemologically all the time. In so doing, he both did it and gave it the stature of doctrine (if only dictum). That is, he revealed that the obscenity standard—and it is not unique—is built on what the male standpoint sees. The problem is, so is pornography. In this way, the law of obscenity reproduces the pornographic point of view of women on the level of constitutional jurisprudence.

Pornography, in the feminist view, is a form of forced sex, a practice of sexual politics, an institution of gender inequality. In this perspective, pornography, with the rape and prostitution in which it participates, institutionalizes the sexuality of male supremacy, which fuses the erotization of dominance and submission with the social construction of male and female. Gender is sexual. Pornography constitutes the meaning of that sexuality. Men treat women as whom they see women as being. Pornography constructs who that is. Men's power over women means that the way men see women defines who women can be. Pornography is that way. In this light, obscenity law can be seen to treat morals from the male point of view, meaning the standpoint of male dominance. The feminist critique of pornography, by contrast, proceeds from women's point of view, meaning the standpoint of the subordination of women to men.

. . .

Obscenity law proposes to control what and how sex can be publicly shown. In practice, its standard centers upon the same features that feminism and pornography both reveal as key to male sexuality: the erect penis and penetration. Historically, obscenity law was vexed by restricting such portrayals while protecting great literature. (Nobody considered protecting women.) Solving this problem by exempting works of perceived value, obscenity restrictions relaxed—some might say collapsed—revealing a significant shift in the last decade. Under the old law, pornography was publicly repudiated yet privately consumed and actualized: do anything to women with impunity in private behind a veil of public denial and civility. Under the new law, in a victory for Freudian derepression, pornography is publicly celebrated. The old private rules have become the new public rules. Women were sex and are still sex. Greater efforts of brutality have become necessary to eroticize the taboo—each taboo being a hierarchy in disguise—since the frontier of the taboo keeps vanishing as one crosses it. Put another way, more and more violence has become necessary to keep the progressively desensitized consumer aroused to the illusion that sex (and he) is daring and dangerous. Making sex with the powerless "not allowed" is a way of keeping "getting it" defined as an act of power, an assertion of hierarchy, which keeps it sexy in a sexual system in which hierarchy is sexy. In addition, pornography has become ubiquitous. Sexual terrorism has become democratized. Pornography has become truly available to women for the first time in history. Among other effects, this central mechanism of sexual subordination, this means of systematizing the definition of women as a sexual class, has now become available to its victims for scrutiny and analysis as an open public system, not just as a private secret abuse. Hopefully, this was a mistake.

. . .

In 1973, obscenity under law came to mean that which "the average person applying contemporary standards, would find that, taken as a whole, appeals to the prurient interest; that [which] depicts or describes, in a patently offensive way, sexual conduct as defined by the applicable state law; and that which, taken as a whole, lacks serious literary, artistic, political, or scientific value." Feminism doubts whether "the average person," gender neutral, exists; has more questions about the content and process of definition of community standards than about deviations from them; wonders why prurience counts but powerlessness does not, why sensibilities are better protected from offense than women are from exploitation; defines sexuality, hence its violation and expropriation, more broadly than does any state law; and wonders why a body of law which cannot in practice tell rape from intercourse should be entrusted with telling pornography from anything less. In feminist perspective, one notices that although the law of obscenity says that sex on streetcorners is not supposed to be legitimated "by the fact that the persons are simultaneously engaged in a valid political dialogue,"[2] the requirement that the work be considered "as a whole" legitimates something very like that on the level of publications such as *Playboy*,[3] even though experimental evidence is beginning to support what victims have long known: legitimate settings diminish the injury perceived to be done to the women whose trivialization and objectification it contextualizes. Besides, if a woman is subjected, why should it matter that the work has other value? Perhaps what redeems a work's value among men enhances its injury to women. Existing standards of literature, art, science, and politics are, in feminist light, remarkably consonant with pornography's mode, meaning, and message. Finally and foremost, a feminist approach reveals that although the content and dynamic of pornography concerns women—the sexuality of women,

women as sexuality—in the same way that the vast majority of "obscenities" refer specifically to women's bodies, women's invisibility has been such that the law of obscenity has never even considered pornography a women's issue.

To appeal to "prurient interest" means to give a man an erection. Men are scared to make it possible for some men to tell other men what they can and cannot have sexual access to, because men have power. Men believe that if you do not let them have theirs, they might not let you have yours. This is why the indefinability of pornography—all the "one man's this is another man's that"—is so central to pornography's definition. It is not because all men are such great liberals, but because those other men might be able to do to them whatever *they* can do to *them*, which may explain why the liberal principle is what it is.

What this frame on the issue obscures, because the fought-over are invisible, is that the fight over a definition of pornography is a fight among men over the terms of access to women, hence over the best means to guarantee male power as a system. The tacit questions become: Whose sexual practices threaten this system? Are they men whose sexual access can be sacrificed in the interest of maintaining it for the rest? Public sexual access by men to anything other than women is far less likely to be protected speech. This is not to say that male sexual access to anything—children, other men, women with women, objects, animals—is not the real rule. The issue is rather how public, hence how express in law, that system will be.

In this light, the "prurient interest" prong of the obscenity standard has a built-in bind. To find prurience as a fact, someone has to admit sexual arousal by the materials; but male sexual arousal signals the importance of protection. Men put themselves in this position and then wonder why they cannot agree. Sometimes it seems that what is obscene is what does not turn on the Supreme Court, or what revolts them more, which is rare, since revulsion is eroticized. Sometimes it seems that what is obscene is what turns on those men whom the men in power think they can afford to ignore. Sometimes it seems that what is obscene is what makes dominant men see themselves as momentary potential targets of male sexual aggression. Sometimes it seems that anything can be done to a woman, but obscenity is sex that makes male sexuality look bad.

Courts' difficulties in framing workable standards to separate "prurient" from other sexual interest, commercial exploitation from art or advertising, sexual speech from sexual conduct, and obscenity from great literature make the feminist point. These lines have proved elusive in law because they do not exist in life. Commercial sex resembles art because both exploit women's sexuality. The liberal slippery slope is the feminist totality. Politically speaking, whatever obscenity may do, pornography converges with more conventionally acceptable depictions and descriptions just as rape does with intercourse, because both are acts within the same power relation. Just as it is difficult to distinguish literature or art against a background, a standard, of objectification, it is difficult to discern sexual freedom against a background, a standard, of sexual coercion. This does not mean that it cannot be done. It means that legal standards will be practically unenforceable, will reproduce this problem rather than solve it, until they address its fundamental issue—gender inequality—directly.

To define the pornographic as the "patently offensive" further misconstrues its harm. Pornography is not bad manners or poor choice of audience; obscenity is. Pornography is also not an idea; obscenity is. The legal fiction whereby the obscene is "not speech" has deceived few; it has effectively avoided the need to adjudicate pornography's social etiology. But obscenity law got one thing right: pornography is more actlike than thoughtlike. The fact that pornography, in a feminist view, furthers the idea of the sexual inferiority of women, a political idea, does not make pornography a political idea. That one can express the idea a practice expresses does not make that practice an idea. Pornography is not an idea any more than segregation or lynching are ideas, although both institutionalize the idea of the inferiority of one group to another. The law considers obscenity deviant, antisocial. If it causes harm, it causes antisocial acts, acts against the social order. In a feminist perspective, pornography is the essence of a sexist social order, its quintessential social act. . . .

The success, therefore the harm, of pornography, is invisible to the male state in its liberal guise and so has been defined out of the customary approach taken to, and the dominant values underlying, the First Amendment. The theory of the First Amendment under which most pornography is protected from governmental restriction proceeds from liberal assumptions that do not apply to the situation of women. First Amendment theory, like virtually all liberal legal theory, presumes the validity of the distinction between public and private: the "role of law [is] to make and guard the line between the sphere of social power, organized in the form of the state, and the arena of private right." On this basis, courts distinguish between obscene billboards ("thrust upon the unwilling viewer") and the private possession of obscenity at home. The problem is that not only the public but also the private is a "sphere of social power" of sexism. On paper and in life, pornography is thrust upon unwilling women in their homes. The distinction between public and private does not cut the same for women as for men. As a result, it is men's right to inflict pornography upon women in private that is protected.

The liberal theory underlying First Amendment law proceeds on the belief that free speech, including pornography, helps discover truth. Censorship, in its view, restricts society to partial truths. Laissez-faire might be an adequate theory of the social preconditions for knowledge in a nonhierarchical society. In a society of gender inequality, the speech of the powerful impresses its view upon the world, concealing the truth of powerlessness under a despairing acquiescence that provides the appearance of consent and makes protest inaudible as well as rare. Pornography can invent women because it has the power to make its vision into reality, which then passes, objectively, for truth. So while the First Amendment supports pornography on the belief that consensus and progress are facilitated by allowing all views, however divergent and unorthodox, it fails to notice that pornography (like the racism, including anti-Semitism, of the Nazis and the Klan) is not at all divergent or unorthodox. It is the ruling ideology. Feminism, the dissenting view, is suppressed by pornography. Thus, while defenders of pornography argue that allowing all speech, including pornography, frees the mind to fulfill itself, pornography freely enslaves women's minds and bodies inseparably, normalizing the terror that enforces silence on women's point of view.

In liberalism, speech must never be sacrificed for other social goals. But liberalism has never understood this reality of pornography: the free so-called speech of men silences the free speech of women. It is the same social goal, just other people. This is what a real inequality, a real conflict, a real disparity in social power looks like. First, women do not simply have freedom of speech on a social level. The most basic assumption underlying First Amendment adjudication is that, socially, speech is free. The First Amendment itself says, "Congress shall make no law . . . abridging the freedom of speech." Free speech exists. The problem for government is to avoid constraining that which, if unconstrained by government, is free. This tends to presuppose that whole segments of the population are not systematically silenced socially, prior to government action. Second, the law of the First Amendment comprehends that freedom of expression, in the abstract, is a system but fails to comprehend that sexism (and racism), in the concrete, are also systems. As a result, it cannot grasp that the speech of some silences the speech of others in a way that is not simply a matter of competition for airtime. That pornography chills women's expression is difficult to demonstrate empirically because silence is not eloquent. Yet on no more of the same kind of evidence, the argument that suppressing pornography might chill legitimate speech has supported its protection.

First Amendment logic has difficulty grasping harm that is not linearly caused in the "John hit Mary" sense. The idea is that words or pictures can be harmful only if they produce harm in a form that is considered an action. Words work in the province of attitudes, actions in the realm of behavior. Words cannot constitute harm in themselves—never mind libel, invasion of privacy, blackmail, bribery, conspiracy, most sexual harassment, and most discrimination. What is saying "yes" in Congress—a word or an act? What is saying "Kill" to a trained guard dog? What is its training? What is saying "You're fired" or "We have enough of your kind around here"? What is a sign that reads "Whites Only"? What is a real estate advertisement that reads "Churches Nearby"? What is a "Help Wanted—Male" ad? What is a letter that states: "Constituent interests dictate that the understudy

to my administrative assistant be a man"? What is "Sleep with me and I'll give you an 'A'"? These words, printed or spoken, are so far from legally protecting the cycle of events they actualize that they are regarded as evidence that acts occurred, in some cases as actionable in themselves. Is a woman raped by an attitude or a behavior? Which is sexual arousal? Which is cross burning? The difficulty of the distinction in the abstract has not prevented the law from acting when the consequences were seen to matter. When words are tantamount to acts, they are treated as acts.

. . .

The dominant view is that pornography must cause harm just as car accidents cause harm, or its effects are not cognizable as harm. The trouble with this individuated, atomistic, linear, exclusive, isolated, narrowly tortlike—in a word, positivistic—conception of injury is that the way pornography targets and defines women for abuse and discrimination does not work like this. It does hurt individuals, just not as individuals in a one-at-a-time sense, but as members of the group women. Individual harm is caused one woman and not another essentially as one number rather than another is caused in roulette; but on a group basis, the harm is absolutely selective and systematic. Its causality is essentially collective and totalistic and contextual. To reassert atomistic linear causality as a sine qua non of injury—you cannot be harmed unless you are harmed through this etiology—is to refuse to respond to the true nature of this specific kind of harm. Such refusals call for explanation. Morton Horowitz has written that the issue of causality in tort law is "one of the pivotal ideas in a system of legal thought that sought to separate private law from politics and to insulate the legal system from the threat of redistribution." Perhaps causality in the law of obscenity is an attempt to privatize the injury pornography does to women in order to insulate the same system from the threat of gender equality.

Women are known to be brutally coerced into pornographic performances. But so far it is only with children, usually male children, that courts see that the speech of pornographers was once someone else's life. Courts and commissions and legislatures and researchers have searched largely in vain for the injury of pornography in the mind of the (male) consumer or in "society," or in empirical correlations between variations in levels of "antisocial' acts and liberalization in obscenity laws. Speech can be regulated "in the interest of unwilling viewers, captive audiences, young children, and beleaguered neighborhoods," but the normal level of sexual force—force that is not seen as force because it is inflicted on women and called sex— has never been a policy issue in the pornography area. Until the last few years experimental research never approached the question of whether pornographic stimuli might support sexual aggression against women or whether violence per se might be sexually stimulating or have sexual sequelae. Research is just beginning on the consequences for women of sexual depictions that show consensual dominance and submission. We know the least about the impact of female-only nudity, depictions of specific acts like penetration, or sex that appears mutual in a social context of gender inequality. We know even less about why sex—that is, women— *must*, seemingly, be experienced through a traffic in pictures and words.

. . .

Because obscenity law so evades the reality of pornography, it is difficult to show that the male state, hegemonically liberal whether in the hands of conservatives or of liberals, actually protects pornography. The deception that the state is hostile to sexual derepression and eager to repress pornography, the fantasy that an authoritarian state restricts pornography rather than protects it, lay clearly exposed when the courts were confronted with the real damage pornography does to women's status and treatment as the basis for making it civilly actionable to its victims. The courts accepted the harm but held the pornography more important than those it harms—hence protected it as speech. In *American Bookseller Assn. Inc. v. Hudnut* the Seventh Circuit Court of Appeals held that an ordinance that makes the injuries of pornography actionable as sex inequality is unconstitutional under the First Amendment because it prohibits expression of a point of view.[4]

Acts became ideas and politics became morals as the court transformed coercion, force, assault, and trafficking in subordination into "thought control" and second-class citizenship on the basis of

gender into "ideas that can be expressed about sexuality."[5] Obscenity law, which is based upon nothing but value judgments about morality, was presented as the standard for constitutional point-of-viewlessness. The court saw legal intervention against acts (most of which are already crimes) as "point of view" discrimination without doubting the constitutionality of state intervention against obscenity, which has no connection with acts and is expressly defined on the basis of point of view about sex. The court saw civil action by individual women as censorship threatening freedom, yet saw no threat to freedom and no censorship in criminal prosecutions of obscenity. When is a point of view not a point of view? When it is yours—especially when your words, like those of the pornographers, are words in power. In the epistemologically hermetic doublethink of the male point of view, prohibiting advances toward sex equality under law is state neutrality. From the male standpoint, it looks neutral because the state mirrors the inequality of the social world. Under the aegis of this neutrality, state protection of pornography becomes official policy.

The law of pornography thus has the same surface theme and the same underlying theme as pornography itself. Superficially both involve morality: rules made and transgressed for purposes of sexual arousal. Actually, both are about power: the equation between the erotic and the control of women by men, *women* made and transgressed for purposes of sexual arousal. It seems essential to the kick of pornography that it be to some degree against the rules, but never truly unavailable or truly illegitimate. Thus obscenity law, like the law of rape, preserves both the value and the ability to get what it purports to devalue and restrict access to by prohibition. Obscenity law helps keep pornography sexy by putting state power—force, hierarchy—behind its purported prohibition on what men can have sexual access to. The law of obscenity is to pornography as pornography is to sex: a map that purports to be a mirror, a practice that pretends to represent a practice, a legitimation and authorization and set of directions and guiding controls that project themselves onto social reality, while purporting merely to reflect an image of what is already there. Pornography presents itself as fantasy or illusion or idea, which can be good or bad as it is accurate or inaccurate while it actually, hence accurately, distributes power. Liberal morality cannot deal with illusions that constitute reality because its theory of reality, lacking a substantive critique of the distribution of social power, cannot get behind the empirical word, truth by correspondence. On the surface, both pornography and the law of obscenity are about sex. But it is the status of women that is at stake.

Endnotes

[1] *Jacobellis v. Ohio,* 378 U.S. 184, 197 (1964) (Stewart, J., concurring).

[2] *Paris Adult Theatre I v. Slayton,* 413 U.S. 49, 67 (1973). See also "a quotation from Voltaire in the fly-leaf of a book will not constitutionally redeem an other-wise obscene publication." *Kois v. Wisconsin,* 408 U.S. 229, 231 (1972), quoted in *Miller v. California,* 413 U.S. at 25 n. 7.

[3] *Penthouse International v. McAuliffe,* 610 F. 2d 1353 (5th Cir. 1980). For a study in enforcement, see *Coble v. City of Birmingham,* 389 Sol. 2d 527 (Ala. Ct. App. 1980).

[4] *American Booksellers Assn., Inc. v. Hudnut,* 771 F. 2d 323 (7th Cir. 1985).

[5] 771 F. 2d at 328.

Study Questions

1. In *Reno v. ACLU,* the Supreme Court rejected the analogy, drawn by defenders of the Communications Decency Act, between the Internet and forms of broadcast media that have long been subject to various kinds of governmental regulation. Why does the Court reject the analogy? Are its reasons convincing?

2. Critics of obscene material on the Internet have urged that providers use filters to regulate access or similar devices to limit minors' access to web pornography. Are such restrictions consistent with the Court's argument in *Reno v. ACLU?*

3. The court in *Hudnut* declares that the Indianapolis antipornography ordinance is a form of "thought-control." How does the court arrive at this conclusion?

4. How does the *Hudnut* court respond to the feminist argument that pornography is a practice whose result is the continuation and deepening of the subordination and domination of women by men? Do you find the court's response convincing?

5. On what grounds does Feinberg criticize the courts' confusion of pornography with obscenity?

6. What, according to Feinberg, are the causal relationships between pornography (especially violent pornography) and the "cult of macho"? Is Feinberg's defense of his view of the causal relationship sound?

7. Imagine a video store run by the Ku Klux Klan. The store sells racist videos, magazines, and films with titles such as *Beat Them Niggers,* in which whites are shown (among other things) verbally abusing, beating, and urinating upon blacks. Should the distribution and sale of such materials be allowed? Is there a difference, relevant for First Amendment purposes, between these kinds of films and the examples of violent pornography described by Feinberg and MacKinnon?

8. Crenshaw agrees with those who argue that 2 Live Crew's obscenity conviction should not have been upheld. What are her reasons?

9. If misogynistic appeals to violence are not obscene, how does Crenshaw think the law of freedom of expression should be modified so as to afford some level of protection to women of color?

10. Some courts have argued for a shift in the law away from an exclusive focus upon the viewers of pornography and toward its participants, who are often victims of the industry that people like MacKinnon want to protect. In a 1982 case, the Supreme Court ruled unanimously that "child pornography"—sexually explicit films depicting children involved in sex acts—deserves no constitutional protec-

tion. The Court's argument summed up a number of factors concerning child pornography that place it outside the protection of the First Amendment: the need to safeguard the physical and psychological well-being of minors; the claim that pornographic material is "intrinsically" related to the sexual abuse of children; and the fact that child pornography has no literary, scientific, or educational value.

Could it be argued that the same factors apply in the case of women who participate in the making of pornography? If not, why not? Could it be argued that the women who participate in the pornography industry are being harmed, even though many of them may not fully realize that fact, just as the children involved in "kiddie porn" are being harmed without their awareness?

D. *Freedom of Religion*

Freedom of Religion and RFRA

In 1997, the Supreme Court ruled that the Religious Freedom Restoration Act (RFRA) was unconstitutional. The Act had been passed in response to an earlier Court ruling (see *Employment Division v. Smith* in the readings for this chapter). RFRA was intended to expand religious freedom by forcing government at all levels to accommodate the free exercise of religion, except where the government had a compelling interest of overriding importance and where the least restrictive means were used in limiting the exercise of religion. Various claims for religious accommodation had been filed under RFRA, including prisoners' arguing for the right to be served special meals or to pray during work details, and a Christian landlady's arguing for the right to refuse to rent to unmarried couples.

Although the Supreme Court ruling against RFRA turned largely on a procedural question, the case revived a contentious debate over the proper limits of religious freedom.

Accommodating Religious Free Expression

Religious freedom is protected by the Constitution in two ways: Under the so-called "Establishment" clause of the First Amendment, no level of government is permitted to designate an official church or religion; under the "Free Exercise" clause, every citizen is guaranteed the right freely to exercise his or her religion. However, general claims hide some tough questions: What constitutes a "religion"? Must a "religion" include a belief in God? Can deeply held moral or ethical convictions constitute a religion? Does government "establish a religion when it (for example) gives financial aid to activities conducted by a religious organization, or when it displays religious symbols during a holiday season? When, if ever, may government exempt a person or group from, or make special accommodations regarding, the requirement of a generally applicable law—for example, laws requiring attendance at school, payment of taxes, or service in the military, as well as those prohibiting drug use or animal sacrifice?

The readings in this section provide a brief introduction to these issues. The *Gobitis* case involved two students, ages ten and twelve, who refused to participate in a daily classroom flag salute. The Gobitis children were Jehovah's Witnesses, and believed, in the words of Billy Gobitis, "that I must not worship anything out of harmony with God's commandments . . . I do not salute the flag because I do not like my country. I love my country but I love God more." The children were expelled from school, and the father brought suit. In a famous opinion (subsequently overturned), Supreme Court Justice Felix Frankfurter upheld the flag salute requirement on the ground that it promotes national unity and that this takes priority over accommodating religious scruple. Frankfurter's justification for limiting the religious freedom of the Jehovah's Witness children should be compared with Patrick Devlin's appeal to "public morality" in the context of freedom of expression.

The *Lukumi* case also raises an issue of the free exercise of religion. In 1987, the city of Hialeah, Florida, passed an ordinance outlawing ritual animal sacrifice. The ordinance was aimed at the worshippers of the church of Santeria, a religious group with roots in the Caribbean. Practitioners of Santeria, it was claimed, believe that animal sacrifices are necessary to cure illnesses and sanctify births, deaths, and marriages. Chickens, goats, turtles, and ducks, among other animals, are killed by being stabbed through the neck. Residents of the city complained that the sacrifices could do psychological harm to children of Santeria worshippers, and the city charged that the animal carcasses were not always properly disposed of. Members of the church asserted that they could not "exercise" their religion without including the sacrificial rituals.

The Supreme Court's ruling in the *Smith* case, included here, sparked the passage of RFRA. *Smith* asks whether a state may prohibit an individual from ingesting an illegal drug when he does so as part of a bona fide religious practice. In an opinion by Justice Antonin Scalia, the Court answers that the state may forbid such religiously based conduct—at least where it does so on the basis of a law designed to apply to everyone, regardless of religious background.

The concluding essay in this section, by legal scholar Stephen Carter, looks at the problem of accommodating religious free exercise by exempting certain people and practices from the requirements of the law. Carter argues that the types of accommodations typically granted by the courts should be expanded.

43. *Minersville School District v. Gobitis*

Mr. Justice Frankfurter delivered the opinion of the Court.

A grave responsibility confronts this Court whenever in course of litigation it must reconcile the conflicting claims of liberty and authority. But when the liberty invoked is liberty of conscience, and the authority is authority to safeguard the nation's fellowship, judicial conscience is put to its severest test. Of such a nature is the present controversy.

Lillian Gobitis, aged twelve, and her brother William, aged ten, were expelled from the public schools of Minersville, Pennsylvania, for refusing to salute the national flag as part of a daily school

310 U.S. 586 (1940)
United States Supreme Court

exercise. The local Board of Education required both teachers and pupils to participate in this ceremony. The ceremony is a familiar one. The right hand is placed on the breast and the following pledge recited in unison: "I pledge allegiance to my flag, and to the Republic for which it stands; one nation indivisible, with liberty and justice for all." While the words are spoken, teachers and pupils extend their right hands in salute to the flag. The Gobitis family are affiliated with "Jehovah's Witnesses," for whom the Bible as the Word of God is the supreme authority. The children had been brought up conscientiously to believe that such a gesture of respect for the flag was forbidden by command of Scripture.[1]

The Gobitis children were of an age for which Pennsylvania makes school attendance compulsory. Thus they were denied a free education, and their parents had to put them into private schools. To be relieved of the financial burden thereby entailed, their father, on behalf of the children and in his own behalf, brought this suit. He sought to enjoin the authorities from continuing to exact participation in the flag-salute ceremony as a condition of his children's attendance at the Minersville school.

We must decide whether the requirement of participation in such a ceremony, exacted from a child who refuses upon sincere religious grounds, infringes without due process of law the liberty guaranteed by the Fourteenth Amendment.

Centuries of strife over the erection of particular dogmas as exclusive or all-comprehending faiths led to the inclusion of a guarantee for religious freedom in the Bill of Rights. The First Amendment, and the Fourteenth through its absorption of the First, sought to guard against repetition of those bitter religious struggles by prohibiting the establishment of a state religion and by securing to every sect the free exercise of its faith. So pervasive is the acceptance of this precious right that its scope is brought into question, as here, only when the conscience of individuals collides with the felt necessities of society.

Certainly the affirmative pursuit of one's convictions about the ultimate mystery of the universe and man's relation to it is placed beyond the reach of law. Government may not interfere with organized or individual expression of belief or disbelief.

Propagation of belief—or even of disbelief—in the supernatural is protected, whether in church or chapel, mosque or synagogue, tabernacle or meetinghouse. Likewise the Constitution assures generous immunity to the individual from imposition of penalties for offending, in the course of his own religious activities, the religious views of others, be they a minority or those who are dominant in government.

But the manifold character of man's relations may bring his conception of religious duty into conflict with the secular interests of his fellow-men. When does the constitutional guarantee compel exemption from doing what society thinks necessary for the promotion of some great common end, or from a penalty for conduct which appears dangerous to the general good? To state the problem is to recall the truth that no single principle can answer all of life's complexities. The right to freedom of religious belief, however dissident and however obnoxious to the cherished beliefs of others—even of a majority—is itself the denial of an absolute. But to affirm that the freedom to follow conscience has itself no limits in the life of a society would deny that very plurality of principles which, as a matter of history, underlies protection of religious toleration. Our present task, then, as so often the case with courts, is to reconcile two rights in order to prevent either from destroying the other. But, because in safeguarding conscience we are dealing with interests so subtle and so dear, every possible leeway should be given to the claims of religious faith.

In the judicial enforcement of religious freedom we are concerned with a historic concept. The religious liberty which the Constitution protects has never excluded legislation of general scope not directed against doctrinal loyalties of particular sects. Judicial nullification of legislation cannot be justified by attributing to the framers of the Bill of Rights views for which there is no historic warrant. Conscientious scruples have not, in the course of the long struggle for religious toleration, relieved the individual from obedience to a general law not aimed at the promotion or restriction of religious beliefs. The mere possession of religious convictions which contradict the relevant concerns of a political society does not relieve the citizen from the discharge of political responsibilities. The necessity for this adjustment has again and again been recognized. In a number of situations the exertion of political authority has been sustained, while basic considerations of religious freedom have been left inviolate. *Reynolds v. United States*, 98 U.S. 145. . . . In all these cases the general laws in question, upheld in their application to those who refused obedience from religious conviction, were manifestations of specific powers of government deemed by the legislature essential to secure and maintain the orderly, tranquil, and free society without which religious toleration itself is unattainable. Nor does the freedom of speech assured by Due Process move in a more absolute circle of immunity than that enjoyed by religious freedom. Even if it were assumed that freedom of speech goes beyond the historic concept of full opportunity to utter and to disseminate views, however heretical or offensive to dominant opinion, and includes freedom from conveying what may be deemed an implied but rejected affirmation, the question remains whether school children, like the Gobitis children, must be excused from conduct required of all the other children in the promotion of national cohesion. We are dealing with an interest inferior to none in the hierarchy of legal values. National unity is the basis of national security. To deny the legislature the right to select appropriate means for its attainment presents a totally different order of problem from that of the propriety of subordinating the possible ugliness of littered streets to the free expression of opinion through distribution of handbills.

. . .

Unlike the instances we have cited, the case before us is not concerned with an exertion of legislative power for the promotion of some specific need or interest of secular society—the protection of the family, the promotion of health, the common defense, the raising of public revenues to defray the cost of government. But all these specific activities of government presuppose the existence of an organized political society. The ultimate foundation of free society is the binding tie of cohesive sentiment. Such a sentiment is fostered by all those agencies of the mind and spirit which may serve to gather up the traditions of a people, transmit them from generation to generation, and thereby create that continuity of a treasured common life which constitutes

a civilization. "We live by symbols." The flag is the symbol of our national unity, transcending all internal differences, however large, within the framework of the Constitution. This Court has had occasion to say that . . . the flag is the symbol of the Nation's power, the emblem of freedom in its truest, best sense. . . . It signifies government resting on the consent of the governed; liberty regulated by law; the protection of the weak against the strong; security against the exercise of arbitrary power; and absolute safety for free institutions against foreign aggression.

. . .

The wisdom of training children in patriotic impulses by those compulsions which necessarily pervade so much of the educational process is not for our independent judgment. Even were we convinced of the folly of such a measure, such belief would be no proof of its unconstitutionality. For ourselves, we might be tempted to say that the deepest patriotism is best engendered by giving unfettered scope to the most crotchety beliefs. Perhaps it is best, even from the standpoint of those interests which ordinances like the one under review seek to promote, to give to the least popular sect leave from conformities like those here in issue. But the courtroom is not the arena for debating issues of educational policy. It is not our province to choose among competing considerations in the subtle process of securing effective loyalty to the traditional ideals of democracy, while respecting at the same time individual idiosyncrasies among a people so diversified in racial origins and religious allegiances. So to hold would in effect make us the school board for the country. That authority has not been given to this Court, nor should we assume it.

. . .

The preciousness of the family relation, the authority and independence which give dignity to parenthood, indeed the enjoyment of all freedom, presuppose the kind of ordered society which is summarized by our flag. A society which is dedicated to the preservation of these ultimate values of civilization may in self-protection utilize the educational process for inculcating those almost unconscious feelings which bind men together in a comprehending loyalty, whatever may be their lesser differences and difficulties. That is to say, the process may be utilized so long as men's right to believe as they please, to win others to their way of belief, and their right to assemble in their chosen places of worship for the devotional ceremonies of their faith, are all fully respected.

Reversed.

Dissent

Mr. Justice Stone, dissenting:

I think the judgment below should be affirmed.

Two youths, now fifteen and sixteen years of age, are by the judgment of this Court held liable to expulsion from the public schools and to denial of all publicly supported educational privileges because of their refusal to yield to the compulsion of a law which commands their participation in a school ceremony contrary to their religious convictions. They and their father are citizens and have not exhibited by any action or statement of opinion, any disloyalty to the Government of the United States. They are ready and willing to obey all its laws which do not conflict with what they sincerely believe to be the higher commandments of God. It is not doubted that these convictions are religious, that they are genuine, or that the refusal to yield to the compulsion of the law is in good faith and with all sincerity. It would be a denial of their faith as well as the teachings of most religions to say that children of their age could not have religious convictions.

The law which is thus sustained is unique in the history of Anglo-American legislation. It does more than suppress freedom of speech and more than prohibit the free exercise of religion, which concededly are forbidden by the First Amendment and are violations of the liberty guaranteed by the Fourteenth. For by this law the state seeks to coerce these children to express a sentiment which, as they interpret it, they do not entertain, and which violates their deepest religious convictions. It is not denied that such compulsion is a prohibited infringement of personal liberty, freedom of speech and religion, guaranteed by the Bill of Rights, except in so far as it may be justified and supported as a proper exercise of the state's power over pub-

lic education. Since the state, in competition with parents, may through teaching in the public schools indoctrinate the minds of the young, it is said that in aid of its undertaking to inspire loyalty and devotion to constituted authority and the flag which symbolizes it, it may coerce the pupil to make affirmation contrary to his belief and in violation of his religious faith. And, finally, it is said that since the Minersville School Board and others are of the opinion that the country will be better served by conformity than by the observance of religious liberty which the constitution prescribes, the courts are not free to pass judgment on the Board's choice.

Concededly the constitutional guaranties of personal liberty are not always absolutes. Government has a right to survive and powers conferred upon it are not necessarily set at naught by the express prohibitions of the Bill of Rights. It may make war and raise armies. To that end it may compel citizens to give military service, and subject them to military training despite their religious objections. It may suppress religious practices dangerous to morals, and presumably those also which are inimical to public safety, health and good order. But it is a long step, and one which I am unable to take, to the position that government may, as a supposed educational measure and as a means of disciplining the young, compel public affirmations which violate their religious conscience.

The very fact that we have constitutional guaranties of civil liberties and the specificity of their command where freedom of speech and of religion are concerned require some accommodation of the powers which government normally exercises, when no question of civil liberty is involved, to the constitutional demand that those liberties be protected against the action of government itself. The state concededly has power to require and control the education of its citizens, but it cannot by a general law compelling attendance at public schools preclude attendance at a private school adequate in its instruction, where the parent seeks to secure for the child the benefits of religious instruction not provided by the public school. And only recently we have held that the state's authority to control its public streets by generally applicable regulations is not an absolute to which free speech must yield, and cannot be made the medium of its suppression, any more than can its authority to penalize littering of the streets by a general law be used to suppress the distribution of handbills as a means of communicating ideas to their recipients.

In these cases it was pointed out that where there are competing demands of the interests of government and of liberty under the Constitution, and where the performance of governmental functions is brought into conflict with specific constitutional restrictions, there must, when that is possible, be reasonable accommodation between them so as to preserve the essentials of both and that it is the function of courts to determine whether such accommodation is reasonably possible. In the cases just mentioned the Court was of opinion that there were ways enough to secure the legitimate state end without infringing the asserted immunity, or that the inconvenience caused by the inability to secure that end satisfactorily through other means, did not outweigh freedom of speech or religion. So here, even if we believe that such compulsions will contribute to national unity, there are other ways to teach loyalty and patriotism which are the sources of national unity, than by compelling the pupil to affirm that which he does not believe and by commanding a form of affirmance which violates his religious convictions. Without recourse to such compulsion the state is free to compel attendance at school and require teaching by instruction and study of all in our history and in the structure and organization of our government, including the guaranties of civil liberty which tend to inspire patriotism and love of country. I cannot say that government here is deprived of any interest or function which it is entitled to maintain at the expense of the protection of civil liberties by requiring it to resort to the alternatives which do not coerce an affirmation of belief.

The guaranties of civil liberty are but guaranties of freedom of the human mind and spirit and of reasonable freedom and opportunity to express them. They presuppose the right of the individual to hold such opinions as he will and to give them reasonably free expression, and his freedom, and that of the state as well, to teach and persuade others by the communication of ideas. The very

essence of the liberty which they guaranty is the freedom of the individual from compulsion as to what he shall think and what he shall say, at least where the compulsion is to bear false witness to his religion. If these guaranties are to have any meaning they must, I think, be deemed to withhold from the state any authority to compel belief or the expression of it where that expression violates religious convictions, whatever may be the legislative view of the desirability of such compulsion.

History teaches us that there have been but few infringements of personal liberty by the state which have not been justified, as they are here, in the name of righteousness and the public good, and few which have not been directed, as they are now, at politically helpless minorities. The framers were not unaware that under the system which they created most governmental curtailments of personal liberty would have the support of a legislative judgment that the public interest would be better served by its curtailment than by its constitutional protection. I cannot conceive that in prescribing, as limitations upon the powers of government, the freedom of the mind and spirit secured by the explicit guaranties of freedom of speech and religion, they intended or rightly could have left any latitude for a legislative judgment that the compulsory expression of belief which violates religious convictions would better serve the public interest than their protection. The Constitution may well elicit expressions of loyalty to it and to the government which it created, but it does not command such expressions or otherwise give any indication that compulsory expressions of loyalty play any such part in our scheme of government as to override the constitutional protection of freedom of speech and religion. And while such expressions of loyalty, when voluntarily given, may promote national unity, it is quite another matter to say that their compulsory expression by children in violation of their own and their parents' religious convictions can be regarded as playing so important a part in our national unity as to leave school boards free to exact it despite the constitutional guarantee of freedom of religion. The very terms of the Bill of Rights preclude, it seems to me, any reconciliation of such compulsions with the constitutional guaranties by a legislative declaration that they are more important to the public welfare than the Bill of Rights.

But even if this view be rejected and it is considered that there is some scope for the determination by legislatures whether the citizen shall be compelled to give public expression of such sentiments contrary to his religion, I am not persuaded that we should refrain from passing upon the legislative judgment "as long as the remedial channels of the democratic process remain open and unobstructed." This seems to me no less than the surrender of the constitutional protection of the liberty of small minorities to the popular will. We have previously pointed to the importance of a searching judicial inquiry into the legislative judgment in situations where prejudice against discrete and insular minorities may tend to curtail the operation of those political processes ordinarily to be relied on to protect minorities. And until now we have not hesitated similarly to scrutinize legislation restricting the civil liberty of racial and religious minorities although no political process was affected. Here we have such a small minority entertaining in good faith a religious belief, which is such a departure from the usual course of human conduct, that most persons are disposed to regard it with little toleration or concern. In such circumstances careful scrutiny of legislative efforts to secure conformity of belief and opinion by a compulsory affirmation of the desired belief, is especially needful if civil rights are to receive any protection. Tested by this standard, I am not prepared to say that the right of this small and helpless minority, including children having a strong religious conviction, whether they understand its nature or not, to refrain from an expression obnoxious to their religion, is to be overborne by the interest of the state in maintaining discipline in the schools.

The Constitution expresses more than the conviction of the people that democratic processes must be preserved at all costs. It is also an expression of faith and a command that freedom of mind and spirit must be preserved, which government must obey, if it is to adhere to that justice and moderation without which no free government can exist. For this reason it would seem that legislation which operates to repress the religious freedom of small minorities, which is admittedly within the scope of the protection of the Bill of Rights, must at least be subject to the same judicial scrutiny as legislation which we have recently held to infringe the constitutional liberty of religious and racial minorities.

With such scrutiny I cannot say that the inconveniences which may attend some sensible adjustment of school discipline in order that the religious convictions of these children may be spared, presents a problem so momentous or pressing as to outweigh the freedom from compulsory violation of religious faith which has been thought worthy of constitutional protection.

Endnotes

[1] Reliance is especially placed on the following verses from Chapter 20 of Exodus:

"3. Thou shalt have no other gods before me.

"4. Thou shalt not make unto thee any graven image, or any likeness of any thing that is in heaven above, or that is in the earth beneath, or that is in the water under the earth:

"5. Thou shalt not bow down thyself to them, nor serve them: . . . "

44. *Church of the Lukumi Babalu Aye v. City of Hialeah*

Justice Kennedy delivered the opinion of the Court.

[This] case involves practices of the Santeria religion, which originated in the nineteenth century. When hundreds of thousands of members of the Yoruba people were brought as slaves from eastern Africa to Cuba, their traditional African religion absorbed significant elements of Roman Catholicism. The resulting syncretion, or fusion, is Santeria, "the way of the saints." The Cuban Yoruba express their devotion to spirits, called orishas. [The] Santeria faith teaches that every individual has a destiny from God, a destiny fulfilled with the aid and energy of the orishas. The basis of the Santeria religion is the nurture of a personal relation with the orishas, and one of the principal forms of devotion is an animal sacrifice. [According] to Santeria teaching, the orishas are powerful but not immortal. They depend for survival on the sacrifice. Sacrifices are performed at birth, marriage, and death rites, for the cure of the sick, for the initiation of new members and priests, and during an annual celebration. Animals sacrificed in Santeria rituals include chickens, pigeons, doves, ducks, guinea pigs, goats, sheep, and turtles. The animals are killed by the cutting of the carotid arteries in the neck. The sacrificed animal is cooked and eaten, except after healing and death rituals. Santeria adherents faced widespread persecution in Cuba, so the religion and its rituals were practiced in secret. The open practice of Santeria and its rites remains infrequent.

[The Church's] announcement of plans to open a Santeria church in Hialeah prompted the city council to hold an emergency public session on June 9, 1987. [The] city council adopted Resolution 87–66, which noted the "concern" expressed by residents of the city "that certain religions may propose to engage in practices which are inconsistent with public morals, peace or safety," and declared that "the City reiterates its commitment to a prohibition against any and all acts of any and all religious groups which are inconsistent with public morals, peace or safety." [In] September 1987, the city council adopted three substantive ordinances addressing the issue of religious animal sacrifice. Ordinance 87–52 defined "sacrifice" as "to unnecessarily kill, torment, torture, or mutilate an animal in a public or private ritual or ceremony not for the primary purpose of food consumption," and prohibited owning or possessing an animal "intending to use such animal for food purposes." It restricted application of this prohibition, however, to any individual or group that "kills, slaughters or sacrifices animals for any type of ritual, regardless of whether or not the flesh or blood of the animal is to be consumed." The ordinance contained an exemption for slaughtering by "licensed establishments" of animals "specifically raised for food purposes." [Ordinance] 87–71 [defined] sacrifice as had Ordinance 87–52, and then provided that "it shall be unlawful for any person, persons, corporations or associations to sacrifice any animal within the corporate limits of the City of Hialeah, Florida." The final Ordinance, 87–72, defined "slaughter" as "the killing of animals for food" and prohibited slaughter outside of areas zoned for slaughterhouse use. The ordinance provided an exemption, however, for the slaughter or processing for sale of "small numbers of hogs and/or cattle per week in accordance with an exemption provided by state law." All ordinances and resolutions passed the city council by unanimous vote. Violations [were] punishable by fines not exceeding $500 or imprisonment not exceeding 60 days, or both.

[At] a minimum, the protections of the Free Exercise Clause pertain if the law at issue discriminates against some or all religious beliefs or regulates or prohibits conduct because it is undertaken for religious reasons. Indeed, it was "historical instances of religious persecution and intolerance

508 U.S. 520, 113 S.Ct. 2217, 124 L.Ed.2d 472 (1993).

that gave concern to those who drafted the Free Exercise Clause." These principles, though not often at issue in our Free Exercise Clause cases, have played a role in some.

[If] the object of a law is to infringe upon or restrict practices because of their religious motivation, the law is not neutral; and it is invalid unless it is justified by a compelling interest and is narrowly tailored to advance that interest. To determine the object of a law, we must begin with its text, for the minimum requirement of neutrality is that a law not discriminate on its face. [Petitioners] contend that three of the ordinances fail this test of facial neutrality because they use the words "sacrifice" and "ritual," words with strong religious connotations. We agree that these words are consistent with the claim of facial discrimination, but the argument is not conclusive. The words "sacrifice" and "ritual" have a religious origin, but current use admits also of secular meanings. [But] facial neutrality is not determinative. [The] Free Exercise Clause protects against governmental hostility which is masked, as well as overt.

[The] record in this case compels the conclusion that suppression of the central element of the Santeria worship service was the object of the ordinances. [The June 9 resolution aimed at] "certain religions" [and] it cannot be maintained that city officials had in mind a religion other than Santeria. It is [also] a necessary conclusion that almost the only conduct subject to ordinances 87–40, 87–52, and 87–71 is the religious exercise of Santeria church members. [Ordinance] 87–71 excludes almost all killings of animals except for religious sacrifice, and the primary purpose requirement narrows the proscribed category even further, in particular by exempting Kosher slaughter. Operating in similar fashion is Ordinance 87–52, which prohibits the "possession, sacrifice, or slaughter" of an animal with the "intent to use such animal for food purposes" [but exempts] "any licensed [food] establishment" with regard to "any animals which are specifically raised for food purposes," if the activity is permitted by zoning and other laws. This exception, too, seems intended to cover Kosher slaughter. [Ordinance] 87–40 incorporates the Florida animal cruelty statute. Its prohibition is broad on its face, punishing "whoever . . . unneces-

sarily . . . kills any animal." The city claims that this ordinance is the epitome of a neutral prohibition. [But the city] deem[s] [k]illings for religious reasons [unnecessary but] deems hunting, slaughter of animals for food, eradication of insects and pests, and euthanasia as necessary. [The city's] application of the ordinance's test of necessity devalues religious reasons for killing by judging them to be of lesser import than nonreligious reasons. Thus, religious practice is being singled out for discriminatory treatment.

[The] legitimate governmental interests in protecting the public health and preventing cruelty to animals could be addressed by restrictions stopping far short of a flat prohibition of all Santeria sacrificial practice. [Counsel] for the city conceded at oral argument that, under the ordinances, Santeria sacrifices would be illegal even if they occurred in licensed, inspected, and zoned slaughterhouses. [With] regard to the city's interest in ensuring the adequate care of animals, regulation of conditions and treatment, regardless of why an animal is kept, is the logical response to the city's concern, not a prohibition on possession for the purpose of sacrifice. . . .

. . . In determining if the object of a law is a neutral one under the Free Exercise Clause, we can also find guidance in our equal protection cases. [Here], as in equal protection cases, we may determine the city council's object from both direct and circumstantial evidence. [The] minutes and taped excerpts of the June 9 session, both of which are in the record, evidence significant hostility exhibited by residents, members of the city council, and other city officials toward the Santeria religion and its practice of animal sacrifice. The public crowd that attended the June 9 meetings interrupted statements by council members critical of Santeria with cheers and the brief comments of [the Church's leader] with taunts. When [a council member supporting the ordinances] stated that in prerevolution Cuba "people were put in jail for practicing this religion," the audience applauded. [One council member said that the] "Bible says we are allowed to sacrifice an animal for consumption," [and] continued, "but for any other purposes, I don't believe that the Bible allows that." [The] chaplain of the Hialeah Police Department told the city council that Santeria was a sin, "foolishness," "an abomination to the Lord," and the worship of "demons." [This] history discloses the object of the ordinances to target animal sacrifice by Santeria worshippers because of its religious motivation.

In sum, [the] ordinances had as their object the suppression of religion. The pattern we have recited discloses animosity to Santeria adherents and their religious practices; the ordinances by their own terms target this religious exercise; the texts of the ordinances were gerrymandered with care to proscribe religious killings of animals but to exclude almost all secular killings; and the ordinances suppress much more religious conduct than is necessary in order to achieve the legitimate ends asserted in their defense.

[A] law burdening religious practice that is not neutral or not of general application must undergo the most rigorous of scrutiny. [It] follows from what we have already said that these ordinances cannot withstand this scrutiny. First, even were the governmental interests compelling, [all] four ordinances are overbroad or underinclusive. [The] absence of narrow tailoring suffices to establish the invalidity of the ordinances. [Moreover,] [w]here government restricts only conduct protected by the First Amendment and fails to enact feasible measures to restrict other conduct producing substantial harm or alleged harm of the same sort, the interest given in justification of the restriction is not compelling.

---

45. *Employment Division, Department of Human Resources of Oregon v. Smith*

Justice Scalia delivered the opinion of the Court.

This case requires us to decide whether the Free Exercise Clause of the First Amendment permits the State of Oregon to include religiously inspired peyote use within the reach of its general criminal prohibition on use of that drug, and thus permits the State to deny unemployment benefits to persons dismissed from their jobs because of such religiously inspired use. . . .

Respondents Alfred Smith and Galen Black were fired from their jobs with a private drug rehabilitation organization because they ingested peyote for sacramental purposes at a ceremony of the Native American Church, of which both are members. When respondents applied to petitioner Employment Division for unemployment compensation, they were determined to be ineligible for benefits because they have been discharged for work-related "misconduct."

. . .

The Free Exercise Clause of the First Amendment, which has been made applicable to the States by incorporation into the Fourteenth Amendment . . . , provides that "Congress shall make no law respecting an establishment of religion, or *prohibiting the free exercise thereof*. . . ." U.S. Const. Am. I (emphasis added). The free exercise of religion means, first and foremost, the right to believe and profess whatever religious doctrine one desires. . . .

But the "exercise of religion" often involves not only belief and profession but the performance of (or abstention from) physical acts: assembling with others for a worship service, participating in sacramental use of bread and wine, proselytizing, abstaining from certain foods or certain modes of transportation. It would be true, we think (though

88-1213; 58 U.S. LW. 4435 (1990)
United States Supreme Court

no case of ours has involved the point), that a state would be "prohibiting the free exercise [of religion]" if it sought to ban such acts or abstentions only when they are engaged in for religious reasons, or only because of the religious belief that they display. It would doubtless be unconstitutional, for example, to ban the casting of "statues that are to be used for worship purposes," or to prohibit bowing down before a golden calf.

Respondents in the present case, however, seek to carry the meaning of "prohibiting the free exercise [of religion]" one large step further. They contend that their religious motivation for using peyote places them beyond the reach of a criminal law that is not specifically directed at their religious practice, and that is concededly constitutional as applied to those who use the drug for other reasons. They assert, in other words, that "prohibiting the free exercise [of religion]" includes requiring any individual to observe a generally applicable law that requires (or forbids) the performance of an act that his religious belief forbids (or requires). As a textual matter, we do not think the words must be given that meaning. It is no more necessary to regard the collection of a general tax, for example, as "prohibiting the free exercise [of religion]" by those citizens who believe support of organized government to be sinful, than it is to regard the same tax as "abridging the freedom . . . of the press" of those publishing companies that must pay the tax as a condition of staying in business. It is a permissible reading of the text, in the one case as in the other, to say that if prohibiting the exercise of religion (or burdening the activity of printing) is not the object of the tax but merely the incidental effect of a generally applicable and otherwise valid provision, the First Amendment has not been offended. . . .

Our decisions reveal that the latter reading is the correct one. We have never held that an individual's religious beliefs excuse him from compliance with an otherwise valid law prohibiting conduct that the State is free to regulate. On the contrary, the record of more than a century of our free exercise jurisprudence contradicts that proposition. As described succinctly by Justice Frankfurter in *Minersville School Dist. Bd. Of Educ. v. Gobitis*, 310 U.S. 586, 594–595 (1940): "Conscientious scruples have not, in the course of the long struggle for religious toleration, relieved the individual from obedience to a general law not aimed at the promotion or restriction of religious beliefs. The mere possession of religious convictions which contradict the relevant concerns of a political society does not relieve the citizen from the discharge of political responsibilities (footnote omitted)." We first had occasion to assert that principle in *Reynolds v. United States*, 98 U.S. 145 (1879), where we rejected the claim that criminal laws against polygamy could not be constitutionally applied to those whose religion commanded the practice. "Laws," we said, "are made for the government of actions, and while they cannot interfere with mere religious belief and opinions, they may with practices. . . . Can a man excuse his practices to the contrary because of his religious belief? To permit this would be to make the professed doctrines of religious belief superior to the law of the land, and in effect to permit every citizen to become a law unto himself."

. . .

The only decisions in which we have held that the First Amendment bars application of a neutral, generally applicable law to religiously motivated action have involved not the Free Exercise Clause alone, but the Free Exercise Clause in conjunction with other constitutional protections, such as freedom of speech and of the press. . . .

The present case does not present such a hybrid situation, but a free exercise claim unconnected with any communicative activity or parental right. Respondents urge us to hold, quite simply, that when otherwise prohibitable conduct is accompanied by religious convictions, not only the convictions but the conduct itself must be free from governmental regulation. We have never held that, and decline to do so now. There being no contention that Oregon's drug law represents an attempt to regulate religious beliefs, the communication of religious beliefs, or the raising of one's children in those beliefs, the rule to which we have adhered ever since *Reynolds* plainly controls.

. . .

Because respondents' ingestion of peyote was prohibited under Oregon law, and because that prohibition is constitutional, Oregon may, consistent with the Free Exercise Clause, deny respondents unemployment compensation when their dismissal results from use of the drug. The decision of the Oregon Supreme Court is accordingly reversed.

It is so ordered.

. . .

Justice Blackmun, with whom Justice Brennan and Justice Marshall join, dissenting. . . .

Until today, I thought this was a settled and inviolate principle of this Court's First Amendment jurisprudence. The majority, however, perfunctorily dismisses it as a "constitutional anomaly." . . . As carefully detailed in Justice O'Connor's concurring opinion, . . . the majority is able to arrive at this view only by mischaracterizing this Court's precedents. The Court discards leading free exercise cases such as *Cantwell v. Connecticut*, 310 U.S. 296 (1940), and *Wisconsin v. Yoder*, 406 U.S. 205 (1972), as "hybrid." . . . The Court views traditional free exercise analysis as somehow inapplicable to criminal prohibitions (as opposed to conditions on the receipt of benefits), and to state laws of general applicability (as opposed, presumably, to laws that expressly single out religious practices). . . . The Court cites cases in which, due to various exceptional circumstances, we found strict scrutiny inapposite, to hint that the Court has repudiated that standard altogether. . . . In short, it effectuates a wholesale overturning of settled law concerning the Religion Clauses of our Constitution. One hopes that the Court is aware of the consequences, and that its result is not a product of overreaction to the serious problems the country's drug crisis has generated.

This distorted view of our precedents leads the majority to conclude that strict scrutiny of a state law burdening the free exercise of religion is a "luxury" that a well-ordered society cannot afford, . . . and that the repression of minority religions is an "unavoidable consequence of democratic government." . . . I do not believe the founders thought their dearly bought freedom from religious persecution a "luxury," but an essential element of liberty—and they could not have thought religious intolerance "unavoidable," for they drafted the Religion Clauses precisely in order to avoid that intolerance. . . .

In weighing respondents' clear interest in the free exercise of their religion against Oregon's asserted interest in enforcing its drug laws, it is important to articulate in precise terms the state interest involved. It is not the State's broad interest in fighting the critical "war on drugs" that must be weighed against respondents' claim, but the state's narrow interest in refusing to make an exception for the religious, ceremonial use of peyote. . . .

. . . Failure to reduce the competing interests to the same plane of generality tends to distort the weighing process in the State's favor. . . .

Similarly, this Court's prior decisions have not allowed a government to rely on mere speculation about potential harms, but have demanded evidentiary support for a refusal to allow a religious exception. . . .

. . . In this case, the State's justification for refusing to recognize an exception to its criminal laws for religious peyote use is entirely speculative.

The State proclaims an interest in protecting the health and safety of its citizens from the dangers of unlawful drugs. It offers, however, no evidence that the religious use of peyote has ever harmed anyone. . . .

The carefully circumscribed ritual context in which respondents used peyote is far removed from the irresponsible and unrestricted recreational use of unlawful drugs. The Native American Church's internal restrictions on, and supervision of, its members' use of peyote substantially obviate the State's health and safety concerns. . . .

Moreover, just as in *Yoder*, the values and interests of those seeking a religious exemption in this case are congruent, to a great degree, with those the State seeks to promote through its drug laws. . . .

. . . Not only does the Church's doctrine forbid nonreligious use of peyote; it also generally advocates self-reliance, familial responsibility, and abstinence from alcohol. . . .

. . . There is considerable evidence that the spiritual and social support provided by the Church has been effective in combating the tragic effects of alcoholism on the Native American population.

Respondents believe, and their sincerity has *never* been at issue, that the peyote plant embodies their deity, and eating it is an act of worship and communion. Without peyote, they could not enact the essential ritual of their religion. . . .

If Oregon can constitutionally prosecute them for this act of worship, they, like the Amish, may be "forced to migrate to some other and more tolerant region." *Yoder*, 406 U.S., at 218. This potentially devastating impact must be viewed in light of the federal policy—reached in reaction to many years of religious persecution and intolerance—of protecting the religious freedom of Native Americans. . . .

For these reasons, I conclude that Oregon's interest in enforcing its drug laws against religious use of peyote is not sufficiently compelling to outweigh respondents' right to the free exercise of their religion. Since the State could not constitutionally enforce its criminal prohibition against respondents, the interests underlying the State's drug laws cannot justify its denial of unemployment benefits. . . .

. . . The State of Oregon cannot, consistently with the Free Exercise Clause, deny respondents unemployment benefits.

I dissent.

---

46. *The Accommodation of Religion*

Stephen L. Carter

To be consistent with the Founders' vision and coherent in modern religiously pluralistic America, the religion clauses should be read to help avoid tyranny—that is, to sustain and nurture the religions as independent centers of power, the democratic intermediaries we have been discussing. To do that, the clauses must be interpreted to do more than protect the religions against explicit discrimination. Nowadays, the government hardly ever adopts laws aimed at burdening particular religions. Consequently, the question of religious freedom arises most frequently when the religious ask for exemptions under the Free Exercise Clause from laws that apply to everybody else. And it must not be missed that those "laws that apply to everybody else" often reflect, albeit implicitly, the values and teachings of the nation's dominant religious traditions.

Consider an example: virtually unnoticed in the brouhaha surrounding George Bush's 1992 Christmas Eve pardons of Caspar Weinberger and other officials implicated in the Iran-Contra scandal were pardons for two Jehovah's Witnesses whose crime was refus-

ing to register for military service in the 1940s and 1950s. The law has long allowed the Witnesses, and others with religious objections to combat, to register and then seek "conscientious objector" status; but it does not exempt from the registration requirement itself those with moral objections to war.

By seeking an exemption from a law that applies to everybody else, the war resisters are asking for what is called an "accommodation" of their religious belief. A few constitutional scholars—not many—believe that granting accommodations violates the Establishment Clause, because it provides to the religious something that others cannot have. President Bush's pardons of the Witnesses, then, might be seen as a version of religious preferment in which the government must not engage.

The Supreme Court, fortunately, has never accepted the idea that all accommodations are unconstitutional. So the government can generally allow religious exemptions, as the Congress did in the statute allowing the religious to wear unobtrusive religious apparel while on active military duty. However, after a brief flowering of judicially created exemptions, the Court has looked increasingly askance at claims of a free exercise right to violate laws that everyone else must obey. The most notable

From *The Culture of Disbelief* by Stephen L. Carter.

recent example is the Court's 1990 decision in *Employment Division v. Smith*, which upheld the application of a state antidrug policy to state employees who, as members of the Native American church, were required to use peyote during religious rituals.

In this [essay], I argue for a broader understanding of religious freedom and, in consequence, a wider set of religious exemptions from laws of general application. In no other way can we enable the religions to stand as intermediaries between sovereign and citizen, thus limiting the prospect of majoritarian tyranny; and in no other way can we translate the Founders' ideal of religious freedom in a relatively simple society into a new ideal for a new era, one characterized by a regulatory regime far more intrusive than the Founders could possibly have contemplated.

What are Accommodations?

The accommodation of a religious group's faith traditions in an otherwise applicable legal framework can best be envisioned as a from of affirmative action. Recognizing both the unique historical circumstances of the religions and the importance of nurturing their continued existence, the state chooses to grant them a form of differential treatment. When President Bush pardoned the Jehovah's Witnesses, he was not endorsing their religious claims, but he was seeking ways to accommodate them within a political structure that generally favors the adherents of the mainstream religions.

Indeed, the domination of our politics by citizens raised in the mainstream religions helps explain why accommodations are so often necessary. Consider for a moment the Supreme Court's 1990 decision in *Employment Division v. Smith*.[1] The case involved the dismissal of two state employees who had violated policy by using a controlled substance, peyote. The employees protested that the Free Exercise Clause was a shield, because they had used peyote as part of a religious ritual. The majority scoffed at this claim, not so much disbelieving it as disregarding it: the fact that the peyote use had religious significance, the Court said, was irrelevant, as long as the state law was not "an attempt to regulate religious beliefs, the communication of religious beliefs, or the raising of one's children in those beliefs"—which, plainly, it was not.[2]

Employment Division v. Smith is a much criticized—and justly criticized—decision, and it shows clearly just where the current Court's Free Exercise jurisprudence is heading: toward a clear separation of church and self, a world in which citizens who adopt religious practices at variance with official state policy are properly made subject to the coercive authority of the state, which can, without fear of judicial intervention, pressure them to change those practices.

Formally, the *Smith* decision turned on the question of whether the Free Exercise Clause imposed the weightiest constitutional burden—the requirement that the state demonstrate a "compelling" interest—before the courts would uphold a seemingly neutral statute that interfered with the practice of a religion. The *Smith* majority lamented that insisting on a heightened standard "would open the prospect of constitutionally required religious exemptions from civic obligations of almost every conceivable kind." One can understand the Court's worry about how to stay off of the slippery slope—*if peyote, why not cocaine? If the Native American Church, why not the Matchbook Cover Church of the Holy Peyote Plant?*—but the implications of the decision are unsettling. If the state bears no special burden to justify its infringement on religious practice, as long as the challenged statute is a neutral one, then the only protection a religious group receives is against legislation directed at that group. But legislation directed at a particular religious group, even in the absence of the Free Exercise Clause, presumably would be prohibited by the Equal Protection Clause.

After *Smith* was decided, critics tumbled all over one another in the rush to be the first to offer the obvious hypothetical situation. Prohibition, implemented by the Volstead Act of 1919, included an exemption for religious use of wine—but suppose it had not. If a Christian or Jew were prosecuted for defiance of the act, would a conviction really be sustained against a free exercise challenge? (At least one dry state, Oklahoma, apparently made no exception during Prohibition for religious use of wine, for the state was dominated by Baptists who did not use wine and who saw it as an indulgence of Catholics and Jews.)

Perhaps the dissenting Christian or Jew would have to go to jail, because a nation prepared to pass a Volstead Act without a religious exemption would be a nation no longer as heavily dominated by its religious mainline. And that, of course, is the point of the story. In America as it is today, the hypothetical case about the prohibition on the religious use of wine is a hypothetical case that would never occur precisely because the nation's dominant religious traditions—Catholic, Protestant, and Jewish—all use wine for religious purpose. The great majority of Americans profess one of these faiths, and they will not countenance a state effort to shut down their religious observances; indeed, the state would never try. As the legal scholar Kathleen Sullivan has pointed out, "not a single religious exemption claim has ever reached the Supreme Court from a mainstream Christian religious practitioner."[3]

The judgment against the Native American Church, however, demonstrates that the political process will protect only the mainstream religions, not the many smaller groups that exist at the margins. It is as though the relevant legal principles have been designed in order to uphold state regulations infringing on faith traditions that lie far from the mainstream; perhaps the courts are unable to appreciate the concern about 'incidental" infringements precisely because judges are not drawn from religious traditions likely to suffer them.

Justice Antonin Scalia, perhaps unknowingly, made this precise point at the conclusion of his opinion for the *Smith* majority:

> It may fairly be said that leaving accommodation to the political process will place at a relative disadvantage those religious practices that are not widely engaged in; but that unavoidable consequence of democratic government must be preferred to a system in which each conscience is a law unto itself or in which judges weigh the social importance of all laws against the centrality of all religious beliefs.[4]

What Justice Scalia misses is that it was in order to avoid this "unavoidable consequence of democratic government" that the Free Exercise Clause was crafted in the first place. The fact that the defense of religious liberty burdens the courts is hardly a reason, as he implies it is, to forbear.

A more practical danger also lurks, one that the legal scholar Frederick Mark Gedicks has

noted: "Without exemptions, some religious groups will likely be crushed by the weight of majoritarian law and culture. Such groups pose no threat to order. However, majoritarian dominance could radicalize some believers into destabilizing, antisocial activity, including violence."[5] Of course, the dominant culture can do what it has always done in the face of threats to order, especially threats from people the nation itself has oppressed, such as Native Americans and slaves: it can declare the marginalized and violent dissenters to be criminals, and thus rid itself of them, their movements, and their religions all at once.

The Reduction of Religion

Smith is part of a recent and unfortunate line of cases that reduce the scope of the Free Exercise Clause until it lacks independent content, forbidding by its own force no more than do the document's other clauses that protect individual rights (here, equal protection, in other cases, free speech or assembly). So, for example, the Court has held that religious people (*not* religions as such) have the rights to proselytize or seek contributions without government permission;[6] to give sermons without an official license;[7] and to meet and worship without first seeking state approval.[8] All of these rights resemble, and perhaps are identical to, rights that would be upheld on free speech grounds even if there were no religious freedom clause. In a sense, this might be seen as a triumph. Justice William Brennan, in a slightly different context, has put the matter this way: "religionists, no less than members of any other group," should "enjoy the full measure of protection afforded speech, association and political activity generally."[9] However, this glowing account of the similarity between speech rights and religion rights masks a danger. The question is whether those are the only rights that religionists hold. For the cases upholding religiously motivated actions that look like other protected speech exemplify what the legal scholar Mark Tushnet has labeled the "reduction principle" of religious freedom, a doctrine holding "that religious belief is indistinguishable from other types of belief, so that neither the free exercise nor the establishment clause constrains governmental action any differently than the free speech clause does."[10]

Indeed, Justice Scalia's focus in his majority opinion on the ability to *communicate* religious beliefs, whether to others or to one's progeny, fits the traditional free speech model so snugly that one can assume that those protections would be available even if there were no Free Exercise Clause. The vision of the clause as protecting communicative acts rather than acts of worship or public acts carries with it precisely the message that the separation of church and self entails: you are free to believe as you like, but, for goodness sake, don't act on it!

Now, one will not find many serious scholars of the Free Exercise Clause who find *Smith* convincingly reasoned, and it does seem inconsistent with earlier cases in which the court did command accommodations of religious belief. For example, the Old Order Amish won a rather spectacular victory when, in *Wisconsin v. Yoder*,[11] the Justices allowed them to cease sending their children to school after the eighth grade. And then there is the challenging line of cases that began with *Sherbert v. Verner*, wherein the Justices ruled that if an employer refuses to accommodate the religious needs of an employee and the employee is subsequently dismissed, the state cannot deny unemployment compensation.[12]

But those decisions seem increasingly shaky. The Justices have refused to extend *Yoder*-type protections to any other group, or, for the Old Order Amish, to any other activity. As for *Sherbert*, the Justices warned, in *Frazee v. Illinois Department of Employment Security* (1989), that the protection of religiously based refusals to work (at least on Sunday) might vanish if "Sunday shopping, or Sunday sporting, for that matter, [would] grind to a halt."[13] In other words, if accommodating a religious tradition is inconvenient, no accommodation is necessary.

In light of reasoning of this kind, it is small wonder the Justices showed such little sympathy for the Yurok, Karok, and Talowa Indians who challenged the Forest Service's decision to allow a road to be built through an area used by the tribes for sacred rituals. [T]he court, in *Lyng v. Northwest Indian Cemetery Protective Association*, ruled that even though road building might have "devastating effects" on the Indians' religious practices, "government simply could not operate" if forced to "satisfy every citizen's religious needs and desires."[14] Again, as in the case of the Native American Church, the court seems to fear the slippery slope. After all, were the Court to require the Forest Service to take account of the Native Americans' religious practices, thus enabling them to block the road, goodness knows who might be next. Hunters, maybe, or the Sunday shoppers who so concerned the justices in *Frazee;* maybe even (gasp!) environmentalists.

The legal distinction, of course, is that the other potential objectors would not be able to call upon the special protection of the Free Exercise Clause. The practical distinction is that none of the other potential objectors represent religious traditions that are on the margin of America's religious culture. It is no coincidence that the losers in these cases are Native Americans, just as, in an earlier era, they were Mormons; after all, only the religions that are political outsiders are likely to object to what the state requires or forbids them to do. And if, as I have been arguing, the religions are at their most useful when they serve as democratic intermediaries and preach resistance, then it is at precisely that moment, the moment when the religious tradition most diverges from the mainstream, that protection is both most needed and most deserved.

"Compelling State Interest"

To say that the courts should pay greater heed to the claims of outsider religions—or perhaps even to the claims of insider religions, on the rare occasions that the state interferes with their traditions—is not to say that the religions should always win and thus always be exempt from the laws that apply to everybody else. Rather, the rule would be that the state, in trying to enforce a law impinging on the religion's ability to sustain itself, would be required to demonstrate a compelling interest in enforcement of the questioned statute. A compelling interest is one of greater weight than is ordinarily demanded to sustain regulation, and the state would be required to demonstrate that its goal is sufficiently weighty and that the goal could not be accomplished through a less intrusive means.

It is possible that the state antidrug law at issue in *Smith* would have been sustained under a higher standard, but it is not likely, because a majority of states *do* in fact exempt Native Americans from certain drug regulations. Similarly, even under a compelling interest test, the Forest Service might have been able to build its road and destroy the sacred lands, and the Air Force officer . . . might properly have been disciplined for wearing a yarmulke. But we can only guess what would have happened under a higher standard of scrutiny, because the Supreme Court has never demanded one in cases calling for accommodations of religion. To apply such a standard, wrote Justice Scalia for the *Smith* majority, "would be courting anarchy." His language recalls the language that the Court chose a century ago in rejecting the claim of Mormons for an exemption from antipolygamy laws. To grant the exemption, the Court wrote then, would be "subversive of good order." In other words, the big religions win and the little religions lose.

The Case for Subversive Anarchy

As a general proposition, order is a good thing. Nobody much likes anarchy. Justice Scalia lists in his opinion many of the modern statutes from which the religious might demand exemptions—everything from traffic laws to environmental laws to child labor laws—but he misses a crucial historical point. When the First Amendment was written, none of those laws existed. None of them existed because the modern concept of a welfare state, a state in which the government's duty was caring for its citizens, did not exist.

Justice Scalia's conception of a free exercise clause that only protects the religious against discrimination is an example of what is called "neutrality" in the legal literature, the idea that the state should not favor religion but also should not oppress it. The ideal of neutrality might provide useful protection for religious freedom in a society of relatively few laws, one in which most of the social order is privately determined. That was the society the Founders knew. In such a society, it is enough to say that the law leaves religion alone. It is difficult, however, to see how the law can protect religious freedom in the welfare state if it does not offer exemptions and special protection for religious devotion. To offer the religions the chance to win exemptions from laws that others must obey obviously carves out a special niche for religion, but that is hardly objectionable: carving out a special place for religion is the minimum it might be said that the Free Exercise Clause does.

Nowadays, the government rarely if ever enacts legislation intended to oppress a particular religion, which is why Michael McConnell has written that the difference between neutrality and accommodation "is the difference between a Free Exercise Clause that is a major restraining device on government action that affects religious practice and a Free Exercise Clause that will rarely have practical application."[15]

That practical distinction is not, however, the important theoretical distinction. What matters more is the different attitudes that neutrality and accommodation evince toward the role of religious belief in a democratic polity. Neutrality treats religious belief as a matter of individual choice, an aspect of conscience, with which the government must not interfere but which it has no obligation to respect. This was the significance of Justice Scalia's almost snide closing reference in *Smith* to a land in which "every conscience is a law unto itself."[16] In this sense, neutrality treats religious belief like any other belief, controlled by the same rules: the choice is free, but it is entitled to no special subsidy, and, indeed, it can be trampled by the state as long as it is trampled by accident.

Accommodation, however, can be crafted into a tool that accepts religion as a group rather than an individual activity. When accommodation is so understood, corporate worship, not individual conscience, becomes the obstacle around which state policy must make the widest possible berth. Accommodation is therefore closer to Tocqueville's (and the Founders') conception of religious groups as autonomous moral and political forces, intermediate institutions, separate heads of sovereignty vital to preventing majoritarian tyranny. Thus, the reason for accommodation becomes not the protection of individual conscience, but the preservation of the religions as independent power bases that exist in large part in order to resist the state. To allow the state, without very strong reason, to enforce policies that interfere with this corporate freedom would be antithetical to the understanding of religious purpose as resistance.

There remains the question of what it means to speak of an accommodation of religion that takes account of the intermediary function of religious autonomy, especially in a nation, as Justice Scalia's opinion reminds us, where the laws are diverse and all-embracing. The problem of making accommodation work in the welfare state is the subject of [another essay].

Endnotes

[1] *Employment Division v. Smith*, 494 U.S. 872 (1990).

[2] *Ibid.*

[3] Kathleen M. Sullivan, "Religion and Liberal Democracy," *University of Chicago Law Review* 59 (1992): 195, 216.

[4] 494 U.S. at 890.

[5] Frederick Mark Gedicks, "Public Life and Hostility to Religion," *Virginia Law Review* 78 (1992): 671, 690.

[6] *Cantwell v. Connecticut*, 310 U.S. 296 (1940).

[7] *Kunz v. New York*, 340 U.S. 290 (1951); *Murdock v. Pennsylvania*, 319 U.S. 105 (1943).

[8] *Widmar v. Vincent*, 454 U.S. 263 (1981) (meeting on a college campus).

[9] *McDaniel v. Paty*, 435 U.S. 618, 641 (1978) (Justice William Brennan, concurring).

[10] Mark Tushnet, *Red, White, and Blue: A Critical Analysis of Constitutional Law* (Cambridge: Harvard University Press, 1988), p. 257.

[11] 406 U.S. 205 (1972).

[12] *Sherbert v. Verner*, 374 U.S. 398 (1963).

[13] *Frazee v. Illinois Department of Employment Security*, 489 U.S. 829, 835 (1989).

[14] *Lyng v. Northwest Indian Cemetery Protective Association*, 485 U.S. 439 (1988).

[15] Michael W. McConnell, "Accommodation of Religion: An Update and a Response to the Critics," *George Washington Law Review* 60 (March 1992): 685, 689.

[16] *Employment Division v. Smith*, 494 U.S. at 890.

Study Questions

1. In *Gobitis*, Justice Frankfurter argues that the interest in free exercise of religion must be subordinated to "the promotion of national cohesion." He also speaks of "national unity."

Are these appeals a convincing justification for the Court's decision? Are there any exceptions to such a rationale that Frankfurter seems prepared to accept? Could any claim to religious free exercise be denied under this reasoning? How much and what kind of religious freedom is compatible with Frankfurter's position?

2. Frankfurter says in *Gobitis* that "government may not interfere with organized or individual expression of belief or disbelief." Suppose I believe that saluting an object such as a national flag is an expression of disbelief in God. How could Frankfurter respond to my refusal to participate in the salute?

3. Some scholars have suggested that the cases in which the courts have permitted states to limit religious freedom nearly always involve activities important to minority religious groups: the use of peyote by Native Americans, the practice of polygamy among Mormons, the refusal to salute the flag among Jehovah's Witnesses, and so on. These critics contend that the courts would not be likely to permit similar restrictions if they impacted "mainstream" religious groups in America, such as Catholics or Jews. Is this criticism fair?

4. If the use of a drug such as peyote is harmful to users, why can't the state ban its consumption, regardless of religious convictions? Why can't antidiscrimination laws be applied to religious believers who hold that segregation is commanded by God?

5. Should the Constitution be interpreted, so as to prohibit members of a religion who believe in animal sacrifice from engaging in such practices?

6. Read *Reynolds v. United States* (in "Cases for Further Reflection," below). What result would the holding of *Reynolds* have if applied to religiously motivated animal sacrifice? Is there a principled way to decide which religious practices must be accommodated and which not? What might John Stuart Mill say of this case? (Note that Mill did write on the persecution of the Mormons in nineteenth-century America.) What about a church whose mem-

bers believe that Scripture commands them to handle poisonous snakes? What of a church whose members refuse to obtain "standard" medical care for children?

7. What argument does Justice Scalia give in *Smith* for the Court's decision? How does he explain the very different result reached by the Court in the Amish school case (see *Yoder* in Cases for Further Reflection, below)? How do the dissenters respond?

8. Do you agree that a state may prohibit an individual from ingesting an illegal drug when he does so as part of a bona fide religious practice?

9. The Pentagon, in 1997, announced that it was considering a policy change that would permit soldiers who are members of the Native American Church to use peyote in religious services. The draft rule would permit the use of peyote on military bases if the soldier has the consent of his or her commanding officer; possession and the use of peyote would be banned on military vehicles, aircraft, and ships. Would you support such a policy change? Why or why not?

10. Critics of the ruling in *Smith* argued that Justice Scalia's position amounts to a return to a stark distinction between religious belief and religious practice. (On that distinction, see the *Reynolds* case in the "Cases for Further Reflection," below). Are the critics right? What is wrong with saying that you may *believe* whatever you want from a religious perspective but that you may not always have the right to put those beliefs into practice?

11. Anderson Jack and George Louie Charlie were members of the Coast Salish people, a group of native Americans from British Columbia, Canada. They were charged with hunting a deer out of season in violation of Canada's Wildlife Act. The defendants alleged that the hunting and killing were part of a religious ceremony of burning food to satisfy the spirits of ancestors. At trial, anthropologists testified that the burning of food for the dead was a kind of memorial, that the use of deer meat was required, and that the ritual was of ancient origin. The defendants were convicted, and they appealed. The appeal was rejected on the grounds that, although "there can be no question as to the existence" of freedom of conscience regarding religious belief, "when it comes to the practices which flow from a religious belief . . . the State has a legitimate interest in restricting them, should it be necessary to do so, in the interest of public order and decency." (*Regina v. Jack and Charlie* British Columbia Court of Appeal, [1982] 5 W.W.R. 193.) Was this case correctly decided, in your view?

12. What criticisms does Stephen Carter raise concerning the *Smith* decision? Do you agree with them?

13. In what ways does Carter think that the courts have failed sufficiently to take account of the free exercise interests of "religious outsiders"? How does Carter propose that such interests be accommodated?

14. In December 1995, Chia Thai Moua, a Hmong immigrant from Laos now living in Fresno, California, pled no contest to a charge of felony animal cruelty. Moua admitted to clubbing a three-month-old German shepherd puppy to death on the front steps of his home. Moua is a Hmong shaman and, like other Hmong, believed that the soul of a dog, when released from its body, can track down and destroy evil spirits that bring disease. Moua contended at trial that his wife had been seriously ill during the time leading up to the incident, and that none of his other treatments had cured her. Moua had previously sacrificed a pig and a chicken and had burned paper money. "But still my wife gets no better. What was I to do? I am a shaman and this is what I believe." Moua unsuccessfully sought to defend himself by arguing that he was exercising his religious beliefs and did not kill the dog with "malice." A lower court refused to allow the religious freedom defense. [*Los Angeles Times,* 16 Dec. 1995, p. A1.] Should Hmong people continue to be prosecuted for practices dictated by their apparently sincere religious convictions?

Cases for Further Reflection

47. *South Florida Free Beaches, Inc., v. City of Miami, Florida*

OPINION: Albert J. Henderson, Circuit Judge:

South Florida Free Beaches, Inc. (South Florida) and Gary Bryant sought a declatory judgment and injunctive relief in the United States District Court for the Southern District of Florida, alleging that various state statues and city of Miami ordinances unconstitutionally infringed on their right to sunbathe in the nude.

After a non-jury trial, the district court, held that nude sunbathing was not a form of expression protected by the first amendment. . . .

We *affirm.*

. . .

The bare facts in the record show that Bryant and other members of South Florida for several years regularly swam and sunbathed in the nude on a public beach within the corporate limits of the city of Miami. Although a number of statues and local ordinances restricted such conduct, they were not consistently enforced. Recently, however, Miami officials expressed an intent to prosecute any person who violates these statutes and ordinances. Dade County and the state of Florida, while disclaiming any current intent to arrest the plaintiffs, contend the laws are valid and enforceable. The plaintiffs assert that the city's threat of prosecution chills the exercise of their first amendment right of expression. Nude sunbathing, the plaintiffs claim, is the practice by which they advocate and communicate their philosophy that the human body is wholesome and that nudity is not indecent.

. . .

As noted above, the district court, in a revealing evaluation, held that "nude sunbathing *per se* is not

734 F.2d 608 (1984)
United States Court of Appeals
Eleventh Circuit

a constitutionally protected activity." Examining the challenged laws for vagueness, the district court noted that although some of the language may be unclear in the abstract, they clearly proscribed nudity. Employing an overbreadth analysis, the district court upheld all the challenged statutes and ordinances, except that part of Fla.Stat. § 877.03 proscribing actions "as of a nature to corrupt the public morals, or outrage the sense of public decency. . . .

South Florida and Bryant initially assign as error the district court's failure to accord constitutional protection to their activities. Because they allegedly are advocating an idea, they maintain that the government cannot absolutely prohibit the form chosen to express it. Although that may be true in other contexts, we agree that nudity is protected as speech only when combined with some mode of expression which itself is entitled to first amendment protection.

All of the reported cases adhere to this view that the constitution does not protect unassociated nudity from exposure to governmental limitations. . . .

The plaintiffs point to a number of cases for the proposition that nudity, as a means of expression, is constitutionally permissible. All of these cases, however, involved nudity in combination with a protected form of expression. Nudity alone does not place otherwise protected material outside the mantle of the First Amendment.

Stripped of constitutional protection, nude sunbathing is subject to legitimate governmental proscriptions. Thus, we hold that the first amendment does not clothe these plaintiffs with a constitutional right to sunbathe in the nude. Neither do they possess a constitutional right of associating in the nude. They remain able to advocate the benefits of nude sunbathing, albeit while fully dressed.

. . .

48. *Texas v. Johnson*

Justice Brennan delivered the opinion of the Court.

After publicly burning an American flag as a means of political protest, Gregory Lee Johnson was convicted of desecrating a flag in violation of Texas law. This case presents the question whether his conviction is consistent with the First Amendment. We hold that it is not.

I

While the Republican National Convention was taking place in Dallas in 1984, respondent Johnson participated in a political demonstration dubbed the "Republican War Chest Tour." As explained in literature distributed by the demonstrators and in speeches made by them, the purpose of this event was to protest the policies of the Reagan administration and of certain Dallas-based corporations. The demonstrators marched through the Dallas streets, chanting political slogans and stopping at several corporate locations to stage "die-ins" intended to dramatize the consequences of nuclear war. On several occasions they spray-painted the walls of buildings and overturned potted plants, but Johnson himself took no part in such activities. He did, however, accept an American flag handed to him by a fellow protestor who had taken it from a flag pole outside one of the targeted buildings.

The demonstration ended in front of Dallas City Hall, where Johnson unfurled the American flag, doused it with kerosene, and set it on fire. While the flag burned, the protestors chanted, "America, the red, white, and blue, we spit on you." After the demonstrators dispersed, a witness to the flag-burning collected the flag's remains and buried them in his backyard. No one was physically injured or threatened with injury, though several witnesses testified that they had been seriously offended by the flag-burning.

Of the approximately 100 demonstrators, Johnson alone was charged with a crime. The only criminal offense with which he was charged was the desecration of a venerated object in violation of Tex. Penal Code Ann. § 42.09(a)(3)(1989).[1] After a trial, he was convicted, sentenced to one year in prison, and fined $2,000. The Court of Appeals for the Fifth District of Texas at Dallas affirmed Johnson's conviction, . . . but the Texas Court of Criminal Appeals reversed, . . . holding that the State could not, consistent with the First Amendment, punish Johnson for burning the flag in these circumstances.

. . .

II

Johnson was convicted of flag desecration for burning the flag rather than for uttering insulting words. This fact somewhat complicates our consideration of his conviction under the First Amendment. We must first determine whether Johnson's burning of the flag constituted expressive conduct, permitting him to invoke the First Amendment in challenging his conviction. . . .

The First Amendment literally forbids the abridgement only of "speech," but we have long recognized that its protection does not end at the spoken or written word. While we have rejected "the view that an apparently limitless variety of conduct can be labeled 'speech' whenever the person engaging in the conduct intends thereby to express an idea," . . . we have acknowledged that conduct may be "sufficiently imbued with elements of communication to fall within the scope of the First and Fourteenth Amendments." . . .

Especially pertinent to his case are our decisions recognizing the communicative nature of conduct relating to flags. Attaching a peace sign to the flag . . . saluting the flag . . . and displaying a

109 S. Ct. 2533 (1989)
United States Supreme Court

red flag . . . we have held, all may find shelter under the First Amendment. . . . Pregnant with expressive content, the flag as readily signifies this Nation as does the combination of letters found in "America."

The State of Texas conceded for purposes of its oral argument in this case that Johnson's conduct was expressive conduct, . . . and this concession seems to us prudent. . . . Johnson burned an American flag as part—indeed, as the culmination—of a political demonstration that coincided with the convening of the Republican Party and its renomination of Ronald Reagan for President. The expressive, overtly political nature of this conduct was both intentional and overwhelmingly apparent. At his trial, Johnson explained his reasons for burning the flag as follows: "The American Flag was burned as Ronald Reagan was being renominated as President. And a more powerful statement of symbolic speech, whether you agree with it or not, couldn't have been made at that time. It's quite a just position [juxtaposition]. We had new patriotism and no patriotism." . . . In these circumstances, Johnson's burning of the flag was conduct "sufficiently imbued with elements of communication" . . . to implicate the First Amendment.

. . . [W]e must decide whether Texas has asserted an interest in support of Johnson's conviction that is unrelated to the suppression of expression. . . . . The State offers two separate interests to justify this conviction: preventing breaches of the peace, and preserving the flag as a symbol of nationhood and national unity. We hold that the first interest is not implicated on this record and that the second is related to the suppression of expression.

A

Texas claims that its interest in preventing breaches of peace justifies Johnson's conviction for flag desecration. However, no disturbance of the peace actually occurred or threatened to occur because of Johnson's burning of the flag. . . .

The State's position, therefore, amounts to a claim that an audience that takes serious offense at particular expression is necessarily likely to disturb the peace and that the expression may be prohibited on this basis. Our precedents do not countenance such a presumption. On the contrary, they recognize that a principal "function of free speech under our system of government is to invite dispute. It may indeed best serve its high purpose when it induces a condition of unrest, creates dissatisfaction with conditions as they are, or even stirs people to anger." . . .

Nor does Johnson's expressive conduct fall within that small class of "fighting words" that are "likely to provoke the average person to retaliation, and thereby cause a breach of the peace." No reasonable onlooker would have regarded Johnson's generalized expression of dissatisfaction with the policies of the Federal Government as a direct personal insult or an invitation to exchange fisticuffs. . . .

We thus conclude that the State's interest in maintaining order is not implicated on these facts. . . .

It remains to consider whether the State's interest in preserving the flag as a symbol of nationhood and national unity justifies Johnson's conviction.

. . . Johnson was not, we add, prosecuted for the expression of just any idea; he was prosecuted for his expression of dissatisfaction with the policies of this country, expression situated at the core of our First Amendment values. . . .

Moreover, Johnson was prosecuted because he knew that his politically charged expression would cause "serious offense." If he had burned the flag as a means of disposing of it because it was dirty or torn, he would not have been convicted of flag desecration under this Texas law: federal law designates burning as the preferred means of disposing of a flag "when it is in such condition that it is no longer a fitting emblem for display," and Texas has no quarrel with this means of disposal. . . . The Texas law is thus not aimed at protecting the physical integrity of the flag in all circumstances, but is designed instead to protect it only against impairments that would cause serious offense to others. . . .

Texas argues that its interest in preserving the flag as a symbol of nationhood and national unity survives this close analysis. Quoting extensively from the writings of this Court chronicling the flag's historic and symbolic role in our society, the State emphasizes the "special place" reserved for the flag in our Nation. . . . The State's argument is not that it has an interest simply in maintaining the flag as a symbol of *something*, no matter what it symbolizes; indeed, if that were the State's position, it would be difficult to see how that interest is endangered by highly symbolic conduct such as Johnson's. Rather, the State's claim is that it has an interest in preserving the flag as a symbol of *nationhood* and *national unity*, a symbol with a determinate range of meanings. . . . According to Texas, if one physically treats the flag in a way that would tend to cast doubt on either the idea that nationhood and national unity are the flag's referents or that national unity actually exists, the message conveyed thereby is a harmful one and therefore may be prohibited.

If there is a bedrock principle underlying the First Amendment, it is that Government may not prohibit the expression of an idea simply because society finds the idea itself offensive or disagreeable.

In short, nothing in our precedents suggests that a State may foster its own view of the flag by prohibiting expressive conduct relating to it.

Texas'[s] focus on the precise nature of Johnson's expression, moreover, misses the point of our prior decisions: Their enduring lesson, that the Government may not prohibit expression simply because it disagrees with its message, is not dependent on the particular mode in which one chooses to express an idea. If we were to hold that a State may forbid flag-burning wherever it is likely to endanger the flag's symbolic role, but allow it wherever burning a flag promotes that role—as where, for example, a person ceremoniously burns a dirty flag—we would be saying that when it comes to impairing the flag's physical integrity, the flag itself may be used as a symbol—as a substitute for the written or spoken word or a "short cut from mind to mind"—only in one direction. We would be permitting a State to "prescribe what shall be orthodox" by saying that one may burn the flag to convey one's attitude toward it and its referents only if one does

not endanger the flag's representation of nationhood and national unity. . . .

. . . To conclude that the Government may permit designated symbols to be used to communicate only a limited set of messages would be to enter territory having no discernible or defensible boundaries. Could the Government, on this theory, prohibit the burning of state flags? Of copies of the Presidential seal? Of the Constitution? In evaluating these choices under the First Amendment, how would we decide which symbols were sufficiently special to warrant this unique status? To do so, we would be forced to consult our own political preferences, and impose them on the citizenry, in the very way that the First Amendment forbids us to do. . . .

There is, moreover, no indication—either in the text of the Constitution or in our cases interpreting it—that a separate juridical category exists for the American flag alone. Indeed, we would not be surprised to learn that the persons who framed our Constitution and wrote the Amendment that we now construe were not known for their reverence for the Union Jack. The First Amendment does not guarantee that other concepts virtually sacred to our Nation as a whole—such as the principle that discrimination on the basis of race is odious and destructive—will go unquestioned in the marketplace of ideas. . . . We decline, therefore, to create for the flag an exception to the joust of principles protected by the First Amendment. . . .

We are tempted to say, in fact, that the flag's deservedly cherished place in our community will be strengthened, not weakened, by our holding today. Our decision is a reaffirmation of the principles of freedom and inclusiveness that the flag best reflects, and of the conviction that our toleration of criticism such as Johnson's is a sign and source of our strength. Indeed, one of the proudest images of our flag, the one immortalized in out own national anthem, is of the bombardment it survived at For McHenry. It is the Nation's resilience, not its rigidity, that Texas sees reflected in the flag—and it is that resilience that we reassert today.

The way to preserve the flag's special role is not to punish those who feel differently about these matters. It is to persuade them that they are wrong. . . .

. . . We can imagine no more appropriate response to burning a flag than waving one's own, no better way to counter a flag-burner's message than by saluting the flag that burns, no surer means of preserving the dignity even of the flag that burned than by—as one witness here did—according its remains a respectful burial. We do not consecrate the flag by punishing its desecration, for in doing so we dilute the freedom that this cherished emblem represents.

Chief Justice Rehnquist, with whom Justice White and Justice O'Connor join, dissenting.

. . .

The American flag, throughout more than 200 years of history, has come to be the visible symbol embodying our Nation. It does not represent the views of any particular political party, and it does not represent any particular political philosophy. The flag is not simply another "idea" or "point of view" competing for recognition in the marketplace of ideas. Millions and millions of Americans regard it with an almost mystical reverence regardless of what sort of social, political, or philosophical beliefs they may have. I cannot agree that the First Amendment invalidates the Act of Congress, and the laws of 48 of the 50 States, which make criminal the public burning of the flag.

. . .

Johnson's public burning of the flag in this case; it obviously did convey Johnson's bitter dislike of his country. But his act . . . conveyed nothing that could not have been conveyed and was not conveyed just as forcefully in a dozen different ways. As with "fighting words," so with flag burning, for purposes of the First Amendment: it is "no essential part of any exposition of ideas, and [is] of such slight social value as a step to truth that any benefit that may be derived from [it] is clearly outweighed" by the public interest in avoiding probable breach of the peace. The highest courts of several States have upheld state statutes prohibiting the public burning of the flag on the grounds that it is so inherently inflammatory that it may cause a breach of public order. . . .

The result of the Texas statute is obviously to deny one in Johnson's frame of mind one of many means of "symbolic speech." Far from being a case of "one picture being worth a thousand words," flag burning is the equivalent of an inarticulate grunt or roar that, it seems fair to say, is most likely to be indulged in not to express any particular idea, but to antagonize others. Only five years ago we said . . . that "the First Amendment does not guarantee the right to employ every conceivable method of communication at all times and in all places." The Texas statute deprived Johnson of only one rather inarticulate symbolic form of protest—a form of protest that was profoundly offensive to many—and left him with a full panoply of other symbols and every conceivable form of verbal expression to express his deep disapproval of national policy. Thus, in no way can it be said that Texas is punishing him because his hearers—or any other group of people—were profoundly opposed to the message that he sought to convey. Such opposition is no proper basis for restricting speech or expression under the First Amendment. It was Johnson's use of this particular symbol, and not the idea that he sought to convey by it or by his many other expressions, for which he was punished.

Endnotes

[1] Tex. Penal Code Ann. § 42.09 (1989) provides in full: "§ 42.09. Desecration of Venerated Object

"(a) A person commits an offense if he intentionally or knowingly desecrates:

"(1) a public monument;

"(2) a place of worship or burial; or

"(3) a state or national flag.

"(b) For purposes of this section, 'desecrate' means deface, damage, or otherwise physically mistreat in a way that the actor know will seriously offend one or more persons likely to observe or discover his action.

"(c) An offense under this section is a Class A misdemeanor."

49. *Herandez v. Commonwealth of Virginia*

Buddy Hernandez was convicted of violating a statute making it illegal for any person over the age of sixteen to appear in public wearing a mask "so as to conceal the identity of the wearer." Hernandez challenged the statute on several grounds: that he did not intend to conceal his identity; that the statute would prohibit many otherwise lawful activities; and that the purpose of the statute was not unrelated to the suppression of expression. What was the purpose of the statute? Was it legitimate and compelling? Could the state have achieved its objective with a different statute?

Barrow, Judge.

In this appeal, the appellant challenges the constitutionality of Code § 18.2–422, which prohibits a person from wearing a mask in public. He contends that the statute is unconstitutional on its face and as applied to him. Appellant also contends that the trial court impermissibly considered his beliefs in imposing punishment. We hold that Code § 18.2–422 is constitutional on its face and as applied to the appellant. Furthermore, we conclude that, the trial court did not consider the appellant's beliefs when it imposed sentence on him.

The appellant is a member of the Ku Klux Klan. Shortly after noon on Sunday, August 13, 1989, he was seen by the police wearing a long, white robe, a hood on his head, and a mask covering his entire face except for his eyes. He was standing on the sidewalk of a public street in Fredericksburg in front of a bank, directly across the street from a church. He had two companions. One was a woman wearing a long, white robe. According to the appellant, she held a hood in her hands but did not wear it. The other companion, a man, was wearing a camouflage jacket. The police arrested the appellant for wearing a mask in public in violation of Code § 182.–411.[1]

At trial, the appellant testified that he wore the hood as "part of the symbolic symbol of the Klan." A witness, Roger Kelly, described himself as the

---

406 S.E. 2d 398 (1991)
Court of Appeals of Virginia

"Grand Dragon" of Virginia's Klan and testified that a Klansman has the option of wearing a mask or not but that "the uniform is set up to wear the mask."

At the conclusion of the evidence, the trial court found that the "mask is not a necessary part of the symbolic speech of this particular organization." The trial judge explained that "this organization and its members can express themselves fully without the need for that liner or that mask to go across the face."

The appellant first argues that Code § 18.2–422 is unconstitutional on its face because it is overbroad. He contends that, regardless of whether his own conduct may constitutionally be regulated, the statute impermissible deters or "chills," constitutionally protected expression. . . .

In order to find this statute facially invalid, we must first determine whether it "reaches a substantial amount of constitutionally protected conduct." . . . The chilling effect on legitimate expression must be both "real and substantial." . . . However, the statue "should not be deemed facially invalid unless it is not readily subject to a narrowing construction by the state courts."

The appellant argues that the statute prohibits persons from wearing ski masks in the winter, Muslim women from wearing traditional outfits covering their faces, widows from wearing black veils, and other similar face coverings. He argues that this prohibition is unconstitutional because it criminalizes personal expression. We decline to read Code § 18.2–422 as broadly as the appellant suggests we should.

The statute makes it illegal for any person over the age of sixteen to appear in a public place wearing a mask covering a substantial part of the face "so as to conceal the identity of the wearer." Code § 18.2–422. These words "so as to conceal the identity" express a requirement of intent. Therefore, to violate the statute and individual must *intend* to conceal his identity by covering his face. . . . So construed, this statute does not prohibit the masking of one's face for a purpose other than concealing one's identity, such as protection from cold weather, expression of grief, or practice of a religion.

The appellant contends that the record does not support a finding that he intended to conceal his identity. He contends that the evidence showed only that he wore the mask for symbolic purposes, not concealment. We disagree. A trier of fact may infer that a person intends the natural consequences of his or her acts. . . . Therefore, evidence in this case that the mask covered the appellant's face except for his eyes was sufficient to support the verdict. The trier of fact was free to accept or reject the appellant's testimony or any other evidence concerning a contrary intent.

The appellant also argues that the statute is unconstitutional as applied to him because it penalizes him for engaging in disfavored symbolic speech. This is so only if the appellant's wearing of the mask constitutes expressive activity permitting him to invoke the first amendment. . . . In order for appellant's conduct to fall within the scope of first amendment protection, he must have intended to convey a particularized message by wearing the mask, and there must have been a great likelihood that the message would be understood by those who viewed it. . . .

This record does not support a finding that the wearing of a mask conveyed a particularized message that would have been likely to have been understood by those who viewed it. The record does not establish, as the appellant contends, that the mask is so identified with the Ku Klux Klan that it is a symbol of its identity. The robe and the hood may be such symbols, but the mask is not. The mask worn without the robe and the hood would be meaningless. The mask adds nothing, save fear and intimidation, to the symbolic message expressed by the wearing of the robe and the hood. Without the mask, the social and political message conveyed by the uniform of the Ku Klux Klan is the same as it would be with the mask.

Even if the wearing of the Ku Klux Klan mask constitutes expressive conduct protected by the first amendment, the statute is constitutional if its purpose is unrelated to the suppression of free expression. . . . A statute which restricts expressive conduct because of the message it conveys is subject to "the most exacting scrutiny." . . . On the other hand, a statute which is directed at the "secondary effects" of the regulated speech, and whose justification has nothing to do with that speech is content-neutral. . . . A statute is content-neutral if it is one in which "the governmental interest is unrelated to the suppression of free expression." Such a statute is constitutional so long as it furthers an important governmental interest and "the incidental restriction on alleged First Amendment freedoms is not greater than is essential to the furtherance of the interest."

We acknowledge that the legislature's original motivation for enacting the anti-mask statute may have been to "unmask the Klan." The statute was, after all, created in the same act with statutes prohibiting cross burning and intimidation, activities historical associated with the Klan. . . .However, whatever motivation might have prompted the anti-mask statute's enactment, the purpose of the statute is no more than what appears in the plain language of the statute. . . . The statute simply forbids the wearing of masks under certain circumstances. An obvious justification for such a prohibition is the prevention of violence, crime and disorder by the unmasking of potential criminals. For example, a potential rapist or bank robber wearing a mask could just as easily be prosecuted under this statute as a Klansman. . . .

The plain language of Code § 18.2–422 indicates no purpose to stifle the Klan's freedom of expression. Further, nothing in the record shows an indiscriminate enforcement of the statute against members of the Klan. The justification for prosecuting an individual under this statute is the same whether or not that individual is a Klansman. The incidental effect of preventing a Klansman, such as the appellant, from wearing his "full costume" is minor when compared to the government's interest in keeping communities safe and free from violence. We conclude therefore, that Code § 18.2–422 is not unconstitutional as applied to the appellant.

Finally, the appellant contends that a comment by the trial court at the sentencing hearing demonstrated that the court impermissibly punished the appellant for his disfavored views. Before sentencing the defendant, the trail judge stated that, "[despite the fact that I disagree with [the appellant's beliefs] wholeheartedly, I am not going to punish him unduly because of those beliefs."

The appellant misinterprets the trail judge's comment. The appellant would read the remark to mean that the trial judge was going to punish the appellant because of his beliefs, but not to an extent to which the appellant was not due. We, however, read this remark to mean that the trial court would not punish him because of his beliefs to an extent to which he would not otherwise be deserving. Neither the record nor the sentence which was imposed (a thirty day jail sentence suspended and a $1,000 fine) reflects that the appellant's unpopular views in any way were considered by the trial court in its imposition of sentence.

For these reasons, we conclude that the judgment of conviction should be affirmed.

Affirmed

Endnote

[1] Code § 18.2–422:
It shall be unlawful for any person over sixteen years of age while wearing any mask, hood or other device whereby a substantial portion of the face is hidden or covered so as to conceal the identity of the wearer, to be or appear in any public place, or upon any private property in this Commonwealth without first having obtained from the owner or tenant thereof consent to do so in writing.

---

50. *Reynolds v. United States*

This is an indictment found in the District Court for the third judicial district of the Territory of Utah, charging George Reynolds with bigamy, in violation of sect. 5352 of the Revised Statutes, which, omitting its exceptions, is as follows:—

"Every person having a husband or wife living, who marries another, whether married or single, in a Territory, or other place over which the United States have exclusive jurisdiction, is guilty of bigamy, and shall be punished by a fine of not more that $500, and by imprisonment for a term of not more than five years."

. . .

---

98 U.S. 145 (1878)
United States Supreme Court

On the trial, the plaintiff in error, the accused, proved that at the time of his alleged second marriage he was, and for many years before had been, a member of the Church of Jesus Christ of Latter-Day Saints, commonly called the Mormon Church, and a believer in its doctrines; that it was an accepted doctrine of that church "that it was the duty of male members of said church, circumstances permitting, to practise polygamy; . . . that this duty was enjoined by different books which the members of said church believed to be to divine origin, and among others the Holy Bible, and also that the members of the church believed that the practice of polygamy was directly enjoined upon the male members thereof by the Almighty God, in a revelation to Joseph Smith, the founder and prophet of said church; that the failing or refusing to practise polygamy by such male members of said church, when circumstances would admit, would be punished, and the penalty for such failure and refusal would be damnation in the life to come." He also proved "that he had received permission from the recognized authorities in said church to enter into polygamous marriage; . . . that Daniel H. Wells, one having authority in said church to perform the marriage ceremony, married the said defendant on or about the time the crime is alleged to have been committed, to some woman by the name of Schofield, and that such marriage ceremony was performed under and pursuant to the doctrines of said church."

Upon this proof he asked the court to instruct the jury that if they found from the evidence that he "was married as charged—if he was married—in pursuance of and in conformity with what he believed at the time to be a religious duty, that the verdict must be 'not guilty.'" This request was refused, and the court did charge "that there must have been a criminal intent, but that if the defendant, under the influence of a religious belief that it was right—under an inspiration, if you please, that it was right—deliberately married a second time, having a first wife living, the want of consciousness of evil intent—the want of understanding on his part that he was committing a crime—did not excuse him; but the law inexorably in such case implies the criminal intent."

Upon this charge and refusal to charge the question is raised, whether religious belief can be accepted as a justification of an overt act made criminal by the law of the land. The inquiry is not as to the power of Congress to prescribe criminal laws for the Territories, but as to the guilt of one who knowingly violates a law which as been properly enacted, if he entertains a religious belief that the law is wrong.

Congress cannot pass a law for the government of the Territories which shall prohibit the free exercise of religion. The first amendment to the Constitution expressly forbids such legislation. Religious freedom is guaranteed everywhere throughout the United States, so far a congressional interference is concerned. The question to be determined is, whether the law now under consideration comes within this prohibition.

Polygamy has always been odious among the northern and western nations of Europe, and, until the establishment of the Mormon Church was almost exclusively a feature of the life of Asiatic and of African people. At common law, the second marriage was always void (2 Kent, Com. 79), and from the earliest history of England polygamy has been treated as an offence against society. After the establishment of the ecclesiastical courts, and until the time of James I., it was punished through the instrumentality of those tribunals, not merely because ecclesiastical rights had been violated, but because upon the separation of the ecclesiastical courts from the civil the ecclesiastical were supposed to be the most appropriate for the trial of matrimonial causes and offences against the rights of marriage, just as they were for testamentary causes and the settlement of the estate of Deceased persons.

By the statute of 1 James I. (c. 11), the offence, if committed in England or Wales, was made publishable in the civil courts, and the penalty was death. As this statute was limited in its operation to England and Wales, it was at a very early period re-enacted, generally with some modifications, in all the colonies. In connection with the case we are now considering, it is a significant fact that on the 8th of December, 1788, after the passage of the act establishing religious freedom, and after the convention of Virginia had recommended as an amendment to the Constitution of the United States the declaration in a bill of rights that "all men have an equal, natural, and unalienable right to the free exercise of religion, according to the dictates of conscience," the legislature of that State substantially enacted the statute of James I., death penalty included, because, as recited in the preamble, "it hath been doubted whether bigamy or polygamy be punishable by the laws of this Commonwealth." 12 Hening's Stat. 691. From that day to this we think it may safely be said there never has been a time in any State of the Union when poligamy has not been an offence against society, cognizable by the civil courts and punishable with more or less severity. In the face of all this evidence, it is impossible to believe that the constitutional guaranty of religious freedom was intended to prohibit legislation in respect to this most important feature of social life. Marriage, while from its very nature a sacred obligation, is nevertheless, in most civilized nations, a civil contract, and usually regulated by law. Upon it society may be said to be built, and out of its fruits spring social relations and social obligations and duties, with which government is necessarily required to deal. In fact, according as monogamous or polygamous marriages are allowed, do we find the principles on which the government of the people to a greater or less extent, rests.

. . .

[T]he only question which remains is, whether those who make polygamy a part of their religion are excepted from the operation of the statute. If they are, then those who do not make polygamy a part of their religious belief may be found guilty and punished, while those who do, must be acquitted and go free. This would be introducing a new element into criminal law. Laws are made for the government of actions, and while they cannot interfere with mere religious belief and opinions,

they may with practices. Suppose one believed that human sacrifices were a necessary part of religious worship, would it be seriously contended that the civil government under which he lived could not interfere to prevent a sacrifice? Or if a wife religiously believed it was her duty to burn herself upon the funeral pile of her dead husband, would it be beyond the power of the civil government to prevent her carrying her belief into practice?

So here, as a law of the organization of society under the exclusive dominion of the United States, it is profited that plural marriages shall not be allowed. Can a man excuse his practices to the contrary because of his religious belief? The permit this would be to make the professed doctrines of religious belief superior to the law of the land, and in effect to permit every citizen to become a law unto himself. Government could exist only in name under such circumstances.

51. *Wisconsin v. Yoder*

A landmark decision in the law of the "free exercise" clause, this case illustrates the conflict between the right of individuals to entertain beliefs on religious grounds and to educate their children accordingly, and the authority of the state to override the claims of these beliefs by working to instill certain values and attitudes in the classroom. To what other religious groups might the Court's reasoning here apply? What would Mill and Kendall say of this case?

[Mr. Chief Justice Burger delivered the opinion of the Court.]

[We granted certiorari] to review a decision of the Wisconsin Supreme Court holding that respondents' convictions of violating the State's compul-

_____

406 U.S. 205 (1972)
United States Supreme Court

sory school-attendance law were invalid under the Free Exercise Clause. [We *affirm*.]

Respondents Jonas Yoder and Wallace Miller are members of the Old Order Amish Religion, and respondent Adin Yutzy is a member of the Conservative Amish Mennonite Church. . . . Wisconsin's compulsory school-attendance law required them to cause their children to attend public or private school until reaching age 16 but the respondents declined to send their children, ages 14 and 15, to public school after they completed the eighth grade. [Respondents were convicted under the compulsory-attendance law and were fined $5 each.] Trial testimony showed that they believed that by sending their children to high school, they [would] endanger their own salvation and that of their children. The State stipulated that respondents' religious beliefs were sincere. . . .

Formal high school education beyond the eighth grade is contrary to Amish beliefs, not only because it places Amish children in an environment hostile to Amish beliefs with increasing emphasis on competition in class work and sports and with pressure to conform to the styles, manners, and ways of the peer group, but also because it takes them away from their community, physically and emotionally, during the crucial and formative adolescent period of life. During this period, the children must acquire Amish attitudes favoring manual work and self-reliance and the specific skills needed to perform the adult role of an Amish farmer or housewife. . . .

[An expert] testified that compulsory high school attendance could not only result in great psychological harm to Amish children, because of the conflicts it would produce, but would also, in his opinion, ultimately result in the destruction of the Old Order Amish church community as it exists in the United States today. The testimony of [another expert] also showed that the Amish succeed in preparing their high school children to be productive members of the Amish community. [The] evidence also showed that the Amish have an excellent record as law-abiding and generally self-sufficient members of society. . . .

[A] State's interest in universal education, however highly we rank it, is not totally free from a balancing process when it impinges on fundamental rights and interests, such as those specifically protected by the Free Exercise Clause of the First Amendment, and the traditional interest of parents with respect to the religious upbringing of their children. . . . It follows that in order for Wisconsin to compel school attendance beyond the eighth grade against a claim that such attendance interferes with the practice of a legitimate religious belief, it must appear either that the State does not deny the free exercise of religious belief by its re-

quirement, or that there is a state interest of sufficient magnitude to override the interest claiming protection under the Free Exercise Clause. [O]nly those interests of the highest order and those not otherwise served can overbalance legitimate claims to the free exercise of religion. . . .

. . . In evaluating [respondents'] claims we must be careful to determine whether the Amish religious faith and their mode of life are, as they claim, inseparable and interdependent. A way of life, however virtuous and admirable, may not be interposed a barrier to reasonable state regulation of education if it is based on purely secular considerations; to have the protection of the Religion Clauses, the claims must be rooted in religious belief. Although a determination of what is a "religious" belief or practice entitled to a constitutional protection may present a most delicate question, the very concept of ordered liberty precludes allowing every person to make his own standards on matters of conduct in which society as a whole has important interests. Thus, if the Amish asserted their claims because of the subjective evaluation and rejection of the contemporary secular values accepted by the majority, much as Thoreau rejected the social values of his time and isolated himself at Walden Pond, Their claim would not rest on a religious basis. Thoreau's choice was philosophical and personal rather than religious, and such belief does not rise to the demands of the Religion Clause.

Giving no weight to such secular considerations, however, we see that the record in this case abundantly supports the claim that the traditional way of life of the Amish is not merely a matter of personal preference, but one of deep religious conviction, shared by an organized group, and intimately related to daily living. That the Old Order Amish daily life and religious practice stem from their faith is shown by the fact that it is in response to their literal interpretation of the Biblical injunction from the Epistle of Paul to the Romans, "be not conformed to this world. . . ." This command is fundamental to the Amish faith. Moreover, for the Old Order Amish, religion is not simply a matter of theocratic belief. As the expert witnesses explained, the Old Order Amish religion pervades and determines virtually their entire way of life, regulating it with the detail of the Talmudic diet through the strictly enforced rules of the church community. . . .

The impact of the compulsory-attendance law on respondents' practice of the Amish religion is not only severe, but inescapable, for the Wisconsin law affirmatively compels them, under threat of criminal sanction, to perform acts undeniably at odds with fundamental tenets of their religious beliefs. Nor is the impact of the compulsory-attendance law confined to grave interference with important Amish religious tenets from a subjective point of view. It carries with it precisely the kind of objective danger to the free exercise of religion which the First Amendment was designed to prevent. [It raises] a very real threat of undermining the Amish community and religious practice as they exist today; they must either abandon belief and be assimilated into society at large, or be forced to migrate to some other and more tolerant region. [In sum], enforcement of the State's requirement of compulsory formal education after the eighth grade would gravely endanger if not destroy the free exercise of respondents' religious beliefs.

. . . [The State does not challenge] the claim that the Amish mode of life and education is inseparable from a part of the basic tenets of their religion— indeed, as much a part of their religious belief and practices as baptism, the confessional, or a sabbath may be for others. The Court must not ignore the danger that an exception from a general obligation of citizenship on religious grounds may run afoul of the Establishment Clause, but that danger cannot be allowed to prevent any exception no matter how vital it may be to the protection of values promoted by the right of free exercise. . . .

The State advances two primary arguments in support of its system of compulsory education. It notes, as Thomas Jefferson pointed out early in our history, that some degree of education is necessary to prepare citizens to participate effectively and intelligently in our open political system if we are to preserve freedom and independence. Further, education prepares individuals to be self-reliant and self-sufficient participants in society. We accept these propositions.

However, the evidence adduced by the Amish in this case is persuasively to the effect that an additional one or two years of formal high school for Amish children in place of their long-established

program of informal vocational education would do little to serve those interests. . . . It is one thing to say that compulsory education for a year to two beyond the eighth grade may be necessary when its goal is the preparation of the child for life in modern society as the majority live, but it is quite another if the goal of education be viewed as the preparation of the child for life in the separated agrarian community that is the keystone of the Amish faith.

The State attacks respondents' position as one fostering "ignorance" from which the child must be protected by the State. [But] this record strongly shows that the Amish community has been a highly successful social unit within our society, even if apart from the conventional "mainstream." Its members are productive and very law-abiding members of society; they reject public welfare in any of its usual modern views. The Congress itself recognized their self-sufficiency by authorizing exemption of such groups as the Amish from the obligation to pay social security taxes. A way of life that is odd or even erratic but interferes with no rights or interests of others is not to be condemned because it is different.

The State, however, supports its interest in providing an additional one or two years of compulsory high school education to Amish children because of the possibility that some such children will choose to leave the Amish community, and that if this occurs they will be ill-equipped for life. . . . However, on this record, that argument is highly speculative. . . .

Contrary to the suggestion [in Justice Douglas's dissent], our holding today in no degree depends on the assertion of the religious interest of the child as contrasted with that of the parents. It is the parents who are subject to prosecution here [and] it is their right of free exercise, not that of their children, that must determine Wisconsin's power to impose criminal penalties on the parent. The dissent argues that a child who expresses a desire to attend public high school in conflict with the wishes of his parents should not be prevented from doing so. There is no reason for the Court to consider that point since it is not an issue in the case. The children are not parties to this litigation. The State has at no point tried this case on the theory that respondents were preventing their children from attending school against their expressed desires, and indeed the record is to the contrary. . . .

Our holding in no way determines the proper resolution of possible competing interests of parents, children, and the State in an appropriate state court proceeding in which the power of the State is asserted on the theory that Amish parents are preventing their minor children from attending high school despite their expressed desires to the contrary. Recognition of the claim of the State in such a proceeding would, of course, call into question traditional concepts of parental control over the religious upbringing and education of their minor children recognized in this Court's past decisions. It is clear that such an intrusion by a State into family decisions in the area of religious training would give rise to grave questions of religious freedom. . . .

On this record we neither reach nor decide those issues.

. . . It cannot be over-emphasized that we are not dealing with a way of life and mode of education by a group claiming to have recently discovered some "progressive" or more enlightened process for rearing children for modern life. [In light of the" convincing showing" by the Amish here,] one that probably few other religious groups or sects could make, and weighing the minimal difference between what the State would require and what the Amish already accept, it was incumbent on the State to show with more particularity how its admittedly strong interest in compulsory education would be adversely affected by granting an exemption to the Amish. . . .

Chapter III

Equality and the Law

The ideals of equality and justice are among the most powerful of those by which we purport to live. Many believe that the highest purpose of our law is to bring about justice and to treat persons equally; the central place given to these principles in the Constitution and the Declaration of Independence is testament to their importance. Yet, as with the guarantees of freedom of speech and religion, the aspiration to equality brings with it a host of deep and perplexing philosophical problems. Chapter Three introduces us to them.

Just what is the condition of "equality"? And can the law bring it about? The material in Section A investigates these questions, focusing on the constitutional requirement of "equal protection" and its implementation through antidiscrimination law and programs of preferential treatment or "affirmative action." What kind of equality does the Constitution guarantee? Should it tolerate any differences in treatment based on race or sex? Should it be "color-blind"? Gender-blind? The *Bakke* and *Hopwood* cases frame the legal issues involved and set up the discussion pursued by the contributors to this section.

Section B looks at discrimination based on sex and gender. What concept of sexual equality does the Constitution endorse? What forms of gender bias exist in the law? And should all distinctions based upon sex be impermissible? The section begins with the Supreme Court's recent decision disallowing formerly all-male military academies from excluding women. This is followed by the unusual claim made by the defendant in *Michael M. v. Superior Court of Sonoma County*. The section ends with one contributor's concept of a society of complete gender equality.

A. Constitutional Equality and Preferential Treatment

Introduction

The idea of equality is deceptively simple. Consider this question: Should everyone have an equal opportunity to be a Boy Scout? The immediate thought is to say "Sure, why not. As long as you abide by their rules." But what if the rules themselves do not treat everyone equally? In 1998 the California Supreme Court decided two cases in which discrimination claims had been brought against the Boy Scouts of America (BSA). In one case, the court ruled that two brothers from Anaheim could be ejected from the BSA for refusing to recite a required oath to God; in the other case, the court said that the BSA could deny a former Eagle Scout a job as a scoutmaster because he was gay. Current civil rights law prohibits businesses from discriminating on grounds of religion or sexual orientation, but the BSA, the court reasoned, is "an expressive social organization whose primary function is the inculcation of values in its youth members"; hence it has broad authority to discriminate against atheists, agnostics, and gays. The ruling also has implications for suits currently pending by girls who wish to join. Is this equal treatment? How can we know?

It is surprising to many to learn that the original Constitution of 1789 makes no mention of "equality." Nor does the term appear in any of the first ten Amendments—the so-called "Bill of Rights." The original document arguably does address religious discrimination, at least indirectly, in the form of the "Establishment" and "Free Exercise" clauses of the First Amendment. (See Chapter Two for more on these notions.) And the Constitution prohibits "titles of nobility." These aspects of the original Constitution very much reflect the aspirations and concerns of its Enlightenment authors, who believed in the equal opportunity to pursue happiness without the impediment of legal restrictions based on heredity or religious affiliation. It was not until the aftermath of the Civil War, however, that equality became part of the amended Constitution.

Today, the ultimate source and focus for the philosophically difficult legal issues regarding equality is the Fourteenth Amendment to the Constitution, and in particular, the so-called *equal protection* clause, guaranteeing that no state shall "deny to any person within its jurisdiction the equal protection of the laws." A brief discussion of the background to and subsequent development of this clause will set the stage for an understanding of the difficulties it poses.

The Fourteenth Amendment

Following the Civil War, the Congress passed a number of constitutional amendments with the aim of "reconstructing" the South and healing the union. The Thirteenth Amendment prohibited slavery and gave Congress the power to take steps to eradicate it. In response, many of the Southern states passed harsh and restrictive laws applying to Blacks, curtailing their civil rights in various ways, though short of an outright return to slavery. To eliminate these "Black Codes," Congress enacted the Civil Rights Act of 1866. This act granted to newly freed Blacks a small number of specifically enumerated but limited rights: to enter into contracts, to sue, to hold and convey property, to move about without threat of arrest. While the original draft language of the act apparently included a reference to general "civil rights and immunities," this was later dropped.

According to some scholars, the majority of the supporters of the 1866 act were against the idea of full political and social equality for Blacks, and this may have been a factor in the passage of the Fourteenth Amendment. According to legal historian Raoul Berger, one group of legislators, concerned that the act have a proper foundation in the Constitution, proposed the Fourteenth Amendment to serve that purpose; and it was their view that the equal protection clause guaranteed to Blacks no more than the few specific rights listed in the act. Other factions, however, seemingly had larger ambitions and may have intended that "equal protection of the law" be broadly read to ensure full political and social equality for Blacks.

Throughout the rest of the nineteenth century and well into this one, the narrow conception of equality predominated in the courts. In 1896, in *Plessy v. Fergusen*,[1] the Supreme Court held that the segregation of Blacks and Whites on public transit facilities (and by implication in various other public facilities) did not violate the guarantee of equal protection, provided that such separate facilities were roughly similar; and the Court noted that many of the states that supported the Fourteenth Amendment had, for example, segregated their schools and prohibited racial intermarriage. This "separate-but-equal" doctrine prevailed until 1954 and the landmark case *Brown v. Board of Education*.[2] Finding that the practice of segregation stamped Blacks with "a badge of inferiority," the Court concluded that separate but equal "is inherently unequal." Later cases prohibited racial segregation in a whole variety of public facilities and settings.

The significance for us of the history just sketched is twofold. First, it seems clearly to show that the understanding of equality now endorsed by the courts, and presumably by the great majority of Americans, moves well beyond any views reasonably attributable to the framers of the Fourteenth Amendment; they, it appears, may well have regarded *Plessy* as correctly decided and *Brown* as a misinterpretation of the amendment's language.

---

[1] 163 U.S. 537 (1986).
[2] 347 U.S. 483 (1954).

Second, the fact of two such divergent interpretations as *Plessy* and *Brown* reveals just how flexible and open-ended the language of the equal protection clause is. If we acknowledge that the guarantee of equality may mean more than its authors took it to mean, and if we recognize the breadth and sweep of the text itself, we are brought to the edge of a basic issue in social and political philosophy: What is equality? What concept of equality should we understand our law to endorse? Why is equality desirable?

The Concept of Equality

Thinking about the idea of equality quickly leads to puzzlement. This fact is demonstrated in the selection reprinted here by Peter Westen. Westen employs a series of illustrations to show that treating people equally is not as easy as it seems. What, for example, can it mean to treat people equally when making them equal in one way has the effect of making them unequal in another respect? Westen's aim is to raise this and similar questions.

Even assuming that we understand what equality means, why is it important to treat people equally? Suppose that you and I are both hungry. We have both gone without food for the same length of time and for the same reasons. We are physically quite alike and both extremely weak. What gives each of us an equal claim to a piece of food? The answer given by many philosophers going back to Aristotle invokes a basic moral principle that has been thought by some to be self-evidently true: *Those who are the same in relevant respects ought to be treated the same with regard to those respects;* or, *Those similarly situated should be similarly treated.* This *formal principle of equality* reveals an important feature of the concept of equality: When we ask whether two things or two people are "equal," we must always be assumed to be asking this question relative to an aspect of the things or people that we judge to be relevant. It is not enough simply to ask "Are A and B equal?" The question makes no sense until we further specify the traits in which A and B are to be judged equal or unequal. Are A and B equal in respect of height, weight, shoe size, intelligence, bravery, moral worth? We must have in mind, in other words, the parameters within which they are to be judged similar or dissimilar, the relevant respects in which they are the same or different.

One way to understand the equal protection clause of the Constitution is as a confirmation or implementation of the formal principle of equality: The clause says that legislatures must treat similarly those who are similarly situated with respect to the purposes of the laws they pass. After a legislature decides which people are to be affected by a new law, for example, it must further ensure that those people are treated equally with respect to that law.

The problem in all of this, of course, is that the formal principle of equality and the equal protection clause understood simply as a guarantee of formal equality say nothing by themselves about which are the traits that matter. They merely lay down a requirement of fair administration, prohibiting differences in treatment among those who have already been determined to be the same in the relevant way. In one crucial respect, however, the equal protection clause of the Fourteenth Amendment is not merely a guarantee of formal equality, for that clause actually rules out altogether, as ever relevant to how people should be treated, one trait or characteristic: the fact of being Black.

It is obvious that people differ from each other in a variety of ways, for example, in their physical characteristics and abilities and in their talents, aptitudes, and interests. And it is also apparent that when people notice or recognize ways in which others are different from themselves, they often use that recognition as a reason for treating the others less well. The recognition of difference both supports and further reinforces prejudicial attitudes and biases. The concept of equality, however, demands that law preclude the acknowledgment of at least some differences from becoming prejudicial practices, and the law does this by disallowing that certain differences matter. In this way, the concept of equality is connected to the idea of *justice*. In one sense, treating people justly means that all are given a fair share of the goods, services, and opportunities that society has to offer. If I am denied an opportunity based on an irrelevant difference, I am the victim of injustice. In another sense, justice may demand that I be compensated for something of

which I have been unfairly deprived. If I have been wrongly treated on the basis of an irrelevant characteristic, I may demand compensation from those who wronged me. As we will see, both of these forms of justice are relevant to the debate over programs of affirmative action.

But the problem remains: How do we specify the differences among people that matter or are relevant to how people should be treated? Generally speaking, the law has sought to solve this problem through a negative process of elimination: Instead of trying to settle on all of the ways in which, ideally, people should be regarded as similarly situated, the law has contented itself with seeking to identify and root out the respects that should *not* matter, the traits or characteristics that do not justify differences in treatment. This approach derives support from the basic aim of the post–Civil War amendments to the Constitution: to prohibit at least some forms of discrimination against Blacks; "race, color, or previous condition of servitude" are traits on which the Constitution says it is unfair or unjust to base differences in treatment. Other parts of the Constitution, and of our law generally, would add national origin, religious affiliation, and status as an illegitimate child to the list of proscribed traits. Any law that classifies people on the basis of these traits automatically becomes "suspect" and must be subjected to "strict scrutiny" to determine whether it is justified by a "compelling" interest of the state. To treat people differently or unequally on the basis of these characteristics without such a compelling reason is to practice discrimination.

Many of us think of discrimination on the basis of race or religion as the most fundamental violation of equality, yet the concept of discrimination is not without its own difficulties. How is discrimination to be identified and remedied? When does a practice that disadvantages a particular population or group become "discriminatory"? School districts in many parts of the country were at one time racially segregated by law, yet even when such deliberately discriminatory efforts were ended, their effects lingered through segregated housing patterns and school attendance zones. Is this "de facto" segregation a violation of the equal protection of the laws that should be remedied by, for example, forced busing of students? Or is it the conconsequence of private "choice" for which government is not responsible? Consider the example of a state that enacts a law requiring a passing score on a literacy test as a prerequisite to registration as a voter. The test has the effect of disqualifying almost all of the Latinos in the state, but nearly all Whites pass the exam. How should a law that has a disproportionate racial impact but is nonetheless nondiscriminatory "on its face" be viewed? Should it automatically be presumed invalid? Should it be taken as evidence of racial prejudice operating behind the scenes? Should the fact that it is color-blind on its face be sufficient to let it stand? Finally, there is the issue of remedies for discrimination. Should the victims of past discrimination be given some kind of favored treatment? Should a firm or other employer shown to have discriminated in the past be required to hire a fixed percentage of its workforce from among members of the minority group against which it discriminated? Should it matter if the actual minority persons hired were not the individuals originally turned down for a job?

The Bakke Case

Among the most hotly contested issues concerning equality is the use of race as a basis for differential treatment. Is it *always* impermissible to use traits such as ethnic or national origin as factors on the basis of which to treat people differently or unequally? This query has been given sharp focus in recent years by the proliferation of "preferential treatment" or "affirmative action" policies in education and employment. Supporters argue that such programs are required by ideas of fairness and the greater social good; opponents contend that such practices disserve the ideal of equality.

Although it was decided some years ago, the *Bakke* case remains a useful introduction to the legal dimensions of the preferential treatment controversy. The medical school at the University of California at Davis ran two admissions programs, one for "regular" applicants and one for "special," disadvantaged students. Sixteen of the 100 seats in the entering class were set aside for students from the special program, which had a lower minimum grade point average requirement than the regular

program. Alan Bakke was twice rejected under the regular program, although students with lower overall scores were admitted through the special program. Bakke sued the university, alleging that he was unjustifiably excluded from the medical school in violation of both the equal protection clause of the Constitution and the Civil Rights Act of 1964. The trial court agreed with Bakke but refused to order the school to admit him; this was done by the Supreme Court of California.

The United States Supreme Court split badly on the issues involved in *Bakke*, with Justice Powell emerging as the key figure. (Powell voted against "quotas" but in favor of using race as a factor in medical school admissions. Four other justices held that the Civil Rights Act, and by implication the equal protection clause, prohibits any consideration of race as a relevant factor, joining with Powell to make a majority against quotas; another four justices held that Davis-type preferential treatment programs are permissible under both the act and the Constitution, joining with Powell in asserting that consideration of race and ethnicity is allowable.) Because Powell was the key vote, our selection focuses upon his opinion.

As we saw earlier, the courts have long held that any ordinance, policy, or practice that treats a person's race as a factor relevant to how he or she is to be treated by the government must be subjected to "strict scrutiny," meaning that the law must be shown necessary to the realization of a "compelling" objective if it is to have any hope of being upheld. Justice Powell argues that such scrutiny must be applied to the Davis program, and he carefully reviews the various arguments given by Davis to support preferential treatment: to increase the representation of minority students in medical school; to "cure" societal discrimination; to better serve the health needs of the minority community. Powell rejects these as constitutionally permissible grounds for preferential treatment but argues that another purpose—to promote diversity—is legitimate and may permit the use of race as one factor among many in admissions decisions. The Constitution will not tolerate, however, policies that unduly burden the rights of particular, innocent individuals such as Bakke simply to further the social standing of certain groups.

The Hopwood Case

In June 1996, the U.S. Supreme Court, in a move widely viewed as further repudiation of affirmative action, refused to hear an appeal from a lower federal court ruling in the case of Cheryl Hopwood. Hopwood worked about twenty hours a week to pay her way through college. Her father left the family when she was small, and her mother worked at several jobs to support the family; Hopwood raised a severely disabled child of her own. In 1992 Hopwood applied for admission to the University of Texas law school. She had a 3.8 grade point average (GPA) and scored in the 83rd percentile on the LSAT. The Texas law school admits 500 students a year, accepting students who score better than 85 percent of all college graduates who take the LSAT and have a 3.5 GPA. Texas, like other law schools, seeks to recruit a "diverse" class on incoming students. In 1992, however, only eighty-eight African-American and fifty-two Mexican-American students in the entire nation satisfied these standards. To achieve diversity, Texas therefore segregated its admissions process, reviewing separately applications from African-American and Mexican-American students. Hopwood, who is white, was denied admission and filed suit, alleging racial discrimination by the law school.

Hopwood argued that only one of the forty-one African-American students and three of the Mexican-American students admitted to Texas in 1992 had scores that matched hers. Hopwood insisted that the university operated a virtual "quota-system" for certain students. University officials countered that the African-American and Mexican-American students it admitted were qualified, with average GPAs of around 3.3. It also pointed out that the population of the state of Texas is nearly 50 percent African- and Mexican-American, and that the university would not be doing its job if it enrolled students on the numbers alone. In March 1996, the Fifth U.S. Circuit Court of Appeals accepted Hopwood's arguments and struck down the University of Texas plan on the grounds that it failed to pass the test of "strict scrutiny." The court argued that *Bakke* should no longer be followed. Part of the court's argument is excerpted in our readings for this section.

Equality and Preferential Treatment

Two of the arguments most commonly offered in support of preferential treatment programs are based on the idea of justice. The first argument appeals to the obvious inequalities of material condition and opportunity presently existing between Whites and members of certain minority groups and claims that such differences are the result of *distributive injustice,* an unequal distribution of benefits stemming from the use of race as a relevant factor in the distribution of social wealth: jobs, educational opportunities, and so forth. Preferences are therefore needed now to place Blacks and other minorities in positions they would have had but for the discrimination, positions they would presumably have attained under conditions of fair competition.

Those favoring affirmative action point to significant evidence of the continued underrepresentation of Blacks and women in both labor and educational institutions. *Fortune* magazine, for example, found only one Black CEO among its Fortune 1,000 and only one Black among its top 500 industrial firms in 1988.[3] *Business Week*'s directory of 1,000 publicly held companies lists only one Black and two female executive officers.[4] Of two million engineers in America, only 2 percent are Hispanic. Of 225,000 physical scientists, 3 percent are Black and less than 2 percent are Hispanic. Blacks and Hispanics comprise less than 2½ percent of the lawyers in the nation's largest law firms. According to another recent survey, seven out of ten Blacks and Latinos remain in low-level jobs and only one architect in five is a woman. Nearly 80 percent of all skilled jobs are still held by White males.[5] Nor have women fared much better. Many women continue to be relegated to poor-paying "pink-collar" jobs or are stranded in entry-level positions at the bottom of the corporate ladder. According to one university study, one quarter of the 1,300 women polled earn a poverty-level income. It is estimated by a Rand Corporation study that women can expect to

---

[3] See *Fortune,* January 19, 1988.

[4] See *Business Week,* October 19, 1990.

[5] See *Los Angeles Times,* Sept. 10, 1995.

earn 75 percent of the average for working men by the year 2000.[6] The Department of Education estimates that male full professors outnumber female full professors by almost six to one; in 1988, Blacks and Latinos constituted just 15 percent of the total nationwide college enrollment.

The foregoing figures are taken to reveal significant and continuing disparities in material resources and prestige between Whites and non-whites, and between men and women. The reasons for these disparities are rarely overt or blatant discrimination; proponents of affirmative action suggest that the disparities are much more likely the result of institutional barriers: the use of qualification requirements, employment networks and tradition, and the aftereffects of previous legal segregation. Employers who use race- or gender-neutral qualifications as the basis of their hiring practices might create a disadvantage for minorities. Nearly all employers insist that they want to hire the most qualified candidates; yet qualifications justifiable on grounds of ensuring productivity may also put at a comparative disadvantage individuals whose education was second-rate. This problem is particularly acute for Blacks in the labor force who attended legally segregated schools in which there was likely a presumption of Black inferiority, or for women who were taught that analytical and scientific reasoning are unfeminine and that their proper role in society is to get married and become a housewife.

Another argument maintains that the case for preferential treatment rests on the notion of *reparation.* We must institute such programs to aid minorities not because we want to achieve some ideal of equal opportunity but because the present condition of Blacks in America is a direct result of a history of injustices committed against them by Whites and because reparation, so understood, is owed by Whites as a group to Blacks as a group.

Those opposed to affirmative action programs also make arguments of justice. Recall the formal principle of equality, which affirms that individuals who are equal under the law should be treated in the same manner. This principle means that people who are governed by the same laws must have the same rights and obligations; the fact that some may possess greater economic power than others should have no bearing on whether and how the law applies to each. Critics of affirmative action argue that the demands of formal justice require that one's race and gender (and perhaps other characteristics as well) be deemed irrelevant to possession of the opportunity to participate equally in the benefits and burdens of society. Yet affirmative action programs seem to entail a violation of this very requirement. For if it was a violation of equality to discriminate *against* people in the past, it is also wrong to discriminate *in favor* of them now by means of programs that give preferential treatment. Affirmative action destroys equality under the law, say the opponents, and in so doing might even open the door to further discrimination. Members of groups not preferred by special admissions or hiring programs are themselves treated unjustly by being denied access to schools or jobs based on *their* race. The guarantee of equality is a promise of neutrality and color blindness, and this applies no matter what policy or whose race is at stake.

Arguments based upon the notion of social utility, or overall social good, frequently complement arguments for or against preferential treatment based on considerations of justice. Utilitarian supporters of preferential treatment have urged, for example, that such programs are necessary to bring larger numbers of minorities into the professions, thereby enriching and benefiting the lives of those who participate in them. The presence of women and people of color in universities and professional schools, for example, enhances the likelihood that important perspectives on life will not go unrepresented in the classroom. It is further claimed, as by U.C. Davis in *Bakke,* that greater numbers of minorities in medical, law, and business schools will result in improved service to minority communities currently underserved by these professions. And it is asserted that "successful" minority persons who have been aided by preferential treatment can serve as valuable role models for young people from disadvantaged backgrounds. Opponents of affirmative action respond that such programs will not bring about the greatest good for society as a whole. They point to the potential for

---

[6] *Ibid.*

resentment among those members of nonpreferred groups who, like Bakke, are passed over in favor of minority individuals, and they raise the concern that minority graduates of professional schools who are admitted with lower grade averages and test scores may not be as qualified to dispense beneficial, and sometimes vital, services as the rejected applicants would be.

In his selection included here, law professor Richard Epstein is critical of the direction taken by current laws against discrimination, particularly as they relate to employment. The "antidiscrimination principle," which holds that employers are forbidden to discriminate in a variety of ways, represents, according to Epstein, the wrong approach to the social problems of bigotry and inequality. Antidiscrimination law interferes too deeply with freedom of contract—the ability to make and enforce private arrangements. Furthermore, antidiscrimination law has perverted the original meaning of civil rights and attempts to impose understandings of ideas such as merit and qualifications, which cannot be defended legitimately.

Philosopher Thomas Nagel gives a guarded defense of affirmative action policies. Nagel begins by distinguishing efforts to enhance the diversity of applicant pools and training programs to make minority candidates competitive, what he calls "weak affirmative action," from definite preferences in employment and education given to members of minority groups over other equally or even better-qualified candidates, what he calls "strong affirmative action." Nagel evaluates three objections to programs of strong affirmative action, concluding that only significant moral arguments in favor of affirmative action can overcome these objections. He concludes by presenting his own arguments seeking to justify strong affirmative action. Nagel argues that such programs are justified in the short term but only for Blacks, whose unique history of oppression justifies extraordinary measures.

Women and members of other minority groups, however, have not suffered in the same way as Blacks, Nagel believes, and therefore strong affirmative action in their case is unjustified.

In the final selection, writer Shelby Steele makes a case against affirmative action. Steele believes that programs of affirmative action have done more to harm Blacks than to help them, and in the selection included here he tries to establish this. Affirmative action, Steele asserts, has shifted from simply ensuring equality of opportunity to proportional representation of races in schools and professions without regard for whether those who benefit were victims of past discrimination. Nor has achieving proportionate representation ameliorated the social and economic disparities between Blacks and Whites. Steele rejects the argument that preferential treatment is justified on the basis of reparations owed by Whites to Blacks. On another level, Steele insists, affirmative action preferences actually harm Blacks by sustaining the assumption that Blacks are inferior and wouldn't be able to make it without reliance upon preferences. Preferential treatment encourages them to play the role of victim and to rely on others instead of doing for themselves.

The "Cases for Further Reflection" at the end of the chapter look at a variety of Supreme Court cases dealing with difficult issues of equality, discrimination, and fairness: Does it discriminate against either partner in an interracial relationship to forbid them to marry? Does a preference for hiring minorities or veterans discriminate against those who lose out on the basis of such a preference? Does a state discriminate against gays when it forbids gays and lesbians from enjoying the same protected status as members of racial or religious groups?

52. Regents of the University of California v. Bakke

Summary by the Reporter of Decisions:

The Medical School of the University of California at Davis (hereinafter Davis) had two admissions programs for the entering class of 100 students—the regular admissions program and the special admissions program. Under the regular procedure, candidates whose overall undergraduate grade point averages fell below 2.5 on a scale of 4.0 were summarily rejected. About one out six applicants was then given an interview, following which he was rated on a scale of 1 to 100 by each of the committee members (five in 1973 and six in 1974), his rating being based on the interviewers' summaries, his overall grade point average, his science courses grade point average, and his Medical College Admissions Test (MCAT) scores, letters of recommendation, extracurricular activities, and other biographical data, all of which resulted in a total "benchmark score." The full admissions committee then made offers of admission on the basis of their review of the applicant's file and his score, considering and acting upon applications as they were received. The committee chairman was responsible for placing names on the waiting list and had discretion to include persons with "special skills." A separate committee, a majority of whom were members of minority groups, operated the special admissions program. The 1973 and 1974 application forms, respectively, asked candidates whether they wished to be considered as "economically and/or educationally disadvantaged" applicants and members of a "minority group" (blacks, Chicanos, Asians, American Indians). If an applicant of a minority group was found to be "disadvan-

taged," he would be rated in a manner similar to the one employed by the general admissions committee. Special candidates, however, did not have to meet the 2.5 grade point cut-off and were not ranked against candidates in the general admissions process. About one-fifth of the special applicants were invited for interviews in 1973 and 1974, following which they were given benchmark scores, and the top choices were then given to the general admissions committee, which could reject special candidates for failure to meet course requirements or other specific deficiencies. The special committee continued to recommend candidates until 16 special admission selections had been made. During a four-year period 63 minority students were admitted to Davis under the special program and 44 under the general program. No disadvantaged whites were admitted under the special program, though many applied.

Respondent, a white male, applied to Davis in 1973 and 1974, in both years being considered only under the general admissions program. Though he had a 468 out of 500 score in 1973, he was rejected since no general applicants with scores less than 470 were being accepted after respondent's application, which was filed late in the year, had been processed and completed. At that time four special admission slots were still unfilled. In 1974 respondent applied early, and though he had a total score of 549 out of 600, he was again rejected. In neither year was his name placed on the discretionary waiting list. In both years special applicants were admitted with significantly lower scores than respondent's. After his second rejection, respondent filed this action in state court for mandatory injunctive and declaratory relief to compel his admission to Davis, alleging that the special admissions program operated to exclude him on the basis of his race in violation of the Equal Protection Clause of the Fourteenth Amendment, a provision of the California Constitution, and §60I of Title VI of the Civil Rights Act of 1964. . . .

438 U.S. 265 (1978)
United States Supreme Court

Powell, [Justice].

Although many of the Framers of the Four-teenth Amendment conceived of its primary function as bridging the vast distance between members of the Negro race and the white "major-ity," . . . supra, the Amendment itself was framed in universal terms, without reference to color, ethnic origin, or condition of prior servitude. . . .

Indeed, it is not unlikely that among the Framers were many who would have applauded a reading of the Equal Protection Clause that states a principle of universal application and is responsive to the racial, ethnic, and cultural diversity of the Nation.

Over the past 30 years, this Court has em-barked upon the crucial mission of interpreting the Equal Protection Clause with the view of assuring to all persons "the protection of equal laws" . . . in a Nation confronting a legacy of slavery and racial discrimination. . . .

Petitioner urges us to adopt for the first time a more restrictive view of the Equal Protection Clause and hold that discrimination against mem-bers of the white "majority" cannot be suspect if its purpose can be characterized as "benign." The clock of our liberties, however, cannot be turned back to 1868. It is far too late to argue that the guar-antee of equal protection to *all* persons permits the recognition of special wards entitled to a degree of protection greater than that accorded others. . . . The concepts of "majority" and "minority" neces-sarily reflect temporary arrangements and political judgments. As observed above, the white "major-ity" itself is composed of various minority groups, most of which can lay claim to a history of prior discrimination at the hands of the State and private individuals. Not all of these groups can receive preferential treatment and corresponding judicial tolerance of distinctions drawn in terms of race and nationality, for then the only "majority" left would be a new minority of white Anglo-Saxon Protes-tants. There is no principled basis for deciding which groups would merit "heightened judicial so-licitude" and which would not. . . .

Moreover, there are serious problems of justice connected with the idea of preference itself. First, it may not always be clear that a so called preference is in fact benign. . . . Second, preferential programs may only reinforce common stereotypes holding that certain groups are unable to achieve success without special protection based on a factor having no relationship to individual worth. Third, there is a measure of inequity in forcing innocent persons in respondent's position to bear the burdens of re-dressing grievances not of their making. . . .

We have held that in "order to justify the use of a suspect classification, a State must show that its purpose or interest is both constitutionally per-missible and substantial, and that its use of the classification is 'necessary . . . to the accomplish-ment' of its purpose or the safeguarding of its interest." . . . The special admissions program pur-ports to serve the purposes of: (i) "reducing the historic deficit of traditionally disfavored mi-norities in medical schools and the medical profession," (ii) countering the effects of societal discrimination; (iii) increasing the number of physicians who will practice in communities cur-rently underserved; and (iv) obtaining the educa-tional benefits that flow from an ethnically diverse student body. It is necessary to decide which, if any, of these purposes is substantial enough to support the use of a suspect classification.

If petitioner's purpose is to assure within its student body some specified percentage of a partic-ular group merely because of its race or ethnic ori-gin, such a preferential purpose must be rejected not as insubstantial but as facially invalid. Prefer-ring members of any one group for no reason other than race or ethnic origin is discrimination for its own sake. This the Constitution forbids.

The State certainly has a legitimate and sub-stantial interest in ameliorating, or eliminating where feasible, the disabling effects of identified discrimination. . . .

We have never approved a classification that aids persons perceived as members of relatively victimized groups at the expense of other innocent individuals in the absence of judicial, legislative, or administrative findings of constitutional or statu-tory violations. After such findings have been made, the governmental interest in preferring members of the injured groups at the expense of others is substantial, since the legal rights of the victims must be vindicated. In such a case, the ex-tent of the injury and the consequent remedy will have been judicially, legislatively, or administra-tively defined. Also, the remedial action usually remains subject to continuing oversight to assure that it will work the least harm possible to other innocent persons competing for the benefit. . . .

Petitioner does not purport to have made, and is in no position to make, such findings. Its broad mission is education, not the formulation of any legislative policy or the adjudication of particular claims of illegality. For reasons similar to those stated [earlier], isolated segments of our vast governmental structures are not competent to make those decisions, at least in the absence of legislative mandates and legislatively determined criteria. . . . Before relying upon these sorts of findings in establishing a racial classification, a governmental body must have the authority and capability to establish, in the record, that the classification is responsive to identified discrimination. . . .

Petitioner simply has not carried its burden of demonstrating that it must prefer members of particular ethnic groups over all other individuals in order to promote better health-care delivery to deprived citizens. Indeed, petitioner has not shown that its preferential classification is likely to have any significant effect on the problem.

The fourth goal asserted by petitioner is the attainment of a diverse student body. This clearly is a constitutionally permissible goal for an institution of higher education. Academic freedom, though not a specifically enumerated constitutional right, long has been viewed as a special concern of the First Amendment. The freedom of a university to make its own judgments as to education includes the selection of its student body. . . .

The atmosphere of "speculation, experiment and creation"—so essential to the quality of higher education—is widely believed to be promoted by a diverse student body. . . .

Thus, in arguing that its universities must be accorded the right to select those students who will contribute the most to the "robust exchange of ideas," petitioner invokes a countervailing constitutional interest, that of the First Amendment. In this light, petitioner must be viewed as seeking to achieve a goal that is of paramount importance in the fulfillment of its mission.

It may be argued that there is greater force to these views at the undergraduate level than in a medical school where the training is centered primarily on professional competency. But even at the graduate level, our tradition and experience lend support to the view that the contribution of diversity is substantial. . . . Physicians serve a heterogeneous population. An otherwise qualified medical student with a particular background—whether it be ethnic, geographic, culturally advantaged or disadvantaged—may bring to a professional school of medicine experiences, outlooks, and ideas that enrich the training of its student body and better equip its graduates to render with understanding their vital service to humanity.

. . . As the interest of diversity is compelling in the context of a university's admissions program, the question remains whether the program's racial classification is necessary to promote this interest.

. . . The diversity that furthers a compelling state interest encompasses a far broader array of qualifications and characteristics of which racial or ethnic origin is but a single though important element. Petitioner's special admissions program, focused *solely* on ethnic diversity, would hinder rather than further attainment of genuine diversity. . . .

The experience of other university admissions programs, which take race into account in achieving the educational diversity valued by the First Amendment, demonstrates that the assignment of a fixed number of places to a minority group is not a necessary means toward that end. An illuminating example is found in the Harvard College program:

> In recent years Harvard College has expanded the concept of diversity to include students from disadvantaged economic, racial and ethnic groups. Harvard College now recruits not only Californians or Louisianans but also blacks and Chicanos and other minority students. . . .
>
> In practice, this new definition of diversity has meant that race has been a factor in some admission decisions. When the Committee on Admissions reviews the large middle group of applicants who are "admissible" and deemed capable of doing good work in their courses, the race of an applicant may tip the balance in his favor just as geographic origin or a life spent on a farm may tip the balance in other candidates' cases. A farm boy from Idaho can bring

something to Harvard College that a Bostonian cannot offer. Similarly, a black student can usually bring something that a white person cannot offer. . . .

In Harvard college admissions the Committee has not set target-quotas for the number of blacks, or of musicians, football players, physicists or Californians to be admitted in a given year. . . . But that awareness [of the necessity of including more than a token number of black students] does not mean that the Committee sets a minimum number of blacks or of people from west of the Mississippi who are to be admitted. It means only that in choosing among thousands of applicants who are not only "admissible" academically but have other strong qualities, the Committee, with a number of criteria in mind, pays some attention to distribution among many types of and categories of students.

In such an admissions program, race or ethnic background may be deemed a "plus" in a particular applicant's file, yet it does not insulate the individual from comparison with all other candidates for the available seats. The file of a particular black applicant may be examined for his potential contribution to diversity without the factor of race being decisive when compared, for example, with that of an applicant identified as an Italian-American if the latter is thought to exhibit qualities more likely to promote beneficial educational pluralism. Such qualities could include exceptional personal talents, unique work or service experience, leadership potential, maturity, demonstrated compassion, a history of overcoming disadvantage, ability to communicate with the poor, or other qualifications deemed important. In short, an admissions program operated in this way is flexible enough to consider all pertinent elements of diversity in light of the particular qualifications of each applicant, and to place them on the same footing for consideration, although not necessarily according them the same weight. Indeed, the weight attributed to a particular quality may vary from year to year depending upon the "mix" both of the student body and the applicants for the incoming class.

This kind of program treats each applicant as an individual in the admissions process. The applicant who loses out on the last available seat to another candidate receiving a "plus" on the basis of ethnic background will not have been foreclosed from all consideration for the seat simply because he was not the right color or had the wrong surname. It would mean only that his combined qualifications, which may have included similar nonobjective factors, did not outweigh those of the other applicant. His qualifications would have been weighed fairly and competitively, and he would have no basis to complain of unequal treatment under the Fourteenth Amendment.

It has been suggested that an admissions program which considers race only as one factor is simply a subtle and more sophisticated—but no less effective—means of according racial preference than the Davis program. A facial intent to discriminate, however, is evident in petitioner's preference program and not denied in this case. No such facial infirmity exists in an admissions program where race or ethnic background is simply one element—to be weighed fairly against other elements—in the selection process. "A boundary line," as Mr. Justice Frankfurter remarked in another connection, "is none the worse for being narrow." . . . And a court would not assume that a university, professing to employ a facially nondiscriminatory admissions policy, would operate it as a cover for the functional equivalent of a quota system. . . .

In summary, it is evident that the Davis special admissions program involves the use of an explicit racial classification never before countenanced by this Court. It tells applicants who are not Negro, Asian, or Chicano that they are totally excluded from a specific percentage of the seats in an entering class. No matter how strong their qualifications, quantitative and extracurricular, including their own potential for contribution to educational diversity, they are never afforded the chance to compete with applicants from the preferred groups for the special admissions seats. At the same time, the preferred applicants have the opportunity to compete for every seat in the class.

The fatal flaw in petitioner's preferential program is its disregard of individual rights as guaranteed by the Fourteenth Amendment. . . .

In enjoining petitioner from ever considering the race of any applicant, however, the courts below failed to recognize that the State has a substantial interest that legitimately may be served by a properly devised admissions program involving the competitive consideration of race and ethnic origin. For this reason, so much of the California court's judgment as enjoins petitioner from any consideration of the race of any applicant must be reversed.

With respect to respondent's entitlement to an injunction directing his admission to the Medical School, petitioner has conceded that it could not carry its burden of proving that, but for the existence of its unlawful special admissions program, respondent still would not have been admitted. *Hence, respondent is entitled to the injunction, and that portion of the judgment must be affirmed.*

53. *Cheryl J. Hopwood v. State of Texas*

Opinion:

Jerry E. Smith, Circuit Judge:

With the best of intentions, in order to increase the enrollment of certain favored classes of minority students, the University of Texas School of Law ("the law school") discriminates in favor of those applicants by giving substantial racial preferences in its admissions program. The beneficiaries of this system are blacks and Mexican Americans, to the detriment of whites and non-preferred minorities. The question we decide today is whether the Fourteenth Amendment permits the school to discriminate in this way.

We hold that it does not. The law school has presented no compelling justification, under the Fourteenth Amendment or Supreme Court precedent, that allows it to continue to elevate some races over others, even for the wholesome purpose of correcting perceived racial imbalance in the student body. . . .

The University of Texas School of Law is one of the nation's leading law schools, consistently rank-

78 F.3d 932 (1996)
United States Court of Appeals, Fifth Circuit

ing in the top twenty. Accordingly, admission to the law school is fiercely competitive, with over 4,000 applicants a year competing to be among the approximately 900 offered admission to achieve an entering class of about 500 students. Many of these applicants have some of the highest grades and test scores in the country.

Numbers are therefore paramount for admission. In the early 1990's, the law school largely based its initial admissions decisions upon an applicant's so-called Texas Index ("TI") number, a composite of undergraduate grade point average ("GPA") and Law School Aptitude Test ("LSAT") score. The law school used this number as a matter of administrative convenience in order to rank candidates and to predict, roughly, one's probability of success in law school. Moreover, the law school relied heavily upon such numbers to estimate the number of offers of admission it needed to make in order to fill its first-year class. . . .

Because of the large number of applicants and potential admissions factors, the TI's administrative usefulness was its ability to sort candidates. For the class entering in 1992 the admissions group at issue in this case the law school placed the typical applicant in one of three categories according to his TI scores: "presumptive admit," "presumptive deny," or a middle "discretionary zone." An applicant's TI category determined how extensive a review his application would receive. . . .

Blacks and Mexican Americans were treated differently from other candidates, however. First, compared to whites and non-preferred minorities, the TI ranges that were used to place them into the three admissions categories were lowered to allow the law school to consider and admit more of them. In March 1992, for example, the presumptive TI admission score for resident whites and non-preferred minorities was 199. Mexican Americans and blacks needed a TI of only 189 to be presumptively admitted. The difference in the presumptive-deny ranges is even more striking. The presumptive denial score for "nonminorities" was 192; the same score for blacks and Mexican Americans was 179. . . .

These disparate standards greatly affected a candidate's chance of admission. For example, by March 1992, because the presumptive denial score for whites was a TI of 192 or lower, and the presumptive admit TI for minorities was 189 or higher, a minority candidate with a TI of 189 or above almost certainly would be admitted, even though his score was considerably below the level at which a white candidate almost certainly would be rejected. Out of the pool of resident applicants who fell within this range (189–192 inclusive), 100% of blacks and 90% of Mexican Americans, but only 6% of whites, were offered admission. . . .

In addition to maintaining separate presumptive TI levels for minorities and whites, the law school ran a segregated application evaluation process. Upon receiving an application form, the school color-coded it according to race. If a candidate failed to designate his race, he was presumed to be in a nonpreferential category. Thus, race was always an overt part of the review of any applicant's file. . . .

Cheryl Hopwood, Douglas Carvell, Kenneth Elliott, and David Rogers (the "plaintiffs") applied for admission to the 1992 entering law school class. All four were white residents of Texas and were rejected.

The plaintiffs were considered as discretionary zone candidates. Hopwood, with a GPA of 3.8 and an LSAT of 39 (equivalent to a three-digit LSAT of 160), had a TI of 199, a score barely within the presumptive-admit category for resident whites, which was 199 and up. She was dropped into the discretionary zone for resident whites (193 to 198), however, because Johanson decided her educational background overstated the strength of her GPA. Carvell, Elliott, and Rogers had TI's of 197, at the top end of that discretionary zone. Their applications were reviewed by admissions subcommittees, and each received one or no vote. . . .

The central purpose of the Equal Protection Clause is to prevent the States from purposefully discriminating between individuals on the basis of race. . . .

Strict scrutiny is necessary because the mere labeling of a classification by the government as "benign" or "remedial" is meaningless. . . .

Under the strict scrutiny analysis, we ask two questions: (1) does the racial classification serve a compelling government interest, and (2) is it narrowly tailored to the achievement of that goal?

With these general principles of equal protection in mind, we turn to the specific issue of whether the law school's consideration of race as a factor in admissions violates the Equal Protection Clause. The district court found both a compelling remedial and a non-remedial justification for the practice.

First, the court approved of the non-remedial goal of having a diverse student body, reasoning that "obtaining the educational benefits that flow from a racially and ethnically diverse student body remains a sufficiently compelling interest to support the use of racial classifications." Second, the court determined that the use of racial classifications could be justified as a remedy for the "present effects at the law school of past discrimination in both the University of Texas system and the Texas educational system as a whole." . . .

Here, the plaintiffs argue that diversity is not a compelling governmental interest under superseding Supreme Court precedent. Instead, they believe that the Court finally has recognized that only the remedial use of race is compelling. In the alternative, the plaintiffs assert that the district court misapplied Justice Powell's *Bakke* standard, as the law school program here uses race as a strong determinant rather than a mere "plus" factor and, in any case, the preference is not narrowly applied. The law school maintains, on the other hand, that Justice Powell's formulation in *Bakke* is law and must be followed at least in the context of higher education.

We agree with the plaintiffs that any consideration of race or ethnicity by the law school for the purpose of achieving a diverse student body is not a compelling interest under the Fourteenth Amendment. Justice Powell's argument in *Bakke* garnered only his own vote and has never represented the view of a majority of the Court in *Bakke* or any other case. Moreover, subsequent Supreme Court decisions regarding education state that non-remedial state interests will never justify racial classifications. Finally, the classification of persons on the basis of race for the purpose of diversity frustrates, rather than facilitates, the goals of equal protection.

Justice Powell's view in *Bakke* is not binding precedent on this issue. While he announced the judgment, no other Justice joined in that part of the opinion discussing the diversity rationale. In *Bakke*, the word "diversity" is mentioned nowhere except in Justice Powell's single-Justice opinion. In fact, the four-Justice opinion, which would have upheld the special admissions program under intermediate scrutiny, implicitly rejected Justice Powell's position.

Thus, only one Justice concluded that race could be used solely for the reason of obtaining a heterogeneous student body. As the *Adarand* Court states, the *Bakke* Court did not express a majority view and is questionable as binding precedent.

Since *Bakke*, the Court has accepted the diversity rationale only once in its cases dealing with race. Significantly, however, in that case, *Metro Broadcasting, Inc. v. Federal Communications Comm'n*, (1990), the five-Justice majority relied upon an intermediate scrutiny standard of review to uphold the federal program seeking diversity in the ownership of broadcasting facilities. In *Adarand*, the Court squarely rejected intermediate scrutiny as the standard of review for racial classifications, and *Metro Broadcasting* is now specifically overruled to the extent that it was in conflict with this holding. No case since *Bakke* has accepted diversity as a compelling state interest under a strict scrutiny analysis.

Indeed, recent Supreme Court precedent shows that the diversity interest will not satisfy strict scrutiny. Foremost, the Court appears to have decided that there is essentially only one compelling state interest to justify racial classifications: remedying past wrongs. . . .

Within the general principles of the Fourteenth Amendment, the use of race in admissions for diversity in higher education contradicts, rather than furthers, the aims of equal protection. Diversity fosters, rather than minimizes, the use of race. It treats minorities as a group, rather than as individuals. It may further remedial purposes but, just as likely, may promote improper racial stereotypes, thus fueling racial hostility.

The use of race, in and of itself, to choose students simply achieves a student body that looks different. Such a criterion is no more rational on its own terms than would be choices based upon the physical size or blood type of applicants. Thus, the Supreme Court has long held that governmental actors cannot justify their decisions solely because of race.

Accordingly, we see the caselaw as sufficiently established that the use of ethnic diversity simply to achieve racial heterogeneity, even as part of the consideration of a number of factors, is unconstitutional. Were we to decide otherwise, we would contravene precedent that we are not authorized to challenge.

While the use of race per se is proscribed, state-supported schools may reasonably consider a host of factors—some of which may have some correlation with race—in making admissions decisions. The federal courts have no warrant to intrude on those executive and legislative judgments unless the distinctions intrude on specific provisions of federal law or the Constitution. A university may properly favor one applicant over another because of his ability to play the cello, make a downfield tackle, or understand chaos theory. An admissions process may also consider an applicant's home state or relationship to school alumni. Law schools specifically may look at things such as unusual or substantial extracurricular activities in college, which may be atypical factors affecting undergraduate grades. Schools may even consider factors such as whether an applicant's parents attended college or the applicant's economic and social background. . . .

For this reason, race often is said to be justified in the diversity context, not on its own terms, but as a proxy for other characteristics that institutions of higher education value but that do not raise similar constitutional concerns. Unfortunately, this approach simply replicates the very harm that the Fourteenth Amendment was designed to eliminate.

The assumption is that a certain individual possesses characteristics by virtue of being a member of a certain racial group. This assumption, however, does not withstand scrutiny. . . .

To believe that a person's race controls his point of view is to stereotype him. . . .

[I]ndividuals, with their own conceptions of life, further diversity of viewpoint. Plaintiff Hopwood is a fair example of an applicant with a unique background. She is the now-thirty-two-year-old wife of a member of the Armed Forces stationed in San Antonio and, more significantly, is raising a severely handicapped child. Her circumstance would bring a different perspective to the law school. The school might consider this an advantage to her in the application process, or it could decide that her family situation would be too much of a burden on her academic performance.

We do not opine on which way the law school should weigh Hopwood's qualifications; we only observe that "diversity" can take many forms. To foster such diversity, state universities and law schools and other governmental entities must scrutinize applicants individually, rather than resorting to the dangerous proxy of race.

The Court also has recognized that government's use of racial classifications serves to stigmatize. While one might argue that the stigmatization resulting from so-called "benign" racial classifications is not as harmful as that arising from invidious ones, the current Court has now retreated from the idea that so-called benign and invidious classifications may be distinguished. . . .

Finally, the use of race to achieve diversity undercuts the ultimate goal of the Fourteenth Amendment: the end of racially motivated state action. Justice Powell's conception of race as a "plus" factor would allow race always to be a potential factor in admissions decisionmaking. While Justice Blackmun recognized the tension inherent in using race-conscious remedies to achieve a race-neutral society, he nevertheless accepted it as necessary. . . .

In sum, the use of race to achieve a diverse student body, whether as a proxy for permissible characteristics, simply cannot be a state interest compelling enough to meet the steep standard of strict scrutiny. These latter factors may, in fact, turn out to be substantially correlated with race, but the key is that race itself not be taken into account. Thus, that portion of the district court's opinion upholding the diversity rationale is reversibly flawed. . . .

The Supreme Court repeatedly has warned that the use of racial remedies must be carefully limited, and a remedy reaching all education within a state addresses a putative injury that is vague and amorphous. It has "no logical stopping point."

The district court's holding employs no viable limiting principle. If a state can "remedy" the present effects of past discrimination in its primary and secondary schools, it also would be allowed to award broad-based preferences in hiring, government contracts, licensing, and any other state activity that in some way is affected by the educational attainment of the applicants. . . .

Strict scrutiny is meant to ensure that the purpose of a racial preference is remedial. Yet when one state actor begins to justify racial preferences based upon the actions of other state agencies, the remedial actor's competence to determine the existence and scope of the harm and the appropriate reach of the remedy is called into question. . . .

Here, however, the law school has no comparative advantage in measuring the present effects of discrimination in primary and secondary schools in Texas. Such a task becomes even more improbable where, as here, benefits are conferred on students who attended out-of-state or private schools for such education. Such boundless "remedies" raise a constitutional concern beyond mere competence. In this situation, an inference is raised that the program was the result of racial social engineering rather than a desire to implement a remedy.

No one disputes that in the past, Texas state actors have discriminated against some minorities in public schools. In this sense, some lingering effects of such discrimination is not "societal," if that term is meant to exclude all state action. But the very program at issue here shows how remedying such past wrongs may be expanded beyond any reasonable limits.

Even if, arguendo, the state is the proper government unit to scrutinize, the law school's admissions program would not withstand our review. For the admissions scheme to pass constitutional muster, the State of Texas, through its legislature, would have to find that past segregation has present effects; it would have to determine the magnitude of those present effects; and it would need to limit carefully the "plus" given to applicants to remedy that harm. A broad program that sweeps in all minorities with a remedy that is in no way related to past harms cannot survive constitutional scrutiny. Obviously, none of those predicates has been satisfied here. . . .

In sum, the law school has failed to show a compelling state interest in remedying the present effects of past discrimination sufficient to maintain the use of race in its admissions system. Accordingly, it is unnecessary for us to examine the district court's determination that the law school's admissions program was not narrowly tailored to meet the compelling interests that the district court erroneously perceived.

54. *Puzzles About Equality*

Peter Westen

One day, while on vacation in Guatemala, I go to a *campesino* market to buy food for dinner. I ask a vendor for one pound of black beans. He puts a brass weight marked "one pound" in one pan of a hand-held balance and pours beans into the other pan until the two come into balance. "Bueno," he says, "ya son iquales" ("Good, now they're equal").

What does the vendor mean when he says that the two pans of the scale are "equal"? Does he mean that they are absolutely identical in weight? Does he mean that they are highly similar in weight? Or does 'equal' mean something different from—something in between—'identical', on the one hand, and 'similar', on the other?

I try to buy a newspaper, but the vendor cannot make change for a $10 bill. I ask the pharmacist for change. She takes the $10 bill and gives me two $5 bills, while counting aloud, "5 + 5 = 10."

What does the pharmacist mean by saying "5 + 5 = 10"? Does 'equal' have the same meaning in arithmetic as it does for the *campesino*? If the pharmacist means something different, where does the

difference lie—in the meaning of the word 'equal' or in something to which the 'equal' refers? Is there any core meaning of 'equality' that remains constant in both usages?

After buying snacks for my three children, I sit in a cafe and read the newspaper. I read that the people of Guatemala have recently adopted a new constitution, which states that "in Guatemala, all people are free and equal." What does it mean to say in law that all people are equal? Does the legal equality of one Guatemalan to another differ from the mathematical equality of "5 + 5 = 10" and the descriptive equality of the two pans of the balance scale? Is there any sense in which the meaning of equality remains the same in all three instances? Why does the concept of equality in the Guatemalan constitution seem more elusive, more complex, and more controversial than the equality of "5 + 5 = 10"? And if the former equality is more enigmatic than the latter, where does the enigma lie—in the concept of equality itself, or somewhere else?

I return home with the snacks for the children—chocolate for my son, gum for my daughters. "Because I want to treat you all equally," I say, "I have brought each of you your favorite treat." My son likes the chocolate but not my explanation. "I agree that you're treating us fairly," he says, "but you're not treating us equally because you're bringing us different things." Who is right? Am I right that I treated my children equally, or is my son right that I did not? Or is it possible that both of us are right?

My older daughter has a different problem with the gum. Like her younger sister she would rather have gum than chocolate, but unlike her sister, she does not care much for any kind of sweet. She would rather have the money than the gum. "I know you're trying to be fair," she says, "but it's not really equal to give the same thing to both of us if it's something she likes more than I do."

Am I right in thinking that I am treating my daughters equally by giving the same quantity of gum to each without further distinguishing between them? Or is the older child right when she says that no distribution is really equal which has a disparate impact on them by giving one more pleasure than the other? Are we both right? Or does the answer lie in the distinction some commentators draw between treating people "equally," on the one hand, and treating them "as equals," on the other? Have I succeeded in treating the girls equally and yet failed to treat them as equals? Or is it sophistic to distinguish between equal treatment and treatment as equals?

The older daughter's complaint also raises a question about the relationship between fair treatment and equal treatment. What is the connection between treating a person fairly and treating her equally? Why does she regard it as a form of moral criticism to call the treatment "unequal"? Is unequal treatment a moral concept, or is it a purely descriptive concept? Is it both?

I am still thinking about the relationship between equal treatment and fair treatment when my wife calls us to dinner. My wife serves the meal to the children by giving the largest portion to our son, who is a teenager and has the largest appetite, the next largest portion to the older daughter, who is going through a growth spurt, and the smallest portion to the youngest, who never eats much at dinner. She also gives everyone a glass of water. Everything goes smoothly until I suggest that we have treated the children equally by treating them in accordance with their needs. My son does not like my use of 'equal'.

"I don't get it," he says. "The more you talk about equality, the less I understand it. 'Equal' means giving us each the same amount: It means taking food and dividing it by the number of people at the table. What Mom did with the glasses of water was equal. What she did with the meal was proportional—dividing the meal in proportion to our needs. "Equal' is equal; it's not proportional."

I resist the temptation to say that while some commentators agree with him, others (including Aristotle) disagree. Some agree that per-capita distributions are the only truly equal distributions. Others believe that, while per-capita distributions differ in substance from distributions in accord with needs (or in accord with merit, or effort, or wants), per capita distributions are no more inherently equal than other principled distributions.

Nor do I tell my son that some commentators would question the proposition he regards as self-evident, namely, that his mother treated him and his sisters equally by giving them each a glass of water. Whether it is truly equal, they would say, depends upon her *reason* for giving him a glass of water. If she gave him the glass of water because (and *only* because) she had already given water to his sisters, then she treated him equally. If, however, she gave him the glass of water because she believes every child is entitled to at least one glass of water per meal (and not because she had already given glasses of water to his sisters), then she did not treat him equally with his sisters. This is so, they say, because treatment is equal if and only if it is treatment to which a person is entitled only by virtue of its having already been given to others.

After dinner several children from the neighborhood come to the door soliciting contributions for their parish church's Lenten celebration. Each holds out a tin can asking that we favor him with our donation. Our girls both want to give a portion of their allowance, but they don't know how they should distribute it. My wife, not seeing any basis for distinguishing among the children, feels we should divide the donation among them equally. "Unless someone gives me a good reason for preferring one child over the others," she says, "I really think we have to treat them the same."

My son, who is embarrassed by the throng of children, doesn't feel presumptively obliged to treat them equally. "I don't see why it's up to us to find reasons for treating them differently; it's up to them to show us reasons for treating them the same. Why do we have to resolve doubts in their favor?"

The difference of opinion between my wife and son is the difference between competing normative propositions—competing maxims—regarding equality. My wife is proceeding in accord with what some call "the presumption of equality," that is, the normative proposition that "people ought to be treated equally unless there are good reasons for treating them differently." My son, feeling no presumption one way or the other, may be unconsciously proceeding in accord with what is sometimes called the "principle of equality," namely, the principle that "equals should be treated equally, and unequals should be treated unequally."

Which of the two propositions of equality is the more persuasive? Are they consistent with one another? What do they both mean in the context at hand? Who are the "people" who are to be treated equally within the meaning of the "presumption of equality"—only those children who are soliciting contributions at our door, or all the door-to-door solicitors in town? What would constitute a "good reason" for treating the children unequally within the meaning of the presumption? Is a personal preference for redheads a good reason? Who are the "equals" who are to be treated equally within the meaning of the "principle of equality"—the first child to approach us, or the one we wish most to please? And what is the meaning of "equal treatment" within both propositions of equality—to donate to the most courteous child, or to all the children per capita?

I turn on the evening news to hear about a controversial campaign by Guatemalan women in favor of affirmative action. Advocates on both sides of the controversy adopt the language of equality. I am reminded of other controversies in which both sides invoke 'equality' in support of their contrary positions—controversies over the use of sex tables in computing life insurance, the use of height and strength requirements for fire departments, and the maintenance of separate athletic events for men and women. How does the concept of equality accommodate such mutually exclusive positions, and what is the source of its compelling rhetorical force? Why is it easier to argue in favor of equality than against it? Why is inequality always on the defensive? Is it because equality is inherently desirable, or presumptively desirable? If either, how can equality also lend itself to the most controverted of social causes? How can equality be simultaneously both desirable and controversial?

In one sense, these questions regarding equality differ significantly. Some involve descriptive statements of equality, others involve prescriptive statements of equality. Some look to whether rules are equal on their face, others to whether rules are equal as applied. Some concern the meaning of 'equals', others the meaning of 'equal treatment'. Some probe the relationship between equality and rights of nondiscrimination. Some involve propositions of equality. Yet in another sense the questions are also the same. They all call for an analysis of language—an inquiry into ordinary usages of the word 'equality'. Their answers turn not on contested moral propositions but on linguistic analysis of the concept of equality in moral and legal discourse.

It is fitting that these questions of equality should differ from one another and yet be the same, for equality is itself a relationship that uniquely straddles the gap between "different" and "same": things that are equal, being distinct things, are necessarily different; and yet, being equal, they are also the same. Moreover, the general concept of equality that underlies particular relationships of equality has both a fixed element, which remains the same in all its usages (at least regarding persons and things we perceive through the sense), and a variable term, which can differ greatly from one statement of equality to another. The key to understanding the meaning and rhetorical force of 'equality' in law and morals, I believe, lies in identifying the kinds of variable terms that enter into moral and legal statements of equality.

55. The Case Against Antidiscrimination Law

Richard A. Epstein

. . .

There is little question that a broad antidiscrimination principle lies at the core of American political and intellectual understandings of a just and proper society, not only in employment but also in housing and public accommodations, medical care, education, indeed in all areas of public and private life. The consensus in favor of the principle is as wide as it is deep. Its implications profoundly influence the shape and efficiency not merely of American labor markets but also of our basic social institutions.

The cultural and historical reasons for this social consensus on discrimination provide powerful leitmotifs for the present legal discourse, especially on issues of race. The history of official and private discrimination in American life covers slavery in the South, the Civil War, Reconstruction, Jim Crow, segregation in the military, massive resistance to school desegregation, sit-ins and lunch counters, and struggles for the ballot. The enormous successes in changing a misguided, and often hateful, pattern of race relations have all come through sustained government action, which often depended on the use of force. Even today frequent outbreaks of racial violence, conflict, boycotts, and demonstrations have ushered in a new spate of racial tensions greater than any that have existed in the previous twenty years. The symbolic role of an antidiscrimination statute in this context is not something that can be easily ignored or cast aside.

The history of sex discrimination is not as searing as that of race relations, but the transformation of the legal rights of women in both the public and private sphere has been accompanied by extensive social unrest that has often spilled over into violence. Limitations on the civil capacity for ordinary social and business transactions form a part of our nation's history, and the same is true of the long battle over women's suffrage. The full complex of women's issues is still very much in the forefront. In my judgment, feminism is the single most powerful social movement of our time, one that addresses every aspect of human and social life. But in this realm too we have not reached closure. There are continuing signs of unrest, with reports of widespread uneasiness about women in the military, and a series of incidents over such matters as whether women reporters should be barred from men's locker rooms after sporting events.

The scope of the antidiscrimination norm has its most powerful appeal in matters of race and sex, but it has been extended to other areas. When the 1964 Civil Rights Act was passed, there was little, if any, public sentiment to regulate discrimination on the basis of either age or handicap. But within a matter of a few years, protection against these forms of discrimination by analogy and extension became a dominant theme within our legal culture. . . .

In undertaking this critique of the antidiscrimination laws in employment, I have engaged in a process of relentless disaggregation by looking closely at the application of each form of law as it applies to existing employment markets. My work follows in the steps of others who have expressed uneasiness about the desirability or operation of these laws. Yet several of these authors did their major work in the early period of the civil rights movement, and none of them has urged the outright rejection of the antidiscrimination principle in private employment or the repeal of Title VII of the 1964 Civil Rights Act, as I do. I am under no illusion about the magnitude of the enterprise of seeking to undo the legal status quo, given the enormous support that it commands from the intellectual, business, and political elites in this country. . . .

The unchallenged social acceptance of the antidiscrimination principle has far-reaching conse-

Reprinted by permission of the publisher from *Forbidden Grounds: The Case Against Employment Discrimination Law* by Richard Epstein, Cambridge, MA: Harvard University Press, © 1992 by the President and Fellows of Harvard College.

quences. At stake is the basic choice of legal regimes under which social life is ordered. An antidiscrimination law is the antithesis of freedom of contract, a principle that allows all persons to do business with whomever they please for good reason, bad reason, or no reason at all. Under this contractual regime, the chief job of the state is to ensure that all persons enjoy the civil capacity to own property, to contract, to sue and be sued, and to give evidence. The rights that the state thereby recognizes and protects are easily made universal, and can be held simultaneously by all persons. There is no effort to form separate codes of conduct for particular trades, professions, or businesses. There are no special status-based rules that limit the power to contract of employers, landlords, manufacturers, or suppliers of any form of goods or services. The state secures for all persons a zone of freedom against aggression and fraud in which voluntary transactions for business, personal, charitable, and religious activities of all kinds and descriptions occur. The legal system does not take it upon itself to specify the trading partners for any person or the terms and conditions under which trade takes place. Individuals themselves decide which contracts are made and on what terms.

With regard to commerce and trade, freedom of contract confines the state to functions that are both facilitative and reactive: facilitative because it provides the forms and mechanisms that allow people to exchange and trade as they please, and reactive because it enforces the trades so made. The law allows all people to enter into private agreements with the modest confidence that they will be able to enforce these agreements when the other side is in breach, but subject to the sober recognition that the power of the state will be turned against them if they themselves are in breach. Only where the state acts as an employer are there substantive limitations on the kinds of contracts that can be formed.

The antidiscrimination principle operates as a powerful brake against this view of freedom of contract and the concomitant but limited role of the state. By its nature the antidiscrimination principle is interventionist for reasons that have nothing to do with the prevention of force and fraud. Rather, the principle rests on the collective social judgment (often born out of wrenching historical experience) that some grounds for private decision are so improper that it is both immoral and illegal for the

government to allow employers to use them in deciding whether to hire, retain, or promote workers. The list of forbidden grounds includes race, sex, age, national origin, religious belief, handicap, and in some cases sexual orientation. Decisions made "on the merits" are allowed, but, subject to a broad and controversial exception of affirmative action, any private reliance on these socially extraneous criteria is prohibited. The defenders of the antidiscrimination principle often treat that principle as though it were a self-evident truth that certain grounds for decision should be banned for moral reasons. On other occasions they treat the principle not as a good in itself but as a means to other ends: to creating an open and equal society with full participation, or to increasing the overall wealth of society by ensuring that all productive labor may be put to its highest use.

Whatever the precise rationale, the antidiscrimination principle is tenacious in labor markets. Only on rare occasions may the principle be overridden by a powerful showing of business necessity. Any person may refuse to contract for no reason at all, or even for bad reasons that lie outside the reach of the antidiscrimination principle. But refusal to deal for reasons forbidden by statute renders an employer's conduct illegal, and exposes the employer to heavy legal sanctions. Nor can an antidiscrimination statute bring about fundamental changes in labor markets if its application is confined only to refusals to deal., Employers could always make offers on terms so unattractive that they would not be accepted. Once those "terms and conditions" cases are covered by the statute, then by degrees it becomes necessary to scrutinize each and every aspect of any transaction in the employment arena.

During its 1988–89 term, the Supreme Court handed down a number of critical decisions that imposed some new limits on the reach of the antidiscrimination principle in the private sector and breathed new life into the principle in the public sector.[1] These cases have been interpreted by many in the civil rights establishment as marking a judicial retreat from two generations of unwavering support for the antidiscrimination principle. The decisions themselves are all worthy of close examination, but at the outset it is sufficient to say that none of these Supreme Court cases challenges, or even questions, the basic antidiscrimination principle, now embodied in Title VII of the 1964 Civil

Rights Act. Instead, these cases are directed at collateral questions: the interaction of different statutory schemes, the proof of discrimination by statistical inference, the ability of consent decrees to bind or otherwise limit the rights of nonsigning parties, and the constitutionality of minority set-asides. At no point has the Court ever stated, or even intimated, that the basic antidiscrimination principle is not an essential part of the fabric of modern American law and social life. The debates within the Supreme Court mirror those of the larger society: they concern the reach and application of a principle that is accorded quasi-sacred status, not its essential soundness. Needless to say, under current law any constitutional attack against the antidiscrimination principle is wildly inconceivable.

Indeed, given its institutional role, the Supreme Court would be foolhardy to take any other view on the subject, even if it were inclined to do so, which it is not. The strength of the political and intellectual consensus on behalf of the existing law is so strong, I doubt that the Court would be able to withstand the pounding that would result if it undertook a frontal assault on the basic antidiscrimination norm. Academics and scholars are not so situated or constrained, however. . . . I advance a position that is well outside the mainstream of American political thought. I develop a defense of the traditional common law approach to the regulation of labor markets. My target is the social consensus that supports one or another version of the modern antidiscrimination principle. My method is a frontal intellectual assault on that consensus. . . .

The underlying problem with Title VII runs far deeper than it would appear at first. The Civil Rights Act necessarily involves a different conception of value and contracting from that found in market settings. The market model assumes that all elements of gain and loss are subjective, and that explicit measurement by external parties is not possible but is obtainable only be indirect inference. There is in a market exchange no objective test of merit on which any external observer can rely. There is only the subjective test of desire manifested in consent. Those things that tend to make a worker more desirable to the employer (and the employer more desirable to the worker) count as meritorious, while those that do not are not meritorious. In most cases an employer will value intelligence, initiative, honesty, reliability, and the like, so

the conventional accounts of merit carry substantial weight in individual personnel decisions. It looks, therefore, as though the civil rights statutes do not limit in the slightest the ability to discriminate on the strength of those universally desirable (because universally desired) characteristics.

. . .

The idea, then, that workers are "qualified," or that only merits are taken into account, is not drawn from the theory of private contract on which the market system operates. On the contrary, these ideas all assume that there is some objective measure that can be administered by an external agent who decides which types of agreements meet some standard of social acceptability and which do not. For these purposes it does not matter whether the prohibited grounds are defined in terms of race, sex, eye color, or anything else. What does matter is that the government makes the effort to define those prohibited grounds at all and enforces its judgments by coercive means. The argument here is, moreover, perfectly general: there is no independent objective standard of what package of benefits is right for all workers. There are only offers that can be accepted or rejected at will, and these reveal the benefits that are desired by the parties.

Once certain grounds for judgment are ruled out of bounds, the legal system must respond to a fresh round of imperatives. How does any court or administrative tribunal decide whether a personnel decision was made on the strength of one of the prohibited criteria, such as race or sex? The obvious case is easy to state and relatively easy to control. The employer who places a sign over the entrance to the workplace reading, "No blacks, women, or Jews allowed" (or "No whites, men, or Christians—or, as lately in Chicago, Arabs allowed"), is in violation of Title VII, without any further probing. In these disparate treatment cases the stated grounds for rejection, which were unquestionably legal in the common law world, now become the paradigmatic wrong within the regulatory framework, But the system of civil rights enforcement cannot stop with the obvious violations as long as some employers treat regulation as a burden that they try to evade. If the overt forms of discrimination are prohibited, then some recalcitrant employers will go underground, at a price. Given the prior commitment to the universal antidiscrimination norm, it therefore becomes necessary, albeit costly, to impose restric ttions as well upon the *covert* schemes and devices whereby employers seek by indirection the objective of the "no blacks" (or "no whites") sign. At this point the government prosecutor or aggrieved individual can no longer use a firm's public admission to establish its guilt; rather, it becomes necessary to collect the circumstantial evidence needed to justify criminal punishment or civil liability.

How does a trier of fact come by that evidence? One possible source is discarded memos or overheard discussions that indicate that decisions made on ostensibly neutral, or merit, grounds were in fact made on prohibited ones. The confidential admission is thus the "smoking gun" that takes the place of the defiant public refusal to deal. But these statements themselves are not easy to uncover, and cases of this sort are "relatively unusual." Once it is clear that powerful consequences attach to using forbidden criteria, some parties will abandon them. But for others the preferred alternative will be to burrow in deeper so as to keep their true grounds concealed. Memos to the file, far from being candid, will now be phrased in language that tracks the statute. Candidate X was not hired or promoted because he or she failed on grounds related to merit and to merit only. Much of the enforcement of Title VII on race or sex would grind to a halt if explicit evidence of motive were required to show that a refusal or failure to hire or promote was made "because of race, color, religion, sex or national origin." But it should not be supposed that the statute would have no effect at all. The explicit "whites only" provisions once common in union charters would, for example, be a thing of the past, and so would the explicit affirmative action programs of such rising popularity today.

Nonetheless, a strong commitment to a color-blind system of employment requires a sustained and systematic level of interference in the business place. The demands of enforcement are such that some types of external proof are needed to show whether the employer operated with the wrong type of mental state. It then becomes necessary to ask just what form the public evidence has to take. The current literature customarily distinguishes between the disparate treatment cases mentioned earlier and the disparate impact cases, which focus on the effects of hiring practices rather than on their motivation. At one level it may appear that the distinction is overdrawn, for both sets of cases raise

basically the same question: Where there is no admission, public or private, of guilt, what evidence can the plaintiff introduce in order to prevail, and what types of evidence can the defendant introduce to rebut the claim? The disparate treatment cases involve shorter chains of inference than the disparate impact cases.

Given the evolution of the legal system, however, the line between disparate treatment and disparate impact becomes the essence of the modern law. These structural similarities should not be allowed to obscure the massive differences in degree, which are often very pronounced. In practice Title VII in race relations would be a modest show of itself if plaintiffs were confined to the disparate treatment framework.

. . .

There seems to be little doubt that the civil rights movement is one of the most powerful political and social movements to surface in modern times. From its modest aspirations with the 1964 Civil Rights Act, it has continued to redefine its roles and to expand its goals, until today it represents a complete and consistent world view that permeates all areas of our collective social life. The imperialism of the movement is such that there is no issue within the realm of employment, and indeed within the larger realm of social endeavor, on which the civil laws do not exert a heavy, and baleful, influence. A movement with this power and this influence does not arise and flourish on the strength of political power or legal coercion alone. At some level it responds to deep-seated social conditions and powerful social symbols. . . .

If there is one image that drives the movement it is the specter of exclusion on grounds of race and sex. It is the image of "no blacks or women allowed" prominently displayed in businesses and firms throughout the nation. There is a powerful belief that these practices are so odious and their consequences so devastating that we as a nation should be willing to pay a very high price for their elimination, and should not be reluctant to use state force in order to achieve that collective goal. Does a rejection of Title VII mean that whites should be allowed to refuse to deal with blacks and men with women? As stated, the question captures part of the issue but misses other aspects of equal importance. Thus the verb *mean* has two separate meanings. First, it could suggest that the two assertions are identical, and that only whites can discriminate against blacks and only men against women. But the repudiation of the antidiscrimination norm for private affairs does not carry that meaning. A second implication of the general rule is that blacks may refuse to deal with whites (or with other blacks), and women may refuse to deal with men (or with other women). The principle of formal equality of all persons is respected fully when the antidiscrimination principle is accepted. There is of course no *duty* on the part of any person to discriminate against any other person, and there are many situations in which the discrimination will not occur, if only because it is against the interests of the party that might engage in it.

It would be a mistake to insist that all forms of discrimination would disappear in a competitive marketplace. Nonetheless, the antidiscrimination law does not satisfy any condition of formal equality because some forms of discrimination are allowed while others are forbidden. It is possible for organizations to post signs that say "no whites admitted," or "no males admitted," and there is no question that the groups that post such signs believe themselves better able to achieve their collective goals and missions if those policies are observed. The nature of interactions among individuals depends heavily on who is present. The women and blacks who post these signs do not necessarily wish to cut off all contacts with men and with whites, but they do want to have a sanctuary of their own where they can discuss their common concerns about "them" with a level of candor they do not believe to be possible in mixed company. There are gains from having certain groups with select criteria for admission. But there is no reason to believe that people who join one exclusive group thereby insist that *all* groups in which they participate must operate under identical rules of selection.

Once we can see the benefits of exclusion for ourselves, we should be prepared to recognize that these could exist for other people as well, for they too have desires and needs that cannot always be satisfied in mixed groups. Coherence is necessary for the perpetuation and success of voluntary organizations. And exclusion underlies the success of most religious organizations, clubs, and businesses, indeed any organization that has criteria for admission that mark them off from common carriers. Given their ubiquity, the fear of exclusion should lose some of its sting, when it is recognized that the

option should be available to all private groups, with no questions asked, and that the freedom to form additional groups leads to a broader range of opportunities across the board. It is not possible to create a world in which all people simultaneously have the right to join any organization that they choose and the right to keep others out of any organization that they form. The key question worth asking about the right to exclude in private settings is whether we are better off with its generalization or its repudiation. I can see no strong case for the latter. The right to exclude, and the correlative rejection of the antidiscrimination principle, is not a license to kill or an invitation for abuse, insult, or defamation. It is part of the right to be left alone with the people of one's choice.

It will be argued that there are strong externalities from exclusion. Some will say, "I don't wish to live in a society in which other people practice exclusion on grounds of race or sex." But when that claim is made by those who are opposed to the current pattern of state-supported discrimination, they are told that the justifications for the existing practices outweigh any private regret they might feel. It is never explained why one set of needs may be fully satisfied while the other must go completely unanswered. It is very easy to develop rules that give us exactly what we want if the only preferences and desires that are taken into account are those of people with whom we agree on moral or political grounds. The problem of social governance, however, requires that we make peace not with our friends but with our enemies, and that can be done only if we show some respect for their preferences even when we detest them. Using the principle of exclusion allows both groups to go their separate ways side by side. The antidiscrimination laws force them into constant undesired interaction. The totalitarian implications become clear only when one realizes the excessive steps that must be taken to enforce the antidiscrimination principle in favor of some groups while it is overtly ignored relative to other groups. It is not the least of the ironies of the study of Title VII that it has brought in its wake more discrimination (and for less good purpose) than would exist in an unregulated system.

In part the explanation rests on the substantial weight often attached to symbols relative to other forms of gains and losses both for society as a whole and for the individuals who compose it.

Thus it is frequently said that even if the employment discrimination laws do bring in their wake major economic dislocations, these costs should be cheerfully borne because they are more than offset by the substantial social and symbolic gains to the larger society. The initial difficulty with this position is that its defenders are no more skillful than its opponents in trading off symbolic losses against economic gains. How much of a symbolic gain is necessary to offset any economic loss? The paralysis induced by the broader analysis is one that infects both the supporters and the critics of the employment discrimination laws. If this were all that there was to the matter, then the best we could say was that there is some unfortunate standoff that advances the case for, even if it does not fully justify, the employment discrimination laws.

This ostensible tension between symbolic gains and economic losses itself seriously understates the difficulty of formulating any intelligent social policy based on the symbolic values of a society writ large. The major breakthrough of the economic analysis of social welfare rests mainly on the insight that the gains and losses to a society can be determined only by first calculating and then combining the gains and losses to its individual members. There are no shortcuts to the social interest that allows any analyst to avoid the inevitable difficulties that arise in implementing the enterprise. Does one measure wealth or utility? Can the gains to one person offset the losses to the next? Do sentiments of empathy or envy count? And so on. None of these difficulties with the aggregation problem are avoided when symbolic issues dominate the agenda. Just as with economic goods, determining social preferences from individual ones is easy only where there is *unanimous* agreement as to what the symbolic values are; and should that improbable state of affairs be achieved, it is likely that we could forge an equally strong consensus on the other economic and moral issues within the employment discrimination laws.

The critical problem, however, is that symbols also speak with many voices. To some an employment discrimination law that speaks of protected classes and affirmative action represents a strong social commitment to rectify the sins of the past, or a special solicitude for the concerns of the weakest and most disadvantaged among us. To those who are excluded or hurt by this body of rules, it could speak in a different voice—that of partisan politics

and ordinary special-interest lobbying. To some who benefit economically by it, these policies are regarded as a backhanded insult, as an implicit statement by persons in power that women and minorities cannot today (and will not ever in the future) make it on their own. The civil rights law thus speaks of a perpetual state of dependence, of a group of people who need constant state intervention to redress what would otherwise be their permanent inferior status in the marketplace.

These variations can easily be expanded, and the richer the mosaic, the greater the difficulties. Symbols therefore offer no trump to normative analysis, for the national divisions on economic issues carry over to the symbolic realm as well. If there is no way to trade off symbolic issues against economic ones, neither is there any easy way to trade off symbol against symbol, or different symbolic views of the same legal rules against one another. Given the limits of our own knowledge, I believe that the best way to take into account the full range of symbols, good and bad, noble and vain, is for the legal system to *ignore* them all—mine and yours alike. The symbols that then will prevail are those that can garner the highest level of support in the population at large. No one's symbolic aspirations can be achieved by passing laws that force others to adhere to a set of symbolic meanings and understandings they do not accept. Our strong tradition of freedom of speech, which allows persons to say thoughtless and hurtful things about the symbols held dear by others—think only of the flag-burning cases—is eminently defensible even though these hurts are real to the persons who bear them. The decision to keep off represents a profound social judgment that the business of weighing and trading symbolic meanings is one in which the state should never inject its collective judgment. What is true about speech itself should carry over to other laws, even those with manifest symbolic import. Their adoption or rejection should depend on their capacity to allow individuals to develop a sphere of personal control in which they can lead their own lives. Symbols are, in a sense, too important and too volatile to be either the subject of, or the justification for, direct government regulation.

This position leaves me securely outside the mainstream. The success and dangers of the modern civil rights movement rest in part on the elaborate set of social symbols and meanings that have allowed it to achieve its current dominance. Identifying these symbols reveals, however, a persistent ironic pattern. The most powerful symbols of the civil rights movement often make an implicit appeal to the libertarian tradition of private property and limited government that is in reality the polar opposite of its substantive positions. The dominant language of the modern civil rights movement allows it to draw its symbolic strength from the very principles of the legal order that it has come to undermine.

The first of the critical terms here is of course *civil rights* itself. In its original conception the term referred to civil capacity to contract, to own property, to make wills, to give evidence, and to sue and be sued. These are rights all individuals can enjoy simultaneously against the state and against one another. Their accurate definition and faithful protection is indispensable for any regime of limited government and individual freedom, and for all persons regardless of race, creed, religion, sex, or national origin. The great tragedy of the American experience with segregation was that our nation lost sight of that principle, and substituted an expansive regime of government activity, constitutionally sanctioned under the police power, which injected government influence and government favoritism into every transaction. Private markets respond to the external structures within which they operate; often in the past they took the path of least resistance and adopted explicit discriminatory practices that reflected these external constraints. To the extent that the civil rights movement is dedicated to the elimination of these formal and coercive barriers to entry, there is no conflict between civil rights in its traditional sense and civil rights in its modern incarnation.

Victory on this front was slow in coming, but it was achieved during the period culminating in passage of the Civil Rights Act of 1964. At that time, however, the movement changed its objectives, and civil rights changed its meaning. In the modern context it has become a term that refers to limits on freedom of association. It has thus repeated the fundamental official mistake of earlier generations by sanctioning active and extensive government interference in private markets. Civil rights quickly assumed an imperial air. It now allows the state (or some group within the state) to force others to enter into private arrangements that they would prefer to avoid. Although the traditional use of the police power allowed certain associations and exchanges to be forced, as with innkeepers and common carriers, it was always understood that this limitation on liberty was a way to diffuse the exercise of monopoly power, and it was subject to quid pro quo in that the party so regulated remained entitled, even as a matter of constitutional principle, to earn a just rate of return on its investment after the imposition of government restraint.

The modern civil rights movement cares little about the overall allocative consequences of its intervention, and often proceeds as if the misallocations that it brings about simply did not exist at all. It redescribes the patterns of routine business operations. If one assumes that firms are not moderately rational in the way in which they make their employment decisions, there is little efficiency cost to government interference that forces firms to restructure the way in which they do business. Similarly, if all firms are more or less homogeneous in their internal composition and identical in their internal modes of operation, then all firms can adapt equally well to a single and rigid system of external regulation, such as that propounded under modern civil rights legislation. Reliable enforcement of a system can then come at reasonably low cost. Finally, if quality differences between employees are, regardless of circumstances and roles, regarded as trivial, there is little net loss to the firm from the legislative limitation on its common law power to hire and fire. The gains from substituting one worker for another are thought to be small enough that productivity will not suffer. It is as though all choices were between productivity differentials of one or two points rather than large magnitudes and there were no high costs from subjecting all personnel decisions to external review.

This approach to business does have its high costs. Progress in business often comes from the cumulation of small edges and incremental advantages brought about by persons with extensive local knowledge. Imperfect information—hunch, intuition, experience—is often all that we have, and it is surely better than no information at all. But it is the kind of information that is greeted with scorn and hostility in the enforcement of a civil rights law that demands the highest level of proof to justify existing business practices that have survived in the market, while offering no proof that its own prescriptions will have their desired effects, or will do so at reasonable cost. Modern civil rights enforcement is thus legitimated because its defenders have flattened the world in order to reduce the apparent costs of regulation.

The civil rights movement has also changed its measures of social success and failure. Its mission today is defined not in terms of any overall standard of social welfare that takes into account the preferences and desires of all persons within society, but solely in terms of the various classes of protected parties. The refusal to take into account wide ranges of consumer preference is but one illustration of how certain individual losses are simply written off the ledger in the name of civil rights enforcement. Although the movement speaks in terms of rights, it suppresses the question of correlative duties, and of overall economic effect. In practice the antidiscrimination laws impose an elaborate set of disguised subsidies, and these distort resource allocation just like any other sort of subsidies. The civil rights statutes are not exempt from the usual critiques of wage and price regulation that point out their unresponsiveness to changes in supply, demand, and external circumstances. There is no reason to believe that in this area, unlike any other, we can be confident that the wisdom and self-restraint of government administrators will limit the excesses of the law. To the contrary, aggressive enforcement is the norm, a norm that is encouraged by the belief that certain losses do not count because they are borne by persons whose preferences do not count.

Civil rights is not the only term that has been ripped from its original libertarian moorings. We are often told that the goal of the civil rights movement is *diversity*. Diversity as it is traditionally understood means that no one should put all his or her eggs into a single basket. Invest in a broad-based fund and not in a single stock in order to diversify your losses and gains. The very term speaks of a toleration of differences and of a willingness to allow other individuals, or other institutions, to go their separate ways when they do not agree with you. With respect to government, diversity speaks of the importance of decentralization in the control of decision-making power, and necessarily directs us to limitations on government authority.

Within the modern civil rights discourse, however, diversity does not have that defensive orientation. Instead, it becomes yet another buzzword in the campaign for political conformity to a state-imposed ideal. Institutions that do not hire the right number of women or minorities are deemed to be not politically correct; therefore they should be exposed to government action, be it by private suit for discrimination, by enforcement actions from the EEOC, or by being hauled before accreditation committees. Unpacked, diversity today amounts to little more than a call for race-conscious and sex-conscious hiring, and in some circumstances even the more extreme position of proportionate representation by race and by sex. In the name of diversity all institutions have to follow the same policies or face the wrath of the state. A true sense of diversity would allow different institutions to explore different policies with respect to race and sex, including a color-blind and sex-blind policy, so often dismissed as a naive anachronism championed only by those who are ignorant of the sordid truth of the American past. But institutional diversity is not what is meant. Institutional rigidity is what is required in the name of diversity.

The call for diversity rests in large measure on the capacity of a new elite to tell the difference between invidious and benevolent forms of discrimination. Whereas the older common law rules stressed the need to set fixed and clear boundaries that established a perimeter of rights within which individuals could create their own autonomous systems, the newer rules make the *motive* from which acts are performed critical in the assessment of their legality. Yet we should always beware of claims of benevolence made in the political context. Even if certain practices are introduced from benevolent motives, the forces of individual self-interest and political action are never far from the scene, and these can easily become dominant no matter how lofty and disinterested the rationale of some defenders of the new practice. The durability of political institutions rests on their ability to resist domination by a few, and no test of good and motive is likely to prove strong enough over the long haul to resist the ravages of self-interest. The claims for diversity may properly be taken into account within private institutions, which can give them great weight if they so choose. But they offer no justification for any system of external coercion or state control. The presumption of distrust should always accompany the use of coercion, and that lesson too has been forgotten in the enforcement of the civil rights laws.

The drive for institutional conformity is further buttressed by pointing to practices of unconscious racism or sexism, which it is said must be rooted out at all costs. But there is scant recognition that much of today's underground resentment of the civil rights movement arises from the conscious racism and sexism that is so visible, powerful, and formalized in modern institutions. Freudian sophistication and Freudian naiveté go hand in hand. People who are quick to impugn the motives and the integrity of others, to find racial or sexual innuendo in innocent and everyday actions and speech, find it all too easy to make race and sex the dominant if not the sole determinants of their institutional decisions. It is as though unconscious racism and sexism were said to justify the formal, explicit, and conscious racism and sexism that so often run the other way. Anyone who works in academic circles, and I dare say elsewhere, knows full well that *all* the overt and institutional discrimination comes from those who claim to be the victims of discrimination imposed by others. It is a sad day when any effort to defend the traditional norms of a discipline, profession, trade, or craft exposes the defender to withering political attack for a covert form of discrimination under the guise of excellence and neutral standards. In all too many cases honorable people are attacked as racist or sexist when the charges often apply with far greater truth to the persons who make these charges than to the persons about whom they are made.

The appeal to unconscious racism is backed up by other powerful notions, which have no libertarian underpinnings. One of these is the condemnation of racial and sexual stereotypes. But the definition of *stereotype* does not refer solely to *false* generalizations about any group of persons. It refers as well to *true* generalizations. But lest one learn to accept and to live with the important differences between groups and individuals, we must dismantle other features of our common social life. The antidiscrimination laws thus play havoc with the use of any standard insurance principles, whether they deal with longevity or health, or any other aspect of human behavior. In a similar vein the antidiscrimination laws lead to a systematic Orwellian campaign of disinformation. One is not allowed to ask about age, about prior disability or handicap, about marital status, about individual abilities. Tests that have modest predictive value are rejected in favor of universal generalizations that have no predictive value at all. And this systematic campaign to discredit accurate statistical generalizations is punctuated by the self-congratulatory pronouncement that we have done all this not for our benefit but for yours. The current legislative view is that perfect information may be used (precisely because it can never be acquired), but nothing less will do.

This constant attack on statistical methods and insurance rests on a larger view of culture that is doubtless false as well. We are constantly instructed that differences between the sexes and among the various races are always *socially constructed*. The use of the term *gender* instead of *sex* is an effort to make it appear as though the differences between the sexes were mere accidents of biology that have no social relevance in employment settings and no long-term consequences for the welfare of either men or women. Similarly, differences along racial, ethnic, or religious lines are regarded as superficial and transient, so persons are to be treated as perfectly fungible with one another —unless, of course, the appeal to these same differences is made on behalf of, it not by, persons who fall into the appropriate protected categories. Then the differences are always relevant if not decisive.

It is difficult to see how discourse can go on in the present circumstances, when the use of language so constrains the nature of the debate that it is quite impossible to have an honest dialogue about the costs and benefits that derive from the present civil rights law. In the civil rights literature there is but scant, passing reference to intellectual excellence, personal dedication, effort, entrepreneurial zeal. It is as though all benefits were a result of luck or impersonal social forces, and none the result of intelligence, initiative, creativity, or plain hard work. One hears only constant complaints about why it is that some vague set of external forces, far short of state coercion and power, holds large classes of persons in its thrall. There is a pervasive ethos of victimology, and an eagerness to destroy standards, to make excuses. Taken together, the defeatist attitude and the lack of self-esteem sap the individual self-reliance that is necessary to ensure the safety and prosperity of a free and self-reliant nation.

A strong undercurrent today suggests that something has gone badly amiss with the civil rights law, that a great cause has become diverted from its central mission, that its excesses have overwhelmed its virtues. People are uneasy about the reach of the disparate impact tests in race and sex cases; they are troubled by the impact of the law on pensions and insurance; they think that a kind word could be said for mandatory retirement; they fret over the high costs associated with complying with rules for disabled employees. But they insist on finding small causes for their uneasiness. They seek errors in application, some explanation of how it is that sound principles have somehow gone awry.

My own examination of the subject has convinced me that the difficulties are far more fundamental. The root difficulty of the statute is that it maintains that a qualified norm of forced association is better than a strong norm of freedom of association. It is dangerous to assume that whatever conduct is thought to be wise or enlightened can and should be forced on society by the public speaking with one voice. There is little understanding of why the proscribed differences might matter, and little appreciation of the enormous political risks that come with concentrating power over employment decisions in the hands of a bureaucracy that operates under its own set of expansionist imperatives. There is also a failure to understand that the first question that should be asked in any public debate is *who* shall decide, not *what* should be decided. On the question of association, the right answer is the private persons who may (or may not) wish to associate, and not the government or the public at large. But having given the wrong collective answer to the "who" question, we find the "what" question receiving an extended elaboration that has resulted in the extensive and disruptive coercive structure that is civil rights enforcement today. More than I had anticipated, my study of the employment discrimination laws has persuaded me of the bedrock social importance of the principles of individual autonomy and freedom of association. Their negation through the modern civil rights law has led to a dangerous form of government coercion that in the end threatens to do more than strangle the operation of labor and employment markets. The modern civil rights laws are a new form of imperialism that threatens the political liberty and intellectual freedom of us all.

Endnote

[1] See *Martin v. Wilks,* 490 U.S. 755 (1989) (consent decrees); *Wards Cove Packing Co., Inc. v. Atonio,* 490 U.S. 642 (1989) (disparate impact); *City of Richmond v. J. A. Croson Co.,* 488 U.S. 469 (1989) (minority set-asides); *Patterson v. McLean Credit Union,* 491 U.S. 164 (1989) (relationship of §1981 of 1866 Civil Rights Act to the 1964 act).

---

56. A *Defense of Affirmative Action*

THOMAS NAGEL

The term "affirmative action" has changed in meaning since it was first introduced. Originally it referred only to special efforts to ensure equal opportunity for members of groups that had been subject to discrimination. These efforts included public advertisement of positions to be filled, active recruitment of qualified applicants from the formerly excluded groups, and special training programs to help them meet the standards for admission or appointment. There was also close at-

Reprinted by permission of the author.

tention to procedures of appointment, and sometimes to the results, with a view to detecting continued discrimination, conscious or unconscious.

More recently the term has come to refer also to some degree of definite preference for members of these groups in determining access to positions from which they were formerly excluded. Such preference might be allowed to influence decisions only between candidates who are otherwise equally qualified, but usually it involves the selection of women or minority members over other candidates who are better qualified for the position.

Let me call the first sort of policy "weak affirmative action" and the second "strong affirmative action." It is important to distinguish them, because the distinction is sometimes blurred in practice. It is strong affirmative action—the policy of preference—that arouses controversy. Most people would agree that weak or precautionary affirmative action is a good thing, and worth its cost in time and energy. But this does not imply that strong affirmative action is also justified.

I shall claim that in the present state of things it is justified, most clearly with respect to blacks. But I also believe that a defender of the practice must acknowledge that there are serious arguments against it, and that it is defensible only because the arguments for it have great weight. Moral opinion in this country is sharply divided over the issue because significant values are involved on both sides. My own view is that while strong affirmative action is intrinsically undesirable, it is a legitimate and perhaps indispensable method of pursuing a goal so important to the national welfare that it can be justified as a temporary, though not short-term, policy for both public and private institutions. In this respect it is like other policies that impose burdens on some for the public good.

Three Objections

I shall begin with the argument against. There are three objections to strong affirmative action: that it is inefficient; that it is unfair; and that it damages self-esteem.

The degree of inefficiency depends on how strong a role racial or sexual preference plays in the process of selection. Among candidates meeting the basic qualifications for a position, those better qualified will on the average perform better, whether they are doctors, policemen, teachers, or electricians. There may be some cases, as in preferential college admissions, where the immediate usefulness of making educational resources available to an individual is thought to be greater because of the use to which the education will be put or because of the internal effects on the institution itself. But by and large, policies of strong affirmative action must reckon with the costs of some lowering in performance level: the stronger the preference, the larger the cost to be justified. Since both the costs and the value of the results will vary from case to case, this suggests that no one policy of affirmative action is likely to be correct in all cases, and that the cost in performance level should be taken into account in the design of a legitimate policy.

The charge of unfairness arouses the deepest disagreements. To be passed over because of membership in a group one was born into, where this has nothing to do with one's individual qualifications for a position, can arouse strong feelings of resentment. It is a departure from the ideal—one of the values finally recognized in our society—that people should be judged so far as possible on the basis of individual characteristics rather than involuntary group membership.

This does not mean that strong affirmative action is morally repugnant in the manner of racial or sexual discrimination. It is nothing like those practices, for though like them it employs race and sex as criteria of selection, it does so for entirely different reasons. Racial and sexual discrimination are based on contempt or even loathing for the excluded group, a feeling that certain contacts with them are degrading to members of the dominant group, that they are fit only for subordinate positions or menial work. Strong affirmative action involves none of this: it is simply a means of increasing the social and economic strength of formerly victimized groups, and does not stigmatize others.

There is an element of individual unfairness here, but it is more like the unfairness of conscription in wartime, or of property condemnation under the right of eminent domain. Those who benefit or lose out because of their race or sex cannot be said to deserve their good or bad fortune.

It might be said on the other side that the beneficiaries of affirmative action deserve it as compensation for past discrimination, and that compensation is rightly exacted from the group that has benefited from discrimination in the past. But this is a bad argument, because as the practice usually works, no effort is made to give preference to those who have suffered most from discrimination, or to prefer them especially to those who have benefited most from it, or been guilty of it. Only candidates who in other qualifications fall on one or the other side of the margin of decision will directly benefit or lose from the policy, and these are not necessarily, or even probably, the ones who especially deserve it. Women or blacks who don't have the qualifications even to be considered are likely to have been handicapped more by the effects of discrimination than those who receive preference. And the marginal white male candidate, who is turned down can evoke our sympathy if he asks, "Why me?" (A policy of explicitly *compensatory* preference, which took into account each individual's background of poverty and discrimination, would escape some of these objections, and it has its defenders, but it is not the policy I want to defend. Whatever its merits, it will not serve the same purpose as direct affirmative action.)

The third objection concerns self-esteem, and is particularly serious. While strong affirmative action is in effect, and generally known to be so, no one in an affirmative action category who gets a desirable job or is admitted to a selective university can be sure that he or she has not benefited from the policy. Even those who would have made it anyway fall under suspicion, from themselves and from others: it comes to be widely fit that success does not mean the same thing for women and minorities. This painful damage to esteem cannot be avoided. It should make any defender of strong affirmative action want the practice to end as soon as it has achieved its basic purpose.

Justifying Affirmative Action

I have examined these three objections and tried to assess their weight, in order to decide how strong a countervailing reason is needed to justify such a policy. In my view, taken together they imply that strong affirmative action involving significant preference should be undertaken only if it will substantially further a social goal of the first importance. While this condition is not met by all programs of affirmative action now in effect, it is met by those which address the most deep-seated, stubborn, and radically unhealthy divisions in the society, divisions whose removal is a condition of basic justice and social cohesion.

The situation of black people in our country is unique in this respect. For almost a century after the abolition of slavery we had a rigid racial caste system of the ugliest kind, and it only began to break up twenty-five years ago. In the South it was enforced by law, and in the North, in a somewhat less severe form, by social convention. Whites were thought to be defiled by social or residential proximity to blacks, intermarriage was taboo, blacks were denied the same level of public goods—education and legal protection—as whites, were restricted to the most menial occupations, and were barred from any positions of authority over whites. The visceral feelings of black inferiority and untouchability that this system expressed were deeply ingrained in the members of both races, and they continue, not surprisingly, to have their effect. Blacks still form, to a considerable extent, a hereditary social and economic community characterized by widespread poverty, unemployment, and social alienation.

When this society finally got around to moving against the caste system, it might have done no more than to enforce straight equality of opportunity, perhaps with the help of weak affirmative action, and then wait a few hundred years while things gradually got better. Fortunately it decided instead to accelerate the process by both public and private institutional action, because there was wide recognition of the intractable character of the problem posed by this insular minority and its place in the nation's history and collective consciousness. This has not been going on very long, but the results are already impressive, especially in speeding the advancement of blacks in the middle class. Affirmative action has not done much to improve the position of poor and unskilled blacks. That is the most serious part of the problem, and it requires a more direct economic attack. But increased access to higher education and upper-level jobs is an essential part of what must be achieved to break the structure of drastic separation that was left largely undisturbed by the legal abolition of the caste system.

Changes of this kind require a generation or two. My guess is that strong affirmative action for blacks will continue to be justified into the early decades of the next century, but that by then it will have accomplished what it can and will no longer be worth the costs. One point deserves special emphasis. The goal to be pursued is the reduction of a great social injustice, not proportional representation of the races in all institutions and professions. Proportional racial representation is of no value in itself. It is not a legitimate social goal, and it should certainly not be the aim of strong affirmation action, whose drawbacks make it worth adopting only against a serious and intractable social evil.

This implies that the justification for strong affirmative action is much weaker in the case of other racial and ethnic groups, and in the case of women. At least, the practice will be justified in a narrower range of circumstances and for a shorter span of time than it is for blacks. No other group has been treated quite like this, and no other group is in a comparable status. Hispanic-Americans occupy an intermediate position, but it seems to me frankly absurd to include persons of oriental descent as beneficiaries of affirmative action, strong or weak. They are not a severely deprived and excluded minority, and their eligibility serves only to swell the numbers that can be included on affirmative action reports. It also suggests that there is a drift in the policy toward adopting the goal of radical proportional representation for its own sake. This is a foolish mistake, and should be resisted. The only legitimate goal of the policy is to reduce egregious racial stratification.

With respect to women, I believe that except over the short term, and in professions or institutions from which their absence is particularly marked, strong affirmative action is not warranted and weak affirmative action is enough. This is based simply on the expectation that the social and economic situation of women will improve quite rapidly under conditions of full equality of opportunity. Recent progress provides some evidence for this. Women do not form a separate hereditary community, characteristically poor and uneducated, and their position is not likely to be self-perpetuating in the same way as that of an outcast race. The process requires less artificial acceleration, and any need for strong affirmative action for women can be expected to end sooner than it ends for blacks.

I said at the outset that there was a tendency to blur the distinction between weak and strong affirmative action. This occurs especially in the use of numerical quotas, a topic on which I want to comment briefly.

A quota may be a method of either weak or strong affirmative action, depending on the circumstances. It amounts to weak affirmative action—a safeguard against discrimination—if, and only if, there is independent evidence that average qualifications for the positions being filled are no lower in the group to which minimum quota is being assigned than in the applicant group as a whole. This can be presumed true of unskilled jobs that most people can do, but it becomes less likely, and harder to establish, the greater the skill and education required for the position. At these levels, a quota proportional to population, or even to representation of the group in the applicant pool, is almost certain to amount to strong affirmative action. Moreover it is strong affirmative action of a particularly crude and indiscriminate kind, because it permits no variation in the degree of preference on the basis of costs in efficiency, depending on the qualification gap. For this reason I should defend quotas only where they serve the purpose of weak affirmative action. On the whole, strong affirmative action is better implemented by including group preference as one factor in appointment or admission decisions, and letting the results depend on its interaction with other factors.

I have tried to show that the arguments against strong affirmative action are clearly outweighed at present by the need for exceptional measures to remove the stubborn residues of racial caste. But advocates of the policy should acknowledge the reasons against it, which will ensure its termination when it is no longer necessary. Affirmative action is not an end in itself, but a means of dealing with a social situation that should be intolerable to us all.

57. *Affirmative Action*

SHELBY STEELE

In a few short years, when my two children will be applying to college, the affirmative action policies by which most universities offer black students some form of preferential treatment will present me with a dilemma. I am a middle-class black, a college professor, far from wealthy but also well-removed from the find of deprivation that would qualify my children for the label "disadvantaged." Both of them have endured racial insensitivity from whites. They have been called names, have suffered slights, and have experienced firsthand the peculiar malevolence that racism brings out in people. Yet, they have never experienced racial discrimination, have never been stopped by their race on any path they have chosen to follow. Still their society now tells that if they will only designate themselves as black on their college applications they will likely do better in the college lottery than if they conceal this fact. I think there is something of a Faustian bargain in this.

Of course, many blacks and a considerable number of whites would say that I was sanctimoniously making affirmative action into a test of character. They would say that this small preference is the meagerest recompense for centuries of unrelieved oppression. And to these arguments other very obvious facts must be added. In America, many marginally competent or flatly incompetent whites are hired everyday—some because their white skin suits the conscious or unconscious racial preference of their employer. The white children of alumni are often grandfathered into elite universities in what can only be seen as a residual benefit of historic white privilege. Worse, white incompetence is always an individual matter, while for blacks it is often confirmation of ugly stereotypes. The Peter Principle was not concerned with only blacks in mind. Given that unfairness cuts both ways, doesn't

Reprinted by permission of St. Martin's Press.

it only balance the scales of history that my children now receive a slight preference over whites? Doesn't this repay, in a small way, the systematic denial under which their grandfather lived out his days?

So, in theory, affirmative action certainly has all the moral symmetry that fairness requires—the injustice of historical and even contemporary white advantage is offset with black advantage; preference replaces prejudice, inclusion answers exclusion. It is reformist and corrective, even repentant and redemptive. And I would never sneer at these good intentions. Born in the late forties in Chicago, I started my education (a charitable term in this case) in a segregated school and suffered all the indignities that come to blacks in a segregated society. My father, born in the South, only made it to the third grade before the white man's fields took permanent priority over his formal education. And though he educated himself into an advanced reader with an almost professorial authority, he could only drive a truck for a living and never earned more than ninety dollars a week in his entire life. So yes, it is crucial to my sense of citizenship, to my ability to identify with the spirit and the interests of America, to know that this country, however imperfectly, recognizes its past sins and wishes to correct them.

Yet good intentions, because of the opportunity for innocence they offer us, are very seductive and can blind us to the effects they generate when implemented. In our society, affirmative action is, among other things a testament to white goodwill and to black power, and in the midst of these heavy investments, its effects can be hard to see. But after twenty years of implementation, I think affirmative action has shown itself to be more bad than good and that blacks—whom I will focus on in this essay—now stand to lose more from it than they gain.

In talking with affirmative action administrators and with blacks and whites in general, it is clear that supporters of affirmative action focus on its good intentions while detractors emphasize its negative effects. Proponents talk about "diversity" and "pluralism"; opponents speak of "reverse discrimination," the unfairness of quotas and set-asides. It was virtually impossible to find people outside either camp. The closest I came was a white male manager at a large computer company who said, "I think it amounts to reverse discrimination, but I'll put up with a little of that for a little more diversity." I'll live with a little of the effect to gain a little of the intention, he seemed to be saying. But this only makes him a halfhearted supporter of affirmative action. I think many people who don't really like affirmative action support it to one degree or another anyway.

I believe they do this because of what happened to white and black Americans in the crucible of the sixties when whites were confronted with their racial guilt and blacks tasted their first real power. In this stormy time white absolution and black power coalesced into virtual mandates for society. Affirmative action became a meeting ground for these mandates in the law, and in the late sixties and early seventies it underwent a remarkable escalation of its mission from simple anti-discrimination enforcement to social engineering by means of quotas, goals, timetables, set-asides and other forms of preferential treatment.

Legally, this was achieved through a series of executive orders and EEOC guidelines that allowed racial imbalances in the workplace to stand as proof of racial discrimination. Once it could be assumed that discrimination explained racial imbalances, it became easy to justify group remedies to presumed discrimination, rather than the normal case-by-case redress for proven discrimination. Preferential treatment through quotas, goals, and so on is designed to correct imbalances based on the assumption that they always indicate discrimination. This expansion of what constitutes discrimination allowed affirmative action to escalate into the business of social engineering in the name of anti-discrimination, to push society toward statistically proportionate racial representation, without any obligation of proving actual discrimination.

What accounted for this shift, I believe, was the white mandate to achieve a new racial inno-cence and the black mandate to gain power. Even though blacks had made great advances during the sixties without quotas, these mandates, which came to a head in the very late sixties, could no longer be satisfied by anything less than racial preferences. I don't think these mandates in themselves were wrong, since whites clearly needed to do better by blacks and blacks needed more real power in society. But, as they came together in affirmative action, their effect was to distort our understanding of racial discrimination in a way that allowed us to offer the remediation of preference on the basis of mere color rather than actual injury. By making black the color of preference, these mandates have reburdened society with the very marriage of color and preference (in reverse) that we set out to eradicate. The old sin is reaffirmed in a new guise.

But the essential problem with this form of affirmative action is the way it leaps over the hard business of developing a formerly oppressed people to the point where they can achieve proportionate representation on their own (given equal opportunity) and goes straight for the proportionate representation. This may satisfy some whites of their innocence and some blacks of their power, but it does very little to truly uplift blacks.

A white female affirmative action officer at an Ivy League university told me what many supporters of affirmative action now say: "We're after diversity. We ideally want a student body where racial and ethnic groups are represented according to their proportion in society." When affirmative action escalated into social engineering, diversity became a golden word. It grants whites an egalitarian fairness (innocence) and blacks an entitlement to proportionate representation (power). *Diversity* is a term that applies democratic principles to races and cultures rather than to citizens, despite the fact that there is nothing to indicate that real diversity is the same thing as proportionate representation. Too often the result of this on campuses (for example) has been a democracy of colors rather than of people, an artificial diversity that gives the appearance of an educational parity between black and white students that has not yet been achieved in reality. Here again, racial preferences allow society to leapfrog over the difficult problem of developing blacks to parity with whites and into a cosmetic diversity that covers the blemish of disparity—a full six years after admission, only about 26 percent of black students graduate from college.

Racial representation is not the same thing as racial development, yet affirmative action fosters a confusion of these very different needs. Representation can be manufactured; development is always hard-earned. However, it is the music of innocence and power that we hear in affirmative action that causes us to cling to it and to its distracting emphasis on representation. The fact is that after twenty years of racial preferences, the gap between white and black median income is greater than it was in the seventies. None of this is to say that blacks don't need policies that ensure our right to equal opportunity, but what we need more is the development that will let us take advantage of society's efforts to include us.

I think that one of the most troubling effects of racial preferences for blacks is a kind of demoralization, or put another way, an enlargement of self-doubt. Under affirmative action the quality that earns us preferential treatment is an implied inferiority. However this inferiority is explained—and it is easily enough explained by the myriad deprivations that grew out of our oppression—it is still inferiority. There are explanations, and then there is the fact. And the fact must be borne by the individual as a condition apart from the explanation, apart even from the fact that others like himself also bear this condition. In integrated situations where blacks must compete with whites who may be better prepared, these explanations may quickly wear thin and expose the individual to racial as well as personal self-doubt.

All of this is compounded by the cultural myth of black inferiority that blacks have always lived with. What this means in practical terms is that when blacks deliver themselves into integrated situations, they encounter a nasty little reflex in whites, a mindless, atavistic reflex that responds to the color black with alarm. Attributions may follow this alarm if the white cares to indulge them, and if they do, they will most likely be negative—one such attribution is intellectual ineptness. I think this reflex and the attributions that may follow it embarrass most whites today, therefore, it is usually quickly repressed. Nevertheless, on an equally atavistic level, the black will be aware of the reflex his color triggers and will feel a stab of horror at

seeing himself reflected in this way. He, too, will do a quick repression, but a lifetime of such stabbings is what constitutes his inner realm of racial doubt.

The effects of this may be a subject for another essay. The point here is that the implication of inferiority that racial preferences engender in both the white and black mind expands rather than contracts this doubt. Even when the black sees no implication of inferiority in racial preferences, he knows that whites do, so that—consciously or unconsciously—the result is virtually the same. The effect of preferential treatment—the lowering of normal standards to increase black representation—puts blacks at war with an expanded realm of debilitating doubt, so that the doubt itself becomes an unrecognized preoccupation that undermines their ability to perform, especially in integrated situations. On largely white campuses, blacks are five times more likely to drop out than whites. Preferential treatment, no matter how it is justified in the light of day, subjects blacks to a midnight of self-doubt, and so often transforms their advantage into a revolving door.

Another liability of affirmative action comes from the fact that it indirectly encourages blacks to exploit their own past victimization as a source of power and privilege. Victimization, like implied inferiority, is what justifies preference, so that to receive the benefits of preferential treatment one must, to some extent, become invested in the view of one's self as a victim. In this way, affirmative action nurtures a victim-focused identity in blacks. The obvious irony here is that we become inadvertently invested in the very condition we are trying to overcome. Racial preferences send us the message that there is more power in our past suffering than our present achievements—none of which could bring us a *preference* over others.

When power itself grows out of suffering, then blacks are encouraged to expand the boundaries of what qualifies as racial oppression, a situation that can lead us to paint our victimization in vivid colors, even as we receive the benefits or preference. The same corporations and institutions that give us preference are also seen as our oppressors. At Stanford University minority students—some of whom enjoy as much as $15,000 a year in financial aid—recently took over the president's office demanding, among other things, more financial aid. The power to be found in victimization, like any power, is intoxicating and can lend itself to the creation of a new class of supervictims who can feel the pea of victimization under twenty mattresses. Preferential treatment rewards us for being underdogs rather than for moving beyond that status—a misplacement of incentives that, along with its deepening of our doubt, is more a yoke than a spur.

But, I think, one of the worst prices that blacks pay for preference has to do with an illusion. I saw this illusion at work recently in the mother of a middle-class black student who was going off to his first semester of college. "They owe us this, so don't think for a minute that you don't belong there." This is the logic by which many blacks, and some whites, justify affirmative action—it is something "owed," a form of reparation. But this logic overlooks a much harder and less digestible reality, that it is impossible to repay blacks living today for the historic suffering of the race. If all blacks were given a million dollars tomorrow morning it would not amount to a dime on the dollar of three centuries of oppression, nor would it obviate the residues of that oppression that we still carry today. The concept of historic reparation grows out of man's need to impose a degree of justice on the world that simply does not exist. Suffering can be endured and overcome, it cannot be repaid. Blacks cannot be repaid for the injustice done to the race, but we can be corrupted by society's guilty gestures of repayment.

Affirmative action is such a gesture. It tells us that racial preferences can do for us what we cannot do for ourselves. The corruption here is in the hidden incentive *not* to do what we believe preferences will do. This is an incentive to be reliant on others just as we are struggling for self-reliance. And it keeps alive the illusion that we can find some deliverance in repayment. The hardest thing for any sufferer to accept is that his suffering excuses him from very little and never has enough currency to restore him. To think otherwise is to prolong the suffering.

Several blacks I spoke with said they were still in favor of affirmative action because of the "subtle" discrimination blacks were subject to once on the job. One photojournalist said, "They have ways of ignoring you." A black female television producer said, "You can't file a lawsuit when your

boss doesn't invite you to the insider meetings without ruining your career. So we still need affirmative action." Others mentioned the infamous "glass ceiling" through which blacks can see the top positions of authority but never reach them. But I don't think racial preferences are a protection against this subtle discrimination; I think they contribute to it.

In any workplace, racial preferences will always create two-tiered populations composed of preferreds and unpreferreds. This division makes automatic a perception of enhanced competence for the unpreferreds and of questionable competence for the preferreds—the former earned his way, even though others were given preference, while the latter made it by color as much as by competence. Racial preferences implicitly mark whites with an exaggerated superiority just as they mark blacks with an exaggerated inferiority. They not only reinforce America's oldest racial myth but, for blacks, they have the effect of stigmatizing the already stigmatized.

I think that much of the "subtle" discrimination that blacks talk about is often (not always) discrimination against the stigma of questionable competence that affirmative action delivers to blacks. In this sense, preferences scapegoat the very people they seek to help. And it may be that at a certain level employers impose a glass ceiling, but this may not be against the race so much as against the race's reputation for having advanced by color as much as by competence. Affirmative action makes a glass ceiling virtually necessary as a protection against the corruptions of preferential treatment. This ceiling is the point at which corporations shift the emphasis from color to competency and stop playing the affirmative action game. Here preference backfires for blacks and becomes a taint that holds them back. Of course, one could argue that this taint, which is, after all, in the minds of whites, becomes nothing more than an excuse to discriminate against blacks. And certainly the result is the same in either case—blacks don't get past the glass ceiling. But this argument does not get around the fact that racial preferences now taint this color with a new theme of suspicion that makes it even more vulnerable to the impulse in others to discriminate. In this crucial yet gray area of perceived competence, preferences make whites look better than they are and blacks worse, while doing nothing whatever to stop the very real discrimination that blacks may encounter. I don't wish to justify the glass ceiling here, but only to suggest the very subtle ways that affirmative action revives rather than extinguishes the old rationalizations for racial discrimination.

In education, a revolving door; in employment, a glass ceiling.

I believe affirmative action is problematic in our society because it tries to function like a social program. Rather than ask it to ensure equal opportunity we have demanded that it create parity between the races. But preferential treatment does not teach skills, or educate or instill motivation. It only passes out entitlement by color, a situation that in my profession has created an unrealistically high demand for black professors. The social engineer's assumption is that this high demand will inspire more blacks to earn Ph.D.'s and join the profession. In fact, the number of blacks earning Ph.D.'s has declined in recent years. A Ph.D. must be developed from preschool on. He requires family and community support. He must acquire an entire system of values that enables him to work hard while delaying gratification. There are social programs, I believe, that can (and should) help blacks *develop* in all these areas, but entitlement by color is not a social program; it is a dubious reward for being black.

It now seems clear that the Supreme Court, in a series of recent decisions, is moving away from racial preferences. It has disallowed preferences except in instances of "identified discrimination," eroded the precedent that statistical racial imbalances are *prima facie* evidence of discrimination, and in effect granted white males the right to challenge consent degrees that use preference to achieve racial balances in the workplace. One civil rights leader said, "Night has fallen on civil rights." But I am not so sure. The effect of these decisions is to protect the constitutional rights of everyone rather than take rights away from blacks. What they do take away from blacks is the special entitlement to more rights than others that preferences always grant. Night has fallen on racial preferences, not on the fundamental rights of black Americans. The reason for this shift, I believe, is that the white mandate for absolution from past racial sins has weakened considerably during the eighties. Whites are now less willing to endure unfairness to themselves in order to grant special entitlements to blacks, even when these entitlements are justified in the name of past suffering. Yet the black mandate for more power in society has remained unchanged. And I think part of the anxiety that many blacks feel over these decisions has to do with the loss of black power they may signal. We had won a certain specialness and now we are losing it.

But the power we've lost by these decisions is really only the power that grows out of our victimization—the power to claim special entitlements under the law because of past oppression. This is not a very substantial or reliable power, and it is important that we know this so we can focus more exclusively on the kind of development that will bring enduring power. There is talk now that Congress will pass new legislation to compensate for these new limits on affirmative action. If this happens, I hope that their focus will be on development and anti-discrimination rather than entitlement, on achieving racial parity rather than jerry-building racial diversity.

I would also like to see affirmative action go back to its original purpose of enforcing equal opportunity—a purpose that in itself disallows racial preferences. We cannot be sure that the discriminatory impulse in America has yet been shamed into extinction, and I believe affirmative action can make its greatest contribution by providing a rigorous vigilance in this area. It can guard constitutional rather than racial rights, and help institutions evolve standards of merit and selection that are appropriate to the institution's needs yet as free of racial bias as possible (again, with the understanding that racial imbalances are not always an indication of racial bias). One of the most important things affirmative action can do is to define exactly what racial discrimination is and how it might manifest itself within a specific institution. The impulse to discriminate *is* subtle and cannot be ferreted out unless its many guises are made clear to people. Along with this there should be monitoring of institutions and heavy sanctions brought to bear when actual discrimination is found. This is the sort of affirmative action that America owes to blacks and to itself. It goes after the evil of discrimination itself, while preferences only sidestep the evil and grant entitlement to its *presumed* victims.

But if not preferences, then what? I think we need social policies that are committed to two goals: the educational and economic development of disadvantaged people, regardless of race, and the eradication from our society—through close monitoring and severe sanctions—of racial, ethnic, or gender discrimination. Preferences will not deliver us to either of these goals, since they tend to benefit those who are not disadvantaged—middle-class white women and middle-class blacks—and attack one form of discrimination with another. Preferences are inexpensive and carry the glamour of good intentions—change the numbers and the good deed is done. To be against them is to be unkind. But I think the unkindest cut is to bestow on children like my own an advantage while neglecting the development of those disadvantaged children on the East Side of my city who will likely never be in a position to benefit from a preference. Give my children fairness; give disadvantaged children a better shot at development—better elementary and secondary schools, job training, safer neighborhoods, better financial assistance for college, and so on. Fewer blacks go to college today than ten years ago; more black males of college age are in prison or under the control of the criminal justice system than in college. This despite racial preferences.

The mandates of black power and white absolution out of which preferences emerged were not wrong in themselves. What was wrong was that both races focused more on the goals of these mandates than on the means to the goals. Blacks can have no real power without taking responsibility for their own educational and economic development. Whites can have no racial innocence without earning it by eradicating discrimination and helping the disadvantaged to develop. Because we ignored the means, the goals have not been reached, and the real work remains to be done.

Study Questions

1. Do the reasons leading us to believe that racial discrimination against Blacks and others is wrong and unconstitutional also apply in the case of the discrimination involved in affirmative action practices? Should the classifications utilized in such programs (being a Black, being a woman, etc.) be subjected to "strict scrutiny"? What would be the result?

2. Does Justice Powell in his opinion in *Bakke* really apply strict scrutiny? Would even the Harvard Plan pass such scrutiny? Powell seems to think that it makes a difference whether an applicant is turned down for medical school because of a quota system or because race is used as a factor in an admissions policy. Is he right? Why should that matter to someone like Bakke who, after all, loses out either way and apparently as a consequence of his race?

3. On what grounds does the court in *Hopwood* assert that Justice Powell's rationale in *Bakke* is not a precedent for the case presented by the University of Texas law school? Do you agree with the arguments of the court in *Hopwood* that the interest in obtaining a diverse student body cannot pass the test of "strict scrutiny"? Should such a purpose be subjected to that test?

4. Why does the *Hopwood* court reject the claim that a person's race can serve as a "proxy" for other traits that a university might value and thus want to have reflected in its student body?

5. Why does Epstein think that existing antidiscrimination law is the antithesis of the free market?

6. Is it reasonable to expect that discrimination based on race, gender, age, and other traits will be ameliorated by reliance upon the free market? Is Epstein committing himself to that view?

7. James O'Connor worked for Consolidated Coin Caterers from 1978 until August 19, 1990, when at age 56 he was fired. Believing that he had been fired because of his age, O'Connor filed a suit in federal court, alleging that Coin Caterers had violated the Age Discrimination in Employment Act (ADEA). The court dismissed his suit. The ADEA limits its protection to individuals forty years of age and older and this, the court reasoned, meant that, to prove

discrimination, plaintiffs such as O'Connor must show that they were replaced by someone with comparable qualifications who was *under* forty years old. Because the person who replaced O'Connor was exactly forty, a *prima facie* case of discrimination could not be made. O'Connor appealed to the U.S. Supreme Court. In April of 1996, the Court ruled in O'Connor's favor. According to Justice Scalia, writing for the majority, "the fact that one person in the protected class [40 or older] has lost out to another person in the protected class is . . . irrelevant, so long as he has lost out *because of his age*. . . . There can be no greater inference of *age* discrimination (as opposed to "40 or over" discrimination) when a 40-year-old is replaced by a 39-year-old than when a 56-year-old is replaced by a 40-year-old." Do you agree with Justice Scalia's argument? How much of a disparity in ages must be present before you would be persuaded that discrimination on the basis of age has occurred? Is ten years'

difference sufficient? Five? Three? Suppose O'Connor had been thirty-five years old and that he was fired and replaced by someone who was twenty. Would this suggest age discrimination?

8. What, for Nagel, distinguishes "weak" from "strong" affirmative action policies?

9. What three objections to strong affirmative action does Nagel consider?

10. Why does Nagel think that strong affirmative action is not justified in the case of women? Are you convinced?

11. What does Steele mean when he says of affirmative action programs that "the old sin is reaffirmed in a new guise"?

12. What does Steele think is wrong with the appeal to one's status as a victim of past injustice as a way of justifying preferential treatment?

B. *Sex, Gender, and Equality*

Women at All-Male Military Academies

In 1993 The Citadel, South Carolina's formerly all-male military academy, accepted—and then tried to reject—Shannon Faulkner, a female high-school student. (The school apparently mistook Faulkner's name for that of a male.) Faulkner filed suit, alleging that The Citadel's policy of excluding women was an equal-protection violation. Faulkner won the suit, but left The Citadel only two days after the beginning of the school year, al-

leging that she was the victim of brutal hazing and sexual harassment. Faulkner's story paralleled that of several women who sought admission to Virginia Military Institute (VMI), another state-supported, single-sex academy. In that case, the federal government filed suit against VMI. After a lower court had ruled in the school's favor, a federal appellate court reversed. It found that VMI had a unique program that would be significantly affected by coeducation. It ruled, however, that Virginia had failed convincingly to justify having such a unique military academy for men only. The appellate court ordered that plans be drawn either to admit women to VMI or to establish a separate but equal academy for women. In response to the ruling, Virginia created Virginia Women's Institute for Leadership (VWIL), intended to be an all-female version of VMI. Alleging that VWIL was not an equal facility, the government again brought a challenge, which made its way to the Supreme Court. The opinion by Justice Ruth Ginsburg, which opens the readings for this section, ruled that VMI had no justification for refusing to admit women and that VWIL does not substitute for that exclusion.

The Case of Michael M.

In 1978 a jury in Sonoma County, California, convicted a young man named Michael M. (his last name being withheld to shield his identity) for violating the section of the California Penal Code then defining statutory rape: unlawful sexual intercourse "accomplished with a female not the wife of the perpetrator, where the female is under the age of eighteen years." California, like most states, criminalizes "statutory rape," so called because the act is unlawful even if both parties consent to it. Appealing to reverse his conviction, Michael M. made an unusual and intriguing argument: The California law is unconstitutional and violates the guarantee of equal protection since only men can be held criminally liable for its violation. California's statutory rape law is an example of sex discrimination. Although California has since changed its law on statutory rape to incorporate a gender-neutral definition of the crime, the issues posed by *Michael M.* are, as we shall see, still very much a part of the law.

In his opinion for the United States Supreme Court, included in our readings, Chief Justice Rehnquist began by stating what the Court (and California) took to be the purpose of the statute: to prevent illegitimate teenage pregnancy. The Court found that this is an important objective (citing statistics regarding teenage pregnancy and its attendant social effects). Can the state seek to meet this objective by punishing only the male? The court answered yes, since most of the burden of the pregnancy falls on the female. A gender-neutral statute, permitting the punishment of the female as well as

the male, would frustrate the law's enforcement since the female is unlikely to notify the authorities if she, too, faces a penalty. The statute therefore does not violate the equal protection guarantee. Males and females are not similarly situated with respect to the risks of sex and pregnancy, and therefore it is not a violation of equal protection to treat them differently.

Justice Brennan, in a dissenting opinion, countered that even if the goal here is an important one, the statute is not "substantially related"—does not come close enough—to the achievement of that goal. Other states have switched to gender-neutral statutes without much difficulty, and a gender-neutral law might well have a greater deterrent effect, because both participants would be liable. It is irrational, the dissenters seem to believe, to take illicit sexual activity so seriously and yet exempt from punishment 50 percent of the violators.

Critics of the Court's decision in *Michael M* are suspicious of the declared purpose in retaining the statutory rape law. Is it to prevent teenage pregnancy? If so, why not punish both people involved? They suggest a more sinister purpose. On a deeper level, they claim, the statute reinforces a range of damaging and morally unacceptable sexual stereotypes: that men are always the aggressors in sexual encounters, that women are submissive and naive, that women need to have their chastity protected. In short, the Court assumes that the problem of teenage pregnancy is important and thereby acquiesces in a sexist law. The Court invokes the physiological difference of pregnancy, together with socially imposed sex-role expectations, with the consequence that deeper and potentially more damaging prejudices against women are retained.

Sexism in the Law

The *Michael M.* and *VMI* cases serve as useful points of departure for an exploration of the whole question of "equality between the sexes" and what that means (or should mean) under our Constitution and laws. Any discussion of sexual equality must begin, however, with the history of legalized sexual discrimination, justified by what were thought to be "legitimate" or "real" differences between the sexes. Throughout the nineteenth century and the early part of this century, the law treated women as separate and distinct from men. Women were thought to possess a separate, distinct, and immutable "nature" that made them unfit for many of the positions and occupations traditionally held by men; women properly belonged to a separate social and legal sphere, consisting primarily if not exclusively of domestic life and child rearing. The law excluded women from many aspects of public life and left them unprotected within the private, domestic world. This ideology was succinctly expressed by the Supreme Court in 1873 when it ruled that Myra Bradwell could not be admitted to the practice of law in Illinois. Concurring in the court's decision, Justice Bradley wrote:

> [T]he civil law as well as nature itself, has always recognized a wide difference in the respective spheres and destinies of man and woman. Man is, or should be woman's protector and defender. The natural and proper timidity and delicacy which belongs to the female sex evidently unfits it for many of the occupations of civil life. . . . The paramount destiny and mission of woman are to fulfill the noble and benign offices of wife and mother. This is the law of the Creator.[1]

With increasing industrialization, many states passed legislation regulating a variety of working conditions for women. Typical was a law challenged in *Muller v. Oregon*,[2] which upheld restrictions on the number of hours women could work.

> [T]hat woman's physical structure and the performance of maternal functions place her at a disadvantage in the struggle for subsistence is obvious. . . . Differentiated by these matters from the other sex, she is properly placed in a class by herself, and legislation designed for her protection may be sustained, even when the legislation is not necessary for men.[3]

As late as 1948, the Supreme Court upheld a Michigan law forbidding a woman to work as a bartender unless she was the "wife or daughter of the male owner."[4] The blatant stereotyping of and discrimination against women exemplified by the foregoing cases is now no longer legal. However, despite legal protections and gains in such areas as employment, many women still encounter barriers reflecting sexist assumptions and prejudices. For example, some women perceive that their work is still undervalued relative to that of men. Traditional women's professions, such as nursing, teaching, and social work, have become targets of recent efforts to cut budgets and trim spending; and more women than men are relegated to part-time work with little job security and few benefits. Stereotyped views about women also still prevail. In the late 1980s, for example, a group of female workers at Johnson Controls, a Milwaukee-based manufacturer of automotive batteries, accused the company of sex discrimination.[5] Car batteries are made with lead, and studies had shown that exposure to certain levels of lead can seriously impair female reproductive abilities and injure developing fetuses. Johnson Controls, along with many other large manufacturing corporations, instituted a fetal protection policy. Under the policy, all female employees, unless they provided proof of sterility, were barred from any job with a level of lead exposure alleged to pose reproductive hazards; no such restrictions were placed on male employees, regardless of their fertility and level of lead exposure. The policy had the effect of excluding women workers from virtually all of the typically higher-paying assembly-line positions in the company. The women who challenged the company in court claimed that the policy reflected some of the same paternalistic and condescending attitudes toward women prevalent a century ago, evident, for example, in the assumption that women, unlike men, are not capable of deciding for themselves whether to accept a job that poses certain risks.

Only recently have the courts begun consistently to strike down gender-based classifications as violative of women's equal-protection rights. Even here, however, the courts have generally refused to

---

[1] *Bradwell v. Illinois* 83 U.S. 130 (1873).
[2] 208 U S. 412 (1908).
[3] 208 U.S 412 (1908) at 421–22.

[4] See *Goesaert v. Cleary* 335 U.S. 464 (1948).
[5] *International Union, UAW v. Johnson Controls* 111 S. Ct. 1196 (1991)

require that laws that distinguish between people on the basis of their sex must be "strictly scrutinized." Instead, they have settled on a weaker, intermediate standard of review: It is enough if such laws are "substantially related to an important governmental objective."

To many, these rulings are morally indefensible; nonetheless, they do raise important questions: Does rejecting these rulings mean that *any* laws that differentiate between the sexes are impermissible? Is it a violation of equal protection to prohibit women from serving as guards at male, maximum-security prisons?[6] To ban women from military combat? To refuse to admit women to all-male military academies or the Boy Scouts? These questions are explored in this section.

Difference and Sameness

In what ways are men and women the same? What are the "real" differences between men and women? Given that judgments about the relevance of differences can vary, how are so-called "real" differences to be distinguished from the effects of stereotypes and sexist assumptions that have been or should be rejected? Recent literature on this topic, much of it by feminist legal scholars, struggles with two contrasting views of "sameness" and "difference." The "equal treatment" view reasons that treating men and women equally means treating them the same. There are no "real" differences between the sexes that matter, only ways in which society and culture have made differences matter when they shouldn't. Legal equality, therefore, means behaving the same toward each sex. The contrasting view says that ensuring true sexual and gender equality requires giving women (and conceivably men as well) "special treatment." The law should recognize and accommodate the real, biological differences between men and women so that women are not disadvantaged relative to men with regard to employment and education. The distinction between these two views can best be seen through an illustrative case.

Company C offers all employees, regardless of sex, a benefits package that includes insurance benefits covering a variety of disabilities. Mr. M. is an employee who requires prostate surgery and will be off work for ten weeks. Another employee, Ms. W., is pregnant; with delivery and postnatal care she will also be out for ten weeks. The company's disability insurance package covers prostate surgery but excludes disabilities incident to normal pregnancy. Has the company treated Ms. W. and Mr. M. equally? The company can argue that it has given equal treatment here because it offers the same benefits package to all employees—women are not discriminated against in terms of being covered as much by the policy as are men. This argument by the company was supported by the Supreme Court in *Geduldig v. Aiello*,[7] in which the Court upheld the exclusion of pregnancy from a disability insurance scheme. "There is no risk from which men are protected and women are not," the Court wrote, and "there is no risk from which women are protected and men are not." The Court's reasoning in this case followed the "equal treatment" model, arguing that "equality" just means giving the same benefits to men and women. Ms. W., on the other hand, can argue that Company C is in reality imposing a double standard: it limits the disabilities for which women employees may receive coverage, and from which they alone suffer, while extending full coverage to male employees, even for specifically male conditions such as prostate surgery. This has happened, Ms. W. can claim, because the entire benefits package was arrived at in a gender-biased manner in that it was created with men in mind, with the model of the male employee as its standard or norm. Women were then covered to the degree that they conformed to or were "like" men. But women are not the same as men; women have special capacities and burdens, and "equal protection" means adjusting for these through law. Ms. W. thus relies on the "special treatment" model.

The argument between Company C and Ms. W. can be examined on another level. Suppose the state forbids employers to refuse granting preg-

---

[6] See *Dothard v. Rawlinson* 433 U. S. 321 (1977).

[7] 417 U.S. 484 (1974).

nancy leaves of up to four months (as some states now do). Company C does refuse to grant Ms. W. a pregnancy leave, relying on the principle that "equal protection" means that all forms of workplace discrimination based on pregnancy are impermissible. In court, Company C argues that its decision is evenhanded and deals with all workers equally—it doesn't give men any comparable extended disability leave either. All it has to do, says the company, is give leaves to everyone or no one. But, responds Ms. W., the company's choice is not equitable, for it is still assuming that where women really do have different needs from men, those differences don't count, and this is a form of bias against women.

Underlying both of these theories of difference and sameness is the problem of fixing the standard or norm used to determine in what ways men and women are similar or different. Suppose the military requires that all fighter pilots be at least 5' 11" in height, arguing that fighter-plane cockpits necessitate that the pilot be this tall to reach and work the controls for the aircraft properly. If the military permits both men and women to apply for fighter-pilot positions, has it treated them equally even if the height requirement disqualifies many more women than men? The military can insist that it denies no one a spot as a pilot merely on the grounds of sex. But suppose it can be shown that the height requirement is not just "the way things are," but that the cockpit requires a pilot at least 5' 11" in height because for years cockpit dimensions have been normed after men, most of whom average 5' 11"? A solution here would be to use *androgynous* norms as the appropriate standards against which to judge men and women, that is, norms not arrived at by reference to traits specific to either gender. This might be accomplished in the jet-fighter case by reconfiguring cockpits around a height dimension close to average for men *and* women. Knowing how to identify the appropriate androgynous standard, however, might not be as apparent in other cases.

The Dilemma of Difference

In her selection included here, legal scholar Martha Minow explains and illustrates what she considers the central problem in the legal and conceptual understanding of equality, what she terms the "dilemma of difference." The dilemma arises because both recognizing and failing to recognize a way in which people are different can perpetuate prejudice and stigma attached to that difference, thus frustrating the goal of achieving equality. As we have already seen, some contend that the *Michael M.* case exemplifies this difficulty: California's statutory rape law, in recognizing the difference of pregnancy and seeking to deal with both sexes fairly by treating women and men dissimilarly with regard to the risk of pregnancy, may at the same time serve to reinforce stereotypes that undercut the very fairness and equality at which the law aims in the first place. Minow thinks dilemmas of difference occur throughout the law as a result of hidden or unconscious assumptions about the nature and significance of difference that have worked their way into the fabric of the law. Minow carefully explains and illustrates each of these assumptions with the aim of clarifying the challenges confronting the laws' effort to ensure equality, especially equality between the sexes.

The Assimilationist Ideal

Philosopher and lawyer Richard Wasserstrom explores a broader question: In what way would differences in race and sex be viewed in an "ideal" society? Wasserstrom investigates and compares three possibilities.

The first, or "assimilationist," ideal seeks a society in which differences among the races or between the sexes are treated as are differences in eye color. Because no one thinks that eye color should be relevant in any way to the distribution of social benefits or burdens, the assimilationist society would be one in which nothing turns on one's race or sex. The second ideal, that of "diversity," analogizes sex and race to the current legal status of religion. One's religious identity, we believe, should make no difference to political rights and benefits; yet we still permit (and encourage) people to recognize and celebrate their differing religious identities. Similarly, in this view people could still define themselves in terms of gender differences, although no political or social stigma would be attached to doing so. The last of the three ideals would take sexual equality much as we have it now, with considerable sex-role differentiation.

Which ideal is the most attractive? Would assimilationism be too radical a break with our current set of beliefs and traditions? These questions cannot be answered, Wasserstrom thinks, without facing the further question of whether the "differences" between the sexes are "natural" or "social." Wasserstrom argues that they are largely, if not entirely, social in origin because almost none of the obvious physical differences between men and women really make a difference in our technologically advanced society. He then constructs a positive case for the assimilationist ideal: The assimilationist society allows all of its members a degree of individual autonomy that cannot be present in a society that, like ours, defines people's prospects and limits their possibilities ahead of time, simply by confining them to "preprogrammed" sex roles.

Intersectionality and the Experience of Black Women

In the final reading for this section, Kimberle Crenshaw examines the issues of gender equality and discrimination from the standpoint of Critical Race Theory (CRT) (see Chapter One for background on CRT). Crenshaw argues that the dominant perspective of the law of equal protection toward gender issues systematically excludes the situation of those who are both black and female. The dominant framework must be modified, Crenshaw maintains, to ensure genuinely equal protection to people at the "intersection" of two dimensions of discrimination: racial and sexual.

---

58. *United States v. Virginia*

Justice Ginsburg delivered the opinion of the Court.

Virginia's public institutions of higher learning include an incomparable military college, Virginia Military Institute (VMI). The United States maintains that the Constitution's equal protection guarantee precludes Virginia from reserving exclusively to men the unique educational opportunities VMI affords. We agree.

Founded in 1839, VMI is today the sole single-sex school among Virginia's 15 public institutions of higher learning. VMI's distinctive mission is to produce "citizen-soldiers," men prepared for leadership in civilian life and in military service. VMI pursues this mission through pervasive training of a kind not available anywhere else in Virginia, an "adversative method" [that] constantly endeavors to instill physical and mental discipline in its cadets and impart to them a strong moral code. [Neither] the goal of producing citizen-soldiers nor VMI's implementing methodology is inherently unsuitable to women. And the school's impressive record in producing leaders has made admission desirable to some women. Nevertheless, Virginia has elected to preserve exclusively for men the advantages and opportunities a VMI education affords.

From its establishment in 1839, [VMI] has remained financially supported by Virginia. [Today, it] enrolls about 1300 men as cadets. [Its] "adversative, or doubting, model of education" [features]

518 U.S. 515 116 S.Ct. 2264, 135 L.Ed.2d 735 (1996)

"physical rigor, mental stress, absolute equality of treatment, absence of privacy, minute regulation of behavior, and indoctrination in desirable values." [VMI] cadets live in spartan barracks where surveillance is constant and privacy nonexistent; they wear uniforms, eat together in the mess hall, and regularly participate in drills. Entering students are incessantly exposed to the rat line, "an extreme form of the adversarial model," comparable in intensity to Marine Corps boot camp. Tormenting and punishing, the rat line bonds new cadets to their fellow sufferers and, when they have completed the 7-month experience, to their former [tormentors]. In 1990, prompted by a complaint filed [by] a female high-school student seeking admission to VMI, the United States sued, [alleging] that VMI's exclusively male admission policy violated [equal protection]. The District Court ruled in favor of VMI, [but the Court of Appeals reversed and remanded, suggesting] these options for the State: Admit women to VMI; establish parallel institutions or programs; or abandon state support, leaving VMI free to pursue its policies as a private institution. [In response,] Virginia proposed a parallel program for women: Virginia Women's Institute for Leadership (VWIL). The 4-year, state-sponsored undergraduate program would be located at Mary Baldwin College, a private liberal arts school for women, and would be open, initially, to about 25 to 30 students. Although VWIL would share VMI's mission—to produce "citizen-soldiers"—the VWIL program would differ, as does Mary Baldwin College, from VMI in academic offerings, methods of education, and financial resources. [The] District Court [decided] the plan met the requirements of [equal protection]. [A] divided Court of Appeals [affirmed].

The cross-petitions in this case present two ultimate issues. First, does Virginia's exclusion of women from the educational opportunities provided by VMI—extraordinary opportunities for military training and civilian leadership development—deny to women "capable of all of the individual activities required of VMI cadets" the equal protection of the [laws]? Second, if VMI's "unique" situation—as Virginia's sole single-sex public institution of higher education—offends the Constitution's equal protection principle, what is the remedial requirement?

Parties who seek to defend gender-based government action must demonstrate an "exceedingly persuasive justification" for that action. Today's skeptical scrutiny of official action denying rights or opportunities based on sex responds to volumes of history. [Since] Reed, the Court has repeatedly recognized that neither federal nor state government acts compatibly with the equal protection principle when a law or official policy denies to women, simply because they are women, full citizenship stature—equal opportunity to aspire, achieve, participate in and contribute to society based on their individual talents and capacities. Without equating gender classifications, for all purposes, to classifications based on race or national origin, the court, in post-Reed decisions, has carefully inspected official action that closes a door or denies opportunity to women (or to men). . . .

. . . Measuring the record in this case against the review standard just described, we conclude that Virginia has shown no "exceedingly persuasive justification" for excluding all women from the citizen-soldier training afforded by VMI. We therefore affirm the Fourth Circuit's initial judgment. [Because] the remedy proffered by Virginia—the Mary Baldwin VWIL program—does not cure the constitutional violation, [we] reverse the fourth Circuit's final judgment in this case.

[Virginia] asserts two justifications in defense of VMI's exclusion of women. First, "[single-sex] education provides important educational benefits," and the option of single-sex education contributes to "diversity in educational approaches." Second, "[the] unique VMI method of character development and leadership training," the school's adversarial approach, would have to be modified were VMI to admit women. We consider these [in] turn.

Single-sex education affords pedagogical benefits to at least some students, Virginia emphasizes, and that reality is uncontested in this litigation. Similarly, it is not disputed that diversity among public educational institutions can serve the public good. But Virginia has not shown that VMI was established, or has been maintained, with a view to diversifying, by its categorical exclusion of women, educational opportunities within the State. In cases of this genre, our precedent instructs that "benign" justifications proffered in defense of categorical exclusions will not be accepted automatically; a tenable justification must describe actual state purposes, not rationalizations for actions in fact differently grounded. [Neither] recent nor distant history bears out Virginia's alleged pursuit of diversity through single-sex educational options. . . .

[In] sum, we find no persuasive evidence in this record that VMI's male-only admission policy "is in furtherance of a state policy of 'diversity.'" [A] purpose genuinely to advance an array of educational options [is] not served by VMI's historic and constant plan—a plan to "afford a unique educational benefit only to males." However "liberally" this plan serves the State's sons, it makes no provision whatever for her daughters. That is not equal protection.

Virginia next argues that VMI's adversative method of training provides educational benefits that cannot be made available, unmodified, to women. Alterations to accommodate women would necessarily be [so] "drastic," Virginia asserts, as to transform, indeed "destroy," VMI's program. Neither sex would be favored by the transformation, Virginia maintains: Men would be deprived of the unique opportunity currently available to them; women would not gain that opportunity because their participation would "eliminate the very aspects of [the] program that distinguish [VMI from] other institutions of higher education in Virginia." The District Court forecast from expert witness testimony, and the Court of Appeals accepted, that coeducation would materially affect "at least these three aspects of VMI's program—physical training, the absence of privacy, and the adversative approach." And it is uncontested that women's admission would require accommodations, primarily in arranging housing assignments and physical training programs for female cadets. It is also undisputed, however, that "the VMI methodology could be used to educate women." The District Court even allowed that some women may prefer it to the methodology a women's college might pursue. The parties, furthermore, agree that "some women can meet the physical standards [VMI] now imposes on men." [In] support of its initial judgment for Virginia, [the] District Court made "findings" on "gender-based developmental differences" [that] restate the opinions of Virginia's

expert witnesses, opinions about typically male or typically female "tendencies." For example, "males tend to need an atmosphere of adversativeness," while "females tend to thrive in a cooperative atmosphere." [The] United States emphasizes that [we] have cautioned reviewing courts to take a "hard look" at generalizations or "tendencies" of the kind pressed by [Virginia]. State actors controlling gates to opportunity [may] not exclude qualified individuals based on "fixed notions concerning the roles and abilities of males and females."

It may be assumed [that] most women would not choose VMI's adversative method. [However,] it is also probable that "many men would not want to be educated in such an environment." (On that point, even our dissenting colleague might agree.) [The] issue, however, is not whether "women—or men—should be forced to attend VMI" [but] whether the State can constitutionally deny to women who have the will and capacity, the training and attendant opportunities that VMI uniquely affords. The notion that admission of women would downgrade VMI's stature, destroy the adversative system and, with it, even the school, is a judgment hardly proved, a prediction hardly different from other "self-fulfilling prophecies" once routinely used to deny rights or opportunities. When women first sought admission to the bar and access to legal education, concerns of the same order were [expressed]. Medical faculties similarly resisted men and women as partners in the study of medicine. [Surely,] the State's great goal [of producing citizen-soldiers] is not substantially advanced by women's categorical exclusion, in total disregard of their individual merit, from the State's premier "citizen-soldier" corps. Virginia, in sum, "has fallen far short of establishing the 'exceedingly persuasive justification'" that must be the solid base for any gender-defined classification.

In the second phase of the litigation, Virginia presented its remedial plan—maintain VMI as a male-only college and create VWIL as a separate program for women. . . . The constitutional violation in this case is the categorical exclusion of women from an extraordinary educational opportunity afforded men. A proper remedy for an unconstitutional exclusion, we have explained, aims to "eliminate [so far as possible] the discriminatory effects of the past" and to "bar like discrimination in the future." [VWIL] affords women no opportunity to experience the rigorous military training for which VMI is famed. Instead, the VWIL program "deemphasizes" military education, and uses a "cooperative method" of education "which reinforces self-esteem." VWIL students participate in ROTC and a "largely ceremonial" Virginia Corps of Cadets, but Virginia deliberately did not make VWIL a military institute. The VWIL House is not a military-style residence and VWIL students need not live together throughout the 4-year program, eat meals together, or wear uniforms during the school day. VWIL students thus do not experience the "barracks" life "crucial to the VMI experience," the spartan living arrangements designed to foster an "egalitarian ethic." [VWIL] students receive their "leadership training" in seminars [etc.] lacking the "physical rigor, mental stress, [minute] regulation of behavior, and indoctrination in desirable values" made hallmarks of VMI's citizen-soldier training. Kept away from the pressures, hazards, and psychological bonding characteristic of VMI's adversative training, VWIL students will not know the "feeling of tremendous accomplishment" commonly experienced by VMI's successful cadets. Virginia maintains that these methodological differences are "justified pedagogically," based on "important differences between men and women in learning and developmental needs," "psychological and sociological differences" [that] Virginia describes as "real" and "not stereotypes." [Generalizations] about "the way women are," estimates of what is appropriate for most women, no longer justify denying opportunity to women whose talent and capacity place them outside the average description. [In] contrast to the generalizations about women on which Virginia rests, we note against these dispositive realities: VMI's "implementing methodology" is not "inherently unsuitable to women," "some women [do] well under [the] adversative model," "some women, at least, would want to attend [VMI] if they had the opportunity," "some women are capable of all of the individual activities required of VMI cadets," and "can meet the physical standards [VMI] now imposes on men." It is on behalf of these women that the United States has instituted this suit, and it is for them that a remedy must be crafted, a remedy that will end their ex-

clusion from a state-supplied educational opportunity for which they are [fit].

In myriad respects other than military training, VWIL does not qualify as VMI's equal. VWIL's student body, faculty, course offerings, and facilities hardly match VMI's. Nor can the VWIL graduate anticipate the benefits associated with VMI's 157-year history, the school's prestige, and its influential alumni network. Virginia, in sum, while maintaining VMI for men only, has failed to provide any "comparable single-gender women's institution." Instead the Commonwealth has created a VWIL program fairly appraised as a "pale shadow" of VMI in terms of the range of curricular choices and faculty stature, funding, prestige, alumni support and influence. . . . We rule here that Virginia has not shown substantial equality in the separate educational opportunities the State supports at VWIL and VMI. [The] Fourth Circuit plainly erred in exposing Virginia's VWIL plan to a deferential analysis, for "all gender-based classification today" warrant "heightened scrutiny." Valuable as VWIL may prove for students who seek the program offered, Virginia's remedy affords no cure at all for the opportunities and advantages withheld from women who want a VMI education and can make the grade. In sum, Virginia's remedy does not match the constitutional violation; the State has shown no "exceedingly persuasive justification" for withholding from women qualified for the experience premier training of the kind VMI affords.

. . .

Justice Scalia, dissenting.

Today the Court shuts down an institution that has served the people of [Virginia] with pride and distinction for over a century and a half. To achieve that desired result, it [rejects] the factual findings of two courts below, sweeps aside the precedents of this Court, and ignores the history of our people. As to facts: it explicitly rejects the finding that there exist "gender-based developmental differences" supporting Virginia's restriction of the "adversative" method to only a men's institution, and the finding that the all-male composition of [VMI] is essential to that institution's character. As to precedent: it drastically revises our established standards for reviewing sex-based classifications. And as to history: it counts for nothing the long tradition [of] men's military [colleges]. Much of the

Court's opinion is devoted to deprecating the closed-mindedness of our forebears with regard to women's [education]. Closed-minded they were—as every age is, including our [own]. The virtue of a democratic system [is] that it readily enables the people, over time, to be persuaded that what they took for granted is not so, and to change their laws accordingly. That system is destroyed if the smug assurances of each age are removed from the democratic process and written into the Constitution. Since [the Constitution]—the old one—takes no sides in this educational debate, I dissent.

I shall devote most of my analysis to evaluating the Court's opinion on the basis of our current equal-protection [jurisprudentce]. [I] have no problem with a system of abstract tests such as rational-basis, intermediate, and strict scrutiny (though I think we can do better than applying strict scrutiny and intermediate scrutiny whenever we feel like it). [But] the function of this Court is to preserve our society's values, [not] to revise them; to prevent backsliding from the degree of restriction the Constitution imposed upon democratic government, not to prescribe, on our own authority, progressively higher degrees. [Whatever] abstract tests we may choose to devise, they cannot supersede—and indeed ought to be crafted so as to reflect—those constant and unbroken national traditions that embody the people's understanding of ambiguous constitutional texts. [The] tradition of having government-funded military schools for men is as well rooted in the traditions of this country as the tradition of sending only men into military combat. The people may decide to change the one tradition, like the other, through democratic processes; but the assertion that either tradition has been unconstitutional through the centuries is not law, but politics-smuggled-into-law. And the same applies, more broadly, to single-sex education in general which [is] threatened by today's decision with the cut-off of all state and federal support. Today, however, change is forced upon Virginia, and reversion to single-sex education is prohibited nationwide, not by democratic processes but by order of this Court. Even while bemoaning the sorry, bygone days of "fixed notions" concerning women's education, the Court favors current notions so fixedly that it is willing to write them into the [Constitution] by application of custom-built "tests." This is not the interpretation of a Constitution, but the creation of one.

. . .

[I] now proceed to describe how the analysis should have been conducted. The question to be answered [is] whether the exclusion of women from VMI is "substantially related to an important governmental objective." A. It is beyond question that Virginia has an important state interest in providing effective college education for its citizens. That single-sex instruction is an approach substantially related to that interest should be evident enough from the long and continuing history in this country of men's and women's colleges. [But] beside its single-sex constitution, VMI is different from other colleges [in employing] a "distinctive educational method." [A] State's decision to maintain within its system one school that provides the adversative method is "substantially related" to its goal of good education. Moreover, it was uncontested that "if the state were to establish a women's VMI-type [i.e., adversative] program, the program would attract an insufficient number of participants to make the program work"; and it was found by the District Court that if Virginia were to include women in VMI, the school "would eventually find it necessary to drop the adversative system altogether." Thus, Virginia's options were an adversative method that excludes women or no adversative method at all. [Virginia's] election to fund one public all-male institution and one on the adversative model—and to concentrate its resources in a single entity that serves both these interests in diversity—is substantially related to the State's important educational interests.

. . .

As is frequently true, the Court's decision today will have consequences that extend far beyond the parties to the case. What I take to be the Court's unease with these consequences, and its resulting unwillingness to acknowledge them, cannot alter the reality. [Under] the constitutional principles announced and applied today, single-sex public education is unconstitutional. By going through the motions of applying a balancing test—asking whether the State has adduced an "exceedingly persuasive justification" for its sex-based classification—the Court creates the illusion that government officials in some future case will have a clear shot at justifying some sort of single-sex public education. Indeed, the Court seeks to create even a greater illusion than that: It purports to have said nothing of relevance to other public schools at all. "We address specifically and only an educational opportunity recognized [as 'unique']." [But] the rationale of today's decision is sweeping: for sex-based classifications, a redefinition of intermediate scrutiny that makes it indistinguishable from strict scrutiny. Indeed, the Court indicates that if any program restricted to one sex is "unique," it must be opened to members of the opposite sex "who have the will and capacity" to participate in it. [T]he single-sex program that will not be capable of being characterized as "unique" [is] nonexistent. [R]egardless of whether the Court's rationale leaves some small amount of room for lawyers to argue, it ensures that single-sex public education is functionally dead. [The] enemies of single-sex education have won; by persuading only seven Justices [that] their view of the world is enshrined in the Constitution, they have effectively imposed that view on all 50 States.

There are few extant single-sex public educational programs. The potential of today's decision for widespread disruption of existing institutions lies in its application to *private* single-sex education. Government support is immensely important to private educational institutions. Charitable status under the tax law is also highly significant for private [colleges,] and it is certainly not beyond the Court that rendered today's decision to hold that a donation to a single-sex college should be deemed contrary to [public policy]. The Court adverts to private single-sex education only briefly, and only

to make the assertion that "we address specifically and only an educational opportunity recognized by the District Court and the Court of Appeals as 'unique.'" As I have already remarked, [the Court's] assurance [that this case concerns only a "unique" educational opportunity] assures nothing, unless it is to be taken as a promise that in the future the Court will disclaim the reasoning it has used today to destroy VMI. The Government, in its briefs to this Court, at least purports to address the consequences of its attack on VMI for public support of private single-sex education. It contends that private colleges which are the direct or indirect beneficiaries of government funding are not thereby necessarily converted into state actors to which [equal protection] is then applicable. That is true. It is also virtually meaningless. The issue will be not whether government assistance turns private colleges into state actors, but whether the government itself would be violating the Constitution by providing state support to single-sex colleges. [The] only hope for state-assisted single-sex private schools is that the Court will not apply in the future the principles of law it has applied today. That is a substantial hope, I am happy and ashamed to say. [It] will certainly be possible for this Court to write a future opinion that ignores the broad principles of law set forth today, and that characterizes as utterly dispositive the opinion's perceptions that VMI was a uniquely prestigious all-male institution, conceived in chauvinism, etc., etc. I will not join that [opinion].

59. *Michael M. v. Superior Court of Sonoma County*

Justice Rehnquist announced the judgment of the Court and delivered an opinion, in which The Chief Justice, Justice Stewart, and Justice Powell joined.

The question presented in this case is whether California's "statutory rape" law, § 261.5 of the Cal. Penal Code Ann . . . violates the Equal Protection Clause of the Fourteenth Amendment. Section 261.5 defines unlawful sexual intercourse as "an act of sexual intercourse accomplished with a female not the wife of the perpetrator, where the female is under the age of 18 years." The statute thus makes men alone criminally liable for the act of sexual intercourse.

In July 1978, a complaint was filed in the Municipal Court of Sonoma County, Cal., alleging that petitioner, then a 17½-year-old male, had had unlawful sexual intercourse with a female under the age of 18, in violation of § 261.5. The evidence adduced at a preliminary hearing showed that at approximately midnight on June 3, 1978, petitioner and two friends approached Sharon, a 16½-year-old female, and her sister as they waited at a bus stop. Petitioner and Sharon, who had already been drinking, moved away from the others and began to kiss. After being struck in the face for rebuffing petitioner's initial advances, Sharon submitted to sexual intercourse with petitioner. Prior to trial, petitioner sought to set aside the information on both state and federal constitutional grounds, asserting that § 261.5 unlawfully discriminated on the basis of gender. The trial court and the California Court of Appeal denied petitioner's request for relief and petitioner sought review in the Supreme Court of California.

The Supreme Court held that "section 261.5 discriminates on the basis of sex because only females may be victims, and only males may violate the section." . . . The court then subjected the classi-

fication to "strict scrutiny," stating that it must be justified by a compelling state interest. It found that the classification was "supported not by mere social convention but by the immutable physiological fact that it is the female exclusively who can become pregnant." . . . Canvassing "the tragic human costs of illegitimate teenage pregnancies," including the large number of teenage abortions, the increased medical risk associated with teenage pregnancies, and the social consequences of teenage childbearing, the court concluded that the State has a compelling interest in preventing such pregnancies. Because males alone can "physiologically cause the result which the law properly seeks to avoid," the court further held that the gender classification was readily justified as a means of identifying offender and victim. For the reasons stated below, we affirm the judgment of the California Supreme Court.

As is evident from our opinions, the Court has had some difficulty in agreeing upon the proper approach and analysis in cases involving challenges to gender-based classifications. . . .

. . . Unlike the California Supreme Court, we have not held that gender-based classifications are "inherently suspect" and thus we do not apply so-called "strict scrutiny" to those classifications. . . . Our cases have held, however, that the traditional minimum rationality test takes on a somewhat "sharper focus" when gender-based classifications are challenged. See *Craig v. Boren* 429 U.S. 190, 210 (1976). . . . In *Reed v. Reed*, 404 U.S. 71 (1971), for example, the Court stated that a gender-based classification will be upheld if it bears a "fair and substantial relationship" to legitimate state ends, while in *Craig v. Boren*. . . . the Court restated the test to require the classification to bear a "substantial relationship" to "important governmental objectives."

Underlying these decisions is the principle that a legislature may not "make overbroad generalizations based on sex which are entirely unrelated to any differences between men and women or which

450 U.S. 464 (1981)
United States Supreme Court

demean the ability or social status of the affected class." . . . But because the Equal Protection Clause does not "demand that a statute necessarily apply equally to all persons" or require "'things which are different in fact . . . to be treated in law as though they were the same,'" . . . this Court has consistently upheld statutes where the gender classification is not invidious, but rather realistically reflects the fact that the sexes are not similarly situated in certain circumstances. . . . As the Court has stated, a legislature may "provide for the special problems of women." . . .

Applying those principles to this case, the fact that the California Legislature criminalized the act of illicit sexual intercourse with a minor female is a sure indication of its intent or purpose to discourage that conduct. Precisely why the legislature desired that result is of course somewhat less clear. This Court has long recognized that "[i]nquiries into congressional motives or purposes are a hazardous matter." . . .

. . . Here, for example, the individual legislators may have voted for the statute for a variety of reasons. Some legislators may have been concerned about preventing teenage pregnancies, others about protecting young females from physical injury or from the loss of "chastity," and still others about promoting various religious and moral attitudes towards premarital sex.

The justification for the statute offered by the State and accepted by the Supreme Court of California, is that the legislature sought to prevent illegitimate teenage pregnancies.

. . .

We are satisfied not only that the prevention of illegitimate pregnancy is at least one of the "purposes" of the statute, but also that the State has a strong interest in preventing such pregnancy. At the risk of stating the obvious, teenage pregnancies, which have increased dramatically over the last two decades, have significant social, medical, and economic consequences for both the mother and her child, and the State.

. . .

. . . Of particular concern to the state is that approximately half of all teenage pregnancies end in abortion. And of those children who are born, their illegitimacy makes them likely candidates to become wards of the State.

We need not be medical doctors to discern that young men and young women are not similarly situated with respect to the problems and the risks of sexual intercourse. Only women may become pregnant, and they suffer disproportionately the profound physical, emotional, and psychological consequences of sexual activity. The statute at issue here protects women from sexual intercourse at an age when those consequences are particularly severe.

The question thus boils down to whether a State may attack the problem of sexual intercourse and teenage pregnancy directly by prohibiting a male from having sexual intercourse with a minor female. We hold that such a statute is sufficiently related to the State's objectives to pass constitutional muster.

Because virtually all of the significant harmful and inescapably identifiable consequences of teenage pregnancy fall on the young female, a legislature acts well within its authority when it elects to punish only the participant who, by nature, suffers few of the consequences of his conduct. It is hardly unreasonable for a legislature acting to protect minor females to exclude them from punishment. Moreover, the risk of pregnancy itself constitutes a substantial deterrence to young females. No similar natural sanctions deter males. A criminal sanction imposed solely on males thus serves to roughly "equalize" the deterrents on the sexes.

We are unable to accept petitioner's contention that the statute is impermissibly underinclusive and must, in order to pass judicial scrutiny, be *broadened* so as to hold the female as criminally liable as the male. It is argued that this statute is not *necessary* to deter teenage pregnancy because a gender-neutral statute, where both male and female would be subject to prosecution, would serve that goal equally well. The relevant inquiry, however, is not whether the statute is drawn as precisely as it might have been, but whether the line chosen by the California Legislature is within constitutional limitations. . . .

In any event, we cannot say that a gender-neutral statute would be as effective as the statute California has chosen to enact. The State persuasively contends that a gender-neutral statute would frustrate its interest in effective enforcement. Its view is that a female is surely less likely to report violations of the statute if she herself would be subject to criminal prosecution. In an area already fraught with prosecutorial difficulties, we decline to hold that the Equal Protection Clause requires a legislature to enact a statute so broad that it may well be incapable of enforcement.

We similarly reject petitioner's argument that § 261.5 is impermissibly overbroad because it makes unlawful sexual intercourse with prepubescent females, who are, by definition, incapable of becoming pregnant. Quite apart from the fact that the statute could well be justified on the grounds that very young females are particularly susceptible to physical injury from sexual intercourse . . . , it is ludicrous to suggest that the Constitution requires the California Legislature to limit the scope of its rape statute to older teenagers and exclude young girls.

There remains only petitioner's contention that the statute is unconstitutional as it is applied to him because he, like Sharon, was under 18 at the time of sexual intercourse. Petitioner argues that the statute is flawed because it presumes that as between two persons under 18, the male is the culpable aggressor. We find petitioner's contentions unpersuasive. Contrary to his assertions, the statute does not rest on the assumption that males are generally the aggressors. It is instead an attempt by a legislature to prevent illegitimate teenage pregnancy by providing an additional deterrent for men. The age of the man is irrelevant since young men are as capable as older men of inflicting the harm sought to be prevented.

In upholding the California statute we also recognize that this is not a case where a statute is being challenged on the grounds that it "invidiously discriminates" against females. To the contrary, the statute places a burden on males which is not shared by females. But we find nothing to suggest that men, because of past discrimination or peculiar disadvantages, are in need of the special solicitude of the courts. Nor is this a case where the gender classification is made "solely for . . . administrative convenience" . . . , or rests on "the baggage of sexual stereotypes." . . . As we have held, the statute instead reasonably reflects the fact that the consequences of sexual intercourse and pregnancy fall more heavily on the female than on the male. . . .

Accordingly the judgment of the California Supreme Court is

Affirmed.

. . .

Justice Brennan, with whom Justices White and Marshall join, dissenting. . . . It is disturbing to find the Court so splintered on a case that presents such a straightforward issue: Whether the admittedly gender-based classification in Cal. Penal Code Ann. § 261.5 . . . bears a sufficient relationship to the State's asserted goal of preventing teenage pregnancies to survive the "mid-level" constitutional scrutiny mandated by *Craig v. Boren.* . . . Applying the analytical framework provided by our precedents, I am convinced that there is only one proper resolution for this issue: the classification must be declared unconstitutional. I fear that the plurality opinion . . . reach[es] the opposite result by placing too much emphasis on the desirability of achieving the State's asserted statutory goal—prevention of teenage pregnancy—and not enough emphasis on the fundamental question of whether the sex-based discrimination in the California statute is *substantially* related to the achievement of that goal.

. . .

The State of California vigorously asserts that the "important governmental objective" to be served by § 261.5 is the prevention of teenage pregnancy. It claims that its statute furthers this goal by deterring sexual activity by males—the class of persons it considers more responsible for causing those pregnancies. But even assuming that prevention of teenage pregnancy is an important governmental objective and that it is in fact an objective of § 261.5 . . . , California still has the burden of proving that there are fewer teenage pregnancies under its gender-based statutory rape law than there would be if the law were gender-neutral. To meet this burden, the State must show that because its statutory rape law punishes only males, and not females, it more effectively deters minor females from having sexual intercourse.

The plurality assumes that a gender-neutral statute would be less effective than § 261.5 in deterring sexual activity because a gender-neutral statute would create significant enforcement problems. . . .

. . . However, a State's bare assertion that its gender-based statutory classification substantially furthers an important government interest is not enough to meet its burden of proof under *Craig v. Boren*. Rather, the State must produce evidence that will persuade the court that its assertion is true. . . .

The State has not produced such evidence in this case. Moreover, there are at least two serious flaws in the State's assertion that law enforcement problems created by a gender-neutral statutory rape law would make such a statute less effective than a gender-based statute in deterring sexual activity. . . .

. . . There are now at least 37 States that have enacted gender-neutral statutory rape laws. . . .

. . . California has introduced no evidence that those States have been handicapped by the enforcement problems the plurality finds so persuasive. . . .

The second flaw in the State's assertion is that even assuming that a gender-neutral statute would be more difficult to enforce, the State has still not shown that those enforcement problems would make such a statute less effective than a gender-based statute in deterring minor females from engaging in sexual intercourse. Common sense, however, suggests that a gender-neutral statutory rape law is potentially a *greater* deterrent of sexual activity than a gender-based law, for the simple reason that a gender-neutral law subjects both men and women to criminal sanctions and thus arguably has a deterrent effect on twice as many potential violators. Even if fewer persons were prosecuted under the gender-neutral law, as the State suggests, it would still be true that twice as many persons would be *subject* to arrest. The state's failure to prove that a gender-neutral law would be a less effective deterrent than a gender-based law, like the State's failure to prove that a gender-neutral law

would be difficult to enforce, should have led this court to invalidate § 261.5. . . .

. . . Until very recently, no California court or commentator had suggested that the purpose of California's statutory rape law was to protect young women from the risk of pregnancy. Indeed, the historical development of § 261.5 demonstrates that the law was initially enacted on the premise that young women, in contrast to young men, were to be deemed legally incapable of consenting to an act of sexual intercourse. Because their chastity was considered particularly precious, those young women were felt to be uniquely in need of the State's protection. In contrast, young men were assumed to be capable of making such decisions for themselves; the law therefore did not offer them any special protection.

It is perhaps because the gender classification in California's statutory rape law was initially designed to further these outmoded sexual stereotypes, rather than to reduce the incidence of teenage pregnancies, that the State has been unable to demonstrate a substantial relationship between the classification and its newly asserted goal. . . . But whatever the reason, the State has not shown that Cal. Penal Code § 261.5 is any more effective than a gender-neutral law would be in deterring minor females from engaging in sexual intercourse. It has therefore not met its burden of proving that the statutory classification is substantially related to the achievement of its asserted goal.

I would hold that § 261.5 violates the Equal Protection Clause of the Fourteenth Amendment, and I would reverse the judgment of the California Supreme Court.

60. *The Dilemma of Difference*

MARTHA MINOW

. . .

[W]hen does treating people differently emphasize their differences and stigmatize or hinder them on that basis? And when does treating people the same become insensitive to their difference and likely to stigmatize or hinder them on *that* basis?

I call this question "the dilemma of difference." The stigma of difference may be recreated both by ignoring and by focusing on it. Decisions about education, employment, benefits, and other opportunities in society should not turn on an individual's ethnicity, disability, race, gender, religion, or membership in any other group about which some have deprecating or hostile attitudes. Yet refusing to acknowledge these differences may make them continue to matter in a world constructed with some groups, but not others, in mind. The problems of inequality can be exacerbated both by treating members of minority groups the same as members of the majority and by treating the two groups differently.

The dilemma of difference may be posed as a choice between integration and separation, as a choice between similar treatment and special treatment, or as a choice between neutrality and accommodation. Governmental neutrality may be the best way to assure equality, yet governmental neutrality may also freeze in place the past consequences of differences. Do the public schools fulfill their obligation to provide equal opportunities by including all students in the same integrated classroom, or by offering some students special programs tailored to their needs? Special needs arise from "differences" beyond language proficiency and physical or mental disability. Religious differences also raise questions of same versus different treatment. Students who belong to religious minorities may seek exemption from courses in sex education or other subjects that conflict with their religious teachings. Religiously observant students may ask to use school time and

facilities to engage in religious activities, just as other students engage in other extra-curricular activities. But the legal obligation of neutrality is explicit here, in policy committed to separating church and state. Do the schools remain neutral toward religion by balancing the teaching of evolution with the teaching of scientific arguments about creation? Or does this accommodation of a religious viewpoint depart from the requisite neutrality?

The difference dilemma also arises beyond the schoolhouse. If women's biological differences from men justify special benefits in the workplace—such as maternity leave—are women thereby helped or hurt? Are negative stereotypes reinforced, in violation of commitments to equality? Or are differences accommodated, in fulfillment of the vision of equality? Members of religious groups that designate Saturday as the Sabbath may desire accommodation in the workplace. Is the commitment to a norm of equality advanced through such an accommodation, or through neutral application of a Saturday work requirement that happens to burden these individuals differently from others?

. . .

Dilemmas of difference appear unresolvable. The risk of nonneutrality—the risk of discrimination—accompanies efforts both to ignore and to recognize difference in equal treatment and special treatment. Difference can be recreated in color or gender blindness and in affirmative action; in governmental neutrality and in governmental preferences; and in discretionary decisions and in formal constraints on discretion. Why does difference seem to pose choices each of which undesirably revives difference or the stigma or disadvantage associated with it?

In this last question lies a clue to the problem. The possibility of reiterating difference, whether by acknowledgment or nonacknowledgment, arises as long as difference itself carries stigma and precludes equality. Buried in the questions about difference are assumptions that difference is linked to stigma or deviance and that sameness is a prerequisite for equality. Perhaps these assumptions themselves must be identified and assessed if we are to escape or transcend the dilemmas of difference.

If to be equal one must be the same, then to be different is to be unequal or even deviant. But any assignment of deviance must be made from the vantage point of some claimed normality: a position of equality implies a contrasting position used to draw the relationship—and it is a relationship not of equality and inequality but of superiority and inferiority. To be different is to be different in relationship to someone or something else—and this point of comparison must be so taken for granted, so much the "norm," that it need not even be stated.

At least five closely related but unstated assumptions underlie difference dilemmas. Once articulated and examined, these assumptions can take their proper place among other choices about how to treat difference, and we can consider what we might do to challenge or renovate them.

Five Unstated Assumptions

Assumption 1: Difference Is Intrinsic, Not a Comparison

Can and should questions about who is different be resolved by a process of discovering intrinsic differences? Is difference something intrinsic to the different person or something constructed by social attitudes? By posing legal claims through the difference dilemma, litigants and judges treat the problem of difference as what society or a given decision-maker should do about the "different person"—a formulation that implicitly assigns the label of difference to that person.

The difference inquiry functions by pigeonholing people in sharply distinguished categories based on selected facts and features. Categorization helps people to cope with complexity and to understand one another. Devising categories to simplify a complicated world may well be an inevitable feature of human cognition.

When lawyers and judges analyze difference and use categories to do so, they import a basic method of legal analysis. Legal analysis, cast in a judicial mode, typically asks whether a given situation "fits" in a category defined by a legal rule or, instead, belongs outside it. Questions presented for review by the Supreme Court, for example, often take the form "Is this a that?" For example, are Jews a race? Is a contagious disease a handicap? Other questions take the form "Is doing x really doing y?" For example, is offering a statutory guarantee of job reinstatement after maternity leave really engaging in gender discrimination? Is denying unemployment benefits to someone who left work because of pregnancy also really discriminating on the basis of gender? . . .

. . .

Some have argued that the assignment of differences in Western thought entails not just relationships and comparisons but also the imposition of hierarchies. To explore this idea, we need the next unstated assumption: the implicit norm or reference point for the comparison through which difference is assigned.

Assumption 2: The Norm Need Not be Stated

To treat someone as different means to accord him treatment that is different from the treatment of someone else, to describe someone as "the same" implies "the same as" someone else. When differences are discussed without explicit reference to the person or trait on the other side of the comparison, an unstated norm remains. Usually, this default reference point is so powerful and well established that specifying it is not thought necessary.

When women argue for rights, the implicit reference point used in discussions of sameness and difference is the privilege accorded some men—typically, white men who are well established in the society. . . . Unfortunately for the reformers, embracing the theory of "sameness" meant that any sign of difference between women and the men used for comparison could be used to justify treating women differently from those men.

A prominent "difference" assigned to women by implicit comparison with men, is pregnancy—especially pregnancy experienced by women working for pay outside their homes. The Supreme Court's treatment of issues concerning pregnancy and the workplace highlights the power of the unstated norm in analyses of problems of difference. In 1975 the Court accepted an appeal to a male norm in striking down a Utah statute that disqualified a woman from receiving unemployment compensation for a specified period surrounding childbirth, even if her reasons for leaving work were unrelated to the pregnancy. Although the capacity to become pregnant is a difference between women and men, this fact alone did not justify treating women and men differently on matters unrelated to pregnancy. Using men as the norm, the Court reasoned that any woman who can perform like a man can be treated like a man. A woman could not be denied unemployment compensation for different reasons than a man would.

What, however, is equal treatment for the woman who is correctly identified within the group of pregnant persons, not simply stereotyped as such, and temporarily unable to work outside the home for that reason? The Court first grappled with these issues in two cases that posed the question of whether discrimination on the basis of pregnancy—that is, employers' denial of health benefits—amounted to discrimination on the basis of sex. In both instances the Court answered negatively, reasoning that the employers drew a distinction not on the forbidden basis of sex but only on the basis of pregnancy; and since women could be both pregnant and nonpregnant, these were not instances of sex discrimination. Only from a point of view that regards pregnancy as a strange occurrence, rather than an ongoing bodily potential, would its relationship to female experience be made so tenuous; and only from a vantage point that regards men as the norm would the exclusion of pregnancy from health insurance coverage seem unproblematic and free from gender discrimination.

Congress responded by enacting the Pregnancy Discrimination Act, which amended Title VII (the federal law forbidding gender discrimination in employment) to include discrimination on the basis of pregnancy within the range of impermissible sex discrimination. Yet even under these new statutory terms, the power of the unstated male norm persists in debates over the definition of discrimination. Indeed, a new question arose under the Pregnancy Discrimination Act: if differential treatment on the basis of pregnancy is forbidden, does the statute also forbid any state requirement for pregnancy or maternity leaves—which are, after all, distinctions drawn on the basis of pregnancy, even though drawn to help women?

A collection of employers launched a lawsuit in the 1980s arguing that even favorable treatment on the basis of pregnancy violated the Pregnancy Discrimination Act. The employers challenged a California statute that mandated a limited right to resume a prior job following an unpaid pregnancy disability leave. The case—*California Federal Savings & Loan Association v. Guerra,* which became known as "Cal/Fed"[1]—in a real and painful sense divided the community of advocates for women's rights. Writing briefs on opposing sides, women's rights groups went public with the division. Some maintained that any distinction on the basis of pregnancy—any distinction on the basis of sex—would perpetuate the negative stereotypes long used to demean and exclude women. Others argued that denying the facts of pregnancy and the needs of new mothers could only hurt women; treating women like men in the workplace violated the demands of equality. What does equality demand—treating women like men, or treating women specially?

What became clear in these arguments was that a deeper problem had produced this conundrum: a work world that treats as the model worker the traditional male employee who has a full-time wife and mother to care for his home and children. The very phrase "special treatment," when used to describe pregnancy or maternity leave, posits men as the norm and women as different or deviant from that norm. The problem was not women, or pregnancy, but the effort to fit women's experiences and needs into categories forged with men in mind.

The case reached the Supreme Court. Over a strenuous dissent, a majority of the justices reconceived the problem and rejected the presumption of the male norm which had made the case seem like a choice between "equal treatment" and "special treatment." Instead, Justice Marshall's opinion for the majority shifted from a narrow workplace comparison to a broader comparison of men and women in their dual roles as workers and as family members. The Court found no conflict between the Pregnancy Discrimination Act and the challenged state law that required qualified reinstatement of women following maternity leaves, because "California's pregnancy disability leave statute allows women, as well as men, to have families without losing their jobs." The Court therefore construed the federal law to permit states to require that employers remove barriers in the workplace that would disadvantage pregnant people compared with others. Moreover, reasoned the majority, if there remains a conflict between a federal ban against sex-based discrimination and a state law requiring accommodation for women who take maternity leaves, that conflict should be resolved by the extension to men of benefits comparable to those available to women following maternity or pregnancy leaves. Here, the Court used women's experiences as the benchmark and called for treating men equally in reference to women, thus reversing the usual practice. The dissenters, however remained convinced that the federal law prohibited preferential treatment on the basis of pregnancy; they persisted in using the male norm as the measure for equal treatment in the workplace. . . .

Assumption 3: The Observer Can See Without a Perspective

This assumption builds on the others. Differences are intrinsic, and anyone can see them; there is one true reality, and impartial observers can make judgments unaffected and untainted by their own perspective or experience. The facts of the world, including facts about people's traits, are knowable truly only by someone uninfluenced by social or cultural situations. Once legal rules are selected, regardless of prior disputes over the rules themselves, society may direct legal officials to apply them evenhandedly and to use them to discover and categorize events, motives, and culpability as they exist in the world. This aspiration to impartiality in legal judgments, however, is just that—an aspiration, not a description. The aspiration even risks obscuring the inevitable perspective of any given legal official, or of anyone else, and thereby makes it harder to challenge the impact of perspective on the selection of traits used to judge legal consequences.

The ideal of objectivity itself suppresses the coincidence between the viewpoints of the majority and what is commonly understood to be objective or unbiased. For example, in an employment discrimination case the defendant, a law firm, sought to disqualify Judge Constance Baker Motley from sitting on the case because she, as a black woman who had once represented plaintiffs in discrimination cases, would identify with those who suffer race or sex discrimination. The defendant assumed that Judge Motley's personal identity and her past political work had made her different, lacking the ability to perceive without a perspective. Judge Motley declined, however, to recuse herself and explained; "If background or sex or race of each judge were, by definition, sufficient grounds for removal, no judge on this court could hear this case, or many others, by virtue of the fact that all of them were attorneys, of a sex, often with distinguished law firm or public service backgrounds."[2]

Because of the aspiration to impartiality and the prevalence of universalist language in law, most observers of law have been reluctant to confront the arguments of philosophers and psychologists who challenge the idea that observers can see without a perspective. Philosophers such as A. J. Ayer and W. V. Quine note that although we can alter the theory we use to frame our perceptions of the world, we cannot see the world unclouded by preconceptions. What interests us, given who we are and where we stand, affects our ability to perceive.

The impact of the observer's unacknowledged perspective may be crudely oppressive. When a municipality includes a nativity creche in its annual Christmas display, the majority of the community may perceive no offense to non-Christians in the community. If the practice is challenged in court as a violation of the Constitution's ban against establishment of religion, a judge who is Christian may also fail to see the offense to anyone and merely conclude, as the Supreme Court did in 1984, that Christmas is a national holiday. Judges may be peculiarly disabled from perceiving the state's message about a dominant religious practice because judges are themselves often members of the dominant group and therefore have the luxury of seeing their perspectives mirrored and reinforced in major social and political institutions. Similarly, members of a racial majority may miss the impact of their own race on their perspective about the race of others.

. . .

Assumption 4: Other Perspectives Are Irrelevant

. . . Many people who judge differences in the world reject as irrelevant or relatively unimportant the experience of "different people." William James put it this way: "We have seen the blindness and deadness to each other which are our natural inheritance."[3] People often use stereotypes as though they were real and complete, thereby failing to see the complex humanity of others. Stereotyped thinking is one form of the failure to imagine the perspective of another. Glimpsing contrasting perspectives may alter assumptions about the world, as well as about the meaning of difference.

. . .

A perspective may go unstated because it is so unknown to those in charge that they do not recognize it as a perspective. Judges in particular often presume that the perspective they adopt is either universal or superior to others. Indeed, a perspective may go unstated because it is so powerful and pervasive that it may be presumed without defense. It has been said that Aristotle could have checked out—and corrected—his faulty assertion that women have fewer teeth than men. He did not do so, however, because he thought he knew. Presumptions about whose perspective ultimately matters arise from the fifth typically unarticulated assumption, that the status quo is the preferred situation.

Assumption 5: The Status Quo Is Natural, Uncoerced, and Good

Connected with many of the other assumptions is the idea that critical features of the status quo—general social and economic arrangements—are natural and desirable. From this assumption follow three propositions. First, the goal of governmental neutrality demands the status quo because existing societal arrangements are assumed to be neutral. Second, governmental actions that change the status quo have a different status from omissions, or failures to act, that maintain the status quo. Third, prevailing societal arrangements are not forced on anyone. Individuals are free to make choices and to assume responsibility for those choices. These

propositions are rarely stated, both because they are deeply entrenched and because they treat the status quo as good, natural, and freely chosen—and thus not in need of discussion.

Difference may seem salient, then, not because of a trait intrinsic to the person but because the dominant institutional arrangements were designed without that trait in mind—designed according to an unstated norm reconfirmed by the view that alternative perspectives are irrelevant or have already been taken into account. The difference between buildings built without considering the needs of people in wheelchairs and buildings that are accessible to people in wheelchairs reveals that institutional arrangements define whose reality is to be the norm and what is to seem natural. Sidewalk curbs are not neutral or natural but humanly constructed obstacles. Interestingly, modifying what has been the status quo often brings unexpected benefits as well. Inserting curb cuts for the disabled turns out to help many others, such as bike riders and parents pushing baby strollers. (They can also be positioned to avoid endangering a visually impaired person who uses a cane to determine where the sidewalk ends.)

Yet the weight of the status quo remains great. Existing institutions and language already shape the world and already express and recreate attitudes about what counts as a difference, and who or what is the relevant point of comparison. Assumptions that the status quo is natural, good, and uncoerced make proposed changes seem to violate the commitment to neutrality, predictability, and freedom.

. . .

. . . An extensive dispute about the role of women's choices in the gender segregation of the workplace arose in a sex discrimination charge pursued by the federal Equal Employment Opportunity Commission against Sears, Roebuck & Co.[4] Did the absence of women from jobs as commission salespersons result from women's own choices and preferences, or from societal discrimination and employers' refusals to make those jobs available? The legal framework in the case seemed to force the issue into either/or questions: women's work-force participation was due either to their own choices or to forces beyond their control; women's absence from certain jobs was either due to employers' discrimination or not; either women lacked the interest and qualifications for these jobs, or women had the interest and qualifications for the jobs.

Would it be possible to articulate a third view? Consider this one: choices by working women and decisions by their employers were both influenced by larger patterns of economic prosperity and depression and by shifting social attitudes about appropriate roles for women. These larger patterns became real in people's lives when internalized and experienced as individual choice. Assuming that the way things have been resulted either from people's choices or from nature helps to force legal arguments into these alternatives and to make legal redress of historic differences a treacherous journey through incompatible alternatives.

Sometimes, judges have challenged the assumption that the status quo is natural and good; they have occasionally approved public and private decisions to take difference into account in efforts to alter existing conditions and to remedy their harmful effects. But for the most part, unstated assumptions work in subtle and complex ways. They fill a basic human need to simplify and make our world familiar and unsurprising, yet by their very simplification, assumptions exclude contrasting views. Moreover, they contribute to the dilemma of difference by frustrating legislative and constitutional commitments to change the treatment of differences in race, gender, ethnicity, religion, and handicap.

. . .

Endnotes

[1] 107 S. Ct. 683 (1987).

[2] *Blank v. Sullivan & Cromwell,* 418 F. Supp. 1 (S.D.N.Y. 1975); accord *Commonwealth v. Local Union 542,* Int'l Union of Operating Eng'rs, 388 F. Supp. 115 (F.D.Pa. 1974)(Higginbotham, J.)(denying defendant's motion to disqualify the judge from a race discrimination case because of the judge's racial identity as a black person). Judge Higginbotham noted that "black lawyers have litigated in federal courts almost exclusively before white judges, yet they have not urged the white judges should be disqualified on matters of race relations" (id. at 177).

[3] James, "What Makes a Life Significant," in *On Some of Life's Ideals,* pp. 49, 81. I want to acknowledge here that "blindness" as a metaphoric concept risks stigmatizing people who are visually impaired.

[4] 628 F. Supp. 1264 (N.D. Ill. 1986).

---

61. *The Assimilationist Ideal*

RICHARD WASSERSTROM

Just as we can and must ask what is involved in our or any other culture in being of one race or one sex rather than the other, and how individuals are in fact viewed and treated, we can also ask a different question, namely, what would the good or just society make of an individual's race or sex, and to what degree, if at all, would racial and sexual distinctions ever properly be taken into account there? Indeed, it could plausibly be argued that we could not have a wholly adequate idea of whether a society was racist or sexist unless we had some conception of what a thoroughly nonracist or nonsexist society would look like. This question is an extremely instructive as well as an often neglected one. Comparatively little theoretical literature that deals with either racism or sexism has concerned itself in a systematic way with this issue, but as will be seen it is in some respects both a more important and a more

Reprinted by permission of The University of Notre Dame Press.

complicated one where sex is concerned than where race is involved. Moreover, as I shall argue, many discussions of sexual differences which touch upon this question do so inappropriately by concentrating upon the relatively irrelevant question of whether the differences between males and females are biological rather than social in origin.

The inquiry that follows addresses and seeks to answer two major questions. First, what are the major, plausible conceptions of what the good society would look like in respect to the race and sex of individuals, and how are these conceptions to be correctly characterized and described? And second, given a delineation of the alternatives, what is to be said in favor or against one or another of them? . . .

. . .

[O]ne conception of a nonracist society is that which is captured by what I shall call the assimilationist ideal: a nonracist society would be one in which the race of an individual would be the functional equivalent of the eye color of individuals in our society today. In our society no basic political rights and obligations are determined on the basis of eye color. No important institutional benefits and burdens are connected with eye color. Indeed, except for the mildest sort of aesthetic preferences, a person would be thought odd who even made private, social decisions by taking eye color into account. It would, of course, be unintelligible, and not just odd, were a person to say today that while he or she looked blue-eyed, he or she regarded himself of herself as really a brown-eyed person. Because eye color functions differently in our culture than does race, there is no analogue to passing for eye color. Were the assimilationist ideal to become a reality, the same would be true of one's race. In short, according to the assimilationist ideal, a nonracist society would be one in which an individual's race was of no more significance in any of these three areas than is eye color today.

What is a good deal less familiar is an analogous conception of the good society in respect to sexual differentiation—one in which an individual's sex were to become a comparably unimportant characteristic. An assimilationist society in respect to sex would be one in which an individual's sex was of no more significance in any of the three areas than is eye color today. There would be no analogue to transsexuality, and, while physio-

logical or anatomical sex differences would remain, they would possess only the kind and degree of significance that today attaches to the physiologically distinct eye colors persons possess.

It is apparent that the assimilationist ideal in respect to sex does not seem to be as readily plausible and obviously attractive here as it is in the case of race. In fact, many persons invoke the possible realization of the assimilationist ideal as a reason for rejecting the Equal Rights Amendment and indeed the idea of women's liberation itself. . . .

To begin with, it must be acknowledged that to make the assimilationist ideal a reality in respect to sex would involve more profound and fundamental revisions of our institutions and our attitudes than would be the case in respect to race. On the institutional level we would, for instance, have to alter significantly our practices concerning marriage. If a nonsexist society is a society in which one's sex is no more significant than eye color in our society today, then laws which require the persons who are getting married to be of different sexes would clearly be sexist laws.

More importantly, given the significance of role differentiation and ideas about the psychological differences in temperament that are tied to sexual identity, the assimilationist ideal would be incompatible with all psychological and sex-role differentiation. That is to say, in such a society the ideology of the society would contain no proposition asserting the inevitable or essential attributes of masculinity or femininity; it would never encourage or discourage the ideas of sisterhood or brotherhood; and it would be unintelligible to talk about the virtues or the disabilities of being a woman or a man. In addition, such a society would not have any norms concerning the appropriateness of different social behavior depending upon whether one were male or female. There would be no conception of the existence of a set of social tasks that were more appropriately undertaken or performed by males or by females. And there would be no expectation that the family was composed of one adult male and one adult female, rather than, say, just two adults—if two adults seemed the appropriate number. To put it simply, in the assimilationist society in respect to sex, persons would not be socialized so as to see or understand themselves or others as essentially or significantly who they were or what their lives would be like because they were either male or female. And no political rights or social institutions, practices, and norms would mark the physiological differences between males and females as important.

Were sex like eye color, these kinds of distinctions would make no sense. Just as the normal, typical adult is virtually oblivious to the eye color of other persons for all significant interpersonal relationships, so, too, the normal, typical adult in this kind of nonsexist society would be equally as indifferent to the sexual, physiological differences of other persons for all significant interpersonal relationships. Bisexuality, not heterosexuality or homosexuality, would be the typical intimate, sexual relationship in the ideal society that was assimilationist in respect to sex.

To acknowledge that things would be very different is, of course, hardly to concede that they would thereby be undesirable—or desirable for that matter. But still, the problem is, perhaps, with the assimilationist ideal. And the assimilationist ideal is certainly not the only possible, plausible ideal.

There is, for instance, another one that is closely related to, but distinguishable from that of the assimilationist ideal. It can be understood by considering how religion rather than eye color tends to be thought about in our culture today and incorporated within social life today. If the good society were to match the present state of affairs in respect to one's religious identity, rather than the present state of affairs in respect to one's eye color, the two societies would be different, but not very greatly so. In neither would we find that the allocation of basic political rights and duties ever took an individual's religion into account. And there would be a comparable indifference to religion even in respect to most important institutional benefits and burdens—for example, access to employment in the desirable vocations, the opportunity to live where one wished to live, and the like. Nonetheless, in the good society in which religious differences were to some degree socially relevant, it would be deemed appropriate to have some institutions (typically those which are connected in an intimate way with these religions) which did in a variety of ways properly take the religion of members of the society into account. . . .

. . .

[I]t may be that in respect to sex, and conceivably, in respect to race, too, something more like this ideal of diversity in respect to religion is the right one. But one problem then—and it is a more substantial one than is sometimes realized—is to specify with a good deal of precision and care what the ideal really comes to in the matter of sexual or racial identity and degree of acceptable sexual or racial differentiation. Which institutional and personal differentiations would properly be permissible and which would not be? Which attitudes, beliefs, and role expectations concerning the meaning and significance of being male or female would be properly introduced and maintained in the good society and which would not be?

. . .

. . . Some persons might think the right ideal was one in which substantially greater sexual differentiation and sex-role identification were retained than would be the case within a good society of that general type. Thus, someone might believe, for instance, that the good society was, perhaps, essentially like the one they think we now have in respect to sex: equality of basic political rights, such as the right to vote, but all of the sexual differentiation in both legal and nonlegal, formal and informal institutions, all of the sex-role socialization and all of the differences in matters of temperament that are characteristic of the way in which our society has been and still is ordered. And someone might also believe that the prevailing ideological concomitants of these arrangements are the correct and appropriate ones to perpetuate. . . .

[T]he next question is that of how a choice is rationally to be made among these different, possible ideals. One general set of issues concerns the empirical sphere, because the question of whether something is a plausible and attractive ideal does turn in part on the nature of the empirical world. If it is true, for example, that any particular characteristic, such as an individual's race or sex, is not only a socially significant category in our culture but that it is largely a socially created one as well, then for many people a number of objections to the assimilationist ideal appear immediately to disappear. The other general set of issues concerns the relevant normative considerations. Here the key questions concern the principles and considerations by which to assess and evaluate different conceptions of how persons ought to be able to live and how their social institutions ought to be constructed and arranged. I begin with the empirical considerations and constraints, although one heuristic disadvantage in doing so is that this decision may appear to give them greater weight than, as I shall argue, they in fact deserve.

What opponents of assimilationism and proponents of schemes of strong sexual differentiation seize upon is that sexual difference appears to be a naturally occurring category of obvious and inevitable relevance for the construction of any plausible conception of the nature of the good society. The problems with this way of thinking are twofold. To begin with, a careful and thorough analysis of the social realities would reveal, I believe, that it is the socially created sexual differences which constitute most of our conception of sex differences and which tend in fact to matter the most in the way we live our lives as persons of one sex or the other. For, it is, I think, sex-role differentiation and socialization, not the physiological and related biological differences—if there are any— that make men and women as different as they are from each other, and it is these same sex-role-created differences which are invoked to justify the necessity or the desirability of most sexual differentiation proposed to be maintained at any of the levels of social arrangements and practices described earlier.

It is important, however, not to attach any greater weight than is absolutely necessary to the truth or falsity of this causal claim about the source of the degree of sexual distinctions that exist[s] in our or other cultures. For what is significant, although seldom recognized, is the fact that the answer to that question almost never goes very far in settling the question of what the good society should look like in respect to any particular characteristic of individuals. And the answer certainly does not go as far as many persons appear to believe it does to settle that question of the nature of the good society.

Let us suppose that there are what can be called "naturally occurring" sexual differences and even that they are of such a nature that they are in some sense of direct prima facie social relevance. It is essential to see that this would by no means settle the question of whether in the good society sex

should or should not be as minimally significant as eye color. Even if there are major or substantial biological differences between men and women that are in this sense "natural" rather than socially created, this does not determine the question of what the good society can and should make of these differences—without, that is, begging the question by including within the meaning of "major" or "substantial" or "natural" the idea that these are things that ought to be retained, emphasized, or otherwise normatively taken into account. It is not easy to see why, without begging the question, it should be thought that this fact, if it is a fact, settles the question adversely to anything like the assimilationist ideal. Persons might think that truths of this sort about nature or biology do affect, if not settle, the question of what the good society should look like for at least two different reasons.

In the first place, they might think the differences are of such a character that they substantially affect what would be *possible* within a good society of human persons. Just as the fact that humans are mortal necessarily limits the features of any possible good society, so, they might argue, the fact that males and females are physiologically or biologically different limits in the same way the features of any possible good society.

In the second place, they might think the differences are of such a character that they are relevant to the question of what would be *desirable* in the good society. That is to say, they might not think that the differences determine or affect to a substantial degree what is possible, but only that the differences are appropriately taken into account in any rational construction of an ideal social existence.

The second reason seems to be a good deal more plausible than the first. For there appear to be very few, if any, respects in which the ineradicable, naturally occurring differences between males and females *must* be taken into account. The industrial revolution has certainly made any of the general differences in strength between the sexes capable of being ignored by the good society for virtually all significant human activities. And even if it were true that women are naturally better suited than men to care for and nurture children, it is also surely the case that men can be taught to care for and nurture children well. Indeed, the one natural or biological fact that seems *required* to be taken into account is the fact that reproduction of the human species requires that the fetus develop *in utero* for a period of months. Sexual intercourse is not necessary, for artificial insemination is available. Neither marriage nor the nuclear family is necessary either for conception or child rearing. Given the present state of medical knowledge and what might be termed the natural realities of female pregnancy, it is difficult to see why any important institutional or interpersonal arrangements are constrained to take the existing biological differences as to the phenomenon of *in utero* pregnancy into account.

But to say all this is still to leave it a wholly open question to what degree the good society *ought* to build upon any ineradicable biological differences, or to create ones in order to construct institutions and sex-roles which would thereby maintain a substantial degree of sexual differentiation. The way to answer that question is to consider and assess the arguments for and against doing so. What is significant is the fact that many of the arguments for doing so are less persuasive than they appear to be upon the initial statement of this possibility.

It might be argued, for instance, that the fact of menstruation could be used as a premise upon which to base the case for importantly different social roles for females than for males. But this could only plausibly be proposed if two things were true: first, that menstruation would be debilitating to women and hence relevant to social role even in a culture which did not teach women to view menstruation as a sign of uncleanliness or as a curse; and, second, that the way in which menstruation necessarily affected some or all women was in fact necessarily related in an important way to the role in question. But even if both of these were true, it would still be an open question whether any sexual differentiation ought to be built upon these facts. The society could still elect to develop institutions that would nullify the effect of these natural differences and it would still be an open question whether it ought to do so. Suppose, for example, what seems implausible—that some or all women will not be able to perform a particular task while menstruating, e.g., guard the border of a country. It would be possible, even easy, if the society wanted

to, to arrange for substitute guards for the women who were incapacitated. We know that persons are not good guards when they are sleepy, and we make arrangements so that persons alternate guard duty to avoid fatigue. The same could be done for menstruating women, even given the implausibly strong assumptions about menstruation.

The point that is involved here is a very general one that has application in contexts having nothing to do with the desirability or undesirability of maintaining substantial sexual differentiation. It has to do with the fact that humans possess the ability to alter their natural and social environment in distinctive, dramatic, and unique ways. An example from the nonsexual area can help bring out this too seldom recognized central feature. It is a fact that some persons born in human society are born with congenital features such that they cannot walk or walk well on their legs. They are born naturally crippled or lame. However, humans in our society certainly possess the capability to devise and construct mechanical devices and institutional arrangements which render this natural fact about some persons relatively unimportant in respect to the way they and others will live together. We can bring it about, and in fact are in the process of bringing it about, that persons who are confined to wheelchairs can move down sidewalks and across streets because the curb stones at corners of intersections have been shaped so as to accommodate the passage of wheelchairs. And we can construct and arrange buildings and events so that persons in wheelchairs can ride elevators, park cars, and be seated at movies, lectures, meetings, and the like. Much of the environment in which humans live is the result of their intentional choices and actions concerning what that environment shall be like. They can elect to construct an environment in which the natural incapacity of some persons to walk or walk well is a major difference or a difference that will be effectively nullified vis-à-vis the lives that they, too, will live. . . .

There are, though, several other arguments based upon nature, or the idea of the "natural" that also must be considered and assessed. First, it might be argued that if a way of doing something is natural, then it ought to be done that way. Here, what may be meant by "natural" is that this way of doing the thing is the way it would be done if culture did not direct or teach us to do it differently. It is not clear, however, that this sense of "natural" is wholly intelligible; it supposes that we can meaningfully talk about how humans would behave in the absence of culture. And few if any humans have ever lived in such a state. Moreover, even if this is an intelligible notion, the proposal that the natural way to behave is somehow the appropriate or desirable way to behave is strikingly implausible. It is, for example, almost surely natural, in this sense of "natural," that humans would eat their food with their hands, except for the fact that they are, almost always, socialized to eat food differently. Yet, the fact that humans would naturally eat this way, does not seem in any respect to be a reason for believing that that is thereby the desirable or appropriate way to eat food. And the same is equally true of any number of other distinctively human ways of behaving.

Second, someone might argue that substantial sexual differentiation is natural not in the sense that it is biologically determined nor in the sense that it would occur but for the effects of culture, but rather in the sense that substantial sexual differentiation is a virtually universal phenomenon in human culture. By itself, this claim of virtual universality, even if accurate, does not directly establish anything about the desirability or undesirability of any particular ideal. But it can be made into an argument by the addition of the proposition that where there is a widespread, virtually universal social practice or institution, there is probably some good or important purpose served by the practice or institution. Hence, given the fact of substantial sex-role differentiation in all, or almost all, cultures, there is on this view some reason to think that substantial sex-role differentiation serves some important purpose for and in human society.

This is an argument, but it is hard to see what is attractive about it. The premise which turns the fact of sex-role differentiation into any kind of a strong reason for sex-role differentiation is the premise of conservatism. And it is no more or less convincing here than elsewhere. There are any number of practices or institutions that are typical and yet upon reflection seem without significant social purpose. Slavery was once such an institution; war perhaps still is.

. . .

If the chief thing to be said in favor of something like the assimilationist society in respect to sex is that some arguments against it are not very relevant, that does not by itself make a very convincing case. Such is not, however, the way in which matters need be left. There is an affirmative case of sorts for something like the assimilationist society.

One strong, affirmative moral argument on behalf of the assimilationist ideal is that it does provide for a kind of individual autonomy that a substantially nonassimilationist society cannot provide. The reason is because any substantially nonassimilationist society will have sex roles, and sex roles interfere in basic ways with autonomy. The argument for these two propositions proceeds as follows.

Any nonassimilationist society must have some institutions and some ideology that distinguishes between individuals in virtue of their sexual physiology, and any such society will necessarily be committed to teaching the desirability of doing so. That is what is implied by saying it is nonassimilationist rather than assimilationist. And any substantially nonassimilationist society will make one's sexual identity an important characteristic so that there will be substantial psychological, role, and status differences between persons who are male and those who are female. That is what is implied by saying that it is substantially nonassimilationist. Any such society will necessarily have sex roles, a conception of the places, characteristics, behaviors, etc., that are appropriate to one sex or the other but not both. That is what makes it a *sex* role.

Now, sex roles are, I think, morally objectionable on two or three quite distinct grounds. One such ground is absolutely generic and applies to all sex roles. The other grounds are less generic and apply only to the kinds of sex roles with which we are familiar and which are a feature of patriarchal societies, such as our own. I begin with the more contingent, less generic objections.

We can certainly imagine, if we are not already familiar with, societies in which the sex roles will be such that the general place of women in that society can be described as that of the servers of men. In such a society individuals will be socialized in such a way that women will learn how properly to minister to the needs, desires, and interests of men; women and men will both be taught that it is right and proper that the concerns and affairs of men are more important than and take precedence over those of women; and the norms and supporting set of beliefs and attitudes will be such that this role will be deemed the basic and appropriate role for women to play and men to expect. Here, I submit, what is objectionable about the connected set of institutions, practices, and ideology—the structure of the prevailing sex role—is the role itself. It is analogous to a kind of human slavery. The fundamental moral defect—just as is the case with slavery—is not that women are being arbitrarily or capriciously assigned to the social role of server, but that such a role itself has no legitimate place in the decent or just society. As a result, just as is the case with slavery, the assignment on *any* basis of individuals to such a role is morally objectionable. A society arranged so that such a role is a prominent part of the structure of the social institutions can be properly characterized as an *oppressive* one. It consigns some individuals to lives which have no place in the good society, which restrict unduly the opportunities of these individuals, and which do so in order improperly to enhance the lives and opportunities of others.

But it may be thought possible to have sex roles and all that goes with them without having persons of either sex placed within a position of general, systemic dominance or subordination. Here, it would be claimed, the society would not be an oppressive one in this sense. Consider, for example, the kinds of sex roles with which we are familiar and which assign to women the primary responsibilities for child rearing and household maintenance. It might be argued first that the roles of child rearer and household maintainer are not in themselves roles that could readily or satisfactorily be eliminated from human society without the society itself being deficient in serious, unacceptable ways. It might be asserted, that is, that these are roles or tasks that simply must be filled if children are to be raised in a satisfactory way. Suppose this is correct, suppose it is granted that society would necessarily have it that these tasks would have to be done. Still, if it is also correct that, relatively speaking, these are unsatisfying and unfulfilling ways for humans to concentrate the bulk of their

energies and talents, then, to the degree to which this is so, what is morally objectionable is that if this is to be a *sex* role, then women are unduly and unfairly allocated a disproportionate share of what is unpleasant, unsatisfying, unrewarding work. Here the objection is the degree to which the burden women are required to assume is excessive and unjustified vis-à-vis the rest of society, i.e., the men. Unsatisfactory roles and tasks, when they are substantial and pervasive, should surely be allocated and filled in the good society in a way which seeks to distribute the burdens involved in a roughly equal fashion.

Suppose, though, that even this feature were eliminated from sex roles, so that, for instance, men and women shared more equally in the dreary, unrewarding aspects of housework and child care, and that a society which maintained sex roles did not in any way have as a feature of that society the systemic dominance or superiority of one sex over the other, there would still be a generic moral defect that would remain. The defect would be that any set of sex roles would necessarily impair and retard an individual's ability to develop his or her own characteristics, talents, capacities, and potential life-plans to the extent to which he or she might desire and from which he or she might derive genuine satisfaction. Sex roles, by definition, constitute empirical and normative limits of varying degrees of strength—restrictions on what it is that one can expect to do, be, or become. As such, they are, I think, at least prima facie objectionable.

To some degree, all role-differentiated living is restrictive in this sense. Perhaps, therefore, all role differentiation in society is to some degree troublesome, and perhaps all strongly role-differentiated societies are objectionable. But the case against sex roles and the concomitant sexual differentiation they create and require need not rest upon this more controversial point. For one thing that distinguishes sex roles from many other roles is that they are wholly involuntarily assumed. One has no choice about whether one shall be born a male or female. And if it is a consequence of one's being born a male or a female that one's subsequent emotional, intellectual, and material development will be substantially controlled by this fact, then it is necessarily the case that substantial, permanent, and involuntarily assumed restraints have been imposed on some of the most central factors concerning the way one will shape and live one's life. The point to be emphasized is that this would necessarily be the case, even in the unlikely event that substantial sexual differentiation could be maintained without one sex or the other becoming dominant and developing oppressive institutions and an ideology to support that dominance and oppression. Absent some far stronger showing than seems either reasonable or possible that potential talents, abilities, interests, and the like are inevitably and irretrievably distributed between the sexes in such a way that the sex roles of the society are genuinely congruent with and facilitative of the development of those talents, abilities, interests, and the like that individuals can and do possess, sex roles are to this degree incompatible with the kind of respect which the good or the just society would accord to each of the individual persons living within it. It seems to me, therefore, that there are persuasive reasons to believe that no society which maintained what I have been describing as *substantial* sexual differentiation could plausibly be viewed as a good or just society.

What remains more of an open question is whether a society in which sex functioned in the way in which eye color does (a strictly assimilationist society in respect to sex) would be better or worse than one in which sex functioned in the way in which religious identity does in our society (a nonoppressive, more diversified or pluralistic one). For it might be argued that especially in the case of sex and even in the case of race much would be gained and nothing would be lost if the ideal society in respect to these characteristics succeeded in preserving in a nonoppressive fashion the attractive differences between males and females and the comparably attractive differences among ethnic groups. Such a society, it might be claimed, would be less bland, less homogeneous and richer in virtue of its variety.

I do not think there is any easy way to settle this question, but I do think the attractiveness of the appeal to diversity, when sex or race are concerned, is less alluring than is often supposed. The difficulty is in part one of specifying what will be preserved and what will not, and in part one of preventing the reappearance of the type of systemic dominance and subservience that produces the injustice of oppression. Suppose, for example, that it were suggested that there are aspects of being male and aspects of being female that are equally attractive and hence desirable to maintain and perpetuate: the kind of empathy that is associated with women and the kind of self-control associated with men. It does not matter what the characteristic is, the problem is one of seeing why the characteristic should be tied by the social institutions to the sex of the individuals of the society. If the characteristics are genuinely ones that all individuals ought to be encouraged to display in the appropriate circumstances, then the social institutions and ideology ought to endeavor to foster them in all individuals. If it is good for everyone to be somewhat empathetic all of the time or especially empathetic in some circumstances, or good for everyone to have a certain degree of self-control all of the time or a great deal in some circumstances, then there is no reason to preserve institutions which distribute these psychological attributes along sexual lines. And the same is true for many, if not all, vocations, activities, and ways of living. If some, but not all persons would find a life devoted to child rearing genuinely satisfying, it is good, surely, that that option be open to them. Once again, though, it is difficult to see the argument for implicitly or explicitly encouraging, teaching, or assigning to women, as opposed to men, that life simply in virtue of their sex. Thus, while substantial diversity in individual characteristics, attitudes, and ways of life is no doubt an admirable, even important feature of the good society, what remains uncertain is the necessity or the desirability of continuing to link attributes or behaviors such as these to the race or sex of individuals. And for the reasons I have tried to articulate there are significant moral arguments against any conception of the good society in which such connections are pursued and nourished in the systemic fashion required by the existence and maintenance of *sex* roles.

. . .

62. A *Black Feminist Critique of Antidiscrimination Law*

Kimberle Crenshaw

One way to approach the problem at the intersection of race and sex is to examine how courts frame and interpret the stories of Black women plaintiffs. Indeed, the way courts interpret claims made by Black women is itself part of Black women's experience; consequently, a cursory review of cases involving Black female plaintiffs is quite revealing. To illustrate the difficulties inherent in judicial treatment of intersectionality, I will consider three employment discrimination cases: *DeGraffenreid v. General Motors, Moore v. Hughes Helicopter* and *Payne v. Travenol.*[1]

In *DeGraffenreid*, five Black women brought suit against General Motors, alleging that the employer's seniority system perpetuated the effects of past discrimination against Black women. Although General Motors did not hire Black women prior to 1964, the court noted that "General Motors has hired . . . female employees for a number of years prior to the enactment of the Civil Rights Act of 1964." Because General Motors did hire women—albeit *white women*—during the period that no Black women were hired, there was, in the court's view, no sex discrimination that the seniority system could conceivably have perpetuated. Moreover, reasoning that Black women could choose to bring either a sex or a race discrimination claim, but not both, the court stated:

> The legislative history surrounding Title VII does not indicate that the goal of the statute was to create a new classification of "black women" who would have greater standing than, for example, a black male. The prospect of the creation of new classes of protected minorities, governed only by the mathematical principles of permutation and combination, clearly raises the prospect of opening the hackneyed Pandora's box.

The court's conclusion that Congress did not intend to allow Black women to make a compound claim arises from its inability to imagine that discrimination against Black women can exist independently from the experiences of white women or of Black men. Because the court was blind to this possibility, it did not question whether Congress could have meant to leave this form of discrimination unredressed. Assuming therefore that there was no distinct discrimination suffered by Black women, the court concluded that to allow plaintiffs to make a compound claim would unduly advantage Black women over Black men or white women.

This negative conclusion regarding Black women's ability to bring compound claims has not been replicated in another kind of compound discrimination case—"reverse discrimination" claims brought by white males. Interestingly, no case has been discovered in which a court denied a white male's reverse discrimination claims on similar grounds—that is, that sex and race claims cannot be combined because Congress did not intend to protect compound classes. Yet, white males challenging affirmative action program that benefit minorities and women are actually in no better position to make a race and gender claim than the Black women in *DeGraffenreid:* If white men are required to make their claims separately, they cannot prove race discrimination because white women are not discriminated against, and they cannot prove sex discrimination because Black males are not discriminated against. One would think, therefore, that the logic of *DeGraffenreid* would complicate reverse discrimination cases. That Black women's claims raise the question of compound discrimination while white males' reverse discrimination claims do not suggests that the notion of "compound class" is somehow relative or contingent on some presumed norm rather than definitive and absolute. If that norm is understood to be white male, one can understand how Black women, being "two steps removed" from being white men, are deemed to be a compound class while white men are not. Indeed, if assumptions about objectivity of law are replaced with the subjective perspective of white males, one can understand better not only why Black women are viewed as compound classes and white men are not, but also why the boundaries of sex and race discrimination doctrine are defined respectively by the experiences of white women and Black men. Consider first that when a white male imagines being a female, he probably imagines being a white female. Similarly, a white male who must project himself as Black will no doubt imagine himself to be a Black male, thereby holding constant all other characteristics except race.

Antidiscrimination law is similarly constructed from the perspective of white males. Gender discrimination, imagined from the perspective of white men, is what happens to white women; race discrimination is what happens to Black men. The dominance of the single-axis framework, most starkly represented by *DeGraffenreid,* not only marginalizes Black women but simultaneously privileges the subjectivity of white men. Under this view, Black women are protected only to the extent that their experiences coincide with those of either of the two groups. Where their experiences are distinct, Black women will encounter difficulty articulating their claims as long as approaches prevail which completely obscure problems of intersectionality.

Moore v. Hughes Helicopters, Inc. presents a different way in which courts fail to understand or recognize Black women's claims. *Moore* is typical of cases in which courts refused to certify Black females as class representative in race *and* sex discrimination actions. In *Moore,* the plaintiff alleged that the employer, Hughes Helicopter, practiced race and sex discrimination in promotions to upper-level craft positions and to supervisory jobs. Moore introduced statistical evidence establishing a significant disparity between men and women, and somewhat less of a disparity between Black and white men in supervisory jobs.

Affirming the district court's refusal to certify Moore as the class representative in the sex discrimination complaint on behalf of all women at Hughes, the Ninth Circuit noted approvingly:

. . . Moore had never claimed before the EEOC that she was discriminated against as a female, *but only* as a Black female. . . . [T]his raised serious doubts as to Moore's ability to adequately represent white female employees.

The curious logic in *Moore* reveals not only the narrow scope of antidiscrimination doctrine and its failure to embrace intersectionality, but also the centrality of white female experiences in the conceptualization of gender discrimination. The court rejected Moore's bid to represent all females apparently because her attempt to specify her race was seen as being at odds with the standard allegation that the employer simply discriminated "against females." However, the court failed to see that the absence of a racial referent does not necessarily mean that the claim being made is a more inclusive one. A white woman claiming discrimination against females may be in no better position to represent all women than a Black woman who claims discrimination as a Black female and wants to represent all females. The court's preferred articulation of "against females" is not necessarily more inclusive—it just appears to be so because the racial contours of the claim are not specified.

The court's preference for "against females" rather than "against Black females" reveals the implicit grounding of white female experiences in the doctrinal conceptualization of sex discrimination. For white women, claiming sex discrimination is simply a statement that but for gender, they would not have been disadvantaged. For them there is no need to specify discrimination as *white* females because their race does not contribute to the disadvantage for which they seek redress. The view of discrimination that is derived from this grounding takes race privilege as a given.

Discrimination against a white female is thus the standard sex discrimination claim; claims that diverge from this standard appear to present some sort of hybrid claim. More significantly, because Black females' claims are seen as hybrid, they sometimes cannot represent those who may have "pure" claims of sex discrimination. The effect of this approach is that even though a challenged policy or practice may clearly discriminate against all females, the fact that it has particularly harsh consequences for Black females places Black plaintiffs at odds with white females.

The *Moore* court also denied the plaintiffs' bid to represent Black males, leaving Moore with the task of supporting her race and sex discrimination claims with statistical evidence of discrimination against Black females alone. Because she was unable to represent white women or Black men, she could not use overall statistics on sex disparity at Hughes, nor could she use statistics on race. Proving her claim using statistics on Black women alone was no small task, due to the fact that she was bringing the suit under a disparate impact theory of discrimination.

The court's rulings on Moore's sex and race claim left her with such a small statistical sample that even if she had proved that there were qualified Black women, she could not have shown discrimination under a disparate impact theory. *Moore* illustrates yet another way that antidiscrimination doctrine essentially erases Black women's distinct experiences and, as a result, deems their discrimination complaints groundless.

Finally, Black female plaintiffs have sometimes encountered difficulty in their efforts to win certification as class representatives in some race discrimination actions. This problem typically arises in cases where statistics suggest significant disparities between Black and white workers and further disparities between Black men and Black women. Courts in some cases have denied certification based on logic that mirrors the rationale in *Moore*: The sex disparities between Black men and Black women created such conflicting interests that Black women could not possibly represent Black men adequately. In one such case, *Payne v. Travenol*, two Black female plaintiffs alleging race discrimination brought a class action suit on behalf of all Black employees at a pharmaceutical plant. The court refused, however, to allow the plaintiffs to represent Black males and granted the defendant's request to narrow the class to Black women only. Ultimately, the district court found that there had been extensive racial discrimination at the plant and awarded back pay and constructive seniority to the class of Black female employees. But, despite its finding of general race discrimination, the court refused to extend the remedy to Black men for fear that their conflicting interests would not be adequately addressed; The Fifth Circuit affirmed.[2]

Even though *Travenol* was a partial victory for Black women, the case specifically illustrates how antidiscrimination doctrine generally creates a dilemma for Black women. It forces them to choose between specifically articulating the intersectional aspects of their subordination, thereby risking their ability to represent Black men, or ignoring intersectionality in order to state a claim that would not lead to the exclusion of Black men. When one considers the political consequences of this dilemma, there is little wonder that many people within the Black community view the specific articulation of Black women's interests as dangerously divisive.

In sum, several courts have proved unable to deal with intersectionality, although for contrasting reasons. In *DeGraffenreid*, the court refused to recognize the possibility of compound discrimination against Black women and analyzed their claim using the employment of white women as the historical base. As a consequence, the employment experiences of white women obscured the distinct discrimination that Black women experienced.

Conversely, in *Moore*, the court held that a Black woman could not use statistics reflecting the overall sex disparity in supervisory and upper-level labor jobs because she had not claimed discrimination as a woman, but "only" as a Black woman. The court would not entertain the notion that discrimination experienced by Black women is indeed sex discrimination—provable through disparate impact statistics on women.

Finally, courts such as the one in *Travenol* have held that Black women cannot represent an entire class of Blacks due to presumed class conflicts in cases where sex additionally disadvantaged Black women. As a result, in the few cases where Black women are allowed to use overall statistics indicating racially disparate treatment, Black men may not be able to share in the remedy.

Perhaps it appears to some that I have offered inconsistent criticisms of how Black women are treated in antidiscrimination law: I seem to be saying that in one case, Black women's claims were rejected and their experiences obscured because the court refused to acknowledge that the employment experience of Black women can be distinct from that of white women, while in other cases, the interests of Black women were harmed because Black women's claims were viewed as so distinct from the claims of either white women or Black men that the court denied to Black females representation of the larger class. It seems that I have to say that Black women are the same and harmed by being treated differently, or that they are different and harmed by being treated the same. But I cannot say both.

This apparent contradiction is but another manifestation of the conceptual limitations of the single-issue analyses that intersectionality challenges. The point is that Black women can experience discrimination in any number of ways and that the contradiction arises from our assumptions that their claims of exclusion must be unidirectional. Consider an analogy to traffic in an intersection, coming and going in all four directions. Discrimination, like traffic through an intersection, may flow in one direction, and it may flow in another. If an accident happens in an intersection, it can be caused by cars traveling from any number of directions and, sometimes, from all of them. Similarly, if a Black woman is harmed because she is in the intersection, her injury could result from sex discrimination or race discrimination or both.

Providing legal relief only when Black women prove that their claims are based on race or on sex is analogous to calling an ambulance for the victim only after the driver responsible for the injuries is identified. But it is not always easy to identify the driver: sometimes the skid marks and the injuries simply indicate that they occurred simultaneously, frustrating efforts to determine which driver caused the harm. In these cases the tendency seems to be that no driver is held responsible, no treatment is administered, and the involved parties simply get back in their cars and zoom away.

I am suggesting that Black women can experience discrimination in ways that are both similar to and different from those experienced by white women and Black men. Black women sometimes experience discrimination in ways similar to white women's experiences; sometimes they share very similar experiences with Black men. Yet often they experience double discrimination—the combined effects of practices which discriminate on the basis of race, and on the basis of sex. And sometimes, they experience discrimination as Black women— not the sum of race and sex discrimination, but as Black women.

DeGraffenreid, Moore, and *Travenol* are doctrinal manifestations of a common political and theoretical approach to discrimination which operates to marginalize Black women. Unable to grasp the importance of Black women's intersectional experiences, not only courts, but feminist and civil rights thinkers as well have treated Black women in ways that deny both the unique compoundedness of their situation and the centrality of their experiences to the larger classes of women and Blacks. Consequently, their needs and perspectives have been relegated to the margin of the feminist and Black liberationist agendas. While it could be argued that this marginalization represents an absence of political will to include Black women, I believe that it reflects an uncritical and disturbing acceptance of dominant ways of thinking about discrimination.

Underlying dominant conceptions of discrimination, which have been challenged by a developing approach called critical race theory, is a view that the wrong which antidiscrimination law addresses is the use of race or gender factors to interfere with decisions that would otherwise be fair or neutral. This process-based definition is not grounded in a bottom-up commitment to improve the substantive conditions for those who are victimized by the interplay of numerous factors. Instead, the dominant message of antidiscrimination law is that it will regulate only the limited extent to which race or sex interferes with the process of determining outcomes. This narrow objective is facilitated by the top-down strategy of using a singular "but for" analysis to ascertain the effects of race or sex. Because the scope of antidiscrimination law is so limited, sex and race discrimination have come to be defined in terms of the experiences of those who are privileged *but for* their racial or sexual characteristics. Put differently, the paradigm of sex discrimination tends to be based on the experiences of white women; the model of race discrimination tends to be based on the experiences of the most privileged Blacks. Notions of what constitutes race and sex discrimination are, as a result, narrowly tailored to embrace only a small set of circumstances which do not explicitly include the experiences of Black women.

To the extent that this general description is accurate, the following analogy can be useful in describing how Black women are marginalized in the interface between antidiscrimination law and race and gender hierarchies: imagine a basement which contains all people who are disadvantaged on the basis of race, sex, class, sexual preference, age and/or physical ability. These people are stacked—feet standing on shoulders—with those on the bottom being disadvantaged by the full array of factors, up to the very top, where the heads of all those disadvantaged by a singular factor brush up against the ceiling. Their ceiling is actually the floor above which only those who are *not* disadvantaged in any way reside. In efforts to correct some aspects of domination, those above the ceiling admit from the basement only those who can say that "but for" the ceiling, they too would be in the upper room. A hatch is developed through which those placed immediately below can crawl. Yet this hatch is generally available only to those who—due to the singularity of their burden and their otherwise privileged position relative to those below—are in the position to crawl through. Those who are multiply burdened are generally left below unless they can somehow pull themselves into the groups that are permitted to squeeze through the hatch.

As this analogy translates for Black women, the problem is that they can receive protection only to the extent that their experiences are recognizably similar to those whose experiences tend to be reflected in antidiscrimination doctrine. If Black women cannot conclusively say that "but for" their race or "but for" their gender they would be treated differently, they are not invited to climb through the hatch but told to wait in the unprotected margin until they can be absorbed into the broader, protected categories of race and sex.

Despite the narrow scope of this dominant conception of discrimination and its tendency to marginalize those whose experiences cannot be described within its tightly drawn parameters, this approach has been regarded as the appropriate framework for addressing a range of problems. In much of feminist theory and, to some extent, in antiracist politics, this framework is reflected in the belief that sexism or racism can be meaningfully discussed without paying attention to the lives of those other than the race-, gender-, or class-privileged. As a result, both feminist theory and an-

tiracist politics have been organized, in part, around the equation of sexism with what happens to white women and the equation of racism with what happens to the Black middle class or to Black men.

Looking at historical and contemporary issues in both the feminist and the civil rights communities, one can find ample evidence of how both communities' acceptance of the dominant framework of discrimination has hindered the development of an adequate theory and praxis to address problems of intersectionality. Not only does this adoption of a single-issue framework for discrimination marginalize Black women within the very movements that claim them as part of their constituency but it also makes the illusive goal of ending racism and patriarchy even more difficult to attain.

. . .

Endnotes

[1] 673 F.2d 798 (5th Cir. 1983). These are all statutory cases pursuant to Title VII of the Civil Rights Act of 1964, 42 U.S.C. §2000e, *et seq.* as amended (1982).

[2] 416 F. Supp. 248 (N.D. Miss. 1976), aff'd., 673 F.2d 798 (5th Cir. 1982).

Study Questions

1. In what ways is California's statutory rape law "sexist"? Reread the text of the statute (in Rehnquist's opinion in *Michael M.*) and then consider the following: Under the statute, intercourse with a female under the age of eighteen is criminal but intercourse with a male under eighteen is not. Therefore, any female under eighteen who has sex with an older male participates in an unlawful activity (even though she cannot be punished for it); whereas any male under eighteen, as long as he has sex with a woman above that age, participates in a perfectly lawful activity. Teenage boys, in other words, seem to have more sexual freedom than teenage girls. Was this an intended consequence of the statute? How can we tell? Is this further evidence of prejudice against women?

2. VMI won its case initially at appellate level, though this verdict was overturned by the Supreme Court. The appellate court had found that coeducation at VMI would change the nature of the educational experience furnished there, and had therefore concluded that it is not "maleness" that justifies the program but "the homogeneity of gender . . . regardless of which sex is considered." Does the state have an interest in restricting such "adversative" training to men only?

3. Why does the Supreme Court reject Virginia's argument that the "adversative" method of military training at VMI requires an all-male environment? Why, according to the Court, is an education at VWIL not comparable to one at VMI?

4. On what grounds does Justice Scalia dissent in the VMI case?

5. What does Minow mean by the "dilemma of difference"? Can you think of an example of such a dilemma other than those given by Minow?

6. According to Minow, dilemmas of difference rest on five unacknowledged assumptions. What are these assumptions? Are these assumptions made only by courts, or do we all make them?

7. Why does Wasserstrom think the assimilationist ideal is less attractive in the case of sex than in the case of race?

8. How does Wasserstrom respond to the objection against assimilationism that sex-role differentiation is necessary because it is almost universally present throughout the range of human culture?

9. Is sex discrimination bad or wrong for the same reasons as racial discrimination? Is sex discrimination rooted in assumptions of inferiority and prejudice? Do the various familiar stereotypes of women (that they are weak, overly emotional, dependent, less intellectual than men) add up to the suspicion that laws that maintain (or even encourage) these stereotypes are motivated by a hatred of women, similar to race hatred in the case of Blacks?

10. In 1972 the Congress proposed an amendment to the Constitution stating that "equality of rights under the law shall not be denied or abridged by the United States or by any State on account of sex." Because it was not ratified by a sufficient number of states (some even withdrew their initial support), the Equal Rights Amendment (ERA) failed to become part of the Constitution. What changes might it have made to the law of sex discrimination? If you had been a judge faced with interpreting the amendment, what would you have taken to be its meaning? It is worth noting that some opponents of the ERA sought to defeat it by arguing that it would lead ultimately to some of the same consequences that Wasserstrom says would follow in an "assimilationist" society. Would the ERA have required an assimilationist society? Does the equal protection clause of the Fourteenth Amendment require assimilationism?

11. Hooters of America, Inc. operates a chain of restaurants. For years, the company has had a strict policy of hiring only women to work as servers in its restaurants. The women hired by the company are called "Hooters Girls," and are chosen (among other things) for their large bust size and how good they look in a skimpy uniform. In late 1995, the Equal Employment Opportunity Commission filed a gender bias complaint against Hooters. The company reportedly was willing to invest as much as $10 million in resisting the complaint. "A little good clean wholesome female sexuality," according to a company spokesperson, "is what our customers come for." Company supporters argue that the EEOC's bias suit was misplaced and that its reasoning would dictate that "men would have to be allowed to try out for the Dallas

Cheerleaders." Critics of Hooters respond that similar arguments were once used by airlines to justify hiring only women as flight attendants (women's unique "nurturing" abilities were essentially to comfort passengers); they also argue that female waitresses make up a disproportionately large segment of servers in the poorly paying fast-food sector. Should customer preferences be used to justify sex-based hiring? And does such hiring necessarily reflect a negative stereotype?

12. Many states are currently experiencing a sharp rise in prison populations; many new prisons are under construction, and states are hiring to fill a variety of jobs associated with these facilities. Imagine that a number of women have recently applied with the state department of corrections for positions as correctional officers, whose basic role is to serve as prison guards. Correctional officer jobs are highly sought after, since they are much better compensated than other positions with the department. The state, however, refuses to hire the female applicants, pointing to a state policy that assigns guards to maximum-security facilities based upon their gender; since the overwhelming majority of the state's prisoners are men, women are virtually excluded from correctional officer positions. The state defends its policy by arguing that the essence of a correctional officer's job is to maintain prison security and that this job simply could not be adequately performed by a woman, regardless of her size, strength, and ability. Sex offenders, for example, who have assaulted women before might well do so again if access to female guards were possible; and other inmates, "deprived of the normal heterosexual environment," might assault women guards "just because they were women." The female applicants insist that the state's reasoning is simply a rationalization for its perpetuation of sexist thinking: namely, that women are unwitting sex objects who need to be protected from male inmates. Does the state policy at issue here discriminate against women? How would you decide that question? Suppose the job of a correctional officer were to include observing prisoners as they took showers. Is it justifiable to limit this duty to members of the same sex as the prisoners?

13. In the 1980s, the Equal Employment Opportunity Commission (EEOC) brought charges against the Sears, Roebuck corporation, alleging that the giant retailer had, over a period of a decade or more, engaged in a nationwide pattern of discrimination against women by failing to promote its female employees into commission sales positions on the same basis as males and by paying female management employees less than similarly situated male employees. Commission selling at Sears typically involved high-cost merchandise such as major appliances, furnaces, and roofing, whereas merchandise sold on a noncommission basis was generally low-cost and included such items as clothing, jewelry, and cosmetics. Noncommission salespeople were paid a straight hourly wage. Commission sales offered greater financial reward. The EEOC relied heavily upon statistical evidence revealing a significant gender disparity among Sears' sales positions, with the great majority of the commission sales positions being held by men. Such a disparity went beyond what would be expected under fair employment conditions. Sears admitted these facts but contested the EEOC explanation, arguing instead that women had little interest in commission sales. Women generally prefer to sell soft-line products, such as clothing and housewares, rather than fencing, refrigeration equipment, or tires. Women also like jobs that are less stressful, risky, and competitive than commission selling tends to be, Sears claimed, because women prefer social contact and the cooperative aspects of the workplace. Does evidence of the disparity between men and women in commission sales jobs reflect a sexist bias on the part of Sears, resulting in far fewer opportunities presented to women than to men? Or does the evidence merely reflect the general preferences of most women in society? Sears had developed a statement of

qualifications for commission sales: the salesperson should be aggressive and competitive, have lots of drive, and have technical knowledge and fluency. Does this profile accurately state the qualifications necessary for the job? Or does it describe the type of people who had been doing the job up to that point, almost all of whom were men?

14. A federal court ruled in 1997 that the Alabama prison system does not violate the Equal Protection clause by placing only male inmates in chain gangs. The court held that excluding women from working while shackled is not unconstitutional, due to the low ratio of female to male prisoners in Alabama: of 20,000 state prisoners, only 776 are female. Is this a convincing argument? Can male prisoners make an equal protection argument that *they* are being treated unequally?

Cases for Further Reflection

63. Loving v. Virginia

The following case, *Loving v. Virginia,* involved an antimiscegenation law, that is, a law forbidding racial intermarriage. The Supreme Court unanimously struck down the law as a violation of the "equal protection" clause of the Fourteenth Amendment. When reading the brief excerpt from the Court's ruling, consider the following: The Virginia law did not prohibit all racial intermarriage—it prohibited those who were White from marrying anyone who was not White. Passed in 1924, during the peak of the eugenics movement in the United States, the law was entitled "An Act to Preserve Racial Integrity." Its stated intention was to prevent the "corruption of blood" and a "mongrel breed of citizens." The Court found that the law drew a "racial classification" and lacked a rational basis.

Although blatantly racist, such a law raises interesting questions: Did the law classify on the basis of race in a way that disadvantaged racial minorities? Whites could not marry non-Whites; Blacks, Asians, Latinos, and other non-White persons could intermarry without restriction. Given that fact, how can it be argued that the law reflects racial prejudice? *Loving* involved a Black woman and a White man. The Virginia law, "on its face, " applied equally to Blacks and to Whites: neither could marry the other. If Blacks can't marry Whites and Whites can't marry Blacks, why isn't everyone being treated equally? Could these facts be used to argue that the law actually treated Whites *unequally* with respect to members of other racial groups?

Opinion

Mr. Chief Justice Warren delivered the opinion of the Court.

This case presents a constitutional question never addressed by this Court: whether a statutory scheme adopted by the State of Virginia to prevent marriages between persons solely on the basis of racial classifications violates the Equal Protection and Due Process Clauses of the Fourteenth Amendment. For reasons which seem to us to reflect the central meaning of those constitutional commands, we conclude that these statutes cannot stand consistently with the Fourteenth Amendment.

In June 1958, two residents of Virginia, Mildred Jeter, a Negro woman, and Richard Loving, a white man, were married in the District of Columbia pursuant to its laws. Shortly after their marriage, the Lovings returned to Virginia and established their marital abode in Caroline County. At the October Term, 1958, of the Circuit Court of Caroline County, a grand jury issued an indictment charging the Lovings with violating Virginia's ban on interracial marriages. On January 6, 1959, the Lovings pleaded guilty to the charge and were sentenced to one year in jail; however, the trial judge suspended the sentence for a period of 25 years on the condition that the Lovings leave the State and not return to Virginia together for 25 years. He stated in an opinion that:

"Almighty God created the races white, black, yellow, malay and red, and he placed them on separate continents. And but for the interference with his arrangement there would be no cause for such marriages. The fact that he separated the races shows that he did not intend for the races to mix."

The Supreme Court of Appeals upheld the constitutionality of the antimiscegenation statutes, and, after modifying the sentence, affirmed the convictions. The Lovings appealed this decision, and we noted probable jurisdiction. . . .

The two statutes under which appellants were convicted and sentenced are part of a comprehen-

388 U.S. 1 (1967)
United States Supreme Court

sive statutory scheme aimed at prohibiting and punishing interracial marriages. The Lovings were convicted of violating § 20–58 of the Virginia Code:

"Leaving State to evade law.—If any white person and colored person shall go out of this State, for the purpose of being married, and with the intention of returning, and be married out of it, and afterwards return to and reside in it, cohabiting as man and wife, they shall be punished as provided in § 20–59, and the marriage shall be governed by the same law as if it had been solemnized in this State. The fact of their cohabitation here as man and wife shall be evidence of their marriage."

Section 20–59, which defines the penalty for miscegenation, provides:

"Punishment for marriage.—If any white person intermarry with a colored person, or any colored person intermarry with a white person, he shall be guilty of a felony and shall be punished by confinement in the penitentiary for not less than one nor more than five years."

Other central provisions in the Virginia statutory scheme are § 20–57, which automatically voids all marriages between "a white person and a colored person" without any judicial proceeding, and §§ 20–54 and 1–14 which, respectively, define "white persons" and "colored persons and Indians" for purposes of the statutory prohibitions. The Lovings have never disputed in the course of this litigation that Mrs. Loving is a "colored person" or that Mr. Loving is a "white person" within the meanings given those terms by the Virginia statutes.

Virginia is now one of 16 States which prohibit and punish marriages on the basis of racial classifications. Penalties for miscegenation arose as an incident to slavery and have been common in Virginia since the colonial period. The present statutory scheme dates from the adoption of the Racial Integrity Act of 1924, passed during the period of extreme nativism which followed the end of the First World War. The central features of this Act, and current Virginia law, are the absolute prohibition of a "white person" marrying other than another "white person," a prohibition against issuing marriage licenses until the issuing official is satisfied that the applicants' statements as to their race are correct, certificates of "racial composition" to be kept by both local and state registrars, and the carrying forward of earlier prohibitions against racial intermarriage. . . .

[T]he State does not contend in its argument before this Court that its powers to regulate marriage are unlimited notwithstanding the commands of the Fourteenth Amendment. . . . Instead, the State argues that the meaning of the Equal Protection Clause, as illuminated by the statements of the Framers, is only that state penal laws containing an interracial element as part of the definition of the offense must apply equally to whites and Negroes in the sense that members of each race are punished to the same degree. Thus, the State contends that, because its miscegenation statutes punish equally both the white and the Negro participants in an interracial marriage, these statutes, despite their reliance on racial classifications, do not constitute an invidious discrimination based upon race. The second argument advanced by the State assumes the validity of its equal application theory. The argument is that, if the Equal Protection Clause does not outlaw miscegenation statutes because of their reliance on racial classifications, the question of constitutionality would thus become whether there was any rational basis for a State to treat interracial marriages differently from other marriages. On this question, the State argues, the scientific evidence is substantially in doubt and, consequently, this Court should defer to the wisdom of the state legislature in adopting its policy of discouraging interracial marriages.

Because we reject the notion that the mere "equal application" of a statute containing racial classifications is enough to remove the classifications from the Fourteenth Amendment's proscription of all invidious racial discriminations, we do not accept the State's contention that these statutes should be upheld if there is any possible basis for concluding that they serve a rational purpose. The mere fact of equal application does not mean that our analysis of these statutes should follow the approach we have taken in cases involving no racial discrimination. . . .

The State argues that statements in the Thirty-ninth Congress about the time of the passage of the Fourteenth Amendment indicate that the Framers did not intend the Amendment to make unconsti-tutional state miscegenation laws. . . . While these statements have some relevance to the intention of Congress in submitting the Fourteenth Amendment, it must be understood that they pertained to the passage of specific statutes and not to the broader, organic purpose of a constitutional amendment. As for the various statements directly concerning the Fourteenth Amendment, we have said in connection with a related problem, that although these historical sources "cast some light" they are not sufficient to resolve the problem;" [at] best, they are inconclusive. . . .

There can be no question but that Virginia's miscegenation statutes rest solely upon distinctions drawn according to race. The statutes proscribe generally accepted conduct if engaged in by members of different races. Over the years, this Court has consistently repudiated distinctions between citizens solely because of their ancestry as being odious to a free people whose institutions are founded upon the doctrine of equality. At the very least, the Equal Protection Clause demands that racial classifications, especially suspect in criminal statutes, be subjected to the most rigid scrutiny, and, if they are ever to be upheld, they must be shown to be necessary to the accomplishment of some permissible state objective, independent of the racial discrimination which it was the object of the Fourteenth Amendment to eliminate. . . .

There is patently no legitimate overriding purpose independent of invidious racial discrimination which justifies this classification. The fact that Virginia prohibits only interracial marriages involving white persons demonstrates that the racial classifications must stand on their own justification, as measures designed to maintain White Supremacy. We have consistently denied the constitutionality of measures which restrict the rights of citizens on account of race. There can be no doubt that restricting the freedom to marry solely because of racial classifications violates the central meaning of the Equal Protection Clause.

These statutes also deprive the Lovings of liberty without due process of law in violation of the Due Process Clause of the Fourteenth Amendment. The freedom to marry has long been recognized as one of the vital personal rights essential to the orderly pursuit of happiness by free men.

Marriage is one of the "basic civil rights of man," fundamental to our very existence and survival. To deny this fundamental freedom on so unsupportable a basis as the racial classifications embodied in these statutes, classifications so directly subversive of the principle of equality at the heart of the Fourteenth Amendment, is surely to deprive all the State's citizens of liberty without due process of law. The Fourteenth Amendment requires that the freedom of choice to marry not be restricted by invidious racial discriminations. Under our Constitution, the freedom to marry, or not marry, a person of another race resides with the individual and cannot be infringed by the State.

These convictions must be reversed.

It is so ordered.

64. *Adarand Constructors v. Pena*

In 1989 the federal Department of Transportation awarded a contract for a Colorado highway construction project to Mountain Gravel & Construction Company. Mountain Gravel solicited bids from a variety of subcontractors specializing in guardrail work. Among the firms submitting subcontracting bids were Adarand Constructors and Gonzales Construction. Adarand submitted the lowest bid; but Mountain awarded the guardrail work to Gonzales. Gonzales had been certified by the Small Business Administration (SBA), a federal agency, as a business 51 percent controlled by "socially and economically disadvantaged individuals," and under the terms of federal law, Mountain Gravel would receive extra federal money if it hired an SBA-certified concern. The SBA presumed that "Black, Hispanic, Asian Pacific, Subcontinent Asian, and Native Americans" are "socially and economically disadvantaged." After losing the guardrail subcontract to Gonzales, Adarand filed suit against various federal officials, claiming that the SBA's presumptions of disadvantage based on race violated Adarand's right to "equal protection of the laws," guaranteed by the Fifth and Fourteenth Amendments to the U.S. Constitution. Lower federal courts, relying on some of the Supreme Court's recent rulings, denied Adarand's claim. But the Supreme Court reversed the lower courts and held that Adarand had a legitimate complaint under the Constitution. The lower courts had rejected Adarand's claim because they found that the SBA rules were designed to achieve the "significant governmental purpose" of providing subcontracting opportunities for small disadvantaged business enterprises. O'Connor argued that Adarand had to be given another day in court, this time focusing on whether the ways in which the government uses subcontracting compensation rules can meet the test of strict scrutiny.

Writing for the majority of the court, Justice O'Connor explained that a central point of controversy in *Adarand* turned on the level of scrutiny appropriate to racial classifications included in the federal subcontracting law. As O'Connor explained, any local, state, or federal law classifying people according to their racial identity is automatically suspect because of the risk that the law may be the result of bigotry and prejudice. Consequently, the courts must look carefully at such laws to ensure their validity. How carefully the courts must scrutinize or examine such laws, however, has been unclear. Two differing levels of examination, or standards of review, had previously been endorsed by the courts, according to O'Connor. One standard was articulated by the Supreme Court in *Richmond v. Croson,* decided in 1989. As O'Connor wrote in *Adarand,*

> [a] majority of the Court in *Croson* held that the standard of review under the Equal Protection Clause is not dependent on the race of those burdened or benefited by a particular classification and that the single standard of review for racial classifications should be 'strict scrutiny,'

meaning that the law in question must be shown to be necessary to the furtherance of a "compelling governmental objective," something of such overriding importance that it outweighs the dangers of race-based laws. The *Croson* opinion held

> that the Fourteenth Amendment requires strict scrutiny of all race-based action by state and local governments. But *Croson* . . . had no occasion to declare what standard of review the Fifth Amendment requires for such action taken by the Federal Government.

A competing interpretation of the appropriate standard of review had been announced by the Court in the year following *Croson.* The decision in that case, O'Connor argued, was a mistake.

> *Metro Broadcasting, Inc. v. FCC* involved a Fifth-Amendment challenge to race-based policies of the Federal Communications Commission. In *Metro Broadcasting,* the Court repudiated the long-held notion that it would be unthinkable that the same Constitution would impose a lesser duty of the Federal Government than it does on a State to afford equal protection of the laws. . . . It did so by holding that "benign" federal racial classifications need only satisfy intermediate scrutiny, even though *Croson* had recently concluded that such classifications must satisfy strict scrutiny. "Benign" federal racial classifications, the Court said, "even if those measures are not 'remedial' in the sense of being designed to compensate victims of past governmental or societal discrimination—are constitutionally permissible to the extent that they serve *important* governmental objectives within the power of Congress and are *substantially related* to achievement of those objectives."

This more relaxed standard of review, O'Connor argued, which some courts had used to justify programs of preferential treatment, is inappropriate in all cases where people are being distinguished by race. This conclusion and its implications for programs of affirmative action were hotly debated among members of the Court.

Although the Court in *Adarand* did not actually invalidate any federal affirmative action laws, it did clearly announce its intention in the future to subject such programs to the strictest possible scrutiny—a level of examination which, as Justice O'Connor noted, has a reputation for being "strict in theory but fatal in fact." On this view, existing programs that do not seek to redress specific instances of past, overt discrimination and look merely to the nonremedial goal of expanding diversity [may well] be illegal under *Adarand*. A memorandum issued by the Department of Justice in 1995 states that affirmative action programs justified "solely by reference to general societal discrimination, general assertions of discrimination in a particular sector or industry, or a statistical underrepresentation of minorities in a sector or industry . . . without more" will be "impermissible bases for affirmative action."[1]

Justice O'Connor

. . . [According to precedent] the basic principle is that the Fifth and Fourteenth Amendments to the Constitution protect persons, not groups. It follows from that principle that all governmental action based on race—a group classification long recognized as "in most circumstances irrelevant and therefore prohibited" . . . should be subjected to detailed judicial inquiry to ensure that the personal right to equal protection of the laws has not been infringed. These ideas have long been central to this Court's understanding of equal protection, and holding "benign" state and federal racial classifications to different standards does not square with them. [A] free people whose institutions are founded upon the doctrine of equality . . . should tolerate no retreat from the principle that government may treat people differently because of their race only for the most compelling reasons. Accordingly, we hold today that all racial classifications, imposed by whatever federal, state, or local governmental actor, must be analyzed by a reviewing court under strict scrutiny. In other words, such classifications are constitutional only if they are narrowly tailored measures that further compelling governmental interests.

---

132 L. Ed. 2d 158 (1995)
United States Supreme Court

Justice Scalia, concurring in part and concurring in the judgment.

. . . In my view, government can never have a "compelling interest" in discriminating on the basis of race in order to "make up" for past racial discrimination in the opposite direction. . . . Individuals who have been wronged by unlawful racial discrimination should be made whole; but under our Constitution there can be no such thing as either a creditor or a debtor race. That concept is alien to the Constitution's focus upon the individual . . . and its rejection of dispositions based on race. . . . To pursue the concept of racial entitlement—even for the most admirable and benign of purposes—is to reinforce and preserve for future mischief the way of thinking that produced race slavery, race privilege and race hatred. In the eyes of government, we are just one race here. It is American. . . .

Justice Thomas, concurring in part and concurring in the judgment.

. . . I believe that there is a "moral [and] constitutional equivalence" . . . between laws designed to subjugate a race and those that distribute benefits on the basis of race and those that distribute benefits on the basis of race in order to foster some current notion of equality. Government cannot make us equal; it can only recognize, respect, and protect us as equal before the law.

That these programs may have been motivated, in part, by good intentions cannot provide refuge from the principle that under our Constitution, the government may not make distinctions on the basis of race. As far as the Constitution is concerned, it is irrelevant whether a government's racial classifications are drawn by those who wish to oppress a race or by those who have a sincere desire to help those thought to be disadvantaged. There can be no doubt that the paternalism that appears to lie at the heart of this program is at war with the principle of inherent equality that underlies and infuses our Constitution. . . .

These programs not only raise grave constitutional questions, they also undermine the moral basis of the equal protection principle. . . .

. . . [T]here can be no doubt that racial paternalism and its unintended consequences can be as poisonous and pernicious as any other form of discrimination. So-called "benign" discrimination teaches many that because of chronic and apparently immutable handicaps, minorities cannot compete with them without their patronizing indulgence. Inevitably, such programs engender attitudes of superiority or, alternatively, provoke resentment among those who believe that they have been wronged by the government's use of race. These programs stamp minorities with a badge of inferiority and may cause them to develop dependencies or to adopt an attitude that they are "entitled" to preferences. . . .

In my mind, government-sponsored racial discrimination based on benign prejudice is just as noxious as discrimination inspired by malicious prejudice. . . . In each instance, it is racial discrimination, plain and simple.

Justice Stevens, with whom Justice Ginsburg joins, dissenting.

. . . There is no moral or constitutional equivalence between a policy that is designed to perpetuate a caste system and one that seeks to eradicate racial subordination. Invidious discrimination is an engine of oppression, subjugating a disfavored group to enhance or maintain the power of the majority. Remedial race-based preferences reflect the opposite impulse: a desire to foster equality in society. No sensible conception of the Government's

constitutional obligation to "govern impartially" . . . should ignore this distinction. . . .

The consistency that the Court espouses would disregard the difference between a "No Trespassing" sign and a welcome mat. It would treat a Dixiecrat Senator's decision to vote against Thurgood Marshall's confirmation in order to keep African Americans off the Supreme Court as on a par with President Johnson's evaluation of his nominee's race as a positive factor. . . . An attempt by the majority to exclude members of a minority race from a regulated market is fundamentally different from a subsidy that enables a relatively small group of newcomers to enter that market. An interest in "consistency" does not justify treating differences as though they were similarities.

. . . As a matter of constitutional and democratic principle, a decision by representatives of the majority to discriminate against the members of a minority race is fundamentally different from those same representatives' decision to impose incidental costs on the majority of their constituents in order to provide a benefit to a disadvantaged minority. . . .

Justice Souter, with whom Justice Ginsburg and Justice Breyer join, dissenting.

. . . When the extirpation of lingering discriminatory effects is thought to require a catch-up mechanism, like the racially preferential inducement under the statutes considered here, the result may be that some members of the historically favored race are hurt by that remedial mechanism, however innocent they may be of any personal responsibility for any discriminatory conduct. When this price is considered reasonable, it is in part because it is a price to be paid only temporarily; if the justification for the preference is eliminating the effects of a past practice, the assumption is that the effects will themselves recede into the past, becoming attenuated and finally disappearing. . . .

Justice Ginsburg, with whom Justice Breyer joins, dissenting.

. . . The statutes and regulations at issue, as the Court indicates, were adopted by the political branches in response to an "unfortunate reality": "[t]he unhappy persistence of both the practice and the lingering effects of racial discrimination against minority groups in this country. . . . " The United States suffers from those lingering effects because, for most of our Nation's history, the idea that "we are just one race" was not embraced. For generations, our lawmakers and judges were unprepared to say that there is in this land no superior race, no race inferior to any other. In *Plessy v. Ferguson*, 163 U.S. 537 (1896), not only did this Court endorse the oppressive practice of race segregation, but even Justice Harlan, the advocate of a "color-blind" Constitution, stated: "The white race deems itself to be the dominant race in this country. And so it is, in prestige, in achievements, in education, in wealth and in power. So, I doubt not, it will continue to be for all time, if it remains true to its great heritage and holds fast to the principles of constitutional liberty. . . ." Not until *Loving v. Virginia*, 388 U.S. 1 (1967), which held unconstitutional Virginia's ban on interracial marriages, could one say with security that the Constitution and this Court would abide no measure "designed to maintain White Supremacy. . . ."

. . . [The lingering effects of discrimination], reflective of a system of racial caste only recently ended, are evident in our workplaces, markets, and neighborhoods. Job applicants with identical resumes, qualifications, and interview styles still experience different receptions, depending on their race. . . . White and African-American consumers still encounter different deals. . . . People of color looking for housing still face discriminatory treatment by landlords, real estate agents, and mortgage lenders. . . . Minority entrepreneurs sometimes fail to gain contracts though they are the low bidders, and they are sometimes refused work even after winning contracts. . . . [B]ias both conscious and unconscious, reflecting traditional and unexamined habits of thought . . . keeps up barriers that must come down if equal opportunity and nondiscrimination are ever genuinely to become this country's law and practice. . . .

Endnote

[1] See *National Law Journal,* July 17, 1995, A12.

65. *Personnel Administrator of Massachusetts v. Feeney*

The facts of this case raise a number of issues discussed in this chapter: What is discrimination? When does a practice that unequally affects a given group or population, disadvantaging it relative to others, become discriminatory and thus impermissible? To be illegal, must such unequal treatment be motivated by a desire to bring it about? Or is the unequal state of affairs enough by itself? Do you agree with Justice Stewart that an intent to exclude women was not present in this case?

Feeney, a woman who was not a veteran, worked for twelve years as a state employee. She had taken and passed a number of civil service exams for better jobs, but because of Massachusetts's veterans' preference law, she was each time ranked below male veterans who had earned lower test scores than herself. Under the Massachusetts law, all veterans who qualified for state civil service jobs had to be considered for appointment ahead of any qualified nonveteran. The law defined a veteran as "any person, male or female, including a nurse," who was honorably discharged from the armed forces after at least ninety days of active service, at least one day of which was during "wartime." The law operated to the overwhelming advantage of males. Feeney brought suit in federal court, alleging that the state's absolute preference for veterans constituted discrimination and thus violated the equal protection clause of the Fourteenth Amendment. The federal district court agreed with Feeney; Massachusetts then appealed to the Supreme Court.

Stewart, [Justice]. . . .

Notwithstanding the apparent attempts by Massachusetts to include as many military women as possible within the scope of the preference, the statute today benefits an overwhelmingly male class. This is attributable in some measure to the variety of federal statutes, regulations, and policies that have restricted the number of women who could enlist in the United States Armed Forces, and largely to the simple fact that women have never been subject to a military draft.

When this litigation was commenced, then, over 98% of the veterans in Massachusetts were male; only 1.8% were female. And over one-quarter of the Massachusetts population were veterans.

442 U.S. 256 (1979)
United States Supreme Court

During the decade between 1963 and 1973 when the appellee was actively participating in the State's merit selection system, 47,005 new permanent appointments were made in the classified official service. Forty-three percent of those hired were women, and 57% were men. Of the women appointed, 1.8% were veterans, while 54% of the men had veteran status. A large unspecified percentage of the female appointees were serving in lower paying positions for which males traditionally had not applied.

At the outset of this litigation appellants conceded that for "many of the permanent positions for which males and females have competed" the veterans' preference has "resulted in a substantially greater proportion of female eligibles than male eligibles" not being certified for consideration. The impact of the veterans' preference law upon the public employment opportunities of women has thus been severe. This impact lies at the heart of the appellee's federal constitutional claim.

II

The sole question for decision on this appeal is whether Massachusetts, in granting an absolute lifetime preference to veterans, has discriminated against women in violation of the Equal Protection Clause of the Fourteenth Amendment.

A

The equal protection guarantee of the Fourteenth Amendment does not take from the States all power of classification. . . .

Certain classifications, however, in themselves supply a reason to infer antipathy. Race is the paradigm. A racial classification, regardless of purported motivation, is presumptively invalid and can be upheld only upon an extraordinary justification. This rule applies as well to a classification that is ostensibly neutral but is an obvious pretext for racial discrimination. But, as was made clear in *Washington v. Davis,* 426 U.S. 229, and *Arlington Heights v. Metropolitan Housing Dev. Corp.,* 429 U.S. 252, even if a neutral law has a disproportionately adverse effect upon a racial minority, it is unconstitutional under the Equal Protection Clause only if that impact can be traced to a discriminatory purpose.

Classifications based on gender, not unlike those based upon race, have traditionally been the touchstone for pervasive and often subtle discrimination. This Court's recent cases teach that such classifications must bear a close and substantial relationship to important governmental objectives, and are in many settings unconstitutional. . . . [A]ny state law overtly or covertly designed to prefer males over females in public employment would require an exceedingly persuasive justification to withstand a constitutional challenge under the Equal Protection Clause of the Fourteenth Amendment.

The cases of *Washington v. Davis, supra,* and *Arlington Heights v. Metropolitan Housing Dev. Corp., supra,* recognize that when a neutral law has a dis-

parate impact upon a group that has historically been the victim of discrimination, an unconstitutional purpose may still be at work. But those cases signaled no departure from the settled rule that the Fourteenth Amendment guarantees equal laws, not equal results. . . .

When a statute gender-neutral on its face is challenged on the ground that its effects upon women are disproportionably adverse, a twofold inquiry is thus appropriate. The first question is whether the statutory classification is indeed neutral in the sense that it is not gender based. If the classification itself, covert or overt, is not based upon gender, the second question is whether the adverse effect reflects invidious gender-based discrimination. In this second inquiry, impact provides an "important starting point," but purposeful discrimination is "the condition that offends the Constitution." . . .

If the impact of this statute could not be plausibly explained on a neutral ground, impact itself would signal that the real classification made by the law was in fact not neutral. But there can be but one answer to the question whether this veteran preference excludes significant numbers of women from preferred state jobs because they are women or because they are nonveterans. Apart from the fact that the definition of "veterans" in the statute has always been neutral as to gender and that Massachusetts has consistently defined veteran status in a way that has been inclusive of women who have served in the military, this is not a law that can plausibly be explained only as a gender-based classification. Indeed, it is not a law that can rationally be explained on that ground. . . . Too many men are [adversely] affected by ch. 31, §23, to permit the inference that the statute is but a pretext for preferring men over women. . . .

The dispositive question, then, is whether the appellee has shown that a gender-based discriminatory purpose has, at least in some measure, shaped the Massachusetts veterans' preference legislation. . . . [S]he points to two basic factors which in her view distinguish ch. 31, §23, from the neutral rules at issue in the *Washington v. Davis* and *Arlington Heights* cases. The first is the nature of the preference, which is said to be demonstrably gender-biased in the sense that it favors a status reserved under federal military policy primarily to men. The second concerns the impact of the absolute lifetime preference upon the employment opportunities of women, an impact claimed to be too inevitable to have been unintended. The appellee contends that these factors, coupled with the fact that the preference itself has little if any relevance to actual job performance, more than suffice to prove the discriminatory intent required to establish a constitutional violation. . . .

To the extent that the status of veteran is one that few women have been enabled to achieve, every hiring preference for veterans, however modest or extreme, is inherently gender-biased. If Massachusetts by offering such a preference can be said intentionally to have incorporated into its state employment policies the historical gender-based federal military personnel practices, the degree of the preference would or should make no constitutional difference. Invidious discrimination does not become less so because the discrimination accomplished is of a lesser magnitude. Discriminatory intent is simply not amenable to calibration. It either is a factor that has influenced the legislative choice or it is not. The District Court's conclusion that the absolute veterans' preference was not originally enacted or subsequently reaffirmed for the purpose of giving an advantage to males as such necessarily compels the conclusion that the State intended nothing more than to prefer "veterans." Given this finding, simple logic suggests that an intent to exclude women from significant public jobs was not at work in this law. To reason that it was, by describing the preference as "inherently nonneutral" or "gender-biased," is merely to restate the fact of impact, not to answer the question of intent.

To be sure, this case is unusual in that it involves a law that by design is not neutral. The law overtly prefers veterans as such. As opposed to the written test at issue in *Davis,* it does not purport to define a job-related characteristic. To the contrary, it confers upon a specifically described group—perceived to be particularly deserving—a competitive headstart. . . .

The appellee's ultimate argument rests upon the presumption, common to the criminal and civil law, that a person intends the natural and foreseeable consequences of his voluntary actions. . . .

The decision to grant a preference to veterans was of course "intentional." So, necessarily, did an adverse impact upon nonveterans follow from that decision. And it cannot seriously be argued that the Legislature of Massachusetts could have been unaware that most veterans are men. It would thus be disingenuous to say that the adverse consequences of this legislation for women were unintended, in the sense that they were not volitional or in the sense that they were not foreseeable.

"Discriminatory purpose," however, implies more than intent as volition or intent as awareness of consequences. It implies that the decision-maker, in this case a state legislature, selected or reaffirmed a particular course of action at least in part "because of," not merely "in spite of," its adverse effects upon an identifiable group. Yet nothing in the record demonstrates that this preference for veterans was originally devised or subsequently re-enacted because it would accomplish the collateral goal of keeping women in a stereotypic and predefined place in the Massachusetts Civil Service.

To the contrary, the statutory history shows that the benefit of the preference was consistently offered to "any person" who was a veteran. That benefit has been extended to women under a very broad statutory definition of the term veteran. . . . When the totality of legislative actions establishing and extending the Massachusetts veterans' preference are considered, the law remains what it purports to be: a preference for veterans of either sex over nonveterans of either sex, not for men over women.

. . .

Marshall, [Justice], joined by Brennan, [Justice], dissenting.

Although acknowledging that in some circumstances, discriminatory intent may be inferred from the inevitable or foreseeable impact of a statute, the Court concludes that no such intent has been established here. I cannot agree. In my judgment, Massachusetts' choice of an absolute veterans' preference system evinces purposeful gender-based discrimination. And because the statutory scheme bears no substantial relationship to a legitimate governmental objective, it cannot withstand scrutiny under the Equal Protection Clause. . . .

That a legislature seeks to advantage one group does not, as a matter of logic or of common sense, exclude the possibility that it also intends to disadvantage another. Individuals in general and lawmakers in particular frequently act for a variety of reasons. . . . [T]he critical constitutional inquiry is not whether an illicit consideration was the primary or but-for cause of a decision, but rather whether it had an appreciable role in shaping a given legislative enactment. . . .

. . . [S]ince reliable evidence of subjective intentions is seldom obtainable, resort to inference based on objective factors is generally unavoidable. To discern the purposes underlying facially neutral policies, this Court has therefore considered the degree, inevitability, and foreseeability of any disproportionate impact as well as the alternatives reasonably available.

In the instant case, the impact of the Massachusetts statute on women is undisputed. . . . Because less than 2% of the women in Massachusetts are veterans, the absolute preference formula has rendered desirable state civil service employment an almost exclusively male prerogative.

As the District Court recognized, this consequence follows foreseeably, indeed inexorably, from the long history of policies severely limiting women's participation in the military. Although neutral in form, the statute is anything but neutral in application. . . . Where the foreseeable impact of a facially neutral policy is so disproportionate, the burden should rest on the State to establish that sex-based considerations played no part in the choice of the particular legislative scheme.

Clearly, that burden was not sustained here. The legislative history of the statute reflects the Commonwealth's patent appreciation of the impact the preference system would have on women, and an equally evident desire to mitigate that impact only with respect to certain traditionally female occupations. Until 1971, the statute and implementing civil service regulations exempted from operation of the preference any job requisitions "especially calling for women." In practice, this exemption, coupled with the absolute preference for veterans, has created a gender-based civil service hierarchy, with women occupying low-grade clerical secretarial jobs and men holding more responsible and remunerative positions.

Thus, for over 70 years, the Commonwealth has maintained, as an integral part of its veterans' preference system, an exemption relegating female civil service applicants to occupations traditionally filled by women. Such a statutory scheme both reflects and perpetuates precisely the kind of archaic assumptions about women's roles which we have previously held invalid particularly when viewed against the range of less discriminatory alternatives available to assist veterans. Massachusetts' choice of a formula that so severely restricts public employment opportunities for women cannot reasonably be thought gender-neutral. . . .

66. *Romer v. Evans*

In *Romer v. Evans*, the Supreme Court invalidated a law passed by the voters of Colorado. The law, popularly considered an "anti–gay rights" measure, would have made it illegal for any agency of the state to treat gays and lesbians as a "protected class" or "minority," or in any way to extend special protections to or preferences in favor of them. The Court found that the state's purpose could only be to make homosexuals "unequal to everyone else," by declaring gays alone ineligible for protection from discrimination. Consider the Court's argument in light of *Bowers v. Hardwick* (in Chapter One), a point brought out by Justice Scalia's dissent: "If it is rational to criminalize the conduct," Scalia wrote, "surely it is rational to deny special favor and protection to those with a self-avowed tendency or desire to engage in the conduct." Is that a fair criticism?

Justice Kennedy delivered the opinion of the Court.

The enactment challenged in this case is an amendment to the Constitution of the State of Colorado, adopted in a 1992 statewide referendum. The parties and the state courts refer to it as "Amendment 2," its designation when submitted to the voters. The impetus for the amendment and the contentious campaign that preceded its adoption came in large part from ordinances that had been passed in various Colorado municipalities. For example, the cities of Aspen and Boulder and the City and County of Denver each had enacted ordinances which banned discrimination in many transactions and activities, including housing, employment, education, public accommodations, and health and welfare services. What gave rise to the statewide controversy was the protection the ordinances afforded to persons discriminated against by reason of their sexual orientation. Amendment 2 repeals these ordinances to the extent they prohibit discrimination on the basis of "homosexual, lesbian or bisexual orientation, conduct, practices or relationships." Yet Amendment 2, in explicit terms, does more than repeal or rescind these provisions. It prohibits all legislative, executive or judicial ac-

513 U.S. 1146, 116 S.Ct. 1620, 134 L.Ed.2d 855 (1996)

tion at any level of state or local government designed to protect the named class, a class we shall refer to as homosexual persons or gays and lesbians. The amendment reads:

"No Protected Status Based on Homosexual, Lesbian, or Bisexual Orientation. Neither the State of Colorado, through any of its branches or departments, nor any of its agencies, political subdivisions, municipalities or school districts, shall enact, adopt or enforce any statute, regulation, ordinance or policy whereby homosexual, lesbian or bisexual orientation, conduct, practices or relationships shall constitute or otherwise be the basis of or entitle any person or class of persons to have or claim any minority status, quota preferences, protected status or claim of discrimination. This Section of the Constitution shall be in all respects self-executing." . . .

The State's principal argument in defense of Amendment 2 is that it puts gays and lesbians in the same position as all other persons. So, the State says, the measure does no more than deny homosexuals special rights. This reading of the amendment's language is implausible. . . .

Sweeping and comprehensive is the change in legal status effected by this law. So much is evident from the ordinances that the Colorado Supreme Court declared would be void by operation of

Amendment 2. Homosexuals, by state decree, are put in a solitary class with respect to transactions and relations in both the private and governmental spheres. The amendment withdraws from homosexuals, but no others, specific legal protection from the injuries caused by discrimination, and it forbids reinstatement of these laws and policies.

The change that Amendment 2 works in the legal status of gays and lesbians in the private sphere is far-reaching, both on its own terms and when considered in light of the structure and operation of modern anti-discrimination laws. . . .

. . . Amendment 2 bars homosexuals from securing protection against the injuries that these public-accommodations laws address. That in itself is a severe consequence, but there is more. Amendment 2 [nullifies] specific legal protections for this targeted class in all transactions in housing, sale of real estate, insurance, health and welfare services, private education, and employment.

Not confined to the private sphere, Amendment 2 also operates to repeal and forbid all laws or policies providing specific protection for gays or lesbians from discrimination by every level of Colorado government. The State Supreme Court cited two examples of protections in the governmental sphere that are now rescinded and may not be reintroduced. The first is [the] Colorado Executive Order [which] forbids employment discrimination against "'all state employees, classified and exempt' on the basis of sexual orientation." Also repealed, and now forbidden, are "various provisions prohibiting discrimination based on sexual orientation at state colleges." The repeal of these measures and the prohibition against their future reenactment demonstrates that Amendment 2 has the same force and effect in Colorado's governmental sector as it does elsewhere and that it applies to policies as well as ordinary legislation.

Amendment 2's reach may not be limited to specific laws passed for the benefit of gays and lesbians. It is a fair, if not necessary, inference from the broad language of the amendment that it deprives gays and lesbians even of the protection of general laws and policies that prohibit arbitrary discrimination in governmental and private settings. . . .

. . . [E]ven if, as we doubt, homosexuals could find some safe harbor in laws of general applica-

tion, we cannot accept the view that Amendment 2's prohibition on specific legal protections does no more than deprive homosexuals of special rights. To the contrary, the amendment imposes a special disability upon those persons alone. Homosexuals are forbidden the safeguards that others enjoy or may seek without constraint. They can obtain specific protection against discrimination only by enlisting the citizenry of Colorado to amend the state constitution or perhaps, on the State's view, by trying to pass helpful laws of general applicability. This is so no matter how local or discrete the harm, no matter how public and widespread the injury. We find nothing special in the protections Amendment 2 withholds. These are protections taken for granted by most people either because they already have them or do not need them; these are protections against exclusion from an almost limitless number of transactions and endeavors that constitute ordinary civic life in a free society.

The Fourteenth Amendment's promise that no person shall be denied the equal protection of the laws must co-exist with the practical necessity that most legislation classifies for one purpose or another, with resulting disadvantage to various groups or persons. We have attempted to reconcile the principle with the reality by stating that, if a law neither burdens a fundamental right nor targets a suspect class, we will uphold the legislative classification so long as it bears a rational relation to some legitimate end.

Amendment 2 fails, indeed defies, even this conventional inquiry. First, the amendment has the peculiar property of imposing a broad and undifferentiated disability on a single named group, an exceptional and, as we shall explain, invalid form of legislation. Second, its sheer breadth is so discontinuous with the reasons offered for it that the amendment seems inexplicable by anything but animus toward the class that it affects; it lacks a rational relationship to legitimate state interests.

Taking the first point, even in the ordinary equal protection case calling for the most deferential of standards, we insist on knowing the relation between the classification adopted and the object to be attained. [In] the ordinary case, a law will be sustained if it can be said to advance a legitimate government interest, even if the law seems unwise or works to the disadvantage of a particular group, or if the rationale for it seems tenuous. [By] requiring that the classification bear a rational relationship to an independent and legitimate legislative end, we ensure that classifications are not drawn for the purpose of disadvantaging the group burdened by the law.

Amendment 2 confounds this normal process of judicial review. It is at once too narrow and too broad. It identifies persons by a single trait and then denies them protection across the board. The resulting disqualification of a class of persons from the right to seek specific protection from the law is unprecedented in our jurisprudence. It is not within our constitutional tradition to enact laws of this sort. Central both to the idea of the rule of law and to our own Constitution's guarantee of equal protection is the principle that government and each of its parts remain open on impartial terms to all who seek its assistance. [Respect] for this principle explains why laws singling out a certain class of citizens for disfavored legal status or general hardships are rare. A law declaring that in general it shall be more difficult for one group of citizens than for all others to seek aid from the government is itself a denial of equal protection of the laws in the most literal sense.

A [related] point is that laws of the kind now before us raise the inevitable inference that the disadvantage imposed is born of animosity toward the class of persons affected. [Even] laws enacted for broad and ambitious purposes often can be explained by reference to legitimate public policies which justify the incidental disadvantages they impose on certain persons. Amendment 2, however, in making a general announcement that gays and lesbians shall not have any particular protection

from the law, inflicts on them immediate, continuing, and real injuries that outrun and belie any legitimate justifications that may be claimed for it. We conclude that, in addition to the far-reaching deficiencies of Amendment 2 that we have noted, the principles it offends, in another sense, are conventional and venerable; a law must bear a rational relationship to a legitimate governmental purpose, and Amendment 2 does not.

The primary rationale the State offers for Amendment 2 is respect for other citizens' freedom of association, and in particular the liberties of landlords or employers who have personal or religious objections to homosexuality. Colorado also cites its interest in conserving resources to fight discrimination against other groups. The breadth of the Amendment is so far removed from these particular justifications that we find it impossible to credit them. We cannot say that Amendment 2 is directed to any identifiable legitimate purpose or discrete objective. It is a status-based enactment divorced from any factual context from which we could discern a relationship to legitimate state interests; it is a classification of persons undertaken for its own sake, something the Equal Protection Clause does not permit. [We] must conclude that Amendment 2 classifies homosexuals not to further a proper legislative end but to make them unequal to everyone else. This Colorado cannot do. A State cannot so deem a class of persons a stranger to its laws. Amendment 2 violates the Equal Protection Clause, and the judgment of the Supreme Court of Colorado is affirmed.

. . .

Chapter IV

Criminal Law

Many of us are better acquainted with the basic language and aims of the criminal law than with any other part of our jurisprudence. Unfortunately, most of that familiarity fails to extend much beyond the latest TV show or movie mystery. Sensational criminal trials, such as those of O.J. Simpson and Theodore Kaczynski, the confessed Unabomber, also distort the public's perception of the criminal process. All of this is regrettable, for the criminal law raises some of the most troubling and yet fascinating philosophical difficulties anywhere in the law—problems sharpened in their urgency by the obvious extent to which the criminal law can affect the course of a human life, or, in the extreme case, end it.

In 1995, a New York jury awarded Darrell Cabey $43 million in his suit against Bernhard Goetz. Goetz had shot and paralyzed Cabey in a notorious clash in a New York subway. A few days before Christmas 1984, the slightly built Goetz entered a subway car in New York City. Four youths, apparently looking for trouble, asked him for money. Goetz responded with a .38-caliber revolver, wounding each of the four and paralyzing one of them. The media quickly branded Goetz the "subway vigilante," and his eventual trial on multiple

counts of assault and attempted murder raised difficult issues: Did Goetz intend to kill the youths? Could he be convicted of "attempted" murder? Did he act in self-defense? Did he endanger others unjustifiably? Should he be punished? These questions prompt larger ones: Under what conditions should a person be held responsible for his or her acts? Under what conditions may one be excused? Suppose I simply made a mistake? Or was merely careless? Or was mentally unstable? Is it fair to punish me for a harm I caused but did not intend? If I try but fail to commit a crime, should I be punished as severely as if I had succeeded? What is the aim of punishment in the first place? Must the punishment always "fit" the crime? Is that always possible? If, for example, my crime consists in subjecting you to a chance of injury, would it be fair to subject me in similar fashion to a risk of harm? Are there punishments that ought never to be inflicted?

Section A begins our exploration of these issues through a study of liability for criminal "attempts." George Fletcher identifies two different approaches to the question of attempts and relates them to the specific issues raised in the Goetz case. Two further cases, one real and one by legal scholar Leo Katz, explore how attempts to commit a crime should be punished.

Section B examines the role of the "mental element" in crime and how it relates to the concepts of excuse and justification. The burgeoning variety of excuses advanced by criminal defendants is reviewed, and two specific excuses are discussed in detail. The court's opinion in the case of Janice Leidholm and the essay by Cathryn Jo Rosen each weigh the arguments for and against the battered-woman's defense; the remaining selections examine the role of mental illness and the insanity defense, with Norval Morris arguing for its abolition and Sanford Kadish for its retention.

Section C turns to larger issues about punishment and sentencing. James Q. Wilson outlines the case for a utilitarian approach to the justification of punishment; Michael Moore seeks to defend the retributive theory. The focus then shifts to the perspective of the vic-

tims of crime. *Payne v. Tennessee* looks at the role of victim-impact statements in criminal sentencing, and Randy Barnett proposes an alternative to traditional theories of punishment by imagining a criminal justice system built around the notion of restitution.

Section D examines the complex issues of the death penalty. Two Supreme Court cases address the constitutional issues posed by capital punishment: whether it is "cruel and unusual," and whether it is imposed in a discriminatory way. The moral and policy dimensions of these issues are debated by Ernest van den Haag, Hugo Bedau, and Randall Kennedy.

The "Cases for Further Reflection" deal with issues ranging from the meaning of "cruel and unusual punishment" to the death penalty, habitual offender statutes, and even a case involving the criminal punishment of a dog.

A. *What Is a Crime?*

The Elements of Criminality

Bernhard Goetz was accused of having committed at least four separate and distinct crimes, all arising out of his use of a gun on the subway that morning: possessing a loaded gun in public, recklessly endangering the lives of others, criminal assault, and attempted murder. How can one action produce

such a wealth of "crimes"? The answer is that each offense was based upon one or another aspect of Goetz's conduct together with his state of mind at the time of the incident, as these were defined by the relevant laws. Notorious as Goetz's case was, it nonetheless illustrates both procedural and substantive aspects of the criminal law. Because these concepts figure prominently in the material for this section, it will be useful to pause a moment over them.

You will recall from Chapter One that *procedural* law is concerned with the rules governing how civil and criminal cases are begun, conducted, and resolved. In a criminal case, the procedural aspects begin with the apprehension of a person (or persons) suspected of wrongdoing. Although criminal procedure is complex and the precise steps followed may differ greatly from one case to the next, all criminal cases resulting in a conviction must pass through some basic steps, illustrated in the following chart:[1]

Procedural Elements of Conviction and Punishment

1. Defendant 's (D's) allegedly wrongful conduct is detected or is confessed.
2. D is apprehended by, or otherwise comes into the custody of authorities.
3. D is indicted and arraigned, with charges formally presented and a plea entered.
4. D pleads guilty and is sentenced, *or* D's plea results in a trial.
5. D is tried and convicted.
6. D is sentenced by the judge .
7. D's sentence is carried out.

Goetz initially fled, later to turn himself in to authorities and offer a confession. He was indicted (as we have seen) for committing multiple crimes and entered a plea of "not guilty." The subsequent trial resulted in a conviction on one count (illegal possession of a firearm). He was then sentenced and served 250 days in jail. Years later, Darrell Cabey, the young man whom Goetz paralyzed with his final shot, sued Goetz in civil court for damages. This is not an unknown state of affairs, because a criminal conviction (or acquittal) does not bar a private lawsuit concerning injuries sustained by victims of crime.

Although procedural law raises important issues, this section focuses largely on problems raised by the *substantive* law. What are the elements of *substantive* law in a case such as Goetz's? What is involved in showing that a defendant is guilty of

---

[1] I would like to thank Prof. Jim Nickel for the charts used here.

having committed a crime? The following is a list of some of the basic elements:

Substantive Elements of a Crime

1. A valid, publicly known, and nonretroactive law prohibits a given act (A).
2. Defendant (D) committed A.
3. D committed A with the state of mind defined by the law prohibiting A.
4. D has neither a justification nor an excuse for committing A (i.e., D is responsible for committing A).

Several aspects of this list of conditions are important. The first element or condition seems to state the obvious, but some significant principles are in play here. One is the *Principle of Legality,* which requires that people subject to the law be given clear and adequate notice of what the law expects of them so that they can have a fair opportunity to conform their conduct to its requirements. As interpreted by the courts, the demand of legality is a component of *due process* and requires that statutes and other enactments be sufficiently definite to provide both a standard of conduct for the average citizen to follow, and a clear standard for police enforcement. Statutes have been found to violate this principle. In *Lanzetta v. New Jersey* (306 U.S. 451 [1939]), for example, the defendants were arrested pursuant to a statute that read: "any person not engaged in any lawful occupation, known to be a member of a gang consisting of two or more persons, who has been convicted of any crime in . . . any state" has violated the law. The Supreme Court held that this statute was "repugnant" to the *Due Process* clause of the Constitution because of its vagueness: It simply isn't clear what one is not supposed to do here. Not be unemployed? Not associate with two other people? *Lanzetta* also illustrates another important aspect of conditions (1) and (2), above: namely, that the law prohibits what people *do* (e.g., shooting a police officer; reckless driving), not *who they are* (e.g., an unemployed "gangster"). The reference in (1), above, to retroactivity also has a constitutional dimension: the Constitution explicitly forbids laws that are *"ex post facto,"* that is, laws making illegal actions that took place before the law was enacted. Clearly such laws cannot pass the test of legality, because no one can conform his or her conduct to a law that has yet to exist.

Conditions (2) and (3), above, together express the core of the substantive notion of a crime: the central feature of the criminal law is its attempt to rest liability upon the conjunction of these two elements, outward behavior and inner state of mind.

Act and Intent

These two basic elements of criminality are marked by their Latin names: *actus reus* and *mens rea*. *Actus reus* refers to an act of wrongdoing: running a red light, shooting someone, taking a television set without the owner's permission (and not returning it). The criminal law is concerned with conduct, with things people *do*. You might wonder why this is so. Must something be *done* before the criminal law can respond? Why not (for example) focus on thoughts or emotions? Why not subject to punishment those who possess, though they have not yet manifested, "poor character"? Why can't a person be punished for having "evil thoughts"? (Consider in this connection that several centuries ago, it was a criminal offense in England to "imagine the King's death.") It is of course difficult to prove what thoughts or feelings people have (unless they are willing to tell you), and perhaps thoughts, by themselves, are less dangerous than actual conduct. Certainly they are difficult to control, whereas acts are, at least usually, something over which we have some power.

Even if we agree that the criminal law should confine its attention to acts, this still leaves the problem of understanding what an "act" is. Acts can be difficult to define. How many "acts" did Bernhard Goetz commit? Is imagining the King's death an "act"? The Model Penal Code (MPC), a proposed uniform criminal statute written by a number of lawyers and legal scholars, defines an "act" as a "muscular movement under conscious control." Is "possessing a loaded gun" an "act" under this definition?

The expression *mens rea* literally means "guilty mind" or "evil mind," and is generally taken to refer to the *mental* element of a crime. The basic idea is that one must have had a culpable or blameworthy state of mind before one can be said to have committed a crime. This requirement is frequently explained in terms of the idea that a criminal acts

with the *intent to commit the offense*. It doesn't take much reflection to see that this requirement raises a whole range of fresh difficulties and problems: How can it be determined what X intended or thought or believed or wanted? Aren't there different states of mind that a person can have when he or she performs an action that constitutes an *actus reus*? Should all states of mind be regarded as equally culpable? If not, how can we distinguish between the relevant states of mind and grade them appropriately? What states of mind excuse people from liability altogether?

Plainly there are some conditions under which a person cannot be held accountable for an act of wrongdoing. This ties *mens rea* to the last of the conditions, (4), noted above. An *excuse* is a factor that, if proven, establishes that the actor did not have the required state of mind and is therefore not properly subject to the sanctions of the criminal law. Typical excuses include infancy (being a minor), duress (being forced or pressured by another), mistake (being unaware of crucial facts or circumstances), and insanity (suffering from some kind of mental disability or defect). To say that a defendant has a *justification* for his conduct makes even a stronger claim: namely, that the defendant made the correct choice, all things considered.

Strict Criminal Liability

For all rules there are exceptions, and this holds true for the conditions defining a substantive criminal offense. One important exception worth noting applies to condition (3), the requirement that the defendant acted with a certain state of mind with regard to the offense charged. Common as this principle is, there are important and controversial exceptions to it, such as the doctrine of *felony-murder*.

Generally speaking, to be convictable of murder, one must either have acted with the intent to kill or have exhibited extreme recklessness with regard to human life (for example, by emptying a revolver into a crowded room). To be convicted of first-degree murder it is usually necessary to have acted in a premeditated fashion or to have committed the crime under circumstances presumed to be premeditated, for example, by administering poison. The felony-murder doctrine is an exception to these requirements. This doctrine says that if, in the course of the commission of a felony a killing occurs, all accomplices in the felony can be charged with murder. X, Y, and Z decide to rob a bank. Z waits in the getaway car while X and Y commit the holdup. A security guard makes a menacing gesture, and Y shoots him. Z is guilty of felony-murder even if he was nowhere near the scene and did not pull the trigger.

The felony-murder concept has numerous permutations and complexities. Suppose that, after X and Y leave the bank, one of the tellers dies of a fright-induced heart attack. California has held that Z is guilty of felony-murder.[1] What if X turns on Y in the bank and shoots him? Some states, again including California, have held that Z can be convicted for this murder as well.[2] Finally, what if neither the person killed nor the person doing the killing is one of the felons? Should felony-murder still apply?

Other crimes are similar to felony-murder in a critical respect: Statutory rape (unlawful intercourse with a female minor), bigamy (being married to more than one person at a time), and various "public welfare" offenses (for example, mishandling or mislabeling drug products), along with the felony-murder rule, have traditionally been among the offenses imposing *strict criminal liability,* the defining feature of which is the refusal to require proof of the actor's state of mind as a prerequisite to liability.

The principal justifications offered for the creation of strict liability offenses have been utilitarian in nature, appealing to the supposed good consequences of imposing such liability. Those who favor strict criminal liability on these grounds argue that it will deter crime by inducing those contemplating felonious conduct to think again, and that it will protect the public by provoking those who engage in dangerous but socially beneficial activities (such as drug manufacture) to be especially cautious. Others argue that strict liability is more efficient than the traditional emphasis upon the requirement of *mens rea* since it is burdensome

to inquire into a defendant's state of mind. It has also been argued that that a person who begins a series of events that terminates in the death of another incurs a kind of moral stain or taint that must then be expiated through punishment appropriate to the crime of murder. Alternatively, it might be urged that those who commit felonies run the risk that things might turn out worse than they expected.

Opponents of strict liability offenses object that it is wrong and unfair to thus use the defendant as an expedient to promote the greater good. People should be punished, the critics insist, only when they manifest a culpable state of mind for the offense with which they have been charged.

The Model Penal Code

To have before us a useful framework for the analysis of problems having to do with states of mind, consider the manner in which the drafters of the Model Penal Code sought to handle the mental element. The code proposes that every criminal offense be specified in terms of a breakdown of its constituent elements. Take burglary as an example. Most jurisdictions define burglary in this way: Knowingly breaking and entering the dwelling house of another with the intent to commit a felony therein. This crime has several elements: (1) breaking and entering; (2) dwelling house; (3) of another; (4) intent to commit a felony. The code proposes that, to be convictable of this offense, I must have the requisite state of mind with respect to each element of the offense. In this case, that means that I must, with intent or conscious purpose, have broken in and entered property; have done so in the awareness that it was a dwelling house, and the dwelling house of another; and have intended to commit a felony when I got inside. Failure to possess the relevant state of mind in conjunction with any of the elements would mean that I could not be convicted of the offense. Suppose I leave my house late at night, intending to burglarize some homes down the street. It is unusually dark and foggy; I break into my own house. Have I committed burglary? No. Although I acted with the purpose or conscious intent to enter, I did not do so with respect to the dwelling house of *another.* (I may be

---

[1] *People v. Stampe* 2 Cal. App. 3d 203 (1969).
[2] *People v. Cabaltero* 31 Cal. App. 2d 52 (1939).

convictable of *attempting* burglary, of course, but that is a separate matter.) Frustrated, I try again the next night. Hours of effort and no success wear me out and I decide to return home. It is dark and even foggier than the night before. I walk through the unlocked door of what I think is my house. But it is not my house. Have I committed burglary? No. I entered the dwelling of another, but I did not act with the "purpose to enter the house of another"; I acted with the purpose to go home, even though that's not where I wound up.

Conflicting Conceptions of Criminal Wrongdoing

In the issues posed by the Goetz case, law professor George Fletcher sees a clash between two general approaches to understanding the aims and purposes of the criminal law. The debate formed by that conflict turns on a basic question: Why should consequences matter in defining a criminal offense? Recall the substantive elements of a crime listed above. Conditions (1) and (2) refer to an act prohibited by law. As we saw in the discussion of the enforcement of morality in Chapter Two, there is a lively debate about what specific kinds of acts should be so proscribed. Should they, for example, always be acts that cause harm? And if so, what about acts that pose a *risk* of harm, even if they do not actually bring it about? Fletcher contrasts two approaches to theorizing about substantive criminal law that reflect conflicting answers to these questions.

The traditional approach focuses upon the *suffering* of the crime victim, the actual harm done. This concern was reflected in the charges brought against Goetz for assault. The traditional view is less inclined to consider, for example, the imposition of a risk of harm—reflected in the reckless endangerment charge—as deserving of criminal punishment. But if an injury occurs, even if it was not specifically intended by the perpetrator, the suffering of the victim demands a response. In this way, the traditional view construes the mental element or "intent" requirement broadly: If the "natural and probable" consequence of shooting at a man at close range is that you might sever his spinal cord, and if that happens, you "intended" it, even if there was no con-

scious aim to bring about that consequence. The traditional approach, Fletcher points out, is also closely linked with a *retributive* conception or understanding of the aim of punishment: The suffering of the victim demands that the perpetrator "pay" for his wicked deed. (Retributivism is discussed in detail in Section C, below.)

In contrast to the traditional view, the newer or modern approach, as Fletcher refers to it, is reflected in the charges brought against Goetz for attempted murder and reckless endangerment. Here the concern is not with the harm done to the victim but with the assailant's act itself, with the act that caused the harm, and with the degree of control the assailant had over that act. If I shoot at you, intending to kill you, but I miss, why should the absence of a victim mitigate the seriousness of what I have done? Am I not just as guilty of endangering your life, putting you at risk? The modern view thus settles on a rationale for punishing the *attempt* to commit a crime and for punishing such attempts with severity equal to that for successfully completed crimes.

Which approach to defining and responding to criminality is best? Which is morally right? Fletcher is worried about the headlong flight of the law in the direction set by the modern approach, and his concerns can be most easily understood in terms of the category of attempted crimes. It is to these that the other readings in this section turn.

Liability and Punishment for Attempts

How should people who *attempt* to break the law, but who don't succeed, be dealt with by the law? Focusing on the law of attempts usefully brings many of the questions we have been examining into focus.

The common law position for some time has been that those who (unsuccessfully) attempt to commit a crime should be punished less severely than those who succeed in the commission of the crime. That this has been the general practice of our law is indisputable, but the reasons for it are less clear. Imagine that two people shoot at me. One hits me; the other misses by inches. Both tried equally hard and acted with equal malice (evil intent). Insofar as we want to punish the wicked or deter the dangerous, both of my attackers would seem to merit equal punishment. Does it make sense to punish less harshly the person who missed the target than the one who got the "bull's eye"? Doesn't this seem to make guilt or innocence a function of luck? Is the one who missed more likely to try again? Does the fact that both tried and only one succeeded show that the successful attempter tried harder—was "wholehearted" in his efforts—so he deserves more punishment or manifests greater danger?

Dlugash and the "Impossible" Attempt

The facts of *People v. Dlugash* raise a further question: Should attempts to commit crimes be punished at all if what the actor sought to do was impossible under the circumstances? During an argument in the early morning hours, Joe Bush shoots Mike Geller three times in the chest. Roughly five minutes later, Bush's companion, Dlugash, walks over the prone Geller and empties five shots into and about his head and vital organs. Dlugash later testifies that he acted because he was "afraid of Joe Bush." Dlugash is convicted of murder; but an appellate court reverses the conviction on the grounds that the state did not prove beyond a reasonable doubt that Geller was alive at the time Dlugash pulled the trigger. However Dlugash is also convicted of the "lesser included offense" of attempted murder. Dlugash now presents the appellate court with an unusual question: Can you attempt to murder a man who is already dead?

The common law of England—many of the central principles and distinctions of which were adopted by the early states in this country—made it a criminal offense to attempt to commit a crime: the unsuccessful effort to bring about the intended harm. Like most crimes, attempt has both *actus reus* and *mens rea* components. The *mens rea* requirement for attempts is fairly straightforward: One must have acted with the purpose of committing the object crime. (There are some difficult cases here, though. If I throw a bomb at a car, hoping and desiring to kill the driver but killing the passenger instead, did I intend the passenger's death?) The

actus reus requirement for attempts is more complex, the principal difficulty being how to draw a line successfully between merely *preparing* to commit a crime (for example, buying burglar's tools) and *beginning the attempt* (heading off to the bank with the tools in my backpack). How much do I have to do, how far do I have to go, in order to have "made the attempt"?

Certainly the thorniest problem in the law of attempts, however, has been that posed by the following question: If what you are trying to do would constitute a crime if completed, should you be convicted of attempt if the crime was impossible to commit? Should it matter why the crime could not be committed? One obvious sort of reason for the "impossibility" involved here is that the facts might not be as you take them to be. X shoots at a shape lying under the blankets on a bed, intending to kill the person he believes to be asleep on it, but the lump under the sheets is merely a pile of pillows. Y is a pickpocket looking for easy prey; he reaches into your pocket, intending to steal your wallet, but the pocket is empty. Has X attempted murder or simply engaged in target practice with the bedclothes? Should Y be convicted of attempted robbery or merely admonished to keep his hands to himself?

What if the facts that make it impossible to complete your attempt relate to the legal definition or classification of a thing? Z tries to buy what he thinks are stolen goods from a "fence"; yet the goods are not stolen but really Z's own. Must Z be acquitted on the grounds that no amount of effort exerted in "buying" one's own things will make that conduct into the crime of receiving stolen property? Or should Z be judged guilty, since only an unforeseeable contingency (no thanks to him) kept his act from being a crime? If we let every such contingency exonerate the attempter, does that mean that the only attempts punishable will be (paradoxically) the successful ones? Traditionally, the law called the impossibility faced by X and Y "factual" and that facing Z "legal." The grounds for this distinction are not clear; they are explored by the court in *Dlugash*.

In *Dlugash*, the court notes that the law of attempt in New York has been modified to reflect the position adopted by the Model Penal Code. MPC section 5.01 effectively does away with the legal–factual impossibility distinction. It focuses on what the defendant intended or believed, not what actually happened. How does this approach apply to Dlugash? If he believed the victim to be alive at the moment of the shooting, he is guilty of attempted murder, even if Geller was in fact dead at the time. And, the Court holds, there is evidence here to support the claim that Dlugash *did* believe Geller to be alive. (It is also worth noting that the MPC, unlike the code in many states, would punish Dlugash's attempt with the same degree of severity as the crime that was his object.)

The Crime That Never Was

In the final reading of this section, law professor Leo Katz treats us to a hypothetical case of a forged work of art and a crime that, at least in some sense, could not have occurred. Katz uses that case to explore various proposed solutions to the problem of the "impossible" attempt and some of the larger factors at work in shaping the substantive criminal law.

67. The Significance of Suffering

GEORGE P. FLETCHER

[In New York City on] December 22, 1984, the Saturday before Christmas, about 1:00 P.M., Bernhard Goetz leaves his apartment at 55 West 14th Street and walks to the subway station at the corner of Seventh Avenue and 14th Street. He enters a car on the number 2 line, the IRT express running downtown, and sits down close to four black youths. The youths, seeming drifters on the landscape of the city, are noisy and boisterous, and the 15 to 20 other passengers have moved to the other end of the car. Goetz is white, 37 years old, slightly built, and dressed in dungarees and a windbreaker. Something about his appearance beckons. One of the four, Troy Canty, lying nearly prone on the long bench next to the door, asks Goetz as he enters, "How are ya?" Canty and possibly a second youth, Barry Allen, then approach Goetz, and Canty asks him for five dollars. Goetz asks him what he wants. Canty repeats: "Give me five dollars." Suddenly,

the moving car resounds with gunshots, one aimed at each of the young blacks.

At this point the story becomes uncertain. According to Goetz's subsequent confession, he pauses, goes over to a youth sitting in the two-seater by the conductor's cab at the end of the car, looks at him, and says, "You seem to be [doing] all right; here's another," and fires a fifth shot that empties his five-shot Smith & Wesson .38 revolver. The bullet enters Darrell Cabey's body on his left side, traverses the back, and severs his spinal cord. There are other interpretations of these events, particularly an argument that Goetz hit Cabey on the fourth rather than the fifth shot, but in the early days after the shooting these alternative accounts are not widely disseminated.

Someone pulls the emergency brake and the train screeches to a halt. The passengers flee the car, but two women remain, immobilized by fear. Goetz says some soothing words to the fearful women, and then a conductor approaches and asks him whether he is a cop. The gunman replies, "They tried to rip me off." He refuses to hand over his gun and quietly walks to the front of the car, enters the platform be-

---

Reprinted by permission of Simon & Schuster, Inc.

tween cars, patiently unfastens the safety chain, jumps to the tracks below, and disappears into the dark of the subway tunnel. Three young black kids lie bleeding on the floor of the train; Darrell Cabey sits wounded and paralyzed in the end seat.

A mythical figure is born—an unlikely avenger for the fear that both unites and levels all urban dwellers in the United States. If the four kids had mugged a passenger, newspaper reporters would have sighed in boredom. There are, on the average, 38 crimes a day on the New York subways. If a police officer had intervened and shot four kids who were hassling a rider for money, protests of racism and police brutality would have been the call of the day. This was different. A common man had emerged from the shadows of fear. He shot back when others only fantasize their responses to shakedowns on the New York subways.

Like the Lone Ranger, the mysterious gunman subdues the criminals and disappears into the night. If he had been apprehended immediately, the scars and flaws of his own personality might have checked the public's tendency to romanticize him. The analogy to Charles Bronson's avenging crime in *Death Wish* is on everyone's lips. The *Times* remains cautious, but the *Post*, from the beginning, dubs the unknown gunman the "subway vigilante." The police participate in this posturing of the case by setting up an "avenger hotline." They expect to receive tips leading to an arrest and eventually they get one, but at first they are swamped with calls supporting the "avenger." Though Mayor Ed Koch condemns the violence, he too inflates the incident by describing it as the act of a vigilante. No common criminal, this one. An everyman had come out of the crowd and etched his actions, right or wrong, in the public imagination.

With no offender to bear down on, the press has only the four black kids to portray in the news; the picture they present is not attractive. Uneducated, with criminal records, on the prowl for a few dollars, they exemplify the underclass of teenage criminals feared by both blacks and whites. In October of the same year, Darrell Cabey, age 19, had been arrested in the Bronx on charges of armed robbery. In 1983, James Ramseur, age 18, and Troy Canty, age 19, had both served short sentences for petty thievery. Barry Allen, age 18, had twice pled guilty to charges of disorderly conduct. James

Ramseur and Darrell Cabey are found with a total of three screwdrivers in their pockets—the tools of their petty thievery. The few witnesses who come forward describe the behavior of the four youths before Goetz entered the car as "boisterous."

The emerging information supports the picture that frustrated New Yorkers want to believe in. Four stereotypical muggers who harass and hound a frail-looking middle-class "whitey." That he should turn out, against all odds, to be armed confirms the extraordinary nature of true, spontaneous justice. It is not often that things turn out right, and here in the season of religious miracles comes an event in which good triumphs over evil.

A willingness to accept a rumor of "sharpened screwdrivers" testifies to the widespread bias in favor of the romanticized gunman. The *Times* reported the day after the shooting that two of the victims were found with screwdrivers in their jackets. There was no suggestion that they were "sharpened." Somehow, however, the story got abroad that the screwdrivers were sharpened weapons rather than merely tools for opening sealed metal boxes. On the "Donahue" show, a week after the event, the discussion was of "sharpened" screwdrivers. In an article in the *Times* surveying the first week's events, the writer reports the supposed fact: "three of the youths were found to be carrying sharpened screwdrivers." Some journalists resist the popular rumor that the screwdrivers were specially prepared weapons of assault. On the whole, however, the press and the public want to believe the worst about the subway victims.

Goetz makes an effort to go underground. On the day of the shooting he rents a car and drives north to Vermont and New Hampshire. As he later describes it, "heading north, is the way to go if there's a problem." The countryside in New England may remind him reassuringly of his early years in rural upstate New York. He thinks "the system would interpret it as one more crime. I just figured I'd get away for two days, I wanted to come back." When he does come back to New York a few days later, he learns that the police, acting on a tip that Goetz meets the description of the slight blond gunman, left notes for him in his mailbox and on his door. They want to talk to him, but they are far from having singled him out as a serious suspect. Nonetheless, he fears apprehension and returns to

Vermont and New Hampshire. He agonizes for almost two days and then walks into the police station in Concord, New Hampshire, shortly after noon on December 31.

He delivers several lengthy confessions. One two-hour interview with the New Hampshire police is recorded on audiotape; another of equal length, with New York authorities, is videotaped. Neither of these is fully disclosed to the public until after the trial begins. Goetz is turned over to the New York authorities on January 3, 1985, and spends a few days at Rikers Island prison. When he is released January 7 on $50,000 bail, his popular support is at its peak.

From the very beginning, the Goetz proceedings are caught in a political dialectic between the rush of popular support for the "subway vigilante" and the official attitude of outrage that anyone would dare usurp the state's task of keeping law and order. While the public calls into the newly established police hotline to express support for the wanted man, public officials, ranging from President Reagan to black leaders to Mayor Koch, come out strongly against "vigilantism" on the streets. The general public might applaud a little man's striking back against uncontrolled violence, but the President speaks of the "breakdown of civilization" when people like Bernhard Goetz "take the law into their own hands." Hazel Dukes of the NAACP calls Goetz a 21st-century version of a Ku Klux Klan "nightrider."

These pitted, hostile forces eventually find their way into well-prepared channels of legal argument and customary patterns of legal maneuvering. The legal system converts our ill-understood rage into a stylized mode of debate about broader issues of criminal responsibility and fair procedure. The "breakdown of civilization" never comes to pass, precisely because the issue of defending oneself against a threat in the subway can be formulated as a question beyond passion and instinctual conflict.

. . .

The second grand jury concluded that the prosecution had a sound basis for bringing Goetz to trial and convincing the jury beyond a reasonable doubt that Goetz's responses in the subway were unreasonable under the circumstances. Thus they indicted Goetz for a variety of crimes, 10 dis-

tinct offenses in all, based not only on the possession of the gun but on shooting the four youths without justification. If there was no self-defense, Goetz committed a crime by pulling his gun and firing five shots, injuring each of the youths once. But precisely what was the crime? There is no crime called "shooting in a subway" nor even a crime of shooting a gun. The criminal law seeks to specify particular aspects of violent and aggressive behavior that make the conduct wrongful and worthy of punishment.

In a single act of shooting at Troy Canty, Goetz might have committed three distinct offenses, each offense focusing on a different aspect of the violent outburst. The crime of attempted murder stresses Goetz's allegedly murderous intent in shooting. The crime of assault zeroes in on the actual suffering inflicted on Troy Canty. The newly devised crime of "reckless endangerment" consists exclusively in creating a risk of harm to Canty as well as the other passengers on the train. These three perspectives are hardly consistent. If the essence of the crime is Goetz's shooting with murderous intent, why should it matter whether the bullet rips through Canty's flesh? And if the crime inheres in wounding Canty, why should we inquire whether, in addition, Goetz endangered him by creating a risk of wounding him?

A single volley of shots generated nine felony charges, one count of attempted murder and of assault against each of the four victims and an additional charge of endangering others. It makes good sense to distinguish among the four victims, to recognize the humanity of each and thus to hinge distinct offenses on each of the wounding shots. It is far more questionable to apply three overlapping offenses to each of these shots.

The multiplicity of charges camouflages basic uncertainty in the legal system about why an act of shooting should be treated as a crime. Two conflicting schools of thought have emerged about the essential nature of criminal wrongdoing. A traditional approach emphasizes the victim's suffering and the actor's responsibility for bringing about irreversible damage. A modern approach to crime takes the act—the range of the actor's control over what happens—as the core of the crime. It is a matter of chance, the modernists say, whether a shot intended to kill actually hits its target. It is purely fortuitous, as the argument goes, that Goetz failed to kill one of his four intended victims. It is a matter of providence, as Gregory Waples later argued to the jury, that the volley of shots did not injure an innocent bystander on the train.

The traditionalists root their case in the way we feel about crime and suffering. Modernists hold to arguments of rational and meaningful punishment. Despite what we might feel, the modernist insists, reason demands that we limit the criminal law to those factors that are within the control of the actor. The occurrence of harm is beyond his control and therefore ought not to have weight in the definition of crime and fitting punishment. The tension between these conflicting schools infects virtually all of our decisions in designing a system of crime and punishment.

Historically, it is hard to deny the relevance of actual harm and suffering in our thinking about crime. The criminal law would never have come into being unless people actually harmed each other. Our thinking about sin and crime begins with a change in the natural order, a human act that leaves a stain on the world. The sin of Eden was not looking at the apple, not possessing it, but eating it. Oedipus's offense against the gods was not lusting, but actually fornicating with his mother. Cain's crime was not endangering Abel, but spilling his blood. The notions of sin and crime are rooted in the harms that humans inflict on each other.

The classical conception of retributive punishment, the *lex talionis*, reenacts the crime on the person of the offender. This is expressed metaphorically in the biblical injunction to take an eye for an eye, a tooth for a tooth, and life for a life. In *Discipline and Punish*, the philosopher Michel Foucault argues that classically, punishment symbolically *expiated* the crime by replicating on the body of the criminal the harm he inflicted on another. It is hard even to think about punishment without perceiving the relationship between the harm wrought by the criminal and the harm he suffers in return.

From this perspective the salient fact in Goetz's crime, then, is his actually injuring the four youths. And the greater the injury, the greater the crime. If one of the four youths had died, even a year later, the crime would have fallen into a different category. Causing death is the ultimate evil, at least in the prevailing secular worldview. Homicide is the only crime for which, in some of its variations, capital punishment is still constitutional. The feature of homicide that makes it so heinous is not only the intention, not only the risk implicit in the defendant's act, but the inescapable fact of death. We no longer speak about the victim's blood crying out for revenge. But sensitivity to death and other irreversible harms represents an enduring afterglow of the biblical passion for punishing violations of the natural order.

This is not the way many or perhaps most policy makers think about crime in the modern world. Sometime in the last two or three centuries, our scientific thinking about crime began to shift from the harm done to the act that brings about the harm. The fortuitous connection between acts and their consequences did not trouble the great jurists of the past, but today, in the thinking of the moderns, a great divide separates the actor and his deed from the impact of his act on others. "There is many a slip 'twixt the cup and the lip." And all those slips, all those matters of chance, have undermined the unity we once felt between a homicidal act and the death of the victim.

The notions of risk, probability, and chance circumscribe the modern way of thinking about action and harm. Instead of seeing harm first and the action as the means for bringing about the harm, we are now inclined to see the action first and the harm as a contingent consequence of the action. And if we see the action first and the harm second, we invite the question, Why should we consider the harm at all in assessing the criminal evil of shooting someone in the subway? Many radical reformers hold that indeed the harm is totally irrelevant. If you shoot and miss, you should be punished as though you had killed someone. All that matter are the acts that you can control. And you cannot control the bullet after it leaves the barrel. Power may come from the barrel of a gun, as Chairman Mao said, but according to the modernists, you exhaust your power as soon as you fire the gun.

Modernists pride themselves on the rationality of their theory. If the purpose of punishment is *either* to punish wickedness *or* to influence and guide human behavior, the criminal law should limit its sights to conduct and circumstances within human control. There is nothing wicked about the way things fortuitously turn out. The actor's personal culpability is expressed in his actions—not in the accidents of nature that determine the consequences of his actions. And so far as the purpose of punishment is to set an example and deter future offenders, the only conduct that can be deterred is that within our control. The arguments of reason seem almost unbeatable.

The shift toward arresting and prosecuting those who merely attempt crimes reflects a practical concern as well. The legal system should arguably not only react to crimes already committed, but should intervene before the harm is done. The police should arrest the would-be offender before he has a chance to realize the harm his conduct bespeaks. Crimes should be defined and jail sentences inflicted not only to expiate previous wrongs and deter future offenders, but to prevent harm from occurring. This makes a good deal of sense in a world in which we try to manage the resources of government in order to maximize the welfare of all. This approach to punishment is typically called "preventive" as opposed to the traditional "retributive" practice of punishing past crimes, measure for measure.

The rationalists have held sway over English and American criminal law for most of the period since World War II. The prevailing view is that criminal law should serve social goals, rationally determined and efficiently pursued. Punishment should serve the goal of control either by rehabilitating offenders or, when we despair of changing criminals with doses of therapy, by deterring people in the future from choosing crime as a profitable career. The modern approach to crime dismisses as subrational the argument that people simply *feel* that actually killing someone is far worse than trying to kill. The Model Penal Code, a rationalist document that reflects the attitudes of reform-minded lawyers in the 1950s, goes so far as to recommend punishing attempted murder the same way we punish murder. Yet the concern for the suffering of victims is too deep-seated to be rejected simply because the reformers have so limited a conception of fair and decent punishment.

We punish convicted criminals not only because as social planners we see a need to deter crime in the future, but because we recognize the irrepressible need of victims to restore their faith in

themselves and in the society in which they live. The imperative to do justice requires that we heed the suffering of the victims, that we inquire at trial whether the defendant is responsible for that suffering, and we adjudge him guilty, if the facts warrant it, not for antiseptically violating the rules of the system, but for inflicting a wrong on the body and to the dignity of the victim. If Goetz was guilty for having shot at Troy Canty, Barry Allen, James Ramseur, and Darrell Cabey, his guilt consisted primarily in having brought these young men to their knees in pain, in leaving lead in their flesh and scars on their bodies, and, in Darrell Cabey's case, in severing his spinal cord, causing him to be paralyzed and to suffer brain damage for the rest of his life.

Whether the defendant actually causes the harm to the victim becomes, therefore, a pivotal question in every trial responding to the fact of suffering. Usually there is no particular problem in establishing the toll a gunshot takes on its victim, but unexpectedly, the question whether Goetz's shooting Cabey actually caused Cabey's brain damage became a hotly contested issue in the Goetz trial.

. . .

The question that united these two debates is why consequences should matter at all in defining a criminal offense. The traditional approach to crime, stressing the consequences more than the actor's intention, still shapes the law of New York, and even more significantly, it controls the way ordinary people sitting as jurors make decisions about how wrong, how criminal, a shooting should be regarded. A shooting that results in brain damage is worse than one that merely wounds. And a shot that inflicts permanent injuries is harder to justify on grounds of self-defense than one that misses altogether.

Each of the two competing theories, the traditional and modern, generated one of the primary charges levied against Goetz. The traditional theory expresses itself in the crime of assault, which is hinged to the harm, the serious physical injury, suffered by each of the victims. The modern theory comes to the fore in the charge of attempted murder, a crime that inheres in an unsuccessful effort to bring about an intended harm. The attempter is liable even if he has not caused harm to anyone. He can stab and miss, put poison in the food that is never eaten, point a gun that unbeknownst to him is unloaded—in all of these cases he can be guilty of attempted murder. The charge of attempted murder against Goetz did not require proof that his bullets struck anyone.

The crime of assault, traditionally called assault and battery, dates back to the earliest stages of the common law of crimes. The core of the crime is the physical injury inflicted on the victim. The actor must act in some way to bring about this injury, and it cannot be the case that the injury is purely accidental. In a general way, we can say that the injury must be intentional.

The crime of attempt is an innovation of the early 19th century. It comes into the law in the same period that the preventive theory of crime takes hold in the minds of reformers and the use of the modern prison replaces forms of punishment like flogging and modes of execution that reenacted the crime on the body of the criminal. As homicide and assault embody the old order, the crime of attempt is the flagship of modern, rational penology.

The external aspects of both assault and attempted murder—apart from the question of Goetz's intention, motive, and subjective state—lent themselves to easy proof. Assault merely requires that the actor cause physical harm to the victim. It is true the New York statute distinguishes among levels of injury. Reflecting the influence of the traditional school, the statute requires a "serious physical injury" for the crime of assault in the first degree. Causing mere "physical injury" can never be worse than assault in the third degree. There is not much learning about the difference between regular and serious physical injury, but presumably, a gunshot would be serious under anyone's definition.

The external side of attempted murder was equally easy to prove. The New York statute defines a criminal attempt in general terms suitable to any offense. All that is required is "any conduct which tends to effect the commission" of the crime. There is no doubt that shooting represents some conduct tending . . . "to effect the commission" of homicide.

Generally we can determine when particular crimes occur. An assault occurs when injury sets in—in Goetz's case, when the bullet strikes the flesh of each of the victims. Attempted crimes are different, for there is no way, in theory or in fact, to know when the actor crosses the threshold of punishable, criminal conduct. Let us suppose that Goetz decided in 1981, after being mugged and beaten, that he would arm himself and shoot the first group of black kids who made any move at all toward harassing him. That act of arming himself would not, everyone would agree, be sufficient to constitute attempted murder. But then let us consider the events of December 22, 1984. At what point did Goetz commit the crime of attempt—when did he complete the act that "tended to effect the commission" of homicide? When he entered the subway car? When he sat down amid the four youths? When he stood up in response to Cabey's asking him for five dollars? When he pulled the gun? When he aimed it? There is simply no way of drawing the line, even in theory. Unmoored from the traditional anchor of criminality—the suffering of the victim—the boundaries of attempted crime have remained hopelessly vague.

. . .

The vague contours of attempted murder also trigger increased attention to the intention required for it to be said that someone attempts to kill. Both the traditional crime of assault and the modern offense of attempted murder require intentional conduct, but the requirement is construed more narrowly for the latter. The difference between the narrow view and broad view of intention emerges from reflecting about the intention of Lee Harvey Oswald in firing two shots in the apparent aim of assassinating President Kennedy. One shot hit Governor Connally, who was sitting in front of Kennedy. Oswald knew that it was likely that he would hit Connally as well as the President. Did he intend to kill, or at least to injure, Connally as well as to kill Kennedy? Many lawyers would say yes. Others would insist that Oswald was, at most, reckless in hitting Connally, that he did not intend to injure him.

The moral doctrine of double effect distinguishes between two results of an action—the conscious object of the action and an expected side effect on the basis of what is important to the actor. The actor *intends* only the result in which his desires and personality are invested. Expected but undesired side effects are therefore not within the scope of the actor's intention. Accordingly, killing a fetus as an undesired side effect of removing it from a fallopian tube would not be an intentional killing. Destroying a schoolhouse and killing children as the by-product of bombing a railroad depot would not qualify as an intentional killing. Nor would injuring Connally be regarded as intentional. Oswald had neither an interest in injuring Connally nor a desire to injure him; in this strict sense he did not intentionally hit him with the shot intended for Kennedy.

The intention required for common law assault and battery has always been more expansive than this narrow linking of intention with the desired end of one's action. Intentional assault includes knowingly causing harm as a side effect. If the required intent is understood in this broader sense, Oswald was guilty of an intentional assault against Connally. Lawyers capture this point by saying that the intent required for assault need not be specific or purposeful, but may be general.

In contrast, the intention required for attempted murder is narrowly construed. Because attempted murder lacks the element of harm inflicted on a specific victim, the burden of the wrong is expressed in a pointed, narrowly construed intent to kill. The required intention is so demanding because that is all there is to the crime. Accordingly, few lawyers would say that Oswald intended to kill Connally. The notion of an assault is compatible with lesser degrees of focus on causing harm, such as the element of recklessness sufficient for assault in the second degree. But the law of attempts remains linked to intended wrongdoing, narrowly understood.

This restrictive approach to liability makes sense, for the crime of attempted murder has already gone far toward an innovative, atypical form of liability. It insists neither on the suffering of a specific victim nor on a precisely defined boundary as a fair warning to those who might trespass on the interests of others. The least that the law can require is a precisely defined intention.

From a moral perspective as well, the crime of attempted murder demands a more rigorous intention than does the traditional crime of assault. Assault requires an intent to injure; murder officially requires an intent to kill. Jurors might well be inclined, however, to take the name of the attempted crime—murder—as the object of the required in-

tent. A critical conceptual difference divides killing from murder. The sixth commandment does not say: thou shalt not kill. It says: thou shalt not murder. Killing in self-defense underscores the difference. If justified by self-defense, a killing is not murder, but it is a killing nonetheless.

If the jurors thought about attempted murder as turning on an intent to murder, they might well think that Goetz's claim of self-defense precluded his having this vicious intent. If, in his own view of what was going on, he was motivated by a desire to save himself, then one could not say that he desired to kill as an end in itself. His end would not be to murder, but to save himself from a threatened attack. If his intent was morally sound and not evil in itself, jurors might balk at treating it as an intent to murder or even to kill.

This way of thinking about attempted murder makes perfectly good sense, even though New York judges would be loath to instruct a jury to integrate the issue of self-defense with the analysis of intention. The standard instruction in New York defines intention, dryly, as merely the "conscious end or object" of the act. Even a killing in self-defense is the conscious end of the defense act, and therefore the killing is intended—even if thought to be necessary to personal survival. Yet, in the final analysis, lay jurors invariably follow their commonsense understanding of an intent to murder. If the jurors thought of this intent as necessarily vicious, they might well take any belief in the necessity of self-defense as logically incompatible with the required intent.

The irony of this logic would be that they would, in effect, bring in the subjective standard of self-defense by the back door. The prolonged pretrial appeal in the Goetz case rejected the subjective standard in favor of the standard of reasonableness, but conceptualizing viciousness as an element of the required intent to kill turns out to have the same logical implications as the subjective standard of self-defense. Both imply that a good faith belief in self-defense precludes liability for attempted murder, in one case because the intent is not vicious and in the other because the claim of self-defense is subjectively sound.

The charges levied against Bernhard Goetz reflect the traditional harm-oriented as well as the modern act-oriented approaches to crime. The grand jury faulted him both for causing suffering (assault in the first degree) and for acting with the potential of causing even greater intended suffering (attempted murder).

The tension between these two philosophical positions reappears in the field of reckless conduct. As intentional conduct can be considered criminal, with or without resulting harm, so reckless conduct can be faulted, apart from the harm that may eventuate. When harm occurs, the proper charges are reckless homicide or reckless assault—depending, of course, on the victim's fate. If no one is hurt, the reckless act itself might support a charge of reckless endangerment.

Intentional crimes are admittedly more serious than reckless offenses; in the former case, the offender identifies himself with the evil he tries to bring about. He chooses it; he wants it. The evil is his. But in a case of recklessness, the actor chooses only to create a *risk* of injury. He does not identify with the harm that may eventuate from the risk. He chooses merely the risk.

Obviously some risks are beneficial. We choose to create and expose ourselves and others to risks of driving, flying, using fireplaces, smoking, and, these days, of sexual intercourse. In order to talk about reckless behavior, we need to distinguish the bad risks that render conduct reckless from the good risks we accept as the price of modern living. The conventional approach to this distinction is to insist that a reckless risk be both substantial and unjustifiable. The point of the "substantiality" requirement is simply to set a threshold of seriousness. The issue of "justifiable" risk speaks to the question whether the risk was worth running under the circumstances.

On the charges of recklessly assaulting the four youths, there was not much question at the trial whether the risk was substantial. After all, Goetz shot at them. The burden of analysis on those charges fell on the question whether the risk was "justified" under the circumstances. As self-defense could justify an intentional assault, it could do the same for reckless assault. Thus the issue of self-defense would control liability for reckless as well as for intentional assault.

As 19th-century penology generated the crime of attempt, 20th-century thinking yielded a crime of recklessness in which no one is hurt. This crime of pure risk-taking first crystallized in American legal thought in the 1950s, when the Model Penal Code proposed its adoption. In 1965 the New York legislature improvised on the theme introduced in the model code by distinguishing misdemeanor and felony versions of reckless endangerment. The former, reckless endangerment in the second degree, requires merely that the actor recklessly create a "substantial risk of serious physical injury to another person." The latter, the first-degree charge, is more demanding in several respects and most significantly in requiring that the defendant's act evince "a depraved indifference to human life."

These two offenses closely track the wording of manslaughter in the second degree and murder in the second degree. Take manslaughter in the second degree, committed by "recklessly causing the death of another person," then subtract the element of suffering and death. The remainder is the misdemeanor of reckless endangerment. Take murder in the second degree without the consequence of actual harm, and the balance is reckless endangerment in the first degree.

This offense aptly captured the alleged danger that Goetz's shooting generated toward the other passengers on the train. Though the felony of reckless endangerment technically speaks to the risk Goetz created to the four youths as well as the other passengers, the prosecution treated the offense as addressing the potential harm to the noninvolved bystanders. It was a matter of "providence," Gregory Waples argued, that shooting five times in a crowded subway car did not injure one of the other passengers. In contrast, the defense maintained that the bullets were fired either directly into the bodies of the victims or, in the case of the one stray bullet, into the steel side panel of the car. Despite the suggestion of one witness, no bullet ricocheted through the car; no one except the four targets, the defense maintained, was in fact endangered by the shooting.

These argumentative forays never, as lawyers say, "joined issue." With Waples relying on the potential of harm and the defense stressing what actually happened, these arguments passed each other by. Waples relied on an abstract conception of risk-taking, defined generally as shooting in a crowded subway car. Baker and Slotnick relied on a more concrete notion of the relevant risk, defined by this suspect's shooting under these unique circumstances.

There are in fact an infinite number of ways of describing the risk that Goetz created. It would also be correct to say that he fired the gun in a crowded place, without specifying that it was a moving train, or that he fired a weapon, without distinguishing between a machine gun and a pistol. One could get more concrete and fill in details about where the passengers were sitting, the speed of the train, and the force of air currents at the time of the shooting. All these factors are relevant to the likelihood that a bystander would be hit. In the end, the danger of Goetz's shooting posed a problem of physics not of providence.

Yet as soon as we pin down all the physical variables and predict the path of the bullets, a paradox arises. It turns out that bullets that do not strike innocent bystanders *could not* have struck them, for the path of the bullet is physically determined at the moment of firing. If a bullet did not in fact strike a particular passenger, it was physically impossible that it strike him. According to this logic, if the bullet did not strike a bystander, it did not endanger him. In a physically determined world (that we can know in principle) it is not clear that it makes sense to talk about recklessly endangering but not injuring another.

The only way to avoid this paradox is to retreat from the quest for a total description of the physical variables. We have to think about classes of cases, such as those of firing in the direction of a passenger, or in the vicinity of a passenger or in the same subway car the passenger is sitting in. In these cases, the marksman's accuracy may vary. The physical forces may vary. An element of chance enters into the analysis. And in a world of chance, we can say that perhaps someone could have been hit who was not hit.

As with many other theoretical conundrums raised by the Goetz case, Justice Crane never had to cut through to the core of the problem. He rejected the defense's motion to dismiss on the ground that there was no risk at all to anyone other than the four kids, but he never had to formulate a view on the correct description of the risk. He avoided the issue by instructing the jury in the language of the statute. It was up to the jury to decide precisely what risk Goetz took by firing the gun under those circumstances.

Even those who sympathized with Goetz in his struggle to vindicate himself relative to the four youths thought that he might have a weak case on the charge of reckless endangerment. That he was justified relative to four apparent aggressors does not mean that he was justified in scaring the daylights out of the 15 to 20 other passengers in the car. They, after all, were totally innocent bystanders. How can the provocative behavior of four youths on the train justify depriving innocent people of their peace and security on the subway? The prosecution developed an ingenious argument about why the argument of justification as to bystanders could not be based on the criteria of self-defense.

Waples argued that self-defense should be limited to cases of justification relative to the alleged aggressors. So far as a risk is justified relative to innocent bystanders, the argument should be grounded in the statutory provision on necessity, an innovation in the 1965 Penal Law. The difference between the two provisions, as Waples developed his theory, is that the provision on self-defense generates a full justification any time the defender reasonably believes that he is under attack—whether in fact he is being attacked or not. The provision on necessity seems to require that an "imminent public or private injury" actually be "about to occur." If the four youths were not in fact about to attack Goetz, that fact would not preclude a claim of self-defense, but it would bar—at least under Waples's plausible reading of the statute—a claim of necessity. Thus Waples sensed an important advantage in seeking a ruling that the proper justification in cases of reckless endangerment is not self-defense, but necessity.

Neither the defense nor Justice Crane adequately responded to Waples's argument on this point. The defense never countered the theoretical thrust of the argument and they never had to; for tactical reasons, Waples decided midtrial that he preferred that the question whether the four youths were actually committing a robbery not be treated as a relevant issue in the case.

The defense may have sensed that they had a weak case on the charge of reckless endangerment, for after the impaneling of the jury in the trial, they approached Gregory Waples with an offer to plead guilty to two felony charges, possessing a loaded gun in public and reckless endangerment in the first degree. This plea would have seemed to vindicate Goetz in his confrontation with the four youths and yet satisfy the public interest in condemning and deterring violent conduct on the subway. But the District Attorney refused the deal. It was too important, in his view, to try the case and let a jury of ordinary New Yorkers resolve the issues.

The law remains ambivalent about the relevance of human suffering in defining criminal conduct. Both kinds of charges—those of actual harm and those of potential harm—were levied against Bernhard Goetz. There would be no plea bargain, no plea of guilty. The jury would have to make the ultimate decision about whether Goetz acted in self-defense and, if he did not, how his victims' suffering should be gauged.

The relevance of the victim's suffering in the criminal law poses a serious hurdle to the struggle for reasoned principles in the law. Generations of theorists have sought to explain why we punish actual homicide more severely than attempted homicide, the real spilling of blood more severely than the unrealized intent to do so. Our combined philosophical work has yet to generate a satisfactory account of why the realization of harm aggravates the penalty. Yet the practice persists in every legal system of the Western world. We cannot adequately explain why harm matters, but matter it does.

The law can and should go only so far to implement a rule of reason abstracted from the sensibilities of common people. It is after all common people, speaking in the voice of the jury, who ultimately decide whether an accused offender is guilty under the law. This is not to say that the law should surrender to the irrational passions that thrive in racial antagonism and the lust for vengeance. But neither should the drive for reason in the law make us forget that the law serves human beings. Oliver Wendell Holmes captured this elementary point in the best-known aphorism of American law: "The life of the law has not been logic; it has been experience." The collected wisdom of tradition is expressed in the learned arguments of those who seek to refine the law on the basis of reason, but it also demands continual reinforcement from the jurors who bring to criminal trials their common sense and intuitive sense of justice.

. . .

68. *People v. Dlugash*

Jasen, Judge.

The criminal law is of ancient origin, but criminal liability for attempt to commit a crime is comparatively recent. At the root of the concept of attempt liability are the very aims and purposes of penal law. The ultimate issue is whether an individual's intentions and actions, though failing to achieve a manifest and malevolent criminal purpose, constitute a danger to organized society of sufficient magnitude to warrant the imposition of criminal sanctions. Difficulties in theoretical analysis and concomitant debate over very pragmatic questions of blameworthiness appear dramatically in reference to situations where the criminal attempt failed to achieve its purpose solely because the factual or legal context in which the individual

363 N. E. 2d 1155 (1977)
Court of Appeals of New York

acted was not as the actor supposed them to be. Phrased somewhat differently, the concern centers on whether an individual should be liable for an attempt to commit a crime when, unknown to him, it was impossible to successfully complete the crime attempted. For years, serious studies have been made on the subject in an effort to resolve the continuing controversy when, if at all, the impossibility of successfully completing the criminal act should preclude liability for even making the futile attempt. The 1967 revision of the Penal law approached the impossibility defense to the inchoate crime of attempt in a novel fashion. The statute provides that, if a person engages in conduct which would otherwise constitute an attempt to commit a crime, "it is no defense to a prosecution for such attempt that the crime charged to have been attempted was, under the attendant circumstances, factually or legally impossible of commission, if such crime could have been committed had the attendant circumstances been as such person believed them to be." (Penal Law, §110.10.) This appeal presents to us, for the first time, a case involving the application of the modern statute. We hold that, under the proof presented by the People at trial, defendant Melvin Dlugash may be held for attempted murder, though the target of the attempt may have already been slain, by the hand of another, when Dlugash made his felonious attempt.

On December 22, 1973, Michael Geller, 25 years old, was found shot to death in the bedroom of his Brooklyn apartment. The body, which had literally been riddled by bullets, was found lying face up on the floor. An autopsy revealed that the victim had been shot in the face and head no less than seven times. Powder burns on the face indicated that the shots had been fired from within one foot of the victim. Four small caliber bullets were recovered from the victim's skull. The victim had also been critically wounded in the chest. One heavy caliber bullet passed through the left lung, penetrated the heart chamber, pierced the left ventricle of the heart upon entrance and again upon exit, and lodged in the victim's torso. Although a second bullet was damaged beyond identification, the bullet tracks indicated that these wounds were also inflicted by a bullet of heavy caliber. A tenth bullet, of unknown caliber, passed through the thumb of the victim's left hand. The autopsy report listed the

cause of death as "[m]ultiple bullet wounds of head and chest with brain injury and massive bilateral hemothorax with penetration of [the] heart." Subsequent ballistics examination established that the four bullets recovered from the victim's head were .25 caliber bullets and that the heart-piercing bullet was of .38 caliber.

Detective Joseph Carrasquillo of the New York City Policy Department was assigned to investigate the homicide. On December 27, 1973, five days after the discovery of the body, Detective Carrasquillo and a fellow officer went to the defendant's residence in an effort to locate him. The officers arrived at approximately 6:00 P.M. The defendant answered the door and, when informed that the officers were investigating the death of Michael Geller, a friend of his, defendant invited the officers into the house. Detective Carrasquillo informed defendant that the officers desired any information defendant might have regarding the death of Geller and, since defendant was regarded as a suspect, administered the standard preinterrogation warnings. The defendant told the officers that he and another friend, Joe Bush, had just returned from a four- or five-day trip "upstate someplace" and learned of Geller's death only upon his return. Since Bush was also a suspect in the case and defendant admitted knowing Bush, defendant agreed to accompany the officers to the station house for the purposes of identifying photographs of Bush and of lending assistance to the investigation. Upon arrival at the police station, Detective Carrasquillo and the defendant went directly into an interview room. Carrasquillo advised the defendant that he had witnesses and information to the effect that as late as 7:00 P.M. on the day before the body was found, defendant had been observed carrying a .25 caliber pistol. Once again, Carrasquillo administered the standard preinterrogation statement of rights. The defendant then proceeded to relate his version of the events which culminated in the death of Geller. Defendant stated that on the night of December 21, 1973, he, Bush and Geller had been out drinking. Bush had been staying at Geller's apartment and, during the course of the evening, Geller several times demanded that Bush pay $100 towards the rent on the apartment. According to defendant, Bush rejected these demands, telling Geller that "you better shut up or you're going to get a bullet." All three returned to Geller's apartment at approximately midnight, took seats in the bedroom, and continued to drink until sometime between 3:00 and 3:30 in the morning. When Geller again pressed his demand for rent money, Bush drew his .38 caliber pistol, aimed it at Geller and fired three times. Geller fell to the floor. After the passage of a few minutes, perhaps two, perhaps as much as five, defendant walked over to the fallen Geller, drew his .25 caliber pistol, and fired approximately five shots in the victim's head and face. Defendant contended that, by the time he fired the shots, "it looked like Mike Geller was already dead." After the shots were fired, defendant and Bush walked to the apartment of a female acquaintance. Bush removed his short, wrapped the two guns and a knife in it, and left the apartment, telling Dlugash that he intended to dispose of the weapons. Bush returned 10 or 15 minutes later and stated that he had thrown the weapons down a sewer two or three blocks away.

After Carrasquillo had taken the bulk of the statement, he asked the defendant why he would do such a thing. According to Carrasquillo, the defendant said, "gee, I really don't know." Carrasquillo repeated the question 10 minutes later, but received the same response. After a while, Carrasquillo asked the question for a third time and defendant replied, "well, gee, I guess it must have been because I was afraid of Joe Bush."

At approximately 9:00 P.M., the defendant repeated the substance of his statement to an Assistant District Attorney. Defendant added that at the time he shot at Geller, Geller was not moving and his eyes were closed. White he did not check for a pulse, defendant stated that Geller had not been doing anything to him at the time he shot because "Mike was dead."

Defendant was indicted by the Grand Jury of Kings County on a single count of murder in that, acting in concert with another person actually present, he intentionally caused the death of Michael Geller. At the trial, there were four principal prosecution witnesses: Detective Carrasquillo, the Assistant District Attorney who took the second admission, and two physicians from the office of the New York City Chief Medical Examiner. For proof of defendant's culpability, the prosecution relied upon defendant's own admissions as related by the detective

and the prosecutor. From the physicians, the prosecution sought to establish that Geller was still alive at the time defendant shot at him. Both physicians testified that each of the two chest wounds, for which defendant alleged Bush to be responsible, would have caused death without prompt medical attention. Moreover, the victim would have remained alive until such time as his chest cavity became fully filled with blood. Depending on the circumstances, it might take 5 to 10 minutes for the chest cavity to fill. Neither prosecution witness could state, with medical certainty, that the victim was still alive when, perhaps five minutes after the initial chest wounds were inflicted, the defendant fired at the victim's head. The defense produced but a single witness, the former Chief Medical Examiner of New York City. This expert stated that, in his view, Geller might have died of the chest wounds "very rapidly" since, in addition to the bleeding, a large bullet going through a lung and the heart would have other adverse medical effects. "Those wounds can be almost immediately or rapidly fatal or they may be delayed in there, in the time it would take for death to occur. But I would say that wounds like that which are described here as having gone through the lungs and the heart would be fatal wounds and in most cases they're rapidly fatal."

The jury found the defendant guilty of murder. The defendant then moved to set the verdict aside. He submitted an affidavit in which he contended that he "was absolutely, unequivocally and positively certain that Michael Geller was dead before [he] shot him." This motion was denied.[1]

On appeal, the Appellate Division reversed the judgment of conviction on the law and dismissed the indictment. The court ruled that "the People failed to prove beyond a reasonable doubt that Geller had been alive at the time he was shot by defendant; defendant's conviction of murder thus cannot stand." Further, the court held that the judgment could not be modified to reflect a conviction for attempted murder because "the uncontradicted evidence is that the defendant, at the time that he fired the five shots into the body of the decedent, believed him to be dead, and . . . there is not a scintilla of evidence to contradict his assertion in that regard."

While the defendant admitted firing five shots at the victim approximately two to five minutes after Bush had fired three times, all three medical expert witnesses testified that they could not, with any degree of medical certainty, state whether the victim had been alive at the time the latter shots were fired by the defendant. Thus, the People failed to prove beyond a reasonable doubt that the victim had been alive at the time he was shot by the defendant. Whatever else it may be, it is not murder to shoot a dead body.

The distinction between "factual" and "legal" impossibility is a nice one indeed and the courts tend to place a greater value on legal form than on any substantive danger the defendant's actions pose for society. The approach of the draftsmen of the Model Penal Code was to eliminate the defense of impossibility in virtually all situations. Under the code provision, to constitute an attempt, it is still necessary that the result intended or desired by the actor constitute a crime. However, the code suggested a fundamental change to shift the locus of analysis to the actor's mental frame of reference and away from undue dependence upon external considerations. The basic premise of the code provision is that what was in the actor's own mind should be the standard for determining his dangerousness to society and, hence, his liability for attempted criminal conduct.

In the belief that neither of the two branches of the traditional impossibility arguments detracts from the offender's moral culpability, the Legislature substantially carried the code's treatment of impossibility into the 1967 revision of the Penal Law. Thus, a person is guilty of an attempt when, with intent to commit a crime, he engages in conduct which tends to effect the commission of such crime. (Penal Law, §110.10.) Thus, if defendant believed the victim to be alive at the time of the shooting, it is no defense to the charge of attempted murder that the victim may have been dead.

Turning to the facts of the case before us, we believe that there is sufficient evidence in the record from which the jury could conclude that the defendant believed Geller to be alive at the time defendant fired shots into Geller's head. Defendant admitted firing five shots at a most vital part of the victim's anatomy from virtually point blank range. Although defendant contended that the victim had already been grievously wounded by another, from the defendant's admitted actions, the jury could

conclude that the defendant's purpose and intention was to administer the coup de grace.

Defendant argues that the jury was bound to accept, at face value, the indications in his admissions that he believed Geller dead. Certainly, it is true that the defendant was entitled to have the entirety of the admissions, both the inculpatory and the exculpatory portions, placed in evidence before the trier of facts.

However, the jury was not required to automatically credit the exculpatory portions of the admissions. The general rule is, of course, that the credibility of witnesses is a question of fact and the jury may choose to believe some, but not all, of a witness' testimony.

In this case, there is ample other evidence to contradict the defendant's assertion that he believed Geller dead. There were five bullet wounds inflicted with stunning accuracy in a vital part of the victim's anatomy. The medical testimony indicated that Geller may have been alive at the time defendant fired at him. The defendant voluntarily left the jurisdiction immediately after the crime with his coperpetrator. Defendant did not report the crime to the police when left on his own by Bush. Instead, he attempted to conceal his and Bush's involvement with the homicide. In addition, the other portions of defendant's admissions make his contended believe that Geller was dead extremely improbable. Defendant, without a word of instruction from Bush, voluntarily got up from his seat after the passage of just a few minutes and fired five times point blank into the victim's face, snuffing out any remaining chance of life that Geller possessed. Certainly, this alone indicates a callous indifference to the taking of a human life. His admissions are barren of any claim of duress[2] and reflect, instead, an unstinting co-operation in efforts to dispose of vital incriminating evidence. Indeed, defendant maintained a false version of the occurrence until such time as the police informed him that they had evidence that he lately possessed a gun of the same caliber as one of the weapons involved in the shooting. From all of this, the jury was certainly warranted in concluding that the defendant acted in the belief that Geller was yet alive when shot by defendant.

The jury convicted the defendant of murder. Necessarily, they found that defendant intended to kill a live human being. Subsumed within this finding is the conclusion that defendant acted in the belief that Geller was alive. Thus, there is no need for additional fact findings by a jury. Although it was not established beyond a reasonable doubt that Geller was, in fact, alive, such is no defense to attempted murder since a murder would have been committed "had the attendant circumstances been as [defendant] believed them to be." (Penal Law, §110.10.) The jury necessarily found that defendant believed Geller to be alive when defendant shot at him.

The Appellate Division erred in not modifying the judgment to reflect a conviction for the lesser included offense of attempted murder. An attempt to commit a murder is a lesser included offense of murder and the Appellate Division has the authority, where the trial evidence is not legally sufficient to establish the offense of which the defendant was convicted, to modify the judgment to one of conviction for a lesser included offense which is legally established by the evidence.

Endnotes

[1] It should be noted that Joe Bush pleaded guilty to a charge of manslaughter in the first degree. At the time he entered his plea, Bush detailed his version of the homicide. According to Bush, defendant Dlugash was a dealer in narcotic drugs and Dlugash claimed that Geller owed him a large sum of money from drug purchases. Bush was in the kitchen alone when Geller entered and threatened him with a shotgun. Bush pulled out his .38 caliber pistol and fired five times at Geller. Geller slumped to the floor. Dlugash then entered, withdrew his .25 caliber pistol and fired five shots into the deceased's face. Bush, however, never testified at Dlugash's trial.

[2] Notwithstanding the Appellate Division's implication to the contrary, the record indicates that defendant told the Assistant District Attorney that Bush, after shooting Geller, kept his gun aimed at Geller, and not at Dlugash. As defendant stated, "this was after Joe had his .38 on him, I started shooting on him."

69. *The Crime That Never Was*

Leo Katz

Before Newson, C. J., Henchard, Hardy, Farfrae, Middlebury, J.

Newson, C. J.

The defendant, Jan Omeira, is charged with attempting to export illegally "valuable artifacts of the native culture" in violation of Section 901.34(1) of the Wessex Code.

A Fake Opinion in a Fake Case Involving Fakes
Commonwealth v. Omeira
Supreme Court of Wessex
Reprinted by permission of the University of Chicago Press.

To protect our national patrimony, the Wessex legislature twenty years ago passed a law making it illegal to export native art works produced before 1920 and worth more than 100,000 pounds. This sweeping prohibition is subject to only one ill-defined exception. The Arts Council, an agency of the Interior Department, has broad discretion to grant exemptions, that is, special licenses, when it finds that "unusual circumstances so warrant." Licenses are typically granted when a work of art cannot be sold in Wessex except at a very small fraction of its world market price or when the applicant promises to secure another "native" work of comparable worth currently in foreign hands.

The defendant is a retired businessman of considerable wealth. He owns a farm in Casterbridge, Wessex, where he spends half of the year, and a rancho in Cuernavaca, Mexico, where he spends the other half. He is a zealous aficionado of the arts; indeed, since his retirement the acquisition of expensive paintings has become his chief preoccupation. He has opened art galleries both in his house in Casterbridge and in his villa in Cuernavaca, the one in Casterbridge for the public at large, the one in Cuernavaca almost exclusively for his own use and that of his guests.

The Constabulary has been aware for some time that not all native paintings Mr. Omeira is known to have acquired at public auctions in Wessex have made their appearance in his Casterbridge gallery and suspected him therefore of having illegally transported many of them to his gallery in Cuernavaca. Since few people have gained access to that gallery, no direct confirmation has been possible. For several years Mr. Omeira was systematically strip-searched on every one of his departures for Mexico. The searches turned up nothing and were discontinued.

In January of this year, the Constabulary received an anonymous tip that some time in March, Omeira would personally be smuggling a picture by the famous eighteenth-century landscape painter Ignacius Decameron out of the country. The picture, *Seminole Falls,* had for several years been hanging in Omeira's Casterbridge gallery and had recently been taken down for "cleaning." When Omeira left for Mexico in March, Customs scoured his luggage. They found a false bottom in one of his trunks and inside it, tightly rolled up, *Seminole Falls.*

Omeira's case was about to go to trial, when something very unusual happened. A well-known Belgian landscape painter named Flammarion remarked in an interview with the French monthly *Paris Match* that he thought it "rather amusing" that a Wessex art collector was being prosecuted for smuggling a Decameron landscape when in fact the painting was a forgery. How did he know it was a forgery, the astonished journalist asked. Because, replied Flammarion, he had painted it himself.

The government to whom Omeira had forfeited the smuggled picture immediately invited a panel of experts to test Flammarion's claim. They found that the painting's age crackle had a different structure from that of genuine eighteenth-century paintings.

Moreover, the crackle seemed to have been artificially produced. They found that the dirt in the painting's crevices wasn't dirt at all. It had crept into the crevices very unevenly and had a different homogeneity from dirt. They suspected it was ink. With the help of radiographic studies they discovered a residue of a prior painting underneath the landscape, suggesting that this was an eighteenth-century canvas that had been recycled for forgery. They also noticed some of the paints used contained pigments not known in Decameron's day. Finally, one of the experts was struck by the reddish tinge of the painting's sky. He had been to Seminole Falls and he knew that tinge. But he was almost certain it was due to factory smoke and could not have been present in the eighteenth century. The group concluded that Flammarion was right: the picture was a fake.

Why had Flammarion forged a Decameron? When Flammarion was still a young, struggling painter living in Wessex, he entered into a feud with the influential art critic Arcadius Breitel. Breitel had published some scathing reviews of Flammarion's work, which had sent the painter into a fit of impotent rage. He wrote a letter to the magazine *Kaleidoscope,* which Breitel edited. Breitel was a snob, he wrote, who had never yet dared to praise a painting by an unknown. His sole basis for judging a painting was its age and signature. "What a delightful prank it would be," the letter concluded, "to confront this nincompoop with a picture by an unknown in the style and name of an 'Old Master,' hear him pronounce it a masterpiece, and see him squirm when the true author is revealed." The prank, tossed in at the end of the letter more as a figure of speech than a real suggestion, captured his fancy. He resolved to give it a try.

Flammarion bought a real eighteenth-century painting depicting the Last Supper by a mediocre and forgotten artist. He carefully ground the original painting off the canvas and now had a genuine eighteenth-century canvas to work on. He had taken care not to remove the painting's base which was cracked in many places, since he planned to use it when he began to age his own superimposed painting. He then retired to an inn near Seminole Falls, where he produced a rendition of the famous spot in the distinctive style of Ignacius Decameron. When he was done, he rolled it around in a cylinder to induce the age crackle. He covered the entire surface with India ink, letting it seep into the painting's cracks to simulate the fine dust that collects on an old canvas over time. Once it had dried, he removed the ink and added another layer of light brown varnish. He was ready to sell the picture.

He approached an art dealer–friend with an involved story about a former mistress of his, descended from an impoverished aristocratic Wessex family that now made its home in Uruguay. The family had only recently discovered the painting in its vaults, thought it might be a real Decameron, and wish to sell it without divulging their identity, since the sale of expensive works of art abroad was frowned upon by the government of Uruguay. The art dealer accepted the story unquestioningly and took the painting, as Flammarion expected, to none other than Arcadius Breitel for authentication. Breitel was known to be an expert on Decameron. In fact, Flammarion had painted the picture so as to fall in nicely with some of Breitel's pet theories about the painter.

Breitel not only authenticated the painting but pronounced it a major, if not *the* major work of Decameron. He praised it as the "ultimate synthesis of the romanticist yearnings of Decameron's early years and the naturalistic sobriety of his more mature years, the sort of synthesis I argued he was on the verge of attaining when his life was so tragically cut short by that riding accident. I was wrong. *Seminole Falls* proves that he did attain it before he died." He gushed about the way "the hard facts of topography are diffused behind pearly films of colour," found the colors "purer, more prismatic" than any other of Decameron's work, and concluded that for its brilliancy and iridescence this was perhaps the finest Decameron yet.

This was the point at which Flammarion had originally intended to step forth and expose Breitel. He didn't. A man named VanDamm had offered one million pounds for the painting. Faced with this offer and with the opportunity to see his painting forever after celebrated as a sublime example of Wessex art, he could no longer bring himself to admit the hoax. For nearly ten years the painting remained a part of the VanDamm collection. Then VanDamm, who found himself in financial straits, decided to sell it. He applied to the Arts Council for an export license so that he would be able to offer it

up through Sotheby's. An expert from the Arts Council inspected the painting and concluded that it was probably a fake, worth at best 50,000 pounds. Although under the circumstances no license would have been necessary, the council issued one anyway, simply because the painting's status was still unclear.

VanDamm, however, had lost all appetite for having it sold at Sotheby's. If the painting really was a forgery, a public auction would bring that to light all too quickly. Instead, he discreetly search for buyers among his colleagues in the business. He finally sold it to Jan Omeira for 1,200,000 pounds. Needless to say, he mentioned nothing about the painting's suspect provenance or even about the export license.

The discovery that *Seminole Falls* was a forgery put the trial judge in this case in a delicate quandary. Omeira was charged with attempting illegally to export a valuable native painting. But it is perfectly legal to export a forged Decameron. How then was the defendant guilty of any wrongdoing? The trial judge chose to slight the issue. In a disturbingly desultory opinion, he simply noted that the "defendant believed he was smuggling a real Decameron. Therefore he is guilty of attempting to export a 'valuable artifact of native culture'" and sentenced the defendant to three years in prison. The defendant appealed. I believe his appeal has merit.

A failed crime can still be a crime. That's why we have the law of attempts. The assassin who is prevented from firing a bullet by an alert bodyguard, the safecracker who is stopped short of opening the vault by an unsuspected alarm system, the rapist who is frustrated in his aim by an obstreperous victim, all have failed in completing their intended crime; yet they are guilty of a crime nonetheless, the crime of criminal attempt.

But not all failed crimes are crimes. "Suppose a man takes away an umbrella from a stand with intent to steal it, believing it not to be his own, but it turns out to be his own, could he be convicted of attempting to steal?" Baron Bramwell, who posed this hypothetical more than a century ago in a case called *Regina v. Collins*, rightly considered the question purely rhetorical.[1]

When is a failed crime not an attempt? It behooves us to make a brief foray through some of the more typical cases and to see what general principle is to be extracted from them.

In *Commonwealth v. Dunaway* a man was charged with attempting to rape and engage in incestuous relations with his daughter. He had apparently advanced quite far in this undertaking when his wife called the police to arrest him. In the course of the trial it turned out that the girl was the man's stepdaughter. Wessex law makes consanguinity a prerequisite of incest. The defendant did not, of course, know that; he thought he was committing incest. He was convicted. On appeal the attempted rape conviction was upheld, the attempted incest conviction overturned. The court observed that even if the man had succeeded in his undertaking, even if he had actually completed an act of intercourse with his stepdaughter, he would only be guilty of rape, not incest. Stephen's *Digest of the Criminal Law* defines an attempt to commit a crime as "an act done with intent to commit that crime, and forming part of a series of acts which would constitute its actual commission if it were not interrupted."[2] The defendant's acts, even if not interrupted, would not have constituted incest. Hence, the court reasoned, he could not be guilty of the attempt to commit incest.

The defendant in *Stephens v. Abrahams* wanted to import a certain item into Victoria (Australia) without paying the duty on it.[3] To this end he presented the customs officer with a fake invoice for the item. Unbeknownst to him, the item was not dutiable anyway. A bill was pending in Parliament that proposed to tax such items, but it had not yet been passed. The Customs Office discovered the defendant's deception and charged him with attempt to "defraud the revenue contrary to the Commonwealth Customs Act." The Supreme Court acquitted him. Even "if the accused had succeeded in his object, he would not have succeeded in defrauding the revenue," it argued. Even if the defendant had managed to deceive the Customs office with his fake invoice, he would not have cheated them out of any money they were entitled to. So there could be no attempt to defraud them either.

Wilson received a check for $2.50. The upper right-hand corner of the check read: $2^{50}/_{100}$." The body of the check read: "two and $^{50}/_{100}$ dollars." The top of the check read: "Ten Dollars or Less." Undaunted, Wilson inserted a "1" in front of the "2

50/100" hoping to cash the check in for $12.50. Needless to say, the pathetic ploy foundered and Wilson was charged with attempting to commit check forgery. Check forgery, however, requires an alteration of a material part of the check. The number on a check itself is immaterial. Whenever there is a discrepancy between number and words, the words control. Since Wilson had done all he meant to do and it did not amount to check forgery, how, the court asked, could he be guilty of attempted check forgery? Wilson was acquitted.[4]

In *People v. Dlugash* the defendant was charged with attempted murder because he had shot a corpse.

> Defendant stated that, on the night of December 21, 1973, he, Bush and Geller had been out drinking. Bush had been staying at Geller's apartment and, during the course of the evening, Geller several times demanded that Bush pay $100 towards the rent on the apartment. According to defendant, Bush rejected these demands, telling Geller that "you better shut up or you're going to get a bullet." All three returned to Geller's apartment at approximately midnight, took seats in the bedroom, and continued to drink until sometime between 3:00 and 3:30 in the morning. When Geller again pressed his demand for rent money, Bush drew his .38 caliber pistol, aimed it at Geller and fired three times. Geller fell to the floor.[5]

Then, to confuse the police and to buy the defendant's silence, Bush ordered him to fire some extra bullets into Geller's body. The somewhat frightened defendant did just that, believing that Geller was still alive. The autopsy, however, revealed that Geller was almost certainly already dead. In an arcanely reasoned opinion, the New York Court of Appeals somehow reached the conclusion that the defendant could indeed be found guilty of attempted murder. Few courts, I venture to say, would accept that conclusion. Lord Reid in *Haughton v. Smith* some years ago contemplated just such a case and gave what I think is the definitive answer: "A man lies dead. His enemy comes along and thinks he is asleep, so he stabs the corpse. The theory [advanced by some] inevitably required us to hold that the enemy has attempted to murder the dead man. The law may sometimes be an ass but it cannot be so asinine as that."[6]

The defendant in *People v. Jaffe* had bought what he thought were stolen goods from some undercover policemen.[7] He could not be charged with buying stolen goods since the goods weren't stolen. Instead, he was charged with attempting to buy stolen goods. The courts acquitted him: "If all which an accused person intends to do would if done constitute no crime it cannot be a crime to attempt to do with the same purpose a part of the thing intended."

In *State v. Clarissa* the defendant, a black slave, was charged with attempting to murder two white men by feeding them a substance called Jamestown weed, which she believed to be poisonous.[8] The prosecution failed to allege or prove that it was. The Supreme Court of Alabama reversed the conviction, explaining:

> [The] administration of a substance not poisonous, or calculated to cause death, though believed to be so by the person administering it, will not be an attempt to poison, within the meaning of the [murder] statute. From this analysis of the statute, it follows, that the indictment should allege, that the substance administered was a deadly poison, or calculated to destroy human life, as it is necessary that every indictment should warrant the judgment that is rendered upon it. Yet every allegation in this indictment may have been proved, and the life of the persons against whom the supposed attempt to poison was made, never have been in jeopardy; as it cannot be known as a matter of law, that the seed of the Jamestown weed is a deadly poison. The moral guilt, it is true, is as great in the one case as in the other, but that is not the offense which the law intended to punish; but the actual attempt to poison, by means calculated to accomplish it.

A notable curiosity occurred in our own jurisdiction only very recently in *Commonwealth v. Jejune.*[9] The defendant and his wife were Haitian immigrants. The defendant's wife had grown very sick shortly after coming to this country. At the behest of a neighbor a doctor visited her. She told him that she could not be helped because her husband had cast a spell over her. Two days earlier she had found in his shaving cabinet a doll bearing her likeness with pins in it. The doctor ordered her taken to the hospital, where she quickly recovered. No organic cause for her illness was ever discovered. The woman's husband did not deny having tried to kill her by magic. He was charged with attempted murder. The trial court rightly dismissed the charge and acquitted the man. It observed, "To try to kill someone by sticking pins in a doll is to try the impossible. Even if the man had continued sticking pins in the doll for the rest of his life he could not have killed his wife. How then can we brand such an inherently innocent activity attempted murder?"

These cases establish a simple yet powerful principle. An act which, unless interrupted, constitutes a crime is a criminal attempt. But an act which, even if completed, wouldn't be a crime, is not.

The defendant in all of these cases is morally heinous. But why is he morally heinous? Because of what he did? No, because of what he thought he did. In that case to convict him "would be to convict him not for what he did but simply because he had a guilty intention." It is a fundamental tenet of our criminal law that a man cannot be convicted for his thoughts, only for his acts.

My disposition of Omeira's case should now be clear. Even if Jan Omeira had succeeded in smuggling his painting across the border, he would not have violated the export ban, since *Seminole Falls* is a forgery. If the completed act was no crime, the attempt could not possible be one either. The trial court's verdict should be reversed.

Henchard, J.

I disagree sharply with the reasoning of Justice Newson. He would have us endorse what I think is a rather strange principle: that an "act which, although intended to be a crime, would not have amounted to one, even if it had not been interrupted, is not a criminal attempt." Taken seriously, this principle would have absurd implications. Justice Newson concedes that the assassin who is overpowered by a bodyguard, the safecracker who is caught by an unsuspected alarm system, the rapist who is stymied by a resistant victim all are guilty of a criminal attempt. But suppose that given the way the assassin aimed his gun, he would have missed his target anyway. Justice Newson's principle would have the man acquitted. Suppose the gold bars in the vault were too heavy for the safecracker to move, even if he had gotten to them. Justice Newson's principle would have the man acquitted. Suppose the rapist was impotent and could not have achieved an erection. Justice Newson's principle would have the man acquitted. I do not see how Justice Newson can propose a principle with such consequences.

Nor can I approve of many of the decisions that seem to have endorsed this principle. If the defendant in *Jaffe* thought he was buying stolen goods, he was attempting to buy stolen goods. If the defendant in *Jejune* thought what he did would tend to kill his wife, he was attempting murder. By contrast, the decision of the *Dlugash* court was exactly right: If the defendant in *Dlugash* thought he was shooting a human being, he was attempting murder. In each of these cases, what the defendants were attempting was impossible only because of some unforeseen contingency. That makes them no different from the assassin, the safecracker, the rapist. They, too, failed because some unforeseen contingency stopped them in their tracks.

Justice Newson contends that to punish the defendants in cases like *Dlugash, Jaffe*, and *Jejune* is to punish evil thoughts, not evil acts. But that's not so. We punish the defendants there not because they wanted to commit an evil act but because they took what they thought were substantial steps toward putting those thoughts into practice. I think I can pinpoint the source of Justice Newson's confusion. He thinks that when but for the defendant's evil thought he would not be punished we are punishing him for the evil thought. That's a mistaken idea. We would not convict a murderer but for the act that he intended to kill a human being. Yet it can hardly be said that we are punishing him only for his evil thoughts.

I do no think, therefore, than Jan Omeira is innocent of a criminal attempt to violate the export ban on art merely because what he took to be a real Decameron turned out to be a forgery. But I think there are other reasons for acquitting him.

Suppose two men furtively engage in homosexual intercourse thinking that it is illegal. In fact, state law has nothing against mutually consented-to homosexual intercourse. Are they guilty of a criminal attempt? Evidently not. You cannot invent the law against yourself. Just because you think something is illegal and then attempt to do it, you haven't yet done anything illegal. The crime you attempt is, we might say, "legally impossible" because there isn't such a crime. This is very different from the case where what you are attempting to do isn't really criminal because the facts, not the law, are different from what you took them to be: because the man you attempt to shoot is already dead, because the goods you attempt to buy are not really stolen, because the method you adopt for killing someone won't really work. We might call these cases of "factual impossibility." In sum, attempting the legally impossible is not a crime, attempting the factually impossible *is*. In a way, this is a corollary to the principle that ignorance of law is no excuse. Just as thinking something is legal when it isn't won't get a defendant out of a bind, thinking it is illegal when it isn't won't get him into one.

This principle, rather than the one endorsed by Justice Newson, serves to make sense of the three cases cited in his opinion with which I agree. I agree that the defendant in *Dunaway* who thought he was committing incest should have been acquitted of the charge of attempting incest. What he attempted was legally impossible. The law does not make intercourse with one's stepdaughter part of incest. Thinking that the law does cannot make the defendant guilty of attempted incest.

I also agree that the defendant in *Stephens v. Abrahams* who thought he was smuggling a dutiable item past customs should have been acquitted of the charge of attempting to "defraud the revenue." He, too, attempted the legally impossible, since Victoria did not make the item he smuggled dutiable. Thinking that it did could not have made the defendant guilty of attempted smuggling.

Finally, I agree that the defendant in *State v. Wilson* who thought he was forging a check when he altered its numerals should have been acquitted of the charge of attempting check forgery. He thought that what he did was forgery. The law happens to define forgery differently. Thus, he, too, attempted the legally impossible. Thinking that the law prohibited what he did as forgery did not make him guilty of attempted forgery.

When the Decameron was still in Mr. Van-Damm's possession, he applied for an export license to the Arts Council. The Arts Council granted him the license. In effect, they amended the export law so as to exempt this particular painting from its sway. Thus what Mr. Omeira attempted to do was to smuggle out of the country a painting under the mistaken belief that the law prohibited him from exporting it. In fact, the law specifically exempted that painting. What he was attempting to do was not merely factually impossible (because he was dealing with a forgery) but legally impossible (because the painting had been exempted from the export ban). The case is thus on all fours with *Dunaway, Stephens*, and *Wilson*. It is for that reason that I too would acquit Mr. Omeira, notwithstanding my wholehearted disagreement with the reasoning of Justice Newson's opinion.

Farfrae, J., with whom Hardy, J., concurs.

I agree in spirit with Justice Newson's approach. I agree with him that many of the so-called impossible attempt cases should be resolved in the defendant's favor. I disagree with the particulars of his argument, for many of the reasons given in Justice Henchard's opinion. And I disagree with his resolution of this case.

I disagree both in spirit and substance with Justice Henchard's approach, and, of course, with his resolution of this case in particular. The approach hinges on a distinction that strikes me as both obscure and unimportant, that between law and fact, legal impossibility and factual impossibility.

The distinction between "law" and "fact" has proved obscure wherever it is employed. For instance, the common law used to require that a plaintiff's complaint in a civil action only state the "facts" of his case, not any "legal conclusions." Unfortunately, no one has ever been able to tell whether the allegation that "on November 9, the defendant negligently ran over the plaintiff with his car at the intersection of State Street and Chestnut Street" is a statement of fact or a legal conclusion. In fact, the distinction between law and fact is just the legal version of the philosophical distinction between "empirical" and "analytical" statements, a distinction on whose existence philosophers have been unable to agree to this day.

The distinction is an unimportant as it is obscure. It distinguishes between cases that are really alike. [Here Justice Farfrae retells the story of Mr. Law and Mr. Fact, which the reader already encountered in chap. 1.] The present case shows neatly just how unimportant it is. The defendant Omeira made two mistakes. First, he mistakenly thought the picture was authentic. Second, he mistakenly thought it hadn't been licensed for export. Under Justice Henchard's rule, the first mistake fails to exonerate him, but the second mistake does. The first is a mistake of fact, the second a mistake of law. Yet I fail to see any profound difference between the two kinds of mistake. If Omeira's ignorance of the painting's authenticity doesn't exonerate him, then neither should his ignorance of the export license.

The proper way to approach cases like the present is to ask two questions. Let me ask them in turn, explain why they are important, show how one goes about answering them, and answer them for the present case. The first question is this: Did the defendant really attempt something criminal?

An attempt is often mistakenly thought of as the fragment of a completed offense. Of course, that isn't so. The driver who hurtles down a slippery road at breakneck speed may be inviting a deadly accident that would qualify as involuntary manslaughter if it occurred. Nevertheless, he is not attempting to commit the crime of involuntary manslaughter. To attempt something one must not merely be on one's way to committing it, one must intend to commit it. The reckless driver clearly is not.

This obvious point has subtle implications. It means that a defendant may be thinking he is committing a crime, without actually attempting to commit it. He knows the bomb he plans to hurl into the queen's carriage will kill not only the queen, but her bodyguard, but he is only attempting to kill the queen, not the bodyguard. Killing the bodyguard is an unintended by-product of killing the queen. Of course, determining whether somebody is actually attempting something or merely engaging in conduct which he thinks will bring it about, often is hard. It depends on whether the commission of the crime is his desired end or a means toward such an end (in which case we have an attempt) or whether it is rather a by-product of bringing about some desired end. To find out which it is, one has to ask whether the defendant would change his course of conduct if he thought the commission of the crime was not tied to the achievement of his desired end.

If we apply this analysis, we will see that many defendants charged with impossible attempts are not in fact attempting the crime they are charged with attempting. They merely think they are committing a crime. The rapist in *Commonwealth v. Dunaway* is not guilty of attempted incest, because he was not intending to commit incest. He only thought he was committing incest. Had he been told that incest requires consanguinity, he would have been relieved. He would certainly not have desisted from his actions. The "smuggler" in *Stephens v. Abrahams* is not guilty of attempted smuggling because he was not intending to smuggle. He merely thought he was smuggling. Had he been told that the items he was importing weren't dutiable, he would have been relieved. He would certainly not have abstained from importing them. The "killer" in *People v. Dlugash* is not guilty of attempting murder, because he was not intending to kill the already-dead man. He merely thought he was killing him. Had he been told that he was shooting a corpse, he would have been relieved. He would certainly not have avoided shooting it. The "fence" in *People v. Jaffe* is not guilty of attempting to buy stolen goods because he was not intending to buy stolen goods. He merely thought he was buying stolen goods. Had he been told that the goods were not stolen, he would have been relieved. He would certainly not have eschewed buying them.

What now of this case? Was the defendant intending to export an authentic Decameron? Or was he merely thinking he was exporting an authentic Decameron? That depends: Had he been told that the Decameron was fake, would he have cared? Would he have changed his course of conduct? Would he not have exported it? The defendant will, of course, argue that although he thought the painting was a genuine Decameron, that was not the reason he wanted to export it. He will argue that he liked the painting for its artistic merits, not its provenance, and that he would still have wanted to take it to Cuernavaca, even if it was a forgery. That's a tough argument to reckon with.

The record indicates that the defendant liked to keep his most exclusive and prized possessions in his Cuernavaca gallery. It also indicates that the defendant did not collect art as an investment. Very few paintings he acquired he ever resold. He collected them purely and simply for the aesthetic pleasure they afforded. Asking whether the defendant would have tried to export a forged Decameron to Cuernavaca amounts to asking whether his aesthetic enjoyment of the painting would have been diminished by his discovery that it was a fake? Should it have been? Is it rational to enjoy a painting as long as you think it is a Decameron and on learning it is a mere Flammarion-imitating-Decameron cease to do so?

Some decades ago it was discovered that a widely hailed Vermeer depicting *Christ and the Disciples at Emmaus*, exhibited for many years at Rotterdam's Boymans Museum, was a forgery by a twentieth-century painter named van Meegeren. Hundreds of thousands of visitors, many of them connoisseurs and critics, had enjoyed the painting. When the fraud was discovered, the picture was immediately removed from view. Was that rational? The philosopher Alfred Lessing argues that it wasn't:

> What is the difference between a genuine Vermeer and a van Meegeren forgery? It is of little use to maintain that one need but look to see the difference. The fact that *The Disciples* is a forgery (if indeed it is) cannot, so to speak, be read off from its surface, but can finally be proved or disproved only by means of extensive scientific investigations and analyses. Nor are the results of such scientific investigations of any help in answering our question, since they deal exclusively with nonaesthetic elements of the picture, such as its chemical composition, its hardness, its crackle, and so on. . . .
>
> The plain fact is that aesthetically it makes no difference whether a work of art is authentic or a forgery, and, instead of being embarassed at having praised a forgery, critics should have the courage of their convictions and take pride in having praised a work of beauty. . . .

The fact that a work of art is a forgery is an item of information about it on a level with such information as the age of the artist when he created it, the political situation in the time and place of its creation, the price it originally fetched, the kind of materials used in it, the stylistic influences discernible in it, the psychological state of the artist, his purpose in painting it, and so on. All such information belongs to areas of interest peripheral at best to the work of art as aesthetic object, areas such as biography, history of art, sociology, and psychology. I do not deny that such areas of interest may be important and that their study may even help us become better art appreciators. But I do deny that the information which they provide is of the essence of the work of art or of the aesthetic experience which it engenders.

It would be merely foolish to assert that it is of no interest whatever to know that *The Disciples* is a forgery. But to the man who has never heard of either Vermeer or van Meegeren and who stands in front of the *Disciples* admiring it, it can make no difference whether he is told that it is a seventeenth-century Vermeer or a twentieth-century van Meegeren in the style of Vermeer. And when some deny this and argue vehemently that, indeed, it does make a great deal of difference, they are only admitting that *they* do know something about Vermeer and van Meegeren and the history of art and the value and reputation of certain masters. They are only admitting that *they* do not judge a work of art on purely aesthetic grounds but also take into account when it was created, by whom, and how great a reputation it or its creator has.[10]

Is Lessing right to suggest that we are being snobbish and irrational if we permit our pleasure in a painting to be decisively influenced by its identity? I will offer two examples to show that he is not. (To be sure, a bit of irrational self-suggestion is involved. The art critic takes to a famous signature like many a patient to a placebo. He will find virtues in the painting that really aren't there. This doesn't prove that all virtues in all paintings are the invention of the art critics, just as the reaction of the patient doesn't prove that the real medicine is superfluous. For unlike the forgery and the placebo, the real painting and the real medicine do their job without suggestion—which is why the medicine works for many not susceptible to the placebo's suggestive power.)

My first example is the plot of a film made some time ago by the American director Martin Ritt, written by Walter Bernstein and starring Woody Allen. It was called *The Front*. The story takes place sometime in the 1950s. Howard Prince, a man in his late twenties or early thirties, works as a cashier in a diner. He is a bright college dropout and sometime bum. One day Al Miller, a childhood pal who has become a well-known TV scriptwriter, drops in. The man is depressed. He had been ordered to appear before the House Committee on Un-American Activities, had taken the Fifth Amendment, and had been blacklisted as a result. On seeing Howard he hits upon a ruse for salvaging something of his dwindling livelihood. He proposes that Howard (Woody Allen) submit his manuscripts for him, representing himself to be their author. In return, he promises Howard 10 percent of the proceeds. Howard is delighted. He is pleased to help. Besides he likes the adventure, the money, and the glamor of holding himself up as a television scriptwriter. The first, second, and third scripts are accepted without much questioning and with much acclaim. But the charade doesn't always go smoothly. Howard is not very well read and therefore hard-pressed to make conversation on literary subjects. Nor is he much good at explaining and "selling" his own scripts. Finally, disaster threatens when the director asks him to rewrite a scene on the spot. Howard finesses all of these obstacles, and so successful is the scheme that several more blacklisted authors are brought in to take advantage of Howard's ability as a front. Howard Prince soon becomes known as one of the most prolific TV scriptwriters around.

On the set Howard meets a young directorial assistant named Florence Barret, a tall, pretty, young woman with long, brunette hair and soulful eyes. Florence is involved with a stockbroker but cannot resist the charms of this outwardly rather clumsy but yet so clever and creative writer. She is a friendly, warmhearted, open-minded person, but it is clear that Howard Prince would not have had a chance with her but for his new persona—but for his reputation as an immensely talented, prolific new writer.

Months later Howard confesses his real identity to Florence. She is shocked and angry, she feels duped, and she wonders whether she really knows him. But she doesn't break with Howard. As things stand when the movie ends the two are likely to be married soon.

Why does Florence love Howard? He doesn't have the attributes she was looking for in a man. He only seemed, at some point, to have those attributes. Why does she not discard him when she discovers he doesn't? Because she has grown to love him. But why has she grown to love him? Because of attributes he doesn't have. In other words, she continues to love him for no other reason than that he is identical with the person she loved in the past. Even if a man came along who genuinely epitomized the attributes she had been looking for in a man, she would not abandon Howard for him. Do we consider her snobbish or irrational for placing such emphasis not on Howard's real attributes but the fact that he happens to be identical with someone she loved in the past? Not in the least. We might consider her snobbish if she did otherwise. Identity then is a crucial concern not only to the snob.

Evidently it doesn't much matter that the person we love possess certain attributes making him suitable for loving, but only that he be identical with a person we once considered suitable for such loving.

My second example: ABC corporation, a car-manufacturing company, is being prosecuted for negligent homicide. One of its buses has caused the death of thirty school children. The bus model, the state's attorney argues, was thrown on the market quite recklessly with only a modicum of testing. As a result, its tendency to explode readily after a head-on collision with another vehicle was never discovered and corrected. Before the indictment is officially announced, the company is reorganized top to bottom. Almost all of the management and personnel involved in the production of the fatal model

are fired. Two-thirds of the board of directors, the real culprits, are tossed out. The fired and dismissed managers, employees, and board members coalesce into a new corporation of their own, called the XYZ company and also begin to produce cars. Which of the two companies will be liable for the misdeeds of the ABC corporation? Why, clearly the ABC corporation. Evidently, we don't punish the entity because we think it particularly deserving a punishment, but because it happens to be identical with an entity which sometime in the past was particularly deserving of punishment.

Why then should we only admire a Decameron painting for the aesthetic qualities it now possesses rather than because it is identical with the work of a man whose work we have come to admire? I don't think there is anything snobbish about such an attitude. A man is not irrational or unreasonable for behaving in this fashion. And I don't feel we are imputing any irrational, unreasonable or implausible trait to Mr. Omeira when we assume that he cared very much that his picture be a real Decameron rather than merely "another pretty picture."

We have established that the defendant really attempted to export an authentic Decameron. But that is not enough to show that he is guilty of a criminal attempt. Before finding him liable for that, we need to answer a second question: Did the defendant really create an unreasonable risk of a crime being committed? Why do I think this question needs to be asked?

Before we convict someone for recklessly or negligently causing harm, we require that his conduct be "unreasonable," that it be the sort a reasonable man would take exception to. In a sense, that introduces an element of luck into the law. The defendant may think that what he is doing creates an unreasonable risk, but if in fact it does not, he will not be convicted. The law does not want to trouble itself with conduct that wouldn't bother a reasonable man.

We should impose the same requirement of unreasonableness before we convict someone for intentionally or knowingly causing harm. Indeed, I think we already do. It's just that, typically, when a defendant intentionally brings about harm, there is no doubt that his conduct was such as would have bothered a reasonable man. If it wouldn't have bothered a reasonable man, the prosecutor usually decides not to press charges. That has the unfortunate effect of making us overlook this potentially important point.

Let me elucidate with an example. Suppose a father wants to kill his five-year-old son. He decides to do so by sending him to summer camp, not, as he did in past years, by train, but by plane instead. He is under the mistaken impression that plane crashes are a lot more frequent than train crashes. He hopes such a crash will occur. And indeed it does. Clearly, the father has intentionally caused his son's death. (He intended his son to die in just the manner he did, and the son wouldn't have died, if he hadn't been on that plane.) But should we convict him of murder? I don't think so. Why? Because the father did nothing a reasonable man would object to: It was not unreasonably risky to send the boy to summer camp by airplane.

Suppose the plane never crashed. But the police learn of the father's evil intentions and charge him with attempted murder. Should we convict him? I don't think so. Why? Because the father did nothing a reasonable man would object to: To repeat, it is not unreasonably risky to send the boy to summer camp by airplane.

The same analysis applies to many cases of impossible attempts. The man who tried to kill his wife by witchcraft was engaging in conduct a reasonable man would not object to. It is not unreasonably risky to stick pins into someone's likeness. Hence the defendant should be acquitted. Whether the slave who tried to kill someone with the harmless Jamestown weed created an unreasonable risk depends on the facts of that case. From what I know of the case, I cannot say. In any event, the decision is one for the jury. Whether Wilson, who tried to forge a check with ludicrous ineptitude, created an unreasonable risk is a close call.

In the present case, did the defendant Omeira create an unreasonable risk that valuable artifacts of the native culture would be exported? Would a reasonable man have objected to his conduct? I believe so. The forgery was near-perfect. A reasonable man would certainly have been worried that what Omeira was trying to export was a real Decameron. Of course, if the forgery were terribly crude, so

crude that any reasonable man could detect it, the answer would be different.

I conclude that the defendant's conviction should be affirmed.

The court being evenly divided, Justice Middlebury will cast the deciding vote. I leave it to the reader to make Justice Middlebury's decision for him. But first read on.

A Possible Solution of the Impossible Problem of Impossible Attempts

The three opinions in the *Omeira* case present two views of impossibility—two, not three, because the third opinion is really a refined version of the first. The first represents the "English" approach, the second the "American" approach. The third is designed to show that the English approach, properly argued, isn't as silly or incoherent as its critics often claim. Which of these perspectives is the right one?

Why do we hesitate to punish impossible attempts? Why do we have such a thing as an "impossibility defense"? It seems to make the defendant's guilt dependent on luck. Everyone who attempts a crime intends to succeed. Some fail because of impossibility. They seem no less evil than those who succeed. Why do we acquit them on grounds of impossibility? To sharpen the issue: We punish attempts to reduce the role of luck in the criminal law—to treat all would-be assassins alike, whether their bullet happens to hit or miss its mark. Why do we reintroduce luck by allowing the impossibility defense?

Some practical reasons have been offered for the impossibility defense: First, it is said that if we allowed the law to punish someone for attempting something he thinks is a crime, even though it isn't (e.g., homosexual intercourse when it isn't forbidden), we would be violating the "principle of legality: *nulla poena sine lege*, "no punishment without law." (Glanville Williams writes: "If the legislature has not seen fit to prohibit the consummated act, a mere approach to consummation should *a fortiori* be guiltless. Any other view would offend against the principle of legality; in effect the law of attempt would be used to manufacture a new crime, when the legislature has left the situation outside the ambit of the law.")[11] Second, it is said that if we allowed the law to punish someone whenever he mistakenly thought he was committing a crime, we would be making it very easy for a malicious prosecutor to convict the innocent. After all, he only needs to fabricate some evidence suggesting that certain innocent conduct in fact served some sinister purpose.

The real reason for the impossibility defense, I believe, is more fundamental, less pragmatic. It is for logical reasons impossible to design a system of criminal law that doesn't have some kind of impossibility defense. To be sure, one can give the defense a broad or a narrow scope, but one cannot wipe it out. It is an inevitable by-product of the inherent vagueness of rules.

Why are rules inherently vague? They are vague because all of language is vague. Language is vague because it rests on human perception and human perception is of limited acuity. The word "red" is vague because we can't distinguish close shades of color. There is a substantial range of colors in the color spectrum of whose redness we are unsure. It might seem that we could eliminate this vagueness by using scientific instruments with potentially unlimited perceptual acuity, but a human has to read those instruments. The point is neatly made by the philosopher Michael Polanyi:

> The award of the winner's place in a horse race in England used to be a highly skilled performance entrusted to the stewards of the Jockey Club, until the advent of the photofinish camera which seemed to render the decision altogether obvious. However, some years ago, the late A. M. Turing showed me the print of a photo finish where one horse's nose is seen a fraction of an inch ahead of another's, but the second horse's nose extends forward by six inches or so well ahead of that of its rival by virtue of the projection of a thick thread of saliva. Since such a situation was not foreseen by the rules, the case had to be referred to the stewards and the award made on the grounds of their personal judgment. Turing gave me this as an example for the ultimate vagueness of even the most objective methods of observation.[12]

How does vagueness lead to the impossibility defense? Vagueness means that for any rule there are numerous cases in which the applicability of the rule is uncertain. Now suppose we wanted to implant in the criminal law an "anti-impossibility" rule, a rule designed to eradicate the impossibility defense. Such a rule would have to say something like this: Whenever the defendant is certain that he is committing a crime, rightly or wrongly, he is at least guilty of a criminal attempt. This anti-impossibility rule is itself vague. There are cases in which its applicability is uncertain. Consider such a case. The defendant is uncertain whether, under the anti-impossibility rule, he is committing a crime. Since he is not certain that he is committing a crime, under the rule he is not committing a crime. But that contradicts the original assumption that it is uncertain whether he is committing a crime. Nor can the rule be rewritten to avoid this difficulty. You might think that adding a provision stating that the rule should not be applied to itself, might resolve the problem. But it doesn't, because that provision too is inherently vague. What this means is that an anti-impossibility rule, if rigorously applied, is self-contradictory.

The argument is rather analogous to that used by Bertrand Russell to show that the notion of certain sets is conceptually incoherent. He asked us to imagine the set of all sets that don't have themselves as a member. It seems like a perfectly coherent notion, at first. The set would comprise most sets we are familiar with, like the set of numbers and the set of desks, and would exclude certain others, like the set of mathematical objects. But would the set have itself as a member? If it does, then it doesn't. If it doesn't, then it does. The idea of such a set turns out to be self-contradictory.

Interestingly, there is a principle related to the impossibility defense which can be rationalized in an analogous manner, the principle that ignorance of the law is no defense. The principle is usually justified by saying that permitting ignorance to be a defense would encourage willful ignorance of the law. But again the reason lies deeper. Ignorance of the law is no defense because we couldn't draft a rule that would always make it a defense. Suppose we had a rule that said: When a person is uncertain whether something is illegal, he is innocent of any crime. This rule, too, is unavoidably vague. There are cases in which its applicability is uncertain. Consider such a case. The defendant thinks that he may or may not be committing a crime. Thus, according to the rule, he is innocent. But that contradicts the assumption that it is uncertain whether the rule applies. What this means is that an "ignorance rule," if rigorously applied, is self-contradictory.

So the impossibility defense cannot be rooted out. As noted, however, it can be given a small or a large role to play. Which of these one prefers depends on what role one thinks luck should play in the law of attempt.

The American approach assigns luck a small role. It takes its cue from the principle that ignorance of the law is no defense. Whether a defendant who doesn't think he is doing anything wrong has violated the law depends on whether he was lucky enough to be correct. The American approach assigns luck a similar role in the law of attempt. Whether a defendant who thinks he is doing something wrong has violated the law should depend on whether he is lucky enough to be incorrect.

The English approach assigns luck a larger role. It takes its cue from negligence law. Whether a defendant who thinks he has done something negligent has violated the law depends on whether he was unlucky enough, first, actually to have caused some harm and, second, actually to have created an unreasonable risk. The English approach thinks luck should play a similar role in the law of attempt. To begin with, in cases other than attempts, in the narrowest truest sense, it would impose no liability except for the completed crime. Even in genuine attempts, it would impose no liability unless an unreasonable risk was created.

Which approach is right? Neither strikes me as wrong. I think both are legitimate. The choice between them belongs to Justice Middlebury.

Endnotes

[1] *Regina v. Collins*, 9 Cox C.C. 497, 498 (1864).

[2] Stephens, *Digest of Criminal Law*, 5th ed. (1894), art. 50, quoted in *Haughton v. Smith* [1975] A.C. 476, 491.

[3] *Stephens v. Abrahams*, 27 V.L.R. 753, 768 (1902).

[4] *State v. Wilson*, 38 So. 46 (Mississippi, 1905).

[5] *People v. Dlugash*, 363 N.E. 2d 1155, 1157 (Ct. of App. of N.Y., 1977).

[6] *Haughton v. Smith*, [1975] A.C. 500.

[7] *People v. Jaffe*, 78 N.E. 169–70 (N.Y. Ct. of App., 1906).

[8] *State v. Clarissa*, 11 Ala. 57, 60 (Ala., 1847).

[9] Invented case.

[10] Alfred Lessing, "What Is Wrong with a Forgery," in D. Dutton, ed., *The Forger's Art* (Berkeley: University of California Press, 1983), 58–59, 62–64.

[11] Glanville Williams, *Criminal Law: The General Part* (London: Stevens & Sons, 1961), 633–34.

[12] Michael Polanyi, *Personal Knowledge* (Chicago: University of Chicago Press, 1962), p. 20 n.l.

Study Questions

1. How does Fletcher define the "traditional" and "modern" approaches to the theory of crimes?

2. What is Fletcher's response to the arguments of the modernist?

3. Why, according to the court in *Dlugash*, can't Dlugash be convicted of murder?

4. What evidence convinced the court that Dlugash did believe Geller was alive at the time Dlugash fired his shots?

5. *Hyam v. Director of Public Prosecutions* involved a British woman who was charged with murder. Hyam went to the apartment of her former lover, stuffed gasoline-soaked newspapers through a mail slot in the door, and ignited them. A fire resulted, in which two children inside the apartment died. Hyam testified that she had intended only to scare off a woman who had taken up with Hyam's ex-boyfriend, and that she had no idea that a fire would result or that any children were inside the apartment. To be guilty of murder, Hyam had to have acted with the "intent to kill." Was that her intention? How would you decide that question? More generally, do people intend only the things that they have immediately in mind (e.g., scaring off the new girlfriend)? What about the means one uses and the ultimate consequences of one's acts? If I act through means that lead to consequences I did not foresee (even though others might have), did I "intend" those consequences?

6. Mildred Pruner, a sixty-seven-year-old woman, was robbed at gunpoint. When Pruner appeared to testify at the trail of her alleged assailant, she became so distraught at describing the assault that she suffered a heart attack on the witness stand and died on the floor of the courtroom. The state's chief medical examiner determined that Pruner was literally "scared to death." The court subsequently ruled Pruner's death a homicide. Should the defendant be held responsible for the witness's death? Did he perform an "act" of killing her? Is some kind of strict criminal liability being imposed here?

7. Philosopher David Lewis has argued that punishing (unsuccessful) attempters less harshly than those who complete the crime is justified as a form of *penal lottery*, subjecting a person to a risk of harm. Attempts to commit a crime, whether or not they succeed, do impose risks (perhaps of death) on their intended victims. So, Lewis proposes, our law appropriately deals with attempters in the same way, exposing *them* to a risk of greater punishment (perhaps even death): the risk that they may hit the target, rather than miss, and wind up in the electric chair rather than a jail cell. Lewis proposes that we make the element of chance operating in the law of attempt more explicit and overt by instituting a penal lottery in which those convicted of attempt draw lots, the loser perhaps being executed. The worse the crime you attempt, the worse the odds for you. [See Lewis, "The Punishment that Leaves Something to Chance," *Philosophy and Public Affairs*, Vol. 18 (1989), pp. 53–67.] Is a penal lottery unfair or unjust? If so, how? Is it fair to subject all attempters, successful or not, to a risk of death? Does it matter that we subject them *equally* to such a risk of death? If people's lives are affected by chance in a whole variety of other ways (which they indisputably are), why not in this way?

8. Victor is unhappily married to Esmeralda. In fact, Victor so despises his wife that he has on more than one occasion seriously thought of killing her. Victor was raised on a small island in the Caribbean and, as a young boy, was initiated into the black-magic cults of the native peoples. Victor still retains deep beliefs in the power of voodoo magic. One day, when he feels he can stand his wife no longer, Victor retires to his secret workshop, where he has over the years meticulously collected the accoutrements of the black arts. Carefully he prepares a tiny, doll-like replica of the despised Esmeralda. When at last the doll is finished, Victor takes a deep breath and, with nervous fingers and a look of hatred, viciously and repeatedly stabs the doll with "sacred" needles. Exhausted by his deed, Victor collapses. When he awakens, he is overcome with remorse and disgust at what he has done. He promptly leaves his workshop, marches to the local police station, and turns himself in, believing with all sincerity that he has murdered his wife. Question: Is Victor guilty of attempted murder? Why not? Consider the language of the Model Penal Code, section 5.01:

(1) *Definition of Attempt.* A person is guilty of an attempt to commit a crime if, acting with the kind of culpability otherwise required for commission of the crime, he:

(a) purposely engages in conduct which would constitute the crime if the attendant circumstances were as he believes them to be; or

(b) when causing a particular result is an element of the crime, does or omits to do anything with the purpose of causing or with the belief that it will cause such result without further conduct on his part; or

(c) purposely does or omits to do anything which, under the circumstances as he believes them to be, is an act or omission constituting a substantial step in a course of conduct planned to culminate in his commission of the crime.

Is Victor convictable of attempt under this language? If so, does this make sense?

B. *Justification and Excuse*

"*It Wasn't Really My Fault*"

Theodore Kaczynski, Robert Alton Harris, Jeffrey Dahmer, Lyle and Erik Menendez. Each of these defendants, central figures in some of the most highly publicized and notorious criminal trials of the last decade, enraged many by seeking, to one degree or another, to *excuse* their violent conduct.

In everyday life, most of us are willing to excuse a friend who arrives late for an important meeting or a student who turns in a late paper, but only if the excuse is reasonable under the circumstances (the teacher gets to decide what's reasonable!). The law is willing to listen to excuses, too. But under what circumstances and for what reasons should it do so? This is the central question examined in this section.

The Cases of Theodore Kaczynski and Robert Harris

Theodore Kacznyski, the confessed "Unabomber," pled guilty in January 1998 to thirteen charges, including murder. Kaczynski was overwhelmingly implicated in a string of attacks dating back to the 1970s, which resulted in three deaths and twenty-nine injuries. Excerpts from his own journals revealed that Kaczynski intended "to start killing people" and referred to his mail bombs as "experiments." Of one of the attacks, Kaczynski's journal entry reported that his experiment was a "success at last" and that he was "producing good results."

Aided by his brother, authorities found Kaczynski living in a rustic, one-room cabin in a remote part of Montana. Fearful that they would seek to portray him as "sick," Kaczynski fought with his court-appointed lawyers and even threatened to act in his own defense. A key issue confronting the judge and the lawyers in the case turned on Kaczynski's mental state. Defense experts argued that Kaczynski was a paranoid schizophrenic who had lived for years as a hermit; had no electricity, phone, or running water; and ate squirrel and porcupine roasted over a fire. The lawyers cited Kaczynksi's erratic behavior concerning his own case and how it should be handled, as well as an apparent suicide attempt while in police custody. The judge in the case, however, initially found the former math professor to be lucid, calm, and intelligent, with a clear understanding of the legal issues at stake in his own case.

Kaczynski's case presented the court with several questions: Does he suffer from mental illness? Did he suffer from mental illness at the time of the crimes? Were his intentions, although clearly apparent from his diaries, nonetheless the product of mental disease?

Robert Alton Harris was convicted of brutally murdering two teenage boys (after which he casually ate the remainder of their lunches). Harris had a ghastly childhood. His father was an abusive alcoholic who beat his wife and children and sexually molested his daughters. Harris was born prematurely after the father kicked Harris's mother in the stomach. Harris was repeatedly kicked, hit, and emotionally abused. He was slated for execution in California's gas chamber when the horror of his upbringing was used in making a plea for clemency to then governor Pete Wilson. Wilson denied the clemency request with these words:

> It is argued on his behalf that Robert Harris must be judged to be in effect a child who cannot be held accountable under California law. . . . Experts contend that Harris has

suffered organic brain damage both as a result of his mother's abuse of alcohol during pregnancy and as a result of trauma inflicted by his parents, mostly by an especially vicious father. . . . The application for clemency adequately demonstrates that Mr. Harris' childhood was a living nightmare. He suffered monstrous child abuse that would have a brutalizing effect on him. . . . But victimized though he may have been, Harris was not deprived of the capacity to premeditate, to plan or to understand the consequences of his actions. . . . For the protection of its most vulnerable members, society must hold accountable and hold to a minimum level of personal responsibility Robert Harris and all members of society— excepting only those who have been clearly shown to lack the capacity to meet that minimum level of responsibility. . . . Harris' own conduct [includes] clear and chilling evidence of his capacity to think, to conceive a plan, to understand the consequences of his actions, to dissemble and deceive and destroy evidence to avoid apprehension and punishment. . . . He was capable of planning to do wrong, and taking precautions to conceal his wrongdoing. . . . Robert Harris, the child, had no choice. He was a victim of serious and inexcusable abuse. Robert Harris, the man, did have a choice. He chose to take a life, two lives. . . . The decision of the jury was correct. . . . Clemency is denied.

Excuse and Justification

The Kaczynski and Harris cases illustrate ways in which the law of excuse and justification involve serious questions concerning a defendant's responsibility for his or her actions. Suppose that I am charged with the robbery of an elderly man in a city park. Recognized defenses or legitimate excuses under the law to such a charge would be that I was *entrapped* into committing the crime, a police officer having planted the idea of it in my mind, an idea to which I was not otherwise predisposed; I was *coerced* into the robbery through a threat of death or

serious bodily harm; I was a *minor* under the age of seven. *In Richardson v. U.S.*,[1] the defendant was charged with robbery for having stopped a man named Snowden and removing $98 from his (Snowden's) wallet. On appeal of his conviction, Richardson told that Snowden owed him (Richardson) a long-standing gambling debt, amounting to $270, which Richardson had been seeking to collect for some time. Richardson's conviction was reversed on the grounds that he had made an honest mistake: he thought that, as a result of the outstanding debt, the money in Snowden's wallet was his (Richardson's) property. To engage in robbery, one must act with the intent (purpose) to take the property of another; since Richardson thought the property belonged to him, his mistake negated the *mens rea* required for the offense. Mistakes can excuse.

A distinction long made in the criminal law is the distinction between conditions or circumstances *excusing* a defendant's conduct and those serving as *a justification* for that conduct. In both cases, the defendant admits to causing a result forbidden by law but argues nonetheless that she should not be punished. The defendant can claim justification in situations in which she did something the law forbids under circumstances that did no harm to society but actually advanced a social interest in a way society wishes to encourage. The actor can claim excuse when she did cause harm to society but did so under conditions that mark her as less deserving of punishment. As noted above, coercion or duress are traditionally regarded as excuses; acting in self-defense is often classified as a justification, although, as the readings in this section explore, this is not a classification without critics.

The Proliferation of Excuses

The last twenty years have seen a dramatic expansion in both the kinds of excuses and justifications offered by criminal defendants and their successful deployment in high-profile cases. Among the recent entrants is the so-called "abuse excuse." Lyle and Erik Menendez, accused in the shotgun slayings of their wealthy parents, won a deadlocked

---

[1] 403 F. 2d 574 (1968).

jury and a mistrial with their claim of excuse that the killings were fear-induced, brought on by years of sexual abuse and molestation on the part of their father. Lorena Bobbit, charged with mutilating her husband's genitals while he slept, insisted that her marriage was an abusive "reign of terror" that provoked her to act in self-defense. Recent cases invoking other excuses include the following: (1) In May 1979, while working at a pub in England, the defendant, a woman, got into a fight with a barmaid and stabbed her to death. Charged with murder, her record indicated a history of uncontrolled behavior resulting in nearly thirty convictions in the preceding ten years. It was noticed that her uncontrollable disruptive behavior followed a definite monthly pattern. Doctors later diagnosed her condition as "premenstrual syndrome" [PMS].[2] (2) In 1984 a defendant was charged with attempted bank robbery and larceny. In defense, he pled insanity in the form of "pathological gambling disorder."[3] (3) Ann Green was charged with murder in the suffocation deaths of her two infants. She testified that she had seen hands she did not recognize holding pillows over the infants' faces. In 1989 a jury found Ms. Green "not responsible" for the deaths on the grounds that she suffered from "postpartum psychosis." (4) In 1989 Terrence Frank successfully avoided a conviction for first-degree murder in the shooting deaths of two people on the Navajo reservation in Arizona. Mr. Frank's attorney convinced the jury that his client was temporarily insane at the time of the killing as a result of brain damage he had sustained from childhood exposure to uranium radiation leaking from mines surrounding his home. Frank's father and grandfather had both died from radiation-induced cancer, and an abnormally high rate of birth defects was recorded in the area. (Frank was convicted of second-degree, unpremeditated murder.)[4] (5) In April 1994, a Texas jury returned no verdict against a defendant accused of shooting two unarmed men who had pur-

portedly threatened him. The defense argued that "urban survival syndrome," created by life on the inner-city streets, led to the shooting. As yet, few of these excuses have received widespread acceptance. Which, if any, should be acknowledged?

Can Everything Be Excused?

Legal philosopher Michael Corrado opens this section with a selection that explores the limits of the law's recognition of excuses. Corrado looks at this problem: If the causes of someone's conduct can be traced to things in a person's background or makeup that are in some sense outside that person's control and thus not his or her "fault," does that mean that he or she should be excused? Corrado is particularly concerned with the implications of the philosophical theory that all human choice and conduct are determined by antecedent causes over which none of us has any power. If the practice of excusing those who break the law rests on an acknowledgment of this theory, how can we avoid the conclusion that everyone should be excused for everything? Corrado looks at several ways of meeting the challenge to retain the practice of excusing consistent with retaining as well the practice of subjecting wrongdoers to punishment.

Battered-Woman's Defense

One excuse that has increasingly been recognized by many jurisdictions involves the tragic spread of domestic violence and spousal abuse. "Battered-woman's syndrome" has been invoked by female defendants, victims of repeated physical and emotional abuse, who injure or kill their abusers. Women exhibiting the syndrome frequently lack self-esteem. They want to leave abusive relationships but feel they cannot, often because they are unable to support themselves and fear that their abusers will track them down and beat them worse than before should they attempt to leave. Battered-woman's syndrome is often treated as a justification, analogous to self-defense. But as Cathryn Jo Rosen points out in her essay, this choice raises some problems.

---

[2] See D. Brahams, "Premenstrual Syndrome: A Disease of the Mind." *The Lancet*, Vol. 11 (Nov. 28, 1981), pp. 1238–1240.

[3] *U.S. v. Gould* 741 F. 2d 45 (4th Cir. 1984).

[4] See "'Toxin Defense' Successful," *The National Law Journal*, May 1, 1989, p. 5.

The exercise of force to repel an attacker in self-defense has traditionally been regarded as a full-fledged justification, rather than an excuse. To defend an immediate threat to your life where no other option exists, the law has said, is the "right " thing to do. (Whether a convincing moral argument can be given to support this position is explored in our readings.) Historically, the use of defensive force has been evaluated in terms of the criteria outlined as follows:

Traditional Criteria for the Use of Defensive Force

1. There must be an imminence of violent attack threatening death or great bodily injury
2. Only the immediate context of the situation may be used to justify self-defense.
3. The force used to repel the attack can be no greater than the attacking force itself.
4. The previous three criteria are to be judged from the standpoint of the objective,"reasonable person."

Taken together, these criteria show that the law of self-defense typically has been conceived by the law on the model of the momentary, face-to-face encounter between armed strangers, where the defendant has a reasonable belief that he is in imminent danger to which he must respond in kind. However, this model often fails to describe the realities of spousal abuse or women's responses to it. Lorena Bobbit claimed she acted in self-defense in mutilating her husband because he had threatened to track her down and rape her if she left him. Yet Mr. Bobbit was asleep when attacked, not brandishing a gun. If an abused woman chooses a moment when she is most likely to prevail over her victimizer, can she still argue that her action was justified? Those who think so maintain that the law must take account of the woman's perspective, and they point to the law of rape as an example of how and why this is to be done.

Feminist theorists such as Susan Estrich[5] have argued that for too long the law's understanding of whether a woman consented to sex was to be as-

sessed in terms of how hard she resisted, how seriously her life was threatened, or how reasonable her belief was that she was in mortal danger. But, say critics of rape law, what counts as resistance or force, what is understood to be a threat, and what is taken to be unreasonable about a belief—all are substantially, if not entirely, *gendered:* they are conceived (in the case of existing law) from a male point of view and reflect distorted images of women and of sexuality.

The widely discussed *Rusk*[6] case from the early 1980s drives home the point. The defendant met his victim at a bar and asked her for a ride home. She agreed. When they arrived, it was late at night in a neighborhood unfamiliar to the woman. The defendant asked her up to his apartment; she refused. He asked again. After her second refusal, he reached over and took her car keys. She accompanied him upstairs, where he pulled her by the arms onto the bed and began to undress her. Crying, she testified "I was really scared, because I can't describe, you know, what was said. It was more the look in his eyes . . . and I said 'If I do what you want, will you let me go without killing me?' . . . He said yes and I proceeded to do what he wanted me to."[7] Although ultimately his conviction was sustained, many of the judges hearing this case found, in the words of one judge, "no conduct by the defendant reasonably calculated to make the victim so fearful that she should fail to resist."[8] No force was employed; the victim's alleged fear sprang from nothing of substance. In this view, the defendant committed not rape but a seduction; his belief that she "went

---

[5] See Susan Estrich, *Real Rape* (Cambridge: Harvard University Press; 1987).

[6] 289 Md. 230, 424 A. 2d 720 (1981).

[7] *Ibid.*, p. 722.

[8] *Ibid.*, p. 733 (Cole, J., dissenting). The dissent further observes:

She also testified that she was afraid of 'the way he looked,' and afraid of his statement, 'come on up, come on up.' But what can the majority conclude from this statement coupled with a 'look' that remained undescribed? There is no evidence whatsoever to suggest that this was anything other than a pattern of conduct consistent with the ordinary seduction of a female acquaintance who at first suggests her disinclination. (*Ibid.*, p. 733.)

The majority cites the lower court, finding that "'the way he looked' fails utterly to support the fear required by [law]." (*Ibid,* p. 724.)

along with it" was not unreasonable from *his* point of view. Requiring that juries examine a similar series of events from the standpoint of the *reasonable woman,* however, might well lead to very different results.

Asking juries to consider what a reasonable woman would do when faced with an assailant like Rusk or an abusive husband will, in the view of some, introduce a much-needed corrective into the criminal law. With regard to the battered-woman's defense, however, Cathryn Jo Rosen is not fully convinced. Rosen focuses on this question: Will looking only at the subjective perspective of the female victim result in justifying any killing she believes necessary to defend herself? Neither the battered-woman's defense nor self-defense more generally, Rosen argues, should be regarded as justification for what would otherwise be criminal conduct. Rosen shows how her concerns regarding the battered-woman's defense connect with deeper questions about how to justify any form of self-defense in the law. She concludes that evidence of spousal abuse should be cautiously considered, and then only as an excuse, not a justification.

Cultural Defenses

Recent changes in the law of rape and sexual harassment and the introduction of the battered-woman's defense stem from the awareness that women experience the world, and especially sexuality, in ways different from men. In the same fashion but on a much broader scale, peoples of differing cultures may regard as excusable, or even fully justified, conduct proscribed by the criminal law.

In 1997 a California court, sentenced a Korean missionary, Sung Soo Choi, to involuntary manslaughter in the death of a woman upon whom Sung had performed an exorcism ritual. Sung believed the woman to be possessed by demons that made her disobedient to her husband. Sung and the husband agreed that the woman should be treated with a ritual combining prayer and a laying on of hands. The victim was discovered to have suffered sixteen broken ribs, deep bruises, and internal injuries resulting from the five-hour ritual. In 1985 a woman of Japanese ancestry walked into the ocean near Santa Monica, California, with her two children after learning that her husband was having an affair. She survived, but the children drowned. Experts testified at trial that the woman's actions were consistent with the traditional practice of *oyako-shinju,* or parent–child suicide, for which she would be charged with involuntary manslaughter in Japan today. The first-degree murder charge initially filed against her was dropped, and she was allowed to plead guilty to voluntary manslaughter. She received five years' probation with psychiatric treatment.[9] A Yoruban woman who immigrated to England from Nigeria was arrested after she scarred her child's face with a razor to initiate the child into their tribe. She argued in her defense that it would be abuse *not* to practice this ritual.[10] A Hmong man, tried by California for kidnapping and rape after abducting a woman at a college campus, defended himself by arguing that in Hmong culture, *zij poj niam,* or "marriage by bride-capture," was considered an acceptable way of obtaining a bride.[11]

Should a person's cultural background be invocable to show that he or she did not have the *mens rea* for a crime with which he or she is charged? Should the introduction of evidence bearing on a defendant's culture be permitted as an excusing condition in mitigation of punishment?

The Insanity Plea

As the case of Theodore Kaczynski, the admitted Unabomber, reveals, no claim of excuse has provoked such contentious debate as the claim that a defendant must be acquitted, even for a wrongdoing he plainly committed, because at the time of the offense he was *insane.*

Lorena Bobbit's jury acquitted her on grounds of temporary insanity, finding that an "irresistible impulse" provoked her to attack her husband; yet in Wisconsin, a jury refused to accept an insanity

---

[9] See "'Cultural' Defenses Draw Fire," *The National Law Journal,* April 17, 1989, pp. 3, 28.

[10] See "Judges Debate Cultural Defense," *American Bar Association Journal,* December 1992, p. 28.

[11] See "Cultural Defense—A Legal Tactic," *L.A. Times,* 15 July 1988, pt. I, p. 1.

plea by Jeffrey Dahmer, accused (and eventually convicted) of killing, dismembering, and even eating the body parts of fifteen young men and boys. To understand these results, we conclude this section with a discussion of two prominent issues: How is "insanity" to be understood, and why should it be an excuse at all? The Cameron case serves as a point of departure for these questions.

The facts of Marie Cameron's gruesome murder need no elaboration. Marie's stepson, Gary, was arrested and charged with the crime. At trial he raised the defense that he was insane at the time of the murder, and evidence was introduced to show he was a "paranoid schizophrenic." As is always the case in a criminal proceeding before a jury, the closing arguments of the prosecution and the defense are followed by the phase of the trial in which the judge "instructs" the jury, that is, informs the jury of the rules of the law that they must apply to their determination of the facts of the case. In *Cameron,* the trial judge instructed the jury regarding the rules governing the defense of insanity, as these rules were then structured by the law of Washington state. Applying the judge's instructions, the jury convicted Cameron. The appellate court affirmed the conviction. Cameron appealed to the Supreme Court of Washington, alleging that the instructions given to the jury incorrectly stated the "law" governing the insanity plea. Before we delve more deeply into the issues raised by Cameron's appeal, we must understand something of the broader history of the insanity defense and the various attempts to fashion and define an appropriate test for insanity.

Insanity is a legal rather than a medical term, and the efforts to clarify its meaning have been many and varied. The modern law of insanity begins with the famed *M'Naghten case,* decided by the British House of Lords in 1843. Daniel M'Naghten had been charged with shooting and killing Edward Drummond, whom M'Naghten mistakenly believed to be the prime minister of England, Sir Robert Peel. M'Naghten pled not guilty, his lawyer insisting that M'Naghten suffered from delusions that undermined his perception of right and wrong. Upon considering the matter, the House of Lords articulated what came to be called the *M'Naghten Rule,* as intended to govern pleas of insanity. They held that:

in all cases a man is presumed to be sane and to possess sufficient degree of reason to be responsible for his crimes, until the contrary be proved to the juror's satisfaction; and to establish a defense on the grounds of insanity it must be clearly proved that, at the time of committing the act, the party accused was laboring from such a defect of reason, from a disease of the mind, as not to know the nature and quality of the act he was doing; or, if he did know it, that he did not know he was doing what was wrong.[12]

The substance of the M'Naghten Rule can be reduced to four elements: (1) defect of reason; (2) disease of the mind; (3) failure to know the nature and quality of one's act; and (4) failure to know that the act was wrong. As the rule is generally interpreted, elements 1 and 2 are necessary for a determination of insanity; either 3 or 4, together with 1 and 2, is sufficient. Typically, the "mental disease" spoken of in 2 must be a comparatively permanent condition, including such things as congenital defects and traumatic injury. There are at least two divergent interpretations of "know" as it is employed in 3 and 4. One view holds that "know" refers only to formal cognition or intellectual awareness (as in "I know that two plus two equals four"); the other holds that "know" is to be understood in a wider sense to mean that one appreciates the total setting (including the feelings and emotions of oneself and others) in which one's actions take place, and that one can evaluate the impact of one's actions upon others (as in "He knew that the match would cause a fire and the people would be burned").

The M'Naghten Rule was widely adopted throughout the jurisdictions of the common law world as the appropriate test for legal insanity, and many states, including Washington state at the time of *Cameron,* rely on some variant of it. Yet the M'Naghten Rule has been subjected to severe criticism over the years. Contemporary criminologists and jurists argue that it relies heavily on an outmoded psychology according to which the mental life of a person can be neatly divided into "cognitive," "affective," and "volitional" components. Such a model ignores the complexity of our psychic

---

[12] 8 Eng. Rep. 718 (1843).

lives, the degree to which how we seek to understand the world and what we believe about it both influence and are influenced by our deepest desires, goals, and feelings. Other critics point out that *M'Naghten* stresses only cognitive impairment as relevant to insanity, with the result that the insanity defense often is unavailable to those who are seriously disturbed even though cognitively they may function on a near-normal level. A person suffering from kleptomania, for instance, would be such a case. It was for these reasons that, early on, some jurisdictions sought to supplement *M'Naghten* with an "irresistible impulse" test: One is exempt from criminal liability if one either fits the *M'Naghten* definition or at the time of the offense could not control the urge to act as one did. This ancillary test was not without critics of its own. Is it really possible for a jury to ascertain whether a given "impulse" was irresistible? How can we tell when someone could have resisted if only he or she had tried a little harder? How do we know that he or she *could* have tried harder?

An alternative test for insanity was proposed by federal judge David Bazelon in 1954 in *Durham v. U.S.*[13] Durham was a habitual offender who underwent numerous psychiatric treatments, none of which seemed to be effective. When Durham was arrested and convicted for yet another offense, Judge Bazelon took advantage of Durham's appeal to state a new test: The accused is not criminally responsible if his or her unlawful act was the "product of mental disease or mental defect." The court believed this rule to be superior to those it supplanted because it treated the mind as a functional unit, thus bringing the legal standards up-to-date with developments in modern psychiatry and psychology and allowing experts to present the relevant scientific and medical data to the jury. *Durham* represented a sharp departure from the old tests of criminal insanity; nevertheless, several jurisdictions adopted it. The rule created problems, however, and was ultimately rejected by the U.S. Supreme Court. The most frequent criticism of the rule was that it gave no standards or guidelines to the jury. As a result of its breadth, inordinate weight was given to the testimony of "ex-

perts," whose conflicting testimony often left juries in a state of bewilderment. Is the defendant crazy or not?

The test for insanity proposed by the Model Penal Code is rapidly gaining acceptance as a remedy for the defects of the *M'Naghten, Durham,* and irresistible impulse tests. Section 4.01 of the code provides that "a person is not responsible for criminal conduct if at the time of such conduct as a result of mental disease or defect he lacks substantial capacity either to appreciate the criminality [wrongfulness] of his conduct or to conform his conduct to the requirements of the law."

The central issue in *Cameron* has to do with the applicability of the M'Naghten Rule to the defendant's conduct and, in particular, to the third and fourth elements of the test: Did Cameron understand the nature and quality of his actions? Plainly, he understood in some sense what he was doing and comprehended its implications (why else would one stab a victim more than seventy times?). On the other hand, he may have thought he was killing Satan. Did Cameron know that what he was doing was wrong? The narrow issue in the case centers on the trial court's definition of "wrong," which it took to be knowledge that the act was "contrary to law." Did Cameron realize that what he was doing violated the law? Perhaps. The Supreme Court of Washington reversed Cameron's conviction, holding that one who believes he is acting under a divine command is no less insane because he knows or realizes (in some sense) that murder is against the law.

Should the Insanity Defense Be Abolished?

Some people are outraged that a person such as Cameron should be found "not guilty by reason of insanity." The deliberate and vicious nature of the crime seems to them to demand a guilty verdict. Dissatisfaction with the realities of the insanity defense, together with the obvious difficulty in framing an acceptable and workable test for it, have moved some to condemn the defense as misconceived from the outset and to push for its abolition. The debate over abolition is joined here in the selections by Norval Morris and Sanford Kadish.

---

[13] 214 F. 2d 862 (D.C. Cir. 1954).

Morris defends the abolitionist position. What does this actually amount to, and what are the arguments for it? Under existing law, a plea of insanity is a special defense. This means that it excuses an individual from responsibility for conduct that otherwise satisfies the (*actus reus* and *mens rea*) requirements for a crime. Morris proposes that the special defense of insanity be eliminated. In his view, mental illness would be relevant to a person's guilt or innocence only insofar as it might show that the defendant lacked the specific *mens rea* for the offense with which he or she is charged. An example serves to illustrate Morris's scheme and how it would differ from the current regime: In *People v. Wetmore*,[14] the victim of a burglary returned home after a three-day absence to find the defendant living in his (the victim's) apartment. The defendant, Wetmore, was wearing the victim's clothes and cooking his food. The lock on the door had been broken, and the place was a shambles. Psychiatric examiners found that the homeless Wetmore suffered from the delusion that he "owned" the property and that he was "directed" to the victim's apartment, where he promptly moved in. Wetmore's conviction on burglary charges was reversed, the court finding that Wetmore could not be held accountable for breaking and entering the house of another if he thought it was his own.

Wetmore's mental illness precluded his having the state of mind necessary for the offense with which he was charged. However, mental illness does not always have this effect, and Cameron's case shows us why: In spite of his illness, it is beyond dispute that Cameron acted with the intent and purpose to kill. Under the abolitionist proposal, then, Wetmore is acquitted but Cameron is not. This is the difference between eliminating and retaining the insanity plea as a special defense.

Should the law distinguish in this way between Wetmore and Cameron? Why should the special defense be abolished? As Morris indicates, the principal argument made for eliminating the defense asserts that it is simply unworkable. "Insanity" defies any attempt at a meaningful definition; it confuses judges and juries; and it is very costly. Moreover, Morris alleges, the special defense

is rarely raised and then only in connection with particularly heinous crimes. Morris concludes on a larger theme: The very idea of attempting to draw a bright line between the sick and the bad is misguided because it obscures the reality that social factors and determinants of behavior impair the capacity of people to conform to the law much more severely than insanity ever does.

What are the objections to Morris's proposal? As Kadish claims, the abolition of the special defense of insanity will have the consequence that people like Cameron are convicted. But, one might ask, what is the real difference here? After all, whether or not he is found "guilty," Cameron is not likely simply to "go free." Mentally ill individuals who are acquitted, like Wetmore, frequently are taken into custody again under the procedure of "civil commitment" and subjected to treatment. If they wind up in custody in either case, what is the difference between the law's handling of Wetmore and Cameron? Kadish replies that the difference is this: Criminal conviction and a verdict of guilty, unlike civil commitment, carry with them a *moral stigma;* they represent a judgment that the individual's conduct is evil or wicked, properly deserving of blame and condemnation. This way of understanding a guilty verdict is reflected elsewhere in our law, for instance, in the refusal to permit convicted felons to vote. Yet if people such as Cameron truly are "sick," Kadish reasons, they should not be blamed or condemned in this way. Cameron is not a proper object of that kind of moral response. And all of this is quite independent of whether Cameron should be detained for his and others' safety.

To better appreciate the intuition animating Kadish's position, consider the following: It seems that for many centuries in Europe, from the early Middle Ages through the close of the eighteenth century, animals were routinely tried, convicted, and punished for a variety of "crimes," including eating crops, destroying livestock, and attacking humans.[15] Typical of these animal cases is that of the dog Provetie. (See "Cases for Further Reflection" at the conclusion of this chapter.) On May 5

---

[14] 149 Cal. Rptr. 265 (1978).

[15] For a thorough and entertaining discussion, see E. P. Evans, *The Criminal Prosecution and Capital Punishment of Animals* (London: Faber and Faber, 1987).

1595, Provetie bit the hand of a young child who was carrying a piece of meat. The child died, and Provetie was apprehended, tried, and convicted of murder. In passing sentence, the judge proclaimed that Provetie must be severely punished "as an example to others and more especially to evilly disposed dogs," and in consequence he ordered Provetie to be hanged "at the plain of Gravesteijn . . . where evildoers are customarily punished." (In this case the dog got off easily; other punishments routinely involved torture.)

Various hypotheses have been offered to explain this bizarre chapter of legal history but its relevance for us lies in this: Although many of us might want this dog off the streets, few if any of us would regard the procedure of charging and convicting the dog, condemning it as an evildoer, and hanging it in order to deter other dogs as anything but silly. Most of us would find something peculiarly inappropriate about such treatment of a dog. Such conduct is inappropriate because it reflects a way of regarding dogs that seems simply to be mis-

taken: Dogs are not capable of understanding the requirements of law or good morals, nor are they able to conform their behavior to such standards. Those opposing the abolition of the insanity defense ask us to imagine a case involving a person who, with respect to the law, is in substantially the same position as the dog, that is, someone who is unable either to understand fully its requirements or to conform his or her behavior to them.

Morris concedes that there is something to the claim that conviction in a case such as *Cameron* is inappropriate, but he regards this claim as vague and ill-founded. Every day we punish people whose capacity to conform their behavior to the law is impaired by a variety of factors: parental neglect, social and economic deprivation, and the like. Yet no one thinks, he points out, that we should have a special defense of "growing up in a ghetto."

---

70. *Excuses in the Criminal Law*

Michael L. Corrado

I. *The Problem: Drawing the Line*

To begin with, consider the following argument:

Argument #1

1. The principle of justice that underlies our practice of excusing wrongdoers is this:
   (A.) Someone who, through no fault of her own, could not help breaking the law should not be punished.
2. But persons from a deprived and abusive background may not be able to avoid breaking the law, precisely because of that background.

3. When that is so, the principle of justice that underlies excuses requires that they not be punished for their crimes.

. . .

Peering out from around the edges of this argument is the specter of a possibility that most of us would find unacceptable. What the argument suggests is that the principle of justice that underlies the practice of excusing wrongdoers, if consistently applied, requires us to excuse many of these whom we assume ought to be punished. Indeed, it may be that it requires us to excuse everyone who breaks the law. That is the issue here: How can we prevent principle (A) from leading us to a bizarre and perhaps universal extension of the doctrine of excuse?

Suppose, for example, that Jones is captured by a terrorist group and that (through no fault of her own) she is subjected to some advanced technology, perhaps involving the use of drugs, all of which imbues in her an intense hatred of some local politician. The belief is also forced upon her that only the assassination of that man will save the country from a horrible fate. She is turned loose with a weapon, and she kills him. Shortly afterwards the technology wears off and she "comes to herself." She is stunned by what she has done. She would never have done it "in her right mind." Scientists study the technology used and agree that, yes, it is effective in implanting beliefs and desires against the will of the victim. Should this woman be punished for what she has done? We would agree, I believe, that she was a victim carrying out the wishes of someone else. If the feelings implanted in her were intense enough, it would have been extremely difficult for her to have avoided doing what she did. We would be sympathetic; and it would not be unreasonable to conclude that she ought to be excused for what she has done (if it is proper to say that she has done it at all).

But change the story a bit, and our feelings about it will be different. This time, as before, Jones has an overwhelming hatred of and desire to kill that same politician, and does kill him. The desire and the hatred are precisely those she had in the first example. The difference is in the way Jones came by her hatred and desire. In *this* story Jones (through no fault of her own) came by her feelings through the education provided by years growing up in a ghetto. Perhaps intense frustration found its outlet in her hatred; perhaps she had some more or less realistic foundation for her desire. In any case, they are exactly the same as the feelings she was given in the first example. If Jones should not be punished in the first story, why should she be punished here? Is she not acting, in both stories, upon beliefs and desires that make it difficult to avoid the killing?

Notice that in the first story no one forced her to kill; she was given certain beliefs and desires, and simply turned loose. She then acted upon the beliefs and desires. Is she not acting, in both stories, upon beliefs and desires she is not responsible for? If she should be punished in the second story but not the first, on what grounds? Because of the way in which she acquired the beliefs and desires in each story? But of course acquiring those beliefs and desires was not her doing in either story. What is the morally relevant difference? If there is none, then she should be excused in both cases, or in neither.

Consider, again, the following pair of stories. The same terrorists, instead of imbuing her with overpowering hatred, imbue her (through no fault of her own) with an overwhelming lust for power, and they teach her that killing the politician is the only way to achieve that power. After killing the politician she "comes to herself." She is stunned by what she has done. She had been made over into a power hungry monster, and she has done the unthinkable. Might we not excuse her? She could not help herself. She was a mere puppet of the terrorists.

Change the story once more: Suppose that she comes by the same overwhelming lust for power "naturally." She comes by it by upbringing (which may be a warm and loving upbringing in a family with ample resources), and be genetic disposition perhaps, but certainly through no fault of her own. And suppose that that trait leads her to kill the politician. If we would excuse in the last case, what is the principle in accordance with which we would refuse to excuse in this case? What difference does it make where the traits or feelings come from, so long as they drive her to crime, and are acquired through no fault of her own?

What these last two stories bring to the debate is this: even if you are willing to suppose that anger or hatred nurtured by deprivation and abuse might go some way toward excusing crime, you should be unwilling to excuse those who act out of greed or a lust for power. But how can the case of naturally acquired greed be distinguished from the case of the artificial implantation of greed that went before; and how should that be distinguished from cases involving hatred and anger?

Someone who commits a violent crime has sufficient motivation to commit the crime; if he did not, he would not have committed the crime. If the Joneses in whom terrorists artificially implant sufficient motivation ought to be excused, it must be because of principle (A) above; so why should the other Joneses not be excused on that ground as well? In each of the stories, the difficulty of avoiding the crime was (by hypothesis) exactly the same. And in this way the argument from principle (A) appears to lead to a wide and unacceptable extension of the applicability of excuses.

It would be bad enough if it ended there; that would give us plenty to deal with. But it is even worse than that. To say that someone could have avoided committing a crime entails that he could have done otherwise. What if, as may well be the case, *determinism* is true? What if every event, including every human choice, is caused by prior events? If that is true, then no one who chooses to do something could have chosen to do otherwise. And if that is true, then no one could ever have helped himself, or could have avoided doing what he did.

Does it follow, then, if we start from principle (A) above, that everyone ought to be excused for everything? We could, of course, avoid that conclusion by rejecting principle (A) and by denying that anyone at all ought to be excused. If that is the only alternative, then either we must give up the practice of excusing, along with the principle that appears to lie behind it, or we must give up the practice of punishing criminals. Anyone who thinks that both the institution of punishment and the institution of excuse are worth saving will see this reasoning as a slide into the absurd, and will look for a way to prevent it. But how are we to go about it? Three answers, not entirely independent of one another, are associated with three controversial doctrines that dominate the discussion . . . utilitarianism; compatibilism; and the character theory of excuse.

II. *Utilitarianism*

The utilitarian theory of punishment is well known; but what is a utilitarian theory of excuse? If the utility of punishment is a necessary condition for its justification, then an *absence* of utility would be a sufficient condition for excusing from punishment. Thus we have Bentham's account, according to which excuses are circumstances in which it is useless to punish.

Now the utilitarian has an answer to our argument and the universal extension of excuses that it seems to entail. The utilitarian gives a meaning to "could not help himself" that she hopes will keep us off that slippery slope. The utilitarian takes "He could not help himself" to mean something very much like "He could not have been deterred." And that is why we do not punish in circumstances identified with the excuses. It is useless—a wasted infliction of pain—to punish someone who belongs to a class of individuals who cannot be deterred. What is the point? Put them away if they are dangerous, but don't waste time trying to use them to deter the undeterrable.

Notice that this interpretation purports to explain principle (A) above. Someone who cannot help himself—someone who is insane, for example—may well be undeterrable. (If he is not, then the utilitarian ought not to excuse him.) Someone who cannot help himself because it would be unreasonably difficult for him to do otherwise—someone who acts under duress, for example—may likewise be undeterrable. In both cases the utilitarian would find it pointless to punish. If the utilitarian is right about this, then we never get onto the slippery slope at all. Most people, including those with a rotten social background and those who suffer from overwhelming hatred or overwhelming greed, can be deterred by the threat of punishment.

And determinism does not complicate this picture at all. To say that a person's choices, and therefore his actions, are determined is to say that they are caused by prior events. And the question whether a person can be deterred is just the question whether adding a threat of punishment to those prior events would have changed the outcome. If it would have, then the action in question is deterrable; it could have been avoided; the agent can help himself. The mere fact that he *was not* deterred does not mean that people with a similar make-up, in similar circumstances, cannot be deterred. On the utilitarian view, punishment is aimed at the future; it works by deterring and should be reserved for those cases in which it can deter. If there is a class of people who cannot be deterred, then it is pointless to punish them, and they should be excused.

The fact that someone finds it very *difficult* to comply with the law may mean that he cannot be deterred and therefore should not be punished, but it need not. For it may be that he could have been deterred by increasing the penalty. If he could have been, then perhaps he should not be excused at all. That doesn't commit the utilitarian to increasing punishment without limit. There is, according to utilitarianism, an optimal measure of punishment for any crime. We do not want to prevent all crime, only those crimes that do not promote utility. Breaking the law out of necessity, for example, may actually increase utility. Thus whether someone ought to be excused must be a function of how much punishment it would take to deter him, and what the optimal punishment is. If he can be deterred by increasing punishment, then punishment ought to be increased—but only up to the level at which it becomes counterproductive.

This account is intended to explain much of the existing structure of legal excuses and justifications without at the same time warranting their universal extension. The insane and incompetent and the involuntarily intoxicated should be excused because the threat of punishment will not work on such individuals (but only, note, to the extent that it will not work). One who acts under duress may or may not be excused on this account. It turns in part on deterrability, and in part on the optimal level of punishment. Do we want punishments so severe that people will abandon themselves or family members to harm rather than harm another? The greedy, on the other hand, can be deterred, as can the lustful for power: they are precisely the ones who respond best to calculations of reward and punishment. And the hateful can succeed in punishing their hated object only if they themselves are not punished in turn; if they are capable of plotting and calculating against another they are capable of taking into account the possibility of punishment.

To return to the four cases we considered in the preceding section, describing artificially and naturally implanted feelings of hatred, on the one hand, and a lust for power, on the other, we can see how the utilitarian might draw the line. Those who acquire the motivation for crime over a lifetime have done so in spite of a threat of punishment sufficient to deter the person of appropriate firmness—that is, the person whose motivation we

think serves to maximize utility, judged by the level that crime reaches given that level of punishment.

But those who were all at once implanted with the motivation to commit a crime have not been given a chance to take the threat of punishment into account; their normal development has been bypassed, in the course of which the threat of punishment (along with other kinds of education) had its desired effect. They are therefore a special case; punishing them would have no point, since the normal development of our attitudes toward the law does not give us a way to anticipate the effect of technology that would entirely transform it. And thus although the utilitarian might argue against punishment in cases one and three, where motivation was manipulated artificially, she need not so argue in cases two and four, where motivation is the product of a lifetime's experience. And so (on this line of reasoning) if we understand principle (A) correctly it does not lead to an undesirable increase in the cases that must be excused.

But even if that reasoning is valid, its soundness depends upon the acceptability of a utilitarian theory of excuses. Here are several objections.

(1) Why wouldn't punishing the undeterrable promote utility? If the way punishment promotes utility is by reducing crime, then is there really no benefit from punishing the insane? Perhaps such punishment would reduce borderline crimes—crimes committed by people who, though they have it in their power to do otherwise, feel that they can make a strong enough case for insanity to get away with the crime. Perhaps, in addition, the very barbarity of such punishment would deter criminal behavior and so increase happiness.

Utilitarians disagree on this point. Some argue that a strict liability system—that is, a system without excuses—could not possibly promote happiness. Therefore, they insist, excuses are an essential part of the theory of punishment. But that claim is an empirical one, subject to refutation in the real world. How do we respond if we find that a system without excuses *does* increase happiness, even if only marginally? Isn't the utilitarian committed to saying that under those circumstances we should punish the insane, among others?

Other utilitarians accept the conclusion of our *reductio ad absurdum*: they believe that we would be better off without excuses. They would round up everyone whose behavior breaks the law, including the insane, the incapacitated, and others who in our system would be excused, and subject them to some combination of punishment and treatment. But this solution is no more attractive than excusing everyone, and it is a proposal whose time appears to be past.

(2) As a philosophy of punishment, utilitarianism is subject to apparently fatal objections. For example, if the moral justification of punishment lies in its ability to increase happiness in the future, *and that alone*, then it is morally acceptable (indeed it is morally required) to punish innocent people, wherever punishing innocent people would promote happiness better than any alternative.

Of course, a utilitarian theory of excuses does not presuppose a utilitarian theory of punishment. All it requires is that utility be a necessary condition of punishment. Many who reject utility as a complete moral justification of punishment accept it as one of the necessary conditions for justified punishment. That is, they accept a mixed theory in which both utility and retribution play a role. No one is to be punished, according to such a theory, unless he is guilty and deserves punishment. That is the retributive element. But no one is to be punished either unless it serves some morally acceptable purpose; no one may be punished pointlessly. That is the utilitarian element. So even if, for example, Jones has murdered and deserves to be punished, if the effect of punishing her would be to make things worse (suppose it greatly increased the incidence of murder to punish murderers), then she may not be punished.

But although an absence of utility should provide a sufficient condition for excuse, on a mixed theory it is not the only sufficient condition. A mixed retributive-utilitarian theory should provide two classes of excusing conditions: those conditions in which punishment would be pointless, and those in which it is not deserved. Those whom it would be useful to punish but who do not deserve punishment should not be punished any more than those who deserve to be punished, but whom it would be pointless to punish. And though the utilitarian condition might call punishment into question only when the accused belongs to a class of

individuals who are undeterrable, it is obvious that not everyone who belongs to a class of individuals who are deterrable deserves to be punished. And if the bright line between conditions that make people undeterrable and those that do not should fail us as a way to separate punishability from excuse, how should we separate them? For it seems unlikely that we will be able to distinguish among the four cases we considered in the preceding section simply on the basis of what the actor deserves.

For example, it may be that the more difficult it is to avoid a crime, the less punishment is *deserved* for committing it. Suppose on a certain occasion Jones finds herself in circumstances in which it is difficult to avoid a crime, and she succumbs to the difficulty and commits the crime. Our question is whether the circumstances that made it difficult to avoid should excuse her. She *could* have avoided it, and she does not deserve to get off the hook entirely; but our intuition is that she doesn't deserve the full punishment for the crime, let us suppose. She doesn't deserve the punishment that would be deserved by someone who committed the same crime but was not subject to the same constraints. At the same time, we notice that she could have been deterred by a greater degree of punishment, and that it therefore might have increased utility. Punishment in the degree that we feel she deserved would not deter people in her position.

Consider a crime of impulse. . . . On retributive grounds we should treat the provoking circumstances as mitigating and reduce punishment (as provocation might reduce murder to manslaughter, for example). But so long as the impulse could have been deterred by the threat of punishment, and so long as it would promote utility to do so, utilitarianism would call for increased punishment.

Since there are cases in which utility and retribution give different results, and since if either retribution or utility is lacking there should be no punishment, we cannot rely on the fact that under some conditions persons may be undeterrable to explain the line between cases that ought to be punished and cases that ought to be excused. Utilitarianism does not help us to draw the line unless it is, all by itself, an adequate account of punishment. So long as the justification of punishment requires us to talk about desert, we cannot count on utility to impede the threatened advance of excusing circumstances.

III. *Compatibilism*

We saw, in the last section, that determinism would not be a problem for a utilitarian theory of excuses. But if we reject the utilitarian theory, determinism reappears as a problem. If determinism is true, then it would seem to be the case that punishment is never deserved; and thus a theory that has desert as a necessary condition would never justify punishment if determinism is true.

The argument would go like this:

ARGUMENT #2

1. Someone who, through no fault of her own, could not help breaking the law should not be punished. (Principle (A) from argument #1).
2. If determinism is true, then every event occurs under conditions that make it causally impossible for that event not to occur. (Definition of determinism.)
3. Thus if determinism is true, then every choice an agent makes is made under conditions that make it causally impossible for that choice not to have been made.
4. Thus if determinism is true, no one who acted in a certain way could have helped herself.
5. If determinism is true, therefore, no one should be punished for anything she does.

. . .

If the argument is sound, then if determinism is true, punishment is never justified. Detention may be; treatment and rehabilitation may be; but punishment will never be. And to say that punishment is never justified because no one can ever help himself is to say that everything is excused.

Since we do not *know* that determinism is true, of course, the conclusion of the argument must remain hypothetical. But new learning eats away at our ignorance, and as we learn the causes of more and more kinds of behavior, it becomes less and less plausible to suppose that human actions, alone among observable events, have a gap in their causal history. Should our belief that human beings deserve punishment diminish at the same rate? If not, which of the steps in the argument above should we reject?

Line 2 is merely a definition of determinism. Line 3 pre-supposes only that making a choice is an event like any other; it is not clear what it would mean to deny that. If making a choice is in fact an event, then line 3 follows from line 2.

Line 1 is denied by those who believe that character, and not choice, is the basis of desert; we will take up that argument in the next section. In this section we are concerned with line 4, or rather with the inference from 3 to 4. Is it really true that if all of an agent's choices are causally determined, she could not have avoided doing what she did? One of the important efforts to rescue the theory of excuses from being universally extended is grounded on a denial of that inference. The denial is labeled "compatibilism," and it asserts that even if an agent's choices were fully determined by prior events, it still makes sense to say that he could have helped himself, or could have done otherwise, and therefore it makes sense to say that he deserves punishment. The thesis of compatibilism is that determinism is compatible with criminal responsibility and desert.

According to the compatibilist, to say that someone could have done A simply means that, had he chosen to do A, he would have done A; and saying someone could have avoided doing A simply means that, had he chosen to avoid doing A, he would have avoided doing A. The compatibilist admits that if determinism is true then when someone chooses to do A there is a sufficient causal condition for his choosing to do A, and choosing to avoid doing A would be causally impossible. Nevertheless, in the sense required for criminal desert, breaking the law can be said to be avoidable so long as there is not some *external* force that would prevent the agent from avoiding it. Just because someone is so constituted that he could not choose to resist beating his wife, it does not follow that he couldn't have avoided it. Nothing (external) stopped him from refraining from beating her, so he could have refrained. He therefore deserves punishment. And therefore the conclusion of Argument #2 can be rejected. The error, says the compatibilist, is in moving from 3 to 4.

To go at it in a slightly different way, the compatibilist idea is this: to say that an agent could have done otherwise means, for the purposes of discussion of legal and moral responsibility, that had he chosen to do otherwise, he would have succeeded—nothing stood in his way. It does not mean that he could have chosen to do otherwise; if determinism is true, his choice is determined just like any other event, and so he could not have chosen otherwise. And since to say, "He could have avoided doing what he did," only means, "Had he chosen to avoid doing what he did, he would have succeeded," it may be true of a person that he could have avoided breaking the law even though *he could not have chosen to avoid breaking the law*. The avoidability relevant to criminal liability has to do with whether there are impediments to action *after* a choice has been made, not with whether the choice itself could have been avoided. Even if determinism is true, punishment as retribution makes sense, according to the compatibilist.

What should we say, then, about this attempt to limit excuses? One of the main objections to compatibilism is that it is implausible on its face. Those who adopt the position invariably describe it as capturing the ordinary sense of free and responsible action: You obviously act unfreely and do not deserve punishment, they say, only when some outside circumstance prevents you from doing otherwise, or makes it unreasonably difficult for you to avoid breaking the law. But I have never known anyone who, on encountering the theory for the first time, recognized it as capturing what *she* meant when she said that someone could have done otherwise.

Of course that is sometimes true of very difficult concepts; speakers often don't understand the philosophical implications of the words they use. But I don't think that is the whole story here. Compatibilism is simply a defective thesis. . . .

It is sometimes said, in support of compatibilism, that if our choices are not caused by prior events, then they are merely randomly occurring events, inexplicable, and thus we cannot be held responsible for them. And it is true that a picture of the universe in which human actions are random events is not an acceptable explanation of responsibility. But we should not infer that because that picture is unacceptable, the compatibilist picture must be acceptable.

Nevertheless, compatibilism is widely accepted among philosophers today, and it has found its way into the law as a bulwark against the implications of determinism. It has another, related, benefit: it gives us a way to avoid the slippery slope of Argument # 1, with which this essay began. If only external forces make actions unavoidable in the sense relevant to excuses, we are not excused for choices that we make simply because we are caused to make them by our own internal makeup. Thus a crime caused by my own greed or lust for power is not to be excused; it was not the result of external constraints. On the other hand, a crime caused by a threat of harm from someone else may be excused; it was caused by external constraints, and therefore may be unavoidable in the requisite sense. A crime caused by the hatred I bear someone cannot be excused; it was avoidable though caused. (What of poor Jones, though, who had someone else's hatred temporarily implanted in her, and killed as a result? We are inclined to excuse her, I think; but how would the compatibilist deal with that? Would he subsume her case to that of the person acting under duress? But how does he distinguish her case from that of the person who came by the hatred naturally?)

All of this depends, of course, upon accepting the view that determinism is compatible with desert, a view that remains, for me at least, implausible on its face.

IV. *Character and Choice*

There is, however, one other way that has been suggested to avoid the conclusion of Argument # 2. That is to reject line 1 and argue that desert does not depend upon a person's ability to avoid committing the crime. This is the position taken by proponents of the character theory of excuse.

According to the character theory (or at least the most prominent version of the character theory), we cannot accept without qualification the principle that someone who could not help breaking the law should not be punished. We must qualify it in this way: There are various sorts of condition that make it difficult or impossible for someone to avoid breaking the law. Some of these conditions are part of the *character* of the actor himself. Someone who is by nature a glutton (to use the words of a dated psychology) may not be able to, or may find it very difficult to, avoid eating to excess. But we do not excuse him for overeating because of the difficulty; and in general we do not excuse when the difficulty of avoidance is due to the actor's character. We excuse only when the difficulty has another source; for example, when I commit a crime because someone has threatened to shoot me if I do not.

For what *deserves* punishment, on this theory, is bad character, and not the choice to do something bad. If a bad character is what makes it difficult to avoid breaking the law, all the more reason to punish. But if the circumstances prevent us from inferring a bad character from the fact that the agent has broken the law, then there is no basis for saying that he deserves punishment. And that is how excuses are explained on the character theory: they are circumstances that interfere with the inference that the violation was caused by bad character. That is what difficulties that arise from external sources do: they prevent us from attributing the crime to a bad character.

Thus, if someone commits a crime in order to protect her child, or to save her home, or in self-defense, or as a result of involuntary intoxication, it does not follow that she has a bad character and ought to be punished. Difficulties that stem from character itself, on the other hand, far from blocking the inference support it. If someone commits a crime out of greed, or cowardice, or excessive irritability, it is his character that is at fault. And since it is bad character that deserves punishment, it follows that we should excuse crimes that are unavoidable for reasons other than character, but not for those attributable to character.

By distinguishing between various sources of unavoidability, the character theory would seem to block the slide toward universal excuse. And since the character theorist rejects line 1 of Argument # 2, determinism itself would also not seem to be a worry. If indeed it is bad character that deserves punishment, then people should be punished for breaking the law whenever it is an indication of bad character, regardless of how one acquired one's

character; regardless, that is, of the causal background of character.

The character theory gets along moderately well with utilitarianism. Perhaps the usefulness of punishment is mediated through the formation of character. But how does it fare with retributivism? I am afraid that if we admit retribution into our theory of punishment, as it seems we must, we will have difficulty with the character theory. Why should bad character *deserve* punishment? To some extent our characters are within our control, it is true; but by and large they are not. To put the question another way, why should we be held responsible for actions made unavoidable by our characters, when we are not by and large responsible for our characters?

Consider again the sort of example considered in section I. Imagine that Jones committed a crime, and that because of her character she could not have avoided it; she couldn't help herself. The character theory says she is not to be excused. But what if, just before the crime, she had had a character-implant: someone changed her and gave her the character traits that led to the crime. Should she be punished for it? We are talking here about a crime that her character made it difficult or impossible for her to avoid. Nevertheless, and apparently in opposition to what the character theory would seem to imply, the answer must be that she should not be punished for it; she was overwhelmed just as if the difficulty had had an external source.

Of course, in a sense the difficulty did have an external source: the technician who changed her character traits. But in that sense most character traits have external sources: education, training, genetics, experiences with family and community. We are back to this: Why should we excuse the one who has an instantaneous character transformation, and not the one who acquired her character over many years (though without any more responsibility for it than the implant victim had)?

Conventional wisdom would seem to support the view that character is not something we can do something about, and that therefore character is not something for which we can be punished. Of course, that is just to reassert what the character theory denies, that we can be punished only for what we could have avoided. Still, that principle of justice has firm roots, and the character theorist will have to say more if he means to deny it. Our tentative judgment must be: So far not proven.

V. *Alternatives?*

Utilitarianism, compatibilism, and character would each of them resolve the issue [of] whether there should be an excuse of rotten social background. For the utilitarian, the threat of punishment would be one way of countering the effects of a rotten background. For the compatibilist, the mere fact that crime was caused by background would not be enough to excuse it. For the character theorist, it would be immaterial how character is formed; a bad character is a bad character, however it is acquired. Yet none of the three theories is free from serious problems, so the issue can hardly be said to be resolved.

If we reject utilitarianism, compatibilism, and the character theory, are we committed to excusing every crime? Is there any reasonable alternative to these theories? The most plausible theory, I think, is also the riskiest. It is a retributivism that would punish only for actions freely chosen, where to choose freely means that the choice was not caused by prior events. Now of course that requires us to make sense of uncaused and yet responsible actions. As I noted above there is a great deal of skepticism about such a project: Is an uncaused event one that is merely random? And are we responsible for random actions? And even if it finds a way to answer that criticism, it faces this problem: if such a theory is correct, then determinism would indeed

lead to a requirement of universal excuse. That is why I call it the riskiest theory; it puts punishment itself at risk.

Nevertheless I believe that there is a great deal of preanalytic support for this view. Setting aside the problem raised by the need to appeal to uncaused actions, and the problem raised by the possibility of determinism (if that is indeed a problem for the theory), it leads to the following problem: All four of the cases in section I should be treated the same. For given that Jones really had a choice in each case, her right to an excuse is determined by the difficulty she would have had in trying to do otherwise. If Jones should be excused when her anger is attributable to the action of the terrorists, then it should be excused when attributable to her background. To some extent that conflicts with our intuitions about the case.

More importantly, though, on this theory there is no reason of principle to enable us to distinguish between the first set of cases, involving hatred and frustration, and the second set of cases involving a greed for power. So long as the degree of difficulty created is the same, the cases must be treated the same. But that seems to fly in the face of the law's experience, which is that the more greed and similar traits are evident, the more punishment may be deserved. This is something that the character theory handles admirably well; but the character theory cannot tell us how the other cases are different.

I believe it is safe to say, therefore, that there are great difficulties, and no simple solutions, in this undertaking. . . .

71. State v. Leidholm

Leidholm is one of the early cases recognizing the admissibility of the "battered-woman's syndrome." The court's reasons for recognizing the syndrome as a corollary to the law of self-defense should be compared with the arguments of Cathryn Jo Rosen.

Vande Walle, Justice.

Janice Leidholm was charged with murder for the stabbing death of her husband, Chester Leidholm, in the early morning hours of August 7, 1981, at their farm home near Washburn. She was found guilty by a McLean County jury of manslaughter and was sentenced to five years' imprisonment in the State Penitentiary with three years of the sentence suspended. Leidholm appealed from the judgment of conviction. We reverse and remand the case for a new trial.

I

According to the testimony, the Leidholm marriage relationship in the end was an unhappy one, filled with a mixture of alcohol abuse, moments of kindness toward one another, and moments of violence. The alcohol abuse and violence was exhibited by both parties on the night of Chester's death.

Early in the evening of August 6, 1981, Chester and Janice attended a gun club party in the city of Washburn where they both consumed a large amount of alcohol. On the return trip to the farm, an argument developed between Janice and Chester which continued after their arrival home just after midnight. Once inside the home, the arguing did not stop; Chester was shouting, and Janice was crying.

At one point in the fighting, Janice tried to telephone Dave Vollan, a deputy sheriff of McLean County, but Chester prevented her from using the phone by shoving her away and push-

334 N.W. 2d 811 (1983)
Supreme Court of North Dakota

ing her down. At another point, the argument moved outside the house, and Chester once again was pushing Janice to the ground. Each time Janice attempted to get up, Chester would push her back again.

A short time later, Janice and Chester re-entered their home and went to bed. When Chester fell asleep, Janice got out of bed, went to the kitchen, and got a butcher knife. She then went back into the bedroom and stabbed Chester. In a matter of minutes Chester died from shock and loss of blood.

II

. . . The first, and controlling, issue we consider is whether or not the trial court correctly instructed the jury on self-defense.

. . .

A defense of justification is the product of society's determination that the *actual existence* of certain circumstances will operate to make proper and legal what otherwise would be criminal conduct. A defense of excuse, contrarily, does not make legal and proper conduct which ordinarily would result in criminal liability; instead, it openly recognizes the criminality of the conduct but excuses it because the actor believed that circumstances actually existed which would justify his conduct when in fact they did not. In short, had the facts been as he supposed them to be, the actor's conduct would have been justified rather than excused. . . .

In the context of self-defense, this means that a person who believes that the force he uses is necessary to prevent imminent unlawful harm is *justified* in using such force if his belief is a *correct* belief; that is to say, if his belief corresponds with what actually is the case. If, on the other hand, a person *reasonably* but incorrectly believes that the force he uses is necessary to protect himself against imminent harm, his use of force is *excused.*

. . .

Courts have traditionally distinguished between standards of reasonableness by characterizing them as either "objective" or "subjective." An objective standard of reasonableness requires the factfinder to view the circumstances surrounding the accused at the time he used force from the standpoint of a hypothetical reasonable and prudent person. Ordinarily, under such a view, the unique physical and psychological characteristics of the accused are not taken into consideration in judging the reasonableness of the accused's belief.

This is not the case, however, where a subjective standard of reasonableness is employed. See *State v. Wanrow*, 88 Wash. 2d 221, 559 P.2d 548 (1977). Under the subjective standard the issue is not whether the circumstances attending the accused's use of force would be sufficient to create in the mind of a reasonable and prudent person the belief that the use of force is necessary to protect himself against immediate unlawful harm, but rather whether the circumstances are sufficient to induce in the accused an honest and reasonable belief that he must use force to defend himself against imminent harm.

. . .

Because (1) the law of self-defense as developed in past decisions of this court has been interpreted to require the use of a subjective standard of reasonableness, and (2) we agree with the court in *Hazlett* that a subjective standard is the more just, and (3) our current law of self-defense . . . does not require a contrary conclusion, that is to say, our current law of self-defense is consistent with either a subjective or objective standard, we now decide that the finder of fact must view the circumstances attending an accused's use of force from the standpoint of the accused to determine if they are sufficient to create in the accused's mind an honest and reasonable belief that the use of force is necessary to protect himself from imminent harm. . . .

The practical and logical consequence of this interpretation is that an accused's actions are to be viewed from the standpoint of a person whose mental and physical characteristics are like the accused's and who sees what the accused sees and knows what the accused knows. For example, if the accused is a timid, diminutive male, the factfinder must consider these characteristics in assessing the reasonableness of his belief. If, on the other hand, the accused is a strong, courageous, and capable female, the factfinder must consider these characteristics in judging the reasonableness of her belief.

In its statement of the law of self-defense, the trial court instructed the jury:

> The circumstances under which she acted must have been such as to produce in the mind of reasonably prudent persons, regardless of their sex, similarly situated, the reasonable belief that the other person was then about to kill her or do serious bodily harm to her.

In view of our decision today, the court's instruction was a misstatement of the law of self-defense. A correct statement of the law to be applied in a case of self-defense is:

> [A] defendant's conduct is not to be judged by what a reasonably cautious person might or might not do or consider necessary to do under the like circumstances, but what he himself in good faith honestly believed and had reasonable ground to believe was necessary for him to do to protect himself from apprehended death or great bodily injury.

The significance of the difference in viewing circumstances from the standpoint of the "defendant alone" rather than from the standpoint of a "reasonably cautious person" is that the jury's consideration of the unique physical and psychological characteristics of an accused allows the jury to judge the reasonableness of the accused's actions against the accused's subjective impressions of the need to use force rather than against those impressions which a jury determines that a hypothetical reasonably cautious person would have under similar circumstances. . . .

Hence, a correct statement of the law of self-defense is one in which the court directs the jury to assume the physical and psychological properties peculiar to the accused, viz., to place itself as best it can in the shoes of the accused, and then decide whether or not the particular circumstances surrounding the accused at the time he used force were sufficient to create in his mind a sincere and reasonable belief that the use of force was necessary to protect himself from imminent and unlawful harm. . . .

Leidholm argued strongly at trial that her stabbing of Chester was done in self-defense and in reaction to the severe mistreatment she received from him over the years. Because the court's instruction in question is an improper statement of the law concerning a vital issue in Leidholm's defense, we conclude it amounts to reversible error requiring a new trial.

. . .

The expert witness in this case testified that Janice Leidholm was the victim in a battering relationship which caused her to suffer battered woman syndrome manifested by (1) a psychological condition of low self-esteem and (2) a psychological state of "learned helplessness." . . .

The instruction on battered woman syndrome was designed to support Leidholm's claim of self-defense by focusing the jury's attention on the psychological characteristics common to women who are victims in abusive relationships, and by directing the jury that it may consider evidence that the accused suffered from battered woman syndrome

in determining whether or not she acted in self-defense. The instruction correctly points out that battered woman syndrome is not of itself defense. In other words, "The existence of the syndrome in a marriage does not of itself establish the legal right of the wife to kill the husband, the evidence must still be considered in the context of self-defense." . . .

There is nothing in the proposed instruction at issue which would add to or significantly alter a correct instruction on the law of self-defense. The jury's use of a subjective standard of reasonableness in applying the principles of self-defense to the facts of a particular case requires it to consider expert testimony, once received in evidence, describing battered woman syndrome and the psychological effects it produces in the battered spouse when deciding the issue of the existence and reasonableness of the accused's belief that force was necessary to protect herself from imminent harm. If an instruction given is modeled after the law of self-defense which we adopt today, the court need not include a specific instruction on battered woman syndrome in its charge to the jury. . . .

The judgment of conviction is reversed and the case is remanded . . . for a new trial.

---

72. *The Battered Woman's Defense*

Cathryn Jo Rosen

Defining the battered woman's defense is not an easy task. The literature is full of claims that the defense is misconceived. Yet, even those authors who bemoan the misconceptions have difficulty arriving at a co-

gent definition of the term. Indeed, use of the term at all is widely disparaged. A number of writers repeatedly emphasize that the theory should be denominated "women's self-defense," perhaps to dispel the notion that there is a special exception to the normal rules of self-defense for battered women. Nonetheless, courts and the media relentlessly choose to adhere to the battered woman's defense phraseology.

Reprinted by permission of American University Law Review.

One explanation for some of the confusion between "self-defense," "women's self-defense," and "battered woman's defense" may lie in the defense's historical development. The best descriptions of the battered woman's defense are by feminist lawyers who based their strategy on lessons learned while representing women who defended themselves against male aggression under circumstances that fell outside the setting of traditional self-defense. Self-defense rules were developed to acquit a man who kills to protect himself or his family against a threatened attack from a man of similar size and strength with whom the defender usually has had only a single encounter. Rules requiring like force, imminency of the threatened harm, consideration of only the circumstances surrounding the single encounter, and use of an objective reasonable man standard are more than adequate in such circumstances. Women, however, usually use deadly force to protect themselves under very different circumstances. Usually their male victims are larger and stronger and are not strangers. The woman's fear of the man will be influenced by her knowledge of his character and reputation for violence. Rules requiring like force, imminency, consideration of only the circumstances immediately surrounding the killing, and use of an objective reasonable man standard necessarily defeat the woman's claim.

The first successes for the notion of women's self-defense were not battered women's cases. In the early 1970s, feminists rallied to support the defense of Joan Little, a prisoner in a North Carolina jail who stabbed and killed a male guard. Little claimed that she stabbed the unarmed guard because he threatened to rape her. Ms. Little was acquitted on the theory of self-defense despite the arguable absence of equal force.

Two years later, Inez Garcia was acquitted by a jury after her second trial on homicide charges. She claimed a self-defense. Garcia was physically and sexually assaulted by two male acquaintances. Before leaving the scene, the men threatened to return and rape Garcia again. She took her shotgun and went to search for her assailants. Several hours later she found one of the men on a street and shot and killed him. Judged by an objective standard of reasonableness, Garcia's motive appeared to be vengeance rather than self-defense. The jury, however, was permitted to consider the defendant's ethnic background, her rape, and the men's threat to repeat their attack when determining whether she reasonably believed that the use of deadly force was necessary to avoid an imminent threat of serious bodily harm.

Soon acquittals of women, including battered women, who pleaded self-defense became common in many jurisdictions. The most important appellate victory for the feminist advocates of women's self-defense was in a case that did not involve a battered woman. In 1977, the Washington Supreme Court reversed Yvonne Wanrow's second degree murder conviction in a decision holding that use of the reasonable man objective standard of self-defense violated Wanrow's right to equal protection of the law. Wanrow shot an intoxicated, unarmed man whom she knew had a reputation for violence when he approached her in a threatening manner. At the time, Wanrow, who was five-foot-four, had a broken leg and was using a crutch. Recognizing that Wanrow's fear and perception of danger was affected by her status as a woman, the court held that use of the reasonable man standard in the jury instruction was improper because it deprived Wanrow of the right to have the jury consider her conduct in light of her own perceptions. The court directed that the jury on retrial should be instructed to apply a subjective, sex-specific standard of reasonableness.

Little, *Garcia*, and *Wanrow* involved situations in which an objectively reasonable observer of the confrontation would not have perceived that the aggressor threatened imminent death or serious bodily harm to the defendant nor have believed that defensive use of deadly force was the only alternative available. Application of traditional rules of self-defense inevitably would lead to a murder conviction. Defense counsel were able to persuade the courts that their mistaken beliefs that the circumstances justified self-help were subjectively reasonable given the particular experiences and perceptions of the defendants.

The same problems occur in battered women's cases, often in more extreme forms. In the late 1970s, feminist lawyers began to outline a defense strategy for battered women who kill their abusers. They combined the women's self-defense theory developed in cases like *Little*, *Garcia*, and *Wanrow* with the use of expert testimony on the psychological impact of an abusive relationship on battered women. The feminists assumed from the start that homicides committed by women are equally reasonable as homicides committed by men. The defense strategy is to persuade the judge and jury that a variety of social factors cause women to perceive imminent, lethal danger in situations where men would not. Although stemming from unique factors, women's perceptions of danger demand equal recourse to deadly force. This argument is necessary because traditional self-defense, permeated as it is by male experience, does not acknowledge that a woman's response to a set of circumstances could be reasonable even though it was different than a man's response to the same set of circumstances. Rather than requesting that battered women receive special treatment from the law, the creators of the defense hoped to encourage application of the law of self-defense in a sex-neutral, individualized manner to all women, including those who kill their abusers.

The feminists proposed to obtain equality under the law by removing stereotypical myths and misconceptions about battered women from the trial process. Yet their self-defense theory for battered women who kill depends upon persuading the judge and the jury to accept an alternate set of factual generalizations about women in general, battered women in particular, the efficacy of the criminal justice system, and society. These assumptions, which serve to remedy the failure of battered women who kill to prove the traditional elements of self-defense, include the following:

1. Women find it necessary to resort to self-help because the courts and police do not provide them with adequate protection from their abusers. Therefore, even in the absence of an imminent or immediate threat of harm, their belief that self-defense is necessary may be reasonable.
2. A woman's perception of danger will be affected by her smaller size, socialization regarding passive attributes of femininity, and poor physical training. Therefore, it is perfectly reasonable for a woman to believe an unarmed man may be able to kill her.
3. A woman may reasonably feel the need to use a weapon to protect herself from an unarmed assailant.
4. Consideration of surrounding circumstances should not be limited to the time immediately preceding the killing. Prior conduct of the victim toward defendant will influence her perception of the dangerous nature of his behavior at the time of the homicide. Prior specific acts of violence should be admissible as well as the victim's general reputation for violence.
5. Defendant's rage and desire for revenge is not inconsistent with self-defense.

These assumptions widen the scope of relevant testimony and constitute the framework for the argument that the defendant's belief that self-defense was necessary was subjectively reasonable. Borrowing from Fletcher's writings, the feminists argued that the reasonableness of the woman's act of self-help should be adjudged in a sex-neutral, individualized manner in which the individual defendant's characteristics and culpability are relevant. The jurors should be instructed to place themselves in defendant's shoes and determine under all the circumstances, including defendant's history as a battered woman, the reasonableness of defendant's belief that use of deadly force was necessary.

Among the trial tactics the creators of the battered woman's defense recommend is the careful and strategic use of lay and expert testimony to neutralize stereotypical prejudices and ideas that may interfere with the jury's ability to perceive the defendant's conduct as a reasonable act of self-defense. Although the expert testimony may take numerous forms, many defense attorneys have used expert psychiatrist or psychological testimony. Often it consists primarily of a description of Dr. Lenore E. Walker's cycle of violence and learned helplessness theories which together constitute the battered woman syndrome. The expert will describe the battered woman syndrome in general terms after which she may be permitted to testify that the defendant suffers from battered woman syndrome.

Expert testimony is used to show why, under the particular circumstances of the case, the defendant's conduct was reasonable and, therefore, justified. Theoretically, the woman's defensive action will be proved necessary and proportionate by showing how the defendant could perceive a threat of imminent danger in verbal threats alone, in a nondeadly attack from an unarmed spouse, or from a sleeping man. The testimony explains why the woman stayed with her spouse despite the abusive relationship and why, on the occasion in question, she may not have run away or sought assistance from friends, relatives, or the police despite an apparent opportunity to do so. Finally, the testimony explains why the woman cannot be faulted for becoming involved in an abusive relationship. Rather, she is a victim of her social reality, responding to circumstances in accordance with the values of femininity and life-long marriage to which she was acculturated.

The problem is that such an inquiry is inconsistent with the theory of justification which assumes that anyone who does the same act under the same external circumstances has done the right thing. By including a certain psychological trait of the individual in the circumstances, we have moved closer to the theory of excuse than to justification. Nonetheless, the feminist theory is based on the premise that explanation of the reasonableness of defendant's belief that use of deadly force was proportionate and necessary will establish that the woman's act was justified rather than excused. Feminists argue that recognition of the woman's act as justified rather than excused is crucial.

> [E]xcusable self-defense would imply that her response was typically and idiosyncratically emotional. The doctrine would perpetuate the views that the woman could not have been rational in assessing the danger and that the legal system must compensate for her mental and physical weaknesses. . . .
>
> Justification, on the other hand, would assume that society values a woman's and a man's lives equally, and thus considers women's lives worthy of self-defense. It would recognize that a woman has the capacity to correctly and reasonably perceive that the act is warranted, legitimate, and justified. Justification would encourage, indeed would compel, a legal recognition that a woman's capacity for reasonable judgment—comparable to that of a man's—can be the basis for engaging in the "correct behavior" of self-defense.[1]

This doctrinaire insistence on treatment of the battered woman's defense as a justification is un-

necessary and may be fatal to widespread and successful use of the battered woman's defense. Most battered woman's defense cases involve situations in which the defendant was not, in fact, in imminent danger of death or serious bodily harm at her victim's hands. The defense relies on persuading the jury that the defendant suffered from an identifiable psychological syndrome that caused her to assess the dangerousness of the situation in a different manner than an average, ordinary person—including a woman who does not suffer from battered woman syndrome. In other words, acquittal is dependent upon proving that defendant had . . . a disability that caused a mistaken, but reasonable, belief in the existence of circumstances that would justify self-defense. It is a theory of excuse rather than of justification. Because defendant responded to internal and external coercive pressures, for which she was not responsible but which were created by her social reality as a battered woman, she is not to blame for her conduct. A person who did not suffer from battered woman syndrome, however, would be culpable under identical external circumstances. Indeed, successful use of the battered woman's defense theory depends in part on defense counsel's ability to persuade the court and jury that a person who did not suffer from battered woman syndrome would not be justified under identical objectively identifiable circumstances. This, however, is inherently inconsistent with the concept of justification.

Efforts to characterize artificially the battered woman's defense as a justification must ultimately lead to some of the current misapprehensions as to its nature and the fears that its adoption will ultimately lead to justification of all killings that the defendant subjectively believed were necessary and proportionate. Conversely, it may explain, in part, the tendency to incorrectly view battered women as bearing a special right to self-defense based on their victimized status alone. Recognition that the defense is categorized properly as an excuse rather than a justification may enhance the ability of battered women who kill to win acquittals. To present a complete defense, a defendant would still have to show that her belief that justificatory circumstances existed was subjectively reasonable. Because the defendant is excused rather than justified, however, there would be no chance that the conduct will be encouraged.

The fact that the battered woman's defense is more consistent with excuse theory does not answer the feminist concern that excusing battered women who kill, in circumstances they believe create a right of self-defense, may perpetuate undesirable views that women are by nature irrational and that their lives are unworthy of self-defense against a man. First, however, these concerns are overblown. Treatment of the battered woman's defense as an excuse does not preclude justifying women who kill men under objectively identifiable circumstances more akin to traditional self-defense. Second, for the same reasons that battered women should be excused for killing their spouses, men who kill under mistaken beliefs as to justifying circumstances should also be excused. Third, even if treatment of the battered woman's defense as an excuse does lead to perpetuation of sex discrimination under the current law, it may be that the problem should be cured in a different manner than the feminists recommend. All self-defense should be treated as excused rather than justified conduct. Indeed, the difficulties that the courts and commentators have encountered with the battered woman's defense vividly illustrate the need for such a reconceptualization of the defense. Excused self-defense would better meet the needs of battered women, of the criminal justice system, and of society in general.

. . .

Today, most American jurisdictions classify self-defense as a justification even though it traditionally developed as an excuse. As a result, principles of excuse have become merged with principles of justification in the law of self-defense. Consequently, results in some cases are illogical and inconsistent with basic principles of criminal law. The problem is particularly apt to arise when demands are made to justify self-help behavior that is harmful to society in instances where the actor cannot fairly be held blameworthy because of circumstances particular to that individual. Battered women who kill their abusers present the paradigm example of such cases. Although the defendant's conduct is understandable, and absolving her from moral blame is not difficult, we are hesitant to proclaim that the act was justified and therefore to be encouraged. Even in traditional cases, self-defense is, at most, permissible and tolerated.

Treatment of all self-defense as an excuse would further the criminal justice system's interest in discouraging self-help, promote society's interest in preserving the sanctity of human life, and fulfill the feminist goal of absolving battered women who kill of guilt without proclaiming that such women are inferior to men.

Justification requires that the actor chose to violate the criminal law only because it was the lesser of a necessary choice of evils. Classification of self-defense as a justification, therefore, requires that the defender's interest in life be regarded as superior to that of the unlawful aggressor's. The act is accordingly one that is encouraged because it was beneficial to society or at least created no harm. The qualitative balancing act required to justify killings in self-defense, however, is not easy to perform.

The law's prohibition against intentional killing coincides with contemporary society's emphasis on the importance of human life as the most valuable interest protected by the criminal law. Clearly, however, there are also circumstances when intentional killing is justified because of the benefit it confers upon society as a whole. The intentional killings originally justified by the criminal law illustrate such situations. For example, one who kills a military enemy in battle is justified, as is the officer who kills to prevent an act of terrorism or to apprehend a person who has taken others hostage. Similarly, if we assume for the moment that capital punishment is acceptable, the executioner's act of killing the condemned is certainly justified. In all of these circumstances (the list is not exclusive), one life is taken to save many lives and to enhance the power of the rule of law. And, except in the instance of war, arguably the person whose life has been taken already has been shown to be dangerous and a threat to society as a whole.

A classic self-defense case involves a situation in which the actor takes the life of another to save the actor's life. One life has been chosen over one other life and the choice has been made in contravention of the legal rule generally prohibiting intentional killings. In the best of cases, it is difficult to identify any benefit that might accrue to society in general as a result of the killing. Moreover, the common law has always had great difficulty making judgments that one human life is more valuable than another. The result is the rule that a person can only defend against unlawful force. Yet, even this rule, the basis of which is uncertain, does not entirely solve the problem. First, modern criminal codes, for the most part, classify at least those cases in which the mistake was reasonable as justified self-defense. The closer the law moves toward a subjective standard of reasonableness, the greater the threat to the attacker's basic human rights. The extent of the attacker's rights would be defined solely by the victim's judgment of what was the right response under the circumstances. Indeed, cases involving mistake regarding the perception that the victim was threatening unlawful deadly force could result in the taking of an entirely innocent life. The killing of an innocent victim cannot be justified rationally. Society has been harmed by the taking of an innocent life and the actor can only be acquitted under an excuse theory. Second, even an unlawful aggressor is not necessarily a threat to all society. The attacker may only be a threat to one other person, the defender. Therefore, self-defense can only be the lesser evil if the interests of the defender that the aggressor threatens are greater than the aggressor's interest in life.

A variety of theories have been suggested to support the relative devaluation of the unlawful aggressor's life. Robinson[2] postulates that, although the relative physical harms to be suffered by the defender and the aggressor are equal, the defender also has an interest in bodily integrity. When the right to bodily integrity is added to the defender's right to be free from physical injury, the aggressor's interest in freedom from physical injury is outweighed. This view, however, is problematic because it blithely ignores the fact that the aggressor must also have a right to bodily integrity.

Essentially, Robinson's theory is a forfeiture theory. The idea behind the moral forfeiture theory that self-defense is correctly classified as a justification is that by virtue of his act of aggression, the aggressor forfeits some interest or right he would otherwise have had—such as the right to bodily integrity, his interest in life, or his right to freedom from aggression. The forfeiture theories cannot withstand a number of difficulties. If the defender is mistaken as to the unlawfulness of the aggression, his act will still be justified. Yet, it is difficult to say that one whose aggression was not unlawful has waived any rights. Even when the aggressor's conduct is actually unlawful there are difficulties. The criminal law generally does not permit express consent to one's own death. Yet, any forfeiture theory presumes that the victim's act of aggression constitutes implied consent to the use of defensive force.

Ultimately, there probably is no acceptable calculus to support treatment of self-defense as a justification. Its modern classification as such is likely the product of historical accident. If the law were to recognize that even traditional self-defense is properly considered an excuse, the nonculpable defensive acts of many more people could be excepted from punishment without the threat of escalating societal violence.

The difficulty in devaluing the life of the aggressor is particularly acute in some battered women's cases. Many men who abuse their spouses never display aggressive or violent behavior outside the confines of their homes. Certainly, perpetrators of domestic violence are not nice people. Yet, it is doubtful that anyone seriously could argue that ridding society of people merely because they are not nice benefits all. Feminists assert that the abuser's intent to kill or seriously injure his wife makes his death nonharmful rather than his character as a wife-beater. A victim of battered woman syndrome, however, may be mistaken as to the true nature of her spouse's threats on a particular occasion. Even if the mistake is reasonable or if there is no mistake, the difficulty with the calculus remains. Proponents of the battered woman's defense sympathize so much with the defendant that they have a tendency to focus exclusively on the psychological and physical harm suffered by the woman while forgetting the abuser. His right to life, though, is equally important as the woman's.

One of the most difficult problems confronted by legal theorists is the question of whether killing a legally insane aggressor in self-defense can be justified. Forfeiture theories of self-defense that rely on devaluing the aggressor's interest in life, freedom from aggression, or bodily integrity because of his wrongful conduct disintegrate in cases where the aggressor is not culpable. This problem is particularly acute in battered woman's defense cases. If we sympathize with the women as being victims of their social reality, we must sympathize with the batterers as well. Abusers are not entirely morally reprehensible. According to psychological and sociological literature, they also are victims of "disease" or of their social reality. This makes it even more difficult for the legal system to determine that the abuser's life is less valuable than his victim's.

The most that can be said in battered woman's defense cases, as in all self-defense cases, is that society is neutral with respect to the killing. By treating such cases as instances of excuse rather than justification, the difficulties created by weighing qualitative values of human lives and according a lesser interest to a potentially "innocent" person can be avoided. An excuse analysis would lead to identical results—acquittal—but do so by focusing on the pressure confronted by the defendant and the lack of available options.

It is difficult to identify a positive benefit that accrues to anyone other than the killer from the taking of an aggressor's life in self-defense. Thus, there is no reason for the law affirmatively to encourage such conduct. To the contrary, classification of self-defense as a justification may be detrimental to society. The early common law failed to recognize self-defense as either a justification or an excuse because self-help was inimical to the goal of creating respect for the rule of law and, in turn, for governmental authority. Although lack of respect for properly constituted legal authority is not generally a problem today, the law still serves a vital function of discouraging self-help.

There are a number of reasons why self-help is contrary to the interests of modern society. Reliance on self-help tends to diminish respect for the rule of law. Self-help in the form of self-defense carries the additional problem of increasing the quantum of violence in an already violent society. More troublesome is the possibility that the more widespread resort to self-help becomes, the more often innocent people may be killed erroneously.

It is troublesome even when a person who is guilty of a crime becomes the victim of proper self-help. The constant decline in the number of capital crimes throughout American history attests to the

general view that only the most vicious of intentional killers deserve to die for their deeds. We cling to the hope that criminals can be reformed, or at least deterred, if only they are subjected to incarceration, institutionalization, or community corrections. Most persons killed in self-defense would not have been eligible for capital punishment if duly convicted of their threatened crimes. This is particularly true of many of the abusive husbands in battered woman's defense cases.

The proportionate force, necessity, and imminence prerequisites for self-defense are designed to quiet the law's uneasiness about encouraging self-help. The requirement that deadly force only be used to counter deadly force is geared to ensure that the aggressor, in fact, will commit an intentional homicide if not met with defensive force. One must suffer nondeadly harm if use of deadly force would be the only way to avoid it. The necessity rule seeks to limit the use of self-help to circumstances in which there is absolutely no other alternative to striking back against the aggressor. It is intended to encourage the defendant to seek, in the first instance nonviolent or nondeadly defensive means. By requiring strict necessity, it is hoped that use of deadly force in self-defense will be considered only as a last resort. Finally, the imminence requirement is meant to restrict self-defense to those situations where there is no time to turn to actors in the criminal justice system to do their designated job and save the defendant from the need to resort to self-defense. Relaxation of any of these strict, narrow requirements raises the specter of justifying, and thus encouraging, self-help—conduct that the law and society prefer to discourage.

The battered woman's defense requires relaxation of all of these requirements. Rather than limiting the determination of whether these elements of the defense have been met to very limited, objectively ascertainable circumstances, defenders of battered women ask the courts to consider circumstances that would be unknown to the casual observer. Factors such as relative strength, the defendant's physical training, and the defendant's prior experiences with and knowledge about her victim are neither external nor objectively identifiable. Consideration of such circumstances is not compatible with the notion of self-defense as behavior that is justified and should be encouraged.

Even more worrisome, however, is the assumption underlying the battered woman's defense that self-defense is necessary in some situations—even when the threatened attack is not imminent—because the criminal justice system has not adequately protected women. This assertion supports the feminist demand that the concepts of imminence and necessity be broadened. Yet, it is exactly this notion that the law must suppress. For the logical corollary is that any person who believes, reasonably or unreasonably, that the criminal justice system does not offer adequate protection can resort to self-help even though there may have been sufficient time to summon the aid of lawful authority. Even when we understand the actor's unusual need to resort to self-help, the actor's behavior may still be dangerous to society. If self-defense is a justification and if justified conduct is conduct we consistently encourage because it benefits society whenever similar circumstances arise, the defense cannot rationally be expanded to encompass the battered woman's defense. Indeed, it may be that if those who suffer from battered woman syndrome or other psychological trauma induced by their social reality are more likely to kill in self-help, the criminal law should be doing even more than it currently does to prevent them from doing so. Domestic abuse is a serious societal problem but promotion of vigilantism is certainly not the solution. Treatment of self-defense as an excuse allows the judge to make a determination that it would be unjust to convict the defendant while at the same time avoiding a determination that the defendant did the right and just thing and the consequent risk of increasing the quantum of violence in an all too violent society.

Just as the early common law's difficulty with condoning self-help has survived into late twentieth century America, the conflicting recognition that an individual whose life is threatened cannot be expected to die meekly also has survived. When self-defense is categorized as an excuse, it reflects the community's understanding that, under all circumstances, the defendant understandably believed that she had no option but to kill or be killed.

Although self-help should not be affirmatively encouraged, the pressure to resort to self-help can be understood. A person who submits to these pressures is not culpable and should not be convicted of any crime.

. . .

Battered women who kill their abusers in perceived self-defense present a special challenge to the criminal justice system, especially to the evolution of the law of self-defense. Although self-defense first appeared in the common law as an excuse, in the twentieth century it has been classified as a justification. Justified conduct is otherwise criminal conduct that under particular external, objectively identifiable circumstances did not harm society. Under these circumstances it was the exact opposite of a discouraged criminal act; it was an encouraged desirable course of conduct. Few cases in which self-defense is claimed, however, fit the model of a justification. The problem is that self-defense constitutes self-help, and self-help is inimical to the rule of law.

Battered woman's defense cases are illustrative of this policy conflict. Often battered women use deadly force in self-defense under external circumstances where their act is not objectively reasonable. The woman's status as a battered woman makes her resort to deadly force understandable; it is subjectively reasonable. It is, therefore, easy to conclude that the woman is not to be blamed for her actions and should not be convicted of homicide. To hold that she acted in self-defense, however, is a determination that her act was justified. To justify such conduct may result in the encouragement of self-help as the preferred solution to domestic abuse. On the other hand, to convict or to excuse women who act in self-defense is to treat women as inferior to men whose defensive acts are justified.

The solution to this dilemma is to return self-defense to its original theoretical basis as an excuse in all cases. Excuse recognizes that, even though self-help may not be desirable and may harm society, such conduct often results from a person's understandable inability to choose an alternative course of action due to overwhelming external or internal pressures. Treatment of self-defense as an excuse accommodates the defensive needs of battered women and other individuals who act in subjectively reasonable fear given their social reality. It allows the fact-finder to consider the defender's subjective beliefs without risking the possibility that all bona fide defensive acts, no matter how objectively unreasonable, will be condoned by the criminal law. Concomitantly, it furthers the criminal law's goals of preserving life and discouraging self-help.

Endnotes

[1] Crocker, "The Meaning of Equality for Battered Women Who Kill Men in Self-Defense," 8 *Harvard Women's Law Journal* 121 (1985), no. 20 at 131 (footnotes omitted).

[2] Paul Robinson, "Criminal Law Defenses: A Systematic Analysis," 82 *Columbia Law Review* (1982): 199–291.

73. *State v. Cameron*

Petitioner, Gary Cameron, was charged with the premeditated first degree murder of his step-mother, Marie Cameron. His principal defense was that he was insane at the time he committed the offense. The Court of Appeals affirmed a guilty verdict and this court granted Cameron's petition for review. We reverse the trial court and the Court of Appeals. In doing so, we shall discuss only those issues on which reversal is granted.

At the outset it should be noted that petitioner does not challenge the charge that he stabbed Marie Cameron numerous times or that she died as a result of those wounds. Further, there does not seem to be any serious question that, except for the defense of insanity, the stabbing was done with an intent to kill. Rather, the challenge focuses on three errors alleged to have denied him a fair trial: (1) the definition of insanity in such a way as to prevent the jury's consideration of his insanity defense; (2) the admission of foreign pubic hairs found on the victim's body; and (3) the admission of hearsay evidence of an alleged statement made by the victim 2 months prior to her murder. . . .

Turning first to the insanity defense, it is clear there is evidence running counter to petitioner's

100 Wash. 2d 520 (1983)
Supreme Court of Washington

contention. This however, does not detract from petitioner's challenge to the trial court's insanity instruction. The question is whether there is evidence of insanity which the jury could have considered but for the court's instruction. We hold there is.

The basic facts reveal that on the morning of June 9, 1980, petitioner stabbed Marie Cameron in excess of 70 times, leaving the knife sticking in her heart. The body was left in the bathtub with no apparent attempt to conceal it. Later that day a police officer saw petitioner in downtown Shelton wearing only a pair of women's stretch pants, a woman's housecoat, a shirt and no shoes. He was stopped and questioned. After first giving a false name, he corrected it and explained he was dressed that way because "I just grabbed what I could . . . My mother-in-law turned vicious." He also stated he was headed for California. Having no known reason to detain petitioner, the officer released him to continue hitchhiking.

The next day petitioner was detained by the Oregon State Police as he wandered along the shoulder of Interstate 5 near Salem. Since he was wearing only the stretch pants and one shoe he was thought to be an escapee from a nearby mental hospital. A check revealed petitioner was wanted in Shelton for the death of Marie Cameron.

Petitioner was arrested and informed of his constitutional rights. He then gave two confessions, the first being a tape-recorded oral confession and the second a signed written confession. Neither is challenged by petitioner.

In the oral confession petitioner stated generally that he was living in or about the home of his father and stepmother. He left home dressed as he was because his stepmother had become violent. "[S]he's into different types of sorcery. She's just strictly a very evil person . . . and she became very violent with me, with a knife in her hand, and so, uh, I don't deny that I'm the one that did what went on out there." He indicated that when he walked into the bathroom he had not expected her. When he saw her, she had the knife which he was able to take from her easily by bending her wrist back. Then, as he stated, "I took the knife and really stabbed her."

In describing the stabbing, petitioner related: "I just kept stabbing her and stabbing her, because she wasn't feeling . . . it was as if she was laughing . . . as if she was up to something that morning, and I don't know . . . she plays around with witchcraft and that stuff . . ." The last place he saw her was in the bathtub about which he said "she kept moving and moving and moving, and kind of grabbed me like this, but laughing, as if she was enjoying . . . and it was kind of sickening, but it was really maddening to me, because of her offense towards me, it was like . . . you know, it was almost like she was mechanical . . . I mean, the thing was set up that, that's what she wanted to happen. . . . I feel that deep inside she was asking somebody to put her out of her misery . . . she was very symbolic with the 'Scarlet Whore Beast' she was very much into sorcery very, uh, anti-God, not really anti-God but takes the God's truth and twists it into sorcery."

Concerning his feelings about the incident petitioner said: "I felt confused . . . I felt no different from the beginning than the end there was no difference . . . legally I know, that it is against the law, but as far as right and wrong in the eye of God, I would say I felt no particular wrong."

When asked further about the incident petitioner responded: "I washed the blood off me, and I changed clothes, and then I looked back at her and she was, uh, she was still moving around, after being stabbed, what I thought was in the heart, and the throat . . . about seven or eight times, and she just . . . she kept moving. It was like . . . there was a

smile on her face, she kept lunging for me, while she was dead . . . I wasn't trying to be vicious . . . it would look that way, but that wasn't the intent, but she kept lunging at me, over and over again, and the nature of her attack, I was, ah, mad enough I wanted to kill her. I felt that I was justified in self-defense at that point . . ." The last petitioner saw of the knife "I tried to stick it in her heart . . . she's some kind of an animal."

Petitioner explained further "she's into a very strong sorcery trip, and that's why so many stab wounds . . . I'm not a goring [sic] person . . . I've never been violent in my life, but for some reason . . . there was some evil spirit behind her that was . . . it was like, it was like there was some thing within her that, that wasn't really part of her body . . . she was smiling . . . she was almost like enjoying playing and it was disgusting."

When petitioner subsequently gave the written confession he added: "My attack wasn't a vicious attack the first time. I was trying to stop the spirit that was moving in her. She kept saying, 'Gary, Gary, Gary,' as if she was enjoying it." When she stopped moving he washed himself, changed his clothes and then "My stepmother started moving again as if a spirit was in her. I took the knife and started stabbing her again. When I realized there was something in her that wouldn't stop moving, I started stabbing her in the head and heart. I wanted to kill the spirit that seemed to be attacking my spirit." Once again he changed his clothes but again found her moving and again stabbed her numerous times until all movement stopped. He then changed clothes once more and left.

As with the petitioner's testimony we note the testimony of the psychiatrists and psychologists is not without some disparity. Nevertheless, there is ample evidence which, under a proper insanity instruction, could have been considered by the jury as a matter of defense.

Prior to trial, petitioner made a motion to acquit on the ground of insanity pursuant to RCW 10.77.080. Three psychiatrists, Doctors Jarvis, Allison and Bremner and a psychologist, Dr. Trowbridge, were called to testify. They agreed petitioner suffered from paranoid schizophrenia both at the time of the killing and at the time of trail. Although stating it differently, all four appeared to agree that petitioner believed he was an agent of

God, required to carry out God's directions. They also agreed that petitioner believed God commanded him to kill his stepmother and that he was therefore obligated to kill the "evil spirit." Consequently, all doctors concurred he was legally insane at the time of the murder.

The trail court denied the motion for acquittal and submitted the issue of insanity to the jury. At trial, the four doctors repeated their earlier testimony. All agreed that at the time of the killing, and at the time of trial, petitioner suffered from the mental disease of paranoid schizophrenia. While expressing their views in slightly different ways, they agreed petitioner understood that, as a mechanical thing, he was killing his stepmother and knew it was against the laws of man. They stressed, however, that at the time, he was preoccupied with the delusional belief that his stepmother was an agent of satan who was persecuting him, as were others like Yasser Arafat and the Ayatollah Khomeini. He believed he was being directed by God to kill satan's angel and that by so doing, he was obeying God's higher directive or law. At this time he believed himself to be a messiah and in fact compared himself with Jesus Christ.

The doctors pointed out, in different ways, that because of his delusional beliefs, petitioner felt God had directed him to send her from this life to another. He had no remorse over the killing. He felt it was justified by God and that he was merely doing a service. "He felt he would generally be protected from any difficulties . . . because 'God would not allow it to happen.'"

Concerning the legal tests for insanity the mental health experts opined that while he understood it was against the law to kill, he believed he was responding to God's directive and thus had an obligation to rid the world of this "demon," "sorceress" or "evil spirit." Thus, while technically he understood the mechanical nature of the act he did not have the capacity to discern between right and wrong with reference to the act. Some of the doctors expressed the clear view that at the time of the killing, he was unable to appreciate the nature and quality of his acts. No doctor contended otherwise.

Concerning petitioner's insanity defense the trial court gave standard . . . pattern jury instruction . . . but, over petitioner's exception, added a last paragraph which defines "right and wrong."

In addition to the plea of not guilty, the defendant has entered a plea of insanity existing at the time of the act charged.

Insanity existing at the time of the commission of the act charged is a defense.

For a defendant to be found not guilty by reason of insanity you must find that, as a result of mental disease or defect, the extent that the defendant was unable to perceive the nature and quality of the acts with which the defendant is charged or was unable to tell right from wrong with reference to the particular acts with which defendant is charged.

What is meant by the terms "right and wrong" refers to knowledge of a person at the time of committing an act that he was acting contrary to the law. (Italics ours.)

Petitioner, on the other hand, proposed the use of [an alternative] jury instruction . . . which does not contain the last paragraph.

Petitioner argues that the trial court should have left the term "right and wrong" undefined as provided by the Legislature in RCW 9A.12.010. At the very least, it is urged, "right and wrong" should not have been defined in such a way as to exclude from the jury's deliberation the consideration of "right and wrong" in terms of one's ability to understand the moral qualities of the act.

[The court held that the instruction was wrong.]

At the time this case was tried, the Court of Appeals had just issued *State v. Crenshaw* . . . 617 P.2d 1041 (1980) which approved the instruction challenged herein. Subsequent thereto this court affirmed the Court of Appeals opinion. . . .

Insofar as the instant case is concerned, however, our discussion of *Crenshaw* also recognized an exception to the alternative grounds set forth therein. That exception is controlling here:

A narrow exception to the societal standard of moral wrong has been drawn for instances wherein a party performs a criminal act, knowing it is morally and legally wrong, but believing, because of a mental defect, that the act is ordained by God: such would be the situation with a mother who kills her infant child to whom she is devotedly attached, believing that God has spoken to her and decreed the act. Although the woman knows that the law and society condemn the act, it would be unrealistic to hold her responsible for the crime, since her free will has been subsumed by her belief in the deific decree.

. . . Consequently, as we held in *Crenshaw*, one who believes that he is acting under the direct command of God is no less insane because he nevertheless knows murder is prohibited by the laws of man. Indeed, it may actually emphasize his insanity. . . .

In the instant case there is considerable evidence (although not unanimous) from which the jury could have concluded that petitioner suffered from a mental disease; that he believed his step-mother was satan's angel or a sorceress; that he believed God directed him to kill his stepmother; that because of the mental disease it was impossible for him to understand that what he was doing was wrong; and . . . that his free will had "been subsumed by [his] belief in the deific decree." The last paragraph of the trail court's challenged instruction precluded the jury's consideration of these factors and thus runs afoul of the *Crenshaw* exception. In short, the instruction prevented the jury from considering those essential relevant facts that formed the petitioner's theory of the case. To this extent the trial court erred by adding the definitional paragraph to the instruction.

---

74. *The Abolition of the Insanity Defense*

Norval Morris

Abolition of the defense of insanity has received exhaustive attention in the literature; the informed reader is entitled, therefore, to be notified of where the argument leads so that he may avoid the sharper irritations of redundancy. In accordance with the thesis of separation of the mental health law and the criminal-law powers to incarcerate, I propose the abolition of the special defense of insanity. A fallback alternative position, in no way conflicting with the separation thesis, is for the abolition of the special defense and for legislative substitution of a qualified defense of diminished responsibility to a charge of murder having the effect, if successful, of a conviction of manslaughter with the usual sentencing discretion attached to that crime.

The argument will be presented in broad perspective, the nuances of difference between the competing defenses of insanity being glossed over. The sequence will be (a) the general argument for abolition, (b) an analysis of how the law would operate under the proposed abolition and the alternative substitution of diminished responsibility, and (c) a consideration and repudiation of the main criticisms of the abolition proposal.

The problem is to cut through the accumulated cases, commentaries, and confusions to the issues of principle underlying the responsibility of the mentally ill for conduct otherwise criminal. The issues are basically legal, moral, and political, not medical or psychological, though, of course, the developing insights of psychiatry and psychology are of close relevance to those legal, moral, and political issues.

. . .

Reprinted by permission of The University of Chicago Press.

I must stress that in advocating the abolition of the special defense of insanity, the nuances of difference among the *McNaughtan* Rules, the *Durham* Rule, the rules offered by the American Law Institute and accepted in *Brawner* and in many state criminal codes, the irresistible impulse test, the recommendations of the Group for the Advancement of Psychiatry, and other suggested special defenses, though important in practice and meriting close analysis, are not essential to the present discussion. All vary around the following structure: a definition of mental illness, as a threshold to the invocation of the defense, and a statement of a required causal relationship between that "mental illness" and the otherwise criminal behavior of the accused. My thesis stands, whatever definition of illness and whatever language to capture a causal relationship are offered. And, of course, variations on where the burdens of proof are placed on those two issues, and on how heavy are those burdens, are also irrelevant.

. . .

Why, then, go beyond the simple rule, to give mental illness the same exculpatory effect as, say, blindness or deafness? Evidence of the latter afflictions may be admitted as indicative of lack of both the *actus reus* (prohibited act) and the *mens rea* of a crime. Why go further? The answer lies in the pervasive moral sense that when choice to do ill is lacking, it is improper to impute guilt. And hence there is pressure for a special defense of insanity, just as there is pressure for a special defense of infancy or duress.

. . .

One is left . . . with the feeling that the special defense is a genuflection to a deep-seated moral sense that the mentally ill lack freedom of choice to guide and govern their conduct and that therefore blame should not be imputed to them for their otherwise criminal acts nor should punishment be imposed. To the validity of this argument we will several times return, but it is important not to assume that those who advocate the abolition of the special defense of insanity are recommending the wholesale punishment of the sick. They are urging rather that mental illness be given the same exculpatory effect as other adversities that bear upon criminal guilt. And they add the not unfair criticism of the conventional position that they observe the widespread conviction and punishment of the mentally ill, the special defense being an ornate rarity, a

tribute to our capacity to pretend to a moral position when pursuing profoundly different practices.

The number held as not guilty by reason of insanity in the United States as a whole and in some states will illustrate the relative rarity of the special defense. Nationally, in the 1978 census of state and federal facilities, 3,140 persons were being held as not guilty by reason of insanity.[1] In Illinois, at the time of writing 127 are so held. In New York, between 1965 and 1976 inclusive, 278 persons were found not guilty by reason of insanity (53 in the first five years, 225 in the second six years—the increase being explicable presumably by constitutionally imposed relaxation of the *Brawner* rules for, and processes of, releasing those found not guilty by reason of insanity). No one acquainted with the work of the criminal courts can think that these numbers remotely approximate the relationship between serious mental illness and criminal conduct. The defense is pleaded only where it may be advantageous to the accused and that balance of advantage fluctuates with sentencing practice and rules and practices relating to the release of those found not guilty by reason of insanity. Hence statistics will not lead us to principle in this matter; a more fundamental inquiry is necessary.

A useful entering wedge to principle is to inquire, What is the irreducible minimum relationship between mental illness and criminal guilt? What is the least the criminal law could do in this matter?

It is unthinkable that mental illness should be given a lesser reach than drunkenness. If a given mental condition (intent, recklessness) is required for the conviction of a criminal offense, then, as a proposition requiring no discussion, in the absence of that mental condition there can be no conviction. This holds true whether the absence of that condition is attributable to blindness, deafness, drunkenness, mental illness or retardation, linguistic difficulties, or, if it could be established, hypnotic control. But this states basic principles of criminal law, not a special defense. The main reasons for defining a "special defense" beyond the traditional common-law relationship between mental illness and the *actus reus* and *mens rea* of crime are, I think, twofold: expediency in crime control and fairness.

The expediency rationale can be quickly advanced and disposed of; the fairness rationale is more difficult.

In an important article in 1963, "Abolish 'The Insanity Defense'—Why Not?"[2] J. Goldstein and J. Katz accurately perceived that "the insanity defense is not a defense, it is a device for triggering indeterminate restraint"[3] of those who were mentally ill at the time of the crime but are not civilly committable now. In considerable part, that has been its role since 1800 when the emergence of the special defense in England led to the Criminal Lunatics Act of 1800, which provided indeterminate custody for those found not guilty by reason of insanity, with similar legislation spreading in the states and federal systems in this country.

Few are prepared any longer to justify the special defense on this crime control basis, as a means of confining the dangerous though not civilly committable. It would be a strange "defense," an unusual benevolence, whose purpose is confinement of those who could not otherwise be confined.

Hence we are brought to the central issue—the question of fairness, the sense that it is unjust and unfair to stigmatize the mentally ill as criminals and to punish them for their crimes. The criminal law exists to deter and to punish those who would or who do choose to do wrong. If they cannot exercise choice, they cannot be deterred and it is a moral outrage to punish them.[4] The argument sounds powerful but its premise is weak.

Choice is neither present nor absent in the typical case where the insanity defense is currently pleaded; what is at issue is the degree of freedom of choice on a continuum from the hypothetically entirely rational to the hypothetically pathologically determined—in states of consciousness neither polar condition exists.

The moral issue sinks into the sands of reality. Certainly it is true that in a situation of total absence of choice it is outrageous to inflict punishment; but the frequency of such situations to the problems of criminal responsibility becomes an issue of fact in which tradition and clinical knowledge and practice are in conflict. The traditions of being possessed of evil spirits, of being bewitched, confront the practices of a mental health system which increasingly fashions therapeutic practices to hold patients responsible for their conduct. And suppose we took the moral argument seriously and eliminated responsibility in those situations where we thought there had been a substantial impairment of the ca-

pacity to choose between crime and no crime (I set aside problems of strict liability and of negligence for the time being). Would we not have to, as a matter of moral fairness, fashion a special defense of gross social adversity? The matter might be tested by asking which is the more criminogenic, psychosis or serious social deprivation? In an article in 1968 on this topic I raised the question of whether there should be a special defense of dwelling in a black ghetto.[5] Some literal-minded commentators castigated me severely for such a recommendation, mistaking a form of argument, the *reductio ad absurdum*, for a recommendation. But let me again press the point. If one were asked how to test the criminogenic effect of any factor in man or in the environment, the answer would surely follow empirical lines. . . .

Hence, at first blush, it seems a perfectly legitimate correlational and, I submit, causal inquiry, whether psychosis, or any particular type of psychosis, is more closely related to criminal behavior than, say, being born to a one-parent family living on welfare in a black inner-city area. And there is no doubt of the empirical answer. Social adversity is grossly more potent in its pressure toward criminality, certainly toward all forms of violence and street crime as distinct from white-collar crime, than is any psychotic condition. As a factual matter, the exogenous pressures are very much stronger than the endogenous.

But the argument feels wrong. Surely there is more to it than the simple calculation of criminogenic impact. Is this unease rationally based? I think not, though the question certainly merits further consideration. As a rational matter it is hard to see why one should be more responsible for what is done to one than for what one is. Yet major contributors to jurisprudence and criminal-law theory insist that it is necessary to maintain the denial of responsibility on grounds of mental illness to preserve the moral infrastructure of the criminal law.[6] For many years I have struggled with this opinion by those whose work I deeply respect, yet I remain unpersuaded. Indeed, they really don't try to persuade, but rather affirm and reaffirm with vehemence and almost mystical sincerity the necessity of retaining the special defense of insanity as a moral prop to the entire criminal law.

And indeed I think that much of the discussion of the defense of insanity is the discussion of a myth rather than of a reality. It is no minor debating point that in fact we lack a defense of insanity as an operating tool of the criminal law other than in relation to a very few particularly heinous and heavily punished offenses. There is not an operating defense of insanity in relation to burglary or theft, or the broad sweep of index crimes generally; the plea of not guilty on the ground of insanity is rarely to be heard in city courts of first instance which handle the grist of the mill of the criminal law—though a great deal of pathology is to be seen in the parade of accused and convicted persons before these courts. As a practical matter we reserve this defense for a few sensational cases where it may be in the interest of the accused either to escape the possibility of capital punishment (though in cases where serious mental illness is present, the risk of execution is slight) or where the likely punishment is of a sufficient severity to make the indeterminate commitment of the accused a preferable alternative to a criminal conviction. Operationally the defense of insanity is a tribute, it seems to me, to our hypocrisy rather than to our morality.

To be less aggressive about the matter and to put aside anthropomorphic allegations of hypocrisy, the special defense of insanity may properly be indicted as producing a morally unsatisfactory classification on the continuum between guilt and innocence. It applies in practice to only a few mentally ill criminals, thus omitting many others with guilt-reducing relationships between their mental illness and their crime; it excludes other powerful pressures on human behavior, thus giving excessive weight to the psychological over the social. It is a false classification in the sense that if a team of the world's most sensitive and trained psychiatrists and moralists were to select from all those found guilty of felonies and those found not guilty by reason of insanity any given number who should not be stigmatized as criminals, very few of those found not guilty by reason of insanity would be selected. How to offer proof of this? The only proof, I regret, is to be found by personal contact with a flow of felony cases through the courts and into the prisons. No one of serious perception will fail to recognize both the extent of mental illness and retardation among the prison population and the overwhelming weight of adverse social circumstances on criminal behavior. This is, of course, not an argument that so-cial adversities should lead to acquittals; they should be taken into account in sentencing. And the same is true of the guilt and sentencing of those pressed by psychological adversities. The special defense is thus a morally false classification. And it is a false classification also in the sense that it does not select from the prison population those most in need of psychiatric treatment.

. . .

There are three points to be made in favor of a legislatively introduced rule of "diminished responsibility" in this country of the type now well tested by English juries.

First, for some exceptional murder charges *mens rea* principles and even rules like the Illinois 9-2-(b) may not suffice to reduce murder to manslaughter in cases where such a reduction is desirable. I hypothesize an accused who is clearly psychotic and paranoiac believing he is commanded by God to kill, as Hadfield and some others have believed. He has heard voices to that effect and is in no doubt of his moral duty. He probably does not fall within any *mens rea* provisions which would reduce his crime from murder to manslaughter (unless one sets out on the unacceptable path of California case law) and does not fall within analogues of Illinois section 9-2-(b) since he does not believe he has a defense to a criminal charge. Yet such cases are, it is submitted, better treated and sentenced as manslaughter than as murder. A legislative provision modeled on the English Homicide Act of 1957 would achieve that result.

Secondly, where states impose mandatory sentences on those convicted of murder, some escape mechanisms from those sentences for the mentally ill (other than frustration by charge bargaining) are desirable. The evil to be remedied here lies in the mandatory sentence, not in the criminal law relating to mentally ill criminals; but the only politically acceptable remedy may be legislative enunciation of a doctrine of diminished responsibility.

Thirdly, diminished responsibility is, on close analysis, apart from the two special problems in the two previous paragraphs, a shift of sentencing discretion to a degree from judge to jury, the jury under diminished responsibility lowering the maximum (and sometimes the minimum) sentencing range within which the judge will impose sentence.

In some states there may be advantages in such a limitation of judicial discretion.

I now try to draw the analysis to a close. For the reasons offered above I urge the legislative abolition of the special defense of insanity. For those who find persuasive the three reasons last offered for a special legislatively introduced doctrine of diminished responsibility to flush out ordinary *mens rea* doctrines I recommend a formula akin to that in the English Homicide Act of 1957 with the accused who falls within it being convicted of and sentenced for manslaughter, his sentence taking into account his mental illness at the time of the crime.

. . .

Endnotes

[1] Steadman, Monahan, Hartstone, Davis & Clark, "Mentally Disordered Offenders: A National Survey of Patients and Facilities," *Law and Human Behavior.*

[2] 72 *Yale L. J.* 853 (1963).

[3] *Id.* at 868.

[4] Arguments for the retention of the special defense of insanity as a moral foundation of the criminal law are offered by Herbert Wechsler (see, for example, 37 F.R.D. 365 (2d Cir. 1964)) and by Sanford Kadish ("The Decline of Innocence," 26 *Camb. L. J.* 273 (1968)). A more cautious support of retention is advanced by Francis A. Allen (*Law, Intellect and Education*, at 114–18 (1979)). Contrary views, generally supporting the abolitionist position taken in this chapter, are advanced by H. L. A. Hart, Chief Justice Weintraub, Lady Barbara Wooton, Joel Feinberg, Dr. Seymour Halleck, and Dr. Thomas Szasz. (Their views are summarized in the appendix to N. Morris, "Psychiatry and the Dangerous Criminal," 41 *S. Cal. L. Rev.* 514 (1968), prepared by Gary Lowenthal; see n. 13 of that article). The lists of those favoring abolition lengthens with the Butler Committee Report . . . and the Carnahan Report . . . as well as the apparently unending debates of the various proposals for a Federal Criminal Code. [Report of the Committee on Mentally Abnormal Offenders, Cmd. 6244 (1975).]

[5] Morris, note 4 *supra.*

[6] See note 4 *supra.*

75. *The Decline of Innocence*

SANFORD KADISH

The criminological positivist at the turn of the century started a good deal of creative rethinking about the criminal law. Some of their proposals have gained widespread acceptance in the criminal law as we know it today. Others made no headway at all. One particular proposal, and a very fundamental one indeed, began a controversy which has ebbed and flowed regularly since. That is the proposal to eliminate from the criminal law the whole apparatus of substantive principles, or at least some of them, such as the legal insanity defense, which owe their presence to the law's traditional concern for distinguishing the guilty and the innocent in terms of their blameworthiness. The essence of the proposal is that innocence in this sense, moral innocence, if you will, should not disqualify a person from the consequences of the penal law. Moral innocence should, it is urged, give way to social dangerousness as the basis for a criminal disposition.

In recent years there has been a resurgence of the controversy produced by serious proposals to eliminate the defense of legal insanity and, more radical

Reprinted by permission of Cambridge University Press and the author.

still, to eliminate across the board the requirements of *mens rea* from the definition of criminal offenses and defenses. If I may raise my colors at the outset, I am frankly a friend to neither proposal. In this brief paper I would like to discuss the implications of these suggested reforms and to develop my reasons for believing that the case has not been made.

The term *"mens rea"* is rivaled only by the term "jurisdiction" for the varieties of senses in which it has been used and for the quantity of obfuscation it has created. A few introductory paragraphs on usage is inescapable if minds are to meet on the genuine issues.

The criminal law constitutes a description of harms which a society seeks to discourage with the threat of criminal punishment for those who commit those harms. At the same time the criminal law comprises an elaborate body of qualifications to these prohibitions and threats. It used to be common, and it still is not unknown, to express all of these qualifications to liability in terms of the requirement of *mens rea*. This is the thought behind the classic maxim, *"Actus non facit reum, nisi mens sit rea."* Or in Blackstone's translation, "An unwarrantable act without a vicious will is no crime at all." The vicious will was the *mens rea*. Reduced to its essence it referred to the choice to do a blameworthy act. The requirement of *mens rea* was rationalized on the common sense view of justice that blame and punishment were inappropriate and unjust in the absence of that choice.

It is more helpful (and also more usual today) to speak more discriminatingly of the various classes of circumstances in which criminal liability is qualified by the requirement of blameworthiness. Putting aside the circumstances of justification and excuse (they are relevant but not central to the controversy) there are two principal categories of *mens rea* which should be distinguished.

The *first* category we can call *mens rea* in its special sense. In this special sense *mens rea* refers only to the mental state which is required by the definition of the offense to accompany the act which produces or threatens the harm. An attempt to commit a crime consists of an act which comes close to its commission done *with the purpose that the crime be committed.* Unlawful assembly is joining with a group in a public place *with intent to commit unlawful acts.* Larceny consists of the appropriation of another's property *knowing* it is not your own with *intent* to deprive the

owner or possessor of it permanently. Receiving stolen goods is a crime when one receives those goods *knowing they are stolen.* Manslaughter is the killing of another by an act done with *awareness* of a substantial and unjustifiable risk of doing so.

That the absence of the *mens rea*, in this special sense of the required mental state, precludes liability in all of these cases is of course the merest tautology. This is the way these crimes are defined. But it is important to see that they are so defined because the special *mens rea* element is crucial to the description of the conduct we want to make criminal. And description is crucial in so far as it is regarded as important to exclude from the definition of criminality what we do not want to punish as criminal. To revert to the examples just given, it would not be regarded as appropriate to make criminal the taking of another's property where the taker believed honestly that he was taking his own property. Neither would it make sense to make a person guilty of receiving stolen goods where he neither knew nor had occasion to know that the goods were stolen. And surely we should see nothing criminal in joining a group in a public place, apart from the intent to commit unlawful acts.

The *second* category of *mens rea* qualifications to liability is that of legal responsibility, which includes the familiar defenses of legal insanity and infancy. These qualifications differ in several particulars from the *mens rea* qualifications of the first category. In requiring *mens rea* in the first, special, sense the law is saying that it does not hold a person where he has shown himself by his conduct, judged in terms of its totality, including his mental state, to be no different than the rest of us, or not different enough to justify the criminal sanction. In requiring *mens rea* in the sense of legal responsibility, the law absolves a person precisely because his deficiencies of temperament, personality or maturity distinguish him so utterly from the rest of us to whom the law's threats are addressed that we do not expect him to comply.

Proposals to eliminate the defense of legal insanity entail the abolition of *mens rea* in this latter sense of legal responsibility. The elimination of *mens rea* in its special sense raises more radical challenges to the traditional criminal law. Let me start with legal insanity.

I

Devising an appropriate definition of legal insanity has been the subject of most of the argument concerning this defense. The modern starting point in England and the United States is the M'Naghten test formulated in 1843 which asks whether at the time of the act the accused was laboring under such a disease of the mind as not to know the nature and quality of the act he was doing, or that it was wrong.

The justification for this formulation is that it does in fact exclude from liability a category of persons who by definition could not be deterred by the prospect of punishment, simply because they were incapable of choice, and whom, in consequence, it would be futile as well as unjust to punish. The definition of the exculpation, therefore, coincides with the rationale of the traditional requirement of *mens rea*. Nonetheless, the M'Naghten test has been vigorously and consistently criticized since its formulation. One can roughly identify four major themes of criticism, which, half-seriously, I want to refer to as the themes of reaction, liberal reform, radical reform and neo-reaction.

The reactionary criticism is based on the premise that the defense of legal insanity provides a loophole through which those who deserve punishment can too easily manage to escape. Therefore, the protection of the public requires that the defense be eliminated altogether, or at least be made so difficult to establish (for example, by placing the burden upon the defendant to prove his insanity beyond reasonable doubt) that very few will escape.

The liberal reform criticism is that the M'Naghten test does not go far enough. Inconsistently with its own premise of exculpating the blameless the test fails to cover classes of defendants who merit exculpation as much as those it does exculpate. The major class of such defendants comprises those whose ability to choose to conform is destroyed even though their cognitive capacity is sufficiently intact to disqualify them under M'Naghten. Another class consists of those who *knew* on a superficial intellectual level what they were doing and that it was wrong, but did not really understand with the full emotional affect that gives meaning to knowledge. This criticism produced a

number of changes in the legal insanity defense in American jurisdictions, notably the addition of the irresistible impulse defense and a broadening in the conception of the requirement of knowledge. It has also produced the increasingly influential proposal of the American Law Institute's Model Penal code: "A person is not responsible for criminal conduct if at the time of such conduct as a result of mental disease or defect he lacks substantial capacity either to appreciate the criminality of his conduct or to conform his conduct to the requirements of law."

The radical critique of M'Naghten is that it is wrongheaded, not simply inadequate, because it is based upon particular symptoms of mental disease in large part meaningless in the medical conception of mental illness. In short, it is a mistake to attempt to impose a legal definition upon what is inevitably a medical phenomenon. As a consequence of this criticism such proposals emerged as those of the Royal Commission on Capital Punishment in 1953 which put the test of legal insanity in terms of whether an accused was suffering from mental disease or deficiency to such a degree that he ought not to be held responsible. It also produced the famous Durham test in 1954 which inquires whether the unlawful act of the accused was the product of mental disease or defects. Such proposals have found virtually no acceptance either in England or in the United States.

The neo-reactionary criticism recommends that efforts to find improved definitions of the test of legal insanity be abandoned and that legal insanity as a defense be eliminated from the criminal law. The justification for this view differs from the reactionary case for abolition. Both end up proposing undiscriminating penalisation of the sick and the bad. But the new criticism, or much of it, does so as a first step toward penalizing neither. This more sophisticated proposal for abolition has been advanced by a variety of persons for a variety of reasons. Let me try to summarize what I understand to be the major arguments.

The first is that the administration of the tests of insanity—all tests—have been a total failure. It has proven impossible to administer the defense rationally and equitably. In the end the jury's determination is largely governed by the credentials and presentation of the psychiatric experts; and the defendant's ability to pay determines the quality of the psychiatric evidence he can present. Moreover, psychiatric testimony is worth little—it is the softest of the soft sciences, psychiatrists disagree on key concepts and their conclusions and analyses turn on their own value judgments. Finally, the whole enterprise is an elaborate search after something that does not exist—there is not and cannot be a workable distinction between the responsible and the irresponsible, particularly when the distinction is drawn in terms of the issue of volitional capacity.

Secondly, it is argued that the defense of legal insanity is of little practical importance. To be sure the defense has real bite in cases of capital punishment. But the death penalty has been abolished in England and is fast becoming otiose in the United States. In the United States legal insanity is pleaded in no more than about 2 percent of the jury cases which go to trial. In England the situation is similar. With increasing frequency, issues of the mental abnormality of the offender are being taken into account after conviction rather than before. For example, mental abnormality questions in England are taken into consideration in probation orders with mental treatment as a condition, in hospital orders under section 60 or 65 of the Mental Health Act of 1959 and in transfers of prisoners from prisons to mental hospitals. As a consequence of these developments in recent years only in about 1 or 2 percent of cases is the mental abnormality of an offender taken into account by finding the defendant not guilty because of legal insanity.

Finally, and of central importance, it is believed that the retention of the distinction between those to be punished and those only to be treated is unfortunate and invidious because in point of fact it is in all cases, not only in some, that persons who do harms should be treated and held in the interest of the public protection. The incidence of gross psychopathy among criminal offenders is enormous, ranging over the widest classes of offenders, and only the smallest fraction are covered by the legal insanity tests. The effect of maintaining the dichotomy between the sick and the bad (essentially a false one anyway) is to block public and legislative perception that in most crimes psychical and social determinants inhibit the capacity of the actors to control their behavior. As a consequence effective develop-

ment and use of psychiatric therapeutic resources for the vast majority of offenders are thwarted.

In the last analysis this case for abolition makes two claims—the first, that the present situation is bad; the second, that abolition would make it better. My own view is that the first claim is supportable although somewhat overdrawn. The second claim I believe is unfounded.

I am ready to concede that the record of the administration of the legal insanity defense is very bad indeed. And to some extent I am inclined to believe that the softness of psychiatry as a science and the inherent difficulty of the issue which the defense presents are partly responsible. But several necessary qualifications tend to blunt the point made by this criticism. The insanity defense is scarcely the only feature of our criminal justice system which is badly administered in practice. For example, inefficiency and inequity are endemic to a system committed to an adversary process but not committed to supplying the resources of legal contest to the typically penurious who make up the bulk of criminal defendants. But I would hope that the lesson of all this would not be to abandon the adversary method on that score, but to improve its operation. Likewise with the insanity defense, improvement of its operation rather than its abolition would seem the more appropriate response. The difficulty is not all produced by psychiatrists and the nature of the issue. To the extent that the difficulty is due to inadequate defense resources, to persistent, if not perverse, misunderstandings by psychiatrists of what the law's concern is, to unjustifiable restrictions on the scope of psychiatric testimony—and I believe it is due to all of these factors to some extent—it seems at least equally plausible to address those causes as to eliminate the feature of the law which allows them to operate. And even to the extent that the causes of the difficulty are incorrectible because inherent in the insanity defense, the case for abolition is not made out, any more than the case for abolishing the jury or the defense of unintentionality or ignorance would be made out by pointing to the grave problems of administration they produce. This dispositive issue is whether we would achieve a net gain in doing without the troublesome element in the law. And this I will come to shortly.

As to the argument founded on the infrequency of the defense, in one sense it cuts the other way. For to the extent that the case for abolition rests on the inequitableness and irrationality of its administration, the very infrequency of the invocation of that defense reduces the import of the criticism. But in any event the infrequency of a defense is not an argument for its elimination. The defenses of necessity or duress surely are invoked in a minute fraction of criminal cases. Yet few would regard this as a reason for abandoning them. The function of a legal defense is not measured by its use but by its usefulness in the total framework of the criminal justice system.

Finally, we face the claim that the perpetuation of the insanity defense has tended to reduce the flow of psychiatric and other resources for treatment of the great mass of offenders. Certainly the flow has been far too small. We need more research and more resources in the effective treatment of offenders. But whether the presence of the insanity defense has contributed to this situation (and substantially so, according to the charge) is a question of fact which I have not seen the slightest evidence to support. Indeed there is evidence to the contrary—witness the proliferation in England of alternative routes for the disposition of psychologically disturbed offenders which abolitionists often use to show the otioseness of the defense of legal insanity.

Now for the second claim. Would we achieve a net advantage in eliminating the defense? As a start let us try to get clear what would follow if the defense of legal insanity were abolished. Certainly what would follow would depend on the formulation of the defense. But for present purposes we can confine ourselves to M'Naghten. Since other tests include the cases which it covers, what is true of eliminating the M'Naghten defense is true of eliminating the other formulations as well.

It will be remembered that M'Naghten authorizes the defense of legal insanity when the effect of the defendant's mental disease is to destroy his cognitive capacity, to make him unable to know the nature and quality of his act. When this is so the defense of legal insanity is made out and the defendant becomes subject to the variety of provisions governing commitment of the criminally insane. Now if this defense were eliminated what would be the position of a defendant charged with a crime? Apparently it would depend upon the *mens rea*, in the special sense, required by the definition of the crime. If the crime were one like attempt, requiring a purpose by the defendant to achieve an object; or if it were one like larceny, requiring knowledge of a particular matter of fact; or if it were one like manslaughter, requiring knowledge of a particular risk, would it not be the case that the defendant has a complete defense? A total inability to know the nature and quality of the act quite plainly precludes convicting a defendant of any crime whose definition requires that he have that knowledge. And any crime which requires intent, or knowledge or recklessness surely posits that knowing. If it were not for the special, preemptive defense of legal insanity, therefore, the defendant would have a complete defense on the merits to any such crime—namely, the lack of *mens rea*. What the insanity defense does is to deprive a defendant of his normal *mens rea* defense (which would be unqualified and lead to discharge) and to require that he be acquitted on this special ground with its consequences for indeterminate commitment.

If, on the other hand, the crime required only negligence, the absence of an insanity defense would leave the defendant with no defense at all, since all that is required is that the defendant has fallen substantially below the standard of the reasonable man, and this, by definition, a M'Naghten defendant has done. (Except, of course, to the extent that the subjective feature of the concept of negligence—requiring that *some* special characteristics of the defendant be considered in defining the standard, as, for example, his inability to see or to hear—were enlarged to embrace his special cognitive disabilities.)

Now precisely these consequences are apparently intended, or at least accepted, by some abolitionists. But it is difficult to see the force of their case. The whole spirit of the proposal is to put social defense on a surer ground; to assure that those who constitute threats to personal and social security be effectively channeled into a preventive system which authorizes the state to subject them to restraint in the public interest and to provide them with a therapeutic regimen both in the public interest and in their own. The effect of eliminating the insanity defense is to do the opposite precisely for those offenders who have done the greatest harm—those defined by crimes requiring *mens rea* of intent, knowledge or recklessness. (As for crimes of negligence, to which insane defendants might still be liable, this objection does not apply, of course. Here the difficulty created is the conviction of the innocent, a matter I will consider subsequently.)

This self-defeating consequence of eliminating the insanity defense simpliciter has moved other abolitionists to add another branch to their proposal. This entails enactment of a provision which would preclude all evidence bearing on the absence of *mens rea* which is founded on the mental abnormality of the accused. This was the form, for example, that the earliest abolitionist enactment in the United States took. In 1909 the State of Washington amended its law to provide that it should no longer be a defense that the defendant by reason of his insanity was unable to comprehend the nature and quality of the act committed. But the statute then continued: "nor shall any testimony or other proof thereof be admitted in evidence." In addition, it is interesting to note, the statute, consistent with the positivist premise and with more modern proposals, provided for indeterminate commitment in a state hospital for the insane or "the insane ward of the state penitentiary" for those convicted who are found by the judge to meet the M'Naghten test of insanity.

To the abolitionist proposal on this footing there are two principal objections—the first technical, the second fundamental.

The technical objection is this. For the reasons put earlier evidence of the defendant's mental abnormality may be directly relevant to the presence of the *mens rea* of the crime charged, without of which a conviction is not possible. If *some* evidence which is relevant to the issue of *mens rea* is excluded the judge must have a standard to distinguish the admissible from the inadmissible evidence. This standard, of course, under the Washington statute, as well as under similarly grounded formulations, would presumably be whether the evidence goes to establish the inability of the defendant, as the result of a mental disease, to understand the nature and the quality of his acts. The upshot would be, therefore, that the test of legal insanity having been ejected through one door would re-enter through another, now presenting itself as a rule of evidence rather than as a substantive defense. And a good deal, if not all, of the messy and unsettling business

of bringing psychiatrists into the courtroom and in exposing the guilt-innocent determination to those inherently inconclusive medical arguments over the operation of men's minds, which it is one of the important objectives of the abolitionist proposals to eliminate, would not be eliminated after all. For how else could the parties address themselves to the issue of whether certain *mens rea* evidence, somehow touching the defendant's mental abnormality, is or is not part of the forbidden case bearing on legal insanity?

And there is another consideration which makes the picture even darker for the success of this proposal. That is the unlikelihood of finally working to screen out any substantial amount of psychiatric evidence from the trail on the issue of guilt or innocence. California's experience with the bifurcated trial teaches a dismaying lesson. In order to clarify and simplify the issues before the jury, the California law was amended in 1927 to require separate trials whenever the defendant raises defenses on the merits as well as the defense of legal insanity. At the first trial, the defendant's sanity is presumed, and evidence bearing on legal insanity is excluded. The lower courts struggled for years in an attempt to distinguish between admissible and inadmissible evidence at the first trial. But it was hopeless. Evidence of mental insanity tending to establish legal insanity will usually do double service as also tending to establish the absence of the specific *mens rea* required. Finally the Supreme Court ended the agony by holding that any evidence of defendant's mental abnormality was admissible at the trial of the issue of his guilt, so long as it was relevant to the existence of a mental state required by the crime. The experiment was a failure—issues of guilt and of mental condition proved to be inseparable. Abolishing the legal insanity defense is no more likely to keep the trial free of psychiatry and its preceptors and their probing into the mental condition of the accused than is the requirement of the separate trial of the issue of insanity. You can change the name of the game, but you cannot avoid playing it so long as *mens rea* is required.

I turn now to what I referred to as the fundamental objection to this proposal. Essentially it is that it opens to the condemnation of a criminal conviction a class of persons who, on any common-sense notion of justice, are beyond blaming and ought not to be punished. The criminal law as we know it today does associate a substantial condemnatory onus with conviction for a crime. So long as this is so a just and humane legal system has an obligation to make a distinction between those who are eligible for this condemnation and those who are not. It is true, as has been argued, that a person adjudicated not guilty but insane suffers a substantial social stigma. It is also true that this is hurtful and unfortunate, and indeed, unjust. But it results from the misinterpretation placed upon the person's conduct by people in the community. It is not, like the conviction of the irresponsible, the paradigmatic affront to the sense of justice in the law which consists in the deliberative act of convicting a morally innocent person of a crime, of imposing blame when there is no occasion for it.

This sentiment of justice has attained constitutional stature in decisions of the United States Supreme Court. Obviously I do not bring the Supreme Court into this for its legal authority in the U.K. What is relevant is that in these decisions the court was responding to a fundamental sense of justice, which, unlike the mandate of the court, does not stop at national boundaries. The animating principle in several recent decisions was that to convict a person of a crime in circumstances in which it was impossible for him to conform violates a fundamental principle of justice. It was this principle which led the court to hold that it constituted an unconstitutional imposition of cruel and unusual punishment to make it a crime for a person "to be" a narcotic addict. The same principle persuaded the court in another case to find a violation of due process of law in the conviction of a person for failing to register as a previously convicted offender upon arrival in Los Angeles in the absence of any circumstances calculated to give notice of her obligation to do so. As observed recently by Mr. Justice Fortas: "Our morality does not permit us to punish for illness. We do not impose punishment for involuntary conduct, whether the lack of volition results from 'insanity,' or addition to narcotics, or from other illnesses."[1]

Of course the spirit behind these proposals to abolish the insanity defense is humane rather than punitive: what is contemplated is that persons, once convicted, who are insane would them receive all the care and treatment appropriate to their condition, as indeed would all persons who commit crime. The answer was given by the Washington Supreme Court when it declared unconstitutional the abolition amendment to which I earlier referred: "Yet the stern and awful fact still remains, and is patent to all men, that the status and condition in the eyes of the world, and under the law, of one convicted of crime is vastly different from that of one simply adjudged insane. We cannot shut our eyes to the fact that the element of punishment is still in our criminal laws."[2]

A common rejoinder is that we convict and punish persons daily whose ability to conform is impaired by a variety of circumstances—by youthful neglect, by parental inadequacy, by the social and psychical deprivations of growing up in a grossly underprivileged minority subculture, or by countless other contingencies of life. This is perfectly true, but I fail to see that it supports eliminating the insanity defense. First, the argument logically is an argument for extension of the defense of lack of responsibility, not for its abolition. It is never a reason for adding to injustice that we are already guilty of some. Second, confining the defense to patent and extreme cases of irresponsibility is not a whimsical irrationality. There may well be an injustice in it, but it rests upon the practical concern to avoid vitiating the deterrent impact of the criminal law upon those who are more or less susceptible to its influences. As Professor Wechsler has observed: "The problem is to differentiate between the wholly non-deterrable and persons who are more or less susceptible to influence by law. The category must be so extreme that to the ordinary man burdened by passion and beset by large temptations, the exculpation of the irresponsibles bespeaks no weakness in the law. He does not identify with them; they are a world apart."[3] We may accept as a necessary evil—necessary, that is, given our commitment to a punishment system—the criminal conviction of persons whose ability to conform is somewhat impaired and still protest that it is unacceptable for a society to fail to make a distinction for those who are utterly and obviously beyond the reach of the law.

At the heart of a good deal of the argument for abolition is, and must be, the rejection of the punishment system altogether. To the extent this is the case the rejoinder I have just been discussing makes more sense. The refusal to punish defined classes of offenders is an assertion of the propriety of punishing the rest. As Professor Morris has rightly observed, "one group's exculpation from criminal responsibility confirms the inculpation of other groups."[4] On this footing my reservations to the abolitionist proposal is twofold. In the first place it is far from self-evident that the best way to achieve the end of penalisation is by penalizing all rather than by expanding the definition of the irresponsible. Secondly, and more fundamentally, the decline of guilt—which is what penalization is about—also means, and necessarily, the decline of innocence.

. . .

Endnotes

[1] *Budd v. California*, 385 U.S. 909, 912–913 (1966) (dissenting opinion).

[2] *State v. Strasburg*, 110 Pac. 1020, 1025 (1910).

[3] "The Criteria of Criminal Responsibility" (1955) 22 *Univ. of Chi. L. Rev.* 367, 374.

[4] N. Morris, "Psychiatry and the Dangerous Criminal" (1968) 41 *So. Calif. L. Rev.* 514.

Study Questions

1. According to Corrado, what is the utilitarian theory of excuses? What problems does Corrado set out for the utilitarian claim that the "deterrability" of an offender should be the key determinant in whether that person is excused?

2. What is the "character" theory of excuse, according to Corrado? What is an example of an act that the character theorist would excuse? What kinds of acts would such a theorist not excuse?

3. According to Rosen, what rationales are typically given in support of treating self-defense as a justification?

4. How does Rosen respond to the objection that simply excusing women who kill their abusers, rather than justifying their conduct as appropriate self-defense, will reinforce stereotypes of women as irrational?

5. In 1990 nine children of Hmong parents died from cardiac arrest after contracting measles. The parents had initially sought the aid of shamans and had waited until the children were near death before taking them to a hospital. In other incidents, Hmong immigrants have refused corrective surgery or chemotherapy for their children. In one case, a shaman told the family that the child's condition was to atone for sins committed by ancestors, and that medical intervention would pass these sins on to the next generation. Assuming that the parents in such cases were to face criminal charges relating to medical neglect of their children, should they be able to invoke their sincerely held religious beliefs and cultural practices as an excuse?

6. What is the argument for a cultural defense to criminal liability? Is the assumption that members of a minority subculture are ignorant of the applicable law? Although ignorance of governing law is generally not an excuse, should it be for those raised in a foreign culture? If cultural factors are presented to the jury in an effort to show that the defendant should be excused for breaking the law, what limits should be placed upon such an excuse? Should people always be judged by the standards of their native culture?

7. In *Regina v, Machekequonabe* (28 O.R. 309 [1897]), a Native American was charged with manslaughter for killing what he took to be an evil spirit clothed in human form, called a "Wendigo," which the defendant believed would eat a human being. The defendant saw what appeared to be a tall human being running in the distance, gave chase, challenged the victim, and then fired. The defense argued that the defendant lacked the "intention even to harm a human being much less to kill." Did the court correctly refuse to consider the defendant's argument?

8. What does it mean to say that a plea of insanity should be retained by the law as a "special defense"?

9. What two arguments does Morris think support retention of the special defense of insanity? How does he seek to counter each of these arguments?

10. In his essay, Kadish tries to clarify the issues surrounding the insanity defense by distinguishing between two different kinds of *mens rea* or two different ways in which *mens rea* is relevant. What are these two senses?

11. What is Kadish's fundamental objection to the abolition of the insanity plea?

12. In response to growing frustration with the existing tests for insanity, some jurisdictions, rather than abolish the defense altogether, have created a new verdict—"guilty but mentally ill"—as an alternative to the traditional options, "guilty" and "not guilty by reason of insanity." This verdict allows the jury to find that a person was sufficiently culpable to be said to have committed the crime, but at the same time to have suffered from a mental illness. Under this verdict, the accused is convicted and sentenced as a normal offender. He or she may then be moved to a treatment facility for all or part of the sentence, and any time remaining after the completion of treatment must be spent back in prison. Does this compromise verdict make sense? Is it morally defensible?

13. In March 1991, a jury convicted Norma Valentin on drug possession charges despite a defense based on the claim that she suffered from multiple personality disorder. According to Ms. Valentin, her other personalities include "Vicki," a drug dealer; "Ayessa," an Indian fortune-teller; and "Virginia," the personality involved in relationships with men. Ms. Valentin's counsel contended that her "core" personality should not be criminally liable for crimes committed by one of her "secondary" personalities (see "Don't Try This Defense," *The National Law Journal*, March 25, 1991, p. 6). Assuming that Ms. Valentin's multiple personality disorder is genuine, as attested by psychiatrists, should the law attempt to apportion responsibility among the various personalities "housed" within a single body? Why or why not?

C. *Punishment and Responsibility*

The Justification of Punishment

Criminal defendants who are indicted and convicted of an offense are then subject to punishment. Most of the time we simply assume that those who are convicted are properly subject to punishment, although we often disagree on what that punishment should be. What does justify the legal infliction of punishment? What, for example, would you say of the following items?

1. Under California's "three-strikes" law, a stiff, habitual offender statute approved by voters in 1994, an offender who commits a felony and who has two prior convictions for "serious" felonies must be sentenced to a minimum of twenty-five years to life imprisonment. In 1995

a Los Angeles man faced a twenty-five year sentence on petty theft for stealing a slice of pepperoni pizza; a parolee who broke into a restaurant and stole four chocolate chip cookies received twenty-six years.

2. California recently became the only state in the nation to require that convicted child molesters be punished through chemical castration. Under the law, molesters with two convictions will be forced to receive weekly injections of a synthetic hormone called Depo-Provera, which is intended to suppress their sex drive.

Are the punishments inflicted or proposed in these cases justifiable? If so, on what grounds?

The question of how to justify the infliction of punishment is not simply an academic one: punishment seems by its very nature to involve hard treatment—the coercive infliction of pain and suffering. Normally, such a way of treating another person would be wrong. What makes it right when punishment is involved?

Courts and lawmakers have traditionally considered a variety of social goals and moral claims in addressing the question of how to justify the institution of criminal punishment. Some argue that the only legitimate concern of the criminal justice system is the *rehabilitation* of the offender. The purpose of fixing responsibility, in this view, is simply to locate individuals who need preventive detention and therapy. Others contend that the aim of the law is to *deter* crime, by either incapacitating or specifically deterring an individual, thus preventing him or her from engaging in further criminality, or by generally deterring others, seeking to induce them to avoid acting as the offender did. Finally, some insist that the practice of punishment is grounded in the *retributive* idea that punishment is what the offender deserves and may be inflicted only on that ground, not on the theory that punishment will benefit society in some way. Retributivists maintain that their view is not to be equated with a primitive and thinly disguised lust for vengeance; rather, the motivation is the desire to do justice, to see that the moral balance is restored and the criminal's debt repaid.

As Michael Moore explains in his selection, the goals and principles appealed to in the effort to jus-

tify criminal punishment tend to align themselves with one or the other of the two general moral and social theories reviewed at the beginning of Chapter I: *utilitarianism* and *deontology*. As we saw in Chapter I, utilitarianism on the most abstract level is one of a family of views that takes the *consequences* or results produced or likely to be produced by an act or a policy to be the measure of its moral correctness. Deontological ethics, in contrast, measures the rightness or correctness of conduct by the degree to which it conforms to the duties or obligations we have to treat others in appropriate ways. The deontologist Kant held a deontological theory of punishment called *retributivism*, which can be formulated more precisely as the view that punishing a person is justifiable only if it gives to him or her what he or she deserves. Let's examine these theories more fully.

Theories of Punishment

Recall that a consequentialist says that an action is right or wrong depending upon its overall consequences. To justify a system of criminal punishment, in this view, would require showing that punishment does some good or prevents some evil, and that it does so better than any alternative for handling criminal behavior. As we saw in Chapter I, proponents of consequentialism differ among themselves as to the precise nature of the "good" to be promoted, and this difference spills over into consequentialist reasoning about punishment. Consequentialists have argued that legal punishment is necessary to achieve the greatest happiness or to secure the maximum degree of liberty for all citizens; more specifically, they have contended that punishment is aimed at incapacitating identified wrongdoers, rehabilitating those with criminal propensities, and deterring potential offenders. Deterrence, incapacitation, and so on, are, according to consequentialists, *goals,* to which a system of punishment is (supposedly) the most effective *means.* The goals of utilitarian consequentialists have in the past had an important impact on actual penological practice: sentencing reform and experiments with various rehabilitative programs are but two of the ways in which utilitarians since Bentham have sought to align the penal system more closely with legitimate consequentialist goals.

Advocates of the retributive conception of punishment make at least two basic claims: (1) Only those who are guilty should be subject to punishment, and (2) Punishment may be inflicted only if it gives to the guilty person what he or she deserves. These basic principles are, again, fleshed out in various ways by various retributivists. Some argue that giving an offender his or her "just desserts" is a way of removing an unfair advantage that the wrongdoer has taken over those who obey the law; other retributivists assert that the moral censure or opprobrium represented by the infliction of punishment is the essential factor. It is important to note that retributivists who refer to registering moral censure or erasing an unfair advantage are insisting that the imposition of censure or annulment of an advantage are *intrinsic features* of punishment itself, not simply goals achievable through the means of punishment, as the consequentialists would have it. Retributivism has also had a significant effect on criminal justice, particularly in the form of calls to lessen the discretion of courts by requiring determinate sentencing, and in the enactment of stiff sentencing guidelines at both the state and federal levels.

Utilitarianism vs. Retributivism

As an initial matter, both the utilitarian and the retributive conceptions of punishment possess some degree of attractiveness. A utilitarian holds that for an instance of punishment to be justified it is necessary that it do some good. Suppose an old man steals some bread from a supermarket to feed his hungry children. A utilitarian asks us to temper the reaction to punish the man for his choice and to consider the larger circumstances within which he acted: What good will it do to penalize him? The problem with Kant's retributivism, the utilitarian might say, is that it requires that we punish such persons even when it clearly won't do any good, and this is inconsistent with a humane and enlightened approach to criminality. A Kantian, on the other hand, claims that it is necessary that punishment be deserved, and, he claims, this is an imper-

ative that the utilitarian will not always observe. Suppose we inform you that we have decided to punish you with life imprisonment for the crime of running a stop sign. We are doing this not because you deserve or merit such a punishment, but rather to use you as an example to others (tired of the widespread failure to obey stop signs, we reason that the frequency of such lawlessness will decrease dramatically at the sight of your awful plight). Even assuming that subjecting you to such punishment would serve the goal of deterrence, surely you would demand to know what gives us the right to use you in this way—and it is this demand that lies at the heart of the retributivist insistence that punishment must be deserved. The difficulty with the utilitarian preoccupation with deterrence, it seems, is that it may allow people to be punished out of all proportion to their guilt, or even in the absence of any guilt whatever, when it serves the interests of society.

"Scarlet-Letter" Punishments

Many crimes are punished through the imposition of jail sentences, payment of fines, or a combination of both. An interesting test case for utilitarian and retributivist theories of punishment concerns more novel forms of punishment with which courts in various parts of the United States have begun to experiment. Windell McDowell was convicted in a California court of purse snatching and was placed on probation on the condition that he not go out of his house without wearing shoes with metal taps on the soles.[1] In Oregon Thomas Kirby pled guilty to a charge of first-degree burglary and was placed on probation on the condition that he publish, at his own expense, an advertisement, accompanied by a picture, in the local newspaper. The ad was to read "Criminal's Apology."[2] Richard Bateman was convicted on two counts of first-degree sexual abuse in 1985. He faced a maximum sentence of five years' imprisonment and a large fine, but an Oregon court

---

[1] *People v. McDowell* 59 Cal. App. 3d 807 (1976).
[2] *State v. Kirby* No. 85–1649 (Or. Cirt. Ct. for Lincoln County, Oregon [1986]).

instead suspended his sentence and placed him on probation. As one of the conditions of his sentence, Bateman was required to place on the door of his residence and on both doors of any vehicle he might drive, in three-inch lettering, the words "DANGEROUS SEX OFFENDER—NO CHILDREN ALLOWED."[3] In other cases, offenders have been asked to wear sandwich boards proclaiming their guilt or place "DUI" on their license plates; one man convicted of murder was required to place family photos of his victim on the walls of his cell.

In one of his most famous stories, nineteenth-century American author Nathaniel Hawthorne described the punishment inflicted upon an adulteress in early America: She was forced for the rest of her days to wear on her chest a scarlet letter A, plainly visible to all, as a sign of her crime. Judicial "scarlet letters" are becoming increasingly common, and they raise troublesome questions: Is humiliation a useful form of punishment? Is subjecting a person to disgrace and public ridicule justifiable in a utilitarian theory of punishment? In a retributive view? Do such sentences constitute "cruel and unusual" punishment"? Even more broadly, are there some forms of punishment that our law should never inflict?

Readings on Punishment

The details of the debate between these and other approaches to the topic of punishment are explored more fully in the reading selections by James Q. Wilson and Michael Moore.

In his selection, Wilson carefully examines several aspects of the claim that the infliction of punishment deters crime. Uncertainty about apprehension and delays in the administration of penalties undermine the assumption that severe punishments always deter. Wilson also discusses problems in interpreting statistical data on the relationship between crime rates and punishments inflicted. Despite these shortcomings, Wilson defends the assertion that deterrence does work and works in ways that can be measured.

Michael Moore defends the retributive theory of punishment. Moore defines retributivism as the view that "punishment is justified only if the person receiving it deserves it." He contrasts the "pure retributivist" theory with both utilitarianism and a "mixed" theory of punishment that seeks to combine the retributive and utilitarian views. Through an argument by elimination, Moore seeks to show that retributivism is the only viable candidate among the competing theories.

Victims' Rights and Restitution

In the Anglo-American criminal justice system, those victimized by crime play no significant role. They do not prosecute wrongdoers, nor do they carry out a sentence against them. As crime rates have increased, so has the visibility of victims' rights organizations. Because those victimized by crime are often left feeling vulnerable, fearful, and resentful of the perceived failings of the criminal justice system, victims' rights advocates have sought a more meaningful, participatory role for victims in the criminal justice process. Two specific devices that have been urged upon courts by the victims' rights movement are employing *restitution* as a sentencing alternative to traditional punishment and using *victim-impact evidence* at trial, particularly during the sentencing phase of death-penalty cases. Each of these devices is discussed in this section.

Under existing procedure, a defendant convicted of a capital crime (one carrying the death penalty) is brought to a second proceeding in which a separate jury determines whether to impose the death penalty based on the presence or absence of both mitigating and aggravating circumstances. The fact that the defendant had no prior record or was acting under emotional distress might, for example, be considered in mitigation; that the defendant was already a convicted murderer or killed for money (as a "hit-man") might be used as aggravating factors to justify death. Should a death-penalty jury also be permitted to weigh evidence pertaining to the personal characteristics of the victim and the emotional impact of the crime on the victim's family? This is the question raised in *Payne v. Tennessee*, reprinted here.

---

[3] *State v. Bateman* Nos. C85–08–33209 and C85–10–34220 (Or. Cir. Ct. for Multonomah County, Oregon [1986]).

In *Payne,* the Supreme Court overruled two previous cases, *Booth v. Maryland* and *South Carolina v. Gathers,* both of which had forbidden the use of victim-impact evidence. Such evidence, the Court had earlier reasoned, violates the defendant's Eighth Amendment right that sentencing decisions be based on an "individualized determination" reflecting the defendant's characteristics, personal responsibility, and moral guilt. In *Payne,* the members of the Court reconsider this holding and ask a basic question: What are the things about a crime that properly relate to the perpetrator's blameworthiness? The state of Tennessee permitted the jury to hear testimony about Payne's victims and the devastating effect of the crime upon the victims' family, especially on the small boy, Nicholas. The opinion in *Payne* prompts many questions: Should the age, sex, and other traits of one's victim be considered at sentencing? Would doing so encourage comparative judgments between differing victims? Would those who victimize celebrities, for example, potentially be subject to greater punishment than those who attack the homeless? Is victim-impact evidence legitimately considered by a jury, or is it an improper attempt to sway jurors with irrelevant, emotional testimony? If the defendant is permitted to furnish testimony speaking to his "good character," why can't evidence pertaining to the victim's character also be admissible?

In his essay, Randy Barnett maintains that a proper concern for the welfare of victims of crimes argues in favor of substituting for a system of criminal punishment a system of *restitution,* the fundamental principle of which is that victims have a right to be compensated for their injuries by those who injure them. Justice must be done to victims, regardless of whether this will incapacitate or deter an offender. Barnett outlines what he sees as the advantages of a restitutionary system: assistance for crime victims, flexibility in sentencing arrangements, and constructive effects on wrongdoers, among others. Barnett also confronts some serious objections to his proposal: How is restitution to be made? Can it always be made? What does it include? Will it give an undeserved break to those sufficiently wealthy to make restitution easily?

76. *Penalties and Opportunities*

J. Q. WILSON

The average citizen hardly needs to be persuaded of the view that crime will be frequently committed if, other things being equal, crime becomes more profitable compared to other ways of spending one's time. Accordingly, the average citizen thinks it obvious that one major reason why crime has gone up is that people have discovered it is easier to get away with it; by the same token, the average citizen thinks a good way to reduce crime is to make the consequences of crime to the would-be offender more costly (by making penalties swifter, more certain, or more severe), or to make the value of alternatives to crime more attractive (by increasing the availability and pay of legitimate jobs), or both. Such opinions spring naturally to mind among persons who notice, as a fact of everyday life, that people take their hands off hot stoves, shop around to find the best buy, smack their children to teach them not to run out into a busy street, and change jobs when the opportunity arises to earn more money for the same amount of effort.

These citizens may be surprised to learn that social scientists who study crime are deeply divided over the correctness of such views. To some scholars, especially economists, the popular view is also the scientifically correct one—becoming a criminal can be explained in much the same way we explain becoming a carpenter or buying a car. To other scholars, especially sociologists, the popular view is wrong—crime rates do not go up because people discover they can get away with it and will not come down just because society decides to get tough on criminals.

The debate over the effect on crime rates of changing the costs and benefits of crime is usually referred to as a debate over deterrence—a debate, that is, over the efficacy (and perhaps even the propriety) of trying to prevent crime by making would-be offenders more fearful of committing crime. But that is something of a misnomer, because the theory of human nature on which is erected the idea of deterrence (the theory that people respond to the penalties associated with crime) is also the theory of human nature that supports the idea that people will take jobs in preference to crime if the jobs are more attractive. In both cases, we are saying that would-be offenders are reasonably rational and respond to their perception of the costs and benefits attached to alternative courses of action. When we use the word 'deterrence', we are calling attention only to the cost side of the equation. There is no word in common scientific usage to call attention to the benefit side of the equation; perhaps 'inducement' might serve. To a psychologist, deterring persons from committing crimes or inducing persons to engage in non-criminal activities are but special cases of using 'reinforcements' (or rewards) to alter behaviour.

The reason there is a debate among scholars about deterrence is that the socially imposed consequences of committing a crime, unlike the market consequences of shopping around for the best price, are characterized by delay, uncertainty, and ignorance. In addition, some scholars contend that a large fraction of crime is committed by persons who are so impulsive, irrational, or abnormal that, even if there were no delay, uncertainty, or ignorance attached to the consequences of criminality, we would still have a lot of crime.

Imagine a young man walking down the street at night with nothing on his mind but a desire for good times and high living. Suddenly he sees a little old lady standing alone on a dark corner stuffing the proceeds of her recently cashed social security check into her purse. There is nobody else in view. If the boy steals the purse, he gets the money immediately. That is a powerful incentive, and it is available immediately and without doubt. The costs of taking it are uncertain; the odds are at least fourteen to one that the police will not catch a given robber, and even if he is caught the odds are very good that he will not go to prison, unless he has a long record. On the average, no more than three felonies out of one hundred result in the imprisonment of the offender. In addition to this uncertainty, whatever penalty may come his way will come only after a long delay; in some jurisdictions, it might take a year or more to complete the court disposition of the offender, assuming he is caught in the first place. Moreover, this young man may, in his ignorance of how the world works, think the odds in his favour are even greater and that the delay will be even longer.

Compounding the problems of delay and uncertainty is the fact that society cannot feasible reduce the uncertainty attached to the chances of being arrested by more than a modest amount, and though it can to some degree increase the probability and severity of a prison sentence for those who are caught, it cannot do so drastically by, for example, summarily executing all convicted robbers or even by sending all robbers to twenty-year prison terms. Some scholars add a further complication: the young man may be incapable of assessing the risks of crime. How, they ask, is he to know his chances of being caught and punished? And even if he does know, is he perhaps 'driven' by uncontrollable impulses to snatch purses whatever the risks?

As if all this were not bad enough, the principal method by which scholars have attempted to measure the effect on crime of differences in the probability and severity of punishment has involved using data about aggregates of people (entire cities, counties, states, and even nations) rather than about individuals. In a typical study, of which there have been several dozen, the rate at which, say, robbery is committed in each state is 'explained' by means of a statistical procedure in which the analyst takes into account both he socioeconomic features of each state that might affect the supply of robbers (for example, the percentage of persons with low incomes, the unemployment rate, or the population density of the big cities) and the operation of the criminal justice system of each state as it attempts to cope with robbery (for example, the probability of being caught and imprisoned for a given robbery and the length of the average prison term for robbery). Most such studies find, after controlling for socioeconomic differences among the states, that the higher the probability of being imprisoned, the lower the robbery rate. Isaac Ehrlich, an economist, produced the best known of such analyses using data on crime in the United States in 1940, 1950, and 1960. To simplify a complex analysis, he found, after controlling for such factors as the income level and age distribution of the population, that the higher the probability of imprisonment for those convicted of robbery, the lower the robbery rate. Thus, differences in the certainty of punishment seem to make a difference in the level of crime. At the same time, Ehrlich did not find that the severity of punishment (the average time served in prison for robbery) had, independently of certainty, an effect on robbery rates in two of the three time periods (1940 and 1960).

But there are some problems associated with studying the effect of sanctions on crime rates using aggregate data of this sort. One is that many of the most important factors are not known with any accuracy. For example, we are dependent on police reports for our measure of the robbery rate, and these undoubtedly vary in accuracy from place to place. If all police departments were inaccurate to the same degree, this would not be important; unfortunately, some departments are probably much less accurate than others, and this variable error can introduce a serious bias into the statistical estimates of the effect of the criminal justice system.

Moreover, if one omits from the equation some factor that affects the crime rate, then the estimated effect of the factors that are in the equation may be in error because some of the causal power belonging to the omitted factor will be falsely attributed to the included factors. For example, suppose we want to find out whether differences in the number of policemen on patrol among American cities are associated with differences in the rate at which robberies take place in those cities. If we fail to include in our equation a measure of the population density of the city, we may wrongly conclude that the more police there are on the streets, the *higher* the

robbery rate and thus give support to the absurd policy proposition that the way to reduce robberies is to fire police officers. Since robberies are more likely to occur in larger, densely settled cities (which also tend to have a higher proportion of police), it would be a grave error to omit such measures of population from the equation. Since we are not certain what causes crime, we always run the risk of inadvertently omitting a key factor from our efforts to see if deterrence works.

Even if we manage to overcome these problems, a final difficulty lies in wait. The observed fact (and it has been observed many times) that states in which the probability of going to prison for robbery is low are also states which have high rates of robbery can be interpreted in one of two ways. It can mean *either* that the higher robbery rates are the results of the lower imprisonment rates (and thus evidence that deterrence works) *or* that the lower imprisonment rates are caused by the higher robbery rates. To see how the latter might be true, imagine a state that is experiencing, for some reason, a rapidly rising robbery rate. It arrests, convicts, and imprisons more and more robbers as more and more robberies are committed, but it cannot quite keep up. The robberies are increasing so fast that they 'swamp' the criminal justice system; prosecutors and judges respond by letting more robbers off without a prison sentence, or perhaps without even a trial, in order to keep the system from becoming hopelessly clogged. As a result, the proportion of arrested robbers who go to prison goes down while the robbery rate goes up. In this case, we ought to conclude, not that prison deters robbers, but that high robbery rates 'deter' prosecutors and judges. . . .

Some commentators believe that these criticisms have proved that 'deterrence doesn't work' and thus the decks have now been cleared to get on with the task of investing in those programmes, such as job creation and income maintenance, that *will* have an effect on crime. Such a conclusion is, to put it mildly, a bit premature.

People are governed in their daily lives by rewards and penalties of every sort. We shop for bargain prices, praise our children for good behaviour and scold them for bad, expect lower interest rates to stimulate home building and fear that higher ones will depress it and conduct ourselves in public in ways that lead our friends and neighbours to form good opinions of us. To assert that 'deterrence doesn't work' is tantamount to either denying the plainest facts of everyday life or claiming that would-be criminals are utterly different from the rest of us. They may well be different to some degree—they most likely have a weaker conscience, worry less about their reputation in polite society, and find it harder to postpone gratifying their urges—but these differences of degree do not make them indifferent to the risks and gains of crime. If they were truly indifferent, they would scarcely be able to function at all, for their willingness to take risks would be offset by their indifference to loot. Their lives would consist of little more than the erratic display of animal instincts and fleeting impulses.

The question before us is whether feasible changes in the deferred and uncertain penalties of crime (and, as we shall see, in the deferred and uncertain opportunities for employment) will affect crime rates in ways that can be detected by the data and statistical methods at our disposal. Though the unreliability of crime data and the limitations of statistical analysis are real enough and are accurately portrayed by the Panel of the National Research Council, there are remedies and rejoinders that, on balance, strengthen the case for the claim that not only does deterrence work (the panel never denied that), it probably works in ways that can be measured, even in the aggregate.

The errors in official statistics about crime rates have been addressed by employing other measures of crime, in particular reports gathered by Census Bureau interviewers from citizens who have been victims of crime. While these victim surveys have problems of their own (such as the forgetfulness of citizens), they are not the same problems as those that affect police reports of crime. Thus, if we obtain essentially the same findings about the effect of sanctions on crime from studies that use victim data as we do from studies using police data, our confidence in these findings is strengthened. Studies of this sort have been done by Itzhak Goldberg at Stanford and by Barbara Boland and myself, and the results are quite consistent with those from research based on police reports. As sanctions become more likely, crime becomes less common.

There is a danger that important factors will be omitted from any statistical study of crime in ways

that bias the results, but this problem is no greater in studies of penalties than it is in studies of unemployment rates, voting behaviour, or any of a hundred other socially significant topics. Since we can never know with certainty everything that may affect crime (or unemployment, or voting), we must base our conclusions not on any single piece of research, but on the general thrust of a variety of studies analyzing many different causal factors. The Panel of the National Research Council took exactly this position. While noting that 'there is the possibility that as yet unknown and so untested' factors may be affecting crime, 'this is not a sufficient basis for dismissing' the common finding that crime goes up as sanctions become less certain because 'many of the analyses have included some of the more obvious possible third causes and they still find negative associations between sanctions and crimes'.[1]

It is possible that rising crime rates 'swamp' the criminal justice system so that a negative statistical association between, say, rates of theft and the chances of going to prison for theft may mean not that a decline in imprisonment is causing theft to increase, but rather that a rise in theft is causing imprisonment to become less likely. This might occur particularly with respect to less serious crimes, such as shoplifting or petty larceny; indeed, the proportion of prisoners who are shoplifters or petty thieves has gone down over the last two decades. But it is hard to imagine that the criminal justice system would respond to an increase in murder or armed robbery by letting some murderers or armed robbers off with no punishment. There is no evidence that convicted murderers are any less likely to go to prison today than they were twenty years ago. Moreover, the apparent deterrent effect of prison on serious crimes, such as murder and robbery, was apparently as great in 1940 or 1950, when these crimes were much less common, as it is today, suggesting that swamping has not occurred.

The best studies of deterrence that manage to overcome many of these problems provide evidence that deterrence works. Alfred Blumstein and Daniel Nagin studied the relationship between draft evasion and the penalties imposed for evading the draft. After controlling for the socioeconomic characteristics of the states, they found that the higher the probability of conviction for draft evasion, the lower the evasion rates. This is an especially strong finding because it is largely immune to some of the problems of other research. Draft evasion is more accurately measured than street crime, hence errors arising from poor data are not a problem. And draft evasion cases did not swamp the federal courts in which they were tried, in part because such cases (like murder in state courts) make up only a small fraction of the courts' workload (7 per cent in the case of draft evasion) and in part because the attorney general had instructed federal prosecutors to give high priority to these cases. Blumstein and Nagin concluded that draft evasion is deterrable.[2]

Another way of testing whether deterrence works is to look, not at differences among states at one point in time, but at changes in the nation as a whole over a long period of time. Historical data on the criminal justice system in America is so spotty that such research is difficult to do here, but it is not at all difficult in England where the data are excellent. Kenneth I. Wolpin analysed changes in crime rates and in various parts of the criminal justice system (the chances of being arrested, convicted, and punished) for the period 1894 to 1967, and concluded that changes in the probability of being punished seemed to cause changes in the crime rate. He offers reasons for believing that this causal connection cannot be explained away by the argument that the criminal justice system was being swamped.[3]

Given what we are trying to measure—changes in the behaviour of a small number of hard-to-observe persons who are responding to delayed and uncertain penalties—we will never be entirely sure that our statistical manipulations have proved that deterrence works. What is impressive is that so many (but not all) studies using such different methods come to similar conclusions. . . . Even after wading through all this, the sceptical reader may remain unconvinced. Given the difficulties of any aggregate statistical analysis, that is understandable. But if unconvinced, the reader cannot conclude that criticisms of the statistical claims for deterrence have by implication enhanced the statistical claims for job creation. This is one time when, if you throw out the bath water, you will have to throw out the baby as well.

. . .

Ideally, we would like to know how the probability of severity of a possible punishment will affect the behaviour of persons who *might* commit a serious crime. Such persons constitute only a small fraction of the total population, but they are an important fraction. Most of us would not commit a serious crime because of the operation of internal controls on our behaviour, reinforced by the fear or embarrassment should our misconduct be detected. A few of us may commit serious crimes with only small regard to the risks, unless those risks can be made great and immediate. For example, most men would never dream of killing their wives, and a few men might kill them (perhaps in an alcoholic rage) unless a police officer were standing right next to them. But for a certain fraction of men, the idea of doing away with their wives is strongly conditioned by their perception of the risks. Wives, and in particular feminist organizations, concede this when they demand, as they have with increasing vigour, the strict enforcement of laws against wife-abuse. (Not long ago, the New York Police Department was obliged to promise in writing to arrest and prosecute wife-beating men who previously had been handled in a more conciliatory fashion.)

I mention wife-abuse and murder because some people think of such actions as inevitably the result of a deranged or irrational mind, and thus of one insensitive to the risks attendant on actions. Sometimes this may be so, but more often it is not, as is evident by the fact that the arrival of a police officer usually results in the end of the fight, at least in its physical phase. Even when no officer is there, people pay attention to some costs when engaged in even the most emotional behaviour. . . .

If the consequences of even emotional and impulsive acts are given some weight by most people, then the consequences of less emotional acts (such as shoplifting, auto theft, robbery, and burglary) are likely to play an even larger role in affecting the willingness of people to engage in them. What we would like to know is how changes in the prospective costs of crime and the prospective benefits of pursuing legitimate alternatives to crime affect, at the margin, the behaviour of those individuals who are 'at risk'.

Persons who are 'at risk' are those who lack strong, internalized inhibitions against misconduct, who value highly the excitement and thrills of breaking the law, who have a low stake in conformity, who are willing to take greater chances than the rest of us, and who greatly value quick access to ready cash. Such persons tend, disproportionately, to be young males. As Philip J. Cook has argued, it is not necessary for those would-be offenders to be entirely rational or fully informed for the criminal justice system (or the legitimate labour market) to have an effect on them.[4] It is only necessary that they attach some value to the consequences of their actions (since we know they attach a positive value to the loot, it is reasonable to suppose they also attach some value—a negative one, that is—to the chances of being caught) and that they operate on the basis of at least a crude rule of thumb about how great or small those risks are, a rule of thumb that can be affected by society.

Most of us are probably not very well informed about the true costs of crime; being law-abiding, we probably imagine that the chances of being caught are higher than in fact they are and that the severity of the sentence (measured in years in prison) is greater than it really is. But most of us depend for our information on newspaper stories, detective programmes on television, and our own deep fear of being exposed as a disreputable person. But persons at risk (young men hanging around on street corners and thieves who associate with other thieves) have quite different sources of information. These are the accounts of other young men and other thieves who have had a run-in with the police or the courts and who therefore can supply to their colleagues a crudely accurate rule of thumb: 'the heat is on' or 'the heat is off', Judge Bruce MacDonald* is either 'Maximum Mac' or 'Turn 'Em Loose Bruce', the prosecutor will let you 'cop out' to a burglary charge so that it gets marked down to a misdemeanour larceny or will 'throw the book at you' and demand 'felony time'.

It is the behaviour of these persons, thus informed, that we wish to observe. But how? As we have seen, we cannot easily do it with aggregate statistical studies in which the behaviour of these persons is often buried in the 'noise' generated by the behaviour of the majority of people who do not

---

* A fictional name.

commit crimes whatever the advantages. There have in fact been only a few efforts to measure the deterrent effect of the sanctions of the criminal justice system on individuals, as opposed to cities or states (though some of the studies of rehabilitation can be reinterpreted as studies of deterrence). One such effort was made by Ann Witte, who followed for about three years the activities of 641 men released from prison in North Carolina. She gathered information not only about their subsequent brushes with the law (80 per cent were rearrested) but also about their experiences with the law before being imprisoned (their prior risk of being arrested, convicted, and imprisoned), the time it took them to find a job after release and the amount it paid in wages, and such aspects of their life-style as their involvement with alcohol and drugs.

Witte could not find out directly how these ex-convicts evaluated their chances of being caught if they broke the law in the future, but she could observe how frequently in the past (that is, before being imprisoned the last time) their arrests had led to a conviction and their convictions had led to imprisonment. Her assumption was that these men might be influenced in their future conduct by their past experience with the criminal justice system. The results of her analysis based on this assumption were complex and not entirely consistent, but in general she found that 'deterrence works'—the higher the probability of being punished in the past, the lower the number of arrests per month free on the street in the future. She also found that deterrence works differently for different kinds of offenders. For persons who engaged in violent offences or drug use, the severity of the prior sentence seemed to have the greatest effect, whereas for persons who engaged in less serious property offences the certainty of imprisonment seemed to be most significant. Deterrence may not work, judging from her data, for thieves who were also drug addicts. The availability of jobs had no consistent effect on subsequent criminality.[5]

There are some obvious limitations to this study. One is that, as Witte notes, it is a study of 'losers'—older men (the average age was thirty-two) who had already been in prison, often many times. What we would prefer knowing is whether differences in sanctions or job availability affect the behaviour of persons not yet involved in crime or young men involved for the first time. Because her group consisted of older, ex-cons, it is quite possible her findings understate the true effect of either sanctions or jobs.

A comparable study was carried out in Cook County, Illinois, and this was aimed at the young offender. Charles A. Murray and Louis A. Cox, Jr., followed the criminal careers (measured by the number of times they were arrested per month free on the street) of 317 Chicago boys who had been incarcerated for the first time by the Illinois Department of Corrections. Though young (their average age was sixteen), they were scarcely novices at crime: they had been arrested an average of thirteen times each before receiving this, their first prison sentence. Nor were their offences trivial: as a group, they had been charged with fourteen homicides, twenty-three rapes, over three hundred assaults and a like number of auto thefts, nearly two hundred armed robberies, and over seven hundred burglaries. The patience of the court finally exhausted, they were sent off to a correctional institution, where they served an average sentence of ten months. Murray and Cox followed them for (on the average) seventeen months after their release. During this period, the frequency with which they were arrested (that is, arrests per month per one hundred boys) declined by about two-thirds. To be exact, the members of this group of hard-core delinquents were arrested 6.3 times each during the year before being sent away but only 2.9 times each during the seventeen months on the street after release.[6]

Murray and Cox refer to this as the 'suppression effect'; namely, the tendency of the first exposure to prison to suppress the rate at which delinquents are arrested and, presumably, the rate at which they actually were committing crimes.

The Murray and Cox study, one of the few of its kind that has been carried out, adds some support to the deterrence theory. But it still focuses on persons who have already committed crimes; we remain uncertain about the effect of changes in the criminal justice system on would-be offenders. It is almost impossible to study behaviour that does not occur except to ask, as some scholars have done, various persons, often students, whether they would commit or have committed a crime when they perceived the penalties to be of a given severity and a given probability. One such study was done among students at an eastern college,[7] and another among high school students in Arizona.[8] Both found that the students who believed there was a high probability of being punished for a particular criminal act were less likely to report (anonymously) having committed the act than were students who thought there was a low probability of being punished. Both studies are broadly consistent with the view that deterrence works, but both are also difficult to interpret. It is hard to be confident that the number of offences the students reported bears any relationship to the number they actually committed. More important, the studies raise the possibility that what actually deters these students (very few of whom commit any serious acts with any frequency) is not what they guess to be the chances of being caught, but the moral opprobrium with which such acts are viewed. For most people in most circumstances, the moral nature of the act and the internalized inhibitions on misconduct arising out of that moral code are probably the major deterrents to crime. Interviewing students may highlight that fact, but it cannot tell us what happens, at the margin, when society alters the certainty or severity of punishment for a given offence. And for purposes of public policy, that is exactly what we want to know.

The relationship between crime on the one hand and the rewards and penalties at the disposal of society on the other is complicated. It is not complicated, however, in the way some people imagine. It is not the case (except for a tiny handful of pathological personalities) that criminals are so unlike the rest of us as to be indifferent to the costs and benefits of the opportunities open to them. Nor is it the case that criminals have no opportunities. . . .

It is better to think of both people and social controls as arrayed on a continuum. People differ by degrees in the extent to which they are governed by internal restraints on criminal behaviour and in the stake they have in conformity; they also differ by degrees in the extent to which they can find, hold, and benefit from a job. Similarly, sanctions and opportunities are changeable only within modest limits. We want to find out to what extent feasible changes in the certainty, swiftness, or severity of penalties will make a difference in the behavior of those 'at the margin'—those, that is, who are neither so innocent nor so depraved as to be prepared to ignore small changes (which are, in fact, the only feasible changes) in the prospects of punishment. By the same token, we want to know what feasible (and again, inevitably small) changes in the availability of jobs will affect those at the margin of the labour market—those, that is, who are neither so eager for a good job nor so contemptuous of 'jerks' who take 'straight jobs' as to ignore modest changes in job opportunities. I am aware of no evidence supporting the conventional liberal view that while the number of persons who will be affected by changing penalties is very small, the number who will be affected by increasing jobs is very large; nor am I aware of any evidence supporting the conventional conservative view, which is the opposite of this.

I believe that the weight of the evidence—aggregate statistical analyses, evaluations of experiments and quasi-experiments, and studies of individual behaviour—supports the view that the rate of crime is influenced by its costs. This influence is greater—or easier to observe—for some crimes and persons than for others. It is possible to lower the crime rate by increasing the certainty of sanctions, but inducing the criminal justice system to make those changes is difficult, especially if committing the offence confers substantial benefits on the perpetrator, if apprehending and punishing the offender does not provide substantial rewards to members of the criminal justice system, or if the crime itself lacks the strong moral condemnation of society. In theory, the rate of crime should also be sensitive to the benefits of non-crime—for example, the value and availability of jobs—but thus far efforts to show that relationships have led to inconclusive results. Moreover, the nature of the connection between crime and legitimate opportunities is complex: unemployment (and prosperity!) can cause crime, crime can cause unemployment (but probably not prosperity), and both crime and unemployment may be caused by common third factors. Economic factors probably have the greatest influence on the behaviour of low-rate, novice offenders and the least on high-rate, experienced ones. Despite the uncertainty that attaches to the connection between the economy and crime, I believe the wisest course of action for society is to try simultaneously to increase both the benefits of non-crime and the

costs of crime, all the while bearing in mind that no feasible change in either part of the equation is likely to produce big changes in crime rates.

Some may grant my argument that it makes sense to continue to try to make those marginal gains that are possible by simultaneously changing in desirable directions both the costs of crime and benefits of non-crime, but they may still feel that it is better to spend more heavily on one side or the other of the cost–benefit equation. I have attended numerous scholarly gatherings where I have heard learned persons subject to the most searching scrutiny any evidence purporting to show the deterrent effect of sanctions but accept with scarcely a blink the theory that crime is caused by a 'lack of opportunities'. Perhaps what they mean is that, since the evidence on both propositions is equivocal, then it does less harm to believe in—and invest in—the 'benign' (that is, job-creation) programme. If so, they are surely wrong. If we try to make the penalties for crime swifter and more certain, and it should turn out that deterrence does not work, then all we have done is increase the risks facing persons who commit a crime. If we fail to increase the certainty and swiftness of penalties, and it should turn out that deterrence *does* work, then we have needlessly increased the risk of innocent persons being victimized.

There is one objection to this line of analysis with which I do agree. If we try to improve on deterrence by sharply increasing the severity of sentences, and we are wrong, then we may spend a great deal of money and unnecessarily blight the lives of offenders who could safely be punished for much shorter periods of time. Reaching a sound judgment about how severe penalties should be is a much more difficult matter than deciding how certain they should be; indeed, one cannot reach such a judgment at all on purely empirical grounds. The problem of severity is inextricably bound up with the problem of justice.

Endnotes

[1] Alfred Blumstein, Jacqueline Cohen, and Daniel Nagin (eds), *Deterrence and Incapacitation: Estimating the Effects of Criminal Sanctions on Crime Rates* (Washington, DC: National Academy of Sciences, 1978), 23.

[2] Alfred Blumstein and Daniel Nagin, 'The Deterrent Effect of Legal Sanctions on Draft Evasion', *Stanford Law Reviews*, 28 (1977), 241–75.

[3] Kenneth I. Wolpin, 'An Economic Analysis of Crime and Punishment in England and Wales, 1894–1967', *Journal of Political Economy*, 86 (1978), 815–40.

[4] Philip J. Cook, 'Research in Criminal Deterrence: Laying the Groundwork for the Second Decade', in Norval Morris and Michael Tonry, *Crime and Justice*, ii (Chicago: University of Chicago Press, 1980), 219.

[5] Ann Dryden Witte, 'Estimating the Economic Model of Crime with Individual Data', *Quarterly Journal of Economics*, 94 (1980), 57–84.

[6] Charles A. Murray and Louis A. Cox, Jr., *Beyond Probation: Juvenile Correlations and the Chronic Delinquent* (Beverly Hills, Calif.: Sage Publications, 1979).

[7] Matthew Silberman, 'Toward a Theory of Criminal Deterrence', *American Sociological Review*, 41 (1976), 442–61.

[8] Maynard L. Erickson, Jack P. Gibbs, and Gary F. Jensen, 'The Deterrence Doctrine and the Perceived Certainty of Legal Punishment', *American Sociological Review*, 42 (1977), 305–17. See also Charles R. Tittle, *Sanctions and Social Deviance: The Question of Deterrence* (New York: Praeger, 1980).

77. The Argument for Retributivism

MICHAEL MOORE

A Taxonomy of Purposes of Punishment

The Prima Facie Justifications of Punishment

. . .

Retributivism, the final theory used to justify punishment, is the view that punishment is justified by the desert of the offender. The good that is achieved by punishing, in this view, has nothing to do with future states of affairs, such as the prevention of crime or the maintenance of social cohesion. Rather, the good that punishment achieves is that someone who deserves it gets it.

Retributivism is quite distinct from a view that urges that punishment is justified because a majority of citizens feel that offenders should be punished. Rather, retributivism is a species of objectivism in ethics that asserts that there is such a thing as desert

and that the presence of such a (real) moral quality in a person justifies punishment of that person. What a populace may think or feel about vengeance on an offender is one thing; what treatment an offender deserves is another. And it is only this last notion that is relevant to retributivism.

Retributivism is also distinct from what it sometimes called "revenge utilitarianism." This is the view that the state must punish because private citizens otherwise will take the law into their own hands and that such private vengeance leads to chaos and disorder. Punishment in such a view is justified by its ability to prevent these bad things. Retributivism has nothing to do with this essentially forward-looking justification. Moreover, this "prevention of private vengeance" theory is to my mind not even a prima facie justifying reason for punishment. The obvious thing to do if citizens are going to violate the law by taking it into their own hands, is to deter those citizens by punishing them, not by punishing someone else. It places retributivism in an unnecessarily bad light to think that it justifies pun-

Reprinted by permission of the author.

ishment only because of the shadow cast by a threat of illegal violence by vengeful citizens.

The Two Pure Theories of Punishment

It is common to reduce the survivors on this list of prima facie justifications of punishment to two general theories, the utilitarian theory and the retributive theory. To see how this is done, one need only consider the good state of affairs that is to be achieved by incarceration, special deterrence, general deterrence, and rehabilitation (to the extent that it is of the first sort of rehabilitative theory, and not the second). For all four of these rationales for punishment share the prevention of crime as the beneficial end that justifies punishment. In each case, the ultimate justification for inflicting the harm of punishment is that it is outweighed by the good to be achieved, namely, the prevention of future crimes by that offender or by others. This justification of an institution by the social welfare it will enhance make all such theories instances of the utilitarian theory of punishment.

Thus, the denunciation theory of punishment is a second kind of utilitarian theory of punishment, insofar as the good it seeks to achieve is not simply the prevention of crime. To the extent one grants intrinsic value to social cohesion, and does not regard that as a value only because it contributes to the maintenance of public order, the denunciation theory can be distinguished from the other utilitarian theories just considered by the differing social good it seeks to achieve. Nonetheless, it is still a utilitarian theory, since it outweighs the harm that is punishment by some form of net social gain that punishment achieves.

Both crime prevention and the maintenance of social cohesion are types of collective good. The general utilitarian theory of punishment is one that combines these and other forms of collective good that punishment might achieve, and calls them all a "social gain." Whenever the social gain outweighs the harm punishment causes to offenders or their families, such a theory would say that there is a net social gain. Such a vocabulary allows us a succinct definition of any form of utilitarian theory: Punishment is justified if and only if some net social gain is achieved by it.

A retributivist theory is necessarily nonutilitarian in character, for it eschews justifying punishment by its tendency to achieve any form of net social gain. Rather, retributivism asserts that punishment is properly inflicted because, and only because, the person deserves it. That some people deserve punishment in such a theory is both a necessary and a sufficient condition justifying criminal sanctions. A succinct definition of the retributivist theory of punishment, paralleling that given of the utilitarian theory, is that punishment is justified if and only if the persons receiving it deserve it.

The Mixed Theory of Punishment

Once one grants that there are two sorts of prima facie justifications of punishment—effecting a net social gain (utilitarian) and giving just deserts (retributivist)—one can also see that in addition to the two pure theories of punishment there can also be mixed theories. There are two logically possible mixed theories, although only one of these merits any serious attention. There is first of all the popular form of mixed theory that asserts that punishment is justified if and only if it achieves a net social gain *and* is given to offenders who deserve it. Giving just deserts and achieving a net social gain, in such a case, are each individually necessary but only jointly sufficient conditions justifying punishment. The second logically possible mixed theory would be one asserting that punishment is justified if and only if it achieves a net social gain, *or* if it is given to offenders who deserve it. Such a theory has no name, because there is no one, to my knowledge who has ever adopted it. Such a theory is unnamed and unclaimed because it shares the defects of each of the pure theories, utilitarianism and retributivism. I shall accordingly put this "mixed theory" aside from further consideration.

The first kind of mixed theory itself has two branches. By far the most usual and popular form of the theory asserts that we do not punish people *because* they deserve it. Desert enters in, this theory further asserts, only as a limit on punishment: We punish offenders *because* some net social gain is achieved, such as the prevention of crime, but only if such offenders deserve it. It is, in other words, the achieving of a net social gain that justifies punishment, whereas the desert of offenders serves as a limiting condition on punishment but as not part of its justification. The alternative branch of the mixed theory is just the converse: One would urge that we punish *because* offenders deserve it, but *only if* some net social gain is achieved by doing so. In such a case, the roles of net social gain and desert are simply reversed: Giving offenders their just deserts serves as the justification of punishment, and the achieving of a net social gain as the limiting condition.

A cynic might view these two branches of the mixed theory as nothing more than an uncomfortable shuffle by mixed theorists. When accused of barbarism for punishing persons for retributivist reasons, they assert the first branch of the theory (they punish not because some persons deserve it, but because of a collective good that is achieved). When accused of immorality for imposing harsh treatment on someone as a means of making everyone else better off, such theorists shift to the other foot, and claim they do not punish someone to achieve a net social gain, but only to give offenders their just deserts. The cynic has a point here, because there is a sense in which the two branches of the theory are the same, namely, the sense that they justify exactly the same kinds of treatment for all cases. The only difference in theories is in the motivations of those who hold them. And while that may make a difference in our moral judgments of those who hold the different branches of the mixed theory of punishment, it does not make a difference in terms of the actual social institutions and judgments such theories will justify. I shall accordingly lump both of these branches together and call them the mixed theory of punishment.

The Argument for Retributivism

The Argument Against the Pure Utilitarian Theory

In exploring one's thoughts about punishment, it is perhaps easiest to start with some standard kinds of thought experiments directed against a pure utilitarian theory of punishment. A though experiment is essentially a device allowing one to sort out one's true reasons for believing that certain propositions are true. To be successful, such a thought experiment need not involve any actual case or state of affairs, nor need the cases envisioned even be very likely; they only need be conceivable in order to test our own thoughts.

It is standard fare in the philosophy of punishment to assert, by way of several thought experiments, counterexamples to the utilitarian thesis that punishment is justified if and only if some net social gain is achieved. I mention only two such counterexamples: scapegoating and preventive detention. With regard to the first, it might be recalled that D. B. Cooper successfully skyjacked an aircraft some years ago, and that this successful, unsolved crime apparently encouraged the mass of skyjackings that have cost so much in terms of dollars, lives, and convenience. Cooper wore large sunglasses in his escapade, and there was accordingly only a very limited description available of him. Imagine that shortly after his skyjacking we had the benefit of the knowledge we now have by hindsight, and we decided that it would be better to punish someone who looked like Cooper (and who had no good alibi) in order to convince others that skyjacking did not pay. For a consistent utilitarian, there is a net social gain that would be achieved by punishing such an innocent person, and there is no a priori reason that the net social gain in such a case might not outweigh the harm that is achieved by punishing an innocent person.

The preventive detention kind of counterexample is very similar: Imagine that a psychiatrist discovers that a patient has extremely dangerous propensities. The patient is also the accused in a criminal trial. It turns out, however, that the accused is not guilty of the crime for which he is charged and in fact has committed no crime whatsoever. Should a judge who, we may suppose, is the only one who knows that the man is both dangerous and innocent find the accused guilty? Doing so will prevent the defendant's predicted criminal behavior because he will be incarcerated. In a utilitarian theory, it is difficult to see why such a judgment would not be perfectly appropriate, as long as the prediction is reliable enough, and as long as the crimes predicted are sufficiently serious that the good of their prevention outweighs the harm of punishing that person, even though he has committed no crime as yet.

The general form of the argument arising from these kinds of thought experiments is that of a reductio ad absurdum argument. The argument has three premises:

1. Punishment should be inflicted if and only if doing so achieves a net social gain.
2. A net social gain would be achieved in this case by the infliction of punishment.
3. Punishment should not be inflicted in this case.

Each of these premises corresponds to steps in both of the foregoing thought experiments. The first premise is simply a restatement of the utilitarian theory of punishment. The second premise presupposes that there are some cases where a net social gain can be achieved by punishing an innocent person and asserts that this is such a case. The third premise asserts our intuition that such persons ought not to be punished.

All three premises together yield a contradiction:

4. Punishment should not be inflicted and punishment should be inflicted.

The first two premises have as their joint conclusion that the person should be punished; this conclusion, when conjoined with the third premise, produces the contradictory conclusion.

The strongest possible form of a reductio ad absurdum argument is one that ends in a formal contradiction. To avoid the contradiction, there are only three possibilities, corresponding to each of the three premises. One could give up the third premise and simply admit that in such cases the persons should be punished, despite their innocence. This move is a rather implausible one, inasmuch as it commits one to admitting that one will punish an entirely innocent person. The second possibility is to deny that there will be cases where there will be a net social gain from punishing an innocent person. This move is usually associated with the name of rule utilitarianism and involves the idea that one cannot make a general practice of punishing the innocent, because then the harm of so doing (in terms of demoralization costs in society and the like) will outweigh any possible good to be achieved, even the prevention of skyjacking. The problem with this response, popular as it is, is

that it fails to deal fairly with the nature of the thought experiment. That is, suppose there are some risks of detection of punishment of innocent persons, and, thus, some risks of demoralization costs; such risk will only allow utilitarians to say that the number of cases in which punishment of the innocent will maximize utility is somewhat diminished. It does not foreclose as somehow impossible that there are such cases. Such cases are conceivable, and if in them one is still not willing to punish, one thereby shows oneself not to be a utilitarian about punishment.

This brings us to the third possibility: One can simply give up the first premise, that is, one can repudiate the utilitarian theory of punishment. Such thought experiments, I think, when clearly conceived and executed, show almost all of us that we are not pure utilitarians about punishment.

Arguments Against the Mixed Theory of Punishment

The arguments against the pure utilitarian theory of punishment do not by themselves drive one into retributivism. For one can alleviate the injustice of the pure utilitarian theory of punishment by adopting the mixed theory. Since under the mixed theory the desert of the offender is a necessary condition of punishment, it will follow from the mixed theory that in each of the kinds of counterexamples considered (where punishment is not deserved), punishment should not be given. No contradictions will be generated, because the premises are consistent:

1. Punishment should be inflicted if and only if doing so achieves both a net social gain and gives an offender his just deserts.
2. A net social gain would be achieved in this case by the infliction of punishment.
3. It is not the case that punishment would give an offender his just deserts in this case.
4. Punishment should not be inflicted.

From the first three of these premises, the conclusion is deducible that there should be no punishment. This is also what the fourth premise asserts, so that there is no contradiction when one substitutes the mixed theory for the utilitarian theory of punishment.

There is, nonetheless, another sort of thought experiment that tests whether one truly believes the mixed theory, or is in fact a pure retributivist. Such thought experiments are the kind that fill the editorial pages where outrage is expressed at the lightness of sentence in a particular case, or the lightness of sentencing generally in the courts of some communities. An example is provided by *State v. Chaney* wherein the defendant was tried and convicted of two counts of forcible rape and one count of robbery. The defendant and a companion had picked up the prostitute at a downtown location in Anchorage. After driving the victim around in their car, the defendant and his companion beat her and forcibly raped her four times, also forcing her to perform an act of fellatio with the defendant's companion. During this same period of time, the victim's money was removed from her purse, and she only then was allowed to leave the vehicle after dire threats of reprisals if she attempted to report the incident to the police.

Despite this horrendous series of events, the trial judge imposed the minimum sentence on the defendant for each of the three counts and went out of his way to remark that he (the trial judge) was "sorry that the (military) regulations would not permit keeping (defendant) in the service if he wanted to stay because it seems to me that is a better setup for everybody concerned than putting him in the penitentiary." The trial judge also mentioned that as far as he was concerned, there would be no problem for the defendant to be paroled on the very first day of his sentence, if the parole board should so decide. The sentence was appealed by the state under a special Alaska procedure, and the attorney general urged the Alaska Supreme Court to disapprove the sentence.

The thought experiment such a case begins to pose for us is as follows: Imagine in such a case that after the rape but before sentencing the defendant has gotten into an accident so that his sexual desires are dampened to such an extent that he presents no further danger of rape; if money is also one of his problems, suppose further that he has inherited a great deal of money, so that he no longer needs to rob. Suppose, because of both of these facts, we are reasonably certain that he does not present a danger of either forcible assault, rape, robbery, or related crimes in the future. Since

Chaney is (by hypothesis) not dangerous, he does not need to be incapacitated, specially deterred, or reformed. Suppose further that we could successfully pretend to punish Chaney, instead of actually punishing him, and that no one is at all likely to find out. Our pretending to punish him will thus serve the needs of general deterrence and maintain social cohesion, and the cost to the state will be less than if it actually did punish him. Is there anything in the mixed theory of punishment that would urge that Chaney nonetheless should really be punished? I think not, so that if one's conclusion is that Chaney and people like him nonetheless should be punished, one will have to give up the mixed theory of punishment.

The argument structure is again that of a reductio and is as follows:

1. Punishment should be inflicted if and only if doing so both achieves a net social gain and gives an offender his just deserts.
2. A net social gain would not be achieved in this case by the infliction of punishment.
3. Punishment should be inflicted.

Again, these three premises generate a contradiction:

4. Punishment should not be inflicted and punishment should be inflicted.

From the first two premises, it follows that there should be no punishment; this contradicts the third premise that there nonetheless should be punishment.

One again has the choice of giving up one of the three premises of the argument. To give up the third premise is very unappealing to most people; doing so requires that people like Chaney should not be punished at all. Again, the tempting move is to assert that there will be no cases in which one will be sure enough that the danger is removed, or the ends of general deterrence served, that one can ever successfully assert the second premise. But as in the earlier case, this is simply to misunderstand the nature of the thought experiment. One only need think it conceivable that such dangers could be removed, or such ends of deterrence served, in order to test one's theory of punishment. And nothing in utilitarianism can guarantee that utility is always maximized by the punishment of the guilty. The only other way to avoid the contradiction is to give up the first premise. Yet this means that one would have to give up the mixed theory of punishment.

The Argument for Retributivism

If one follows the predicted paths through these thought experiments, the end result is that one finds oneself, perhaps surprisingly, to be a retributivist. We might call this an argument through the back door for retributivism, because the argument does not assert in any positive way the correctness of retributivism. It only asserts that the two theories of punishment truly competitive with retributivism, namely, the pure utilitarian theory and the mixed theory, are each unacceptable to us. That leaves retributivism as the only remaining theory of punishment we can accept.

It has seemed to some theorists that there is a limited amount of positive argument that can be given in favor of a retributivist theory and still have the theory remain truly retributivist. Hugo Bedau has recently reminded us, for example, that the retributivist faces a familiar dilemma:

> Either he appeals to something else—some good end—that is accomplished by the prac-

tice of punishment, in which case he is open to the criticism that he has nonretributivist, consequentialist justification for the practice of punishment. Or his justification does not appeal to something else, in which case it is open to the criticism that is circular and futile.[1]

In this respect, however, retributivism is no worse off than any other nonutilitarian theories in ethics, each of which seeks to justify an institution or practice not by the good consequences it may engender, but rather by the inherent rightness of the practice. The justification for any such theories is one that appeals to both our particular judgments and our more general principles, in order to show that the theory fits judgments that on reflection we are sure of, and principles that on reflection we are proud of.

. . .

Endnote

[1] Hugo Bedau, "Retribution and the Theory of Punishment," *Journal of Philosophy*, vol. 75 (1978): 601–20.

78. *Payne v. Tennessee*

Chief Justice Rehnquist delivered the opinion of the court.

In this case we reconsider our holdings in *Booth v. Maryland*, 482 U.S. 496, . . . (1987), and *South Carolina v. Gathers*, 490 U.S. 805 (1989), that the Eighth Amendment bars the admission of victim impact evidence during the penalty phase of a capital trial.

501 U.S. 808 (1991)
United States Supreme Court

The petitioner, Pervis Tyrone Payne, was convicted by a jury on two counts of first-degree murder and one count of assault with intent to commit murder in the first degree. He was sentenced to death for each of the murders, and to 30 years in prison for the assault.

The victims of Payne's offenses were 28-year-old Charisse Christopher, her 2-year-old daughter Lacie, and her 3-year-old son Nicholas. The three lived together in an apartment in Millington, Tennessee, across the hall from Payne's girlfriend,

Bobbie Thomas. On Saturday, June 27, 1987, Payne visited Thomas' apartment several times in expectation of her return from her mother's house in Arkansas, but found no one at home. . . .

. . . Sometime around 3 p.m., Payne returned to the apartment complex, entered the Christophers' apartment, and began making sexual advances towards Charisse. Charisse resisted and Payne became violent. A neighbor who resided in the apartment directly beneath the Christophers, heard Charisse screaming, "'Get out, get out,' as if she were telling the children to leave." The noise briefly subsided and then began, "'horribly loud.'" The neighbor called the police after she heard a "blood curdling scream" from the Christopher apartment. . . .

Inside the apartment, the police encountered a horrifying scene. Blood covered the walls and floor throughout the unit. Charisse and her children were lying on the floor in the kitchen. Nicholas, despite several wounds inflicted by a butcher knife that completely penetrated through his body from front to back, was still breathing. Miraculously, he survived, but not until after undergoing seven hours of surgery and a transfusion of 1700 cc's of blood—400 to 500 cc's more than his estimated normal blood volume. Charisse and Lacie were dead.

. . .

During the sentencing phase of the trial, Payne presented the testimony of four witnesses: his mother and father, Bobbie Thomas, and Dr. John T. Huston, a clinical psychologist specializing in criminal court evaluation work. Bobbie Thomas testified that she met Payne at church, during a time when she was being abused by her husband. She stated that Payne was a very caring person, and that he devoted much time and attention to her three children, who were being affected by her marital difficulties. She said that the children had come to love him very much and would miss him, and that he "behaved just like a father that loved his kids." She asserted that he did not drink, nor did he use drugs, and that it was generally inconsistent with Payne's character to have committed these crimes.

Dr. Huston testified that based on Payne's low score on an IQ test, Payne was "mentally handicapped." Huston also said that Payne was neither psychotic nor schizophrenic, and that Payne was the most polite prisoner he had ever met. Payne's par-

ents testified that their son had no prior criminal record and had never been arrested. They also stated that Payne had no history of alcohol or drug abuse, he worked with his father as a painter, he was good with children, and that he was a good son.

The State presented the testimony of Charisse's mother, Mary Zvolanek. When asked how Nicholas had been affected by the murders of his mother and sister, she responded:

"He cries for his mom. He doesn't seem to understand why she doesn't come home. And he cries for his sister Lacie. He comes to me many times during the week and asks me, Grandmama, do you miss my Lacie. And I tell him yes. He says, I'm worried about my Lacie."

In arguing for the death penalty during closing argument, the prosecutor commented on the continuing effects of Nicholas' experience, stating:

"But we do know that Nicholas was alive. And Nicholas was in the same room. Nicholas was still conscious. His eyes were open. He responded to the paramedics. He was able to follow their directions. He was able to hold his intestines in as he was carried to the ambulance. So he knew what happened to his mother and baby sister.

"There is nothing you can do to ease the pain of any of the families involved in this case. There is nothing you can do to ease the pain of Bernice or Carl Payne, and that's a tragedy. There is nothing you can do basically to ease the pain of Mr. and Mrs. Zvolanek, and that's a tragedy. They will have to live with it the rest of their lives. There is obviously nothing you can do for Charisse and Lacie Jo. But there is something you can do for Nicholas.

"Somewhere down the road Nicholas is going to grow up, hopefully. He's going to want to know what happened. And he is going to know what happened to his baby sister and his mother. He is going to want to know what type of justice was done. He is going to want to know what happened. With your verdict, you will provide the answer."

. . .

The jury sentenced Payne to death on each of the murder counts.

. . .

We granted certiorari . . . to reconsider our holdings in *Booth* and *Gathers* that the Eighth Amendment prohibits a capital sentencing jury from considering "victim impact" evidence relating to the personal characteristics of the victim and the emotional impact of the crimes on the victim's family.

In *Booth*, the defendant robbed and murdered an elderly couple. As required by a state statute, a victim impact statement was prepared based on interviews with the victims' son, daughter, son-in-law, and granddaughter. The statement, which described the personal characteristics of the victims, the emotional impact of the crimes on the family, and set forth the family members' opinions and characterizations of the crimes and the defendant, was submitted to the jury at sentencing. The jury imposed the death penalty. The conviction and sentence were affirmed on appeal by the State's highest court.

. . .

This Court held by a 5-to-4 vote that the Eighth Amendment prohibits a jury from considering a victim impact statement at the sentencing phase of a capital trial. The Court made clear that the admissibility of victim impact evidence was not to be determined on a case-by-case basis, but that such evidence was *per se* inadmissible in the sentencing phase of a capital case except to the extent that it "related directly to the circumstances of the crime." In *Gathers*, decided two years later, the Court extended the rule announced in *Booth* to statements made by a prosecutor to the sentencing jury regarding the personal qualities of the victim.

The *Booth* Court began its analysis with the observation that the capital defendant must be treated as a "'uniquely individual human bein[g],'" and therefore the Constitution requires the jury to make an individualized determination as to whether the defendant should be executed based on the "'character of the individual and the circumstances of the crime.'" The Court concluded that while no prior decision of this Court had mandated that only the defendant's character and immediate characteristics of the crime may constitutionally be considered, other factors are irrelevant to the capital sentencing decision unless they have "some bearing on the defendant's 'personal responsibility and moral guilt.'" To the extent that victim impact evidence presents "factors about which the defendant was unaware, and that were irrelevant to the decision to kill," the Court concluded, it has nothing to do with the "blameworthiness of a particular defendant." Evidence of the victim's character, the Court observed,

"could well distract the sentencing jury from its constitutionally required task [of] determining whether the death penalty is appropriate in light of the background and record of the accused and the particular circumstances of the crime." The Court concluded that, except to the extent that victim impact evidence relates "directly to the circumstances of the crime," the prosecution may not introduce such evidence at a capital sentencing hearing because "it creates an impermissible risk that the capital sentencing decision will be made in an arbitrary manner."

Booth and *Gathers* were based on two premises: that evidence relating to a particular victim or to the harm that a capital defendant causes a victim's family do not in general reflect on the defendant's "blameworthiness," and that only evidence relating to "blameworthiness" is relevant to the capital sentencing decision. However, the assessment of harm caused by the defendant as a result of the crime charged has understandably been an important concern of the criminal law, both in determining the elements of the offense and in determining the appropriate punishment. Thus, two equally blameworthy criminal defendants may be guilty of different offenses solely because their acts cause differing amounts of harm. "If a bank robber aims his gun at a guard, pulls the trigger, and kills his target, he may be put to death. If the gun unexpectedly misfires, he may not, His moral guilt in both cases is identical; but his responsibility in the former is greater." *Booth*, 482 U.S., at 519 (Scalia, J., dissenting). The same is true with respects to two defendants, each of whom participates in a robbery, each of whom acts with reckless disregard for human life; if the robbery in which the first defendant participated results in the death of a victim, he may be subjected to the death penalty, but if the robbery in which the second defendant participates does not result in the death of a victim, the death penalty may not be imposed.

The principles which have guided criminal sentencing—as opposed to criminal liability—have varied with the times. The book of Exodus prescribes the *Lex talionis*, "An eye for an eye, a tooth for a tooth." Exodus 21:22–23. In England and on the continent of Europe, as recently as the 18th century crimes which would be regarded as quite minor today were capital offenses. Writing in the

18th century, the Italian criminologist Cesare Beccaria advocated the idea that "the punishment should fit the crime." He said that "[w]e have seen that the true measure of crimes is the injury done to society." J. Farrer, *Crimes and Punishments*, 199 (London, 1880).

Gradually the list of crimes punishable by death diminished, and legislatures began grading the severity of crimes in accordance with the harm done by the criminal. The sentence for a given offense, rather than being precisely fixed by the legislature, was prescribed in terms of a minimum and a maximum, with the actual sentence to be decided by the judge. With the increasing importance of probation, as opposed to imprisonment, as a part of the penological process, some States such as California developed the "indeterminate sentence," where the time of incarceration was left almost entirely to the penological authorities rather than to the courts. But more recently the pendulum has swung back. The Federal Sentencing Guidelines, which went into effect in 1987, provided for very precise calibration of sentences, depending upon a number of factors. These factors relate both to the subjective guilt of the defendant and to the harm caused by his acts.

Wherever judges in recent years have had discretion to impose sentence, the consideration of the harm caused by the crime has been an important factor in the exercise of that discretion:

> The first significance of harm in Anglo-American jurisprudence is, then, as a prerequisite to the criminal sanction. The second significance of harm—one no less important to judges—is as a measure of the seriousness of the offense and therefore as a standard for determining the severity of the sentence that will be meted out." S. Wheeler, K. Mann, and A. Sarat, Sitting in Judgment: The Sentencing of White-Collar Criminals 56 (1988).

Whatever the prevailing sentencing philosophy, the sentencing authority has always been free to consider a wide range of relevant material. In the federal system, we observed that "a judge may appropriately conduct an inquiry broad in scope, largely unlimited as to the kind of information he may consider, or the source from which it may come." . . .

The Maryland statute involved in *Booth* required that the presentence report in all felony cases include a "victim impact statement" which would describe the effect of the crime on the victim and his family. Congress and most of the States have, in recent years, enacted similar legislation to enable the sentencing authority to consider information about the harm caused by the crime committed by the defendant. The evidence involved in the present case was not admitted pursuant to any such enactment, but its purpose and effect was much the same as if it had been. While the admission of this particular kind of evidence—designed to portray for the sentencing authority the actual harm caused by a particular crime—is of recent origin, this fact hardly renders it unconstitutional. . . .

"We have held that a State cannot preclude the sentencer from considering 'any relevant mitigating evidence' that the defendant proffers in support of a sentence less than death." *Eddings v. Oklahoma*, 455 U.S. 104, 114 (1982). Thus we have, as the Court observed in *Booth*, required that the capital defendant be treated as a "'uniquely individual human bein[g].'" But it was never held or even suggested in any of our cases preceding Booth that the defendant, entitled as he was to individualized consideration, was to receive that consideration wholly apart from the crime which he had committed. The language quoted from *Woodson* in the *Booth* opinion was not intended to describe a class of evidence that *could not* be received, but a class of evidence which *must* be received. Any doubt on the matter is dispelled by comparing the language in *Woodson* with the language from *Gregg v. Georgia*, quoted above, which was handed down the same day as *Woodson*. This misreading of precedent in *Booth* has, we think, unfairly weighted the scales in a capital trial; while virtually no limits are placed on the relevant mitigating evidence a capital defendant may introduce concerning his own circumstances, the State is barred from either offering "a glimpse of the life" which a defendant "chose to extinguish," *Mills*, 486 U.S. at 397, (REHNQUIST, C. J., dissenting), or demonstrating the loss to the victim's family and to society which have resulted from the defendant's homicide.

Booth reasoned that victim impact evidence must be excluded because it would be difficult, if not impossible, for the defendant to rebut such evidence without shifting the focus of the sentencing hearing away from the defendant, thus creating a "'mini-trial' on the victim's character." *Booth, supra*, at 506–507. In many cases the evidence relating to the victim is already before the jury at least in part because of its relevance at the guilt phase of the trail. But even as to additional evidence admitted at the sentencing phase, the mere fact that for tactical reasons it might not be prudent for the defense to rebut victim impact evidence makes the case no different than others in which a party is faced with this sort of a dilemma. As we explained in rejecting the contention that expert testimony on future dangerousness should be excluded from capital trials, "the rules of evidence generally extant at the federal and state levels anticipate that relevant, unprivileged evidence should be admitted and its weight left to the fact-finder, who would have the benefit of cross examination and contrary evidence by the opposing party." *Barefoot v. Estelle*, 463 U.S. 880, 898 (1983).

Payne echoes the concern voiced in *Booth*'s case that the admission of victim impact evidence permits a jury to find that defendants whose victims were assets to their community are more deserving of punishment than those whose victims are perceived to be less worthy. As a general matter, however, victim impact evidence is not offered to encourage comparative judgments of this kind— for instance, that the killer of a hardworking, devoted parent deserves the death penalty, but that the murderer of a reprobate does not. It is designed to show instead *each* victim's "uniqueness as an individual human being," whatever the jury might think the loss to the community resulting from his death might be. The facts of *Gathers* are an excellent illustration of this: the evidence showed that the victim was an out of work, mentally handicapped individual, perhaps not, in the eyes of most, a significant contributor to society, but nonetheless a murdered human being.

Under our constitutional system, the primary responsibility for defining crimes against state law, fixing punishments for the commission of these crimes, and establishing procedures for criminal trials rests with the States. The state laws respecting crimes, punishments, and criminal procedure are of course subject to the overriding provisions of the United States Constitution. Where the State imposes the death penalty for a particular crime, we have held that the Eighth Amendment imposes special limitations upon that process. . . . But, as we noted in *California v. Ramos*, 463 U.S. 992, 1001 (1983), "[b]eyond these limitations . . . the Court has deferred to the State's choice of substantive factors relevant to the penalty determination."

. . . The States remain free, in capital cases, as well as others, to devise new procedures and new remedies to meet felt needs. Victim impact evidence is simply another form or method of informing the sentencing authority about the specific harm caused by the crime in question, evidence of a general type long considered by sentencing authorities. We think the *Booth* Court was wrong in stating that this kind of evidence leads to the arbitrary imposition of the death penalty. In the majority of cases, and in this case, victim impact evidence serves entirely legitimate purposes. In the event that evidence is introduced that is so unduly prejudicial that it renders the trial fundamentally unfair, the Due Process Clause of the Fourteenth Amendment provides a mechanism for relief. Courts have always taken into consideration the harm done by the defendant in imposing sentence, and the evidence adduced in this case was illustrative of the harm caused by Payne's double murder.

We are now of the view that a State may properly conclude that for the jury to assess meaningfully the defendant's moral culpability and blameworthiness, it should have before it at the sentencing phase evidence of the specific harm caused by the defendant. "[T]he State has a legitimate interest in counteracting the mitigating evidence which the defendant is entitled to put in, by reminding the sentencer that just as the murderer should be considered as an individual, so too the victim is an individual whose death represents a unique loss to society and in particular to his family." By turning the victim into a "faceless stranger at the penalty phase of a capital trial," *Booth* deprives the State of the full moral force of its evidence and may prevent the jury from having before it all the information necessary to determine the proper punishment for a first-degree murder.

The present case is an example of the potential for such unfairness. The capital sentencing jury heard testimony from Payne's girlfriend that they met at church, that he was affectionate, caring, kind to her children, that he was not an abuser of drugs or alcohol, and that it was inconsistent with his character to have committed the murders. Payne's parents testified that he was a good son, and a clinical psychologist testified that Payne was an extremely polite prisoner and suffered from a low IQ. None of this testimony was related to the circumstances of Payne's brutal crimes. In contrast, the only evidence of the impact of Payne's offenses during the sentencing phase was Nicholas' grandmother's description—in response to a single question—that the child misses his mother and baby sister. Payne argues that the Eighth Amendment commands that the jury's death sentence must be set aside because the jury heard this testimony. But the testimony illustrated quite poignantly some of the harm that Payne's killing had caused; there is nothing unfair about allowing the jury to bear in mind that harm at the same time as it considers the

mitigating evidence introduced by the defendant.

. . .

We thus hold that if the State chooses to permit the admission of victim impact evidence and prosecutorial argument on that subject, the Eighth Amendment erects no *per se* bar. A State may legitimately conclude that evidence about the victim and about the impact of the murder on the victim's family is relevant to the jury's decision as to whether or not the death penalty should be imposed. There is no reason to treat such evidence differently than other relevant evidence is treated.

. . .

We accordingly affirm the judgment of the Supreme Court of Tennessee.
Affirmed.

---

79. *Restitution:* A *New Paradigm of Criminal Justice*

Randy E. Barnett

Outline of a New Paradigm

The idea of restitution is actually quite simple. It views crimes as an offense by one individual against the rights of another. The victim has suffered a loss. Justice consists of the culpable offender making good the loss he has caused. It calls for a complete refocusing of our image of crime. Kuhn would call it a "shift of worldview." Where we once saw an offense against society, we now see an offense against an individual victim. In a way, it is a common sense

Reprinted by permission of The University of Chicago Press.

view of crime. *The armed robber did not rob society, he robbed the victim.* His debt, therefore, is not to society; it is to the victim. There are really two types of restitution proposals: a system of "punitive" restitution and a "pure" restitutional system.

1. Punitive Restitution

"Since rehabilitation was admitted to the aims of penal law two centuries ago, the number of penological aims has remained virtually constant. Restitution is waiting to come in."[1] Given this view, restitution should merely be added to the paradigm of punishment. Stephen Schafer outlines the proposal: "[Punitive] restitution, like punishment,

must always be the subject of judicial consideration. Without exception it must be carried out by
personal performance by the wrong-doer, and
should even then be equally burdensome and just
for all criminals, irrespective of their means,
whether they be millionaires or laborers."[2]

There are many ways by which such a goal
might be reached. The offender might be forced to
compensate the victim by his own work, either in
prison or out. If it came out of his pocket or from the
sale of his property this would compensate the victim, but it would not be sufficiently unpleasant for
the offender. Another proposal would be that the
fines be proportionate to the earning power of the
criminal. Thus, "A poor man would pay in days of
work, a rich man by an equal number of days' income or salary."[3] Herbert Spencer made a proposal
along similar lines in his excellent "Prison-Ethics,"
which is well worth examining.[4] Murray N. Rothbard
and others have proposed a system of "double payments" in cases of criminal behavior.[5] While closer to
pure restitution than other proposals, the "double
damages" concept preserves a punitive aspect.

Punitive restitution is an attempt to gain the
benefits of pure restitution, which will be considered shortly, while retaining the perceived advantages of the paradigm of punishment. Thus, the
prisoner is still "sentenced" to some unpleasant-
ness—prison labor or loss of X number of days' income. That the intention is to preserve the "hurt" is
indicated by the hesitation to accept an out-of-
pocket payment or sale of assets. This is considered
too "easy" for the criminal and takes none of his
time. The amount of payment is determined not by
the *actual harm* but by the *ability of the offender to pay*.
Of course, by retaining the paradigm of punishment this proposal involves many of the problems
we raised earlier. In this sense it can be considered
another attempt to salvage the old paradigm.

2. Pure Restitution

"Recompense or restitution is scarcely a punishment
as long as it is merely a matter of returning stolen
goods or money. . . . The point is not that the offender
deserves to suffer, it is rather that the offended party
desires compensation."[6] This represents the complete
overthrow of the paradigm of punishment. No longer
would the deterrence, reformation, disablement, or
rehabilitation of the criminal be the guiding principle
of the judicial system. The attainment of these goals
would be incidental to, and as a result of, reparations
paid to the victim. No longer would the criminal deliberately be made to suffer for his mistake. Making
good that mistake is all that would be required. What
follows is a possible scenario of such a system.

When a crime occurred and a suspect was apprehended, a trial court would attempt to determine
his guilt or innocence. If found guilty, the criminal
would be sentenced to make restitution to the victim. If a criminal is able to make restitution immediately, he may do so. This would discharge his liability. If he were unable to make restitution, but were
found by the court to be trustworthy, he would be
permitted to remain at his job (or find a new one)
while paying restitution out of his future wages.
This would entail a legal claim against future wages.
Failure to pay could result in garnishment or a new
type of confinement.

If it is found that the criminal is not trustworthy,
or that he is unable to gain employment, he would
be confined to an employment project. This would
be an industrial enterprise, preferably run by a private concern, which would product actual goods or
services. The level of security at each employment
project would vary according to the behavior of the
offenders. Since the costs would be lower, inmates at
a lower security project would receive higher wages.
There is no reason why many workers could not be
permitted to live with their families inside or outside
the facility, depending, again, on the trustworthiness
of the offender. Room and board would be deducted
from the wages first, then a certain amount for restitution. Anything over that amount the worker could
keep or apply toward further restitution, thus hastening his release. If a worker refused to work, he
would be unable to pay for his maintenance, and
therefore would not in principle be entitled to it. If
he did not make restitution he could not be released.
The exact arrangement which would best provide
for high productivity, minimal security, and maximum incentive to work and repay the victim cannot
be determined in advance. Experience is bound to
yield some plans superior to others. In fact, the ex-
perimentation has already begun.[7]

While this might be the basic system, all sorts
of refinements are conceivable, and certainly many
more will be invented as needs arise. A few exam-

ples might be illuminating. With such a system of repayment, victim *crime insurance* would be more economically feasible than at present and highly desirable. The cost of awards would be offset by the insurance company's right to restitution in place of the victim (right of subrogation). The insurance company would be better suited to supervise the offender and mark his progress than would the victim. To obtain an earlier recovery, it could be expected to innovate so as to enable the worker to repay more quickly (and, as a result, be released that much sooner). The insurance companies might even underwrite the employment projects themselves as well as related industries which would employ the skilled worker after his release. Any successful effort on their part to reduce crime and recidivism would result in fewer claims and lower premiums. The benefit of this insurance scheme for the victim is immediate compensation, conditional on the victim's continued cooperation with the authorities for the arrest and conviction of the suspect. In addition, the centralization of victim claims would, arguably, lead to efficiencies which would permit the pooling of small claims against a common offender.

Another highly useful refinement would be *direct arbitration* between victim and criminal. This would serve as a sort of healthy substitute for plea bargaining. By allowing the guilty criminal to negotiate a reduced payment in return for a guilty plea, the victim (or his insurance company) would be saved the risk of an adverse finding at trial and any possible additional expense that might result. This would also allow an indigent criminal to substitute personal services for monetary payments if all parties agreed. . . .

Something analogous to the medieval Irish system of *sureties* might be employed as well.[8] Such a system would allow a concerned person, group, or company to make restitution (provided the offender agrees to this). The worker might then be released in the custody of the surety. If the surety had made restitution, the offender would owe restitution to the surety who might enforce the whole claim or show mercy. Of course, the more violent and unreliable the offender, the more serious and costly the offense, the less likely it would be that anyone would take the risk. But for first offenders, good workers, or others that charitable interests

found deserving (or perhaps unjustly convicted) this would provide an avenue of respite.

Restitution and Rights

These three possible refinements clearly illustrate the flexibility of a restitutional system. It may be less apparent that this flexibility is inherent to the restitutional paradigm. Restitution recognizes rights in the victim, and this is a principal source of its strength. The nature and limit of the victim's right to restitution at the same time defines the nature and limit of the criminal liability. In this way, the aggressive action of the criminal creates a *debt* to the victim. The recognition of rights and obligations make possible many innovative arrangements. Subrogation, arbitration, and suretyship are three examples mentioned above. They are possible because this right to compensation[9] is considered the property of the victim and can therefore be delegated, assigned, inherited, or bestowed. One could determine in advance who would acquire the right to any restitution which he himself might be unable to collect.

The natural owner of an unenforced death claim would be an insurance company that had insured the deceased. The suggestion has been made that a person might thus increase his personal safety by insuring with a company well known for tracking down those who injure its policy holders. In fact, the partial purpose of some insurance schemes might be to provide the funds with which to track down the malefactor. The insurance company, having paid the beneficiaries would "stand in their shoes." It would remain possible, of course, to simply assign or devise the right directly to the beneficiaries, but this would put the burden of enforcement on persons likely to be unsuited to the task.

If one accepts the Lockean trichotomy of property ownership,[10] that is, acquiring property via exchange, gifts, and homesteading (mixing one's labor with previously unowned land or objects), the possibility arises that upon a person's wrongful death, in the absence of any heirs or assignees, his right to compensation becomes unowned property. The right could then be claimed (homesteaded) by anyone willing to go to the trouble of catching and prosecuting the criminal. Firms might specialize in this sort of activity, or large insurance companies might make the effort as a kind of "loss leader" for public relations purposes.

This does, however, lead to a potentially serious problem with the restitutional paradigm: what exactly constitutes "restitution"? What is the *standard* by which compensation is to be made? Earlier we asserted that any such problem facing the restitutional paradigm faces civil damage suits as well. The method by which this problem is dealt with in civil cases could be applied to restitution cases. But while this is certainly true, it may be that this problem has not been adequately handled in civil damage suits either.

Restitution in cases of crimes against property is a manageable problem. Modern contract and tort doctrines of restitution are adequate. The difficulty lies in cases of personal injury or death. How can you put a price on life or limb, pain or suffering? Is not any attempt to do so of necessity arbitrary? It must be admitted that a fully satisfactory solution to this problem is lacking, but it should also be stressed that this dilemma, though serious, has little impact on the bulk of our case in favor of a restitutional paradigm. It is possible that no paradigm of criminal justice can solve every problem, yet the restitutional approach remains far superior to the paradigm of punishment or any other conceivable rival.

This difficulty arises because certain property is unique and irreplaceable. As a result, it is impossible to approximate a "market" or "exchange" value expressed in monetary terms. Just as there is no rational relationship between a wrongfully taken life and ten years in prison, there is little relationship between the same life and $20,000. Still, the nature of this possibly insoluble puzzle reveals a restitutional approach theoretically superior to punishment. For it must be acknowledged that a real, tangible loss has occurred. The problem is only one of incommensurability. Restitution provides some tangible, albeit inadequate, compensation for personal injury. Punishment provides none at all.[11] . . .

Advantages of a Restitutional System

1. The first and most obvious advantage is the assistance provided to victims of crime. They may have suffered an emotional, physical, or financial loss. Restitution would not change the fact that a possibly traumatic crime has occurred (just as the award of damages does not undo tortious conduct). Restitution, however, would make the resulting loss easier to bear for both victims and their families. At the same time, restitution would avoid a major pitfall of victim compensation/welfare plans: Since it is the criminal who must pay, the possibility of collusion between victim and criminal to collect "damages" from the state would be all but eliminated.

2. The possibility of receiving compensation would encourage victims to report crimes and to appear at trial. This is particularly true if there were a crime insurance scheme which contractually committed the policyholder to testify as a condition for payment, thus rendering unnecessary oppressive and potentially tyrannical subpoenas and contempt citations. Even the actual reporting of the crime to police is likely to be a prerequisite for compensation. Such a requirement in auto theft insurance policies has made car thefts the most fully reported crime in the United States. Furthermore, insurance companies which paid the claim would have a strong incentive to see that the criminal was apprehended and convicted. Their pressure and assistance would make the proper functioning of law enforcement officials all the more likely.

3. Psychologist Albert Eglash has long argued that restitution would aid in the rehabilitation of criminals. "Restitution is something an inmate does, not something done for or to him. . . . Being reparative, restitution can alleviate guilt and anxiety, which can otherwise precipitate further offenses."[12] Restitution, says Eglash, is an active effortful role on the part of the offender. It is socially constructive, thereby contributing to the offender's self-esteem. It is related to the offense and may thereby redirect the thoughts which motivated the offense. It is reparative, restorative, and may actually leave the situation better than it was before the crime, both for the criminal and victim.[13]

4. This is a genuinely "self-determinative" sentence. The worker would know that the length of his confinement was in his own hands. The harder he worked, the faster he would make restitution. He would be the master of his fate and would have to face that responsibility. This would encourage useful, productive activity and instill a conception of reward for good behavior and hard work. Compare this with the current probationary system and "indeterminate sentencing" where the decision for release is made by the prison bureaucracy, based only (if fairly administered) on "good behavior"; that is, passive acquiescence to prison discipline. Also, the fact that the worker would be acquiring *marketable* skills rather than more skillful methods of crime should help to reduce the shocking rate of recidivism.

5. The savings to taxpayers would be enormous. No longer would the innocent taxpayer pay for the apprehension and internment of the guilty. The cost of arrest, trial, and internment would be borne by the criminal himself. In addition, since now-idle inmates would become productive workers (able, perhaps, to support their families), the entire economy would benefit from the increase in overall production.

6. Crime would no longer pay. Criminals, particularly shrewd white-collar criminals, would know that they could not dispose of the proceeds of their crime and, if caught, simply serve time. They would have to make full restitution plus enforcement and legal costs, thereby greatly increasing the incentive to prosecute. While this would not eliminate such crime it would make it rougher on certain types of criminals, like bank and corporation officials, who harm many by their acts with a virtual assurance of lenient legal sanctions. It might also encourage such criminals to keep the money around for a while so that, if caught, they could repay more easily. This would make a full recovery more likely.

A restitutional system of justice would benefit the victim, the criminal, and the taxpayer. The humanitarian goals of proportionate punishment, rehabilitation, and victim compensation are dealt with on a *fundamental* level making their achievement more likely. In short, the paradigm of restitution would benefit all but the entrenched penal bureaucracy and enhance justice at the same time. What then is there to stop us from overthrowing the paradigm of punishment and its penal system and putting in its place this more efficient, more humane, and more just system? The proponents of punishment and others have a few powerful counterarguments. It is to these we now turn.

Objections to Restitution

1. Practical Criticisms of Restitution.

It might be objected that "crimes disturb and offend not only those who are directly their victim, but also the whole social order."[14] Because of this, society, that is, individuals other than the victim, deserves some satisfaction from the offender. Restitution, it is argued, will not satisfy the lust for revenge felt by the victim or the "community's sense of justice." This criticism appears to be overdrawn. Today most members of the community are mere spectators of the criminal justice system, and this is largely true even of the victim. One major reform being urged presently is more victim involvement in the criminal justice process. The restitution proposal would necessitate this involvement. And while the public generally takes the view that officials should be tougher on criminals, with "tougher" taken by nearly everyone to mean more severe in punishing, one must view this "social fact" in light of the lack of a known alternative. The real test of public sympathies would be to see which sanction people would choose: incarceration of the criminal for a given number of years or the criminal's being compelled to make restitution to the victim: While the public's choice is not clearly predictable, neither can it be assumed that it would reject restitution. There is some evidence to the contrary.

This brings us to a second practical objection: that monetary sanctions are insufficient deterrents to crime. Again, this is something to be discovered, not something to be assumed. There are a number of reasons to believe that our *current* system of punishment does not adequately deter. . . . In fact, many have argued that the deterrent value of sanctions has less to do with *severity* than with *certainty*, and the preceding considerations indicate that law enforcement would be more certain under a restitutional system. In the final analysis, however, it is irrelevant to argue that more crimes may be committed if our proposal leaves the victim better off. It must be remembered: *Our goal is not the suppression of crime; it is doing justice to victims.*

A practical consideration which merits considerable future attention is the feasibility of the employment project proposal. A number of questions can be raised. At first blush, it seems naively optimistic to suppose that offenders will be able or willing to work at all, much less earn their keep and pay reparations as well. On the contrary, this argument continues, individuals turn to crime precisely because they lack the skills which the restitutional plan assumes they have. Even if these workers have the skills, but refuse to work, what could be done? Would not the use of force to compel compliance be tantamount to slavery?

. . . [O]ne can advance several responses. First, the problem as usually posed assumes the offender to be highly irrational and possibly mentally unbalanced. There is no denying that some segment of the criminal population fits the former description. What this approach neglects, however, is the possibility that many criminals are making rational choices within an irrational and unjust political system. Specifically I refer to the myriad laws and regulations which make it difficult for the unskilled or persons of transitory outlook to find legal employment. I refer also to the laws which deny legality to the types of services which are in particular demand in economically impoverished communities. Is it "irrational" to choose to steal or rob when one is virtually foreclosed from the legal opportunity to do otherwise? Another possibility is that the criminal chooses crime not because of foreclosure, but because he enjoys and obtains satisfaction from a criminal way of life. Though morally repugnant, this is hardly irrational.

Furthermore, it no longer can be denied that contact with the current criminal justice system is itself especially damaging among juveniles. The offenders who are hopelessly committed to criminal behavior are not usually the newcomers to crime but those who have had repeated exposure to the penal system. In Kuhn's words, "Existing institutions have ceased to meet the problems posed by an environment *they have in part created.*" While a restitutionary system might not change these hard-core offenders, it could, by the early implementation of sanctions perceived by the criminal to be just, break the vicious cycle which in large part accounts for their existence.

Finally, if offenders could not or would not make restitution, then the logical and just result of their refusal would be confinement until they could

or would. Such an outcome would be entirely in their hands. While this "solution" does not suggest who should justly pay for this confinement, the problem is not unique to a restitutionary system. In this and other areas of possible difficulty we must seek guidance from existing pilot programs as well as from the burgeoning research in this area and in victimology in general.

2. *Distributionary Criticisms of Restitution.*

There remains one criticism of restitution which is the most obvious and the most difficult with which to deal. Simply stated, it takes the following form: "Doesn't this mean that rich people will be able to commit crimes with impunity if they can afford it? Isn't this unfair?" The *practical* aspect of this objection is that whatever deterrent effect restitution payments may have, they will be less for those most able to pay. The *moral* aspect is that whatever retributive or penal effect restitution payments may have they will be less for those who are well off. Some concept of equality of justice underlies both considerations.

Critics of restitution fail to realize that the "cost" of crime will be quite high. In addition to compensation for pain and suffering, the criminal must pay for the cost of his apprehension, the cost of the trial, and the legal expenditures of *both* sides. This should make even an unscrupulous wealthy person think twice about committing a crime. The response to this is that we cannot have it both ways. If the fines would be high enough to bother the rich, then they would be so high that a project worker would have no chance of earning that much and would, therefore, have no incentive to work at all. If, on the other hand, you lower the price of crime by ignoring all its costs, you fail to deter the rich or fully compensate the victim.

This is where the option of arbitration and victim crime insurance becomes of practical importance. If the victim is uninsured, he is unlikely to recover for all costs of a very severe crime from a poor, unskilled criminal, since even in an employment project the criminal might be unable to earn enough. If he had no hope of earning his release, he would have little incentive to work very hard beyond paying for his own maintenance. The victim would end up with less than if he had "settled" the case for the lesser amount which a project worker could reasonably be expected to earn. If, however, the victim had full-coverage criminal insurance, he would recover his damages in full, and the insurance company would absorb any disparity between full compensation and maximal employment project worker's output. This cost would be reflected in premium prices, enabling the insurance company which settled cases at an amount which increased the recovery from the criminal to offer the lowest rates. Eventually a "maximum" feasible fine for project workers would be determined based on these considerations. The "rich," on the other hand, would naturally have to pay in full. This arrangement would solve the practical problem, but it should not be thought of as an imperative of the restitutional paradigm.

The same procedure of varying the payments according to ability to pay would answer the moral considerations as well (that the rich are not hurt enough) and this is the prime motive behind *punitive* restitution proposals. However, we reject the moral consideration outright. The paradigm of restitution calls not for the (equal) hurting of criminals, but for restitution to victims. Any appeal to "inadequate suffering" is a reversion to the paradigm of punishment, and by varying the sanction for crimes of the same magnitude according to the economic status of the offender it reveals its own inequity. *Equality of justice means equal treatment of victims.* It should not matter to the victim if his attacker was rich or poor. His plight is the same regardless. Any reduction of criminal liability because of reduced earning power would be for practical, not moral, reasons.

Equality of justice derives from the fact that the rights of men should be equally enforced and respected. Restitution recognizes a victim's right to compensation for damages from the party responsible. Equality of justice, therefore, calls for equal enforcement of each victim's right to restitution. *Even if necessary or expedient, any lessening of payment to the victim because of the qualities of the criminal is a violation of that victim's rights and an inequality of justice.* Any such expedient settlement is only a recognition that an imperfect world may make possible only imperfect justice. As a practical matter, a resti-

tutional standard gives victims an enormous incentive to pursue wealthy criminals since they can afford quick, full compensation. Contrast this with the present system where the preference given the wealthy is so prevalent that most victims simply assume that nothing will be done.

The paradigm of restitution, to reiterate, is neither a panacea for crime nor a blueprint for utopia. Panaceas and utopias are not for humankind. We must live in a less than perfect world with less than perfect people. Restitution opens the possibility of an improved and more just society. The old paradigm of punishment, even reformed, simply cannot offer this promise.

Endnotes

[1] Gerhard O. W. Mueller, "Compensation for Victims of Crime: Thought before Action," *Minnesota Law Review* 50 (1965): 221.

[2] Schafer, p. 127.

[3] *Ibid.*

[4] Herbert Spencer, "Prison-Ethics," in *Essays: Scientific, Political and Speculative* (New York: D. Appleton & Co., 1907), 3:152–91.

[5] Murray N. Rothbard, *Libertarian Forum* 14, no. 1 (January 1972): 7–8.

[6] Kaufmann, p. 55.

[7] For a recent summary report, see Burt Calaway, "Restitution as an Integrative Punishment" (paper prepared for the Symposium on Crime and Punishment: Restitution, Retribution, and Law, Harvard Law School, March 1977).

[8] For a description of the Irish system, see Joseph R. Peden, "Property Rights in Medieval Ireland: Celtic Law versus Church and State" (paper presented at the Symposium on the Origins and Development of Property Rights, University of San Francisco, January 1975); for a theoretical discussion of a similar proposal, see Spencer, pp. 182–86.

[9] Or, perhaps more accurately, the compensation itself.

[10] For a brief explanation of this concept and several of its possible applications, see Murray N. Rothbard. "Justice and Property Rights," in *Property in a Humane Economy*, ed. Samuel L. Blumenfeld (La Salle, Ill.: Open Court Publishing Co., 1974), pp. 101–22.

[11] That the "spiritual" satisfaction which punishment may or may not provide is to be recognized as a legitimate form of "compensation" is a claim retributionists must defend.

[12] Albert Eglash, "Creative Restitution: Some Suggestions for Prison Rehabilitation Programs," *American Journal of Correction* 40 (November–December 1958): 20.

[13] *Ibid.*; see also Eglash's "Creative Restitution: A Broader Meaning for an Old Term," *Journal of Criminal Law and Criminology* 48 (1958): 619–22; Burt Galaway and Joe Hudson, "Restitution and Rehabilitation—Some Central Issues," *Crime and Delinquency* 18 (1972): 408–10.

[14] Del Vecchio, p. 198.

Study Questions

1. Which of the following does Wilson argue will likely have a greater deterrent effect on criminal behavior: changing the levels of penalties to which wrongdoers are subjected or making changes to increase the probability the wrongdoers will be apprehended and convicted?

2. Wilson admits that a variety of social factors (parenting; educational and employment opportunities) are significant in the causal explanation of criminal behavior. If this is true, is it morally justifiable to assume that wrongdoers are "rational economic actors" whose incentives to criminal conduct can be effectively altered by appropriate penalties? Is this what a deterrence-oriented theory assumes?

3. What two kinds of counterexamples does Moore develop as arguments against the utilitarian theory of punishment?

4. What argument does Moore use to reject the mixed theory of punishment?

5. In 1996, the California State Assembly narrowly defeated a bill that would have reinstituted corporal punishment for youthful offenders. The bill provided that juveniles found to have vandalized property with graffiti would be whacked on the bottom up to ten times with a wooden paddle wielded by a parent. If the parent refused to mete out the punishment or to deliver a sufficient blow, the judge could empower the bailiff to administer the punishment. Proponents argued that the measure would give the judge an additional tool in the effort to combat vandalism; opponents claimed that corporal punishment would backfire by breeding anger and resentment. Can corporal punishment be justified on utilitarian grounds? What assumptions would be necessary in the utilitarian view to show the justifiability of such punishment? Could corporal punishment be justified on retributive grounds? Would you have endorsed the bill? Why or why not?

6. The Women's Coalition of Pasadena, California, proposed in 1997 to seek legislation requiring permanent, lifetime cuffs to be affixed to sexual offenders after they leave prison. The cuffs would contain an antitampering microchip to avoid removal. Children could then be taught to recognize the bracelet and avoid those who wear it. Do you think such restraints would be justified, assuming that the cuffs could be shown to reduce the rate of child molestation?

7. According to the majority of the Supreme Court in *Payne,* upon what two assumptions did the rulings in the earlier *Booth* and *Gathers* cases rely?

8. How does the majority in *Payne* respond to the argument that the use of victim-impact evidence will encourage juries to assign degrees of punishment to criminal defendants based on the status (wealth, social standing, etc.) of their victims?

9. How does Barnett explain the distinction between "punitive" and "pure" restitution? Which one of these does Barnett favor? Why?

10. According to Barnett, how would restitution by the wrongdoer to the victim be assured when the wrongdoer is unable or unwilling to provide it?

11. How does Barnett propose that restitution be handled in cases in which the victim has been killed?

12. In 1995, two Native American teenagers of the Tlingit tribe were convicted in the beating and

robbery of a pizza deliveryman. Rather than sentence them for the crime, however, the Washington state judge turned the youths over to tribal authorities who proposed to deal with the offenders in a way more consistent with their tribal traditions. The two eighteen-year-olds were given the punishment of banishment: provided with the basics, a Bible, and a book on Tlingit culture, the boys were sent to live for a year on uninhabited islands in Alaska. Tribal authorities argued that banishment is integral to a process of rehabilitation. Restitution was also to be a part of the punishment: the families of the teenagers gave money to the victim, and the boys were forced to carve objects for sale toward restitution. Is such a form of punishment justifiable? If so, on what grounds?

13. In a recent essay, Randy Barnett applied the arguments for restitution to the case of O.J. Simpson. The Simpson case presented a strong *prima facie* argument against restitution, Barnett maintained, for "here was an accused murderer who really could write a check to the victim's family and presumably walk away free and clear." Barnett responded to this criticism by insisting that "while it is true that a wealthy person could make restitution, by the same token a wealthy person can use his or her wealth to avoid being punished" by hiring expensive lawyers who will help them avoid or delay punishment. "Under the prevailing system," Barnett claimed, "wealthy defendants can claim vindication they would have been denied if they had been compelled to make restitution." (Barnett, "Harshest Sentence Is Restitution," *National Law Journal*, January 7, 1997, p. A22.) Are Barnett's arguments here convincing? Why or why not?

14. Growing frustration with drug-related crimes has prompted several state legislators to introduce bills with harsh punishments. One such bill, introduced recently in the Texas legislature, would have punished convicted drug dealers by cutting off their fingers, one finger for each conviction. A bill introduced in Delaware would have required felony drug offenders to receive "no fewer than five nor more than 40 lashes well laid on" on a bare back. Should either mutilation or flogging be permissible punishments for such offenses?

D. *The Death Penalty*

The Case of Karla Faye Tucker

One out of every three executions in the United States occurs in the state of Texas. In early February 1998, one scheduled execution drew intense scrutiny from both opponents and proponents of the death penalty. Karla Faye Tucker was sched-uled to die as punishment for her participation in a double murder. In 1983 Tucker, then twenty-three-years-old, along with her boyfriend, broke into the apartment of an acquaintance to steal motorcycle parts. Tucker killed the acquaintance with a pickax, claiming that she experienced an orgasm with each blow; a woman found in the apartment was killed by Tucker's boyfriend. Subsequent to her capture, Tucker confessed her crimes and testified against her boyfriend. She expressed remorse—even to the point of admitting that she should die for her wrongdoing. Central to Tucker's cooperation was a religious conversion, which Tucker claimed she underwent while awaiting trial. Fourteen years later, on the eve of her execution, supporters described Tucker as a caring, repentant, and deeply religious person; she had married the prison minister in 1993. Tucker, along with those opposed to her execution, argued that she could help save troubled youth through spiritual counseling. Some objected to leniency for Tucker, alleging that the public outcry on her behalf was due to her gender and race (Tucker was White). Texas had not executed a woman since the Civil War, the critics contended, and had Tucker been a Black male (as are the majority of death row inmates across the country), no one would have cared. Tucker died in the Texas death chamber on February 3, 1998, after Governor George W. Bush refused to commute her sentence.

The Complexity of Capital Punishment

The Tucker case acted as a lens to focus public attention on the death penalty and the legal and moral questions it raises. Among these questions are: What purpose is capital punishment supposed to serve? Does it deter crime? Is it a form of just retribution? Should a genuinely repentant person be executed? Is capital punishment administered in a racially or sexually discriminatory fashion?

The debate concerning capital punishment is complex in that it blends issues at once constitutional, moral, and empirical. Of constitutional importance is the question of whether death is a "cruel and unusual" punishment. Morally, the death penalty involves questions about the sanctity of life, the power of the state, and the justice of fitting crime to punishment. Empirically, the controversies over the death penalty turn on whether and to what extent credible evidence shows capital punishment to be a greater deterrent than life-imprisonment and on how statistical evidence of disproportionality between White and non-White

defendants sentenced to death is to be explained. These issues are explored in the readings for this section.

Cruelty, Proportionality, and the Eighth Amendment

Hours before his scheduled execution in 1992, Robert Alton Harris made a last-minute plea to the Supreme Court of the United States. His argument was simple: death in California's gas chamber, which exposes the condemned to cyanide gas, is an unconstitutional form of cruel and unusual punishment. The Court refused to stay the execution, but two justices dissented, arguing in part that when California began use of the gas chamber,

> it was considered a humane method of execution. Fifty-five years of history and moral development have superseded that judgment. The barbaric use of cyanide gas in the Holocaust, the development of cyanide agents as chemical weapons, our contemporary understanding of execution by lethal gas, and the development of less cruel methods of execution all demonstrate that execution by cyanide gas is unnecessarily cruel.[1]

After his execution, Harris's argument won over state legislators, who modified the law to permit the alternative of lethal injection. The Harris case nonetheless raises questions about the humaneness of certain forms of punishment, and about the meaning of the Eighth Amendment. Because these notions also relate importantly to the debate concerning capital punishment, it is worth exploring them a bit further.

What kinds of punishment does the Eighth Amendment ban? How can we flesh out the meaning of "cruel and unusual" punishments? A number of possibilities exist. It might be suggested, for example, that the language simply be taken at face value: only punishments that are painful and infrequently administered are forbidden. But this won't work; a punishment does not become licit if done only painlessly and often. Another suggestion turns to the constitu-

---

Gomez v. U.S. District Court 112 S. Ct. 1652 (1992).

tional theory of original intent (see the discussion in Chapter I) and urges that "cruel and unusual" means whatever the framers of the Constitution thought it meant, that is, whatever *they* would have deemed cruel and unusual. This interpretation, however, is subject to all of the problems confronting originalism as a general interpretive method (See Chapter I). Nor, some would argue, is it reasonable to let the meaning of "cruel and unusual" reflect the consensus of public opinion at any one time. The Eighth and similar amendments were supposed to serve as a check or constraint on the sentiments of the majority, not an implementation of them. A utilitarian might argue that a punishment is "cruel and unusual" just in case it levies a penalty in excess of what is warranted by the goal of bringing about the greatest happiness, say, by deterring others. But here the problem is that the language and subsequent interpretation of the clause make it clear that it was meant to rule out certain punishments altogether, even if they would have an extra deterrent effect if carried out. Finally, others propose that the meaning of "cruel and unusual" punishment be interpreted in light of the Kantian, retributive conception of punishment. Cruel and unusual punishments are those that may not be inflicted, no matter how advantageous to society, because they are inconsistent with a proper regard for human dignity and a respect for people as autonomous and responsible beings. The clause thus acts as a "side constraint," setting the permissible outer boundaries of social policy.

Central both to the retributive theory and to the approach of many courts to the Eighth Amendment is the *principle of proportionality.* This states that the severity of the punishment inflicted must be proportional to the gravity of the offense; the punishment, in other words, must "fit the crime." Familiar as this saying is, the principle it represents is not entirely clear.

In early 1993, the state of Washington executed convicted triple-murderer Westley Allan Dodd by hanging. Because he had hanged one of the three boys he confessed to killing, Dodd insisted that his own execution be by hanging rather than the available alternative of lethal injection. Dodd evidently felt that this mode of punishment "fit" his crime. In his writings on the state of Virginia, Thomas Jefferson recorded, among other things, some proposed revisions to the state's criminal code.[2] The revised code assigned specific punishments to types of of-

fenses: treason and murder were to be punished with death, rape and sodomy with "dismemberment," and maiming and disfiguring with "retaliation." The proposed penal code constituted an attempt to carry out the retributive requirement that the punishment fit the crime on at least two levels. First, the schedule of proposed punishments attempted to ensure that the mode or kind of punishment be appropriate to the crime committed: reparation for larceny, physical beatings for battery, and so on. Second, this principle was applied concretely to the specific manner in which crimes and their matching punishments were to be carried out: murder by poison, for example, was to be punished with death by poison.

How closely must punishment match crime? Would it be possible to carry out the logic of the Virginia Code across the board? In some cases, this would be impossible; for example, a blind man who attacks and blinds another can't be blinded in return. But are there certain punishments that must remain unacceptable even if they are literally workable as a return of like for like? May we torture the torturer? Rape the rapist? (Neither Kant nor the Virginia Code is willing to insist upon literal sameness here; both recommend castration as a punishment for rape.) Some retributivists answer that their theory should be understood to recommend only that crimes and punishments be ranked in severity, with the most serious crimes getting the most serious punishment, the second most serious crime getting the second most serious punishment, and so on, with no further requirement that the crime be precisely mirrored, detail for detail, in the punishment.

The Death Penalty and the Eighth Amendment

Is the death penalty a constitutionally permissible punishment? This question is taken up in our readings by the Supreme Court's opinion in *Gregg v.*

---

[2] Thomas Jefferson, *Notes on the State of Virginia: Proposed Revised Code of Virginia,* reprinted in S. Presser and J. Zainalden (eds.) *Law in American History: Cases and Materials* (St. Paul, Minn.: West, 1980)

Georgia. A brief review of the background to *Gregg* will help clarify the terrain of the debate.

It is widely agreed that the Constitution itself certainly contemplates the death penalty, which was commonly used in the eighteenth century, even for crimes other than murder. The document says, for example, that no one shall be held "to answer for a capital . . . crime" except upon indictment, and it insists that no one shall be deprived of "life" without due process of law. In 1972, however, the Supreme Court, in *Furman v. Georgia*,[3] struck down all state capital punishment laws as they then operated. Differing explanations were given for the ruling. Some justices took the position that death, for whatever crime, is always cruel and unusual because it fails to comport with "evolving standards of decency." The plurality took the view that death is not unconstitutional *per se*, but that the unbridled discretion then given to juries to impose death as a punishment had resulted in a racially prejudicial administration of the penalty, making its imposition "arbitrary and capricious" and violating the Eighth Amendment on that ground.

Subsequent to *Furman*, most states enacted statutes to control jury deliberations in death-penalty cases, providing for "guided discretion." These new procedural laws created a separate "penalty phase" in any trial resulting in conviction for a capital offense, permitting juries to recommend execution only if they found "aggravating circumstances" (for example, that the murder was committed for monetary gain or by a prisoner under a sentence of life imprisonment). It is these laws that were upheld by the Court in *Gregg*. Subsequent to the ruling in *Gregg*, the Court has refused to allow states to limit the kinds of mitigating circumstances that juries can consider in deliberating on whether to impose death; and it has been held that no crime can carry a mandatory death penalty—execution can result only when a jury has been permitted to weigh the considerations for and against death.[4]

The plurality opinion in *Gregg* echoes the views of pro-death-penalty advocates like Ernest

van den Haag: the constitutional judgment that a punishment is or is not excessive or inhumane must be based on the public consensus. Because most people favor the death penalty, execution cannot be *per se* unconstitutional. Accordingly, the plurality opinion in the *Gregg* case argues that whether a punishment is consistent with "evolving standards of decency" is a judgment to be made on the basis of "objective indicia" reflecting the "public attitude toward a given sanction." The Court observes that the re-enactment of capital punishment statutes by most states after the *Furman* decision reveals that the majority of Americans believe death to be an appropriate punishment for some crimes. Execution does not violate the proportionality constraint of the retributive theory of punishment, the Court argues, at least where the defendant has been convicted of taking a life himself (as was the case with *Gregg*); and whether the death penalty is an effective deterrent is a judgment to be left to legislators. Two dissenting opinions, by Justice Brennan and Justice Marshall, are sharply critical of the Court's reasoning.

The Argument for the Death Penalty

Both retributive and utilitarian arguments are made to support the death penalty. Famous among retributive arguments is that made by Kant, who insisted that one who murders must be punished with death. There is no "sameness of kind" between death (of the victim) and continued life (of the murderer). No amount of imprisonment for the living, Kant maintained, would "equal" being dead. Van den Haag suggests a similar argument in our readings: wanton murder is the worst of offenses and thus deserves the worst punishment. And, although it is true that a mistaken execution would be irredeemable, this does not distinguish death from life imprisonment, for lost years cannot be restored to one unjustly imprisoned any more than life can to those who are gone.

The retributive claim is not that death is imposed as an act of revenge; it is, rather, that justice

---

[3] 408 U.S. 238 (1972).

[4] See *Lockett v. Ohio* 438 U.S. 586 (1978); *Woodson v. North Carolina* 428 U.S. 280 (1976).

demands it. Nor is execution inconsistent with respect for the "sanctity of life," say retributive supporters of capital punishment. Kant, for example, reasoned that part of what it means to treat a condemned murderer as an autonomous person is that society must give to that person what he or she deserves (death)—to do less would be to use that person's fate (which she has chosen) as a vehicle for our own needs (for example, to lessen our own discomfort at the thought of execution).

The utilitarian argument in support of capital punishment turns on the various "goods" that execution is supposed to confer. Chief among these alleged goods are the ideas that the death penalty is an efficient *preventive* and a better *deterrent* than alternative forms of punishment, such as life imprisonment. The notions of prevention and deterrence are fraught with confusion, however, and it is important to consider carefully what these concepts mean in their application to capital punishment. To say that any form of punishment is *preventive* of crime just means that the infliction of punishment makes it impossible for the individual punished to commit the crimes that he or she would have committed had the punishment not been inflicted. To say that a form of punishment is a *deterrent* is to assert that the example of inflicting punishment in a given case will induce others inclined toward criminal acts to refrain from criminality.

It is a frequently made but often unsubstantiated claim that capital punishment is a perfect preventative measure. After all, dead people don't commit crimes. This is true, of course, but it doesn't follow simply from this fact that in executing someone you have thereby prevented any crimes. To license this claim you would have to know whether the person executed would have committed further crimes had he or she been allowed to live. Because this kind of "counterfactual" statement can never be known with certainty, it is false to insist that capital punishment is in every case necessarily a crime preventive measure. Capital punishment may be definitively *incapacitative* (since the dead person is powerless), but that is a different claim from the assertion that it prevents future crime.

Is the death penalty a more effective deterrent than any alternative—for example, life imprisonment? Here, again, it is tempting to try to answer this question *a priori* by insisting that death *must* be a deterrent, given that everyone is afraid to die. However, the question that must be answered is whether the fear of death will affect the incentives that criminals might have to commit capital crimes. This issue must be assessed on the basis of the empirical evidence. As the readings by van den Haag and Hugo Bedau make clear, the evidence relating to the deterrence value of the death penalty is highly contested. Van den Haag and Bedau debate the results of numerous studies that have been done—studies comparing crime rates in jurisdictions with capital punishment with those that do not impose it, and studies comparing crime rates in a single jurisdiction both before and after capital punishment was imposed (or abandoned).

The Argument Against the Death Penalty

Both the utilitarian and the retributive grounds for the institution of the death penalty have been challenged by opponents. To begin with, the opponents say, the existing research has not convincingly shown capital punishment to be a significantly more effective deterrent than life imprisonment without parole. But even aside from that problem, the critics caution, capital punishment brings with it negative costs that utilitarians must face. First, capital punishment is extremely expensive. Currently more than 3,000 people are on death row nationwide, and the number is growing by roughly 200 per year. Because of the lengthy appeals frequently pursued by death-row inmates, the average time spent on death row is six years. Long-term incarceration, attorneys' fees, and the laborious procedures required by law to put someone to death have pushed the cost of some executions well into the millions. A different type of cost, according to death-penalty foes, is in human terms. Innocent people have been and will continue to be executed, and life cannot be restored once taken. Finally, opponents of capital punishment such as Bedau contend that the deterrence arguments, if correct, prove too much: even supposing that torture were found to be an extremely effective deterrent, that would not legitimate its use. Bedau observes in this connection that neither Kant nor van den Haag approves death-by-torture.

The primary objection to the retributive case for capital punishment turns on the requirement of proportionality. Ensuring that the punishment "fit the crime" is not something that retributivists are willing to do in all cases (as noted above), but if it is not permissible to dismember one who killed others by dismemberment, why is it permissible to kill at all? Retributivists are unwilling to follow the dictates of proportionality in every case, so why must death be punished with death? Wouldn't proportionality be satisfied as long as the most severe crime was linked to the most severe sanction short of capital punishment, namely, life imprisonment without parole? Critics also worry that retributivists wrongly assume that murderers autonomously choose to kill and thus "will" their own deaths. The reality, they contend, is that a high proportion of murders are correlated with drug use and mental disorders, thereby undermining the moral imperative that those who commit murder must die.

Race and the Death Penalty

The claim that the death penalty is administered arbitrarily and capriciously—the claim at the center of the Court's ruling in *Furman v. Georgia*—has not gone away. Years after capital punishment was reinstated, many of those opposed to it maintain that death is meted out in a deeply discriminatory fashion. Various researchers have claimed to discover disturbing patterns in the ways juries and judges impose capital punishment.[5] The facts cited by the researchers include these: that more than 48 percent of inmates in death row are non-White, even though minorities make up less than 20 percent of the total United States population; that the number of Blacks put to death since 1930 is greater than that of Whites executed, although Blacks account for less

than 12 percent of the total population; that in some states a murderer of a White person is more than ten times more likely to be sentenced to death than the murderer of a Black person. Critics of capital punishment allege that these and similar statistical results cannot be explained on any ground other than race. Judges and juries, they contend, clearly value White lives more than Black lives, and this bias leads them to execute a disproportionate number of Blacks and spare a disproportionate number of murderers of Blacks. Are these allegations warranted? These questions are taken up in the *McCleskey* case and in the essay by Randall Kennedy.

McCleskey involved a Black defendant convicted and sentenced to death for a murder committed during an armed robbery. McCleskey argued that Georgia's capital punishment statute violated the Equal Protection clause of the Fourteenth Amendment to the Constitution. McCleskey relied upon an extensive study of death-penalty convictions in Georgia. That study had purported to find many racial disparities in the imposition of the death penalty in Georgia. McCleskey argued that those who murder Whites are more likely to be sentenced to death, and that Black defendants are more likely to be sentenced to death than White defendants convicted of the same offense. The Supreme Court rejected McCleskey's argument, insisting that proof of discrimination in capital sentencing cannot be merely general and statistical, but must demonstrate that those involved in McCleskey's own case acted with racial bias. No such proof, according to the Court, was forthcoming.

In his essay, Randall Kennedy subjects the Court's reasoning in *McCleskey* to careful scrutiny. Kennedy is critical of the Court's refusal to concede that racial bias has been shown to be a likely factor in McCleskey's fate, given that the disparities confirmed by researchers can be explained in no other way. Kennedy then looks at a deeper issue: Assuming that it had ruled in favor of McCleskey, what should the Court have done? What follows from the discrimination argument upon which the critics of the death penalty rely? That all forms of capital punishment should be abolished? Or that states be required to increase the number of people executed for murdering Blacks? Kennedy examines these and several other responses to the inequality of capital punishment.

---

[5] See, for example, Gross and Mauro, "Patterns of Death," 37 *Stanford Law Review* (1984), pp. 27–101; Bowers and Pierce, "Aribitrariness and Discrimination under Post-*Furman* Capital Statutes," 26 *Crime and Delinquency* (1980), pp. 563–635.

80. *Gregg v. Georgia*

Mr. Justice Stewart, with Justices Powell and Stevens concurring:

We address initially the basic contention that the punishment of death for the crime of murder is, under all circumstances, "cruel and unusual" in violation of the Eighth and Fourteenth Amendments of the Constitution. [Later in] this opinion, we will consider the sentence of death imposed under the Georgia statutes at issue in this case.

The Court on a number of occasions has both assumed and asserted the constitutionality of capital punishment. . . . But until *Furman v. Georgia*, 408 U.S. 238 (1972), the Court never confronted squarely the fundamental claim that the punishment of death always, regardless of the enormity of the offense or the procedure followed in imposing the sentence, is cruel and unusual punishment in violation of the Constitution. Although this issue was presented and addressed in *Furman*, it was not resolved by the Court. Four Justices would have held that capital punishment is not unconstitutional *per se*; two Justices would have reached the opposite conclusion; and three Justices, while agreeing that the statutes then before the Court were invalid as applied, left open the question whether such punishment may ever be imposed. We now hold that the punishment of death does not invariably violate the Constitution. . . .

. . .

It is clear from the foregoing precedents that the Eighth Amendment has not been regarded as a static concept. As Mr. Chief Justice Warren said, in an oft-quoted phrase, "[t]he Amendment must draw its meaning from the evolving standards of decency that mark the progress of a maturing society." . . . Thus, an assessment of contemporary values concerning the infliction of a challenged sanction is relevant to the application of the Eighth Amendment. As we develop below more fully, . . . this assessment does not call for a subjective judgment. It requires, rather, that we look to objective indicia that reflect the public attitude toward a given sanction.

But our cases also make clear that public perceptions of standards of decency with respect to criminal sanctions are not conclusive. A penalty also must accord with "the dignity of man," which is the "basic concept underlying the Eighth Amendment." *Trop v. Dulles*. . . . This means, at least, that the punishment not be "excessive." When a form of punishment in the abstract (in this case, whether capital punishment may ever be imposed as a sanction for murder) rather than in the particular (the propriety of death as a penalty to be applied to a specific defendant for a specific crime) is under consideration, the inquiry into "excessiveness" has two aspects. First, the punishment must not involve the unnecessary and wanton infliction of pain. . . . Second, the punishment must not be grossly out of proportion to the severity of the crime. . . .

The imposition of the death penalty for the crime of murder has a long history of acceptance both in the United States and in England. The common-law rule imposed a mandatory death sentence on all convicted murderers. . . . And the penalty continued to be used into the 20th century by most American States, although the breadth of the common-law rule was diminished, initially by narrowing the class of murders to be punished by death and subsequently by widespread adoption of laws expressly granting juries the discretion to recommend mercy. . . .

It is apparent from the text of the Constitution itself that the existence of capital punishment was accepted by the Framers. At the time the Eighth Amendment was ratified, capital punishment was a common sanction in every State. Indeed, the First Congress of the United States enacted legislation providing death as the penalty for specified crimes. . . .

428 U.S. 153 (1976)
United States Supreme Court

Four years ago, the petitioners in *Furman* and its companion cases [predicated] their argument primarily upon the asserted proposition that standards of decency had evolved to the point where capital punishment no longer could be tolerated. The petitioners in those cases said, in effect, that the evolutionary process had come to an end, and that standards of decency required that the Eighth Amendment be construed finally as prohibiting capital punishment for any crime regardless of its depravity and impact on society. This view was accepted by two Justices. Three other Justices were unwilling to go so far; focusing on the procedures by which convicted defendants were selected for the death penalty rather than on the actual punishment inflicted, they joined in the conclusion that the statutes before the Court were constitutionally invalid.

The petitioners in the capital cases before the Court today renew the "standards of decency" argument, but developments during the four years since *Furman* have undercut substantially the assumptions upon which their argument rested. Despite the continuing debate, dating back to the 19th century, over the morality and utility of capital punishment, it is now evident that a large proportion of American society continues to regard it as an appropriate and necessary criminal sanction.

The most marked indication of society's endorsement of the death penalty for murder is the legislative response to *Furman*. The legislatures of at least 35 States have enacted new statutes that provide for the death penalty for at least some crimes that result in the death of another person. . . .

. . . [H]owever, the Eighth Amendment demands more than that a challenged punishment be acceptable to contemporary society. The Court also must ask whether it comports with the basic concept of human dignity at the core of the Amendment. . . .

The death penalty is said to serve two principal social purposes: retribution and deterrence of capital crimes by prospective offenders.

In part, capital punishment is an expression of society's moral outrage at particularly offensive conduct. This function may be unappealing to many, but it is essential in an ordered society that asks its citizens to rely on legal processes rather than self-help to vindicate their wrongs. . . . "Retribution is no longer the dominant objective of the criminal law," *Williams v. New York*, 337 U.S. 241, 248 (1949), but neither is it a forbidden objective nor one inconsistent with our respect for the dignity of men. . . . Indeed, the decision that capital punishment may be the appropriate sanction in extreme cases is an expression of the community's belief that certain crimes are themselves so grievous an affront to humanity that the only adequate response may be the penalty of death.

Statistical attempts to evaluate the worth of the death penalty as a deterrent to crimes by potential offenders have occasioned a great deal of debate. The results simply have been inconclusive. . . .

Although some of the studies suggest that the death penalty may not function as a significantly greater deterrent than lesser penalties, there is no convincing empirical evidence either supporting or refuting this view. We may nevertheless assume safely that there are murderers, such as those who act in passion, for whom the threat of death has little or no deterrent effect. But for many others, the death penalty undoubtedly is a significant deterrent. There are carefully contemplated murders, such as murders for hire, where the possible penalty of death may well enter into the cold calculus that precedes the decision to act. And there are some categories of murder, such as murder by a life prisoner, where other sanctions may not be adequate.

The value of capital punishment as a deterrent of crime is a complex factual issue the resolution of which properly rests with the legislatures, which can evaluate the results of statistical studies in terms of their own local conditions and with a flexibility of approach that is not available to the courts. . . . Indeed, many of the post-*Furman* statutes reflect just such a responsible effort to define those crimes and those criminals for which capital punishment is most probably an effective deterrent.

In sum, we cannot say that the judgment of the Georgia Legislature that capital punishment may be necessary in some cases is clearly wrong. Considerations of federalism, as well as respect for the ability of a legislature to evaluate, in terms of its particular State, the moral consensus concerning the death penalty and its social utility as a sanction, require us to conclude, in the absence of more convincing evidence, that the infliction of death as a punishment for murder is not without justification and thus is not unconstitutionally severe.

Finally, we must consider whether the punishment of death is disproportionate in relation to the crime for which it is imposed. There is no question that death as a punishment is unique in its severity and irrevocability. . . . When a defendant's life is at stake, the Court has been particularly sensitive to insure that every safeguard is observed. . . . But we are concerned here only with the imposition of capital punishment for the crime of murder, and when a life has been taken deliberately by the offender, we cannot say that the punishment is invariably disproportionate to the crime. It is an extreme sanction, suitable to the most extreme of crimes.

We hold that the death penalty is not a form of punishment that may never be imposed, regardless of the circumstances of the offense, regardless of the character of the offender, and regardless of the procedure followed in reaching the decision to impose it.

. . .

For the reasons expressed in this opinion, we hold that the statutory system under which Gregg was sentenced to death does not violate the Constitution. Accordingly, the judgment of the Georgia Supreme Court is affirmed.

It is so ordered.

Mr. Justice Brennan, dissenting:

. . .

This Court inescapably has the duty, as the ultimate arbiter of the meaning of our Constitution, to say whether, when individuals condemned to death stand before our Bar, "moral concepts" require us to hold that the law has progressed to the point where we should declare that the punishment of death, like punishments on the rack, the screw, and the wheel, is no longer morally tolerable in our civilized society. . . . I emphasize only that foremost among the "moral concepts" recognized in our cases and inherent in the Clause is the primary moral princi-

ple that the State, even as it punishes, must treat its citizens in a manner consistent with their intrinsic worth as human beings—a punishment must not be so severe as to be degrading to human dignity. A judicial determination whether the punishment of death comports with human dignity is therefore not only permitted but compelled by the Clause. . . .

The fatal constitutional infirmity in the punishment of death is that it treats members of the human race as nonhumans, as objects to be toyed with and discarded. [It is] thus inconsistent with the fundamental premise of the Clause that even the vilest criminal remains a human being possessed of common human dignity. As such it is a penalty that subjects the individual to a fate forbidden by the principle of civilized treatment guaranteed by the [clause]. I therefore would hold, on that ground alone, that death is today a cruel and unusual punishment prohibited by the Clause. Justice of this kind is obviously no less shocking than the crime itself, and the new "official" murder, far from offering redress for the offense committed against society, adds instead a second defilement to the first.

Mr. Justice Marshall, dissenting:

In *Furman* I concluded that the death penalty is constitutionally invalid for two reasons. First, the death penalty is excessive. And second, the American people, fully informed as to the purposes of the death penalty and its liabilities, would in my view reject it as morally unacceptable.

Since the decision in *Furman*, the legislatures of 35 States have enacted new statutes authorizing the imposition of the death sentence for certain crimes, and Congress has enacted a law providing the death penalty for air piracy resulting in death. . . . I would be less than candid if I did not acknowledge that these developments have a significant bearing on a realistic assessment of the moral acceptability of the death penalty to the American people. But if the constitutionality of the death penalty turns, as I have urged, on the opinion of an *informed* citizenry, then even the enactment of new death statutes cannot be viewed as conclusive. In *Furman*, I observed that the American people are largely unaware of the information critical to a judgment on the morality of the death penalty, and concluded that if they were better informed they would consider it shocking, unjust, and unacceptable. A recent study, conducted after the enactment of the post-*Furman* statutes, has confirmed that the American people know little about the death penalty, and that the opinions of an informed public would differ significantly from those of a public unaware of the consequences and effects of the death penalty.

Even assuming, however, that the post-*Furman* enactment of statutes authorizing the death penalty renders the prediction of the views of an informed citizenry an uncertain basis for a constitutional decision, the enactment of those statutes has no bearing whatever on the conclusion that the death penalty is unconstitutional because it is excessive. An excessive penalty is invalid under the Cruel and Unusual Punishments Clause "even though popular sentiment may favor" it. . . . The inquiry here, then, is simply whether the death penalty is necessary to accomplish the legitimate legislative purposes in punishment, or whether a less severe penalty—life imprisonment—would do as well. . . .

The two purposes that sustain the death penalty as nonexcessive in the Court's view are general deterrence and retribution. In *Furman*, I canvassed the relevant data on the deterrent effect of capital punishment. . . . The state of knowledge at that point, after literally centuries of debate, was summarized as follows by a United Nations Committee:

> It is generally agreed between the retentionists and abolitionists, whatever their opinions about the validity of comparative studies of deterrence, that the data which now exist show no correlation between the existence of capital punishment and lower rates of capital crime.[1]

The available evidence, I concluded in *Furman*, was convincing that "capital punishment is not necessary as a deterrent to crime in our society." . . .

The other principal purpose said to be served by the death penalty is retribution. . . . It is this notion that I find to be the most disturbing aspect of today's unfortunate decisions.

The concept of retribution is a multifaceted one, and any discussion of its role in the criminal law must be undertaken with caution. On one level, it can be said that the notion of retribution or reprobation is the basis of our insistence that only those who have broken the law be punished, and in this sense the notion is quite obviously central to a just system of criminal sanctions. But our recognition that retribution plays a crucial role in determining who may be punished by no means requires approval of retribution as a general justification for punishment. It is the question whether retribution can provide a moral justification for punishment—in particular, capital punishment—that we must consider.

My Brothers Stewart, Powell, and Stevens offer the following explanation of the retributive justification for capital punishment:

> "The instinct for retribution is part of the nature of man, and channeling that instinct in the administration of criminal justice serves an important purpose in promoting the stability of a society governed by law. When people begin to believe that organized society is unwilling or unable to impose upon criminal offenders the punishment they 'deserve,' then there are sown the seeds of anarchy—of self help, vigilante justice, and lynch law."

This statement is wholly inadequate to justify the death penalty. As my Brother Brennan stated in *Furman*, "[t]here is no evidence whatever that utilization of imprisonment rather than death encourages private blood feuds and other disorders." It simply defies belief to suggest that the death penalty is necessary to prevent the American people from taking the law into their own hands.

In a related vein, it may be suggested that the expression of moral outrage through the imposition of the death penalty serves to reinforce basic moral values—that it marks some crimes as particularly offensive and therefore to be avoided. The argument is akin to a deterrence argument, but differs in that it contemplates the individual's shrinking from antisocial conduct, not because he fears punishment, but because he has been told in the strongest possible way that the conduct is wrong. This contention, like the previous one, provides no support for the death penalty. It is inconceivable that any individual concerned about conforming his conduct to what society says is "right" would fail to realize that murder is "wrong" if the penalty were simply life imprisonment.

The foregoing contentions—that society's expression of moral outrage through the imposition of the death penalty pre-empts the citizenry from taking the law into its own hands and reinforces moral values—are not retributive in the purest sense. They are essentially utilitarian in that they portray the death penalty as valuable because of its beneficial results. These justifications for the death penalty are inadequate because the penalty is, quite clearly I think, not necessary to the accomplishment of those results.

There remains for consideration, however, what might be termed the purely retributive justification for the death penalty—that the death penalty is appropriate, not because of its beneficial effect on society, but because the taking of the murderer's life is itself morally good. Some of the language of the opinion of my Brothers Stewart, Powell, and Stevens in No. 74–6257 appears positively to embrace this notion of retribution for its own sake as a justification for capital punishment. They state:

> [T]he decision that capital punishment may be the appropriate sanction in extreme cases is an expression of the community's belief that certain crimes are themselves so grievous an affront to humanity that the only adequate response may be the penalty of death.

They then quote with approval from Lord Justice Denning's remarks before the British Royal Commission on Capital Punishment:

> "The truth is that some crimes are so outrageous that society insists on adequate punishment, because the wrong-doer deserves it, irrespective of whether it is a deterrent or not."

Of course, it may be that these statements are intended as no more than observations as to the popular demands that it is thought must be responded to in order to prevent anarchy. But the implication of the statements appears to me to be quite different—namely, that society's judgment that the murderer "deserves" death must be respected not simply because the preservation of order requires it, but because it is appropriate that society make the judgment and carry it out. It is this latter notion, in particular, that I consider to be fundamentally at odds with the Eighth Amendment. . . . The mere fact that the community demands the murderer's life in return for the evil he has done cannot sustain the death penalty, for as Justices Stewart, Powell, and Stevens remind us, "the Eighth Amendment demands more than that a challenged punishment be acceptable to contemporary society." . . . To be sustained under the Eighth Amendment, the death penalty must "compor[t] with the basic concept of human dignity at the core of the Amendment," ibid.; the objective in imposing it must be "[consistent] with our respect for the dignity of [other] men." . . . Under these standards, the taking of life "because the wrongdoer deserves it" surely must fall, for such a punishment has as its very basis the total denial of the wrongdoer's dignity and worth.

The death penalty, unnecessary to promote the goal of deterrence or to further any legitimate notion of retribution, is an excessive penalty forbidden by the Eighth and Fourteenth Amendments. I respectfully dissent from the Court's judgment upholding the sentences of death imposed upon the petitioners in these cases.

Endnote

[1] United Nations, Department of Economic and Social Affairs, Capital Punishment, pt. II, I 159, p. 123 (1968).

81. The Death Penalty Once More

Ernest van den Haag

People concerned with capital punishment disagree on essentially three questions: (1) Is it constitutional? (2) Does the death penalty deter crime more than life imprisonment? (3) Is the death penalty morally justifiable?

I. Is *the Death Penalty Constitutional?*

The fifth amendment, passed in 1791, states that "no person shall be deprived of life, liberty, or property, without due process of law." Thus, with "due process of law," the Constitution authorizes depriving persons "of life, liberty or property." The fourteenth amendment, passed in 1868, applies an identical provision to the states. The Constitution, then, authorizes the death penalty. It is left to elected bodies to decide whether or not to retain it.

The eighth amendment, reproducing almost verbatim a passage from the English Bill of Rights of 1689, prohibits "cruel and unusual punishments." This prohibition was not meant to repeal the fifth amendment since the amendments were passed simultaneously. "Cruel" punishment is not prohibited unless "unusual" as well, that is, new, rare, not legislated, or disproportionate to the crime punished. Neither the English Bill of Rights, nor the eighth amendment, hitherto has been found inconsistent with capital punishment.

This work was originally published in 29 U.C. Davis L. Rev. 957 (1985). © 1985 by The Regents of the University of California. Reprinted by permission.

A. Evolving Standards

Some commentators argue that, in *Trop v. Dulles*, the Supreme Court indicated that "evolving standards of decency that mark the progress of a maturing society" allow courts to declare "cruel and unusual," punishments authorized by the Constitution. However, *Trop* was concerned with expatriation, a punishment that is not specifically authorized by the Constitution. The death penalty is. *Trip* did not suggest that "evolving standards" could de-authorize what the Constitution repeatedly authorizes. Indeed, Chief Justice Warren, writing for the majority in *Trop*, declared that "the death penalty . . . cannot be said to violate the constitutional concept of cruelty."[1] Furthermore, the argument based on "evolving standards" is paradoxical: the Constitution would be redundant if current views, enacted by judicial fiat, could supersede what it plainly says. If "standards of decency" currently invented or evolved could, without formal amendment, replace or repeal the standards authorized by the Constitution, the Constitution would be superfluous.

It must be remembered that the Constitution does not force capital punishment on the population but merely authorizes it. Elected bodies are left to decide whether to use the authorization. As for "evolving standards," how could courts detect them without popular consensus as a guide? Moral revelations accepted by judges, religious leaders, sociologists, or academic elites, but not by the majority of voters, cannot suffice. The opinions of the most organized, most articulate, or most vocal might receive unjustified deference. Surely the eighth amendment was meant to limit, but was not meant to replace, decisions by the legislative branch, or to enable the judiciary to do what the voters won't do. The general consensus on which the courts would have to rely could be registered only by elected bodies. They favor capital punishment. Indeed, at present, more than seventy percent of the voters approve of the death penalty. The state legislatures reflect as much. Wherefore, the Supreme Court, albeit reluctantly, rejected abolition of the death penalty by judicial fiat. This decision was subsequently qualified by a finding that the death penalty for rape is disproportionate to the crime, and by rejecting all mandatory capital punishment.

B. Caprice

Laws that allowed courts too much latitude to decide, perhaps capriciously, whether to actually impose the death penalty in capital cases also were found unconstitutional. In response, more than two-thirds of the states have modified their death penalty statutes, listing aggravating and mitigating factors, and imposing capital punishment only when the former outweigh the latter. The Supreme Court is satisfied that this procedure meets the constitutional requirements of noncapriciousness. However, abolitionists are not.

. . . Professor Charles Black contends that the death penalty is necessarily imposed capriciously, for irremediable reasons. If he is right, he has proved too much, unless capital punishment is imposed more capriciously now than it was in 1791 or 1868, when the fifth and fourteenth amendments were enacted. He does not contend that it is. Professor Black also stresses that the elements of chance, unavoidable in all penalization, are least tolerable when capital punishment is involved. But the irreducible chanciness inherent in human efforts does not constitutionally require the abolition of capital punishment, unless the framers were less aware of chance and human frailty than Professor Black is. . . .

C. Discrimination

Sociologists have demonstrated that the death penalty has been distributed in a discriminatory pattern in the past: black or poor defendants were more likely to be executed than equally guilty others. This argues for correction of the distributive process, but not for abolition of the penalty it distributes, unless constitutionally excessive maldistribution ineluctably inheres in the penalty. There is no evidence to that effect. Actually, although we cannot be sure that it has disappeared altogether, discrimination has greatly decreased compared to the past.

However, recently the debate on discrimination has taken a new turn. Statistical studies have found that, *ceteris paribus*, a black man who murders a white has a much greater chance to be executed than he would have had, had his victim been black. This discriminates against black *victims* of murder: they are not as fully, or as often, vindicated as are white victims. However, although unjustified per se, discrimination against a class of victims need not, and here does not, amount to discrimination against their victimizers. The pattern discriminates *against* black murderers of whites and *for* black murderers of blacks. One may describe it as discrimination for, or discrimination against, just as one may describe a glass of water as half full or half empty. Discrimination against one group (here, blacks who kill whites) is necessarily discrimination in favor of another (here, blacks who kill blacks).

Most black victims are killed by black murderers, and a disproportionate number of murder victims is black. Wherefore the discrimination in favor of murderers of black victims more than offsets, numerically, any remaining discrimination against other black murderers.

D. Comparative Excessiveness

Recently lawyers have argued that the death penalty is unconstitutionally disproportionate if defendants, elsewhere in the state, received lesser sentences for comparable crimes. But the Constitution only requires that penalties be appropriate to the gravity of the crime, not that they cannot exceed penalties imposed elsewhere. Although some states have adopted "comparative excessiveness" reviews, there is no constitutional requirement to do so.

Unavoidably, different courts, prosecutors, defense lawyers, judges and juries produce different penalties even when crimes seem comparable. Chance plays a great role in human affairs. Some offenders are never caught or convicted, while others are executed; some are punished more than others guilty of worse crimes. Thus, a guilty person, or group of persons, may get away with no punishment, or with a light punishment, while others receive the punishment they deserve. Should we let these others go too, or punish them less severely? Should we abolish the penalty applied unequally or discriminatorily?

The late Justice Douglas suggested an answer to these questions:

> A law that . . . said that blacks, those who never went beyond the fifth grade in school, those who made less than $3,000 a year, or those who were unpopular or unstable should be the only people executed [would be wrong]. A law which in the overall view reaches that result in practice has no more sanctity than a law which in terms provides the same.[2]

Justice Douglas' answer here conflates an imagined discriminatory law with the discriminatory application of a non-discriminatory law. His imagined law would be inconsistent with the "equal protection of the laws" demanded by the fourteenth amendment, and the Court would have to invalidate it ipso facto. But discrimination caused by uneven application of non-discriminatory death penalty laws may be remedied by means other than abolition, as long as the discrimination is not intrinsic to the laws.

Consider now, albeit fleetingly, the moral as distinguished from the constitutional bearing of discrimination. Suppose guilty defendants are justly executed, but only if poor, or black and not otherwise. This unequal justice would be morally offensive for what may be called tautological reasons: if any punishment for a given crime is just, then a greater or lesser punishment is not. Only one punishment can be just for all persons equally guilty of the same crime. Therefore, different punishments for equally guilty persons or group members are unjust: some offenders are punished more than they deserve, or others less.

Still, equality and justice are not the same. "Equal justice" is not a redundant phrase. Rather, we strive for two distinct ideals, justice and equality. Neither can replace the other. We want to have justice and, having it, we want to extend it equally to all. We would not want equal injustice. Yet, sometimes, we must choose between equal injustice and unequal justice. What should we prefer? Unequal justice is justice still, even if only for some, whereas equal injustice is injustice for all. If not every equally guilty person is punished equally, we have unequal justice. It seems preferable to equal injustice—having no guilty person punished as deserved. Since it is never possible to punish equally

all equally guilty murderers, we should punish, as they deserve, as many of those we apprehend and convict as possible. Thus, even if the death penalty were inherently discriminatory—which is not the case—but deserved by those who receive it, it would be morally just to impose it on them. If, as I contend, capital punishment is just and not inherently discriminatory, it remains desirable to eliminate inequality in distribution, to apply the penalty to all who deserve it, sparing no racial or economic class. But if a guilty person or group escaped the penalty through our porous system, wherein is this an argument for sparing others?

If one does not believe capital punishment can be just, discrimination becomes a subordinate argument, since one would object to capital punishment even if it were distributed equally to all the guilty. If one does believe that capital punishment for murderers is deserved, discrimination against guilty black murderers and in favor of equally guilty white murderers is wrong, not because blacks receive the deserved punishment, but because whites escape it.

Consider a less emotionally charged analogy. Suppose traffic police ticketed all drivers who violated the rules, except drivers of luxury cars. Should we abolish tickets? Should we decide that the ticketed drivers of nonluxury cars were unjustly punished and ought not to pay their fines? Would they become innocent of the violation they are guilty of because others have not been ticketed? Surely the drivers of luxury cars should not be exempted. But the fact that they were is no reason to exempt drivers of nonluxury cars as well. Laws could never be applied if the escape of one person, or group, were accepted as ground for not punishing another. To do justice is primarily to punish as deserved, and only secondarily to punish equally.

Guilt is personal. No one becomes less guilty or less deserving of punishment because another was punished leniently or not at all. That justice does not catch up with all guilty persons understandably is resented by those caught. But it does not affect their guilt. If some, or all, white and rich murderers escape the death penalty, how does that reduce the guilt of black or poor murderers, or make them less deserving of punishment, or deserving of a lesser punishment?

Some lawyers have insisted that the death penalty is distributed among those guilty of murder as though by a lottery and that the worst may escape it. They exaggerate, but suppose one grants the point. How do those among the guilty selected for execution by lottery become less deserving of punishment because others escaped it? What is wrong is that these others escaped, not that those among the guilty who were selected by the lottery did not.

Those among the guilty actually punished by a criminal justice system unavoidably are selected by chance, not because we want to so select them, but because the outcome of our efforts largely depends on chance. No murderer is punished unless he is unlucky enough both to be caught and to have convinced a court of his guilt. And courts consider evidence not truth. They find truth only when the evidence establishes it. Thus they may have reasonable doubts about the guilt of an actually guilty person. Although we may strive to make justice as equal as possible, unequal justice will remain our lot in this world. We should not give up justice, or the death penalty, because we cannot extend it as equally to all the guilty as we wish. If we were not to punish one offender because another got away because of caprice or discrimination, we would give up justice for the sake of equality. We would reverse the proper order of priorities.

II. Is the Death Penalty More Deterrent Than Other Punishments?

Whether or not the death penalty deters the crimes it punishes more than alternative penalties—in this case life imprisonment with or without parole—has been widely debated since Isaac Ehrlich broke the abolitionist ranks by finding that from 1933–65 "an additional execution per year . . . may have resulted on the average in seven or eight fewer murders."[3] Since his article appeared, a whole cottage industry devoted to refuting his findings has arisen. Ehrlich, no slouch, has been refuting those who refuted him. The result seems inconclusive. Statistics have not proved conclusively that the death penalty does or does not deter murder more than other penalties. Still, Ehrlich has the merit of being the first to use a sophisticated statistical analysis to tackle the problem, and of defending his

analysis, although it showed deterrence. . . . His predecessors cannot be accused of mathematical sophistication. Yet the academic community uncritically accepted their abolitionist results. I myself have no contribution to make to the mathematical analyses of deterrent effects. Perhaps this is why I have come to believe that they may becloud the issue, leading us to rely on demonstrable deterrence as though decisive.

Most abolitionists believe that the death penalty does not deter more than other penalties. But most abolitionists would abolish it, even if it did. I have discussed this matter with prominent abolitionists. . . . Each told me that, even if every execution were to deter a hundred murders, he would oppose it. I infer that, to these abolitionist leaders, the life of every murderer is more valuable than the lives of a hundred prospective victims, for these abolitionists would spare the murderer, even if doing so would cost a hundred future victims their lives.

Obviously, deterrence cannot be the decisive issue for these abolitionists. It is not necessarily for me either, since I would be for capital punishment on grounds of justice alone. On the other hand, I should favor the death penalty for murderers, if probably deterrent, or even just possibly deterrent. To me, the life of any innocent victim who might be spared has great value; the life of a convicted murderer does not. This is why I would not take the risk of sacrificing innocents by not executing murderers.

Even though statistical demonstrations are not conclusive, and perhaps cannot be, I believe that capital punishment is likely to deter more than other punishments because people fear death more than anything else. They fear most death deliberately inflicted by law and scheduled by the courts. Whatever people fear most is likely to deter most. Hence, I believe that the threat of the death penalty may deter some murderers who otherwise might not have been deterred. And surely the death penalty is the only penalty that could deter prisoners already serving a life sentence and tempted to kill a guard, or offenders about to be arrested and facing a life sentence. Perhaps they will not be deterred. But they would certainly not be deterred by anything else. We owe all the protection we can give to law enforcers exposed to special risks.

Many murders are "crimes of passion" that, perhaps, cannot be deterred by any threat. Whether or not they can be would depend on the degree of passion; it is unlikely to be always so extreme as to make the person seized by it totally undeterrable. At any rate, offenders sentenced to death ordinarily are guilty of premeditated murder, felony murder, or multiple murders. Some are rape murderers, or hit men, but, to my knowledge, no one convicted of a "crime of passion" is on death row. Whatever the motive, some prospective offenders are not deterrable at all, others are easily deterred, and most are in between. Even if only some murders were, or could be, deterred by capital punishment, it would be worthwhile.

Sometimes an anecdote, invented in the 19th Century, is told to suggest that the threat of the death penalty does not deter. Some pickpockets are said to have gone eagerly about their business in a crowd assembled to see one of them hang. We are not told what the level of their activity was, compared to the level in crowds of similar size assembled for different purposes. Thus, the anecdote merely shows that the death penalty does not deter some criminals. This never was contested.

Almost all convicted murderers try to avoid the death penalty by appeals for commutation to life imprisonment. However, a minuscule proportion of convicted murderers prefer execution. It is sometimes argued that they murdered for the sake of being executed, of committing suicide via execution. More likely, they prefer execution to life imprisonment. Although shared by few, this preference is not irrational per se. It is also possible that these convicts accept the verdict of the court, and feel that they deserve the death penalty for the crimes they committed, although the modern mind finds it hard to imagine such feelings. But not all murderers are ACLU humanists.

Because those sentenced to death tend to sedulously appeal the verdict of the trial courts, executions are correctly said to be costly. It is doubtful, however, that they are most costly than life imprisonment. Contrary to widely shared assumptions, life prisoners spend much of their time preparing habeas corpus appeals (not to speak of other lawsuits) just as prisoners condemned to death do. But even if execution were more costly than life imprisonment, it should not be abandoned if it is just. If unjust, execution should not occur, even if it were cheap and imprisonment costly. But execution probably is less costly than life imprisonment.

III. Is *the Death Penalty Moral?*

A. Miscarriages

Miscarriages of justice are rare, but do occur. Over a long enough time they lead to the execution of some innocents. Does this make irrevocably punishments morally wrong? Hardly. Our government employs trucks. They run over innocent bystanders more frequently than courts sentence innocents to death. We do not give up trucks because the benefits they produce outweigh the harm, including the death of innocents. Many human activities, even quite trivial ones, foreseeably cause wrongful deaths. Courts may cause fewer wrongful deaths than golf. Whether one sees the benefit of doing justice by imposing capital punishment as moral, or as material, or both, it outweighs the loss of innocent lives through miscarriages, which are as unintended as traffic accidents.

B. Vengeance

Some abolitionists feel that the motive for the death penalty is an un-Christian and unacceptable desire for vengeance. But though vengeance be the motive, it is not the purpose of the death penalty. Doing justice and deterring crime are the purposes, whatever the motive. Purpose (let alone effect) and motive are not the same.

The Lord is often quoted as saying "Vengeance is mine." He did not condemn vengeance. He merely reserved it to Himself—and to the government. For, in the same epistle He is also quoted as saying that the ruler is "the minister of God, a revenger, to execute wrath upon him that doeth evil." The religious notion of hell indicates that the biblical God favored harsh and everlasting punishment for some. However, particularly in a secular society, we cannot wait for the day of judgment to see murderers consigned to hell. Our courts must "execute wrath upon him that doeth evil" here and now.

C. Charity and Justice

Today many religious leaders oppose capital punishment. This is surprising, because there is no biblical warrant for their opposition. The Roman Catholic Church and most Protestant denominations traditionally have supported capital punishment. Why have their moral views changed? When sharing secular power, the churches clearly distinguished between justice, including penalization as deserved, a function of the secular power, and charity, which, according to religious doctrine, we should feel for all those who suffer for whatever reasons. Currently, religious leaders seem to conflate justice and charity, to conclude that the death penalty and, perhaps, all punishment, is wrong because uncharitable. Churches no longer share secular power. Perhaps bystanders are more ready to replace justice with charity than are those responsible for governing.

D. Human Dignity

Let me return to the morality of execution. Many abolitionists believe that capital punishment is "degrading to human dignity" and inconsistent with the "sanctity of life." Justice Brennan, concurring in *Furman*, stressed these phrases repeatedly. He did not explain what he meant.

Why would execution degrade human dignity more than life imprisonment? One may prefer the latter; but it seems at least as degrading as execution. Philosophers, such as Immanuel Kant and G. F. W. Hegel, thought capital punishment indispensable to redeem, or restore, the human dignity of the executed. Perhaps they were wrong. But they argued their case, whereas no one has explained why capital punishment degrades. Apparently those who argue that it does degrade dignity simply define the death penalty as degrading. If so, degradation (or dehumanization) merely is a disguised synonym for their disapproval. Assertion, reassertion, or definition do not constitute evidence or argument, nor do they otherwise justify, or even explain, disapproval of capital punishment.

Writers, such as Albert Camus, have suggested that murderers have a miserable time waiting for execution and anticipating it. I do not doubt that. But punishments are not meant to be pleasant. Other people suffer greatly waiting for the end, in hospitals, under circumstances that, I am afraid, are at least as degrading to their dignity as execution. These sufferers have not deserved their suffering by committing crimes, whereas murderers have. Yet, murderers suffer less on death row, unless their consciences bother them.

E. Lex Talionis

Some writers insist that the suffering the death penalty imposes on murderers exceeds the suffering of their victims. This is hard to determine, but probably true in some cases and not in other cases. However, the comparison is irrelevant. Murderers are punished, as are all offenders, not just for the suffering they caused their victims, but for the harm they do to society by making life insecure, by threatening everyone, and by requiring protective measures. Punishment, ultimately, is a vindication of the moral and legal order of society and not limited by the *Lex Talionis*, meant to limit private retaliation for harms originally regarded as private.

F. Sanctity of Life

We are enjoined by the Declaration of Independence to secure life. How can this best be achieved? The Constitution authorizes us to secure innocent life by taking the life of murderers, so that any one who deliberately wants to take an innocent life will know that he risks forfeiting his own. The framers did not think that taking the life of a murderer is inconsistent with the "sanctity of life" which Justice Brennan champions. He has not indicated why they were wrong.

G. Legalized Murder?

Ever since Cesare Bonesana, Marchese di Beccaria, wrote *Die Delitti e Delle Pene*, abolitionists have contended that executing murderers legitimizes murder by doing to the murderer what he did to his victim. Indeed, capital punishment retributes, or pays back the offender. Occasionally we do punish offenders by doing to them what they did to their victims. We may lock away a kidnapper who wrongfully locked away his victim, and we may kill the murderer who wrongfully killed his victim.

To lawfully do to the offender what he unlawfully did to his victim in no way legitimizes his crime. It legitimizes (some) killing, and not murder. An act does not become a crime because of its physical character, which, indeed, it may share with the legal punishment, but because of its social, or, better, antisocial, character—because it is an unlawful act.

H. Severity

Is the death penalty too severe? It stands in a class by itself. But so does murder. Execution is irreparable. So is murder. In contrast, all other crimes and punishments are, at least partly or potentially, reparable. The death penalty thus is congruous with the moral and material gravity of the crime it punishes.

Still, is it repulsive? Torture, however well deserved, now is repulsive to us. But torture is an artifact. Death is not, since nature has placed us all under sentence of death. Capital punishment, in John Stuart Mill's phrase, only "hastens death"—which is what the murderer did to his victim. I find nothing repulsive in hastening the murderer's death, provided it be done in a nontorturous manner. Had he wished to be secure in his life, he could have avoided murder.

To believe that capital punishment is too severe for any act, one must believe that there can be no act horrible enough to deserve death. I find this belief difficult to understand. I should readily impose the death penalty on a Hitler or a Stalin, or on anyone who does what they did, albeit on a smaller scale.

Conclusion

The death penalty has become a major issue in public debate. This is somewhat puzzling, because quantitatively it is insignificant. Still, capital punishment has separated the voters as a whole from a small, but influential, abolitionist elite. There are, I believe, two reasons that explain the prominence of the issue.

First, I think, there is a genuine ethical issue. Some philosophers believe that the right to life is equally imprescriptible for all, that the murderer has as much right to live as his victim. Others do not push egalitarianism that far. They believe that there is a vital difference, that one's right to live is lost when one intentionally takes an innocent life, that everyone has just the right to one life, his own. If he unlawfully takes that of an other he, *eo ipso*, loses his own right to life.

Second, and perhaps as important, the death penalty has symbolic significance. Those who favor it believe that the major remedy for crime is punishment. Those who do not, in the main, believe that the remedy is anything but punishment. They look at the causes of crime and conflate them with compulsions, or with excuses, and refuse to blame. The majority of the people are less sophisticated, but perhaps they have better judgment. They believe that everyone who can understand the nature and effects of his acts is responsible for them, and should be blamed and punished, if he could know that what he did was wrong. Human beings are human because they can be held responsible, as animals cannot be. In that Kantian sense the death penalty is a symbolic affirmation of the humanity of both victim and murderer.

Endnotes

[1] 356 U.S. 86 (1958) at 99.

[2] *Furman v. Georgia*, 408 U.S. 238, 256 (1972) (Douglas, J., concurring).

[3] Ehrlich, *The Deterrent Effect of Capital Punishment: A Question of Life or Death*, 65 Am. Econ. Rev. 397, 414 (1975).

82. A *Reply to van den Haag*

H. A. BEDAU

Ernest van den Haag divides his defense of the death penalty into three sections: its constitutionality, its preventive effects, and its moral status. It will be convenient to address his criticisms in the order in which he presents them, even though that may make for somewhat tedious reading. . . .

I

Van den Haag argues five different issues on the constitutionality of the death penalty, the first of which rests on the text of the Fifth Amendment in the Bill of Rights (1791). Since "due process of law" is mentioned there in connection with lawful deprivation of "life, limb, or liberty," he concludes that "the Constitution . . . authorizes the death penalty." But this is triply wrong.

First, the text in question does not *authorize* the death penalty; instead, it presents us with a conditional proposition: *If* life is to be taken as a punishment, then it *must* be done with due process of law. In effect, this text presents the government with a choice: Either repeal the death penalty or carry it out according to the requirements of due process. As for any "authorization" of the death penalty, or any other punishment, that depends on the exercise of legislative power within the constraints of the Constitution. As for this mention of the death penalty in the Fifth Amendment, I agree that it shows that the Framers did not consider the possibility that there might be an inconsistency between permitting this mode of punishment under the constraint of due process and any of the other provi-

From *Death Penalty in America: Current Controversies* by Hugo Adam Bedau. © 1997 by Hugo Adam Bedau. Used by permission of Oxford University Press, Inc.

sions of the Bill of Rights. In any case, it is essential to realize that this conditional proposition is consistent with the rejection of the death penalty (in standard logic, the truth of a conditional neither depends upon nor implies accepting the antecedent).

Second, van den Haag passes over the crucial question whether our current procedures for imposing the death penalty really do satisfy the requirements of due process. I take his silence on the point to imply that he has no qualms here. Well, I do. . . . To be sure, due process of law is a complex and contested concept, and reasonable people can disagree over its requirements. Former Supreme Court Justice Harry Blackmun is not the only erstwhile supporter of the death penalty in America who has abandoned hope that "the machinery of death" can be operated according to the requirements of due process of law.

Finally, by parity of reasoning to van den Haag's own argument, if a state legislature were to enact corporal punishments of extreme cruelty, say cutting off the hand of a thief after his third felony conviction, the legislature could count on the reference to deprivation of "limb" in this clause of the Fifth Amendment to enable such a punishment to pass the Supreme Court's scrutiny—so long as the maiming were done with "due process of law." Are we seriously to believe that the Court would endorse such reasoning? I cannot; nothing in the Fifth Amendment precludes the Court from relying on the Eighth Amendment, prohibiting "cruel and unusual punishments," to rule out as unconstitutional any punishments that maim. The same is true of punishments that kill.

Van den Haag next attacks the argument that the Eighth Amendment prohibition against "cruel and unusual punishments" undermines the legitimacy of the death penalty in our day, even if it did not do so when the amendment was passed, because the clause must be interpreted (in the language of the Court's ruling in *Trop v. Dulles* [1958]) according to "evolving standards of decency." He dismisses this judicial language as "paradoxical" if used to interpret the Constitution in order to repeal punishments having statutory authority, since it would make the Constitution as written "superfluous." Van den Haag seems to think *Trop* was nonetheless correctly decided because the punishment ruled out by the Court in that case was "expatriation, a punishment not specifically authorized by the Constitution." But the Eighth Amendment nowhere mentions (and certainly doesn't "authorize") capital punishment, either.

The issue here is twofold: how to interpret the "cruel and unusual punishment" clause of that amendment, and how to apply that interpretation to the death penalty in light of the relevant facts. As the ratification discussions in 1789 show, it was even then anticipated that at some future date this language might plausibly be used to strike down the death penalty. Nothing in either the Fifth or the Eighth Amendments prohibits the Supreme Court from concluding that two hundred years of experience with capital punishment reveals that it is, after all, cruel and unusual, that its administration makes a mockery of due process of law, and that it also violates "the equal protection of the law" (Fourteenth Amendment).

In this regard it is important to notice that van den Haag mentions in passing (though without implying his approval) that the Supreme Court has declared the death penalty for rape (in *Coker v. Georgia* [1977]) and the mandatory death penalty for murder (in *Woodson v. North Carolina* [1976]) to be in violation of the Eighth Amendment. Consistent with his prior argument here, he must reject the legitimacy of these rulings. On his view, any legislature that wants to have the death penalty for rape is constitutionally "authorized" to do so, whether or not it is "disproportionate" to the crime. And the same is true of any other crime—armed robbery, kidnapping, treason, espionage, arson, train robbery, desecration of a grave—each of them punishable by death earlier in this century in one or another American jurisdiction. But by van den Haag's reasoning, since disproportionality is nowhere mentioned in the Eighth Amendment (having been invented by the Supreme Court in *Weems v. United States* [1910] as an appropriate interpretive principle to explain what a "cruel and unusual punishment" is), he must infer that courts have no authority to invoke disproportionality as a ground

for declaring *any* penalties unconstitutional. Thus, he implicitly rejects the Supreme Court's authority to nullify the death penalty for murder by means of an argument that prevents the Court from applying the Eighth Amendment to invalidate *any* penalty, so long as that penalty is carried out by "due process of law" and was tolerated by the Framers.

Van den Haag next addresses the objection that the death penalty as administered is too capricious to be tolerated on constitutional grounds. (As his essay preceded the Court's decision in *McCleskey v. Kemp* by two years, he had no opportunity to mention that this decision supports his own views.) He replies in two steps: First, he endorses the Supreme Court's decision in *Gregg* that the post-*Furman* statutory reforms have eliminated whatever caprice infected the administration of pre-*Furman* death penalties. This judgment simply will not withstand scrutiny. The good-faith hopes of the *Gregg* majority in 1976 (especially evident in the concurring opinion by Justice White) have simply not been borne out in practice in the two decades since then. No serious and informed student of the administration of the death penalty believes these statutes have so far accomplished more than cosmetic reforms, however well-intentioned they may have been when enacted.

The next objection van den Haag raises is that unless we are to believe the administration of the death penalty today is *more* capricious than it was in the previous century, its capriciousness today fails to show any constitutionally relevant defect. This is a bad argument because it ignores the holding in *Furman*, which was based above all on the capricious, arbitrary, and discriminatory administration of the death penalty of that day. Unless there is *less*—indeed, little or no—caprice in the death penalty as administered today, in contrast to what there was when *Furman* was decided, the post-*Furman* statutes ought to be invalidated by the reasoning that prevailed in *Furman*. One way around this, of course, is to argue that *Furman* was wrongly decided in the first place and ought to be overruled—an argument I am sure van den Haag would want to make. The fact that the Supreme Court has so far failed to reverse its ruling in *Gregg*, or to hold the states on a short tether where the death penalty is concerned, tells us more about the ideology and politics of the majority of the Court since 1975 than it does about the constitutionality of the death penalty.

Van den Haag devotes two paragraphs to attacking the claim that racial discrimination in administering the death penalty establishes that penalty's unconstitutionality. (Subsequent to his essay, David Baldus and his two coauthors published *Equal Justice and the Death Penalty: A Legal and Empirical Analysis* [1990], amply establishing just such discrimination.) Van den Haag concedes that there is some racial discrimination in the way this penalty is administered. The importance of this concession is not to be underestimated; few defenders of the death penalty today are willing to concede as much. Van den Haag probably attaches little weight to it because he probably would also concede that the whole criminal justice system is tilted slightly against nonwhites, thus reducing to relative insignificance whatever racial discrimination the death penalty involves. He insists that the remedy is not to abolish the death penalty but to abolish the discrimination (which, he adds, favor murderers of blacks and therefore favors blacks over whites, since most black murder victims are killed by blacks). When this is taken as an abstract proposition, one must agree with van den Haag: Since capital statutes as they are written do not discriminate on racial grounds, they ought not to be repealed just because they are administered with discriminatory results.

But this remedy of nondiscrimination, which van den Haag so easily proposes, simply flies in the face of everything we know about the history of the death penalty in this nation, and especially in the South. Are we seriously to think that in Texas or Alabama or South Carolina (or even outside the South, in California, Illinois, or New York) prosecutors and trial juries will remedy their history of racial discrimination by meting out death penalties regardless of the race of the victim or the offender? No, we are not. Van den Haag's argument is simply beside the point; it is a frivolous appeal to an abstract possibility that two centuries of experience tell us will not be put into practice, not in our lifetimes and not in those of our children or their children. If we really want to improve on the rough justice of our current practices involving the death penalty, the only way to do so is to abolish it and sentence *all* convicted murderers to prison, whatever their race and the race of their victim(s). No doubt inequities will

remain, but their magnitude will have been dramatically reduced.

Van den Haag's final and lengthiest constitutional consideration takes up proportionality review. A year after his essay was published, the Supreme Court ruled in *Pulley v. Harris* (1984) as he would have wished, rejecting the argument to make proportionality review a constitutional requirement in capital cases. However, nowhere in his discussion does he address the equal protection clause of the Fourteenth Amendment and what relevance it may have, although that ought to be his chief, if not his sole, concern here. Instead, he invites us to consider which is worse—giving some murderers their just deserts (a death penalty) even when we do not give it to all murderers, or giving it to none because we cannot give it to all. Van den Haag favors, he says, justice over equality if we cannot have both. Again, taken abstractly, his position here is plausible.

But, also once again, why take the matter so abstractly? We have ample empirical evidence, based on actual research on prosecutorial decision making, the deliberations of capital juries, and the conduct of clemency hearings in capital cases, to believe that the disproportionality in sentencing is *not* the result of a random "lottery" or of mere "chance" (van den Haag's favorite explanatory factors). Rather, it is due to illegitimate factors of race, class, and social policy. This is why the decision to execute a given capital offender is vulnerable to criticism on equal protection grounds.

. . .

II

With constitutional issues disposed of, van den Haag addresses deterrence and the empirical research on which judgments of deterrence are and ought to be made. Oddly, he says nothing explicit about incapacitation, although the special incapacitative effects of the death penalty are usually touted by those of its defenders who attach importance to deterrence. He concludes that the results of all the empirical research are "inconclusive," and so he is inclined to advise partisans on each side of the death penalty debate to distrust reliance on research of this sort. This is a minimalist interpretation of the evidence if ever there was one, since it wrongly encourages the inexperienced student of this subject to think that the empirical pros and cons about the special deterrent effects of the death penalty are at a standoff. Van den Haag and others who support the death penalty on deterrent grounds need to ponder [other research] to see just how completely without foundation is any belief in the deterrent efficacy of the death penalty in the United States during the past half century.

Van den Haag then insists that despite the lack of empirical evidence he still believes the death penalty is a better deterrent. Why? "[B]ecause people fear death more than anything else." Perhaps they would say they do, if they were asked to answer the question, Which do you fear more, a death penalty or life in prison? But armed robbers, gangland hit men, kids in cars hell-bent on drive-by shootings, and other persons really interested in murdering someone are not thinking about that question. They are thinking instead about this question: "What's the best way for me to commit the crime and not get caught?" Van den Haag also argues that the death penalty must be a better deterrent because death row convicts would rather have their sentences commuted to life in prison. This preference tends to show that life imprisonment is believed to be a less *severe* punishment than death. It does not show that death is a better *deterrent*—unless you accept as an axiom that the more severe a punishment is thought to be, the better a deterrent it is. The truth of that belief matters not at all if rational people will be deterred from murder as well by a long prison sentence as by a death sentence.

Van den Haag concedes that many murderers are undeterrable but adds: "Even if only some murders were, or could be, deterred by capital punishment, it would be worthwhile." Many agree with him. But one must ask, What cost are you prepared to pay to gain this elusive extra deterrence? The dollar costs, as Richard Dieter has shown, are mounting rapidly, with no end in sight. Quite apart from these costs are the moral costs, chief of which is the great risk of executing the innocent (I will return to this later).

Before turning to his third category of issues, van den Haag addresses the relative costs of execution versus imprisonment. He argues that imprisonment is the more costly of the two and that, even if it weren't we should pay the extra cost of jus-

tice—which involves putting to death all who are sentenced to death, preferably with more dispatch than we currently do. We all should agree with him about paying what justice costs, but it remains to be shown that executing prisoners *is* what justice requires (an issue to which I will return in the following). And on the empirical question of the relative costs, the best current information and research, summarized by Dieter, suggest van den Haag is simply wrong—just as he is wrong in claiming that it is primarily the postconviction appeals that run up the economic costs of capital punishment.

Throughout his discussion of deterrence, van den Haag fails to address a crucial question: If the death penalty is to be defended on grounds of its superior deterrence (or incapacitation), what stops us from defending even more savage penalties if they prove (or seem likely to prove) to be an even better deterrent than the death penalty as currently used? Later in his essay, he dismisses torture on the subjective ground that it is "repulsive to us." Well, it is not repulsive to torturers, and to them van den Haag evidently has nothing to say except to express his personal disapproval. It's of no use to his argument that everyone agrees the Constitution prohibits such "cruel and unusual punishments" as boiling in oil or crucifixion or burning at the stake. He has to explain, consistent with his endorsement of the importance of extra deterrence, how and why he respects the moral basis of the constitutional prohibition. He fails to do that; his ethical subjectivism prevents him from doing so. Like every other defender of the death penalty on deterrent grounds, van den Haag has nursed an asp to his bosom that will destroy whatever limits he thinks might be morally appropriate on cruel punishments—limits that in any case he can treat as nothing more than collective subjective preferences.

I complete my criticism of van den Haag's view on deterrence by responding to his claim that I and other abolitionists who oppose the death penalty on principle would evidently tolerate the murder of hundreds rather than execute any convicted murderers even if we knew that by doing so we could have prevented those murders by the extra deterrence the death penalty provides. I cannot speak for the others whom van den Haag mentions in this connection. . . . But speaking only for myself, I would point out two things.

First, my unwillingness to execute (or to have the state hire someone to execute) a convicted murderer is not the same as someone else's decision to commit murder. Neither is it in any sense the cause of such a decision. My refusal to authorize killing the guilty is not equivalent to my authorizing the death of the innocent. So my refusal to authorize executions does not make me responsible for murder, even if those executions would have deterred murderers that imprisonment would not.

Second, as is evident from contemporary philosophical discussion, it is extremely difficult to resist the lure of torture, murder, and other dark deeds when it can be argued that without such acts thousands, or millions, of innocents will surely die. Where the death penalty today is concerned, however, any version of this dilemma is so conjectural that worrying about it is as implausible as worrying about sharks on dry land. Van den Haag is right that I oppose the death penalty in principle and without exceptions; he is wrong in implying that I would tolerate with equanimity the deaths of innocents simply to avoid lawful execution of one who is guilty. I favor abolition, not least because I am confident that zero deterrence would be lost.

III

In the final and most important (but briefest and least coherent) part of his argument, van den Haag raises eight scattered issues collected under the heading of the morality of the death penalty. On the first of these, miscarriages of justice, he concedes that in the long run the death penalty "lead[s] to the execution of some innocents." This is another important concession. . . . But these losses are rare and worth it, he argues, because of the offsetting advantages that *only* the death penalty provides— at which point he recycles his belief in the deterrent superiority of the death penalty. As for his analogy (we tolerate high-speed highways despite our knowledge that they increase traffic deaths), all one can say is that there is *no* analogy between a morally defensible practice in which lethal accidents do occur that take statistical lives and a morally dubious practice in which lethal events are designed for particular individuals in the mistaken belief that they deserve it.

Van den Haag turns next to the role of "vengeance." [H]is interest in this concept arises from its role in Judeo-Christian religious morality. . . . I am troubled by van den Haag's endorsement of vengeance as a legitimate "motive" for the death penalty, even if not its real "purpose." Insofar as vengeance is the motive, does he want us to believe that only supporters of the death penalty *can* act from this motive? Or that only they are *entitled* to act from it? Neither is plausible. That to one side, vengeance is too eruptive and violent an emotion to encourage in ourselves and others. It cannot be confined and channeled to tolerate, much less support, due process of law in punishment, and is likely to spill over into private violence. However, as van den Haag rightly notes, subjective "motives" such as vengeance are not what is at issue in evaluating punitive policy; it is the objective "purposes" that govern the discussion. So, asking us to tolerate vengeance as a legitimate motive for the death penalty is really a red herring, and a dangerous one.

Van den Haag rebukes Christian religious leaders who oppose the death penalty, reminding them that "there is no biblical warrant for their opposition." However, even if van den Haag is right about how to read and interpret the Bible, all he has done is put in question the legitimacy of professing Christians opposing the death penalty on narrowly biblical (constructing "biblical" to mean "literally textual") grounds. This does nothing to undermine any nonreligious moral arguments against the death penalty, which Jews and Christians are as entitled to advance as well as anyone else.

Van den Haag next tackles the concept and role of "human dignity" and denies that there is any mileage for abolitionists to be gained by invoking this value. He adds that "no one has explained why capital punishment degrades" human dignity, and he implies that no one can. In an essay published some years after his and designed to explain the idea of the death penalty as a violation of human dignity, I began by using the four principles Justice Brennan introduced in his concurring opinion in *Furman* in order to explain why the death penalty was an affront to human dignity and thus in violation of the Eighth Amendment's prohibition of "cruel and unusual punishments." The essential part of my argument, taken out of the context of a rather long discussion, was this:

Let us reformulate Brennan's four principles in a more uniform manner that emphasizes their connection to human dignity. Taking them in the order in which he mentions them, this is what we get: First, it is an affront to the dignity of a person to be forced to undergo catastrophic harm at the hands of another when, before the harm is imposed, the former is entirely at the mercy of the latter, as is always the case with legal punishment. Second, it offends the dignity of a person who is punished according to the will of a punisher free to pick and choose arbitrarily among offenders so that only a few are punished very severely when all deserve the same severe punishment if any do. Third, it offends the dignity of a person to be subjected to a severe punishment when society shows by its actual conduct in sentencing that it no longer regards this severe punishment as appropriate. Finally, it is an affront to human dignity to impose a very severe punishment on an offender when it is known that a less severe punishment will achieve all the purposes it is appropriate to try to achieve by punishing anyone in any manner whatsoever.

These reformulation link the concept of human dignity explicitly with the concept of "cruel and unusual punishments" via the notion of appropriate limits to the permissible severity of punishments. This is easily seen if we recall several of the constitutive elements of human dignity discussed earlier: Respect for the autonomy of rational creatures forbids its needless curtailment in the course of deserved punishment. Respect for the equal worth of persons forbids inequitable punishments of convicted offenders equally guilty. The fundamental equal rights of persons, including convicted offenders, precludes treating some offenders as if they had ceased to be persons.

Van den Haag turns to the law of retaliation, *lex talionis*, only to reject its authority. This is another important concession because it deprives him of arguing from this general principle of retaliatory punishments to the special case of the death penalty for murder, in which we take "a life for a life." (Of course, his disavowal of *lex talionis* also spares him the embarrassment of trying to cope with the inapplicability and absurdity of this law for a wide range of crimes, just as it frees him to defend the death penalty, should he wish to, for crimes that include no murder.) Instead, he argues that "[p]unishment, ultimately, is a vindication of the moral and legal order of society." No doubt it ought to be, although it behooves those who would defend punishment in these terms to convince us that the current moral and legal order is sufficiently just to warrant our punitive practices. But of course one can grant van den Haag's claim about the nature or ultimate purpose of state punishment without for one moment suggesting that law and moral order can be vindicated *only* or *best* by the use of death penalties or any other unnecessary punishment. This is precisely what I would deny and what van den Haag apparently believes and ought to defend. But he doesn't.

Before turning to the next of van den Haag's moral considerations, we should notice how the fundamental principle of much of his overall argument is badly neglected. He makes it clear in passing that murderers *deserve* to die, and that the principal justification of the death penalty is *justice*. He seems to believe that *desert* tells us *whom* to punish (guilty criminals), *what* they deserve as their punishment (murderers deserve death), and *why* this is what they deserve (justice). Yet his position on these issues is incomplete and unsatisfactory, for at least two reasons. First, he does not defend a mandatory death penalty; in principle that ought to prevent the arbitrariness, which he concedes, of our current discretionary death penalty, just as it ought to increase deterrence and retribution. So why doesn't he support it? Because a mandatory death penalty "risks jury cancellations." Historically, there is evidence to support this worry, but it is a silly reason for him to endorse, unless he believes that the future death penalties likely to be canceled by this route are so many that they vastly exceed in number the future death penalties not meted out under the current discretionary system, with the result that a return to mandatory death penalties would achieve less deterrence and retribution than the current system. Why van den Haag would believe this, when he believes the public overwhelmingly favors the death penalty and when he knows that opponents of the death penalty are routinely excluded from capital trial juries, beats me. And how our current arbitrary and discretionary death penalty system "vindicates the moral and legal order" in a manner of which we can be proud remains a mystery.

Second, what are we to make of his fundamental proposition that *murderers deserve the death penalty?* Is it supposed to be a necessary moral truth that anyone can see to be true simply by understanding the concepts used to express it, an analytic a priori proposition? I hope van den Haag would not take this route to defend this proposition because it will be difficult to prevent turning it into a mere prejudice. To avoid that, this proposition must be somehow established by derivation from more fundamental norms. What are they? Since he has rejected *lex talionis*—the obvious if unsatisfactory answer—and supplied no alternative, we are left to guess. It is interesting to note that in the face of a resurgent approval among philosophers during the past two decades for a retributive justification of punishment, only a few have gone on to endorse a purely or primarily retributive defense of capital punishment.

The next target of his critique is the ideal of "the sanctity of life," which some abolitionists (notably, Justice Brennan) insist the death penalty violates. He does not try to explain this ideal or why one might think it is inconsistent with the death penalty. Instead, he recycles constitutional considerations, purporting to show that the Framers, who accepted this ideal, did so in a manner that did not rule out capital punishment. But none of this really speaks to the moral issues involved. For my part, I would put this ideal to one side in the present discussion because the *sanctity* of life (all life? only human life? only innocent human life?) is not a secular concept but a religious one—unlike the *right* to life, which is a secular concept. For some reason, van den Haag has virtually nothing to say about this idea (but see my penultimate paragraph below). Whatever role the sanctity of life properly plays in a religiously based morality, it really cannot be used as a building block for a secular morality. Nor can it be properly used to evaluate from a secular perspective such controversial issues as suicide, euthanasia, abortion,

war—or the death penalty. Since van den Haag does not discuss the bearing of our right to life on the morality of the death penalty, I will excuse myself from doing so here.

Van den Haag's penultimate barb is directed at those abolitionists who think that executing murderers "legitimizes murder by doing to the murderer what he did to his victim." He rejects this objection because it confuses the legitimate killing of convicted murderers with the illegitimate killing by murderers. This strikes me as completely begging the question. The point of the objection he wishes to refute is that where the legitimacy of killing lies in the eye of the killer, we must be very careful what killings we are prepared to permit.

Consider by contrast for a moment the idea of killing in self-defense. Opponents of the death penalty do not condemn such killings, arguing that killing in self-defense legitimates murder. (Notice, by the way, that van den Haag nowhere claims that when society uses the death penalty, it does so in self-defense. Perhaps he would grant that this is an implausible claim for defenders of the death penalty to advance, because nowhere in Europe today, or in Michigan for a century and a half, to cite but one local example, has social defense required reliance on the death penalty.) The reason abolitionists believe the death penalty legitimates murder in the eyes of some is that the grounds on which the government acts in deciding whom to prosecute for a death sentence, whom to convict of capital murder, whom to sentence to death, whom to refuse clemency, looks suspiciously vindictive, arbitrary, and illegitimate. This invites some to reason as follows: "If the government is permitted to kill for its reasons, then I should be permitted to kill for mine." Van den Haag's argument is not with abolitionists, who do not endorse this reasoning, but with whoever does reason in the manner. Simply declaring that murder is wrong and the death penalty legitimate is hardly sufficient.

Finally, van den Haag turns to the question whether the death penalty is "too severe" and concludes that it is not. Yes, it is "irreparable"—but so is murder. No, it is not "repulsive"—since we all must die someday. And he ends by informing us how readily he would put to death a Hitler, a Stalin, or "anyone who does what they did, albeit on a smaller scale." But whether the death penalty is too severe depends on what one thinks the purpose and rationale of its severity is. Whatever that purpose or rationale, I think it is unnecessary for deterrence or incapacitation, arbitrary and discriminatory in the retribution it inflicts, and therefore an affront to our civilized sensibilities.

As to whether the death penalty is repulsive, I suggest that van den Haag inform himself more vividly about what happens during a typical electrocution—a pretty ugly affair at best . . . and as demonstrated by the repulsive 1990 electrocution of Jesse Tafero in Florida. I would grant . . . that the physical act of execution by lethal injection is not repulsive typically or necessarily—no doubt, a widely shared belief and a significant factor in explaining the popularity of lethal injection with American legislatures during the past twenty years. But this emphasis on the details of particular executions or on techniques for carrying out the death penalty obscures what is arguably repulsive about executions as such: It is not only that the prisoner dies, or dies in agony, or dies with ugly disfigurement, but that the lethal act itself is the result of calculated planning by the impersonal state in which the state's overwhelming power is on display against the helplessness of the prisoner.

When van den Haag reminds us that death is inevitable in the nature of things, he does not make a very persuasive point. Human disappointment, pain, loneliness, bereavement, and other forms of misery and suffering are part of the human condition and virtually inevitable for each of us. Yet is that a good reason for complacency in their face if it is within our power to remedy or mitigate, even if only briefly or slightly, these inevitabilities? Van den Haag does not address this question.

As for Hitler and Stalin, they are often the trump card used by modern defenders of the death penalty who cannot believe that anyone really would oppose *all* executions. The trouble is that appealing to Hitler and Stalin sheds no light on whether to execute all or some or none of the more than three thousand prisoners on American death rows today. For myself, I would be glad to make an exception to my absolute rejection of the death penalty by permitting van den Haag to destroy tyrants such as these if he would give me the lives

of those actually under sentence of death today, whose crimes are pathetically insignificant if measured against genocide, aggressive warfare, and the other crimes against humanity of which these dictators and their henchmen were guilty.

Van den Haag ends his essay by making two points with which abolitionists ought to agree—in part. First, he insists that the national debate over the death penalty is important because it involves "a genuine ethical issue." He is right, but what is this issue as he sees it? It is whether "the right to life" extends to all humans and cannot ever be forfeited. He thinks it can be; I think it cannot. Even if I am right, I suggest that this is not the important ethical issue in the debate. The paramount ethical issue posed by the death penalty is this: Whether or not everyone has an unforfeitable right to life, do *we* do the right thing in authorizing killing some criminals when we know there is an adequate alternative punishment (imprisonment), or do we do the right thing when we refuse to kill any, no matter how guilty they are? The issue, in short, is not the right to life; it is the right to *kill*.

Second, van den Haag insists that we are rightly concerned about the death penalty because it has important "symbolic significance," a significance far beyond its practical import. Again, this is correct. For him, however, this symbolic significance lies in its "affirmation of the humanity of both victim and murderer." Van den Haag here has the support of no less a philosopher than Immanuel Kant, though he does not mention this. I, on the other hand, think the whole idea is bizarre. The very thought that I affirm the humanity of a murderer by treating him more or less as he treated his innocent and undeserving victim would be funny were it not so momentous. For me, the death penalty symbolizes *unlimited impersonal power* over the individual, with dramatically final and irreversible results whenever it is expressed. As long as we choose to hang this moral albatross around our necks, I see no way for us to enjoy, much less help the rest of the world to enjoy, the benefits of a truly human community.

83. McCleskey v. Kemp, Superintendent
Georgia Diagnostic and Classification Center

Justice Powell delivered the opinion of the Court, in which Rehnquist, C. J., and White, O'Connor, and Scalia, J. J., joined.

This case presents the question whether a complex statistical study that indicates a risk that racial considerations enter into capital sentencing determinations proves that petitioner McCleskey's capital sentence is unconstitutional under the Eighth of Fourteenth Amendment.

I

McCleskey, a black man, was convicted of two counts of armed robbery and one count of murder in the Superior Court of Fulton County, Georgia, on October 12, 1978. McCleskey's convictions arose out of the robbery of a furniture store and the killing of a white police officer during the course of the robbery. The evidence at trial indicated that McCleskey and three accomplices planned and carried out the robbery. All four were armed. McCleskey entered the front of the store while the other three entered the rear. McCleskey secured the front of the store by rounding up the customers and forcing them to lie face down on the floor. The other three rounded up the employees in the rear and tied them up with tape. The manager was forced at gunpoint to turn over the store receipts, his watch, and $6. During the course of the robbery, a police officer, answering a silent alarm, entered the store through the front door. As he was walking down the center aisle of the store, two shots were fired. Both struck the officer. One hit him in the face and killed him.

Several weeks later, McCleskey was arrested in connection with an unrelated offense. He confessed that he had participated in the furniture store robbery, but denied that he had shot the police officer. At trial, the State introduced evidence that at least one of the bullets that struck the officer was fired from a .38 caliber Rossi revolver. This description matched the description of the gun that McCleskey had carried during the robbery. The State also introduced the testimony of two witnesses who had heard McCleskey admit to the shooting.

The jury convicted McCleskey of murder. At the penalty hearing, the jury heard arguments as to the appropriate sentence. Under Georgia law, the jury could not consider imposing the death penalty unless it found beyond a reasonable doubt that the murder was accompanied by one of the statutory aggravating circumstances. . . . The jury in this case found two aggravating circumstances to exist beyond a reasonable doubt: the murder was committed during the course of an armed robbery . . . ; and the murder was committed upon a peace officer engaged in the performance of his duties. . . . McCleskey offered no mitigating evidence. The jury recommended that he be sentenced to death on the murder charge and to consecutive life sentences on the armed robbery charges. The court followed the jury's recommendation and sentenced McCleskey to death.

On appeal, the Supreme Court of Georgia affirmed the convictions and the sentences. . . .

McCleskey next filed a petition for a writ of habeas corpus in the Federal District Court for the Northern District of Georgia. His petition raised 18 claims, one of which was that the Georgia capital sentencing process is administered in a racially discriminatory manner in violation of the Eighth and Fourteenth Amendments to the United States Constitution. In support of his claim, McCleskey proffered a statistical study performed by Professors David C. Baldus, Charles Pulaski, and George Woodworth (the Baldus study) that purports to show a disparity in the imposition of the death sentence in Georgia based on the race of the murder victim and, to a lesser extent, the race of the defendant. The Baldus study is actually

481 U.S. 279 (1986)
United States Supreme Court

two sophisticated statistical studies that examine over 2,000 murder cases that occurred in Georgia during the 1970's. The raw numbers collected by Professor Baldus indicate that defendants charged with killing white persons received the death penalty in 11% of the cases, but defendants charged with killing blacks received the death penalty in only 1% of the cases. The raw numbers also indicate a reverse racial disparity according to the race of the defendant: 4% of the black defendants received the death penalty, as opposed to 7% of the white defendants.

Baldus also divided the cases according to the combination of the race of the defendant and the race of the victim. He found that the death penalty was assessed in 22% of the cases involving black defendants and white victims; 8% of the cases involving white defendants and white victims; 1% of the cases involving black defendants and black victims; and 3% of the cases involving white defendants and black victims. Similarly, Baldus found that prosecutors sought the death penalty in 70% of the cases involving black defendants and white victims; 32% of the cases involving white defendants and white victims; 15% of the cases involving black defendants and black victims; and 19% of the cases involving white defendants and black victims.

Baldus subjected his data to an extensive analysis, taking account of 230 variables that could have explained the disparities on nonracial grounds. One of his models concludes that, even after taking account of 39 nonracial variables, defendants charged with killing white victims were 4.3 times as likely to receive a death sentence as defendants charged with killing blacks. According to this model, black defendants were 1.1 times as likely to receive a death sentence as other defendants. Thus, the Baldus study indicates that black defendants, such as McCleskey, who kill white victims have the greatest likelihood of receiving the death penalty.

The District Court . . . denied the petition insofar as it was based upon the Baldus study. . . . The Court of Appeals affirmed the denial. . . .

We . . . now affirm.

II

McCleskey's first claim is that the Georgia capital punishment statute violates the Equal Protection Clause of the Fourteenth Amendment. He argues that race has infected the administration of Georgia' statute in two ways: persons who murder whites are more likely to be sentenced to death than persons who murder blacks, and black murderers are more likely to be sentenced to death than white murderers. As a black defendant who killed a white victim, McCleskey claims that the Baldus study demonstrates that he was discriminated against because of his race and because of the race of his victim. In its broadest form, McCleskey's claim of discrimination extends to every actor in the Georgia capital sentencing process, from the prosecutor who sought the death penalty and the jury that imposed the sentence, to the State itself that enacted the capital punishment statute and allows it to remain in effect despite its allegedly discriminatory application. We agree with the Court of Appeals, and every other court that has considered such a challenge, that this claim must fail.

A

Our analysis begins with the basic principle that a defendant who alleges an equal protection violation has the burden of proving "the existence of purposeful discrimination." . . . Thus, to prevail under the Equal Protection Clause, McCleskey must prove that the decisionmakers in his case acted with discriminatory purpose. He offers no evidence specific to his own case that would support an inference that racial considerations played a part in his sentence. Instead, he relies solely on the Baldus study. McCleskey argues that the Baldus study compels an inference that his sentence rests on purposeful discrimination. McCleskey's claim that these statistics are sufficient proof of discrimination, without regard to the facts of a particular case, would extend to all capital cases in Georgia, at least where the victim was white and the defendant is black.

The Court has accepted statistics as proof of intent to discriminate in certain limited contexts. First, this Court has accepted statistical disparities as proof of an equal protection violation in the selection of the jury venire in a particular district. . . . Second, this Court has accepted statistics in the form of multiple-regression analysis to prove statutory violations under Title VII of the Civil Rights Act of 1964. . . .

But the nature of the capital sentencing decision, and the relationship of the statistics to that decision, are fundamentally different from the corresponding elements in the venire-selection or Title VII cases. Most importantly, each particular decision to impose the death penalty is made by a petit jury selected from a properly constituted venire. Each jury is unique in its composition, and the Constitution requires that its decision rest on consideration of innumerable factors that vary according to the characteristics of the individual defendant and the facts of the particular capital offense. . . . Thus, the application of an inference drawn from the general statistics to a specific decision in a trial and sentencing simply is not comparable to the application of an inference drawn from general statistics to a specific venire-selection or Title VII case. In those cases, the statistics relate to fewer entities, and fewer variables are relevant to the challenged decisions. . . .

Because discretion is essential to the criminal justice process, we would demand exceptionally clear proof before we would infer that the discretion has been abused. The unique nature of the decisions at issue in this case also counsels against adopting such an inference from the disparities indicated by the Baldus study. Accordingly, we hold that the Baldus study is clearly insufficient to support an inference that any of the decisionmakers in McCleskey's case acted with discriminatory purpose.

B

McCleskey also suggests that the Baldus study proves that the State as a whole has acted with a discriminatory purpose. He appears to argue that the State has violated the Equal Protection Clause by adopting the capital punishment statute and allowing it to remain in force despite its allegedly discriminatory application. But "'discriminatory purpose' . . . implies more than intent as volition or intent as awareness of consequences. It implies that the decisionmaker, in this case a state legislature, selected or reaffirmed a particular course of action at least in part 'because of,' not merely 'in spite of,' its adverse effects upon an identifiable group." . . . For this claim to prevail, McCleskey would have to prove that the Georgia Legislature enacted or maintained the death penalty statute because of an an-

ticipated racially discriminatory effect. In *Gregg v. Georgia*, . . . this Court found that the Georgia capital sentencing system could operate in a fair and neutral manner. There was no evidence then, and there is none now, that the Georgia Legislature enacted the capital punishment statute to further a racially discriminatory purpose. . . . Nor has McCleskey demonstrated that the legislature maintains the capital punishment statute because of the racially disproportionate impact suggested by the Baldus study. . . .

Accordingly, we reject McCleskey's equal protection claims. . . .

Justice Brennan, with whom Justice Marshall joins, and with whom Justice Blackmun and Justice Stevens join in all but Part I, dissenting.

III

A

It is important to emphasize at the outset that the Court's observation that McCleskey cannot prove the influence of race on any particular sentencing decision is irrelevant in evaluating his Eighth Amendment claim. Since *Furman v. Georgia*, . . . The Court has been concerned with the risk of the imposition of an arbitrary sentence, rather than the proven fact of one. . . . This emphasis on risk acknowledges the difficulty of divining the jury's motivation in an individual case. In addition, it reflects the fact that concern for arbitrariness focuses on the rationality of the system as a whole, and that a system that features a significant probability that sentencing decisions are influenced by impermissible considerations cannot be regarded as rational. . . . As we said in *Gregg v. Georgia* . . . , "the petitioner looks to the sentencing system as a whole (as the Court did in Furman and we do today)": a constitutional violation is established if a plaintiff demonstrates a "pattern of arbitrary and capricious sentencing." . . .

Defendants challenging their death sentences thus never have had to prove that impermissible considerations have actually infected sentencing decisions. We have required instead that they establish that the system under which they were sentenced posed a significant risk of such an occurrence. Mc-Cleskey's claim does differ, however, in one respect from these earlier cases: it is the first to base a challenge not on speculation about how a system might operate, but on empirical documentation of how it does operate.

The Court assumes the statistical validity of the Baldus study, and acknowledges that McCleskey has demonstrated a risk that racial prejudice plays a role in capital sentencing in Georgia. . . . Nonetheless, it finds the probability of prejudice insufficient to create constitutional concern. . . . Close analysis of the Baldus study, however, in light of both statistical principles and human experience, reveals that the risk that race influenced McCleskey's sentence is intolerable by any imaginable standard.

B

The Baldus study indicates that, after taking into account some 230 nonracial factors that might legitimately influence a sentencer, the jury more likely than not would have spared McCleskey's life had his victim been black. The study distinguishes between those cases in which (1) the jury exercises virtually no discretion because the strength or weakness of aggravating factors usually suggests that only one outcome is appropriate; and (2) cases reflecting an "intermediate" level of aggravation, in which the jury has considerable discretion in choosing a sentence. McCleskey's case falls into the intermediate range. In such cases, death is imposed in 34% of white-victim crimes and 14% of black-victim crimes, a difference of 139% in the rate of imposition of the death penalty. . . . In other words, just under 59%—almost 6 in 10—defendants comparable to McCleskey would not have received the death penalty if their victims had been black. . . .

Of the more than 200 variables potentially relevant to a sentencing decision, race of the victim is a powerful explanation for variation in death sentence rates—as powerful as nonracial aggravating factors such as a prior murder conviction or acting as the principal planner of the homicide. . . .

C

Evaluation of McCleskey's evidence cannot rest solely on the numbers themselves. We must also ask whether the conclusion suggested by those numbers is consonant with our understanding of history and human experience. Georgia's legacy of a race-conscious criminal justice system, as well as this Court's own recognition of the persistent danger that racial attitudes may affect criminal proceedings, indicates that McCleskey's claim is not a fanciful product of mere statistical artifice. . . .

IV

The Court cites four reasons for shrinking from the implications of McCleskey's evidence: the desirability of discretion for actors in the criminal justice system, the existence of statutory safeguards against abuse of that discretion, the potential consequences for broader challenges to criminal sentencing, and an understanding of the contours of the judicial role. While these concerns underscore the need for sober deliberation, they do not justify rejecting evidence as convincing as McCleskey has presented.

The Court maintains that petitioner's claim "is antithetical to the fundamental role of discretion in our criminal justice system." . . . It states that "where the discretion that is fundamental to our criminal process is involved, we decline to assume that what is unexplained is invidious." . . . Reliance on race in imposing capital punishment, however, is antithetical to the very rationale for granting sentencing discretion. Discretion is a means, not an end. It is bestowed in order to permit the sentencer to "trea[t] each defendant in a capital case with that degree of respect due the uniqueness of the individual." . . . Considering the race of a defendant or victim in deciding if the death penalty should be imposed is completely at odds with this concern that an individual be evaluated as a unique human being. . . .

The Court also declines to find McCleskey's evidence sufficient in view of "the safeguards designed to minimize racial bias in the [capital sentencing] process." . . . [T]he Court cannot rely on the statutory safeguards in discounting Mc-Cleskey's evidence, for it is the very effectiveness of those safeguards that such evidence calls into question. While we may hope that a model of procedural fairness will curb the influence of race on sentencing, "we cannot simply assume that the model works as intended; we must critique its performance in terms of its results." . . .

The Court next states that its unwillingness to regard petitioner's evidence as sufficient is based in part on the fear that recognition of McCleskey's claim would open the door to widespread challenges to all aspects of criminal sentencing. . . . Taken on its face, such a statement seems to suggest a fear of too much justice. . . . In fairness, the Court's fear that McCleskey's claim is an invitation to descend a slippery slope also rests on the realization that any humanly imposed system of penalties will exhibit some imperfection. Yet to reject McCleskey's powerful evidence on this basis is to ignore both the qualitatively different character of the death penalty and the particular repugnance of racial discrimination, considerations which may properly be taken into account in determining whether various punishments are "cruel and unusual." Furthermore, it fails to take account of the unprecedented refinement and strength of the Baldus study. . . .

Finally, the Court justifies its rejection of McCleskey's claim by cautioning against usurpation of the legislatures' role in devising and monitoring criminal punishment. The Court is, of course, correct to emphasize the gravity of constitutional intervention and the importance that it be sparingly employed. The fact that "capital punishment is now the law in more than two thirds of our States,". . . however, does not diminish the fact that capital punishment is the most awesome act that a State can perform. The judiciary's role in this society counts for little if the use of governmental power to extinguish life does not elicit close scrutiny. . . . Those whom we would banish from society or from the human community itself often speak in too faint a voice to be heard above society's demand for punishment. It is the particular role of courts to hear these voices, for the Constitution declares that the majoritarian chorus may not alone dictate the conditions of social life. The Court thus fulfills, rather than disrupts, the scheme of separation of powers by closely scrutinizing the imposition of the death penalty, for no decision of a society is more deserving of "sober second thought." . . .

84. *Homicide, Race and Capital Punishment*

Randall Kennedy

No issues concerning race and criminal law are more sobering than those raised by allegations that racial selectivity affects the administration of capital punishment. First, sentencing a person to death as punishment for crime is a unique flexing of state power that inevitably reflects the society's deepest values, emotions, and neuroses. Second, the legal system has shown itself to be largely incapable of acknowledging the influence of racial sentiment in the meting out of punishment even in circumstances in which the presence of such bias is obvi-

ous. In no other area of criminal law have judges engaged in more obfuscation, delusion, evasion, and deception. Third, addressing racial discrimination in capital sentencing poses a daunting task for those seeking to craft appropriate remedies.

If a jurisdiction tends to punish more harshly murderers of whites than murderers of blacks, is the appropriate response to abolish capital punishment, to more narrowly limit the circumstances in which capital punishment is imposed, or to execute more people who murder blacks? Even if such a tendency exists, should it be the basis for granting relief to a convicted murderer who fails to show that racial discrimination affected the punishment meted out in his particular case? Is such a tendency a remediable wrong or, instead, an inevitable social trait whereby people unavoidably identify more with the victimization of "their own" as opposed to the victimization of "others"? If this tendency is a wrong, is remedying it within the capacity of courts or is remedying this wrong best left to the legislative and executive branches of government?

. . .

The Supreme Court decided *Coker* at a critical moment in the history of capital punishment. In 1972, in *Furman v. Georgia*, a closely divided (5 to 4) Court invalidated most existing state laws authorizing the death sentence on the grounds that they violated the Eighth Amendment's prohibition against cruel and unusual punishments. All nine justices wrote opinions in *Furman*. . . . Amid the cacophony, however, a main chord is discernible—that the principal failing of then-existing capital sentencing regimes was the absence of a meaningful basis for distinguishing the few cases in which [capital punishment] is imposed from the many cases in which it is not. "These death sentences," Justice Potter Steward complained, were "cruel and unusual in the same way that being struck by lightning is cruel and unusual."

Furman suggested to some observers that the United States might join the trend of other advanced, Western, industrial democracies toward disavowal of capital punishment. Many state legislatures responded to *Furman*, however, by enacting new death penalty statutes which they believed might overcome the Court's objections. In 1976, in yet another case from Georgia, *Gregg v. Georgia*, the Supreme Court affirmed the constitutionality of at least some of these new "improved" capital punishment laws. The Court validated capital punishment as long as it was implemented by procedures that, in its view, "suitably directed and limited" the discretion of sentencers to preclude arbitrary or capricious punishment. The most salient and significant feature of the approved death penalty statutes is the bifurcaton of trials into a phase directed solely to determining whether the defendant is guilty and then a phase directed solely to determining whether he should be sentenced to death.

At the sentencing phase, the defendant is given wide latitude to argue to a judge or jury that his life should be spared. The state, on the other hand, must persuade the judge or jury that the crime meets certain statutorily defined criteria that distinguish it from other crimes, and therefore justifies a death sentence.

In the aftermath of *Gregg*, and particularly as states began aggressively to seek the execution of condemned prisoners, civil rights activists redoubled their efforts. A central feature of their attack, in courts of public opinion as well as courts of law, was and remains their allegation that death sentences tend to be applied in a racially discriminatory fashion. The Court declined to adjudicate the issue on several occasions but finally agreed to consider it in 1987 in yet a third landmark case from Georgia, *McCleskey v. Kemp*.

On May 13, 1978, Warren McCleskey, a black man, helped to rob the Dixie Furniture Store in Atlanta, Georgia. A white police officer, Frank Schlatt, attempted to foil the robbery but was killed by a shot to the head. Sometime later, McCleskey was arrested in connection with another armed robbery. Under questioning, he admitted to participating in the furniture store heist but denied shooting Officer Schlatt. After further investigation, it emerged that McCleskey had stolen a revolver capable of shooting the type of bullet that killed Officer Schlatt. McCleskey also reportedly admitted shooting Schlatt to both a codefendant and a neighboring inmate in jail, both of whom later testified against him.

A jury of eleven whites and one black sentenced McCleskey to life imprisonment for the robbery and death for the murder. His subsequent appeals followed the normal, dreary route of postconviction proceedings in capital cases. An aspect of his appeal, however, contained a challenge to the entire system of capital punishment in Georgia and beyond. Supported by the most comprehensive statistical analysis ever done on the racial demographics of sentencing in a single state, McCleskey's attorneys argued that their client's sentence should be invalidated because there was a constitutionally impermissible risk that both his race and that of his victim had played a significant role in the decision to sentence him to death.

McCleskey's claim was largely predicated on a study organized and overseen by David C. Baldus, an expert in the application of statistics to legal problems. The Baldus study was derived from records involving the disposition of more than two thousand murder cases between 1973 and 1979. The Georgia Department of Pardons and Paroles and other state agencies provided Baldus with police reports, parole board records, prison files, and other items that evidenced the process by which state authorities handled criminal homicides.

Three findings of the Baldus study are especially pertinent. First, viewing the evidence on a statewide basis, Baldus found "neither strong nor consistent" evidence of discrimination directed against black defendants because of their race. That did not prevent McCleskey's attorneys from asserting that the race of the defendant—especially when the defendant is black and victim white—influences Georgia's capital sentencing process. In their argument to the Supreme Court, however, McCleskey's attorneys clearly subordinated the claim of race-of-the defendant discrimination to the claim of race-of-the-victim discrimination.

Second, Baldus found that among the variables that might plausibly influence capital sentencing— age, level of education, criminal record, military record, method of killing, motive for killing, relationship of defendant to victim, strength of evidence, and so forth—the race of the victim emerged as the most consistent and powerful factor. Initially, simple correlations suggested the importance of this variable. Without attempting to control for the possible effects of competing variables, Baldus found that perpetrators in white-victim cases were eleven times more likely to be condemned to death than perpetrators in black-victim cases.

Professor Baldus and his associates subjected this striking correlation to extensive statistical analysis to test whether the seemingly racial nature of this disparity was explainable in terms of hidden factors confounded with race. He eventually took into account some 230 nonracial variables that might have influenced the pattern of sentencing. He concluded that even after accounting for every nonracial variable that might have mattered substantially, the race of the victim continued to have a statistically significant correlation with the imposition of capital sentences. Applying a statistical model that included the thirty-nine nonracial variables believed most likely to play a role in capital

punishment in Georgia, the Baldus study concluded that the odds of being condemned to death were 4.3 times greater for defendants who killed whites than for defendants who killed blacks, a variable nearly as influential as a prior conviction for armed robbery, rape, or even murder.

Third, Baldus concluded that racial disparities in capital sentencing are most dramatic in that category containing neither the most aggravated nor the least aggravated homicides. Racial disparities are greatest, he argued, in the middle range of aggravated homicides. In the most aggravated cases, decisionmakers typically impose the death sentence regardless of racial variables, and in the least aggravated cases decisionmakers typically spare the defendant regardless of racial variables. In the middle range of aggravation, however, where a decision could go either way, the influence of racial variables emerges more powerfully. This hypothesis is particularly relevant to *McCleskey* because, in Baldus's view, McCleskey's crime was situated in the middle range of aggravated homicide.

After an evidentiary hearing, U.S. District Judge J. Owen Forrester rejected McCleskey's race discrimination claim primarily on the ground that the Baldus study did not represent "good statistical methodology." He objected to what he viewed as significant omissions, errors, and inconsistencies in Baldus's data base and inadequacies in the design of Baldus's statistical models. Judge Forrester's findings were subsequently eclipsed because the court of appeals and the Supreme Court resolved the case without reviewing them; the appellate courts assumed arguendo that the Baldus study was valid. Judge Forrester's findings, however, continue to be relevant insofar as much of the criticism of *McCleskey* and support for legislative responses to it is premised on a belief in the validity of the Baldus study.

. . .

The factual core of the Baldus study withstands even a skeptical analysis, however. To some extent I am moved to this conclusion by the study's evident carefulness and its authors' insistence on making their data, premises, and calculations available and transparent to the public. I am also influenced by the sworn testimony of respected experts in Baldus's field, notwithstanding the risk of ideological taint identified above. The Baldus study, moreover, is consistent with findings published by a large body of prior research. Even commentators who generally deride allegations of racial discrimination in the administration of criminal law concede that in the context of capital punishment the race of the victim consistently influences sentencing decisions.

. . .

The Court of Appeals for the Eleventh Circuit assumed the validity of the Baldus study but nevertheless affirmed the district court's race discrimination holding on the grounds that the statistical disparities and supplemental evidence failed to prove a constitutional violation.

Justice Lewis Powell's opinion for a bare majority (5 to 4) of the Supreme Court largely followed the Eleventh Circuit's analysis. The Supreme Court, too, assumed, arguendo, the validity of the Baldus study. Similarly, the Court insisted that the constitutionality of McCleskey's sentence must be determined by asking whether officials in *his* case purposefully discriminated on the basis of race. The Court concluded that no such inference could be drawn from the Baldus statistics. Justice Powell noted that in some contexts a "stark" pattern of statistical disparities may create a prima facie case which shifts onto the state the burden of rebutting an allegation of racial discrimination. He observed, however, that in the context of capital sentencing, "decisions at the heart of the State's criminal justice system," the Court would demand "exceptionally clear proof" before inferring that a sentencing authority had abused its discretion. In the Court's view, the racial correlations revealed by the Baldus study did not meet that standard. Powell declared that "because of the risk that the factor of race may enter the criminal justice process, [the Court has] engaged in 'unceasing efforts' to eradicate racial prejudice from our criminal justice system." In this instance, though, no clear showing had been made that racial prejudice animated the death sentence imposed upon McCleskey. Nor, according to Powell, did the Baldus statistics even show that racial prejudices played a significant role in other cases in Georgia. "At most," Powell averred, "the Baldus study indicates a discrepancy that appears to correlate with race."

Justice Powell noted several reasons of policy that pushed the Court to rule as it did. One was the need to give ample latitude for sentencers to use their discretion in making the unique decision as to whether to end the life of a human being as punishment for a crime. Another concern was that accepting McCleskey's challenge would open a Pandora's box of litigation. "McCleskey's claim, taken to its logical conclusion," Powell remarked with alarm, "throws into serious question the principles that underlie our entire criminal justice system," because, if accepted, the Court "could soon be faced with similar claims as to other types of penalty" from members of other groups alleging bias. Finally, Powell invoked considerations of judicial competence and judicial restraint as reasons for avoiding intervention. "McCleskey's arguments," he declared, "are best presented to legislative bodies. . . . It is the legislatures, the elected representatives of the people, that are constituted to respond to the will and consequently the moral values of the people."

With the exception of Thurgood Marshall, each of the dissenting justices (William J. Brennan, Harry A. Blackmun, and John Paul Stevens) wrote opinions explaining their disagreement with the Court. Maintaining that "we cannot pretend that in three decades we have completely escaped the trap of a historical legacy spanning centuries," Justice Brennan declared that "Warren McCleskey's evidence confronts us with the subtle and persistent influence of the past." Crediting the Baldus study "in light of both statistical principles and human experience," Brennan concluded that "the risk that race influenced McCleskey's sentence is intolerable by any imaginable standard." Responding to the Court's concern that accepting McCleskey's claim would open the door to challenges attacking all aspects of criminal sentencing, Brennan remarked that it displayed "a fear of too much justice. . . . The prospect that there may be more widespread abuse than McCleskey documents may be dismaying, but it does not justify complete abdication of [the] judicial role."

In his dissent, Justice Blackmun wrote that he was "disappointed with the Court's action not only because of its denial of constitutional guarantees to petitioner McCleskey individually, but also because of its departure from . . . well-developed constitutional jurisprudence." Blackmun concluded that "the Court . . . sanctions the execution of a man despite his presentation of evidence that establishes a constitutionally intolerable level of racially based discrimination leading to the imposition of his death sentence." . . .

. . .

A sign of the difficulties posed by *McCleskey* is that none of the justices' opinions is altogether satisfactory. The worst of the lot is also the one backed by the most power: Justice Powell's opinion for the Court. Powell strives to convey the impression that the conclusion he and his four associates reached is the only sensible alternative. He therefore gives the false impression that the case is easy. He responds to the parties' briefs, which one expects to be one-sided, with yet another tendentious brief, although his is styled an "opinion" and thus part of the constitutional law of the United States.

Two features of Powell's opinion are especially troubling. One is his minimization of the facts behind McCleskey's claim. Confronted by statistics indicating that people who kill whites in Georgia are four times more likely to be sentenced to death than people who kill blacks, Powell blandly remarked that "at most [this] indicates a discrepancy that appears to correlate with race"—a statement as vacuous as one declaring, say, that "at most" studies on lung cancer indicate a discrepancy that appears to correlate with smoking. Another example of the resolute evasiveness that emerges time and again in Powell's opinion is his statement that the Court should "decline to assume that what is unexplained is invidious." The petitioner, of course, was not asking the Court to make any such assumption. Rather, McCleskey's attorneys offered into evidence a comprehensive study showing that certain patterns in capital sentencing cannot plausibly be explained by any variable other than race. . . .

The second outstanding feature of Powell's opinion is his resolute unwillingness to recognize the uniqueness of two distinctions that the Court had previously periodically acknowledged. One was that *McCleskey* involved a peculiarly irrevocable punishment; as various justices have noted, "death is different." The other is that the case involved an allegation that capital punishment in Georgia was systematically meted out according to an especially toxic social demarcation, the race line. Powell refused to recognize these two distinctions as limiting boundaries, probably because doing so

would undercut his demagogic assertion that accepting McCleskey's claim would necessarily open a Pandora's box from which limitless disruption would ensue. Fretting that an acceptance of Mc-Cleskey's racial claim would invite members of other groups—"even" women—to launch equal protection challenges, Powell and the Court majority resolutely shut the door to any statistics-driven, class-based challenge to the administration of punishment. To justify this action in the context of a case involving blacks, the paradigmatic "out-group" in American political culture, Powell argued that no "logical" reason exists for distinguishing racial or gender bias from any other sort of bias—a bias, for instance, against facial unattractiveness. The life of the law, however, includes not only logic but also experience, and experience teaches that in the United States, racial sentiment displays an intensity and persistence that is distinguishable from all other biases. There exists, moreover, a textual warrant in the Constitution for distinguishing racial and, to a lesser extent, gender bias from other sorts of preference and prejudice.

A similar slamming of the door greeted the oft-voiced claim that allegations of unfairness with respect to death penalties are entitled to special judicial solicitude. As Blackmun complained in dissent, Powell's opinion for the Court gave "new meaning" to the notion that death is different by applying *lesser* scrutiny to the decisionmaking process that leads to death sentences than to decisions affecting employment or the selection of juries.

Powell's *McCleskey* opinion was haunted by anxiety over the consequences of acknowledging candidly the large influence of racial sentiment in the administration of capital punishment in Georgia. Powell did not want to concede facts that might prompt the Court to question the racial fairness of capital sentencing, trigger additional *McCleskey*-like challenges, and perhaps even lead to judicially directed reforms of sentencing in general. Nor did he want to concede facts that indicate that the Court was knowingly willing to countenance a regime of capital punishment in which race significantly influenced decisions as to who would be spared and who would be killed. So Powell and his associates acted as if the Baldus study uncovered a minor discrepancy as opposed to an alarming anomaly. It would have been better if the Court openly declared that, for reasons of policy, it declined to grant relief to McCleskey notwithstanding the disturbing facts revealed by the Baldus study. Doing so would have performed the tremendous benefit of educating the public about the real world of capital sentencing and the real world of Supreme Court decisionmaking.

The dissenters rebuked the *McCleskey* Court for what they saw as its betrayal of established traditions. Justice Blackmun maintained, for instance, that he was "disappointed with the Court's action . . . because of its departure from . . . well-developed constitutional jurisprudence." There is much in the claim of disappointment, however, that smells of rank sentimentality. True, the Court could have decided differently; had there been the will, available precedent could have lit the way. In the context of equal protection challenges to jury commissioners authorized to select jury pools on the basis of vague standards, for example, the Supreme Court has shown a marked skepticism toward unexplained racial disparities. It has shifted the burden of explanation to the state when presented with evidence indicating significant discrepancies between the percentage of the population of eligible racial minorities in a given jurisdiction and the percentage of racial minorities selected for possible jury service. The Court could have deployed this same methodology in *McCleskey*—if it had possessed the will to do so. On the other hand, Powell's opinion for the Court was well within the ambit of expectations reasonably derived from prior rulings. *McCleskey* did not begin the Supreme Court's deregulation of the death penalty; it reflected and accelerated a process that had already begun and developed momentum. Although some justices had intimated that the Court should subject to special rigor death sentences challenged on grounds of racial fairness, a stronger tradition, exemplified by the Martinsville Seven case, favored the ethos that prevailed.

If *McCleskey* disappoints, it should do so on some basis other than tradition, for the majority cannot rightly be accused of promulgating a startling ruling. To the contrary, *McCleskey* was all too predictable. Its critics must face the fact that, as far as reported cases disclose, defendants rarely, verging on never, succeed in challenging punishments using arguments of the sort voiced by Warren McCleskey's attorneys.

The central concern that dictated the Court's resolution of *McCleskey* was anxiety about what judges might have to face if it acknowledged that the influence of racial sentiment in sentencing represents a distortion and unfairness of constitutional dimension. Pretend for a moment, however, that the Supreme Court reversed the district court's rejection of the Baldus study and, based on the study's conclusions, declared a violation of the Equal Protection Clause. Assuming that the Court could have reached this point, what should it have done next?

One alternative would have been to abolish capital punishment entirely on the grounds that racial selectivity is an inextricable part of the administration of capital punishment in the United States and that it would be better to have no death penalty than one unavoidably influenced consistently by racial sentiment.

A more reserved variant would have involved vacating all death sentences in Georgia. Such a response would have fallen short of the ultimate aim of abolitionists since it would apply only to a single state. However, this response would surely have given a tremendous boost to the abolitionist movement by placing a large question mark over the legitimacy of any death penalty system generating unexplained racial disparities of the sort at issue in *McCleskey*. Since studies suggest that *McCleskey*-like statistics exist in several death penalty states, especially those with the largest death rows, the implementation of even a limited abolitionist remedy would have been significant indeed.

For those opposed to capital punishment anyway, abolishing it to vindicate the norms of equal protection is a costless enterprise. Abolition, however, is a costly prospect to the extent that one views the death penalty—as most Americans do—as a useful and highly valued public good. Polls indicate that, at least since the 1980s, upwards of 70 percent of Americans indicate that they favor capital punishment. Moreover, since 1988, the number of crimes punishable by death has increased dramatically, mainly as a result of federal legislation. From the perspective of a proponent of capital punishment, abolition as a remedy for race-of-the-victim discrimination is equivalent to reducing to darkness a town in which streetlights have been provided on a racially unequal basis. From this perspective, it would make more sense to remedy the inequality by installing lights in the parts of town which have been wrongly deprived of illumination. Carrying on the analogy, it would be better to remedy the problem outlined by the Baldus statistics by leveling up—increasing the number of people executed for murdering blacks—rather than leveling down—abolishing capital punishment altogether.

Before turning to the level-up solution, however, notice should be paid to still other possibilities. One is the idea, embraced by Justices Stevens and Blackmun, of limiting the class of persons eligible for execution to those who commit only the most aggravated homicides. The problem with this proposal is that it seems merely to replicate what the Court sought to accomplish by permitting the revival of capital punishment pursuant to procedures that, theoretically, limited and informed sentencers so that similarly situated criminals would be punished according to some tolerably coherent pattern. One point upon which both death penalty deregulators and death penalty abolitionists agree is that the task of selecting in some objective way those persons who should be condemned to die . . . remains beyond the capacities of the criminal justice system. The facts of *McCleskey* itself highlight this problem with the Stevens and Blackmun proposal. According to Professor Baldus, McCleskey's murder was located in the middle range of aggravated murders. In his view, the crime was not among the most heinous murders for which people have been condemned to death in Georgia. It is difficult, however, to see why this is so. McCleskey's crime involved, after all, the murder of a policeman during a robbery by a recidivist who is said to have boasted of the killing. Surely there are many, including potential judges and jurors, who would rank this crime in the same category of heinousness as some of the murders which Professor Baldus does place in the "worst case" category.

Another alternative would be for the Court to retract its rejection of mandatory death sentences. As we have seen, in 1972 the Court struck down all existing state death penalty statutes on the grounds that, by delegating unguided discretionary power to sentencing authorities, they provided insufficient protection against arbitrariness or discrimination. Ten states responded by enacting statutes prescribing capital punishment as the mandatory

sentence for the commission of certain crimes. In 1976, the Court invalidated these laws on the grounds that they were inconsistent with fundamental trends in social mores, encouraged juries to shape their verdicts to avoid the harshness of mandatory sentences, and that the procedures established by mandatory sentencing failed to consider each defendant in a sufficiently individualized manner. The justices imposed a constitutional requirement that sentences in capital trial be provided with discretion to extend mercy. Yet it is precisely this power to grant leniency that opens the door to the *McCleskey* problem. . . .

It is by no means clear, moreover, that mandatory capital sentencing would affect racial disparities. First, even if mandatory capital sentencing were allowed, there would remain the possibility that juries would continue to extend relatively more leniency to the killers of blacks, declining more frequently to convict such killers of crimes that trigger automatic death sentences. Second, and probably more important, the institutional actors who have the most to do with the prevalence and incidence of capital sentences are prosecutors, not jurors. Prosecutors decide whether and for what to charge a defendant. Prosecutors further decide whether to charge a person with a capital crime or to accept a plea bargain for a noncapital offense. That prosecutors can be strongly influenced by racial bias is clear. Yet mandatory sentencing schemes do little to address the problem of race-dependent leniency on the part of prosecutors. Although mandatory sentencing provisions would limit, to some extent, the discretion of jurors or judges in responding to choices framed by prosecutors, such laws would do nothing to constrain the prior exercise of prosecutorial discretion. . . .

The level-up solution to the *McCleskey* problem would entail purposefully securing more death sentences against murderers of blacks. One way to pursue this aim would be to impose a choice upon jurisdictions with *McCleskey*-like sentencing patterns: Either respond as vigorously to the murders of blacks by condemning perpetrators of such crimes to death (as is done to murderers of whites), or relinquish the power to put anyone to death.

One problem with using race-conscious measures to reform the administration of capital punishment is that to many observers doing so will seem bizarre at first blush. That reaction, however, is likely to be based, at least in part, upon an exaggerated perception of the extent to which notions of individual dessert currently infuse sentencing practices. Sentencing is typically keyed not only to the perceived moral dessert of individual defendants but also to utilitarian calculations regarding society's needs. Punishment is used by those pronouncing sentence upon convicted defendants to instruct an onlooking society.

Another problem with the level-up alternative is that even those who favor, or at least tolerate, race-conscious remedies in some contexts reach a point where they find that such remedies are simply too severe to impose upon individuals who themselves played no direct part in inflicting the initial injury. The Supreme Court, for instance, has drawn a bright line of prohibition against affirmative action in the context of employment layoffs. Affirmative action for racial minorities that decreases the chances that white applicants will be *hired* is sometimes allowable, because the burden to be borne "is diffused to a considerable extent among society generally." Affirmative action that results in the *layoff* of white workers, however, is deemed a burden that is "too intrusive" to accept. Transposed to the death penalty pursuant to a race-conscious plan to equalize the provision of death penalty services is simply too harsh a social tax to impose even upon convicted murderers who are, because of their own conduct, "eligible" for execution.

This argument, however, rests heavily upon the "death is different" distinction. It loses considerable force to the extent that one sees the death penalty as part of a continuum of punishments rather than a unique phenomenon occupying a wholly different moral plane. For those who eschew the "death is different" idea, it is not self-evident why, if race can and should be taken into account in redressing racial injustice in employment, housing, voting, and education, race cannot also be taken into account in reforming capital sentencing. They might well recognize the real danger of creating incentives to sentence certain defendants to death primarily to create "good" statistics. They might conclude, however, that this is a danger worth risking in order to encourage officials to take more seriously the security and suffering of black communities and in order to symbolize the affirma-

tive constitutional obligation to insure some rough measure of substantive racial equality in every sphere of American life—including the provision of law enforcement resources.

. . .

Study Questions

1. The Court in *Gregg* argued that a punishment is cruel and unusual if it is "excessive." What are the two ways in which a punishment can be excessive, according to the Court?

2. According to Justice Brennan, why is the death penalty uniquely degrading to human dignity?

3. In a famous passage in his *Metaphysics of Morals,* Kant gave the following argument to demonstrate the necessity of death as a punishment for murder:

   If . . . he has committed a murder, he must die. In this case, there is no substitute that will satisfy the requirements of legal justice. There is no sameness of kind between death and remaining alive even under the most miserable conditions, and consequently there is also no equality between the crime and the retribution unless the criminal is put to death. . . . Even if a civil society were to dissolve itself by common agreement of all its members (for example, if the people inhabiting an island decided to separate and disperse themselves around the world), the last murderer remaining in prison must first be executed, so that everyone will duly receive what his actions are worth. (John Ladd, trans., *The Metaphysical Elements of Justice* [Indianapolis, Ind.: Bobbs-Merrill, 1965], p. 102)

   In what respects is this argument convincing? In what respects not?

4. Which crimes should be punished with death, according to van den Haag? Why those and not others?

5. How does van den Haag respond to the argument that the death penalty is administered in

a way that is arbitrary? In a way that is discriminatory? Are his responses adequate in your view?

6. Does van den Haag's case for the death penalty place greater weight on utilitarian or on retributive reasons?

7. What criticisms does Bedau raise of van den Haag's claim that murderers deserve the death penalty? Does Bedau dismiss this claim too quickly? Why or why not?

8. Bedau claims that he favors abolition of capital punishment, "not the least because I am confident that zero deterrence would be lost." Does Bedau adequately defend this claim, in your judgment?

9. According to Bedau, "nothing [in the Constitution] prohibits the Supreme Court from concluding that two hundred years of experience with capital punishment reveals that it is, after all, cruel and unusual punishment. . . ." Assume that the majority of Americans consistently votes for and supports the death penalty. Would a moral consensus on the permissibility of capital punishment undermine Bedau's claim about its constitutionality?

10. Can the Court's language concerning "evolving standards of decency" be interpreted in a way that does not invoke a societal consensus? In *Thompson v. Oklahoma* (487 U.S. 815 [1988]) the Court held that there was a clear social consensus that executing a person under the age of sixteen violates evolving standards of decency. (Thompson had been sentenced to death for a murder he committed when he was fifteen.) Do you agree? What if there is no clear consensus on an age limit? Does that mean that executing a nine-year-old would not violate the Constitution?

11. Should the death penalty, if it is to be used at all, ever be imposed for crimes other than murder? If so, what crimes and why?

12. Do you agree that statistical evidence of racial disparities in the imposition of capital punishment in a given jurisdiction is sufficient to prove racial discrimination in a death sentence handed down in a particular case?

13. What problems does Kennedy see with what he calls the "level-up" solution to the recognition of discriminatory imposition of the death penalty?

14. What specific criticisms does Kennedy lodge against the majority opinion in the *McCleskey* case? Do you agree?

15. Horace Kelly was sentenced to death in a California court for the 1984 murder of two women and an eleven-year-old boy. Kelly's scheduled execution in April 1998 was stayed by a federal judge, pending a review of arguments by Kelly's lawyers that he had become insane while on death row. Under current doctrine, a criminal cannot be subjected to capital punishment if he or she is insane at the time of execution. When asked whether he felt guilty or bad, Kelly is reported to have replied: "the word guilty goes to litification examination. You also can defend a person. Guilt runs three different words and magnatize self." Court-appointed psychiatrists described Kelly's thinking as "illogical and bizarre," and his speech as an incomprehensible "word salad." Kelly's lawyers asserted that he was unable to understand the punishment he was slated to suffer or why he was to suffer it. (See *Los Angeles Times*, 10 April, 1998, p. A1.) In your view, should someone in Kelly's mental condition be executed? Why should the inability of a death-row inmate to understand why he is being executed matter? Is the only explanation for this requirement a retributive one? If this requirement is appropriate, why shouldn't it be required that the condemned individual not only understand why he is being executed, but agree that he should be?

Cases for Further Reflection

85. Goldschmitt v. Florida

Arthur Goldschmitt was convicted of driving under the influence of alcohol. The trial court placed Goldschmitt on probation (releasing him into the community under the supervision of a court officer) but on the grounds that he comply with a condition: that he place on his car a bumper sticker reading "CONVICTED D.U.I.—RESTRICTED LICENSE." Goldschmitt objected to this condition on several grounds, relying primarily on the claim that the humiliation and disgrace of being forced to display such a message on his car amounted to a form of "cruel and unusual" punishment, in violation of the Eighth Amendment to the Constitution. For what reasons does the court in *Goldschmitt* reject the defendant's argument that the condition of his probation amounted to cruel and unusual punishment? What aims does the court find are furthered by such shaming sanctions?

Per Curiam.

Appellant, Arthur Goldschmitt, was convicted of driving under the influence of alcohol to the extent his normal faculties were impaired (D.U.I.). Goldschmitt appeals the trial court's order placing him on probation and requiring as a special condition of probation that he affix to his personal vehicle a bumper sticker reading "Convicted D.U.I.—Restricted License."

. . . We first consider whether section 316.193(4)(a), Florida Statutes (1985), permits the imposition of this or any other special conditions of probation. Goldschmitt urges that the statute authorizes probation for first-time D.U.I. offenders solely to ensure compliance with the concomitant statutory provision that the offender perform fifty hours of community service. Appellee responds that while the community service condition is a special, additional penalty created by the legislature, D.U.I. probation otherwise is no different than any other form of probation. We agree. Section

948.03(4), Florida Statutes (1985), which permits the sentencing court to fashion special conditions of probation, does not distinguish between felony, misdemeanor, and criminal traffic offenses, or between county and circuit courts.

. . . Goldschmitt's argument that the bumper sticker constitutes a judicially developed, new penalty finds additional basis in the fact that this particular condition has become standard for all first-time D.U.I. offenders sentenced by two of the county's four judges. We would be quicker to accept his argument if we could be persuaded that any of the judges felt duty bound by local custom or rule to require the sticker despite their personal desire to the contrary. However, this obviously is not the case since half the local judiciary disdain the use of the sticker. While we are skeptical of special probation conditions imposed across-the-board, as opposed to being tailored to the needs and circumstances of the individual probationer, we cannot say that a judge may not impose a special condition of probation any time he or she chooses if that special condition otherwise is lawful. Those who do require the bumper sticker apparently are of the opinion the sticker serves some

490 So. 2d 123 (Fla. App. 2 Dist. 1986)
District Court of Appeal of Florida, Second District

useful purpose and that every first-time offender should have one.

. . . Next, we turn to the various constitutional objections raised by Goldschmitt. First, he advances the theory that the trial court has infringed upon his first amendment rights by forcing him to broadcast an ideological message via the bumper sticker. His principal authority for this proposition is *Wooley v. Maynard*, 430 U.S. 705, 97 . . . (1977), wherein a New Hampshire Jehovah's Witness found objectionable and taped over the "Live Free or Die" motto on his automobile license plate. Suffice it to say we agree with appellee that the message involved in the present case is "no more ideological than a permit to park in a handicapped parking space" as required by section 320.0848, Florida Statutes (1985). Further, in *Wooley v. Maynard*, the issue was whether New Hampshire's interest in broadcasting its state motto sufficiently overrode the defendant's objections to the motto that criminal penalties could be imposed for defacing the tag. Here, the criminal behavior has already been committed prior to the requirement that the message be displayed as a form of penance and a warning to other potential wrongdoers.

. . . Goldschmitt's second constitutional argument is that the bumper sticker constitutes cruel and unusual punishment and is therefore violative of the eighth amendment. He likens the sticker to the pillory of colonial times, a form of publicly suffered punishment that most would agree is cruel and unusual by modern standards. . . . However, the differences between the degrading physical rigors of the pillory and a small strip of colorful adhesive far outweigh the similarities. The mere requirement that a defendant display a "scarlet letter" as part of his punishment is not necessarily offensive to the Constitution.

The deterrent, and thus the rehabilitative, effect of punishment may be heightened if it "inflicts disgrace and contumely in a dramatic and spectacular manner." *United States v. William Anderson Co., Inc.*, 698 F.2d 911, 913 (8th Cir. 1983). The court in William Anderson expressed approval of behavioral sanctions imposed as conditions of probation for certain white-collar criminals, including speeches before civic groups on the evils of price fixing. "Measures are effective which have the impact of the 'scarlet letter' described by Nathaniel Hawthorne or the English equivalent of 'wearing papers' in the vicinity of Westminster Hall like a sandwich-man's sign describing the culprit's transgressions." . . . And, in *United States v. Carlston*, 562 F.Supp. 181 (N. D. Cal.1983), a defendant convicted of tax evasion was ordered to purchase computers and teach their use to probationers and parolees, the court noting that by association with street criminals he would be "constantly reminded that his conduct was legally and socially wrong." . . . Appellee refers to this philosophy, in the context of the present case, as "Pavlovian conditioning."

Of course, such innovative dispositions can be carried to extremes which might offend constitutional standards. In *Bienz v. State*, 343 So.2d 913 (Fla. 4th DCA 1977), a probationer was ordered into a halfway house with directions to obey all instructions. A supervisor accused him of behaving like a baby and directed him to wear diapers over his regular clothing. While the case was resolved on other grounds, the court commented: "[S]uffice it to say that a command . . . that an adult male wear diapers in public would certainly be demeaning in the minds of so-called reasonable men . . . not surprisingly, prior decisions involving such bizarre incidents are sparse." . . . On the other hand, the requirement that a purse snatcher wear taps on his shoes whenever he left his residence was approved in *People v. McDowell*, 59 Cal. App.3d 807 . . . (1976), despite the defendant's plea that this was tantamount to a sign saying "I am a thief."

In the final analysis, we are unable to state as a matter of law that Goldschmitt's bumper sticker is sufficiently humiliating to trigger constitutional objections or, perhaps more to the point, that the lower court's belief that such a sticker is "rehabilitative" is so utterly without foundation that we are empowered to substitute our judgment for its.

Accordingly, we affirm the judgment and order of probation of the trial court.

86. *The Case of the Dog "Provetie"*

As explained in Section B, the following case is one among many "animal trials" recorded throughout Europe from the late middle ages up to the eighteenth century. What does our reaction to such cases say about the objectives of criminal punishment? (Also, how did they make the dog "confess"?)

Claim and Conclusion made and taken in the matter of Lot Huygens Gael, Schout of the Town of Leiden, against and in respect of the dog of Jan Jansse van der Poel, named Provetie, with moreover the sentence of the court.

Lot Huygens Gael, Schout of the Town of Leiden, prosecutor on behalf of his lordship [the Count of Holland] in criminal matters, accuses in the open Court of the Schepenes of the Town of Leiden the dog of Jan Jansse van der Poel, named Provetie, or by whatsoever other name he may be called, now a prisoner, and says that he, the said Provetie, did not scruple on Sunday last, being the 5th of May, 1595, to bite the child of Jan Jacobsz van der Poel, which child was then playing at his uncle's house and had a piece of meat in his hand, and the said Provetie snapping at it did bite the said child and thus inflicted a wound in the second finger of the right hand, going through the skin to the flesh in such manner that the blood flowed therefrom, and the child a few days after died in consequence of fright, for which cause the prosecutor apprehended the said Provetie, all of which appears from the prisoner's own confession, made by him without torture or being put in irons. . . .

Sentence: The Schepenen of Leiden, having seen the claim and conclusion made and taken by Lot Huygens Gael, Schout of this town, against and to the charge of the dog of Jan Jansse van der Poel, named Provetie, or by whatsoever other name or surname he may be known, the prisoner being present, having seen, moreover, the information obtained by the prosecutor for the purpose, besides the prisoner's own confession made without torture or being placed in irons, doing justice in the name of, etc., have condemned and hereby do condemn him to be led and taken to the plain of Gravesteijn in this town, where evildoers are customarily punished, and that he be there hanged by the executioner to the gallows with a rope until death ensues, that further his dead body be dragged on a hurdle to the gallows-field, and that he there remain hanging to the gallows, to the deterring of other dogs and to all as an example; moreover, they declare all his goods, should he have any, to be confiscated and forfeited for the benefit of the countship.

This done in the open court, all schepenen being present, the 15th May, 1595.

Reported in *The South African Law Journal*, Vol. 24 (1907): 232–234.

87. Coker v. Georgia

While serving time in prison for murder and other violent crimes, Ehrlich Coker escaped from a Georgia facility and raped a woman. He was tried, convicted, and sentenced to death on the rape charge, the jury finding death to be an appropriate punishment given the presence of certain "aggravating factors." The Supreme Court overturned Coker's conviction, arguing that death as a punishment for rape is grossly disproportionate and thus violative of the Eighth Amendment. The case should be read with an eye to how to understand and apply the retributive requirement of proportionality. This problem surfaces in the Court's opinion in at least two forms. First, should the aggravating factors here, including the previous crimes Coker had committed, bear on the appropriate punishment for his act of rape? And second, does death itself "fit the crime," Should it matter for these purposes that, though rape is a brutal and violent crime, it does not involve taking a life?

Syllabus [of Majority Opinion][1]

While serving various sentences for murder, rape, kidnaping, and aggravated assault, petitioner escaped from a Georgia prison and, in the course of committing an armed robbery and other offenses, raped an adult woman. He was convicted of rape, armed robbery, and the other offenses and sentenced to death on the rape charge, when the jury found two of the aggravating circumstances present for imposing such a sentence, *viz*, that the rape was committed (1) by a person with prior capital-felony convictions and (2) in the course of committing another capital felony, armed robbery. The Georgia Supreme Court affirmed both the conviction and sentence. *Held: The judgment upholding the death sentence is reversed and the case is remanded.*

Mr. Justice White, joined by Mr. Justice Stewart, Mr. Justice Blackmun, and Mr. Justice Stevens, concluded that the sentence of death for the crime of rape is grossly disproportionate and exces-

433 U.S. 584 (1977)
United States Supreme Court

sive punishment and is therefore forbidden by the Eighth Amendment as cruel and unusual punishment.

(a) The Eighth Amendment bars not only those punishments that are "barbaric" but also those that are "excessive" in relation to the crime committed, and a punishment is "excessive" and unconstitutional if it (1) makes no measurable contribution to acceptable goals of punishment and hence is nothing more than the purposeless and needless imposition of pain and suffering; or (2) is grossly out of proportion to the severity of the crime.

(b) That death is a disproportionate penalty for rape is strongly indicated by the objective evidence of present, public judgment, as represented by the attitude of state legislatures and sentencing juries, concerning the acceptability of such a penalty, it appearing that Georgia is currently the only State authorizing the death sentence for rape of an adult woman, that it is authorized for rape in only two other States but only when the victim is a child, and that in the vast majority (9 out of 10) of rape convictions in Georgia since 1973, juries have not imposed the death sentence.

(c) Although rape deserves serious punishment, the death penalty, which is unique in its severity and irrevocability, is an excessive penalty for the rapist who, as such and as opposed to the murderer, does not unjustifiably take human life.

(d) The conclusion that the death sentence imposed on petitioner is disproportionate punishment for rape is not affected by the fact that the jury found the aggravating circumstances of prior capital felony convictions and occurrence of the rape while committing armed robbery, a felony for which the death sentence is also authorized, since the prior convictions do not change the fact that the rape did not involve the taking of life, and since the jury did not deem the robbery itself deserving of the death penalty, even though accompanied by the aggravating circumstances of prior capital felony convictions.

(e) That under Georgia law a deliberate killer cannot be sentenced to death, absent aggravating circumstances, argues strongly against the notion that, with or without such circumstances, a rapist who does not take the life of his victim should be punished more severely than the deliberate killer.

Mr. Justice Brennan concluded that the death penalty is in all circumstances cruel and unusual punishment prohibited by the Eighth and Fourteenth Amendments.

Mr. Justice Marshall concluded that the death penalty is a cruel and unusual punishment prohibited by the Eighth and Fourteenth Amendments.

Mr. Justice Powell concluded that death is disproportionate punishment for the crime of raping an adult woman where, as here, the crime was not committed with excessive brutality and the victim did not sustain serious or lasting injury.

Dissenting Opinion

Mr. Chief Justice Burger, with whom Mr. Justice Rehnquist joins, dissenting.

In a case such as this, confusion often arises as to the Court's proper role in reaching a decision. Our task is not to give effect to our individual views on capital punishment; rather, we must determine what the Constitution permits a State to do under its reserved powers. In striking down the death penalty imposed upon the petitioner in this case, the Court has overstepped the bounds of proper constitutional adjudication by substituting its policy judgment for that of the state legislature.

I accept that the Eighth Amendment's concept of disproportionality bars the death penalty for minor crimes. But rape is not a minor crime; hence the Cruel and Unusual Punishment Clause does not give the Members of this Court license to engraft their conceptions of proper public policy onto the considered legislative judgments of the States. Since I cannot agree that Georgia lacked the constitutional power to impose the penalty of death for rape, I dissent from the Court's judgment.

1

On December 5, 1971, the petitioner, Ehrlich Anthony Coker, raped and then stabbed to death a young woman. Less than eight months later Coker kidnapped and raped a second young woman. After twice raping this 16-year-old victim, he stripped her, severely beat her with a club, and dragged her into a wooded area where he left her for dead. He was apprehended and pleaded guilty to offenses stemming from these incidents. He was sentenced by three separate courts to three life terms, two 20-year terms, and one eight-year term of imprisonment. Each judgment specified that the sentences it imposed were to run consecutively rather than concurrently. Approximately one and one-half years later, on September 2, 1974, petitioner escaped from the state prison where he was serving these sentences. He promptly raped another 16-year-old woman in the presence of her husband, abducted her from her home, and threatened her with death and serious bodily harm. It is this crime for which the sentence now under review was imposed.

The Court today holds that the State of Georgia may not impose the death penalty on Coker. In so doing, it prevents the State from imposing any effective punishment upon Coker for his latest rape. The Court's holding, moreover, bars Georgia from guaranteeing its citizens that they will suffer no further attacks by this habitual rapist. In fact, given the lengthy sentences Coker must serve for the crimes he has already committed, the Court's holding assures that petitioner—and others in his position—will henceforth feel no compunction whatsoever about committing further rapes as frequently as he may be able to escape from confinement and indeed even within the walls of the prison itself. To what extent we have left States "elbow room" to protect innocent persons from depraved human beings like Coker remains in doubt.

2

My first disagreement with the Court's holding is its unnecessary breadth. The narrow issue here presented is whether the State of Georgia may constitutionally execute this petitioner for the particular rape which he has committed, in light of all the facts and circumstances shown by this record. The plurality opinion goes to great lengths to consider societal mores and attitudes toward the generic crime of rape and the punishment for it; however, the opinion gives little attention [to] the special circumstances which bear directly on whether imposition of the death penalty is an appropriate societal response to Coker's criminal acts: (a) On account of his prior offenses, Coker is already serving such lengthy prison sentences that imposition of additional periods of imprisonment would have no incremental punitive effect; (b) by his life pattern Coker has shown that he presents a particular danger to the safety, welfare and chastity of women, and on his record the likelihood is therefore great that he will repeat his crime at first opportunity; (c) petitioner escaped from prison, only a year and a half after he commenced serving his latest sentences; he has nothing to lose by further escape attempts; and (d) should he again succeed in escaping from prison, it is reasonably predictable that he will repeat his pattern of attacks on women—and with impunity since the threat of added prison sentences will be no deterrent.

Unlike the Court, I would narrow the inquiry in this case to the question actually presented: Does the Eighth Amendment's ban against cruel and unusual punishment prohibit the State of Georgia from executing a person who has, within the space of three years, raped three separate women, killing one and attempting to kill another, who is serving prison terms exceeding his probable lifetime and who has not hesitated to escape confinement at the first available opportunity? Whatever one's view may be as to the State's constitutional power to impose the death penalty upon a rapist who stands

before a court convicted for the first time, this case reveals a chronic rapist whose continuing danger to the community is abundantly clear.

Mr. Justice Powell would hold the death sentence inappropriate in this case because "there is no indication that petitioner's offense was committed with excessive brutality or that the victim sustained serious or lasting injury." Apart from the reality that rape is inherently one of the more egregiously brutal acts one human being can inflict upon another, there is nothing in the Eighth Amendment that so narrowly limits the factors which may be considered by a state legislature in determining whether a particular punishment is grossly excessive. Surely recidivism, especially the repeated commission of heinous crimes, is a factor which may properly be weighed as an aggravating circumstance, permitting the imposition of a punishment more severe than for one isolated offense. . . . As a factual matter, the plurality opinion is correct in stating that Coker's "prior convictions do not change the fact that the instant crime being punished is rape not involving the taking of life," . . . however, it cannot be disputed that the existence of these prior convictions make Coker a substantially more serious menace to society than a first-time offender.

. . .

In sum, once the Court has held that "the punishment of death does not invariably violate the Constitution," *Gregg v. Georgia*, 428 U.S., at 169 . . . it seriously impinges upon the State's legislative judgment to hold that it may not impose such sentence upon an individual who has shown total and repeated disregard for the welfare, safety, personal integrity and human worth of others, and who seemingly cannot be deterred from continuing such conduct. I therefore would hold that the death sentence here imposed is within the power reserved to the State and leave for another day the question of whether such sanction would be proper under other circumstances. . . .

. . .

The question of whether the death penalty is an appropriate punishment for rape is surely an open one. It is arguable that many prospective rapists would be deterred by the possibility that they could suffer death for their offense; it is also arguable that the death penalty would have only minimal deterrent effect. It may well be that rape victims would become more willing to report the crime and aid in the apprehension of the criminals if they knew that community disapproval of rapists was sufficiently strong to inflict the extreme penalty; or perhaps they would be reluctant to co-operate in the prosecution of rapists if they knew that a conviction might result in the imposition of the death penalty. Quite possibly, the occasional, well-publicized execution of egregious rapists may cause citizens to feel greater security in their daily lives, or, on the contrary, it may be that members of a civilized community will suffer the pangs of a heavy conscience because such punishment will be perceived as excessive. We cannot know which among this range of possibilities is correct, but today's holding forecloses the very exploration we have said federalism was intended to foster. It is difficult to believe that Georgia would long remain alone in punishing rape by death if the next decade demonstrated a drastic reduction in its incidence of rape, and increased cooperation by rape victims in the apprehension and prosecution of rapists, and a greater confidence in the rule of law on the part of the populace.

. . .

The subjective judgment that the death penalty is simply disproportionate for the crime of rape is even more disturbing than the "objective" analysis discussed *supra.* The plurality's conclusion on this point is based upon the bare fact that murder necessarily results in the physical death of the victim, while rape does not. . . . However, no Member of the Court explains why this distinction has relevance, much less constitutional significance. It is, after all, not irrational—nor constitutionally impermissible—for a legislature to make the penalty more severe than the criminal act it punishes in the hope it would deter wrongdoing. . . .

It begs the question to state, as does the plurality opinion:

"Life is over for the victim of the murderers; for the rape victim, life may not be nearly so happy as it was, but is not over and normally is not beyond repair." . . .

Until now, the issue under the Eighth Amendment has not been the state of any particular victim after the crime, but rather whether the punishment imposed is grossly disproportionate to the evil committed by the perpetrator. See, *Gregg v. Georgia,* 428 U.S., at 173 . . . ; *Furman v. Georgia,* 408 U.S. . . . (Powell, J., dissenting). As a matter of constitutional principle, that test cannot have the primitive simplicity of "life for life, eye for eye, tooth for tooth." Rather States must be permitted to engage in a more sophisticated weighing of values in dealing with criminal activity which consistently poses serious danger of death or grave bodily harm. If innocent life and limb is to be preserved I see no constitutional barrier in punishing by death all who engage in such activity, regardless of whether the risk comes to fruition in any particular instance. . . .

. . . Rape thus is not a crime "light-years" removed from murder in the degree of its heinousness; it certainly poses a serious potential danger to the life and safety of innocent victims—apart from the devastating psychic consequences. It would seem to follow therefore that, affording the States proper leeway under the broad standard of the Eighth Amendment, murder is properly punishable by death, rape should be also, if that is the considered judgment of the legislators.

. . .

Endnote

[1] The syllabus constitutes no part of the opinion of the Court but has been prepared by the Reporter of Decisions for the convenience of the reader.

88. *Rummell v. Estelle*

The opposing evaluations of the punishment given in this case should be read in light of the discussion of cruel and unusual punishments in Section D. What purpose is Texas's "three-time-loser" statute supposed to serve? Is there evidence that it works? "Recidivist" statutes, such as this one, are directed at "habitual criminals." Is it reasonable to expect to deter such persons? Does the moral and constitutional requirement of proportionality apply only to types of crimes and punishments (so that, for example, death is proportional to murder, though not to rape) but not to particular sentences within a given type (so that any length of imprisonment is permissible as long as some imprisonment is proportional)? Is the majority in Rummel making this argument?

Mr. Justice Rehnquist delivered the opinion of the Court.

Petitioner William James Rummel is presently serving a life sentence imposed by the State of Texas in 1973 under its "recidivist statute," . . . which provided that "[w]hoever shall have been three times convicted of a felony less than capital shall on such third conviction be imprisoned for life in the penitentiary." On January 19, 1976, Rummel sought a writ of habeas corpus in the United States District Court for the Western District of Texas, arguing that life imprisonment was "grossly disproportionate" to the three felonies that formed the predicate for his sentence and that therefore the sentence violated the ban on cruel and unusual punishments of the Eighth and Fourteenth Amendments. The District Court and the United States Court of Appeals for the Fifth Circuit rejected Rummel's claim, finding no unconstitutional disproportionality. We granted certiorari . . . and now affirm.

In 1964 the State of Texas charged Rummel with fraudulent use of a credit card to obtain $80 worth of goods or services. Because the amount in question was greater than $50, the charged offense was a felony punishable by a minimum of 2 years

445 U.S. 263 (1980)
United States Supreme Court

and a maximum of 10 years in the Texas Department of Corrections. Rummel eventually pleaded guilty to the charge and was sentenced to three years' confinement in a state penitentiary.

In 1969 the State of Texas charged Rummel with passing a forged check in the amount of $28.36, a crime punishable by imprisonment in a penitentiary for not less than two nor more than five years. Rummel pleaded guilty to this offense and was sentenced to four years' imprisonment.

In 1973 Rummel was charged with obtaining $120.75 by false pretenses. Because the amount obtained was greater than $50, the charged offense was designated "felony theft," which, by itself, was punishable by confinement in a penitentiary for not less than 2 nor more than 10 years. The prosecution chose, however, to proceed against Rummel under Texas'[s] recidivist statute, and cited in the indictment his 1964 and 1969 convictions as requiring imposition of a life sentence if Rummel were convicted of the charged offense. A jury convicted Rummel of felony theft and also found as true the allegation that he had been convicted of two prior felonies. As a result, on April 26, 1973, the trial court imposed upon Rummel the life sentence mandated by Art. 63 [of the Texas Penal Code].

. . .

This Court has on occasion stated that the Eighth Amendment prohibits imposition of a sentence that is grossly disproportionate to the severity of the crime. In recent years this proposition has appeared most frequently in opinions dealing with the death penalty.

. . .

Because a sentence of death differs in kind from any sentence of imprisonment, no matter how long, our decisions applying the prohibition of cruel and unusual punishments to capital cases are of limited assistance in deciding the constitutionality of the punishment meted out to Rummel.

Outside the context of capital punishment, successful challenges to the proportionality of particular sentences have been exceedingly rare. In *Weems v. United States* [217 U.S. 349 (1910)], a case coming to this Court from the Supreme Court of the Philippine Islands, petitioner successfully attacked the imposition of a punishment known as "cadena temporal" for the crime of falsifying a public record. . . . The mandatory "remedy" for this offense was *cadena temporal*, a punishment described graphically by the Court:

> Its minimum degree of confinement in a penal institution for twelve years and one day, a chain at the ankle and wrist of the offender, hard and painful labor, no assistance from friend or relative, no marital authority or parental rights or rights of property, no participation even in the family council. These parts of his penalty endure for the term of imprisonment. From other parts there is no intermission. His prison bars and chains are removed, it is true, after twelve years, but he goes from them to a perpetual limitation of his liberty. He is forever kept under the shadow of his crime, forever kept within voice and view of the criminal magistrate, not being able to change his domicil without giving notice to the "authority immediately in charge of his surveillance," and without permission in writing. Id., at 366. . . .

Although Rummel argues that the length of Weems's imprisonment was, by itself, a basis for the Court's decision, the Court's opinion does not support such a simple conclusion. The opinion consistently referred jointly to the length of imprisonment and its "accessories" or "accompaniments."

. . .

In an attempt to provide us with objective criteria against which we might measure the proportionality of his life sentence, Rummel points to certain characteristics of his offenses that allegedly render them "petty." He cites, for example, the absence of violence in his crimes. But the presence or absence of violence does not always affect the strength of society's interest in deterring a particular crime or in punishing a particular criminal. A high official in a large corporation can commit undeniably serious crimes in the area of antitrust, bribery, or clean air or water standards without coming close to engaging in any "violent" or short-term "life-threatening" behavior. Additionally, Rummel cites the "small" amount of money taken in each of his crimes. But to recognize that the State of Texas could have imprisoned Rummel for life if he had stolen $5,000, $50,000, or $500,000, rather than the $120.75 that a jury convicted him of stealing, is virtually to concede that the lines to be drawn are indeed "subjective," and therefore properly within the province of legislatures, not courts. Moreover, if Rummel had attempted to defraud his victim of $50,000, but had failed, no money whatsoever would have changed hands; yet Rummel would be no less blameworthy, only less skillful, than if he had succeeded.

In this case, however, we need not decide whether Texas could impose a life sentence upon Rummel merely for obtaining $120.75 by false pretenses. Had Rummel only committed that crime, under the law enacted by the Texas Legislature he could have been imprisoned for no more than 10 years. In fact, at the time that he obtained the $120.75 by false pretenses, he already had committed and had been imprisoned for two other felonies, crimes that Texas and other States felt were serious enough to warrant significant terms of imprisonment even in the absence of prior offenses. Thus the interest of the State of Texas here is not simply that of making criminal the unlawful acquisition of another person's property; it is in addition the interest, expressed in all recidivist statutes, in dealing in a harsher manner with those who by repeated criminal acts have shown that they are simply incapable of conforming to the norms of society as established by its criminal law. By conceding the validity of recidivist statutes generally, Rummel himself concedes that the State of Texas, or any other State, has a valid interest in so dealing with that class of persons.

. . .

. . . Thus, under Art. 63, a three-time felon receives a mandatory life sentence, with possibility of parole, only if commission and conviction of each succeeding felony followed conviction for the preceding one, and only if each prior conviction was followed by actual imprisonment. Given this necessary sequence, a recidivist must twice demonstrate that conviction and actual imprisonment do not deter him from returning to crime once he is released. One in Rummel's position has been both graphically informed of the consequences of lawlessness and given an opportunity to reform, all to no avail. Article 63 thus is nothing more than a societal decision that when such a person commits yet another felony, he should be subjected to the admittedly serious penalty of incarceration for life, subject only to the State's judgment as to whether to grant him parole.

. . .

Mr. Justice Powell, with whom Mr. Justice Brennan, Mr. Justice Marshall, and Mr. Justice Stevens join, dissenting.

. . .

The scope of the Cruel and Unusual Punishments Clause extends not only to barbarous methods of punishment, but also to punishments that are grossly disproportionate. Disproportionality analysis measures the relationship between the nature and number of offenses committed and the severity of the punishment inflicted upon the offender. The inquiry focuses on whether a person deserves such punishment, not simply on whether punishment would serve a utilitarian goal. A statute that levied a mandatory life sentence for overtime parking might well deter vehicular lawlessness, but it would offend our felt sense of justice. The Court concedes today that the principle of disproportionality plays a role in the review of sentences imposing the death penalty, but suggests that the principle may be less applicable when a noncapital sentence is challenged. Such a limitation finds no support in the history of Eighth Amendment jurisprudence.

The principle of disproportionality is rooted deeply in English constitutional law. The Magna Carta of 1215 insured that "[a] free man shall not be [fined] for a trivial offense, except in accordance with the degree of the offense; and for a serious offense he shall be [fined] according to its gravity." By 1400, the English common law had embraced the principle, not always followed in practice, that punishment should not be excessive either in severity or length.

. . .

In sum, a few basic principles emerge from the history of the Eighth Amendment. Both barbarous forms of punishment and grossly excessive punishments are cruel and unusual. A sentence may be excessive if it serves no acceptable social purpose, or is grossly disproportionate to the seriousness of the crime. The principle of disproportionality has been acknowledged to apply to both capital and noncapital sentences.

. . .

Examination of the objective factors traditionally employed by the Court to assess the proportionality of a sentence demonstrates that petitioner suffers a cruel and unusual punishment. Petitioner has been sentenced to the penultimate criminal penalty because he committed three offenses defrauding others of about $230. The nature of the crimes does not suggest that petitioner ever engaged in conduct that threatened another's person, involved a trespass, or endangered in any way the peace of society. A comparison of the sentence petitioner received with the sentences provided by habitual offender statutes of other American jurisdictions demonstrates that only two other States authorize the same punishment. A comparison of petitioner to other criminals sentenced in Texas shows that he has been punished for three property-related offenses with a harsher sentence than that given first-time offenders or two-time offenders convicted of far more serious offenses. The Texas system assumes that all three-time offenders deserve the same punishment whether they commit three murders or cash three fraudulent checks.

The petitioner has committed criminal acts for which he may be punished. He has been given a sentence that is not inherently barbarous. But the relationship between the criminal acts and the sentence is grossly disproportionate. For having defrauded others of about $230, the State of Texas has deprived petitioner of his freedom for the rest of his life. The State has not attempted to justify the sentence as necessary either to deter other persons or to isolate a potentially violent individual. Nor has petitioner's status as a habitual offender been shown to justify a mandatory life sentence. My view, informed by examination of the "objective indicia that reflect the public attitude toward a given sanction," is that this punishment violates the principle of proportionality contained within the Cruel and Unusual Punishments Clause.

. . .

Chapter V

Tort Law

In 1983 a young woman named Connie Daniell tried to commit suicide by locking herself in the trunk of a 1973 Ford LTD, where she remained for nine days. After being rescued, Daniell took Ford to court, alleging that the company was responsible for the psychological and physical injuries she suffered in the ordeal because the company had not built the trunk with an internal latch.[1] Daniell sought to enlist the law in naming Ford the responsible party. What is the legal basis for such a claim?

To answer this question imagine the following scenario: You have just landed a new job downtown. As the first day at the new office approaches, you become excited and a bit nervous. The night before your first meeting with the boss, you check that the alarm clock is set to go off early because you must be at the office on time to make a good first impression. As fate would have it, the clock malfunctions during the night, the alarm doesn't go off, and you leap out of bed in the morning with only a few minutes to get downtown. You catch an "express" bus to the business district. The bus driver seems to be in a hurry,

too; in fact, the bus is traveling at an illegal speed. This is all for the good, you think, until the bus approaches a major intersection, rounding the corner at the precise moment when a construction crew lifting a steel beam with a crane loses control of the rig and sends the beam crashing through the side of the bus at exactly where you are seated.

Fanciful as this may seem, accidents equally bizarre and equally costly occur daily. Now recovering in Mercy Hospital—with broken bones, intravenous tubes, and a mounting medical bill—you have lost your job. Is anyone but you responsible for your plight? The construction crew? The bus company? The driver? The alarm clock manufacturer? If any of them is responsible in some way, what can you do about it? Have you been wronged by any or all of these parties in a way that the law might recognize? The answer is yes. Any one of these parties (with the probable exception of the alarm clock maker) may have committed a *tort*: a personal harm or wrong to an individual for which the law provides redress.

Connie Daniell alleged that Ford was liable in tort for her injuries because it was careless in the design of the trunk on one of its cars. When consumer goods fail to perform as expected or cause injuries, tort suits

---

[1] See *Daniell v. Ford Motor Co., Inc.*, 581 F.Supp 728 (1984).

often result. Goods ranging from oral contraceptives and silicon breast implants to car batteries and drain cleaners have been the subject of alleged torts, but the field of tort is by no means restricted to actions brought for defective consumer products. A great many types of injuries, to person or to property, can be the basis for a tort claim: infliction of emotional distress, medical malpractice, environmental damage, and invasions of privacy are all "actionable" (the basis for a suit) in tort. Not everyone agrees that such tort actions always have merit. For example, many in the business world were outraged when, in a widely publicized case, a woman was awarded nearly $3 million from McDonald's for burns she suffered after spilling a cup of McDonald's coffee in her lap. The coffee, she claimed, was too hot.[2] Holding the company responsible for consumers' clumsiness, critics argued, is unjustifiable.

Many tort cases raise important questions about responsibility and fairness. Given the inevitability of injuries and accidents in a crowded, highly technological society, who should bear the burden of the costs those injuries and accidents incur? Who should be responsible for the costs of defective merchandise or products, disease caused by ground water pollution, or the negligence of an unsafe driver? Is it fair to leave these costs to those unlucky enough to incur them, or is there a morally defensible basis for shifting the costs to someone other than the injured party? These larger questions of social policy and public morality lead to critical legal issues. Was Connie Daniell correct in asserting that Ford was careless in the design of its cars?

How careful is Ford required to be? Should Ford have foreseen that someone might be injured by doing what Connie Daniell did? Was the risk of injury from being trapped in the trunk so obvious that no warning was necessary? Did Ford cause the injuries Daniell sustained, or did she cause them herself? These questions are the subject of the cases and essays included in this chapter.

The *Hammontree* case and the readings by Dan Dobbs, Jules Coleman, and Roger Cramton in Section A explore the basic aims of tort law and discuss how these aims have been debated in such contexts as no-fault auto insurance and so-called "mass tort" cases. The discussion centers on what the law of tort is to accomplish. Is it to minimize the costs of injuries and accidents, or to rectify the wrongdoing of "faulty" defendants? The selections in Section B pursue questions about causation in the law of tort. The *Lynch* and *Palsgraf* cases present contrasting perspectives on the question of when one thing can be said to have caused another. The essays by H. L. A. Hart and A. M. Honoré, and Judith Thomson examine a range of further questions: What determines whether my conduct has caused your injury? Am I responsible for all of the harm that I cause? How relevant to my responsibility for your harm is the fact that I caused it? How relevant is the fact that I was at fault or blameworthy in acting as I did? The readings in Section C take up a more specific related issue: liability for omissions, or failures to act, and the legal status of a duty to rescue.

"Cases For Further Reflection" close the chapter with some well-known cases in which courts have grappled with the puzzles of causation, duty, negligence, and other elements of tort.

---

[2] See *Lieback v. McDonald's Restaurants, Jury Verdict Research,* #CV 932419.

A. *Justice, Compensation, and Tort*

Grounds for Liability in Tort

What sort of "wrong" is a tort? Why doesn't the accident in our bus case amount to a *criminal* wrong—crimes that the bus driver and the construction crew have committed and for which they deserve to be punished? The answer is that although these individuals also may have committed certain crimes being convictable of a crime is not the same thing as being liable under the law of tort. In the criminal law, the state (the "people") collectively seeks to enforce basic standards of behavior by acting to pay back a wrongdoer for his wrongful deed and by working to discourage similar future conduct. In the law of tort, it is the individual victim of another's wrongdoing who brings a suit against the perpetrator. This difference between crime and tort marks a deeper difference in the fundamental purposes of the two branches of law.

The aim of the criminal law is, broadly, to ensure compliance with the rules and standards deemed essential to the preservation of society as a whole. When these rules are broken, people are often hurt. However, the criminal law concerns itself with that hurt only insofar as it is reflected in the disrespect shown for society's rules. It is not a necessary condition of criminality that there be an identifiable "victim" in the sense that you in your hospital bed believe that you have been made a victim.

Some crimes (conspiracy, illegal possession, unsuccessful attempts) do not have victims who suffer loss in this way, and even crimes that do have victims (robbery, rape, sexual abuse) do not concern themselves with addressing that loss. Thus arises the need for a body of law specifically concerned with determining where the burden of losses created intentionally or even unintentionally should fall. This role is fulfilled by tort law. You, the plaintiff, seek to have the losses or burdens that have befallen you (medical bills, lost wages, "pain and suffering") shifted to and compensated by someone else. A central question is when and under what circumstances this should be done.

Initially, losses "lie where they fall," and the law does not shift them to others without a good reason. These reasons are framed in terms of *liability rules*, which state what an injured plaintiff must show in order to force someone else to pay for his or her injuries. The two main types of liability rules in tort are *strict liability* and *negligence*. Let's look at each in turn.

Strict Liability in Tort

In a case covered by strict liability, the plaintiff must show that (1) the defendant did something, (2) the plaintiff was injured, and (3) the injury was caused by what the defendant did. The defining feature of strict liability is the absence of any requirement that the defendant has been somehow *at fault* in his conduct. Traditionally, the common law imposed liability in this strict sense on property owners whose livestock trespassed on the property of adjacent landowners, causing damage. Strict liability was also imposed for abnormally dangerous conditions or activities such as storing explosives or flammable liquids or engaging in blasting or pumping that resulted in a flood. Today the strict liability rule is widely used in product liability cases, in which a consumer is injured by a defectively designed or manufactured product. Strict product liability claims dominate the current landscape of consumer protection litigation. A seller may be strictly liable for defective products introduced into the stream of commerce even though the seller was in no way negligent.

Section 402(A) of the *Restatement of Torts, Second*, is a source of much modern strict liability law. It states that a seller may be held liable when it makes and sells a product in a "defective" condition, "unreasonably dangerous" to the consumer. What do these terms mean? It is generally accepted that a product is defective if it was manufactured incorrectly, for example with screws missing or parts not in the right place. Manufacturers can also be liable for defects in the design or concept of a product. For example, a company that made buses for commercial transit was held liable when a woman riding in one of its buses fell to the floor and was injured as the bus made a sharp right turn. The bus was said to be defectively designed as there was no "grab bar" or vertical pole for passengers to hold on to next to the plaintiff's seat.[1] Courts have employed at least two criteria to determine whether a design is defective:

1. The product is more dangerous than would be contemplated by an ordinary consumer using common knowledge—in other words, it falls below reasonable consumer expectations.
2. The product sold creates such a risk of serious injury that the cost to make it safe would outweigh the benefits to society.

It is important to see that these tests may yield different results. Recall the case of Connie Daniell, who locked herself in the trunk of an old car. There was no latch or other device with which the trunk could be opened from the inside. Had the car's trunk been defectively designed? To prove her claim under the first test, Daniell would have had to show that most consumers could not have foreseen the type of injury she suffered. Because most people would readily see the danger, however, this would be difficult. Still, this test has limitations: How should we handle cases in which consumers simply don't have any clear expectations about how a product should behave or how safe it is? For this and other reasons, some courts have preferred to ask a different question: Do trunks without inside latches create such a danger that the risk outweighs the utility or value of having such items available at all? The answer here is somewhat less clear and would probably depend on how much inside trunk latches would add to the cost of cars. Assessments of risk and utility are not easy. After all, such common household items as knives and scissors cause many accidents each year, yet few people would argue that we would be better off without them. Some products, of course, cannot be made completely safe. "Unavoidably unsafe" goods such as vaccines nonetheless have great utility.

Sellers of goods have also been held strictly liable in tort for failing to inform or to warn consumers adequately about the possible dangers of their products. Here the question facing producers is how best to transmit such information. How much of the risk must be disclosed? How vivid must a warning be? A woman taking birth-control pills was told by the maker, Ortho Pharmaceutical, that there could be side effects from use, "the most severe of which is abnormal blood-clotting." After several years of taking the pills, the woman suffered a stroke and sued Ortho, arguing that the risk of a "stroke" had not been fully and adequately conveyed to her.[2] Those in favor of holding manufacturers strictly liable in these cases argue that the firm is in the best position to understand the hazards posed by its products and warn of them; others contend that holding companies liable in all cases in which a product user has not understood the warnings will sharply increase the cost of the products in question, such that consumers who use products safely will wind up subsidizing the careless users.

More generally, advocates of strict tort liability argue that mass production of standardized products and the rapidly growing technological complexity of goods available to the public have left consumers increasingly ill-equipped to evaluate the safety and quality of the goods they purchase. The magnitude of harm presented by products increases as our capacity to assess the risks they impose diminishes. For these and other reasons,

---

[1] See *Campbell v. General Motors,* 32 Cal.3d 112 (1982).

[2] See *Macdonald v. Ortho Pharmaceutical Corp.,* 475 N.E.2d 65 (1985).

courts and legislators have felt it fair to impose strict liability on manufacturers, insisting that they pay for injuries sustained by those who use their products even though the seller has exercised all possible care in the design, manufacture, and sale of its products.

Plaintiff's Fault and Product Misuse

Although the producer of a good may be responsible if the item is dangerous or defective, it seems unfair to insist that the producer be held liable even when its commodity is misused by a consumer. A ladder that has been poorly constructed is the builder's problem, but most would say that a ladder placed on obviously uneven ground or clearly overbalanced by the user is the user's problem. Suppose that a plaintiff in a tort suit is injured by a fall from a ladder or from scaffolding after she was warned not to stand on it because it was unstable. If the plaintiff's own carelessness was the immediate cause of her injury, the defendant who supplied the ladder or scaffolding might be able to assert that fact in its defense. Such a claim was traditionally known as the doctrine of *contributory negligence* because, the allegation went, the plaintiff contributed to her own accident. Consumer misconduct is a frequently invoked defense to product liability lawsuits although this defense has been questioned in some cases. Suppose that Seller markets a car capable of traveling at tremendous speeds. Seller can foresee that at least some buyers of its cars will drive them at the dangerous speeds of which they are capable. Should such "foreseeable misuses" of a product be Seller's problem?

The old common law rule held that contributory negligence was a "complete bar" to the award of damages: even if the plaintiff's carelessness was less significant or obvious than that of the defendant, the plaintiff received nothing. Most jurisdictions have now supplanted the common law rule with a regime of *comparative fault*, according to which the plaintiff's overall compensation is diminished, but not entirely eliminated, by an amount proportional to her part in the accident.

Negligence

Contrasting with the rule of strict liability is the rule of *negligence*. Liability in negligence is established when the plaintiff shows each of the following: (1) the defendant did something, (2) the plaintiff was injured, (3) the injury was caused by what the defendant did, and (4) the defendant was at fault. The last requirement is sometimes referred to as a *breach of duty* to exercise due care or regard for the safety of others, thereby exposing them to an unreasonable risk of harm. To say that a person is negligent is not necessarily to say that he or she is forgetful or inattentive (even though this may be the case). Rather, to be negligent means to fall below the acceptable level of care for the welfare of others that society expects of us all. As such, "fault" in the law of tort is not always equivalent to moral blame or censure. As one commentator has said, negligence may be the result of "ignorance, lack of intelligence, or an honest mistake"; thus the kind of "fault" required "means nothing more than a departure from a standard of conduct required of a person by society for the protection of his neighbors."[3]

According to the standard doctrine of tort, a defendant is liable for negligent conduct if he or she failed to act as a *reasonable* person would have acted. Courts have typically resolved tort disputes with the device of a hypothetical "reasonable person" whose conduct serves as a measure of what is reasonable behavior under the circumstances. The obvious vagueness of the term "reasonable" is regarded by the law as a benefit, not a drawback, for it allows the jury to consider all of the factors present in a given case in light of what a person of average intelligence and prudence would do. Driving at 70 miles an hour down a slick road may be "unreasonable" conduct for teenagers out for a thrill, but it may be reasonable for paramedics trying to get a dying patient to the hospital.

It is important to see that, with few exceptions, the law evaluates a defendant's conduct based on what was in fact reasonable under the circum-

---

[3] W. Page Keeton, *Prosser and Keeton on Torts, 5th ed.* (St. Paul: West Publishing Co., 1984), p. 535.

stances, not on what the defendant herself may have believed to be reasonable. The distinction here is sometimes marked by saying that the law employs an *objective,* rather than a *subjective,* test of negligence or fault. Suppose you leave a banana peel on the stairway. I slip on the peel and am injured. When the law asks whether you acted negligently, it does not assess the faultiness of your conduct exclusively from your own (subjective) point of view, taking into account your particular weaknesses or inabilities or beliefs. It doesn't inquire into whether you personally realized the danger presented by the banana peel—perhaps you are slow and just never thought about it. Instead it asks whether a reasonable person would have appreciated the danger. Even though you may have thought that depositing the banana peel on the steps was "reasonable," what matters is whether your actions were reasonable from an objective standpoint. Tort law does make allowances for some individual physical limitations: for example, a blind person cannot be expected to conform to the standards of the sighted, and a child cannot always be expected to act as an adult would.

Why should negligence be measured by an objective test? After all, it may seem unfair to judge people by standards that do not necessarily reflect their individual level of blameworthiness or culpability. Many jurists answer, in utilitarian fashion, that cooperative social life requires a certain minimum standard of average care upon which everyone can rely. People who, because of their constitution, cannot live up to this standard may be forgiven by an enlightened conscience, but because their conduct still poses a threat or danger, they must be held to that average, objective standard.

We can now return to the construction crew in the hypothetical case sketched at the opening of this chapter. Suppose the crew was required by industry standards (in addition to common sense) to hoist the steel beams with a cable of sufficient tensile strength to handle the load, but they were using a cheaper, substandard cable. This is an example of a failure to exercise proper care for the safety of others by exposing workers and pedestrians (and transit passengers) to a risk of serious harm. Does this mean that you can sue the company for its negligence? Not of itself. To establish a *prima facie* case of negligent harm, the law requires a plaintiff to prove,

by a preponderance (majority) of the evidence, that: (1) the defendant (here the construction company) had a duty to exercise reasonable care in the context within which it acted (lifting heavy steel girders), (2) the defendant violated or breached that duty (using cheap, unsafe cable and thereby creating a genuine hazard), and (3) the breach of that duty caused harm to you (permitting the girder to escape and strike you, resulting in injuries), and (4) the defendent was at fault, having exposed you to danger through its carelessness.

Strict Liability vs. Negligence

The central questions in the law of tort concern what kinds of unintended harms or accidents should be dealt with under strict liability and what kinds under negligence, and whether one or the other rule should become the uniform rule for all tort cases or neither rule should govern and the tort system should be modified or abandoned.

One of the principal justifications often advanced in support of a regime of strict tort liability is that such an approach has the effect of taking a cost that initially falls on an individual and *spreading that cost out* by asking manufacturers of defective products or those involved in dangerous activities to absorb the cost. More generally, those who support strict liability appeal to the good consequences that the adoption of such a liability rule will have. To see what this means, imagine a company that manufactures and sells explosives used in mining and construction. What are the costs of placing such items on the market? Clearly one such cost is the expense incurred by the company in the process of manufacture: what it costs to buy the raw materials, to process and assemble the explosives, and so on. It also costs the company money to advertise and market its goods. Just as plainly, however, another cost of having explosives on the market is that they may injure those who use them. Because such costs would not otherwise appear on the ledger books of the company, economists call them *externalities*. The basic idea behind a policy of strict liability, say its defenders, is to make the explosives industry (in this case) cover its own costs or absorb its own externalities—pay its own way in the world. By holding the explosives business liable for injuries caused by its products, society gives the industry an incentive to make its goods as safe as possible. Strict liability makes sense economically as well since, with its knowledge and expertise, the industry can eliminate or avoid accident costs more cheaply (efficiently) than can consumers. Finally, strict liability affords an effective way of insuring against the costs of accidents; the industry can simply add the costs of covering injuries to the price of its goods, thus spreading the costs out among the large base of consumers rather than leaving the burden concentrated on the few who are injured.

Those who support a negligence theory of tort law challenge each of the foregoing arguments. Strict liability is poor economic policy since it will generate more costs than its proponents acknowledge. Plaintiffs do not have to shoulder the responsibility and the costs of injuries under a system of strict tort liability, so they will tend to be less careful, with the result that the number of accidents and court cases will rise steadily. Insurance premiums will increase. Consumers will be less mindful of product instructions and warnings and will have less incentive to use the products safely. Supporters of a negligence-based theory of tort often rest their case on the moral claim that liability should never be imposed except where there is a finding of fault, even if fault is measured objectively. Even if it could be shown that strict liability will lower the number of accidents or will spread costs more efficiently, why is it fair to use a defendant in that way? If a company that makes explosives or chainsaws is as careful as possible in the design and construction of its wares, why is it nonetheless fair to force it to pay for harm to consumers? Sometimes, say the critics of strict liability, bad things just happen to consumers and are not the manufacturers' fault.

As should now be apparent, the debate over negligence and strict liability is both broad and abstract, and for this reason several of the readings in this section try to approach that debate by looking at a specific class of losses—auto injuries—and asking who should bear the costs of such losses and why.

Automobile Accidents and No-Fault

The readings for this section begin with an illustrative automobile injury case, *Hammontree v. Jenner*.

Plaintiffs Mr. and Mrs. Hammontree were injured when motorist Jenner careened into their store after suffering an epileptic seizure at the wheel. The jury found for the defendant and the Hammontrees appealed. The dispute here pitted negligence against absolute or strict liability. The Hammontrees argued that Jenner should be strictly liable despite his explanations for causing the accident; Jenner, on the other hand, claimed that he should be judged against a negligence standard and that his conduct was reasonable because he had no warning of the seizure. The court ruled in favor of Jenner and explained why the negligence standard should continue to govern auto accidents.

The *Hammontree* case is followed by a brief essay by Dan Dobbs. Dobbs lays out the basic framework of tort law and reviews the differences between torts and crimes. He examines the claim that those who are wronged by others should be compensated, and he shows that a system of tort law is not the only way of dealing with the cost of injuries.

Jules Coleman's essay defends a no-fault scheme for losses arising out of auto accidents. Typical no-fault plans provide that drivers insure themselves against loss, even for accidents caused by the "faulty" driving of others. Coleman first identifies the various costs associated with accidental harm. "Primary costs" involve the number and severity of the accidents themselves, "secondary costs" are the costs of compensation for harm sustained by accidents, and "tertiary costs" are those that must be paid to maintain the expensive legal and business machinery necessary to administer the insurance system. Coleman argues that the traditional fault system of tort law, as applied to auto accidents, is not cost effective. He also argues that a no-fault scheme will reduce primary costs by reducing the frequency of accidents.

Coleman then turns to a key argument in favor of a fault-based tort system: that liability for accidents should be assigned, not to minimize costs but to do justice, either by penalizing those somehow at fault (retributive justice) or by nullifying wrongful gain by ensuring that recompense for losses is made by those at fault. Coleman argues that the fault-based tort system cannot be explained on retributive grounds, because (1) the "objective" standard of negligence in tort means that some drivers will be liable even though they really aren't blameworthy in a retributive sense and (2) some who drive carelessly (and are thus "faulty" from a retributive standpoint) will escape liability as long as they don't actually cause injury. Corrective justice says that those injured have a right to compensation, but must the compensation come from the person who caused the injury, as the fault system would require? Coleman answers by maintaining that corrective justice requires only that the injured person receive compensation and that, as with repaying the debt of another, there is no requirement that the repayment come from the injurer who, after all, hasn't really "benefited" from the accident.

The final reading for this section turns away from auto accidents to examine problems raised by a new area of tort law. Law professor Roger Cramton outlines the challenges to existing law posed by the emergence of so-called "mass exposure torts." Some of the most difficult legal and moral issues to arise from the expansion of strict liability are raised by society's efforts to handle tens of thousands of similar product-related injuries. Many courts now permit manufacturers of tobacco, asbestos, IUDs, and breast implants to be sued by both actual and prospective victims in a single proceeding. Cramton examines the tension between the societal goals of such "class action" lawsuits and the need for each individual victim to seek compensatory justice. Cramton believes that the current system for dealing with large-scale consumer injuries leaves many questions unanswered.

---

89. *Hammontree v. Jenner*

Lillie, J. [Judge]

Plaintiffs Maxine Hammontree and her husband sued defendant for personal injuries and property damage arising out of an automobile accident. The cause was tried to a jury. Plaintiffs appeal from judgment entered on a jury verdict returned against them and in favor of defendant.

The evidence shows that on the afternoon of April 25, 1967, defendant was driving his 1959 Chevrolet home from work; at the same time plaintiff Maxine Hammontree was working in a bicycle shop owned and operated by her and her husband; without warning defendant's car crashed through the wall of the shop, struck Maxine and caused personal injuries and damage to the shop.

Defendant claimed he became unconscious during an epileptic seizure losing control of his car.

---

20 Cal. App. 3d 528 (1971)
Court of Appeal of California

He did not recall the accident but his last recollection before it, was leaving a stop light after his last stop, and his first recollection after the accident was being taken out of his car in plaintiffs' shop. Defendant testified he has a medical history of epilepsy and knows of no other reason for his loss of consciousness except an epileptic seizure; prior to 1952 he had been examined by several neurologists whose conclusion was that the condition could be controlled and who placed him on medication; in 1952 he suffered a seizure while fishing; several days later he went to Dr. Benson Hyatt who diagnosed his condition as petit mal seizure and kept him on the same medication; thereafter he saw Dr. Hyatt every six months and then on a yearly basis several years prior to 1967; in 1953 he had another seizure, was told he was an epileptic and continued his medication; in 1954 Dr. Kershner prescribed dilantin and in 1955 Dr. Hyatt prescribed phelantin; from 1955 until the accident occurred (1967) defendant had used phelantin on a regular basis which controlled his condition; defendant has continued to take medication as prescribed by his physician and has done everything his doctors told him to do to avoid a seizure; he had no inkling or warning that he was about to have a seizure prior to the occurrence of the accident.

In 1955 or 1956 the Department of Motor Vehicles was advised that defendant was an epileptic and placed him on probation under which every six months he had to report to the doctor who was required to advise it in writing of defendant's condition. In 1960 his probation was changed to a once-a-year report.

Dr. Hyatt testified that during the times he saw defendant, and according to his history, defendant "was doing normally" and that he continued to take phelantin; that "[t]he purpose of the [phelantin] would be to react on the nervous system in such a way that where, without the medication, I would say to raise the threshold so that he would not be as subject to these episodes without the medication, so as not to have the seizures. He would not be having the seizures with the medication as he would without the medication compared to taking medication"; in a seizure it would be impossible for a person to drive and control an automobile; he believed it was safe for defendant to drive.

Appellants' contentions that the trial court erred in refusing to grant their motion for summary judgment on the issue of liability and their motion for directed verdict on the pleadings and counsel's opening argument are answered by the disposition of their third claim that the trial court committed prejudicial error in refusing to give their jury instruction on absolute liability.[1]

Under the present state of the law found in appellate authorities . . . the trial judge properly refused the instruction. The . . . cases generally hold that liability of a driver, suddenly stricken by an illness rendering him unconscious, for injury resulting from an accident occurring during that time rests on principles of negligence. However, herein during the trial plaintiffs withdrew their claim of negligence and, after both parties rested and before jury argument, objected to the giving of any instructions on negligence electing to stand solely on the theory of absolute liability. The objection was overruled and the court refused plaintiffs' requested instruction after which plaintiffs waived both opening and closing jury arguments. Defendant argued the cause to the jury after which the judge read a series of negligence instructions. . . .

Appellants seek to have this court override the established law of this state which is dispositive of the issue before us as outmoded in today's social and economic structure, particularly in the light of the now recognized principles imposing liability upon the manufacturer, retailer and all distributive and vending elements and activities which bring a product to the consumer to his injury, on the basis of strict liability in tort. . . . These authorities hold that [a] manufacturer [or retailer] is strictly liable in tort when an article he places on the market, knowing that it is to be used without inspection for defects, proves to have a defect that causes injury to a human being. . . . Drawing a parallel with these products liability cases, appellants argue, with some degree of logic, that only the driver affected by a physical condition which could suddenly render him unconscious and who is aware of that condition can anticipate the hazards and foresee the dangers involved in his operation of a motor vehicle, and that the liability of those who by reason of seizure or heart failure or some other physical condition lose the ability to safely operate and control a motor vehicle resulting in injury to an innocent person should be predicated on strict liability.

We decline to superimpose the absolute liability of products liability cases upon drivers under the circumstances here. The theory on which those cases are predicated is that manufacturers, retailers and distributors of products are engaged in the business of distributing goods to the public and are an integral part of the over-all producing and marketing enterprise that should bear the cost of injuries from defective parts. This policy hardly applies here and it is not enough to simply say, as do appellants, that the insurance carriers should be the ones to bear the cost of injuries to innocent victims on a strict liability basis. In *Maloney v. Rath*, 69 Cal. 2d 442 . . . appellant urged that defendant's violation of a safety provision (defective brakes) of the Vehicle Code makes the violator strictly liable for damages caused by the violation. While reversing the judgment for defendant upon another ground, the California Supreme Court refused to apply the doctrine of strict liability to automobile drivers.

The situation involved two users of the highway but the problems of fixing responsibility under a system of strict liability are as complicated in the instant case as those in *Maloney v Rath* (p. 447), and could only create uncertainty in the area of its concern. As stated in *Maloney,* at page 446: "To invoke a rule of strict liability on users of the streets and highways, however, without also establishing in substantial detail how the new rule should operate would only contribute confusion to the automobile accident problem. Settlement and claims adjustment procedures would become chaotic until the new rules were worked out on a case-by-case basis, and the hardships of delayed compensation would be seriously intensified. Only the Legislature, if it deems it wise to do so, can avoid such difficulties by enacting a comprehensive plan for the compensation of automobile accident victims in place of or in addition to the law of negligence."

The instruction tendered by appellants was properly refused for still another reason. Even assuming the merit of appellants' position under the facts of this case in which defendant knew he had a history of epilepsy, previously had suffered seizures and at the time of the accident was attempting to control the condition by medication, the instruction does not except from its ambit the driver who suddenly is stricken by an illness or physical condition which he had no reason whatever to anticipate and of which he had no prior knowledge.

The judgment is affirmed.

Endnote

[1] "When the evidence shows that a driver of a motor vehicle on a public street or highway loses his ability to safely operate and control such vehicle because of some seizure or health failure, that driver is nevertheless legally liable for all injuries and property damage which an innocent person may suffer as a proximate result of the defendant's inability to so control or operate his motor vehicle.

"This is true even if you find the defendant driver had no warning of any such impending seizure or health failure."

---

90. *Torts and Compensation*

Dan B. Dobbs

a. *What is Tort Law?*

Torts, roughly speaking, are "wrongs," recognized by law as grounds for a lawsuit. These wrongs include an intentional punch in the nose and also a negligent car wreck. They include medical malpractice and some environmental pollution. Other torts include such wrongs as libel or slander, fraud, and interference with contract. The list is very long.

In all these cases the defendant's wrong results in harm to another person (or corporation), a harm the law is willing to say constitutes a legal injury. The injured person is said to have a "cause of action" or claim against the person who committed the tort and caused the harm. This claim can be pursued in court. These are the claims adjudicated in this essay.

Torts and Crimes

Some torts are also crimes. The punch in the nose is a tort called battery, but it may also be a crime. It would be possible that a defendant who attacked the plaintiff would be prosecuted criminally and sentenced to jail or given a fine and that he would also be held liable to the plaintiff for the tort. The two fields of law often overlap and often serve similar purposes. However, they are not identical. Criminal prosecutions are aimed at vindicating public interests, not private harms. For this reason, some acts that cause no harm at all to individuals might be crimes. For example, a state might make it a crime to shoot a gun at a person, even if the person is not hurt and even if the person is wholly unaware of the shooting. The public interest in suppressing violence might justify such a rule. But if the individual who was the intended victim was not in fact hurt and not even in apprehension of danger, there is no reason to say this crime is also a tort for which the individual could sue.

Tort Damages

What is characteristic of the tort claim, then, is that a person is, in the eyes of the law, harmed. Occasionally such a person sues for an injunction, a court order forbidding the tortious conduct. Usually, however, the tort is a single act and the plaintiff only sues for damages as compensation for the harm already done. [Here, we will be concerned with] torts that cause physical injury to persons or to property, often with accompanying emotional harm. It is a good idea to see immediately the general kinds of damages a plaintiff can recover when there is physical injury to an individual.

The *amount* of damages to be recovered by an injured plaintiff may vary from case to case, depending on how serious the injury is. But the *measure* of damages for compensation is the same, regardless how the injury came about. The injured plaintiff is entitled to recover:

1. Loss of earning capacity (or wage loss).
2. Reasonable medical expenses.
3. A payment for pain and suffering, including mental pain and suffering.

The law generally provides for one and only one legal action, and for this reason the plaintiff recovers not only the damages already suffered, but also all future expected damages. For example, a plaintiff who is paralyzed as the result of a tort will probably be unable to work as productively in the future, and will also have future medical expenses

and future pain. He will be entitled to recover under all three heads.

In cases of especially bad conduct by the defendant, the plaintiff may also be permitted to recover punitive or exemplary damages, as a kind of punishment or example. Although such damages serve a purpose of criminal law, the individual plaintiff is allowed to recover these damages in special cases.

As you might suspect, there is a good deal more to the law of damages than is outlined here. . . . It is important to understand at the beginning, however, that damages recovered in tort cases may range from trivial or nominal to sums of several million dollars. Even an injury that sounds on the surface like a moderate one may result in a jury verdict of $50,000 or $100,000. When large sums of money are awarded, the most usual reason is that the jury has been influenced by the claim of "pain," which cannot be quantified. Much turns, then, on the seriousness of the injury and the persuasiveness of the lawyers and, unavoidably, on the sympathies of any particular jury for any particular plaintiff.

Bases of Liability in Tort

Tort law is distinguished from criminal law partly because its purposes are compensatory rather than punitive. But there are some other distinctions. One of these is that crimes almost always involve some kind of intent, often an intent to cause harm or to do something people in general consider to be wrong. Some torts are also like this, but not all of them. The law of torts has recognized three distinct bases of tort liability:

1. *Intent.* For example, an intentional striking of another person.
2. *Negligence.* For example, driving too fast or failing to keep a proper lookout with a resulting collision.
3. *Strict liability.* For example, selling a consumer product that is "defective" and causes harm, even though the seller acted with reasonable care. This is sometimes called liability without fault and it may be imposed whenever it is thought that the defendant's activity, whatever it is, should "pay its own way," even though the defendant is guilty of no fault.

Roughly speaking, these three bases of liability will be considered in the order just given.

Although there are cases in which courts have consciously imposed liability upon a defendant who is said not to be at fault, in the great majority of cases judges have said the defendant must be guilty of some kind of fault before he can be held responsible. Fault may be defined in ways that will seem peculiar at times, but fault, according to the prevailing orthodoxy, is required in some degree. As we will see shortly in more detail, this fault usually appears as "intent," or as "negligence"—both terms that will require some considerable definition.

b. *Economic and Dignitary Torts*

Tort law is not limited to cases of *physical* injury. Some legally recognized injuries involve pure economic harm—that is, harm that costs the plaintiff money without causing him physical injury. Other injuries recognized by law involve "dignitary" harm—that is, harm that neither costs money nor causes physical injury, but may cause emotional harm or demean the plaintiff as a human being.

For example, it may be a tort to say that the plaintiff has a venereal disease, or to lie about the existence of termites in a house being sold, or to discharge the plaintiff from employment for highly improper reasons. The accusation of venereal disease may not cause any economic harm, but even if it does not, it denigrates the plaintiff as a human being (or so the law has said) and may involve emotional distress. The lie about the termites may cause the house buyer pure economic harm, since the house will require repairs or will be worth less because of the termites. The wrongful discharge of the plaintiff from employment will cause economic harm, and, given that improper reasons were behind the discharge, may also cause emotional harm to the plaintiff, as where the plaintiff is discharged because of race or gender. In none of these cases is there physical injury; yet all these cases are torts.

These economic and dignitary torts are often quite different from physical injury torts. For instance, most of the "pocketbook" torts involve some form of communication between people and therefore they involve, at least potentially, the First Amendment's protection for free speech. Because of such differences—of which the free speech concern is only one—it is useful to separate the economic and many of the dignitary torts for consideration late in the course, devoting the first and largest part of the course to torts that involve physical injury to person or property, or at least to acts that risk such injuries.

c. *Physical Injury and the Law*

Though physical injury is not the exclusive concern of tort law, it is a major one. Injury is also a very large social problem and society responds to that problem in a number of different ways, of which tort law is only one. . . .

Injury is a problem most obviously for the injured person, who may suffer a complete disruption of life, loss of income, excruciating pain, continuous medical costs, and a loss of emotional give and take with those around him. These are grounds enough for treating injury seriously, but the loss does not stop with the injured person. Those immediately around such a person usually also suffer. For example, a serious injury may disrupt a marriage or deprive it of its emotional or sexual content. It may also disrupt the larger family, too, and children of a seriously injured person appear at times to engage in antisocial activities, the least of which is vandalism. The radiating effects of injury may lessen the children's chances of adequate education, which in turn will have future disruptive effects on society at large.

Society at large suffers many costs from injury. There are something like 200,000 deaths a year from injury in the United States, and literally millions of disabling injuries from accidents in work, home and automobiles. The costs of these injuries is almost beyond grasp. Lost production, medical costs, loss of wages, and property damage runs to many billions. The radiating costs and their distribution to the non-injured also pose a problem. For example, if injury is uncompensated, public assistance may be required or creditors may go unpaid. If compensation is provided to an injured person, insurance rates may rise. Injury is costly to everyone in society. It is thus not merely an individual problem but also a social problem.

Tort law deals with physical injury mostly in terms of right and wrong. If the injury was wrongfully caused, the wrongdoer—tortfeasor, he is called—must pay compensation. But if the defendant caused harm without committing a legal wrong, or if he has a defense, he will pay nothing and the injury will go uncompensated, no matter how horrible or permanent it is. Each case is judged on its own merits with careful investigation of the facts, professional supervision of inferences to be drawn from the facts and professional application of legal rules, many of which are complex or difficult. This investment in each case is so great that it is likely to improve the chances of doing justice. On the other hand, given the millions of injuries, it is costly. Furthermore, it leaves many injured persons uncompensated. If injury itself is not merely an individual problem, uncompensated injury presents a social concern.

This concern has led many reformers to seek alternatives to tort law, not for all purposes, but for purposes of physical injury cases. Several schemes have been developed for providing compensation on a more massive—and procedurally more efficient—basis than tort law provides. One of these, workers' compensation, provides that when a worker is injured "on the job," he or she will be entitled to certain benefits. These benefits do not include any recovery for pain or suffering, but do cover most medical and most wage loss, at least in the average case. The worker is deprived of a tort action as well as a claim for pain and suffering. In exchange for this loss, however, the worker has the assurance that when injury comes, there will be compensation—an assurance tort law definitely does not give.

Another possible method of handling the injury problem is to respond in a massive way to serious but not to minor injury. It would be possible, for example, to say that if one is permanently disabled by an injury, that is equivalent to an early, forced retirement and the injured person should be entitled to his or her retirement fund. This, in effect, is the rule for social security disability payments.

Still other possibilities include the idea that each person should be compelled to provide for himself a certain minimum insurance protection against some of the more serious risks, such as automobile injury, and that, to the extent that protection is required, no tort action should be permitted at all. This is the essence of the "basic protection" or "no-fault auto plan," now in force in about half the states in some form or another.

These alternatives to the tort method of dealing with injury have several points in common. They envision very little room for factual dispute since they do not turn on "fault," or wrongdoing. They also contemplate *no* payment for pain and suffering damages—one of the mainstays of tort litigation—but seek instead to be sure that all persons within the scope of coverage are assured of recovering actual out-of-pocket losses.

All of these means of dealing with injury are a part of this course, to be considered after the tort system of dealing with injury is first mastered. The tort system, as we will see, is complicated, bristling with puzzles and issues. This system, with its long trials, detailed examination of facts, careful analysis of arguments, is very expensive compared to some of the alternatives. Yet it has its advantages.

d. *Freedom, Accountability and Social Responsibility*

The tort system of dealing with injury emphasizes individual accountability—at least in theory and episodically. The defendant who has done "wrong" is liable to those whom he injures, and is thus held accountable. Just as important, the plaintiff is also accountable—if he causes his own injury he will not be allowed to recover damages from the defendant. Like most statements in this introduction, this one will be qualified at various places in these materials, but the trust of it is correct. Although accountability is a complex idea—and so is "wrongdoing," by the way—the law of torts seeks to make it meaningful in these cases, and thus appeals to a strong moral sense.

The law of torts also protects the freedom of individuals to act as they please so long as they are not legal wrongdoers. As already indicated, there are some cases in which one commits a legal wrong even though one is not in any way morally at fault, and some commentators believe that this strict ability approach is or should be quite prevalent. The courts and the orthodox commentators, however, have traditionally taken the view for the last 130 years or so that liability for tort turns on a finding that the defendant was at fault in some important sense. One who is *not* at fault is not to be held liable in tort even if he causes an injury. This is the freedom side of the accountability coin, and of course it has its own appeal.

Against the strong historical preference in this country for letting each person work out his or her own destiny, holding each accountable for wrongs but free to act in the absence of wrongs, there is also a strong thread of social concern. For example, when it became apparent in the 19th century that railroad workers were injured in great numbers and that other people generally were not, the Congress enacted a statute requiring railroads in interstate commerce to provide certain safety equipment to protect workers. Conceivably the railroads were not negligent by standards of the times in failing to provide safety appliances; workers could have been expected to be "accountable" for their own safety. Yet the Congress acted, imposing on railroads an expense not imposed on everyone else. Similarly today some reformers have felt that tort law is not sufficient protection for large numbers of people who are injured in automobile accidents.

There is a great deal of conflict here. If people who are injured are allowed to recover even though they themselves are at fault, the idea of accountability is sacrificed. Yet if millions of injuries go uncompensated, society as a whole may suffer. This conflict furnishes one of the great themes of the modern course in tort law. Is accountability a goal we can achieve at all? If it is, can we hope to achieve both accountability and a reasonable degree of concern for what is "good for us all"?

The conflict just described can be described in other terms. Philosophers could talk in terms of a conflict between Kantian notions of right-and-wrong and the Utilitarian notions of doing, not what is right for right's sake, but doing what is best for the society as a whole. Economists can cast the issues in terms of efficiency, in the narrow economic sense. But for the moment it is sufficient to see that, whatever the terms, tort law today represents only *one* of the ways of dealing with physical injury.

As we proceed with the course, then, tort law should be evaluated. Does it seek and does it achieve accountability? Is it efficient? Might alternatives be better? The generation of lawyers represented in part by those now in law school will have much to say about the future of tort law and other solutions to the problem of injury.

. . .

91. *Justice and the Costs of Automobile Accidents*

JULES COLEMAN

Which members of the community should bear the costs of automobile accidents? The answer to this question depends first on whether one is to consider traffic accident costs on an individual case basis or as they accumulate over a specified period of time. Should one maintain that those individuals who ought to bear the cumulative costs of traffic accidents are precisely those who are at fault in causing particular ones, the distinction between particular and cumulative costs seems to conflate. This need not be the case, however, since one could maintain that the faulty parties in particular accidents should bear the cumulative costs without committing oneself to the position that each faulty party ought to be responsible for the costs of all and only those accidents that is his fault. After determining that the cumulative costs of accidents should be spread among those at fault in causing particular ones, one could then consult some other criterion to determine what percentage of the total costs, or the costs of which particular accidents, each should bear, for example the criterion of prior capacity to bear loss. What constitutes sufficient reason for shifting the burden of automobile accident costs depends on the goals of accident law. This point is well made by Guido Calabresi in his important and provocative book, *The Costs of Accidents:*

> it is a policy question whether accident costs should be (1) borne by particular victims; (2) paid on a one to one basis by those who injure a particular victim; (3) borne by those broad categories of people who are likely to be victims; (4) paid by those broad categories of people who are likely to be injurers; (5) paid by those who in some sense violate our moral codes (in some sense are *at fault*) according to the degree of their wrongdoing; (6) paid by those who in some actuarial sense are most likely to violate our moral codes; (7) paid from the general coffers of the state or by particular industry groups in accordance with criteria (such as wealth) that may be totally unrelated to accident involvement; or (8) paid by some combination of these methods.[1]

Calabresi suggests that accident law should satisfactorily secure two independent goals. "First [accident law] must be just or fair; second it must reduce the costs of accidents."[2] Thus, whether liability for traffic accident costs ought to be decided on a case-by-case basis in a civil court according to the criterion of fault—as it is in the fault system—depends on whether or not doing so constitutes the most plausible means of *justly* achieving accident cost avoidance. In this section I want to explore briefly some of the ways in which allocating traffic accident costs on a no-fault basis can maximize cost avoidance, and defend the no-fault concept against the charge that it secures cost reduction only at the expense of justice.

Within the goal of cost avoidance, Calabresi includes (1) the reduction in number and severity of accidents, what he calls "primary cost reduction"; (2) the reduction of compensation costs, what he calls "secondary cost reduction"; and (3) the reduction of administrative and legal costs that arise in operating cumbersome judicial machinery and/or in administering an insurance system. This last subgoal of cost avoidance he terms "tertiary cost reduction."

The tertiary costs of the fault system are astronomical. As of 1969, nearly 56¢ of every insurance premium dollar was being devoured by administrative and legal costs! This figure compares unfavorably with the same costs in the Social Security System, Blue Cross, and in most health and accident plans, which are 3¢ per dollar, 7¢ per dollar and 17¢ per dollar respectively.[3] The startling fact is that insurance companies return less than 50 percent of the consumers' premium dollars in the form of liability coverage. A sizeable chunk of the remainder of the consumers' dollar goes into the costly machinery—including lawyers, technicians and law courts—necessary to examine conduct to determine if the criterion of fault has been satisfied. Allocating traffic costs on a no-fault basis seems to guarantee a reduction in insurance premiums if only because it eliminates one of the most costly features of the fault system—the courtroom determination of the fault.

One prevalent argument against no-fault is that it does not promote accident deterrence or primary cost avoidance. Underlying this claim is the conviction that faulty conduct is effectively deterred only by penalizing instances of it and, in the case of traffic accidents, only if the penalty takes the form of the insurer being liable for the costs of his victim's injuries. This claim rests on at least two unwarranted assumptions. First, even if faulty driving were deterred only by penalizing instances of it, it would be a mistake to assume that the penalty of liability for accident costs would be the only adequate inducement to safe driving. When the threat of penalty is employed as a deterrent, there is no evidence to suggest that stiff penal fines and the threat of revocation of license are less adequate on that score. Second, the success of vicarious liability statutes and workmen's compensation provisions in the law suggest that in order to secure accident deterrence we need not penalize those at fault (or likely to be at fault) in causing injuries. In the case of workmen's compensation, employers have shown a remarkable facility for improving safety conditions—and thereby reducing the number of accidents—when, regardless of personal culpability, they have been placed in the position of standing to lose in virtue of increased accident costs.

Instead of spreading the risks of an activity among consumers who use a product or employ a service by, for example, having them contract for liability or health insurance, we could distribute the costs among those persons who manufacture products or offer services. According to this extension of traditional products liability law, we might then let the costs of automobile injuries fall on the shoulders of automobile manufacturers. They would presumably purchase costly liability protection for specific automobile-related injuries and then pass the costs of these premiums on to the consumer, probably by increasing the purchase price of automobiles. In addition to being an effective form of secondary cost avoidance—by spreading the costs among all persons who purchase cars—eliminating hidden accident costs may enhance accident deterrence both among consumers and producers by encouraging the production and purchase of safer cars, insofar as their safety is reflected in their lower initial price. A sufficient increase in the cost of automobiles in virtue of the additional "accident costs" would result first in a reduction in the number of cars purchased on a yearly basis. Fewer automobiles will eventually mean fewer accidents.

In addition, as the cost of the cars increases, there will be a group of consumers on the financial borderline of being able to maintain their automobiles. Members of this group, each of whom stands to lose by faulty driving the convenience of an automobile, have a personal incentive to drive safely and to encourage safe driving generally. Finally, car manufacturers who, in virtue of increased costs, stand to lose the consumer of moderate income are encouraged to produce a safer product. Nothing in this approach requires that traffic victims establish the fault either of their injurer or of the appropriate car manufacturer, and accident deterrence as well as compensatory cost reduction are therefore promoted without regard to the criterion of fault.

In the fault system, insurance plays the traditional role of protecting policy holders against spcific losses, thereby promoting secondary cost reduction and helping thereby to maintain an acceptable balance between the burdens and benefits of motoring. One persuasive argument in favor of no-fault is that by abandoning fault as a relevant criterion in compensating traffic victims, we will be able to allocate the costs of accidents in even less burdensome and, perhaps, fairer ways.

Calabresi argues that the most plausible procedures for maximizing secondary cost savings involve distributing costs through either *risk-spreading* or *deep-pocket methods*, both of which aim at reducing the relative impact of those losses on individuals. Insurance schemes usually apply the risk-spreading method. That is, within limits determined by the total number of policy holders, liability insurance maximizes the number of persons and, to an extent, the period of time over which costs are spread. Motorists who fall within the same actuarial categories and hold contracts with the same insurance company pay roughly equal premiums for approximately identical coverage. But it does not follow from the fact that such policy holders pay equal monetary shares that the burdens of bearing those costs are allocated equally among them. Therefore, in contrast with risk-spreading, the deep-pocket method allocates costs according to a sliding ratio of assigned shares based on prior capacity to pay. The major theoretical difference between risk-spreading and deep-pocket methods is that, according to the former, losses are presumed to be least burdensome if they are spread thinly while, according to the latter, losses are considered to be least burdensome if they are borne by those most able to bear them.

In the deep-pocket method, the only relevant qualification for status as a risk-bearer is prior capacity to bear one's loss; one's rank among risk-bearers being determined entirely by how great that capacity is. This feature of the deep-pocket method—its allocating costs without regard to other criteria—has led some to criticize it as unjust in that some persons would seem to be required to pay simply because they could afford to. However, all except the most determined of hermits are engaged in or otherwise benefit from the activity of motoring. Thus, no one contributes *simply* because he or she can afford to. Still, provided we can clearly distinguish between direct and indirect benefits and degrees thereof, an allocation of losses strictly on a deep-pocket basis may yet be unfair in that it may violate the principle of justice that requires burdens to be commensurate with benefits. As a general principle for distributing losses, the deep-pocket principle could endorse allocating automobile accident costs through highly graduated tax structures, for example, income taxes. Such an alternative could escape certain charges of being unjust if it were part of a comprehensive plan designed to protect citizens against loss resulting from all accidentally caused injuries. What makes this proposal prima facie plausible is the fact that while few individuals would be willing to pay the accident costs of activities they neither engage in nor otherwise benefit from, nearly everyone would be anxious to protect himself against accident losses of one sort or another.

But at what cost? It is unlikely that such a plan could work its way into the hearts of an already heavily taxes citizenry—especially one with free market pretensions. It is even less likely that such a plan would be embraced by powerful insurance and trial lawyer lobbies. Moreover, this form of no-fault coverage, which has obvious compensatory cost-avoidance virtues, could prove counterproductive with respect to the goal of accident deterrence. That is because this particular no-fault scheme "hides" the accident costs of some specific activities by offering blanket coverage for all of them through tax dollars. Shielding these costs eliminates one important opportunity for the consumer to associate an activity with its accident costs, and consequently with its risks.

More modest no-fault plans would maintain private insurance and depend on penal fines and the driver's natural concern for his own well-being to promote accident deterrence. These proposals usually obtain secondary cost avoidance by applying risk-spreading methods. We could alter these traditional approaches to no-fault to incorporate, on a small scale, certain virtues of the deep-pocket principle by having premiums within respective actuarial categories reflect prior capacity to pay. Alternatively we could have everyone pay something through their income tax toward the cost of accidents, and have the remainder of the costs distributed either through the costs of automobiles or the purchase of insurance policies. Thus, those who directly benefit from motoring—those who drive—would pay more than those who benefit indirectly.

Nothing in the previous argument suggests the need to introduce the criterion of fault into accident law as a means of securing any of its economic or utilitarian goals. That should be surprising neither to legal theorists nor to consumers who have borne the high costs of the fault system for too long. But the criterion of fault is not present in accident law to enhance cost reduction. Presumably, consulting it enables us to identify those individuals upon whom the cost of accidents ought to fall if *justice* is to be served, not if money is to be saved. Deciding liability on the basis of fault is, on the accepted view, inextricably linked to justice, which, in turn, is seen as requiring that burdens due to individual fault be allocated according to the criterion of fault, and that those burdens be commensurate with the degree of fault. This conception of justice is seen as supporting a fault system and prohibiting contracting for no-fault liability coverage.

Interestingly enough, if justice were to require that fault-related burdens be distributed exclusively according to the criterion of fault, it would be very hard to imagine how such demands could be met by the fault system, at least as we know it. In the first place, all traditional forms of insurance would be ruled out since they would allocate burdens in part among individuals whose records have been (and may remain) spotless, as well as among past and present wrongdoers. The burdens of the faultless would not reflect their desert and would be objectionable on those grounds. In the absence of insurance, the costs of particular accidents would fall either on individual victims or injurers, with victims being ruled out on the same grounds as the faultless: no fault, no penalty. But if the costs of accidents were to fall entirely on individual wrongdoers, they would often prove disproportionate to the wrongdoing involved—slight errors can result in costly accidents—and this would be objectionable on the grounds that the burden would not reflect the degree of fault.

We might attempt to obviate these difficulties first by altering the fault system, and in the event that fails, by compromising the principle. Suppose that instead of allocating costs on an individual-case basis, we were to lump together the costs of all automobile accidents over a specified period of time and then distribute them among particular injurers by assigning relative weights to the different types of wrongdoing exhibited in the conduct of each. Then each injurer would no longer be responsible for the costs of the damages he caused, but would instead be liable for some portion of the whole: that portion reflecting the degree of shortcoming in his or her conduct. One major flaw in this proposal is that it gives each fault a *market* rather than a moral value, and may therefore fail to satisfy the principle in question. It would, after all, hardly carry the day for the forces of justice if legislators attached a lesser sanction to parking violations than to homicide, but decided on decapitation for the latter, and mere amputation for the former.

Alternatively, we might reintroduce traditional forms of insurance and justify this maneuver as required by the need to resolve a conflict between competing moral principles: one requiring the distribution of costs owing to error to reflect fault, and the other supporting the right to contract voluntarily to protect oneself against losses resulting from future untoward events. Any such form of contract requires that some of the costs of untoward events be absorbed by the faultless, somewhat analogously to the way in which medical expenses covered by health insurance policies are paid for in part through premiums of individuals who themselves may never invoke their policies. Introducing insurance of any sort into accident law—fault or no-fault—necessarily compromises this principle of liability for fault. Compromised but not abandoned, it would presumably carry enough weight to require that fault play some role in the allocation of accidents costs. This role would perhaps be satisfied by having the costs of particular accidents fall initially on those at fault, as they do in the fault system.

The argument does not yet establish the relevance of this principle of liability for fault to the goals of accident law. And surely it is on the claim of relevance that the argument stands or falls. For if there is nothing to be gained in terms of the aims of accident law—justice and/or cost avoidance—by satisfying the requirement that degree of liability reflect fault, the fact that the fault system with significant alterations meets these demands could not count in its favor. Underlying this claim to relevance is the prevalent view among defenders of the fault system that distributing losses in this way— by having them fall initially on individual injurers—secures the goal of justice, a legitimate aim of accident law, by penalizing the wrongdoing of

those at fault. The fault system, by penalizing the wrongful conduct, is therefore required by principles of retributive justice. On related grounds, prohibitions against no-fault are supported by principles of compensatory justice, which are said to require that recompense for losses must originate with those at fault. I want to consider both of these arguments in turn.

According to the standard conception of retributive justice, wrongdoing deserves its comeuppance: a measure of pain, suffering, or deprivation should be exacted from wrongdoers, and the deprivation should reflect the nature and magnitude of the wrongdoing. In its most prevalent and, I believe, least acceptable form the retributivist principle is a moral position in a very strong sense that in order for penalization to be deserved, the defective conduct must be morally defective, and the author of it morally at fault. Thus legal fault, insofar as it is based on the moral fault of the actor, ought to be penalized.

One of the most prevalent defenses of a fault system rests on the claim that this principle of retributive justice requires it. The argument usually takes the following form. If an actor's defective conduct is a substantial contributory factor in bringing about harm, we impute the harm to him as his fault. He has, in the legal jargon, satisfied the fault requirement. The fault system, by making those at fault in causing accidents liable for their costs, guarantees that culpable motoring gets its comeuppance and is therefore required by the retributivist principle.

This argument in favor of the fault system does not purport to establish that every time an actor is at fault he is morally blameworthy. It establishes only that he is blameworthy in some sense of the term. And although some faulty driving is morally defective, for example, drunken, reckless driving, most driving faults are not moral shortcomings. If the retributivist principle were to support penalties only for moral wrongdoing, the fault system would justify too much. However, we need not interpret the retributivist principle this narrowly. Perhaps we should understand it as endorsing penalties for nonmoral as well as for moral shortcomings. H. L. A. Hart, for one, has argued persuasively that it is permissible morally to penalize wrongdoing that is an actor's fault—to his genuine discredit—whether or not the flaw in his conduct is a moral one.[4] If Hart is correct, then there exists a moral license to impose penalties on drivers who fail to satisfy the legal standard of due care, provided that failure can be charged against their personal records, that is, is something for which they are to blame. Hart's position does not amount to an endorsement of retributivism since he claims only that genuine wrongdoing may be penalized, while retributivists claim that such penalties are not merely permissible but a matter of right action.

Being at fault, morally or otherwise, has two essential ingredients. One element in fault judgments relates to the character of the act and its relationship to the appropriate standard of conduct, while the other relates to the actor's "state of mind." Most fault judgments are true just in case both the act-regarding and the actor-regarding requirements are satisfied. The essence of these requirements is perhaps best illustrated by the defenses alleged wrongdoers offer to defeat accusations of fault—that is, justifications and excuses. When an actor has a justification for what he has done, he denies that the act, all things considered, fails to satisfy the appropriate norm, or he argues that his conduct is an exception to the rule usually governing that type of conduct, or that it is an exception to the rule that such conduct is wrong. Should he have an excuse for what he has done, he would not be denying that his conduct was substandard, only that it was his fault. The "subjective" or mental element necessary to charge the act against his record, he thus argues, is missing.

If an actor has an excuse for his actions, he is not at fault in the sense appropriate to justify imposing penalties against him on the grounds of retributive justice. That is because retributivism licenses penalties for *genuine* wrongdoing only. Insofar as excuses evidence the nonvoluntary character of the conduct, failure to measure up under excusing conditions cannot be considered something for which the actor is to blame. Though the retributivist principle would not endorse penalties for what would ordinarily count as excusable departures from the standard of due care, the system of awarding liability for accident costs on the basis

of fault often penalizes those who in Hart's words "could not help doing what they did."

This feature of the fault system is well known among lawyers and has led some legal theorists to question if the courts should apply subjective (internal) or objective (external) standards of fault to determine liability in accident law. In other words, should the law require no more of each member of the community than he is capable of (the subjective test of fault) or should it require each to live up to a standard that may exceed the capacities of some (the objective test). The most famous and perhaps still the most compelling defense of the objective test is articulated in Oliver Wendell Holmes:

> If, for instance, a man is borne hasty and awkward, is always having accidents and hurting himself or his neighbors, no doubt his congenital defects will be allowed for in the courts of Heaven, but his slips are no less troublesome to his neighbors than if they sprang from guilty neglect. His neighbors, accordingly require him, at his proper peril, to come up to their standard, and the courts which they establish decline to take his personal equation into account.[5]

Ascriptions of fault that are verified by applying objective criteria of conduct are not defeasible by excuses. That is their distinctive feature. Thus, if an injurer genuinely could do no better than he did—if, in other words, his conduct was, in a suitably narrow sense, nonvoluntary—this would *not* suffice to free him from the burdens of recompense under the present system of accident law, though the nonvoluntary character of his actions would normally constitute excusing conditions and free him from blame.

We could of course amend the fault system to obviate this sort of difficulty by requiring that it apply only subjective criteria of fault. In this way, the fault system would penalize only those whose failure to exercise due care is to their personal discredit. But even if we recommend the application of the subjective test, the fault system would fail to satisfy the retributivist principle. That is because, in the fault system, only accident-causing wrongful driving receives its due—where the penalty is liability for accident costs—leaving unpenalized the class of dangerous and unnecessarily risky, but not harm-causing, wrongful motoring. From the retributivist point of view, this is unacceptable, since suitably culpable conduct without harmful causal upshots falls within its ambit. Thus, in the criminal law, so-called wrongful attempts are punishable, for example, attempted murder, attempted rape, and so on. From the retributivist point of view, the punishment of wrongful attempts is mandatory. The rough civil law analogue of criminal attempts is conduct that is "at fault," that is unreasonably risky, harm-threatening, or dangerous. If securing the goal of retributive justice were the only goal of accident law, and if the penalty of liability for accident costs were the only sort of penalty befitting wrongful conduct of this sort, securing that goal would require that liability be spread among those at fault, not merely among those at fault in causing injuries. But even in this system driving faults are rendered market, not moral, values.

Moreover, the retributivist principle requires only that a fitting penalty be administered to wrongdoers. Nothing in the principle specifies that the penalty be liability for accident costs. Indeed, we have seen some of the difficulties inherent in trying to "fit" the penalty of civil liability to driving faults. An accident law in which liability for accident costs is the penalty for wrongful driving conflates two distinguishable issues: those of retribution and recompense. The fault system may be characterized by the fact that it joins these two issues, since in that system, the retribution for wrongdoing is recompense for injuries that are one's fault. The distinguishing feature of no-fault is the separation of these two concerns. By referring to accident law as a no-fault system, we do not mean to imply that there exist no purposes for which conduct should be examined for fault. Indeed, the criterion of fault is perfectly relevant to contriving penal fines or other penalties themselves suggested by the retributivist principle: penalties more fitting than civil liability in the sense that they are not subject to market fluctuations. All we mean to imply by the label "no-fault" is that the criterion of fault is irrelevant to the issue of recompense. That goal is to be satisfied by ensuring that the traffic victim receives the compensation to which he is entitled. Our notions of retributive justice therefore do not require

that compensation, in order to be just, originate with those at fault. Whether or not our notions of corrective justice do is what I now want to consider.

There are a number of statements or ways of characterizing the requirements of corrective justice. I want to begin with the following conception of corrective justice. On this view, corrective or rectificatory justice is concerned with wrongful gains and losses. Rectification is, on this view, a matter of justice when it is necessary to protect a distribution of holdings (or entitlements) from distortions that arise from unjust enrichments or wrongful losses. The principle of corrective justice requires the annulment of both wrongful gains and losses.

In order to invoke the principle of corrective justice to support eliminating or rectifying a distortion in a distribution of holdings or entitlements, the distribution need not itself be just. Corrective justice is a matter of justice on this view *not* because it promotes justice in the distribution of holdings, but rather because it remedies unjust departures from the prevailing distribution of holdings. However, following the requirements of corrective justice is necessary to maintain a just distribution of holdings. Therefore, any theory of distributive justice must make provisions for a theory of corrective justice. Corrective justice is an independent principle of justice precisely because it may be legitimately invoked to protect or reinstate distributions of holdings that would themselves fail the test of distributive justice.

Under the principle of corrective or compensatory justice, the victim of another's fault may have a right to recompense. The principle of corrective justice does not establish the right of victims to recompense for "faultlessly" caused injuries, and though an insurance scheme that protected policy holders against errorless as well as faultily caused injuries might be preferable, the protection such a scheme could offer would extend beyond what injured parties could claim as their *right*.

If compensation for wrongfully inflicted harms is one's right, against whom does the right bearer hold it? Upon whom does the corresponding obligation fall? In an insurance scheme, the injured party's right to recompense may be against his insurance company or against the insurance company of his injurer. That depends on whether the insurance coverage is a "first" or "third" party plan; that is, whether individuals insure themselves against personal loss owing to the conduct of others (or themselves)—first party—or against liability for the injuries they may cause others—third party. According to the most extensive form of no-fault coverage, the victim's right to recompense is a valid claim he holds against his own insurance company: that right being derived from contract. The underlying moral issue is whether or not such contracts and their corresponding rights and obligations are consistent with principles of corrective justice. Is compensation for accidental harms to be analyzed broadly to require only that victims receive the compensation to which they are entitled, or narrowly to require that recompense for victims must originate with respective injurers.

Suppose now that two individuals, X and Y, were involved in an accident that is Y's fault. X's right to compensation creates a corresponding duty to provide recompense that seems to fall on Y, his injurer. It seems, moreover, that justice would require that Y compensate X. If this is so, it suggests the general conclusion that, in order to be just, compensation must come from those at fault.

Why is it that justice requires that Y bear X's costs? Perhaps, if Y does not compensate X, X will go without compensation. One consequence of this would be that X's conduct would be penalized. Certainly that would be unjust. But that justice is avoidable by guaranteeing that X does not have to bear his own costs. That goal is accomplished when anyone other than X, including, but not necessarily, Y shoulders them. Perhaps by Y not bearing X's costs, Y's wrongdoing would go unpenalized. That would presumably constitute a retributive injustice. But the retributive principle requires only that Y's wrongdoing be penalized, and that goal is accomplished not only when Y is made to compensate X, but also when Y is penalized in some other way, for example, through penal channels.

Both compensation and punishment are concerned with wrongdoing—wrongful gain, advantage, or benefit. But where punishment involves wrongdoers incurring some evil—usually the loss of assorted legal rights—for their wrongfully obtained (or sought) gains or advantages, compensation aims at annulling, rectifying, or eliminating these undeserved or otherwise unjustifiable gains. Where punishment is concerned with victims only secondarily, the overriding concern of compensation is the nullification of the victim's losses; the reordering of his affairs to make him whole again. James Nickel has simply but insightfully captured this feature of compensatory justice as the elimination of unjustifiable *gains and losses* owing to human action—what he aptly terms "distortions."[6]

If compensation involves the elimination of distortions, surely we must acknowledge that not every means of securing that goal would be endorsed by principles of compensatory justice. However seductive the myth of Robin Hood may be, there is little evidence to suggest that such a method for nullifying unwarranted gains and losses would satisfy the demands of compensatory justice. What further distinguishes compensatory from other principles of justice is that, in order to secure the elimination of distortions, it supports a system of correlative rights and duties between respective victims and wrongdoers. In the typical case of compensation, finding for the plaintiff amounts to a recognition of his or her (legal) rights to recompense; a right that imposes a correlative duty upon the defendant to provide compensation. In the typical instance of punishment, a verdict of guilty confers upon the state a right to impose some penalty against the defendant. But this right is a moral license, and unlike a claim right, it does not give rise to a correlative duty; in this case, an obligation on the defendant to be punished or to allow himself to be punished.

But if a distinguishing feature of compensatory justice is this structure of correlative rights and duties, wouldn't principles of compensatory justice therefore prohibit contractual relations that supersede this structure by imposing duties of recompense on the *victim's* insurance company—contractual relations that require the victim's insurance company to discharge what are, in fact, the duties of wrongdoers? Compensation is a kind of repayment, and it is therefore with the category of obligations to repay that we are concerned. In the case of obligations to repay debts or loans, justice does not as a rule require that the repayment originate with the party obligated to repay. Thus, when someone borrows money from the local bank, few protests of injustice are heard above clicking safe locks, provided the money is returned in sufficient quantities and at appropriate intervals, regardless of exactly who is forwarding the payments on whose behalf. My obligation to repay a debt of, say, $100 to you is discharged when my wealthy patron approaches you with that sum, and you accept it as repayment, even if I know nothing of this transaction. Of course some obligations to repay may be described so determinately that they could not justly be discharged by another. Here the requirement that the repayment originate with the obligated party is built into the description of the obligation, and the fact that it cannot justly be discharged by another is a function of the determinacy of the obligation, not of justice.

Though it is a misleading way of talking, we sometimes describe punishment as a kind of repayment. We talk, for example, about criminals as owing "debts to society," which are presumably repaid through incarceration. If there is any merit in viewing punishment as a debt of repayment, then surely it is the sort of debt that in order to be just must be repaid by the "obligated" party, that is, the wrongdoer. Now, is the obligation to provide compensation for accidental torts something that can justly be discharged by intervening parties—in this case, insurance companies—and therefore like obligations to repay debts in this respect, or is it something that can be discharged justly only by wrongdoers—like the purported obligation criminals have to pay back society? If compensation is, in this regard, like punishment, in order to be just, recompense for accidental torts must therefore originate with those at fault.

Unlike the obligation to repay debts, the obligation to compensate traffic victims is not derived from contractual relation or promise. It is derived from wrongdoing. But wrongdoing plays significantly different roles in punishment and in compensation. In compensation, unlike punishment, wrongdoing is not viewed as something in itself worthy of penalty. Instead compensation is concerned with wrongdoing only insofar as it either involves wrongful gain or benefit at another's expense, or it is evidence of the unjustifiable character of the victim's loss. In the absence of wrongful gain, proof of wrongdoing supports the victim's assertion that his losses have been wrongfully ab-

sorbed, and therefore justifies his demanding compensation as a matter of right, rather than requesting it as a matter of benevolence, utility, or welfare.

The distinguishing feature of automobile accidents and of accidental torts generally is that the injurer does not, as a rule, gain from his wrong, nor is it plausible to interpret his conduct as directed at securing some temporary or long-term advantage. It is, after all, the nature of the beast; accidents are unintentional. One does not plan an accident. On the contrary, intentional torts such as fraud are undertaken to secure wrongful advantage at another's expense. A no-fault allocation of losses owing to intentional torts involving gain would not nullify the wrongdoer's gain and would be objectionable on those grounds. Nor would punishing him under the criminal law eliminate the gain, since the penal statute requires only that he suffer some evil for his wrong; nothing in it requires that he forfeit his gain. But in the case of accidental torts there is, in general, no gain on the wrongdoer's behalf that needs to be eliminated. That his conduct is wrongful supports the right of the victim to recompense, nothing more. Of course, his conduct may exhibit sufficient fault to merit penalty, but that is a concern of retributive justice and may best be dealt with by penal fine. Thus, it is my contention that principles of compensatory justice would not support a no-fault allocation of losses owing to certain intentional torts,—i.e., because of the element of wrongful gain—but would not prohibit no-fault accident law precisely because of the absence of wrongful gain.

This conclusion should be especially comforting to legal reformers such as Guido Calabresi and Jeffrey O'Connell, both of whom have recently urged the separation of accident law from the main body of tort law. Such proposals suggest that accident law govern recompense for harms owing primarily to negligence and defective products, and that they do so on a no-fault, no-defect basis. They are usually recommended to us by dint of their cost-saving features. The arguments I have been considering in this section on compensatory justice suggest still further support for their position. It is hoped that support from these quarters will surprise only those who are wedded to the view that justice and utility cannot be achieved except at one another's expense.

Endnotes

[1] Guido Calabresi, *The Costs of Accidents* (New Haven: Yale University Press 1970), 22.

[2] *Ibid.*, 24.

[3] These figures come from Jeffrey O'Connell, "Expanding No-Fault Beyond Auto Insurance: Some Proposals," *University of Virginia Law Review* 59 (May 1973):749–56.

[4] Cf. H. L. A. Hart, "Legal Responsibility and Excuses," in *Punishment and Responsibility* (New York: Oxford, 1968), 39.

[5] O. W. Holmes, *The Common Law* (Boston: Little, Brown and Company, 1963), 86.

[6] James Nickel, "What Is Compensatory Justice?" *William and Mary Law Review,* Vol. 3.

92. Individualized Justice, Mass Torts, and "Settlement Class Actions": An Introduction

Roger C. Cramton

The tension between individual justice (party autonomy in an adversary system) and collective justice (aggregated handling of legal claims) is the basic theme of [this essay]. Nowhere is this tension more evident than in recent efforts to use "settlement class actions" as a means for large-scale resolution of personal injury or property damage claims arising out of exposure to defective products or toxic substances. Important and novel issues of tort law, civil procedure, constitutional due process, and lawyer behavior are presented by settlements resolving the tort claims of future as well as current claimants. Pending cases provide a number of examples: (1) a class containing millions of persons occupationally exposed to asbestos, (2) a class of more than one million women who received breast implants, (3) a class containing all of the owners of Ford Bronco all-terrain vehicles, (4) a class of owners of GM pickups with saddlebag gas tanks, and (5) a class of current and future owners of homes that have a polybutylene plumbing system, an allegedly defective plumbing material that has been installed in three million mobile homes and an estimated four to five million site-built homes.

This use of the class action device, like most other new developments, has both long- and short-term antecedents. Yet, the recent class actions mentioned above, which contain a novel combination of features, illustrate something quite new in degree and kind. For example, the cases were either brought or certified for settlement purposes rather than to be tried; the plaintiff class includes future victims, many of whom have yet to suffer a legally cognizable injury; approved settlements will bind absent class members, many of whom may not have had an effective opportunity to opt out of the class; the settlements affect claims nationwide and may have the effect of a federal decree eliminating claims governed by state law or a state decree eliminating claims governed by federal law; and in some of the cases, the plaintiffs' lawyers representing the class entered into side settlements with the defendants, giving their current clients different and more favorable relief than the class settlement provides to future claimants. A class action settlement with these features would have been unthinkable to lawyers of a decade or so ago. . . .

Recent class action settlements such as those previously mentioned raise several questions.

Some of the most central are:

(1) Is the individual justice provided by tort law in the courts so delayed, erratic, and inefficient that it should be replaced by schemes of collective justice molded by self-interested parties and approved by a single federal district judge? If administrative schemes are to be substituted for the tort system, should this be accomplished by legislation rather than by private settlements approved by a single judge?

(2) Does a federal district court have authority to enter a decree that eliminates or displaces the personal injury rights, otherwise governed by state law, of individuals who have been exposed to a product or substance but have not yet suffered a legal injury (future claimants whose claims have not yet matured when notice is given of the opportunity to opt out)?

(3) How can adequate notice of opportunity to opt out of a class action, required by due process, be provided to "exposure only" persons who do not and cannot know that they will suffer an injury in the future? Is "adequate representation" provided when a lawyer negotiates cash settlements for the lawyer's current clients simultaneously with a class action settlement providing different terms for future claimants? Do the virtues of private settlement and alternative dispute resolution justify departures from general principles of legal ethics?

The American common-law system emphasizes party control of litigation rather than judicial prosecution and investigation. The adversary system presupposes opposing parties who exercise a wide range of choice on whether, where, and when a lawsuit is filed; what claims and defenses are asserted; what resources should be devoted to the litigation; and whether the case is settled or tried. The common-law judge is envisioned as a neutral, relatively passive arbiter of conflicting private interests who rules on questions of law and supervises the conduct of the litigation. Party initiative and the underlying principle of individual autonomy are supported by the constitutional right of trial by jury, which presupposes a detailed evaluation of particularistic facts bearing on the plaintiffs claim and the defendant's defenses.

The American tort system reflects the same values by requiring proof of fault, causation, and harm before one person's loss is shifted to someone else. The injured plaintiff must establish by a preponderance of the evidence that the defendant's wrongful acts caused the plaintiff's harm. Although tort law serves mixed goals—compensating accident victims, deterring conduct that is wrongful or involves unreasonable risks to the health or safety of others, and punishing wrongdoers —the central notion until quite recently has been one of corrective justice—repairing, to the extent possible with a money award, the harm that one individual's wrongful act has caused another. Proof that the defendant's wrongful act has caused the plaintiff's injury inevitably requires a particularistic assessment of the plaintiff's and defendant's conduct, a causal relationship between their actions and the claimed harm, and a valuation of the plaintiff's resulting injury.

Two developments in the twentieth century threaten to displace the traditional model of individual rights and party autonomy. First, many judges participate more actively in the management, conduct, and settlement of litigation. Second, pressures flow from the volume, complexity, cost, and interrelatedness of what are referred to here as "mass exposure torts."

Since the development of negligence doctrine in the nineteenth century, the paradigm case of the traditional tort is an accident in which an actor's vehicle—whether stage coach, railroad, or automobile—has injured a stranger. The individualized approach to adjudicating such disputes seemed a natural, if not inevitable, given the premises of American law and the constitutional right to a jury trial. In today's world, however, America's market economy encourages mass distribution of products of new, and perhaps untested, technology. Thousands of strangers may be injured by the dissemination and use of a single product. Mass exposure to these products or substances creates situations in which a large number of people believe, or are led to believe, that the defendant's product caused their injuries. The resulting volume of litigation poses problems that threaten both the tort system's reliance on individual responsibility and the procedural system's reliance on party initiative and control.

Mass exposure torts threaten these aspects of the tort system for several reasons. First, proving or determining whether exposure to the product or substance caused the claimed injury is difficult. Frequently, the exposure that leads to claims of injury occurs over a substantial period of time, and the injury itself may have a long latency period. Often there is scientific uncertainty as to whether the exposure caused the alleged harm or whether the condition was the result of the individual's conduct (smoking, for example) or the presence obackground substances in the natural environment. Frequently, expert witnesses will be able to testify about causation only in terms of statistical probabilities based on scattered or inconclusive epidemiological studies.

Second, in many cases it is difficult or impossible to determine which of multiple actors caused the claimed injury. If the harm has a long latency period, evidence of whose product or substance caused the harm may be unavailable fifteen or thirty years after the product's distribution and consumption. A related problem arises in cases involving long-term occupational exposure, such as in the asbestos field. The worker may have been exposed to several products, each with somewhat different injury characteristics, manufactured by a number of companies over a lengthy period of time. In such a case, it may be difficult for the plaintiff to establish that the named defendant or defendants were responsible for the plaintiff's harm.

Third, it is doubtful whether individualized justice can be provided when thousands or even millions of claims flow from mass exposure to a product or substance. For example, millions of Americans were exposed occupationally to asbestos products from the 1930s through the 1970s, before regulatory and safety controls reduced the future danger. Many of those exposed have died or suffered injuries, and the exposure will claim further victims well into the twenty-first century. As another example, over one million women had silicone gel breast implants between 1979 and 1994. As of yet, only a small portion of this group has suffered injury, and the causal relationship between implants and some injuries remains uncertain.

The sheer number of claims in cases like these creates troublesome problems of judicial delay, repetitive trials, high transaction costs and an inevitable interrelationship among claimants. As indicated earlier, claimants may suffer from a "disease" rather than the type of immediate physical injury associated with a traumatic accident. Causation may be established only by reliance on probabilistic methods. Publicity given to the dangers of use or exposure to the product gives rise to new claims, such as the emotional harm flowing from fear of contracting the disease in the future, and increases the percentage of victims who assert claims. Evidence that defendants knew of the products' risks but failed to warn those exposed to them supports punitive damage claims that threaten producers with large, unpredictable, and recurring judgments based on the same conduct.

Individual trials that replicate evidence of exposure, causation, and injury in case after case burden the courts, create judicial delay, and carry high transaction costs. In conventional tort litigation, approximately sixty percent of amounts paid go to accident victims. A study of asbestos litigation estimates that plaintiffs only receive about forty percent of each litigation dollar. Critics assert that lawyers, insurance companies, and litigation expenses consume too much of the amounts available to compensate victims. If fault and causation requirements were eliminated entirely from complex, difficult cases of mass tort exposure, as was done in social security disability or workers' compensation cases, transaction costs could be greatly reduced.

The model of individualized justice posits that each claimant should make all relevant decisions with respect to her claim. The existence of a host of other similar claims inevitably affects these decisions because a claimant will "now have to take into account the existence of the other claimants, the extent to which the other claims may deplete the assets of the tortfeasor, and the possible savings which may be achieved by sharing the costs of litigation." If payment of compensatory and punitive damages to early claimants results in a producer's insolvency, future claimants will receive little or nothing. Some courts assume that maintaining the solvency of corporate actors is a desirable objective wholly apart from its effect on future claimants.

The high costs of proving causation in the individual case may be reduced by a collective action that spreads the costs of discovery, expert testimony, and litigation among many claimants. Thus, collective justice appeals to all parties to some degree and to courts and judges almost without exception. Plaintiffs avoid the "free rider" problem by sharing the costs of discovering evidence and proving causation and fault. Defendants benefit from reduced transaction costs and fixed liability, displacing the uncertainty of unpredictable future liability. Courts similarly benefit from reduced caseloads because thousands of individual cases are combined into one large class action, and claims are processed outside the courts.

These characteristics of mass exposure torts produce pressures that result in efforts at aggregative or collective justice. The class action is a procedural technique in which representatives of a group (class representatives) may assert against the defendants both their own claims and similar claims of other persons who share a common interest. [The law] requires that class actions meet four prerequisites, generally referred to as numerosity, commonality, typicality, and adequacy. First, the class must be so numerous that joinder of all members is impracticable. Second, questions of law or fact must be common to the class. Third, the claims or defenses of the representative parties must be typical of the class as a whole. Finally, the representative plaintiffs and their lawyers must "fairly and adequately protect the interests of the class." . . .

Although the legislative history of the [rules creating class actions] states that the class action device is "ordinarily not appropriate" for "[a] 'mass accident' resulting in injuries to numerous persons, federal courts in recent years have authorized class actions in a number of single-incident mass accident cases and a smaller number of mass exposure tort cases. The Agent Orange class action, involving the claimed injuries of Vietnam veterans from battlefield exposure to dioxin manufactured by the defendants, was the first such case. Bankruptcy situations involving a major asbestos defendant and the manufacturer of the Dalkon Shield intrauterine device had class action aspects.

Collective justice . . . has its distinctive vices as well as its virtues. To the extent that compensating victims becomes a major goal, considerations of fault, responsibility, and deterrence are muted or eliminated. Collective action may solve the "free rider" problem of individualized justice—some litigants benefitting from, but not contributing to, the expensive efforts of another litigant in discovering causation and fault. But collective action creates the new and serious problem of the "kidnapped rider," an individual deprived of any freedom of action by being drawn involuntarily into collective litigation. Collective action may also deprive individuals of meaningful control over their own legal claims, pushing them involuntarily into compensation grids and administrative claims-handling processes to whose ministrations they have not consented.

Collective justice also departs from the normal lawyer-client relationship in which the client makes decisions concerning objectives and the client's lawyer makes tactical and procedural decisions. The plaintiff's lawyer in traditional tort litigation is probably more in charge of the case than traditional theory would suggest. But an individual plaintiff represented by a lawyer retained on a contingent-fee basis may discharge the lawyer at will and may decide whether or not to accept a settlement offer. In most class actions, especially those involving large classes of absent persons whose claims are of limited worth or future creation, the lawyers representing the class ("class counsel") are clearly in charge. Class counsel typically pick the class representatives, frame the issues, push or abandon particular claims, and make settlement decisions. Class action law even permits class counsel to submit a settlement to the court that some or all of the class representatives oppose. Class action lawyers, even more than government lawyers who represent an amorphous "public," are their own clients in the sense that their fiduciary responsibilities to class members are what they determine them to be in the absence of court supervision and scrutiny.

During the last year or two, a spate of mass exposure class actions have raised novel and interesting questions. The major current cases [include] two class action settlements in the asbestos field; the settlement of the silicone gel breast implants litigation; the *Ford Bronco II* property damage case; the similar litigation involving General Motors pickup trucks; and the polybutylene plumbing case in a Texas state court. In each of these cases, defendants facing mass tort claims have combined with class action plaintiffs' lawyers in efforts to settle the claims of current and future claimants. Some of these proposed settlements have been approved by district courts as fair and reasonable, but have not been reviewed by appellate courts. The proposed settlements have been rejected in the two motor vehicle cases. The breast implants case and other class action filings are pending before trial courts. Appellate review has occurred in only one case. These legal innovations will be tested over the next few years until authoritative decisions, new procedural rules, or legislative solutions replace conflicting arguments with stable law—innovations which may be a long time coming.

Study Questions

1. On what legal theory did the plaintiffs in *Hammontree* seek damages from the epileptic driver? Why did the court refuse to adopt that theory?

2. Why should it make a difference to the outcome of the *Hammontree* case that the driver knew he was susceptible to seizures? Why shouldn't it simply be enough that he was the cause of the injury?

3. According to Dobbs, how does the purpose of tort law differ from the purpose of criminal law?

4. Dobbs contends that tort law emphasizes accountability. What does he mean by this? Do the alternatives to tort that Dobbs reviews also serve to further accountability?

5. According to Coleman, in what ways will a no-fault system for auto-accident loss promote "primary cost avoidance"?

6. What is the distinction between the "deep-pockets" and "risk-spreading" methods of reducing accident costs, as explained by Coleman?

7. Gwendolyn Robbins suffered a severe hip injury when the car in which she was riding veered off the road after the driver fell asleep at the wheel. The driver died. Robbins sued to recover from the insurance company of the deceased driver. The defendant insurer argued that Robbins should be denied a large part of

her recovery due to her failure to "mitigate damages," that is, to use reasonable efforts to minimize the injuries sustained. Evidence revealed that at the time of the accident, Robbins had refused surgical intervention that in all likelihood would have returned her to a near normal life. Robbins, a devout Jehovah's Witness, insisted that she was obliged by religious teaching to refuse the surgery and the blood transfusions it would have entailed. On appeal, Robbins lost. The trial and appellate courts disagreed as to how the "reasonableness" of Robbins' conduct was to be measured. The trial court instructed the jury to consider whether "it was reasonable for her [Robbins] given her beliefs" to act as she did. The appellate court disagreed, arguing that the proper standard for the jury in such a case is "whether the plaintiff acted as a reasonably prudent person, under all the circumstances confronting her." (See *Williams v. Bright*, 658 N.Y.S2d 910 [1997].) How would you decide this issue?

8. According to Cramton, what are the aspects of mass exposure torts that threaten to undermine what he calls the "traditional" model of product-related tort lawsuits?

9. Consumer advocates have long argued that cigarettes and other tobacco products are dangerous and that the costs associated with tobacco use should be borne by the tobacco industry. Through the late 1980s, tobacco manufacturers argued in court that smoking injuries were the result of "contributory negligence," in effect, the consumer's own fault: if consumers take up smoking despite the obvious and mandated warning, they "assume the risk" of any resulting injury. Users' own personal freedom of choice, not the product, was the cause of injuries sustained. Recent legal actions against cigarette makers have directly attacked the industry's "freedom of choice" defense. These lawsuits do not focus on the alleged addictive qualities of tobacco's central ingredient: nicotine. Plaintiffs in the massive class action case *Castano v. American Tobacco* (95-30725), for example, accused the industry of fraud in connection with a number of allegedly related activities: suppressing

the industry's own research revealing that nicotine is an addictive substance, refusing to fund the development of a "safer" cigarette, attempting to conceal knowledge of the addictiveness of cigarettes, and adjusting or manipulating the level of nicotine in cigarettes to keep smokers "hooked." Although the *Castano* case was not permitted to go forward as a class action suit, arguments quite similar to those advanced in *Castano* are now being used by a number of individual states, each suing the major tobacco manufacturers. Should smoking-related injuries be treated by the law as the plaintiff's own fault? Can a convincing argument be made for holding cigarette manufacturers strictly liable for the harmful results of smoking?

10. By mid-1998 several attempts had been made to achieve a "global settlement" between the tobacco industry and numerous individuals, state, and local governments alleging injuries and financial costs associated with tobacco use. The proposed settlements were criticized as deeply immoral, given that they excluded any current or future overseas victims of smoking-related illnesses, by most estimates the fastest-growing segment of smokers worldwide. Should such settlements be approved? Would such agreements be more fair to consumers injured by tobacco use than permitting them to pursue an individual remedy through a tort suit?

B. *Causation and Liability*

Did the Defendant Cause the Harm?

Two cases involving bizarre events open the readings for this section. In *Lynch v. Fisher,* the defendant ran out of gas while driving his truck down the highway. He negligently parked the truck on the road, failing either to move it completely to the side or to set out flares. He then left the scene in search of a service station. A couple, Mr. and Mrs. Gunter, rounded the corner at excessive speed, were unable to avoid collision with the truck, and were injured, Mrs. Gunter severely. Plaintiff Lynch, traveling in the opposite direction, encountered the accident scene soon after the incident occurred and went to aid the Gunters. Helping Mrs. Gunter out of the car, he then went to the driver's side. When Mr. Gunter got out, Lynch leaned inside to remove the floor pad to use as a cushion. There he found a loaded pistol, which he handed to Mr.

Gunter. As Lynch prepared to tend to the wife, Mr. Gunter, temporarily deranged from shock, mistook Lynch for an assailant and shot him in the foot. Finally, truck driver Fisher returned to find a confusion of wrecked vehicles, an unconscious woman, a trigger-happy madman, and a footsore Good Samaritan, who promptly slapped Fisher with a hefty bill for his injuries.

Helen Palsgraf purchased a ticket to ride the train from Brooklyn to Rockaway Beach. While she waited on the railway platform, various trains to other destinations arrived and departed. As one of these was pulling away, a man carrying a plain-wrapped package emerged from the crowd and sprinted down the platform to catch the train. He appeared to be losing ground when two of the railroad's employees came to his assistance, pulling and pushing him onto the moving train. As they did this, the package—which contained large fireworks—fell to the ground, slid under the tracks, and, ignited by a spark from the train, exploded. Either the explosion of the fireworks or a stampede caused by the explosion (the facts are still unclear, despite what Judge Cardozo says), caused some scales located at the other end of the platform to topple over onto poor Mrs. Palsgraf. She sued the railroad, alleging that it caused her injuries. (Why didn't she sue the man with the package?)

Should the defendants in either of these cases be held liable for the injuries involved? As we have seen, the law of negligence makes the answer to this question turn on another one: Did either of these defendants *cause* the injuries? This is not easy to answer.

Cause in Fact

When is an act or event the cause of some further act or event? Indeed, when is an act or event even relevant to a question of causation? Suppose that you sneeze and that immediately following this, an elderly man in Peoria has a heart attack. Absent any further knowledge of the matter, a reasonable person would surely deny that these two events were in any way causally linked or related. One way both to explain and to support this obvious reaction would be to point out that the injury (heart attack) would certainly have occurred even if you hadn't sneezed. (After all, what possible connection could there be?) This observation strongly suggests that for one act or event, A, to be causally relevant to the occurrence of some other act or event, B, it must at least be the case that A is a *necessary condition* for the occurrence of B; that is, B would not have happened "but for" the occurrence of A. Traditionally, the law refers to a factor that is a necessary condition in this sense as a *cause in fact* or *factual cause*.

Courts have long required that a plaintiff in a tort action establish factual causation as part of his or her *prima facie* tort case. In *Rinaldo v. McGovern*[1], for example, the defendant hit a golf ball but failed to announce his shot by shouting the word "fore." The errant ball traveled some distance to a nearby

road and struck the plaintiff in his car. The court held that the accident could not be traced to the defendant's failure to warn, because no warning could have been heard from a car traveling on the highway. The failure to shout "fore" was thus not a cause in fact of the plaintiff's injuries.

Proving factual causation does raise important concerns. For instance, which party should shoulder the burden of proof with regard to issues of factual causation? Should the law require the plaintiff to prove it more likely than not that, had the defendant not acted, the plaintiff would not have been injured? (How are such "contrary to fact" conditional statements to be proven?) Or should it be enough if the plaintiff can show that the defendant's act substantially increased the likelihood that the plaintiff would be injured? And on a more theoretical level, the idea that one event would not have occurred "but for" another appears to have some serious limitations. Consider this case: Two fires simultaneously converge on your house and burn it to the ground. Either fire would have destroyed the house in the absence of the other. The fires were negligently started by separate defendants. Which defendant caused the destruction of your house? Puzzling as it may seem, the "but for" test exonerates each defendant: each can insist that his actions were *not* necessary for the damage inflicted, because the other guy's fire would have done the job. (This problem is explored further below.)

Of course, such hypothetical scenarios are farfetched; and the requirement of cause in fact makes sense in a good many cases. However, although proving factual causation is a start, reflection shows that by itself, the notion won't get us very far. Consider the tragic circumstances surrounding the death of former president John Kennedy. Many people still believe (whether correctly or incorrectly we may never know) that the pulling of a trigger on a rifle by a man named Lee Harvey Oswald led to Kennedy's death. If they are right, then Oswald's pulling of that trigger at that moment on that day in Dallas was a necessary condition, or *sine qua non* ("that without which there is not") of Kennedy's death. But consider: If the sun hadn't been shining, Oswald would not have been able to see the presidential motorcade; if the motorcade hadn't kept to its prescribed route, it would not have arrived at

---

[1] 78 N.Y.2d 729 (1991).

the point opposite Oswald's location; if the trigger on Oswald's rifle hadn't been working properly . . . if Oswald had not gained entry to the building from which he shot . . . if Kennedy hadn't made it to Dallas or hadn't been elected president . . . if Oswald hadn't been born. . . . The point is obvious enough. If we look into the past of any given event, we will find numerous (perhaps infinitely many?) conditions that, had they not occurred as they did, would have negated the event in question. And for each of these conditions, a seemingly endless number of further events serve as necessary conditions, and on and on. Insofar as each is a necessary condition or *sine qua non* of its successor in the chain, all would seem to have an equal claim to being called a "cause," and we are left with an abundance of causes and of potential defendants.

A related difficulty in understanding legal causation can be seen in a similar way. Presumably, for any given act I perform, that act will continue having consequences indefinitely; that is, it will stand as a necessary condition for the occurrence of an entire series of other acts or events. Take, for example, my act of preparing this book. That act is a necessary condition for your reading it. Suppose, reading this book with such enthusiasm, you stay up too late one night and sleep in too late the next morning, you miss class and the final exam, you flunk the course, your grade point average is ruined, and you can't get into law school as you had planned. Because of this, you don't meet the young attorney who would have been your spouse, and so on. Does it make sense to say that I am responsible for your not having a spouse or a legal career? When do I cease being responsible for what I do, for chains of cause and effect that I initiate?

I start a fire in my fireplace, negligently leaving it unattended. A spark ignites my draperies and spreads from there to the wall; soon the entire house is ablaze. From my home, the fire grows and spreads to neighboring houses and eventually to the entire town. Would it make sense to hold me liable for all of the resulting injury and damage? Plainly, some limitations must be placed on liability for harm that is, loosely speaking, a "consequence" of one's conduct, if for no other reason than that failing to do so would seem to undermine at least one animating purpose of the tort system. If my conduct results in the destruction of an entire town, it would be pointless to hold me liable in tort (although there might be reason for charging me with a crime), because the purpose of fixing liability in tort is to see to it that the victim's losses are compensated. Obviously I can't compensate the entire town. How, then, can these limits be drawn in a philosophically defensible fashion?

Judge Benjamin Cardozo (later to sit on the U.S. Supreme Court), writing for the New York Court of Appeals in *Palsgraf,* puts the central question in the case this way: Was the railroad's act a wrong to *Mrs. Palsgraf* (even if it was a wrong to the man with the package)? Cardozo insists that negligence requires a *relationship* between the parties involved: The negligent act must have been directed to a specific person before that individual may recover from the defendant. To have a "cause of action" (basis for a suit), Mrs. Palsgraf must show that the railroad breached a duty it had to her. Cardozo claims that this did not occur: "The risk reasonably to be perceived defines the duty to be obeyed." Nothing in this case would have suggested to a reasonable person that the parcel wrapped in plain paper posed a risk to the health or safety of the plaintiff. The railroad does, of course, have certain duties to Mrs. Palsgraf, but these all amount to duties not to harm her in *foreseeable* ways. Because she was not harmed in a foreseeable way, none of those duties were violated.

Judge Andrews, dissenting from Cardozo's majority opinion, asserts that negligence is not a relationship between a person and those whom he "might reasonably be expected" to injure but rather to all those whom he "in fact" injures. Andrews rejects the restriction of negligence to the domain of the foreseeable. Such restrictions are vague and ill-defined questions of policy. What we know is that the negligence of the railroad workers was a necessary condition of the resulting harm and that the accident was a direct consequence of the defendant's actions, remote in neither time nor space.

The majority in *Lynch* make much the same argument: Although the injury arose in a bizarre and unforeseeable manner, it remains true that Lynch would not have been injured but for the negligence of Fisher. It is true that Gunter did the shooting, but he cannot be accounted the "cause" of the wounded foot, because he was not acting deliberately or voluntarily at the time. The court, concluding that the "chain [linking Fisher's negligence to Lynch's injuries] is complete and whole—link by link," finds Fisher liable.

Proximate Cause

The question of placing limits upon the consequences of my conduct that, for the purposes of tort law, I can correctly be said to have caused, has been transformed by the law into the requirement that the plaintiff actually prove *two* kinds of cause: *cause in fact* and *proximate cause*. In general, the requirement that the plaintiff show proximate cause marks the concern of the courts to contain the limits of causal liability within reasonable, fair, or just boundaries. D's conduct is the proximate cause of P's injury only if the act and the injury are "closely enough" related to make it fair or just to hold D liable. Over the years, the courts have devised various limiting principles under the heading of proximate cause, appealing, for example, to whether the injury was a foreseeable result of the defendant's conduct or whether another cause "intervened" to bring about the harm. To appreciate fully the philosophical complexities of proximate causation, we have to look briefly at these limiting principles.

As a useful reference point, consider the facts of *Derdiarian v. Felix Contracting Co.*[2] (included in "Cases For Further Reflection" at the end of the chapter). Plaintiff Derdiarian worked as a subcontractor for Felix Contracting. Felix was installing an underground gas main along a highway, and Derdiarian testified that he requested to set up his work area on the side of the pipeline excavation away from oncoming traffic. Felix's foreman instructed Derdiarian to work on the opposite side, only a few feet from the oncoming lane. A passing motorist suffered an epileptic seizure and lost consciousness as he approached the excavation, hitting the plaintiff and throwing him into the air. When he landed, Derdiarian was splattered over his face, head, and body with 400-degree liquid enamel from a kettle struck by the careening auto. Although he reportedly "ignited into a fireball," Derdiarian miraculously survived. Felix disclaimed all responsibility,

arguing that the plaintiff was injured in a freakish accident brought about by the motorist's negligence. (It was determined that the driver was under treatment for seizures but had neglected to take his medication.) Hence, Felix maintained, it had not proximately caused the plaintiff's injuries.

The issue of proximate cause in cases like *Derdiarian* can usefully be analyzed along four dimensions: (1) the type of accident involved, (2) the precise chain of events or causal mechanism, (3) the extent of the damage, and (4) the nature of the victim. A few general principles, corresponding to these dimensions, form the core of the law of proximate cause. However, as we will see, there are unresolved controversies within each area.

Type

A great many courts have held that a plaintiff's injuries are proximately caused by a defendant only if the harm that occurred was of a foreseeable type, meaning that the kind of harm suffered was just the kind of thing the defendant should have been guarding against. According to this rule, the defendant's liability extends only to the foreseeable risks of his or her negligence. In *Derdiarian*, for example, the court concluded that the "foreseeable, normal, and natural result of the risk created by Felix was the injury of a worker by a car," even though the exact sequence of events was unusual. Some courts have read the law differently. In one famous case, the defendant was off-loading planks from a ship's hold. His negligence caused one of the planks to slip and fall into the hold. The plank struck the bottom of the ship, caused a spark, and ignited gas vapors in the hold, resulting in a costly fire. The court acknowledged that a fire is not one of the things one would normally expect a falling plank to cause, but it held the defendant liable anyway, on the grounds that the fire was directly traceable to the defendant's actions.[3]

Causal Mechanism

Related to the foregoing, most courts have said that as long as the harm involved is of a foreseeable

---

[2] 414 N.E.2d 666 (1980).

[3] *In Re Polemis* 3 K.B. 560 (1921).

type, the precise chain of events that lead to it need not be foreseeable by the defendant in order for the defendant to be held liable. In one case, a barge owner had neglected to clean residue from the inside of an oil barge, leaving it full of explosive gas. A storm developed and a lightning bolt struck the ship, exploded the gas, and injured nearby workers. The lightning strike was unforeseeable, but the danger of an explosion should have been apparent to a reasonable person.[4] Similarly, in *Derdiarian,* the sequence of events was bizarre, but the resulting injury was a clearly foreseeable consequence of a vehicle's crashing into the work area. Yet, here again, there is controversy. How, for example, should the court rule if it is discovered that the explosion of gas in the barge was ignited by an arsonist, instead of by lightning? Wouldn't the accident then really have been caused by the arsonist? In some cases, an intervening act has been held to "break the causal chain" linking the defendant's original negligence with the final injuries.

Extent of Damage

Suppose that the plaintiff is struck by the defendant in a fight. The defendant's blow would normally cause a bruise, but the wound would not be serious. However, unknown to the defendant, the plaintiff has a very thin skull, and the glancing blow actually kills him. When the extent of the injury goes beyond what the defendant might have expected, courts frequently impose liability anyway, on the theory that "you take your victim as you find him (her)."

Nature of the Victim

Suppose the defendant sets in motion a chain of events that winds up injuring someone the defendant could not have anticipated to be in danger. In most such cases, the rule adhered to is the one articulated by Judge Cardozo in *Palsgraf*: the defendant's actions can proximately injure only individuals foreseeably within the zone of risk created by the defendant's carelessness. Mrs. Palsgraf was not

a foreseeable victim in this way, although the unfortunate plaintiff in *Derdiarian* certainly was.

What Should be Foreseen?

Clearly the idea that a harm or event is "foreseeable" plays a big role in the analysis of cause and effect in the law of tort. The *Lynch* and *Palsgraf* cases in your reading afford an opportunity to confront further puzzles concerning that notion. Is it always clear, for example, which harms would and which would not be foreseeable by a reasonable person? How are the foreseeable risks to be defined or described? Did Fisher's conduct in *Lynch* impose the clearly recognizable risk of *injury to motorists,* making Lynch's injury directly traceable to Fisher's conduct? If so, Fisher is liable. But why couldn't the facts be described this way: Fisher's actions created an unforeseeable (and very small) risk of *bullet wounds to rescuers of deranged and gun-packing injured motorists.* In that way of describing what Fisher did, it seems clear that he could not be held liable. How should questions like this be resolved?

The Theory of Hart and Honoré

In the excerpt from their book *Causation in the Law,* included in the readings, philosophers H. L. A. Hart and A. M. Honoré take us deeper into the philosophical analysis and justification of causal language in the law. Hart and Honoré begin with the obvious fact that we all use causal language to describe the world: "He broke the window," "Oswald killed Kennedy," and so on. We make these kinds of judgments continually—in assigning responsibility, in reconstructing the past. Hart and Honoré defend the thesis that this ordinary causal language, our everyday, working understanding of "cause," includes distinctions and nuances that place limits on what we can truly be said to have caused. Hence, they reject the conclusion of Judge Andrews in *Palsgraf* that drawing such lines or defining such limits is purely a matter of arbitrary policy. The law both can and ought to reflect these commonsense ways of thinking.

Hart and Honoré begin their search for the implicit limiting principles of causal attribution with

---

[4] *Johnson v. Kosmos Portland Cement Co.* 64 F.2d 193 (1933).

a paradigm case of causation: A throws a lighted match on some dry brush and soon a fire is blazing. Can the fire properly be attributed to A's conduct despite the presence of other factors (oxygen in the air, wind, dryness), each of which were equally necessary to the final result? If so, why? We would all agree that A's conduct caused the fire, but why are we justified in this conviction? Because, Hart and Honoré answer, the wind and other factors are merely part of the background circumstances, part of the total context in which A acted. The wind and oxygen are mere conditions, rather than causes. And what is the difference? Conditions such as oxygen in the air are not unusual or out of the ordinary. Hart and Honoré argue that the same tacit appeal to "normal" background conditions explains the following kind of case: A hits B, who falls to the ground, stunned. At precisely that moment, a tree topples on B and kills him. The collapse of the tree at that precise moment was not a normal condition, but rather a part of an abnormal conjunction of events, a coincidence for which A cannot be blamed. The same idea can be applied in a third kind of case: A throws a lighted match on some dry brush; just before the flames die out, B arrives and creates a blaze by pouring gasoline on the smoldering embers. Here we would not be inclined to classify B's act as a mere condition or circumstance through which A acted. Why? Because B is an independent agent acting in the world. His voluntary and deliberate intervention "breaks" the causal chain linking A to the fire.

In Hart and Honoré's view, then, an act is the cause of harm if it is both necessary to the occurrence of the harm and sufficient to produce it without the cooperation of the voluntary or deliberate acts of others or abnormal conjunctions of events. In other words, if your conduct was a *sine qua non* of some harm, you caused it, unless another person voluntarily and deliberately intervened to produce the harm or an unusual combination of events conspired to give rise to the harm.

The Decline of Cause

As we have seen, the law of tort has traditionally required that a plaintiff who wishes to recover against a defendant establish three things: (1) that

the plaintiff was injured; (2) that the defendant failed to exercise his or her duty of reasonable care; and (3) that, as a result, the defendant caused the plaintiff's injuries.

Exceptions to the second requirement continue to be recognized by the law; these are pockets of strict liability, in which defendants can find themselves liable for injuries brought on by their actions even if they were not "at fault" in failing to act reasonably and to exercise care for the well-being of others. Prominent among cases in which strict tort liability is imposed are those involving "ultrahazardous" activities (such as blasting) and those dealing with the manufacture and distribution of consumer goods (product liability). Strict tort liability endorses a view that Hart and Honoré call "causal maximalism": the view that the question "Who is responsible for this injury" is to be settled exclusively by reference to causal criteria.[5]

What about exceptions to the last of the requirements stated above, the requirement that D caused P's injury? To abandon this requirement would be to embrace "causal minimalism": the idea that judgments about who caused an injury should play little or no role in determining who is to be held responsible or liable for it. You might think that this is a demand the law could not sensibly endorse, but as Judith Thomson chronicles, a small but growing number of recent cases have taken just this position. The *Summers* and *Sindell* cases, explored in detail by Thomson, illustrate this trend. Moreover, as Thomson notes, a growing number of contemporary legal theorists have dismissed the causation requirement as unimportant when the true goals and aims of tort law are placed in proper perspective. The theorists to whom Thomson refers argue that the fundamental purpose of tort law is *economic:* to bring about an efficient allocation of social resources, a cost-justified level of accidents and safety.

Assuming that cause is thus "declining" in the law, is this a good or bad thing from a moral point of view? Thomson's essay sets out to answer this question by taking note of a parallel trend: the decline of cause in moral theory. Thomson is suspi-

---

[5] See *Causation in the Law,* 2nd ed. (Oxford: Clarendon Press, 1985), pp. lxxiii–lxxvii.

cious of both trends and tries to identify the source of her unease.

The ruling in *Summers v. Tice,* Thomson believes, illustrates the declining importance of cause in tort doctrine. The case involved two defendants, Tice and Simonson, who were both hunting quail. A quail was flushed and both defendants fired negligently in the direction of Summers; one shot struck him in the eye. The defendants were roughly equidistant from Summers and were using the same type of gun and shot; it was not possible to determine from which gun the pellet in Summers' eye had come. The Supreme Court of California argued that the standard practice of placing the burden of proof upon the plaintiff to establish that a specific person caused his injury had to be abandoned in this case because to stick with it would leave Summers without a remedy. The burden must be shifted to the defendants to prove that they did not cause the injury. If they cannot, each is liable.

Thomson tries to articulate the moral position of those who agree with *Summers* and similar decisions: It doesn't matter that Tice didn't cause Summers' injury (if in fact it wasn't he) or that Simonson didn't cause Summers' injury (if in fact it wasn't he). What matters is that they both acted (equally) badly; and for that they should each have to pay. Thomson seeks to relate this view to the Kantian position that one's intention, one's "will," and not the results or effects of one's conduct should matter to its moral worth.

Responding to those who support the waning of cause, both in law and in our moral outlook, Thomson attempts to isolate the basis of the conviction that cause does matter. We simply *do* judge more harshly a person who, while acting badly, causes injury or death than a person who, acting equally badly, does not cause injury or death. Why? Because the first, but not the second, is to blame for what he or she has caused. Thomson tries to blunt the criticism that enhancing or enlarging the liability of the bad actor who just happens to hit the target rather than miss makes liability turn on sheer luck. It is more than sheer bad luck that makes one bad actor the cause of the injury and another not: The actor's own negligence helped to produce that result.

93. *Lynch v. Fisher*

Hardy, Judge.

This matter comes before us on appeal from judgment of the Eleventh Judicial District Court of Louisiana sustaining exceptions of no cause or right of action filed on behalf of all defendants and dismissing plaintiff's action as of nonsuit.

The allegations of the petition which are placed at issue as to their sufficiency in setting forth the cause of action in the exceptions referred to,

and which set forth the facts upon which plaintiff's action is based, may be summarized as follows:

That about 9:00 P.M. on July 3, 1945, an employee of the defendants, Wheless and Fisher, (whose insurer is the defendant, Lumbermen's Mutual Casualty Company of Chicago, Ill.) at the time engaged within the general scope and course of his employment, parked a pulpwood truck which he was driving on the right-hand side of highway No. 171, some twelve miles north of Mansfield, De Soto Parish, Louisiana;

That, while said truck was thus parked, a passenger car owned and driven by the defendant,

34 So. 2d 513 (1949)
Louisiana Court of Appeal

Robert Joe Gunter, collided violently with the rear end thereof;

That the driver of the parked truck was guilty of negligence, imputable to his employers, on numerous grounds, specifically in parking the truck entirely on the highway without leaving a clearance of fifteen feet on the pavement; in failing to have warning lights on the parked truck; in leaving the truck parked on the highway, thereby constituting a menace to traffic, and in failing to set out flares, or to have same available and ready for service.

That the negligence of the defendant, Robert Joe Gunter, consisted of driving and operating his automobile at an excessive, unreasonable and unlawful rate of speed; in failing to keep and maintain a proper lookout; operating his vehicle without adequate brakes; and failing to take any action to avoid the collision;

That the concurrent acts of negligence of the driver of the truck and the driver of the passenger car were the proximate causes of the accident;

That plaintiff seeing the collision ran to the scene thereof, succeeded in opening the doors of the badly damaged Gunter car, and, with the aid of another party, extricated both Mrs. Gunter and the defendant, Robert Joe Gunter, from the automobile, which had meanwhile caught fire;

That, in the effort to further assist the fatally injured Mrs. Gunter, plaintiff attempted to pull a floor mat out of the car to be used as a cushion for her head as she lay upon the roadside; that in the performance of this act plaintiff found a pistol on the floor of the car and handed the same to the defendant Gunter, who, being delirious and temporarily mentally deranged by reason of the shock of the accident, fired the pistol at plaintiff, the bullet passing through plaintiff's left ankle and inflicting serious injuries, for which damages are claimed in this action.

. . .

Determination of the issue of proximate cause must of necessity be considered with relation to the allied doctrine of intervening cause which is clearly material under the alleged facts of this case.

It is quite true, as contended by learned counsel for defendants, as a general proposition of law that only that negligence which directly causes the injury is deemed to be proximate. But a resolution of this point must perforce depend upon the particular facts of each case.

In the matter before us there are three elements that must be determined:

(a) Did the original negligence of the driver of the parked truck set in motion a chain of circumstances following consecutively one upon the other which led to plaintiff's injury?

(b) Was the act of original negligence superseded by an intervening act breaking the chain of causation leading to plaintiff's injury?

(c) Is the fact that plaintiff's injuries resulted from an improbable and unforeseeable incident sufficient to eliminate the original act of negligence from consideration as a proximate cause?

The answer to these queries will dispose of all the claims based upon the doctrines of proximate and intervening causes and foreseeability.

Upon the basis of the allegations there is no room for any reasonable contravention of the proposition that the circumstances following the negligent parking of the truck down to the removal of the pistol from the car by plaintiff were natural, probable and reasonably to be expected. But at this point an imponderable enters into consideration. The rescuer hands a pistol to the rescued and is shot by the latter. Certainly under the general rule, this action could not be within the reasonable contemplation of any normal individual and the specific incident therefore could not be imputed to the negligent truck driver as a probable result flowing from his negligence. But, unfortunately, the proposition does not admit of being disposed of so easily, for it is well established in the jurisprudence of the State of Louisiana and a majority of other jurisdictions that the general rule must yield to specific instances.

Of course, no Court could reasonably hold that the driver of a vehicle, no matter how gross his negligence, could have contemplated the shooting of a third party as a normal and natural result of such negligence. Nor, indeed, could the rescuer himself be held to have assumed the risk of such a strange, unnatural and unusual result flowing from his gallant efforts.

But, if the results of accidents were normal, usual and predictable, the burden of both Bar and Bench would be immeasurably lighter.

To determine whether or not the shooting incident is susceptible of being distinguished and set apart from the general law of proximate cause, we must base our conclusions not upon those elements which would be applicable as between parties to the collision itself but as affecting the injury inflicted upon an innocent third party, himself without fault.

Let us assume that plaintiff in this case, rushing to the aid of helpless parties occupying the automobile involved in the collision, in the darkness of night, and wrenching open the door of the vehicle, had been severely bitten by a dog which was accompanying the occupants of the car and which had been so frightened or injured by the shock of the collision as to have lost its accustomed gentleness. Could it be said that such a result was proximately caused by the negligence of the truck driver because such a possibility was normally an expectable or foreseeable result of such negligence? The answer is obvious. Scores of cars might have collided with the rear end of this particular truck on this particularly well-traveled main highway without producing such a result.

Similarly, the laws of probability were overwhelmingly against the occurrence of the character and nature of the incident and resulting injury to plaintiff under the actual facts of this case. But, certainly, plaintiff is without fault, and, certainly, the negligence of some party or the concurrent negligence of several parties combined to set up the unfortunate situation which resulted in his injury.

In our opinion the general doctrine of proximate cause cannot be applied under the alleged facts and chain of circumstances herein presented. Under the tenor of the allegation it is quite clear that plaintiff would not have been shot if originally the truck driver had not negligently parked his truck in such manner as to constitute a menace and hazard to vehicles rightfully traveling the highway.

. . . The proximate cause of the injury to one who voluntarily interposes to save the lives of persons imperiled by the negligence of others is the negligence which causes the peril. . . .

. . . In determining the question as to the efficiency of the intervening act, that is, in this case, the shooting of plaintiff by one of the defendants, we must consider the well-established principle that an intervening cause is not necessarily a su-

perseding cause. The intervening cause, in order to supersede original negligence, must have alone produced injury.

Under paragraph (B) of the Common on Section 440 of the Restatement of the Law of Torts this proposition is set forth: "Therefore, if in looking back from the harm and tracing the sequence of events by which it was produced, it is found that a superseding cause has perated, there is no need of determining whether the actor's antecedent conduct was or was not a substantial factor in bringing about the harm."

In the instant case there is not question but that in tracing back from the point of the actual injury to plaintiff we would ordinarily be compelled to conclude that the shooting by one of the defendants was unquestionably a superseding cause were it not for the allegation that the defendant inflicting the injury at the time was temporarily insane by reason of shock resulting from the collision caused by the initial negligence of the truck driver.

Section 455 of the Restatement of the Law of Torts submits the principle:

"If the actor's negligent conduct so brings about the delirium or insanity of another as to make the actor liable for it, the actor is also liable for harm done by the other to himself while delirious or insane, if his delirium or insanity.

(a) Prevents him from realizing the nature of his act. . . .

. . . We think it must logically and inevitably follow that under such circumstances the actor is not only liable for harm done in a fit of delirium or insanity by such deranged person to himself, but also for any harm caused by him to another."

In discussing proximate cause the opinion in *Cruze v. Harvey & Jones* . . . : "The nearest independent cause which is adequate to, and does, produce the result, is the proximate cause of the accident, and supersedes all remote causes."

From this principle, with respect to the facts applicable to the case under consideration, the opinion stated: "The nearest independent cause which produced the death of this mule was the open, unprotected well, and this supersedes all other remote causes, among which may have been the open gap through which the mule escaped."

In *Lee v. Powell Bros. & Sanders Co.,* . . . the Court said: "For severing the legal connection between the negligence by which such an imminent danger was created and the injury that has resulted from it the intervening voluntary act of some person responsible for his acts would have to be shown."

In every consideration of the point which has come to our attention in the study of this case, the qualities of the relieving or superseding act are repeatedly and unfailingly designated as being intervening and voluntary, by a person responsible for his acts.

. . . Since we must accept the well pleaded allegations of the petition as being true for the purpose of determining the exception, we are constrained to hold that plaintiff has met the requirements established by these several factors and has negatived the possibility that the act which immediately resulted in the harm was the voluntary action of a person responsible for his acts.

Under the allegations of the petition it is inescapable that plaintiff has properly alleged that the defendant Gunter was mentally deranged and rendered temporarily insane as the result of the collision of his car with the parked truck. Plaintiff by his allegations has further definitely asserted that such a condition was brought about by the concurrent negligence of the several defendants. In order to affirm the holding of the lower court it would be necessary for us to find that the temporary insanity of the defendant Gunter, which led to the shooting, was not caused by the collision. Clearly, this is a question of fact to be determined by trial on the merits, and, meanwhile, any conclusion must be governed by the plain allegations of the petition.

Any attempt to determine at what point, with relation to the actual injury to plaintiff, the negligence of the original actor, namely, the driver of the truck, ceased and a new and independent tortious act intervened and superseded the original negligence, conclusively impresses us with the impossibility of such a severance of causes. The chain is complete and whole, link by link, and though tested with the utmost care no break is revealed in the succession of circumstances.

The consecutive order of the related circumstances and events may be briefly outlined:

(1) Negligence of the truck driver in parking his truck on the highway, resulting in
(2) Collision, superinduced by the concurrent negligence of the defendant Gunter, resulting in
(3) (a) Attempted rescue by the plaintiff.
(b) Temporary mental derangement of the defendant Gunter as a result of the shock of the collision, resulting in
(4) The shooting of plaintiff and the injury sustained thereby.

If there is any break in the continuity of the incidents flowing from the original act of negligence, we are unable to point out such a circumstance.

. . .

We make no attempt to minimize the unusual and improbable character of the incident which is alleged to have occurred in the case before us.

The facts set forth are additional evidence of the truth of the adage that "truth is stranger than fiction."

We do not believe that the theory of foreseeability is applicable to the facts of this case. Referring again to the Restatement of the Law of Torts, we find in Section 435 a plain and unambiguous statement of the principle which refutes the requirement of foreseeability: "If the actor's conduct is a substantial factor in bringing about harm to another, the fact that the actor neither foresaw nor should have foreseen the extent of the harm or the manner in which it occurred does not prevent him from being liable."

. . .

94. *Palsgraf v. Long Island Railroad*

Cardozo, [Chief Judge].

Plaintiff was standing on a platform of defendant's railroad after buying a ticket to go to Rockaway Beach. A train stopped at the station, bound for another place. Two men ran forward to catch it. One of the men reached the platform of the car without mishap, though the train was already moving. The other man, carrying a package, jumped aboard the car, but seemed unsteady as if about to fall. A guard on the car, who had held the door open, reached forward to help him in, and another guard on the platform pushed him from behind. In this act, the package was dislodged, and fell upon the rails. It was a package of small size, about fifteen inches long, and was covered by a newspaper. In fact it contained fireworks, but there was nothing in its appearance to give notice of its contents. The fireworks when they fell exploded. The shock of the explosion threw down some scales at the other end of the platform, many feet away. The scales struck the plaintiff, causing injuries for which she sues.

The conduct of the defendant's guard, if a wrong in its relation to the holder of the package, was not a wrong in its relation to the plaintiff, standing far away. Relatively to her it was not negligence at all. Nothing in the situation gave notice that the falling package had in it the potency of peril to persons thus removed. Negligence is not actionable unless it involves the invasion of a legally protected interest, the violation of a right. "Proof of negligence in the air, so to speak, will not do." "Negligence is the absence of care, according to the circumstances." The plaintiff as she stood upon the platform of the station might claim to be protected against intentional invasion of her bodily security. Such invasion is not charged. She might claim to be protected against unintentional invasion by conduct involving in the thought of reasonable men an unreasonable hazard that such invasion would ensue. These, from the point of view of the law, were the bounds of her immunity, with perhaps some rare exceptions, survivals for the most part of ancient forms of liability, where conduct is held to be at the peril of the actor (*Sullivan v. Dunham* . . .). If no hazard was apparent to the eye of ordinary vigilance, an act innocent and harmless, at least to outward seeming, with reference to her, did not take to itself the quality of a tort because it happened to be a wrong, though apparently not one involving the risk of bodily insecurity, with reference to some one else. "In every instance, before negligence can be predicated of a given act, back of the act must be sought and found a duty to the individual complaining, the observance of which would have averted or avoided the injury." "The ideas of negligence and duty are strictly correlative." (Bowen, L. J., in *Thomas v. Quartermaine* . . .). The plaintiff sues in her own right for a wrong personal to her, and not as the vicarious beneficiary of a breach of duty to another.

A different conclusion will involve us, and swiftly too, in a maze of contradictions. A guard stumbles over a package which has been left upon a platform. It seems to be a bundle of newspapers. It turns out to be a can of dynamite. To the eye of ordinary vigilance, the bundle is abandoned waste, which may be kicked or trod on with impunity. Is a passenger at the other end of the platform protected by the law against the unsuspected hazard concealed beneath the waste? If not, is the result to be any different, so far as the distant passenger is concerned, when the guard stumbles over a valise which a truckman or a porter has left upon the walk? The passenger far away, if the victim of a wrong at all, has a cause of action, not derivative, but original and primary. His claim to be protected against invasion of his bodily security is neither greater nor less because the act resulting in the invasion is a wrong to another far removed. In this case, the rights that are said to have been violated, the interests said to have been invaded, are not

248 N.Y. 339 (1928)
New York Court of Appeals

even of the same order. The man was not injured in his person nor even put in danger. The purpose of the act, as well as its effect, was to make his person safe. If there was a wrong to him at all, which may very well be doubted, it was a wrong to a property interest only, the safety of his package. Out of this wrong to property, which threatened injury to nothing else, there has passed, we are told, to the plaintiff by derivation or succession a right of action for the invasion of an interest of another order, the right to bodily security. The diversity of interests emphasizes the futility of the effort to build the plaintiff's right upon the basis of a wrong to some one else. The gain is one of emphasis, for a like result would follow if the interests were the same. Even then, the orbit of the danger as disclosed to the eye of reasonable vigilance would be the orbit of the duty. One who jostles one's neighbor in a crowd does not invade the rights of others standing at the outer fringe when the unintended contact casts a bomb upon the ground. The wrongdoer, as to them is the man who carries the bomb, not the one who explodes it without suspicion of the danger. Life will have to be made over, and human nature transformed, before prevision so extravagant can be accepted as the norm of conduct, the customary standard to which behavior must conform.

The argument for the plaintiff is built upon the shifting meanings of such words as "wrong" and "wrongful," and shares their instability. What the plaintiff must show is "a wrong" to herself, *i.e.*, a violation of her own right, and not merely a wrong to some one else, nor conduct "wrongful" because unsocial, but not "a wrong" to any one. We are told that one who drives at reckless speed through a crowded city street is guilty of a negligent act and, therefore, of a wrongful one irrespective of the consequences. Negligent the act is, and wrongful in the sense that it is unsocial, but wrongful and unsocial in relation to other travelers, only because the eye of vigilance perceives the risk of damage. If the same act were to be committed on a speedway or a race course, it would lose its wrongful quality. The risk reasonably to be perceived defines the duty to be obeyed, and risk imports relation; it is risk to another or to others within the range of apprehension. . . . This does not mean, of course, that one who launches a destructive force is always relieved of liability if the force, though known to be destructive, pursues an unexpected path. It was not necessary that the defendant should have had notice of the particular method in which an accident would occur, if the possibility of an accident was clear to the ordinarily prudent eye. . . . Some acts such as shooting, are so imminently dangerous to any one who may come within reach of the missile, however unexpectedly, as to impose a duty of prevision not far from that of an insurer. Even today, and much oftener in earlier stages of the law, one acts sometimes at one's peril. Under this head, it may be, fall certain cases of what is known as transferred intent, an act willfully dangerous to A resulting by misadventure in injury to B. These cases aside, wrong is defined in terms of the natural or probable, at least when unintentional. The range of reasonable apprehension is at times a question for the court, and at times, if varying inferences are possible, a question for the jury. Here, by concession, there was nothing in the situation to suggest to the most cautious mind that the parcel wrapped in newspaper would spread wreckage through the station. If the guard had thrown it down knowingly and willfully, he would not have threatened the plaintiff's safety, so far as appearances could warn him. His conduct would not have involved, even then, an unreasonable probability of invasion of her bodily security. Liability can be no greater where the act is inadvertent.

Negligence, like risk, is thus a term of relation. Negligence in the abstract, apart from things related, is surely not a tort, if indeed it is understandable at all. Negligence is not a tort unless it results in the commission of a wrong, and the commission of a wrong imports the violation of a right, in this case, we are told, the right to be protected against interference with one's bodily security. But bodily security is protected, not against all forms of interference or aggression, but only against some. One who seeks redress at law does not make out a cause of action by showing without more that there has been damage to his person. If the harm was not willful, he must show that the act as to him had possibilities of danger so many and apparent as to entitle him to be protected against the doing of it though the harm was unintended. Affront to personality is still the keynote of the wrong. Confirmation of this view will be found in the history and development of the action on the case. Negligence as a basis of civil liability was un-known to medieval law. For damage to the person, the sole remedy was trespass, and trespass did not lie in the absence of aggression, and that direct and personal. Liability for other damage, as where a servant without orders from the master does or omits something to the damage of another, is a plant of later growth. When it emerged out of the legal soil, it was thought of as a variant of trespass, an offshoot of the parent stock. This appears in the form of action, which was known as trespass on the case. The victim does not sue derivatively, or by right of subrogation, to vindicate an interest in-vaded in the person of another. Thus to view his cause of action is to ignore the fundamental differ-ence between tort and crime. He sues for breach of a duty owing to himself.

The law of causation, remote or proximate, is thus foreign to the case before us. The question of liability is always anterior to the question of the measure of the consequences that go with liability. If there is no tort to be redressed, there is no occa-sion to consider what damage might be recovered if there were a finding of a tort. We may assume, without deciding, that negligence, not at large or in the abstract, but in relation to the plaintiff, would entail liability for any and all consequences, how-ever novel or extraordinary. There is room for argu-ment that a distinction is to be drawn according to the diversity of interests invaded by the act, as where conduct negligent in that it threatens an in-significant invasion of an interest in property re-sults in an unforeseeable invasion of an interest of another order, as *e.g.*, one of bodily security. Per-haps other distinctions may be necessary. We do not go into the question now. The consequences to be followed must first be rooted in a wrong.

The judgment of the Appellate Division and that of the Trial Term should be reversed, and the complaint dismissed, with costs in all courts.

. . .

Andrews, [Judge] (dissenting).

Assisting a passenger to board a train, the de-fendant's servant negligently knocked a package from his arms. It fell between the platform and the cars. Of its contents the servant knew and could know nothing. A violent explosion followed. The concussion broke some scales standing a consider-able distance away. In falling they injured the plaintiff, an intending passenger.

Upon these facts may she recover the damages she has suffered in an action brought against the master? The result we shall reach depends upon our theory as to the nature of negligence. Is it a rel-ative concept—the breach of some duty owing to a particular person or to particular persons? Or where there is an act which unreasonably threatens the safety of others, is the doer liable for all its prox-imate consequences, even where they result in in-jury to one who would generally be thought to be outside the radius of danger? This not a mere dis-pute as to words. We might not believe that to the average mind the dropping of the bundle would seem to involve the probability of harm to the plaintiff standing many feet away whatever might be the case as to the owner or to one so near as to be likely to be struck by its fall. If, however, we adopt the second hypothesis we have to inquire only as to the relation between cause and effect. We deal in terms of proximate cause, not of negligence.

Negligence may be defined roughly as an act or omission which unreasonably does or may affect the rights of others, or which unreasonably fails to protect oneself from the dangers resulting from such acts. Here I confine myself to the first branch of the definition. Nor do I comment on the word "un-reasonable." For present purposes it sufficiently de-scribes that average conduct that society requires of its members.

There must be both the act or the omission, and the right. It is the act itself, not the intent of the actor, that is important. In criminal law both the in-tent and the result are to be considered. Intent again is material in tort actions, where punitive damages are sought, dependent on actual malice—not on merely reckless conduct. But here neither in-sanity nor infancy lessens responsibility.

As has been said, except in cases of contribu-tory negligence, there must be rights which are or may be affected. Often though injury has occurred, no rights of him who suffers have been touched. A licensee or trespasser upon my land has no claim to affirmative care on my part that the land be made safe. Where a railroad is required to fence its tracks against cattle, no man's rights are injured should he wander upon the road because such fence is absent.

An unborn child may not demand immunity from personal harm.

But we are told that "there is no negligence unless there is in the particular case a legal duty to take care, and this duty must be one which is owed to the plaintiff himself and not merely to others." This, I think too narrow a conception. Where there is the unreasonable act, and some right that may be affected there is negligence whether damage does or does not result. That is immaterial. Should we drive down Broadway at a reckless speed, we are negligent whether we strike an approaching car or miss it by an inch. The act itself is wrongful. It is a wrong not only to those who happen to be within the radius of danger but to all who might have been there—a wrong to the public at large. Such is the language of the street. Such the language of the courts when speaking of contributory negligence. Such again and again their language in speaking of the duty of some defendant and discussing proximate cause in cases where such a discussion is wholly irrelevant on any other theory. As was said by Mr. Justice Holmes many years ago, "the measure of the defendant's duty in determining whether a wrong has been committed is one thing, the measure of liability when a wrong has been committed is another." Due care is a duty imposed on each one of us to protect society from unnecessary danger, not to protect A, B or C alone.

It may well be that there is no such thing as negligence in the abstract. "Proof of negligence in the air, so to speak, will not do." In an empty world negligence would not exist. It does involve a relationship between man and his fellows. But not merely a relationship between man and those whom he might reasonably expect his act would injure. Rather, a relationship between him and those whom he does in fact injure. If his act has a tendency to harm some one, it harms him a mile away as surely as it does those on the scene. We now permit children to recover for the negligent killing of the father. It was never prevented on the theory that no duty was owing to them. A husband may be compensated for the loss of his wife's services. To say the wrongdoer was negligent as to the husband as well as to the wife is merely an attempt to fit facts to theory. An insurance company paying a fire loss recovers its payment of the negligent incendiary. We speak of subrogation—of suing in the right of the insured. Behind the cloud of words is the fact they hide, that the act, wrongful as to the insured, has also injured the company. Even if it be true that the fault of father, wife or insured will prevent recovery, it is because we consider the original negligence not the proximate cause of the injury.

In the well-known *Polemis* case (1921, 3 K. B. 560), Scrutton, L. J., said that the dropping of a plank was negligent for it might injure "workman or cargo or ship." Because of either possibility the owner of the vessel was to be made good for his loss. The act being wrongful the doer was liable for its proximate results. Criticized and explained as this statement may have been, I think it states the law as it should be and as it is.

The proposition is this. Every one owes to the world at large the duty of refraining from those acts that may unreasonably threaten the safety of others. Such an act occurs. Not only is he wronged to whom harm might reasonably be expected to result, but he also who is in fact injured, even if he be outside what would generally be thought the danger zone. There needs to be duty due the one complaining but this is not a duty to a particular individual because as to him harm might be expected. Harm to some one being the natural result of the act, not only that one alone, but all those in fact injured may complain. We have never, I think, held otherwise. Indeed in the *DiCaprio* case we said that a breach of a general ordinance defining the degree of care to be exercised in one's calling is evidence of negligence as to every one. We did not limit this statement to those who might be expected to be exposed to danger. Unreasonable risk being taken, its consequences are not confined to those who might probably be hurt.

If this be so, we do not have a plaintiff suing by "derivation or succession." Her action is original and primary. Her claim is for a breach of duty to herself—not that she is subrogated to any right of action of the owner of the parcel or of a passenger standing at the scene of the explosion.

The right to recover damages rests on additional considerations. The plaintiff's rights must be injured, and this injury must be caused by the negligence. We build a dam, but are negligent as to its foundations. Breaking, it injures property down stream. We are not liable if all this happened because of some reason other than the insecure foundation. But when injuries do result from our unlawful act we are liable for the consequences. It does not matter that they are unusual, unexpected, unforeseen and unforeseeable. But there is one limitation. The damages must be so connected with the negligence that the latter may be said to be the proximate cause of the former.

These two words have never been given an inclusive definition. What is a cause in a legal sense, still more what is a proximate cause, depend in each case upon many considerations, as does the existence of negligence itself. Any philosophical doctrine of causation does not help us. A boy throws a stone into a pond. The ripples spread. The water level rises. The history of that pond is altered to all eternity. It will be altered by other causes also. Yet it will be forever the resultant of all causes combined. Each one will have an influence. How great only omniscience can say. You may speak of a chain, or if you please, a net. An analogy is of little aid. Each cause brings about future events. Without each the future would not be the same. Each is proximate in the sense it is essential. But that is not what we mean by the word. Nor on the other hand do we mean sole cause. There is no such thing.

Should analogy be thought helpful, however, I prefer that of a stream. The spring, starting on its journey, is joined by tributary after tributary. The river, reaching the ocean, comes from a hundred sources. No man may say whence any drop of water is derived. Yet for a time distinction may be possible. Into the clear creek, brown swamp water flows from the left. Later, from the right comes water stained by its clay bed. The three may remain for a space, sharply divided. But at last, inevitably no trace of separation remains. They are so comingled that all distinction is lost.

As we have said, we cannot trace the effect of an act to the end, if end there is. Again, however, we may trace it part of the way. A murder at Sarajevo may be the necessary antecedent to an assassination in London twenty years hence. An overturned lantern may burn all Chicago. We may follow the fire from the shed to the last building. We rightly say the fire started by the lantern caused its destruction.

A cause, but not the proximate cause. What we do mean by the word "proximate" is, that because of convenience, of public policy, of a rough sense of justice, the law arbitrarily declines to trace a series of events beyond a certain point. This is not logic, it is practical politics. Take our rule as to fires. Sparks from my burning haystack set on fire my house and my neighbor's. I may recover from a negligent railroad. He may not. Yet the wrongful act as directly harmed the one as the other. We may regret that the line was drawn just where it was, but drawn somewhere it had to be. We said the act of the railroad was not the proximate cause of our neighbor's fire. Cause it surely was. The words we used were simply indicative of our notions of public policy. Other courts think differently. But somewhere they reach the point where they cannot say the stream comes from any one source.

Take the illustration given in an unpublished manuscript by a distinguished and helpful writer on the law of torts. A chauffeur negligently collides with another car which is filled with dynamite, although he could not know it. An explosion follows. A, walking on the sidewalk nearby, is killed. B, sitting in a window of a building opposite, is cut by flying glass. C, likewise sitting in a window a block away, is similarly injured. And a further illustration. A nursemaid, ten blocks away, startled by the noise, involuntarily drops a baby from her arms to the walk. We are told that C may not recover while A may. As to B it is a question for court or jury. We will all agree that the baby might not. Because, we are again told, the chauffeur had no reason to believe his conduct involved any risk of injuring either C or the baby. As to them he was not negligent.

But the chauffeur, being negligent in risking the collision, his belief that the scope of the harm he might do would be limited is immaterial. His act unreasonably jeopardized the safety of any one who might be affected by it. C's injury and that of the baby were directly traceable to the collision. Without that, the injury would not have happened. C had the right to sit in his office, secure from such dangers. The baby was entitled to use the sidewalk with reasonable safety.

The true theory is, it seems to me, that the injury to C, if in truth he is to be denied recovery, and the injury to the baby is that their several injuries were not the proximate result of the negligence. And here not what the chauffeur had reason to believe would be the result of his conduct, but what the prudent would foresee, may have a bearing. May have some bearing, for the problem of proximate cause is not to be solved by any one consideration.

It is all a question of expediency. There are no fixed rules to govern our judgment. There are simply matters of which we may take account. We have in a somewhat different connection spoken of "the stream of events." We have asked whether that stream was deflected—whether it was forced into new and unexpected channels. This is rather rhetoric than law. There is in truth little to guide us other than common sense.

There are some hints that may help us. The proximate cause, involved as it may be with many other causes, must be, at the least, something without which the event would not happen. The court must ask itself whether there was a natural and continuous sequence between cause and effect. Was the one a substantial factor in producing the other? Was there a direct connection between them, without too many intervening causes? Is the effect of cause on result not too attenuated? Is the cause likely, in the usual judgment of mankind, to produce the result? Or by the exercise of prudent foresight could the result be foreseen? Is the result too remote from the cause, and here we consider remoteness in time and space, where we passed upon the construction of a contract—but something was also said on this subject. Clearly we must so consider, for the greater the distance either in time or space, the more surely do other causes intervene to affect the result. When a lantern is overturned the firing of a shed is a fairly direct consequence. Many things contribute to the spread of the conflagration—the force of the wind, the direction and width of streets, the character of intervening structures, other factors. We draw an uncertain and wavering line, but draw it we must as best we can.

Once again, it is all a question of fair judgment, always keeping in mind the fact that we endeavor to make a rule in each case that will be practical and in keeping with the general understanding of mankind.

Here another question must be answered. In the case supposed it is said, and said correctly, that the chauffeur is liable for the direct effect of the explosion although he had no reason to suppose it would follow a collision. "The fact that the injury occurred in a different manner than that which might have been expected does not prevent the chauffeur's negligence from being in law the cause of the injury." But the natural results of a negligent act—the results which a prudent man would or should foresee—do have a bearing upon the decision as to proximate cause. We have said so repeatedly. What should be foreseen? No human foresight would suggest that a collision itself might injure one a block away. On the contrary, given an explosion, such a possibility might be reasonably expected. I think the direct connection, the foresight of which the courts speak, assumes prevision of the explosion, for the immediate results of which, at least, the chauffeur is responsible.

It may be said this is unjust. Why? In fairness he should make good every injury flowing from his negligence. Not because of tenderness toward him we say he need not answer for all that follows his wrong. We look back to the catastrophe, the fire kindled by the spark, or the explosion. We trace the consequences—not indefinitely, but to a certain point. And to aid us in fixing that point we ask what might ordinarily be expected to follow the fire or the explosion.

This last suggestion is the factor which must determine the case before us. The act upon which defendant's liability rests is knocking an apparently harmless package onto the platform. The act was negligent. For its proximate consequences the defendant is liable. If its contents were broken, to the owner; if it fell upon and crushed a passenger's foot, then to him. If it exploded and injured one in the immediate vicinity, to him also as to A in the illustration. Mrs. Palsgraf was standing some distance away. How far cannot be told from the record—apparently twenty-five or thirty feet. Perhaps less. Except for the explosion, she would not have been injured. We are told by the appellant in his brief "it cannot be denied that the explosion was the direct cause of the plaintiff's injuries." So it was a substantial factor in producing the result—there was here a natural and continuous sequence—direct connection. The only intervening cause was that instead of blowing her to the ground the concussion smashed the weighing machine which in turn fell upon her. There was no remoteness in time, little in space. And surely, given such an explosion as here it needed no great foresight to predict that the natural result would be to injure one on the platform at no greater distance from its scene than was the plaintiff. Just how no one might be able to predict. Whether by flying fragments, by broken glass, by wreckage of machines or structure no one could say. But injury in some form was most probable.

Under these circumstances I cannot say as a matter of law that the plaintiff's injuries were not the proximate result of the negligence. That is all we have before us. The court refused to so charge. No request was made to submit the matter to the jury as a question of fact, even would that have been proper upon the record before us.

The judgment appealed from should be affirmed, with costs.

Pound, Lehman and Kellogg, [Judges], concur with Cardozo, [Chief Judge], Andrews, [Judge], dissents in opinion in which Crane and O'Brien, [Judges], concur.

Judgment reversed, etc.

95. *Tracing Consequences*

H. L. A. HART AND A. M. HONORÉ

Tracing Consequences

'To consequences no limit can be set': 'Every event which would not have happened if an earlier event had not happened is the consequence of that earlier event.' These two propositions are not equivalent in meaning and are not equally or in the same way at variance with ordinary thought. They have, however, both been urged sometimes in the same breath by the legal theorist and the philosopher: they are indeed sometimes said by lawyers to be 'the philosophical doctrine' of causation. It is perhaps not difficult even for the layman to accept the first proposition as a truth about certain physical events; an explosion may cause a flash of light which will be propagated as far as the outer nebulae; its effects or consequences continue indefinitely. It is, however, a different matter to accept the view that whenever a man is murdered with a gun his death was the consequence of (still less an 'effect' of or 'caused by') the manufacture of the bullet. The first tells a perhaps unfamiliar tale about unfamiliar events; the second introduces an unfamiliar, though, of course, a possible way of speaking about familiar events. It is not that this unrestricted use of 'consequence' is unintelligible or never found; it is indeed used to refer to bizarre or fortuitous connections or coincidences: but the point is that the various causal notions employed for the purposes of explanation, attribution of responsibility, or the assessment of contributions to the course of history carry with them implicit limits which are similar in these different employments.

It is, then, the second proposition, defining consequence in terms of 'necessary condition', with which theorists are really concerned. This proposition is the corollary of the view that, if we look into the past of any given event, there is an infinite number of events, each of which is a necessary condition of the given event and so, as much as any other, is its cause. This is the 'cone'[1] of causation, so called because, since any event has a number of simultaneous conditions, the series fans out as we go back in time. The justification, indeed only partial, for calling this 'the philosophical doctrine' of causation is that is resembles Mill's doctrine that 'we have no right to give the name of cause to one of the conditions exclusive of the others of them.' It differs from Mill's view in taking the essence of causation to be 'necessary condition' and not 'the sum total'[2] of the sufficient conditions of an event.

Legal theorists have developed this account of cause and consequence to show what is 'factual,' 'objective,' or 'scientific' in these notions: this they call 'cause in fact' and it is usually stressed as a preliminary to the doctrine that any more restricted application of these terms in the law represents nothing in the facts or in the meaning of causation, but expresses fluctuating legal policy or sentiments of what is just or convenient. Moral philosophers have insisted in somewhat similar terms that the consequences of human action are 'infinite': this they have urged as an objection against the Utilitarian doctrine that the rightness of a morally right action depends on whether its consequences are better than those of any alternative action in the circumstances. 'We should have to trace as far as possible the consequences not only for the persons affected directly but also for those indirectly affected and to these no limit can be set.'[3] Hence, so the argument runs, we cannot either inductively establish the Utilitarian doctrine that right acts are 'optimific' or use it in particular cases to discover what is right. Yet, however vulnerable at other points Utilitarianism may be as an account of moral judgment, this objections seems to rest on a mistake as to the sense of 'consequence.' The Utilitarian assertion that the rightness of an action depends on its consequences is not the same as the assertion that it depends on all those later occurrences which would not have happened had the action not been done, to which indeed 'no limit can be set.' It is important to see that the issue here is not the linguistic one whether the word 'consequence' would be understood if used in this way. The point is that, though we could, we do not think in this way in tracing connections between human actions and events. Instead, whenever we are concerned with such connections, whether for the purpose of explaining a puzzling occurrence, assessing responsibility, or giving an intelligible historical narrative, we employ a set of concepts restricting in various ways what counts as a consequence. These restrictions colour *all* our thinking in causal terms; when we find them in the law we are not finding something invented by or peculiar to the law, though of course it is for the law to say when and how far it will use them and, where they are vague, to supplement them.

No short account can be given of the limits thus placed on 'consequences' because these limits vary, intelligibly, with the variety of causal connection asserted. Thus we may be tempted by the generalization that consequences must always be something intended or foreseen or at least foreseeable with ordinary care: but counter-examples spring up from many types of context where causal statements are made. If smoking is shown to cause lung cancer this discovery will permit us to describe past as well as future cases of cancer as the effect or consequence of smoking even though no one foresaw or had reasonable grounds to suspect this in the past. What is common and commonly appreciated and hence foreseeable certainly controls the scope of consequences in certain varieties of causal statement but not in all. Again the voluntary intervention of a second person very often constitutes the limit. If a guest sits down at a table laid with knife and fork and plunges the knife into his hostess's breast, her death is not in any context other than a contrived one[4] thought of as caused by, or the effect or result of the waiter's action in laying the table; nor would it be linked with this action as its consequence for any of the purposes, explanatory or attributive, for which we employ causal notions. Yet as we have seen there are many other types of case where a voluntary action or the harm it does are naturally treated to the consequence of to some prior neglect or precaution. Finally, we may think that a simple answer is already supplied by Hume and Mill's doctrine that causal connection rests on general laws asserting regular connection; yet, even in the type of case to which this important doctrine applies, reference to it alone will not solve our problem. For we often trace a causal connection between an antecedent and a consequent which themselves very rarely go together: we do this when the case can be broken down into intermediate stages, which themselves exemplify different generalizations, as when we find that the fall of a tile was the cause of someone's death, rare though this be. Here our problem reappears in the form of the question: When can generalizations be combined in this way?

We shall examine first the central type of case where the problem is of this last-mentioned form. Here the gist of the causal connection lies in the general connection with each other of the succes-

sive stages; and is not dependent on the special notions of one person providing another with reasons
or exceptional opportunities for actions. This form
of causal connection may exist between actions and
events, and between purely physical events, and it
is in such cases that the words 'cause' and 'causing'
used of the antecedent action or event have their
most obvious application. It is convenient to refer
to cases of the first type where the consequence is
harm as cases of 'causing harm,' and to refer to
cases where harm is the consequence of one person
providing another with reasons or opportunities
for doing harm as cases of 'inducing' or 'occasion-
ing' harmful acts. In cases of the first type a voluntary act, or a conjunction of events amounting to a
coincidence, operates as a limit in the sense that
events subsequent to these are not attributed to the
antecedent action or event as its consequence even
though they would not have happened without it.
Often such a limiting action or coincidence is
thought of and described as 'intervening': and
lawyers speak of them as 'superseding' or 'extraneous' causes 'breaking the chain of causation.' To see
what these metaphors rest on (and in part obscure)
and how such factors operate as a limit we shall
consider the detail of three simple cases.

(i) A forest fire breaks out, and later investigation shows that shortly before the outbreak A had
flung away a lighted cigarette into the bracken at
the edge of the forest, the bracken caught fire, a
light breeze got up, and fanned the flames in the direction of the forest. If, on discovering these facts,
we hesitate before saying that A's action caused the
forest fire this would be to consider the alternative
hypothesis that in spite of appearances the fire only
succeeded A's action in point of time, that the
bracken flickered out harmlessly and the forest fire
was caused by something else. To dispose of this it
may be necessary to examine in further detail the
process of events between the ignition of the
bracken and the outbreak of fire in the forest and to
show that these exemplified certain types of continuous change. If this is shown, there is no longer any
room for doubt: A's action *was* the cause of the fire,
whether he intended it or not. This seems and is the
simplest of cases. Yet it is important to notice that
even in applying our general knowledge to a case
as simple as this, indeed in regarding it as simple,
we make an implicit use of a distinction between

types of factor which constitute a limit in tracing
consequences and those which we regard as mere
circumstances 'through' which we trace them. For
the breeze which sprang up after A dropped the
cigarette, and without which the fire would not
have spread to the forest, was not only subsequent
to his action but entirely independent of it: it was,
however, a common recurrent feature of the environment, and, as such, it is thought of not as an
'intervening' force but as merely part of the circumstances in which the cause 'operates.' The decision
so to regard it is implicitly taken when we combine
our knowledge of the successive stages of the
process and assert the connection.

It is easy to be misled by the natural metaphor
of a casual 'chain,' which may lead us to think that
the causal process consists of a series of single
events each of which is dependent upon (would not
have occurred without) its predecessor in the
'chain' and so is dependent upon the initiating action or event. In truth in any causal process we have
at each phase not single events but complex sets of
conditions, and among these conditions are some
which are not only subsequent to, but independent
of the initiating action or event. Some of these independent conditions, such as the evening breeze in
the example chosen, we classify as mere conditions
in or on which the cause operates; others we speak
of as 'interventions' or 'causes.' To decide how such
independent elements shall be classified is also to
decide how we shall combine our knowledge of the
different general connections which the successive
stages exemplify, and it is important to see that
nothing *in* this knowledge itself can resolve this
point. We may have to go to science for the relevant
general knowledge before we can assert with
proper confidence that A's action did cause the fire,
but science, though it tells us that an air current was
required, is silent on the difference between a current in the form of an evening breeze and one produced by someone who deliberately fanned the
flames as they were flickering out in the bracken.
Yet an air current in this deliberately induced form
is not a 'condition' or 'mere circumstance' through
which we can trace the consequence; its presence
would force us to revise the assertion that A caused
the fire. Conversely if science helped us to identify
as a necessary factor in producing the fire some condition or element of which we had previously been

totally ignorant, e.g., the persistence of oxygen, this would leave our original judgment undisturbed if this factor were a common or pervasive feature of the environment or of the thing in question. There is thus indeed an important sense in which it is true that the distinction between cause and conditions is not a 'scientific' one. It is not determined by laws or generalizations concerning connections between events.

When we have assembled all our knowledge of the factors involved in the fire, the residual question which we then confront (the attributive question) may be typified as follows: Here is *A's* action, here is the fire: can the fire be attributed to *A's* action as its consequence given that there is also this third factor (the breeze or *B's* intervention) without which the fire would not have happened? It is plain that, both in raising questions of this kind and in answering them, ordinary thought is powerfully influenced by the analogy between the straightforward cases of causal attribution (where the elements required for the production of harm in addition to the initiating action are all 'normal' conditions) and even simpler cases of responsibility which we do not ordinarily describe in causal language at all but by the simple transitive verbs of action. These are the cases of the direct manipulation of objects involving changes in them or their position: cases where we say "He pushed it,' "He broke it,' 'He bent it.' The cases which we do confidently describe in causal language ('The fire was caused by his carelessness,' 'He caused a fire') are cases where no other human action or abnormal occurrence is required for the production of the effect, but only normal conditions. Such cases appear as mere long-range or less direct versions or extensions of the most obvious and fundamental case of all for the attribution of responsibility: the case where we can simply say 'He did it.' Conversely in attaching importance to thus causing harm as a distinct ground of responsibility and in taking certain kinds of factor (whether human interventions or abnormal occurrences), without which the initiating action would not have led to harm, to preclude the description of the case in simple causal terms, common sense is affected by the fact that here, because of the manner in which the harm eventuates, the outcome cannot be represented as a mere extension of the initiating action; the analogy with the

fundamental case for responsibility ('He did it') has broken down.

When we understand the power exerted over our ordinary thought by the conception that causing harm is a mere extension of the primary case of doing harm, the interrelated metaphors which seem natural to lawyers and laymen, in describing various aspects of causal connection, fall into place and we can discuss their factual basis. The persistent notion that some kinds of event required in addition to the initiating action for the production of harm 'break the chain of causation' is intelligible, if we remember that though such events actually *complete* the *explanation* of the harm (and so *make* rather than *break* the causal explanation) they do, unlike mere normal conditions, break the *analogy* with cases of simple actions. The same analogy accounts for the description of these factors as 'new actions' (*nouvus actus*) or 'new causes,' 'superseding,' 'extraneous,' 'intervening forces': and for the description of the initiating action when 'the chain of causation' is broken as 'no longer operative,' 'having worn out,' *functus officio.*[5] So too when the 'chain' is held not to be 'broken' the initiating action is said to be still 'potent,'[6] 'continuing,' 'contributing,' 'operative,' and the mere conditions held insufficient to break the chain are 'part of the background,'[7] 'circumstances in which the cause operates,'[8] 'the stage set,' 'part of history.'

(ii) *A* throws a lighted cigarette into the bracken which catches fire. Just as the flames are about to flicker out, *B,* who is not acting in concert with *A,* deliberately pours petrol on them. The fire spreads and burns down the forest. *A's* action, whether or not he intended the forest fire, was not the cause of the fire: *B's* was.

The voluntary intervention of a second human agent, as in this case, is a paradigm among those factors which preclude the assimilation in causal judgments of the first agent's connection with the eventual harm to the case of simple direct manipulation. Such an intervention displaces the prior action's title to be called the cause and, in the persistent metaphors found in the law, it 'reduces' the earlier action and its immediate effects to the level of 'mere circumstances' or 'part of the history.' *B* in this case was not an 'instrument' through which *A* worked or a victim of the circumstances *A* has created. He has, on the contrary, freely exploited the circumstances and brought about the fire without the co-operation of any further agent or any chance coincidence. Compared with this the claim of A's action to be ranked the cause of the fire fails. That this and not the moral appraisal of the two actions is the point of comparison seems clear. If A and B both intended to set the forest on fire, and this destruction is accepted as something wrong or wicked, their moral wickedness, judged by the criterion of intention, is the same. Yet the causal judgment differentiates between them. If their moral guilt is judged by the outcome, this judgment though it would differentiate between them cannot be the source of the causal judgment; for it presupposes it. The difference just is that B has caused the harm and A has not. Again, if we appraise these actions as good or bad from different points of view, this leaves the causal judgments unchanged. A may be a soldier of one side anxious to burn down the enemy's hide-out: B may be an enemy soldier who has decided that his side is too iniquitous to defend. Whatever is the moral judgment passed on these actions by different speakers it would remain true that A had not caused the fire and B had.

There are, as we have said, situations in which a voluntary action would not be thought of as an intervention precluding causal connection in this way. These are the cases discussed further below where an opportunity commonly exploited for harmful actions is negligently provided, or one person intentionally provides another with the means, the opportunity, or a certain type of reason for wrongdoing. Except in such cases a voluntary intervention is a limit past which consequences are not traced. By contrast, actions which in any of a variety of different ways are less than fully voluntary are assimilated to the means by which or the circumstances in which the earlier action brings about the consequences. Such actions are not the outcome of an informed choice made without pressure from others, and the different ways in which human action may fall short in this respect range from defective muscular control, through lack of consciousness or knowledge, to the vaguer notions of duress and of predicaments, created by the first agent for the second, in which there is no 'fair' choice.

In considering examples of such actions and their bearing on causal judgments there are three dangers to avoid. It would be folly to think that in tracing connections through such actions instead of regarding them, like voluntary interventions, as a limit, ordinary thought has clearly separated out their non-voluntary aspect from others by which they are often accompanied. Thus even in the crude case where A lets off a gun (intentionally or not) and startles B, so that he makes an involuntary movement of his arm which breaks a glass, the commonness of such a reaction as much as its compulsive character may influence the judgment that A's action was the cause of the damage.

Secondly we must not impute to ordinary thought all the fine discriminations that could be made and in fact are to be found in a legal system, or an equal willingness to supply answers to complex questions in causal terms. Where there is no precise system of punishment, compensation or reward to administer, ordinary men will not often have faced such questions as whether the injuries suffered by a motorist who collides with another in swerving to avoid a child are consequences attributable to the neglect of the child's parents in allowing it to wander onto the road. Such questions courts have to answer and in such cases common judgments provide only a general, though still an important indication of what are the relevant factors.

Thirdly, though very frequently non-voluntary actions are assimilated to mere conditions or means by which the first agent brings about the consequences, the assimilation is never quite complete. This is manifested by the general avoidance of many causal locutions which are appropriate when the consequences are traced (as in the first case) through purely physical events. Thus even in the case in which the second agent's role is hardly an 'action' at all, e.g., where A hits B, who staggers against a glass window and breaks it, we should say that A's blow made B stagger and break the glass, rather than that A's blow caused the glass to break, though in an explanatory or attributive context the case would be *summarized* by saying that A's action was the cause of the *damage*.

In the last two cases where B's movements are involuntary in the sense that they are not part of any action which he chose or intended to do, their connection with A's action would be described by saying that A's blow *made* B stagger or *caused* him to stagger or that the noise of A's shot *made* him jump or *caused* him to jump. This would be true, whether A intended or expected B to react in this way or not, and the naturalness of treating A's action as the cause of the ultimate damage is due to the causal character of this part of the process involving B's action. The same is, however, true where B's actions are not involuntary movement but A is considered to have made or caused B to do them by less crude means. This is the case if, for example, A uses threats or exploits his authority over B to make B do something, e.g., knock down a door. At least where A's threats are of serious harm, or B's act was unquestionably within A's authority to order, he too has made or forced or (in formal quasi-legal parlance) 'caused' B to act.

Outside the area of such cases, where B's will would be said either not to be involved at all, or to be overborne by A, are cases where A's act creates a predicament for B *narrowing* the area of choice so that he has either to inflict some harm on himself or others, or sacrifice some important interest or duty. Such cases resemble coercion in that A narrows the area of B's choice but differ from it in that this predicament need not be intentionally created. A sets a house on fire (intentionally or unintentionally): B to save himself has to jump from a height involving certain injury, or to save a child rushes in and is seriously burned. Here, of course, B's movements are not involuntary; the 'necessity' of his action is here of a different order. His action is the outcome of a choice between two evils forced on him by A's action. In such cases, when B's injuries are thought of as the consequence of the fire, the implicit judgment is made that his action was the lesser of two evils and in this sense a 'reasonable' one which he was obliged to make to avoid the greater evil. This is often paradoxically, though understandably, described by saying that here the agent 'had no choice' but to do what he did. Such judgments involve a comparison of the importance of the respective interests sacrificed and preserved, and the final assertion that A's action was the cause of the injuries rests on evaluations about which men may differ.

Finally, the ground for treating some harm which would not have occurred without B's action as the consequence of A's action may be that B acted in ignorance of or under a mistake as to some feature of the situation created by A. Poisoning of-fers perhaps the simplest example of the bearing on causal judgments of actions which are less than voluntary in this Aristotelian sense. If A intending B's death deliberately poisons B's food and B, knowing this, deliberately takes the poison and dies, A has not, unless he coerced B into eating the poisoned food, caused B's death: if, however, B does not know the food to be poisoned, eats it, and dies, A has caused his death, even if he put the poison in unwittingly. Of course only the roughest judgments are passed in causal terms in such cases outside law courts, where fine degrees of 'appreciation' or 'reckless shutting of the eyes' may have to be discriminated from 'full knowledge.' Yet, rough as these are, they indicate clearly enough the controlling principles.

Though in the foregoing cases A's initiating action might often be described as 'the cause' of the ultimate harm, this linguistic fact is of subordinate importance to the fact that, for whatever purpose, explanatory, descriptive, or evaluative, consequences of an action are traced, discriminations are made (except in the cases discussed later) between free voluntary interventions and less than voluntary reactions to the first action or the circumstances created by it.

(iii) The analogy with single simple actions which guides the tracing of consequences may be broken by certain kinds of conjunctions of physical events. A hits B who falls to the ground stunned and bruised by the blow; at that moment a tree crashes to the ground and kills B. A has certainly caused B's bruises but not his death: for though the fall of the tree was, like the evening breeze in our earlier example, independent of and subsequent to the initiating action, it would be differentiated from the breeze in any description in causal terms of the connection of B's death with A's action. It is to be noticed that this is not a matter which turns on the intention with which A struck B. Even if A hit B inadvertently or accidentally his blow would still be the cause of B's bruises: he would have caused them, though unintentionally. Conversely even if A had intended his blow to kill, this would have been an attempt to kill but still not the cause of B's death, unless A knew that the tree was about to fall just at that moment. On this legal and ordinary judgments would be found to agree; and most legal systems would distinguish for the purposes of punishment an attempt with a fatal upshot, issuing by such chance or anomalous events, from 'causing death'— the terms in which the offenses of murder and manslaughter are usually defined.

Similarly the causal description of the case does not turn on the moral appraisal of *A's* action or the wish to punish it. *A* may be a robber and a murderer and *B* a saint guarding the place *A* hoped to plunder. Or *B* may be a murderer and *A* a hero who has forced his way into *B's* retreat. In both cases the causal judgment is the same. *A* had caused the minor injuries but not *B's* death, though he tried to kill him. *A* may indeed be praised or blamed but not for causing *B's* death. However intimate the connection between responsibility and causation, it does not determine causal judgments in this simple way. Nor does the causal judgment turn on a refusal to attribute grave consequences to actions which normally have less serious results. Had *A's* blow killed *B* outright and the tree, falling on his body, merely smashed his watch we should still treat the coincidental character of the fall of the tree as determining the form of causal statement. We should then recognize *A's* blow as the cause of *B's* death but not the breaking of the watch.

The connection between *A's* action and *B's* death in the first case would naturally be described in the language of *coincidence*. 'It was a coincidence: it just happened that, at the very moment when *A* knocked *B* down, a tree crashed at the very place where he fell and killed him.' The common legal metaphor would describe the fall of the tree as an 'extraneous' cause. This, however, is dangerously misleading, as an analysis of the notion of coincidence will show. It suggests merely an event which is subsequent to and independent of some other contingency, and of course the fall of the tree has both these features in relation to *A's* blow. Yet in these respects the fall of the tree does not differ from the evening breeze in the earlier case where we found no difficulty in tracing causal connection. The full elucidation of the notion of a coincidence is a complex matter for, though it is very important as a limit in tracing consequences, causal questions are not the only ones to which the notion is relevant. The following are its most general characteristics. We speak of a coincidence whenever the conjunction of two or more events in certain spatial or temporal re-

lations (1) is very unlikely by ordinary standards and (2) is for some reason significant or important, provided (3) that they occur without human contrivance and (4) are independent of each other. It is therefore a coincidence if two persons known to each other in London meet without design in Paris on their way to separate independently chosen destinations; or if two persons living in different places, independently decide to write a book on the same subject. The first is a coincidence of time and place ('It just happened that we were at the same place at the same time'), and the second a coincidence of time only ('It just happened that they both decided to write on the subject at the same time').

Use of this general notion is made in the special case when the conjunction of two or more events occurs in temporal and/or spatial relationships which are significant, because, as our general knowledge of causal processes shows, this conjunction is required for the production of some given further event. In the language of Mill's idealized model, they form a necessary part of a complex set of jointly sufficient conditions. In the present case the fall of the tree just as *B* was struck down within its range satisfies the four criteria for a coincidence which we have enumerated. First, though neither event was of a very rare or exceptional kind, their conjunction would be rated very unlikely judged by the standards of ordinary experience. Secondly, this conjunction was causally significant for it was a necessary part of the process terminating in *B's* death. Thirdly, this conjunction was not consciously designed by *A*; had he known of the impending fall of the tree and hit *B* with the intention that he should fall within its range *B's* death would not have been the result of any coincidence. *A* would certainly have caused it. The common-sense principle that a contrived conjunction cannot be a coincidence is the element of truth in the legal maxim (too broadly stated even for legal purposes) that an intended consequence cannot be too 'remote.' Fourthly, each member of the conjunction in this case was independent of the other; whereas if *B* had fallen against the tree with an impact sufficient to bring it down on him, this sequence of physical events, though freakish in its way, would not be a coincidence and in most contexts of ordinary life, as in the law, the course of events would be summarized by saying that in this case, unlike that of the coincidence, *A's* act was the cause of *B's* death, since each stage is the effect of the preceding stage. Thus, the blow forced the victim against the tree, the effect of this was to make the tree fall and the fall of the tree killed the victim.

One further criterion in addition to these four must be satisfied if a conjunction of events is to rank as a coincidence and as a limit when the consequences of the action are traced. This further criterion again shows the strength of the influence which the analogy with the case of the simple manipulation of things exerts over thought in causal terms. An abnormal *condition* existing at the time of a human intervention is distinguished both by ordinary thought and, with a striking consistency, by most legal systems from an abnormal event or conjunction of events subsequent to that intervention; the former, unlike the latter, are not ranked as coincidences or 'extraneous' causes when the consequences of the intervention come to be traced. Thus *A* innocently gives *B* a tap over the head of a normally quite harmless character, but because *B* is then suffering from some rare disease the tap has, as we say, 'fatal results.' In this case *A* has caused *B's* death though unintentionally. The scope of the principle which thus distinguishes contemporaneous abnormal conditions from subsequent events is unclear; but at least where a human being initiates some physical change in a thing, animal, or person, abnormal physical states of the object affected, existing at the time, are ranked as part of the circumstances in which the cause 'operates.' In the familiar controlling imagery these are part of 'the stage already set' before the 'intervention.'

Judgments about coincidences, though we often agree in making them, depend in two related ways on issues incapable of precise formulation. One of these is patent, the other latent but equally important. Just how unlikely must a conjunction be to rank as a coincidence, and in the light of what knowledge is likelihood to be assessed? The only answer is: 'very unlikely in the light of the knowledge available to ordinary men.' It is, of course, the indeterminacies of such standards, implicit in causal judgments, that make them inveterately disputable, and call for the exercise of discretion or choice by courts. The second and latent indeterminacy of these judgments depends on the fact that the things or events to which they relate do not have pinned to them some uniquely correct description always to be used in assessing likelihood. It is an important pervasive feature of all our empirical judgments that there is a constant possibility of more or less specific description of any event or thing with which they are concerned. The tree might be described not simply as a 'tree' but as a 'rotten tree' or as a 'fir tree' or a 'tree sixty feet tall.' So too its fall might be described not as a 'fall' but as a fall of a specified distance at a specified velocity. The likelihood of conjunctions framed in these different terms would be differently assessed. The criteria of appropriate description like the standard of likelihood are supplied by consideration of common knowledge. Even if the scientist knew the tree to be rotten and could have predicted its fall with accuracy, this would not change the judgment that its fall at the time when *B* was struck down within its range was a coincidence; nor would it make the description 'rotten tree' appropriate for the assessment of the chances involved in this judgment. There are other controls over the choice of description derived from the degree of specificity of our interests in the final outcome of the causal process. We are concerned with the fall of an object sufficient to cause 'death' by impact and the precise force or direction which may account for the detail of the wounds is irrelevant here.

Opportunities and Reasons

Opportunities. The discrimination of voluntary interventions as a limit is no longer made when the case, owing to the commonness or appreciable risk of such harmful intervention, can be brought within the scope of the notion of providing an opportunity, known to be commonly exploited for doing harm. Here the limiting principles are different. When *A* leaves the house unlocked the range of consequences to be attributed to this neglect, as in any other case where precautions are omitted, depends primarily on the way in which such opportunities are commonly exploited. An alternative formulation of this idea is that a subsequent intervention would fall within the scope of consequences if the likelihood of its occurring is one of the reasons for holding *A's* omission to be negligent.

It is on these lines that we would distinguish between the entry of a thief and of a murderer; the opportunity provided is believed to be sufficiently commonly exploited by thieves to make it usual and often morally or legally obligatory not to provide it. Here, in attributing consequences to prior actions, causal judgments are directly controlled by the notion of the risk created by them. Neglect of such precautions is both unusual and reprehensible. For these reasons it would be hard to separate the two ways in which such neglect deviates from the 'norm.' Despite this, no simple identification can be made of the notion of responsibility with the causal connection which is a ground for it. This is so because the provision of an opportunity commonly taken by others is ranked as the cause of the outcome independently of the wish to praise or blame. The causal judgment may be made simply to assess a contribution to some outcome. Thus, whether we think well or ill of the use made of railways, we would still claim that the greater mobility of the population in the nineteenth century was a consequence of their introduction.

It is obvious that the question whether any given intervention is a sufficiently common exploitation of the opportunity provided to come within the risk is again a matter on which judgments may differ, though they often agree. The courts, and perhaps ordinary thought also, often describe those that are sufficiently common as 'natural' consequences of the neglect. They have in these terms discriminated the entry of a thief from the entry of a man who burnt the house down, and refused to treat the destruction of the house as a 'natural' consequence of the neglect.[9]

We discuss later in Chapter IX the argument that this easily intelligible concept of 'harm within the risk,' overriding as it does the distinctions between voluntary interventions and others, should be used as the general test for determining what subsequent harm should be attributed for legal purposes to prior action. The merits of this proposal to refashion the law along these simple lines are perhaps considerable, yet consequences of actions are in fact often traced both in the law and apart from it in other ways which depend on the discrimination of voluntary interventions from others. We distinguish, after all, as differing though related grounds of responsibility, causing harm by

one's own action and providing opportunities for others to do harm, where the guiding analogy with the simple manipulation of things, which underlies causal thought, is less close. When, as in the examples discussed above, we trace consequences through the non-voluntary interventions of others our concern is to show that certain stages of the process have a certain type of connection with the preceding stages, and not, as when the notion of risk is applied, to show that the ultimate outcome is connected in some general way with the initiating action. Thus, when *A's* shot makes *B* start and break a glass it is the causal relationship described by the expression 'made *B* start' that we have in mind and not the likelihood that on hearing a shot someone may break a glass. Causal connection may be traced in such cases though the initiating action and the final outcome are not contingencies that commonly go together.

Apart from these conceptual reasons for distinguishing these related grounds for responsibility, it is clear that both in the law . . . and apart from it we constantly treat harm as caused by a person's action though it does not fall 'within the risk.' If, when *B* broke the glass in the example given above, a splinter flew into *C's* eye, blinding him, *A's* action is indeed the cause of *C's* injury though we may not always blame him for so unusual a consequence.

Reasons. In certain varieties of interpersonal transactions, unlike the case of coercion, the second action is quite voluntary. *A* may not threaten *B* but may bribe or advise or persuade him to do something. Here, *A* does not 'cause' or 'make' *B* do anything: the strongest words we should use are perhaps that he 'induced' or 'procured' *B's* act. Yet the law and moral principles alike may treat one person as responsible for the harm which another free agent has done 'in consequence' of the advice or the inducements which the first has offered. In such cases the limits concern the range of those actions done by *B* which are to rank as the consequence of *A's* words or deeds. In general this question depends on *A's* intentions or on the 'plan of action' he puts before *B*. If *A* advises or bribes *B* to break in and steal from an empty house and *B* does so, he acts in consequence of *A's* advice or bribe. If he deliberately burns down the house this would not be treated as the consequence of *A's* bribe or advice, legally or otherwise, though it may in some sense be true that the burning would not have taken place without the advice or bribe. Nice questions may arise, which the courts have to settle, where *B* diverges from the detail of the plan of action put before him by *A*.

. . .

Endnotes

[1] Glanville Williams, *Joint Torts and Contributory Negligence*, p. 239.

[2] Mill, Book III, chap. V, s. 2.

[3] Ross, *The Right and the Good*, p. 36.

[4] E.g., if the guest was suspected of being a compulsive stabber and the waiter had therefore been told to lay only a plastic knife in his place.

[5] *Davies v. Swan Motor Co.* [1947] 2 KB 291, 318.

[6] *Minister of Pensions v. Chennell* [1947] KB 250, 256. Lord Wright (1950), 13 MLR 3.

[7] *Norris v. William Moss & Son Ltd.* [1954] 1 WLR 46, 351.

[8] *Minister of Pensions v. Chennell* [1947] KB 250, 256.

[9] *Bellows v. Worcester Storage Co.* (1937) 297 Mass. 188, 7 NE 2d 588.

96. The Decline of Cause

Judith Jarvis Thomson

I

Once upon a time there was a simple way of characterizing tort law. It could in those days be said that the defendant will be declared liable for the plaintiff's loss if and only if the plaintiff proves the following three things: (1) that he suffered a loss, (2) that an act or failure to act on the part of the defendant was proximate cause of the plaintiff's suffering that loss, and (3) that the defendant was at fault in so acting or failing to act. Proximate cause was a messy business, of course, but one thing that was clear was that a person's act or omission was not proximate cause of another person's loss unless it caused the loss.

So much for once upon a time. Fault went first: it began to be possible in certain kinds of cases for a plaintiff to win his suit if he proved (1) that he suffered a loss, and (2) that an act or failure to act on the part of the defendant proximately caused his loss, even though he did not prove (3)

that the defendant was at fault in so acting or failing to act. Now cause is going. In a number of cases in recent years the plaintiff has won his suit on proof (1) that he suffered a loss, and (3) that there was a faulty act or omission on the part of the defendant, but without proving (2) that the defendant's faulty act or omission caused the loss. No doubt the plaintiff has to prove *some* connection between his loss and the defendant's faulty act. If I prove I lost my legs this morning, and that you hit your little brother with a brick yesterday, *that* certainly will not suffice for me to win a suit against you for damages for the loss of my legs. The plaintiff has to connect the faulty act with the loss. But in the kind of case I have in mind, the connection he makes need not be causation.

Which kind of case? A good example is *Sindell v. Abbott Laboratories*,[1] which was decided by the California Supreme Court in 1980. The plaintiff alleged she could prove that she developed cancer as a result of the DES taken by her mother while pregnant; she alleged she could prove also that the defendants—eleven drug companies—knew or should have known that DES would cause cancer in the daughters of mothers who took it. In other words, she alleged she could prove (1) that she was harmed, and (3) that the defendant drug companies were at fault. But she was unable to prove, after the passage of so many years, which drug company had marketed the very DES her mother took, so she was unable to prove about any of the drug companies (2) that *its* acts had caused the harm she suffered. All the same, she won the right to get a jury on the fact she alleged she could prove, and the right to win if she could prove them.

An earlier California case—*Summers v. Tice*,[2] decided in 1948—presented the problem that confronted the plaintiff in *Sindell* much more starkly and cleanly. The plaintiff Summers had gone hunting with the two defendants, Tice and Simonson. A quail was flushed, and, as Summers alleged, the defendants fired negligently in Summers' direction; as he also alleged, one of the two wounded him. But he was unable to prove which, since the defendants had fired similar pellets from similar guns. Loss yes, fault yes, but causality could not be proved. However he too won his suit.

My own impression is that cases like *Summers* and *Sindell*—in which loss and fault are clear, but causality cannot be proved—were very rarely won until recently. Why are they being won now? It is an excellent question, with, I am sure, a great many answers. Chief among them is probably a mix of four things: first, the very fact that causality *is* hard to prove in them; together with, second, the felt need to regulate the increasing number of activities which impose risk as a byproduct of technological advance; third, an increasing public acceptance of egalitarianism; and fourth the absence as yet of a mechanism other than the tort suit to regulate those activities and secure a measure of compensation for those who may be being victimized by them.[3]

II

A related phenomenon—at least I think it really must be related—is the increasing dismissiveness about causality that can be seen in legal theorizing. Here are Landes and Posner in an article published in 1983: "causation in the law is an inarticulate groping for economically sound solutions. . . . "[4] In an article published in 1975, Calabresi defends the idea that certain concepts related to causality have a role to play in law, but his defense of that idea would have puzzled many lawyers fifty years ago. He says:

> [I]n law the term "cause" is used in different guises but always to identify those pressure points that are most amenable to the social goals we wish to accomplish. . . . [U]se of such [causal] concepts has great advantages over explicit identification and separation of the goals. Terms with an historical, common law gloss [like "cause"] permit us to consider goals (like spreading) that we do not want to spell out or too obviously assign to judicial institutions.[5]

This dismissiveness about causality is not visible only in those whose legal theorizing is influenced by economics.[6]

III

I am not competent to speak to the question why the law and legal theory have been developing in these ways, or even to the question exactly what forms these developments have taken. What I want to do instead is to mull over one of the sources of the welcome with which these developments have been received by many of the moral philosophers who have taken note of them.

What I have in mind is that there has been a phenomenon equally entitled to be called " The Decline of Cause" in moral theorizing.

The moral sophisticate nowadays is nowhere near as enamored of causality as the ignorant rest of us. Here is an example. Yesterday, Alfred backed his car out of his driveway without looking. Bad of him!—one ought not do that. Today, Bert backed his car out of his driveway without looking, but lo and behold there was a child at the end of the driveway, and Bert ran over the child and crushed its legs. Horrendous—much worse. Or so many people think.

The moral sophisticate regards that as a vulgar error. "Look," he says, "both Alfred and Bert behaved negligently, indeed equally negligently. Bert crushed a child's legs and Alfred did not, but that was just bad luck for Bert, and good luck for Alfred. After all, it wasn't Bert's fault that there was a child at the foot of his driveway; all Bert was at fault for is exactly what Alfred was at fault for, namely backing his car out of his driveway without looking. So Bert acted no worse than Alfred did and—other things being equal—Bert is no worse a person than Alfred is."

The moral sophisticate may concede that the law does well to mark a difference between Alfred and Bert in the following two ways: (1) imposing a more severe punishment on Bert than on Alfred, and (2) making Bert, and not Alfred, compensate the child's parents. But if so, he says it is for reasons extraneous to the *moral* valuation proper to them and their acts.

It is clear that the moral sophisticate is going to hold this same view in other pairs of cases too. Murder and attempted murder, of course. Yesterday Charles fired a gun at a man, to kill him; Charles'[s] intended victim was wearing a bullet proof vest, so Charles did not kill him. Today David fired a gun at a man, to kill him; David's intended victim was not wearing a bullet proof anything, so David did kill him. David murdered a man, and Charles only attempted murder, but the moral sophisticate says that David acted no worse than Charles did—for after all, it was just bad luck for Charles that his intended victim was wearing that vest, and thus nothing that Charles can take any credit for.

It seems to me three principles lie behind this moral attitude. The first concerns itself with *acts*. What we do in the world depends on the world as well as on us. If you fire a gun at a man to kill him, then the question whether you do not merely fire a gun at him, but also kill him turns on whether the world cooperates—thus on whether the bullet actually reaches him, as it might not if some third party intervenes, and on whether it enters him when it reaches him, as it might not if he is wearing bullet proof clothes. The first principle I have in mind says that the moral value of what you do in the world turns on and only on that part of it which is *entirely* under your control. When you fire a gun at a man, what is under your control is at most such things as the kind of gun you fire, the time

and place at which you fire it, the direction in which you fire it, and the intention with which you fire it—merely to scare your victim, or merely to wound him, or positively to kill him. The rest that happens is up to the world, and is not something that has any bearing on the moral value of your act.

I said "at most." Let us look again at the kind of gun you fire. Is it new? Is it clean? Is it sufficiently powerful to do the work you want it to do? Strictly speaking, that the gun you fire does or does not have these features is not entirely under your control. What is under your control is only that you have made an effort to be sure that you are firing a suitable gun and now think you are: After all, somebody might have secretly replaced your carefully chosen gun with a different one—whether a person did or did not do this is not under your control. Similarly for the time and place at which you fire the gun, and the direction in which you fire it: Somebody might have secretly altered your clocks and roadmaps, and substituted distorting glasses for the glasses you normally wear—whether a person did or did not do this is also not under your control.

Strictly speaking, all that is entirely under your control are your intentions in acting—what you are at any given time setting yourself to be doing. That is not to say that setting yourself to do this or that is all you actually *do*; it is to say that the normal value of what you do *by* setting yourself to act in this or that way turns entirely on the moral value of those settings of yourself to act.

The second of the three principles concerns itself with *failures to act*, or omissions, for short. Consider two switchmen on different railways, Edward and Frank. Both were under a duty to throw a switch at ten this morning, and both failed to do so because they did not want to be bothered. Edward's omission caused a terrible train crash; Frank's omission caused nothing untoward at all, since the train Frank's switch-throwing was to turn had luckily stalled before the fork in the track. If you think murder no worse than attempted murder, you will surely think Edward's omission no worse than Frank's. It was, after all, no credit to Frank, it was merely good luck for him, that his train had stalled. The second principle says that the moral value of an omission—as of an act—turns on and only on what is entirely under the agent's control. If you could have set yourself to do a thing, and ought to have done so, then your failure to do so is equally bad no matter what your omission does or does not cause.

The cases of Alfred and Bert with which I began are cases to which both principles apply. Alfred and Bert both acted, for they backed their cars down their driveways; and both failed to act, for they failed to look while doing so. Given the two principles, the fact that Bert's acting while failing to act caused a child's legs to be crushed has no bearing at all on the moral value of what he did.

The third of the three principles has to do with the moral value of *persons*. We do think of some people as morally better than others; on what does this judgment turn? Presumably in part on the moral value of what a person does or fails to do. Given the first two principles, however, that is a function only of the moral value of a person's settings of himself to do this or that, and his failures to set himself to do this or that.

But only in part, for there is something else that a friend of these ideas should think bears on a person's moral value. What I have in mind is that if you think that good and bad luck has no bearing on the moral value of an act or omission *or* person, then you should grant that the truth or falsehood of certain counterfactuals is relevant. For example, I do not drive, and a fortiori have never backed my car out of my driveway with *or* without looking. If I had driven, would I on occasion have backed my car out of my driveway without looking? Isn't that relevant to the question how good or bad a person I am?

I am sure that all of us have faced temptations to act badly, and that many of those temptations we have resisted, though some we have not. Most people, however, are lucky enough never to be tempted to do something truly dreadful. For example, I am sure that none of us has ever been in a position of power over prisoners in a concentration camp. I am sure that none of us has been lost at sea in a lifeboat with no provisions other than a plump cabin boy. We have been lucky. How would we behave if we were in such situations? Surely that we would or would not behave in this or that way has a bearing on our moral value as people. One reason why Stanley Milgram's experiments[7] were found so shocking was that they uncovered the fact that a lot of perfectly ordinary people were quite ready to set

themselves to cause others a great deal of pain simply on being told by an authority figure in a white coat to do so. Milgram's readers did not think for a moment that the actual absence of pain excused the subjects of the experiments; and they took it that what Milgram had shown was a deep moral failing which may be present in perfectly ordinary people, though without ever in fact showing itself.

How good a person are you? The third principle tells us that to the extent to which you do not know what you would set yourself to do in situations you have been so far lucky as not to have faced, you just do not know how good a person you are.

I described the person who holds these views as the "moral sophisticate," because I think we do think these views more sophisticated than those which tell us to look merely at what happens, more sophisticated even than those which tell us to look *both* at what happens *and* at what is internal to a person—what he sets himself to do, and what he would set himself to do if he were in situations he has never faced. But I might just as well have described the person who holds these views as a Kantian, because it is directly from Kant that they come down to us today. Kant said: "The good will is not good because of what it effects or accomplishes or because of its adequacy to achieve some proposed end; it is good only because of its willing, i.e., it is good of itself. . . . Usefulness or fruitlessness can neither diminish or augment [its] worth."[8] And so similarly for the bad will: it is not bad because of what it causes, but only of itself. We might redescribe the decline of cause in moral philosophy as the triumph of Kant.

That Kant has triumphed seems clear enough. For example, I rather fancy that all of you have at least some inclination to agree with the three principles I drew attention to. I certainly do.

It is of interest to notice that these Kantian ideas are visible even in contemporary defenders of the most un-Kantian moral theory of all. I have Utilitarianism in mind, of course. Classical Utilitarians—such as John Stuart Mill and G. E. Moore—took the view that you have acted wrongly if and only if your act causes there to be less good in the world than you could have caused by choosing some other alternative act which was open to you at the time. Whether you knew it or not. Mill did explicitly grant that a man's intentions in acting do have a bearing on the moral evaluation *proper* to him; but Mill insisted that the morality of a man's *act* turns on, and only on, a comparison between what it does in fact cause, and what his other available alternatives would have caused. But hardly anyone is a Classical Utilitarian nowadays. Those in favor of its spirit say that the morality of a man's act turns, not on what it in fact causes, but on what he expects it to cause. In short, the morality of action turns, not on actual, but on expected utilities.

Now I think that these Kantian ideas are one source of the welcome with which many moral philosophers have received those developments in law and legal theory that I mentioned at the outset. For example, they think that all of the defendants were at fault in *Sindell* and *Summers*—equally at fault, regardless of whoever in fact caused the harm. So they think that no one can object, on *moral* grounds, to the plaintiffs' winning, and to the defendants' therefore having to share in the plaintiffs' costs.⁹

IV

What should *we* think of all this? It is swimming upstream to try to fight it, but my own feeling is that it smells too much of the study and too little of the open air. Adam Smith said, very plausibly, I think,

> But how well soever we may seem to be persuaded of the truth of [these ideas], when we consider [them] after this manner, in abstract, yet when we come to particular cases, the actual consequences which happen to proceed from any action, have a very great effect upon our sentiments concerning its merit or demerit, and almost always either enhance or diminish our sense of both.¹⁰

Alfred backed his car out of his driveway without looking, and luckily for him, nothing untoward happened in consequence. Bad of him, we think. But not horrendous. People do that kind of thing often enough. They ought not, but they do, and it seems no great sin. Bert also backed his car out of his driveway without looking, but *he* ran a child down and crushed its legs. As Adam Smith said,

we just *do* think that what Bert did was worse than what Alfred did. How can any philosophy be right which tells us we are mistaken in thinking this?

On the other hand, I think that Adam Smith's remark would not have been at all plausible if he had not said "almost always." He said: "the actual consequences which happen to proceed from any action, have a very great effect upon our sentiments concerning its merit or demerit, and *almost always* either enhance or diminish our sense of both."¹¹ There seem to me to be two kinds of case in which they do not.

To get at the first kind, let me draw your attention to the fact that in every example I have given, right from the outset, the agent whose act did cause a harm was at fault. In the two court cases I began with, all of the defendants were at fault, the drug companies in *Sindell*, the negligent hunters in *Summers*. Alfred and Bert were both careless. Charles and David, each of whom shot at a man to kill him, were both at least attempting murder. And so on. But what of an agent who causes someone to suffer a harm, but not by negligence or intention or by any wrong at all? A child runs out into the street and is run down by a truck driver who is entirely without fault—he has taken all due care to ensure that his truck, and in particular, his brakes, were in good order, and he was driving with all due care. The child simply ran too suddenly, too close, into the path of his truck. Does the very fact that he caused harm to the child diminish our sense of the merit of his actions? I think not. This example comes from Thomas Nagel, and he says about it: "The driver, if he is entirely without fault, will feel terrible about his role in the event, but will not have to reproach himself."¹² Nor will we reproach him. There is nothing to reproach him for. So here is a case of the first kind I had in mind: it is a case in which an agent was not at fault at all in acting, and that a bad consequence happens to flow from his action does not affect our sense of its merit or demerit. In particular, the bad consequence does not make us think worse of his driving than we would have thought had that bad consequence not flowed from it.

Symmetrically, we might imagine someone who does something of no particular merit, and something good just happens to flow from his doing it. For example, suppose a man is standing at a street corner, waiting for a bus. As he waits, he is idly tapping his foot. Through some freak of nature, his tapping his foot causes three lives to be saved. This good consequence does not affect our sense of the merit or demerit of his tapping his foot. In particular, it does not make us think better of his tapping his foot than we would have thought had that good consequence not flowed from it.

Let us go back to that truck driver, whom I will call Unlucky No Fault Driver. His not having been at fault must be the crucial fact about him which makes him an exception to Adam Smith's remarks. For let us now contrast him with two other truck drivers. Both of them were at fault. They were supposed to check their brakes before leaving the garage, but did not want to be bothered. So both went out with bad brakes. In the case of the first, nothing untoward happened, and I will call him Lucky Fault Driver. I will call the second Unlucky Fault Driver. A child ran in front of Unlucky Fault Driver's truck and he ran it down. I want to have it be clear about Unlucky Fault Driver that he ran the child down not because the child ran too suddenly, too close into the path of his truck, but because his brakes were not in good working order. Had his brakes been in good working order, he would have been able to stop his truck in time; but they were not, so he was not. Lucky Fault Driver acted badly, of course; but I think we do feel that Unlucky Fault Driver acted worse. The fact that a bad consequence flowed from his action does seem to affect our sense of its demerit.

Why? I think the answer is quite simply that Unlucky Fault Driver is to blame for the death he caused. Unlucky No Fault Driver also caused a death; but he is not to blame for it, since he was in no way at fault for causing it. It seems right to say that that is why the bad consequence which flowed from Unlucky No Fault Driver's action does not make us think it worse than we would have thought it had that bad consequence not flowed from it. More generally, it seems right to say that a bad consequence of an action makes that action worse *only* where the agent is to blame for that bad consequence which his action causes.

I am sure that the Kantian moral sophisticate would say at this point, "But surely it was mere bad luck for Unlucky Fault Driver that he caused a child's death. And surely one can't plausibly think

a man to blame for something that he caused merely out of bad luck." There is a mistake here, and I think it the main source of the trouble. For it was not *mere* bad luck for Unlucky Fault Driver that he caused a child's death. We need a clearer grip on how bad luck figures in these cases. Unlucky No Fault Driver was in two ways unlucky. It was a piece of bad luck for him that a child ran into his path; and second, it was a piece of bad luck for him that a child ran into his path; but it was not a piece of bad luck for him that he was unable to stop his truck in time. Unlucky Fault Driver was unlucky in only the first of those two ways. It was a piece of bad luck for him that he was unable to stop his truck in time. His being unable to stop his truck in time was due to his bad brakes, and thus to his own negligence. Lucky Fault Driver did not have that first piece of bad luck, so it remains a counterfactual truth about him that *if* he had had it, then he too would have been unable to stop his truck in time. His being unable to stop would not have been a mere piece of bad luck for him, but would, instead, have been due to his negligence.

And it is the very same thing—namely Unlucky Fault Driver's negligence—that makes it not *mere* bad luck for him that he caused the child's death, that also makes him to blame for the child's death. Unlucky No Fault Driver, by contrast, was not at fault; and that is why it was mere bad luck for him that he caused a child's death, and therefore also why he is not to blame for the death of the child he killed.

The Kantian moral sophisticate could of course insist that a man cannot be thought to blame for something if bad luck entered *in any way at all* into the history of his bringing it about. But that seems to me even on its face implausible. Consider, for example, a man who is brought to trial for murder. "Look," his lawyer says to the court, "I grant that the victim's death is not *mere* bad luck for my client, since my client fired a gun at him with the intention of killing him. But the victim's death is in part due to my client's bad luck. For unbeknownst to my client, the victim almost always wore a bullet proof vest, and it was just bad luck for my client that the victim's bullet proof vest happened to be at the cleaners' on the day my client shot at him. So my client cannot be thought to blame for his victim's death." Whatever else will work in a court, *that* won't.

Let us go back now and look again at the first of the three principles that I said lie behind the moral attitude of the Kantian moral sophisticate. The first principle is: the moral value of what you do in the world turns on and only on that part of it which is entirely under your control. That seems to me to be false, and for the reason I have pointed to. Admittedly the two faulty drivers, Lucky Fault Driver and Unlucky Fault Driver, both acted equally negligently, and the difference between them has its source in the fact that one had good luck, the other bad luck. All the same, the difference which has that source is a moral difference, and of a very grave order. For the one is *by* his negligence to blame for a death, and the other is not.

A similar point surely holds of failures to act. Edward and Frank both failed to throw the switch; Edward's (but not Frank's) negligence caused a crash, for which he is therefore to blame. That, I think, is why we think that what he did was worse than what Frank did.

It seems to me, however, that we should be more sympathetic to the third of the three principles I mentioned, which yields that Unlucky Fault Driver is no worse a person than Lucky Fault Driver is, and that Edward is no worse a person than Frank. Counterfactual truths about what people would have done and been to blame for if they had been in circumstances which they were lucky enough to have avoided really are important to us in assessing how good a person is—as important, I think, as truths about what they in fact did and in fact are to blame for.

This difference between our judgments of acts on the one hand and the people who perform them on the other hand may perhaps be due to the fact that different kinds of consequences flow from our arriving at these two different kinds of judgments. When we learn that someone is a bad person—untrustworthy, unreliable, prone to acting without thought for others—what flows from this judgment? Well, our attitude toward him changes, and in consequences we will behave differently toward him in many more or less delicate ways in the future. This reaction is appropriate whether the judgment is provoked by what he actually did *or* by what we have come to learn he would do if he were in circumstances he has not in fact been in. By contrast, some of the consequences of learning that a person has actually acted badly are backward looking. If we learn he is to blame for a dreadful outcome, we do not merely alter our behavior toward him in future, we may also lock him up for what he did, or exact compensation for it from him, or both.[13]

V

Candor, however, compels me to mention a difficulty for what I have been saying. Let us go back to Adam Smith. He said: "the actual consequences which happen to proceed from any action, have a great effect upon our sentiments concerning its merit or demerit, and *almost always* either enhance or diminish our sense of both."[14] I mentioned one class of exceptions. Unlucky No Fault Driver, for example, was merely unlucky. He caused a child's death, but because this was through no fault of his own, we do not think the worse of his actions. Where there is fault, however, I said that consequences do make a difference. We do think worse of Unlucky Fault Driver's actions than of Lucky Fault Driver's actions, and that is because the one is, and other is not, to blame for a bad outcome.

But there is yet another class of exceptions to Adam Smith's remarks, which makes trouble for any simple treatment of these issues. The simplest examples comes from a case I mentioned at the outset, namely *Summers v. Tice*.[15] (That is a wonderful case. If it had not occurred, we would have had to invent it.) The two defendants, Tice and Simonson, both fired negligently in Summers' direction, and one of them shot Summers, but we cannot tell which. Who should pay Summers' bills? Most people feel it right that Tice and Simonson should split the costs. The actual outcome in court was joint and several liability, but arguably that comes to roughly the same thing given the possibility of a suit for contribution, and in any case there are reasons to think that outcome fairer to Summers than a division of the costs. So far so good, nothing puzzling yet.

Now for the source of the puzzlement. Suppose that during the course of the trial evidence had come forward which made it as certain as empirical matters ever are that the pellet that caused Summers' injury came from Tice's gun, so that it is

Tice who is to blame for Summers' injury. We do, I think, take it to be clear that Simonson should now be dismissed from the suit: no doubt he acted badly, but he is not to blame for the injury, and hence he is not appropriately held liable for its costs.[16] But our *moral* assessment of Tice and Simonson does not shift. We do not think the worse of Tice, or even of Tice's acts, because he, as it turns out, is to blame for the harm; and we do not think the better of Simonson, or of Simonson's acts, because *he*, as it turns out, is not to blame for the harm. Our moral attitude does not shift in any way by virtue of the discovery that it is Tice who actually caused the harm. So we really seem to have a second kind of exception to Adam Smith's remarks.

It could of course be said that it is just irrational on our part to fail to distinguish between Tice and Simonson in the way in which we do distinguish between Lucky and Unlucky Fault Drivers. But it does not *feel* irrational. And the moral views of the man and woman in the street are deserving of great respect: they ought not be dismissed as irrational unless it really does turn out that there is no rationale for them.

What bubbles up in us men-and-women-in-the-street is, I think, this: "Simonson nearly caused the very same harm that Tice caused." It is not true of Lucky Fault Driver that he nearly caused the very same harm that Unlucky Fault Driver caused. Or at least you were not thinking of him as having done so. One driver goes out in one part of town, the other in another; they both have bad brakes; a child runs in front of one, no child runs in front of the other. So far so good. One is to blame for a death and the other is not, and we feel very differently about what they did.

But now let the two drivers set out from the same part of town, down the same street. A child runs in front of both. Both come to a long screeching halt. The child is hit by one truck and not by the other. If the child had been running *ever* so slightly slower, it would have been hit by the other truck. Now the drivers seem to us like Tice and Simonson: we think no worse of what the one did than of what the other did.

This suggests that something else is at work in these cases, possibly two things, in fact.

In the first place, Tice and Simonson did not merely act equally negligently; they each imposed roughly the same risk of harm on a person. Similarly for the two truck drivers who set out from the same part of town, and in front of both of whom one child runs. Not so for two truck drivers who set out from different parts of town. If they both set out with bad brakes, they acted equally negligently; but if a child runs in front of one, and no child so much as gets near the other, they do not in fact impose even roughly the same risk of harm on anyone.

This does make a different to us. Suppose you back your car out of your driveway without looking, but no child was anywhere near you. Perhaps you will feel bad later on thinking the matter over: after all, it is negligent to back out without looking. But you will not *dwell* on what you did; it would be irrational to lie awake at night shuddering at the thought of what you *might* have caused. But suppose you back your car out of your driveway without looking, and there was a child in the vicinity; indeed, you nearly hit it, and would have hit it but for the child's having noticed a penny up ahead and run faster to get to it. Here the shudder is not out of place. We all know what that terrible, nagging thought is like: it is not merely of what you might have caused, but of what you nearly did cause. You do no feel as bad as you would if you had actually hit the child; but you do feel considerably worse than you would if there had been no child in the vicinity at all.

Adam Smith said that the bad consequences of an act affect our sense of its merit or demerit, and I agreed that this is so if the act was faulty: for the bad things an act causes are things that its agent is to blame for, if his act was faulty. What seems to come out here is that it is not merely the actual bad consequences of an act that affect our sense of its demerit: the higher the risk of bad consequences that the act actually imposes on others, the greater the demerit of the act.

It is puzzling that this should be so, however. Your negligence in backing out of your driveway without looking is no greater or worse if there is a child in the vicinity than if there is not; and since you did not actually hit the child, [you] cannot explain [your] feeling that what you did was worse by appeal to the fact that you are to blame for a harm to the child. *Nobody* was harmed. So there is a gap here, and I hope you will find it as interesting a question as I do just how it is to be filled.

I said it is possible that there are two further things at work in these cases. The second of them is this: Tice and Simonson did not merely act equally negligently, and they did not merely each impose roughly the same risk of harm on *a* person; they each imposed roughly the same risk of harm on one and the same person, namely Summers. Similarly for the two truck drivers who set out from the same part of town, and in front of both of whom one child runs. Does *that* matter to us? I do not find it clear that it does. Dickenson fired his shotgun negligently last Wednesday, and nearly hit someone. He feels awful about what he did, and we think it right that he feel awful about it. Do we think worse of what Simonson did, given he nearly hit someone on Thursday, *and* given also that the person Simonson nearly hit was in fact hit by Tice? Perhaps so. But it is even harder, I think, to see why that should be so—if it is.

VI

Let me now try to pull this material together just briefly. I began by drawing attention to two phenomena in law—more precisely, one in law itself, the other in legal theory—which seem to warrant saying that as far as tort law is concerned at any rate, there has been a decline of cause. Many people think that if cause declines in law, law to that extent departs from morality. It therefore seemed to me worth drawing attention to the fact that there has been a decline of cause in moral theory too. That decline in part explains why moral theorists who interest themselves in law have welcomed those developments in law and legal theory. But it is of interest for its own sake. As Adam Smith said, when you think about these matters in the abstract, the philosophers seem to be right; but when you come out of the study, they seem to be wrong. Moral theorists must of course ask themselves why that is, and whether there is a rationale for it; that is the job of the moral theorist. But I hope that lawyers will find these questions of interest too. The law certainly is not, and need not be, an exact reflection of the morality of those governed by it; but responsible government tries to be sure it has a sound rationale whenever it departs from that morality, and therefore does well to try to become clear about what that morality is.

Endnotes

[1] 26 Cal. 3d 88, 163 Cal. Rptr. 132, 607 P.2d 924, *cert. denied*, 449 U.S. 912 (1980).

[2] 33 Cal. 2d 80, 199 P.2d 1 (1948).

[3] For an interesting discussion of these and related matters, which brings out their bearing on a particular case, see P. Shuck, Agent Orange on Trial, Mass Toxic Disasters in the Courts (1986).

[4] Landes & Posner, *Causation in Tort Law: An Economic Approach*, 12 J. L. Stud. 109, 131 (1983).

[5] Calabresi, *Concerning Cause and the Law of Torts: An Essay for Harry Kalven, Jr.*, 43 U. Chi. L. Rev. 69, 106–07 (1975) (emphasis in original).

[6] *See, e.g.*, Kelman, *The Necessary Myth of Objective Causation Judgments in Liberal Political Theory*, 63 Chi-Kent L. Rev. 579 (1987).

[7] *See* S. Milgram, Obedience to Authority (1974)(summarizing results of Milgram's experiments).

[8] I. Kant, Foundations of the Metaphysics of Morals 12–13 (Bobbs-Merrill ed. 1969).

[9] *See, e.g.*, Fischer & Ennis, *Causation and Liability*, 15 Phil. & Pub. Affairs 33 (1986); Kagan, *Causation, Liability, and Internalism*, 15 Phil. & Pub. Affairs 41 (1986).

[10] A. Smith, The Theory of Moral Sentiments 134 (Arlington House ed. 1969).

[11] The emphasis is mine.

[12] T. Nagel, Mortal Question 28–29 (1979).

[13] As I wrote in part III, the moral sophisticate may say that while the law does well to mark a difference between Alfred and Bert (punishing Bert more severely than Alfred, exacting compensation for the injury from Bert), this is for reasons extraneous to the moral valuation proper to them and their acts. I think it is one thing to say the moral valuation proper to *them* does not warrant differential legal consequences: Bert is surely no worse a person than Alfred is. But it is another thing to say the moral valuation proper to *their* acts does not warrant differential legal consequences: Bert, after all, is to blame for a harm and Alfred is not, so there really is a moral difference between what Bert did and what Alfred did.

[14] A. Smith, *supra* note 10, at 134. The emphasis is mine.

[15] 33 Cal. 2d 80, 199 P.2d 1(1948).

[16] Why this should be so is discussed in Thomson, *Remarks on Causation and Liability*, 13 Phil. & Pub. Affairs 101 (1984). Criticism of that discussion may be found in Fischer & Ennis, *supra* note 9, and in Kagan, *supra* note 9.

Study Questions

1. The court in *Lynch* admits that the injury in the case arose in an unforeseeable manner. Why does the court find the defendant liable in spite of this fact? On what does the court rest its reasoning?

2. According to Cardozo, why was the railroad not negligent in regard to Mrs. Palsgraf? What does Cardozo mean by saying that "negligence in the air" is not enough to ground liability? Do you agree?

3. How does Andrews understand the idea of proximate cause? How does Andrews respond to Cardozo's claim about "negligence in the air"?

4. As noted in the text, the *Lynch* and *Palsgraf* cases represent two competing views of causation in tort law. *Lynch* stands for the first and somewhat older principle that my liability for events that would not have occurred except for my negligent conduct extends to any such consequences directly traceable to me, to my causal agency. Under *Lynch*, in other words, I am liable for any consequences of my conduct traceable through a series of events back to me, as long as that chain is unbroken by the causal contribution of an intervening actor. This principle is preserved in the maxim "You take your victim as you find him (or her)": A hits B with a force that would normally only bruise a person, but, unknown to A, B has a very thin skull or is a hemophiliac; B dies. Under the *Lynch* view, A is liable for B's death. The second, newer principle is represented by Cardozo's opinion in *Palsgraf*: My liability extends only to those whom I might foreseeably harm through my negligent conduct. A number of causation cases line up on either side. Which view seems to you to make more sense? Can these principles be reconciled?

5. According to Hart and Honoré, what distinguishes cases in which event A causes event B from cases in which A and B are coincidences?

6. According to Hart and Honoré, what differentiates a cause from a condition?

7. Hart and Honoré argue that human intervention in a causal sequence "breaks the chain" of causation. Why should this be so?

8. Elsewhere in their book, Hart and Honoré maintain that their analysis of causal attribution agrees with the law's position on the "thin-skull" cases (see question 4, above): They distinguish between a state of a person or thing *existing at the time* of a wrongful act and a later or *subsequent* event or state. Existing abnormal states (thin skulls, hemophilia, and so on) are "mere circumstances" or conditions on which the cause operates and do not "break" the chain of causation, so the defendant is liable for the entire harm produced. But, they add, subsequent abnormal events or conditions *do* break the chain. They put it this way:

   > Suppose plaintiff is run over through defendant's negligence. If on the way to the hospital he is hit by a falling tree, that is a coincidence [for which defendant is not liable]. If, just previously to being run over, he had been hit by a [falling] tree and severely injured, that is a circumstance existing at the time of the running over and will not negative the causal connection between the running over and the victim's death, [so the defendant is liable] even if the victim would not have died from the running down but for the previous blow from the tree. (*Causation in the Law*, 2nd ed., p. 161)

   Does this make sense? Is it consistent with the basic outlines of Hart and Honore's analysis?

9. What result would Hart and Honoré's analysis of causal attribution yield in *Lynch*? Does that result seem to you to count for or against their view?

10. Why do the critics whom Thomson attacks think cause is unimportant?

11. According to Thomson, how are the positions of Kant and the "moral sophisticate" linked?

12. Do you agree with Thomson that the decline of cause is an undesirable trend? How would you recommend that the courts handle cases such as *Summers* and *Sindell*?

13. Negligence law takes the position that, with respect to certain qualities—general skill, intelligence, and judgment—everyone is presumed to be equal, and equally reasonable, and is held to that standard. If you fall below that standard, this will not excuse you. However, as Oliver Wendell Holmes notes, certain specific conditions, for example, blindness or other physical disabilities, are such that we adjust our expectations accordingly. Blind people are judged against what a "reasonable blind person" would have done in a given situation. Are there other conditions that should be included on this list? Children, for instance, have traditionally been judged on the standard of reasonable conduct for people of their actual age, intelligence, and experience. What about the elderly? The infirm? Do the fact of these exceptions to the objective test of reasonableness show that the standard is itself suspicious?

14. How would you decide these cases:
    - Defendant, driving while intoxicated, strikes a woman on the side of the road. Severely injured, the victim is taken to the hospital, where a trauma team determines that both surgery and a blood transfusion are necessary to save her life. The victim, a Jehovah's Witness, declines the transfusion and subsequently dies. Did the defendant proximately cause the victim's death, or was her death the result of her own refusal of medical treatment?
    - Plaintiff is severely injured by defendant's negligence. An ambulance is summoned. En route to the hospital, the ambulance driver suffers a heart attack and the ambulance swerves into a tree, killing the plaintiff. Is the defendant liable for plaintiff's death because the ambulance trip was necessitated by defendant's original carelessness? Or is the wreck of the ambulance a "freakish" intervening cause, which relieves the defendant of complete liability?

C. Acts, Omissions, and the Duty to Rescue

"I Didn't Do Anything"

In an incident that aroused widespread moral condemnation, a nineteen-year-old college freshman admitted in 1998 that he witnessed the beginning of what became a murder and did nothing to stop it. David Cash and a friend were at a Nevada casino in 1997. The friend took a seven-year-old girl into a bathroom stall, sexually assaulted, and then strangled her. Cash admitted that he saw his friend in the stall with his hand over the girl's mouth but left the bathroom just before the attack began. The friend was convicted of murder and sentenced to life imprisonment. Nevada authorities questioned and then released Cash, confessing that although they found Cash's conduct "morally reprehensible," it did not violate the law, since Cash neither encouraged nor aided the assailant. The decision not to pursue charges against Cash sparked numerous calls for changes in the law, ranging from a requirement that those who witness a crime must report it to bills that would require adults to come to the aid of a child under attack. Currently only three or four states have any such laws. Throughout the controversy, Cash continued to maintain his innocence: Speaking on a radio talk-show, Cash insisted "I have done nothing wrong."

The Failure to Act

We are all familiar with situations in which the law imposes upon us a duty to *refrain* from acting in ways harmful to other people or their property, with prohibitions on murder, theft, assault, and so on. But what of situations in which the *failure* to act constitutes a breach of duty? Are there such cases? It is true that the law recognizes certain instances in which *omitting* to do something *for* someone, as opposed to *doing* something *to* him, is a breach of duty: for example, when that person is your child or your spouse, or when you have entered into a contract to care for another—In other words, cases involving an otherwise legally recognized relationship.

As a general matter, the law's approach to the question of duty is governed by two principles: Everyone has a general duty of reasonable care for *misfeasance,* but no one (with few exceptions) has a duty of care for *nonfeasance.* What do these terms mean? *Misfeasance* refers to the infliction of harm, or acting in a way that inflicts harm. *Nonfeasance* refers to the failure to prevent harm. All of us are under a general legal duty not to inflict harm upon one another, but none of us (with few exceptions) is under a legal duty to prevent harm from befalling another.

Misfeasance and Nonfeasance

The concepts of misfeasance and nonfeasance are difficult ones. Part of the difficulty, as several of our selections in this section make clear, is that the distinction itself is problematic. The difference between misfeasance and nonfeasance is supposed to mark the difference between *acts* (or *commissions)* and *omissions.* But what makes something one rather than the other? Take this, for example: It is Monday morning, and my daughter has to be ready for school by 7:00 A.M. I wake her up early, even though she did not get much sleep the night

before. Have I performed the *act* of "getting my daughter ready for school"? Or have I *omitted* to perform the act of "letting her sleep in"? (I know how she will see it!) Some who have thought about this question argue that the answer depends upon how the situation is described, and that how we describe it turns on our *evaluation* of the alternatives:

> Unless the defendant has a duty to act, an omission is not culpable. Of course, the line between omissions and commissions is blurry. There is considerable circularity in claiming that a defendant can be culpable only if he had committed an act, when we often describe an event in active conduct terms rather than passively if we have already (somehow) determined that the party is culpable. For instance, a parent who *does not feed* a child may readily be said to *starve* the child—to commit an act—while a stranger would be said to *fail to feed*—a passive nonact.[1]

You would be more inclined to say "Adams (selflessly) got his daughter ready for (a wonderful day at) school" than to say "Adams (inexcusably) forgot to wake his daughter," the more you are inclined to view one positively and the other negatively. This is revealed by the (loaded) way in which each alternative is described.

Another suggestion, defended in our selection from Ernest Weinrib, distinguishes misfeasance from nonfeasance on the ground that the former always involves a situation in which the defendant has played some role in creating the risk to which the plaintiff has been exposed, whereas in situations of pure nonfeasance, this is not the case. Weinrib contrasts these cases:

1. Driver (defendant) fails to apply his brakes in time and Pedestrian (plaintiff) is hurt.
2. One person (defendant) sees another (plaintiff) drowning in a pool and fails to throw him an easily available rope.

Here our conviction that case 1 is an instance of misfeasance whereas case 2 is "mere" nonfeasance

---

[1] Mark Kelman, "Interpretive Construction in the Substantive Criminal Law," *Stanford Law Review,* 33 (1981), p. 637.

can be explained by seeing that Driver plays a role in creating the danger to which Pedestrian is exposed; presumably this is not true of the defendant in case 2.

What significance does the misfeasance/nonfeasance distinction have for the question of which duties the law imposes upon us? The collective meaning of the two principles stated above is this: If you find a stranger in a position of peril, perhaps even of imminent death—a situation you did nothing to create—and you do nothing to help that person (even when this would be no risk to you), your conduct is mere nonfeasance and you generally are *not* legally liable for that person's injuries or death. The law's position is starkly summarized by the language of an older case:

> Actionable negligence is the neglect of a legal duty. The defendants are not liable unless they owed to the plaintiff a legal duty which they neglected to perform. With purely moral obligations the law does not deal. For example, the priest and Levite who passed by on the other side were not, it is supposed, liable at law for the continued suffering of the man who fell among thieves, which they might and morally ought to have prevented or relieved. Suppose A, standing close by a railroad, sees a two-year-old babe on the track and a car approaching. He can easily rescue the child with entire safety to himself, and the instincts of humanity require him to do so. If he does not, he may, perhaps, justly be styled a ruthless savage and a moral monster; but he is not liable in damages for the child's injury, or indictable under the statute for its death. . . . There is a wide difference—a broad gulf—both in reason and in law, between causing and preventing an injury; between doing by negligence or otherwise a wrong to one's neighbor, and preventing him from injuring himself; between protecting him against injury by another and guarding him from injury that may accrue to him from the condition of the premises which he has unlawfully invaded. The duty to do no wrong is a legal duty. The duty to protect against wrong is, generally speaking and excepting certain intimate relations in the nature of a trust, a moral obligation only, not recognized or enforced by law.[2]

McFall v. Shimp

The impact of the misfeasance/nonfeasance distinction as it bears on the scope and limits of the duty of care owed to others is dramatically illustrated in the tragic case of Robert McFall.

Thirty-nine-year-old McFall suffered from aplastic anemia, a disease in which the patient's bone marrow fails to manufacture certain necessary blood components. McFall's condition was diagnosed in July of 1978, and a search was immediately undertaken to locate a bone marrow donor. Transfusions of bone marrow require that there be a high degree of genetic compatibility between patient and donor, so McFall's relatives were looked to first. Initial tests of McFall's immediate family failed to produce a donor, but eventually the medical team located McFall's first cousin, David Shimp. Preliminary tests indicated a high compatibility rating, and Shimp was scheduled for further testing during the third week of July. He failed to appear, stating in a later interview that his wife had asked him to not go through with the procedure. Running out of time and with no one else to turn to, McFall hired an attorney and filed a suit, asking the court for an *injunction* ordering Shimp to submit to the transfusion procedure.

Counsel for McFall could cite little in the way of prior authority dealing with this case, beyond an invocation of the court's equitable powers, and ended its arguments with a plea: "The time for study is over. The exigencies require action in order to save a human life. Our noblest traditions as a free people and our common sense of decency, society and morality all point to the proper result in this case. We respectfully suggest that it is time our law did likewise."

Judge Flaherty denied the injunction on two grounds. First, there is no legal duty to save another, he conceded, and this is perhaps as it should be; to force Shimp to submit to the procedure would be to usher in a new rule with no limitations. Second,

---

[2] *Buch v. Amory Mfg. Co.,* 44 A. 809 (1897).

the forcible intrusion into the body contemplated here is wholly impermissible. Flaherty's ruling was announced on July 26. Robert McFall died on August 10.

The Duty to Rescue

The essay by legal philosopher Ernest Weinrib reviews the legal and moral dimensions of the debate over the "no-duty-to-rescue" rule. Those who defend the law's stance toward rescue raise several points. To the degree that the law is correct in requiring that your liability for another's injuries depends upon whether you *caused* harm to that person, it must follow that there can be no duty to rescue in cases of pure nonfeasance; these are cases in which you have not caused the harm in question. Furthermore, regardless of which of several possible formulations of a general duty to rescue one selects, it remains the case that no principled limits could be placed on the invasion of individual liberty that would follow from the imposition of such a duty. By encroaching upon individual liberties in this way, a general duty of rescue would require "forced exchanges" between people.

As Weinrib indicates, proponents of a legal duty to rescue commonly make the utilitarian argument that a general legal duty to come to the aid of those in peril is required by the goal of promoting the overall welfare. Critics of a legal duty to rescue have sought to build a moral case for their position by aligning themselves with the moral theory of Kant. Kant argued that the moral value of an act depends not upon the consequences or results it produces, but solely upon the motive or "will" from which it springs. The moral worth of an action turns exclusively on the moral acceptability of the principle on the basis of which one acts: doing the right thing because it is the right thing to do. This view seems to imply that to compel acts of rescue through the law would be to destroy their moral worth; my reason for coming to the aid of another would not simply be to "do my duty for duty's sake" but to do so to avoid punishment. Thus the world would in a sense be made a morally worse place for having a legal duty to rescue. Those opposed to requiring rescue also raise a common complaint about utilitarianism: Because the sole

concern of the utilitarian is with producing good results—maximizing the overall welfare—individuals are under a moral obligation to do whatever they can to achieve this maximization. But this, the critics allege, leaves no room in our moral life for "saints" or "heroes," for those who act "above and beyond the call of duty." For a utilitarian, any act that conduces to greater net good is already required; it is not something for which one can be lionized as a hero. The opponents of a duty to rescue regard this as a loss to our collective moral life.

The case for a general duty of rescue is made here by Weinrib. He endeavors to respond to the critics' fundamental objection that to impose upon all a general duty of rescue is to make all help obligatory and destroy individual moral freedom and choice. Why, Weinrib asks, is it more of a deprivation of liberty to be told that you have to call the police if you see a person in obvious danger than to be told that you must stop at a red light? The critics worry that a general duty of rescue might mean that a solvent person could be held civilly liable for refusing to supply the means of subsistence to someone who might otherwise starve. But what is the difference between this and our familiar system of social welfare programs?

More fundamentally, Weinrib tries to show that preoccupation with the infringement of liberty as an objection to a duty to rescue is misplaced. He maintains that the values supporting our deep concern with individual liberty operate most visibly in the law of contract. Contract law assumes that parties can reach agreements incurring only minimal transaction costs, that negotiations are possible and manageable, and that the parties occupy roughly equal bargaining positions. When these conditions hold and when the proposed arrangements are not otherwise illegal, the liberty of the parties to make such agreements as they see fit is accorded maximum scope. But, cautions Weinrib, there are situations—and rescue is one of them—in which these "contract" values are conspicuously absent, so a limited duty of "easy rescue," creating an affirmative obligation to aid another in an emergency when little or no inconvenience is posed for the rescuer, is consistent with liberty values. Weinrib tries to show that a duty of easy rescue could be explained and accounted for on either utilitarian or Kantian grounds.

97. McFall v. Shimp

Flaherty, [Judge].

The Plaintiff, Robert McFall, suffers from a rare bone marrow disease and the prognosis for his survival is very dim, unless he receives a bone marrow transplant from a compatible donor. Finding a compatible donor is a very difficult task, and limited to a selection among close relatives. After a search and certain tests, it has been determined that only the Defendant is suitable as a donor. The Defendant refuses to submit to the necessary transplant, and before the Court is a request for a preliminary injunction which seeks to compel the defendant to submit to further tests, and, eventually, the bone marrow transplant.

Although a diligent search has produced no authority, the Plaintiff cites the ancient statute of King Edward I, St. Westminster 2, 13 Ed., I, c 24, pointing out, as is the case, that this Court is a successor to the English courts of Chancery and derives power from this statute, almost 700 years old. The question posed by the Plaintiff is that, in order to save the life of one of its members by the only means available, may society infringe upon one's absolute right to his "bodily security"?

The common law has consistently held to a rule which provides that one human being is under no legal compulsion to give aid or to take action to save that human being or to rescue. A great deal has been written regarding this rule which, on the surface, appears to be revolting in a moral sense. Introspection, however, will demonstrate that the rule is founded upon the very essence of our free society. It is noteworthy that counsel for the Plaintiff has cited authority which has developed in other societies in support of the Plaintiff's request in this instance. Our society, contrary to many others, has as its first principle, the respect for the individual, and that society and government exist to protect the individual from being invaded and hurt by another. Many societies adopt a contrary view which has the individual existing to serve the society as a whole. In preserving such a society as we have it is bound to happen that great moral conflicts will arise and will appear harsh in a given instance. In this case, the chancellor is being asked to force one member of society to undergo a medical procedure which would provide that part of that individual's body would be removed from him and given to another so that the other could live. Morally, this decision rests with the Defendant, and, in the view of the Court, the refusal of the Defendant is morally indefensible. For our law to *compel* the Defendant to submit to an intrusion of his body would change the very concept and principle upon which our society is founded. To do so would defeat the sanctity of the individual, and would impose a rule which would know no limits, and one could not imagine where the line would be drawn. This request is not to be compared with an action at law for damages, but rather is an action in equity before a Chancellor, which, in the ultimate, if granted, would require the [forcible] submission to the medical procedure. For a society, which respects the rights of *one* individual, to sink its teeth into the jugular vein or neck of one of its members and suck from it sustenance for *another* member, is revolting to our hard-wrought concept of jurisprudence. [Forcible] extraction of living body tissue causes revulsion to the judicial mind. Such would raise the specter of the swastika and the inquisition, reminiscent of the horrors this portends.

The court makes no comment on the law regarding the Plaintiff's right in an action at law for damages, but has no alternative but to deny the requested equitable relief. An Order will be entered denying the request for a preliminary injunction.

No. 78-177711 (July 26, 1978)
10th Penn. District, Allegheny County

98. *The Case for a Duty to Rescue*

Ernest Weinrib

No observer would have any difficulty outlining the current state of the law throughout the common-law world regarding the duty to rescue. Except when the person endangered and the potential rescuer are linked in a special relationship, there is no such duty. This general rule rests on the law's distinction between the infliction of harm and the failure to prevent it. The distinction between misfeasance and nonfeasance in turn reflects deeply rooted intuitions about causation, and it has played a critical role in the development of the common-law notions of contract and tort and of the boundary between them. In large part because this distinction is so fundamental to the common law, the courts have uniformly refused to enunciate a general duty to rescue, even in the face of repeated criticisms that the absence of such a duty is callous. Nonetheless, recent developments, both judicial and academic, justify a reconsideration of the common-law position.

On the judicial side, many of the outposts of the doctrine that there is no general duty to rescue have fallen. Recognizing the meritoriousness of rescue and the desirability of encouraging it, the courts have increasingly accorded favorable treatment to injured rescuers. When a rescuer sues for compensation for his injuries, voluntary assumption of risk cannot be interposed as a defense, contributory negligence comes into play only if the plaintiff has been reckless, and a broad range of rescue attempts are deemed reasonably foreseeable by the defendant. Moreover, the courts have increased the number of special relationships that require one person to aid another in peril. These developments have made the general absence of a duty to rescue seem more eccentric and isolated. They have also raised the possibility that the general rule is in the process of being consumed and supplanted by the widening ambit of the exceptions and that the relationship between the general rule and the exceptions may be fundamentally incoherent.

. . .

Consideration of the utilitarian approach towards rescue must begin with Jeremy Bentham's thought on the problem. "[I]n cases where the person is in danger," he asked, "why should it not be made the duty of every man to save another from mischief, when it can be done without prejudicing himself . . . ?"[1] Bentham supported the implicit answer to this question and several illustrations: using water at hand to quench a fire in a woman's headdress; moving a sleeping drunk whose face is in a puddle; warning a person about to carry a lighted candle into a room strewn with gunpowder. Bentham clearly had in mind a legal duty that would be triggered by the combination of the victim's emergency and the absence of inconvenience to the rescuer—that is, by the features of most of the proposed reforms requiring rescue. Unfortunately, the rhetorical question was the whole of Bentham's argument for his position. With this question, Bentham appealed directly to his reader's moral intuition; he did not show how his proposed duty can be derived through his distinctive felicific calculus.

Can one supply Benthamite justification that Bentham himself omitted? Because the avoidance of injury or death obviously contributes to the greatest happiness of the greatest number, the difficulties revolve not around the basic requirement of rescue but around the limitations placed upon that requirement by the notions of emergency and absence of inconvenience. Those limitations have no parallel with respect to participation in putting others at risk; they apply only in cases of nonfeasance. Indeed, Bentham's comments come in a section of his *Introduction to the Principles of Morals and Legislation* that distinguishes beneficence (increasing another's happiness) from probity (forbearing to diminish another's happiness). Yet Bentham had earlier contended that the distinction between acts of omission and acts of commission was of no significance.[2] The utilitarian's only concern is that an individual bring about a situation that results in a higher surplus of pleasure over pain than would any of the alternative situations that his actions could produce. Consequences are important; how they are reached is not. The distinction between nonfeasance and misfeasance has no place in this theory, and neither would the rescue duty's emergency or convenience limitations, which apply only after that distinction is made.

One solution to the apparent inconsistency between the rescue limitations and Benthamite theory's regard only for consequences is to drop the conditions of emergency and convenience as limitations on the duty to rescue. The position could be taken that there is an obligation to rescue whenever rescuing would result in greater net happiness than not rescuing. This principle, it is important to observe, cannot really be a principle about rescuing as that concept is generally understood. As a matter of common usage, a rescue presupposes the existence of an emergency, of a predicament that poses danger of greater magnitude and imminence than one ordinarily encounters. The proposed principle, however, requires no emergency to trigger a duty to act. The principle, in fact, is one of beneficence, not rescue, and should be formulated more generally to require providing aid whenever it will yield greater net happiness than not providing aid.

Eliminating the limitations regarding emergency and convenience might transform a requirement of rescue conceived along utilitarian lines into a requirement of perfect and general altruism. This demand of perfect altruism would be undesirable for several reasons. First, it would encourage the obnoxious character known to the law as the officious intermeddler. Also, its imposition of a duty of continual saintliness and heroism is unrealistic. Moreover, it would overwhelm the relationships founded on friendship and love as well as the distinction between the praiseworthy and the required; it would thereby obscure some efficient ways, in the utilitarian's eyes, of organizing and stimulating beneficence. Finally, the most fundamentally, it would be self-defeating. The require-

ment of aid assumes that there is some other person who has at least a minimal core of personhood as well as projects of his own that the altruist can further. In a society of perfect and general altruisms, however, any potential recipient of aid would himself be an altruist, who must, accordingly, subordinate the pursuit of his own projects to the rendering of aid to others. No one could claim for his own projects the priority that would provide others with a stable object of their altruistic ministrations. Each person would continually find himself obligated to attempt to embrace a phantom.

Although the utilitarian principle that requires the provision of aid whenever it will result in greater net happiness than failure to aid easily slips into the pure-altruism duty, it need not lead to so extreme a position. The obvious alternative interpretation of the principle is that aid is not obligatory whenever the costs to one's own projects outweigh the benefits to the recipient's. This interpretation avoids the embracing-of-phantoms objection to pure altruism, but it is subject to all the other criticisms of the purer theory. Because the cost-benefit calculus is so difficult to perform in particular instances, the duty would remain ill-defined. In many cases, therefore, it would encourage the officious intermeddler, seem unrealistically to require saintliness, overwhelm friendship and love, and obliterate the distinction between the praiseworthy and the required. Moreover, the vagueness of the duty would lead many individuals unhappily and inefficiently to drop their own projects in preference for those of others.

A different formulation of the rescue duty is needed to harness and temper the utilitarian impulses toward altruism and to direct them more precisely toward an intelligible goal. One important weakness of a too-generally beneficent utilitarianism is that it tempts one to consider only the immediate consequences of particular acts, and not the longer term consequences, the most important of which are the expectations generated that such acts will continue. If, as the classical utilitarians believed, the general happiness is advanced when people engage in productive activities that are of value to others, the harm done by a duty of general beneficence, in either version discussed above, would override its specific benefits. The deadening of industry resulting from both reliance on beneficence and devotion to beneficence would in the long run be an evil greater than the countenancing of individual instances of unfulfilled needs or wants. "In all cases of helping," wrote John Stuart Mill, in a passage concerned only with the reliance costs:

> there are two sets of consequences to be considered: the consequences of the assistance and the consequences of relying on the assistance. The former are generally beneficial, but the latter, for the most part, injurious. . . . There are few things for which it is more mischievous that people should rely on the habitual aid of others than for the means of subsistence, and unhappily there is no lesson which they more easily learn.[3]

Utilitarianism can use the notion of reliance to restrict the requirement of beneficence. If an act of beneficence would tend to induce reliance on similar acts, it should be avoided. If the act of beneficence does not have this tendency, it should be performed as long as the benefit produced is greater than the cost of performance. In the latter case, there are no harmful effects on industry flowing from excessive reliance to outweigh the specific benefits. This rule can account for Bentham's restriction of the duty to rescue to situations of emergency. People do not regularly expose themselves to extraordinary dangers in reliance on the relief that may be available if the emergency materializes, and only a fool would deliberately court a peril because he or others had previously been rescued from a similar one. As Sidgwick put it, an emergency rescue "will have no bad effect on the receiver, from the exceptional nature of the emergency."[4] Furthermore, an emergency is not only a desperate situation; it is also a situation that deviates from society's usual pattern. The relief of an emergency is therefore unlikely to induce reliance on the assistance of others in normal conditions. The abnormality of emergencies also means that rescuers can confidently pursue their own projects under normal circumstances. The motive for industry that Bentham located in each person's needs is not undermined by extraordinary and isolated events.

The role of emergency in the utilitarian obligation to rescue corresponds to, and illuminates, the definition of a legal duty to rescue by reference to the absence of contract values, as set out in the previous section. Utilitarian philosophy and the concept of the market are closely related. Both regard individuals as maximizers of their own happiness, and both see the use of contracts to acquire and to exchange property as conducive to the public good. Contract law's refusal to enforce certain transactions sets them apart from the usual structure of relationships, in which the satisfaction of the parties' needs and desires can legitimately serve as a stimulus to exchange. The person who sees a member of his own family in difficulty and the police officer who notices a hazard on the highway may not act as ordinary members of the market with respect to those endangered. Those pockets of contractual nonenforcement are sufficiently isolated that they are unlikely to be generalized: they will not generate a widespread reliance on assistance or sense of obligation to assist in settings where market exchanges are permitted and common.

An emergency is similar. Contract values are absent in such a situation because the assistance required is of such a kind that it cannot be purchased on ordinary commercial terms. Suspension of contract values in an emergency will not result in a general deadening of individual industry; the utilitarian can therefore confine his calculus to the specific consequences of the rescue. The denial of relief to the Southwark squatters[5] is a case in point. The desperate situation there was a consequence of poverty and not an extraordinary condition that deviated from the ordinary pattern of contemporary existence. The utilitarian must be concerned in that situation that judicially coercing individual assistance to the poor will generate a reliance whose harmful effects will, in the long run and across society as a whole, outweigh the benefits of the specific assistance.

Bentham's intuitive restriction of beneficence to situations of emergency can thus be supported on utilitarian grounds. Is the same true of the inconvenience limitation? As with the emergency restriction, finding utilitarian support requires looking behind the specific action to its social and legal context. For the utilitarian, the enforcement of a duty through legal sanctions is always an evil, which can be justified only to avoid a greater evil. If the sanction is applied, the offender suffers the pain of punishment. If the prospect of the sanction is sufficient to deter conduct, those deterred suffer the detriment of frustrated preferences. Moreover, the apparatus of enforcement siphons off social resources from other projects promoting the general happiness.

Accordingly, a utilitarian will be restrained and circumspect in the elaboration of legal duties. In particular, he will not pitch a standard of behavior at too high a level: the higher the standard, the more onerous it will be to the person subjected to it, the greater the pleasure that he must forego in adhering to it, and the greater his resistance to its demands. A high standard entails both more severe punishment and a more elaborate apparatus of detection and enforcement. Applied to the rescue situation, this reasoning implies that some convenience restriction should be adopted as part of the duty. Compelling the rescuer to place himself in physical danger, for instance, would be ineffacious, to use Bentham's terminology, because such coercion cannot influence the will: "the evil, which he sees himself about to undergo . . . is so great that the evil denounced by the penal clause . . . cannot appear greater."[6] Limiting the duty of rescue to emergency situations where the rescue will not inconvenience the rescuer—as judicial decisions would elaborate that limitation and thus give direction to individuals—minimizes both the interference with the rescuer's own preferences and the difficulties of enforcement that would result from recalcitrance. Bentham's second limitation can thus also be supported on a utilitarian basis.

The utilitarian arguments for the duty to rescue and for the limitations on that duty rest primarily on administrative considerations. The arguments focus not so much on the parties and their duties as persons as on the difficulties that might be created throughout the whole range of societal interactions. The elements of the duty are evaluated in terms of their likely consequences, no matter how remote. In the convenience limitation, for instance, whether the rescuer *ought* to feel aggrieved at the requirements of a high standard is of no concern. The likelihood that he *will* feel aggrieved is all that matters: for the Ben-

thamite utilitarian, general happiness is the criterion of evaluation and not itself an object of evaluation. Moreover, recalcitrance necessitates more costly enforcement, and that consequence must also enter the calculus. The same is true for the emergency limitation. The argument for that limitation focused on the possibility that a particular instance of assistance would, by example, induce socially detrimental general reliance or beneficence. This use of example does not explore either the fairness of singling out particular persons for particular treatment or the consistency and scope of certain principles. Rather, the argument examines the cumulative consequences of repetition, and decides whether a particular person should perform a particular act on the basis of the act's implications for the entire society's market arrangements.

At least one philosopher has argued that administrative considerations of this sort are not moral ones at all, or that they are moral only in a derivative sense.[7] In this view, the administrative and enforcement considerations on which the utilitarian account of rescue rests are irrelevant to the individual's obligations as a moral agent. The individual should ask what he ought to do, not how others can compel him to fulfill his duty. The merit of this view is its observation that any utilitarian version of a duty to rescue has nuances that do not ring true to the moral contours of the situation. The person in need of rescue stands in danger of serious physical injury or loss of life, harms not quite comparable by any quantitative measure to other losses of happiness. Health and life are not merely components of the aggregate of goods that an individual enjoys. Rather, they are constitutive of the individual, who partakes of them in a unique and intimate way; they are the preconditions for the enjoyment of other goods. Moreover, there is something false in viewing an act of rescue as a contribution to the greatest happiness of the greatest number. If there is an obligation to rescue, it is owed to particular persons rather than to the greatest number. Any such duty would require the rescuing not only of the eminent heart surgeon but also of the hermit bachelor; and even the duty to rescue the heart surgeon would be owed primarily to him, not to his present or prospective patients.

Because the utilitarian account of rescue thus appears to lack an important moral ingredient, and because utilitarianism is not the law's only important philosophical tradition, it is worth attempting to outline a non-utilitarian version of the obligation to rescue. Although the two approaches support the same conclusion, the arguments are different in texture. In particular, the non-utilitarian argument recognizes the distinctive importance of avoiding physical injury or death; it resists the assimilation of health and life to other goods. This attention to the centrality of the person avoids the utilitarian dilemma of either demanding excessive beneficence or having recourse to administrative considerations, which shifts the focus away from the rescuer's obligation to a particular endangered individual. In the non-utilitarian argument, or course, administrative considerations are not ignored; to do so would be impossible in elaborating an argument that attempts to provide an ethical foundation for a judicially enforced duty to rescue. Nonetheless, the non-utilitarian's use of administrative considerations differs from the utilitarian's. The utilitarian weaves the fabric of the duty to rescue out of administrative strands; the cost of administration and enforcement are relevant to the very existence of the duty. The non-utilitarian, by contrast, justifies a legal duty to rescue independently of the administrative costs; the mechanisms of enforcement are invoked only to structure and to coordinate the operation of the duty.

The deontological argument begins with the observation that the ideas of an individual's being under a moral duty is intimately related to the notion that health and life are of distinctive importance. The concept of duty applies only to an individual endowed with the capacity to make choices and to set ends for himself. Further, the person, as a purposive and choosing entity, does not merely set physical integrity as one of his ends; he requires it as a precondition to the accomplishment of the purposes that his freedom gives him the power to set. As Kant put it, physical integrity is "the basic *stuff* (the matter) in man without which he could not realize his ends."[8]

A person contemplating the ethical exercise of his freedom of action must impose certain restrictions on that freedom. Because morality is something he shares with all humanity, he cannot claim a preferred moral position for himself. Any moral claim he makes must, by its very nature as a moral claim, be one to which he is subject when others can assert it. Acting on the basis of his own personhood therefore demands recognition of the personhood of others. This recognition, however, cannot be elaborated in the first instance in terms of the enjoyment of ordinary material goods. Because no conception of happiness is shared by everyone and is constant throughtout any individual's life, the universal concept of personhood cannot be reflected in a system of moral duties directed at the satisfaction of unstable desires for such goods. Physical integrity, by contrast, is necessary for the accomplishment of any human aim, and so is an appropriate subject for a system of mutually restraining duties.

An individual contemplating his actions from a moral point of view must recognize that all others form their projects on a substratum of physical integrity. If he claims the freedom to pursue his projects as a moral right, he cannot as a rational and moral agent deny to others the same freedom. Because his claim to that freedom implies a right to the physical integrity that is necessary to its exercise, he must concede to others the right to physical integrity that he implicitly and inevitably claims for himself.

This conception of the right to life and health derives from the notion of personhood that is presupposed by the concept of moral action. So too do the right's natural limitations. The duty of beneficence exacted by this right need not collapse into a comprehensive and self-defeating altruism. Respect for another's physical security does not entail foregoing one's own.[9] The right to life and health, seen to give content to the universal concept of personhood, must be ascribed not only to others, but also to oneself. As Kant put it,

> since all *other* men with the exception of myself would not be *all* men, and the maxim would then not have the universality of a law, as it must have in order to be obligatory, the law prescribing the duty of benevolence will include myself, as the object of benevolence, in the command of practical reason.[10]

Moreover, the universalizing process radiates outward from the actor: it is only one's desire to act that makes necessary the exploration of the action's implicit claims and thus of the rights that he must rationally concede to others.[11] The priority of the actor is thus embedded in the structure of the argument and should be reflected in the concrete duties that the argument yields.

This outline of deontological analysis can be applied to examine the standard suggestion that the common law should recognize a duty to effect an easy rescue. Such a duty would be the judicial analogue of a moral obligation to respect the person of another and to safeguard his physical integrity, which is necessary for whatever aims he chooses to pursue. The emergency and convenience limitations also fit quite readily into the analysis. An emergency is a particularly imminent threat to physical security, and the convenience limitation reflects the rescuer's entitlement to the priority of his own physical security over that of the endangered person. Although the proposed legal duty fits comfortably within the deontological moral duty of beneficence, however, the two are not co-extensive. Emergencies are not the only circumstances in which life and health are threatened; disease, starvation, and poverty can affect the physical substratum of personhood on a routine basis. If legal duties must reflect moral ones, should not a legal duty to rescue be supplemented by a legal duty to alleviate those less isolated abridgments of physical security?

The convenience limitation on the rescue duty might similarly be loosened in a deontological analysis. One tempting extension would be very far-reaching: if the physical substratum is the "basic *stuff* (the matter) in man without which he could not realize his ends," and if we are under a duty to safeguard that substratum in others as in ourselves, the priority that the rescuer can legitimately grant to himself can be only with respect to his physical integrity. Under this extension, a rescuer could—indeed would be obligated to—abstain from acting only if the act would place him in physical danger; if it would not put him in danger, he would be required to attempt a rescue, no matter what the disruption of his life. In Macaulay's famous example, the surgeon would have to travel from Calcutta to Meerut to perform an operation that only he could perform, because the journey, though inconvenient, would not be dangerous. Indeed, he would have to make the trip even if he were about to leave for Europe or to greet members of his family arriving on an incoming ship. The patient's right to physical security would rank ahead of the satisfaction of the surgeon's contingent desires.

The deontological approach to rescue does not compel such a drastic extension. Although every moral person must value physical integrity, its protection is not an end in itself. Rather, physical security is valued because it allows individuals to realize their own projects and purposes. Whatever the reach of the right to physical integrity, therefore, it must allow the rescuer to satisfy his purposes in a reasonably coherent way. Still, though the extension of the moral duty cannot be so drastic as to require the sacrifice of all of a person's projects, it can be substantial. It can require the rescuer to undergo considerable inconvenience short of fundamental changes in the fabric of his life. The deontological duty relaxes both the emergency and convenience limitations of the duty of easy rescue in emergencies: it applies not only in emergencies but whenever physical integrity is threatened, and it applies even when the rescuer might have to undergo considerable inconveniences. The duty might, after all, obligate Macaulay's surgeon to travel from Calcutta to Meerut. Would it also require the wealthy to use at lease some of their resources to alleviate the plight of the starving and the afflicted? For those concerned about the possibility of setting principled limits to a duty of rescue, the question is critical.

The objection to an affirmative answer to the question rests on the premises that even the wealthy are under no obligation to be charitable and that the afflicted have no right to receive charity. Under the deontological theory, those premises are incorrect. The duty of beneficence derives from the concept of personhood; it is therefore not properly called charity, for the benefactor's performance of this duty is no reason for self-congratulation. Although the duty is an imperfect one—"since no determinate limits can be assigned to what should be done, the duty has in it a playroom for doing more or less,"[12] as Kant said—it is nonetheless a duty to the performance of which the recipient is entitled.

The extent of the duty of beneficence, of course, can still be troubling. It is the indeterminateness of the duty, the "play-room," that is particularly relevant to this problem. Kant meant by this expression that the form and the amount of the benefaction would vary, depending on the resources of the benefactor, the identity of the recipient, and the recipient's own conception of happiness. The indeterminateness, however, applies not only to the form of the benefaction but also to the linking of particular benefactors to particular beneficiaries. Why should any particular person be singled out of the whole group of potential benefactors, and why should the benefit be conferred on one rather than another person in need? If a duty "may be *exacted* from a person, as one exacts a debt," it is a debt that leaves unclear the precise terms of discharge as well as the identities of obligor and obligee.

The proper response to this indeterminacy is not to deny that there is a duty. What is required is to set up social institutions to perform the necessary tasks of coordination and determination. Those institutions would ensure that no person is singled out unfairly either for burdens or for benefits, and that the forms of benefaction correlate both with the resources of those who give and with the needs of those who receive. In fact, all Western democracies undertake to perform this task through programs for social assistance. The institutions they establish, however, are primarily legislative and administrative; precisely because a general duty of beneficence is imperfect, it cannot be judicially enforced. The traditional claim-settling function of courts does not permit the transfer of a resource from one person to another solely because the former has it and the latter needs it. Such judicial action would unfairly prefer one needy person over others and unfairly burden one resourceful person over others. Because the duty of beneficence is general and indeterminate, it does not, in the absence of legislative action that specifies and coordinates, yield judicially enforceable moral claims by individuals against others.

The significant characteristic of the emergency and convenience limitations is that, in combination, they eliminate the "play-room" inherent in the duty of beneficence, thus providing a principled response to Kant and to Epstein and rendering the narrower duty to rescue appropriate for judicial enforcement. An emergency marks a particular person as physically endangered in a way that is not general or routine throughout the society. An imminent

peril cannot await assistance from the appropriate social institutions. The provision of aid to an emergency victim does not deplete the social resources committed to the alleviation of more routine threats to physical integrity. Moreover, aid in such circumstances presents no unfairness problems in singling out a particular person to receive the aid. Similarly, emergency aid does not unfairly single out one of a class of routinely advantaged persons; the rescuer just happens to find himself for a short period in a position, which few if any others share, to render a service to some specific person. In addition, when a rescue can be accomplished without a significant disruption of his own projects, the rescuer's freedom to realize his own ends is not abridged by the duty to preserve the physical security of another. In sum, when there is an emergency that the rescuer can alleviate with no inconvenience to himself, the general duty of beneficence that is suspended over society like a floating charge is temporarily revealed to identify a particular obligor and obligee, and to define obligations that are specific enough for judicial enforcement.

Conclusion

The problem of rescue is a central issue in the controversies about the relationships between law and morality, between contract and tort, and between utilitarian and deontological ethics. The argument of this article has been that tort law's adoption of a duty of easy rescue in emergencies would fit a common-law pattern, found principally in contract law, that gives expression to the law's understanding of liberty. This pattern reveals that the common-law is already instinct with the attitude of benevolence on which a duty to rescue is grounded. The attitude of benevolence is accepted by many legal commentators as a basic moral intuition, yet the particular duty proposed in this article can be systematically elaborated in both the utilitarian and deontological traditions. For those who believe that law should attempt to render concrete the notion of ethical dealing between persons, as well as for those concerned about the method of common-law evolution or about the social costs of legal rules, the article provides an argument for changing the common-law rule on rescue.

Endnotes

[1] *See* J. Bentham, An Introduction to the Principles of Morals and Legislation 74–83 (J. Burns & H. Hart eds. 1970); *see* J. Bentham, The Principles of Legislation 85–86 (R. Hildreth ed. 1840).

[2] *See* J. Bentham, *supra* note 1, at 74–83

[3] J. S. Mill, The Principles of Political Economy 967 (W. Ashley ed. 1923).

[4] H. Sidgwick, The Methods of Ethics 219 (7th ed. 1907) at 437.

[5] *London Borough of Southwark v. Williams,* [1971] 2 All E. R. 175 (C.A.).

[6] Bentham, *supra* note 1, at 162 (footnote omitted).

[7] [*See* Fried, *Right and Wrong—Preliminary Considerations,* 5 J. Legal Studies 165, 181–182 (1976).]

[8] I. Kant, *The Metaphysical Principles of Virtue* 49 (M. Gregor trans. 1964), at 112.

[9] [*Id.*] at 53, 122.

[10] *Id.* At 118

[11] [*Id.*] at 112.

[12] *Id.* at 121.

Study Questions

1. Why does Judge Flaherty refuse to order Shimp to undergo the bone marrow donation?

2. What two limitations or qualifications does Weinrib place on the duty to rescue?

3. According to Weinrib, how is the duty of easy rescue consistent with a deontological basis for a duty to rescue?

4. It is a widely followed rule that when you *begin* a rescue, by taking steps upon which the victim or other potential rescuers might rely, you may not legally stop or abort the rescue, saying that you are merely leaving the situation unaltered; the law says that after you have acted, any subsequent abandonment is no longer a mere failure to act. Why is it worse to begin treatment and then abandon the victim than never to have begun in the first place? Can you see how this rule might create perverse incentives for potential rescuers?

5. In *Depue v. Flateau* (111 N.W. 1 [1907]), a traveling cattle buyer called upon a customer and asked to stay for dinner. During the meal, he was overcome by a "fainting spell" and fell seriously ill. He asked permission to stay the night (it being a cold winter evening in Minnesota), but this was refused. Flateau led Depue to his cart, set him in it, handed him the reins (which Depue was too weak to hold), and started the horses on their way. Depue was found in a ditch the following morning, nearly frozen to death. Depue alleged that Flateau was negligent in not allowing him to stay the night. The court, ruling in favor of Depue, articulated the following principle: "Whenever a person is placed in such a position with regard to another that it is obvious that, if he does not use due care in his own conduct, he will cause injury to that person, the duty at once arises to exercise care commensurate with the situation in which he thus finds himself . . . to avoid such danger." Should the law incorporate this language as stating a general duty of rescue? If applied across the board, what consequences would this principle have?

6. Why was the "intrusion" into David Shimp's body requested by McFall an impermissible one? The donation procedure required the insertion of a curved needle into the donor's hip bone and the removal of 5 cc of marrow. Because 500 cc would have been required by McFall, roughly 100 such taps would have been performed on Shimp. Consider that the law not only permits but actually requires some forms of "bodily intrusion," vaccinations, for example. And a few courts have allowed blood transfusions to be performed upon patients who oppose them on religious grounds (*John F. Kennedy Memorial Hospital v. Heston* 58 N.J. 576 [1971]). Why are these cases different from Shimp's? What is an intrusion anyway? Is simply breaking the skin enough? If so, how is a bone marrow transplant more an intrusion than a blood transfusion? Would it make a difference had a scalpel been necessary for the marrow donation procedure?

7. Commentators Alan Meisel and Loren H. Roth argue that Judge Flaherty made the correct

decision in *McFall:* "Despite the high potential benefits to the recipient [and] the relatively low risks . . . to the donor, . . . irreparable harm would be done to the values of individual autonomy, privacy, and bodily and psychic integrity from compelling a transplant of any kind. . . . No matter how idiosyncratic Shimp's reasons for refusal, his mere wish not to donate marrow should not be overridden. . . . [W]e must be willing to respect his decision even if he could articulate no reasons whatsoever for refusing" (Meisel and Roth, "Must a Man Be His Cousin's Keeper?," *Hastings Center Report* (October, 1978): 5–6.) Do you agree? Why or why not?

8. Why should so much weight be placed by the law upon the misfeasance/nonfeasance distinction? Imagine the following (this hypothetical is taken from John Harris, "The Survival Lottery," *Philosophy* 50 [1975]:81–87): Two patients, Y and Z, will each die soon unless they obtain, respectively, a new heart and a new lung. No donor organs are available in the normal way, so Y and Z make a proposal. If just one healthy person, A, were killed, his or her organs could be removed and transplanted into Y and Z, saving two lives at the cost of one. Using this approach, many lives could be saved. To allay the inevitable insecurity that would attend such a proposal (Will I be the next to go?) and to quell the legitimate fear of abuse, Y and Z suggest a "survival lottery": Everyone is given a number; if and when your number is called, you are secretly taken into custody and painlessly killed so that your organs might "give life" to others. To the doctors' objection that killing the innocent A is morally impermissible, Y and Z respond that, should the doctors fail to kill one to save two, *they* (the doctors) will be responsible for the deaths of the two; and even if it is wrong to kill "innocent" persons, Y and Z are just as innocent as A. Is there some morally relevant difference between bringing about the death of A through misfeasance and bringing about the deaths of Y and Z through nonfeasance? Given the assumption that a world in which Y and Z both live is better overall than the one in which A lives, can it matter how that world comes about? Compare the reasoning of Y and Z to the case of Robert McFall. Can it be said that Judge Flaherty, by refusing to grant McFall's request, is responsible for McFall's death? Did McFall die as a result of the inaction by Judge Flaherty or by "natural causes"? Is there a difference?

9. Recent critics of negligence law argue that existing doctrine and its language of "standards of care" for the "safety of others" and "unreasonable" conduct focuses upon abstract categories and cost-benefit calculations in a way unresponsive to real human needs. Preoccupation with a reasoned and distanced analysis of such cases as *McFall v. Shimp* fails, they contend, to show respect for people and to acknowledge their sufferings, forcing out the caring, compassionate human response that the plight of people such as McFall tends to evoke. Rather than appeal to the duties of the "reasonable man," one critic has suggested that the law "measure the conduct of a tortfeasor [one who commits a tort] by the care that would be taken by a . . . responsible person with conscious care and concern for another's safety," the way one would act "out of care for a neighbor or friend" (Leslie Bender, "A Lawyer's Primer on Feminist Theory and Tort," *Journal of Legal Education* 38 [1988]: 25). The duty to act with the conscious care and concern of a responsible neighbor would require an affirmative duty to rescue "under appropriate circumstances," measured by one's "ability to aid and one's proximity to the need" (*ibid,* p. 36). Does this language state a workable standard? Does the proposed standard represent an improvement over the existing reasonable-man standard? Why or why not?

10. An early proposal for changing the legal doctrine concerning rescue is due to James Barr Ames "Law and Morals," 22 *Harvard Law Review* 97 [1908]). Ames proposed that the rule should be as follows:

> One who fails to interfere to save another from impending death or great

bodily harm, when he might do so with little or no inconvenience to himself, and the death or great bodily harm follows as a consequence of his inaction, shall be punished criminally and shall make compensation to the party injured or to his widow and children in case of death.

Is this an acceptable formulation of a duty to rescue? What implications might it have? Why should rescue be limited to situations in which there is "little or no inconvenience" to the would-be rescuer? Couldn't one make a utilitarian argument that even significant inconvenience is likely to be a lesser cost than the loss of life resulting from a failure to rescue?

Cases for Further Reflection

99. *Derdiarian v. Felix Contracting Corp.*

This case was discussed in the introduction to Section B of this chapter on Causation and Liability. As noted there, this case nicely raises a number of issues dealing with the concept of proximate cause in the law of tort. When reading this case, consider these questions: What is it that made the actions of Felix Contracting negligent? On what grounds did Felix argue that the accident was "freakish"? Even if it was freakish, why should that relieve Felix of liability? How would you assess the responsibility of the motorist, Dickens? Suppose Dickens had crashed because he was drunk? Would that change the way the causal analysis works out?

Plaintiff obtained a judgment after a jury verdict. The appellate division affirmed. The facts are set forth in the opinion.

Chief Judge Cooke.

. . .

The order of the Appellate Division should be affirmed. As a general rule, the question of proximate cause is to be decided by the finder of fact, aided by appropriate instructions. There is no basis on this record for concluding, as a matter of law, that a superseding cause or other factor intervened

to break the nexus between defendant's negligence and plaintiff's injury.

During the fall of 1973 defendant Felix Contracting Corporation was performing a contract to install an underground gas main in the City of Mount Vernon for defendant Con Edison. Bayside Pipe Coaters, plaintiff Harold Derdiarian's employer, was engaged as a subcontractor to seal the gas main.

On the afternoon of November 21, 1973, defendant James Dickens suffered an epileptic seizure and lost consciousness, allowing his vehicle to

414 N.E.2d 666
Court of Appeals of New York

careen into the work site and strike plaintiff with such force as to throw him into the air. When plaintiff landed, he was splattered over his face, head and body with 400 degree boiling hot liquid enamel from a kettle struck by the automobile. The enamel was used in connection with sealing the gas main. Although plaintiff's body ignited into a fire ball, he miraculously survived the incident.

At trial, plaintiff's theory was that defendant Felix had negligently failed to take adequate measure to insure the safety of workers on the excavation site. Plaintiff's evidence indicates that the accident occurred on Oak Street, a two-lane, east-west roadway. The excavation was located in the eastbound lane, and ran from approximately one foot south of the center line to within 2 or 3 feet of the curb. When plaintiff arrived on the site, he was instructed by Felix' foreman to park his truck on the west side of the excavation, parallel to the curb. As a result, there was a gap of some 7½ feet between the side of the truck and the curb line. Derdiarian testified that he made a request to park his truck on the east side of the hole, so he could set up the kettle away from the oncoming eastbound traffic. The Felix foreman instructed him to leave his truck where it was, and plaintiff then put the kettle near the curb, on the west side of the excavation.

James Dickens was driving eastbound on Oak Street when he suffered a seizure and lost consciousness. Dickens was under treatment for epilepsy and had neglected to take his medication at the proper time. His car crashed through a single wooden horse-type barricade that was set up on the west side of the excavation site. As it passed through the site, the vehicle struck the kettle containing the enamel, as well as the plaintiff, resulting in plaintiff's injuries.

To support his claim of an unsafe work site, plaintiff called as a witness Lawrence Lawton, an expert in traffic safety. According to Lawton, the usual and accepted method of safe-guarding the workers is to erect a barrier around the excavation. Such a barrier, consisting of a truck, a piece of heavy equipment or a pile of dirt, would keep a car out of the excavation and protect workers from oncoming traffic. The expert testified that the barrier should cover the entire width of the excavation. He also stated that there should have been two flagmen present, rather than one, and that warning

signs should have been posted advising motorists that there was only one lane of traffic and that there was a flagman ahead.

. . . Defendant Felix now argues that plaintiff was injured in a freakish accident, brought about solely by defendant Dickens' negligence, and therefore there was no causal link, as a matter of law, between Felix' breach of duty and plaintiff's injuries.

The concept of proximate cause, or more appropriately legal cause, has proven to be an elusive one, incapable of being precisely defined to cover all situations. . . . This is, in part, because the concept stems from policy considerations that serve to place management limits upon the liability that flows from negligent conduct (e.g., *Ventricelli v. Kinney System Rent A Car*, 45 N.Y.2d 950, 952; *Palsgraf v. Long Is. R. R. Co.*, 248 N.Y. 339, 352 [Andrews, J., dissenting]). Depending upon the nature of the case, a variety of factors may be relevant in assessing legal cause. Given the unique nature of the inquiry in each case, it is for the finder of fact to determine legal cause, once the court has been satisfied that a prima facie case has been established. . . . To carry the burden of proving a prima facie case, the plaintiff must generally show that the defendant's negligence was a substantial cause of the events which produced the injury. . . . Plaintiff need not demonstrate, however, that the precise manner in which the accident happened, or the extent of injuries, was foreseeable. . . .

Where the acts of a third person intervene between the defendant's conduct and the plaintiff's injury, the causal connection is not automatically severed. In such a case, liability turns upon whether the intervening act is a normal or foreseeable consequence of the situation created by the defendant's negligence. . . . If the intervening act is extraordinary under the circumstances, not foreseeable in the normal course of events, or independent of or far removed from the defendant's conduct, it may well be a superseding act which breaks the causal nexus. . . . Because questions concerning what is foreseeable and what is normal may be the subject of varying inferences, as is the question of negligence itself, these issues generally are for the fact finder to resolve.

There are certain instances, to be sure, where only one conclusion may be drawn from the established facts and where the question of legal cause may be decided as a matter of law. Those cases generally involve independent intervening acts which operate upon but do not flow from the original negligence. Thus, for instance, we have held that where an automobile lessor negligently supplies a car with a defective trunk lid, it is not liable to the lessee who, while stopped to repair the trunk, was injured by the negligent driving of a third party. Although the renter's negligence undoubtedly served to place the injured party at the site of the accident, the intervening act was divorced from and not the foreseeable risk associated with the original negligence. And the injuries were different in kind than those which would have normally been expected from a defective trunk. In short, the negligence of the renter merely furnished the occasion for an unrelated act to cause injuries not ordinarily anticipated.

By contrast, in the present case, we cannot say as a matter of law that defendant Dickens' negligence was a superseding cause which interrupted the link between Felix' negligence and plaintiff's injuries. From the evidence in the record, the jury could have found that Felix negligently failed to safeguard the excavation site. A prime hazard associated with such dereliction is the possibility that a driver will negligently enter the work site and cause injury to a worker. That the driver was negligent, or even reckless, does not insulate Felix from liability. . . . Nor is it decisive that the driver lost control of the vehicle through a negligent failure to take medication, rather than a driving mistake. . . . The precise manner of the event need not be anticipated. The finder of fact could have concluded that the foreseeable, normal and natural result of the risk created by Felix was the injury of a worker by a car entering the improperly protected work area. An intervening act may not serve as a superseding cause, and relieve an actor of responsibility, where the risk of the intervening act occurring is the very same risk which renders the actor negligent.

In a similar vein, plaintiff's act of placing the kettle on the west side of the excavation does not, as a matter of law, absolve defendant Felix of responsibility.[1] Serious injury, or even death, was a foreseeable consequence of a vehicle crashing through the work area. The injury could have occurred in numerous ways, ranging from a worker being directly struck by the car to the car hitting an object that injures the worker. Placement of the kettle, or any object in the work area, could affect how the accident occurs and the extent of injuries. That defendant could not anticipate the precise manner of the accident or the exact extent of injuries, however, does not preclude liability as a matter of law where the general risk and character of injuries are foreseeable.

. . .

Endnote

[1] Plaintiff testified that a Felix foreman had directed him to park his truck on the west side of the excavation. From this, and other related testimony, the jury could have concluded that Felix effectively dictated the location of the kettle, obviating any question of plaintiff's own conduct breaking the causal nexus.

100. *Harper v. Herman*

This is a recent case involving the questions of liability for omissions and the no-duty-to-rescue doctrine. Is the age difference between the plaintiff (twenty years of age) and the defendant (sixty-four years) relevant? Suppose the ages were reversed. Would that change your assessment of the case? If Herman did owe a duty to Harper to "rescue" him by warning him of the shallow water, why didn't that duty also extend to others on the boat who also might realize the danger of diving in that location?

Page, Justice.

This case arises upon a reversal by the court of appeals of summary judgment in favor of the defendant. The court of appeals held that defendant, the owner and operator of a private boat on Lake Minnetonka, had a duty to warn plaintiff, a guest on the boat, that water surrounding the boat was too shallow for diving. We reverse and reinstate judgment in favor of defendant.

The facts are undisputed for the purpose of this appeal. On Sunday, August 9, 1986, Jeffrey Harper ("Harper") was one of four guests on Theodore Herman's ("Herman") 26-foot boat, sailing on Lake Minnetonka. Harper was invited on the boat outing by Cindy Alberg Palmer, another guest on Herman's boat. Herman and Harper did not know each other prior to this boat outing. At the time Herman was 64 years old, and Harper was 20 years old. Herman was an experienced boat owner having spent hundreds of hours operating boats on Lake Minnetonka similar to the one involved in this action. As owner of the boat, Herman considered himself to be in charge of the boat and his passengers. Harper had some experience swimming in lakes and rivers, but had no formal training in diving.

After a few hours of boating, the group decided to go swimming and, at Herman's suggestion, went to Big Island, a popular recreation spot. Herman was familiar with Big Island, and he was

499 N.W.2d 472 (1993)
Supreme Court of Minnesota

aware that the water remains shallow for a good distance away from its shore. Harper had been to Big Island on one previous occasion. Herman positioned the boat somewhere between 100 to 200 yards from the island with the bow facing away from the island in an area shallow enough for his guests to use the boat ladder to enter the water, but still deep enough so they could swim. The bottom of the lake was not visible from the boat. After positioning the boat Herman proceeded to set the anchor and lower the boat's ladder which was at its stern.

While Herman was lowering the ladder, Harper asked him if he was "going in." When Herman responded yes, Harper, without warning, stepped onto the side of the middle of the boat and dove into approximately two or three feet of water. As a result of the dive, Harper struck the bottom of the lake, severed his spinal cord, and was rendered a C6 quadriplegic.

Harper then brought suit, alleging that Herman owed him a duty of care to warn him that the water was too shallow for diving. [The trial court granted defendant's motion for summary judgment on the ground that defendant owed plaintiff no duty to warn. The court of appeals held that defendant voluntarily assumed such a duty when he allowed Harper onto his boat.]

The sole issue on appeal is whether a boat owner who is a social host owes a duty of care to warn a guest on the boat that the water is too shallow for diving.

Harper alleges that Herman owed him a duty to warn of the shallowness of the water because he was an inexperienced swimmer and diver, whereas Herman was a veteran boater. Under those circumstances, Harper argues, Herman should have realized that Harper needed his protection.

We have previously stated that an affirmative duty to act only arises when a special relationship exists between the parties. "The fact that an actor realizes or should realize that action on his part is necessary for another's aid or protection does not of itself impose upon him a duty to take such action . . . unless a special relationship exists . . . between the actor and the other which gives the other the right to protection." . . . Accepting, *arguendo*, that Herman should have realized that Harper needed protection, Harper must still prove that a special relationship existed between them that placed an affirmative duty to act on the part of Herman.

Harper argues that a special relationship requiring Herman to act for his protection was created when Herman, as a social host, allowed an inexperienced diver on his boat. Generally, a special relationship giving rise to a duty to warn is only found on the part of common carriers, innkeepers, possessors of land who hold it open to the public, and persons who have custody of another person under circumstances in which that other person is deprived of normal opportunities of self-protection. . . . Under this rule, a special relationship could be found to exist between the parties only if Herman had custody of Harper under circumstances in which Harper was deprived of normal opportunities to protect himself. These elements are not present here.

The record before this court does not establish that Harper was either particularly vulnerable or that he lacked the ability to protect himself. Further, the record does not establish that Herman held considerable power over Harper's welfare, or that Herman was receiving a financial gain by hosting Harper on his boat. Finally, there is nothing in the record which would suggest that Harper expected any protection from Herman; indeed, no such allegation has been made.

The court of appeals found that Herman owed Harper a duty to warn him of the shallowness of the water because Herman knew that it was "dangerously shallow." We have previously stated that "[a]ctual knowledge of a dangerous condition tends to impose a special duty to do something about that condition." . . . However, superior knowledge of a dangerous condition by itself, in the absence of a duty to provide protection, is insufficient to establish liability in negligence. Thus, Herman's knowledge that the water was "dangerously shallow" without more does not create liability. . . . In this case, Harper was not deprived of opportunities to protect himself, and Herman was not expected to provide protection.

"There are many dangers, such as those of fire and water, . . . which under ordinary conditions may reasonably be expected to be fully understood and appreciated by any child . . . If a child is expected to understand the inherent dangers of water, so should a 20-year-old adult. Harper had no reasonable expectation to look to Herman for protection, and we hold that Herman had no duty to warn Harper that the water was shallow.

Reversed and judgment in favor of defendant reinstated.

101. *Summers v. Tice*

A classic case in the annals of tort, *Summers* should be read in conjunction with a review of the essay by Judith Thomson. In this case, a sole reliance upon the idea of *sine qua non* or "factual" causation yields not only an indeterminate result but what seems to be precisely the wrong result: namely, that neither defendant caused the injury. Can you see why?

Actions by Charles A. Summers against Harold W. Tice and against Ernest Simonson for negligently shooting plaintiff while hunting. From judgments for plaintiff, defendants appeal. . . .

Carter, Justice.

Each of the two defendants appeals from a judgment against them in an action for personal injuries. Pursuant to stipulation the appeals have been consolidated.

Plaintiff's action was against both defendants for an injury to his right eye and face as the result of being struck by bird shot discharged from a shotgun. The case was tried by the court without a jury and the court found that on November 20, 1945, plaintiff and the two defendants were hunting quail on the open range. Each of the defendants was armed with a 12 gauge shotgun loaded with shells containing 7 ½ size shot. Prior to going hunting plaintiff discussed the hunting procedure with defendants, indicating that they were to exercise care when shooting and to "keep in line." In the course of hunting, plaintiff proceeded up a hill, thus placing the hunters at the points of a triangle. The view of defendants with reference to plaintiff was unobstructed and they knew his location. Defendant Tice flushed a quail which rose in flight to a ten foot elevation and flew between plaintiff and defendants. Both defendants shot at the quail, shooting in plaintiff's direction. At that time defendants were 75 yards from plaintiff. One shot struck plaintiff in his eye and another in his upper lip. Fi-

nally it was found by the court that as the direct result of the shooting by defendants the shots struck plaintiff as above mentioned and that defendants were negligent in so shooting and plaintiff was not contributorily negligent.

. . . First, on the subject of negligence, defendant Simonson contends that the evidence is insufficient to sustain the finding on that score, but he does not point out wherein it is lacking. There is evidence that both defendants, at about the same time or one immediately after the other, shot at a quail and in so doing shot toward plaintiff who was uphill from them, and that they knew his location. That is sufficient from which the trial court could conclude that they acted with respect to plaintiff other than as persons of ordinary prudence. . . .

Defendant Tice states in his opening brief, "we have decided not to argue that insufficiency of negligence on the part of defendant Tice." It is true he states in his answer to plaintiff's petition for a hearing in this court that he did not concede this point but he does not argue it. Nothing more need be said on the subject.

. . . Defendant Simonson urges that plaintiff was guilty of contributory negligence and assumed the risk as a matter of law. He cites no authority for the proposition that by going on a hunting party the various hunters assume the risk of negligence on the part of their companions. Such a tenet is not reasonable. It is true that plaintiff suggested that they all "stay in line," presumably abreast, while hunting, and he went uphill at somewhat of a right angle to the hunting line, but he also cautioned that they use care, and defendants knew plaintiff's position. We hold, therefore, that the trial court was justified in finding that he did not assume the risk

199 P. 2d 1 (1948)
Supreme Court of California

or act other than as a person of ordinary prudence under the circumstances. . . .

The problem presented in this case is whether the judgment against both defendants may stand. It is argued by defendants that they are not joint tort feasors, and thus jointly and severally liable, as they were not acting in concert, and that there is not sufficient evidence to show which defendant was guilty of the negligence which caused the injuries—the shooting by Tice or that by Simonson. Tice argues that there is evidence to show that the shot which struck plaintiff came from Simonson's gun because of admissions allegedly made by him to third persons and no evidence that they came from his gun. Further in connection with the latter contention, the court failed to find on plaintiff's allegation in his complaint that he did not know which one was at fault—did not find which defendant was guilty of the negligence which caused the injuries to plaintiff.

. . . Considering the last argument first, we believe it is clear that the court sufficiently found on the issue that defendants were jointly liable and that thus the negligence of both was the cause of the injury or to that legal effect. It found that both defendants were negligent and "That as a direct and proximate result of the shots fired by *defendants, and each of them,* a birdshot pellet was caused to and did lodge in plaintiff's right eye and that another birdshot pellet was caused to and did lodge in plaintiff's upper lip." In so doing the court evidently did not give credence to the admissions of Simonson to third persons that he fired the shots, which it was justified in doing. It thus determined that the negligence of both defendants was the legal cause of the injury—or that both were responsible. Implicit in such finding is the assumption that the court was unable to ascertain whether the shots were from the gun of one defendant or the other or one shot from each of them. The one shot that entered plaintiff's eye was the major factor in assessing damages and that shot could not have come from the gun of both defendants. It was from one or the other only.

It has been held that where a group of persons are on a hunting party, or otherwise engaged in the use of firearms, and two of them are negligent in firing in the direction of a third person who is injured thereby, both of those so firing are liable for the injury suffered by the third person, although the negligence of only one of them could have caused the injury. . . . *Oliver v. Miles,* Miss., 110 So. 666, 50 A.L.R. 357. . . . The same rule has been applied in criminal cases . . . and both drivers have been held liable for the negligence of one where they engaged in a racing contest causing an injury to a third person. . . . These cases speak of the action of defendants as being in concert as the ground of decision, yet it would seem they are straining that concept and the more reasonable basis appears in *Oliver v. Miles,* supra. There two persons were hunting together. Both shot at some partridges and in so doing shot across the highway injuring plaintiff who was traveling on it. The court stated that they were acting in concert and thus both were liable. The court then stated . . . : "We think that . . . each is liable for the resulting injury to the boy, although no one can say definitely who actually shot him. *To hold otherwise would be to exonerate both from liability, although each was negligent, and the injury resulted from such negligence."*

. . .

. . . When we consider the relative position of the parties and the results that would flow if plaintiff was required to pin the injury on one of the defendants only, a requirement that the burden of proof on that subject be shifted to defendants becomes manifest. They are both wrongdoers—both negligent toward plaintiff. They brought about a situation where the negligence of one of them injured the plaintiff, hence it should rest with them each to absolve himself if he can. The injured party has been placed by defendants in the unfair position of pointing to which defendant caused the harm. If one can escape the other may also and plaintiff is remediless. Ordinarily defendants are in far better position to offer evidence to determine which one caused the injury. This reasoning has recently found favor in this Court. In a quite analogous situation this Court held that a patient injured while unconscious on an operating table in a hospital could hold all or any of the persons who had any connection with the operation even though he could not select the particular acts by the particular person which led to his disability. *Ybarra v. Spangard* . . . 154 P.2d 687. . . . There the Court was considering whether the patient could avail himself of res ipsa loquitur, rather than where the burden of proof lay, yet the effect of the decision is that plaintiff has made out a case when he has produced evidence which gives rise to an inference of negligence which was the proximate cause of the injury. It is up to defendants to explain the cause of the injury. It was there said: "If the doctrine is to continue to serve a useful purpose, we should not forget that 'the particular force and justice of the rule, regarded as a presumption throwing upon the party charged the duty of producing evidence, consists in the circumstance that the chief evidence of the true cause, whether culpable or innocent, is practically accessible to him but inaccessible to the injured person.'" . . . Similarly in the instant case plaintiff is not able to establish which of defendants caused his injury.

The foregoing discussion disposes of the authorities cited by defendants . . . , stating the general rule that one defendant is not liable for the independent tort of the other defendant, or that ordinarily the plaintiff must show a causal connection between the negligence and the injury. There was an entire lack of such connection in the Hernandez case and there were not several negligent defendants, one of whom must have caused the injury.

Defendants rely upon *Christensen v. Los Angeles Electrical Supply Co.,* 112 Cal.App. 629, 297 P. 614, holding that a defendant is not liable where he negligently knocked down with his car a pedestrian and a third person then ran over the prostrate person. That involves the question of intervening cause which we do not have here. Moreover it is out of harmony with the current rule on that subject and was properly questioned in *Hill v. Peres,* 136 Cal.App. 132, 28 P.2d 946 (hearing in this Court denied), and must be deemed disapproved.

Cases are cited for the proposition that where two or more tort feasors acting independently of each other cause an injury to plaintiff, they are not joint tort feasors and plaintiff must establish the portion of the damage caused by each, even though it is impossible to prove the portion of the injury caused by each. . . .

. . . In view of the foregoing discussion it is apparent that defendants in cases like the present one may be treated as liable on the same basis as joint tort feasors, and hence the last cited cases are distinguishable inasmuch as they involve independent tort feasors.

. . . In addition to that, however, it should be pointed out that the same reasons of policy and justice shift the burden to each of [the] defendants to absolve himself if he can—relieving the wronged person of the duty of apportioning the injury to a particular defendant, apply here where we are concerned with whether plaintiff is required to supply evidence for the apportionment of damages. If defendants are independent tort feasors and thus each liable for the damage caused by him alone, and, at least, where the matter of apportionment is incapable of proof, the innocent wronged party should not be deprived of his right to redress. The wrongdoers should be left to work out between themselves any apportionment. . . . Some of the cited cases refer to the difficulty of apportioning the burden of damages between the independent tort feasors, and say that where factually a correct division cannot be made, the trier of fact may make it the best it can, which would be more or less a guess, stressing the factor that the wrongdoers are not in a position to complain of uncertainty. . . .

. . . It is urged that plaintiff now has changed the theory of his case in claiming a concert of action; that he did not plead or prove such concert. From what has been said it is clear that there has been no change in theory. The joint liability, as well as the lack of knowledge as to which defendant was liable, was pleaded and the proof developed the case under either theory. We have seen that for the reasons of policy discussed herein, the case is based upon the legal proposition that, under the circumstances here presented, each defendant is liable for the whole damage whether they are deemed to be acting in concert or independently.

The judgment is affirmed.

102. *Yania v. Bigan*

Frequently cited as among the more egregious examples of the "no-duty-to-rescue" rule, this case should be read with these questions in mind: Did Bigan cause Yania's death? How would Hart and Honorés theory handle this case? Would it change the outcome of these theories if Bigan knew Yania to be especially susceptible to dares or to attacks upon his manliness and prowess? Why didn't Bigan have a legal duty to rescue Yania once the latter was in the water? Might the answer to this question turn on whether Bigan caused Yania to be in the water? Is Bigan's conduct misfeasance or nonfeasance, according to Weinrib's definitions?

Benjamin R. Jones, Justice.

A bizarre and most unusual circumstance provides the background of this appeal.

On September 25, 1957 John E. Bigan was engaged in a coal strip-mining operation in Shade Township, Somerset County. On the property being stripped were large cuts or trenches created by Bigan when he removed the earthen overburden for the purpose of removing the coal underneath. One cut contained water 8 to 10 feet in depth with side walls or embankments 16 to 18 feet in height; at this cut Bigan had installed a pump to remove the water.

At approximately 4 p.m. on that date, Joseph F. Yania, the operator of another coal strip-mining operation, and one Boyd M. Ross went upon Bigan's property for the purpose of discussing a business matter with Bigan, and, while there, were asked by Bigan to aid him in starting the pump. Ross and Bigan entered the cut and stood at the point where the pump was located. Yania stood at the top of one of the cut's side walls and then jumped from the side wall—a height of 16 to 18 feet—into the water and was drowned.

Yania's widow, in her own right and on behalf of her three children, instituted wrongful death and survival actions against Bigan contending Bigan was responsible for Yania's death. Preliminary ob-

155 A. 2d 343 (1959)
Supreme Court of Pennsylvania

jections, in the nature of demurrers, to the complaint were filed on behalf of Bigan. The court below sustained the preliminary objections; from the entry of that order this appeal was taken.

. . . Since Bigan has chosen to file preliminary objections, in the nature of demurrers, every material and relevant fact well pleaded in the complaint and every inference fairly deducible therefrom are to be taken as true. . . .

The complaint avers negligence in the following manner: (1) "The death by drowning of . . . [Yania] was caused entirely by the acts of [Bigan] . . . in *urging, enticing, taunting and inveigling* [Yania] to jump into the water, which [Bigan] knew or ought to have known was of a depth of 8 to 10 feet and dangerous to the life of anyone who would jump therein" (emphasis supplied); (2) ". . . [Bigan] violated his obligations to a business invitee in not having his premises reasonably safe, and not warning his business invitee of a dangerous condition and to the contrary urged, induced and inveigled [Yania] into a dangerous position and a dangerous act, whereby [Yania] came to his death"; (3) "After [Yania] was in the water, a highly dangerous position, having been induced and inveigled therein by [Bigan], [Bigan] failed and neglected to take reasonable steps and action to protect or assist [Yania], or [extricate Yania] from the dangerous position in which [Bigan] had placed him." Summarized, Bigan stands charged with three-fold negligence: (1) by urging, enticing, taunting and inveigling Yania to jump into the water; (2) by failing to warn Yania of a dangerous condition on the land, i.e., the cut wherein lay 8 to 10 feet of water; (3) by failing to go to Yania's rescue after he had jumped into the water.[1]

. . . The Wrongful Death Act . . . and the Survival Act . . . really confer no more than rights to recover damages growing out of a single cause of action, namely, *the negligence of the defendant* which caused the damages suffered. . . . While the law presumes that Yania was not negligent, such presumption affords no basis for an inference that Bigan was negligent. . . . Our inquiry must be to ascertain whether the well-pleaded facts in the complaint, assumedly true, would, if shown, suffice to prove negligent conduct on the part of Bigan.

. . . Appellant initially contends that Yania's descent from the high embankment into the water and the resulting death were caused "entirely" by the spoken words and blandishments of Bigan delivered at a distance from Yania. The complaint does not allege that Yania slipped or that he was pushed or that Bigan made any *physical* impact upon Yania. On the contrary, the only inference deducible from the facts alleged in the complaint is that Bigan, by the employment of cajolery and inveiglement, caused such a *mental* impact on Yania that the latter was deprived of his volition and freedom of choice and placed under a compulsion to jump into the water. Had Yania been a child of tender years or a person mentally deficient then it is conceivable that taunting and enticement could constitute actionable negligence if it resulted in harm. However, to contend that such conduct directed to an adult in full possession of all his mental faculties constitutes actionable negligence is not only without precedent but completely without merit. . . .

. . . Appellant next urges that Bigan, as the possessor of the land, violated a duty owed to Yania in that his land contained a dangerous condition, i.e., the water-filled cut or trench, and he failed to warn Yania of such condition. Yania was a business invitee in that he entered upon the land for a common business purpose for the mutual benefit of Bigan and himself. . . . As possessor of the land, Bigan would become subject to liability to Yania for any physical harm caused by any artificial or natural condition upon the land (1) if, and only if, Bigan knew or could have discovered the condition which, if known to him he should have realized in-

volved an unreasonable risk of harm to Yania, (2) if Bigan had no reason to believe Yania would discover the condition or realize the risk of harm and (3) if he invited or permitted Yania to enter upon the land without exercising reasonable care to make the condition reasonably safe or give adequate warning to enable him to avoid the harm. . . . The inapplicability of this rule of liability to the instant facts is readily apparent.

The *only* condition on Bigan's land which could possibly have contributed in any manner to Yania's death was the water-filled cut with its high embankment. Of this condition there was neither concealment nor failure to warn, but, on the contrary, the complaint specifically avers that Bigan not only requested Yania and Boyd to assist him in starting the pump to remove the water from the cut but "led" them to the cut itself. If this cut possessed any potentiality of danger, such a condition was as obvious and apparent to Yania as to Bigan, both coal strip-mine operators. Under the circumstances herein depicted Bigan could not be held liable in this respect.

. . . Lastly, it is urged that Bigan failed to take the necessary steps to rescue Yania from the water. The mere fact that Bigan saw Yania in a position of peril in the water imposed upon him no legal, although a moral, obligation or duty to go to his rescue unless Bigan was legally responsible, in whole or in part, for placing Yania in the perilous position. Restatement, Torts, § 314. Cf. Restatement, Torts, § 322. The language of this Court in *Brown v. French*, 104 Pa. 604, 607, 608, is apt: "If it appeared that the deceased, by his own carelessness, contributed in any degree to the accident which caused the loss of his life, the defendants ought not to have been held to answer for the consequences resulting from that accident. . . . He voluntarily placed himself in the way of danger, and his death was the result of his own act. . . . That his undertaking was an exceedingly reckless and dangerous one, the event proves, but here was no one to blame for it but himself. He had the right to try the experiment, obviously dangerous as it was, but then also upon him rested the consequences of that experiment, and upon no one else; he may have been, and probably was, ignorant of the risk which he was taking upon himself, or knowing it, and trusting to his own skill, he may have regarded it as easily superable. But in either case, the result of his ignorance, or of his mistake, must rest with himself—and cannot be charged to the defendants." The complaint does not aver any facts which impose upon Bigan legal responsibility for placing Yania in the dangerous position in the water and, absent such legal responsibility, the law imposes on Bigan no duty of rescue.

Recognizing that the deceased Yania is entitled to the benefit of the presumption that he was exercising due care and extending to appellant the benefit of every well pleaded fact in this complaint and the fair inferences arising therefrom, yet we can reach but one conclusion: that Yania, a reasonable and prudent adult in full possession of all his mental faculties, undertook to perform an act which he knew or should have known was attended with more or less peril and it was the performance of that act and not any conduct upon Bigan's part which caused his unfortunate death.

Order affirmed.

Endnote

[1] So far as the record is concerned we must treat the 33-year-old Yania as in full possession of his mental faculties at the time he jumped.

Appendix 1

Legal Citations
and Law Reports

This appendix provides a brief explanation of the system currently in use for collecting, publishing, and citing judicial opinions and decisions. We'll begin with an example of a typical case citation, of the sort found throughout this text. Take the citation to the *Hudnut* case in Chapter One:

American Bookseller's Association
v. Hudnut
771 F. 2d 323 (1985)
United States Court of Appeals,
Seventh Circuit

The first line of the citation lists the last names of the parties involved. If the case is a civil rather than a criminal case, the first name appearing in the citation normally is that of the *plaintiff* in the case, the individual filing the complaint. If there is more than one plaintiff, the name of the first plaintiff (listed in alphabetical order) is given. In a criminal case, the complaining party is the state; hence a criminal case situation typically reads *State v. Bradbury* or *People v. Burroughs*. The second name appearing in the first line is that of the person responding to a suit or charged with a crime: the *defendant.*

Occasionally, a citation will refer to a case that is being heard on *appeal.* This means that the party who lost at the lower or trial court level, where evidence is presented and a judgment rendered, is requesting that a higher or appellate court review the record of the trial court proceedings to determine if an error occurred in the definition or application of the rules of law applicable to the case. If the citation refers to a case being heard on appeal, the order of the names—plaintiff/defendant—is the same if the plaintiff is the party instituting the appeal (called the *appellant*); a few states, however, reverse the names when the defendant is the appellant or "plaintiff in error."

The publication of court opinions is sanctioned by statute throughout the states and by the federal government. *United States Reports* (cited as *U.S.*), for example, is the official collection of opinions issued by the United States Supreme Court. Opinions and decisions are also collected and published by private firms: *The Supreme Court Reporter* (cited as *S. Ct.*) is the collection of the Supreme Court's decisions published by the West Publishing Company.

Court reports are organized in several ways: by jurisdiction of the court issuing the opinion (for example, *California Reports* contains the opinions of the Supreme Court of California); by geography (for example, West's *Pacific Reporter* includes opinions by appellate courts in a number of Western states); and by subject matter (for example, the *Military Justice Reporter* reports the decisions of Court of Military Appeals).

The second line of the situation for *Hudnut* reads:

771 F.2d 323 (1985)

This refers to volume 771 of the *Federal Reporter, Second Series.* The *Hudnut* case appears beginning on page 323. The case was decided in 1985. The *Federal Reporter*, published by West, collects opinions handed down by all the various "circuits" or divisions of the United States Court of Appeals. West's *Federal Supplement* (cited as *F. Supp.*) does the same for United States district courts (the trial courts of the federal system). (A table outlining the federal system and a typical state court system appears in the figure below.) The last line of the citation for *Hudnut* indicates that the case was heard by the Seventh Circuit of the United States Court of Appeals.

Many judicial opinions are easily obtained through West's National Reporter System, consisting of a set of volumes reporting both state and federal cases. The United States has seven regional reporters: Atlantic, North Eastern, North Western, Pacific, South Eastern, Southern, and South Western. (Abbreviations for many of the regional and federal reporters are given below.)

In addition to the regional reporters, West publishes special reporters for two states: the *California Reporter* and the *New York Supplement*.

Abbreviations for Selected State, Regional, and Federal Reporters

Cal., Cal 2d, Cal. 3d	*California Reports*
Cal. Rptr.	*West's California Reporter*
Cal. App., Cal. App. 2d, Cal. App. 3d	*California Appellate Reports*
Ill., Ill. 2d	*Illinois Reports*
N.Y., N.Y. 2d	*New York Reports*
A.D., A.D. 2d	*Appellate Division Reports (N.Y.)*
N.Y. Sup. Ct.	*Supreme Court Reports (N.Y.)*
N.Y.S. 2d	*West's New York Supplement*
Atl.	*Atlantic Reporter*
A. 2d	*Atlantic Reporter, Second Series*
N.E.	*North Eastern Reporter*
N.W.	*North Western Reporter*
Pac.	*Pacific Reporter*
P. 2d	*Pacific Reporter, Second Series*
S.E.	*South Eastern Reporter*
So.	*Southern Reporter*
S.W.	*South Western Reporter*
U.S.	*United States Reports*
S. Ct.	*Supreme Court Reporter*

The U.S. Court System

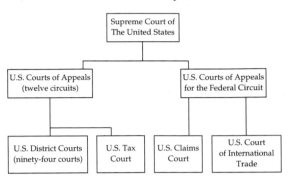

California State System

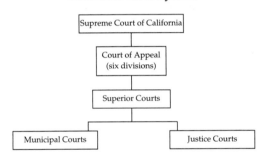

Appendix 2

The Constitution of the United States

Amendment I [1791]

Congress shall make no law respecting an establishment of religion, or prohibiting the free exercise thereof; or abridging the freedom of speech, or of the press; or the right of the people peaceably to assemble, and to petition the Government for a redress of grievances.

Amendment II [1791]

A well regulated Militia, being necessary to the security of a free State, the right of the people to keep and bear Arms, shall not be infringed.

Amendment III [1791]

No Soldier shall, in time of peace be quartered in any house, without the consent of the Owner, nor in time of war, but in a manner to be prescribed by law.

Amendment IV [1791]

The right of the people to be secure in their persons, houses, papers, and effects, against unreasonable searches and seizures, shall not be violated, and no Warrants shall issue, but upon probable cause, supported by Oath or affirmation, and particularly describing the place to be searched, and the persons or things to be seized.

Amendment V [1791]

No person shall be held to answer for a capital, or otherwise infamous crime, unless on a presentment or indictment of a Grand Jury, except in cases arising in the land or naval forces, or in the Militia, when in actual service in time of War or public danger; nor shall any person be subject for the same offense to be twice put in jeopardy of life or limb; nor shall be compelled in any criminal case to be a witness against himself, nor be deprived of life, liberty, or property, without due process of law; nor shall private property be taken for public use, without just compensation.

Amendment VI [1791]

In all criminal prosecutions, the accused shall enjoy the right to a speedy and public trial, by an impartial jury of the State and district wherein the crime shall have been committed, which district shall have been previously ascertained by law, and to be informed of the nature and cause of the accusation; to be confronted with the witnesses against him; to have compulsory process for obtaining witnesses in his favor, and to have the Assistance of Counsel for his defense.

Amendment VII [1791]

In Suits at common law, where the value in controversy shall exceed twenty dollars, the right of trial by jury shall be preserved, and no fact tried by a jury, shall be otherwise re-examined in any Court of the United States, than according to the rules of the common law.

Amendment VIII [1791]

Excessive bail shall not be required, nor excessive fines imposed, nor cruel and unusual punishments inflicted.

Amendment IX [1791]

The enumeration in the Constitution, of certain rights, shall not be construed to deny or disparage others retained by the people.

Amendment X [1791]

The powers not delegated to the United States by the Constitution, nor prohibited by it to the States, are reserved to the States respectively, or to the people.

Amendment XI [1798]

The Judicial power of the United States shall not be construed to extend to any suit in law or equity, commenced or prosecuted against one of the United States by Citizens of another State, or by Citizens or Subjects of any Foreign State.

Amendment XII [1804]

The Electors shall meet in their respective states and vote by ballot for President and Vice-President, one of whom, at least, shall not be an inhabitant of the same state with themselves; they shall name in their ballots the person voted for as President, and in distinct ballots the person voted for as Vice-President, and they shall make distinct lists of all persons voted for as President, and of all persons voted for as Vice-President, and of the number of votes for each, which lists they shall sign and certify, and transmit sealed to the seat of the government of the United States, directed to the President of the Senate;—The President of the Senate shall, in the presence of the Senate and House of Representatives, open all the certificates and the votes shall then be counted;—The person having the greatest number of votes for President, shall be the President, if such number be a majority of the whole number of Electors appointed; and if no person have such majority, then from the persons having the highest numbers not exceeding three on the list of those voted for as President, the House of Representatives shall choose immediately, by ballot, the President. But in choosing the President, the votes shall be taken by states, the representation from each state having one vote; a quorum for this purpose shall consist of a member or members from two thirds of the states, and a majority of all the states shall be necessary to a choice. And if the House of Representatives shall not choose a President whenever the right of choice shall devolve upon them, before the fourth day of March next following, then the Vice-President shall act as President, as in the case of the death or other constitutional disability of the President.—The person having the greatest number of votes as Vice-President, shall be the Vice-President, if such number be a majority of the whole number of Electors appointed, and if no person have a majority, then from the two highest numbers on the list, the Senate shall choose the Vice-President; a quorum for the purpose shall consist of two-thirds of the whole number of Senators, and a majority of the whole number shall be necessary to a choice. But no person constitutionally ineligible to the office of President shall be eligible to that of Vice-President of the United States.[1]

Amendment XIII [1865]

Section I. Neither slavery nor involuntary servitude, except as a punishment for crime whereof the party shall have been duly convicted, shall exist within the United States, or any place subject to their jurisdiction.

Section 2. Congress shall have power to enforce this article by appropriate legislation.

Amendment XIV [1868]

Section 1. All persons born or naturalized in the United States, and subject to the jurisdiction thereof, are citizens of the United States and of the State wherein they reside. No State shall make or enforce any law which shall abridge the privileges or immunities of citizens of the United States; nor shall any State deprive any person of life, liberty, or property, without due process of law, nor deny to any person within its jurisdiction the equal protection of the laws.

Section 2. Representatives shall be apportioned among the several States according to their respective numbers, counting the whole number of persons in each State, excluding Indians not taxed. But

---

[1] Superseded by section 3 of the Twentieth Amendment.

when the right to vote at any election for the choice of electors for President and Vice-President of the United States, Representatives in Congress, the Executive and Judicial officers of a State, or the members of the Legislature thereof, is denied to any of the male inhabitants of such State, being twenty-one years of age, and citizens of the United States, or in any way abridged, except for participation in rebellion, or other crime, the basis of representation therein shall be reduced in the proportion which the number of such male citizens shall bear to the whole number of male citizens twenty-one years of age in such State.

Section 3. No person shall be a Senator or Representative in Congress, or elector of President and Vice-President, or hold any office, civil or military, under the United States, or under any State, who, having previously taken an oath, as a member of Congress, or as an officer of the United States, or as a member of any State legislature or as an executive or judicial officer of any State, to support the Constitution of the United States, shall have engaged in insurrection or rebellion against the same, or given aid or comfort to the enemies thereof. But Congress may by a vote of two-thirds of each House, remove such disability.

Section 4. The validity of the public debt of the United States, authorized by law, including debts incurred for payment of pensions and bounties for services in suppressing insurrection or rebellion, shall not be questioned. But neither the United States nor any State shall assume or pay any debt or obligation incurred in aid of insurrection or rebellion against the United States, or any claim for the loss of emancipation of any slave; but all such debts, obligations and claims shall be held illegal and void.

Section 5. The Congress shall have power to enforce, by appropriate legislation, the provisions of this article.

Amendment XV [1870]

Section 1. The right of citizens of the United States to vote shall not be denied or abridged by the United States or by any State on account of race, color, or previous condition of servitude.

Section 2. The Congress shall have power to enforce this article by appropriate legislation.

Amendment XVI [1913]

The Congress shall have power to lay and collect taxes on incomes, from whatever source derived, without apportionment among the several states, and without regard to any census or enumeration.

Amendment XVII [1913]

[1] The Senate of the United States shall be composed of two Senators from each State, elected by the people thereof, for six years; and each Senator shall have one vote. The electors in each State shall have the qualifications requisite for electors of the most numerous branch of the State legislatures.

[2] When vacancies happen in the representation of any State in the Senate, the executive authority of such State shall issue writs of election to fill such vacancies: *Provided*, That the legislature of any State may empower the executive thereof to make temporary appointments until the people fill the vacancies by election as the legislature may direct.

[3] This amendment shall not be so construed as to affect the election or term of any Senator chosen before it becomes valid as part of the Constitution.

Amendment XVIII [1919]

Section 1. After one year from the ratification of this article the manufacture, sale, or transportation of intoxicating liquors within, the importation thereof into, or the exportation thereof from the United States and all territory subject to the jurisdiction thereof for beverage purposes is hereby prohibited.

Section 2. The Congress and the several States shall have concurrent power to enforce this article by appropriate legislation.

Section 3. This article shall be inoperative unless it shall have been ratified as an amendment to the Constitution by the legislatures of the several States, as provided in the Constitution, within seven years from the date of the submission hereof to the States by the Congress.[2]

---

[2] Repealed by the Twenty-first Amendment.

Amendment XIX [1920]

[1] The right of citizens of the United States to vote shall not be denied or abridged by the United States or by any State on account of sex.

[2] Congress shall have power to enforce this article by appropriate legislation.

Amendment XX [1933]

Section 1. The terms of the President and Vice President shall end at noon on the 20th day of January, and the terms of Senators and Representatives at noon on the 3d day of January, of the years in which such terms would have ended if this article had not been ratified; and the terms of their successors shall then begin.

Section 2. The Congress shall assemble at least once in every year, and such meeting shall begin at noon on the 3d day of January, unless they shall by law appoint a different day.

Section 3. If, at the time fixed for the beginning of the term of the President, the President elect shall have died, the Vice President elect shall become President. If a President shall not have been chosen before the time fixed for the beginning of his term, or if the President elect shall have failed to qualify, then the Vice President elect shall act as President until a President shall have qualified; and the Congress may by law provide for the case wherein neither a President elect nor a Vice President elect shall have qualified, declaring who shall then act as President, or the manner in which one who is to act shall be selected, and such person shall act accordingly until a President or Vice President shall have qualified.

Section 4. The Congress may by law provide for the case of the death of any of the persons from whom the House of Representatives may choose a President whenever the right of choice shall have devolved upon them, and for the case of the death of any of the persons from whom the Senate may choose a Vice President whenever the right of choice shall have devolved upon them.

Section 5. Sections I and 2 shall take effect on the 15th day of October following the ratification of this article.

Section 6. This article shall be inoperative unless it shall have been ratified as an amendment to the Constitution by the legislatures of three-fourths of the several States within seven years from the date of its submission.

Amendment XXI [1933]

Section 1. The eighteenth article of amendment to the Constitution of the United States is hereby repealed.

Section 2. The transportation or importation into any State, Territory, or possession of the United States for delivery or use therein of intoxicating liquors, in violation of the laws thereof, is hereby prohibited.

Section 3. This article shall be inoperative unless it shall have been ratified as an amendment to the Constitution by conventions in the several States, as provided in the Constitution, within seven years from the date of the submission hereof to the States by the Congress.

Amendment XXII [1951]

Section 1. No person shall be elected to the office of the President more than twice, and no person who has held the office of President, or acted as President, for more than two years of a term to which some other person was elected President shall be elected to the office of the President more than once. But this Article shall not apply to any person holding the office of President when this Article was proposed by the Congress, and shall not prevent any person who may be holding the office of President, or acting as President, during the term within which this Article becomes operative from holding the office of President or acting as President during the remainder of such term.

Section 2. This article shall be inoperative unless it shall have been ratified as an amendment to the Constitution by the legislatures of three-fourths of the several States within seven years from the date of its submission to the States by the Congress.

Amendment XXIII [1961]

Section 1. The District constituting the seat of Government of the United States shall appoint in such manner as the Congress may direct:

A number of electors of President and Vice President equal to the whole number of Senators and Representatives in Congress to which the District would be entitled if it were a State, but in no event more than the least populous State; they shall be in addition to those appointed by the States, but they shall be considered, for the purposes of the election of President and Vice President, to be electors appointed by a State; and they shall meet in the District and perform such duties as provided by the twelfth article of amendment.

Section 2. The Congress shall have power to enforce this article by appropriate legislation.

Amendment XXIV [1964]

Section 1. The right of citizens of the United States to vote in any primary or other election for President or Vice President, for electors for President or Vice President, or for Senator or Representative in Congress, shall not be denied or abridged by the United States or any State by reason of failure to pay any poll tax or other tax.

Section 2. The Congress shall have power to enforce this article by appropriate legislation.

Amendment XXV [1967]

Section 1. In case of the removal of the President from office or of his death or resignation, the Vice President shall become President.

Section 2. Whenever there is a vacancy in the office of the Vice President, the President shall nominate a Vice President who shall take office upon confirmation by a majority vote of both Houses of Congress.

Section 3. Whenever the President transmits to the President pro tempore of the Senate and the Speaker of the House of Representatives his written declaration that he is unable to discharge the powers and duties of his office, and until he transmits to them a written declaration to the contrary, such powers and duties shall be discharged by the Vice President as Acting President.

Section 4. Whenever the Vice President and a majority of either the principal officers of the executive departments or of such other body as Congress may by law provide, transmit to the President pro tempore of the Senate and the Speaker of the House of Representatives their written declaration that the President is unable to discharge the powers and duties of his office, the Vice President shall immediately assume the powers and duties of the office as Acting President.

Thereafter, when the President transmits to the President pro tempore of the Senate and the Speaker of the House of Representatives his written declaration that no inability exists, he shall resume the powers and duties of his office unless the Vice President and a majority of either the principal officers of the executive department or of such other body as Congress may by law provide, transmit within four days to the President pro tempore of the Senate and the Speaker of the House of Representatives their written declaration that the President is unable to discharge the powers and duties of his office. Thereupon Congress shall decide the issue, assembling within forty-eight hours for that purpose if not in session. If the Congress, within twenty-one days after receipt of the latter written declaration, or, if Congress is not in session, within twenty-one days after Congress is required to assemble, determines by two-thirds vote of both Houses that the President is unable to discharge the powers and duties of his office, the Vice President shall continue to discharge the same as Acting President; otherwise, the President shall resume the powers and duties of his office.

Amendment XXVI [1971]

Section 1. The right of citizens of the United States, who are eighteen years of age or older, to vote shall not be denied or abridged by the United States or by any State on account of age.

Section 2. The Congress shall have power to enforce this article by appropriate legislation.

Appendix 3

Legal Resources
on the Internet

Many of the legal issues explored in this text concern areas of constitutional, criminal, and civil law that develop and change constantly. One of the best ways to explore the latest developments in any part of the law is to use the legal research tools now available on the Internet and World Wide Web. The following list is a guide to some of the most useful sites available as of the time of writing. These sites can be used to search for a vast array of information: updates on cases covered in the text, appeals of rulings mentioned in the text and readings, new rulings on particular topics (e.g. hate speech or the death penalty), recent legislative activity (state and federal), and law journal and law review essays on all aspects of the law.

The Internet sites listed below can serve as useful starting points for those who wish to research topics of interest. The sites are grouped into several categories, beginning with general sites with links to numerous, more specific sites. Following are all-purpose search engines which can help users look up court rulings, legislative enactments, and other legal texts; federal government sites; university law school libraries; and a few single-focus sites. The list is hardly exhaustive, but it should provide enough information to get you started.

General Legal Information Sites

On-line Catalogs

Following are a few of the best networks for links to legal sites on the Internet:

Hieros Gamos Internet Law Library
http://www.hg.org
Includes: Bar and legal associations, law schools, publishers, law firms, legal education, law library.

The Legal List
http://www.lcp.com/The-Legal-List/index.html
Includes: General assistance on searching for legal materials on the internet.

Lawlinks.com
http://lawlinks.com
Includes: Law library; areas of law; case law; commercial resources; constitutions, statutes, and codes; international resources; law journals and law reviews.

Library of Congress
http://www.loc.gov
Includes: Comprehensive collection of federal, state, and local government web sites.

U.S. House of Representatives Internet Law Library
http://law.house.gov
Includes: Member, Committee, and House organizational information; U.S. federal laws; U.S. state and territorial laws; treaties and international law; law school law library catalogs.

World Wide Web Virtual Law Library
http://www.law.indiana.edu/law/lawindex.html
Includes: Federal and state government web servers, law journals and law reviews, legal information by topic.

General Legal Search Engines

Two of the best all-purpose legal search tools are:

Cornell Legal Information Institute
http://www.law.cornell.edu
Comprehensive search capabilities for state and federal statutes, case law, administrative law, international law, and academic law journals and law reviews.

Findlaw
http://www.findlaw.com
Comprehensive search capabilities for state and federal statutes, case law, and academic law journals and law reviews.

Other useful engines:

LawCrawler
http://www.lawcrawler.com
Affiliated with Findlaw.

Fastsearch
http://www.fastsearch.com

Federal Legislation

U.S. Legislative Information at the Library of Congress (Thomas)
http://thomas.loc.gov

Code of Federal Regulations
http://www.access.gpo.gov/nara/cfr
Official site for searching the CFR.

Federal Court Locator
http://www.law.vill.edu/Fed-Ct/fedcourt.html
Useful portal site to federal courts.

Governmental Agencies

Equal Employment Opportunity Commission (EEOC)
http://gsa.gov/eeo

Federal Trade Commission (FTC)
http://www.gopher.ftc.gov

Environmental Protection Agency (EPA)
http://www.epa.gov

Occupational Safety and Health Administration (OSHA)
http://www.osha-slc.gov

Consumer Product Safety Commission
http://www.epsc.gov

Law School Libraries

Following are some of the most useful sites:

Chicago-Kent College of Law
http://www.kentlaw.edu

Emory University School of Law
http://www.law.emory.edu

Georgetown University Law Center
http://www.ll.georgetown.edu

Indiana University Law School
http://www.law.indiana.edu

New York University Law School
http://www.nyu.edu/law

University of Chicago Law School
http://www-law.lib.uchicago.edu

University of Southern California Law Center
http://www.use.edu/dept/law-lib/index.html

Washburn University Law School
http://lawlib.wuacc.edu

Internet Resources on Specific Areas of Law

Civil Rights/Human Rights

American Civil Liberties Union
http://www.aclu.org

Privacy International
http://www.privacy.org

Amnesty International
http://www.amnesty.org

Cato Institute
http://www.cato.org

Criminal Law

U.S. Dept. of Justice
http://www.usdoj.gov

Death Penalty Information Center
http://essential.org/dpic/dpic.html

Victims of Crime, National Criminal Justice Reference Service
http://www.ncjrs.org/victhome.htm

Employment Law

Equal Employment Opportunity Commission
http://www.eeoc.gov

First Amendment/Freedom of Expression

Cato Institute
http://www.cato.org

American Civil Liberties Union
http://www.aclu.org

Gender, Sexual Orientation, and the Law

Women's Rights and Resources
http://sunsite.unc.edu/cheryb/women/wresources.html

National Organization for Women
http://www.now.org

National Right to Life
http://www.nrlc.org

Lambda Legal Defense and Education Fund
http://www.thebody.com/lambda/lambda.html

International Law

Statute of the International Court of Justice
http://www.us.org/overview/statute/content.html

United Nations
http://www.un.org

Other Sites of Interest

Legal News
http://www.ljx.com

Glossary of Legal Terms

Acquittal: The verdict in a criminal trial in which the **defendant** is found not guilty.

Actus Reus: The "guilty act" or "deed of crime"; an act of wrongdoing that is forbidden by the law and that, when committed in conjunction with a specified state of mind (*mens rea*), constitutes a **crime.**

Amici: see **amicus curiae.**

Amicus Curiae: "Friend of the court"; a person or group who files a brief with the court, supplying relevant information bearing on the case or urging a particular result. While not parties in a case, *amici* typically are third parties who will be indirectly affected by the court's decision.

Answer: The legal document by which a **defendant** responds to the allegations contained in the **complaint** of the **plaintiff.**

Appeal: The resort to a superior or *appellate* court to review the decision of an inferior or *trial* court.

Appellant: The party or person who appeals a decision (usually, but not always, the loser in the lower court).

Appellee: The party or person against whom an **appeal** is taken (usually, but not always, the winner in the lower court).

Brief: A written statement prepared by an attorney arguing a case in court; a summary of the facts of the case, relevant laws, and an argument of how the law applies to the facts in support of the attorney's position.

Cause of Action: A claim in law based on facts sufficient to bring the case to court; the grounds of an action against another (e.g., a suit in **negligence**).

Certiorari: A writ issued by a superior court to an inferior court requiring the latter court to produce the records of a particular case heard before it. Most often used with regard to the U.S. Supreme Court, which uses "cert." as a means of deciding which cases it wishes to hear.

Citation: A reference to an authority used (e.g., a prior case, a statute) to substantiate the validity of one's argument or position.

Common Law: The origin of the Anglo-American legal systems; the system of law originally based on the customary and unwritten laws of England and developed by the doctrine of **precedent** as opposed to legislative enactments. In theory, law that is not created by the courts but rather discovered in the customs, habits, and basic principles of justice acknowledged by society.

Complaint: The legal document (also called a **petition**) that informs a **defendant** of the grounds on which he or she is being sued.

Crime: A wrongful act against society as defined by law; a wrong that is prosecuted by a public official and punishable by fine, imprisonment, or death.

Damages: Monetary compensation awarded by a court for an injury caused by the act of another. Damages may be *actual* or *compensatory* (equal to the amount of loss proven) or *exemplary* or *punitive* (in excess of the actual damages given as a form of punishment to the wrongdoer).

Decedent: One who has ceased to live; in criminal law, the victim of a **homicide.**

Defendant: The person against whom a lawsuit (**cause of action**) or criminal action is brought.

Dictum: A statement or remark, not necessary for the decision of a case, made by the judge in the judge's opinion; a statement not binding as **precedent.**

Discovery: That set of procedures through which the parties to a suit obtain information about matters relevant to the case.

Dissent: An **opinion** given by a judge in a case which differs from that given by the majority of the court. A dissent typically points out the deficiencies of the majority position and states reasons for arriving at a different conclusion.

Equity: Justice administered according to fairness as opposed to the strictly formulated rules of the common law; a system of principles that originated in England as an alternative to the perceived harshness of rigidly applying the rules of the common law in every case.

Ex Post Facto: "After the fact"; a law that makes illegal an action which was done before the law was passed. Such laws violate Article I, Sections 9 and 10 of the United States Constitution.

Felony: Any of a group of "high" or "serious" crimes (as distinguished from minor offenses called **misdemeanors**) generally punishable either by death or imprisonment.

Felony-Murder: An unlawful **homicide** occurring during the commission of (or attempt to commit) a **felony** and which (under this doctrine) is considered first-degree **murder.**

"Fighting Words": Words that, given their nature and the context in which they are uttered, are very likely to provoke their hearer to an immediate breach of the peace. Such words have been held not protected by the First Amendment to the U.S. Constitution.

First Impression: A case that presents a question of law never before considered by any court within the relevant **jurisdiction** and that is therefore not controlled by the doctrine of **precedent.**

Guilty: The condition of having been found to have committed the crime charged.

Holding: A declaration or statement of the law as it applies to the facts of a specific case and given by the court in its **opinion.**

Homicide: Any killing of a human being by another human being. Homicide does not necessarily constitute a crime; to be a crime, homicide must be an **unlawful** killing (e.g., **murder**).

Ignoratia Legis Non Excusat: "Ignorance of the law is no excuse"; the fact that the defendant did not think her or his act was against the law does not prevent the law from punishing the prohibited act.

Infancy: The state of being a minor; not yet having attained the age of majority.

Injunction: A judge's order that a person do, or more commonly, refrain from doing a certain act.

The court's power to issue an injunction is based in equity.

Instruction: Directions the judge gives to the jury, informing them of the law that they are to apply to the facts of the case in order to reach a **verdict.**

Judgment: The final decision of the court in a case, resolving the dispute and determining the rights and obligations of the parties involved.

Jurisdiction: The power of a court to make legally binding decisions over certain persons or property; the geographical area in which a court's decisions or a legislature's enactments are binding.

Liability: The condition of being responsible for **damages** resulting from an injurious act, for discharging an obligation or debt, or for paying a penalty for wrongdoing.

Malum In Se: "That which is wrong in itself"; refers to an act that would be thought evil or wrong even without a specific criminal prohibition (e.g., **murder**).

Malum Prohibitum: "That which is wrong because prohibited"; refers to an act that is wrong only because it is made so by statute (e.g., failure to file for income tax).

Miscegenation: "The mixing of the races"; older statutes (now invalid) typically defined miscegenation as marriage between a Caucasian (white) and a member of another race.

Misdemeanor: That class of criminal offenses less serious than felonies and punished with lesser severity.

Misfeasance: The doing of a wrongful or injurious act.

Moot Case: A case that no longer presents an actual controversy, either because the issues involved have ceased to exist or they have been rendered "academic" by the circumstances.

Motion: A formal request made to a judge pertaining to any issue arising during a lawsuit.

Movant: The party who requests a motion.

Murder: The unlawful killing of a human being. Modern law distinguishes between several degrees of murder. *First degree murder* is a deliberate and premeditated homicide; *second degree murder* is a homicide committed with malice but without premeditation.

Negligence: The failure to exercise due care for the safety and welfare of others; failure to exercise that degree of care which, under the circumstances, a **reasonable person** would take.

Nonfeasance: Nonperformance of an act that one has a duty to perform; neglect of a duty; failure to act so as to prevent harm.

Nuisance: An unreasonable or unwarranted use by a person of his or her own property that produces such annoyance, inconvenience, or discomfort as to interfere with the rights of others to use and enjoy their property.

Obiter Dictum: *see* **dictum.**

On the Merits: A decision or judgment based upon the essential facts of the case rather than upon a "technicality" such as improper jurisdiction.

Opinion: A statement of the reasons why a certain decision or **judgment** was reached in a case. A *majority opinion* is usually written by one judge and represents the principles of law that a majority of the members of a court regard as central to the **holding** in the case. A *concurring opinion* agrees with the ultimate judgment of the majority but disagrees with the reasons leading to that result. A *plurality opinion* is agreed to by less than a majority so far as reasoning is concerned but is agreed to by a majority as stating the correct result. A *per curiam opinion* is an opinion expressing the decision of the court but whose author is not identified. *See also* **dissent.**

Ordinance: The equivalent of a municipal **statute** passed by a city council and dealing with matters not already covered by federal or state law.

Overbreadth: A situation in which a law not only prohibits that which may constitutionally be prohibited but also prohibits conduct which is constitutionally protected (e.g., the freedom of speech under the First Amendment).

Overrule: To overturn or invalidate the **holding** of a prior case. A decision can be overruled only by the same court or by a higher court within the same **jurisdiction.**

Petition: A formal, written application to a court requesting judicial action on a particular matter.

Petitioner: The person presenting the petition to a court; one who starts an equity proceeding; one who takes an appeal from a judgment.

Plaintiff: The person who brings a lawsuit or *cause of action* against another.

Plea: In the law of procedure, an **answer** or response to a **complaint** or allegation of fact; in criminal procedure, the response of the **defendant** in answer to the charge made against him or her.

Pleadings: The **complaint** and the **answer** in a civil suit.

Precedent: The doctrine of Anglo-American law whereby once a court has formulated a principle of law as applied to a given set of facts, it will follow that principle and apply it in future cases where the facts are substantially similar. *See also* **stare decisis.**

Preponderance of the Evidence: The general standard of proof in a civil case (i.e., one involving a lawsuit); to prevail, a party must show that the preponderance of the evidence (better than 50 percent) weighs in her or his favor.

Prima Facie Case: A case that, at first view or "on its face," is supported by enough evidence to entitle a party to have the case go to a jury.

Probation: A procedure whereby a **defendant** found guilty of a crime is released into society subject to conditions laid down by the court and under the supervision of a probation officer.

Proceeding: The form and manner of conducting legal business before a court or judicial officer; the series of events constituting the process through which judicial action takes place.

Prosecution: The act of pursuing a lawsuit or criminal trial; the party initiating a criminal suit, i.e., the state.

Proximate Cause: An event without which injury or damage would not have occurred and which is closely enough related to the occurrence of the injury to make it fair, reasonable, or just to hold the **defendant** liable for that injury.

Ratio Decidendi: The point in a case that determines the result or judgment; the basis or reason for the decision.

Reasonable Doubt: The degree of certainty required of a juror before the juror may find a **defendant guilty;** innocence is to be presumed unless the guilt of the defendant is so clearly proven that the jury can see that no reasonable doubt remains as to the guilt of the defendant.

Reasonable Person: A phrase used to refer to that hypothetical person who exercises those qualities of attention, knowledge, intelligence, and judgment which society requires of its members for the protection of their own interest and the interests of others.

Recidivist: A "habitual criminal," often subjected to extended terms of imprisonment under habitual offender statutes.

Relief: That assistance, redress, or benefit sought by a person filing a **complaint** before a court.

Remand: To send back for further proceedings, as when a higher court sends a case back to a lower court.

Remedy: The means by which a right is enforced or the violation of a right is redressed or compensated. The most common remedy at law consists of money **damages.**

Respondent: The party who contends against an appeal; the party who makes an answer to a complaint in an equity proceeding.

Reversal: The invalidating or setting aside of the contrary decision of a lower court.

Scienter: The **defendant's** "guilty knowledge"; refers to the defendant's alleged previous knowledge of the cause that led to the injury complained of.

Sentence: The punishment a court orders to be inflicted upon a person convicted of a crime.

Sine Qua Non: "That without which there is not"; in tort law, the act of the **defendant** without which there would not have been a **tortious** injury to the **plaintiff.**

Stare Decisis: "Let the decision stand"; refers to the doctrine that courts should follow **precedent,** the authority of earlier, analogous cases.

Statute: An act of a legislature, consistent with constitutional authority and in such proper form that it becomes the law governing the conduct to which it refers.

Statute of Wills: Those statutory provisions of a particular jurisdiction stating the requirement for a valid will.

Strict Liability: Liability without proof of fault. In civil law, one who engages in activity that carries an inherent risk of injury or is ultra-hazardous (e.g., blasting) is often liable for all injuries proximately caused by that activity; in criminal law, strict liability offenses are those that do not require proof of *mens rea* (criminal intent).

Subpoena: A court order compelling a witness to appear and testify in a **proceeding.**

Suit: Any **proceeding** before a court in which a person pursues that **remedy** which the law affords as redress for the injury that person has suffered.

Summary Judgement: A judgment in a civil **suit,** granted on the basis of the **pleadings** and prior to trial, holding that there is no genuine factual dispute between the parties regarding the legal issues involved and that the case need not therefore go before a jury.

Testator: One who is disposing of property by **will.**

Tort: A civil wrong, other than a breach of contract, for which a court will provide a **remedy.**

Tortfeasor: One who commits a **tort.**

Tortious: Used to describe conduct that subjects a person to **tort liability.**

Trial: A judicial examination and determination of issues between parties to action.

Ultra Vires: An act beyond the scope of one's powers or authority, as, for example, by a corporation.

Verdict: The decision of a jury following the trial of a civil or criminal case.

Vicarious Liability: The imputation of **liability** upon one person for the actions of another person.

Void: That which is entirely null, having no legal force.

Volenti Non Fit Injuria: "To one who consents, no harm is done"; in **tort,** the doctrine that one generally cannot claim **damages** when one has consented to the activity which caused an injury.

Will: A document executed with specific legal formalities containing a person's instructions about the disposition of his or her property upon death.